ERRATUM

UNITERM INDEX: The statement on page 718 of this Encyclopedia that publication of the UNITERM INDEX was discontinued in 1964 is completely in error. The UNITERM INDEX is a specialized index system of over 130,000 U.S. chemical and chemically related patents issued from 1950 to date. The Index is done from original patent documents and averages 40-45 technical references per patent. It is published bimonthly in book format and annually on magnetic tapes programmed for use on a variety of computers. [Information for Industry, Inc., Washington, D.C. 20036.]

The Encyclopedia of

PATENT PRACTICE AND INVENTION MANAGEMENT

Main entrance to the United States Patent Office bearing the words of Abraham Lincoln who was himself a patentee.

The Encyclopedia of

PATENT PRACTICE
and
INVENTION MANAGEMENT

*A Comprehensive Statement of the
Principles and Procedures in Solicitation, Enforcement and Licensing of Patents and Recognition and
Utilization of Inventions, Written
by an Eminent Staff of Contributing Authors*

Edited by

ROBERT Peyton CALVERT

*The Borden Company
New York*

REINHOLD PUBLISHING CORPORATION, New York

Chapman & Hall, Ltd., London

Dedication

To scientists, who press onward beyond the frontier of existing knowledge and return with useful discoveries;

To patent practitioners, who organize the data into complete and convincing disclosures, obtain and enforce the patents and become counselors and friends;

To able patent examiners, who diligently search the art and impartially determine patentability;

To erudite judges, who by wise interpretations not only keep the patent system moving forward in the swift and often conflicting currents of technological progress and changing public opinion but also impart a measure of flexibility, so that the patent structure weathers temporary political storms by yielding slightly without breaking;

And, most gratefully, to the contributing authors of high distinction and dedication, who have given freely of themselves and their cumulative experiences to the cause of a worthwhile contribution to the reader and our patent system.

THE EDITOR

Foreword

As education is both a necessary preliminary and a continuing part of life, it is always appropriate and helpful to make available to interested persons the information which they need in order to reach their goals.

This book is more than an encyclopedia of information on United States patent practice. It is also a disclosure of American experience in stimulating the flow of inventions, preparing and prosecuting applications, enforcing patents, and realizing maximum profit from them. The beginner will find here the elementary information which he may seek; the student, a comprehensive textbook; the research director, information of daily applicability; and the practitioner, a most complete and convenient book of reference to which he may turn for information about any subject or procedure that is new to him.

Because of the broad and varied experiences of the hundred contributors—many of whom I have come to regard as distinguished scholars in the law or in science and esteemed personal friends—and because of the forward thinking as well as current procedures that they have written into the Encyclopedia the value of it should persist for many years and contribute support for the United States patent system in its present, effective form.

It is safe to say that the contributors to this volume firmly believe that this system has been and is presently effective in meeting the objectives for which it was established. If this were not so, their names would not appear as contributors to the volume, the tone of which as a whole is one of general approval of those solutions to our specific problems which have been worked out over the years. This is not to say that any one of the contributors opposes all changes in the system; many may actually have proposals in mind. But their comments as well as their participation in the project indicate their conclusion that, as of this time, our patent system works and will continue to be a great public asset if allowed to function in the future substantially as in the past.

The system has served successfully to stimulate the lone inventors of the recent as well as distant past. It has survived the rise of the corporate group to dominance in the field of invention. It has adjusted itself to the processing of the startling technological innovation of this age. At the same time, it has not neglected the simple contribution which immediately benefits the average consumer. We do not live by automation alone, and we receive gladly an improvement in belt buckles.

Naturally, as scientific discoveries of importance appear and as technology, which closely follows, advances into new and more complicated fields, greater knowledge is necessary on the part of all who participate in protecting the discoveries. The judge, with a patent case pending before him, may suddenly face a complex technical problem and need help; the advocacy of referral of such problems to the Patent Office, for advice, is understandable. So also is the need by the Office of more examiners to accomplish its work promptly, certainly until the time when mechanical searching mechanism becomes an effective aid. Interference proceedings should and probably can be expedited and other details of procedure altered to suit modern needs, all without disturbing the foundation upon which our system rests.

We must continue to encourage those with inventive ability to spend the time and treasure necessary to make inventions, in spite of the possibility of failure and loss. We must make the reward commensurate with the risk assumed and the advancement effected, the public being not only the chief beneficiary but also the ultimate judge of the magnitude of the contribution and of the size of the reward.

Since law is a rule of human action and since human characteristics do not change rapidly, the patent law, to be as effective in the future as it has been in the past (and to be made even more effective if possible), must be consistent with reality. It must stand solidly on a tried and tested basis, despite the innovations proposed by pressure groups and politicians and the urgings of some well-meaning but unrealistic friends.

There probably has never been a time when all those having knowledge of the nature of the patent system have held it to be absolutely perfect, but all agree that it is vastly superior to the secrecy practice which the system has replaced. Certain phases of it have been examined, reexamined and adjusted and, no doubt, will be considered critically again in the future, with improvement as the objective. Within the Patent Office, for instance, suggestions for procedural improvement have sometimes gone full cycle—through various phases and back to the starting points, experience having proven the initial positions to have been the best.

It is interesting to observe that our offer of a patent to anyone who contributes to technology in a substantial way is and has been open to all our people and also to the citizens of all countries, since the time when George Washington recommended and Congress enacted the first patent law. As a result, the American economy continues to benefit from technological contributions developed not only at home but also in many foreign nations, some 20 per cent of the applications received presently by our Patent Office being for patents on inventions made in countries other than our own.

In each of a large number of foreign lands, including both Free World and Iron Curtain countries, dedicated men of skill, experience and honesty of purpose, such as our own faithful and able Patent Examiners, are carefully scrutinizing applications for patents filed by their own citizens and by citizens of this nation. They are applying to the concepts submitted a single standard of measurement, alike to their fellow countrymen and foreigners, rejecting those applications which do not measure up and granting patents on the others, wholly regardless of the source of the applications. The various patent systems thus work in the most democratic manner conceivable and for the benefit of the entire world.

It is true, on the other hand, that our patent system differs in certain details from the systems of most other countries. We insist, for instance, in rewarding the inventors who are first in point of time in making their inventions rather than those first in filing applications for patents.

It is to be hoped that those who come after us will examine with the greatest care and caution any and all proposals to modify our patent laws for the purpose of bringing them into accord with those of other countries. Despite international currents tending to world-wide conformity, our successors should sacrifice no advantage which our present system provides.

The Editor is to be congratulated upon having secured the cooperation of so many leaders of the patent profession, providing a suitable forum for them and assembling in one volume so much experience and informative comment upon the different facets of patent practice and invention management.

ROBERT C. WATSON

Preface

Although the principal titles are alphabetically arranged, the reader desiring information on a specific point should turn to the Index for the various aspects of the subject relating most closely to his problem. Those with no previous patent experience may well read first the article *Information for the Independent Inventor*.

You would expect that no person or small group would have the knowledge or time available to bring to you the necessary information and personal knowledge of the whole range of subjects relating to patent practice. Recognizing the difficulty from the start, we obtained the cooperation of just over a hundred contributing authors, selected for their special qualifications and abilities as lawyers or scientists and for experiences estimated, from representative data, to total collectively more than 2500 years and to include authorship of more than 50 books and many journal articles. These contributing authors show an evident dedication to the cause of improving the practice at all levels—for the research worker and director, for the executive seeking a more effective and profitable patent policy, and for the beginner as well as the most experienced patent practitioner.

The authors, numerous as they are, represent only a small fraction of those who would have honored us by appearing as contributors. These others are now invited to submit brief suggestions regarding either the present or a supplementary volume, especially additional unusual features to be presented, with the assurance that the suggestions will be carefully considered.

No doubt the authors would want it understood that their statements herein are not legal opinions regarding situations that may arise in the future. No two cases are ever exactly alike. The decision in a given suit will rest on the particular set of facts, not on general principles laid down by even the most able jurists under similar but necessarily different circumstances.

The decisions reviewed or cited do point the way out of difficulties in many instances. It is significant, however, that these cases involve conditions under which the contending parties have been willing usually to go to bar and continue the prosecution and defense to a conclusion. The implication is that the circumstances may have been on the borderline between favorable and unfavorable, a narrow ledge between proper and improper upon which the parties have dared to walk and from which only one of them ordinarily has fallen in defeat. The cases are not to be construed as invitations to others to take deliberately an unnecessary risk which another may have assumed unwittingly and from which he ultimately escaped.

Gratitude and thanks are due and gratefully extended to the contributing authors; to The Borden Company for allowing the editor to accept this responsibility; to those scholars and gentlemen, including Mr. Reynold Bennett, Mr. William E. Currie, Professor Walter J. Derenberg, Mr. George S. Hastings, Dr. Donald Babcock Keyes, Mr. Charles E. McTiernan, Dr. Joseph Rossman, Mr. John L. Sigalos, Dr. Worth Wade, Mr. Virgil E. Woodcock, and several officials whom the editor is not privileged to name but will long remember, all of whom made fortunate suggestions of writers or reviewed a limited number of the manuscripts prepared by the editor; to Mr. Gessner G. Hawley, Executive Editor for Reinhold Publishing Corporation, friend and able guide on this project from its inception; to my efficient secretary Mrs. Marge D. Albrecht; Mr. Gerrit V. Crouse for editorial assistance; and to my wife, Mary, for recognizing and tolerating the obligations and limitations on normal life imposed by a project of this scope.

As three years of exacting but all-absorbing work draw to a close, I express this earnest and abiding hope: May this Encyclopedia make your work more convenient, accurate and effective. May it lengthen your days in this most difficult but also rewarding and exciting profession in which nothing is old, day after day, but novelty.

Scarsdale, New York   ROBERT CALVERT

Abbreviations for Selected Literature and Citations

Publications marked with an asterisk (*) are available from the U.S. Government Printing Office, Washington 25, D.C.

CA—Court of Appeals, e.g., CA 8 for the U.S. Court of Appeals for the 8th Circuit.

CCPA—U.S. Court of Customs and Patent Appeals in Patent Cases.

C.D.—Decisions of the Commissioner of Patents and selected decisions of the U.S. courts in Patent and Trademark cases. Published annually.*

DC—District Court, e.g., DC SNY for the District Court for the Southern District of New York.

Fed.—Federal Reporter, First Series. See below.

F.2d—Federal Reporter, Second Series. Twelve volumes a year. Decisions in the U.S. courts on cases of all classes. West Publishing Co., St. Paul 2, Minn.

F. Supp.—Supplement to the above, giving additional decisions of U.S. District Courts and U.S. Customs Court. West Publishing Co., supra.

JPOS—Journal of the Patent Office Society, Box 685, Washington 4, D.C. Published monthly.

L.Ed.—U.S. Supreme Court Reports (Lawyers Edition). Lawyers Cooperative Publishing Co., Rochester, N.Y.

M.P.E.P. (or Manual)—Manual of Patent Examination Procedure, third edition, Ernest A. Faller, Editor.*

O.G.—Official Gazette of the U.S. Patent Office. Published weekly.*

PO BdApp—Board of Appeals of U.S. Patent Office.

PTC J—Patent, Trademark, and Copyright Journal of Research and Education. The Patent, Trademark and Copyright Institute (previously Foundation), The George Washington University, Washington 6, D.C.

Rivise and Caesar—Charles W. Rivise and A. D. Caesar, Interference Law and Practice, four volumes. Michie Co., Charlottesville, Va., 1940.

Roster—Roster of Attorneys and Agents Registered to Practice before the U.S. Patent Office, with addresses.*

Rules—Rules of Practice of the United States Patent Office in Patent Cases.*

S.Ct.—Supreme Court Reporter. West Publishing Co., supra.

Shepard—Shepard's Federal Reporter Citations. Cases on Patents, Trademarks, Court Rules, etc. A compilation of citations. Shepard's Citations, Inc., Colorado Springs, Colo.

USPQ—The United States Patents Quarterly. Report of Cases Relating to Patents, Trademarks and Copyrights. Issued weekly and as four bound volumes and a Digest annually. Bureau of National Affairs, Inc., Washington 7, D.C.

Underwood—Card Digest of Patent and Trademark Cases. R. L. Underwood, Washington, D.C.

U.S.—U.S. Supreme Court Reports (of decisions by that Court).*

35 U.S.C.—U.S. Code of Laws, Title 35, Patents. The Patent Act of 1952.*

U.S.C.A.—U.S. Code Annotated. West Publishing Co., supra.

Walker—Walker on Patents, Deller's 2d ed., seven volumes, 1964-65. Baker, Voorhis and Co., Mount Kisco, N.Y.

Contents

The asterisk following the name of an author refers to his identification previously.

A

ABANDONMENT OF INVENTION AND TRADE SECRET

George S. Hastings

Abandonment by intent is relatively rare. Far more frequently abandonment occurs through acts omitted or performed too late by the inventor or owner. It is important, therefore, to know what causes abandonment and how to avoid it.

The Supreme Court has summarized the principal circumstances under which abandonment occurs in the following paragraph (from which case citations have been omitted):

"A patent is not validly issued if the invention is proved to have been abandoned. Abandonment may be evidenced by the express and voluntary declaration of the inventor; it may be inferred from negligence or unexplained delay in making application for patent; it may be declared as a consequence of the inventor's concealing his invention and delaying application for patent in an endeavor to extend the term of the patent protection beyond the period fixed by the statute. In any case the question whether the invention has been abandoned is one of fact." *Electric Storage Battery* v. *Shimadzu et al.,* 41 USPQ 155, 159, 1939.

Abandonments are considered here under the following main headings:
1. Abandonment to the public
2. Abandonment to other persons
3. Loss of rights by delay
4. Abandonment of trade secrets

Abandonment to the Public

35 U.S.C. 102 sets forth that a person meeting certain requirements, "[shall] be entitled to a patent unless . . .

"(b) the invention was patented or described in a printed publication in this or a foreign country or in public use or on sale in this country, more than one year prior to the date of the application for patent in the United States, or

"(c) he has abandoned the invention, or

"(d) the invention was first patented or caused to be patented by the applicant or his legal representatives or assigns in a foreign country prior to the date of the application for patent in this country on an application filed more than twelve months before the filing of the application in the United States. . . ."

Publication, Public Use or Sale over a Year before Filing. Under Section 102(b) any invention is abandoned to the public unless an application for patent is filed thereon within one year of the invention's being patented or described in a printed publication in any country or in public use or on sale in this country, whether by the inventor or another. For instance, a printed publication available only in a foreign language in a foreign library for more than a year before filing is sufficient to bar a patent. To prevent this kind of abandonment, corporate publicity and sales departments should make certain that company publications disclosing new or improved product details are considered by the patent attorneys before the material is released, so that patent applications may be filed within the one year period. In some countries known as "absolute novelty countries," such as France and Italy, an application must be filed, to secure a valid patent, before the date of the publication or public use in any country. On the other hand, public use or sale in a foreign country does not bar a U.S. applicant even though he files more than a year thereafter.

The abandonment referred to in 35 U.S.C. 102(b) is an absolute bar; once it is settled that there was publication anywhere or public use or sale in this country more than one year before filing, no amount of diligence or excuse can remedy the abandon-

1

ment. A possible solution in such a case is to study carefully the details of the alleged public use, publication or sale to determine whether it was in fact a true public use, whether it did disclose the invention as a whole and whether it actually came more than one year before the date of filing.

Public Use. In one case, an inventor sold a fabric treated with paraffin in a manner to restrict passage of water therethrough but not to waterproof the fabric entirely. He sold the product for use in making seeping, self-cooling water bags. More than a year later, another independent inventor filed for and obtained patent on this type of material. In the suit for infringement of the patent, it was urged by the patent owner that the product previously sold had failed, as shown by discontinuance of sale of it after two years. The Court said:

"When the defendant failed to patent his discovery [apply for patent] within one year after the bag had been sold commercially, the wax-impregnated cotton self-cooling water bag had been abandoned as a patentable device by either inventor or anyone else; and the discovery had been dedicated to the public domain." *H. Wenzel Tent and Duck Co.* v. *White Stag Mfg. Co. et al.,* 96 USPQ 25, CA 9 1952.

Another case of illustrating public use is that of an inventor who permitted use of his new stay in the corset of one whom he later married. She wore the corset with the new steels a long time. When it wore out, she transferred them to a new corset. Holding the use to be public, the Supreme Court said in part:

"... [To] constitute the public use of an invention it is not necessary that more than one of the patented articles should be publicly used....

"An invention may consist of a lever or spring, hidden in the running gear of a watch, or of a ratchet, shaft, or cog-wheel covered from view in the recesses of a machine for spinning or weaving. Nevertheless, if its inventor sells a machine of which his invention forms a part, and allows it to be used without restriction of any kind, the use is a public one. So, on the other hand, a use necessarily open to public view, if made in good faith solely to test the qualities of the invention, and for the purpose of experiment, is not a public use within the meaning of the statute." *Egbert* v. *Lippman,* 104 U.S. 333, 1881.

Ordinarily sale for profit is considered public use. On the other hand, use of an invention involving primarily the development of additional experimental data, as in a plant scale test of the invention, may be considered to be not public but experimental use.

Experimental Use Permissible. An extreme case of use held permissible is illustrated in the instance of wooden pavement laid on a toll road in the Boston area and driven upon by public vehicles for a period of several years. The inventor, who lived nearby, examined the pavement almost daily, walked across and tapped the pavement with his cane to determine, he said, the behavior of the pavement under load. He did not place the invention on sale for general use. The Supreme Court held the use to have been experimental. *Elizabeth* v. *The American Nicholson Pavement Co.,* 97 U.S. 126, 1878.

Secret Use More than Year before Filing. The status of an invention used secretly for profit for many years before being filed upon was decided in the *Macbeth-Evans Glass* case. The essential facts were as follows:

In 1903 George A. Macbeth discovered and perfected a process of making illuminating glass. In the fall of that year the company bearing his name began manufacture of the glass and continued to make and sell it up to and including filing the application for patent in 1913, the process being operated in secret. In 1910, however, one of the employees having the secret left the company and disclosed the process to the Jefferson Glass Co. Macbeth obtained a court order enjoining further manufacture by Jefferson.

The filing of the application for patent in 1913, long after manufacture by Macbeth had begun, came after Macbeth became apprehensive that the secret was about to be lost.

These facts were set forth as a defense by General Electric whom Macbeth later sued for infringement.

Attempting to offset this set of facts, Macbeth urged that the use was *not public* and that there was clearly *no intent to abandon* the invention. In fact, Macbeth had taken unusual precautions to preserve the secrecy of it. The court noted that:

"The question is whether one who has discovered and perfected an invention can employ it secretly for more than nine years for purposes only of profit, and then, upon encountering difficulty in preserving his secret, rightfully secure a patent, and thus in effect extend his previous monopoly for the further period fixed by the patent laws."

The court answered the question in the negative. It held the patent void because of abandonment through secret use for profit for more than a year before filing of the application. *Macbeth-Evans Glass Co.* v. *General Electric Co.*, 1918 C.D. 239; 246 F.2d 695, CA 6 1917.

Abandonment through Failure to Claim. Probably the greatest source of abandoned inventions to the public results from failure to claim all that is inventive in the disclosure of the patent. That which is disclosed but not claimed is abandoned. Quite often, such abandonment results because the inventor does not understand his invention fully. Sometimes things may be lost in communication between the inventor and his attorney; or through insufficient study, claims are drawn to that which is not patentable, while what is patentable is overlooked. In general, if something not obvious to those of ordinary skill in the art and not shown in the prior art is disclosed and *not claimed* in an application, there is a dedication or abandonment of the unclaimed part to the public. Under some circumstances this can be remedied by reissue within the two year period for broadened reissue (see *Reissues*). But the better remedy is a search of the art and a thorough understanding of what the invention is all about, by the inventor and the attorney, before filing the application.

Abandonment in Prosecution. Another common way of inadvertently dedicating inventions to the public occurs during prosecution. Subject matter cancelled as whole claims or by limitation of claims during prosecution of an application is abandoned unless the applicant files another case claiming such subject matter, before his first patent disclosing it issues. *Cf. Traitel Marble*

Co. v. *Hungerford Brass and Copper Co.*, 22 F.2d 259, 261, CA 2 1927.

Some courts hold that the applicant is not estopped by his arguments, if he makes or argues certain limitations or interpretations of a claim in order to get it allowed even though they may not be necessary to the claim. Other courts hold him to the limitation or interpretation (see *File Wrapper Estoppel*). It is important that practitioners in amending a claim and arguing the amendment, consider the effect on a court construing the claim. If a claim is cancelled, it is desirable to point out that the subject matter is embodied in other claim(s) or in another application of the inventor and thus seek to avoid the impression that the particular subject matter is being abandoned.

Express Abandonment (35 U.S.C. 102[c]). Generally express abandonment is for some ulterior purpose. Sometimes it is in favor of a continuation application, filed to better the invention of the first application. In such case there is abandonment of an application but not the invention. When a government employee dedicates his patent for free use by the government or the public, he abandons whatever rights he has against the government or the public.

Another type of dedication is express abandonment or disclaimer of whole claim or claims, either to terminate an interference proceeding or to cancel a claim that has been held invalid. Under the statutes, the patentee must abandon the claims known from the record to be invalid before he can sustain a suit on the other claims. 35 U.S.C. 253 permits the disclaimer of a whole claim but not a part of a claim. (See *Disclaimers*)

Another, less obvious express abandonment occurs when a contractor enters into an R&D contract with a U.S. Government agency, which requires that the contractor abandon all rights against the government to inventions of contractor made under the contract, as in Section 9-107 of the Armed Services Procurement Regulations. Some agencies require all title be abandoned except for a non-exclusive license to the contractor.

Letter of Abandonment Received after Application Is Allowed. "When the final fee has been paid and the patent to issue has received its date and number, the abandonment may not be accepted without a showing of the reasons for such a late abandonment. Approval of the Commissioner is necessary." M.P.E.P. 711.05.

This becomes important when, after payment of the final fee, it is decided that the invention is insufficiently covered and it is desired to file a continuation. Presumably, a timely and specific showing that the invention was not covered adequately should be sufficient to secure such approval.

Dedication or Abandonment through Misfiling. An invention can be permanently lost to the public through double patenting, that is, claiming *the same invention* in two patents, resulting generally in the later one being held invalid. The theory is that the public should not be put twice in jeopardy on the same invention and that the monopoly granted in the first should not be prolonged by later issuance of the second. Two copending applications, one on the generic invention and another on a species or a specific subcombination disclosed in the generic case, do not necessarily result in loss of the patent on the genus even if the copending genus application is issued later; the applicant should be prepared, however, to point out clearly the specific patentable differences between the *claims* of the two applications. *Pierce* v. *American Communications Co., Inc.*, 97 USPQ 60, DC Mass 1953. Safer practice is to file the generic case first and where possible, issue it first or simultaneously with the species case, to avoid prolonging the monopoly. (See *Double Patenting*)

Abandonment because Patented Abroad by Inventor. The U.S. application should be filed within the twelve month Convention period following the first foreign filing or the inventor delay issuance of the foreign patent until after filing his U.S. application. The former procedure is obviously the safer.

Invalidation for Violation of Secrecy Requirements. A secrecy order against filing an application abroad in effect prohibits the export of information on subjects considered to involve the national security. If no such order is issued within six months after filing an application, the Patent Office having had this time to examine and determine whether the nature of the information is such as to justify a secrecy order, the applicant is free to file abroad.

In case an applicant (1) violates a secrecy order, or (2) files abroad within six months of the U.S. filing date, without getting a license for the foreign filing, any patent that may issue to him in this country on the same subject matter "shall be invalid" and thus, in effect, is abandoned. There is also a fine for violation of a secrecy order. In case of inadvertent filing and in the absence of such order, a retroactive license to file abroad may be requested. 35 U.S.C. 181-187. Rules of Practice of U.S. Patent Office in Patent Cases 5.1-5.18.

Abandonment through Failure to Record an Agreement Terminating an Interference. Under the amendment to 35 U.S.C. 135 of October 15, 1962 (Public Law 87-831), failure to record with the Commissioner of Patents an agreement terminating an interference "shall render permanently unenforceable such agreement or understanding and any patent of such parties involved in the interference or any patent subsequently issued on any application of such parties so involved."

Abandonment in Favor of Another Person or Inventor

35 U.S.C. 102 states

"A person shall be entitled to a patent unless...

"(g) before the applicant's invention thereof the invention was made in this country by another who had not abandoned, suppressed, or concealed it. In determining priority of invention there shall be considered not only the respective dates of conception and reduction to practice of the invention, but also the reasonable diligence of one who was first to conceive and last to reduce to practice, from a time prior to conception by the other."

Abandonment before Reduction to Practice. An invention becomes abandoned when work upon it terminates before the invention is reduced to practice either (1) physically or (2) constructively by filing an application for patent disclosing the invention. This is not however the absolute bar type of abandonment since the inventor can at any time file an application for patent and obtain a patent to the invention provided no other person has filed who meets the requirements as to priority of invention under 35 U.S.C. 102(g). (See *Interference*)

Actual reduction to practice has been defined by Chief Justice Taft in the *Rubber Accelerator* case as follows:

"A process is reduced to practice when it is successfully performed. A machine is reduced to practice when it is assembled, adjusted and used. A manufacture is reduced to practice when it is completely manufactured. A composition of matter is reduced to practice when it is completely composed." *Corona Cord Tire Co.* v. *Dovan Chemical Corp.,* 276 U.S. 358 1927.

Test under Service Conditions. For actual reduction to practice, it is necessary in many instances not only to complete a workable form of the invention but also to test it with satisfactory results under service conditions.

Such a test, under circumstances that bring into play the various conditions that arise in the commercial use of the article, is frequently more persuasive in proving reduction to practice than more informative tests with laboratory apparatus. However, if testing is done under conditions which make it obvious that the device would work for commercial use, the testing has been held adequate.

In a leading case, the invention was a "cut out" variety of automobile lighter for cigars or the like. In 1933 Sinko and his assistants, experts in the lighter field, made the lighter in form that, a few years later, was manufactured extensively and used successfully. But they did not test the lighter in an automobile at the date which they claimed for reduction to practice. In this case that fine Judge Learned Hand said:

"... [A] test under service conditions is necessary in those cases, and in those cases only in which persons qualified in the art would require such test before selling the invention, as it stands." *Sinko Tool and Mfg. Co.* v. *Automatic Devices Corp.,* 71 USPQ 199, CA 2 1946.

Sinko won the case. Nevertheless, it would have been safer for Sinko to have tested the lighter in an automobile.

The conclusion is that the inventor relying on actual reduction to practice should not only make a physical embodiment of

his invention but test it under conditions as near service or commercial as practical. If such reduction to practice is not practical, the remedy is to reduce to practice constructively by promptly filing an application for patent.

Abandonment after Reduction to Practice. After actual reduction to practice, there is then no "race of diligence" in filing the application. Yet early filing is desirable, if only to avoid the heavy burden of proof on the junior party in an interference.

A delay of five years after making the invention and before filing the application was held not to constitute abandonment when the testimony showed that the period "was one of continuous activity, primarily centered around Gross' [the plaintiff's] efforts to overcome certain technical objections of plaintiff's merchandising department." *Johnson and Johnson* v. *C. B. Stenvall, Inc.,* 129 USPQ 120, DC SNY 1961.

The intent during the period is controlling. Objective factors of significance would seem to include such conditions as lack of customer interest, unavailability of a necessary material, military service of the inventor during the period of delay, or any circumstance negativing the implication that the inventor intended to withhold the invention permanently from the public.

Research results and invention, being of a confidential nature, are ordinarily not disclosed at the time outside the inventor's organization. When nondisclosure for a considerable period of time is coupled with resumption of activity only after learning of the entrance of another into the field, the result is the combination of *suppression or concealment and stimulation.* This combination of conditions occurred in the case in which Mason invented a clip for a gun, tested it and then laid it aside for many years until learning that another party, Hepburn, had independently made the same invention and obtained a patent on it. *Mason* v. *Hepburn,* 1898 C.D. 510, Comr. Pats., 12 App DC 96. The Commissioner said:

"Considering, then, this paramount interest of the public in its bearing upon the question as presented here, we think it imperatively demands that a subsequent inventor of a new and useful manufacture or improvement who had diligently pursued his labors to the procurement of a patent in good faith and without any knowledge of the preceding discoveries of another shall, *as against that other, who has deliberately concealed the knowledge of his invention from the public, be regarded as the real inventor* and as such entitled to his reward." (Emphasis added.)

The question remains as to how an inventor may avoid such abandonment of a set-aside invention so long as he has a good reason for not making his invention available to the public. While he is perfecting it, studying the market, or endeavoring to raise capital, he reduces the danger of abandonment under the doctrine of *Mason* v. *Hepburn* and similar cases. The passage of a relatively long period of time, after all activity has ceased, is likely to be considered suppression or concealment, with resulting abandonment. When all activity with respect to a completed invention has been discontinued, the safe procedure is to file upon it. To promote such disclosure to the public is, in fact, a primary object of the patent system.

Loss of Rights to Public or Individual through Delay—Intervening Rights

Delay in Claiming. Let us consider the case in which the application disclosed the subject matter in good time but did not claim the device, later alleged to infringe, until said device had been in use more than a year before a claim covering it was inserted into the application. On this point it has been held

"The claims in suit [for infringement] in Patent No. 2,695,028 were not presented until more than one year after plaintiff's accused containers were in public use or on sale in this country and after Dulberg [the patentee] had knowledge thereof and are therefore invalid." *Scoville Mfg. Co.* v. *Dulberg* [and consolidated cases], 129 USPQ 134, 145, DC SNY 1960.

See *Delay in Claiming* and *Reissues—Intervening Rights.*

Acquiescence in Continued Infringement. Acquiescence in continued known infringement leads to abandonment of the patent through what is commonly known as laches (q.v.) or sleeping on one's rights.

An example of this is the case in which the patentee and patent owner sold the product for the alleged infringer, his employer, prior to filing the application and after issuance of the patent. The court said:

"The failure of the defendant to assert patent rights against the plaintiff, his employer, for four years, during all of which time he was selling for plaintiff the goods which he now claims infringes his patent, shows that he abandoned such rights." *Victor Talking Mach. Co.* v. *Brunswick-Balke-Collender Co.,* 290 F. 565, 575; aff. 8 F.2d 41, CA 8 1926; *Rubenstein* v. *Slobotkin,* 33 F.2d 603, 608, DC ENY 1929.

Abandonment of Trade Secrets

The question of abandonment of trade secrets often arises in cases involving patent rights. Trade secrets are abandoned to the general public when openly disclosed by the supplier of the secret information, by the issuance of a patent or by a label that discloses the secret. Such disclosure is useless, however, as a defense to a party who (a) has obtained the information illegally to the extent of his use of it in advance of such disclosure, or (b) is under a contract containing no provision for termination of payments on such disclosure. *Warner Lambert Pharmaceutical Co., Inc.* v. *John J. Reynolds, Inc. et al.,* 123 USPQ 431; aff. 126 USPQ 3, CA 2 1960.

When a patent on the secret is held valid, the question of continuing obligation to pay for use of the information may be moot, as the patentee may then rely on his patent rights.

The question of abandonment of trade secrets upon issuance of patent disclosing them arose in the foaming shaving cream case. Here the defendant in the infringement suit, Colgate-Palmolive, had employed Fine, a former employee of Foster D. Snell, Inc., consultants who had developed the cream for Carter Products. Fine was under secrecy contract and was one of the patentees of the product for Carter. He began with Colgate about three years before the patent issued. The court held that Colgate had wrongly appropriated confidential information. The court further said,

"... [It] was held by the Second Circuit Court of Appeals [in an earlier case] that a contract binding the employee to secrecy imposed secrecy only until the issue of the patent involved.... in the Sixth and Seventh circuits however, it has been held otherwise.... We believe that the rule followed by the Second Circuit is the correct one...."

Occasionally, the trade secrets are of such a nature that adequate patent claims cannot be obtained or would be difficult to enforce because of the problem of detection if used by an infringer in his own plant. To avoid such abandonment, it is sometimes desirable, paradoxically, to abandon the patent application, in order to avoid abandoning the trade secret.

Conclusion

Timing is of the essence in avoiding abandonments. The statutes, courts and Patent Office hold the applicant for a patent to a time table more closely probably than any other branch of law.

The rewards for prompt and complete compliance with the statutes, rules and decisions above set forth are high; the penalties for failure to do so are harsh.

Where there is a statutory time limit for an action, allow time for correction of slip-ups such as delays in the mail, wrong addressing, lack of response, inadvertent omission of papers and payments, errors and the like.

Reference

Meigs, J. V., "Time, the Essence of Patent Law," New York, Baker Voorhis & Co., Inc., 1940.

Cross-references: *Dedication, Delay in Claiming, Disclaimers, Interferences.*

ACCOUNTING AFTER INFRINGEMENT SUITS—DAMAGES, ATTORNEYS' FEES, COURT COSTS

Alfred E. Wilson and Edward A. Craig

Elements of Recovery in a Patent Infringement Suit

The statute, Title 35 U.S.C., defines the elements of recovery in a patent infringement suit. Section 281 provides for civil action by the patentee; Section 283 for an injunction to prevent further infringement; Section 284 for recovery by the patentee (actually the patent owner at the time) of damages not less than a reasonable royalty, together with interest and costs, and for total damages that may be increased by the court up to three times the amount found; Section 285 for award by the court, in exceptional cases, of reasonable attorney fees to the prevailing party; Section 286 for limitation of the period for recovery to not more than 6 years prior to filing the claim or counterclaim for infringement; and Section 289 for additional remedy in design patent cases.

The decisions indicate that the courts may apply, as a measure of damages, a "reasonable royalty," the defendant's profits gained as a result of the infringement or the plaintiff's lost business.

Reasonable Royalty

A reasonable royalty may be either an established royalty or a judicial determination of what a reasonable royalty would be.

An established royalty generally is one which has been provided for in licenses granted by the patent owner, but the licenses must meet the qualifications enumerated in several cases in order to be considered as establishing a standard for a royalty rate. The following are the principal criteria:

1. More than one license must have been granted before the infringement.

2. The licenses must have provided for uniform royalties.

3. The licenses must relate to rights infringed.

4. The license must have been granted under circumstances which show that the royalty was representative of the value of the patent.

In *Faulkner* v. *Gibbs*, 199 F.2d 635, CA 9 1952 plaintiff sued on a patent for a game device consisting of a plurality of electrically interconnected game units arranged in banks. A single unit was operated by separate players who competed with players operating other units in the multiple assembly.

Defendant operated two 16-bank units which infringed plaintiff's patent. The court stated that where an established royalty is shown it is the best measure of the value of what was taken by the infringement. The court further indicated that in order to establish a royalty it must be acquiesced in by a number of persons to indicate general acceptance of its reasonableness, and it must be uniform at the places where the licenses were issued. Royalties paid in connection with a threat of litigation are not taken as a standard of reasonable royalty. The court further stated that if an established royalty cannot be proved, damages may be ascertained by proving what would have been a reasonable royalty.

Items to be considered in establishing a reasonable royalty are the nature of the invention, its utility and advantages, and the extent of the use involved. A reasonable royalty is stated to be a question of fact. It is the amount which a person who desires to use the patent would be willing to pay as a royalty and still make a profit. There is no exact mathematical formula for the determination of a reasonable royalty. The facts vary, and the courts are conservative in fixing the amount because of the guesswork involved. They consider gross receipts or profits of the infringer and royalties paid in similar circumstances.

In the Faulkner case, supra, ten written license agreements had been entered into. Of these, one had been made in settlement of an accounting proceeding and five in compromise of infringement suits or claims. Only two were in effect when the defendant began his infringement litigation. These licenses were not accepted as being sufficient to prove an established royalty.

In another case, *United States National Bank* v. *Fabri-Valve Co.*, 235 F.2d 565, CA 9 1956, plaintiff sued for infringement of a patent relating to a gate valve. The patent was found to be valid and infringed. The trial court decided that a reasonable royalty would be 1½ per cent. The plaintiff had granted licenses at a 5 per cent rate, and the Court of Appeals raised the 1½ per cent figure to 5 per cent, the established royalty which is the ordinary, correct measure of damages. The trial court's reduction to 1½

per cent was based on the fact that the patented structure was only a minor improvement in a highly developed art. The Circuit Court said that although it might be a minor improvement, the plaintiff could still get 5 per cent on the open market which gave a good indication of its value.

In another case, *Hartford National Bank & Trust Co.* v. *E. F. Drew & Co.*, 188 F. Supp. 353, DC Del 1960, the defendant sold vitamin products which included vitamin D_3 produced in accordance with plaintiff's patented process. The Special Master decided damages on the basis of an established royalty, but applied the royalty to only a portion of the product because the D_3 formed only a portion of the final product. The court applied the royalty to the whole product because the sale of the product containing D_3 was believed to have resulted solely because the D_3 was present. The court rejected what appeared to be an established royalty because this royalty was not reasonable. It was lower than it might have been if defendant had not ignored plaintiff's patent.

Judicially Determined Royalty

If an established royalty does not exist, a reasonable royalty may be determined by the court. The general statement is made that a reasonable royalty is an amount which the parties would probably have agreed on if plaintiff were willing to grant a license and defendant wished to obtain one, neither party being compelled to do so, and where both parties were trying to reach an agreement.

In *Laskowitz* v. *Marie Designer Inc.*, 119 F. Supp. 541, DC Calif 1954, several problems were involved (infringement of patent, trademark and trade name, and unfair competition). The plaintiff asked for an injunction and damages. Defendant filed a counterclaim seeking damages for infringement of copyrighted advertising material. The court found in favor of the plaintiff on the issue of patent infringement of a design patent, and stated on page 554:

"The award of compensatory damages for patent infringement is mandatory under the statute, and while the court may increase them and also award punitive damages when oppression or fraudulent conduct on the part of the defendant is shown to exist, the exercise of this power is discretionary. Whatever may have been the practice prior to the recent statutory amendments, the general damages now recoverable are the detriment suffered by the plaintiff through the infringement. The profits of the infringer may be the measure when no other is adequate. Whichever determinative method is used, the aim is to 'compensate (the plaintiff) for the infringement,' as the statute declares specifically. And when the profits or a reasonable royalty is chosen as a basis, there is no room for the award of other damages. In ascertaining damages, the object has always been to approximate, as nearly as possible, the actual loss suffered by the patentee."

An example of dividing the infringement into separate periods is shown in *Russell Box Co.* v. *Grant Paper Box Co.*, 203 F.2d 177, CA 1 1953. Defendant was found to have infringed claim 3 of a patent owned by plaintiff for a moisture-vapor proof container wall for the packaging of materials. It consisted essentially of two sheets of paper bonded together by a sheet or film of amorphous petroleum. The court divided the infringement into three time periods. Plaintiff issued no licenses during the first period, consequently the damages were calculated on the basis of a judicially determined royalty. Plaintiff had been paying the inventor a royalty of $8.30 per ton with a minimum yearly payment of $5,000.00. These payments were accepted as the basis for a reasonable royalty. During the second time period, licenses had been issued but the court found them to be "so specialized in character as not to constitute an established royalty." However, the court used the royalties fixed in these licenses as the basis for establishing a reasonable royalty of $5.00 per ton with a minimum annual payment of $5,000.00. Licenses issued during the third time period were found to constitute the basis of an established royalty of $3.00 per ton with a minimum annual payment of $1,000.00. The court also increased the damages by an amount equal to 50 per cent plus an award of attorney's fees. This was done even though defendant believed it was not infringing because this belief was "due to carelessness in ascertaining the facts,

carelessness in construing claim 3 or a combination of the two."

The significance of the improvement wrought by the invention may also be considered in establishing a reasonable royalty. In *Randolph Laboratories, Inc.* v. *Specialties Development Corp.*, 213 F.2d 873, CA 3 1954, Randolph was found to have infringed Specialties' patent relating to recoil prevention safety devices on carbon dioxide fire extinguishers. The Master found that a reasonable royalty would be 7 per cent of total sales or $263,312.40. The Court of Appeals reduced this figure to 2 per cent or $75,232.12 because the patented device did not dominate the use or salability of fire extinguishers. Plaintiff had offered defendant a license at 3 per cent. The Court of Appeals found that 3 per cent was established in the industry as a reasonable royalty for the use of the essential device of a patent dominating the field. Plaintiff's patent, although not dominating the field, was superior to the ball check valve with which it competed.

In *Filtex Corporation* v. *Amen Atiyeh*, 216 F.2d 443, CA 9 1954, plaintiff (appellee) invented a device to be used as a nozzle for cleaners. The court found that the defendant (appellant) produced an infringing nozzle and that the infringement was willful and deliberate, that the patented device of the plaintiff was disclosed to the defendant in confidence and that the defendant appropriated it to his own use. The Master determined that a reasonable royalty would be 10 per cent. Defendant claimed that this was too high. The court stated that there are many factors which determine a reasonable royalty other than the precise improvement. But when the defendant is a wrongdoer, the court is not required to exercise meticulous care to avoid hardship on him. The court also awarded plaintiff reasonable attorney's fees.

A reasonable royalty is usually stated as a per cent of the price received by the infringer on the sale of the patented device. However, the patented device may be integrated with other unpatented features to form the complete unit. The question then arises as to whether the value of the patented and unpatented features should be divided. This created a complicated problem of apportionment of profits under the old law. A good examination of this problem and statement of the applicable law was given in *Swan Carburetor Co.* v. *Nash Motors Co.*, 133 F.2d 562, CA 4 1943.

In this case, defendant infringed plaintiff's patent relating to the inlet manifold of an internal combustion engine. The court found that the profits due to the manifold could not be apportioned from those due to the sale of the entire car. Therefore, a reasonable royalty was decreed. The court stated that the rule of placing the burden on the defendant when profits cannot be apportioned between a patented device used with unpatented structures does not apply when he uses the patented structure without change as part only of a larger machine and there is no practicable way in which apportionment records may be kept. The court stated that 20 outstanding licenses established a royalty which was a proper basis for damages. $80,250.20 was granted as damages for 349,019 manifolds mounted as part of motor cars.

However, the apportionment rule is not being applied in the later cases. The rule seems to be that the royalty rate will apply to the entire value of the structure incorporating the infringing feature as defined by the claims. The nature of the patented invention and its relationship to the entire structure as a whole is taken into consideration when fixing a reasonable royalty. The percentage of royalties should be scaled down in accordance with these principles. *Enterprise Mfg. Co.* v. *Shakespeare Co.*, 141 F.2d 916, CA 6 1944.

Profits of Defendant

Under the law in effect prior to the 1946 Act, the plaintiff was entitled to either the damages he sustained or the profits made by the infringer. A large body of law developed relative to methods of determining plaintiff's loss or defendant's profit. Part of this body of law concerns using a reasonable royalty as a measure of damages. A reasonable royalty was awarded only in cases where profits or loss could not be definitely ascertained. Profits and loss were the primary measure of the infringer's liability.

The 1946 Act apparently was designed to eliminate infringer's profits as an element of damages. However, several cases hold to the contrary. In a recent case, *Ric-Wil Co.* v. *E. B. Kaiser Co.*, 179 F.2d 401 CA 7 1950, the court stated that while profits per se could not form the basis of damages, they might be included as an element of "general damages" depending on the circumstances of the case. The same rule was stated in *Faulkner* v. *Gibbs*, supra.

In *Graham* v. *Jeoffroy Mfg.*, 253 F.2d 72, CA 5 1958, the court stated that "the profits made by the infringer from his improper use of the infringing device may be the measure of damages suffered, even though the statute does not prescribe that profits are to be recovered as such." The court then proceeded to award the plaintiff $64,407.59 which was the exact profit made in defendant's manufacture and sale of 1,863 plows.

In another case, *Zysset* v. *Popeil Brothers, Inc.*, 134 USPQ 222, DC Ill 1962, the court made the bald statement that "it is well established that a patent owner in a patent infringement action is entitled to recover the profits which the infringer has made by reason of his infringement."

There is therefore some confusion as to what the significance of the defendant's profits should be in determining damages. The trend seems to be to determine damages on the basis of a reasonable royalty. Whether this is due to the court's reluctance to accept any other measure or to the practical difficulty presented by the problem of establishing other damages is not clear.

In *U.S. National Bank* v. *Fabri-Valve Co.*, supra, the court made the broad statement, citing Section 284, that the primary method of assessing damages for infringement of a patent is using the patentee's established royalties as a measure of those damages.

Plaintiff's Lost Business

It would seem clear that, in a proper case, the damages may be determined by some standard other than royalties or defendant's profits, e.g., business loss by the plaintiff or destruction of his competitive position. *Krieger* v. *Colby*, 106 F. Supp. 124, DC

Calif 1952, indicates that a reasonable royalty is not necessarily the measure of damages. The patentee was awarded damages for infringement of his design patent which damages were higher than a reasonable royalty would have been.

In the Krieger case, the court stated that Section 284 which provides that a successful plaintiff in a patent infringement action may recover compensation for the making, using, or selling his invention, of not less than a reasonable royalty therefor, is applicable to design patents. A successful plaintiff in such an action is not limited to recovery of $250.00 under Section 289 which specifically refers to design patents. This Section provides that the violator shall be liable in an amount of $250.00 and the excess of profits over $250.00 if the total profit from manufacture and sale exceeds $250.00. The defendant in this case paid a third person $1,000.00 for the right to use a certain name on the infringing cap. The court held that the use of the design would be worth as much as the use of the name. The plaintiff was awarded general damages of $1,000.00 rather than being awarded a reasonable royalty which in this case was found to be 10 per cent of gross sales. This would have been a smaller amount.

Increased Damages

The award of increased damages under Section 284, up to three times the amount found, is within the discretion of the court and will not be disturbed unless it can be shown that this discretion was abused. The cases indicate that the courts will not apply this provision unless the infringement was conscious, deliberate and wilful.

For example, in *E-I-M Company* v. *Philadelphia Gear Works*, 223 F.2d 36, CA 5 1955, defendant violated an injunction restraining him from further infringement of a patent for a valve operator owned by the plaintiff. The District Court held the defendant in contempt and awarded the patentee double damages. The Court of Appeals stated that ordinarily an award of double damages for wilful and deliberate infringement of patents is within the sound discretion of the District Court. However,

the finding that the infringement was wilful and deliberate should be delayed until final judgment after an accounting has been had so that the nature and extent of the infringement can be disclosed.

Merely questioning the validity of a patent or making an honest mistake as to whether there is a reasonable question of validity is usually not found to be grounds for applying increased damages. (*Enterprise Mfg. Co.* v. *Shakespeare Co.*, 141 F.2d 916, CA 6 1944). However, the question of increased damages rests in the discretion of the court. In *Russell Box Co.* v. *Grant Paper Co.*, supra, damages were awarded where the defendant's belief that it was not infringing was found to be due to carelessness. The defendant in this case also failed to preserve its records and cooperate on the issue of damages.

A somewhat different view is stated in *Armstrong* v. *Emerson Radio & Phonograph Corp.*, 132 F. Supp. 176, DC NY 1955, where it was held that the provision for treble damages is remedial, and damages may be increased whether the infringement was intentional or unwitting. However, this view does not seem to have been followed. In the same District at a later date, wilful infringement was indicated as being necessary to justify increased damages and the court was reluctant to find the infringement wilful. In *Upjohn Co.* v. *Italian Drugs Importing Co.*, 190 F. Supp. 361, DC NY 1961, the holding was that there must be a deliberate purpose to infringe and such a purpose is not found where the validity of the patent and any possible infringement is open to honest doubt.

Interest

The rule as stated in *Swan Carburetor Co.* v. *Nash Motor Co.*, supra, citing authorities, is that interest on damages ascertained on the basis of an established royalty runs from the time the royalty should have been paid, while interest on damages calculated on the basis of a judicially determined reasonable royalty does not begin to run, in the absence of special circumstances, until the amount of the damages has been judicially ascertained and liquidated. The rule as to interest on unliquidated damages was recently reaffirmed in *Randolph Laboratories Inc.* v. *Specialties Development Corp.,* supra.

Special circumstances which will start interest running on damages before they become liquidated depend on the facts peculiar to each case. In *Samson United Corp.* v. *F. A. Smith Mfg. Co.,* 68 USPQ 266, interest was applied to the damages at a point before judicial determination of the damages where the defendant continued to infringe after notice of infringement and after obtaining knowledge that the Court of Appeals had sustained the infringed patent in two other suits.

Special circumstances were also found in *Chesapeake & O. Ry. Co.* v. *Kaltenbach,* 124 F.2d 375, CA 4 1941, where the defendant appropriated the unique features of plaintiff's invention from blue prints accompanying a bid submitted by the plaintiff to the defendant on the building of a dumper. Exceptional circumstances were also found in *Mathey* v. *United Shoe Machinery Corp.,* 54 F. Supp. 694, DC Mass 1944, where the infringer offered its infringing machine to customers at such low prices that it would ruin the patentee as the only competitor in a distinctive field over which the patentee would have had a monopoly except for the defendant's tortuous conduct.

Costs

Costs may amount to a substantial sum in a lengthy trial. Federal Rules of Civil Procedure 54 (d), 28 U.S.C.A., provides for the allowance of costs: "Except when express provision therefor is made either in a statute of the United States or in these rules, costs should be allowed as of course to the prevailing party unless the court otherwise directs." Title 28, Section 1920 provides as follows for the items comprising costs:

"A judge or clerk of any court of the United States may tax as costs the following:

"1. Fees of the clerk or marshal;

"2. Fees of the court reporter for all or any part of the stenographic transcript necessarily obtained for use in the case;

"3. Fees and disbursements for printing and witnesses;

"4. Fees for exemplification and copies of papers necessarily obtained for use in the case;

"5. Docket fees under Section 1923 of this Title.

"A bill of costs shall be filed in the case and, upon allowance included in the judgment or decree."

In *Texas Co.* v. *Globe Oil & Refining Co.,* 114 F. Supp. 144, DC Ill 1953, the statutory costs amounted to $64,068.53. They consisted principally of Master's fees, court reporter charges and printing bills. Plaintiff's patent was found valid but not infringed. Plaintiff had overcome some of defendant's arguments maintained that consequently the costs should be divided. The court held that this was not sufficient reason to vary the statutory direction to award costs to the prevailing party as a matter of course.

The costs were divided between the parties in *Dixie Cup* v. *Paper Container Mfg. Co.,* 174 F.2d 834, CA 7 1949. However, in this case plaintiff had sued on several patents. Plaintiff prevailed on some patents and defendant prevailed on others.

Costs beyond those enumerated in the statute may be taxed in exceptional circumstances under general equity rules. This rule is applied only in cases where fraud, oppression, or bad faith exist or in cases of fiduciary relationship or those in which the prevailing party has helped to create the fund upon which the costs are charged. Costs of a model used by defendant as evidence did not fall under statutory costs nor under the general equity rule in *Specialty Equipment and Machine Corporation* v. *Zell Motor Car Co.,* 193 F.2d 515, CA 4 1952.

Attorney's Fees

As previously indicated, attorney's fees are statutorily provided for in Section 285. The attorney's fees may be allowed to either the plaintiff or the defendant.

The criteria for awarding attorney's fees is somewhat similar to that for awarding increased damages. That is, there must be some conduct on the part of either the plaintiff or the defendant which justifies the award. As stated in part in *Park-In-The-atres* v. *Perkins*, 190 F.2d 137, CA 9 1951:

"The exercise of discretion in favor of such an allowance should be bottomed upon a finding of unfairness or bad faith in the conduct of the losing party, or some other equitable consideration of similar force which makes it grossly unjust that the winner of the particular lawsuit be left to bear the burden of his own counsel fees which prevailing litigants normally bear. The cases support this view."

The court, in *Parker Rust Proof* v. *Ford Motor Co.*, 23 F.2d 502, DC Mich 1928, awarded attorney's fees in the amount of $98,000.00 to the plaintiff because this was expense that was unnecessarily forced upon the plaintiff during the trial. In *Blanc* v. *Spartan Tool Co.*, 178 F.2d 104, CA 7 1949, attorney's fees were awarded to the defendant because of the character of the patent involved, the construction of the defendant's device, and the adverse decisions of other courts in relation to the patents involved prior to the institution of the suit.

Defendant was awarded attorney's fees in *Dubil* v. *Rayford Camp & Co.*, 184 F.2d 899, CA 9 1950 because the plaintiff was guilty of unreasonable prolongation of the trial and was also guilty of fraud in the Patent Office in obtaining the patent. This case has been cited repeatedly for the following propositions:

(1) Award of attorney's fees is within the discretion of the trial court.

(2) When the trial court exercises its discretion, it must give reasons.

(3) The Appellate Court should not interfere with this exercise of discretion except where there is an abuse of the discretion amounting to caprice or an erroneous conception of law.

Where the court finds that the litigation is vexatious and unjustified on the part of the plaintiff, attorney's fees may be awarded to the defendant. For example, in *Seismograph Service Corp.* v. *Offshore Raydist*, 263 F.2d 5, CA 5 1958, attorney's fees were awarded to the defendant where one of the two patents sued on was invalid and the other, though valid, was unenforceable because of plaintiff's unclean hands. These fees were awarded by the Appeal Court

after the trial court had in its discretion refused to award such fees.

Attorney's Fees Awarded—Summary for Ten Cases—Amounts when Prevailing Party Was

Plaintiff	Defendant
$30,000	$ 2,500↑
98,000	500
3,000	22,000
7,500	15,000
	7,500
	5,000

Accounting after Infringement

When the validity of plaintiff's patent has been upheld and the defendant has been found to have infringed, the case is normally referred to a Master for an accounting. The accounting usually involves both the mechanics of "bookkeeping" and a determination of the rule of damages to be applied. Each of these factors may involve difficulties. As will be noted in the cases cited supra, in ascertaining damages the Master may consider the defendant's profits, the plaintiff's loss, and the royalty situation with reference to the particular item or process under consideration. This latter factor will involve considering the established royalty, if any, and the subjective concept of what a reasonable royalty would be.

An excellent example of the problems involved in an accounting is *Hartford Nat. Bank & Trust Co.* v. *E. F. Drew Co.*, supra. After the trial at which validity and infringement were found (133 F. Supp. 653, 1955) the court merely stated "Plaintiffs are also entitled to an award of damages for defendant's infringement. As this opinion contains the required findings and conclusions, an order may now be submitted by plaintiffs after notice." It is assumed that the order was submitted and approved, resulting in the appointment of a Master. The Master had only the opinion relating to the finding of validity and infringement as a guide. It was his job to make a finding relating to the extent of damages to be awarded to plaintiff. The Master's report indicated three theories of damages which might be followed (reasonable royalty, established royalty, and profits earned by the infringer).

The Master applied the theory of the established royalty and awarded plaintiff primary damages of $28,307.47. He then found that defendant's infringement was wilful and concluded that the damages should be doubled and that defendant should pay plaintiffs' reasonable attorney's fees of $19,150.00, disbursements of $1,574.65 and interest from the date when the royalty payments would have been paid had defendant taken the license which he had been offered.

The court subsequently modified the Master's proposed findings of damages. However, it will be appreciated that the Master's task involved considerably more than the problem of bookkeeping.

The court may, of course, indicate to the Master what rule of damages should be followed. For example, in *Berry Bros. Corp.* v. *Sigmon*, 134 USPQ 283, DC NC 1962, the court concluded as a matter of law that the measure of damages that ought to be applied in the case was a reasonable royalty together with interest, that costs should be split between the parties and that there should be no award of attorney's fees. A Master was not appointed and the court merely asked counsel to submit an appropriate judgment in accordance with the opinion.

In conducting the accounting, the plaintiff theoretically must take the initiative in producing evidence upon which the Master can pass. However, the court will normally order the defendant, as in *Bristol Laboratories* v. *Schenley Laboratories*, 117 F. Supp. 67, DC Ind 1953, to attend before the Master and produce the information and documents necessary and to submit to oral examination. The information needed for the determination of damages is necessarily in the hands of the defendant, and as a practical matter, he is the one who must supply the Master with the needed evidence. The rule that the defendant must bring in his accounts was first established *In re Beckwith*, 203 F.45 CA 7 1913. The plaintiff may question the defendant's statement, and in so doing may orally examine the defendant and introduce affirmative evidence. *Computing Scale Co.* v. *Toledo Computing Scale Co.*, 279 F.648, CA 7 1921.

Either plaintiff or defendant may take exceptions to the Master's findings as was done by both parties in *Hartford Nat. Bank & Trust Co.* v. *E. F. Drew & Co.*, supra. If exceptions are taken, the court may, as in the *Hartford* case, decide the entire issue and modify the Master's findings or the matter may be referred back to the Master.

We are indebted to Mr. Dwight A. Lewis for his contribution to the section on Attorney's Fees, much of the information of which was published in an article by Alfred E. Wilson and Dwight A. Lewis, 42 JPOS 742, 1960.

Cross-references: *Infringement Suits, Royalty— Rate and Basis.*

APPENDIX

"Reasonable Royalties"

Case, Court & Year	Nature of Invention	Royalty Rate & Total Am't	Case, Court & Year	Nature of Invention	Royalty Rate & Total Am't
Parker Rust Proof v. Ford 23 F.2d 502 DC Mich '28	Ravenizing process	12.6 a lb of acid used in process, $244,588	Rockwood v. Gen. Fire Extinguisher 37 F.2d 62 CA 2 '30	Dry pipe valve for automatic sprinkler	$33/ valve, $205,260
U.S. Godwin v. Internat. Steel Tie 29 F.2d 476 CA 6 '28	Angle iron for edge of concrete pavement	10% of selling price of iron	Van Meter v. U.S. 37 F.2d 111 (Mod. 47 F.2d 192) DC NY '31	Parachute apparatus	3½% ($12.50 per unit), $46,137

Case, Court & Year	Nature of Invention	Royalty Rate & Total Am't	Case, Court & Year	Nature of Invention	Royalty Rate & Total Am't
Standard Brands v. Fed. Yeast 38 F.2d 314 DC Md '30	Process for making baker's yeast	2½¢/ lb $92,010	C & O Ry. v. Kaltenbach 124 F.2d 375 CA 4 '41	Machine for handling coal	½¢/ ton of coal
Nat. Brake & Electric v. Christensen 38 F.2d 721 CA 7 '30	Pump & motor for air brakes	5% for entire unit, 10% for repair parts, $260,750	Austral Sales v. Jamestown 45 F. Supp. 360 DC NY '42	Metallic school wardrobes	12½% of gross sales, $34,370
Overman Cushion Tire v. Goodyear 66 F.2d 361 CA 2 '33	Cushion tire	$5.00/ tire	Marconi Wireless Tel. v. U.S. 53 USPQ 246 Mod. 87 L.Ed. 731 Ct. Cls. '42	Selective tuning of antenna for transmitting station	10% of gross sales, $34,607
Duplate v. Triplex 81 F.2d 352 Mod. 80 L. Ed. 1274 CA 3 '35	Process for manufacture of laminated glass	10¢/ sq. ft. $414,120	Swan Carburetor v. Nash 133 F.2d 562 CA 4 '43	Manifold for internal combustion engine	$80,250
Power Specialty v. Conn. L. & P. 80 F.2d 874 CA 2 '36	Economizer for steam generating plant	15% of cost of entire installation	Enterprise Mfg. v. Shakespeare 141 F.2d 916 CA 6 '44	Mechanism for bait-casting reels	2½% of gross sales, $37,919
General Motors v. Daily 93 F.2d 938 CA 6 '37	Supporting rods for automobile curtains	15¢/car, 3¾¢/ rod for replacement	Mathey v. United Shoe Mach. 54 F. Supp. 694 CC Mass '44	Heel flap trimming machine	$5.00/ month for machine, $39,610
Horvath v. McCord Radiator 100 F.2d 938 CA 6 '38	Machine for making radiator tubes	¾¢/ linear ft, $120,502	Dixie Cup v. Paper Container 169 F.2d 645 CA 7 '49	Spiral machine for making paper cups	5% of selling price of cups, $21,608
Reynolds Spring v. L.A. Young 101 F.2d 257 CA 6 '39	Automobile upholstering spring construction	5¢/ spring construction, $92,196	Faulkner v. Gibbs 199 F.2d 635 CA 9 '52	Game device	$95.00/ unit/ year, $15,000
Autographic Reg. v. Sturgis Reg. 110 F.2d 883 CA 6 '40	Paper feed device for autographic register	10% of selling price to jobbers, $6,622	Russell Box v. Grant Paper 203 F.2d 177 CA 1 '53	Moisture-vapor proof paper board	$8.30-$3 per ton of paper, various periods, $170,259 (increased damages)
Wedge v. Waynesboro 31 F. Supp. 638, DC WVa	Plant packages	10¢/ package, $2,438			

Case, Court & Year	Nature of Invention	Royalty Rate & Total Am't
Excel Auto Radiator v. Bishop & Babcock 212 F.2d 586 CA 6 '54	Combined automobile heater and windshield defrosting device	7% of gross sales
Randolf Labs. v. Specialties Development 213 F.2d 873 CA 3 '54	Recoil prevention device for fire extinguishers	2% of gross sales, $75,232
Filtex v. Amen Atiyeh 103 USPQ 197 CA 9 '54	Nozzle for vacuum cleaner	10% of gross sales
U.S. Nat. Bank v. Fabri 235 F.2d 565 CA 9 '56	Self cleaning gate valve	5% of gross sales
Hartford Nat. Bank & Tr. v. Drew 188 F. Supp. 353 DC Del '60	Vitamin	10% of gross sales, $358,082
Zysset v. Popeil Bros. 134 USPQ 222 DC Ill '62	Vegetable chopper	10¢/ device

ACT OF 1952—PATENTS

Judge Giles S. Rich

Judge Rich, when an attorney, was a member of the Drafting Committee which largely wrote the 1952 Patent Statute, Title 35 U.S. Code. Because of his first-hand knowledge of the origin of certain passages therein, a condensation is presented, with his approval, minor revisions, and addenda, of his address before the New York Patent Law Association on November 6, 1952 in which he discussed the changes being made. The sections included here have been selected by the Editor on the basis of need of interpretation, newness of subject matter over the old statutes, or value as a preview at this point of certain features of our patent system. There is no attempt to be complete, as a large part of this Encyclopedia is in effect a discussion in detail of the Act and its implementation, the Act

being the first complete rewriting of the patent statutes since 1870. (Ed.)

This Act, which took effect on the 1st of January, 1953, applies to all patent applications filed after that date and to all patents granted on such applications.

Section 101—Inventions Patentable

The old familiar language, "art, machine, manufacture or composition of matter" is the same except that "art" has been changed to "process." So one of the first things that the definition of "process" in Section 100 does is to say that "process" means "art." To quote it in full, it says " 'process' means process, art or method." This is how the courts have construed the term "art." The next phrase is the one which raises questions: "and includes a new use of a known process, machine, manufacture, composition of matter, or material." Now, to those of us who wrote it, it is very simple. It is a declaration of existing law, and nothing more. New uses are no more patentable *as such* than under the old law.

I suppose some of the trouble has come from the fact that there was a great deal of discussion in the Committee gatherings on this bill about whether or not we should permit new uses to be patentable as such—label claims such as, "I claim D.D.T. [an old material] as an insecticide"—and the Coordinating Committee decided against it on the ground that it is impractical and would create too much confusion. The merits were outweighed by the demerits.

Now, of course you appreciate that although a new use is not patentable *as such*, a new use has always been patentable if it involves "invention" [i.e., is unobvious under Section 103] and if it is claimed in terms of process.

Section 102(d)—Bar Created by Issuance of Foreign Patent

It will be sufficient, in a non-convention U.S. case based upon an earlier filed foreign case, to *file the application* before the foreign patent issues rather than to have to rush your United States patent out before the foreign patent issues.

Section 103—Non-obvious Subject Matter Required

Section 103 is one of those matters of major importance: The statutory inclusion of a requirement for invention, which has never before been dealt with in the statutes. Since it is firmly established as a prerequisite to patentability, it was felt that it was desirable to include it in the codification. And in doing so, certain troublesome matters were dealt with, but without any attempt to define "invention," the undefinable.

First of all, Section 103 is a statement that a patent cannot be granted if invention is wanting, and want of invention is stated in terms of obviousness, obviousness in view of the prior art. And the prior art includes that art which is prior according to Section 102. This obviousness must, first of all, be determined as of the time when the invention was made. And it must be determined with reference to a person having ordinary skill in the art.

Addendum. Thus spake a patent lawyer of a decade ago who, with hindsight wisdom, would now clarify his earlier explanation.

In 1952 there was a requirement for "invention," a judge-made "law" over a century old. All patent lawyers thought in terms of this undefined mystery.

Section 103 put a requirement into the statute, the purpose of which was to "codify" the requirement for "invention." What was put into the statute, however, was *not* a requirement for "invention" but a provision that *the* invention could *not* be patented if "the subject matter as a whole (i.e., the claimed invention) would have been *obvious* at the time the invention was made *to a person having ordinary skill in the art* to which the subject matter pertains." Clearly the law is not that there must be "invention" but that there must be statutory *unobviousness*. To say, as some courts are still doing, that unobviousness is indicative of "invention" is tautological, not to say confusing.

When unobviousness has been found, there is no need to go further. Only confusion in thinking can result from referring to the less definite term "invention," which Section 103 displaced. Reading the section will show that it contains no reference to a requirement for "invention." The drafters of the section, in fact, assiduously avoided that term for the very purpose of liberating the law from the moss which it had gathered and providing a clearer

and more workable concept free from the clouding of the issue by old cases. (G.S.R.)

Flash of Genius. Finally, the last clause of Section 103 is intended to lay the ghost of the "flash of genius" furore. It says, "Patentability shall not be negatived by the manner in which the invention was made." That is, long toil stands on an equal footing with flashes.

Section 104—Knowledge Abroad

Section 104 is not new. It forbids the use of knowledge or activity abroad in establishing an invention date in all cases, either in the courts or the Patent Office. It derives from Section 9 of the Boykin Act, which has been repealed, and is somewhat broader.

Section 112—Means Claims

The third paragraph, the last, authorizes claiming an element of a combination, not any element but only an element of a combination, in terms of means plus function. The language is such as to include a combination of steps, as in a process. And I would assume that this is authorized even if the particular element or step is at the exact point of novelty. You will recognize its applicability to *Halliburton Oil Well Cementing Co.* v. *Walker et al.,* 64 USPQ 278, CA 9 1945; aff. 329 U.S. 1, 1946. But there is a string to this: If you adopt this practice, that element or step is to be construed—shall be construed (it is mandatory)—to cover corresponding structure, material, or acts described in the specification and equivalents thereof.

Section 121—Restriction

Section 121 is a tightening up of the law on division in favor of the patentees. Note the conjunctive expression "independent and distinct inventions." Requiring that the inventions be both independent and distinct makes it easier to keep two of them in one case. Rule 142. What is now called a requirement for division will hereafter be a "requirement for restriction."

There is an innovation in Section 121, in that it provides that neither the parent nor the divisional patent, where there is co-pendency, can be used as a reference against the other application or patent. This is directed at those annoying rejections that one of your own inventions is not patentably distinguishable from another of your inventions. To take advantage of this section it would be well to let the Patent Office decide on restriction in doubtful cases.

Sections 154 and 163—Rights of Patent Owner

Section 154 at long last brings about a realistic and accurate statement of the patent right, "the right to exclude others."

The plant patent right also has been clarified by saying that it is "the right to exclude others from asexually reproducing the plant or selling or using the plant so reproduced."

Section 251—Reissues

Section 251 on reissue drops that famous old provision "inadvertence, accident, or mistake," and substitutes for it very broad language. It says that reissue may be had if the patent is inoperative or invalid, "through error without any deceptive intention." Query: Is this broad enough to cover the ill-advised, slipshod or stupid cancellation of claims from an application by an attorney? Is his act going to be binding on a subsequent attorney? I don't see why it shouldn't be broad enough to cover that situation.

Realistically, unlike the present statute, Section 251 says that you can reissue where the defect is due to the fact that the patentee has claimed either more *or less* than he had a right to claim.

Now, the changes that you can make in a reissue are stated in rather involved language in the present statute, but here it merely refers to filing a "new and amended application," and the only restriction on it is that there shall be "no new matter."

Another innovation is that an assignee may apply for reissue without the inventor and may swear to the application, if it is not a broadening reissue. If it is a broadening reissue, the inventor's signature is required. Rule 172.

The last paragraph codifies two years as the maximum time within which to apply for a broadening reissue, and no excuses will extend that maximum because it is no longer merely a court-made rule, derived by analogy from other statutes. It is written into the law in positive form. (For a discussion of intervening rights and other subjects relating to reissues, see *Reissue Patents*. Ed.)

Section 253—Disclaimers

You will recall that the old law (R. S. 4922) says: "But no patentee shall be entitled to the benefits of this section if he has unreasonably neglected or delayed to enter a disclaimer." That is gone. There is no longer any sanction whatsoever for failing to disclaim, promptly or otherwise, except the provision in Section 288 that you will not recover costs in a suit if you sue on a patent with a claim known to be invalid without filing your disclaimer before you start the suit.

A further change is that only a complete claim can be disclaimed. Rules 321 and 263.

An innovation of some interest is that you can disclaim any part of the terminal portion of a patent. You can lop off the last two months or two years or two days, or whatever you like, including the entire term which amounts to dedication. Why would you want to do that? Well, if you are in a double-patenting situation, solely because one of your patents will extend the monopoly in a manner which you think would be illegal, you can cut back the younger patent to have the same term as the older one. Rule 321.

Section 255—Correction of Applicants' Mistakes

Section 255 is a new provision which provides for the correction of certain limited classes of mistakes made by applicants or their attorneys or their attorneys' stenographers. You can apply for a certificate of correction for such mistakes on payment of a ten dollar fee, as provided in Section 41 (8). (Rule 323 specifically prohibits "new matter" or matter requiring reexamination. See also Rule 325.)

Section 271—Infringement

Oddly, the statutes up to this time have never said a word about infringement. They have simply created the patent right and left it to the courts to enforce it. So here we have paragraph (a) saying what infringement is. Paragraph (b) is a sort of hybrid, in my opinion. The note says that it deals with contributory infringement, and in a sense it does, since active inducement, provided for in (b), is not, strictly speaking, a direct infringement under (a). But (b) goes on to say that the active inducer shall be held liable *as an infringer*. Its intention is to hold liable the mastermind who plans the whole infringement and sits back and watches it happen, somehow himself managing to avoid either making, using or selling. This can happen in a variety of ways. The architects of a structure may be responsible, or a firm of engineers, or the vendor of a kit sold with instructions or of a machine which can operate only to perform a patented process. The possibilities are unlimited. These people are, legally speaking, joint tort feasors, and they ought to be held liable. So the active inducer is made and denoted an infringer.

Under paragraph (c), to prove a case of contributory infringement (1) a patentee must establish that the thing sold is a component of a patented machine, etc., or material, etc., for use in a patented process. (2) It must constitute a material part of the invention. (3) It must be especially made or especially adapted for use in an infringement, and the infringer must know that fact. (4) It must not be a staple article. And (5) it must not be a commodity of commerce suitable for substantial non-infringing use. Thost last two points are more or less alternatives.

Misuse Doctrine and Contributory Infringement

Now if you have such a case, you will still not recover unless you can escape from what has now become the overriding misuse doctrine.

You will remember the opinion in the Mercoid cases: We have two doctrines: contributory infringement, on the one hand, and misuse, on the other, and where these doctrines conflict, the misuse doctrine must prevail on grounds of public policy.

So from the very beginning of the legislative effort on this subject, back in 1948, in order to make contributory infringement stick, once it has been defined, there has always been coupled with it the equivalent of paragraph (d) to deal with the misuse doctrine, making exceptions to it which correspond in scope to the rights of the owner of the cause of action for contributory infringement.

Stated briefly, paragraph (d) merely excepts from the misuse doctrine acts of the patentee predicated on the existence of a cause of action, actual or potential, for contributory infringement as defined in (c) such as relying upon, licensing, or enforcing his patent right with respect to actual or potential contributory infringers. Such acts shall not be misuse. Unless such exceptions are made we would have the anomalous situation in which there is contributory infringement by statute but no way to stop it.

Section 292—Marking

Section 292, on False Marking, illegitimatizes our old friend "Pat. Pending." He mustn't be mentioned any more unless there is a pending application. Whenever an application becomes abandoned there is an obligation to cease using the term. In addition to the old *qui tam* or informer action, we now have a criminal provision implicit in the words "shall be fined not more than $500."

A Tribute

A monument ought to be erected to Mr. P. J. Federico of the Patent Office for the work that he did on this law over the years and the contributions he made from his vast knowledge of patent law. But knowing him, I am sure he will be satisfied to treat this Act as the monument. *Cf.* his "Commentary on the New Patent Act," U.S. Code Annotated, Title 35 Patents, pp. 1-70, 1954.

ADJUDICATION OF PATENTS UNDER THE 1952 ACT

C. Marshall Dann

A patent which has been issued by the Patent Office enjoys a statutory presumption of validity (35 U.S.C. Sect. 282). That this presumption is rebuttable, however, is regularly demonstrated by the courts. The true strength and scope of a patent is known only when it has been adjudicated.

Low Proportion of Patents Sued Upon

The great majority of patents are never sued on and most of those which are do not remain in litigation long enough to receive an adjudication of their merit. Some idea of the relative numbers involved may be gained from the following table which is based on information for the period from 1948 through 1954, compiled by P. J. Federico.[1]

	Approximate Average Number of Patents per Year	Percentage of Total
Issued	41,000	100.00
Sued on	780	1.90
Adjudicated in:		
District Courts	140	0.34
Courts of Appeals	61	0.15
Supreme Court	1	0.002
Total adjudicated, % of issued		0.34

Trend of Decisions

For at least the last thirty years a patent which has been adjudicated has been more likely to be held invalid than valid and infringed. The trend in recent years, however, has been in the direction of a higher proportion being held valid. Fig. 1 illustrates this trend. This graph is based on the decisions of the federal courts of appeals. It plots by years the percentage of patents adjudicated in which at least one claim was held to be both valid and infringed.[2] In order to smooth the curve somewhat so as to give a better idea of the trend of the decisions, a three-year moving average has

been plotted. The point shown for any given year represents the number of patents held valid and infringed during the year shown, the preceding year and the following year, divided by the total number adjudicated in the same three years. A patent was not counted as valid and infringed if it was held valid but not infringed, infringed but not valid, misused, or invalid and not infringed.

It will be seen that between 1926 and 1931 34 to 40 per cent of the adjudicated patents were upheld and found to be infringed. Thereafter the percentage dropped rather steadily until the early 40's, when it reached a figure of about 15 per cent. After a rise to 25 per cent in the late 40's, the percentage again fell to about 15 per cent in 1952 and 1953. Since that time it has risen rapidly and has reached for the year 1961 (which actually counts the decisions in 1960, 1961 and 1962 through those reported in the December 31 issue of USPQ) a figure of 36 per cent, or only slightly less than in the late 1920's.

As has been pointed out previously,[3] court of appeals decisions are most useful for indicating statistical trends of this sort, since they are essentially all published, relatively numerous, and in most cases represent the final word on the validity of the patent. Too few patents are adjudicated in the Supreme Court to give useful statistics, and in any event the lower courts promptly reflect the principles enunciated by that court. Although the federal district courts decide somewhat more than twice as many patent cases as do the courts of appeals, many of these decisions are not published, many are later contested in the appellate courts, and presumably most follow the law established by the courts of appeals.

Meaning of Statistics

Can it be inferred from these statistics that as of 1961 approximately 35 per cent of the patents in force would be upheld if litigated? The best answer would seem to be that the evidence is too meager to justify such an inference. It has been argued that the proportion of all patents which are valid is considerably higher than in the case of

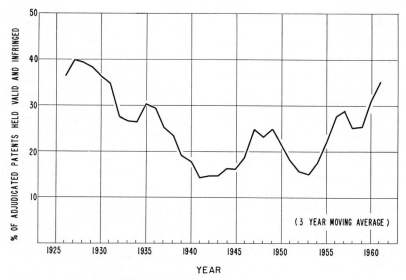

Fig. 1. Patents adjudicated by Courts of Appeals.

the adjudicated patents, since strong patents are respected and only the weak or borderline patents are contested by infringers. On the other hand, many patents certainly exist which are not litigated because the owner considers them too weak to stand a reasonable chance of being upheld in court. It does not seem possible to establish that the percentage of validity is much different for all patents than for the adjudicated patents, yet any conclusion that the percentages are the same must rest on a 700-fold extrapolation from the data.

It is interesting to speculate on the reasons for the substantial changes through the years in the probability of a patent's being upheld in the courts. The sharp decline in this probability through the 1930's is unquestionably related to the depression and the increase in anti-monopoly sentiment which it produced. The New Deal, the T.N.E.C. hearings, and the judges appointed at that time all had a hand in giving the patent owner who wished to enforce his patent a difficult time. During the decade between 1935 and 1944, the Supreme Court supplied considerable guidance to the lower courts on patent matters, adjudicating an average of more than five patents per year in contrast to the subsequent 17 years from 1945 through 1961 when only 16, slightly less than one per year, were passed on.

The dip in the curve for 1952 and 1953 is probably due to the Supreme Court's decisions in *The Great Atlantic and Pacific Tea Co.* v. *Supermarket Equipment Corp.*, 340 U.S. 147, 87 USPQ 303, 1950, and in *Crest Specialty* v. *Trager et al.*, 341 U.S. 912, 89 USPQ 175, 1951. The decision in the *A & P* case suggested a strict standard of inventiveness for claims to combinations, while *Crest* v. *Trager* disposed summarily of a simple gadget-like device. Both cases were frequently cited and relied on by the lower courts.

The rise in the curve since 1953 is to some extent attributable to the Patent Act of 1952, 35 U.S.C., although other factors may be equally important. The principal feature of that act which has tended to improve the chances of a patent in litigation is the last sentence of Section 103 which says that: "Patentability shall not be negatived by the manner in which the invention was made." This was intended and has generally been construed [4] as eliminating the "flash of genius" doctrine announced by Mr. Justice Douglas in *Cuno Engineering Corp.* v. *Automatic Devices Corp.*, 314 U.S. 84, 51 USPQ 272, 1941. According to the Congressional report accompanying the bill, this sentence makes it immaterial whether the invention results "from long toil and experimentation or from a flash of genius." [5]

Grounds for Invalidation

The most frequent grounds for invalidating patents are lack of invention or anticipation, prior public use or sale, double patenting, indefiniteness, inoperativeness, undue breadth, impropriety in reissuing and incorrect inventorship. By far the most common ground is lack of invention over or anticipation by the prior art. A study by P. J. Federico[1] of 50 patents held invalid in 1954 and 1955 showed this to be a ground in 43 cases, or 86 per cent. A less careful examination, by the present writer, of the decisions in which 358 patents were held invalid between 1953 and 1962 showed lack of invention or anticipation to be a ground relied on in 88 per cent of the cases. Both studies showed prior public use or sale to be the ground next most frequently relied on, occurring on the order of 10 per cent of the time.

(For additional studies in this area, reference is made to the next article which analyzes the data by circuits and by arts represented in the patent at bar. Ed.)

Litigation Time-Consuming

While it appears from the statistics that the odds are by no means insuperable against being able to enforce a patent covering an invention thought to be a substantial advance in the art, it should be mentioned that patent litigation has become an unfortunately time-consuming and expensive business. This is particularly true when the invention is the product of extensive and complicated research, where innumerable laboratory notebooks, reports and items of correspondence may be thought to contain evidence for or against the patent and hence to be subject to discovery. The time and expense involved in patent litigation has undoubtedly operated to reduce the number of patents which are tested in the courts.

References

1. Report appearing at pages 176 to 185 of "American Patent System, Hearings before the Subcommittee on Patents, Trademarks, and Copyrights of the Committee on the Judiciary, United States Senate, 84th Congress, 1st session"; reprinted in 38 JPOS 233.

2. Basic data for years 1925 through 1952 taken from compilation by P. J. Federico, supra; for years 1953 through 1962 compiled from decisions reported in USPQ. A somewhat similar graph based on much of the same data appears in "Dynamics of the Patent System," p. 55, New York, Central Book Co., 1960.

3. Federico, supra; "Dynamics of the Patent System," supra, note 2, at page 54.

4. See *Pacific Contact Laboratories* v. *Solex Laboratories*, 100 USPQ 12, CA 9 1953; *Lyon* v. *Bausch & Lomb Optical Co.*, 106 USPQ 1, CA 2 1955; *R. M. Palmer Co.* v. *Luden's Inc.*, 111 USPQ 1, CA 3 1956; *Emerson* v. *National Cylinder Gas Co.*, 116 USPQ 101, CA 1 1958.

5. H. R. Rep. No. 1923, 82nd Congress, 2nd session, May 12, 1952.

Cross-references: *Adjudications by Circuits and Arts Involved, Infringement, Infringement Suits, Patentability, Validity.*

ADJUDICATIONS BY CIRCUITS AND ARTS INVOLVED

Richard J. Dearborn and R. Bradlee Boal

Supplementing the preceding article (*Adjudication of Patents under the 1952 Patent Act*), the following tables show how the circuit courts have stood, collectively and severally, on the issue of validity and infringement of issued patent in the past decade. They show also the grounds for invalidity and the holdings on patents in five major arts considered separately.

Table 1 shows the total number of patents adjudicated, the percentage held (1) valid and infringed, (2) invalid and (3) valid but not infringed by all Circuit Courts of Appeals for each year from 1953 to 1963.

Table 2 shows like data for *each circuit* for all years from 1953 to 1963. The table indicates that the first, second, third and eighth circuits have been the most strict with respect to validity and the fourth, fifth and tenth the most liberal in this respect. Such comparisons cannot be expected to hold for the future nor avoid the need for reappraisals from time to time.

Table 3 shows the material of Tables 1 and 2 broken down by subject matter. It indicates that the particular art to which

TABLE 1. ALL CIRCUIT COURTS OF APPEALS, 1953-1963.

Year Reported	Total No. of Patents Adjudicated	Valid and Infringed %	Invalid %	Valid but not Infringed %
1953	66	24.2	62.2	13.6
1954	61	14.7	75.5	9.8
1955	44	18.2	63.6	18.2
1956	80	32.5	51.3	16.2
1957	74	29.7	64.9	5.4
1958	60	26.6	66.7	6.7
1959	70	25.7	57.1	17.2
1960	62	30.7	51.6	17.7
1961	59	45.8	42.4	11.8
1962	62	40.3	48.3	11.3
1963	96	28.1	53.2	18.8
Total and Averages	734	29.0	57.4	13.6

TABLE 2. COURTS OF APPEALS BY CIRCUIT.

Circuit No.	Total No. of Patents Adjudicated	Valid and Infringed %	Invalid %	Valid but not Infringed %
1	49	20.4	57.1	22.5
2	90	14.4	73.4	12.2
3	71	16.9	77.5	5.6
4	62	43.6	45.1	11.3
5	82	43.8	40.3	15.9
6	93	26.9	60.2	12.9
7	119	35.3	47.9	16.8
8	30	10.0	76.7	13.3
9	112	29.5	58.0	12.5
10	21	57.2	38.1	4.7
D.C.	5	0	60.0	40.0
Total and Averages	734	29.0	57.4	13.6

TABLE 3. VALIDITY BY ARTS, 1953-63.

Subject Matter of Patents	Total No. of Patents Adjudicated	Valid and Infringed %	Invalid %	Valid but not Infringed %
Chemical	98	32.7	52.0	15.3
Design	42	23.8	69.1	7.1
Electrical	108	30.6	50.8	18.5
Mechanical	482	28.6	58.9	12.5
Plant	4	0	75.0	25.0
Total and Averages	734	29.0	57.4	13.6

TABLE 4. GROUNDS FOR ALL CIRCUITS, 1953-1963.

Year	Total No. of Patents Adjudicated	Invalid %	Invalid for lack of Invention		Invalid on Other Grounds	
			% of Total	% of those Invalid	% of Total	% of those Invalid
1953	66	62.2	53.1	85.4	9.1	14.6
1954	61	75.5	60.7	80.4	14.9	19.6
1955	44	63.6	50.0	78.6	13.6	21.4
1956	80	51.3	42.5	82.8	8.8	17.2
1957	74	64.9	50.0	77.1	14.9	22.9
1958	60	66.7	55.0	82.5	11.7	17.5
1959	70	57.1	50.0	87.5	7.1	12.5
1960	62	51.6	32.3	62.4	19.3	37.6
1961	59	42.4	25.4	60.0	17.0	40.0
1962	62	48.3	41.8	86.6	6.5	13.4
1963	96	53.2	35.5	66.7	17.7	33.3
Total and Averages	734	57.4	44.6	77.7	12.8	22.3

the patent relates has had relatively little effect on validity, except possibly in the field of plant patents where the number litigated by the circuit courts is too small to establish a pattern. (See article *Plant Patents*)

Table 4 divides the grounds for adjudications of invalidity by the Courts of Appeals into two categories, (1) lack of invention and (2) other grounds than lack of invention, for 1953-1963.

For the purpose of compiling the data appearing in Tables 4 and 5, if there were several different independent grounds for holding a patent invalid and one of these grounds was lack of invention, the patent was classified as being 'invalid for lack of invention" rather than "invalid on other grounds."

Table 5 shows the same information as Table 4 but for the entire period from 1953 to 1963 for three representative circuits only, the second, fourth and fifth. Statistics of the type presented here are of limited quantitative value only. In the first place, during the entire period from 1953 to 1963 only 734 patents were adjudicated by the United States Circuit Courts of Appeals. During that same period, hundreds of thousands of patents were in effect. Secondly, there is probably some truth in the proposition that it is mostly patents of doubtful

TABLE 5. GROUNDS OF INVALIDITY BY CIRCUIT, 1953-1963.

Circuit No.	Total No. of Patents Adjudicated	Invalid %	Invalid for Lack of Invention		Invalid on Other Grounds	
			% of Total	% of those Invalid	% of Total	% of those Invalid
First	49	57.1	34.7	60.6	22.4	39.4
Second	90	73.4	65.6	89.4	7.8	10.6
Third	71	77.5	57.8	74.5	19.7	25.5
Fourth	62	45.1	35.5	78.5	9.6	21.5
Fifth	82	40.3	26.9	66.7	13.4	33.3
Sixth	93	60.2	53.8	89.3	6.4	10.7
Seventh	119	47.9	37.0	77.2	10.9	22.8
Eighth	30	76.7	56.7	73.8	20.0	26.2
Ninth	112	58.0	42.0	72.3	16.0	27.7
Tenth	21	38.1	33.3	87.5	4.8	12.5
D.C.	5	60.0	40.0	66.7	20.0	33.3
Total and Averages	734	57.4	44.6	77.7	12.8	22.3

validity that are litigated. A patentee who has a weak patent is unlikely to risk the costs of litigation. The patentee with a strong patent, on the other hand, may not have to go into litigation since the industry is likely to respect his patent without recourse to litigation. Therefore, any attempt to extrapolate from the statistics presented here to all issued patents is to a large extent unwarranted.

In the majority of those cases in which the patent has been held invalid, the basis has been lack of invention. The reason for the prevalence of this ground is probably the fact that this is the most subjective of the various usual patent defenses. Accordingly, a judge holding a patent invalid is less likely to be reversed when his holding is based on Section 103 than on a more technical ground. The practical significance of this fact, to the person who is against the patent, is that he should always raise the issue of lack of invention.

For further discussion of the significance of such statistics, see *Patentability*.

Cross-references: *Adjudication under 1952 Patent Act, Infringement, Validity*

ADVANCE INFORMATION FROM FOREIGN PATENT FILINGS

Leonard J. Robbins and Joseph H. Handelman

In many foreign countries, the initial act of filing a patent application (unless it is abandoned before a certain stage is reached) leads inevitably to some sort of publication of its subject matter, either partial or complete, in typescript or printed form, before the patent itself is issued. This is true whether or not the latter is finally printed.

Such foreign patent publications constitute a specialized and important sector of the technical literature, giving access to early information concerning the activities of competitors and knowledge that may generate ideas and avoid duplication of effort. In a number of active fields, involving exports, foreign manufacturing, or licensing programs, it is not uncommon to file patent applications on a more or less world-wide scale, to protect a new invention. Investigation of appropriate foreign patent publications provides, therefore, a most useful and timely supplement to the material available in scientific journals.

Apart from such searching activities, information concerning foreign patent publications, even though not fully revealing all technical subject matter, is of interest for many other purposes, including prosecution and litigation of U.S. and foreign patents.

Also foreign filing programs are often conducted in stages. An understanding of expected publication resulting from knowledge of existing filings is an important guide for the timing of further filings, so that they can be completed before any estoppel is created by such publication.

Early Publication Countries

Certain countries are of particular interest to searchers as providing complete or partial description of the subject matter of a patent application relatively soon after filing. This is due either to publications prescribed by law or to a simple nonexamination patent office procedure leading to prompt grant.

Shortly after being filed, the entire typescript specification can be inspected in Costa Rica, Honduras, Nicaragua, Panama, Ecuador, Uruguay and Venezuela. In Portugal the claims are printed promptly. Applications filed in Ireland and South Africa under the International Convention are open to public inspection 12 and 18 months, respectively, from the Convention date.

Belgium is the principal major country where patents are granted very promptly. Full information in typescript form is available 6 months or less from filing. Other countries with prompt grant furnishing typescript publication include Turkey, Luxembourg, Jamaica and Trinidad.

Kinds of Publications

This chapter sets out in convenient tabular form, for the principal foreign countries, all the various kinds of publications resulting from the filing of patent applications and indicates the stage at which they become available, including printed particulars in official Government journals and gazettes; typescript documents open to public inspection in patent offices; and printed specifications available both before or after grant of the patent.

In spite of the many differences in foreign patent office procedures, the progressive publications resulting from the filing of foreign patent applications can be classified in three broad categories :

(1) Information available on or after filing.

(2) Information available on or after acceptance.

(3) Information available on or after grant.

In the following alphabetical list of countries, details are given for those categories in which publications occur. Only a few countries provide information in all three categories. In those countries where applications are accepted as a separate procedural step prior to grant, this is usually for the purpose of enabling oppositions to be filed by third parties. *The numbers show the stage at which the information becomes available.*

The publications may be simple notices giving such particulars as names, titles, and serial numbers, partial disclosures or summaries of subject matter, or complete disclosures. Because of the nature of foreign patent office procedures, it is not possible in most instances to give any precise dates after filing when subsequent publications occur. In those countries having full novelty examination, acceptance and grant may not take place for a number of years. Early publication of the subject matter of patent applications therefore, occurs mainly in those countries in which patents are granted without examination or with only formal examination.

No reference is made to patents of confirmation or importation, which necessarily imply the existence of patents already issued in other countries, or to registration patents in British colonies and possessions which are based on prior British patents.

Argentina. (3). Typescript specification open to public inspection on grant; notice of grant including main claim and principal drawings published

in *Boletin Oficial* some time after grant; patent specification not printed. (The number 3 shows the category, as stated above, into which the publication policy falls.)

Australia. (1). Notice of filing published in *Official Journal* soon after filing. (2) Notice of acceptance including one or more claims published in *Official Journal;* typescript specification open to public inspection after acceptance or 18 months from filing, whichever is earlier; notice of unaccepted specifications that are open to public inspection published in *Official Journal* and abstracts printed separately; printed copies of published specification available after notice of acceptance published; amendments of a published specification are printed on a slip which is attached to the existing stock of printed specifications, or, if the amendments are extensive, the specification may be reprinted.

Austria. (2). Notice of acceptance published in *Patentblatt;* typescript specification open to public inspection on acceptance. (3). Patent specification printed several months after grant.

Bahamas. (2). Notice of acceptance published in *Official Gazette;* typescript specification open to public inspection shortly after acceptance; patent specification not printed.

Barbados. (2). Notice of acceptance published in *Official Gazette;* typescript specification open to public inspection on acceptance; patent specification not printed.

Belgium. (1). Notice of filing available at the Patent Office soon after filing; filing particulars also available soon after filing in unofficial publications *Revue des Brevets Belges* and *Répertoire des Brevets Belges Récents*. (3). Typescript specification open to public inspection either 3 months after grant (which normally occurs soon after filing) or 6 months after filing date if deferment of grant has been applied for; notice of grant including abstract and drawing published about one year after filing date in *Recueil des Brevets d'Invention* (N.b., the typescript specification is thus open to public inspection before any notice of grant is published); patent specification printed usually several years after filing date.

Bermuda. (2). Notice of acceptance published in *Official Gazette;* typescript specification open to public inspection on acceptance; patent specification not printed.

Bolivia. (1). Notice of filing including abstract (claim 1) published in *Gaceta Oficial de Bolivia* some time after filing and typescript specification then open to public inspection; patent specification not printed.

Brazil. (1). After conclusion of normal examination procedure, claims are printed in *Diario Oficial* (recent practice is to print only claim 1); published claims which are subsequently amended are reprinted in *Diario;* typescript specification open to public inspection upon printing of claim; patent specification not printed.

British Guiana. (2). Notice of acceptance published in *Official Gazette* and typescript specification then open to public inspection; patent specification not printed.

British Honduras. (2). Notice of acceptance published in *Government Gazette* and typescript specification then open to public inspection; patent specification not printed.

Canada. (3). Notice of grant including one or more claims and drawing published in *The Canadian Patent Office Record* on grant; printed patent specification available on grant.

Ceylon. (2). Notice of acceptance including one or more claims published in *The Ceylon Government Gazette* shortly after acceptance and typescript specification then open to public inspection; patent specification not printed.

Chile. (1). Notice of filing published in *Diario Oficial* soon after filing including title which is usually brief but sometimes amplified into an abstract of main claim. (3). Typescript specification open to public inspection one year from date of grant; patent specification not printed.

Colombia. (1). Notice of filing published in *Gaceta de la Propiedad Industrial* soon after filing. (3). Notice of grant published in *Gaceta* soon after grant; typescript specification open to public inspection only after term of patent has expired (term is 10, 15 or 20 years); patent specification not printed.

Costa Rica. (1). Notice of filing published in *La Gaceta* shortly after filing and typescript specification then open to public inspection; patent specification not printed.

Cuba. (1). Notice of filing published in a mimeographed list issued by Patent Office; upon completion of prosecution, title and abstract of claims printed in *Boletin Oficial de la Propiedad Industrial* and typescript specification then open to public inspection; patent specification not printed.

Czechoslovakia. (2). Notice of acceptance including abstract of main claim published in *Věstnik Úřadu pro Patenty a Vynálezy* and typescript specification then open to public inspection. (3). Notice of grant published in *Věstnik;* patent specification printed about a year after grant.

Denmark. (2). Notice of acceptance published in *Dansk Patenttidende;* typescript specification open to public inspection on aceptance. (3). Patent specification printed several months after grant.

Dominican Republic. (3). Notice of grant published in *Revista de Trabajo e Industria* after grant; typescript specification open to public inspection on grant; patent specification not printed.

Ecuador. (1). Notice of filing including abstract published in *Registro Oficial* and in two local newspapers shortly after filing; typescript specification open to public inspection 3 months after publication of abstract; patent specification not printed.

Egypt. (2). Notice of acceptance published in *Official Gazette* and typescript specification then open to inspection; printed specifications available after grant.

Finland. (2). Notice of acceptance published in *Patenttilehti* and typescript specification then open to public inspection. (3). Notice of grant including main claim published in *Patenttilehti* after grant; patent specification printed about a year after grant.

France. (3). Notice of grant including abridgment published in *Bulletin Officiel de la Propriété Industrielle* 5 or 6 weeks after date of grant and typescript specification then open to public inspection; patent specification printed some months after grant.

Germany, East. (3). Notice of grant published in *Bekanntmachungen des Amtes für Erfindungs-und Patentwesen;* typescript specification open to public inspection on grant; patent specification printed after grant.

Germany, West. (2). Notice of accepted applications which are open to public inspection published in *Patentblatt* and printed copies of published specification are available (the published specification is printed on green paper and is called an "Auslegeschrift"). (3). Notice of grant published in *Patentblatt;* patent printed several months after grant (the patent specification is printed on white paper and will differ from the "Auslegeschrift" if amendments were made after publication—however, a notice on the front page of the printed patent specification indicates whether or not it corresponds to the "Auslegeschrift").

Great Britain. (1). Notice of filing published in *Official Journal* shortly after filing. (2). Notice of acceptance published in *Official Journal;* typescript specification open to public inspection on publication date; printed copies of published specification available on or shortly after publication date (about 2 months after acceptance); amendments of a published specification are printed on a slip which is attached to the existing stock of printed specifications, or, if the amendments are extensive, the specification may be reprinted; some time after printing of specification, abstract and drawing printed in *Illustrated Abridgments of Specifications.*

Greece. (3). Notice of grant published in *Official Bulletin* on grant and typescript specification then open to public inspection; patent specification not printed.

Guatemala. (1). Notice of filing published in *El Guatemalteco Diario Oficial* shortly after filing.

(3). Notice of grant published in *Diario;* typescript specification open to public inspection on grant; patent specification not printed.

Haiti. (3). Notice of grant including abstract printed in *Le Moniteur* after grant; patent specification not printed.

Holland. (1). Application open to public inspection and patent specification reproduced 18 months from filing date or Convention priority date. (2) Notice of acceptance published in *De Industriële Eigendom* and printed copies of published specification available. (However, this second publication may not take place for 7 years if deferred examination is requested.) (3) Patent specification printed about one month after grant and may differ from the printed published specification.

Honduras, Republic of. (1). Notice of filing published in *La Gaceta* shortly after filing and typescript specification then open to public inspection; patent specification not printed.

Hungary. (2). Notice of acceptance published in *Szabadalmi Közlöny* and typescript specification then open to public inspection. (3). Notice of grant including abstract published in *Szabadalmi;* patent specification printed about one year after grant.

India. (1). Notice of filing published in *Gazette of India* shortly after filing. (2). For applications claiming priority under reciprocal arrangements existing between India and certain Commonwealth countries, i.e., claiming a priority date earlier than the actual filing date, typescript specification open to public inspection either upon acceptance or 18 months from the priority date claimed, whichever is earlier (N.b., where such an application was filed in India nearly 12 months after the filing date of the basic application, typescript specification thus may be open to public inspection as early as 6 months after the actual filing date in India); for nonpriority applications, typescript specification open to public inspection on acceptance; acceptance must occur within a maximum of 21 months (inclusive of extensions) from the filing date; notice of acceptance including a short summary published in *Gazette* soon after acceptance; printed copies of specification available some years after grant.

Iran. (3). Notice of grant published in *Official Gazette* on grant; typescript specification open to public inspection after grant; patent specification not printed.

Iraq. (3). Notice of grant including a short summary published in *Official Gazette* after grant and typescript specification then open to public inspection; patent specification not printed.

Ireland, Republic of. (1). Notice of filing published in *Official Journal of Industrial and Commercial Property* soon after filing; applications claiming Convention priority are laid open to public inspection 12 months after priority date claimed (N.b., when an application is filed shortly before the end of the Convention priority period, typescript specification thus becomes open to public inspection shortly after the actual filing date in Ireland); notice of Convention applications open to public inspection published in *Official Journal.* (2). Typescript specification of a non-Convention application open to public inspection on acceptance; for both Convention and non-Convention applications, notice of acceptance including abstract and drawing published in *Official Journal* shortly after acceptance; for applications having a corresponding British application in existence, acceptance occurs after acceptance of British application. For other cases, acceptance must normally occur within maximum of 18 months (inclusive of extensions) from filing date; printed copies of specification available several months or more after acceptance.

Israel. (2). Notice of acceptance including abridgment published in *Patents Journal* and typescript specification then open to public inspection; patent specification not printed.

Italy. (1). Register of patent applications can be inspected at Patent Office to obtain filing particulars. (3). Notice of grant including abridgment published in *Bollettino dei Brevetti per Invenzioni* and typescript specification open to public inspection 3 months after grant (6 months after grant on special request of applicant); patent specification printed 1 or 2 years after grant.

Jamaica. (1). Notice of filing published in *The Jamaica Gazette* and in a local newspaper shortly after filing. (2). Typescript specification open to public inspection on grant; patent specification not printed.

Japan. (2). Printed copies of published specification available, those of the same class being bound together in groups of 50 in *Tokkyo-koho* (Patent Gazette). (3). Patent specification printed after grant with a serial number different from that of the printed published specification; the text of the printed patent specification may differ from the printed published specification.

Jordan, Hashemite Kingdom of. (2). Notice of grant published in *Official Gazette* shortly after grant; typescript specification open to public inspection on grant; patent specification not printed.

Jugoslavia. (2). Notice of acceptance including main claim and drawing printed in *Patentni Glasnik* and typescript specification then open to public inspection; patent specification not printed.

Korea (South). (2). Notice of acceptance including abstract published in *Patents Gazette* and typescript specification then open to public inspection; patent specification not printed.

Liberia. (3). Notice of grant published in *The Liberia Official Gazette* soon after grant; typescript specification open to public inspection after grant; patent specification not printed.

Luxembourg. (3). Notice of grant published in *Memorial* after grant; typescript specification open to public inspection on grant; patent specification not printed.

Malta. (2). Notice of acceptance published in *The Malta Government Gazette* and in a local newspaper. (3). Typescript specification open to public inspection after grant; patent specification not printed.

Mexico. (3). Notice of grant including abstract and drawing published in *Gaceta de la Propiedad Industrial* after grant; typescript specification open to public inspection after grant; patent specification not printed.

Morocco. (3). Typescript specification open to public inspection shortly after grant; notice of grant published in *Official Gazette* considerably after grant; patent specification not printed.

New Zealand. (1). Notice of filing published in *New Zealand Patent Office Journal* shortly after filing. (2). Notice of acceptance including abstract and drawing published in *Journal* soon after acceptance and typescript specification then open to public inspection; patent specification not printed.

Nicaragua. (1). Notice of filing published in *La Gaceta* and typescript specification then open to public inspection; patent specification not printed.

Norway. (2). Notice of acceptance published in *Norsk Tidende for det Industrielle Rettsvern* and typescript specification then open to public inspection. (3). Notice of grant published in *Norsk Tidende;* main claim and drawing of previously granted patents published in *Norsk Tidende;* patent specification printed shortly after grant.

Pakistan. (1). Notice of filing published in *The Gazette of Pakistan.* (2). Notice of acceptance including a claim published in *Gazette* and typescript specification then open to public inspection. (3). Printed copies of specification available after a considerable delay after grant.

Panama. (1). Typescript specification open to public inspection on filing; after filing, notice of filing published in *Gaceta Oficial;* patent specification not printed.

Paraguay. (3). Notice of grant including one claim printed in local newspaper after grant; typescript specification open to public inspection after grant; patent specification not printed.

Peru. (1). Notice of filing including abstract published for 10 days in *El Peruano* starting soon after filing; claims open to public inspection from filing date until 30 days after last publication of notice of filing. (3). Notice of grant published in *El Peruano;* typescript specification open to public inspection on grant; patent specification not printed.

Philippines, Republic of the. (3). Notice of grant including a claim and drawing published in *Official Gazette* and typescript specification then open to public inspection; patent specification not printed.

Poland. (3). Notice of grant including short abstract published after grant in *Wiadomości Urzedu Patentowego;* patent specification printed about 1 year after grant.

Portugal. (1). Notice of filing including complete text of claims printed in *Diário do Governo* soon after filing. (3). Notice of grant published in *Diário;* typescript specification open to public inspection after expiration of 3 years from date of grant or upon working the patent; patent specification not printed.

Rhodesia and Nyasaland, Federation of. (1). Notice of filing published in *Patent Journal.* (2). Notice of acceptance published in *Patent Journal* and typescript specification then open to public inspection; acceptance must normally occur within a maximum of 21 months (inclusive of extensions) from filing date; patent specification not printed.

Rumania. (3). Notice of grant published in *Information Bulletin of the Chamber of Commerce;* patent specification printed after grant.

Salvador, El. (1). Notice of filing published in *Diario Oficial* after filing and a party in interest may then be able to inspect the typescript specification. (3). Notice of grant published in *Diario* and typescript specification open to public inspection after grant; patent specification not printed.

South Africa, Republic of. (1). Notice of filing published shortly after filing in *Patentjoernaal.* (2). Notice of acceptance including one or more claims published shortly after acceptance; typescript specification open to public inspection after acceptance; acceptance must occur within a maximum of 21 months (inclusive of extensions) after filing date; however, for Convention applications, typescript specification open to public inspection 18 months from Convention priority date or on acceptance, whichever is earlier (N.b., a Convention application in some cases thus may be open to inspection as soon as 6 months after actual filing); patent specification not printed.

Spain. (1). If Official Action issues during prosecution, notice including title and grounds of the Action published in *Boletin Oficial de la Propiedad Industrial.* (3). Notice of grant published in *Boletin;* typescript specification open to public inspection upon payment by applicant of official issue fees after grant (fees must be paid within a maximum of 7 months after notice of grant is published); patent specification not printed.

Sweden. (2). Notice of acceptance published in *Postoch Inrikes Tidningar;* typescript specification open to public inspection after acceptance. (3). Main claim and drawing printed in *Svensk Tidskrift for Industriellt Rattsskydd* (appendix of *Industritidningen Norden*) after grant; patent specification printed several months after grant.

Switzerland. (2). For most applications there is no publication of subject matter on acceptance, but for applications subject to novelty preexamination (applications concerning the textile or watchmaking arts), notice of acceptance including one or more of the Main Claims published in *Feuille Suisse des Brevets.* (3). Notice of grant published in *Feuille Suisse;* patent specification printed several months after grant.

Syria. (3). Notice of grant published in *Bulletin of the Patent and Trademark Department;* typescript specification open to public inspection on grant; patent specification not printed.

Taiwan (China). (2). Notice of acceptance including claims published in *Official Gazette of the National Bureau of Standards* after acceptance; patent specification not printed.

Trinidad. (3). Notice of grant published in *Gazette* and typescript specification open to public inspection on grant; patent specification not printed.

Tunisia. (2). Notice of acceptance published in *Official Journal* and typescript specification then open to public inspection; patent specification not printed.

Turkey. (3). Notice of grant including abstract and drawings published after grant in *Resmî Sinai Mülkiyet Gazetesi;* typescript specification open to public inspection on grant; patent specification not printed.

Uruguay. (1). Typescript specification open to public inspection on filing; after filing, notice of filing published in *Diario Oficial;* patent specification not printed.

U.S.S.R. (3). Notice of grant including one or more claims published in *Byulleteń Izobreteniǐ;* patent specification printed after grant.

Venezuela. (1). Notice of filing including short abstract published in *Boletin de la Propiedad Industrial y Comercial* and in local newspapers after filing and typescript specification then open to public inspection. (3). Notice of grant published in *Boletin;* patent specification not printed.

Cross-references: *Anticipation, Foreign Patents, Searching.*

ADVERTISING. See ATTORNEYS AND AGENTS

ADVOCACY IN PATENT CAUSES

Judge Arthur M. Smith

This article discusses principles and techniques that assist the advocate in properly presenting the issues and the court in reaching the correct decision. While these fundamentals apply to court room presentations in general, they are illustrated by pleading of patent causes, particularly in the U.S. Court of Customs and Patent Appeals.

Preliminary Observations

Some twenty years ago, the late John W. Davis said:

"The need for an appellate process arises from the innate realization of mankind that the human intellect and human justice are frail at best. It is necessary, therefore, to measure one man's mind against another in order to purge the final result, so far as may be, of all passion, prejudice or infirmity."

This observation is particularly valid in patent cases where the constant danger that personal prejudices, arising from such general matters as philosophical attitudes towards patents and monopolies, may supplant or replace the more mature judicial approach required to give an objective determination of issues involving patents arising either in the Patent Office or in the courts. Astute patent advocates frequently prepare themselves for trials before a particular tribunal with this thought in mind. They study and chart its opinions in previous patent cases. Particularly, if the judge is new, they scrutinize his professional background for clues as to his "patent philosophy." They try to ascertain whether he is "pro" or "anti" patent. They canvass his previous experience with patents. The results of such studies can influence the entire trial strategy. Unless the trial judge is an exceptionally astute person, there is danger he may be unduly influenced by the skillful advocate who, by the time the trial is concluded, may have subtly translated the initial bias of the judge into a matter of "public policy."

In the judicial determination of disputes one litigant is certain to be less happy than the other. The appellate procedure permits a review of the proceeding of the lower tribunal so that if an error has occurred it may be corrected.

While an appellate tribunal is somewhat removed from the passions and prejudices engendered in a spirited trial, it is a mistake to consider that this tribunal is entirely free from them.

Lasswell and McDougal [1] have recognized the need for a basis to predict judicial decisions. They suggest that it may be done by applying the formula $\frac{E}{P} = R$. Here E symbolizes "typical environmental factors" such as testimony, exhibits, briefs and arguments; P the "predispositions" of the court before the lawsuit began, i.e., the judge's bias or attitudes; and R the court's response to E. Thus, the decision of the court results from the impact of E on P. The astute advocate is not misled by the apparent certainty implied in such a formula for he knows these symbols represent, at best, unpredictables.

If this formula is a helpful tool in the trial of a patent case before a single judge without a jury, its applicability to the prediction of appellate decisions is not so clear. On appeal, E has become a relatively fixed or known factor, but the uncertainty inherent in the multiple of P there involved can complicate the aspect of certainty in R, even though many of the uncertainties in the E factor may have been resolved. In the Court of Customs and Patent Appeals the P factor is normally 5. In other appellate courts its numerical value will vary. Thus, the impact of E on 5 P can, and many times does, lead to something other than a single R.

Types of Appeals

Any discussion of patent appellate processes must begin with mention of the two types of appeals which are provided by our judicial system. Actions involving the validity and infringement of issued patents follow the normal course of appeals from the trial court. This means that any one of the ten Circuit Courts of Appeals as well as the Court of Appeals for the District of Columbia may be involved, depending upon the location of the trial court. A judicial review of the administrative proceedings in the Patent Office may be by a direct appeal to the Court of Customs and Patent Appeals *or* a *de novo* proceeding under 35 U.S.C. 145 or 146.

While the importance of an appellate review by the U.S. Supreme Court on Writ of Certiorari cannot be minimized, I shall discuss primarily the other appellate processes since they account for the greatest numbers of appeals in patent litigation.

Choosing the Venue

The problem of "venue shopping" in patent litigation arises by reason of the differences in the attitudes toward patents as reflected in the holdings of the various Circuit Courts of Appeals. While statistics on this difference are impressive, they must be viewed carefully, not as absolute, but as indicators of "probabilities." Mr. P. J. Federico studied this point (see article *Adjudications*). Reporting data for the courts of appeals for ten circuits and for the period 1948-54, he showed that one circuit held valid and infringed only 2.6 per cent of the 39 patents before it while another circuit so held 37 per cent of 46 patents. As long as such differences exist, "venue shopping" will continue to be an important part of the duties of the astute advocate in patent litigation. Remember however, that such statistical differences due to the P factor in judicial decisions may change with the judges in the various circuits.

Attitude of the Attorney

If we are to succeed in the high calling of the law, we must start with a clear understanding that justice is far more important than either winning or losing a law suit. Precedents may be made in appellate decisions which can go far beyond the facts of a particular case, influence another court, or determine rights yet to be adjudicated. It must be remembered, particularly on every appeal, that the case won today may establish a legal principle which tomorrow may defeat the end sought in another case. It is important, therefore, that in presenting a case, particularly to the appellate tribunal, the attorney do so not only with a clear appreciation of the applicable law but also with a deep respect for the justice inherent in the situation.

This will require acting with candor. It

may even require an occasional admission of error. Here some consolation is to be found in Alexander Pope's observation that, "A man should never be ashamed to own that he has been in the wrong, which is but saying, in other words, that he is wiser today than he was yesterday."

Expediting Work of the Court

The congested condition of all appellate dockets makes it imperative that counsel do everything possible to expedite the work of the court. Speaking before the American Law Institute in 1961, Chief Justice Warren reported that in the Federal Courts of Appeal, the appeals taken from 1950 to 1959 increased nearly 33 per cent to a total of 3,754. During the same period, he pointed out, the appeals pending and undisposed of increased 21 per cent to a total of 2,374. During this same period, only three additional circuit judgeships were created.

In terms of the sheer bulk of printed materials which the Court of Customs and Patent Appeals has had to study, the records and briefs of the cases decided during the October 1961 term occupy about 9 lineal feet of shelf space. For the period of 1949-1959, inclusive, patent appeals to the Court of Customs and Patent Appeals averaged about *82* per year. Currently, patent appeals are running at the rate of about 250 per year and the expectation is that this rate will continue to increase for some time to come.

One way counsel can assist the court in handling this rapidly increasing case load and more effectively "compete" against all the other cases is by carefully sifting the facts and presenting only the *material* and *determinative* facts in the briefs and arguments.

An appellate court can be led astray by the failure of counsel to base his arguments and his citation of authority upon facts. Familiarity with the facts should be such as to enable counsel to determine those which are material and determinative of the issues on the basis of the precedents. This requires thorough familiarity with the precedents, not only for the "rules of law" to be extracted from them but also for evaluating the essential facts which must be established before the decision relied upon as authority will be persuasive.

Appellate courts need time for study and reflection before they can write sound opinions. This is especially true of all appellate courts handling patent matters. While the problem of expediting the appeal work load is primarily a problem for the courts, astute counsel will realize that they are competing for the attention of the court in their particular case against the many other appeals and many other lawyers involved therein.

While judges in the isolation of their chambers like to think that they "decide" the cases which come before them, it is my growing conviction that these decisions are made by the lawyers who therefore deserve much of the credit for those which are "right" and who must share at least some of the responsibility for decisions which are "wrong." A decision we recently rendered was apparently more "wrong" than "right" as we learned from reading the appellant's Petition for Rehearing, which we granted. On the reargument I was impressed by the soundness in the observation of the young lawyer, who had fallen heir to this "lost cause." He was open and candid in stating in his argument that when our initial decision had been received, there had been a conference in which, for the most part, the remarks about the competence of our court in such a case were less than flattering. As he told the story in argument he said "someone" asked the question, "Was that particular point brought out *for* the court?" When subsequent research and study showed that it had not been presented, it became the focal point in the Petition for Rehearing. When this point was persuasively argued on the rehearing, our previous opinion was withdrawn and the opposite conclusion was reached.

The moral of this story is that the quality of decisions of a court frequently depends on the quality of work of the advocate.

Presentation of an Appeal

In this and the following sections, I shall direct my remarks primarily to those attorneys who have occasion to appear in oral argument in appellate proceedings. My reason for venturing into this phase of the subject with what at best is a limited judicial experience is my certain knowledge that, at the end of my first day as a judge, I knew how to be a better appellate lawyer. From the other side of the bench I saw, with greater impartiality than I had as an advocate, the issues of the particular appeals presented. Being freed from the problem of advocating a particular point of view, I was able to observe impartially the weaknesses and strengths of the lawyers who appeared as advocates. With this as a preliminary justification, I propose to share with you briefly some observations in the hope that they may be useful in raising the standards of advocacy. I know that the quality of the appellate processes, particularly in patent litigation, will be improved in direct proportion to the greater effectiveness with which the advocates present their cases on appeal.

The Record. In successful appeals we find that the record shows careful preparation and development at the trial level so that all appealed issues are fully supported. It is important for you to familiarize yourself with the rules of the particular court to which you are appealing and it is essential that you conform to such rules. Insist upon good printing and good reproduction of such exhibits as you are going to reproduce in the record. Present your record fully but cut out of it the hundred and one things which occurred below and which have lost their significance on the appeal. We have too much to read as it is and will appreciate anything you can do to cut out the unessential and unnecessary parts of the record. Do not, however, take this so literally that you omit much that you may want to refer to and then be required to come in, either on the day of the argument or a few days before, and ask us to take note of something not in the record.

Remember, it is a cardinal rule of all appellate courts that briefs and arguments based on matters outside the record are not effective in winning an appeal.

Remember also that we read only what is in the record and do not interpolate into it things which may have occurred below or what may have been in your mind. You may read into the record some of these matters if you like, but do not make the mistake of assuming that we will do so.

In every patent case, the record starts with the patent application. Inept specifications, inaccurate drawings and faulty claims, if present, will appear clearly wherever and whenever the patent is drawn into litigation. The patent bar generally recognizes its responsibilities in these early stages but in view of the stringent legal requirements and the increasingly strict judicial interpretation of the patent document, the bar must continually improve its skills in this all important area. Symposia in the application of writing skills to the preparation of better patents have been sponsored by the Practising Law Institute in New York City and by The Lawyers Institute of the John Marshall Law School in Chicago. The Practising Law Institute has published as a monograph a paper by Harry C. Hart and one by the present writer under the headings, respectively, of "The Art of Communicating Complex Patent Matters" and "The Art of Writing Readable Patents." Many of the suggestions therein will be found helpful.

A word about the importance of the Patent Office prosecution of the application is in order. All too often, this record shows failure in joining the issue with the examiner or Board of Appeals. Thus, the grounds of rejection may not be clearly stated by the examiner, or the attorney may not respond to the stated grounds. It is the obligation of the attorney to force the examiner to state clearly the precise grounds of rejection and his duty to his client so to prosecute the application that the file wrapper will show at all times the applicant's true position. A file wrapper which fails to show such a prosecution becomes a very weak foundation upon which to build an appellate record. A very large number of the patent appeals which have come before the Court of Customs and Patent Appeals since I have been sitting as a judge have revealed this weakness.

Many of the appeals which come to us because of a failure of the applicant to comply with some aspect of 35 U.S.C. 112 have involved U.S. applications based upon a non-complying foreign application. Since our patent laws make no exceptions in such cases, attorneys handling such matters must start their appellate record by doing whatever may be necessary to assure that the disclosure of the invention in the U.S. application will meet the requirements of 35 U.S.C. 112.

Basically, no appeal can be better than its record. Too many times attorneys try to cover up or conceal weaknesses in their record by arguments and by reliance on inferences which they would have us draw from omissions in the record. *There is nothing which takes the place of facts properly established in the record.*

The astute lawyer who tries his case in the lower court on the assumption that it may finally be decided in an appellate court will take the necessary steps to build his record on appeal as he proceeds at the trial level. He will here lay the factual foundations for the points of law which he will present to the appellate court. He will present his proofs in such a manner that their force and effect will survive transcription to the printed page.

Exhibits. Where the case permits, the advocate will rely in part upon physical exhibits and models, and he should be certain to have them certified to the appellate court. Such exhibits and models can be very helpful and will save much time in the presentation of the case to the appellate court. He should be sure that the exhibits and models are an aid to his presentation and not a distraction which wastes the time allowed for oral argument. In selecting the materials to be so presented and in presenting them, do so as *an aid to,* rather than as a *substitute for* argument. In other words, they are and should be illustrative of something which is established in the brief and presented in the argument. An improperly presented physical exhibit, demonstration, or model can introduce a false note into the most carefully prepared argument.

The Brief. John J. Duff [2] has given a picture of Lincoln as an appellate lawyer. In characterizing Lincoln's work in the appellate courts, Mr. Duff gives us a word picture of the advocate which every appellate lawyer should strive to be. "Gifted with a mind that never rattled or panicked," says Duff. "and with his remarkable power of lucid expression," Lincoln "bore a deserved reputation, at the time, as one of the most skillful appellate lawyers in the whole state. He thought straight and spoke clearly; he did not . . . traffic in subtleties."

In commenting on the written briefs which Lincoln filed, Mr. Duff was impressed by what he calls their "tight prose." The conciseness of Lincoln's way of "putting down his thoughts on paper" are, writes Mr. Duff, "significant of the clarity of Lincoln's thinking." Lincoln's formula, as stated by Mr. Duff, was "The simplest words in the simplest order, and not too many of them." In writing appellate briefs, every attorney can profit by adopting the principles which were so characteristic of Lincoln's literary output: *conciseness, brevity, clarity.* The lawyer who can write his brief with these ends as his guide and who will then argue his appeal in the same manner is not only a good lawyer, he is also a worthy servant of the court and of the law.

A good brief has its beginning in a careful analytical study of the record to formulate the issue on appeal. The importance of properly stating it early in Appellate Briefs cannot be overstated.

It was my privilege as a practicing attorney to have had a considerable professional association with Frank E. Cooper, Esq., both as a practicing attorney in Detroit, Michigan, and as a Professor of Law at the University of Michigan. He has practiced "Effective Legal Writing," has taught the subject to law students and has written extensively on the subject. The February 1963 issue of the *American Bar Association Journal* (Vol. 49, p. 180) contains an excellent article based on a chapter in his then forthcoming book "Writing in Law Practice." This article gives six tests for checking what one has written in formulating the issue. From my experience both at the bar and as a judge, I recommend the extensive use of these tests.

Mr. Cooper's six tests for most effectively stating the issue in Appellate Briefs are:

(1) The issue must be stated in terms of the facts of the case.

(2) The statement must eliminate all unnecessary detail.

(3) It must be readily comprehensible on first reading.

(4) It must eschew self-evident propositions.

(5) It must be so stated that the opponent has no choice but to accept it as an accurate statement of the question.

(6) It should be subtly persuasive.

In appeals involving the complicated technical terminology of patents, I would add a seventh test. It is:

(7) The statement should tell the court about the issue in language which "even a judge" can understand.

The presentation of the legal issues in terms of the technical facts in language which is understandable only to another technician is a futile exercise in rhetoric. No judge can understand the intensely specialized language of all the technologies which come before him unless the lawyer first explains it in common terms of language with which the judge has had prior contact. Do not hesitate to lead the court step by step into an understanding of the technical aspects of the issue. No judge is insulted by an attorney who thus simplifies the technical aspects of the case.

The most effective briefs I have read are those which are concise, brief and clear. Such a brief tells the judge early in his study of the case what issue is involved in the appeal. Statement of the issue against the background of the facts and of the authorities applicable to those facts is an essential step before any argument is advanced. After the issue is stated, use the statement to select and organize the argument to be presented.

Perhaps it is rather elementary to comment here on such things as proper spelling, punctuation and grammar. Yet, I would be less than candid if I did not say that all too often the failure to be correct in such fundamentals as these will weaken the best of briefs. Also, be very careful as to the accuracy of all citations given. We have had instances in which the name of the case as well as its citation have been wrong. It's a major job of legal research to find such cases and every judge will appreciate anything which can be done to make it unnecessary.

A short word is in order about what we do with your citations. We read them. Citations included as intellectual "window dressing" on the assumption that we will not take the time to read them will do far more harm than good. Also, beware of citing a case on the basis of its head notes—we read the opinions and there can be a vast difference between the opinion and the head notes.

In learning to write more effective briefs, the able appellate lawyer will read and profit by the adoption of the many excellent suggestions under the heading Briefing the Appeal in Wiener's recent book.[3]

Avoid in your brief the narrow legalistic approach which relies heavily upon "authorities." "Authorities" are important as precedent but judges are interested first in the facts of the case and then in reaching a right result on those facts. Thus, it's only after the judge understands these facts that he is ready to consider the precedents and authorities.

A good brief is first and last the end product of good thinking. A technically well-written brief may go a long way in masking shoddy thinking, it never can be a substitute for the long and arduous work required of an attorney in "thinking through" his case.

While a court is a true "captive" audience for the literary efforts of the brief writer, this should not lessen the writer's main purpose of making us *want* to read the brief. So, learn to write well. If you were educated as an engineer, read some books and plays. School yourself in the techniques of the poets for precise word usage, of the newspaper writer who understands the effective use of lead paragraphs and interesting headlines, of the short story writer who is expert in plot development and pacing. Last, but by no means least, gain from the novelist and the dramatist their special skills with characters and in the creation of the backgrounds and environment in which the characters move. Gain from them also the importance of the central theme and its development in the light of the experience of the past, the realities of the present and the hopes for the future. Get some drama out of your fact situation.

In short, write your brief interestingly and write it well. Write it as you would like to read it. Give paragraphs, phrases and sentences which will look well and read well in the court's opinion. Courts have been known to adopt some of them.

The Oral Argument. In his foreword to Wiener, "Effective Appellate Advocacy," [4] John W. Davis asserts that "of all the demands his calling makes of an advocate, none is more weighty than the preparation and argument of an appeal. For one thing, it represents the last chance for a client who has lost below. Or, if he has been fortunate enough to win, it is the last effort necessary to save the advantage he has gained. The argument of the appeal is, therefore, a breathless moment for the lawyer and the client alike."

Since appellate court decisions are apt to establish precedents upon which some future case may be decided, it is important, as Mr. Davis points out, that the work of the advocate "be well and skillfully done and especially that he lend to the court all the assistance in his power."

You, therefore, owe it to yourselves, your clients and the courts to learn the skills of appellate advocacy. In this connection I recommend Wiener's books to you. Perhaps I can best encourage you to study these works by referring to some portions which I think are particularly relevant to patent litigation before appellate courts.

What Wiener says about the state of advocacy today and the need for better advocacy is a truism which judges of appellate courts often have observed. Wiener says:

"Too many, far too many, lawyers burden courts of appeal with poorly prepared, poorly presented, and thoroughly unhelpful arguments—for which they receive, and clients pay, substantial and not infrequently handsome fees. Lawyers, like other professional men, can be divided into the classic three-fold scale of evaluation as able, unable and lamentable. Nonetheless, and after making due allowance for the frailties of mankind, it is really amazing how few good arguments are presented and heard, quite irrespective of the tribunal concerned."

It is a basic premise of our judicial system that the way to the ascertainment of truth and the doing of justice lies in adversary proceedings before an impartial tribunal. The conflicting contentions of the opposing parties must be skillfully and forcefully presented if the court is to be led to a just result based on a sound knowledge of the issues and the facts which give rise to those issues. If the opposing positions are not so stated, the court is less likely to reach a sound result. Thus, any lawyer who fails to brief and argue his case in the most effective manner fails not only his client but the court as well.

A fallacy which is altogether too prevalent to be ignored is that there is no use in arguing an appeal; that the issues will all be decided on the brief. Whitman Knapp of the New York Bar delivered an address before the Association of the Bar of New York entitled "Why Argue An Appeal? If So, How?" It was condensed and published in the May-June 1960 issue of *Case and Comment*. Those who have the feeling that an appellate argument is not worthwhile will profit from reading the address.

"The twin objective of an appeal," says Mr. Knapp, "is to arouse the emotion of the judge so that he will be moved to act (if he is not so moved, the judgment will be affirmed without opinion); and to satisfy the intellect so that he will feel it correct to take action favorable to your client." Do not be misled by his use of the word "emotion" and associate it with the judicial prejudice noted earlier. "Emotion" as used by Mr. Knapp means "nothing more nor less than that part (however defined and wherever located) of the human organism which moves it to act."

You can determine your best approach to the oral argument if you know something of the mechanics of the appellate process, which varies in the different appellate courts. If you are to do your best possible job as an advocate, you will make it your business to learn the way the appellate court which is to hear your case goes about its work. This will include 1) the practice of reading or not reading the briefs before oral argument, 2) the way in which cases are assigned to particular judges for writing the opinion, 3) the method of voting on decisions and, 4) the procedure with which the final decisions are arrived at.

Wiener in his "Effective Appellate Advocacy" has devoted Chapter 2 to Methods of Appellate Courts in Considering Appeals. There you will find a somewhat detailed analysis of these methods.

When the judges leave the robing room and occupy their positions back of the bench, each judge is particularly receptive and wants to be informed about the facts and issues of the cases. The time is peculiarly right for counsel to make his best impression. Here, the ability to speak effectively is most important. Too often this important tool of communication is overlooked in the crowded curricula of the schools which train engineers and lawyers. There are, however, excellent opportunities still available to acquire the skills of effective speaking. In most areas the YMCA "Toastmasters" clubs are available. Evening classes in the schools and opportunities such as the Dale Carnegie courses can do much to help one become proficient in public speaking.

The observations made during the something more than 400 oral arguments in which I have thus far participated as a judge prompts me to make a few specific suggestions in this area which I hope will be helpful.

Organize Your Argument. You have a limited time to present it and the court may appropriate a part of this time with its questions. Make every sentence and every gesture count. Also, there is no law against making your argument interesting and challenging. A few well-chosen remarks giving the background of the particular invention in issue can excite the interest of the court. They need take but a few minutes of your time and, if properly presented, can give the court an interesting insight into the background of the art against which it is required to evaluate your client's contribution. We need such information early in the argument, for it is unlikely that we have had the opportunity to acquire it previously. Above all else do not assume that the court has the same level of technical understanding of the invention as you may have acquired in working on the case. I know all too well how difficult it is to erase the acquired technical knowledge from one's mind and to start an argument with fundamental,

elementary propositions. One effective technique I employed when seeking to avoid this problem was to present the technical argument to my wife. I found that if I had so presented it that she could understand it, I was well on the way to a presentation which a judge could understand. Above all else, forget the old adage that "If an invention is made to look so simple a judge can understand it, it's unpatentable!" If judges do not understand your client's invention, how can we be expected to pass intelligently on the appeal?

Opening the Argument. State the facts impartially and fairly. Help the court to know what your case is all about. We may have glanced at your brief before the argument, or we may come into the argument having been able to give your case little or no preliminary study. We depend upon the lawyers to tell us about these facts which are significant for an understanding of the issues. Do not expect us to jump into the middle of a case and follow an argument which assumes that we have an advanced level of knowledge of the facts.

Seek the Right Action. The oral argument should be designed not only to make us want to act, but more specifically to want to act in the way most advantageous to your client. In stating the facts, they should be presented, Mr. Knapp says, in a non-argumentative fashion with both the favorable and unfavorable facts stated. Only when this has been done should you proceed to a statement of the issues and your argument. He advises that you state the issues themselves, not the attorneys' views of the issues. I would add here that the application of this principle to an appeal from the Patent Office requires that the attorney understand the issue of the appeal, i.e., whether the claim is allowable over the reasons given for its rejection, not whether his client is entitled to a patent. This seems trivial, but it makes a great difference in thought processes as the attorney analyzes the case and organizes his argument.

Mr. Knapp also advises that an oral argument is not the time to try to convince the court that your side of the case is the "right" side. He points out that the court cannot possibly in the course of an oral argument find out whether or not you are right. All it can do is to try and understand your side of the case and then make the "right and wrong" evaluation of it later.

Talk, Don't Read. To draw again from the world of literature, consider your brief as a book you are reviewing in your oral argument for the purpose of convincing the judges that they should read the book. *Do not read your brief,* or a mere paraphrase of it. Preferably, do not read anything. Instead, use your time to point out significant parts of the brief which we should read. Tell what is in the brief and make us want to read it. If you accomplish nothing more than this, your oral argument will have been successful.

In presenting your argument, talk naturally. Use emphasis and change of pace whenever possible. Avoid reading a prepared speech to us. Give us the page numbers for all references you make to the Record and Briefs. Then page your arguments to enable us to find them.

While it may interrupt the set plan of your argument, the questions asked by the judges should, if possible, be answered when they are asked. No advocate can hope to know the thought processes or just what blind groping in the record or the briefs may have prompted the question.

Avoid Distractions in Your Oral Argument. I have yet to see the most experienced advocate approach the lectern before a court without some display of nervousness. As a lawyer, I found consolation on this point in talking with seasoned public performers. All of them had "butterflies" when they began their performances. They lost their "amateur" status and gained composure only when they completely lost themselves in the performance at hand. They could do this because and only because of the hours, days, weeks and even years of preparation which had preceded their performance. All of them told me that a good performer without "butterflies" has yet to be invented.

Psychologists have told me that it is this nervous drive, channeled into a creative performance which gives it life. So, expect your hand to shake a bit, your throat to tighten up and your mouth to go dry. Accept these symptoms as a part of the price you pay for being an advocate. However, if the argument is well organized and based on careful preparation, nervousness will disappear shortly after the first raspy "may it please your honors." Once in command of the situation, some lawyers may become so much "at ease" in the argument that they may revert to little unconscious yet annoying and diverting habits. Such mannerisms and habits as the repeated removing and replacing of eye glasses, false or abortive gestures, an awkward stance, leaning on the lectern, or the idle shuffling of papers can all detract from the effectiveness of the best argument.

Fumbling through the briefs or the record to find something to which the attorney wishes to refer takes time and breaks the pace of the argument. Try marking the passages and putting tabs on the pages to which reference is most likely to be made. Many times the judges on our court can supply the desired page references before the arguing lawyer can do so simply because in advance of the argument we have put index tabs and marks on those parts of the record and briefs which our experience has indicated are most likely to be referred to. You should do no less.

Wherever and whenever the argument lends itself to support from models, schematic diagrams, "chalk talks" or the like, use them. Do not use them as "exhibits" to which an objection can be made that they were not a part of the record below. Present them instead as "illustrative of the argument." They are very helpful to the court and they can do much to simplify an argument. During my years of practice I frequently used enlarged charts mounted on paper board. They were hard to carry on planes and trains and frequently difficult to set up and use in court. Yet they performed a much needed function. Even though I have at times prided myself on my ingenuity I was humbled indeed during recent arguments when one of the attorneys eliminated the rigid mountings of his charts and prepared them as the ancient scrolls with a rigid header and bottom rail. Such scroll type charts can be rolled for ease in handling and carrying and they hang very well from the top of an easel.

If an outline has been prepared for use in

presenting the argument, give each judge and opposing counsel a copy of it. It will prove to be an effective and helpful technique.

In our court we tape record all oral arguments. Frequently we play them back as we work on the opinions. The oral argument therefore is much more effective and helpful if instead of referring to "this" or "that" as a drawing or exhibit is referred to, a proper reference is made to it.

Check List of Essential Points. Wiener's book "Briefing and Arguing Federal Appeals," supra, contains an excellent discussion of the "Hows, Whys and Techniques of Oral Arguments." It is full of practical suggestions drawn from a mature lawyer's extensive trial practice.

I agree with Wiener that the really essential features of an oral argument are:

"(a) Not reading the argument
(b) Application of the fundamentals of good public speaking
(c) An effective opening
(d) Clear statement of facts
(e) Complete knowledge of the record
(f) Thorough preparation
(g) Attitude of respectful intellectual equality
(h) Flexibility"

Judicial Procedure Following Oral Argument

Since my own judicial experience is limited to the Court of Customs and Patent Appeals, I will describe the methods we currently use and leave it to you to follow up on this lead as it may apply to the methods employed by other appellate courts.

When appeals are placed on the docket for oral argument, the current practice in our court is to assign the cases to a particular judge for the opinion. The cases on the calendar are assigned by numerical rotation. Thus, each judge is assigned the case opposite his number regardless of subject matter. Some judges read the briefs and records in the cases assigned to them prior to the argument. Others feel that it is better to hear the argument with a completely open mind on the case and so do not read the briefs or records until after the oral argument. Even those who try to read briefs

before argument sometimes are unable to do so for lack of time.

Each day immediately following the oral arguments, the judges meet in conference and discuss the arguments and the cases. At this time a tentative advisory vote is taken to assist the judge who is to write the opinion. During the time the court is not hearing oral arguments, the judges are writing opinions in the cases assigned to them. It happens frequently that further study of the briefs leads to an opinion directly contrary to the opinion recorded by the vote of the judges at the conference held at the conclusion of the oral argument. Each opinion is circulated to all of the other judges who then determine their agreement or disagreement with it and suggest whatever changes or revisions they wish to see made in the opinion.

After the opinions have been circulated and thus read and edited, the judges meet in a conference at which each opinion is carefully reviewed and reconsidered and a final vote is taken on the opinion. Any judge is free to dissent at any time from such opinion. After review and the final vote, it is necessary that a minimum of three judges agree with a decision before it becomes the opinion of the court.

In any appellate court where an advisory vote is taken after the oral argument, it is significant that Wiener found the final decision to coincide with the tentative decisions after argument in a "majority" to a "great majority" of the cases heard. One judge stated the percentage of coincidence as between 60 and 65 per cent while some of the judges fixed it at 90 per cent. In many of the cases, the first impression, which becomes final in a large majority of the cases, is that created by the oral argument. Need I say more about its importance?

(For additional views of Judge Smith, reference is made to his "Patent Law—Cases, Comments and Materials," 2 vols., Overbeck Co., Ann Arbor, Mich., 1954. Ed.)

References

1. Lasswell and McDougal, 52 *Yale L.J.*, 203.
2. Duff, J. J., "A. Lincoln; Prairie Lawyer," New York, Holt, Rinehart and Winston, Inc., 1960.

3. Wiener, F. B., "Briefing and Arguing Federal Appeals," BNA Incorporated, Washington, 1961.
4. Wiener, F. B., "Effective Appellate Advocacy," New York, Prentice-Hall, Inc., 1950.

Cross-references: *Appeals to Court of Customs and Patent Appeals, Attorneys, Briefs—Planning and Writing, Infringement Suits.*

ANTIBIOTICS. See MICROBIOLOGICAL APPLICATIONS AND PATENTS

ANTICIPATION

Trenton Meredith and
Herbert S. Sylvester

Chapter 10, "Patentability of Inventions" of "Title 35—Patents," of the United States Code is the very heart of the patent laws: within its sections are found a definition of the inventions [1] or discoveries which may be patentable [2] and the conditions under which a patent may *not* be obtained.[3] All the other provisions of Title 35, the patent laws, are directed to the establishment for granting and issuing patents, procedures for obtaining patents and provisions for protecting the patent rights.

This Chapter contains Sections 100 to 104, inclusive, but Anticipation is concerned only with Section 102, and in that section only with Paragraphs (a), (b), (e) and (g). Paragraphs (c) and (d) relate to "loss of right to patent," a portion of the title of Section 102, and Paragraph (f) denies a patent to one who did not "invent the subject matter sought to be patented."

Since there is no legal power for the grant of a patent on an invention which is already in the public domain, Section 102 may be described as that portion of the patent laws which protects the public against the grant of such patents and therefore would not promote the progress of science and useful arts. Section 101 assures an inventor or discoverer that he may obtain a patent "unless" he is excluded from a patent by the conditions of Section 102.

Paragraphs (a), (b), (e) and (g), define the situations in which an actual inventor, who has exercised the highest quality of creative ingenuity worthy to be rewarded

by a patent, nevertheless shall not be entitled to it. These provisions (Paragraphs) thus must be considered as to the meaning of every important word.

An invention which does not fall within the descriptions of Section 102 is legally novel. Legal novelty exists when an invention which is practically operative is not already accessible to the public.[4]

The antithesis of legal novelty (which hereinafter will be termed simply "novelty") is anticipation. Anticipation means in a general sense the act of anticipating or state of being anticipated. The word anticipate has one simple definition, applicable here: "to foresee or do beforehand." In patent law, it has been defined as follows:

"Anticipation means disclosure in the prior art of a thing substantially identical with the art or instrument for which the patent is sought." [5]

Anticipation has also been defined as:

"The existence in the prior art of something which precludes the novelty of the invention." [6]

And

"An invention is not anticipated unless the prior art contains some invention so nearly like it that, in view of all pertinent facts the difference did not require invention, which was completed and perfected and knowledge of which was accessible to the public prior to the date of its completion." [6]

Novelty may be destroyed by any one of the three conditions set out in Section 102, that is,

(1) Prior knowledge or use,
(2) A prior patent, or
(3) A description in a prior printed publication.

"Prior," here, means before the invention by the applicant [Paragraph (a)] or more than one year before the application was filed upon which a patent is sought. [Paragraph (b)]. It is self-evident that if the law ended with Paragraph (a), one who was the first inventor could prolong his rights in the invention by delaying the filing of his application for patent as long as it pleased him to do so; he could not be deprived of his right to a patent because his invention could not be anticipated by "prior art." [7] So, Paragraph (b) protects the public by limiting the period during which he may apply for a patent to one year after the invention has been described in a printed publication or patented (anywhere in the world) or in public use or on sale in this country.

Each of these three "unless" conditions for patentability includes or sets up certain requirements which prohibit or forbid the grant of a (valid) patent. A careful study of the elements of each of these conditions, as has been interpreted by judicial opinions, demonstrates the primary purpose to be protection of the public against unjustified patents. The judicial opinions show equally that the statutes are designed also to carry out the constitutional provision of promoting science and the useful arts by securing rights to the rightful inventors.

Of these three conditions, given above, the one with which the courts have found it necessary to deal with most is the third—description in a prior printed publication of inventions for which patents have been sought thereafter. In view of the vast volume of scientific literature which is in continuous production throughout the world and the great number of printed patents issuing from the patent offices of many countries, this source of anticipation is likely to grow in proportion thereto.

Because it is the most likely to be encountered in patent questions, the judicial guideposts relating to anticipation by description in prior printed publications will be considered first herein.[8]

Prior Printed Publication

The statutory statement "described in a printed publication in this or a foreign country," of which the above heading is a more convenient shortened form, has been the subject of minute study by nearly every court with jurisdiction as well as the Patent Office Board of Appeals. Both "printed" and "publication" appear to have been analyzed from every possible angle, but it is hardly to be hoped that the law is now "well-settled."

The large number of reported cases on this subject indicate that the courts have recognized certain requisites which a printed

publication must meet in order effectively to anticipate a later-filed application for patent. Assuming the prior description of the later invention to be clear, such description must have been

(1) "Printed"
(2) A "publication"
(3) Before the invention was made or more than one year before the application for patent was filed.

The statute does not define "printed." Consequently it has fallen to the lot of the courts to supply this shortcoming. Also, the word "publication" has been subjected to the judicial microscope, though it appears to have presented fewer problems than "printed."

"Printed" — Statutory Development. "Printed publication" did not appear in the patent act of 1790 or in that of 1793, but the latter provided that a defendant in an infringement action could prove that

"The thing thus secured by patent was not originally discovered by the patentee, but had been ... described in some public work anterior to the supposed discovery of the patentee...."

The term "public work" was retained in the act of 1836 (Section 15), but Section 7 thereof first brought in the phrase "printed publication"

"The Commissioner shall make, or cause to be made, an examination of the alleged new invention or discovery; and if, on any such examination, it shall not appear to the Commissioner that the same ... had been patented or described in any *printed publication* in this or any foreign country ... it shall be his duty to issue the patent therefor." (Emphasis added.)

The patent act of 1870 provided that prior public use to invalidate or prohibit a patent was limited to this country and that printed publication could be anywhere in the world. Section 24 (substantially the same as Section 4886 of the Revised Statutes) and Section 62 of that act in substance embodies the same provisions as those of the present law with respect to the printed publication aspect.

What Does "Printed" Mean?

"Standard authorities define 'printed' as
(1) To fix or impress.

(2) To stamp something in or upon; to make an impression or mark by pressure.

(3) To strike off an impression from a set of type or the like.

(4) To take a copy from a negative by the action of light upon a sensitized surface." [9]

No evidence has been found in the reports of cases that this broad definition has influenced judicial thinking on the subject.

One court has said that prior description of an alleged invention in a printed book defeats a patent but the same description in an unprinted book does not.[10] This would suggest that the term "printed" must have been given a specific meaning, but the date of this decision indicates that the meaning of printed could have been on much simpler scale of contrasts then than now. The purpose of the change in the law by the new provisions of 1870 must have been intended by Congress

"to clear away a doubt, and to fix the original and deliberate meaning of the legislature"

as Justice Story said about a much earlier change in the patent statutes.[11]

The law now as applied to typewritten publications is not unanimous. The Patent Office Board of Appeals has repeatedly held that the statutory requirement of printed is satisfied when the "text is fixed or impressed on pages in contradiction to publication by such fugitive means as lectures, gestures, etc." [12]

Support for this view is indicated by the decision in *Hamilton Laboratories* v. *Massengill* [13] where intent to dedicate to the public was considered more important than whether the description was printed or typewritten.

A typewritten document is an anticipation if "made known to the general public" in the view of the Patent Office Board of Appeals in deciding that a thesis which had been placed on the shelves of a university library, was a "printed publication." [14] But the Board of Appeals also has ruled that a foreign (typewritten) patent open to public inspection was not a "printed publication." [15]

The courts have held that a typewritten document available to the public in a for-eign country (a patent) is not anticipation.[16]

The holdings by these courts clearly indicate that a typewritten copy of a patent in a foreign country available to the public is not anticipation.[16] Thus, a typewritten document must not satisfy the requirement that it is "printed." This view is sustained, in effect, in *Ex parte Haller*.[15] Since a prior printed publication in a foreign country, unknown in the U.S.A., is effective to bar a patent,[17] if a typewritten description is equally effective to bar a later patent, it should make no difference whether it is available to the public in this country or in a foreign country. This reasoning is persuasively urged by Robert I. Coulter in "Typewritten Library Manuscripts Are Not Printed Publications." [14]

Microfilm has now been held by the Board of Appeals to constitute a "printed publication." *Ex parte Garbo*, 803 O.G. 315, 1964.

The CCPA [18] has expressed the views that neither a wholly handwritten publication nor an illegible publication (whether "printed" or not) would constitute a "printed publication."

Publication. It is at once obvious that the phrase "printed publication" cannot be divided into "printed" and "publication" with useful purpose or result. The object of the statute can be understood only by the phrase itself rather than by the sum of its parts. It follows, for these reasons, that a comprehensive understanding of the impact of this phrase must be derived from the interpretations by the courts of those situations where a prior written document has been held to be an anticipation, or not to be an anticipation, of a later application for patent.

This section will attempt to consider the various views expressed by the proper tribunals as to the term "publication" or the whole phrase "printed publication" where the meaning of the term "printed" was not primarily or solely the issue.

What is a "publication"?

"Publication means to put into general circulation or on sale, where the work is accessible to the public. See *Reeves* v. *Keystone Bridge Co.*, 5 Fisher 467." [19]

So the condition, accessible to the public, or its equivalent, has become a key requirement in interpreting the meaning of publication. Thus, anything which is printed and made accessible to the public is a printed publication.[20]

"Public disclosure or publication to be effective as such must be a revelation of an invention so publicly published or disclosed as to raise a presumption that the public concerned with the art would know of it."[21]

This quotation is from an opinion in which information contained in the file wrapper but not in the issued patent was held not to have been published.

A thesis (one copy) in a college library "available to students and to other libraries having exchange arrangements with" the repository library was held to be an anticipating publication.

"We think intent that the fruits of research be available to the public is determinative of publication under the statute whether the paper be printed or typewritten."[22]

A single thesis in a library even with a notice forbidding copying of all or part was, nevertheless, held by the Patent Office Board of Appeals to be a printed publication.[23]

A copy of a catalogue in a library has been indicated as satisfying the requirement as to accessibility to the public to constitute anticipation.[24]

The degree (number) of publication has given rise to varying holdings. Some courts say accessibility to the public is sufficient.[25] One court questioned whether a printed copy of a foreign publication available to the public in a New York library which was not supported by public funds should be regarded as prior publication under the statutes.[26] Restricted circulation (of advertising leaflets) is adequate,[27] and intent that the publication should be restricted to a particular class and not available to the whole public constitutes (does not avoid) anticipation.[28]

An oil well supply catalogue was held "not to be a sufficient publication to establish anticipation";[29] in more recent cases, however, a catalogue or booklet, of which 50 to 100 copies were distributed to the trade, was held to be sufficient publication.[33] A printed pamphlet was held to be a publication,[30] and trade catalogues which were distributed were held printed publications.[31] Secret government reports did not become publications when declassified without public announcement.[32]

The description in the printed publication must be of an operative invention[34] and adequate to enable one skilled in the art to put it into operation.[35] The reference must not be ambiguous.[36] Elements essential to the invention and not disclosed in the reference publication may not be added to complete the anticipation,[37] and expert testimony may not supply missing essentials.[38] However, a product clearly disclosed anticipates a later patent on the same product even if the process described in the publication is inoperative,[39] but the opposite view was held by one court.[40] A process may be anticipated by a publication describing an admittedly impractical process.[41]

That the reference publication need not disclose the later invention in the exact terms used to describe the invention sought to be patented is well-recognized.[42] But the description of the reference should enable one skilled in the art to carry into use the invention without help from the patent under consideration.[43]

The invention in question must be disclosed within the prior printed publication to be anticipated[44] and not by addition thereto.

Prior Knowledge or Use

To repeat, inventions which are in the public domain cannot be taken away by a patent obtained by a later inventor, however great the creative effort exercised, or through a patent obtained on an application filed more than one year after the public gains access to the invention. Therefore, if an invention was known or used before it was made by the applicant, or more than one year before the application was filed, a (valid) patent cannot be granted to the applicant.[45]

Certain standards have been established by the courts for prior knowledge or use in order for either to be effective as anticipation. Thus, prior knowledge or use must have been:

(a) In this country
(b) Complete—reduced to practice
(c) Accessible to the public.

Also, it must not have been "lost."

Both knowledge and use are not necessary to anticipate.[46] Prior knowledge alone is sufficient.[47]

Prior Knowledge or Use Must Have Been in This Country. The statute requires that prior knowledge or use must be in this country.[48] Certain decisions have emphasized this by holding that such knowledge or use in a foreign country does not anticipate.[49] And even knowledge in this country of a reduction to practice in a foreign country is itself not anticipation.[50]

Must Have Been of the Complete Invention. That the prior invention must have been complete, that is, reduced to practice, is so well-recognized that there can be no reasonable doubt of it at this time. The reduction to practice must have been actual or constructive (filing of an application which becomes a patent) in order to constitute prior knowledge or use.[51] And the law will not accept the mere unsupported word of the alleged inventor as sufficient proof of prior conception.[52] However, actual construction has been held unnecessary if the publicity is sufficient to enable one skilled in the art to reproduce the invention.[53] A drawing per se has been said to satisfy the requirement,[54] and some devices have been considered so simple that no test was considered necessary to require actual demonstrations of operability.[55] But a mere blue print is not sufficient.[56]

Reduction to practice has been defined, in one of the best known opinions, as follows:

"A process is reduced to practice when it is successfully performed. A machine is reduced to practice when it is assembled, adjusted and used. A manufacture is reduced to practice when it is completely manufactured. A composition is reduced to practice when it is completely composed." [57, p. 383]

"It is a mistake to assume that reduction to use must be a commercial use." [57, p. 384]

Prior knowledge and use by a single person is sufficient to anticipate.[58]

Accessible to the Public. Unless the public has learned, or could have learned of the prior knowledge or use, it has not acquired the operative and necessary information of the invention to have possession for later use. Therefore, a necessary element of prior knowledge or use to constitute anticipation is that it was public or available to the public.[59]

The U.S. Supreme Court in the well-known early opinion in *Pennock* v. *Dialogue* (27 U.S. 1) in 1829 considered the meaning of "known or used before the application" and concluded

"We think, then, the true meaning must be, not known or used by the public, before the application." [45, p. 19]

What is public use? One court has defined public use as that operation of the invention which involves no deliberate attempt at concealment or effort to exclude the public and without instructions of secrecy to employees performing the work.[60] Another has added that "it is public use only if it is neither experimental, secret nor abandoned." [61]

Consequently secret knowledge or use does not anticipate.[62]

What is prior knowledge? It is knowledge of scientists and experts working in the field and not of the general public.[63]

One of the widely known cases in the law relating to anticipation by prior knowledge and use is that of *Alexander Milburn Co.* v. *Davis-Bournonville Co.* (270 U.S. 390, 1926) in which the U.S. Supreme Court held a patent invalid as not issued to the first inventor because an application, describing but not claiming the invention of the patent, was filed a short time before the application of the patent in question. The court did not comment on prior knowledge or reduction to practice but simply held that the patentee (claiming the invention) was not the first inventor.

The Patent Office Board of Appeals has extended the "Milburn Rule" to hold the effective date of an article to be published as the date on which it was received by the publisher, a date much before the date of publication.[64] However, the Court of Custom and Patent Appeals has rejected this extension in a recent decision.[65]

An unpublished manuscript is only a conception and, since reduction to practice is necessary, does not itself anticipate.[66] A report prepared by a research organization to a governmental agency was not prior knowledge since it was not available to the public.[67]

Prior knowledge or use need not be extensive to satisfy the judicial requirement as to "public" and therefore to anticipate;[68] the use of a single device is sufficient to anticipate.[69]

Abandoned Applications. Abandoned applications for U.S. patents have no effect as references against later filed applications for patents unless they are referred to in an issued patent.[70] At most, an abandoned application not mentioned in an issued patent can be evidence only of conception of an invention or corroboration of facts described therein.[71] However, in a recent case the Patent Office Board of Appeals sustained the examiner's view that the specification and drawings of an abandoned application for patent were public knowledge as of the date of publication of an abstract thereof in *Official Gazette,* under the practice temporarily in effect which obligated the applicant to make the application (simultaneously with the abstract) available to the public.[72] The Board held that remarks made in an amendment, inconsistent with the drawings and specification, may not be relied upon as a reference.

In an early U.S. Supreme Court case, an abandoned application for patent was held not to be a reference.[73] It appears that the Board of Appeals may have distinguished *Ex parte Lipkin* from *The Cornplanter Case* on an erroneous ground, since it comments, with reference to the contents of the application in the *Cornplanter Case* "... the contents of the abandoned application never having been made public ... ,"[74] while the practice of the Commissioner at that time of opening abandoned cases to the public was not abandoned until after the decision by the Supreme Court.[75]

The *Ex parte Lipkin* decision is discussed in 44 JPOS 185, 1962.

Patented (Prior Patent)

One of the statutory conditions which, if it exists, prohibits a patent to an applicant is that the invention was patented anywhere in the world "in this or a foreign country" prior to the later application.[76] Thus, if a patent has been granted anywhere which claims the invention of the later application, and the patent has been granted before the invention was made by the applicant, or more than one year before the later application was filed, the later application cannot become a valid patent.

In addition to the two prerequisites, (1) that the patent must have been granted before the date of invention by the later applicant or more than one year before the later application was filed, and (2) for the same invention, the patent must have been accessible to the public. This should not be confused with the situation covered by Section 102(e) where a U.S. patent which does not claim, but does disclose (the invention in question), was granted after the filing date of the application in question on an application filed before its filing date.[77] Here the question is "first inventor" and not that of the invention having been patented prior to the completion of the invention under consideration.[78]

Since the effective anticipatory date of a patent is the date it is granted and becomes accessible to the public, there is no uncertainty in determining the patented date of a U.S. patent. This has not been the case in foreign patents.

Citation Dates of Foreign Patents. For some time the patented date of a Belgian patent was uncertain. Recently it seems to have been settled as being the date the patent becomes available to the public, which is later than the date of grant.[79]

An English patent becomes an anticipation on its publication date, which is before its "sealing" date, the date it becomes a patent.[80]

A French patent is effective as a patent as of its "délivré" date;[81] a German patent as of its "ausgegeben" date.[82]

Helpful information as to the "patenting" dates of foreign patents may be obtained from the Manual of Patent Examining Procedure, Section 901.05(a) and (b).

Citation Date of U.S. Patent Claiming Foreign Priority. Calling the statement in the Manual, 715.01 no longer controlling, Commissioner Brenner's Notice of May 27, 1964, 803 O.G. 305, 1964, says in part:

"When an application claim is rejected on a United States patent, which claims and is entitled to claim a foreign priority date, these decisions hold that to overcome the rejection, it may be necessary for the applicant to carry his date of invention back of the patentee's foreign filing date by an affidavit under Rule 131 or an equivalent thereof.

"The foreign filing date is considered the effective date in those situations where claimed subject matter of the domestic patent (or disclosed matter related thereto) is being used as the basis for rejection, and where no question of interference exists. Where the foreign date is used as the effective date the Examiner must determine from an independent examination of the priority documents in the patent file that the domestic patent is actually entitled to the priority date with respect to the subject matter relied upon for the rejection. Section 102(e) of Title 35 U.S.C. considered with Section 119 determines the effective date of such domestic patents."

References

1. "Invention" includes discovery by definition in Section 100.
2. Section 101.
3. Paradoxically, the title of Section 102 is, in part, "Conditions for patentability," although it sets out those situations in which a person shall not be entitled to a patent.
4. "Legal novelty may be predicated of an invention whenever it is new to the public as a practically operative means. Every invention which is not already accessible to the public is regarded in law as new to the public." "The Law of Patents," by William C. Robinson, Vol. 1, p. 305, 1890.
5. *Interchemical Corporation* v. *Sinclair & Carroll Co.*, 58 USPQ 66, 74, DC SNY 1943.
6. *Ex parte Thomas*, 1918 C.D. 11, 13. See also p. 31.
7. "Prior art" includes prior patents, prior publication and prior invention. *Beverage Ice Marketers, Inc.* v. *Bateman Foundry Machine Co.*, 87 USPQ 425, DC NTex 1950; *Ex parte Thomas*, 1918 C.D. 11, 13.
8. No implication is intended that anticipation by prior printed publication is favored by the courts or is more effective than the other types.
9. "Scope of the Phrase Described in a Printed Publication," Andrew R. Benson, Principal Examiner, Division 28, U.S. Patent Office, Patent Office Papers 1916.
10. *Keane* v. *Wheatley*, 14 Federal cases 1764.
11. *Pennock* v. *Dialogue*, 2 Peters 1, 22, U.S. Sup. Ct. 1829.
12. Majority opinion in *Gulliksen* v. *Halberg* v. *Edgerton* v. *Scott*, 75 USPQ 252, 253, PO BdApp 1937. The dissent is interesting as to the opposite view.
13. 45 USPQ 594, 595, 111 F.2d 584, CA 6 1940; cert. den. 311 U.S. 688, 1940.
14. *Ex parte Hershberger*, 96 USPQ 54, 56, 1953; *Ex parte Brendlein*, 105 USPQ 453, 454, 1955; Robert I. Coulter, "Typewritten Library Manuscripts are Not Printed Publications," 36 JPOS 258, 1954. But see *In re Tenney*, 117 USPQ 348, CCPA.
15. *Ex parte Haller*, 103 USPQ 332, 334, 1954.
16. *Carter Products, Inc. et al.* v. *Colgate-Palmolive Co.*, 104 USPQ 314, 320, DC Md, 1955.
17. *Bone* v. *Marion County, Ind.*, 251 U.S. 134, 144, 1919.
18. *In re Tenney, Frank, and Knox*, 117 USPQ 348, CCPA 1958.
19. *Cottier* v. *Stimson*, 20 Fed. 906, 910, Cir. Ct. Dist. Oregon 1884.
20. *Interchemical Corporation* v. *Sinclair & Carroll Co.*, 325 US 327, 1945.
21. *Camp Bros. & Co.* v. *Portable Wagon Dump & Elevator Co.*, 251 F. 603, 607, CA 9 1917.
22. *Hamilton Laboratories, Inc.* v. *Massengill*, 45 USPQ 594, 595, CA 6 1940; cert. den. 311 US 688, 1940.
23. *Ex parte Hershberger*, 96 USPQ 54, 56, 1953.
24. *Jockmus* v. *Leviton et al.*, 28 F.2d 812, 814, CA 2 1928.
25. *Coburn* v. *Schroeder and others*, 11 Fed. 425, Cir. Ct., SD, NY, 1882, cf. 19 supra.
26. *Alexander Anderson, Inc.* v. *Eastman*, 31 USPQ 110, 114, DC SCalif 1936.
27. *Tampax, Inc.* v. *Personal Products Corp.*, 49 USPQ 311, DC ENY 1941, 51 USPQ 399, CA 2 1941.
28. *Imperial Glass Co.* v. *Heisey*, 294 F. 267, CA 6 1923.
29. *Union Tool Co.* v. *Wilson & Willard Mfg. Co.*, 237 F. 837, DC SCalif 1916.
30. *Browning Manufacturing Co. et al.* v. *Bros, Inc.*, 134 USPQ 231, DC Minn, 4th Div. 1962; 137 USPQ 624, CA 8 1963. Note 27 supra, and also *Bros, Inc.* v. *W.E. Grace Mfg. Co.*, 140 USPQ 324, DC NTex 1964. *McGhee et al.* v. *Le Sage & Co., Inc.*, 32 F.2d 875, 876, CA 9

1929. *Imperial Glass Co. v. A. H. Heisey & Co.,* 294 F. 267, 269, CA 6 1923.

31. *Jockmus* v. *Leviton et al.,* 28 F.2d 812, 814, CA 2 1928. *Sachs* v. *Hartford Electric Supply Co.,* 8 USPQ 302, 304, CA 2 1931.

32. *Ex parte Harris, Hoffman & Flakers,* 79 USPQ 439, 1948.

33. *Jno. T. McCoy Inc.* v. *Schuster,* 53 USPQ 167, DC SNY 1942.

34. *Crown Cork and Seal Co.* v. *Standard Stopper Co.,* 136 F. 199, 204, Cir. Ct., SD, NY, 1904; *Permutit Co.* v. *Harvey Laundry Co.,* 274 F. 937, 949, DC WNY 1921; aff. 279 F. 713, CA 2 1922; *Seymour* v. *Osborne,* 11 Wall. 516, 78 US 516; 1870.

35. *Maibohm* v. *RCA Victor Co.,* 33 USPQ 168, 170, CA 4 1937; *Linde Air Products Co.* v. *Morse Dry Dock & Repair Co.,* 246 F. 834, CA 2 1917; *Permutit Co.* v. *Harvey Laundry Co.,* 274 F. 937, DC WNY 1921; aff. 279 F. 713.

36. *In re Turlay,* 134 USPQ 355, CCPA 1962.

37. *Permutit Co.* v. *Harvey Laundry Co.,* 279 F. 713, CA 2 1922; cert. den. 259 US 588; *Loew Filter Co.* v. *German-American Filter Co. of N.Y.,* 164 F. 855, CA 6 1908.

38. *Badische Anilin & Soda Fabrik* v. *Kalle & Co.,* 104 F. 802, 808, CA 2 1900.

39. *In re Kebrich,* 96 USPQ 411, 414, CCPA 1953; *In re Crosley et al.,* 72 USPQ 499, 501, CCPA 1947.

40. *General Electric Co.* v. *Alexander,* 280 F. 852, CA 2 1922.

41. *In re Krukovsky and Guthrie,* 87 USPQ 110, 111, 1950; *In re McKee et al.,* 37 USPQ 613.

42. *In re Wenzel,* 33 USPQ 30, CCPA 1937.

43. *Wisconsin Alumni Res. Foundation* v. *George A. Breon & Co.,* 85 F.2d 166, CA 8 1936; *Seymour* v. *Osborne,* 11 Wall. 516, 555, 78 US 516; *Midland Flour Milling Co.* v. *Bobbitt,* 70 F.2d 416, 418, CA 8 1934; *Young Radiator Co.* v. *Modine Mfg. Co.,* 55 F.2d 545, CA 7 1932.

44. *Guaranty Trust Co. of N.Y.* v. *Union Solvents Corp.,* 54 F.2d 400, 410, DC Del 1931; aff., 61 F.2d 104; *Alexander Anderson, Inc.* v. *Eastman,* 16 F. Supp. 513, DC SCalif 1936; *Fleischman Yeast Co.* v. *Federal Yeast Corp.,* 8 F.2d 186, 197, DC Md. 1925; aff. 13 F.2d 570, CA 4 1926.

45. *Pennock* v. *Dialogue,* 27 US 1, 1829.

46. *In re Shakell,* 93 USPQ 34, CCPA 1952; *Sayles* v. *Chicago & N.W.R. Co.,* 4 Fisher 584; *Interchemical Corp.* v. *Sinclair & Carroll Co.,* 58 USPQ 66, DC SNY, 1943.

47. *Dovan Chemical Co.* v. *Corona Cord Tire Co.,* 10 F.2d 598, DC WPa. 1926.

48. Title 35, Section 102(a), (b) and (g).

49. *Wilson* v. *Seng Co.,* 92 USPQ 197, CA 7 1952; *Ellis-Foster Co.* v. *Reichhold Chemicals, Inc.,* 94 USPQ 16, CA 3 1952; *In re Schlittler and Uffer,* 110 USPQ 304, CCPA 1956; *Reed* v. *Cutter,* 1 Story 590.

50. *Westinghouse Mach. Co. et al.* v. *General Electric Co. et al.,* 207 Fed. 75, CA 2 1913.

51. *In re Schlittler and Uffer,* 110 USPQ 304, CCPA 1956; *Harper* v. *Zimmerman,* 41 F.2d 261, DC Del 1930; *Lincoln Iron Works* v. *W. H. McWhirter Co.,* 142 F.967, CA 2 1905.

52. *Harper* v. *Zimmerman,* 265, note 51 supra.

53. *Simmons* v. *Hansen,* 117 F.2d 49, 51, CA 8 1941; *In re Beatty,* 94 F.2d 1006, CCPA 1938; *In re Lawson,* 36 F.2d 525, CCPA 1929; *Pickering* v. *McCullough,* 104 US 310.

54. *Jockmus* v. *Leviton et al.,* 28 F.2d 812, CA 2 1928; *Des Rosiers* v. *Ford Motor Co.,* 143 F.2d 907, 911, CA 1 1944.

55. *Stitt Trustee* v. *Eastern R. Co.,* 22 F. 649, Cir. Ct. D. Mass. 1884; Cites *Sayles* v. *Chicago & N. W. R. Co.,* 4 Fisher 584.

56. *Morill* v. *Automatic Industries,* 93 F. Supp. 697, DC, WMo 1950.

57. *Corona Cord Tire Company* v. *Dovan Chemical Corp.,* 276 US 358, 1928.

58. *Coffin* v. *Ogden,* 18 Wall. 120, 1874; *Egbert* v. *Lippman,* 104 US 333, 1881; *Hall* v. *Macneala,* 107 US 90, 1883; *Alexander Milburn Company* v. *Davis-Bournonville Co.,* 270 US 390, 1926.

59. *Gayle* v. *Wilder,* 51 US 477, 1850; *Curtis Co.* v. *Master Metal Strip Service,* 125 F.2d 690, CA 2 1950.

60. *Rosaire* v. *Baroid Sales Division,* 104 USPQ 100, CA 5, 1954.

61. *Lyon* v. *Bausch & Lomb Optical Co.,* 106 USPQ 1, CA 2 1955.

62. *Steinfur Patents Corp.* v. *I. Myerson, Inc.,* 56 F.2d 372, DC ENY 1931; *Gillman* v. *Stern,* 114 F.2d 28.

63. *Radtke Patents Corporation* v. *Coe,* 122 F.2d 937, CA Dist. Col., 1941; *McElrath* v. *Industrial Rayon Corp.,* 123 F.2d 627, CA 4 1941.

64. *Ex parte Speier,* 100 USPQ 169, 1952.

65. *In re Schlittler and Uffer,* 110 USPQ 304, CCPA 1956.

66. *Stearns* v. *Tinker & Rasor,* 220 F.2d 49, CA 9 1955.

67. *Rem-Cru Titanium* v. *Watson,* 152 F. Supp. 282, 114 USPQ 529, DC DC 1957.

68. *Cooper* v. *Robertson,* 38 F.2d 852, DC Md, 1930; *Galion Iron Works & Mfg. Co.* v. *Beckwith Mach. Co.,* 105 F.2d 941, CA 3 1939.

69. *Brush* v. *Condit,* 132 US 39, 1889; *Orrison* v. *C. Hoffberger Co.,* 190 F.2d 787, 1951.

70. *In re Switzer,* 77 USPQ 156, CCPA 1948; *Ex parte Heritage,* 77 USPQ 179, PO BdApp 1948; *Servo Corp. of America* v. *General Electric Co.,* 138 USPQ 195, DC WVa 1963. But see *Ex parte Gresham,* 90 USPQ 350, PO BdApp 1951.

71. *Smith* v. *Hall,* 301 US 216, 1936; *In re Schlittler and Uffer,* 110 USPQ 304, 306, CCPA 1956.

72. *Ex parte Lipkin,* 129 USPQ 427, PO BdApp 1960.

73. *The Cornplanter Case, Brown* v. *Guild,* 90 US 181, 23 Wall. 1874.

74. *Ex parte Lipkin,* 72 Supra, p. 430.

75. "The Use of Abandoned Applications as References," P. J. Federico, 28 JPOS 160, 1946.

76. Title 35, Section 102 (a) and (b).

77. For a discussion and citation of numerous authorities, see *Ex parte Thomas,* 1918 C.D. 11.

78. Note 77, p. 23.

79. *In re Ekenstam,* 118 USPQ 349, CCPA 1958; *Carter Products, Inc. et al.* v. *Colgate-Palmolive Co. et al.,* 104 USPQ 314, DC Md 1955.

80. *A. Schrader's Son, Inc.* v. *Wein Sales Corp.,* 3 F.2d 999, aff., 9 F.2d 306.

81. Note 80 supra.

82. *L. Gessford Handy et al.* v. *American Flyer Manufacturing Co.,* 6 USPQ 294, 297, DC SNY 1930; *Ex parte Glaser,* 56 USPQ 280, PO BdApp 1942.

ANTITRUST LAW AND PATENTS

George E. Frost

In *The Clothworkers of Ipswich,*[1] the Court of the King's Bench held, in 1614, that the king could not grant to a guild the monopoly of a particular trade. Ten years later controversy over the grant of monopolies by the king led to the Statute of Monopolies.[2]

United States patent law began with the 1790 Patent Act.[3] But a full century elapsed before enactment of the first statutory provisions dealing with the historically related subject of restraint of trade. Thus the Sherman Antitrust Act finally came in 1890, after the trust movement and anticompetitive activities in the years following the Civil War had brought about a clear public demand for action. For our purposes the principal features of this Act are the following:

(1) Prohibition of restraints of trade by joint action:

"Every contract, combination in the form of trust or otherwise, or conspiracy, in restraint of trade or commerce among the several States, or with the foreign nations, is declared to be illegal ..." (Section 1)

(2) Prohibition of monopolization and attempts to monopolize:

"Every person who shall monopolize, or attempt to monopolize, or combine or conspire with any other person or persons, to monopolize any part of the trade or commerce among the several States, or with foreign nations, shall be deemed guilty of a misdemeanor...." (Section 2).

(3) Authorization to the Attorney General to institute proceedings in equity "to prevent and restrain such violations."

(4) Provision for the award of treble damages in actions brought by persons injured by violation of the Act.

During the course of the debates leading to the Sherman Act, Senator Sherman himself had said that "A limited monopoly secured by a patent right is an admitted exception, for this is the only way an inventor can be paid for his invention."[4] The "admitted exception" became a substantial loophole. One court squarely held that the Sherman Act did not apply to patented articles.[5] Then in cases involving the United Shoe Machinery Company, the Supreme Court went far to hold that an otherwise illegal combination of competitors would not offend the Act if the products involved were patented.[6] In the very first case involving the relation of patent rights and the Sherman Antitrust Act to reach the Court, the Supreme Court stated:[7]

"...Notwithstanding [certain] exceptions, the general rule is absolute freedom in the use or sale of rights under the patent laws of the United States. The very object of these laws is monopoly, and the rule is, with few exceptions, that any conditions which are not in their very nature illegal with regard to this kind of property, imposed by the patentee and agreed to by the licensee for the right to manufacture or use or sell the article, will be upheld by the courts. The fact that the conditions in the contracts keep up the monopoly or fix prices does not render them illegal."

While the courts were thus narrowly construing the Sherman Act in relation to patents, they also applied an extremely hospitable view towards the enforcement of patent rights in general. The *Paper Bag* case, decided in 1910, was widely regarded as supporting an absolute right to suppress patented inventions, even though the actual decision of the court was far short of any such holding.[8] The Supreme Court had also upheld the enforcement of a patent against the sale of unpatented products on the ground that, when used, they violated a restrictive patent license notice on a patented machine.[9]

The Sherman Act decisions relating to patents, as well as the decisions relating to the enforcement of patent rights, led to a movement for change. In response to this movement, the House Committee on Patents (The Oldfield Committee) held extensive hearings. In 1912, the committee proposed a bill which included compulsory licensing and other provisions designed to curb the abuses. The bill never passed. But the report of the committee included a useful definition of the relation of patent rights and competitive activity.[10]

Rights—Contemplated and Not Contemplated

In considering the antitrust aspects of patent practices, thought should be given to the practice in question in relation to the rights contemplated by the patent law. The acquisition of a patent as the result of an invention through research done by the patent owner is clearly contemplated by the patent law. Also—since there have been many efforts to pass compulsory licensing legislation without success—it seems clear that, in the absence of unusual circumstances, the owner of a patent so acquired is free to refuse to license competitors. In similar fashion, a practice unrelated to the subject matter of the patent in question, such as a license restriction on the sale of competitive devices, must ordinarily stand or fall on whether the practice is legal in the absence of the patent.

In an intermediate group of situations the line between conduct contemplated by the patent law (or at least within the scope of rights granted by patents) and an antitrust law violation is more difficult to draw. These are the cases where the practice challenged, while having some justification in a patent law situation, is not squarely covered by explicit or implicit patent law provisions.

In these cases the courts have generally weighed (1) the significance and reality of the patent law justification and (2) the degree of offense to antitrust law principles. In one leading case,[11] for example, the patents were complementary—that is, the manufacture of the commercially most practical device required licenses under two patents. One patent was held by one competitor and the other patent held by another competitor. The two entered into a price fixing license arrangement under which other competitors were licensed under both patents but to sell only at or above the price of one of the patent owners. This was regarded by the Supreme Court as outside the scope of conduct justified by the patent situation. The emphasis given to the price fixing involved clearly indicated that, if the price fixing was absent, the arrangement would have been approved. In an earlier case,[12] an exceedingly complicated patent situation existed because of overlapping patents and somewhat conflicting patent claims. A group of competitors owning the conflicting patents had entered into a series of licensing arrangements under which each obtained the right to grant licenses under the patents of the others. The licensing arrangements permitted each competitor to issue licenses to its own patents at whatever royalty rate it chose. But when the licenses were granted by any party to patents of others, the licensing arrangements fixed the royalties to be charged. The Government brought an action under the Sherman Act alleging in part that fixing the license royalties was price fixing and that the agreements, therefore, were price fixing agreements in violation of the Sherman Act. This Supreme Court concluded that the arrangements did not violate the Act, reasoning in part that the practical conflict of patent rights compelled some form of practical licensing arrangements and that the agreements were a reasonable arrangement, consistent with continued competition, to accomplish this end.

Dividing Markets. It is additionally settled that intent may play a major role in distinguishing legal use of patent rights and illegal antitrust law violation. The so-called cartel cases are one example. It is settled that individual business concerns may grant licenses or assignments of patents in various countries, even though such licenses or assignments have the effect of territorially limiting competitive activity. But where the intent is simply to divide world markets, such agreements normally violate the Sherman Act. Courts have so held where, on examination of the facts, they have found indications that the parties did not simply intend to transfer patent rights but in fact intended to divide world markets.[13] In a somewhat related type of case, patent rights were acquired by a United States concern from foreign competitors. Finding that the purpose was to eliminate Japanese import competition, the Supreme Court held that the Sherman Act was violated.[14] While the line between illegal intent and purpose and legal intent and purpose is sometimes difficult to draw, the cases are clear that intent and purpose plays a major role in distinguishing licit and illicit conduct.

The antitrust law problems that may arise in connection with the varied transactions that take place with respect to patents are numerous and complex. We shall limit the balance of this article to a topical discussion of the most significant problems and their general antitrust law aspects.

Patent Acquisition

The law is clear that the acquisition of physical assets or of stock ownership of a competitor may be an unreasonable restraint of trade, attempt to monopolize, or act of monopolization under the Sherman Act, or a violation of Section 7 of the Clayton Act. Acquisitions of patents by purchase from a competitor have been attacked on the ground that they have offended the Sherman Act or the Clayton Act. Thus in *United States* v. *United Shoe Machinery Co.*[15] an important part of the findings and conclusions of Judge Wyzanski is a point by point analysis of a number of specific purchases by United Shoe of patent rights of competitors. While this case involved a concern that enjoyed a monopolistic market position, the principles applied in evaluating the separate acquisitions in that case are generally applicable in cases where a lesser market position is involved. They have been summarized as follows: [16]

"(a) the nature, number and value of the patents acquired, in relation to the market for competing patented or unpatented processes or products; (b) whether the inventor is using the patent, or has the ability and plans to use it, as against evidence of the purchaser's actual or intended use; (c) whether the purchase had the purpose and probable effect of resolving patent conflict; (d) the purpose and effect of the purchase on the market position of the purchaser and the increase or decrease in competition in the relevant geographic and product market."

In most instances the purchase of patent rights does not bring to a purchaser sufficient market control to raise major problems or a patent of enough importance to alter significantly that market position. Where this is not true, however, consideration should be given to handling the matter in some fashion that does not foreclose continued competitive activity by the seller of the patent(s). One such way is to acquire a nonexclusive license rather than purchase the patent(s). Another procedure may be to purchase the patent(s), with a nonexclusive license back to the seller.

Where patent rights are obtained by direct grant, the patent law itself sanctions the activity. The point has been expressed as follows: [17]

"... [T]he sound rule [is] that monopoly power individually acquired solely through a basic patent, or aggregation of patent grants should not by itself constitute monopolization in violation of Section 2 [of the Sherman Act]. It would be paradox to encourage individual invention by grant of a patent and then penalize that temporary monopoly by deeming it 'monopolization.' Hence, violation of the Sherman Act should, as the cases suggest, require abuse of the patent grant or proof of intent to monopolize beyond the lawful patent grants."

In the *United Shoe* case mentioned above, Judge Wyzanski noted with approval that about 95 per cent of the patents accumulated by United were the result of its own research. And in the *Hazeltine* case [18] the Supreme Court stated that "the mere accumulation of patents, no matter how many, is not in and of itself illegal."

Grantback License to Licensor. Patent rights are sometimes acquired by so-called grantback. This term is applied to a covenant in a license or other transaction by which all or a part of the consideration for patent rights acquired is an agreement to grant in return some other patent rights. In one leading case where the grantbacks were in the form of exclusive licenses to all future inventions, the Supreme Court held that the grantback undertaking was legal, if reasonable.[19] The case involved the sale of a business with a justification for the grantback in the seller's need to have a security interest. In another case a court found that nonexclusive license grantbacks were part of a patent licensing policy designed to stifle the incentive of other concerns to engage in competitive research endeavors and thereby perpetuate a dominance over the industry. The grantbacks were thereby regarded as part of the pattern of conduct, violation of the Sherman Act.

The nature of the grantback is one of the important considerations in relation to the antitrust problems. Exclusive license grantbacks normally exclude the party obligated to grantback. On the other hand a nonexclusive grantback normally serves to increase the number of concerns free to use the patented invention. Generally speaking, nonexclusive license grantbacks are free from antitrust risk for this reason, but exclusive license grantbacks may be subject to close scrutiny.

Patent Licenses

The patent law gives to the patent owner the right to bring infringements to an end by appropriate legal proceedings. It is contemplated that such proceedings will be brought, or not brought, in the business self-interest of the patent owner. Implicit in this aspect of the patent law is the right of the owner to forego bringing patent infringement suit for an appropriate consideration. Such undertaking in contract form is a patent license.

In the fact of a simple patent license virtually no antitrust law problems can arise. Indeed, in instances where courts have held that patent owners have violated the Sherman Act, decrees have been entered requiring such licensing.[20] Problems do, however,

sometimes arise with respect to specific provisions of patent licenses that are challenged because of purpose or effect.

It is helpful to list the provisions of a patent license that were specifically before the Supreme Court in connection with the decree in the *United States Gypsum* case.[21] The Court there approved decree provisions providing for licenses with the following provisions:

(1) A restriction against transfer of the license.
(2) Payment of a reasonable royalty.
(3) "[R]easonable provisions . . . for periodic inspection of the books and records of the licensee by an independent auditor or any person acceptable to the licensee, who shall report to licensor only the amount of royalty due and payable."
(4) "[R]easonable provision . . . for cancellation of the license upon failure of the licensee to pay the royalty or to permit the inspection of its books and records as hereinabove provided."

The evaluation of any license provision (or entire license) from the antitrust law viewpoint requires a consideration of the extent to which the license provision affects competitive activity in relation to the nature of the patent rights involved. In such an analysis an important consideration may be the extent of restriction by the license provision on the nature of competitive activity or merely a definition of the extent of the activity licensed. Since the former involves a possible remedy in breach of contract action which would not exist in the absence of the license, and the latter involves only the patent infringement remedies that would exist in any event, a license provision that only defines the scope of the license is in theory less likely to create antitrust law problems.[22]

Price Fixing. The most sensitive area of all conduct under the antitrust law is price fixing agreements between competitors. Both express price fixing agreements and conduct designed to raise prices have been struck down as per se violations of the Sherman Act.[23] A patent license with price fixing provisions is, accordingly, subject to the most critical scrutiny as a possible Sherman Act violation.

The classic case upholding price fixing provisions in a patent license is *United States* v. *General Electric Co.*[24] In this case

General Electric had licensed Westinghouse under key patents to the incandescent electric lamp, with a provision that Westinghouse would charge at least the prices charged by General Electric. The Supreme Court—at a time when it was quite hospitable to patent owners—considered the question from the viewpoint of the right of the patent owner not to grant any patent license and said:

"...If a patentee goes further and licenses the selling of the articles, may he limit the selling by limiting the method of sale and the price? We think he may do so provided the conditions of sale are normally and reasonably adapted to secure pecuniary reward for the patentee's monopoly.... When the patentee licenses another to make and vend and retains the right to continue to make and vend on his own account, the price at which his licensee will sell will necessarily affect the price at which he can sell his own patented goods. It would seem entirely reasonable that he should say to the licensee, 'Yes, you may make and sell articles under my patent but not so as to destroy the profit that I wish to obtain by making them and selling them myself.' ..."

The *General Electric* case has not been overruled. However, as the courts (especially the Supreme Court) have become more strict in connection with antitrust law considerations and less hospitable towards patent owners, inroads have been made on the permissible price fixing provisions in patent licenses. Indeed, in the *Line Material* case,[25] the Court failed by only a single vote to overrule the *General Electric* case. Courts have now held that the *General Electric* decision does not apply where (1) two patent owners having complementary patents join in issuing price fixing licenses, (2) there is a pattern of industry effort to find a basis for price control effected through price fixing patent licenses, and (3) the price fixing licenses encompass most of the production of the industry. At least one court has held that the *General Electric* case does not apply where multiple price fixing licenses cover four out of five concerns in the industry.[26]

Limitation of Field of Use. The reasoning of the *General Electric* case was applied by the Court to uphold a field of use limitation

in the *General Talking Pictures* case. In that case Western Electric licensed the manufacture and sale of patented vacuum tube amplifiers by the Transformer Company.[27] The license extended only to the noncommercial field. The defendant purchased from the Transformer Company with knowledge of the license limitation and proceeded to use the amplifier in the commercial field. The Court held that the defendant infringed the patents involved and thereby sustained both the field of use limitation and enforcement of the patents against a purchaser of otherwise licensed apparatus with notice of the license limitation.

A less troublesome case arises where a patent license extends to the manufacture of only certain types of apparatus, or in some other respect permits less than the entire use of the patent rights in question. In such instance problems of the rights of purchasers of patented apparatus are not likely to be involved. Such limited licenses have been upheld and—standing alone—do not represent an area of special antitrust law risk.

Some types of license provisions find support in the specific provisions of the patent laws. One of these is the patent license with a territorial limitation. Under 35 USC 261 the patent owner is authorized to make a "grant," or territorial assignment of the patent right. With this express authorization for a territorially limited assignment, a territorially limited license appears to be implicitly authorized. Such licenses are thus supportable not only under the *General Electric* theory of a grant of less than the whole of the patent rights but in addition on the ground that they are implicit in the assignment provisions of the patent law.

Restriction of Licensee. The particularly sensitive type of license provision is the license restriction on the patentee himself.[28] The *General Electric* case, it will be recalled, proceeds upon the basis that, since the patent owner is free to withhold licenses entirely, he is also free to grant a license to less than the totality of the patent rights. But where the patent owner is himself restrained from some competitive activity, the patent itself affords no justification, since he is then restricted in his own conduct and not just dictating the extent of license to another. In like manner, where the licensee and not the patentee seeks a restrictive license provision (such as a price fixing provision), or the effect of such provision (as by licensee's determining the price fixed), it is the licensee and not the patentee who is determining what should be done and the reasoning of the *General Electric* case cannot be applied.

Attempted Control beyond Scope of Patent. Similarly, license provisions directed to the manufacture, use, and sale of apparatus other than the patented apparatus must be tested by antitrust law considerations. The existence of the patent in such instances does not justify the provisions since the patent is not directed to the subject matter of the license provisions. Thus, price provisions directed to the sales price of articles have been held illegal where the patent related to a tool for the manufacture of the articles or a process for making the articles.[29]

Agreements by licensees not to manufacture products competitive with the patented product have similarly been considered outside of any justification in the patent.[30] In one important case the license contained price fixing provisions directed to the patented product and provisions requiring royalty patents on both patented and unpatented products.[31] The Court regarded such provisions as an important part of the total conduct involving a Sherman Act violation because of the effect of the provisions in driving unpatented products out of the market by reason of the royalty charge.

Exclusive License. An exclusive license restrains the patentee from making, using and selling the patented invention. However, 35 U.S.C. authorizes assignment of the patent. Such assignment gives the assignee the full right title and interest in the patent, and hence the right to exclude the assignor. The restraint on the patentee is the same in the case of an assignment as in the case of an exclusive license. Exclusive licenses are accordingly normally free of antitrust law difficulty despite the restraint on the patentee inherent in their nature.

Tying Practices. Tying practices are second only to price fixing as a sensitive antitrust area. The Supreme Court has stated

that "Tying agreements serve hardly any purpose beyond the suppression of competition." [32] Section 3 of the Clayton Act was specifically framed to reach the practice of the United Shoe Machinery Company of requiring lessees of its patented machines to purchase supplies from it. It is now well settled that where a patent license requires the licensee to use unpatented supplies purchased from the patentee—or in some other respect to give the patentee a business otherwise open to competition—there is a violation of Section 3 of the Clayton Act, the Sherman Act, or the Federal Trade Commission Act in almost every instance. The principal exception applies where the tying arrangement can be justified upon the basis of the need for quality control in relation to the particular facts of the case.[33]

A specific application of the tying doctrine applies in the case of so-called "package" patent licenses. The Supreme Court has held that where a willing licensor and a willing licensee enter into a license agreement giving the licensee freedom to use any, some, or all of the licensor's patents, the fact that the license covers more than one patent brings about no illegality.[34] However, where it is necessary to take a license to an unwanted patent in order to get a license to a patent desired, the licensor is tying the unwanted patent license to the desired patent license.[35] This reasoning was applied to the lease of motion picture films in "blocks" for exhibition, where the Supreme Court regarded this as an important anticompetitive practice forming a part of improper restraint of trade and monopolization. The reasoning was applied in the case of patent licenses to hold that where the same royalty was charged for a license covering a whole group of patents as for any part of the group or any single patent there was an economic coercion giving rise to the necessary insistence that the licensee take an unwanted license to obtain a desired license.[36]

Patent Pools

It will be recalled that the Sherman Act contemplates that individual competitive entities will compete in their own self-interest without agreements or other limitations on competition. It is settled that this applies to research and new product competition as well as other forms of competition. Applied to the field of research and new product competition, this principle would appear to forbid agreements respecting patent rights that have the effect of eliminating competition otherwise present, in the exploitation of rival technologies. In addition, this consideration as applied to patent rights would appear to forbid agreements between patent owners by which their combined patent holdings are collectively used to foreclose competition by others.

The so-called patent "pool" cases have struck down agreements among competitors by which patent rights have been jointly used either to limit competition or foreclose competitors. Many of these cases involve extreme factual circumstances, such as price fixing, agreements not to use patented devices, litigation funds for use against competitors not in the "pool" and the like.[37]

In other instances, the courts have found illegality in efforts by individual concerns designed to preclude the development of inventions by outsiders. In one leading case,[38] the dominant manufacturer used a strong patent position in the electric lamp field to obtain patent license agreements requiring licensees to give licenses under any patents they might obtain. The court looked upon this as a way to foreclose competition by the licensees and an important element in overall conduct violating the Sherman Act.

Other cases involving licensing schemes relating to patents of competitors have been regarded as violating the Sherman Act. In the leading case,[39] two rival concerns with inventions and patent rights in the glass bottle making field entered into agreements that had the effect of limiting their own competition and, in addition, dividing up the field of manufacture of each of the users of the machines. The net effect was considered to be foreclosure of competition otherwise present among the glass bottle manufacturers as well as the machinery manufacturers. The Sherman Act was held to have been violated.

The antitrust law and the patent law both have many facets. This article indicates the approaches involved and generally the nature of the problems that arise.

References

1. 77 *Eng. Rep.* 1218, 11 Coke 53a.
2. 21 Jac. 1, Ch. 3.
3. 1 Stat. 109.
4. 21 Cong. Rec. 2457.
5. Rubber Tire Wheel Co. v. Milwaukee Rubber Works, 154 Fed. 359, CA 7 1907.
6. United States v. United Shoe Machinery Co. of N.J., 247 U.S. 32, 1918; United States v. Winslow, 227, U.S. 202, 1913.
7. Bement v. National Harrow Co., 186 U.S. 70, 91, 1902.
8. Continental Paper Bag Co. v. Eastern Paper Bag Co., 210 U.S. 405, 1908.
9. Henry v. A. B. Dick Co., 224 U.S. 1, 1912.
10. Rep. No. 1161, 62nd Cong. 2d Sess., p. 2.
11. United States v. Line Material Co., 333 U.S. 287, 1948.
12. Standard Oil Co. (Ind.) v. United States, 283 U.S. 163, 1931.
13. E.g. United States v. National Lead Co., 63 Fed. Supp. 513 DC SNY 1945, aff'd. 332 U.S. 319.
14. United States v. Singer Mfg. Co., 83 S.Ct. 1773, 1963.
15. 110 Fed. Supp. 295, DC Mass. 1953.
16. Report of the Attorney General's National Committee to Study the Antitrust Law, p. 227, 1955.
17. *Ibid.*, p. 226.
18. Automatic Radio Mfg. Co. v. Hazelting Research, 339 U.S. 827, 1950.
19. Transparent-Wrap Machine Corp. v. Stokes & Smith Co., 329 U.S. 637, 1947.
20. Report, supra note 17, p. 255.
21. United States v. United States Gypsum Co., 340 U.S. 76, 96-104, 1950.
22. Diggins, Antitrust Problems in the Exploitation of Patents, Staff Report to Subcommittee No. 5, Committee of the Judiciary, House of Representatives, 1956, p. 8.
23. United States v. Trenton Potteries Co., 273 U.S. 392, 1927; United States v. Socony-Vacuum Oil Co., Inc. 310 U.S. 150, 194.
24. 272 U.S. 476, 1926.
25. Supra note 12.
26. Newburgh Moire Co. v. Superior Moire Co., 237 F.2 283, CA 3 1956.
27. General Talking Pictures Corp. v. Western Electric Co., 305 U.S. 124, 1938.
28. Report, supra note 17, at p. 238.

29. United States v. General Electric Co., 80 Fed. Supp. 989, 1004, DC SNY 1948.
30. E.g. National Lockwasher Co. v. Geo. K. Garrett Co., 137 F.2 255, CA 3 1943.
31. United States v. United States Gypsum Co., 333 U.S. 364, 384-5, 1948.
32. Standard Oil Company of California v. United States, 337 U.S. 293, 305, 1949.
33. See, e.g., American Optical Company v. New Jersey Optical Company, 58 Fed. Supp. 601, DC Mass, 1944.
34. Automatic Radio Mfg. Co. v. Hazeltine Research, supra note 19.
35. American Securit Co. v. Shatterproof Glass Corp., 268 F.2 769, CA 3 1959.
36. Id.
37. E.g., Standard Sanitary Mfg. Co. v. United States, 226 U.S. 20 1912.
38. United States v. General Electric Co., 82 Fed. Supp. 753, DC NJ 1949.
39. Hartford-Empire Co. v. United States, 323 U.S. 386, 1945.

Bibliography

Wood, James C., "Patents and the Antitrust Law," 1941.
Nordhaus, Raymond C., and Jurow, Edward F., "Patent Antitrust Law," 1961.
Toulmin, Harry A., "Antitrust Laws," 4 vols., 1950.
Oppenheim, S. C., "Cases on Federal Antirust Laws," Chapter 14, 1959.

Cross-references: *Foreign Licensing and Antitrust Law, Licenses, Licenses—Package, Use Patents, Unfair Competition.*

APPEALS—COURT OF CUSTOMS AND PATENT APPEALS

Chief Judge Eugene Worley

The court, now designated as the United States Court of Customs and Patent Appeals, was created, as the United States Court of Customs Appeals, by an Act of Congress dated August 5, 1909, and was organized for business on April 22, 1910, with quarters in Washington, D.C. Until 1929, the court was known by the latter name and its jurisdiction confined to customs matters.

An Act of March 2, 1929, effective April 7, 1929, conferred on the court the jurisdiction formerly vested in the Court of Appeals of the District of Columbia with respect to appeals from the Patent Office in patent and trademark cases, but not equity cases. That act also changed the title of the court to the United States Court of Customs and Patent Appeals.

The court is presently located in quarters designed for it in the Internal Revenue Building, Washington, D.C., which quarters it has occupied since June 1930. A new courthouse for the United States Court of Customs and Patent Appeals and the United States Court of Claims has now been authorized with construction beginning in 1964. The courthouse is to be located east of and facing Lafayette Square, a park just north of the White House.

The Judges

The Court of Customs and Patent Appeals is composed of a Chief Judge and four Associate Judges, the same number as when the court was established in 1910. As in the case of judges of the courts of appeals and district courts, the judges of this court are appointed by the President, by and with the advice and consent of the Senate, and hold office during good behavior.

The Chief Justice of the United States is authorized, upon presentation of a certificate of necessity by the Chief Judge of the Court of Customs and Patent Appeals, to designate and assign temporarily any circuit or district judge to serve as a judge of the court. A retired judge of any other court of the United States may also be so designated and assigned temporarily to the court.

The court is one created under Article III of the Constitution. Its judges, including those retired, may serve, by designation and assignment of the Chief Justice of the United States, on United States District Courts and Courts of Appeals. *Glidden Co. v. Zdanok et al.*, 370 U.S. 530, 1962.

Employees of the Court

The Court of Customs and Patent Appeals employs a Clerk, a Marshal, and a Reporter of Decisions, all having duties specified by statute, and such other employees as are necessary to the conduct of its work.

Jurisdiction

The jurisdiction and function of the Court of Customs and Patent Appeals in reviewing decisions of Patent Office tribunals are set out in 35 U.S.C. 141, 144, and Section 21 of the Trademark Act of 1946 (Lanham Act) as amended by Section 12 of Public Law 87-772, app. Oct. 9, 1962.

Sections 141 through 144, relating to patent cases, read as follows:

Section 141. Appeal to Court of Customs and Patent Appeals

An applicant dissatisfied with the decision of the Board of Appeals may appeal to the United States Court of Customs and Patent Appeals, thereby waiving his right to proceed under section 145 of this title. A party to an interference dissatisfied with the decision of the board of patent interferences on the question of priority may appeal to the United States Court of Customs and Patent Appeals, but such appeal shall be dismissed if any adverse party to such interference, within twenty days after the appellant has filed notice of appeal according to section 142 of this title, files notice with the Commissioner that he elects to have all further proceedings conducted as provided in section 146 of this title. Thereupon the appellant shall have thirty days thereafter within which to file a civil action under section 146, in default of which the decision appealed from shall govern the further proceedings in the case.

Section 142. Notice of appeal

When an appeal is taken to the United States Court of Customs and Patent Appeals, the appellant shall give notice thereof to the Commissioner, and shall file in the Patent Office his reasons of appeal, specifically set forth in writing, within such time after the date of the decision appealed from, not less than sixty days, as the Commissioner appoints.

Section 143. Proceedings on appeal

The United States Court of Customs and Patent Appeals shall, before hearing such appeal, give notice of the time and place of the hearing to the Commissioner and the parties thereto. The Commissioner shall transmit to the court certified copies of all the necessary original papers and evidence in the case specified by the appellant and any additional papers and evidence specified by the appellee and in an ex parte case the Commissioner shall furnish the court with the grounds of the decision of the Patent Office, in writing, touching all the points involved by the reasons of appeal.

Section 144. Decision on appeal

The United States Court of Customs and Patent Appeals, on petition, shall hear and determine such appeal *on the evidence produced before the Patent Office,* and the decision shall be confined to the points set forth in the reasons of appeal. Upon its determination the court shall return to the Commissioner a certificate of its proceedings and decision, which shall be entered of record in the Patent Office and govern the further proceedings in the case. (Emphasis added)

Taking an Appeal

The statutes provide that the appellant must give notice to the Commissioner of Patents of an appeal to the Court of Customs and Patent Appeals and file his reasons of appeal, in writing, in the Patent Office. Certified copies of all the necessary original papers and the necessary evidence in the case, as specified by the appellant, and, in an interference or other *inter partes* case, any additional papers and evidence specified by the appellee, are transmitted to the court by the Commissioner. The appellant is required to file in the office of the clerk of the court a petition which must show compliance with the requirements of sections 142 and 143.

The clerk of the court causes the record to be printed, the costs being paid by the appellant in *ex parte* cases and also in *inter partes* cases except for certain situations where costs are apportioned under the rules of the court. Briefs of the parties must be submitted in printed form.

Hearings

The court begins its term in October and is open throughout the year for the conduct of all business in connection with appeals other than hearings. Until recently cases on the patent docket, including trademark cases, were generally called for argument beginning on the first Monday of January, March, May and November, and customs cases were heard in February, April, October and December. An increase in the patent and trademark docket in recent years, from

63 appeals in 1956 to 250 in 1963, has made it necessary to call some patent cases for hearing during almost every month of the term. The Commissioner of Patents is always represented by the Solicitor of the Patent Office at oral argument of an *ex parte* case, that is, where the appeal is from the refusal of claims by the Board of Appeals. Otherwise, the parties to an appeal may submit the case on brief if they do not choose to be represented at oral argument. In *ex parte* cases, argument is limited to 30 minutes for each side. In appeals from the decision of the Board of Patent Interferences, the appellant is allowed 45 minutes for argument and the appellee 30 minutes. The Commissioner of Patents is not a party to such *inter partes* appeals. In any appeal, the appellant is permitted to reserve a part of his time for rebuttal.

All five judges customarily sit during the hearing of an appeal. Three judges constitute a quorum and concurrence of three judges is necessary to a decision. 28 U.S.C. 215.

The Decision

Under the provisions of 35 U.S.C. 144, the Court of Customs and Patent Appeals determines the appeal on the evidence produced before the Patent Office and the decision is confined to the points set out in the reasons of appeal filed in the Patent Office. On this point, also note the majority and minority opinions in *In re Gruschwitz et al.*, 138 USPQ 451, CCPA 1963. [Cf. Baechtold, 46 JPOS 373, 1964.] A certificate of the court proceedings and decision is returned to the Commissioner of Patents and entered on record in the Patent Office. The decision governs further proceedings in the case.

While a decision favorable to an applicant in either an *ex parte* or *inter partes* case is not a directive to the Patent Office to issue a patent, such a decision usually does result in the issuance of a patent. However, should the Patent Office subsequently acquire knowledge of reasons, independent of the matters adjudicated in the court's decision on appeal, why a patent should not be granted, it is not barred from taking appropriate action. As pointed out in *Glass*

v. *De Roo et al.*, 44 CCPA 723, 726; 239 F.2d 402, 404; 112 USPQ 62, 64:

"...The decisions of this court, however, do not approve or authorize the actual issuance of patents, even in *ex parte* cases, and are not mandates for their issuance. They are confined to the issues properly raised on appeal, *In re Curley et al.*, 34 CCPA (Patents) 749, 158 F.2d 300, 72 USPQ 116, and their effect is to remand the cases involved to the Patent Office for further proceedings consistent with the court's opinion." *Jeffery Mfg. Co.* v. *Kingsland,* 179 F.2d 35, 83 USPQ 494, 1949.

In this respect, an adjudication of the Court of Customs and Patent Appeals stands in the same position as an adjudication in a civil action under 35 U.S.C. 145, 146. As the Supreme Court stated in *Hoover Co.* v. *Coe,* 325 U.S. 79, 89; 65 USPQ 180, 185, 1945:

"..., where an applicant has succeeded in a bill filed under R. S. 4915 [predecessor of 35 U.S.C. 145 and 146], the courts have not questioned the power of the Patent Office subsequently to disallow the claims for want of invention over a newly discovered reference to the prior art."

Each year, the reporter of decisions publishes the court's opinions in patent and trademark cases in a *Patents* volume of the U.S. Court of Customs and Patent Appeals Reports (CCPA). Each volume covers the term from October to October. The decisions in patent cases are also published in the Federal Reporter, Second Series (F.2d), the United States Patents Quarterly (USPQ), the Official Gazette of the Patent Office (O.G.), and in the Decisions of the Commissioner of Patents (C.D.).

Attorneys

Any attorney who is entitled to practice in the Supreme Court of the United States or in the courts of appeals of the United States or in the court of last resort in any State or Territory or the District of Columbia or in the United States Court of Claims may be admitted to practice in the Court of Customs and Patent Appeals. Admission is usually upon the motion by an attorney of the court made in open court, with the applicant for admission present.

Cross-references: *Advocacy in Patent Causes, Appeals, Validity...Standard of Invention.*

APPEALS IN PATENT SOLICITATION

Edward C. Vandenburgh

Appeals to the Board of Appeals

Time for Appeal—Notice of Appeal. When an applicant believes that claims to an invention have been refused to him without adequate justification, the initial review of the refusal is obtained by way of appeal to the Board of Appeals in the Patent Office. Most attorneys follow the practice of waiting until the "final" rejection before appealing to the Board. However, Rule 191 permits an appeal to be taken after the claims have been twice rejected. This is usually interpreted to mean that all of the existing claims being prosecuted in the application must have been twice rejected. Only rejections of claims are appealable. Rejections based on formalities which do not result in the disallowance of claims are reviewed by way of petition. See *Petitions.*

The applicant has a period of six months following the final rejection within which to appeal. The initial step is quite simple. It requires only the payment of the appeal fee and the filing of a Notice of Appeal. Both of these must be done within the six-month period. As will be seen from the form in the appendix to the Patent Office Rules of Practice, the Notice of Appeal merely identifies the application, states that the applicant is appealing to the Board of Appeals and identifies which claims are included in the appeal. A holding that the appeal is not in proper form is reviewed by way of petition to the Commissioner.

Critical Review of Application Before Appeal. Before filing the Notice of Appeal, it is important that the application, and particularly the claims to be appealed, be reviewed and revised, if necessary, to provide the best possible condition for appeal. One important facet of this review is to list the arguments that are to be employed as a basis for justifying the reversal of the examiner and the allowance of the claims. Each claim then should be checked to make sure that the language of the claim forms a basis for the argumentative distinction between the claimed invention and the prior art. It is surprising how many decisions are affirmed by the Board of Appeals, or by a court reviewing the Board's decision, on the basis that the claims fail to distinguish over the prior art, even though the decision recognizes that the appellant's arguments establish that an invention exists. Except to the extent that a "means" clause is involved, the language in the claims laying a basis for the argument, i.e., point of novelty, should be more than a mere statement of the result sought to be achieved. For the proper claiming of an invention see *Claim Drafting.* If the language of some or all of the claims does not form an adequate basis for the arguments to be employed, an amendment should be filed under Rule 116(a) putting the claims in better condition for appeal before the Notice of Appeal is filed. Such amendment generally, but not necessarily, will be entered. See Section 714.13 of the Manual of Patent Examining Procedure. If entry of the amendment is refused, a review of that refusal can be obtained by way of petition to the Commissioner.

Brief on Appeal and Request for Oral Hearing. Following the filing of the Notice of Appeal and the payment of the appeal fee, the applicant must file a brief to perfect the taking of the appeal. The failure to file a brief will result in a dismissal of the appeal. The brief must be filed by the later of these two dates: (1) sixty days from the date when the Notice of Appeal with the appeal fee was filed or (2) the date of expiration of the response period of the rejection from which an appeal is being taken. (In the case of an appeal from a final rejection, this latter date would be six months from the date of the final rejection.) Upon request made prior to the expiration of the period for filing the brief, the time for filing the brief may be extended. See Rule 192.

The appeal brief should include: (1) a general statement of the invention sought to be protected by the application and including reference to the drawings by means of the numbers employed thereon; (2) a copy of the claims being appealed; and (3) the arguments justifying the allowance of the claims over the rejection (including the citation of prior decisions where pertinent). Only the original, ribbon, copy of the brief need be filed if there is no request for an oral hearing. If a request is made for an oral hearing, the original and two copies (e.g., carbon copies) of the brief must be filed.

The brief should be carefully prepared. Even when an oral argument is requested, the brief will be used by the Board as a principal basis for their consideration of the applicant's arguments that the examiner should be reversed. Furthermore, a well-prepared brief may lead the examiner to conclude that the rejected claims are allowable, thus eliminating the necessity for further proceedings on the appeal. See *Advocacy in Patent Causes; Briefs*. A good discussion of the preparation of briefs will be found also in the article "Briefs Before the Board of Appeals," by T. Price, 30 JPOS 647, 1948.

An applicant's attorney, desirous of orally arguing the appeal before the Board, should make a written request for an oral hearing at the time that his *initial* brief is filed. In the absence of a timely request for an oral hearing, the appeal will be decided by the Board on the basis of the briefs that were filed.

The appeal brief will be reviewed by the examiner previously handling the application. If he or his superiors are not fully convinced that the previous rejection of the claims was sound, it is possible that they will proceed to issue a notice of allowance, which of course ends the matter. As an alternative in some instances, they will call the applicant's attorney, or his Washington associate, and suggest that the claims may be made allowable with certain revisions. In such instance, the applicant is often satisfied to file an amendment incorporating such suggestions to obtain allowance of the claims. It is not inappropriate for the applicant to request an interview with the examiner after the filing of an appeal brief. However, he should allow the examiner sufficient time to review the brief before doing so. Discussions at such an interview, if granted, particularly in the light of the arguments presented in the brief, may re-

sult in an agreement as to a satisfactory form for the allowance of claims.

Examiner's Answer—New Ground of Rejection—Applicant's Reply. Following the filing of the applicant's brief, the examiner will prepare a statement of his position as to the rejection of the claims. A copy of this statement or answer of the examiner is of course mailed to the applicant's attorney. In addition to responding to the arguments made in the applicant's brief, the examiner's answer sets forth the grounds upon which he then relies for the rejection of the claims. Any grounds not included therein, even though they may be set forth in the rejection appealed from, will be deemed to have been withdrawn. See *Ex parte Kaul*, 125 USPQ 70, 73, PO BdApp 1959, and Section 1208 of the Manual of Patent Examining Procedure. If a new ground of rejection is not included in the examiner's answer, the applicant has twenty days from the date of mailing thereof to file a reply to any arguments of the examiner, if the applicant wishes to do so.

In some instances the examiner will present a new ground of rejection, e.g., a new reference, in his answer to applicant's brief. A new ground of rejection need not necessarily involve the citation of a new reference. However, when a new reference is not cited or relied upon, it is not safe to assume that the new argument is a new ground of rejection unless it is specifically labeled as such in the examiner's answer. When a new ground of rejection is made, the applicant has a period of sixty days within which to file a reply thereto. This reply may include a proposed amendment seeking to avoid the new rejection. Similarly, affidavits might be filed seeking to justify the allowance of the claims over the new rejection.

When amendments or affidavits are filed, the subject matter will usually be referred to the examiner by the Board of Appeals for his consideration. If the applicant does not reply to the new ground of rejection, his failure is construed as acquiescence in the rejection and the rejection is automatically sustained. See Section 1208.01 of the Manual.

Hearing and Decision by Board—New Ground of Rejection. While efforts are continually being made to reduce the backlog of cases, the time between the filing of the last brief and the Board's reaching the case for decision is many months. However, if an application has been made "special," that status will continue and it will be reached for action by the Board much more promptly. When an oral hearing has been requested, the applicant's attorney is duly notified of the date and time set for the hearing. Should it subsequently become apparent that no appearance will be made, the attorney should notify the Board as soon as that fact becomes known. Normally the applicant is given thirty minutes for argument. If additional time is desired, it should be requested before the argument commences.

A copy of the decision of the Board is mailed to the applicant's attorney. The applicant has sixty days from the date of the decision in which to seek review thereof outside the Patent Office and thirty days to request reconsideration of the decision. If a request for reconsideration is filed within the thirty-day period, the applicant then has thirty days following the decision on the request for reconsideration within which to seek further review outside the Patent Office.

The Board is not limited merely to affirming or reversing the examiner, in whole or in part. In some instances, the Board may expressly recommend that the claims be allowed if specified action, e.g., amendment, be taken by the applicant. The time period for taking advantage of such express recommendations is limited to the period within which the applicant can obtain review outside the Patent Office following the Board's decision (see the preceding paragraph). Such express recommendations are binding on the examiner unless he presents new art that would tend to destroy the force of the recommendation. The foregoing, however, is applicable only to *express* recommendations and does not include general comments by the Board as to what the applicant has failed to claim.

The Board can reject an *appealed* claim on a new ground differing from any of the grounds utilized by the examiner. In that event, the applicant may (1) proceed with action to review the decision outside the Patent Office, (2) request reconsideration, or (3) file an amendment, affidavit, etc., to establish the patentability of the claims over the new ground of rejection. If the examiner has been otherwise sustained with a new ground of rejection merely being added, the applicant must take the desired action within the period for review of the Board's decision outside the Office (sixty or thirty days as the case may be). However, if the examiner has been otherwise completely reversed, but with a new ground of rejection being supplied by the Board, the applicant has six months from the date of the Board's decision to take the third of the above three courses of action (unless a shortened time is set in the Board's decision). Manual 1214.01. In some instances the Board's decision, particularly with respect to a new ground of rejection, will be based upon an assumed fact, i.e., judicial notice. If this fact is believed to be incorrect, it is appropriate for the applicant to ask the Board for an affidavit under Rule 107. Failure to do so will be construed as an admission of the correctness of the factual statement. *In re Madsen et al.*, 94 USPQ 186, 197 F.2d 536, CCPA 1952. *In re McMurray*, 109 USPQ 46, 230 F.2d 442, CCPA 1956.

In *Ex parte Flowers*, 16 USPQ 125, PO BdApp 1931, it was held that the Board could reject a claim that had stood as allowed at the time of the appeal. However, more recent authority holds that such action by the Board is improper. *Burns* v. *Watson, Comr. Pats.*, 109 USPQ 8, DC 1956, aff. 111 USPQ 324, 239 F.2d 948, CA DC 1956. In this respect note that Rule 196(b) relating to new grounds of rejection applies only to "appealed" claims.

Action After Board's Decision—Withdrawal of Appeal. If the decision of the Board results in a rejection of all claims and the applicant does not take action within the appropriate time periods, as previously discussed, the status of the application is that of being abandoned. No notification is given the applicant. If there are allowed as well as rejected claims and the application is otherwise in condition for allowance, the application is passed to issue with the allowed claims. The examiner cancels the rejected claims as a matter of course and gives no notification to the applicant prior to the issuance of the Notice of Allowance. If there are allowed claims as well as formal objections to the application, an Office Action will issue requiring correction of the formal matters that are objectionable. The comments in this paragraph are applicable not only to the handling of an application by the Patent Office following a decision by the Board of Appeals but also to the procedure following a decision by a court in reviewing the Board's decision.

Substantially the same procedure is followed if an applicant withdraws the appeal before decision by the Board. If there are allowed claims in the application, the withdrawal serves as authorization for the examiner to cancel the rejected claim. With no claims standing as allowed, the application is abandoned. If the applicant has not appealed from the final rejection or has appealed but withdrew the appeal before a decision by the Board of Appeals, the final rejection is not *res judicata* to subsequent claims in another corresponding application. *Ex parte Pflegler*, 131 USPQ 439, PO BdApp 1961. However, see *Mallinckrodt Chemical Works* v. *Watson, Comr. Pats.*, 120 USPQ 264, 169 F. Supp. 851, DC DC 1959.

Decision as *Res Judicata* to Subsequent Claims. Insofar as the applicant subsequently seeks to claim the same invention in a second application having the same disclosure, the decision of the Board is *res judicata*. *In re Application of Carleton Ellis*, 31 USPQ 380, 86 F.d2d 412, CCPA 1936. The same rule applies to decisions by courts in reviewing the Patent Office adjudication. A difference in disclosure may affect the applicability of *res judicata*. *Ex parte Gustavson et al.*, 14 USPQ 332, PO BdApp 1932. When the claims of the subsequent application are patentably distinct from the claims upon which the initial adjudication was made, the rule of *res judicata* does not apply. *In re Prutton*, 97 USPQ 447, 204 F.2d 291, CCPA 1953. *Weeks et al.* v. *Warp et al.*, 105 USPQ 55, 221 F.2d 108, CA DC 1955. The proper test is a comparison of the claims of the two

applications and is not a question of patentability over the prior art insofar as the *res judicata* question is concerned. *In re Lundberg et al.*, 126 USPQ 412, 280 F.2d 865, CCPA 1960. The doctrine of *res judicata* is not made applicable merely by reason of the fact that the claims of the second application *could* have been made in the prior application. *In re Benjamin Gruskin*, 110 USPQ 288, 234 F.2d 493, CCPA 1956. For a further discussion of the subject see "The Doctrine of Res Judicata in Ex Parte Patent Practice—Prototype for a Liberal Approach," R. J. Holton, 39 JPOS 220, 1957.

Review of Patent Office Decisions in the Courts

Alternative Courts for Review—Time for Taking Action—Dissatisfied Party. Following a decision by the Board of Appeals in an ex parte case or by the Board of Interferences in an inter partes case, an applicant who is dissatisfied with the Board's decision may seek review by way of appeal to the Court of Customs and Patent Appeals or by commencing a civil action in federal district court. 35 U.S.C. 141, 145, and 146. These are alternative remedies and are mutually exclusive. *In re Isler*, 68 USPQ 198, 152 F.2d 1002, CCPA 1946. *Jensen et al.* v. *Lorenz et al.*, 34 USPQ 318, 92 F.2d 992, CA DC 1938.

A number of factors should be considered in determining which course of action is to be followed. Among these are: (1) the Court of Customs and Patent Appeals renders its decision on the record made in the Patent Office and the issues presented by the decision of the Board, while in a civil action there is a trial *de novo* with a new record and possibly new issues; (2) the Court of Customs and Patent Appeals sits only in Washington, while in a civil action to review an inter partes decision the proper venue is likely to be in some other part of the country; and (3) the comparative costs are likely to vary, particularly in view of point (1), supra, and the fact that in a civil action to review an ex parte decision, all expenses must be paid by the applicant. These particular points will be discussed in greater detail under the headings of the respective review procedures.

A further point that is to be considered carefully in reaching a decision as to which course of action to follow concerns the precedents, i.e., prior decisions of the respective courts on corresponding legal problems. In a number of instances, the courts will not see eye to eye on particular problems. An extreme example of this is illustrated in the following two decisions, *In re Blaisdell*, 113 USPQ 289, 242 F.2d 779, CCPA 1957 and *Allen* v. *Watson, Comr. Pats.*, 114 USPQ 214 DC DC 1957, aff. 117 USPQ 68, 254 F.2d 342, CA DC 1958. In these cases, the two courts arrived at diametrically opposed positions on the problem of public use and sale based upon the identical sets of facts. While this is an extreme example, legal research may oftentimes disclose more favorable precedents in one court than in the other. See *Adjudications; Advocacy in Patent Causes.*

The time for commencing court action following a decision of the Board is sixty days. However, if there has been a timely request for reconsideration of the Board's decision, the period for court review is thirty days following the decision of the Board on the request for reconsideration. If the calendar date of thirty days from the rehearing decision is earlier than the calendar date of sixty days from the original decision, the latter date is controlling for the filing of the notice and reasons of appeal. *Cincinnati Floor Co.* v. *United States Plywood Corp. et al.*, 115 USPQ 386, Comr. Pats. 1957. Since these time periods are set by rule, rather than by statute, they may be waived or suspended by the Commissioner of Patents. *Eckey* v. *Watson, Comr. Pats.*, 122 USPQ 5, 268 F.2d 891, CA DC 1959. Within this period the appellant must: (1) if appeal is to be taken to the Court of Customs and Patent Appeals, give notice to the Commissioner of his intention to do so and set forth the reasons of appeal, or (2) if review is sought by way of civil action, file his complaint in federal district court. In a civil action, the plaintiff has been permitted to file an amended complaint to correct deficiencies in the original complaint even though this amendment oc-

curred after the period for filing the complaint had expired. *Land-O-Lakes Creameries, Inc.* v. *Oconomowoc Canning Co.*, 131 USPQ 328, 199 F. Supp. 124, DC Wis 1961. Also, where one losing party to an interference commenced an action within the proper time period, naming the winning party and a second losing party as defendants, the second losing party was permitted to counterclaim against the plaintiff and against the winning party defendant, even though the counterclaim was not presented within the statutory period for review of the decision of the Board of Interferences. *Union Carbide Corp.* v. *Traver Investments, Inc. et al.*, 133 USPQ 167, 201 F. Supp. 763, DC Ill 1962.

The statute provides that a "dissatisfied" party may file an appeal to the Court of Customs and Patent Appeals or seek review by way of civil action. The Court of Customs and Patent Appeals has interpreted this to mean that the winning party in an interference, who may be dissatisfied, is entitled to take an appeal. To be dissatisfied, the party need not be the loser in an interference. See *Nenzell* v. *Hutson et al.*, 132 USPQ 635, 299 F.2d 864, CCPA 1962.

The party desiring court review has an initial choice as to whether he desires to appeal to the Court of Customs and Patent Appeals or to file a civil action in federal district court. Having proceeded with either one or the other, he is thereafter precluded from following the alternative course of action upon his own initiative. See the first paragraph of this section. However, if one party to an interference files his Notice of Appeal to the Court of Customs and Patent Appeals following the Board's decision on the merits, any adverse party may elect to have the review by way of civil action rather than by way of appeal to the Court of Customs and Patent Appeals. To effect this election, the adverse party must give notice to the Commissioner of the election within twenty days after the filing of the Notice of Appeal to the Court of Customs and Patent Appeals. This provision does not permit a second losing party (in an interference involving three or more parties), *within the twenty-day period*, to file the notice and require that further review be conducted by way of a civil action. *Adams et. al.* v. *Wolinski*, 128 USPQ 288, 285 F.2d 133, CCPA 1961. When an election has been so made, the appellant is obliged, if he still desires review, to commence a civil action in federal district court within thirty days from the date of the notice of the election. See 35 U.S.C. 141. The decision of the Board of Interferences will control if the appellant fails to commence the civil action within the thirty-day period.

Appeals to the Court of Customs and Patent Appeals

This subject is discussed in the preceding article *Appeals to Court of Customs and Patent Appeals* by Chief Judge Worley, q.v.

Civil Action to Review Patent Office Decisions

Inter Partes Cases—Defendants—Venue. In years past, considerable difficulty was encountered by a plaintiff in naming the proper party defendant in a civil action to review an inter partes decision of the Board of Interferences. A transfer of title of the adverse application, unknown to the plaintiff, would result in the suit being brought against the wrong defendant. Often the plaintiff would not discover this until after the expiration of the period for commencement of the civil action. Thereafter, he could not commence suit against the proper defendant and the original suit would be dismissed for lack of an indispensable party.

In 1952 the statute was amended to correct this situation. The present statute, 35 U.S.C. 146, provides that the civil action to review a decision of the Board of Patent Interferences "may be instituted against the party in interest as shown by the records of the Patent Office at the time of the decision complained of." Thus, even though the owner of record has disposed of his interest by an unrecorded assignment, the civil action is not subject to dismissal for lack of an indispensable party. However, the statute permits the true owner to become a party to the litigation. Conversely, if the civil action is brought against an assignor rather than an assignee, as shown by

the records of the Patent Office, it will be dismissed even though the assignor failed to comply with the Patent Office rule requiring notification of change in title during the pendency of the interference. *Nachtman* v. *Toulmin et al.*, 130 USPQ 151, 196 F. Supp. 367, Ohio 1961.

The Commissioner of Patents is not a necessary party to a suit to review a decision of the Board of Patent Interferences, and a suit brought against him in an inter partes case will be dismissed. *Barr Rubber Products Co.* v. *Burlington Mills, Inc. et al.*, 133 USPQ 617, CA DC 1962. The statute provides, however, that the Commissioner may intervene if he so desires. On this subject, see also the subsequent discussion of issues in inter partes cases.

With respect to venue, the suit should be commenced against a single defendant in the judicial district in which he is a resident. Similarly, if there are a plurality of adverse parties all residing in the same judicial district, it will be commenced in that district. If there are a plurality of adverse parties residing in different judicial districts, or an adverse party residing in a foreign country, the statute provides that the suit be commenced in the District of Columbia.

The term "adverse parties" refers to defendants, and it is not proper to construe the plaintiff and a defendant as being the "adverse parties" for jurisdiction purposes. *Hayes* v. *Livermont*, 125 USPQ 486, 279 F.2d 818, CA DC 1960.

Ex Parte Cases—Defendant—Venue—Expenses. The Commissioner is the proper party defendant in a civil action to review an ex parte decision of the Patent Office. The proper venue is the District of Columbia. The applicant is required to pay all expenses of the proceedings. However, he need only pay the "reasonable" costs. *Watson, Comr. Pats.* v. *Allen*, 123 USPQ 330, 274 F.2d 87, CA DC 1959.

Evidence—Issues—Burden of Proof. A suit to review the Board's decision is an action *de novo,* and the proofs may include evidence not presented in the Patent Office. *Hoover Company* v. *Coe*, 89 L.Ed. 1488, 325 U.S. 79, 65 S.Ct. 955, 1945. As a consequence, the court may not "freeze the record" and grant summary judgment solely upon the record made in the Patent Office. *Royal Crown Cola Co. v. Crown Beverage Corp.*, 130 USPQ 72, 195 F. Supp. 130, NY 1961. However, the Patent Office record will be admitted in evidence and, of course, if that is the only evidence introduced, the decision will be rendered thereon. Evidence intentionally withheld from the Board may not be admitted in the suit. *E. I. duPont de Nemours & Co. et al. v. American Cyanamid Co.*, 101 USPQ 270, 120 F. Supp. 697, DC 1954. Similarly, evidence will not be received by the court where a party was grossly negligent in failing to introduce that evidence in the Patent Office. *Killian v. Watson, Comr. Pats.*, 121 USPQ 497, DC DC 1958. However, where there has been no suppression, bad faith, or gross negligence on the part of the party offering the evidence, it will be received. *Minnesota Mining & Manufacturing Co. v. General Electric Co. et al.*, 119 USPQ 65, 167 F. Supp. 37, DC DC 1958.

The complaint may set forth other causes of action which the plaintiff may have against the defendant other than the propriety of the Patent Office decision. *Century Distilling Co. v. Continental Distilling Co.*, 42 USPQ 348, 351, 106 F.2d 486, CA 3 1939. The defendant may counterclaim on the basis of such other causes of action that he may have against the plaintiff, e.g., patent infringement. *E. I. duPont de Nemours & Co. v. Atlas Powder Co.*, 38 USPQ 383, 24 F. Supp. 263, Del. 1938. *The Durox Co. v. Duron Paint Manufacturing Co., Inc.*, 129 USPQ 180, 193 F. Supp. 829, DC Md 1961.

In inter partes cases, the court will not review an interlocutory decision dissolving an interference (whether or not the basis for the dissolution is ancillary to priority). *American Cable Co. et al. v. John A. Roebling's Sons Co. et al.*, 17 USPQ 451, 65 F.2d 801, CA DC 1933. However, a decision by the Board at the termination of the full interference proceeding, including the taking of testimony, etc., and labeled an award of "priority" in the Board's decision will be reviewed by the court. *Ellis-Foster Co. et al. v. Union Carbide and Carbon Corp.*, 127 USPQ 297, 284, F.2d 917, CA 3 1960. Thus,

patentability, a question normally considered not to be ancillary to the question of priority in an interference, may be raised in the suit. If the party against whom the claims are charged to be unpatentable is otherwise found to be entitled to a patent, the issue of patentability will be resolved by the court. *Sanford v. Kepner*, 97 L.Ed. 12, 344 U.S. 13, 73 S.Ct. 75, 1952. *Hill v. Wooster*, 33 L.Ed. 502, 132 U.S. 693, 10 S.Ct. 228, 1890. But see *Radio Corp. of America v. Philco Corp.*, 131 USPQ 372, 201 F. Supp. 135, DC EPa 1961. As a matter of fact, a failure to raise such issues may make the question *res judicata* as between the parties. *Knutson et al. v. Gallsworthy et al.*, 74 USPQ 324, 164 F.2d 497, CA DC 1947.

Similarly, in a civil action from an ex parte rejection, the Commissioner may raise an additional ground for unpatentability, but the plaintiff should be given ample warning thereof. *Switzer et al. v. Watson, Comr. Pats.*, 125 USPQ 48, 183 F. Supp. 467, DC DC 1960. The plaintiff should be given ample opportunity to introduce evidence to refute any such contention. *Douglas Aircraft Co., Inc. et al. v. Mueller et al.*, 125 USPQ 93, 277 F.2d 351, CA DC 1960. The court cannot remand the case to the Patent Office for review in the light of the new evidence presented. *The General Tire & Rubber Co. et al. v. Watson, Comr. Pats.*, 125 USPQ 628, 184 F. Supp. 344, DC DC 1960.

In suits to review inter partes decisions, the plaintiff has the burden of proof. The finding of fact by the Patent Office as to priority must be accepted as controlling unless the contrary is established by evidence which in character and amount carries thorough conviction. *Esso Standard Oil Co. v. Sun Oil Co. et al.*, 108 USPQ 161, 229 F.2d 37, CA DC 1956. The decision of the Patent Office is given great weight and is overcome only by clear proof of mistake. *Polaroid Corp. et al. v. Clark et al.*, 72 USPQ 67, 159 F.2d 28, CA DC 1947. The same rule is applied in reviewing ex parte decisions from the Patent Office. *Zenith Radio Corp. v. Ladd, Comr. Pats.*, 135 USPQ 216, CA DC 1962. The presumption of correctness of the Patent Office decision is not controlling where material evidence, not before the Office, is presented tending to show patentability. *Stradar et al.* v. *Watson, Comr. Pats.*, 113 USPQ 365, 244 F.2d 737, CA DC 1957. Moreover, where there is a lack of unanimity among the Patent Office employees there may be less weight given to the final Patent Office decision than would be the case when they are all in accord. *The General Tire & Rubber Co. et al.* v. *Watson, Comr. Pats.*, 125 USPQ 628, 184 F. Supp. 344, DC DC 1960.

Cross-references: *Advocacy in Patent Causes; Appeals to Court of Customs and Patent Appeals; Briefs—Planning and Writing; Prosecution of Applications.*

APPLICATION WRITING—ILLUSTRATED BY ELECTRICAL AND ELECTRONIC CASES

Elmer J. Gorn

A well-written application for patent is more than a document that is legally and technically sufficient; it is a work of art in a form to convince the Examiner of patentability, win court support in case of litigation, and interest capital in development of the invention.

These requirements rest so heavily on the attorney's ability as an application writer, as to make him the most important single factor in the entire patent system after the inventor himself.

For the abnormally difficult electrical and electronic cases particularly, the attorney-writer needs certain basic information and skills, as well as familiarity with the patent law and rules of the Patent Office, and the willingness to make the effort necessary to keep abreast of the changing regulations and philosophy of patent practice. He should have facility in the use of lucid, fluent, and accurate language and know or learn the exact meaning of words before he uses them. He should have a probing, inquisitive, perceptive, and keenly analytical mind. He should be able to judge the limits to which an inventive concept may be extended and then to teach those skilled in the art how to make and use all forms of the invention within the expanded limits.

Information Gathering

Prior to preparation of the patent application, the invention involved will have reached a stage justifying the decision to proceed. The writer will then have available preliminary information, such as a written description of the invention, a physical embodiment, or both. In some cases he may have only an oral disclosure of the concept of the invention, so that all knowledge of it exists solely in the minds of one or two persons.

Preliminary Analysis Stage. The writer will now study the data and attempt to obtain a complete understanding of the invention. If the technology is involved, he may wish to refer to textbooks, to expand his knowledge or clarify parts of the technology. He will note questions on which he requires answers from the inventor or others.

During the analysis, he will organize his material into some orderly pattern. He may make some preliminary sketches as a basis for the patent and make notes stating his understanding of the invention.

Development of Complete Invention Description with Inventor. Having gathered and organized his material, the writer should make sure that his understanding of the invention approaches in completeness that of the inventor. To accomplish this, he should interview the inventor and lead him to describe in full detail all he knows about the invention. The attorney-writer should not permit the inventor to pass over any point until he is able to verbalize a description of it in meaningful terms. The writer will usually encounter a very interesting phenomenon: Many inventors have never really tried to describe their inventions in words suitable for the application, and the discussion may open up vistas of invention not previously recognized.

During the discussion, the inventor may try to describe some aspects of his invention in "black-box" terms. The writer may have heard or even used these terms, but he may not understand their full significance. Here again he must insist that the inventor describe more clearly the construction and operation involved.

When the joint exploration is completed

and both the inventor and the writer understand at least one embodiment of the invention, the writer probes more deeply. What new results has the inventor accomplished? Why were these results not obtainable from prior devices? What problems did he encounter in seeking these new results? How did he solve them?

Novelty Search

The tentative decision as to the nature of the invention should be checked against the prior art. Some of this art the writer will have discovered in his study. He will have learned more of it from the inventor's story of the development of the invention. Usually he will want also a search through prior patents and publications in the United States Patent Office, where the best collection of such literature is available and conveniently classified for public search purposes. (See *Searches*)

The writer should familiarize himself with all the prior art material, reach his own decision as to patentability, and explore the differences from the art with the inventor.

Seeking Out the Invention. Often the results of a novelty search will reveal that certain or all features of the invention are old. On the other hand, the search results may be so different from the invention that the writer may expand the tentative scope which he had set. When the prior art is very close, a narrowing of the view which has been taken of the invention may well uncover limited, but nevertheless valuable aspects which previously were overlooked.

During this joint exploration, the writer will be aware of a tendency of many inventors to treat as prior art or as "old" what they themselves may have devised earlier. Sometimes they base their belief of what has been done before on mere rumor or surmise. The writer must insist that only information which has been published, can be proved to be public knowledge, or has been obtained in usable form from another person qualifies as prior art.

Pushing Back the Invention Boundaries. Having decided upon a good statement of what the invention is, the writer is now ready to embark upon one of the most fascinating parts of the application preparation. He starts by posing a problem to the inventor somewhat as follows: "When your patent is published, some of the brightest experts in your field of technology will study its disclosure, analyze it to obtain the maximum of information, ideas, and suggestions from it, and seek to devise a workable modification outside your claims. You are entitled to credit and protection for everything which can be derived from your disclosure but will not have them unless you and I can anticipate what such people will be able to do with your patent."

One procedure on this problem is to go through the details of the invention and ask what alternatives may be used. Could a transistor replace a vacuum tube? Could welding or other fastening means replace a casting? And so on for each element appearing in the invention, the questioner attempts to discover modifications as different from the preferred embodiment as possible.

No one who has ever participated in a session of this kind and seen a truly broad and basic invention grow from the seed of a seemingly limited improvement will doubt that our patent system fulfills a high purpose in stimulating technological advance.

When the writer is satisfied that the inventor has extended his imagination to the fullest in devising alternative forms of his invention, a few of these will be carefully selected to illustrate the various directions in which the invention may be extended and which may be claimed generically.

In the process of pushing back the boundaries, additional formulations of the statement of the invention will occur to the writer and become a part of his store of material for the drafting of claims.

Application as a "Selling" Tool

In addition to teaching the public how to use the invention, the writer should have constantly in mind the severe requirements for patentability. He will strive to create a strong presumption of patentability in the minds of readers. The case should "sell" itself and its invention to the Patent Examiner in the first instance, and eventually to a judge whose erudition is quite properly more legal than scientific. Creating such a presumption increases the chances that the Examiner will allow the application and that the judge will uphold the patent. If the attorney realizes that, in writing the application, he must be convincing as to the merits of the invention, he should produce a more lucid and effective document than if he attempts merely to meet the statutory requirements.

Application Writer as Lexicographer. Although the courts have said that a patentee may "be his own lexicographer" (*Chicago Steel Foundry Company* v. *Burnside Steel Foundry Co.*, 132 F.2d 812, CA 7 1943), this is true only in a limited sense. He should avoid new definitions for technical or other terms having generally accepted meanings but conform in the use of such terms. If, after a conscientious search for an adequate word, however, the writer is at a loss, he may and should devise a term of his own and define it with care and precision.

This is ordinarily unnecessary unless the application writer wishes to use it in one or more of the claims. In order to eliminate extensive language in the claims, the author once recited "electron beam components" for a structure having no commonly accepted, concise expression. He defined his new term as "the phosphor-exciting electron energy generated by a single or a plurality of electron guns, continuous or pulsating." The skillful but sparing use of this technique may solve difficult problems in drafting claims of adequate scope without verbosity.

Starting the Application—What Comes First?

Patent attorneys differ among themselves as to the proper sequence in which the application should be written. Most have the penciled drawings prepared first. Some insist that the claims be drafted before the specification. This, they contend, establishes the scope, crystallizes the theme to be emphasized, and develops vocabulary to be used in the specification. Others proceed with the specification before they attempt to write any claims. Each writer will un-

doubtedly develop a sequence which fits his own pattern of thinking. But one who attempts to "think out" the invention as he writes the specifications is almost certain to produce an application which rambles into unnecessary detours and may obscure the invention by burying it in a mass of irrelevant discussion and details having no direct relation to the claims. Whether or not a particular attorney prefers to write the specifications first, he would do well to have at least some claims prepared so as to give purpose and direction to the writing and establish terminology which the specification must support.

Arrangement of the Specification. Rule 77 sets forth the order of arrangement which should be observed in framing the specification as follows:

(1) Title of the invention
(2) Brief summary of the invention
(3) Brief description of the several views of the drawings if any
(4) Detailed description of the drawings
(5) Claim or claims
(6) Signatures

Title of the Invention. While the title of the invention should be short, the Patent Office will insist that it be somewhat descriptive. A title such as "Electron Beam Conversion Systems," unlike the less specific "Electrical Device," gives considerable information to persons with knowledge of electronics and is of value for indexing purposes and for searching for devices of this kind. The title chosen should most aptly express the nature of the invention to be described without suggesting undue limitation thereof.

Preliminary Passages. In general the presentation proceeds by easy stages from what is old to what is new and surprising, from the simple to the complex. Perhaps it holds back the solution of the problem involved for a paragraph or two, so that the reader may become aware of its complexity.

First comes the field of the invention, that is, the subject to which it relates. Many attorneys then state the particular utility in connection with which the invention will be illustrated.

A brief discussion of the nearest prior art is then in order, with a description of those particular disadvantages which, it will be found later, this invention avoids.

Objects of the Invention. The writer then faces squarely the question as to whether he will or will not list the results to be accomplished, as the "objects" of the invention. In many cases the quality of the invention has been stated without information as to its real nature.

Here there are two schools of thought.

Those for reciting a list of objects no doubt consider the practice more or less conventional and expected. They feel that it directs the attention quickly to what is sought to be accomplished, aids in searching, is somewhat impressive, and perhaps even required.

Those opposed consider the listing no longer required under the latest statute, wish to avoid all wordiness, go as quickly as possible to the invention itself, and prefer to replace the half column or so of objects stated in separate paragraphs by a single paragraph with some such beginning as "The invention provides," followed by its advantages and suitably also with a specific and striking illustration to catch the Examiner's interest.

An attorney interested in this question and favoring the latter approach examined over 100 patents having numbers above 3,000,000 and assigned to corporations. He noted that less than half the chemical patents listed "objects" as such but that almost 90 per cent of the electrical, mechanical and miscellaneous patents so assigned did list them.

Brief Summary of the Invention. The Rules of Practice seem to place more emphasis on the brief summary than on the statement of objects, as follows:

Summary of the Invention. A brief summary of the invention indicating its nature and substance, which may include a statement of the object of the invention, should precede the detailed description. Such summary should, when set forth, be commensurate with the invention as claimed and any object recited should be that of the invention as claimed.

The Manual of Patent Examining Procedure mentions the objects in section 608.01 (d) in the following words:

The brief summary should be more than a statement of the objects of the invention, which is also permissible.

The summary is not only a suggestion by the Patent Office Rule but also an important part of any patent as it comes before a judge or even in prosecution before the Examiner. It gives in convenient form the nature of the invention involved. It reveals the true importance of the invention and discloses clearly and concisely the advance over the state of the art as it existed prior to the invention.

A summary of the invention somewhat broader than the broadest claim is helpful, in case of a reissue application with enlarged claim, to show the originally intended scope of the invention.

Drawings

There are few, if any, applications in the electric, electronic or mechanical arts which do not include drawings. They are usually indispensable in the effective presentation of such inventions.

The drawing is the "dress" which creates the first impression of the patent document. It should be clear and uncluttered. It should present the invention in such concise yet complete form that one reasonably familiar with the art to which it relates will be able to understand the invention in general without reading the specification. These are only a few of the reasons why a capable patent draftsman is an indispensable partner to the writer.

Functional flow diagrams appear in many electrical and electronic applications, as in the reproduction in Fig. 1 from patent 2,987,646. It will be noted that each of the blocks represents a general function and that the influence of one function upon another flows generally in the direction of the arrows on the conductors linking one block to another. It is for this reason that such a drawing is called a "functional flow diagram."

Planning the Drawing. There must be a close correlation between the drawings and the claims. Every element of every claim must be illustrated. In addition, the ar-

June 6, 1961
     H. ZUCKER
     2,987,646

ELECTRON BEAM CONVERSION SYSTEMS

Filed July 6, 1956

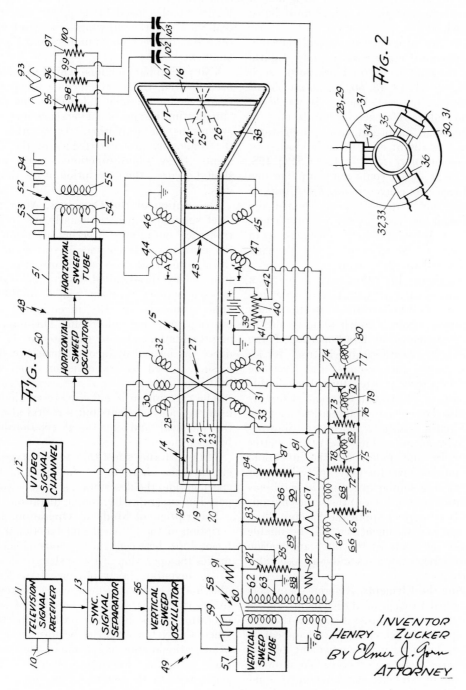

FIG. 1.

69

rangement in the drawings will generally predetermine the sequences of the description of the invention in the specification. If the specification is to proceed in a logical and clear manner, the drawings must be so arranged.

In the case of a diagrammatical showing, the writer must make certain that all parts of the drawing shown in block form, such as elements 11, 12, 13, 50, 51, 56 and 57 of the drawing are well known. It would be good for future reference for him to note, in the file of an important case, publications showing details of each of such blocks. In the case of *In re Hirsch*, 131 USPQ 198, 1959, the applicant could not show that one such block was conventional. The Court of Customs and Patent Appeals denied the application on the ground of insufficient disclosure. When any doubt may arise as to public knowledge of a part, the drawing should detail its construction.

Although the invention may reside in a particular element or detail, it is nevertheless highly desirable to illustrate the whole combination, even if much of it is old, in which that element or detail operates. If the invention is a new form of electrode for an electron tube, for example, the electrode should be shown in such tube, though this need not be illustrated in great detail. A generalized or even diagrammatical showing of old parts is usually adequate. Showing the environment enables the reader better to visualize and understand the invention. Also, another inventor may apply later for a patent on a similar invention in combination with a part at least of the same environment. If the former applicant does not illustrate such environment, he will be unable to make the claim of the later application for interference purposes and may lose valuable rights.

Listing the Elements. Reference numbers are applied to each of the elements shown in the drawing. In order to apply them in the sequence in which they will appear in the specification, it is convenient to add them as the dictation proceeds. To allow for insertions of reference characters later, some writers initially use only even numbers, e.g., 10, 12, 14, etc. Some list the numbers on a sheet of paper with the names of the elements to which they apply to avoid the double use of a number. Some start the reference numbers above that of the highest Figure number used to designate the several views in the drawings, to avoid any confusion between part numbers and Figure numbers.

The preliminary claims, which will have been drafted, frequently include functional terms, as for example, "deflection means," "integrating means," "convergence means," or "means for activating." In addition to the commonly accepted names of the elements, these same functional terms also should occur in the description of the drawings.

Description of the Drawings. After the brief summary, there is usually inserted a transition paragraph directing attention to the drawings. Then comes a statement of the nature of the several Figures which is followed by the detailed description stated in such manner that the reader would be able to understand the invention if the drawings were not before him. This manner of presentation adds to the interest. It reduces the hazard of incompleteness of disclosure caused by an omission from the drawings.

The description is not a mere cataloging of the various elements but a recital also of the physical and functional relationships between them.

Many attorneys feel that to preserve and enhance the character of this part of the specification, the description should be composed uninterruptedly, in one dictation.

Description of Mode of Operation. Description of the physical and functional relationships between the various elements makes the operation of the system or device of the invention fairly obvious. It is desirable and necessary in most cases, however, to insert at this stage an account of such operation. This is particularly important where the system or device performs a series of operational steps upon some material. In such case, the description should follow such steps in the sequence in which they occur, with specific reference to each element involved.

Extending Breadth of the Description

To impart greater breadth to the invention, alternative embodiments, if any, are described in general as stated above.

It is usually impossible to include all the possible variations in detail. The specification usually ends, therefore, with a paragraph attempting to broaden the interpretation to be given to the patent. The Supreme Court has held that such a statement has a favorable influence upon the interpretation of the patent. In considering how broadly the claims were to be construed, the Court said:

"In describing his invention the patentee declared it to be his intention 'to cover all changes and modifications of the example of the invention herein chosen for purposes of the disclosure, which do not constitute departures from the spirit and scope of the invention.'" *Exhibit Supply Co. et al.* v. *Ace Patents Co.*, 315 U.S. 126, 1941; cf. *Katz* v. *Horni Signal Mfg. Corp.*, 63 USPQ 190, CA 2 1944.

The closing paragraph in the transistor patent 2,524,035 to Bardeen and Brattain, reads as follows:

"The invention is not to be construed as limited to the particular forms disclosed herein, since these are to be regarded as illustrative rather than restrictive."

The commonly used closing paragraphs now are or should be those that fit closely into the pattern that has been accepted as having a favorable influence.

Well chosen examples of significant variations are helpful in conveying the impression of breadth for the invention, particularly when shown in the drawings as well as the description.

The Claims

By the time the draft of the specification has been completed, the writer will have developed deeper insight into the nature of the invention and discovered more forms to be claimed. He may add claims and improve those previously written. He will, however, avoid undue multiplication.

Claims in electrical and electronic cases

should avoid the use of limitations in terms of phenomena, the existence of which may be difficult to prove. Whenever possible the basic concept of the invention should be converted into a simple physical picture and expressed as such in the claims.

An example of the writer's use of this method of claim drafting in a complicated electronics case is shown in patent 2,417,789. The claims strip the complex and highly useful structure to fundamentals, for better understanding of the invention. Claim 2 as here given is moderately altered for the teaching purpose of this book.

"2. A magnetron assembly having a cathode and an anode structure adjacent thereto, the anode structure having a plurality of arms, each pair of which forms an inductance and a capacitance adapted to oscillate in predetermined primary mode, and means connecting alternate arms through a path of low impedance, said means comprising a conductor, said conductor being secured to each of said alternate arms and passing freely through grooves in each of the intervening arms."

Claim 1 expresses the invention more narrowly as:

"1. An electron-discharge device comprising an electrode structure including a cathode and an anode adjacent thereto and having a plurality of arms each pair of which bounds a cavity and forms an inductance, each of said pair of arms forming a capacitance, said inductances and capacitances forming tuned circuits which are adapted to have oscillations set up therein during operation, each of said arms having a groove therein, the grooves in alternate arms having a lesser depth than the grooves in intervening arms, and a conductor secured in each of said groves of said alternate arms and passing through the grooves in said intervening arms free of contact therewith."

These simple physical statements of the invention have continued to be applicable to date.

Correlation between Specification and Claims. After the specification and claims have been completed, the writer should study each claim separately and determine that all significant language used therein is to be found also in the specification. If any terminology occurring in the claim is lacking in the specification, the wording is added at the most appropriate point. Indefiniteness and ambiguity in claims are inexcusable and are never to be mistaken as a substitute for true breadth.

Final Polishing

Time demands, real or imaginary, upon the application writer may lead him to end his work when he has met the technical and legal requirements. There remains the correcting and rereading to smooth out the rough spots in the application, sharpen the clarity with which ideas have been expressed, emphasize more the originality of the results, and otherwise polish his work until he is satisfied that it represents the very best of what he is capable. It is perhaps these last coats of polish that distinguish the invention and attorney from the usual or ordinary.

An attorney who has written about a thousand applications estimates that, for every hour he spends in dictating an application, he requires perhaps 15 to 20 hours for the original study of the case, reading, conferring, and final correcting and polishing.

Approval by the Inventor. The writer will deliver a clean copy of the specification and claims and the work copy of the drawings to the inventor or his chief, perhaps after first referring the drawings to the draftsman for revision and to check reference characters.

Many attorneys have all drafts of an application triple spaced for convenience of correction, up to the time that the final form is typed.

During the preparation of an application the writer keeps in touch with the inventor at intervals and discusses various points with him. Some writers even dictate the case, particularly when using dictating machines, with the inventor present. Either way the inventor answers questions as they arise during the dictation or reading. Finally, the triple-spaced draft form of the application invites correction by the inventor. On the other hand, if the inventor is confronted with a neatly typed document together with the drawing completely inked,

he will be reluctant to suggest changes or additions.

When all the changes, if any, agreed upon between the inventor and the attorney (the attorney being the final judge) have been made and the specification and claims have been typed without erasures or interlineations, the completed document is ready for the inventor's signature and notarial acknowledgment. Form 16 set forth for this purpose in the Patent Office Rules of Practice is used.

Cross-references: *Attorneys and Agents; Chemical, General, Mechanical, Design, Plant and Microbiological Applications; Claim Drafting; Fraud—Sec. Inking Drawings.*

APPLICATIONS AND PATENTS. See ATOMIC ENERGY, CHEMICAL, DESIGN, GENERAL AND MECHANICAL, MICROBIOLOGICAL, PHARMACEUTICAL, PLANT

ARBITRATION IN PATENT DISPUTES
Albert S. Davis, Jr.

Arbitration is the procedure in which the parties involved submit a dispute to private individuals for decision, rather than to a court. Arbitration is to be distinguished from compromise or settlement, where the decision is worked out by the parties without an outside arbiter and usually with concessions by each side, and also from mediation in which a third party seeks to bring the disputants to a compromise or settlement.

Arbitration is centuries old in some fields of dispute. It has passed in turn through vigorous opposition and grudging toleration by the courts to helpful legislation in many instances and finally full acceptance under strong supervision as to the impartiality of arbitrators.

Advantages and Disadvantages

The usual arguments for arbitration over court proceedings are that it ordinarily secures a decision more speedily; it can use "judges" chosen for special skill in the technical subject matter or even the particular field of law involved; and it is private, economical and less apt to foster continued ill-feeling between the parties.

The usual arguments against arbitration are that arbitrators are not always trained in decision making; they tend sometimes to ignore important technical legal points; the statute law does not make arbitration easy or practical in all cases; certain procedural steps available in the courts may not be available in arbitration; and the privacy of arbitration may lead to criticism. In addition, many lawyers and laymen tend to oppose it because it is not usual in their experience.

Arbitration, in the field of patent controversies and elsewhere, however, is steadily increasing.

Instituting Arbitration

With rare exceptions, resort to arbitration is the result of a preliminary agreement. Such agreements may take the form of trade association rules extending its facilities to members or even to those who do business with or through members of the association; of a specific understanding that all or certain types of disputes between two or more parties or those controversies arising out of a particular contract or relationship are to be arbitrated; or of a special agreement to submit a specific dispute to arbitration.

Selection of Arbitrators

The method of selection of the arbitrator(s) varies with the will and agreement of the disputants. By agreement, they may bind themselves to use a named individual, or a named permanent or semi-permanent panel. Somtimes the arbitrators are selected by a named agency. Probably a more specific mechanism is provided for the selection when a dispute has arisen or is imminent. An agreement that the parties "will select the arbitrator(s)" presents obvious problems. Sometimes there is obstruction or a genuine inability to settle upon them unless the agreement or statute law permits some third agency, such as a judge of a particular

court or a private administrative agency, to resolve the question of selection.

A second and common method is for each party to appoint an arbitrator, the two then appointing a third. This procedure can lead to a like deadlock. It also often does result in creating two special advocates and an umpire.

Under the Rules of the American Arbitration Association, lists of proposed arbitrators selected from a nationwide panel of qualified individuals are submitted to the parties, and one or more arbitrators are appointed from those individuals remaining after the parties have stricken out unacceptable names.

Application to Patent Controversies

In the field of patent law, the problems to which arbitration may be applied can be conveniently classified as those of interference, title, contract enforcement or interpretation and infringement. The Federal Arbitration Act was late in coming and incomplete, and it is probably accurate to say that the Federal courts are less receptive to the arbitral process in patent matters than are other courts. This is probably due in part to the conservatism, real or fancied, of the patent bar, and in part to a subconscious or expressed feeling that the privacy of arbitration is not entirely fitting in dealing with obtaining, asserting or interpreting a lawful private monopoly and that the privacy might lead to abuse.

Interference Settlements

Early procedures in the Patent Office fully recognized the applicability and use of arbitration to resolve the factual issues in an interference situation. In the last two decades there has been an increasing tendency for parties to an interference to agree to exchange proofs, attempt to agree upon the first and diligent inventor(s) and, failing to agree, to submit the case to the Patent Office as a "case stated," i.e., with stipulated record, sometimes subject to supplementary proof. Upon agreement, action to have the patent issued to the first inventor was taken by disclaimer, abandonment, concession, or simple failure of one party to proceed with the interference. Many attorneys have been assiduous in filing the proofs upon which such actions were based. To this process, essentially one of compromise and settlement, there was often added royalty-free or royalty-bearing licensing or cross-licensing of the parties.

Largely because of the licensing aspect, this procedure led to legislative inquiry and criticism that matured in the interference settlement statutes of 1962, requiring settlement of interference agreements to be submitted to the Patent Office.

Settlement of interference issues between parties, by agreement and concession of priority or the like, probably does not bind the courts, but it is doubtful whether the statutory presumption of validity which may be thus sacrificed is ordinarily of offsetting value.

Title Disputes

Controversies revolving around title to patents and the enforcement and interpretation of agreements which relate to them in whole or part (assignments, licenses, agreements for sale) in most respects are resolved as matters of contract law. There is, therefore, less reason here to feel strangeness in resorting to arbitration or to consider it an inappropriate procedure. An exception comes in cases where questions of patent interpretation are involved—most commonly, where a licensee or assignee argues that particular acts on its part do not come within the scope of claims and hence are not subject to royalty (in effect, that there is no infringement).

Another problem remains as to whether the court in a given jurisdiction will enforce a contractual clause providing that disputes which may arise under the contract or are relevant to it may be referred to the court for enforcement. The judicial and legislative reluctance to enforce prospective arbitration agreements is a survival of much older common law; the trend is slowly to abandon this attitude, but state laws must be still checked, one by one. In general, the current view is that the United States Arbitration Act extends enforcement of agreements for arbitration to patent contract matters.

Infringement

On infringement matters some members of the patent bar feel that arbitrators do not sufficiently understand or properly evaluate the technical and complex points in patent law. In commercial arbitration, the arbitrators tend to arrive at "substantial justice" rather rapidly. Control of this tendency, if it is feared in arbitrating an infringement, would again seem to reside in careful selection of skilled arbitrators such as patent lawyers. There seems to be no substantial question as to the enforceability of the awards.

Summary

Thoughtful students of arbitration believe that, in speed, expertise, economy, and privacy, the process can contribute significantly to solution of legal problems in the field of patents. While they agree that it is by no means a universal or perfect solution for such problems, they generally feel that, when such disputes arise, it is well worthwhile to consider whether they could best be resolved by resorting to arbitration. The arbitration process is improving, and patent lawyers are contributing more to it. Judicial acceptance of arbitration in patent matters is increasing as well.

References

United States Arbitration Act, 9 U.S.C. 1 et seq.
"Interference settlement statute," 35 U.S.C. 135(c), as amended Public Law 87-831, 76 Stat. 958, October 15, 1962.
N.Y.C.P.L.R., Art. 75, ss. 7501 et seq.
Deller, A. W., "The Use of Arbitration in Patent Controversies," 21 JPOS 209, 1939.
Davis, A. S., Jr., "Patent Arbitration," 15 *Arb. Journ.* 127, 1960.
Aeschlimann, C. J., "The Arbitrability of Patent Controversies," 44 JPOS 655, 1962.
Davis, A. S., Jr., "Dialogue Upon the Ramparts," Ohio St. L.J. (to appear).

Cross-references: *Accounting and Recoveries from Infringements, Infringement Suits, Interferences, Licenses, Royalty Rates.*

ASSIGNMENTS

Edward C. Vandenburgh

Basic Distinction between Assignments and Licenses

In preparing contracts dealing with patent rights, the common procedure is to use terminology consonant with the type of interest that the parties intend to convey, e.g., assignment or license and assignor or licensor. The most important aspect in the preparation of patent contracts, too often overlooked, is that the nature and legal effect of the instrument is determined by the rights conveyed rather than by the language employed. A document designated as an "assignment" and employing such terms as assignee and assignor, etc., may in fact be merely a license and vice versa. The importance of this lies in the legal consequences that result, including the right to sue for infringement and the necessity of recording the document in the Patent Office.

The taxation consequences also are significant. Income received as a result of an assignment is treated as capital gain while the income obtained by way of a license is ordinary income. See the article *Taxation*. However, under the tax laws many conveyances that would otherwise be deemed licenses are treated as assignments. As a result, court decisions in tax cases, distinguishing between assignments and licenses, are generally inapplicable to the drawing of a distinction between the two for other purposes. *Etherington* v. *Hardee*, 129 USPQ 205, CA 5 1961.

In *Waterman* v. *MacKenzie*, 138 U.S. 252, 34 L.Ed. 923, 1891, the Supreme Court defined what is necessary to constitute an assignment and to distinguish it from a license. The court said:

"The patentee or his assigns may, by instrument in writing, assign, grant and convey, either, 1st, the whole patent, comprising the exclusive right to make, use and vend the invention throughout the United States; or, 2d, an undivided part or share of that exclusive right; or, 3d, the exclusive right under the patent within and throughout a specified part of the United States.... A transfer of either of these three kinds of interests is an assignment,

properly speaking, and vests in the assignee a title in so much of the patent itself, with a right to sue infringers; ... Any assignment or transfer, short of one of these, is a mere license, giving the licensee no title in the patent, and no right to sue at law in his own name for an infringement."

An example of the first of the above three categories of assignments would be a conveyance of the "entire right, title and interest in and to the patent." Another example would be the conveyance of the "exclusive right to make, use and sell the patented invention" without any reservations of rights to the grantor. If any one of the rights to *make, use* and *sell* is not conveyed in its entirety, the instrument is a license rather than an assignment. *Six Wheel Corp.* v. *Sterling Motor Truck Co. et al., supra.* See the article *Licenses*. An example of the second category would be the conveyance of a percentage, e.g., 5 per cent of the ownership of the patent. An example of the third category would be the conveyance of the exclusive right to make, use and sell throughout the state of New York with no reservation of rights in New York by the grantor.

Express Assignments

Most assignments are in the nature of express contracts conveying the patent rights from one party to another. As such, the usual requisites of a contract, including consideration and capacity to act must be observed.

"No particular form is required for the assignment of a patent interest and patent assignments are subject to the same rules of construction that apply to contracts generally, the intention of the parties being of primary concern in construing them; ..." *United States* v. *Krasnov et al.*, 110 USPQ 411, 422, DC EPa 1956; aff'd., 355 U.S. 5, 2 L.Ed. 2d 21, 1957.

When the assignment is duly acknowledged this constitutes prima facie evidence of its execution. 35 U.S.C. 261.

Assignments may be made of the ownership of future inventions. The fact that the invention is not yet in being does not prevent the assignee from having at least an equitable ownership therein after the invention is made. *Littlefield* v. *Perry*, 88 U.S. 205, 22 L.Ed. 577, 1874; *Guth* v. *Minnesota Mining & Mfg. Co.*, 22 USPQ 89, CA 7 1934. See "Assignments of Future Inventions Particularly as Between Employers and Employees," Knoth, H. M., 31 JPOS 532, 1949.

A conveyance that is otherwise an assignment but which provides for the reversion of title to the grantor at some future date, or upon the occurrence of a future contingency, is in fact an assignment. The grantee has title to the invention until the date of reversion as provided in the contract. *Hook et al.* v. *Hook & Ackerman*, 88 USPQ 267, CA 3 1951.

Territorial Assignments. As pointed out in *Waterman* v. *MacKenzie*, supra, a patentee may assign the ownership of the patent for a specified part of the United States, e.g., one or more states. Product produced and sold by the assignee within the territory granted to him does not become an infringement of the patent when removed from that territory. *Hobbie* v. *Jennison*, 149 U.S. 355, 37 L.Ed. 766, 1893; *Keeler* v. *Standard Folding Bed Co.*, 157 U.S. 659, 38 L.Ed. 848, 1895. Contracts should bind each territorial owner to prevent his exploitation of the patent from interfering with the exclusivity of the patent owner for another territory. See *Hobbie* v. *Jennison*, supra.

Assignment of Undivided Part of Patent. An assignment of an undivided part of the patent results in a co-ownership thereof equivalent to the co-ownership enjoyed by joint inventors. Absent a specific agreement to the contrary, one co-owner can convey all or a part of his rights without the concurrence of the remaining co-owners. Ownership of such an interest is a sufficient defense to a suit for infringement by another co-owner. *Kabbes* v. *Philip Carey Mfg. Co.*, 17 USPQ 56, CA 6 1933. Similarly, a licensee of a co-owner is not an infringer whether the suit be brought by the other co-owner or all co-owners jointly. *Talbot et al.* v. *Quaker-State Oil Refining Co.*, 41 USPQ 1, CA 3 1939. One co-owner need not account to another for profits etc., in the absence of an agreement to the contrary. 35 U.S.C 262.

It will be apparent from the foregoing that in any instance of co-ownership of a patent, it is important that the owners have an agreement among themselves controlling the rights of each as to licensing, litigation, etc. Without such an agreement, each party is at the mercy of the other insofar as the use of the invention and exclusivity are concerned.

Recovery for Past Infringement. The cause of action which a patent owner has to recover damages for past infringement does not automatically pass to an assignee with the assignment of the patent. This right remains with the assignor unless it is specifically conveyed. *Moore* v. *Marsh*, 74 U.S. 515, 19 L.Ed. 39, 1868. This is not to say, however, that the patent owner can convey the right of action for infringement without assigning the patent. *Crown Die & Tool Co.* v. *Nye Tool & Machine Works*, 261 U.S. 24, 67 L.Ed. 516, 1922.

Estoppel of Assignor to Deny Validity. The doctrine that the assignor is not in a position to contend that the assigned patent is invalid is substantially emasculated by the exceptions thereto. This problem will arise when the assignor is sued for infringement by the assignee. In *Westinghouse Electric & Mfg. Co.* v. *Formica Insulation Co.*, 266 U.S. 342, 69 L.Ed. 316, 1924, the court said:

"Of course, the state of the art cannot be used to destroy the patent and defeat the grant because the assignor is estopped to do this. But the state of the art may be used to construe and narrow the claims of the patent, conceding their validity. The distinction may be a nice one, but seems to be workable."

Then in *Scott Paper Co.* v. *Marcalus Mfg. Co., Inc. et al.*, 67 USPQ 193, 325 U.S. 249, 90 L.Ed. 47, 1945, a further limitation on the doctrine was made, to wit:

"[The] doctrine of estoppel so as to foreclose the assignor of a patent from asserting the right to make use of the prior art invention of an expired patent, which anticipates that of the assigned patent, is inconsistent with the patent laws which dedicate to public use the invention of an expired patent. The assignor has a complete defense to an action for infringement where the alleged infringing device is that of an expired patent."

Recording and Notice of Assignments. To protect the assignee, it is important that the assignment be recorded in the Patent Office. This is much the same as the necessity for recording conveyances of title of real estate to protect the purchaser. 35 U.S.C. 261 states in part:

"An assignment, grant or conveyance shall be void as against any subsequent purchaser or mortgagee for a valuable consideration, without notice, unless it is recorded in the Patent Office within three months from its date or prior to the date of such subsequent purchase or mortgage."

This provision applies to both patent applications and patents.

As between the parties to the assignment, the contract is binding even in the absence of recordation. *Fyrac Mfg. Co. et al.* v. *Bergstrom*, 24 F.2d 9, CA 7 1928. The assignee under an unrecorded assignment may sue for infringement. *John Tuman & Sons, Inc.* v. *Basse*, 46 USPQ 302, CA 2 1940. As set forth in the statute, a third party who is a bona fide purchaser for value, without notice of the prior assignment, will obtain good title from the assignor where the prior assignment is not recorded in accordance with the statute. *Paulus* v. *M. M. Buck Mfg. Co.*, 129 Fed. 594, CA 8 1904. The prior assignment need only be recorded prior to the subsequent assignment, not necessarily within any given time period following the original assignment. 35 U.S.C. 261. *Why Corp.* v. *Super Ironer Corp.* 53 USPQ 609, CA 6 1942. A subsequent purchaser who has actual notice of the existence of the unrecorded assignment will not obtain good title. *All Steel Engines, Inc. et al.* v. *Taylor Engines, Inc. et al.*, 85 USPQ 152, DC NCal 1950; aff'd 92 USPQ 35, CA 9 1951.

While the notice provision of the statute pertains only to assignments, the Patent Office will record other papers affecting the title of a patent or an application. See Rule 331. The fact that a document amounting to *something less than an assignment*, e.g., a license, is recorded does not act as constructive notice thereof. *Eastern Dynamite Co.* v. *Keystone Powder Mfg. Co.*, 164 F. 47, DC MPa 1908. However, when an *assignment* is recorded, it gives constructive notice as to the existence of all facts, e.g., the existence of a license, set forth in the recorded assignment. *Waterman* v. *Shipman*, 55 Fed. 982, CA 2 1893.

Rule 331 sets forth a number of requirements of the Patent Office for the recording of assignments. The instrument must be in writing in the English language. It should identify the patent or application to which it relates by the number and date. If an assignment of an application is made before the serial number and filing date are ascertained, it should adequately identify the application, e.g., by its date of execution, the name of the inventor, and the title of the invention.

Some attorneys believe that there is a disadvantage in early recording of assignments of applications because the assignment records are public. In an interference the assignment records may show the approximate filing date of an adversary's application (even though the filing date is not given in the assignment), at a stage in the proceeding when such information otherwise would not be available. To avoid this, some applicants await allowance of the application to record the assignment. This involves the risk, often nominal, that the inventor will convey good title to a bona fide purchaser for value in the absence of a recorded assignment. An alternative is to identify the invention both in the application and in the assignment by a nondescriptive title which will not disclose the subject matter of the application. While the Patent Office will require such title to be changed after the application is filed, the change would not be revealed in a previously filed assignment and an interference adversary would have difficulty in identifying the application with which he is involved in the interference.

Assignments by Operation of Law

Patents having, as they do, the attributes of personal property, 35 U.S.C. 261, are transferred by operation of law as is other personal property under the same circumstances. Upon death of the patentee, his patent rights go to his heirs. See *De La Vergne Refrigerating Machine Co.* v. *Featherstone*, 147 U.S. 209, 37 L.Ed. 138, 1833. Title to patents and patent applications is vested in the trustee of the estate of a bankrupt. With respect to applications, the trustee must agree to prosecute the application to a conclusion. 11 U.S.C. 110. In a receivership, the patent rights will be taken over by the receiver and conveyed. See *Kenyon* v. *Automatic Instrument Co.*, 73 USPQ 21, CA 6 1947.

Equitable title to an invention will pass from the inventor or patentee to another on the basis of an implied contract to assign. A common situation is the hiring of another to invent or do development work. In that event, the employee's work product belongs to the employer. *Standard Parts Co.* v. *Peck*, 264 U.S. 52, 68 L.Ed. 560, 1923. The court will order the patent rights assigned to the employer. *Colgate-Palmolive Co. et al.* v. *Carter Products, Inc. et al.*, 108 USPQ 383, CA 4 1956. The *Standard Parts* case distinguishes the circumstances under which the employer acquires ownership of the invention from those in which he obtains merely a "shopright" i.e., a non-exclusive license to use the invention.

Necessary and Proper Plaintiff in an Infringement Action

35 U.S.C. 281 provides for the bringing of actions for infringement by the "patentee." The assignee of the entire interest is the proper party to bring such action. *Waterman* v. *MacKenzie*, supra. All co-owners must join in an infringement suit. *Switzer Brothers, Inc.* v. *Chicago Cardboard Co. et al.*, 116 USPQ 277, CA 7 1958. It is doubtful if one co-owner can be made a party against his will. *Gibbs* v. *The Emerson Electric Manufacturing Co. et al.*, 43 USPQ 76, DC WMo 1939. The territorial owner is the proper party to sue for infringement within his territory. *Moore* v. *Marsh*, 19 L.Ed. 37, 74 U.S. 515, 1868.

A non-exclusive licensee cannot institute an action for infringement. *Contracting Division, A. C. Horn Corp.* v. *New York Life Insurance Co.*, 46 USPQ 435, CA 2 1940. He is not even a proper party to the infringement action. *Overman Cushion Tire Co., Inc. et al.* v. *Goodyear Tire & Rubber Co., Inc.*, 14 USPQ 104, CA 2 1932.

An exclusive licensee may sue for infringement provided the patentee is a party to the suit. *Waterman* v. *MacKenzie*, supra. *Independent Wireless Telegraph Company* v. *Radio Corporation of America*, 269 U.S.

459, 70 L.Ed. 357, 1926. The exclusive licensee is a proper party to an infringement action brought by the patentee. *Western Electric Company, Inc. et al.* v. *Pacent Reproducer Corporation et al.*, 5 USPQ 105, CA 2 1930. Furthermore, the damages that an exclusive licensee sustains are not recoverable in a suit unless the licensee is a party thereto. *Brookfield* v. *Novelty Glass Mfg. Co.*, 170 Fed. 960, CA 3 1909. *Lawrence-Williams Co.* v. *Societe Enfants Gombault et cie*, 52 F.2d 774, CA 6 1931.

Courts for Determining Questions of Title

While the federal courts have exclusive jurisdiction of all cases arising under the patent laws, state courts may try questions of title to patents. *Cincinnati Shoe Mfg. Co.* v. *Vigorith et al.*, 102 USPQ 99, CA 6 1954. Absent jurisdiction based on diversity, litigation involving questions of title must be brought in state courts. *Vanderveer* v. *Erie Malleable Iron Company*, 111 USPQ 292, CA 3 1956. Federal court jurisdiction is not conferred by the Declaratory Judgments Act. *Cincinnati Shoe* v. *Vigorith*, supra. If the issues raised by the complaint require the court first to adjudicate the plaintiff's title to the patent or to pass on contractual questions before considering the infringement question, then the federal court does not have jurisdiction despite the presence of the subsidiary infringement issue. *Luckett* v. *Delpark, Inc. et al.*, 270 U.S. 496, 70 L.Ed. 703, 1926; *The Dill Mfg. Co.* v. *Goff et al.*, 52 USPQ 517, CA 6 1942.

Patent Office Consequences of Ownership

Filing of Patent Application by Assignee. When the inventor cannot be reached or he refuses to sign an application for patent, the assignee may file in the inventor's name, under circumstances discussed in the article *Inventors*.

Grant of Patent to Assignee. Normally, if there is an assignment of an application of record in the Patent Office and a request is made that the patent issue to the assignee, the Patent Office will comply with this request. Rule 334. However, this will not be done where there are conflicting assignments of record. *In re Moller*, 1904 C.D. 70, Comr. Pats. In a leading case, the Commissioner of Patents said:

"The Office cannot decide between conflicting assignments and can only issue the patent to the inventor, leaving the question of title to be determined by a court of competent jurisdiction." *Ex parte Harrison*, 1925 C.D. 122.

Similarly it will not be done where the application has been signed not by the inventor but by another on his behalf. *In re Schuyler*, 119 USPQ 97, Comr. Pats. 1957. To obtain ownership of the patent that issues on an application not signed by the inventor, it may be necessary for the party claiming ownership to sue the inventor in the courts to establish ownership of the patent or application in question. See Assignments by Operation of Law, above.

Control of and Access to Patent Applications. The right initially to control the prosecution of a patent application, and thus to appoint the attorneys to handle the application, resides in the inventor. *Ex parte Collins*, 1902 C.D. 324, Comr. Pats. Rule 31. This case also holds that the assignment must be recorded before the assignee will be permitted to take control. See also Rule 32. The mere fact that there is a recorded assignment does not act as a revocation of the power of attorney previously given by the assignor. However, the assignee of the entire interest may, if he chooses, take over prosecution of the application. Rules 32 and 36. Only the assignee of the entire interest will be permitted to take over prosecution. Rule 32. *Ex parte Harrison*, 1925 C.D. 122, Comr. Pats. This case also holds that the Patent Office will not pass on the question of ownership as between conflicting assignees of the entire interest. The Patent Office will recognize the assignee holding the earlier assignment as entitled to control prosecution. *Sparkes* v. *Small*, 1904 C.D. 547, Comr. Pats.

The death of the inventor normally acts to revoke any powers of attorney previously given by him. The fact that the application has been assigned in the interim (to other than the attorney) and that the attorney has continued to act under authorization (not recorded) of the assignee does not prevent the inventor's death from terminating his power to act with respect to the application. A new power of attorney executed by the assignee should be made of record promptly, and any action taken by the attorney between the date of the death of the inventor and the filing of the new power of attorney from the assignee should be ratified. M.P.E.P. 409.01.

Normally patent applications are maintained in secrecy and no one is entitled to access thereto without authorization from the party entitled to control the prosecution. Rules 14 and 34. Even after an assignment, the inventor will be permitted access to the application unless the assignee specifically requests that the Patent Office refuse such access. *In re Kellogg Switchboard & Supply Co.*, 1906 C.D. 274, Comr. Pats. M.P.E.P. 106. While an assignee of a part interest or an exclusive licensee is not entitled to control the prosecution of an application, either will be permitted to inspect the application in the Patent Office. M.P.E.P. 106.01. *Ex parte Harrison*, 1925 C.D. 122, Comr. Pats. But see *Ex parte Superior Brass Securities Co.*, 1925 C.D. 92, Comr. Pats.

Consideration of problems of access and control are obtained by way of Petitions to the Commissioner.

Cross-references: *Employees Inventions and Agreements, Forms—Assignment Form, Licenses, Taxation.*

ASSOCIATIONS AND THE PATENT SYSTEM

Reynold Bennett

Various associations have flourished due to their interest and concern with patents, trademarks and copyrights.

In 1894, the American Bar Association established the first of its special sections, the *Patent Section*, to deal with a specific branch of the law.

Subsequently the *American Patent Law Association* was organized to consider patents, trademarks and copyrights. This Association wields a large influence for the good of the patent system, with its Bulletin, conventions, committees, and national office with an Executive Director in Washington.

It has a Code of Ethics for the members, in the interest of protecting the public, the confidences of clients, the patent office and the courts, and other attorneys, all as presented in a panel discussion by John Rex Allen, J. V. Martin and W. Houston Kenyon, Jr., with Virgil E. Woodcock as Chairman, in A.P.L.A. Bull. for January and February 1956, pp. 13 and 66, respectively.

The *National Inventors Council*, established in 1940, is a semi-official government agency with the task of bringing to the attention of the military any inventive idea of potential value to national defense. The Council also refers to other government departments or agencies any invention which might contribute to the national welfare. The membership of the Council has included many distinguished American inventors, scientists, editors and public servants. Approximately 20 individuals are now members, all of whom are leading experts and executives serving without pay. Periodically, it publishes a valuable booklet entitled "Inventions Wanted by the Armed Forces and Other Government Agencies."

The *Patent Office Society* is another effective organization. For a modest sum it offers a monthly Journal, the JPOS, which carries articles on various topics in patent law, discussions of current legislation, decisions of significance, news of the Patent Office, correspondence from readers, and employment advertisements.

There is an active *Association of Registered Patent Attorneys and Agents*, with headquarters in New York which considers matters of interest to the patent system and particularly to its members.

Major population centers have their *local associations*. These groups ordinarily deal with trademarks and copyrights as well as patents and have as members those practising in any of these fields. The *New York Patent Law Association*, with more than a thousand members, conducts meetings at regular intervals, has an annual banquet honoring the federal court judges of the area and elsewhere, publishes a brief but effective Bulletin, and has a Board of Governors and the following standing committees: Nominations, Professional Ethics and Grievances, Meetings and Forums, Patent

Law and Practice, Trademarks, Foreign Patents and Trademarks, Copyrights and Designs, Admissions, Library, and Employment. There are many subcommittees and special committees at this time on Antitrust, Legal Aid, Economic Matters Affecting the Profession, Public Information and Education, and Publications.

The *Patent, Trademark and Copyright Foundation of the George Washington University* is devoted to the study and publication of scientific research papers regarding the principles, facts and operations of patent, trademark and copyright systems around the world. Its Journal of Research and Education appears quarterly and reports on thorough studies and investigations in its field areas.

During the 1930's, when industrial and intellectual property rights were being closely scrutinized by the federal government, such organizations as the *National Association of Manufacturers* first established patents committees to act as spokesmen for industry's viewpoint on the subject.

In recent years, the increased interest of the federal government in research and the patentable inventions growing out of government sponsorship has generated increased activity by business and trade associations in patent rights. Various segments of industry such as automobile manufacturers and electronics companies have formed groups to deal with patent matters.

The *U.S. Trademark Association*, organized in 1878, has a worldwide membership and publishes a Bulletin.

The *Copyright Society of the U.S.A.* has published for a number of years an authoritative bimonthly Bulletin dealing with copyright matters.

Associated patent agents, attorneys and groups have presented views to Congress and various federal administrative agencies on matters relating to industrial and intellectual property. Congressional committees have sought out the support and opinion of these groups on such subjects as compulsory licensing proposals, patent rights under government contracts and other pressing matters of the day. The associations have been highly influential in securing needed legislation such as the Patent

Act of 1952, the Trademark Act of 1946, and ratification by the United States of the Universal Copyright Convention.

During the 1961 celebration in Washington of the 125th anniversary of the 1836 statute, which established our present patent system in its essential features, many associations and individuals from the United States and abroad, who were concerned with industrial property protection, participated in the symposium and week of conferences. President Kennedy hailed the event. He noted that the patent files of nations "can serve the aims of peace and help encourage the development of new emerging and backward nations."

The United Nations initiated studies of inventions and patents around the world. It has received aid from competent organizations such as the *International Chamber of Commerce* and *International Patent and Trademark Association* (A.I.P.P.I. in French). The "Common Market" countries have sought to devise new types of patent protection and have received assistance in this regard from the work of various associations including American-based groups.

During 1964, the *Inter-American Association of Industrial Property* (A.S.I.P.I. in Spanish) was formed to consider the growing hemispheric problems relating to patents, trademarks, copyrights and other pertinent matters.

A number of the associations supply booklets, films, and other material to schools, colleges, and organizations that desire to know more about our system of incentives for inventions and protection of industrial and intellectual property.

Cross-references: *Attorneys and Agents, Government Patent Policies, Public Relations.*

ATOMIC ENERGY PATENTS

Roland A. Anderson *

This article is not intended to review those practices, which although applying to

* Assistant General Counsel for Patents, United States Atomic Energy Commission. This Article has been prepared in the course of performance of the author's official duties. Any copyright in this Article is specifically disclaimed.

Atomic Energy patents, are general under the patent law, but to point up the differences in the processing and handling of inventions, discoveries, patent applications, and patents in the atomic energy field, under the Atomic Energy Acts.

Exclusions and Privileges under 1946 Act

The Atomic Energy Act of 1946 (Public Law 585—79th Congress, 755-775) caused much concern about the invention areas that were excluded from patenting under Section 11(a) of said Act. It was asserted even that the Act excluded the whole area of atomic energy from private patenting.[1] However, subsections 11(a),(1) and (2)[2] excluded patenting inventions or discoveries and revoked patents in only two areas, i.e., when (1) useful solely, or (2) to the "extent... used," (i) in the production of fissionable material, or (ii) in the utilization of fissionable material or atomic energy for a military weapon.

The issuance of approximately 325 patents to the Atomic Energy Commission alone in the field of atomic energy[3] between 1946 and 1954 attests that not all atomic energy developments were excluded.

Act of 1954

In the revision of 1954, the area of exclusion was narrowed further. Under Section 151 (Public Law 83-703; 42 U.S.C., Section 2181) of the Atomic Energy Act of 1954, patents may be obtained on all atomic energy inventions or discoveries except those (a) useful solely, and (b) to the "extent... used" in the utilization of special nuclear material[4] or atomic energy[5] in an atomic weapon.[6]

Note that, after 1954, inventions or discoveries pertaining to *production* of special nuclear material or atomic energy are no longer excluded, and the area of exclusion in utilization is restricted to utilization of special nuclear material or atomic energy in an atomic weapon. Thus a power reactor used as the source of power for a missile, where the invention pertains to the separable power source of the missile and not the weapon component, would appear patentable today.[7] Similarly, the nuclear power generating equipment for a submarine or battleship is within the scope of patenting if other tests of patentability are met. The excluded area of patenting is deemed very limited, particularly since the Government is the only entity which may manufacture, produce, or own "atomic weapons" and an inventor of a weapon may maintain an application for an award under Section 157 of the Atomic Energy Act.[8] Because the Government is the only weapons user, an inventor, if there were no weapon exclusion, would have to secure a patent before he could maintain an action against the Government under Section 1498, Title 28 U.S.C. In all probability an inventor would not be able to secure a patent, since such an invention would undoubtedly carry a security classification and the patent application would be under Secrecy Order. No patent would issue and the inventor would have expended monies for filing and prosecution for a patent. Under the present 1954 Atomic Energy Act, as amended, an inventor may, without such expenditure, in attempting to secure a patent, file a timely report on his invention with the Commission and thereafter make application for award.

The 1954 Atomic Energy Act, 42 U.S.C., as amended,[9] hereinafter referred to as the Act, in addition establishes the statutory framework for the U.S. Patent Policy in the atomic energy field. The Act sets forth, in sections shown below, certain procedures and treatments of inventions, discoveries, and patents in the atomic energy field which differ from those for ordinary inventions and patents in that

(1) (a) Any invention or discovery useful in the production or utilization of special nuclear material or atomic energy (hereinafter referred to as the atomic energy field), is to be reported to the U.S. Atomic Energy Commission (hereinafter referred to as Commission) under Section 151 (c). 2181 (c).

(b) The U.S. Commissioner of Patents, pursuant to Section 151 (d) of the Act, is to notify the Commission of all patent applications disclosing inventions or discoveries required to be reported under the Atomic Energy Act. 2181 (d).

(2) The Commission under Section 152 is vested with all rights in any invention or discovery useful in the production or utilization of special nuclear material or atomic energy, made or conceived in the course of or under any contract, subcontract, or arrangement entered into with or for the benefit of the Commission, unless the Commission waives the rights. 2182.

(3) No patent for any invention or discovery, useful in the production or utilization of special nuclear material or atomic energy shall issue unless the Applicant, in accordance with Section 152 of the Act, files a statement under oath setting forth the full facts surrounding the making or conception of the invention or discovery described in the application. A procedure is established for the determination of Government rights in any such invention or discovery made or conceived in the course of or under any contract, subcontract, or arrangement entered into with or for the benefit of the Commission. 2182.

(4) The Commission may, pursuant to Section 153 of the Act, after hearing, declare certain patents affected with the public interest, and thereafter the Commission may use and license private parties upon specific terms. Further, certain private parties are empowered to initiate proceedings to compel the licensing of atomic energy patents under special circumstances. 2183.

(5) The Courts are enjoined under Section 154 of the Act from granting injunctions as respects the use of any invention or discovery by a licensee licensed under the compulsory provisions of the Atomic Energy Act. 2184.

(6) Patents are not to issue, according to Section 155 of the Act, if any invention or discovery was known or used before, even though such knowledge or use was under secrecy. 2185.

(7) The Commission is authorized under Sections 156 and 161 (g) to acquire inventions and discoveries and hold patents, and directed to sell, dispose of patents, and grant licenses with respect thereto. 2186 and 2201 (g).

(8) The Commission is authorized to establish a Patent Compensation Board under Section 157 of the Act to consider applications for reasonable royalty, just compensa-

tion, or an award as to specified inventions and discoveries. 2187.

(9) If the owner of a patent, the primary use of which is in atomic energy, is held by a court to have violated the antitrust laws, such owner may be compelled, pursuant to Section 158 of the Act, to license the patent. 2188.

(10) If the Commission communicates to any foreign nation "restricted data" based on any patent application not belonging to the United States, the owner is entitled to just compensation under Section 173 of the Act. 2213.

The foregoing listing would appear to indicate considerable differences in the handling and treatment of atomic energy inventions and patents. However, close examination, as hereinafter discussed, reveals that several of the procedures are similar to existing practices and treatment of other inventions. It is understood that several of the departures from previous patent practices were incorporated to:

(a) Protect the general public and the United States Government position in the field of military and civilian application of atomic energy;

(b) Avoid the establishment of a preferred patent position in the atomic energy field by contractors based on Government sponsored work, which might inhibit the growth of peaceful uses of atomic energy; and

(c) Prevent the creation of patent monopoly rights in and to inventions and discoveries developed with public funds.

Patentability of Chemical Elements. Two interesting cases have recently arisen, involving the AEC, in which the Court of Customs and Patent Appeals in 1964 reversed the position of the Patent Office and the Board of Appeals. The decisions involved the preparation of two new artificially produced transuranic elements, curium and americium by Dr. Glenn T. Seaborg under Government contract. *In re Seaborg,* 140 USPQ 659, 662. The inventions are assigned to the United States Government.

During the course of prosecution, the Patent Office had taken the initial position that the subject matter was not patentable since it involved elements available in nature which were inherently produced in a reactor of the Fermi type. During the proceedings, the issue of the subject matter being available in nature was dropped but the rejection was based on the sole issue of inherency. The Patent Office Board of Appeals affirmed the Examiner on the basis that the elements americium and curium were inherently produced in the reactor. Judge Arthur M. Smith in reversing stated

"We also agree with the summary statement in appellant's brief that ... there is no positive evidence that americium was produced inherently in the natural uranium fuel by the operation of the reactor for the times and at the intensity mentioned in the exemplary statement relied upon by the Patent Office. The calculations, however, that the maximum amount of americium-241 which could have been produced by the operation of the reactor disclosed in the Fermi Patent for 100 days at 500 kilowatts would have been one billionth of one gram (1/1,000,000,000 gram), show that the element, if produced, was produced in the most minute quantities. If the one billionth of a gram were produced, it would have been completely undetectable, since it would have been diluted with the 40 tons of intensely radioactive uranium fuel which made up the reactor. The possibility that, although a minute amount of americium may have been produced in the Fermi reactor, it was not identified (nor could it have been identified) would preclude the application of the Fermi patent as a reference to anticipate the present invention."

Reporting of Atomic Energy Inventions

Invention Reports. The statutory provision, Section 151(c) of the Act,[10] requires any person who makes any invention or discovery useful in the production or utilization of special nuclear material or atomic energy to file a report with the Commission containing a complete description within 180 days after the inventor first discovers, or first has reason to believe, that the invention or discovery is useful in atomic energy, unless the invention or discovery is described in a United States Patent Application filed within the time required for filing the aforesaid report.[11]

Reports of Filed U.S. Patent Applications. If an atomic energy invention or discovery is described in a filed United States

Patent Application, the Commissioner of Patents, pursuant to Section 151(d) of the Act,[12] provides access to such patent application to the Commission, for review in the Patent Office, or forwards a copy to the Commission.

Secrecy. The Reports or Patent Applications submitted or made available to the Commission are confidential, and no information concerning them is given without the authority of the inventor or owner, unless necessary to carry out a provision of an Act of Congress. This latter requirement was added in 1961 as Section 151(e).[13] This section assures that the Reports and Patent Applications are held in confidence by the Commission, in a manner similar to the secrecy accorded Patent Applications by the United States Patent Office.

The Commission reviews the reports and patent applications from technical and security aspects to ascertain whether secrecy is required and whether the subject matter is of general technical interest to the program of the Commission. If security classification of the subject matter in a report is required, the submitter is notified of the appropriate security classification as well as the prescribed regulations as to security handling. If the subject matter embraced in a filed patent application is deemed to warrant security handling, the Commissioner of Patents is requested by the Commission[14] to issue a Secrecy Order under Section 181, Title 35 U.S.C.

In view of the unclassified nature of most atomic energy work, very seldom has it been necessary to impose secrecy restrictions on subject matter submitted in a report or to request issuance of a Secrecy Order on privately filed patent applications. Even on Commission-generated inventions and patent applications, Secrecy Orders have been imposed on less than 5 per cent of the patent applications filed by or under the auspices of the Commission in the last five years.

AEC Contract Inventions

Under Section 152 of the Atomic Energy Act of 1954, as amended, the Commission is vested with all rights, unless it elects to waive them, in and to any invention or discovery useful in the production or utilization of special nuclear material or atomic energy made or conceived in the course of or under any contract, subcontract, or arrangement entered into with or for the benefit of the Commission.[15]

The Commission, to carry out this statutory policy, has employed patent provisions under which the Commission is in position to acquire all rights in and to inventions and dissoveries resulting from any research, development, or experimental work conducted under contract. Where the work under a contract pertains indirectly to a primary AEC activity and relates to a general field of activity of the contractor, the patent clause employed provides for the contractor's retention of a nonexclusive license for use of the invention in fields other than production or utilization of special nuclear material or atomic energy. Where the contract work pertains only incidentally to research and development in which AEC is interested and relates directly to a field of activity in which the contractor has an established industrial and patent position, the provisions utilized by the Commission provide for the contractor's retention of a sole license for use in fields other than production or utilization of special nuclear material or atomic energy. All of the provisions[16] provide for the prompt reporting of inventions to the Commission.

In addition to the retention of rights pursuant to the contract clause of a contract, the Commission has waived rights in inventions in various types of arrangements and relationships, including:

(a) Inventions resulting from the sale or distribution of stable or radioactive materials, or from irradiation, or other services publicly available;[17]

(b) Inventions resulting from the Gamma Radiation Facility at the National Reactor Testing Station;[18] and

(c) Inventions resulting from Access Permits.[19]

The General Counsel in an opinion of February 1, 1956,[20] concluded that a license from the Commission was not a contract arrangement or other relationship within the meaning of Section 152 of the Atomic Energy Act of 1954, as amended.

The Commission has in other special circumstances waived rights in inventions and discoveries in the atomic energy field, except to retain limited rights in the Government as to:

(1) Inventions or discoveries made under certain research grants to educational institutions and training programs;

(2) Inventions in the apparatus or process for the production of fuel elements and fuel core cartridge assemblies in research and development contracts for such items; and

(3) Rights in the field of atomic energy in foreign patents, waived by AEC after January 11, 1961, as respects inventions arising out of Commission research and development contracts where the work is performed at privately owned and operated facilities as distinguished from Government-owned and operated facilities, subject to certain reservations, including:

(a) A non-exclusive license to the Government in any foreign patents secured by the contractor, with the right of the Government to grant licenses to foreign governments for purposes of use, pursuant to treaty or agreement;

(b) The granting of royalty-free licenses to United States citizens and United States corporations; and

(c) If after five years the contractor cannot demonstrate practical application of the patented subject matter, the Commission may request the grant of licenses on such foreign patents to others at reasonable royalties.[21]

Special Patent Office Procedures— Issuance of Patents

Section 152 of the Act provides that no patent for any invention or discovery, useful in the production or utilization of special nuclear material or atomic energy, shall be issued unless the applicant files with the application, or within thirty days after request therefor by the Commissioner of Patents, a statement under oath setting forth the full facts surrounding the making or conception of the invention. This provision was modified in 1961 by the addition of a caveat that, where the Commission advises the Commissioner of Patents that its rights have been determined, the Commissioner of Patents need not require a statement.[22]

Since inventors may be out of the country or otherwise not able, within thirty (30) days after the official notice, to file a full factual statement, the Patent Office has initiated a preliminary notice procedure. Under this, it gives a preliminary notice advising the applicant that a thirty day official notice will be issued in forty-five days unless an affidavit is filed before the expiration of the forty-five days. If the applicant deems that he will be unable to secure an affidavit within thirty days after the expiration of the forty-five days, the Patent Office will grant further extensions, for good cause, before the initial forty-five days expire. However, after the official thirty day notice has been issued, the Commissioner of Patents does not appear to have jurisdiction to extend the statutory period, and the Patent Office has taken such position.

The statement and copies of the patent application are made available to the Commission by the Commissioner of Patents, pursuant to the Statute, when the application is "otherwise in condition for allowance." Thus, even if the affidavit is filed before requested by the Patent Office, the Patent Office does not furnish the information to the Commission until the patent application is in allowable condition. The Patent Office, in the initial instance, determines the sufficiency of the statement. One requirement insisted upon by the Patent Office is a concluding statement, following the phraseology of present Section 152, to the effect that the invention or discovery was not "made or conceived in the course of or under any contract, subcontract, or arrangement entered into with or for the benefit of the Commission."

The Commission,[23] after the receipt of the patent application, has ninety days [24] within which to file a directive with the Commissioner of Patents to issue the patent to the Commission. If the applicant does not agree with such Commission action and deems that the invention was not made or conceived in the course of or under any contract, subcontract, or arrangement with or for the benefit of the Commission, the applicant has thirty days to file a request for hearing.[25]

If the Commission has filed a direction for the issuance of the patent to the Commission and the applicant fails to file any request for hearing, the Patent Office will proceed to issue the patent to the Commission.[26]

Subsequent to the applicant's request for hearing, the Interference Division of the Patent Office forwards a statement to the applicant and to the Commission, advising of the times for any motions and taking of testimony by the respective parties, as well as setting a date for a hearing. The times for such actions parallel the regular interference practice and interference rules governing the proceedings.[27] Following the practice in regular interferences, the times set by the Board of Interferences for motions, the taking of testimony, and hearing have been extended from time to time by stipulation, and thus far no case has gone to final hearing. The cases have been settled by stipulations disposing of the proceeding or by the Commission, after completion of its investigation, withdrawing the directive.[28]

If a statement filed by an applicant should at any time thereafter be found to contain "false material statements," any notification by the Commission that it has no objection to the issuance of a patent shall not be deemed a waiver of the provisions of Section 152, and the Commissioner may have the title to the patent transferred, pursuant to said Section, to the Commission.[29]

An appeal from the Board of Interference final order in Section 152 proceedings may be taken to the Court of Customs and Patent Appeals.[30]

Compulsory Licensing of Atomic Energy Patents

Section 153 of the Atomic Energy Act of 1954, as amended, provides for the Commission to declare a patent affected with the public interest (as a preliminary step to compulsory licensing) after hearing and findings that the invention or discovery is:

(1) of "primary importance" in the atomic energy field, and

(2) the licensing is "of primary impor-

tance to effectuate the policies and purposes" of the Act.

The Commission may, under subsection (a) of this Section, notify the patent owner of intent to initiate a proceeding to declare a patent affected with the public interest. The Commission's Regulations [31] provide for the Commission's serving a written Notice of Intent to declare a patent to be affected with the public interest, and the patent owner has thirty (30) days after service of the notice to request a hearing. The Commission has, in testimony before the Joint Committee on Atomic Energy of the Congress, indicated that it considers this provision as to compulsory licensing to be a reserve power.[32] The Commission has never invoked the authority of Section 153.[33]

After the Commission has declared a patent affected "with the public interest," the Commission is licensed to use the invention, and any person whose activity is of primary importance to the conduct of an activity authorized under the Atomic Energy Act may request a nonexclusive license.[34] The Regulations provide for the initiation of an application for a license by filing a petition with the Secretary of the Commission [35] before the Commission issues a license.[36] The patent owner may request a hearing [37] before any such license is issued.

The Atomic Energy Act, in addition to offering the Commission an opportunity to declare atomic energy patents affected with the public interest and thereafter license certain persons, also provides that persons are entitled to initiate proceedings for a patent license, where such persons are required to use the invention or discovery in the production or utilization of special nuclear material or atomic energy [38] and have made applications to the Commission for a license to conduct activities under certain specified sections or are licensees under said sections [39] or whose activities or proposed activities are authorized under Section 31.[40]

Each applicant must set forth the nature and purpose of the use intended to be made of the subject matter of the patent, the steps taken by the applicant to obtain a license from the owner of the patent, and the effects as estimated by the applicant on the authorized activities if the license is not granted.[41] The Rules governing filing the application and notices necessary in addition to those set forth in Section 153(d),[42] are stated in the Commission's Regulations.[43] To date [44] no private person has filed an application for a license pursuant to this section of the Atomic Energy Act of 1954, as amended.

The Commission, before the issuance of any such license, must accord the owner an opportunity for hearing, hold the hearing within sixty days [Section 154(d)], and find, pursuant to Section 153(e),[45] that

(1) the invention covered by the patent is of "primary importance" in the production or utilization of special nuclear material or atomic energy;

(2) the licensing is of "primary importance" to the conduct of the activities of the applicant;

(3) the activities to which the license is to be applied are of "primary importance" to the furtherance of the policies and purposes of the Atomic Energy Act; and

(4) the applicant cannot otherwise obtain a patent license from the owner on the terms that the Commission deems reasonable.[46]

If the Commission finds all four conditions to subsist, the Commission may license on terms it deems equitable.[47] The Commission cannot grant a license under Section 153(e) (1) for any purpose other than that stated in the application for a license [48] or (2) to any other applicant without an application being made pursuant to Section 153(c) and without separate notification, hearing and findings.[49] The owner shall be entitled to a reasonable royalty fee, and in the absence of an agreement, the royalty fee may be fixed pursuant to the provisions of Section 157(c) of the Atomic Energy Act of 1954, as amended.[50] An appeal may be taken to the Courts from the Commission's decision according a license pursuant to Section 189 [51] of the Atomic Energy Act of 1954, as amended.

No Injunctions on Patents Licensed Pursuant to Section 153

Section 154 of the 1954 Atomic Energy Act [52] specifically enjoins any court from granting an injunction where the use of the patent is licensed after the patent has been declared affected with the public interest under Section 153(b) or where the Commission has granted a license to a private party after proceedings under Section 153(e). In other words, the sole remedy of the patent owner in such situation is for damages in the nature of royalties determined pursuant to Section 157(c), together with costs as fixed by the court.

Secret Prior Knowledge or Use

Whereas ordinarily prior knowledge or use, to bar patenting of an invention or discovery, must be public, pursuant to Section 155 of the Atomic Energy Act of 1954,[53] even though the prior knowledge or use was under secrecy within the atomic energy program of the United States, it shall constitute a bar to the patenting of an invention or discovery. The principal use by the U.S. Patent Office of this section has been to apply it in those instances where technical reports or papers which at one time were classified are, at the time of the prosecution of the patent application in the U.S. Patent Office, declassified. When the Patent Office cites such declassified reports, which bear earlier dates than the date of the patent application, filing an affidavit under Rule 131 [54] of the Patent Office, to attempt to overcome the cited declassified publication, may meet with success. The United States Patent Office has applied the same standards to overcome such declassified publications or reports as applied to Rule 131 affidavits when the earlier printed publication was never classified.

Licensing of Commission-Owned Patents

The Commission has specific statutory authority to acquire patents and license Commission-owned patents pursuant to Sections 156 and 161 [55] of the 1954 Act. This is in addition to the authority to declare private patents affected with the public interest and thereafter license them as set forth in Section 153 and as discussed above.

Pursuant to Section 156, the Commission

has established standard specifications for the granting of nonexclusive licenses on patents owned and controlled by the Commission.[56]

The Commission's regulations provide that upon application by any person the Commission will grant nonexclusive, nontransferable, revocable, royalty-free licenses on Commission-owned United States Patents.[57] The license does not constitute a license or authorization under any other provision of the Atomic Energy Act, and the Commission makes no warranty or representation that the exercise of the license will not result in an infringement of any other patent, nor does the Commission assume any liability resulting from the exercise of the license.[58]

Section 156 also provides that the Commission shall establish standards for the grant of licenses on patents affected with the public interest pursuant to subsection 153(a). See Compulsory Licensing Section, supra.

In January 1961 the Commission established a policy of granting licenses for royalties on AEC-owned foreign patents[59] to foreign nationals in those countries where the foreign government or its agencies charge royalties of United States citizens. The AEC will grant free licenses to foreign corporations where the foreign government does not charge United States citizens. In other instances the AEC may or may not charge royalties depending upon what is deemed appropriate in a given situation. The royalty licenses to be granted may be nonexclusive or exclusive for a period of three to five years, with the license authorized to maintain suits on the foreign patents licensed to such party. The AEC will continue to grant free licenses on AEC-owned U.S. patents.[59a]

Reasonable Royalty Fees, Just Compensation, and Awards under the Atomic Energy Act of 1954, as Amended

The Atomic Energy Act of 1946 imposed upon the Commission a function of a quasi-judicial character, which has been continued in Section 157[60] of the Atomic Energy Act of 1954. The Commission, pursuant to the 1946 Act,[61] 60 Stat. 768, 1946 Act, Section 11(e), designated a Patent Compensation Board to consider the applications for awards, just compensation and reasonable royalties. The 1954 Act designates persons who may be claimants before the Board:

(1) An owner of a patent licensed under Section 158 and Sections 153(b) and 153(e)[62] of the Atomic Energy Act may make application for the determination of a reasonable royalty;[63]

(2) A person whose patent has been revoked, or to the extent the use of a patent has been revoked, under Section 151 may make application for just compensation;[64]

(3) Any person making an invention or discovery[65] useful in the production or utilization of special nuclear material or atomic energy, who is not entitled to compensation or royalty under the Act, and who has complied with the provisions of Section 151(c)[66] may make application to the Commission and the Commission may grant an award.[67]

The standards for determining reasonable royalty or what constitutes just compensation, or for determining the amount of an award, are set forth in some detail and generally include "any defense, general or special, that might be pleaded by a defendant in an action for an infringement," the extent to which a patent has been developed through federally financed research, "the degree of novelty, utility, and importance" of the invention or discovery, the cost to the owner of developing the invention or acquiring the patent, and the actual use of the invention or discovery.[68] A six-year statute of limitations is applicable to Patent Compensation Board proceedings.[69]

The United States Court of Appeals for the District of Columbia Circuit, in *Nellie Pauline Fletcher and William Arthur Fletcher v. U.S. Atomic Energy Comm.*,[70] held:

"In order to justify or require the grant of an award, four conditions must co-exist. The first three are prescribed by the statute, and the fourth is necessarily to be inferred therefrom or is implicit therein. The four conditions are: (1) the claimant must have made an invention or discovery useful in the production of fissionable material or in the utilization of fissionable material or atomic energy for a military weapon; (2) the claimant must be unable to claim just compensation under Section 11(a) because he had and has no patent covering his invention or discovery; (3) the claimant must have complied with Section 11(a)(3) by completely disclosing his invention or discovery to the Commission or the Patent Office; and (4) the Commission must have made use of the claimant's invention or discovery."

The Act, in addition to setting forth who the claimants before the Patent Compensation Board may be, as above outlined, and the standards to be followed, prescribes that the determinations of the Commission are subject to judicial review.[71]

In describing the eligibility of applicants, the Act states that the determinations shall be in accordance with procedures which the Commission may establish.[72] Pursuant to this authority, the Commission initially promulgated regulations on June 18, 1948, entitled "General Rules of Procedure on Applications for the Determination of Reasonable Royalty Fee, Just Compensation or the Grant Of An Award For Patents, Inventions Or Discoveries." [73] The Regulations specifically provide that applicants may be represented by Counsel [74]—appearances of Counsel to be filed with the Clerk of the Board.[75]

An applicant is to file a written, signed, and verified application containing a statement of his interest in the subject matter of the claim, together with a specific statement of all the essential facts upon which the claim is based. The Regulations make several suggestions for details which may be incorporated, and they provide for the filing of multiple copies with the Clerk of the Board.[76] The Regulations specifically provide for an opportunity for negotiation for settlement of a claim between the Commission's staff and the applicant at any time before the final determination.[77] Subsequent to the filing of the application, the Office of the General Counsel of the Commission is, pursuant to the regulation, the respondent in the proceeding,[78] and the response of the Office of the General Counsel is to be filed within four (4) months of the filing of the application, unless the time is extended by

order of the Board.[79] Informal prehearing conferences between the Board and the parties are provided to simplify the issues, to obtain agreement, if possible, as to matters of proof, and to consider any other phases which may facilitate consideration of the claim by the Board,[80] and provision is made in the regulations for Interrogatories.[81]

The Board is required to accord an opportunity for hearing of evidence and to give the parties thirty (30) days notice of the time and place of hearing.[82] The order in which the evidence is submitted is specified.[83] The procedures incorporate largely recognized court procedures. Provision is specifically made for the receipt of evidence in affidavit form at the discretion of the Board.[84] Testimony given at hearings shall be reported verbatim,[85] and copies of transcripts are available at cost.[86]

The Board may authorize oral argument and, at its discretion, may request the parties to submit proposed findings and recommendations.[87]

The manner in which the Board shall reach its decision is specified in that the Board is required to prepare and serve upon the parties proposed findings and proposed determinations with a statement of its reasons.[88] The proposed findings and proposed determinations shall be based upon the entire record and shall be supported by reliable, probative, and substantial evidence, and the Board is required to make a ruling upon each finding and recommendation presented by either party. After the service of the Board's proposed findings and determinations, the parties are given twenty (20) days, or more when ordered by the Board, to file exceptions to any findings of the Board or failure of the Board to include proposed requested findings of the parties.[89]

Upon the expiration of the period for the filing of exceptions, the Board proceeds to final consideration, resolving the questions of fact by what it deems to be the greater weight of the evidence, and it is specifically provided that the findings [90] shall be supported by reliable, probative, and substantial evidence and that rulings shall be made on the exceptions of the parties. The Board's decision constitutes the final action of the Commission sixty (60) days after the date thereof, unless any party shall, within such period, file a petition for review of the decision of the Board.[91]

Any petition for review shall precisely and plainly state the facts on which the petitioner bases his claim that he has been adversely affected or aggrieved by the decision, or that the review is required in the public interest.[92] The respondent has twenty (20) days to file a brief in opposition to the petition for review.[93] The Commission in its consideration of the petition for review may take into consideration, without limitation, the following factors:

(1) The propriety of the compensation, royalty or award;

(2) The compliance with the requirements and standards of applicable Statutes and Regulations; and

(3) Important questions of policy or administration.[94]

If the Commission denies the petition, the decision of the Board becomes the final action of the Commission.[95] If the Commission grants the petition for review, the record is certified by the Clerk of the Board to the Commission and the Commission's order is to fix the time within which the parties may submit exceptions and briefs, after which the Commission may proceed to final decision, with or without oral hearing.[96]

Final decisions of the Commission [97] are subject to judicial review in the manner prescribed in the Act of December 1950, as amended (Chap. 1189, 64 Stat. 1129) and to the provisions of Section 10 of the Administrative Procedure Act, as amended.[98]

Violation of Antitrust Laws

Provision is made in the Atomic Energy Act that whenever the owner of a patent granted for any invention "of primary use in the production or utilization of special nuclear material or atomic energy" is found by a court of competent jurisdiction to have "intentionally used such patent in a manner so as to violate any of the antitrust laws," [99] the court in its discretion, in addition to any other lawful sanctions, may include a requirement for licensing of the patent to any other licensee of the Commission who demonstrates a need. If the court deems that a

reasonable fee should be paid to the owner of the patent, the royalty shall be determined in accordance with 42 U.S.C. 2187.[100]

Communication of Private, Secret Patent Applications

If the Commission communicates to any nation any "restricted data" based on a patent application not belonging to the Government, the Act provides in Section 173 [101] that just compensation shall be paid to the owner, with the initial determination being made by the Commission. If the compensation is unsatisfactory, the applicant may accept 75 per cent of the amount and may sue the United States in the Court of Claims.[102] The Commission's Regulations provide that an initial application for compensation under this provision shall be instituted before the Patent Compensation Board.[103] The same regulations govern this type of proceedings as the proceedings for reasonable royalty, just compensation, or an award as discussed above.

In addition to the subject provision as to applications for compensation for disclosure of private patent applications, the Commission is subject, the same as any other Government Agency, to liability in the nature of compensation for the damage caused by the imposition of a Secrecy Order under the General Patent Statutes.[104] The initial application for compensation under the Secrecy Order provisions of the General Patent Act have also initially been delegated to the Patent Compensation Board [105] pursuant to the Commission's regulation.

References

1. Chemical Engineering (Dec. 1954).
2. 60 Stat. 755; Public Law 79-585, 1946 Atomic Energy Act, Public Law 85-787.
3. Patent Office classes most generally associated with atomic energy: 23/145; 75/84.1; 75/122.7; 204/122.7; 204/154.2; 204/193.2; and 260/429.1.
4. "Special nuclear material" is defined in Section 11(y) of the 1954 Atomic Energy Act to mean "plutonium, uranium enriched in isotope 233 or in the isotope 235, and any other material which the Commission, ... deter-

mines to be special nuclear material," with certain materials excluded. The Commission has not, up to February 1964, determined any other materials to be "special nuclear material." The definition of "fissionable material" under the Atomic Energy Act of 1946 was similar, except that it did not embrace the isotope U[233]. Section 5(a) 1946 Atomic Energy Act.

5. "Atomic energy" is defined in Section 11(c) of the 1954 Atomic Energy Act, 42 U.S.C. 2014(c). For earlier definition see Section 18(a) of the 1946 Atomic Energy Act.

6. Under the 1946 Act, the excluded area had embraced utilization "for a military weapon" which, it is submitted, was a term broader than now used in the 1954 Act. It was deemed to embrace utilization of atomic energy or power for a battleship or military plane. Any such construction is believed ruled out today, as "atomic weapon" is defined in Section 11(d) of the 1954 Atomic Energy Act, 42 U.S.C. 2014(d), to mean "any device utilizing atomic energy, exclusive of the means for transporting or propelling the device (where such means is a separable and divisible part of the device), the principal purpose of which is for use as, or for development of, a weapon, a weapon prototype, or a weapon test device."

7. *Ibid.*

8. 42 U.S.C. 2187, discussed under Reasonable Royalty Fees, Just Compensation and Awards.

9. Public Law 83-703; 69 Stat. 919; 42 U.S.C. 2011-2281.

10. 42 U.S.C. 2181(c).

11. The reports are lodged in the Office of the Assistant General Counsel for Patents, pursuant to Commission delegation.

12. 42 U.S.C. 2181(d).

13. 42 U.S.C. 2181(e) added by Public Law 87-206; 75 Stat. 477.

14. The Assistant General Counsel for Patents has been delegated to act for the Commission in matters pertaining to the United States and foreign Patent offices.

15. 42 U.S.C. 2182.

16. AECPR 9-9.5000; particularly 9-9.5003, 9-9.5004 and 9-9.505. The AEC Regulations and patent clauses are under revision in view of the President's Memorandum of October 10, 1963. See *Government Patent Policies.*

17. 10 CFR, Part 83.

18. *Ibid.*

19. 10 CFR, Part 25.23(b).

20. The General Counsel's Opinion of February 1, 1956 (unpublished).

21. *Fed Reg.,* **26,** 693 (1-24-61).

22. Public Law 87-206, 75 Stat. 477 (1961).

23. Office of the Assistant General Counsel for Patents, AEC, is delegated to act in these matters.

24. As the statutory period of 90 days cannot be extended, the Commission has on occasion filed Directives to preserve the status quo, to permit of completion of its investigation.

25. 42 U.S.C. 2182, third paragraph.

26. See Patent No. 3,084,054.

27. 42 U.S.C. 2182, paragraph three, provides that "The Board shall follow the rules and procedures established for interference cases."

28. Since the inception of Section 152 in 1954 until Feb. 1, 1964, the Commissioner of Patents has referred some 3120 patent applications to the Commission under Section 152. The Commission has filed Directives in some one hundred and ten cases and in approximately sixty-two instances the Commission has acquired rights of one nature or another. In thirty-five cases the Commission has withdrawn the Directives after completion of its investigations. The remainder of the applications are pending.

29. Last paragraph of 42 U.S.C. 2182.

30. 42 U.S.C. 2182 specifically provides that appeals shall be taken to the Court of Customs and Patent Appeals.

31. 10 CFR, Part II, sub-part C., Sec. 2.302.

32. Testimony of Loren K. Olson, 1959, before JCAE.

33. Up to February 1964.

34. 42 U.S.C. 2183(b).

35. 10 CFR, Sub-part C, 2.304-2.306. For the contents of the application for a license on a patent declared affected with the public interest see 10 CFR, Part 81.20.

36. The terms and conditions of each such license are set forth in 10 CFR, Part 81.22.

37. The basis for licensing is set forth in 10 CFR, Part 81.21.

38. 42 U.S.C. 2183(e).

39. Section 153 of the Atomic Energy Act of 1954, 42 U.S.C. 2183(3), describes "any person" as one who has made application to the Commission for a license under Sections 53, 62, 63, 81, 103, or 104, or for a permit or lease under Section 67, or a person to whom such a license, permit, or lease has been issued by the Commission, or who is authorized to conduct an activity under a general license under Section 62 or 81. See also 10 CFR, Part 81.30.

40. Section 31 (42 U.S.C. 2051) is the research assistance section of the Atomic Energy Act of 1954, as amended.

41. 42 U.S.C. 2183(c).

42. 42 U.S.C. 2183(d).

43. 10 CFR, Part II, sub-part C, Section 2.307-2.310, inclusive, and 10 CFR, Part 81.31.
44. February 1, 1964.
45. 42 U.S.C. 2183(d).
46. See 10 CFR, Part 81.32.
47. The specific conditions of any such license are set forth in 10 CFR, Part 81.33.
48. See 10 CFR, Part 81.32.
49. 42 U.S.C. 2183(d).
50. 42 U.S.C. 2183(g).
51. 42 U.S.C. 2183(f).
52. 42 U.S.C. 2184.
53. 42 U.S.C. 2185.
54. Rule 131 Affidavits in Prosecutions of Patent Applications.
55. 42 U.S.C. 2186, 2201(g).
56. 10 CFR, Part 81.
57. 10 CFR, Part 81.12. If the person is a corporation, in addition to setting forth the address, the applicant should show the state of incorporation. There is no charge or fee for the filing for or issuance of the license, or are any fees or royalties payable for the exercise of the license.
58. *Ibid.*
59. 26 Federal Register 693.
59a. *Ibid.*
60. 42 U.S.C. 2187.
61. 42 U.S.C. 1811(e).
62. 42 U.S.C., Sections 2183(b) and (e), and 2188.
63. 42 U.S.C. 2187(b)(1).
64. 42 U.S.C. 2187(b)(2).
65. Reporting under 42 U.S.C. 2181(c) has been held a prerequisite by the Board in *In re Philips,* 131 USPQ 285. But see *Philips* v. *AEC,* 137 USPQ 90.
66. The Board in *In re Kramish,* 123 USPQ 568 held that where applicant has no more "than an interesting, speculative innovation," an award may not be granted.
67. 42 U.S.C. 2187(b)(3); the Commission is also authorized, pursuant to the second sentence of said subsection, upon the recommendation of the General Advisory Committee and with the approval of the President to grant an award for especially meritorious contributions to the development, use, or control of atomic energy. The Commission has established the Fermi Award, which consists of a monetary honorarium of $50,000.00, plus a medal and appropriate scroll, and the E. O. Lawrence Award, carrying a monetary honorarium up to $25,000.00.
68. 42 U.S.C. 2187(c).
69. 42 U.S.C. 2187(h) was added by Public Law 87-206-1961. The Patent Compensation Board held that the regular Statute of Limitation, 42 U.S.C. 2401, was applicable to such proceed-

ings. In *In re Philips,* 131 USPQ 285 and *In re Anderson,* 132 USPQ 695; the Court of Appeals, Seventh Circuit in *Anderson* v. *AEC,* 136 USPQ 401 (1963) reversed and held laches applicable; and the Court of Appeals, D. C., 137 USPQ 90 (1963) also reversed the Board as to this point in *Philips* v. *AEC* and held the Rule of Reasonableness applicable.
70. *Fletcher* v. *AEC,* 90 USPQ 3, 5 (1951).
71. 42 U.S.C. 2239.
72. 42 U.S.C., Section 2187(b)(1) and (2). The predecessor Act of 1946 contains similar provisions—42 U.S.C., Section 1811(a) A and B.
73. The current AEC Regulations are embodied in 10 CFR, Part 80. The initial Regulations appeared in 13 Federal Register 3457, June 24, 1948.
74. 10 CFR, Part 80.2(e).
75. 10 CFR, Part 80.11.
76. 10 CFR, Part 80.11 and 80.12.
77. 10 CFR, Part 80.21. In several instances settlements have been consummated pursuant to this Section.
78. 10 CFR, Part 80.2(e).
79. 10 CFR, Part 80.22.
80. 10 CFR, Part 80.31.
81. 10 CFR, Part 80.32.
82. 10 CFR, Part 80.40.
83. 10 CFR, Part 80.41.
84. 10 CFR, Part 80.42.
85. 10 CFR, Part 80.43.
86. 10 CFR, Part 80.45.
87. 10 CFR, Part 80.44.
88. 10 CFR, Part 80.50.
89. 10 CFR, Part 80.50 and 80.51.
90. 10 CFR, Part 80.60.
91. 10 CFR, Part 80.60(c). Until April 10, 1959, the Board's decision was the final action of the Commission from which Appeals were taken directly to the courts without opportunity for interim appeal to the Commission.
92. 10 CFR, Part 80.61.
93. 10 CFR, Part 80.61(c).
94. 10 CFR, Part 80.61(d).
95. 10 CFR, Part 80.61(e).
96. 10 CFR, Part 80.61(c).
97. The Board's Decision being the final decision of the Commission in the absence of appeal, 10 CFR, Part 80.60(c).
98. 42 U.C.C. 2239(b); 189(b) Atomic Energy Act of 1954. Under the 1946 Act, judicial review from the determination as to an award or reasonable royalty fee were reviewable in the Court of Appeals for the District of Columbia [Section 11(e)(4), 42 U.S.C. 181 (e)(4)] and from determinations as to just compensation to the Court of Claims, or in

any District Court of the United States [Section 13a, 42 U.S.C. 1813(a)].

99. The provision includes 26 Stat. 209, 15 U.S.C. 1-7; 28 Stat. 570, 15 U.S.C. 8-11; 38 Stat. 730, 15 U.S.C. 12-27; 18 U.S.C. 402, 29 U.S.C. 52, 53; 38 Stat. 717, 15 U.S.C. 41-49.

100. Prior to Public Law 87-206, the provision was that the licensee shall pay a reasonable royalty fee to be determined in accordance with said Section 42 U.S.C. 2187.

101. 42 U.S.C. 2223.

102. *Ibid.*

103. 10 CFR, Part 80.1.

104. 35 U.S.C. 181, 183. Secrecy Orders at the request of the Atomic Energy Commission, as well as other Government Agencies, and procedures thereunder are processed in the Patent Office.

105. 10 CFR, Part 80.1. The proceedings are governed by the same rules as govern applications for reasonable royalty, just compensation or an award under 42 U.S.C. 2187.

ATTORNEYS AND AGENTS—REGULATIONS, QUALIFICATIONS AND MANNER OF WORKING

Harry C. Hart

Difficulties of Inventor as Own Attorney

Whether or not an inventor is admitted to practice on behalf of others, he may write, file and prosecute his own application for patent. The procedure is so delicate and the practice so unwise, however, that he rarely attempts to do so. To meet the legal requirements, disclose and claim all that is new and patentable and exclude what is old, requires a high degree of ingenuity and a skill that comes only with experience. Many years ago the Supreme Court put the matter this way:

"The specification and claims of a patent, particularly if the invention be at all complicated, constitute one of the most difficult legal instruments to draw with accuracy ... to describe with requisite certainty the exact invention of the patentee ... (without) claiming that which the patentee had not in fact invented, or ... omitting some element which was a valuable or essential part of his actual invention." *Topliff* v. *Topliff,* 145 U.S. 156, 171, 1892.

In spite of these difficulties, financial considerations occasionally lead an experienced inventor to prepare his specification personally with the plan to have his case refiled later if the invention should show promise.

Applicants not represented by an attorney may be required to state the assistance, other than drafting or secretarial, received in preparing the application and to disclose the name or names of those assisting. Notice in 140 USPQ January 27, 1964.

Qualifications of a Patent Practitioner

A knowledge of law in general, and of the law of patents in particular, is essential for competent service to the client. But as a specialist in one branch of the law, the patent practitioner need claim no special knowledge in other branches such as insurance, taxation, negotiable instruments, etc. He should have been graduated from an accredited law school and should have diligently followed the decisions of the courts in patent cases throughout his career.

Patent Solicitor. In the era of the scythe, the water mill and the plow, the necessary knowledge could be expected of any educated person. But this is not true in the age of steroid chemistry, electronics, nuclear physics and automation. To most persons of general education matters such as these are beyond any detailed understanding. Hence, to carry out his responsibility, the patent solicitor must have undergone an education that is to some extent specialized. Preferably, he has taken a degree in physics, in chemistry, or in some branch of engineering. His knowledge need not be entirely up to date, but it should be such as to enable him to make it so when called upon. It should also be such that he can recognize an invention that may be brought to him as from a field of technology in which he has neither special competence nor the time in which to acquire it. With good fortune he has a partner or an associate to whom he can refer it. If not, he may feel that he should decline the assignment or at least offer to do so.

Trial Lawyer. In contrast to the situation in which the patent solicitor normally finds himself, the sums of money involved in patent litigation are so great that it is usually to the client's advantage to provide his trial lawyer with experts, consultants and instructors to whatever extent seems needed. While the latter's knowledge of the law should be both wider and deeper than is required of the solicitor, the trial lawyer, by virtue of the keen intelligence and industry with which he must be endowed, can usually acquire such knowledge of technology as he needs for a particular case in the course of its preparation. Hence, while an educational background in science is all to the good for the trial lawyer, it is less imperative than for the solicitor, and of much less importance than are the rare skills which make for success in the conduct of litigation.

Subjects Other than Law. Many of the authors of the articles in this encyclopedia have taken science degrees. Among replies to a questionnaire asking them for "Courses other than law specifically recommended for future patent attorneys," engineering or other science headed the list of answers. Second in popularity was English or another language.

It was estimated in 1958 (1) that the patent department of a large chemical company included, among others, 45 practitioners who held degrees in chemistry or chemical engineering, 40 of whom were also graduates or students at the time in law, and (2) that 277 Patent Examiners, the large majority of those engaged in examining chemical applications, had like chemical degrees. (Clark and Hawley, Encyclopedia of Chemistry, Supplement, p. 107.) The figure is representative of patent examiners generally, each in his own field of technology.

In the replies to the same questionnaire, personal qualifications repeatedly suggested were persistence, curiosity, logic, memory and diplomacy. Another is the capacity to become absorbed in the client's problem. A large firm advertising recently for a patent attorney sought one with "creativity, writing ability and imagination."

Registration of Attorneys and Agents

A citizen of the United States who is of good moral character and of good repute and who is possessed of the legal, scientific and technical qualifications necessary to enable him to render applicants for patents valuable service and is competent to advise and assist them in the presentation and prosecution of their application may be admitted to practice before the Patent Office. The requirements are set forth in the Rules of Practice of the United States Patent Office in Patent Cases (1960), established by the Commissioner of Patents. The rules of interest in this connection are in part as follows:

Attorneys at Law

"Any attorney at law in good standing admitted to practice before any United States Court or the highest court of any State or Territory of the United States who fulfills the requirements and complies with the provisions of the Rules of Practice may be admitted to practice before the Patent Office and have his name entered on the register of attorneys." Rule 341 (a).

Agents

"Any citizen of the United States not an attorney at law who fulfills the requirements and complies with the provisions of the Rules of Practice may be admitted to practice before the Patent Office and have his name entered on the register of agents. Note: All persons registered prior to November 15, 1938, were registered as attorneys, whether they were attorneys at law or not, and such registrations have not been changed." Rule 341 (b).

Examination

"In order that the Commissioner may determine whether a person seeking to have his name placed upon either of the registers has the qualifications specified, satisfactory proof of good moral character and repute, and of sufficient basic training in scientific and technical matters must be submitted and an examination which is held from time to time must be taken and passed. The taking of an examination may be waived in the case of any person who has actively served for four years in the examining corps of the Patent Office." Rule 341 (c).

As this rule is presently administered by the Patent Commissioner, membership in the bar of any state or of the District of Columbia constitutes "proof . . . of sufficient basic training in scientific and technical matters . . ." and entitles an applicant to take the examination. In contrast, a non-member of such bar much furnish the Commissioner with evidence that his educational background is sufficient.

Foreign Attorneys. Foreign patent attorneys and agents of proper standing and qualifications may be admitted to practice before the Patent Office provided their countries allow substantially reciprocal privileges to those admitted to practice before our Patent Office. Rule 341 (e).

Limited Recognition

Any person not registered and not entitled to be recognized under rule 341 as an attorney or agent to represent applicants generally, upon a showing of circumstances which render it necessary or justifiable, may be recognized by the Commissioner to prosecute as attorney or agent a specified application or applications, but this limited recognition does not extend further than the application or applications specified. Rule 342.

Restrictions on Non-lawyers

Entry of an individual's name on one of the Patent Commissioner's Rosters as an "attorney" or as an "agent" entitles him only to "represent applicants before the Patent Office in the preparation and prosecution of applications for patent." 35 U.S.C. §31; Rule 341. By contrast, the "practice of law" within any state (or District) is regulated by the laws of that state (or District), as a normal exercise of the police power reserved to the states by the United States Constitution.

Now to prepare and prosecute an application for patent is to engage in the practice of law, albeit a highly specialized form of such practice. Hence, as a registered patent attorney or agent does his work within the geographical area over which a state (or District) has jurisdiction, to that extent the Federal and state laws may collide.

Prior to 1952, registered patent attorneys and agents carried on their activities in their several offices, each located in the state (or District) of his choice without state interference, side by side with members of the state bar and on a live-and-let-live basis. State courts considering the problem agreed that the authority conferred by the Patent Office, in any event if appropriately circumscribed, was either consistent with or preemptive of state law. Thus, in *Chicago Bar Assn.* v. *Kellogg*, 338 Ill. App 618, 83 USPQ 269, 1949, defendant, a non-lawyer but a registered patent attorney, was enjoined from activities such as preparing and construing contracts, deeds and other legal documents; rendering legal opinions on validity, infringement and enforcement of patents; preparing and filing pleadings in suits at law and in equity; and participating as an attorney in legal proceedings. The decree, however, was "without prejudice to defendant's rights to advise and assist applicants for patents in the presentation and prosecution of their applications for patents before the United States Patent Office."

In more recent years, a number of cases have arisen in which this position has been called into question. This line of cases culminated in *State of Florida ex rel. Florida Bar* v. *Sperry*, 133 USPQ 157, in which the earlier cases were considered and discussed. In the Sperry case a practitioner, registered to practice before the United States Patent Office but not admitted to practice before the Florida or any other bar, conducted his activities in Tampa, Florida. The Supreme Court of Florida, after reviewing the facts, concluded that the petitioner's conduct constituted the unauthorized practice of law which the state, acting under its police power, could properly prohibit, and that neither federal statute nor the Constitution of the United States empowered any federal body to authorize such conduct in Florida. Accordingly, it enjoined him from pursuing the following activities in Florida unless and until he became a member of the State Bar:

"1. using the term 'patent attorney' or holding himself out to be an attorney at law in this state in any field or phase of the law (we recognize that the respondent according to the record before us has already voluntarily ceased the use of the word 'attorney');

"2. rendering legal opinions, including opinions as to patentability or infringement on patent rights;

"3. preparing, drafting and construing legal documents;

"4. holding himself out, in this state, as qualified

to prepare and prosecute applications for letters patent, and amendments thereto;

"5. preparation and prosecution of applications for letters patent, and amendments thereto, in this state; and

"6. otherwise engaging in the practice of law."

The United States Supreme Court, having granted the practitioner's petition for certiorari and heard argument, handed down, on May 27, 1963, a unanimous decision in petitioner's favor. *Sperry* v. *State of Florida ex rel. Florida Bar*, 10 L.Ed. 2d 428, 137 USPQ 578, 1963. Chief Justice Warren, speaking for the court, acknowledged that, under Florida Law, to prepare and prosecute an application for patent for others is to engage in the practice of law. He then reviewed the successive Acts of Congress in the light of their legislative histories and the successive revisions of The Commissioners' Rules, made note of the implementation clause (18), as well as the patent clause (2) of Article 1, section 8 of the United States Constitution, concluded that it was, and always has been, the intent of the Congress to govern the conduct of persons such as petitioner in the performance of the activities they are licensed to perform, and held that, under the Supremacy Clause, wherever a conflict arises, the state laws must give way. Accordingly, the injunction against petitioner was vacated "since it prohibits him from performing tasks which are incident to the preparation and prosecution of patent applications before the Patent Office."

Respondent urged that registration of non-lawyer practitioners to practice "before" the Patent Office gave them no more than the right to practice "in the physical presence of the Patent Office and in the District of Columbia, where the Office is now located." Instead of replying directly to this argument, the court, in concluding its review, passed it over lightly with the remark that such registration "confers a right to practice before the Patent Office without regard to whether the *State within which the practice is conducted* would otherwise prohibit such conduct."

Among the "tasks which are incident to the preparation and prosecution of patent applications before the Patent Office," two were specifically alluded to, namely (a) rendering opinions on the patentability of inventions brought to the practitioner for patent protection and (b) consideration of alternative forms of protection which might be available under state law.

Still undecided by the Supreme Court are certain related questions, of much interest to the profession, as to which the decisions of the state courts are in conflict. Among these questions are:

(1) What activities, other than the two specifically mentioned, are "incident to the preparation and prosecution of patent applications before the Patent Office"? As to this, it may be that *Chicago Bar Assn.* v. *Kellogg*, supra, is in part overruled by the Sperry decision.

(2) To what extent, if any, does admission to and membership in the Bar of a state other than that in which a registered practitioner maintains his office soften or broaden the state's restrictions on the unauthorized practice of law within its boundaries?

(3) To what extent does activity by or on behalf of a corporation alter the outcome? As to this, *Battelle Memorial Institute* v. *Green*, 133 USPQ 49 (Ohio Ct. App. 1962), cert. denied, 11 L.Ed. 2d 312, 1963, is relevant. The Institute, a corporation, had been charged with indirectly practicing law in Ohio by hiring lawyers and non-lawyers to work in its legal department and patent section. These men, in turn, furnished legal services to others, notably sponsors of projects of the Institute, in an unauthorized manner. Although carried out in Ohio, the practice extended only to proceedings in the Patent Office.

The Court of Common Pleas of Franklin County had held the practice to be improper and issued an order enjoining it. 127 USPQ 289, 1960. The Court of Appeals reversed, pointing out that membership in the Ohio Bar did not carry with it permission to practice before the Patent Office, holding that such activities as had taken place constituted no invasion of the rights of the members of the Ohio Bar and remarking that the proper parties to have brought the action were those admitted to practice before the Patent Office. 133 USPQ 49, 1962.

Suspension and Disbarment

Decisions upholding the right of the Commissioner of Patents, to disbar or suspend attorneys from practice before it for improper conduct, came many years ago. An 1897 case well illustrates the flagrant character of the activities some might engage in, if not properly disciplined.

An attorney had concocted a scheme for obtaining the submissions of many inventions, ostensibly in an effort to prevent the unsuspecting inventor from being entrapped by unscrupulous (sic) attorneys. On receiving the disclosure from those he would so guard, he would have a letter written to the inventor, about as follows: "The merit of the invention submitted is such that you have been admitted to the 'roll of honor.' Beyond that, you will also be entered for the 'Wedderburn prize' without cost to you other than payment of the fees for prosecution of the application." There would then follow an issue of a publication of seemingly respectable title, reporting that the inventor had been awarded the Sterling Silver "Medal of Merit" as a "Reward of Genius." The inventor, naturally, would hasten to "protect" his remarkable invention. In the proceeding that disbarred the promoter from patent practice, it was noted that he had obtained 33,000 clients but allowances of only 1,600 applications, the figures being approximate. *In re Wedderburn*, 1897 C.D. 77, aff., *Wedderburn* v. *Bliss*, 1898 C.D. 413, CA DistCol.

The present strictness of control of the conduct of attorneys is illustrated by *Dorsey* v. *Ooms, Comr. Pats.*, 72 USPQ 405, (DC DistCol 1947). Dorsey, an attorney of long and honorable standing, sought allowance of an application covering an invention that was considered by its owners to be of great commercial importance. He submitted a laudatory published article, purporting to have been written by a disinterested labor union president, described as a "reluctant" witness. The article had actually been ghost-written for the ostensible author by an employee of the owner of the application. The Commissioner of Patents disbarred Dorsey from practice in the United States Patent Office and the District Court upheld the Commissioner's action. The case stands for the proposition that, in presenting evidence of this kind to the Patent Office, an attorney vouches for the fact that, to the best of his knowledge and belief, it is authentic. After an intermediate appeal the United States Supreme Court upheld the action of the District Court. *Kingsland, Comr. Pats.*, v. *Dorsey*, 338 U.S. 318; 83 USPQ 330, 1949.

Affidavits, unlike journal articles, are recognized as having normally been made by avowedly partisan witnesses and as being couched, in part, in the language of the attorney. They are scrutinized carefully on that account to distinguish facts from conclusions.

Rule 348 gives details of suspension and disbarment proceedings.

Advertising

The Commissioner of Patents has the right to regulate nonfraudulent as well as fraudulent advertising by those admitted to practice before the Patent Office. *Evans* v. *Watson et al.*, 122 USPQ 187, D.C. Cir. 1959. Rule 345 reads as follows:

"**345. Advertising.** (a) The use of advertising, circulars, letters, cards, and similar material to solicit patent business, directly or indirectly, is forbidden as unprofessional conduct, and any person engaging in such solicitation, or associated with or employed by others who so solicit, shall be refused recognition to practice before the Patent Office or may be suspended, excluded or disbarred from further practice.

"(b) The use of simple professional letterheads, calling cards, or office signs, simple announcements necessitated by opening an office, change of association, or change of address, distributed to clients and friends, and insertion of listings in common form (not display) in *a* classified telephone or city directory, and listings and professional cards with biographical data in standard professional directories shall not be considered a violation of this rule. (Emphasis added.)

"(c) No agent shall, in any material specified in paragraph (b) of this section or in papers filed in the Patent Office, represent himself to be an attorney, solicitor or lawyer."

Multi-city telephone directory listing is a form of advertising prohibited by the rule. In a case in which an attorney violated it, not willfully but in accord with his misinterpretation of the rule, the court vacated the Commissioner's order of suspension. The court considered that the Patent Commissioner should have called the matter to the attention of the attorney before instituting the proceeding and thus afforded him an opportunity to achieve compliance with the regulation. *Miller* v. *Watson, Comr. Pats.,* 131 USPQ 435, DC DistCol 1961. It would seem unwise to rely, in the future, on such judicial clemency.

In another case involving advertising and misconduct, it was charged in effect that a patent agent had countenanced the interposition of a lay agency between himself and inventors and had advertised under such names as "Inventions on Demand" and "United States Invention Brokerage." The decision was suspension for a year, with the right of the agent then to apply for reinstatement, on the same basis as a new applicant for registration except that he need not take the examination. *In re Blasius,* 128 USPQ 482, Comr. Pats., 1961.

Attorney's Charges for Services

On the basis of "conversations with experienced lawyers," the Patent Commissioner in 1962 estimated the average charges for the various services most commonly performed by patent practitioners to be as follows:

Service	Charge
1. Preliminary search	$ 50-100
2. Preparation of specification and claims (simple invention)	200-450
3. Preparation of drawings, per sheet	25-45
4. Total legal fees (no appeals or interferences)	450-900
5. Attorney's hourly rate	20-50
6. Infringement study (average complexity)	250-?
7. Validity study	200-?
8. Litigation, counsel fees	200-400
	(per 6-hour day in court)

(From Statement of Commissioner Ladd to Subcommittee of the Committee on the Judiciary, U.S. Senate, September 4, 1962, Table 6.)

(The following sections are largely a condensation of a manuscript written for this Encyclopedia and since published in full by the Bell Telephone Laboratories, Inc., as a monograph under the author's name and the title "From Invention to Patent Application —Analysis, Recollection and Synthesis." Ed.)

Manner of Working

Initial Interview. The inventor expounds his discovery to the attorney. Let us assume that the attorney has some experience in the general field, understands what the inventor sets forth, notes gaps and inconsistencies in the information and cross-questions the inventor in order to clear up doubtful points. The attorney will be particularly attentive to the technological situation with which the inventor starts, the problem he undertook to solve, the initial failures and how he overcame them. The attorney will pick out those features that appear most significant in producing a new result or arriving at an old one by a new route. He will let his mind roam over possible alternatives and question his client as to each one. The understanding as to why some alternatives fail will illuminate those that succeed and make for an early apprehension of an entire class whose members have a common feature that makes for success. If all the members of this class turn out to be new, the invention will, by the same token, have turned out to be of much greater scope than at first appeared either to the attorney or to the client himself and hence, hopefully, of much greater value.

Creativity. When the attorney can think of no more questions to ask (and not before), the initial interview will have reached the point of diminishing returns. But the attorney, if he is wise, does not turn at once to other work; that would scatter the thoughts that have begun to group themselves into a vague pattern in his mind. Rather, he takes time to reflect on what he has just been told, to concentrate on its various aspects and features, to mobilize any dormant knowledge he may have of similar matters and to dredge up parallels that may be stored in the recesses of his memory.

Though the attorney may never have dealt with the particular subject matter, he may well, in the past, have worked with related subjects. He focuses his attention, not so much on the problem as a whole as on the individual features of which it is composed, out of which it grows. When his memory is exhausted, he thumbs through a subject matter index into which, year after year and case after case, he has been stuffing cards on which he has noted patents by number and publications by volume and page. When new recollections begin, they spread and, before long, a respectable sample of the prior art may appear.

But, often, he cannot hit upon the proper category. The recent extraordinary growth and proliferation of science and technology make his index somewhat out of date.

The attorney may now have spent on this case all the time that he can afford at the moment. Also he may realize, on the basis of past experience, that his subconscious mind will continue to grind away on the problem so that, when he returns to it, he will have advanced considerably nearer to the solution, with no conscious effort on his part.

After a night's rest—perhaps not the very first one, but soon—he awakes with the feeling that the fog is lifting; the outlines of his target appear; he has gone as far as he can by himself. He knows what additional prior art he wishes to see and in what commercial contexts he is to find it. He needs a novelty search and has reached the point at which he can ask for it with meaningful questions.

At this point, if he is wise, he will write out a tentative patent claim: "The combination which comprises...."

The likelihood that this claim will ever be presented is small; but this does not mean that the effort of formulating it is a waste of time. On the contrary, it serves two purposes. First, such a claim states, as concisely as possible, the feature or features to be searched. Second, it clarifies the attorney's own thoughts, forces him to distinguish between trivia and essentials, identify and designate the essentials and set forth the causal and logical relations among them. Language not only expresses thoughts; it sharpens them.

The Search. The attorney now arranges for his novelty search. Such a search of United States patents, while of course not complete (the closest prior art may be contained in a printed publication or in a foreign patent) is representative. With the assistance of the Patent Office Manual of Classification, an experienced searcher specialist works expeditiously. Many searchers, with offices in Washington, have developed an uncanny skill in threading their way through the labyrinth of Patent Office classes, to locate a representative group of relevant patents. The attorney, therefore, requests a search. Whether or not he communicates his claim to his searcher, he identifies the field of search with all possible care and bases his questions not alone on what he has learned from his client but on the results of his own cogitations as well.

Study of Prior Art. When the patents uncovered in the search have been received, the attorney examines them. If their disclosures are sufficiently intricate, he may call on the inventor to assist in the examination.

These patents are invariably of interest, in one way or another. First, they may suggest a new question to be asked of the searcher. Second (and this is rare) they may indicate that the novelty, as measured by the available prior art, is exactly as it was at first understood to be in the course of the initial conference. Third, a single reference may negate the novelty of the suggestion entirely; it may reveal all the significant features of the original suggestion combined in the same way. Insignificant features, such as the substitution of brass for steel, a spring for a weight, a curved linkage for a straight one, do not spell patentability. Fourth (and this is the most usual case) one reference may show one feature; a second reference, another feature; a third reference, a combination of features which, while individually differing from those of the client's proposal, might be regarded as equivalent.

It is now the responsibility of the attorney to put these references together in a pattern most unfavorable at first to his client and, having done so, to see what patentable novelty may remain. This is no easy task. It may be accomplished only by revision of his earlier patent claim, as required by the newly acquired knowledge of what is old.

This revision may necessitate a mental leap over the inventor's concepts, reorganizing them into a new relationship, and animating a new theory of presentation. It is this type of mental athletics and ingenuity that may convert a narrow invention in a limited field to one of broad application.

The fame of Sir Isaac Newton rests upon just such an organization of the information available to him. Working much as does the application writer, he organized apparently unrelated facts into a single Law of Universal Gravitation.

The Claim Diagram. When the conscious and subconscious minds of the attorney have completed their preliminary work as outlined above, he is ready to start on the final draft of the broadest claim.

Having formulated his claim he should read it critically and test it against all of the prior art uncovered—especially against the most similar. Are its departures from the prior art insignificant trifles? Does it merely give new reasons why the prior art is, after all, fairly good? Is he as skeptical as he knows how to be, imagining himself to be in the position of a competent and able patent examiner faced with the responsibility of passing on the patentability of this claim?

The language of the claim, the terms in which it is expressed, are important, and its content and its logical development are crucial. No device by which it can be checked should be overlooked. In the case of a claim defining a new combination of elements, individually old, to produce a result that is new in kind, a testing device is found in a "claim diagram." For each element recited in the claim (means for this, means for that, means for the other, a carrier wave source, a message wave source, a modulator, a filter) the attorney draws a box and labels it with its function. He then draws lines interconnecting his boxes, exactly as set forth in the claim. Thus: "In combination with a carrier wave source (box 1) and a message wave source (box 2) a modulator (box 3) having two input ter-

minals and an output terminal, one of said input terminals being connected to said carrier wave source (first interconnection), the other of said input terminals being connected to said message wave source (second interconnection), a filter (box 4) connected in tandem with said output terminal (third interconnection) . . ." and so on to the end. Such a diagram will immediately distinguish any elements that may be refinements, from the essentials, and it will reveal any elements that have been left hanging like tassels, with only one connection, or left high and dry with no connections at all so that they serve no purpose in the claim *as written*. The attorney can now decide whether to omit such elements from his claim entirely or to complete the recitals of their interconnections, thus making them true elements of his claimed combination.

Such a diagram serves also to compel the attorney's attention to another point: whether the embodiment which he has in mind for illustration really represents "the best mode . . . of carrying out the invention." 35 U.S.C. 112. For "the best" is not necessarily the most complete or the most exhaustive. Rather, it is the most effective; and one ingredient of effectiveness is comprehensibility. And just as clarity, lucidity and unity make for a good exposition of the invention in the abstract, so simplicity makes for a good illustrative embodiment. It may be better that the illustrative embodiment be one whose operations, though they falter, are clear, than one which, if constructed of hardware, would work perfectly smoothly though for reasons that can neither be explained nor understood.

Many an attorney, about to commence the preparation of his specification and, having at the last moment, heeded a still small voice urging him to diagram his claim, has thereupon completely revised his illustrative embodiment and reduced its complexity.

If the claim passes all tests, the attorney should make notes of some variants, some as to detail and some basic. At the next opportunity he should explain the prior art to his client and read his patent claim to him. The inventor may read it with his eyes, while the attorney reads aloud pointing out on his diagram each element, each interconnection. The inventor should be required to focus his attention on every word. The attorney should tell him precisely why this limitation is included, why that one. How does the inventor like it? Does it define his invention as he would have defined it had he then known what he now knows? If it does, each of the variants should be considered in the same fashion. Consideration of the variants may reveal that the basic claim can be improved. If it can be, a fresh start is called for: the claim should be revised again. If it cannot be improved, the original view as represented in this third revision of the claim, is confirmed.

Claim Writing before Specification. The reader will have noted, in the typical case outlined above, that the claim has already passed into its third revised form while as yet no single word of the specification has been written. This is precisely as it should be. One should start writing when the time is ripe, and not before. It is a great mistake to start writing a specification until at least one claim has been drafted which the attorney feels is good and the inventor feels is very good. The attorney may be strongly tempted to write at least the introductory part of the specification as his first operation. He may feel irked if time is lost because the inventor cannot meet with him immediately. He may feel that to write at least the first part of the exposition of the invention will clarify his thoughts as to what is claimable matter and what is not. He should resist the temptation. Before a claim has been drafted, the attorney has in his mind nothing but hazy, chaotic ideas, unsuited to exposition. Furthermore, the wrong thoughts, once they are on paper, form a tangled skein that is difficult to unwind. The claim defining the subject matter on which patent protection is to be sought is a target, while the specification is a gun with which to shoot. To write the specification before the claim seems as improper as to start shooting before selecting one's target.

The Type of Invention. The writer's experience over the years, out of which the views here expressed have matured, has been largely with inventors engaged in and

inventions arising out of research in physics and applied mathematics, i.e., electronics, techniques of communication, and the like. The disclosures reach him from the inventors in the form of one or two pages of text, supplemented by one or two sheets of comparatively simple drawings. For the most part the inventions have not been embodied in apparatus. The need to add helpful detail is greater than the need to eliminate unnecessary detail.

An invention, in the sense of the patent law, may be compared with a tree. It has a single trunk, which the attorney has defined in his generic claim. It has a number of branches, each supporting a species claim. It may bear blossoms or fruit which are valuable in their own right as subcombinations. Yet trunk, branches, blossoms and fruit together constitute a unitary, coherent structure.

The information herein is based in part upon the author's "The Art of Communicating Complex Patent Matters," 1955, 1958, Practising Law Institute, New York.

Cross-references: *Advocacy, Attorneys-Enhancement of Capabilities, Application Writing, Associations and the Patent System, Corporate Patent Departments, Liaison, Attorneys—Privileged Relations with Client.*

ATTORNEYS—ENHANCEMENT OF CAPABILITIES

John R. Shipman

The article presents a principle for handling patent attorneys in a corporation to enhance their capabilities and employ them effectively while providing them with a high degree of personal satisfaction. The article then describes a number of procedures that have been used in training new men and enhancing the abilities of other attorneys.

Principle of the Whole Patent Attorney

Though a patent organization and its management must be tailored to fit existing circumstances, a single basic principle of managing attorneys is here suggested as effective, desirable, and generally suitable. This is based on the concept of the "whole patent attorney." Under this principle each patent attorney should be permitted to carry as much individual responsibility for a complete professional job as possible without loss of the minimum necessary corporate control. At the same time he should be in training to carry still more responsibility in the future.

This principle is not suggested as one which must necessarily be used for successful operation. It is proposed because it has many advantages and because its fundamental nature is suitable for widely varying circumstances.

The Human Element. The function of a patent operation is to drive effectively and efficiently toward achievement of the corporate patent objective. This cannot be accomplished by plans, policies and procedures alone, no matter how excellent they may be. The patent department function can be accomplished only by men—by the patent attorneys themselves. It is, therefore, of primary importance to determine how the capabilities of available patent attorneys can be most effectively employed and how they can be increased.

To make such a determination it is necessary to consider patent attorneys as people. Behind their professional demeanor they have normal human desires. As a rule they seem to be slightly introverted and engrossed in their profession to an extent concealing the intensity of some of these desires.

A patent attorney, or any other man, performs best, both quantitatively and qualitatively, when his truly meritorious desires associated with his work have a reasonable chance of being satisfied. This is the normal established relationship between performance and motivation.

Intangibles in Performance. What, then, are the more important desires of a patent attorney? Our experience indicates that he strongly desires to have a sense of personal, individual responsibility for an important task with the corresponding feeling of worthwhile accomplishment when the task is completed. He wishes his accomplishments to be recognizable so as to earn him the respect of his fellow professionals. He wants the

opportunity to become more proficient in both the scientific and the patent aspects of his profession. Certainly, he wants to avoid becoming obsolescent in technology or in patent law and practice. He desires an opportunity to advance in stature in the corporation. As a professional it is particularly important to him to be a complete individual—not just a cog in the wheel.

Since the work must be done by the patent attorneys, it seems apparent that first consideration should be given to obtaining maximum individual patent attorney performance. Mechanically efficient procedures, while very important, should receive second consideration. Therefore, first emphasis should be on providing a reasonable chance for as many as practical of the requirements of the patent attorney to be satisfied.

The difficulty here is in the use of the word "practical." It does not mean limiting any arrangement to the most efficient one from a purely mechanical viewpoint. It does mean applying adequate weight to the intangibles of performance.

It is submitted that most of these important needs of a patent attorney can be effectively met in an efficient, productive arrangement using the principle of "the whole patent attorney."

Scope of Work Assignments. Perhaps a better understanding of the principle can be obtained through a brief description or outline of an actual arrangement used successfully. In the particular case, a large patent department is involved. Each regular patent attorney is, at any particular time, assigned responsibility for a group of engineers or scientists and a primary technology in which such group is working. The capabilities of the patent attorney are matched as nearly as possible in making such assignment, with the requirements of the assignment itself.

The patent attorney is then responsible for essentially all patent matters arising out of or principally concerning his group. It does not mean that he necessarily carries out this responsibility alone. He receives as much help and as much guidance as he requires, from either a supervisor, fellow patent attorneys, a "consulting patent attorney" in the corporate patent operation, or, when appropriate, from outside counsel. A "consulting patent attorney," in this operation, is a highly skilled, highly knowledgeable professional of vast experience whose job in the patent department is simply to act as a consultant for patent attorneys who need help on difficult problems. In all cases, however, the job remains the "baby" of the patent attorney.

For example, if a patent attorney has an interference case but has had little previous experience in interference work, a consulting patent attorney might work with and guide him. But he remains in charge of the interference and he writes the briefs and makes the argument at the hearing.

As another illustration, the license negotiating group may need assistance in planning negotiations as to license matters in an area, or engineering may need assistance in developing a program for avoiding infringement. The patent attorney having that area provides the assistance although, if relatively inexperienced, he may be accompanied by his supervisor.

Thus, the patent attorney acts to the extent to which he is capable as a whole patent attorney within his area. But he is not limited to this area, nor does he quite have absolute and complete exclusivity within it. To do so would involve various risks, including the risk inherent in a "single source of supply" of patent knowledge and service; the risk of loss of perspective in the patent attorney through isolation from the rest of the corporation's activity; and the risk of obsolescence through changing technologies.

The story is told of a patent attorney assigned to work as a specialist in vacuum tubes and "who, as a result, was in patent work for ten years and never succeeded in getting outside the envelope of a vacuum tube." It is easy to see how such a man could lose his perspective and could also suffer substantial obsolescence when solid state technology rather quickly reduced the use of vacuum tubes.

To minimize the risks just expressed, the patent attorney may also be assigned some work in other fields. The amount of such other work varies, depending upon the breadth of his primary area and its estimated life as an important technology. In addition, his assignment will be changed from time to time as his capabilities increase or as technologies change in importance.

Improvement through Challenge. Good men become better men under a challenge. In a patent department there is not always room for frequent promotions to higher organizational positions. But there is certainly room to give a patent attorney more professional responsibility, not only in recognition of his increased capabilities, but as a further effective means of causing him to continue to grow.

It is recognized that the "whole patent attorney" principle does not permit the highest possible degree of specialization. It does, however, permit some controlled specialization in technologies. The value of a high degree of specialization in a narrow field is seriously questioned. One may argue that having a relatively inexperienced man handle an interference under the advice and counsel of an experienced man is wasteful and dangerous. However, experience has shown that the inexperienced man is highly motivated by an opportunity to work on an interference. His interest soars—he increases his work effort—and he is more than willing to check and double-check his work and to seek advice and review. Moreover, in addition to learning something about interferences, he learns the importance of good application preparation and prosecution and gains a much broader understanding of the job of a patent attorney. This results in better all-around patent work in the future. It is believed that the time lost through the sacrifice of some degree of specialization is more than compensated by the greater productivity in both quality and quantity of the "whole patent attorney."

Management of the Whole Patent Attorney. The principle of the "whole patent attorney" does create some additional difficulties for the patent manager. It requires careful analysis and treatment of each man as an individual and a more or less continual review. However, it does not eliminate all benefits of the use of patterns in the treatment of patent attorneys but envisions individual variations for each man.

The management of patent attorneys to utilize fully their individual capabilities and to cause them to improve steadily toward realization of their maximum potential capabilities, is possibly the most important function of the head of a patent department. The "whole patent attorney" principle is recommended as a guide toward satisfactory accomplishment of that function.

Training for Professional Enhancement

Some specific arrangements which have been used by different companies for training new men and for enhancing the professional ability of patent attorneys are particularly interesting.

Training Program for New Men. The more or less conventional training program for a new, technically educated man starting patent work in a large corporation frequently consisted, in the past, of making searches for a Washington office and attending law school at night. After finishing law school he would be transferred from the search office to the regular patent department, working there under the supervision of an experienced patent attorney. If the corporation did not have a Washington search office, the new man started work directly under an experienced patent attorney.

Unfortunately, from a training standpoint, most corporate patent departments have plenty of productive work for their experienced men. Consequently, the new man usually must compete with urgent work pressures for the time of the experienced attorney. Moreover, all good patent attorneys are not good teachers. As a result, in learning while working under supervision, a new man frequently learns only how to handle the particular problems he happens to encounter and does not fully appreciate the reasons behind or the necessity for certain patent laws and practices. It is rather obvious that the results of such a training program will vary widely and often be incomplete and less than satisfactory.

Accordingly, to reduce the training time lag associated with a Washington search office and to obtain better and more uniform training, several corporations have changed their training approach.

One of the more complete training programs utilizes two experienced patent attorneys (one full time and the other part time)

as instructors in a Washington office. They are selected for their aptitude in training young men as well as their knowledge of patent matters and the business of the corporation.

This Washington office is neither a search nor a liaison office, though some searching and liaison are performed. It is a place for training, first and foremost. The program includes classroom work and case studies on patent law and practice, lectures on technologies and products pertinent to the corporation's business, and indoctrination in corporate objectives, policies and practices. It also includes actual productive patent work for men in training under close, expert supervision, work selected to provide balanced experience with a steadily increasing degree of difficulty along with an increasing degree of independence and personal responsibility.

Approximately twelve young men participate in the program at any one time. They are spaced over the four years of law school, so that about three will be finishing each year for transfer to a conventional patent department as three new men start in the program. This provides a group of a manageable size that will supply trained patent attorneys needed annually to fill anticipated openings in the patent department.

For this training program to be successful, it was believed desirable to remove its management from many of the pressures and emergencies associated with ordinary corporate patent life. However, it was also necessary to maintain a good flow of practical productive work. The amount of productive work assigned to a man increases so that in the later portion of the program a man will carry a full workload. Then, his transfer to a patent department is primarily one of geography not involving a new kind of job.

In measuring the value of such a program, the time of the instructors and the program expense must be weighed against the savings in time of other experienced patent attorneys which would otherwise have been devoted to training new men, plus the actual work performed in the program, plus the value of having new men well-trained in both patent fundamentals and knowledge of the corporate business, plus the savings realized in recruitment efforts because of the attractiveness of the program to young men. On the basis of about six years' experience, this particular program has certainly been worthwhile in the opinion of the corporate patent management. It is expected to increase even further in value as the program is refined.

Professional Enhancement. It is a function of patent management to achieve an increase in the professional capabilities of the patent attorneys. Moreover, one of the desires of a patent attorney for consideration is to have the opportunity to become more proficient in his profession. Enhancement programs should then be designed to provide the opportunity and stimulation for general professional improvement.

The direct and individual effects of any specific program, or part of a program, are difficult to measure. They are frequently intangible and intertwined with the effects of other aspects of the corporate patent life. Different individual enhancement projects will certainly be more valuable than others with respect to any particular patent department. It should be remembered, however, that the very fact a real effort toward professional enhancement is made is definitely of substantial benefit to the morale of the patent attorneys.

Some enhancement projects which have been used in different departments are described below.

Periodic Professional Meetings in the Department. Where desired by the patent attorneys, a patent department is encouraged to have periodic meetings to discuss professional patent matters apart from specific corporate problems. In one department, this took the form of a presentation at each meeting by a different one of the patent attorneys of selected patent law cases from recent U.S. Patents Quarterly reports, followed by a group discussion. In another department, one of the patent attorneys presents a short paper on a selected patent subject, followed by a group discussion.

Special Group Meetings. From time to time patent management selects a specific topic which seems particularly worthwhile for discussion to increase the professional capabilities of the patent attorneys. Special

group meetings are then arranged for such discussion, with careful advance preparation. They are led by the more experienced men, or in some cases, by outside counsel particularly expert in the subject. Typical topics have been patent claim drafting, preliminary statements in interferences, and preparation of motions in interferences.

Outside Professional Meetings. Attendance of patent attorneys at meetings of recognized professional groups is promoted and encouraged by an arrangement whereby a patent attorney (in addition to meetings attended at the specific request of the management) is entitled to attend a specified number of such meetings per year, at company expense, with certain limitations on total time and total travel distance. The patent attorney is the judge as to whether it is desirable for him to go. In a case where this is practiced, the privilege has not been abused, and most men do not use their full meeting allotment. But the fact he could go if he believed it proper seems to be most important to the patent attorney.

Professional Information Memos. The patent attorneys are encouraged to write information memos on particularly interesting points of patent law or practice which they may encounter. Provisions are made to distribute such memos to all patent attorneys in the corporation for their information and stimulation.

Corporate Patent Attorney Conferences. In some corporations a conference of all corporate patent attorneys has been held at a place away from the corporation offices. Such conferences have included several small-group, workshop sessions on matters directly related to the corporate patent operation; lectures and talks on patent and related topics; and opportunities for informal discussions and for recreation. One of the major objectives not immediately obvious, is an improvement in communication and coordination resulting from the informal, personal contacts established in a relaxed atmosphere.

Professional Criticism. In one arrangement, a senior professional, with wide experience, is assigned to review the work of the less experienced men on a spot check basis. He then offers constructive criticism of the checked work. When these reviews reveal a common weakness among several men, attention of the entire department is called to the type of situation involved and the correct way to handle it.

In another arrangement, each patent attorney was allocated a sum of money to obtain private, constructive criticism of his own work by outside counsel of his own choice who was experienced in litigation work. Each patent attorney selected one or two of his own work products on problems of substantial difficulty. He submitted these to his chosen outside counsel for detailed, constructive criticism without reference or report to his supervisor.

Another corporate patent department had an outside counsel, experienced in litigation, prepare an invention disclosure based on a selected litigated patent. The case selected was one involving various claim limitations and interpretations. The patent attorneys were divided into small groups and given the invention disclosure. Each group was requested to prepare a set of five or six claims on the disclosure without attempting to look up the case on which it was based. These claims were submitted, without author identification, to the outside counsel who subsequently discussed them with reference to the actual claims which had been in litigation.

Cross-references: *Advocacy, Application Writing, Attorneys and Agents, Corporate Patent Department, Information for the Inventor, Examiners' Training.*

ATTORNEYS' PRIVILEGED RELATION WITH CLIENTS

Arthur S. Tenser

Conflicting Principles and Relationships.

Substantially all litigation involving United States patents arises under the Federal patent law (35 U.S.C.) and is conducted in the Federal courts. The Federal Rules of Civil Procedure, which govern the conduct of such litigation, include broad discovery provisions which are accorded the most lib-

eral construction by the courts. Consonant with this approach, any conflicting doctrine whose effect would be to diminish the scope of discovery is looked upon with disfavor, and the privilege safeguarding clients against disclosure of confidential communications with their lawyers is thus subjected to the strictest examination and interpretation by the courts.

Perhaps more than in other fields of the law, the subject matter of patent litigation further serves to complicate the application of the privilege. Because the technology involved in a patent dispute is primarily a business matter of the client, rather than legal, communications between attorney and client may be either purely business or purely legal in nature or more often than not an intermixture of the two. A similar duality exists in the patent lawyer's role in the affairs of his client. Is he acting as a business man, rather than a lawyer when considering a technical question pertaining to a patent validity or infringement question? Or are all of the lawyer's activities in behalf of his client, as long as they are related to patents, to be considered legal in nature? Resolution of these questions is further complicated by the fact that non-lawyers are authorized to file and prosecute patent applications before the Patent Office.

The divergence of opinion in the courts on these questions has not helped to clarify the application of the attorney-client privilege in patent cases. However, from the varying viewpoints expressed, especially in a number of very recent cases, there may be extracted some general principles of comfort and aid to the patent lawyer in furthering the best interests of his client, both prior to and during litigation.

Nature of the Privilege

The duty of the attorney to preserve his client's confidence is as old as the practice of law itself, and the attorney-client privilege has been in development for hundreds of years.[1] The privilege is recognized throughout the United States, and many states have enacted specific statutes protecting it.

The privilege itself is somewhat difficult

to define. Professor Wigmore [2] characterizes it in the following language:

"(1) Where legal advice of any kind is sought, (2) from a professional legal advisor in his capacity as such, (3) the communications relating to that purpose, (4) made in confidence, (5) by the client, (6) are at his instance permanently protected, (7) from disclosure by himself or by the legal advisor, (8) except the protection be waived."

In one of the leading patent cases involving the question of privilege, it is somewhat more explicitly defined: [3]

"The privilege applies only if (1) the asserted holder of the privilege is or sought to become a client; (2) the person to whom the communication was made (a) is a member of the bar of a court, or his subordinate and (b) in connection with this communication is acting as a lawyer; (3) the communication relates to a fact of which the attorney was informed (a) by his client (b) without the presence of strangers (c) for the purpose of securing primarily either (i) an opinion on law or (ii) legal services or (iii) assistance in some legal proceeding, and not (d) for the purpose of committing a crime or tort; and (4) the privilege has been (a) claimed and (b) not waived by the client."

It has been generally accepted that the privilege attaches to communications *between* the client and his legal advisors, regardless of who originates them, providing the other criteria are met.[4]

The attorney's "work product" rule which grants a privilege to the memoranda, papers, etc. prepared by a lawyer in connection with an action or suit, is distinguished from the attorney-client privilege and appears to be recognized in patent cases.[5]

Which Law Controls?

There appears to be some conflict as to whether applicability of the attorney-client privilege is governed by state or federal law. The Ninth Circuit Court of Appeals has held that since state law creates the status of the attorney and thus gives rise to the existence of the attorney-client relationship, state law should control the privilege doctrine.[6] This holding was followed in a recent patent case.[7]

However, in a case before the 2d Circuit Court of Appeals involving the Federal In-

ternal Revenue laws, the court specifically disagreed with the opinion of the Ninth Circuit and found that federal law dictated the scope and applicability of the privilege since the tax provisions in question were matters of federal law.[8] By analogy, it may be arguable that suits brought under the Patent Statute are likewise matters of federal law and the privilege should be similarly governed.

Consistent with such rationale, a New York state court, in an action relating only to interpretation of a patent licensing agreement and involving no federal law, based its decision on a finding that applicability of the privilege was dependent on state law.[9]

The Seventh Circuit has ruled that the question of privilege is substantive in nature and state laws must be looked to in diversity cases.[10] However, since the jurisdiction of the federal courts in the usual patent litigation is not founded on diversity of citizenship but because the action arises under federal law, this conclusion would seem to be of minor import to the patent lawyer.

It is interesting to note however, that an Illinois federal district court, in a diversity case, ignored state law in reaching a decision on the applicability of the privilege to a corporate client and specifically found that federal law was applicable.[11]

Whether by design or not, most of the reported decisions involving privilege in patent cases make no mention of which law was applied, and it is probably correct to assume that the federal law established by the decisions is controlling. In any event, there appears to be no real difference on this question between the state and federal law in the patent area, and substantially the same criteria for judging a particular communication would seem to apply regardless of which law is deemed pertinent.

Parties to the Communication

To be protected by the privilege, the communication in question must be between the client and his attorney. The client may be a private individual or a corporation.[12] Where a corporate client is involved, the employee actually making the communication, regardless of his rank, must be in a position to control or take substantial part in a corporate decision based on the advice received from the attorney in response to the communication. Alternatively, he may be an authorized member of a control group which acts as the alter ego of the corporation and thus may properly make such a communication to counsel. Communications from employees not so qualified would not be protected by the privilege.[13]

The attorney must be admitted to the Bar of some jurisdiction, but not necessarily the one in which he is acting.[14] It has been held that corporate patent department members cannot qualify as lawyers, regardless of Bar membership, on the theory that their activities are confined primarily to business rather than legal aspects of the corporation's affairs.[15] But this view has not been followed, and it is now generally accepted that both outside counsel and members of corporate patent departments who are admitted to the Bar of some jurisdiction may be considered to be acting as lawyers for purposes of the privilege, in specific instances.[16]

There is some indication of a more favorable view of the courts towards granting the privilege where outside counsel is involved, as opposed to house patent counsel.[17]

The Communication

The privilege may be invoked only with respect to communications involving *confidential* information made by the client to the lawyer for the purpose of securing a legal opinion or legal advice. Thus, correspondence relating to validity investigations based on publicly available documents (e.g., issued patents) and infringement determinations where the accused device is publicly known have been found not to be entitled to the privilege.[18]

It is generally agreed that communications in furtherance or defense of suits in the courts qualify for the privilege. And this extends to the preparation and prosecution of appeals to the Court of Customs and Patent Appeals. But the making of initial preparatory determinations of patentability,

the preparation and prosecution of patent applications and the conduct of interference proceedings before the Patent Office, as well as the general application of patent law to the client's developments or those of his competitors, have been held to be activities of a business, rather than legal nature, and communications arising in the course of these activities have thus been held not entitled to the privilege.[19]

However, at least one court has more recently decided that communications are within the purview of the privilege if they pertain to "a specific patent matter in which the client has reason to believe legal advice is necessary, such as where inquiry is made as to a certain patent application, with respect to litigation, infringement, validity or purchase." [20] In reaching this conclusion, the court appeared to be persuaded, at least to some extent, by recent decisions in unauthorized practice of law actions which have held that the patent attorney's work, including activities before the Patent Office, constitutes the practice of law.[21] The other cases apparently took no notice of these decisions. It is interesting to note that a recent case has held that a trademark infringement report prepared by house counsel of a corporation is entitled to the protection of the privilege.[22]

In determining the applicability of the privilege, the courts consider each communication or document individually.[23] It is conceivable, in light of the different viewpoints presented by the decisions, that the applicability of the privilege could turn on the precise form in which the matter is discussed in the communications. Prudence dictates that both attorney and client see to it that the substance of the legal problem in question be incorporated in each communication between them.

References

1. The policy underlying the privilege is admirably expressed in the *American Law Institutes' Model Code of Evidence,* in the comments on Rule 210:
   "In a society as complicated in structure as ours and governed by laws as complex and detailed as those imposed upon us, expert legal advice is essential. To the furnishing of such

advice the fullest freedom and honesty of communication of pertinent facts is a prerequisite. To induce clients to make such communications the privilege to prevent their later disclosure is said by courts and commentators to be a necessity. The social good derived from the proper performance of the functions of lawyers acting for their clients is believed to outweigh the harm that may come from the suppression of the evidence in specific cases."

2. 8 *Wigmore on Evidence,* 3rd ed. Section 2292.

3. *United States* v. *United Shoe Machinery Corp.,* 89 F. Supp. 357, 85 USPQ 5, DC Mass 1950.

4. "Since communications by the attorney to the client might reveal the substance of a client's communication they are also within the privilege." *Georgia-Pacific Plywood Co.* v. *United States Plywood Corp.,* 108 USPQ 294, 18 FRD 463, DC SNY 1956. See also *Paper Converting Machine Co., Inc.* v. *FMC Corporation,* 215 F. Supp. 249, 136 USPQ 549, DC EWis 1963.

5. *American Cyanamid Co.* v. *Hercules Powder Co.,* 211 F. Supp. 85, 135 USPQ 235, DC Del 1962. For a discussion of the "work product" rule, see *Hickman* v. *Taylor et al.,* 329 U.S. 495, 1946.

6. *Baird* v. *Koerner,* 279 F.2d 623, CA 9 1960.

7. *Garrison* v. *General Motors Corp.,* 213 F. Supp. 515, 136 USPQ 343, DC SCal 1963.

8. *Colton et al.* v. *United States,* 306 F.2d 633, CA 2 162, cert. denied 371 U.S. 951.

9. *Kent Jewelry Corp.* v. *Kiefer,* 93 USPQ 388, N.Y. Sup. Ct. 1952.

10. *Palmer* v. *Fisher,* 228 F.2d 603, CA 7 1955.

11. *Radiant Burners Inc.* v. *American Gas Association,* 207 F. Supp. 771, DC NIll. 1962. Cf. 209 F. Supp. 321. The District Court holding that the attorney-client privilege was not applicable to corporate clients was reversed on appeal, 320 F.2d 314; cert. denied 84 S.Ct. 330.

12. *Radiant Burners Inc.* v. *American Gas Association,* supra, reference 11.

13. *City of Philadelphia* v. *Westinghouse Electric Corp.* (D.C.E.D. Pa. 1962) C.C.H. Trade Reg. Rep Par. 70536; *Garrison* v. *General Motors Corp.,* supra, reference 7.

14. *American Cyanamid Co.* v. *Hercules Powder Co.,* supra, reference 5; *Garrison* v. *General Motors Corp.,* supra, reference 7; *Paper Converting Machine Co., Inc.* v. *FMC Corp.,* supra, reference 4.

15. *United States* v. *United Shoe Machinery Co.,* supra, reference 3. The court found, however, that house general counsel qualify as lawyers for the privilege.

16. "I find myself unable to agree with the implied contention that because an attorney happens to be engaged in the field of patents in which field non-attorneys are authorized to practice, he is ipso facto deprived of his status as a lawyer in every activity in which he operates so long as a patent prosecution is involved." *Ellis-Foster Co., et al.* v. *Union Carbide and Carbon Corp.,* 159 F. Supp. 917, 116 USPQ 576, DC NJ 1958. See also, *Georgia-Pacific Plywood Co.* v. *United States Plywood Corp.,* supra, reference 4; *Zenith Radio Corp.* v. *Radio Corp. of America,* 121 F. Supp. 792, 101 USPQ 316, DC Del 1954; *American Cyanamid Co.* v. *Hercules Powder Co.,* supra, reference 5; *Garrison* v. *General Motors Corp.,* supra, reference 7; *Paper Converting Machine Co., Inc.* v. *FMC Corp.,* supra, reference 4.

17. "The court in the Cyanamid case, supra, held that communications from outside counsel were not privileged because they were opinions on facts gleaned from public documents. This court would not go that far." *Garrison* v. *General Motors Corp.,* supra, reference 7. In *Zenith Radio Corp.* v. *Radio Corporation of America,* supra, reference 16, the court stated: "...outside counsel for corporations almost invariably qualify...under this requirement."

18. *American Cyanamid Co.* v. *Hercules Powder Co.,* supra, reference 5.

19. *Zenith Radio Corp.* v. *Radio Corporation of America,* supra, reference 16.

20. *Garrison* v. *General Motors Corp.,* supra, reference 7.

21. Since the *Garrison* v. *General Motors* decision, the U.S. Supreme Court has had the following to say about practice before the Patent Office: "We do not question the determination that under Florida law the preparation and prosecution of patent applications for others constitutes the practice of law, Grennough v. Tax Assessors, 331 U.S. 486; Murdock v. Memphis, 20 Wall. 590. Such conduct inevitably requires the practitioner to consider and advise his clients as to the patentability of their inventions under the statutory criteria, 35 U.S.C. Sections 101-103, 161, 171 as well as to consider the advisability of relying upon alternative forms of protection which may be available under state law. It also involves his participation in the drafting of the specification and claims of the patent application, 35 U.S.C. Section 112, which this Court long ago noted 'constitute[s] one of the most difficult legal instruments to draw with accuracy,' Topliff v. Topliff, 145 U.S. 156,171. And upon rejection of the application, the practitioner may also assist in the preparation of amendments, 37 CFR Sections 1.11701.126, which frequently requires written argument to establish the

patentability of the claimed invention under the applicable rules of law and in light of the prior art 37 CFR Section 1.119." *Sperry* v. *State of Florida, ex rel The Florida Bar,* 373 U.S. 379, 137 USPQ 578, 1963.

22. *8 In 1 Pet Products, Inc.* v. *Swift & Co.,* 218 F.Supp. 253, 137 USPQ 777, DC SNY 1963.
23. *American Cyanamid Co.* v. *Hercules Powder Co.,* supra, reference 5.

ATTORNEYS' PROFESSIONAL ETHICS

Virgil E. Woodcock, John Rex Allen, J. Vincent Martin and W. Houston Kenyon, Jr.

In 1836 the idealistic and realistic Sharswood wrote in his "Professional Ethics"

"There is, perhaps, no profession after that of the sacred ministry, in which a high-toned morality is more imperatively necessary than that of the law. There is certainly, without any exception, no profession in which so many temptations beset the path to swerve from the lines of strict integrity; in which so many delicate and difficult questions of duty are constantly arising."

Four papers * dealing with the practical ethical problems in patent practice follow hereinafter, in condensed form approved by the authors.

Duties Lawyers Owe Their Clients †

Some twenty canons bear upon the duties which a lawyer owes his client, for example, the duty to give candid advice, to advise settlement when the controversy will admit of fair adjustment, not to withdraw from professional employment except for good cause, and his duty with reference to defending one he knows to be guilty. I shall select two of these canons for discussion for patent lawyers—the two which bear upon conflicting interests and the confidence of a client.

I venture to suggest there is no branch of legal practice where the problems of con-

*These papers appear in the Bulletins of the American Patent Law Association of January and February 1956, beginning at pages 13 and 66, respectively.

† This section by W. Houston Kenyon, Jr.

flict of interest present more difficult and thorny problems, than in the patent practice. The reason is simple. Patent lawyers are commonly entrusted by their clients with more confidential information, over longer periods of time and embracing a wider range of detailed subjects, than any other class or specialty of practicing lawyers. It is the nature of technological research and the way in which inventions are hammered out, that makes this inevitable. A lawyer having the duty of protecting his client's rights in inventions must necessarily share knowledge of frustrations as well as hopes. He must be taken into the inner councils of research management, if he is to serve effectively when his services are needed most. It is a matter of common observation that a lawyer's proficiency in handling patent applications and in licensing and litigation, grows with the years, as he familiarizes himself with prior patents in the art, listens while engineers argue, studies their inventions, and forms his own appraisal of the imagination and intellectual resources of the client or organization which he serves. Small wonder indeed it is that attorney-client relationships of this kind not infrequently last a life-time.

The principal canons dealing with questions of conflict of interest are Canon 6, originally adopted in 1908, and Canon 37, adopted in 1928. They follow.

"6. Adverse Influences and Conflicting Interests

"It is the duty of a lawyer at the time of retainer to disclose to the client all the circumstances of his relations to the parties, and any interest in or connection with the controversy, which might influence the client in the selection of counsel.

"It is unprofessional to represent conflicting interests, except by express consent of all concerned given after a full disclosure of the facts. Within the meaning of this canon, a lawyer represents conflicting interests when, in behalf of one client, it is his duty to contend for that which duty to another client requires him to oppose.

"The obligation to represent the client with undivided fidelity and not to divulge his secrets or confidences forbids also the subsequent acceptance of retainers or employment from others in matters adversely affecting any interest of the client with respect to which confidence has been reposed."

When we seek to determine how this canon affects questions of conflict arising in the practice of the average patent lawyer, the canon is not by itself an altogether clear and sufficient guide. For example, is the injunction against representing conflicting interests limited to situations where a legal assertion of one client is presently in direct collision with a denial of that assertion by another client? Or, if you answer this question by saying that probable or possible future collision may also amount to conflict of interest, as many ethics committee decisions have held, then what about future patent infringement collisions which are potential in the sense that they will or may arise only if a client's business expands into new area or product at some future date? Or, in cases where there is no present controversy or any potential future controversy that can be reasonably foreseen, is the lawyer barred from representing interests which are competitive in the market but not in their lines of research? Finally, in the absence of any direct controversy, does the injunction against divulging a client's confidence prevent the lawyer from making use of them, without disclosure, in serving another client?

The failure of Canon 6 to settle questions analogous to these, arising in general practice, led to adoption by the American Bar Association in 1928 of an additional canon, No. 37, which, without repealing No. 6, now stands beside it. I read its first two sentences:

"37. Confidences of a Client

"It is the duty of a lawyer to preserve his client's confidences. This duty outlasts the lawyer's employment, and extends as well to his employees; and neither of them should accept employment which involves or may involve the disclosure or use of these confidences, either for the private advantage of the lawyer or his employees or to the disadvantage of the client, without his knowledge and consent, and even though there are other available sources of such information."

As one seeks to apply Canons 6 and 37 to the everyday problems of patent lawyers in dealing with their clients, it will be found that five working rules or principles emerge. It is improper:

(1) To accept employment on both sides of a presently existing actual controversy, except with the consent of every interested party.

(2) To accept employment which is likely in the future to lead to representation of both sides of an actual controversy except with a like consent. This rule applies with special force to a lawyer who is currently representing one of the parties in a court action.

(3) To divulge the confidences of a client, except with his consent.

(4) To use the confidences of one client in serving another, even though not divulged, except with the consent of the first.

(5) Not to tell a new client of all the circumstances of the lawyer's relation to, or connection with, the controversy or subject matter, which might influence the client in the selection of counsel.

Duties of Lawyers to the Public and the Courts *

Our chief obligations to the public are to see to it that the Bar is well policed, not to stir up litigation or to aid in the unauthorized practice of the law. The canons directed to these obligations are primarily 28, 29 and 47.

A lawyer having formed a partnership with a patent agent is thereafter precluded from performing legal services, as defined by the law of the state where the partnership does business, and unless he so confines himself, he is engaged in unauthorized practice.

The canons with respect to our duty to the courts are primarily numbers 1, 3, 20, 21, 22, 23, 26 and 39.

These canons provide for a respectful attitude toward the court or the Patent Office officials, forbid attempts to secure an advantage for a client by improper means, and require punctuality and candor and fairness with the court and other lawyers.

With respect to the duty of the lawyer to the court and to the Patent Office we should bear in mind that the old idea that

---

* This section by John Rex Allen.

a lawsuit or a Patent Office proceeding is a duel between opposing lawyers is no longer true. Now it is more and more an endeavor to develop facts from which the court or the Patent Office can make a proper determination and mete out justice according to law.

We are all aware, or we should have become aware, by reason of the decisions in the Keystone Driller and Hazel-Atlas cases that it is completely unethical to suppress testimony. *Keystone Driller Co.* v. *General Excavator Co.*, 290 U.S. 240, 1933; *Hazel-Atlas Glass Co.* v. *Hartford-Empire Co.*, 322 U.S. 238, 1944. It was also recently held that it is improper to obtain evidence from the opposing side by means of misstatements, guile or deceit.

We are all ware of the fact that it is improper to seek to obtain ex parte interviews with judges or Patent Office officials in inter partes cases, but I am not sure that this is not sometimes forgotten.

While there is no canon based on the duty not to employ dilatory tactics, it is an obligation that we all have, should remember and most frequently forget. I am thinking now more of the Patent Office than of the courts and even more of the Trademark Division of the Patent Office than of the Patent Division. Prompt replies to actions aid the Patent Office in reducing its load and help the client in obtaining his trademark registration issue promptly.

One of our most common sins is to ask for an oral hearing in both ex parte and inter partes cases and then not appear.

Duties Lawyers Owe Each Other *

At the outset, we should realize that while many of the services rendered by lawyers in patent practice differ widely from the services rendered by lawyers in other branches of the legal profession, all lawyers owe the same ethical duties to each other. We are not only brethren at the bar, but also counsellors and advocates of the causes of our clients, officers of the courts, attorneys registered to practice before the Patent Office, and servants of the public.

* This section by J. Vincent Martin.

Our duties as such are inseparably interwoven.

As a practical matter, perhaps the two principal instances in which conflicting interests arise are those in which two lawyers wish to represent the same client and those in which two lawyers oppose each other in a contested case.

When two lawyers wish to represent the same client, canons 7 and 27 apply.

Canon 7 condemns efforts, direct or indirect, in any way to encroach upon the professional employment of another lawyer, as unworthy of those who should be brethren at the bar. This canon also sets forth the ethical procedure to be followed when a client offers his attorney the assistance of additional counsel and when two lawyers jointly representing one client find themselves in disagreement.

Canon 27 condemns, as unprofessional, not only advertising but any solicitation of professional employment not warranted by personal relations. The first part of APLA Canon 27, which is a verbatim copy of original ABA Canon 27 reads:

"The most worthy and effective advertisement possible, even for a young lawyer, *and especially with his brother lawyers,* is the establishment of a well-merited reputation for professional capacity and fidelity to trust. This cannot be forced, but must be the outcome of character and conduct."

As to the instances in which two lawyers oppose each other in a contested case, the canons include many provisions.

Canon 9 provides that a lawyer should not in any way communicate upon the subject of controversy with a party represented by counsel; much less should be undertaken to negotiate or compromise the matter with him, but should deal only with his counsel.

Canon 17 reminds us that clients, not lawyers, are the litigants, and that ill-feeling existing between clients should not be allowed to influence counsel in their conduct and demeanor toward each other; that all personalities and unseemly wrangling between counsel should be avoided.

Canon 22 states that the conduct of a lawyer towards other lawyers should be characterized by candor and fairness.

We are assured by Canon 24 that the

lawyer, and not his client, should decide
how opposing counsel is to be treated in
incidental matters pending the trial, not
affecting the merits of the cause, or working substantial prejudice to the rights of
the client.

We are instructed by Canon 25 to give
timely notice to opposing counsel and are
reminded that, while agreements between
counsel should be reduced to writing, it is
dishonorable to avoid performance of an
agreement fairly made because it is not reduced to writing.

Some of the miscellaneous provisions affecting our duties and relations to each
other are:

Canon 12, which was written many years
ago, tells us not to forget that the profession is a branch of the administration of
justice and not a mere money-*getting* trade.
It also provides that no division of fees for
legal services is proper, except with another
lawyer or registered patent attorney and
based upon a division of services or responsibility.

Canon 41 of the ABA, not yet included
in the canons of APLA, as such, makes it
the duty of a lawyer to endeavor to rectify
a fraud or deception unjustly imposed upon
the court or a party by advising his client to
forego the advantage thus unjustly gained.
If his client refuses to do so, it becomes the
lawyer's duty to promptly inform the injured person or his counsel so that they
may take appropriate steps.

Discussion and Summary *

Following the discussion of the above
papers, the panelists, under the leadership
of a moderator [Virgil E. Woodcock] discussed some fifty-one questions, of which
the following are exemplary:

(1) Division of fees by the patent lawyer with a general lawyer.

(2) Inserting inventor's corrections into
an application and inking of drawings after
execution and before filing the application.

(3) Delay in doing work for client, as in
preparing an application four months after
receipt of the information.

* This section by Virgil E. Woodcock.

(4) Urging invalidity of a patent under
which the attorney has secured, for another
client, a nonexclusive license.

(5) Prosecuting for a corporate client an
application on which the client has only an
option to acquire patent rights at issuance
of the patent.

(6) Interviews in Patent Office by a non-
lawyer and non-agent in behalf of an employer who is registered to practice before
the Patent Office.

(7) In litigation, questioning privately
a prospective witness known to be one who
will be called by the other side.

(8) Requesting forwarding fee from a
second patent attorney without the for-
warder accepting any responsibility or performing any service.

(9) Filing applications on subject matter on sale in this country for more than a
year, with only small improvements made
subsequently.

Answers to these and the other questions
appear in the February issue of the Bulletin, pages 66-88.

The Moderator then summarized the discussion as follows:

Viewed against the broad background, a
single lawyer doesn't seem very important
to the system. But he is like a link in a
chain. If he fails to live up to the Canons
of Ethics, the world knows the chain is broken. Credit is rarely given to any of the
good links, as many as there may be.

The panel members have distinguished
above between types of conduct which may
be classified as *malum in se* and types of
conduct which come within the classification of *malum prohibitum;* and then there
are those various rules concerning the duty
of a lawyer to be a gentleman and to be
courteous, to respect others, and to abide
by the amenities.

It is important that we engender out of
these discussions an awareness of the Canons and of our obligations and that we keep
out of the traps and the ensnarements.
Many of us know that some of these questions have come perilously close to our own
practice. We need more discussions of this
kind to develop an understanding of what
is best for the public, what is in the interest
of the courts, and what will guide us along

the professional pathways of our practice.

Sometimes we get careless. We may forget we hold in our hands the conscience of our clients. We may tend to dilute our duties to the Patent Office. The Supreme Court, in the case of *Kingsland* v. *Dorsey*, 83 P.Q. 330; 338 U.S. 318, 1949, said:

"The statute under which the Commissioner acted represents Congressional policy in an important field. It relates to the character and conduct of 'persons, agents, or attorneys' who participate in proceedings to obtain patents. We agree with the following statement made by the Patent Office Committee on Enrollment and Disbarment, that considered this case: 'By reason of the very nature of an application for patent, the relationship of the attorneys to the Patent Office requires the highest degree of candor and good faith. In its relation to applicants, the Office . . . must rely upon their integrity and deal with them in a spirit of trust and confidence. . . . It was the Commissioner, not the courts, that Congress made primarily responsible for protecting the public from the evil consequences that might result if practitioners should betray their high trust."

The Commissioner has, in the Rules of Practice, Rule 344 which requires that attorneys and agents appearing before the Patent Office must conform to the standards of ethical and professional conduct generally applicable to attorneys before the courts of the United States.

Can you recall the oath administered by the Patent Office? Every person admitted to practice now takes the following oath:

"I do solemnly swear that I will observe the laws and rules of practice of the United States Patent Office. I will maintain the respect due the Patent Office and the officials thereof. I will not counsel or maintain any application or proceeding which shall appear to me to be unjust nor will I take any action except such as I believe to be honestly debatable under the law. I will employ for the purpose of maintaining the causes confided to me such means as are consistent with truth and honor, and will never employ political influence nor seek to mislead the officials of the Patent Office by any artifice or false statements of fact or of law.

"I will maintain in confidence and preserve inviolate the secrets of my client and will accept no compensation in connection with his business except from him or with his knowledge or approval. I will abstain from all offense of personality and advance no fact prejudicial to the honor or reputation of a party or witness unless required by justice and the cause with which I am charged. I will not delay any man's cause for lucre or malice."

The oath that follows is the one that Mr. Justice Roberts administered to witnesses appearing before him:

"You do swear by Almighty God, the Searcher of all hearts, that the testimony you shall give in the matter at issue, shall be the truth, the whole truth, and nothing but the truth, and so you shall answer at the last great day."

Cross-references: *Attorneys and Agents; Fraud.*

B

BRIEFS—PLANNING AND WRITING

Clyde A. Norton

One would suppose that every patent attorney is aware of the vital importance of a good brief in any proceeding which permits or requires one. It is his last opportunity to persuade the tribunal to decide the matter in his favor.

Characteristics of a Good Brief

A Good Brief Is Logical. Yet, as important as the brief is, there are too many patent lawyers who either do not know what a good brief should be or are unable to produce one. In one case an opponent rambled, repeated himself endlessly, jumped from one subject to another and back again, made ipse dixit assertions for which there was no foundation in the record, and statements of what the record showed which were contrary to the record. He even cited decisions he said were in his favor but which were actually against him. In short, he violated every known rule of good brief writing.

It appeared that he was pressed for time, had not made a plan or outline of what he wanted to say, but had merely called in a stenographer and "talked" without having checked the record or even read the cases he cited. Later he told me this was exactly what happened.

A Good Brief Is Accurate. Any statement made in the brief which is not supported by the record will be a Banquo's ghost. Your opponent will see that it haunts you.

A Good Brief Is Concise. A judge told of one case tried before him in which the record when printed was several hundred pages long. To his amazement, when the brief was filed it turned out to be as bulky. Actually it was practically a duplicate of the record, repeating the testimony of the witnesses, word for word. His Honor's comment was: "I just dropped that 'brief' in the circular file and never looked at it again."

Format of the Brief

Although the facts of every case are different and each brief must be written around its own particular facts, all briefs should use basically the same format, whether they are in the Patent Office, before the Board of Appeals, the Board of Interference Examiners, or in the courts.

The brief should open with a section describing the subject matter and giving a brief history of what has preceded. This is sometimes called, "Statement of the Case," sometimes "The Subject Matter Here" or something similar. It tells what is dealt with, and how the case got where it is. In an appeal to the Board of Appeals of the Patent Office, the opening might be a statement such as the following:

"This is an appeal to the Board of Appeals from the action of the Examiner finally rejecting claims ____ and ____ (all the claims) of this application of John Doe, Serial No. ____, filed ____, for an improvement in Document Feeding Mechanism.
"The improvement consists essentially of ____ (here briefly describe the invention, how it is constructed, and how it operates)."

In an interference brief on final hearing, we might start by saying:

"The general subject matter of which the counts in this interference form a part is a flux-responsive head which senses a static flux condition or magnetomotive force. One example of a static flux condition is a signal recorded on a magnetic tape and read *without relative motion between the head and the tape.*"

In an appeal to the Board of Appeals, we would go on to quote the finally rejected claims, and the reasons given for their final rejection. If the Examiner has based his rejection on prior art patents, each patent should be analyzed and its disclosure summarized as to subject matter, i.e., how the device of the patent is constructed, and how it operates.

We would next take the rejected claims one by one, pointing out what *structure* each claim calls for, and how the structure called for differs from that of each reference, alone or in combination, and why such differences are believed to be patentable, citing authorities.

In choosing authorities, it is desirable to select from recent decisions of the Board, and, if possible, decisions written by members who are highly regarded by their colleagues. Decisions of the Court of Customs and Patent Appeals should also be included if applicable. While decisions of the Supreme Court, Circuit Courts of Appeal, and U.S. District Courts may, of course, also be used, the Board seems to give more weight to its own decisions and to those of the CCPA than to others.

Briefs in an interference are usually longer, particularly when both parties have taken testimony, and it is necessary to analyze and comment on the testimony. In this respect, a brief for final hearing in an interference bears more resemblance to a brief in an infringement suit than it does to one on appeal to the Board of Appeals in an ex parte case.

A brief may be most carefully prepared, the law well researched, and decisions fully cited, but all the effort that went into it is wasted if it is not read, and read carefully, by the tribunal to which it is addressed. But, you say, you have a captive audience; it is the Court's, or the Examiner's, duty to read the brief. That may be true, but it is beside the point, and we all know of instances, like the one mentioned above, where the judge admitted his failure to read. How, then, are we to assure ourselves that the brief will be read? Only by making it concise and to the point, interesting, helpful to the Court, persuasive, and well written.

The authorities cited must be "Shepardized" by searching in Shepard for any reversals. There is no more devastating reply

to an attorney, who has found a case in point and leaned heavily on it, than to have his opponent say, "But that case, on which my friend relies, was reversed on appeal," or, "Counsel has overlooked the fact that the case on which he relies was overruled by the same court in a later decision, and can no longer be regarded as good law."

Plan the Brief before the Testimony

In a very real sense, the preparation of the brief is not something one starts thinking about after the testimony has all been taken. It is an integral part of the action itself, and must be kept in mind at all times as the action progresses. In fact, the trial will be devoted to providing, in the record, in the form of testimony and exhibits, the basis for the arguments to be used in the brief. I have found it essential for guidance during the trial, to prepare what some attorneys call a "trial brief," at an early stage in the action. This should summarize the testimony to be introduced by each witness, the witnesses who are to give it, and the documentary and physical exhibits to be introduced through each witness. If the attorney tries to work without a trial brief, during the stress of the trial he may forget to introduce a key piece of evidence, which at the least, will be embarrassing, and at worst, may be fatal to his case. After the trial is concluded, the trial brief can be revamped into the main brief.

The attorney representing the defendant in a patent infringement action should first familiarize himself with the patent in suit and its history, if any, in the Patent Office, and in other litigation. A search must be made of patents and literature, and translations made of pertinent foreign patents and publications which are not in the English language. At the same time, the attorney will have been assembling all the material available to show what his client has done and is doing, and what product or products plaintiff charges to infringe what claims.

A Model Brief

When these things have been done, it is time to start planning the brief, even before any testimony has been taken. Usually this opens with the "Statement of the Case," which is a short, concise history of the action. This statement should be factual, noncontroversial, and devoid of argument. A good example is to be found in the brief for defendant-appellee in a suit for patent infringement in the Ninth Circuit, *Bailey v. Sears, Roebuck & Co.*, 44 USPQ 217, 47 USPQ 407.

Following our "statement of the case," we are ready to get into the case itself. In a patent infringement action, whether we are for or against the patent, the best starting point is the patent (or patents) charged to be infringed. If you are doing your work properly, you will have read the patent or patents in suit very carefully a number of times. (Attorneys working in the office of a well-known trial patent lawyer used to say that they had to read the patent in suit a hundred times.) I like to underscore and sidescore significant parts of the specification and claims which I believe will be important, with a colored pencil, and for quick reference, make marginal notes of the points that suggest themselves.

Assuming that the patent may be directed to subject matter within one of the patentable classes, we pass to the next question: is the patent one on which there is little prior art, or is there a considerable amount closely related?

If there is little or no relevant prior art available, both you and your defendant-client are likely to be in serious trouble. You might better be writing a license agreement than a brief. Most Federal judges are not experts in patent law, claim drafting, and claim construction or interpretation. They tend to take a broad lay view of such matters. One judge used to ask of counsel appearing before him, "What did the patentee invent and does the defendant use it?"

Down-to-Earth Language. One well-known successful trial patent lawyer had a special talent for establishing his own definition of what he wanted the Court to think the patentee had invented and the defendant was using. In effect, he ignored the claim wording and described the "invention" in his own down-to-earth language. This was very useful to him, particularly when deal-

ing with a patent which had had a stormy career in the Patent Office, with repeated rejections and amendments introduced to avoid references. He simply ignored Patent Office language and claim limitations, and described the "invention," as he wanted the Court to see it. When defendant's counsel talked about the limitations inserted in the claims to avoid cited references, and "file wrapper estoppel," this put him in the position of setting up a smoke screen of technicalities to try to justify the defendant's appropriation of the "invention."

If there is a considerable amount of closely related prior art, you, for the defense, are in a good position. You will probably make a vigorous attack on the validity of the patent, bring in the best of the prior art and hope for a holding of invalidity for lack of invention or, if not obtained, a holding limiting the patent in such a way as to strengthen your non-infringement defense. To take full advantage of this, you will need to describe and explain the patent in suit, laying the groundwork for your defenses.

Explaining the Patent in Suit. The illustrations to be used in the brief are of particular importance and will require careful thought. Many of the figures in patent drawings do not lend themselves well to reproduction in a brief for various reasons, usually because they are too complicated for a lay judge to understand. In a motion for preliminary injunction I argued before a Federal judge in the Southern District of New York, I discovered part way through the argument that he had no idea what a sectional view was.

Benefit can be derived at times from the introduction of simplified, easily explained and readily understood drawings.

In a representative case, we made simplified enlarged drawings of a number of the prior art patents on which we relied, as well as drawings of the dial and pointer mechanism of the radios charged to infringe. These were all introduced through the testimony of our expert witness and admitted by the master, over plaintiff's objections. Plaintiff urged on appeal that the admission of these simplified drawings of the prior art patents was improper and ground for reversal, but the Court of Appeals in *Bailey v. Sears*, supra, rejected this argument, saying:

"The appellant complains of the introduction of certain drawings explanatory of the very small drawings of the patents involved. The simplified drawings are based upon the patent drawings and the description of the drawings. This was entirely proper. There was no attempt to read into the patents involved something which was absent therefrom. The appellant points out no error in the simplified drawings." *Anglo California Nat'l Bk.* v. *Lazard*, 106 F.2d 693; *Jackson Furniture Co.* v. *McLaughlin*, 85 F.2d 606; *Mammoth Min. Co.* v. *Salt Lake Foundry & Mch. Co.*, 151 U.S. 447.

This is a good illustration of the point that the brief must be kept in mind from the beginning of the action. Had we tried to use our drawings for the first time in our brief without getting them in the record through the testimony of our witness, the other side would certainly have objected to their consideration, as without basis in the record. The Court might very well have disregarded the simplified drawings, and the outcome of the suit might have been different.

Emphasize the Purposes and Objects of the Patent in Suit. Assuming now that you have completed your section of the brief dealing with the patent charged to be infringed, by explaining the construction and operation of its mechanism or circuits, you will want to point out and emphasize its objects and purposes, particularly in so far as they differ from those of the defendant's structure, as under the following topics or key sentences:

1. "The purpose of the Bailey patent [1,907,473] is to measure the movement of the rotor blades in a variable condenser.
2. "The Bailey device was designed to measure rotor movements and not for broadcast receivers.
3. "The Bailey patent does not provide backlash and reduction gearing."

Our purpose in this section was to show that the patented device was not useful for broadcast radio receivers, thus tying in with our defense that we did not use it.

Comment on the Claims in Suit. After explaining the construction and operation of the patent in suit and its purposes and objects, it is appropriate to comment on the claims charged to be infringed. In order to do this, counsel will have obtained and offered in evidence a copy of the file wrapper and contents, and the references cited by the Examiner. He will have studied them, particularly to see what claims were originally presented, whether they were rejected, and, if so, on what references and for what reasons. In most instances he will find that the patent issued with claims differing from those originally presented. Usually, during the prosecution of the application, the attorney cancels some claims and amends or rewrites others. Frequently, if the patentee starts with broad claims, he cancels them, and is finally given a few quite limited claims. The brief for the defendant will review the various amendments and the limitations introduced to avoid the art cited, and may conclude this section of the brief as follows:

"We think that the Patent Office was in error in granting a patent on the narrow difference between a sleeve driven by step-up gearing and a sleeve driven by step-down gearing (both being old), but this will be discussed later, the point here being that the applicant obtained his patent on the alleged difference."

Handling of Prior Art. In discussing the prior art, it is desirable to precede this with a list of the patents on which the defendant relies, and if one or more of the patents were not cited by the Patent Office, to point this out. In the case discussed herein, we relied on eight patents, only one of which was cited by the Patent Office.

It is preferable to discuss each prior art patent and publication individually. It is assumed that you will have put in the record the testimony of your expert explaining how the device of each prior art patent is constructed, how it operates, and what bearing it has on the case.

There was one suit in Michigan in which counsel for the defendant failed to put in any testimony concerning the prior art patents on which he relied. He attempted to explain the patents himself, without being sworn as a witness. Aside from being futile, this procedure is generally frowned on by the Patent Office and the Courts. Courts do not adjudicate cases on statements made in briefs or argument without support in the record. See, for instance, *In re Application of Robert C. Spohn*, 77 F.2d 768, 25 USPQ 409; *In re Application of Herbert A. Burns*, 83 F.2d 292, 29 USPQ 423; and *Dreyer, Jr. v. Haffcke*, 137 F.2d 116, 58 USPQ 545.

The Argument on Validity. This argument will follow the suggestions of a general nature given elsewhere herein. The substance will vary necessarily with the available, favorable facts, including for the defense, for example, the following if true:

(1) The patentee made no substantial contribution to the art, as shown by lack of commercial use in advance of the work of the defendant.

(2) The showing of references was misrepresented or misinterpreted in the consideration of the case in the Patent Office.

(3) Patents not cited by the Patent Office but now of record supply all features absent in the Patent Office citations and that, in any line of reasoning, might be held necessary to complete anticipation.

(4) The facts stated bring the case under the following decisions in which patents were held invalid for like reasons: (List of authorities)

The Argument on Infringement. "The law with respect to infringement is clear and well settled," it can be said. "There is no infringement unless the device as disclosed in the patent and the accused device are substantially the same in construction, mode of operation, and result, and the test is not the wording of the claims, or whether as a matter of language they 'read upon' the accused device, but whether the two devices are substantially identical as a matter of substance." (Here we cite authorities.) It is desirable practice to use some leading cases by the Supreme Court, followed by leading cases by the Court of Appeals *for the circuit in which your suit is being heard*, if they exist. Decisions by Courts of Appeal of other circuits may be used if you can't find what you want in your own circuit, or as confirmation of your own CCA decisions. The District Court decisions from your district are also good if they fit your facts.

Comparison of Claims Sought and Those Granted. Having proceeded this far, we are ready to show the meaning of the claims in suit and that they do not describe the accused device.

Point Out the Differences Between the Patent Device and Those Charged to Infringe. We have yet to describe the construction and operation of the accused device (or devices; in our case there were four) and the differences between the device of the patent and ours. Now our job is done, except we have to supply the conclusion, e.g., as follows:

"The Bailey patent is for alleged improvements and is extremely narrow, relating to details of mechanical gearing. There has been no substantial commercial success. The history of the practical art, in conjunction with the prior patents, negatives the contention that patentable genius was required to devise the so-called 'improvements,' and the patent is invalid for want of invention.

"The patent is not infringed, because the claims do not describe defendant's models, and also because the models are not 'approximate copies' of the patented device.

"The decree below should be affirmed."

While the foregoing brief was written for the defendant to show invalidity of the patent and non-infringement, the same general procedure and format may be used for the plaintiff to show validity and infringement, in interferences, and on appeals in the Patent Office and the Court of Customs and Patent Appeals.

Make-Up of a Successful Brief

No two attorneys whom I know use the same style of writing, yet all winning briefs (and who wants to write any other kind?) seem to have certain things in common. They are:

(1) Supported by citations to the record (most important).

(2) Written by an attorney who knows his case in every detail.

(3) Written in simple and understandable form.

(4) Designed to be helpful to the tribunal in reaching the decision the attorney wants.

(5) Arranged logically and forcefully.

(6) Concise and to the point.

(7) Statements of the latest and most pertinent authorities.

(8) Factual and showing how the law applies.

(9) Generally minimally argumentative.

If you wonder how a brief can help but be argumentative, remember that a clear, logical and forceful presentation of facts, keyed to the record, and buttressed by the best authorities you can find, will carry conviction where pages of argument will not. A great attorney once said, "Facts are your best argument."

Make Your Headings a Summary of the Section

The headings and subheadings should be a short summary of the subject matter developed in detail in each section. For instance, instead of using the general and uninformative heading, "The Prior Art," say, "The Prior Art Invalidates the Patent in Suit." If this is done, a quick reading of the Index will give the tribunal the gist of your case. As an example, the following is the Index to our reply brief in an interference (the names of the parties are fictitious):

Adams is Attempting to Evade the Stipulations

Adams Attempts to Read into the Counts Structure Not Required by Them

Adams' Arguments Are Without Basis in the Record

The Question is not "Could Smith Have Made Tests He did Not" but "Could He Have Got the Results He and His Witnesses Swore He Did"

Adams Attempts to Set Up Fictitious Issues as to the Counts

Issues in Interference:

Stipulated Question 1

The Tests Described in Smith's Exhibits A3, A4 and A5 were a Reduction to Practice

Stipulated Question 2

Smith's Record is Legally Sufficient to Establish Reduction to Practice

Adams' Failure to Cross-Examine Shows He Had No Hope of Successful Cross-Examination

Smith's Disclosure Is Not Inoperative

Stipulated Question 3

The Tests Performed by Smith Constituted Reduction to Practice

In this case, the junior party (Smith) was successful in obtaining an award of priority.

General References

The following will be found helpful in improving style, manner of presentation, and readability:

Wellman, F. L., "The Art of Cross-Examination," New York, The Macmillan Company, 1957.

Cohn, A. A., and Chisholm, J. F., "Take the Witness," New York, Stokes, 1934.

Nevins, A., "Ford: The Times, The Man," New York, Scribners, 1954.

Greenleaf, W., "Monopoly on Wheels," Detroit, Mich., Wayne State University Press, 1961.

Nizer, L., "My Life in Court," New York, Doubleday, 1961.

Bernstein, T. M., "Watch Your Language," Great Neck, N.Y., Channel Press, 1958.

Flesch, R., "The Art of Clear Thinking," New York, Harper & Bros., 1951.

Flesch, R., "The Art of Plain Talk," New York, Harper & Bros., 1946.

Flesch, R., "The Art of Readable Writing," New York, Harper & Bros., 1949.

Flesch, R., and Lass, A. H., "The Way to Write," New York, Harper & Bros., 1949.

Flesch, R., "How To Make Sense," New York, Harper & Bros., 1954.

Flesch, R., "How to Test Readability," New York, Harper & Bros., 1951.

"Webster's New International Dictionary," Second Edition, Unabridged, Springfield, Mass., G. & C. Merriam Co.

"Roget's International Thesaurus," Philadelphia, Penna., Thomas Y. Crowell Co.

Cross-references: *Advocacy, Attorneys and Agents, Appeals—Court of Customs and Patent Appeals, Infringement Suits.*

C

CHEMICAL APPLICATIONS

Robert Calvert

The number of chemical and chemically related patents granted by the United States in 1963 was 12,270. Of these about one-sixth were issued to foreign interests. For the period January 1950 to December 1963, inclusive, the totals were 128,134 domestic and 14,421 to companies in 42 foreign countries. Information for Industry, Inc. For review, see Chem. & Eng. News, Mar. 9, 1964, 28.

New chemical elements were first held patentable in 1964. *In re Seaborg,* 140 USPQ 659, 662, CCPA.

Many of the points here made, while relating particularly to chemical applications, apply also to other arts.

Questions that frequently arise in chemical cases relate to functionality of claims, adequacy of disclosure when a class of alternative materials is claimed, and need for recital of minimal proportion, to distinguish from an inoperative trace. These points are discussed fully in the majority decision and more briefly by the minority in *In re Charles T. Fuetterer,* 795 O. G. 783, CCPA 1963.

End Point of Processing

A term that is easy to remember may crystallize an important concept. It is the "end point," or stage to which a reaction or other treatment is conducted.

An inventor once heated two water-soluble reactants in an aqueous solution until they formed the usual insoluble condensation product. Then he continued the heating until the condensate became again soluble in water on infinite dilution. The recital of this end point of the reaction, the reversal of solubility, brought allowance of the case.

An effort should be made to ascertain the end point to which the significant step or steps in a chemical process are carried and to disclose the point in terms as broad but definite as possible. It may be, for example, the heating of a mixture until something happens that can be recorded—the content of one of the components remaining in unreacted condition falls to a certain low or substantially constant level, the pH rises and becomes constant, by-product salt no longer separates, the viscosity shows a rapid onset, the boiling point of the mixture becomes constant, water does not appear in the distillate or the product gels on cooling.

The statement of such end points may and usually will add to the definiteness of the teaching, provide a basis for distinction from prior art, or generally strengthen the case for validity.

Logical and Psychological Order of Presentation

There is no substitute for an orderly description of the invention, carefully outlined in advance and tailored to fit the claims that have been either written or thought out before starting the specification.

The attorney must cope, however, with the fact that many readers confuse what they can understand, once it has been explained to them, with what they would have considered obvious before having the explanation. He should expect that a skilled examiner or judge, on first reading an application or patent, will be wondering, perhaps subconsciously, whether the solution to the problem is obvious to him. If the reader cannot come up with the answer, the invention will have passed an important psychological test.

With this attitude in mind, an attorney may devote a page or so altogether to a correct discussion of the prior art, the disadvantages of it, the need yet to be met, the applicant's surprising result (what the invention provides), the structure (what his invention comprises), and possibly a few more details of the results or structure. Then, or later, he explains the mechanism by which the invention gives the surprising result.

Language

When the inventor submits a semi-finished application, in place of the more helpful technical report, he will occasionally include legalistic expressions. Those that stand out in patents and receive attention are often just those that are conspicuous by their grammatical clumsiness, attempts to be overly clever, or use of perhaps thirty words where ten would do.

Attorneys should and ordinarily do select the simplest words that convey the exact meaning sought. They use them sparingly.

The inventor should identify, in his disclosure, all trademarked materials by their chemical names. He should assist the attorney in defining any "terms of the trade," e.g., "intrinsic viscosity," so that a judge may not have to depend for understanding of the terms upon testimony of opposed and often contradictory experts.

Mr. Arthur M. Smith, now Judge of the Court of Customs and Patent Appeals, has well said:

"[T]he specialist in patent preparation and prosecution may have lost sight of the fact that ... the patent we prepare and prosecute will be held valid or invalid by judges, who for the most part are non-technically trained. This is a challenge which can be met only by very clear writing addressed to this 'non-technical' audience." 41 JPOS 5, 1959.

Contemplated Procedures

The law permits disclosure of inventions that have not been demonstrated.

"The specification shall ... set forth the best mode *contemplated* by the inventor of carrying out his invention." 35 U.S.C. 112. (Emphasis added)

In chemical cases, the applicant must give alternatives if they are to be claimed. In most instances he cannot try all the modifications that his patent will suggest to others. As a result, many applications expand the list of alternative materials, conditions or both beyond what has been tried, to include what can reasonably be expected to work.

In general, a person having an idea of great promise, unable to test even a single embodiment of it, may make a considerable contribution by recording it in a patent for public information and eventual possible reduction to practice and use. In filing such a speculative or paper application, however, the applicant pays a price; he takes the chance of overlooking and not obtaining protection on the features that are the most unobvious. These are the very ones that he could not have been expected to forecast. It is not surprising, therefore, that "paper" patents are seldom of value to the owners. If an idea is good and can be tried, it should receive experimental support.

In his scholarly Study No. 29 of the Subcommittee on Patents, Trademarks, and Copyrights of the Committee on the Judiciary, U.S. Senate, 86th Congress, 2nd Session, Eugene W. Geniesse discusses this subject in part as follows:

"Two distinct and contrary philosophies have been developed as to speculative descriptions. One of these philosophies is illustrated by *Moffet* v. *Fiske,* 51 F.2d 868 (DC Cir. 1931). Fiske obtained a patent for a method of dive bombing which later came into use. At the time of application for the patent, airplanes had not been developed in strength or maneuverability to the extent capable of carrying out the proposed process, but as is now a matter of common knowledge, such planes were later developed. The patent was held to be invalid ...

"A different philosophy is presented in the recent case of *In re Chilowsky,* 229 F.2d 457, 108 USPQ 321 (1956). In this case, Chilowsky presented an application for a patent on a proposed powerplant wherein the energy was to be derived from nuclear (atomic) fission. The description was couched in general and frankly speculative language, there being no pretense that such a powerplant had been constructed. The decision of the Patent Office Board of Appeals refusing the patent on the grounds that it was based on an insufficient description was reversed by the Court of Customs and Patent Appeals and the application remanded to the Office for further proceedings. The speculative nature of the description and the applicant's failure to demonstrate the construction of an operative powerplant *were held to be no bar to allowance of the patent.* The general nature of the examiner's objections, and his failure to particularize as to deficiencies, or to point to the contravention of accepted scientific laws *were held to prevent affirmance of his rejection.* Since the Court of Customs and Patent Appeals is the controlling tribunal for the Office, *the Office must conform to the views expressed by that court."* Pages 30 to 31. (Emphasis added)

It should be noted that Mr. Geniesse, while recognizing the later decision as controlling, identifies himself personally with the first philosophy, i.e., against granting speculative patents. Mr. S. Wolffe, on the other hand, supports the right of inventors in the chemical arts to constructive reduction to practice by filing applications for patents. 41 JPOS 61, 1959.

While holding in favor of the applicant Chilowsky, supra, the Court in that case said:

"On the other hand, if the alleged operation seems clearly to conflict with a scientific principle as, for example, where an applicant purports to have discovered a machine producing perpetual motion, the presumption of inoperativeness is so strong that very clear evidence is required to overcome it ... [when the device of another case] was of such a nature that it could not be tested by any known scientific principles ... it is incumbent upon the applicant to demonstrate the workability and utility of the device and make clear the principles on which it operates." Decision affirmed on other grounds, 134 USPQ 515, CCPA 1962.

What has been said above regarding perpetual motion could be said almost to apply to the patentability of cancer "cures" today.

Stripping the Invention to Indispensables

The attorney needs to know the minimum combination of materials, proportions and conditions necessary for the workability of the invention and novelty, as well as for commercially satisfactory results and the advantages of also using the additional or optional components or conditions.

A typical disclosure of a coating composition, for example, may show a half dozen classes of components, adding one of them in steps, heating the mix to a certain viscosity after each addition, and admixing a conventional surfactant and a defoamer. If the attorney recites all these limitations in all claims, a competitor may leave to his customers the addition of one of the materials in the hope of avoiding infringement, replace a component or step by an expedient not claimed or omit the component or step altogether.

The attorney will disclose and eventually claim as broadly as possible, i.e., the smallest number of components that will work under any circumstances and still be unobvious. If he errs in this regard, let the error come after consideration and not by oversight. He will then limit the specification and ultimately some but not all claims by including the optional ingredients and conditions, usually one by one, until he reaches finally the "picture" claim reciting all features of reasonable significance.

The "picture" claim may seem valueless. To have even a limited claim held valid in a difficult case is sometimes important, however. It should surely work and it should be novel. Procedures not directly covered by the claim may be held to be equivalent, as in the *Electric Welding* case. *Graver Tank and Mfg. Co.* v. *Linde Air Products Co.,* 336 U.S. 271, 1948.

Reducing Likelihood of File Wrapper Estoppel

The attorney, seeking to keep open the way to broadening the patent by court interpretation, avoids any unnecessary acknowledgment of a need for limitation of the scope of the claims. Others, in turn, will search the file of the case in the Patent Office for evidence of giving up, as nonpatentable, the condition under which they are operating. If they find an amendment deliberately excluding their mode of operation, in order to avoid rejection on the art, they can argue file wrapper estoppel against the extension of the scope of the claims to include what was thus excluded.

A patent, now expired, claimed the use of a certain glycol spray as a disinfectant for the air of schools, hospitals or homes. Each claim in the application *as filed* recited the proportion of the glycol within a range that was very low, perhaps of the order of a gram for a thousand cubic feet of air. The seemingly modest claims may well have covered all operable amounts, from the minimum that would be effective up to the maximum that could be tolerated without hazard to the breather or without the vapor condensing, as a mist. The applicant would have been able to say in court that he was not obliged, in order to avoid art, to limit his claims to the exact numerical proportions stated in the claims.

When the attorney knows positively the ranges of alternative materials or conditions outside which the invention will (1) not work, (2) be unusable because of cost, toxicity or other disadvantage, or (3) lack novelty, he considers limiting all claims from the start. He will thus decrease the need of later inevitable limitation in order to establish patentability over the art or to exclude inoperative conditions.

Length of the Application

Our fourth patent, issued January 31, 1790 has a length of 3 manuscript lines in addition to the formal matter and the signatures at the end of "G. Washington" and "Edm. Randolph, Attorney General of the United States."

One of the shortest United States patents issued subsequent to the 1836 statute, establishing our present type of patent practice, had a one sentence specification of 55 words, padded by the unnecessary use of the word "say" four times. It reads as follows:

"In carrying out my invention I take talc, say 60 parts; silicate of soda, say 20 parts; carbonate of soda, say 10 parts; water, say 10 parts, and thoroughly mix the same, producing a mass which when set may be heated by electric wires or conductors placed therein or thereon, while being nonconductors of electricity." Fraley 606,921; see Ralph B. Stewart, 29 JPOS 766, 1947.

Such a specification cannot give a basis for broad claims or even meet the minimum requirements of the Patent Office today.

References by Commissioner Ladd to a patent of 216 printed pages and 354 sheets of drawings and to another with 900 claims shows the length today in cases of great complexity.

He gives the average size of U.S. patents as follows: Printed pages of specification, 3.70, sheets of drawings, 2.00, independent claims, 4.38, total claims, 6.73. Statement of Sept. 4, 1962, before Senate Subcommittee on Patents, Trademarks and Copyrights, page 39.

Whatever an applicant may say that is later found to weaken his case for validity or infringement may be expected to be accepted by the defense at full value and used against him but what he says of a laudatory nature cannot be expected to receive acceptance without proof. A safe rule is to be complete beyond question in the disclosure of structure or substance and cautious and relatively brief in other comments beyond those required for full understanding of the problem and favorable presentation of the invention.

Both the attorney and the inventor should avoid including in the application unnecessarily long and extensive descriptions of parts or steps that are conventional. An overly lengthy specification serves chiefly to divert attention from the real invention and may indicate failure of the inventor or attorney or both to comprehend what is actually the invention.

There seems to be a mistaken notion in some quarters that, since a certain number of claims can be filed without extra charge, the attorney should use his full privilege. This he may do, even though the same mistakes are repeated throughout a whole series of claims. Also he may have claims that differ at most only in reciting obvious variations or equivalents.

Principle of the Invention

Statement of the principle on which an invention is based contributes to the full disclosure. It may broaden the interpretation to include, as equivalents in a pioneer case, variations that operate on the same principle.

An example of such statement in a complex case appears in patent 2,768,994 (1956) to MacDonald on the acetal resin resulting from polymerization of formaldehyde and understood to be the plastic sold under the trademark name "Delrin." The statement is this:

"It is not fully understood why the processes of this invention accomplish results so strikingly different from the prior art. However, although it is not intended that this invention be bound by the explanation, it is believed that the method of introducing the monomer into a reaction medium, whereby the monomer is polymerized as fast as it contacts the reaction medium, may effect some purification of the monomer, of the reaction medium, or of both." (Col. 2, lines 11-19).

An alternative form of wording that the author has used at times would start in about this manner: "Various theories may be advanced to explain the exact mechanism of the reaction giving the surprising results noted. They are attributed, in part, at least, to...."

While an incorrect theory is to be avoided if possible, there is a line of decisions to the effect that, as in *Fyr-Fyter Co.* v. *International Chemical Extinguisher Corp.*,

"[T]he theory is immaterial if the patent actually works as a new and useful device or method or improvement." 122 USPQ 590, CA 5 1959.

Drawings

Since the majority of chemical applications do not require drawings, it is sufficient here to refer to the article *Drawings,* M.P.E.P. 608,02, and publications on Flow Sheets for Chemical Process Patents by I. Louis Wolk, 30 JPOS 368, 1948 and 31 JPOS 327, 410, 1939.

Statement of Alternatives

Choice of scope, important in presenting all classes of inventions, is particularly difficult in chemical cases as they require statement of alternative components and conditions to be claimed.

In a mechanical case, a bolt holding together members of a machine may usually be recited broadly in the claims as "a fastening element." In a chemical application,

however, disclosing the component ethyl alcohol does not entitle the applicant ordinarily to claim any alcohol.

As a basis for satisfactory claiming, a chemical case should give each class of components and a sufficient number of examples to illustrate the class of the general properties required that will work and suitably support a generic claim. If the alcohol, to be operative in the composition or process, must surely be soluble in water, there is no loss in stating that properly in the specification but a distinct gain in definiteness in so restricting the claims. If, in another case, any monohydric aliphatic C_{1-8} alcohol is satisfactory and higher alcohols are ineffective, then this C_{1-8} range should be stated and illustrated by examples.

Some divisions at least of the Patent Office may be expected to allow claiming a C_{1-3} alcohol when the specification discloses such range and gives only one example, methanol. For a small group so well understood and including only four similar members, the single example adequately illustrates the limited class. If the application discloses only "methyl and ethyl alcohols," without any upper limit as to the number of carbon atoms or other properties, the claim would probably be restricted to the two alcohols named. The larger and more complicated the class, the larger also is the number of examples required for proper illustration.

"Thus, in the case of a small genus such as the halogens, consisting of only four species, a reduction to practice of three, or perhaps even two, might serve to complete the generic invention, while in the case of a genus comprising hundreds of species, a considerably larger number of reductions to practice would probably be necessary." *In re Shokal, Devlin, and Winkler,* 113 USPQ 283, CCPA 1957.

But a range of alternatives stated and claimed too broadly may raise the question of indefiniteness, especially when a claim covers a large number of inoperative members, as in the *Rubber Accelerator* case. *Corona Cord Tire Co.* v. *Dovan Chemical Corp.,* 276 U.S. 358, 1927. Herbert H. Goodman, citing conflicting decisions, in 40 JPOS 745, 1958, says:

"...[I]t has been suggested that claims [including inoperative species] in which the generic term applies to a component that is an unessential portion of the chemical compound are valid. Similarly, where the novelty was found chiefly in the steps rather than the chemicals used in a process, the claims are valid. Where any skilled chemist can recognize the operative species, it has been held that claims which include inoperative species are valid."

Proportions of Materials

While dimensions are not essential in most machine and article patents, proportions in chemical cases are usually necessary for full disclosure of the invention, for operativeness, and frequently for patentability over the art that may be found on examination. Proportions may be stated, first of all, in functional terms if possible. The statement is no problem in some instances, e.g., acid in amount equivalent to (or 1 to 2 times that equivalent to) the amine present, an acid added in amount to establish the pH at the isoelectric point for precipitation of the protein, at pH about 4-6, or a catalytic proportion of the initiator of polymerization. The latter illustrates a statement that may be considered at times as merely functional. In all cases numerical proportions or ranges should be included in the text.

Whether ranges are to be set forth will depend on the circumstances. Usually proportions should be stated as broadly as will work, even uneconomically, without weakening the distinction from the prior art. At some point, at least those necessary for commercially satisfactory operations should be stated. This provides a basis for claiming what one seeking to evade the patent would find necessary to use, in order to be competitive in quality and cost of product. One procedure is to include a table as follows:

Parts by Weight

Component Used	Permissible	For Best Results
Compound AB	100	100
Compound CD	10-70	30-50
Accelerator	0.1-1	0.3-0.6
Stabilizer	0.2-2	0.5-1
Pigments	In amount to establish color desired *	

* When conventional and not critical.

The use of zero in a claim, as the lower limit of the range of a component, has been questioned as being an alternative expression meaning, in effect, either some or none. As to a claim reciting "between zero and 9" parts of calcium, the Board said:

"Although the use of zero as the lower limit of a range has been held to be indefinite and improper when it is essential that more than an infinitesimal amount of the component to which the range refers be present we see no impropriety in the use of zero as the lower limit of the calcium-strontium ratio in this case since, according to the disclosure, no calcium need be employed, in which case the ratio would have the value of zero. Any proportion of calcium greater than 0 and less than 9 would also be operative." *Ex parte Butler,* 116 USPQ 597, PO BdApp 1958.

There seems to be no advantage in reciting, for instance, "a proportion of 0 to 9 parts." Such a claim should be no more easily patented or held valid than one with no reference to the optional component. Such a recital, on the other hand, might weaken a dependent claim stating a finite minimum; some divisions of the Patent Office have held that the argument for criticality of proportions is weakened or destroyed when two claims recite different amounts of a given element.

To support a claim to critical proportions, the inventor will hope to discover a point or points corresponding to the occurrence of a certain phenomenon. In the *Hair Waving* case, the court considered the upper limit 10 for the pH range to be shown as critical by the fact that the waving solution, if above 10, will have a different and damaging action on the hair and actually weaken it. *Helene Curtis Industries, Inc.* v. *Sales Affiliates, Inc.,* 109 USPQ 159, CA 2 1956.

In an instance in which a range was not disclosed, where the issue was invention and the applicant sought to distinguish patentably his pH of "about 8 to about 10" from "about 7.0" in the reference, the court said:

"[W]e are not prepared to accept appellant's insistence that the example...of a pH value 'maintained at about 7.0' means maintenance at precisely 7, said to be the neutrality point." *In re De Vaney,* 1951 C.D. 54, CCPA.

Conditions

It is not uncommon to state such conditions also in two ranges, one as broad as operative and novel and one more narrow to cover commercial conditions. A representative expression might read thus: The composition including accelerator AB is cured at about 80 to 180° C and, for best commercial results as to speed of cure and quality of product, at about 100 to 150°.

The two ranges make possible direction of the claims to either condition, as may later be found appropriate.

It is good practice when a range of conditions is critical and unusual to state briefly the advantages of working within it and the disadvantages outside the range.

Examples

It is customary in chemical cases to describe the invention in general and then more specifically in numbered examples.

The examples will show specific materials, modifications, proportions, and conditions varying as much as permissible while remaining operative and within the scope to be claimed.

A procedure in referring back to a previous example, without repeating all details of apparatus and procedure but giving the composition, is illustrated in the following passage from patent 2,958,634 to Cleaver:

> *"Example II*
>
> "[With use of] the apparatus and procedure of Example I, a mixture of 225 g. of ammonium bifluoride and 48 g. of hydrogen fluoride (0.6 mole of HF per mole of $NH_4F \cdot HF$) was electrolyzed at 100° F, 6 volts and 7 amperes. The reaction product from the anode compartment was found by gas chromatography to contain" [analysis follows].

This example is 9 lines long as compared to 28 for Example I.

Those having the earnestness to study what they may safely omit from the disclosure of the application should have also the judgment to keep on the safe side of the border between (1) doubtful procedure and (2) unquestioned practice. Thus they can expect to remain safe through periods of changing judicial interpretations.

Utility

See article *"Utility."*

When there is a plurality of uses, one that can surely be proven readily should be selected and stated. The inventor of an anticarcinogen that is patentable as a compound would be well advised to omit, in his application for the compound, all dependence on the anticarcinogenic effect to show utility. He should assume that it will be practically impossible for him to amass enough data to prove to the Patent Office at this time that his material is safe, dependable and effective for such therapy. He can ordinarily disclose another use that can be demonstrated relatively simply. In that event, he would leave the subject of cancer treatment for another application, to be filed suitably before the first application issues.

For cases, having a multiplicity of demonstrable uses there will be a choice as to how many to disclose. It goes without saying that all disclosed but not claimed in the patent or in another application filed before issuance of the patent are dedicated to the public. A company expecting to be able to rely for strong protection solely on patenting the compound or composition per se may wish to disclose a long list of uses as a means of preventing others from patenting such uses and of keeping the market open. This may have been the reason, for example, why patent 2,394,910 to Gresham gives an entire page of rather concentrated disclosures of uses for a polydioxolane plastic.

When uses are given and not claimed, there should be a definite decision as to whether (1) use patents are necessary to strengthen what might otherwise be an unenforceable or inadequate patent position and (2) divisional or other cases claiming specific uses are to be filed before the parent case issues and dedicates uses not claimed or filed in another case at the time.

Outline of Application

Whether the attorney has written a hundred or a thousand chemical applications and used essentially the same outline over and over again, he will ordinarily list the key words of his several sections in order, with room between for subtitles and notes. He will usually dictate while looking at the outline and following it strictly.

The outline is the first step in orderly presentation and a time saver in the end. Those not using a written outline no doubt find convenient the mental picture of it.

A suitable outline for a chemical application is about as follows, with variations as required to present unique features of individual inventions in the best light.

Field to which the invention relates (title paragraph).

Utility (in the connection which will be illustrated).

Art (brief statement of what is already known or done, including difficulties or disadvantages which, it will be found, the invention avoids).

Objects (optional). About half or more of the chemical cases seem to omit listing "objects."

What the invention provides. A substitute for "objects." An opportunity to emphasize the most unobvious results and give a brief striking result.

What the invention comprises. A preview and summary somewhat broader than the broadest claim.

General statement of the invention, slightly more detailed than above but ordinarily only a paragraph. (Optional.)

Description of drawings, if any.

Materials (general properties required and several examples for each class, e.g., alcohols, acids, and catalysts).

Proportions (perhaps ranges that will work and those for best results).

Conditions of operation (suitably with ranges as above).

Examples (when a control is used to show failure of the prior art practices, it may be identified as no part of the invention, Example numbers being reserved for illustrations of the invention).

Description of results unless stated previously.

Additional statement of uses if not already given sufficiently fully. At least one Example will show the compounding of the product of the invention, if a composition, into form suitable for use. It will show also the actual application, preferably with surprising results.

Closing paragraph to broaden the interpretation. The majority of chemical patents examined show such a paragraph. One quoted by the Supreme Court is shown under *Applications—Electrical and Electronic. Exhibit Supply Co. et al.* v. *Ace Patents Corp.,* 315 U.S. 126; 1942 C.D. 738, 1942. See also *Katz* v. *Horni Signal Mfg. Co.,* 63 USPQ 190, CA 2 1944; *Monogram Mfg. Co.* v. *Glemby Co., et al.,* 58 USPQ 443, CA 2 1943.

Introductory Clause of Claims

Albert S. Davis tells of an inventor-friend who, in a moment of relaxation, sought to show the importance of an introductory clause in clarifying a claim. He wrote the following "claim":

"1. The process of treating proteinaceous matter which comprises transmitting heat from an aqueous medium through successive calcareous and membranous layers into said proteinaceous matter."

Does this appear to be new?

Careful study of the claim will reveal that every detail is fully met in the old art of boiling an egg within its calcareous shell and inner skin, in the aqueous medium water.

Such wording points up the value of an introductory clause identifying the area to which the invention relates. To have started the claim "In boiling an egg, the process which comprises" would have simplified the search and in fact made it wholly unnecessary.

Furthermore, the introductory clause in a bona fide case excludes remote art as anticipation. A claim reciting the combination of "a body portion, sleeves, collar, and fastening elements" might refer to a steam locomotive. Anticipation by such remote art would be avoided if the claim begins with "A shirt comprising."

Product-by-Process Claims

Where it is possible to define a product by its characteristics, the practice is clearly settled that this should be done.

"When the product is novel and involves invention and cannot be defined except by the process of its creation, there are cases holding such a claim may be allowed, and such a claim has been sustained by the courts." *Ex parte Fesenmeier,* 1922 C.D. 18, for Comr. Pats.

The claim allowed to Fesenmeier follows:

"4. The herein described hop liquid product obtained by subjecting a mixture of fresh cured hops and liquid in a hermetically sealed container to a temperature sufficient to extract all the essential oils, essences, and aromas from the hops and disseminate same through the liquid."

Product-by-process claims are refused when the application contains another claim describing the product in usual manner. The presence of such other claim indicates that the product can be described by its characteristics. *Ex parte Fahrini*, 117 USPQ 199, PO BdApp 1958. See also S. Wolffe, 28 JPOS 852, 1946.

Suggestion by the Examiner of an adequate and acceptable definition shows that identification by the steps in the process of preparation is unnecessary and not permissible. M.P.E.P. 706.03(e).

In reversing the Examiner's refusal of a product-by-process claim, the Board noted the absence in the record of an

"...unequivocal statement by the Examiner that in his opinion the product could be defined by other language than that which describes its process of manufacture...[and that no other language is] apparent to us how the product could be defined...." *Ex parte Donahey*, 126 USPQ 61, PO BdApp 1959.

Recital of the product-by-process, in a Fesenmeier type claim, has been held to be sufficient when there is nothing in the record to indicate that the process in the manner stated will produce any other product than that claimed. The same rule applies "when 'the product of the reaction' encompasses all of that which is produced by the reactions, be the product a mixture of two or a dozen compounds." *In re Ruskin*, 125 USPQ 13, CCPA 1960.

Cf. Jon S. Saxe and Julian S. Levitt, 42 JPOS 528-562, 1960, for a good article on product-by-process claims.

Markush Claims

Alternative forms of statement of two distinct elements ordinarily are not permitted in a chemical claim. If the applicant desires to recite specifically "alcohol, acetone or ether," he must word the claim to avoid the use of the word "or." When all the volatile organic solvents are satisfactory for the purpose and the specification states and illustrates that fact by adequate examples, then these three materials may be covered by a claim reciting "a volatile liquid organic solvent." If, however, not all vola-

tile liquid organic solvents will work, then the claim should recite a solvent selected from the group *consisting of* alcohol, ether *and* acetone. No substantial variation is permissible for the words italicized.

This form of claim was first recognized as proper in an application involving an applicant Markush. *Ex parte Markush*, 51 USPQ 70, PO BdApp 1941. He had no way to claim a number of substances too closely related to support a series of patents, Assistant Commissioner Kinnan ruled, except by coining an expression. The Board held allowable to Markush a claim reciting a "material selected from the group *consisting of* aniline, homologues of aniline, *and* halogen substitution products of aniline." (Emphasis added.)

No variation is permissible in the scope of a Markush group. Thus the group may not consist of four members in one claim and three in another. M. C. Rosa, 34 JPOS 324, 333, 1952. Yet there may be different groups for different features of a claim, e.g., one group for a chemical reactant and another for the catalyst.

A claim to a widely used vitamin solution contains an illustrative Markush group:

"...the solubilizing agent being a water soluble polyalkylene oxide derivative of a partial long chain fatty acid ester of a *compound selected from the group consisting of* polyhydric alcohols *and* their anhydrides" Freedman and Green, 2,417,299. (Emphasis added)

At one time such claims were permissible only when there was no commonly accepted generic term available to describe the group of materials recited in the Markush grouping. Now Markush claims may be included in a patent when a generic claim is present but covers many species. This makes it possible to claim an invention broadly and then in a claim of medium scope of the Markush form.

A further liberalizing, in the form of an explanation of the requirement for a specific example of the use of each member of a Markush group, is found in *Ex parte Byrns*, 81 USPQ 444, PO BdApp 1949. The members were an acid anhydride and the further dehydration product ketene. The decision holds that a specific example for each member of the group is unnecessary when the members are thus closely related.

Each case in this test must stand on its own merits. In a later case, for instance, the applicant had two Markush groups. One "Markush group of urea, thiourea and guanidine," said the Board, "has only urea supported by a specific working example. The Markush group of ketones and aldehydes has only ketone supported by a specific working example." Claims including these groups were rejected as lacking adequate support. *Ex parte Haury*, 127 USPQ 52, PO BdApp 1948. This case provides good argument for including at least brief examples, showing how each member of the group is to be used, particularly when chemical reaction of said member is involved.

At one time the practice required that all members of the Markush group be closely similar. Now *unity of function* may reasonably be expected to meet this requirement. More specifically, the members must either (1) belong to a recognized physical or chemical class or to an *art-recognized class* or (2) possess at least one property in common which is mainly responsible *for their function* in the claimed relationship. Where a Markush expression is applied only to portions of a chemical compound, the propriety of the grouping is determined by a consideration of the *compound as a whole,* and does not depend on a community of properties in said portions recited in the Markush expression. M.P.E.P. 706.03(y).

Oxides of Bi, Pb, Tl, W, Ta, and Cd were held sufficiently closely related for inclusion in a Markush group, even though the metals belong to different families in the periodic table and melt from 759 to 2130° C. Either the bismuth oxide or lead oxide must be present in the claimed composition whereas the other oxides are not essential. See *Ex parte Beck and Taylor*, 119 USPQ 100, PO BdApp 1957, citing cases on permissibility of essential and nonessential members of a Markush group, so long as they are so closely related as to be suggestive of one another in the particular field in which they are used.

A disadvantage of the Markush claim has been the difficulty of showing invention in any member of the group when another member is found in the art. Swearing back of a reference, under Rule 131, for certain members of a Markush group, is ineffective when a reference shows a member before the date established by affidavit for the other members. M.P.E.P. 715.03. For this reason, some attorneys rely initially solely on generic claims, even when the Markush claim is expected to be ultimately desirable; they then *submit the Markush claim only after they learn what species, if any, the art shows.*

A leading decision on equivalence is that written by Judge Rich, *In re Ruff and Dukeshire*, 118 USPQ 340, CCPA 1958. The decision states

"Actual equivalence is not enough to justify refusal of a patent on one member of a group when another member is in the prior art. The equivalence must be disclosed in the prior art or be obvious within the terms of Section 103."

A form of Markush claim that refers back to the specification appears in patent 2,459,746 to Radcliffe. It describes the stabilizer in a composition as a "substance selected from the group consisting of those set forth in Table II hereinabove."

Species Claims

Species claims feature most chemical applications. All but one of the species claims must recite each limitation of the genus claim. Rule 141. It is convenient to write all but the one species claim (and often that also) in dependent form, thus:

The ester of claim 1, said polycarboxylic acid being terephthalic.

In any case there must be a generic claim of scope to embrace all species claimed. A Markush group will suffice.

Sales Appeal in Claims

When there is some extremely unobvious feature of the invention, as in many chemical cases, that feature will be emphasized in the specification.

It is good psychology to recite in one or more of the claims the striking function, if any, of a structure, component, or condition set forth fully in itself. Having the sales feature in the claim calls attention to it at the time the claim is under consideration by the Examiner, Judge or competitor, without his having to refer back to an earlier page.

"Omnibus" or "Catch-All" Claim

Attorneys, often the most experienced, may add a claim of the following type:

"The novel products and processes described in the foregoing specification, including the various features of novelty therein set forth, taken either singly and/or in combination."

Such a claim is recognized as nonstatutory. Its inclusion is intended ordinarily to provide a basis for claiming, in a foreign case filed under the International Convention, all that is disclosed in the U.S. application regardless of the scope of the normal claims.

The need for such a catch-all or omnibus claim *no longer exists*. The rules have been changed, so that the *disclosure* in the domestic application provides an adequate basis for all claims based upon it, with the benefit of the first filing data for subsequent cases filed under the International Convention.

Cross-references: *Application Writing; Claim Drafting; General and Mechanical, Microbiological, Pharmaceutical, Design, and Plant Applications; Prosecution of Patent Applications.*

CLAIM DRAFTING

George V. Woodling

This article first presents in elementary manner the fundamental concepts of claim drafting, then discusses the new formats for claims, and concludes with a summary of rules for guidance and checking performance in writing claims.

The article is based largely on the author's book "Inventions and their Protection," Matthew Bender and Co., Albany 1, N.Y. (This is a widely used text. Ed.)

Protection of an invention by claims is a statutory requirement for the purpose of making the patentee define precisely what his invention is. They are the most impor-

tant parts of the patent. The claims and the claims alone construct a fence around the thing patented and protect it from trespassers. All that which is not enclosed by the fence of the claims is public property.

Section 112 of the Patent Codification Act states that the specification as filed in the Patent Office shall conclude with one or more claims particularly pointing out and distinctly noting the subject matter which the applicant regards as his invention.

The protection afforded by a patent is not defined or measured by the patent drawings and descriptions. Yet they constitute a dictionary for the claims and, in case of doubt, are relied upon to explain the true meaning of the claims.

Example of Claim Drafting

The reader may regard the creation of Adam and Eve as analogous to the creation of a mechanical device and further that Eve constitutes a patentable improvement over Adam. Let it be assumed that A is the inventor of Adam and B the inventor of Eve.

Assume that, when A invented Adam, he applied for a patent, that Adam meets the requirements as to the statutory classification of patentable subject matter, and that the prosecution of the patent application upon Adam would have been the same then as now exists in the United States Patent Office.

Although the reader may suggest other claims, let us assume that A's application upon Adam contained the following four claims:

1. An animal.
2. A vertebrate animal.
3. A man.
4. A brown-eyed man.

A claim is said to "read on" a device, if there can be found in the invention or device the elements or characteristics which the claim recites. Claim 1 "reads on" Adam because he is an animal.

Claim 1 above is called, in patent language, a broad claim. It includes species besides Adam. Claim 2 is also broad, but not so broad as claim 1. Claim 3 is specific and claim 4 still more specific to the particular thing shown and described in A's application.

Basic Concepts

From the above discussion, we can now state the first basic concepts of patent claim drafting:

Concept No. 1. The claims in an application must "read on" the invention shown and described in the application.

Concept No. 2. A claim in order to be valid must not read on the prior art.

Concept No. 3. It is legally proper for a claim to read on, and thereby include within its scope, later made inventions, as long as the claim meets the requirements of Concepts 1 and 2.

This Concept 3 points up the importance of including in an application not only claims directed to the principal invention, but also claims covering variations or future improvements. Thus, the inventor is in the favorable position of legally drafting broad claims which will cover a later improvement (Eve) by a subsequent inventor B.

The real test for the rejection of a claim by the examiner is not whether the scope thereof is broad enough to include later made inventions, but whether the claim reads on the prior art.

Imagination Plays a Vital Role in Patent Claims Drafting. The drafting of allowable broad claims, so that they will read upon the original form of the invention as well as upon subsequent variations or improvements which may be made during the 17-year life of the patent is one of the most difficult tasks a patent attorney has to perform. The exercise of the necessary imagination constitutes a real challenge in the practice of patent law, once referred to by Chief Justice Charles Evans Hughes as "the delight of constant intellectual exercise in the field of scientific effort." If, at the time the application is being prepared, the imagination leads one to conceive (superinvent) a large number of additional variations over and above the original form of the invention, then the problem of drafting sound patent claims resolves itself into the area of logic, grammar, and selection of the proper words for the claims so that they will read on the additional variations or improvements, as well as the original form of the invention, and yet not include or "fence in" any prior art. This requires manipulation of language by the careful choice of the exact words, neither too narrow nor too broad in meaning. If only a few variations have been conceived, indicating a lack of vision at the time the broad claims are being drafted, then the possibility of obtaining a valuable patent is materially reduced.

Broad Claims Stand in Jeopardy of Being Declared Invalid by Courts. An allowable broadened claim holds good against or dominates all later made inventions during the life of the patent. The mere allowance of a broad claim by the examiner does not necessarily mean that the claim will stand up when subjected to the test of validity that it may face during its life. Not infrequently the Patent Office inadvertently allows a broad claim which court may later declare invalid, on the basis that a prior art patent, publication or device anticipates the claim.

In view of this fact, the practice is to write a series of claims of varying scope so that, in the event the broadest of the claims are declared invalid, the remaining claims of lesser scope may still be relied upon.

Inventor Cannot Specifically Claim Later Made Inventions in an Already Filed Application. After an application has been filed in the Patent Office, the inventor frequently finds that his invention as described may be improved, to make it simpler, better, or more economical to manufacture. These additional improvements, which are not shown or described in the already filed application, may be referred to as "afterthoughts"; they cannot be *specifically* claimed in the already filed application, because nothing can be specifically claimed unless it has been shown or disclosed originally.

A fine legal distinction is to be made here in that, while an inventor A cannot claim a later made invention specifically, he may have a basis for claims broad enough in scope to cover generically the later invention.

Although A may be entitled to the broadened claim, which includes in its scope the improvement invention of B, it is *not to be inferred* that he is also entitled to a *detailed claim* which reads specifically on the later made invention.

Concept No. 4. Specific claims which read only upon later made inventions cannot be legally included in an application which does not show and describe the later made inventions.

It behooves an inventor, therefore, to make all possible improvements before he files his application and to show specifically and claim them in his application on the principal invention.

One of the advantages of a preliminary search is preparation of the application with knowledge of what may be included and the prior art to be avoided.

Concept No. 5. It is legally proper for an inventor of a later made improvement invention to obtain specific claims on his improvement so long as his claims do not read on the prior art, even though one or more of the patents of the prior art might contain a claim which is broad enough in scope to read on the later made improvement invention.

The mere fact that a broad claim of a prior patent may read on a later made invention is no indication that the broad claim specifically teaches the particular subject matter of the subsequent invention.

A broad patent claim does not teach as much as a specific patent claim. As a rule, the claims disclose less than the drawings and specification of the patent. The rejection of a claim in an application for a later made invention is based strictly upon what the prior patent *teaches* and not upon the *scope* of the claims of the prior art.

Concept No. 6. *Failure of prior inventor to obtain broad claim does not keep the field open for a subsequent inventor to obtain same or equivalent broad claim.*

Let it be assumed that A failed to obtain in his patent a broad patent claim to which he was entitled. Could B obtain in his later application such a broad claim? The answer is no. The subject matter that A was entitled to claim, but did not, is dedicated by issuance of his patent to the public and is free for use by everybody. Also the teaching of A's patent would constitute anticipation of such a broad claim in B's application.

If an inventor had an opportunity to claim a 1000-acre invention but claimed only 100 acres, then the remaining 900 acres

are in the public domain; a subsequent inventor cannot claim the dedicated area as part of his invention.

Concept No. 7. A later inventor may rightfully obtain a patent containing claims specific to his own improvement invention, if such claims avoid anticipation arising from the teaching of the prior art, but he may not legally be entitled to enjoy his common law right to manufacture, sell and use his patented improvement invention without infringing a prior patent if said prior patent is still alive (less than 17 years old) and has a broad dominating claim which reads on the improvement invention.

The reader may now ask himself, Why does the Patent Office grant a later patent to B if he cannot manufacture, sell and use his invention? *The Patent Office is concerned with "anticipation" and not with "infringement,"* as the latter comes under the jurisdiction of the Federal courts. The "read on" test is used to determine both anticipation and infringement. In the case of anticipation, however, the test determines whether a claim reads on the prior art. In the case of infringement, the test is whether a claim reads on a device which is being manufactured, sold or used without authorization.

Concept No. 8. A prior patent, containing a broad dominating claim which reads on an improvement patented by a later inventor, does not vest in the owner of the prior patent the right to manufacture, sell or use the improvement invention in violation of the patent owned by the later inventor.

This result is typical of a modern patent difficulty where two or more persons have patents and neither can exploit the invention. In this situation, each may grant a license under his patent to the other to manufacture, sell or use the invention. One important advantage of an improvement patent is its use for trading purposes, an advantage often overlooked by some manufacturers. Also B, if he does not desire to manufacture, sell or use his invention, may grant a license under his patent to A and receive royalty.

In the absence of the license agreement, the foregoing example of Adam and Eve may be summarized as follows:

1. Based on the foregoing assumption, neither A nor B can legally manufacture, sell or use Eve without infringing the patent of the other.

2. A, according to the assumption, is free to manufacture, sell or use men, as B's claim does not read on men.

Participation of Inventor-Engineer in Drafting Patent Claims

It is the extra inventive thoughts which makes possible the best claim. The patent attorney is well equipped to take care of the word manipulation of the claim, but the words require backing up by creative thinking, which the inventor-engineer is best able to supply. To help the engineer and the designer in the protection of their creations and in the drafting of patent claims in cooperation with the attorney is the purpose of this section.

Precepts and Examples of Claim Drafting

A Patent Claim Is a Definition of the Invention. A "wheel" may be defined as a circular body mounted on a central axis for rotation. The words "circular body," when taken alone, may "read on" or cover many objects or species besides a wheel. Thus, circular body may cover a rolling log, a coin, a circular picture frame, a dinner plate, a pie pan or a hoop. By reason of the fact that the words "circular body" cover or "read on" a class of objects made up of two or more species, one speaks of such words as the genus of the definition. By adding to the genus the qualifying words "mounted on a central axis for rotation," all the species except the wheel are excluded. The qualifying words form the "difference" which characterizes the wheel from the other species. Accordingly, a definition is evolved by adding the difference to the *genus*. It is the difference which defines or limits the scope of the *extension*.

In drafting patent claims, this general rule is employed. Thus, the following claim 1 for A's knife, shown in Fig. 1, was drafted by adding differences to the genus.

A knife comprising a handle, a relatively thin cutting blade, and means connecting an end of said blade to the handle.

In this claim, the word "knife" is the genus. The handle and a relatively thin cutting blade having one of its ends connected to the handle are the differences that exclude other cutting instruments, such as a hatchet or an ax.

As to the effect of the introductory words "a knife," note the following language from a court decision:

"...While it is true that this (introductory) clause of itself does not describe an element in the combination, it should not for that reason be ignored. Each of the elements of the combination should be read in the light of this clause and should be modified by it. Such a clause by itself may entirely fail to supply a necessary element in a combination...yet it may so affect the enumerated elements as to give life and meaning and vitality to them, as they appear in the combination..." *Schram Glass Co.* v. *Homer Brooke Glass Co.,* 249 Fed. 228, 229, CA 1918.

Each Claim in Patent Must Be Patentably Different from the Other Claims. One may begin the claim drafting by listing the essential or cooperatively associated parts to be set forth in the body of the claim. The listed parts may include:

1. *A handle* (having a recess)

2. *A first blade* (pivoted to one end of the handle and pivotally movable into and out of said recess)

3. *A second blade* (pivoted to the other end of the handle and pivotally movable into and out of said recess).

Suppose the three listed parts are catalogued in a claim like this:

A knife comprising a handle, a first blade, and a second blade.

The Patent Office would reject such a claim as a mere aggregation of parts with no expressed cooperation between the catalogued parts. Insofar as this claim shows, the several parts may not even have reached the point of being assembled. It is important to remember that a claim must set forth a true combination and an operative structure, as opposed to a mere aggregation. One must be able figuratively to "use" the words of the claim which defines the knife the same as the knife itself can be "used." Thus, the words of a claim for defining a device or a machine must be "operably" connected together. The objection as to aggregation may be removed by setting forth the knife parts as before, and in addition explaining how the several parts cooperate with respect to each other to make a complete operative device. The improved claim may read as follows:

A knife comprising, in combination, a handle having a recess, a first blade pivoted to one end of the handle and pivotally movable into and out of the recess, and a second blade pivoted to the other end of the handle and pivotally movable into and out of the recess.

This claim sets forth a combination. It overcomes the objection as to aggregation. It tells how each part cooperates to make the knife, as claimed, an operative device. The phrase "in combination" modifies every element recited thereafter in the body of the claim, yet it must not be inferred that the mere use of the phrase will always make a true combination out of a claim which is otherwise an aggregation.

Instead of "comprising," words of similar import, such as "including" or "consisting of" may be used. Care must be exercised in using these words interchangeably. To illustrate, a wheel may "have" or "include" a hub, but it cannot properly be said that a wheel "consists of" a hub. The words "consist of" are limiting, for when one states that an object *consists of* something, he must name all the parts of the object. The word "comprising" is not limiting.

Broadest Patent Claims Should Recite Only Indispensable Elements. The immediately preceding claim sets forth three principal elements (a handle, a first blade and a second blade) and thus gives a rather detailed word picture of the device. This means that the claim is narrow in extension or scope. Such a claim may easily be designed around, to avoid infringement.

If the alleged infringing device omits any *one* of the recited elements, it would avoid infringement unless it substitutes an equivalent element for the one omitted.

The manner of drafting a claim to avoid designing around it, is further illustrated by the following simple illustration. Let it be supposed that Company A has a patent on a three-legged stool and that a claim thereof reads as follows:

A stool comprising a seat and having three legs supporting said seat.

Now let it be assumed that Company B manufactures and sells a stool having one leg. There is no infringement because there cannot be found in the one-legged stool, the *three* legs called for in the patent claim.

Let it now be assumed that Company C manufactures and sells a stool having four legs. The fact that the four-legged stool has one extra leg does not avoid infringement. In other words, a subsequently designed device which has "additional" features over those recited in a prior patented claim does not necessarily avoid infringement, but a subsequently designed device which omits features recited in a prior patent claim does ordinarily avoid infringement. Simply stated, the *addition* does not avoid infringement of a "comprising" claim, but the *omission* does.

The larger the number of coacting elements recited in a claim of a prior patent, the greater is the opportunity for an adverse party, when constructing his device, to omit one of the recited elements and thus avoid infringement.

Therefore, it is a good practice for the inventor himself, when drafting or checking the allowed claims of his application before the patent is granted, to try designing around his own claims by omitting at least one of the recited parts. If he succeeds, it is likely that his competitor can also avoid infringement. The cure for this defect is to draft a broader claim, if the prior art permits it, with a smaller number of recited elements. A claim covers all that it does not exclude, not just what it recites. A claim that recites one component as "an alcohol" covers all alcohols but may be too broad to be allowable or enforceable. A claim reciting "ethanol" or "an alcohol selected from the group consisting of (naming them)" covers only the alcohols specifically named.

In patent language, a claim of restricted scope is referred to as specific or narrow. Claims which have a wide scope are broad or dominating. There will be a smaller number of things or devices embraced in a specific than in a broad claim.

Public Policy Consideration. The drafting of a patent claim involves something more than mere compliance with certain rules of logical definition. A claim must also be molded in consideration of public policy which may restrict the protection the inventor will receive for the disclosure of his invention through his patent to the public.

A patent is a contract between the public and the inventor, and care must be exercised to see that both of the contracting parties are treated fairly. If public policy is so interpreted as to limit needlessly the scope of the inventor's claim, he is not receiving protection commensurate with his contribution to the art. On the contrary, if his claims are made too broad, they tend to monopolize the art unfairly, discourage further experimentation by others, and thereby violate the general purpose of the patent laws which are designed primarily to promote the progress of science rather than to reward the inventor.

Means Claims

In patent claim drafting, the attorneys make much use of the word "means" to recite a feature broadly. The word "means" usually connotes mechanism and includes all possible types of operative structures. Less use is made of the word "mechanism." Therefore, claims which make a wise use of the word "means" are usually referred to as a "means type of claim." Thus, in a safety razor, there is structure for holding the blade and also structure for ejecting it. In drafting a broad claim covering these features of a safety razor, the patent attorney would claim the holding structure as "means holding the blade." Similarly, he would not specifically limit the ejecting structure in the broad claim but would claim it as "means for ejecting the blade."

The use of "means" plus a statement of the function tends to embrace all operable alternatives.

The claiming of the function or result is not the same, however, as claiming the invention itself. For example, suppose an instrument were invented which, when mounted on an airplane, would give an automatic indication of the speed of the airplane relative to the earth. So far as pure logic alone is concerned, a claim might read:

Means for automatically indicating the speed of an airplane relative to the earth.

Observe that this claim sets forth a *single means* for accomplishing the desired result. In patent language a claim of this nature is referred to as a "single means" claim. Its scope is broad enough to embrace all possible ways "of automatically indicating the speed" of the airplane. If such a claim were enforceable, which it is not, it would dominate all future inventions accomplishing this same result, even though wholly different means were used. Subsequent invention in the field would be stifled rather than encouraged.

"Means Combination" Claims. To comply with the public policy, the claim above must set forth the "combination of means" by which the automatic indication of miles-per-hour of the airplane is accomplished.

Although a single "means" plus a statement of the function, when used alone, is bad, yet when two or more "means" are recited in a claim with the function of each, the form of claim is acceptable.

The "means combination" type of claims, which recite elements by "means for" (followed by the statement of the functions) is expressly authorized by 35 U.S.C. 112:

"An element in a claim for a combination may be expressed as a means or step for performing a specified function without the recital of structure, material, or acts in support thereof, and such claims shall be construed to cover the corresponding structure, material or acts described in the specification and equivalents thereof."

In the day-by-day patent claim drafting by attorneys, the "means combination" type of claim is used almost universally for defining broadly mechanical inventions combining more than one function. In fact, it is possibly the best type of broad claim. However, care must be taken (1) not to limit too narrowly the "statement of the function" and thereby restrict unduly the scope of the invention and (2) to add other claims reciting the specific structure of each patentable "means."

"Whereby Functional" Clauses. It is a fact that use of the word "means" followed

by a functional statement has long been recognized as the proper procedure of stating an element in a claim reciting two or more coacting means. Yet the functional statement must contain sufficient structural body to carry out the function so specified. Not infrequently these functional statements are introduced by the word "whereby"; therefore, they may be referred to as "whereby functional" clauses, but may include other similar clauses, namely, "so that," "thereby," etc. An example of a proper "whereby functional" clause follows.

A knife comprising a handle provided with a recess, a blade, means mounting an end of the blade pivotally on said handle WHEREBY SAID BLADE MAY BE MOVED INTO AND OUT OF SAID RECESS, and a spring forcing said blade in the direction of said recess. (Emphasis added.)

If the "whereby" clause were omitted in the above claim, the claim would still define an operative structure. The fault with some "whereby" clauses in claims is that the structural features recited in the claims are insufficient to support the "functional" clauses. The claim should be complete and define an *operative structure, even without the functional clause.*

Claim Should Be Definite. A claim should define an invention so that no confusion can arise in the minds of those who wish to know whether the claim "reads on" a certain device. As an example of indefiniteness, attention is directed to the following claim which was drafted to cover the balloon tire (U.S. Pat. No. 1,537,879).

Balloon Tire

"*1. A pneumatic tire of normally circular cross-section and designed to carry a predetermined normal load at a substantially reduced inflation pressure, modified from standard practice for the same load by a substantial increase in cross-sectional area and a substantial decrease in ratio of wall thickness to cross-sectional diameter.*"

When the owner of the claim sued for holding of infringement, the court held the claim invalid for lack of a definite standard of practice with regard to tire width and inflation pressure. *Steel Wheel Corp.* v. *B. F. Goodrich Rubber Co.,* 6 USPQ 61, 1930.

There Is No Set Rule as to Order of Introducing Elements in a Claim. The elements of a claim may be introduced in any order so long as the finished claim defines an operative device, thus:

1. A wheel comprising, in combination, a hub, a rim, spokes having inner and outer ends, and means connecting said ends, respectively, to the hub and rim.

A second claim for the same wheel may read:

2. A wheel comprising, in combination, a rim, a hub, spokes, and means . . .

The claims are equally acceptable.

Claims Must Set Forth Principal Element Positively and Not Indirectly. In drafting a claim one should not refer to a principal element indirectly, until he first has set it forth directly or positively. The distinction between *directly* and *indirectly* may be illustrated by the following example.

1. A wheel comprising, in combination, spokes having inner and outer ends respectively connected to the hub and rim.

The claim-drafting rule has been violated because the "hub" and "rim" were referred to indirectly without first being introduced directly. In patent language, the hub and rim in wheel claim 1-A are spoken of as having no "antecedents." This lack of "antecedents" may be avoided by reciting the "hub" and the "rim" directly or positively, as done in a previous wheel claim.

Minor Elements May Be Set Forth Indirectly. If an element is considered as a minor or modifying feature of a principal element, then it may be introduced indirectly. One purpose of allowing minor elements to be listed thus indirectly in a claim without first introducing them directly, is to avoid "overstuffing" the claim with too many directly recited minor details. (See *Intangibles . . .*, infra)

Antecedents May Be Set Forth in Introductory Clause. Suppose the invention is a wheel itself which may be used on any type of axle, the axle being *no part of the actual invention.* Aggregation may be avoided and the antecedent stated by introducing the axle in the introductory clause, thus:

A wheel adapted for rotation about an axle comprising, in combination, spokes hav-

ing inner and outer ends, a hub arranged to rotate about the axle, *means connecting the hub to the inner ends of the spokes, a rim, and means connecting the rim to the outer ends of the spokes.* (Emphasis added.)

The "axle" in the introductory clause is not a positive element of the invention but provides an antecedent for the word axle in the body of the claim.

The "building up" of antecedents in the introductory clause of a claim is a good procedure particularly where the invention applies to an old device. (See *Jepson Claims*)

Intangibles Are Not Claimed Positively. A "hole" is not recited positively because it is the absence of something. The same is true of a recess, groove, or a space. Thus, it is improper to claim "A knife comprising a *recess* in a handle."

The recess should be set forth indirectly. A properly written claim would read:

A knife comprising a handle having a recess therein . . .

A support provided with a hole . . .

A brake mechanism comprising a brake drum, a brake band defining an arcuate space therewith, *a friction element, and means securing said element non-rotatably in said space.* (Emphasis added.)

Claims Should State Elements Positively. A claim must define what the invention is, not what it is not. "Stationary" is better than "nonmovable." "Noncircular," "noncorrosive," and like words, although negative in form, have been accepted, however, as defining positive features.

Claims Must Not State Alternatives Separated by "Or." A claim which states elements in the alternative is objectionable, e.g.:

A machine comprising a shaft and a lever *or* a gear for turning the shaft . . .

This alternative may be avoided by selecting a term generic to both the lever and crank; the claim may properly recite: ". . . an actuating element for turning the shaft."

If the lever and the gear are to be covered specifically, two separate claims should be written, one claiming the lever and the other the gear. The "bridge" claim to the "actuating element" is generic to both species.

If the words in the alternative expression mean substantially the same thing, such as a "cable or wire," then the "or" may be used; it is here a question of phraseology and not of alternative structures.

Drafting Claims in Advance of Specification

It is good practice to draft the claims before writing the description, so that the description may be made to support every provision in the claims.

Bridge Claims

"Bridge" claims connect species claims to two or more embodiments of an invention.

"Bridge" claims will not hold two sets of claims in one application unless there is dependency between the sets. In other words, "bridge" claims will be rejected on the ground of a mere aggregation, if there is no cooperative relationship between the wheel and the axle, recited in separate claims, for instance, where the axle does not affect the operation of the wheel.

Upon the rejection of the "bridge" claims, division, now called "restriction," between the two sets of claims (upon the wheel and axle) is proper. In this event, the applicant must elect which group of claims he wishes to prosecute in his patent application if the requirement of restriction is repeated.

Special Forms of Claims

Recently a new format or arrangement has been suggested by the Patent Office for these long involved claims, allowing the presentation of claims divided into subparagraphs and indented according to structure, ingredients, or process steps contained in the patent specification. This new format or subparagraph arrangement simply involves the breaking up of the claim into its various portions (individual elements of the mechanism in the case of a mechanical patent application) and the portions may be identified by a number or a letter. Following is a model claim employing the new format which appeared in the Official Gazette for September 12, 1961 on page 189:

Claim in Subparagraph Form

"1. A device which is designed to receive fuel and air from suitable sources of supply and to transform said fuel and air into a mixture suitable for combustion, said device comprising in combination:

(a) an air manifold,

(b) a throttle valve located within said air manifold and mounted on an axis, each end of the throttle valve extending a substantial distance from said axis,

(c) said air manifold being of substantially constant cross section in the throttle area,

(d) said throttle valve having a mid portion of considerable thickness as compared with its end portions, whereby a venturi effect is created in said air manifold,

(e) means to move said throttle so that its ends move beyond the center position in each direction through arcuate paths about an axis,

(f) a fuel passageway leading to said manifold,

(g) said fuel passageway merging into an orifice as it enters the air manifold, and

(h) the front portion of said throttle being adapted to move through a first arcuate path toward one side of said air manifold, and the rear portion on said throttle being adapted to move through a second arcuate path toward the other side of said air manifold, said orifice being located between planes drawn through the points where the extensions of said first and second arcuate paths would intersect the inner walls of said air manifold, said planes being normal to the axis of said air manifold."

The Patent Office has stated that "the criteria for the selection of a particular claim format should be the clarity of presentation." In the case of the short claim, little is to be gained by using the new subparagraph form.

Use of the new format for the long, complicated claim serves the purpose of clarification. However, a word of caution is timely here because in using the subparagraph form of claim, there is a tendency to carry to an extreme the break up of the various elements of the claim, which in turn may cause the writer to fall into the error of excessive paragraphing and thereby possibly include needless provisions in the claim. It is these provisions in a claim which make it easy for a competitor to design around them. A competitor may easily avoid infringement of such claims by constructing his device so as to *omit at least one of the needless provisions.* An example of a needless provision can be found in B's claim 1, which states: "... a second blade pivotally connected to the other end of the handle." This provision may be readily omitted in the competitor's device by constructing his knife with a blade on only one end of the handle, and not upon each end of the handle, as called for by the claim.

Jepson Type Claims. There was long a question about including in a claim features that were old but necessary to show the environment of the invention and an operable structure. Assistant Commissioner Clay approved such practice, when the old features are recited as such. *Ex parte Jepson,* 1917 C.D. 62.

Here the applicant placed the old elements in the introductory clause and then claimed the combination of them with what was new, as in the following claim:

"16. In an electrical system of distribution of the class wherein a variable speed generator charges a storage battery and when the battery becomes sufficiently charged a voltage coil becomes effective to regulate the generator for constant potential, the combination with said voltage coil of a coil traversed by current flowing to the battery which is acted upon by decreasing battery current to reduce the potential maintained constant by the voltage coil."

In considering a Jepson claim, the Board of Appeals has suggested that the language "the improvement consisting of," starting the body of the claim as frequently worded, should be changed to—the combination thereof with—as in the claim above. *Ex parte Stacy,* 69 USPQ 264, 1946.

In this type of claim it is important to include every feature that contributes novelty to the invention in the body of the claim, not in the introduction for which no allegation of invention is made. In a case claiming an article (a caster cup) it was held that

"No patentable significance can be accorded to the preamble of said claim, since it constitutes at best merely a statement of environment or intended use." *Ex parte Auer*, 104 USPQ 149, PO Bd App 1954. Cf. *In re Dense*, 70 USPQ 212, CCPA 1946.

It should be noted, however, that such introductory clause is often relied upon successfully in a composition claim, to distinguish a new use by excluding remote art under circumstances making the use patentable in an art not analogous to that of an old use. (See *Use Patents*)

Claims Reciting a Figure of the Drawings. It is customary to claim a design thus —"The ornamental design for a [name of article] as shown." Here there is no utility except ornamentation. Such a claim for an invention of "mechanical" utility or structure has been recognized recently. It is evidently a part of the reform that is moving in the field of permissible types of claims.

The Board of Appeals in *Ex parte Squires*, decided December 28, 1961, held allowable in a mechanical patent claims which refer to a figure in the drawings of the case. These claims as allowed and issued in patent 3,034,806 read as follows:

"1. A font of numerals as shown in Fig. 1.

"2. In an environment of low brightness of red light, a font of numerals as shown in Fig. 1."

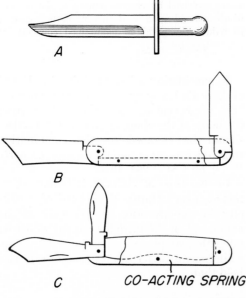

Fig. 1.

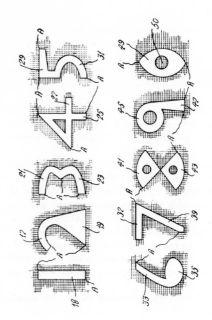

INVENTOR.
PAUL C. SQUIRES

BY

Louis B. Applebaum
ATTORNEY

Fig. 2.

See Fig. 2 and Louis B. Applebaum, 44 JPOS 379, 1962.

The Board of Appeals determined that the two-dimensional subject matter was allowable, holding in substance as follows:

"Claims to a font of numerals having utility in increasing the accuracy with which known types of intelligence can be conveyed—having utility in the shape whereby they can be discerned properly, are allowable as matter comprehended by the Patent Statutes 35 U.S.C. (1952) 101.... While there is no specific thickness ascribed to the numerals, they can reasonably be said to fall within the statutory class of manufacture in that they are something made by the hand of man: they have a particular planar configuration giving an improved result— more accurate readability under adverse conditions. Their alleged utility does not lie in the intelligence they convey, nor in their particular arrangement on a piece of paper, a block of wood or a dial."

What range of equivalents, if any, may be accorded to such a claim as this "One Line Picture Claim" remains to be determined.

Markush Claims. See *Chemical Applications*.

Summary of Rules for Writing Claims

Proficiency in claim drafting is acquired by the correct application of a given set of facts to the general principles. Many rules, which have evolved more from logical expediency than from adherence to some preconceived standard, are not treated herein. The foregoing discussion, however, illustrates principles founded in patent law, the rules of the Patent Office, and well accepted practice.

The following classification of points to be checked in claim drafting present a positive, negative and optional approach, a classification adopted in some instances for the sake of effectiveness and in others because of necessity, with occasional duplication in thought.

Positive Rules

(1) Each claim must be significantly different from each of the others.

(2) A claim must recite an operative structure, telling how the various parts cooperate, i.e., a true combination.

(3) A broad claim should include only the minimum number of elements indispensable for novelty and operability.

(4) A claim must be molded in consideration of public policy.

(5) A claim must set forth the structure or a combination of means by which the result is accomplished rather than the mere result or function.

(6) A "means" claim must recite more than a single means.

(7) Functional claims must contain sufficient structure to carry out the function specified.

(8) A claim should be so definite that no confusion can arise in the minds of those who wish to know whether or not the claim "reads on" a certain device.

(9) A claim must set forth the principal elements positively.

(10) A claim should recite the part provided with a hole rather than the hole itself, such intangible feature being thus set forth indirectly.

(11) Where two or more alternative elements are to be covered, either a term which is broad enough to embrace all of them must be chosen or separate claims drawn to cover each of the elements individually.

(12) Claims must "read on" the invention shown and described in the application.

(13) The claims should be graded in scope, from the broadest claim, reciting the minimum number of features, to claims of intermediate scope including additional limitations, and finally to claim(s) reciting the combination of all features of novelty. This will give a narrow claim maximum likelihood of being held valid in an infringement suit and some possibility of being expanded by court interpretation to include equivalents of some or all of the elements recited.

Negative Rules

(1) A claim must not be merely a catalogue of the parts, with no showing of their inter-associations or coaction.

(2) A claim must not cover merely an aggregation of parts.

(3) Elements which, if omitted, will enable an infringer to design around a claim should not appear in all claims.

(4) Where a single part is new and constitutes the whole of the invention, the recital of this new part, as a "single means plus a statement of function" along with the old elements, does not make a "means combination" type of claim.

(5) A valid claim cannot be drawn to a law of nature, but can to an application of the law or of principle of science.

(6) A claim must not state the elements in the negative when positive language is available.

(7) A claim must not state the elements in the alternative except in rare cases, one of which is use of the Markush type claim.

(8) Claims must not "read on" prior devices.

Optional

(1) A principal element may be set forth indirectly after it is once set forth posi-

tively; thus antecedents may be built up in the first part of the claim and reference to them made later.

(2) Where it is difficult to state the elements in the positive, some negative words (such as "noncircular") may be used.

(3) Antecedents and old environmental features may be set forth in an introductory clause.

(4) A "difference" may be added to claims so that they will not "read on" prior devices.

(5) An allowable generic claim which "reads on" each dependent invention may be employed to bind, into a single application, five species claims that individually "read on" the variations. When two inventions are dependent on each other, they may be tied together also by a "bridge" claim and the two held in a single application.

(6) When intended to mean the same thing, alternative words may be used to describe an element, as "cable or wire," "sheet or plate," and "bolt or stud."

Cross-references: *Chemical, Microbiological Pharmaceutical* and other arts; *Claim Interpretation; Claims—Words and Phrases—Exterior Standards; Delay in Claiming; Validity—Section on Functionality in Claims.*

CLAIM INTERPRETATION AND PATENT CONSTRUCTION

Granville M. Pine

The Patent a Creation of Statute

The most fundamental and reliable rules of interpretation of patents are those which are associated with the legal foundation and function of the patent. They take into account the fact that the patent is wholly a creature of statute. The patent right is granted only in return for a complete and clear written description of the invention in the published patent document so that the public may use the invention after the inventor's exclusive rights have expired. A necessary part of the statutory transaction between the public and the inventor is a careful definition of the invention, so that the exclusive rights granted to the inventor

do not transcend his actual contribution to science and the useful arts.

The patent is to be evaluated on the basis of the extent to which it fulfills its assigned functions and to be interpreted in manner to promote and forward the reasons for its existence.

The Patent Statute

The enabling legislation for patents contains the following provisions defining the legal requirements for the patent document:

Specification

"The specification shall contain a written description of the invention, and of the manner and process of making and using it, in such full, clear, concise, and exact terms as to enable any person skilled in the art to which it pertains, or with which it is most nearly connected, to make and use the same, and shall set forth the best mode contemplated by the inventor of carrying out his invention.

"The specification shall conclude with one or more claims particularly pointing out and distinctly claiming the subject matter which the applicant regards as his invention." 35 U.S.C. 112.

Specification and Claims. The statute defines the specification as including the written description of the invention and also the claims at the end which define the scope of the invention. In the more particular examination and analysis of each of these functionally different parts of the patent, professional usage frequently limits the word "specification" to the descriptive or teaching part of the patent and the word "claim" to the concise definition of the invention at the end of the document. This is the sense in which the words are used in this article.

Drawings. In addition to the textual portion of a patent—the specification and claims—some patents include drawings. "When the nature of the case admits, the applicant shall furnish a drawing." 35 U.S.C. 113.

Drawings are thus always required when the invention is concerned with mechanical structure or electrical circuitry and are helpful in the exposition of such subject matter.

Even in cases of chemical inventions and others not involving physical structures, the Patent Office may require illustrations which will facilitate an understanding of the invention, such as flow sheets and diagrammatic views. Rule 81. The drawings which are a part of the patent application become a part of the issued patent and are thus subject to interpretation along with the specification and claims.

Functions of the Specifications, Claims and Drawings. The function of the specification, as defined by the first paragraph of 35 U.S.C. Section 112 quoted above, is twofold. First, the specification is a part of the patent where the public can get at least a generalized statement by the inventor describing the invention. This function of the specification is the same as that of the claims—to describe and identify that which the inventor has contributed. The second function of the specification is to teach.

The specification therefore needs to be interpreted in the light of its discharge of these two different statutory functions—to describe the invention and to teach how to use it—and the standards and canons of interpretation are such as logically relate to each individual function.

The statutory office of the claim or claims at the end of the patent is to "particularly point out and distinctly" claim "the subject matter which the applicant regards as his invention." This is the place, then, where the statute requires the scope of the inventor's monopoly to be carefully defined, and the interpretation of the claim is made with that statutory purpose in mind.

It will be noted that in the statute the drawings are treated entirely separately from the specification and claims. The drawings are not defined as a part of the written description required in the specification. They cannot of themselves satisfy the statutory necessity for a written description of the invention. Thus, the drawings are referred to as an aid in interpreting the specification and claims. They may be used to explain ambiguities in the patent, but an alleged invention shown only in the drawings but not described in the specification cannot be, except in a design patent, the

invention covered by the claims. *Permutit Co.* v. *Graver Corp.*, 284 U.S. 52, 1931; *Suczek* v. *General Motors Corp.*, 132 F.2d 371, CA 6 1942.

The Patent Interpreted as a Written Instrument

A patent speaks as a written instrument. As such its interpretation is no stranger to the law.

In his opinion in *Doble Engineering Co.* v. *Leeds & Northrop Co.*, 134 F.2d 78, CA 1 1943, Circuit Judge Woodbury discusses at length what he considers to be the principal source of confusion found in precedent and authority on the interpretation of patents. He points out that it is firmly enough established that patents should be interpreted by the rules of construction applicable to all written instruments and that, though they are not contracts strictly speaking, still they are bilateral instruments and the rules for construction of any ordinary contract should be applied to them.

The difficulty in many decided cases arises (Judge Woodbury believes) from the enunciation of minor rules or canons of construction applicable to patents only. These rules in many instances are directly conflicting and fail to incorporate objective standards by which a given set of facts may be judicially decided with reasonable certainty. Judge Woodbury refers as an example to the directly conflicting decisions to be found in the books holding both that the preamble words in a claim *are* and *are not* to be construed as limiting language in the claim definition. He refers also to the canons of interpretation that a pioneer patent should be liberally construed, while one covering a minor step in a crowded art should be narrowly construed; and on the other hand that a patent covering a device enjoying marked practical success should receive liberal construction, while an unused—the so-called "paper" patent—is to be narrowly construed. These rules of interpretation, Judge Woodbury comments, are of no real help and are actually in conflict as in a supposed case of a pioneer patent which is entitled to liberal construction, but which for some reason has never gone into commercial usage and must therefore be narrowly construed.

A Guide to Patent Interpretation

Judge Woodbury's thesis that a patent should be interpreted in accordance with the rules applicable to contracts is one firm guide to interpretation. Another resides in the difference between the patent document and contracts; a patent, in addition to being a written memorial of the intentions of the negotiating patentee and patent examiner, is also subject to the legislative requirements and definitions. Thus, the patent specification should describe the invention and teach how it may be used, and the claims should particularly point out the subject matter which the patentee regards as his invention. The patent specification and claims are to be interpreted in accordance with these statutory directions; a patent which does not meet the imposed functions both fails to qualify under the enabling legislation and misleads the public, which has the right to read it in its statutory context.

Many of the minor canons of the type criticized by Judge Woodbury are objectionable not only because they state rules of uncertain application to a given set of facts, but also because they fail to enforce the requirements of the statute in the reading of patents. The rule that a pioneer patent is to be liberally construed while one covering a minor improvement is narrowly construed, is unserviceable because the standards of what is pioneer and what is improvement are wholly uncertain and to a large extent subjective. The rule is also unreasonable because it permits widely varying standards of interpretation of a document while the statute requires that it be concise and exact in the specification and particular and distinct in the claims, definitions which exclude subjective and fluctuating standards.

A very helpful approach to the interpretation of patents is to apply the applicable rules of contract interpretation but evaluate them in the light of the patent statute. The more reliable precedents are those which follow this approach.

The Claims as the Measure of the Invention

The claims of the patent must satisfy the statutory requirement that they particularly point out the subject matter which the applicant regards as his invention. The object of the statute is the protection of the public against extension of the scope of the patent, *Universal Oil Products Co.* v. *Globe Oil & Refining Co.*, 322 U.S. 471, 1944, so that the public may know which features disclosed in the specification may be used or manufactured and which may not. *Permutit Co.* v. *Graver Corp.*, 284 U.S. 52, 1931. The validity of the claims and their interpretation are both judged upon the basis of their statutory purpose.

If a claim utterly fails to define the invention in the clear and exact terms required by the statute, it will be held invalid. *General Electric Co.* v. *Wabash Appliance Corp.*, 304 U.S. 364, 1938; *United Carbon Co.* v. *Binney & Smith Co.*, 317 U.S. 228, 1942.

The claims are, by statute, the measure of the invention. They are to be interpreted in the words which the inventor has used in clearly and concisely pointing out his invention. They can cover only what their language fairly imports. Even though the inventor has defined in the claims less scope for his invention than he might have, the balance of the invention described in the specification beyond that covered by the claim language is dedicated to the public. *McClain* v. *Ortmayer*, 141 U.S. 419, 1891; *Milcor Steel Co.* v. *George A. Fuller Co.*, 122 F.2d 292, CA 2 1941.

Testimony at trial cannot be taken to vary the plain meaning of the language in the claims. *Kalle & Co.* v. *Multazo Co., Inc.*, 31 F.Supp. 109, DC WMich 1937. The claim language defines the invention, for the purpose both of determining infringement and of comparing the invention with the prior art to measure validity, and must be read in the same way for the two purposes. *DeCew* v. *Union Bag & Paper Corp.*, 57 F.Supp. 388, DC NJ 1944. Where there is no ambiguity in the language of the claims, resort cannot be had to the specification to restrict them from their plain meaning and thus save them from invalidity. *Borg-Warner Corp.* v. *Mall Tool Company*, 217 F.2d 850, CA 7 1954; *Altoona Publix Theatres* v. *American Tri-Ergon Corp.*, 294 U.S. 477, 1935.

Every element in a claimed combination is material. A claim is not infringed unless all claimed elements are found in the accused structure. *Alex Lee Wallau, Inc.* v. *J. W. Landenberger & Co.*, 121 F.Supp. 555, DC SNY 1954. No limitation that the patentee puts into a claim can be ignored. *Cutter Laboratories* v. *Lyophile-Cryochem Corp.*, 179 F.2d 80, CA 9 1949.

The foregoing authorities are examples of the most reasonable and authentic first step in patent claim interpretation. Viewing a patent claim either as a written document to be accorded a legal interpretation as other written instruments or as a writing which the patent statute requires clearly and concisely to define the patentee's invention, the appropriate approach is to read and interpret the claim in the language there used and to depart as little as possible from what is expressed.

The principle has been stated in an early and often-cited opinion of the Supreme Court in *White* v. *Dunbar:*

"Some persons seem to suppose that a claim in a patent is like a nose of wax, which may be turned and twisted in any direction, by merely referring to the specification, so as to make it include something more than, or something different from, what its words express. The context may, undoubtedly, be resorted to, and often is resorted to, for the purpose of better understanding the meaning of the claim; but not for the purpose of changing it, and making it different from what it is. The claim is a statutory requirement, prescribed for the very purpose of making the patentee define precisely what his invention is; and it is unjust to the public, as well as an invasion of the law, to construe it in a manner different from the plain import of its terms. This has been so often expressed in the opinions of this court that it is unnecessary to pursue the subject further." 119 U.S. 47, 1886.

Reading the Claims in the Light of the Specification

The invention which is required to be particularly and distinctly defined in the claims is, of course, that which the patent statute requires to be set forth in a written description in the specification. It is thus entirely reasonable and necessary, as the Supreme Court said in *White* v. *Dunbar*, to resort to the specification for the purpose of better understanding the meaning of the claim. The Rules of the Patent Office recognize that the claims are the legal definitions of the inventions which are to be described and explained in the specification, and that the two should have a clear correspondence with each other. The rules of the Patent Office (present Rule 75) long have provided that terms and phrases used in the claims must find clear support or antecedent basis in the description so that the meaning of the terms in the claims may be ascertainable by reference to the description. It is the frequent failure to observe this obviously salutory rule which gives rise to a very large proportion of the difference of opinion over the scope and meaning of claims which end in litigation.

Since the patentee is one utilizing the patent statute and gaining something under it, and since he has both the duty and opportunity to prepare his specification and claims in terms which accord with the statutory requirements, it is fair and equitable authority that language of doubtful meaning will be construed most strongly against him, as is done in the case of contracts generally. *Hookless Fastener Co.* v. *G. E. Prentice Mfg. Co.*, 68 F.2d 848, CA 2 1934.

The patent claims are to be read in the light of the specification, *Aero Spark Plug Co.* v. *B. G. Corp.*, 130 F.2d 290, CA 2 1942, and are to be construed as one skilled in the art would do from a reading of the entire patent. *Standard Duplicating Mach. Co.* v. *American Business Corp.*, 174 F.2d 101, CA 1 1949.

The patent statute at 35 U.S.C. Section 112 does not require that the specification describe every possible embodiment of the invention, but only that it set forth the best way contemplated by the inventor for carrying it out. The specific disclosure of the invention in the specification is thus made only by way of illustration; the claims need not be construed as confined to the exact disclosure in the specification. *Grant Paper Box Co.* v. *Russell Box Co.*, 154 F.2d 729,

CA 1 1946. As a matter of fact, the claims are rarely so limited as to cover only the exact embodiment shown in the specification.

The claims still must stand on their own terms and scope although the specification may explain and clarify them, and by the same token they may not be enlarged in their scope by any reference made to the specification. *Hutzler Bros. Co.* v. *Sales Affiliates*, 164 F.2d 260, CA 4 1947. It has been held that the claims must be limited as closely as possible to that which the patentee has discovered as demonstrated by the disclosure he has made in the specification. *Kendall Co.* v. *Tetley Tea Co.*, 89 F.Supp. 897, DC Mass 1950. This decision indicates that the claims should, as required by the statute, be construed as drawn to the invention described in the specification, and nothing beyond that.

The patentee may be his own lexicographer and also his own grammarian. *Chicago Steel Foundry Co.* v. *Burnside Steel Foundry Co.*, 132 F.2d 812, CA 7 1943. This means that the patentee may define his own words in any way he likes as he uses them to describe his invention, and the usage which he makes clear will be the accepted definition in the interpretation of the claims, rather than that shown in the dictionary or elsewhere, should there be a difference. *Stuart Oxygen Co.* v. *Josephian*, 162 F.2d 857, CA 9 1947. On the other hand, words used in the patent will be given their ordinary sense, as in dictionaries and scientific works, unless the patentee makes it clear in the patent that he is using them in a different sense. *Universal Oil Products Co.* v. *Globe Oil & Refining Co.*, 137 F.2d 3, CA 7 1943.

Should grammatical construction become important to patent interpretation, it too will be determined by common usage unless the patentee or some technical idiom of the art requires a different interpretation. *Radio Corp. of America* v. *Philco Corp.*, 201 F. Supp. 135, DC EPa 1961.

If a word has two or more ordinary and accustomed meanings, the patentee must make clear what definition he ascribes to the word. *Universal Oil Products* v. *Globe Oil & Refining Co.*, 40 F.Supp. 575, DC NIll 1941. As we have seen above in the *Hookless Fastener* case (68 F.2d 848), where

the patentee does not make clear which of two equally possible meanings he intended in the patent, the document will be construed most strongly against him in any dispute where the meaning becomes important.

Ambiguity in the claim language may be cleared up by reference to the specification and drawings if the matter may thereby be resolved. *Goodman* v. *Paul E. Hawkinson Co.*, 120 F.2d 167, CA 9 1941. But where there is in fact no ambiguity in the claims, the claim language being clearly drawn but too broadly to avoid the prior art, the language will not arbitrarily be restricted to the specification disclosure in order to save the claims from a holding of invalidity. *Wayne* v. *Humble Oil & Refining Co.*, 175 F.2d 230, CA 5 1949.

Doctrine of Claim Differentiation

While the foregoing authorities on patent interpretation accord generally with primary rules of interpretation of contracts, at the same time they emphasize the patent statute as a factor in construction of the document. The rule of interpretation under the present heading is a further example of a fundamental of contract interpretation, namely, to interpret every part with reference to the whole.

Where there are several claims in the patent, as there are in most of the patents issued, the courts have applied a doctrine of interpretation which utilizes a presumption that the claims were issued to cover different inventions. This doctrine is that a limitation not actually present in one claim should not be implied in it if the limitation specifically appears in another claim. *Electric Machinery Mfg. Co.* v. *General Electric Co.*, 88 F.2d 11, CA 2 1937.

It seems reasonable to apply this rule on the basis that two of the several claims of a patent were not intended to cover the identical invention in the identical scope. However, the rule should not be applied beyond this rationalization. Thus, a series of claims in a patent frequently is inserted to cover an invention in definitions of varying degrees of breadth or scope. The same combination of elements or process steps comprise the invention of each claim. In this case there is no reason to conclude that, because the wording of successive claims differs, a different combination of elements or process steps is covered by the several claims.

It is also held that the doctrine of claim differentiation cannot be applied where the result would be to interpret a claim to cover an invention broader than that actually disclosed in the patent. *Burroughs Adding Mach. Co.* v. *Felt & Tarrant Mfg. Co.*, 243 Fed. 861, CA 7 1917. Thus, the rule of claim differentiation is subservient to the statutory requirement that the specification shall contain a written description of the invention, and the claims should distinctly contain that subject matter.

The Drawings as an Aid in Patent Interpretation

When the patent document includes drawings, they may be referred to in about the same way as the specification, in interpretation of claims, specification and ambiguities. *The Wyott Mfg. Co., Inc.* v. *Doran Coffee Roasting Co., Inc.*, 160 F.Supp. 644, DC Colo 1958; *Suczek* v. *General Motors Corp.*, 132 F.2d 371, CA 6 1942. The drawings do not, any more than the specification, purport to show every embodiment of the invention, but only one or more preferred embodiments. Thus, the claims are not limited to the specific disclosure of the drawings. *Cameron Iron Works* v. *Stekoll*, 242 F.2d 17, CA 5 1957. It is the claims, not the drawings, that define the invention. *Binks Mfg. Co.* v. *Ransburg Electro-Coating Corp.*, 281 F.2d 252, CA 7 1960.

File Wrapper Estoppel

See article under that title.

The Inventor's Own Appraisal of His Invention

Statements of the inventor other than those to the Patent Office in obtaining of the patent in question, are sometimes utilized in the interpretation of the patent. This is justified as also applying the patentee's own appraisal or interpretation to his invention. Where the inventor acknowledged in his British patent that certain subject matter was old, the court used it as an admission in construing his U.S. patent. *Jungersen* v. *Baden*, 166 F.2d 807, CA 2 1948.

In *Wood* v. *Peerless Motor Car Corp.*, 75 F.2d 554, CA 6 1935, the interpretation of certain claims of a patent for purposes of infringement was made to depend in part at least upon the action of the patentee in disclaiming another claim.

And, in *Timken Detroit Axle Co.* v. *Cleveland Steel Prod. Corp.*, 148 F.2d 267, CA 6 1945, *cert. denied* 326 U.S. 725, 1945, the court when evaluating validity of the patent over the prior art, utilized a memorandum which the patentee had prepared at one time with respect to the application for the patent as well as arguments entered by the patentee during an interference in the Patent Office, in arriving at the gist of the invention covered by the patent.

Obvious Mistake

Where it is perfectly clear from a reading of the patent that there has been an inadvertent error in the claim language, the claim will be read as if the mistake had not been made. Thus, where the diameter of a hole in the structure was included in a restricted claim of the patent, the specification showed the correct diameter, and the diameter stated in the claim was an inadvertent error, the claims would be read in its corrected form. *Celotex Corp.* v. *Armstrong Cork Co.*, 53 F.Supp. 317, DC EPa 1944.

The Role of the Expert in the Interpretation of Patents

The interpretation of the patent claims is wholly within the province of the court. Patent specifications usually are written in the technical terms of the art to which they pertain, and an expert may be helpful to the court in explaining the terms in colloquial language so that the judge may fully understand the subject matter. *Kohn* v. *Eimer*, 265 Fed. 900, CA 2 1920. But, it is for the trial court to say whether or not it needs the assistance of an expert, *National Transformer Corp.* v. *France Mfg. Co.*, 215 F.2d 343, CA 6 1954, and such testimony may be wholly disregarded by the court if it chooses to do so. *Thabet Mfg. Co.* v. *Kool Vent Metal Awning Corp.*, 226 F.2d 207, CA 6 1955.

Doctrine of Equivalents

The doctrine of equivalents may be mentioned under the heading of patent interpretation because, like language interpretation, it is concerned with the issue of infringement—whether or not the claim covers or dominates a particular device or process. Unlike claim language interpretation, however, the doctrine does not decide infringement upon the basis of what the language does in fact say and cover. Rather, it is a rule of law which begins with the proposition that the claim language does not in fact describe the allegedly infringing subject matter, but holds that the claim nevertheless shall dominate that subject matter. The test by which the rule is applied is whether "two devices do the same work in substantially the same way, and accomplish substantially the same result." *Graver Tank & Mfg. Co.* v. *Linde Air Products Co.*, 339 U.S. 605, 1950. If the two devices are comparable in this way, then infringement is found even though the claims admittedly do not define the accused device or process.

The rule of equivalents is held to be subservient, however, to the doctrine of file wrapper estoppel. Thus, where a patentee clearly has been required to give up subject matter during prosecution in the Patent Office, he may not recapture it later by recourse to the doctrine of equivalents. *Exhibit Supply Co.* v. *Ace Patents Corp.*, 315 U.S. 126, 1942. However, where allowed claims were voluntarily cancelled in the Patent Office, the patentee can cover their subject matter by the doctrine of equivalents. *Musher Foundation* v. *Alba Trading Co.*, 150 F.2d 885, CA 2 1945, *cert. denied* 326 U.S. 770 1945.

The doctrine of equivalents is difficult to square with the statutory requirement that the claims shall particularly point out the invention and with the equally authoritative Supreme Court ruling that this requirement is to be enforced for the protection of the public. A rationalization for its existence may be that, once it is clearly enunciated and uniformly followed, it is as much a known and controlling law of patents as is the patent statute and other pronouncements of the Supreme Court. Whatever its justification, a difficulty with the doctrine is that what is in fact an equivalent in any particular case cannot be standardized, and the doctrine adds indefiniteness to the question of claim definition and infringement which, in the normal case, is already troublesomely unclear.

Doctrine of "Different Animal"

Another rule of law which is not claim language interpretation but which has the same effect is that which might be called the doctrine of the "different animal." This is the rule enunciated by the Supreme Court in *Westinghouse* v. *Boyden Power-Brake Co.*, 170 U.S. 537, 1898, holding that even though the words of a patent claim do in fact clearly describe an accused subject matter, still the invention of the patent and the accused subject matter are so completely different—really entirely different animals— that infringement will not be found.

The basis for this arbitrary departure from the claim language as the measure of the invention is equitable, as in the case of equivalents. The court refuses to hold as an infringement that which it feels was covered only by accident, either through the use of excessively broad claim language by the patentee, or the failure of language itself to be capable of adequately concise definition. The situation in which this doctrine is adopted seems to be where, although the claims are very broadly drawn, suitable prior art to meet and invalidate them has not been adduced, and the court apparently hesitates to hold them invalid as not sufficiently distinct. Instead, it is arbitrarily held that the patented invention and the accused device are quite different.

In the case of this rule of law there is no question of failure, in administering the patent claim to enforce the patent enabling legislation, to protect the public. Rather, it is the patent owner who is aggrieved by lack of definiteness in the law, for he has distinctly claimed the invention to the satisfaction of the Patent Office, nothing in the way of prior art or otherwise is adduced to invalidate his claim, and still he is denied the scope which is admittedly embraced by his claim language. This doctrine, too, introduces lack of certainty into the subject of claim interpretation and enforcement and can only be defended on the ground that, once announced, it qualifies as one of the known rules of the system.

Minor Canons of Patent Construction

The foregoing canons of interpretation and construction provide an approach which should solve most problems of patent claim enforcement. There are numerous other rules stated in the cases which classify under Judge Woodbury's discussion in the *Doble Engineering* case, supra, as minor canons of construction. Some of those which are encountered fairly frequently are discussed below.

The Patent Construed to Secure the Invention to the Patentee. In *Turrill* v. *M. S. & N.I.R.R. Co.*, 68 U.S. 491, 17 L.Ed. 668, 1864, the Supreme Court stated the view that a patent should receive a liberal construction and should be interpreted to uphold rather than destroy the right of the inventor. It was also held that if a claim is fairly susceptible of two constructions, interpretation should be adopted which will secure to the patentee his actual invention rather than to adopt a construction fatal to the grant.

In *Apex Electrical Mfg. Co.* v. *Maytag Co.*, 122 F.2d 182, CA 7 1941, *cert. denied* 314 U.S. 687, 1941, it was held that where language of the claim creates an ambiguity, if the question is equally balanced, then it is the duty of a court to construe the language to preserve the patent and not to destroy it. The issue eliciting this statement of principle by the court was validity of the claim over the prior art. And, in *Cissell* v. *Cleaners Specialties*, 81 F.Supp. 71, DC WMo 1948, the court stated the same canon on construction in a case where the issue

was whether the claims were specific enough to be held valid. The case of *Strong-Scott Mfg. Co.* v. *Weller*, 112 F.2d 389, CA 8 1940, goes so far as to say that if ambiguity were created by differences between the structure as shown in the drawings and that described in the specification and claims, the ambiguity should be resolved in favor of the patentee. Here again, the issue was validity of the patent.

The principle of resolving ambiguities in favor of the patentee seems doubtful in view of the requirement for definition of the invention by the patent statute, and in view of the general canon of document construction that language is to be construed most strongly against the user. It might be thought reasonable to resolve ambiguities in favor of the patentee where the issue is validity, in order to uphold the document and give it the intended legal effect. But, it would never seem reasonable to resolve ambiguities in favor of the patentee where the issue is infringement, if the Supreme Court's repeated pronouncement is to be followed, that the purpose and policy of the patent statute is that the public must be clearly advised of the scope of the patent monopoly.

Any such double standard of interpretation, however, would violate, in spirit at least, the holding that claims should be construed in the same way on the two issues of validity and infringement. Thus, a claim should not be construed in a limited way to avoid prior art and preserve validity, and at the same time in a broad way to cover an accused infringement. *Leeds & Northrup Co.* v. *Doble Engineering Co.*, 159 F.2d 644, CA 1 1947.

Reading Elements into a Claim. It has been held that claims which fail to recite an element necessary to make the claimed combination complete and operative is a void claim. *Daniel Greene Felt Shoe Co.* v. *Dolgeville Felt Shoe Co.*, 210 Fed. 164, CA 2 1913. But on occasion courts will read an element shown in the specification into a claim in order to avoid a holding of invalidity, either because the claim otherwise would be (1) incomplete, *Pacific States Electric Co.* v. *Wright*, 277 Fed. 756, CA 9 1922, or (2) too broad and thus met by the prior art, *Western States Mach. Co. v. S. S. Hepworth Co.*, 147 F.2d 345, CA 2 1945.

This practice seems unsupportable if the patentee is to be required distinctly to claim his invention. It is not particularly harmful in practice, however, since the courts seem invariably to hold that the claims, thus narrowed by reading an element into them, do not cover the accused infringement.

Claims Read in View of the Prior Art. It is said that the claims should be read in view of the prior art. This seems usually to mean that the claims should be construed sufficiently narrowly to preserve their validity over the art. *Penmac Corp. v. Esterbrook Steel Pen Mfg. Co.*, 108 F.2d 695, CA 2 1940. This principle is particularly easy to apply where the claim is of the "means" type, permitting the court to mold the claim more or less specifically to the disclosure and at the same time avoid the prior art. These cases are also examples of those considered under the heading immediately above; the usual result, when an element from the specification is read into the claim in order to avoid the prior art, is the ultimate upholding of validity but non-infringement. *Thompson v. Westinghouse Electric & Mfg. Co.*, 116 F.2d 422, CA 2 1940; *National Development Co. v. Lawson-Porter Shoe Mach. Corp.*, 129 F.2d 255, CA 1 1942.

Effect of Commercial Success. It is held that where a patent is a commercial and practical success, it is entitled to a liberal construction; *Smith v. Snow*, 294 U.S. 1, 1935. On the other hand, where a patent has not gone into commercial use, it should not be expanded beyond what it clearly covers. *Hartford A & B Assoc. v. Puett Elec. Start. Gate Corp.*, 182 F.2d 608, CA 4 1950. In *American Laundry Mach. Co. v. Strike*, 103 F.2d 453, CA 10 1939, it is held that a paper patent in a crowded field should not be aided by a broad interpretation of the claims.

This type of holding departs entirely from any fixed standard as to what a patent claim does or does not cover, predicating claim interpretation and scope of monopoly upon the extent of commercial usage—a logical non-sequitur.

Range of Equivalents. The breadth of the range of equivalents which will be granted in the enforcement of a patent claim is said to be directly proportional to the degree of the invention. Where the patent is a modest improvement in a crowded field, the pressure of the art restricts the effective range of the patent to the four corners of the claims. *Rubinstein v. Silex Co.*, 73 F.Supp. 336, DC SNY 1947. A pioneer patent, on the other hand, will be entitled to a broad range of equivalents. *Hildreth v. Mastoras*, 257 U.S. 27, 1921. The doctrine of equivalents is applicable even to a paper patent, but the claims must be narrowly construed. *Tweedale v. Sunbeam Corp.*, 145 F.Supp. 97, DC EMich 1956.

This, again, is a rule of patent claim enforcement which is of very uncertain application, for no objective determination of the degree of novelty in an invention has ever been developed.

Construction of the Specification as a Teaching of the Invention

As seen earlier, the specification has two statutory functions. The first is that it is to contain a "written description" of the invention which is particularly pointed out at the end of the document in the claims. Therefore one looks first to the specification for the necessary information to interpret the claims. The rules of interpretation applicable to the specification for this purpose have been considered above.

The second function of the specification is to teach the public how to use the invention. The question of interpretation of the specification in this aspect is simply whether the disclosure is sufficient to teach the public how to practice and enjoy the invention. There is relatively less dispute, and hence less litigation and decision authority on the interpretation of the specification, than on its sufficiency as a teaching.

The term person "skilled in the art," to whom the disclosure must be intelligible, does not mean a person who surpasses his fellows in the particular arts or sciences in which they are skilled, but refers merely to men who have ordinary or fair skill in the particular line to which the invention refers. *Application of Beach*, 152 F.2d 981, CCPA 1946.

The disclosure does not have to be detailed as to every last fact. It does not matter that something is left to the skill of the person reading and applying the information. That limited experimentation may still be necessary does not render the specification insufficient. *Minerals Separation* v. *Hyde*, 242 U.S. 261, 1916.

The disclosure is sufficient if it enables the man skilled in the art to practice the invention without the necessity of further experiment which is itself of an inventive nature. *National Latex Products Co.* v. *Sun Rubber Co.*, 274 F.2d 224, CA 6 1959. The court will interpret the specification in the way which both contesting parties do, even though the court itself might read it otherwise. *Dailey* v. *Lipman, Wolfe & Co.*, 88 F.2d 362, CA 9 1937.

Statements in the specification purportedly describing the invention but susceptible to different constructions do not meet the statutory requirement for a "written description" of the invention in "full, clear, concise, and exact terms." *Thompson* v. *Dicke*, 110 F.2d 98, CCPA 1940. The rule in case of ambiguity in the specification thus follows the rule with respect to contracts and which applies to the claims as well, i.e., reading language of doubtful meaning most strongly against the user, who is the patentee. *Hookless Fastener Co.* v. *G. E. Prentice Mfg. Co.*, 68 F.2d 848, CA 2 1934.

Cross-references: *Claim Drafting, Claims ... External Standards, File Wrapper Estoppel, Infringement.*

CLAIMS—WORDS AND PHRASES— EXTERIOR STANDARDS

Leonard Flank

Words and Phrases

This first section deals primarily with words shown by experience to be particularly significant to the patent attorney. They are not those recognizably difficult, for which we turn to the "Glossary" or a dictionary. They are mostly the ostensibly simple terms that we use almost daily and think we understand fully.

In general, terms that broaden the interpretation may dim the clearness of distinction from close art.

"About" and "Approximately." "The use of the qualifying words 'about' and 'approximately' with reference to the moisture content and temperature would seem to be a signal that some range of equivalents is claimed." *Raybestos-Manhattan, Inc.* v. *Texton, Inc.*, 122 USPQ 302, CA 1 1959.

On the other hand, a "molecular formula as qualified by 'approximate' is meaningless as an item of identification of the claimed compound." Such a formula, the Court adds, in effect shows only the kinds of atoms present and variability of their proportions by whole numbers. *Purdue Research Foundation* v. *Watson, Comr. Pats.*, 122 USPQ 445, DC DistCol 1958; aff'd 265 F.2d 107.

There has been informal discussion at times as to whether "about" or "approximately," preceding a range which may or may not have been stretched already to the limit, may make a claim indefinite. This question was at issue in *Ex parte King.* Claims recited "an average molecular weight of from about 70,000 to about 200,000" or a component in amount "equal to from about 65 per cent to 80 per cent by weight...." The Board refused to uphold the rejection of these claims as indefinite, saying:

"The propriety of the use of the expression 'about' in claims to permit 'of some tolerance' is established by long practice in the Patent Office." 82 USPQ 450, PO BdApp 1948.

(To avoid appearing to recommend a wording, the author questions the need grammatically of "from" in stating the ranges. The wording "about 70,000–200,000" seems better.)

"At Least." The statement "at least" part of the germanium is divalent is not indefinite since an extremely small quantity of the divalent element will suffice for the activation desired. *Ex parte Butler*, 116 USPQ 532, PO BdApp 1957.

"Comprising," "Consisting Essentially of," "Consisting of." A group of Primary Examiners has defined these terms for uniformity of usage in the Patent Office. They regard

(1) "Comprising" and "comprising essen-

tially" as leaving the claim open for the inclusion of unspecified ingredients, even in major amounts;

(2) "Consisting of" as closing the claim to the inclusion of materials other than those recited except for impurities ordinarily associated therewith, and

(3) Recital of "essentially" along with "consisting of" as rendering the claim open only for ingredients which do not materially affect the basic and novel characteristics of the composition. Cf. *Ex parte Davis and Tuukkanen*, 80 USPQ 448, PO BdApp 1949.

"A solution 'containing' specified ingredient does not cease to contain it merely because other ingredients are added." *Loukomsky* v. *Gerlich*, 121 USPQ 213, CCPA 1959.

The above definition of "comprising" is not necessarily applicable to patent contracts. See *Deering Milliken Research Corp.* v. *Leesona Corp.*, 133 USPQ 24, DC ENY 1962.

"Improvement." The applicant's calling his invention merely an "improvement disposes of the argument that this was a pioneer invention." *Kenyon* v. *Automatic Instrument Co.*, 88 USPQ 301, CA 6 1961. This decision is difficult to understand in view of the statement in the standard form of Petition for Patent "for the improvement in . . ." Rules, Form 1. What the inventor calls his contribution should, it seems, be less controlling than what he has done and the public acceptance of his invention.

"May." The word "may" carries with it also the meaning "may not." "Can" is stronger and at times a good replacement.

Judge Learned Hand once wrote:

"At the outset I note the use of the word 'may' which recurs throughout the specification substantially to the entire exclusion of the indicative mood. . . . Such equivocation will not avail to amplify what was described only as a possibility. . . . I turn now to the claims . . . the antlike persistence of solicitors has overcome . . . the patience of the Examiners." *Lyon* v. *Boh*, F.2d 48, 49, 1924.

A case bearing on the point is the following: An applicant stated "In practice, I may desire . . . a . . . screen." The expression was held to show that he did not regard the screen as essential and led to rejection of the application. *Smith* v. *Kingsland, Comr. Pats.*, 82 USPQ 353, CA DC 1949.

"May," it should be added, is much used, no doubt properly but never in claims.

"One," "A," "An." Unless otherwise qualified, these terms are read as though preceded by "at least." In interpreting a claim reciting "flow through one of said inlet orifices," the court noted that the claim "does not say 'only one' and so it must be construed as meaning 'at least one.' " *In re Teague*, 117 USPQ 284, CCPA 1958.

"Preferably." "Preferably" suggests that the component, part or condition to which the word relates is optional, not essential, or not necessarily effective in changing the result to a degree constituting a difference of kind. In the absence of supporting data "preferably" may destroy the criticality of the feature. See *In re Ringdal*, 139 USPG 486, 1964. For that reason, it is sometimes desirable and possible to replace the word, for example, by change of "and preferably at a temperature of . . ." to "and, for best results [or best yield, increased water resistance of the product, or rate of curing without discoloration, etc.], at a temperature of . . ."

"Substantially." "Substantially eliminated" as applied to a film was held to be "sufficiently accurate" when the slight portion of the film that remained is negligible. *Ex parte Mallory*, 52 USPQ 297, PO BdApp 1941.

In a mechanical case, the court said:

"The use of the word 'substantially' here is not happy; it is vague and indefinite [in reciting that the hitch point for a tractor to a plow was 'substantially' 59% of a certain distance] . . . And Todd [the inventor] testified that he would rather not state whether 40% or 60% or 75% or 80% would be within the patent. Certainly the use of this word in patent claims has not met with favor at the hands of the federal courts [citing cases]." *Todd* v. *Sears Roebuck and Co.*, 103 USPQ 285, CA 4 1954.

Claims calling for the use of powdered aluminum "substantially" free of waxy coatings were rejected because "it is impossible to tell what degree of purity shall be used." *Ex parte Gardner*, 64 USPQ 137, PO BdApp 1944.

While the term is generally acceptable, the recommended procedure, when "substantially" is to be used in the claims, is to illustrate its meaning in the specification.

"Think," "Believe," "Probably." Such words as "I (or we) think" or "believe" and "probably," seldom if ever, have a place in the disclosure. They make no positive showing. They only call attention to uncertainty, for which they may at times be useful.

Some use the word "consider" as a substitute carrying some degree of conviction, the extent of which would depend on the nature of the remaining parts of the disclosure.

At times the word "attribute" may be used to advantage as a positive manner of saying what may be in some doubt. Thus, "We attribute the surprising stability of the product on exposure to high temperatures, in part at least, to the acceptance of hydrogen chloride by our stabilizer as the hydrogen chloride develops at elevated temperatures."

The following is in part a condensation of an article by the author in 44 JPOS 472-485, 1962.

Exterior Standards or Extrinsic Limitations

Problems arise in claiming those inventions whose elements of structure do not per se point out the invention. These are the claims that rely upon an external standard in recital of the invention.

Clauses such as "so shaped and proportioned as to," "constructed and arranged to," "of sufficient thickness to," and comparative adjectives sometimes employed to recite inventions may be called extrinsic limitations.

Regarding such exterior standard, Judge Arthur M. Smith, 41 JPOS 5, 1959, when an attorney, said:

"...'substantially pure' can mean almost any purity, and 'commercially uniform' is not an absolute characteristic but is a characteristic which is relative to the demands of the buyers of carbon black. Each of the terms in the claims in suit were what I would call relative terms which, in and of themselves, have no definite meaning. Such terms are inherently indefinite because their scope can-not be determined without reference to some *exterior standard*." (Emphasis added.)

The Supreme Court held the claims in suit invalid because of their indefiniteness. *United Carbon Company* v. *Binney and Smith Company*, 317 U.S. 228, 1942.

A good example of an extraneous limitation occurs in claim 1 of Patent 3,085,019 issued to Kueneman *et al.*, in 1963. It reads:

"1. In a process of preparing a mass of precooked potatoes including the steps of [the process is here recited], the product being reconstitutable to said palatable product by the use of an aqueous liquid at a temperature of between about 185 and 212° F, and which product has a *blue value* [iodine test for soluble starch] *below that of an otherwise similar product not subjected to the hereinbefore recited conditions of temperature and relative humidity*." (Emphasis added.)

Such comparison with an extraneous product is acceptable perhaps as a last resort and when not made at the exact point of novelty. But the inventor will usually seek a numerical range for the values recited. He will thus avoid possible controversy as to what is the conventional value.

Guides in Use of Extrinsic Limitations. The first test is whether the extrinsic limitation is used at the point of novelty. The Board of Appeals has said:

"It is not so much what words are used that make a claim good or bad, but what is defined thereby; claims fail to clearly and distinctly point out the invention as required where 'constructed and arranged,' is used at the exact point of novelty." *Ex parte Utz,* 77 USPQ 513, 1948.

Where the inventor's device operates differently from the prior art devices, extrinsic limitations can be properly employed to differentiate broadly over the art. *Ex parte Koch,* PO BdApp, 40 USPQ 672, 1939 held allowable claims calling for "operatively engaging" and "shaped to conform" and pointed out that the terminology used in the claim will be construed in connection with the specification.

The Specification and Extrinsic Limitations. The use of comparative terminology so broad as to be indefinite is to be avoided. As noted in *Angle* v. *Richardson,* 38 USPQ

451, CA 9 1938, "hard tough metal" rendered the claim indefinite because it was not a scientific or trade expression with definite meaning.

However, the Supreme Court held "hard rubber" and "vulcanite" as definite since they fall within a definite range by definition and usage in the trade. *Goodyear Dental Vulcanite Co.* v. *Davis*, 102 U.S. 222, 1954.

A reasonable test of whether extrinsic limitations are proper in a claim is whether the claim defines the invention so adequately as to enable a person of ordinary skill in the art to erect a working model. *Ex parte Wolfskill*, PO BdApp, 97 USPQ 176, 1953.

The general rule, now accepted, is that patentees are allowed great latitude in terminology and their language will be accorded the meaning intended if it can be ascertained from the context. *Smith* v. *Goodyear Dental Vulcanite Co.*, 93 U.S. 486.

Certainty of Description. "Adapted to" and "thereby" clauses are not void for lack of certain description when read with the specifications and drawings which are clear. *Temco Electric Motor Co.* v. *Apco Mfg. Co.*, 275 U.S. 319, 1927. "Heat resistant" is a definite term for use in claim. *Mershon* v. *O'Neil*, 14 USPQ 194, DC NY 1932.

"Hair's breadth" used to measure distance is definite where the specification is clear as to its meaning and application to the invention. *Schick Dry Shaver* v. *R. H. Macy & Co.*, 45 USPQ 454, CA 2 1940.

"Metallic hub," if used to mean any kind of metal structure inside the hub, is not a sufficient disclosure and is too broad. *Texas Rubber* v. *D. & M. Mach. Wks.*, 28 USPQ 182, CA 5 1936.

"A layer of metal wool of sufficient thickness and so positioned" is indefinite where specification fails to define what "thickness" is used or how the metal wool should be positioned in order to accomplish the purpose for which it was intended. *Scheyer* v. *Chicago Motocoil Corp.*, 48 USPQ 618, CA 7 1941.

Indefinite Terms. "Extremely thin." *Schick* v. *General Shaver Corp.*, 44 USPQ 422, DC Conn 1940.

"Low specific gravity." *Slayter* v. *Stebbins-Anderson*, 44 USPQ 231, DC Md 1940.

"Abrupt Bends." *Oxford Varnish Corp.* v. *G.M.C.*, 38 USPQ 42, CA 6 1939; "High, free, independent, low." *Hastings Mfg. Co* v. *Automatic Parts Corp.*, 49 USPQ 547, CA 6 1941; "Relatively long unrefrigerated pipe." *In re Newton & Phelps*, 44 USPQ 458, CCPA 1940; "Clay-like material." *Ex parte Russell et al.*, 43 USPQ 473, PO BdApp 1939; "To effect a material rise in temperature unless restrained." *Standard Oil Co.* v. *Tidewater*, 69 USPQ 41, CA 3 1946; "Having substantially the properties of animal glue." *Holland Furniture Co.* v. *Perkins Glue Co.*, 277 U.S. 245, 1928; 1928 C.D. 266.

Definite Terms. "Substantial space" where relative measurements are given but the space is hardly capable of mathematical determination. *Robertson* v. *Klaver*, 38 USPQ 203, CA 8 1941;

"Guides associated with sides of the diaphragm," not indefinite, merely broad and allowable in absence of prior art. *Ex parte Hendrickson*, 42 USPQ 635, PO BdApp 1939; "High boiling petroleum" with specific definition in the specification. *Ex parte Glover and Heaven*, 42 USPQ 636, PO BdApp 1939; "Lipophillic and hydrophillic." *Ex parte Harris*, 45 USPQ 623, PO BdApp 1940; "Consistently higher yields" where same definition and terminology were accepted in cited prior arts patent. *Ex parte Legg and Stiles*, 47 USPQ 398, PO BdApp 1940;

"Into playing position" fairly means that record is moved on rotary disc although there is nothing in claim to indicate what is meant by "playing position." *Ex parte Freborg*, 49 USPQ 213, PO BdApp 1941; "Long, slender bag," "longer than width of man's palm," "long enough to project at both ends of grasping hand" in description of paper bag. *O.K. Jelks & Son* v. *Tom Huston Peanut Co.*, 10 USPQ 121, CA 5 1931.

Attitude of Courts. The courts exhibit a tendency to weigh commercial success in the determination of validity of extrinsic limitations. *Jelks & Son*, supra; *Diamond Rubber Co.* v. *Consolidated Rubber*, 220 U.S. 428, 1911.

Commercial success is not controlling but is additive to other evidence and, in doubtful cases involving extrinsic limitations, may be the determining factor.

When the trade follows the teaching and produces the claimed invention, this fact assists in showing clarity of the disclosure.

The use of extrinsic limitations is not only valid but, in many instances, desirable. *Ex parte Monson*, PO BdApp, 101 USPQ 472, 1954. Where extrinsic limitations are used and the claim is to be held allowable (by the Patent Office) or valid (by the courts), the following conditions should be met:

(1) The invention operates differently from the prior art. The limitation used (2) is fully explained in the specification or has limits imposed by definition or trade usage, (3) does not extend the claim beyond the scope of the invention, (4) is not at the exact point of novelty although there is growing authority to the contrary as expressed in *Richardson* v. *Bryan,* 110 USPQ 424, DC STex 1956, (5) the comparative words used in the claim are fully explained in the specifications as to use, disposition and physical environment and (6) the invention cannot be claimed properly without resort to extrinsic limitations or an exterior standard.

Cross-references: *Claim Drafting, Claim Interpretation.*

CLEAN HANDS DOCTRINE
AS APPLIED TO PATENT LITIGATION
J. Philip Anderegg

General Principles

A patentee will be denied relief against an infringer or contributory infringer, or against a licensee in a suit for royalties, if he has been guilty of inequitable or unconscionable conduct in obtaining or using his patent.

The phrase "misuse of patents" usually refers to an important class of cases in which the patentee is denied relief because he has employed his patent in an effort to "extend the monopoly of his patent," i.e., an effort to monopolize the market for a product or material whose unlicensed manufacture, use or sale does not constitute infringement of the patent. An example of such misuse is the grant of a license under a patent on condition that the licensee purchase from the licensor unpatented materials needed by the licensee to practice the patent. While these "misuse" cases have been described as originating in the "unclean hands" rule, they represent an extension thereof in that, in contrast to the requirement of the "unclean hands" rule as such, the misuse cases deny relief to the patentee even though his "misuse" has not injured or otherwise affected the infringer and even though the patent is valid, was properly obtained, and is plainly infringed. The misuse cases are treated in a separate article herein.

The "clean hands doctrine," for which paradoxically another name is the "unclean hands doctrine," is a principle of law having wide applicability. It is not limited to cases involving patents. It has its origin in the maxim of equity jurisprudence: "He who comes into equity must come with clean hands."

It meant originally that a litigant seeking from the court the particular kind of relief denominated equitable must come into court with "clean hands." With the disappearance of equity as a separately administered system of law, the maxim is no longer restricted in its application to equitable causes of action such as suits for specific performance of a contract to sell land. The maxim means in substance that if, in respect of the subject matter of the action as it affects the equitable relations of the parties, a suitor has been guilty of unconscionable, unlawful, fraudulent or inequitable conduct, his hands are said to be "unclean," and the court will deny him the relief which he requests even though he shows himself to be otherwise entitled to it. While the maxim may be and often is invoked by the party against whom relief is sought, the court may apply it of its own motion, on learning of the inequitable behavior of the suitor seeking relief. The court thus denies relief to a suitor guilty of unclean hands, not because of the relative merits of the parties to the action, but in order to protect its own integrity and to avoid being employed as the instrument for effectuating a scheme of which the suitor's unconscionable conduct forms a part.

Examples of the Clean Hands Doctrine as Applied to Patent Cases

An example of the clean hands doctrine as applied to a patent case is *Keystone Driller Co.* v. *General Excavator Co.*, 290 U.S. 240, 19 USPQ 228, 1933. In that case, the court denied to a plaintiff damages for past infringement and an injunction against future infringement of a number of patents, all covering parts of a ditching machine. The plaintiff had advanced, in support of the validity of one of the patents in suit, a judgment obtained by him in a prior infringement action, and it was shown that in obtaining that prior judgment, the plaintiff had purchased the suppression of evidence tending to show that the patent was invalid.

The doctrine has been applied also to bar relief to a patentee on facts much less dramatic than these. In *Seismograph Service Corp.* v. *Offshore Raydist*, 263 F.2d 5, 119 USPQ 146, 119 USPQ 452, 120 USPQ 244, CA 5 1958, the patentee had learned of another's development, opened negotiations looking to a joint venture for its exploitation, then decided not to proceed with the joint venture, but continued the negotiations in order to perfect his own patent applications on that development and to purchase for himself exclusive rights in a prior dominating patent. The Court held him guilty of unclean hands and said that the patent issuing on such an application was unenforceable against the originator of the development.

Misconduct of the patentee in obtaining his patent may make it impossible for him to obtain judgment against infringers or to recover in a suit for royalties. If he obtains the patent on misrepresentations of fact concerning either the teachings of the prior art or concerning the time and manner in which he made the invention, his patent may be invalid, even if his misrepresentations were innocent. It may simply be that on the true facts the patent is invalid as a matter of law, irrespective of the motives or good faith of the applicant. See *Corona Cord Tire Co.* v. *Dovan Chemical Corp.*, 276 U.S. 358, 1928. Innocent misrepresentations, however, is not a case of unclean hands, whether the patent is held valid or invalid.

If, on the other hand, the patentee's misrepresentations are known by him to be such and if it is clearly so proven, they may render the patent unenforceable on the ground that the patentee's hands are unclean, whether or not the misrepresentations induced the Patent Office to issue the patent. Thus in *Hazel-Atlas Glass Co.* v. *Hartford-Empire Co.*, 322 U.S. 238, 61 USPQ 241, 1944, a patentee was denied relief in an infringement action on a showing that the patentee had obtained the publication in a magazine of a spurious article praising the invention, by a labor leader purportedly hostile to the use of labor-saving machinery of the type to which the invention related, and had introduced this article into the Patent Office record in support of the application. (Same case below, 137 Fed. 764, 766.)

Again, in *Precision Instrument Mfg. Co.* v. *Automotive Maintenance Machinery Co.*, 324 U.S. 806, 65 USPQ 133, 1945, suits for infringement of patents and for breach of contract were dismissed where it was found that the plaintiff had brought one of those patents to issue when it knew or had good reason to believe that the applicant was not the inventor, and that he had, in an interference, given perjured testimony concerning the time and fact of his invention.

Clear and definite proof is required to establish fraud on the part of a patentee in soliciting his patent. *Armour & Co.* v. *Wilson & Co.*, 274 F.2d 143, 124 USPQ 115, CA 7 1960. Nevertheless, great care and candor should be used in preparing affidavits used in the prosecution of a patent application in order to overcome a prior art reference by showing completion of the claimed invention prior to the effective date of the reference. See *Edward Valves, Inc.* v. *Cameron Iron Works, Inc.*, 286 F.2d 933, 128 USPQ 307, CA 5 1961.

The same care is required in affidavits presenting the results of tests intended to show the inadequacy of a prior art reference on which the Patent Office relies in rejecting claims. This is brought out by the action of the Federal Trade Commission dated August 8, 1963 in *Matter of American Cyanamid Company et al.*, F.T.C. Docket No. 7211. Here the F.T.C takes the position that it is an unfair method of competition, in violation of Section 5 of the Federal Trade Commission Act, to obtain a patent with the aid of material false and misleading representations of fact to the Patent Office in the prosecution of the application for that patent and to assert rights under the patent so obtained, in conjunction with a business operated in interstate commerce. The F.T.C. further takes the position that one who, in an attempt to obtain a patent, makes material false statements concerning the patentability of the subject matter of the application and who thereafter accepts a royalty-bearing license under the patent when issued to a competitor, engages in an illegal attempt to share in the monopoly defined by the patent.

The representations to the Patent Office, here of both the successful and unsuccessful applicants (corporate assignees of the inventors), were essentially to the effect that tetracycline was not inherently produced in the production of chlortetracycline according to the teachings of a prior art patent. The F.T.C. found that it was so inherently produced. The Examiner had told the applicant who ultimately obtained the patent that he would allow claims to tetracycline if the applicant could show by affidavit that tetracycline was not produced in any perceptible or identifiable amount recoverable from the culture media described in a prior art patent on chlortetracycline. Responsive to this indication of the Examiner, the applicant made tests which were negative as to the coproduction of tetracycline in the prior art media, but the F.T.C. found these tests, and the affidavits reporting them to the Patent Office, to be materially false and misleading in that:

(a) The Patent Office was not advised that research personnel of the applicant corporation had previously detected the presence of tetracycline, in concentrations up to about 5 per cent, allegedly recoverable in cultures prepared according to certain examples of the prior art patent other than the one suggested by the Examiner as probably the likeliest to show such co-production.

(b) The cultures forming the basis of the negative conclusion in the affidavits were atypically low in antibiotic potency but were presented in the affidavits as being "representative" of the cultures of the prior art patent.

(c) The Patent Office was not informed that one of the cultures forming the basis of the negative conclusion had been processed for a substantial time outside the optimum pH range of alkalinity-acidity.

(d) The method employed for recovery or isolation of tetracycline from the culture broth was not the best available.

The unsuccessful applicant was found to have denied to the Patent Office, in response to the Examiner's questions, concomitant production of tetracycline in the production of chlortetracycline, whereas the unsuccessful applicant had information in its files that there was such coproduction.

Undoubtedly, the last word has not been heard on this subject and perhaps not on this case. There have, however, been suggestions that even when the applicant is not answering questions of the Examiner, the applicant is under obligation to bring to the attention of the Patent Office pertinent prior art of which he knows, and his failure to do so will render his patent unenforceable. See *Triumph Hosiery Mills, Inc.* v. *Alamance Industries, Inc.*, 191 F. Supp. 652, 128 USPQ 471, DC MD NC 1961, aff. on other grounds 299 F.2d 793, 132 USPQ 414, CA 4 1962; *Admiral Corp.* v. *Zenith Radio Corp.*, 296 F.2d 708, 131 USPQ 456, CA 10 1961; and *U.S.* v. *Standard Electric Time Co.*, 155 F. Supp. 949, 116 USPQ 14, DC Mass. 1957, appeal dismissed by agreement, 254 F.2d 598, 116 USPQ 422, CA 1 1958. In the *Triumph* case, the trial court explicitly held the patent unenforceable on this ground, although valid and infringed. The Court of Appeals, while not rejecting the rule of law thus applied by the trial court, found that there had been no adequate proof of concealment but held the patent invalid for lack of invention.

Cross-references: *Antitrust Law and Patents, Fraud in Patent Matters, Misuse.*

CLIENTS. See ATTORNEYS' PRIVILEGED RELATION

CONFIDENTIAL INFORMATION. See SECRET INFORMATION—EMPLOYEES' RESPONSIBILITIES

CONSTRUCTION OF CLAIMS AND PATENTS. See CLAIM INTERPRETATION

CONSULTANT AND PATENTS

E. Emmet Reid

[This article is written from the viewpoint of the academic consultant. While he was not faced with all the economic exigencies of the private consultant, much of the philosophy resulting from consultations with major companies seems applicable to consultants generally. Ed.]

Attitude Towards Patents

The consultant seeks by discussion to help the research worker attain his objective. Often something turns up which appears to be new and to have commercial value. An application for patent results. In some cases the consultant contributes materially to the invention and his name appears on the patent application. I have always preferred that my suggestions, if I had any, be merged with the thinking of the chemist without any reference being made to me. The chemist who has worked long on a problem should not be called on, it seems, to divide the credit for its solution with a consultant who drops in only once a month.

Consultant as Inventor

There are cases, however, in which the consultant's name should be on the patent. After a conference on the need of a softener for nitrocellulose in lacquer films, thinking dibutyl phthalate a likely material, I made an ounce of it and took it to Wilmington on my next trip. It lay around for about a month. The tests then showed it to be good. Then came further tests and a patent application in my name, as it should have been. This was the first of the plasticizers and the prototype for later ones. Millions of pounds of it have been and are being manufactured.

While consultant for an oil company, I thought of a reaction based on experiences with a compound involved in previous work in no way related to the oil company and told them about it. One of their chemists found that the reaction did work. They applied for a patent in the two names, again quite properly.

As a part of my consultations, totaling 114 years for 4 companies, over a 40-year period, I worked five days a week in the duPont laboratory for a number of summers; patents that resulted from such work properly bore my name but were assigned.

Student Research and Patents

I have known at least one professor who had his students assign in advance all rights to discoveries the students might make. This policy I do not recommend.

At the university I never put a student on a problem in the hope of receiving any financial reward nor undertook a commercial project with a student. There were several reasons.

First, my interest was always on the scientific side and it is impossible, at least for me, to direct work at two diverse objectives; I cannot aim a rifle at two targets without missing one and usually both of them.

Second, I could not face and answer the question of division with a student. Candidates for the Ph.D. degree were supposed to do some of the thinking. Their dissertation problems were devised to delve into the unknown and bring forth something unanticipated. Who would own it? I was neither a partner nor an employer of the student. My services were a part of what he paid for as tuition.

Third, as I made observations which might have had commercial value, none of them appeared at the time worth risking money and effort in patenting. In two cases at least I was mistaken. During the first World War I suggested chloroacetophenone as tear gas. It is believed to be the basis still of all the tear gas used in the whole world. It was old as a compound. I had made it according to literature directions several years before as an intermediate for a synthesis and noted with some dismay its lachrimatory power. When the question of lachrimators came up, I made a new sample and took it to Washington. It proved to be equal to the best known lachrimators and unique among them in being storable in iron. In this case no students were involved. There was no question of division of inventorship. I did not file upon it although at that time a new use of an old compound without modification but with unobvious results was patentable.

In another instance, I was interested in high-speed stirring as an aid to chemical reaction. It had been found that, when ethylene (in place of ethyl chloride formerly used) was passed into benzene containing aluminum chloride, some ethylbenzene formed. I put a student on this as an example of a process in which high-speed stirring might be helpful. With a speed of 10,000 rpm of a special stirrer with small holes through which ethylene issued, we had rapid ethylation of the benzene. Several other students then determined the best conditions and still others studied the chemistry of the products. I never dreamed of any commercial value for ethylbenzene! If I had, who would have been the inventor? Would I have owned 10 per cent or 50 per cent, all or none of it? I just went on publishing articles on the ethylation of benzene. I explained that high-speed stirring with introduction of microscopic bubbles of the gas aided the absorption. Now there are dozens of patents on the ethylation of benzene. I have no interest in any of them.

Patent Rights of Consultant

When employed as a consultant for any long period, I have been asked to assign all inventions and have never declined. Even if engaged for only a day or so I have been willing to sign such an agreement whenever suggested.

As a result, I have never received a cent for my patent rights. The closest to direct compensation involved the publication of a book on aluminum chloride, the catalyst in the ethylation process, by a large firm for which I have not consulted. They had used and are still using the process to an enormous extent. They requested the use of my photograph. Later they gave me a complimentary copy of the book!

As I make my monthly visits to the research laboratories of large clients, go from room to room, sit down and discuss problems with the research men, I recognize and let them realize that I know less about their work than they do and attempt only to direct their thoughts into new channels where they suggest what may be occurring to me at the same time. As I do this my relations must be such that the discussions can proceed free of fear that the men will tell too much to me or I to them. The integrity of the consultant and his motives must be beyond question.

In those instances in which I have had no obligation to any client, I have overlooked discoveries that if patented should have been sources of great income. My policy in such cases is not recommended to others, particularly not to those who lack an underwriting of their living by a generous university or client and not to those who have large salaries and overhead to meet monthly in commercial laboratories.

Cross-references: *Consulting Laboratories' Patent Policies, Expert Testimony, Inventor's Psychology.*

CONSULTING LABORATORIES' PATENT POLICIES

Frank N. Houghton

This article relates to the policies of the consulting laboratory in regard to the acquisition, ownership, exploitation and disposal of rights in inventions.

Agreements with Inventors

First to be considered is the procedure by which the laboratory acquires the patent rights with which we are here concerned. These rights are ordinarily based on inventions made by the laboratory staff members, but they may in some instances be acquired from outside inventors.

Inventions Made by Staff Members. Agreements with staff members must be such as to give the laboratory complete freedom in the handling and disposal of all inventions which they may make. This enables the laboratory to assign to its clients inventions and patent rights thereto, in accordance with its agreements with those clients. It also makes it possible for the laboratory to acquire inventions not connected with work currently under way for clients, but which the laboratory may exploit in any of several ways.

A suitable form of agreement with staff members is as follows:

(Date)

IN CONSIDERATION of my employment by (Laboratory) , I agree to communicate to the President of said Corporation and such other officers or representatives as he may from time to time designate, all inventions, discoveries, or improvements (whether or not patentable) which I may make either solely or jointly with others at any time during the term of my employment. Under the direction of said Corporation, I agree to do whatever is necessary to take out patents on such inventions, discoveries, or improvements in all or any countries and agree to assign the same, and all patents and applications relating to them, to said Corporation, as and when requested before or after leaving its employ, it being understood that the necessary costs of making such assignments and procuring such patents shall be paid by said Corporation.

I recognize that by reason of my employment I will be engaged in, or have contact with or knowledge of, developments, research projects, manufacturing or trade secrets, or business confidences of said Corporation, its clients and other persons. Accordingly, I agree to hold confidential both during and after my said employment all such matters relating to said employment over and above the ordinary skill of my profession, the disclosure of which might prejudicially affect the business or interests of such persons.

Witness my hand and seal.

Signature_____(seal)

Witness_____

This agreement should be signed by every employee of the laboratory. Although most inventions will come from the professional staff, they may on occasion come from nonprofessional personnel. The likelihood of this of course depends to some extent upon the nature and scope of the laboratory's work. This agreement is limited in time to the duration of the staff member's employment by the laboratory. It does not extend beyond his termination date, as any such extension would impair or even preclude his ability to work for any other employer for the duration of the extension, due to the breadth of the commitment. The agreement does, however, apply to every invention made during employment, regardless of subject matter or on whose time it was made. The minds of the more inventive-minded staff members do not stop working at 5 o'clock.

Inventions Acquired from Outside Sources. The laboratory may be in a position to exploit inventions through the licensing, sale, or other disposal of patent rights. These inventions may originate with its own staff, or be acquired from outside sources. Chief among such sources are independent inventors who bring their ideas to the laboratory for exploitation. These ideas may be in a rather embryonic state, or they may have been worked out on at least bench-scale and have been covered by patent applications or issued patents.

The precise form of agreement between the laboratory and the inventor will depend upon many things. It may, for example, be in the form of a license from the inventor to the laboratory, with prescribed division of royalties obtained from sublicensing. It may be an outright assignment, rather than a license, depending upon tax considerations. Or it may be an agency agreement. If no patent applications have yet been filed by the inventor, there should be appropriate provisions in regard to disclosure of confidential information. Failure to make such provisions can lead to embarrassment or injustice to the inventor or the laboratory. More seriously, it can also lead to trouble between the inventor and another client when the laboratory is already working on the same confidential subject. See *Secret Information.*

Client-Laboratory-Inventor Relationships

Since the consulting laboratory's work is primarily for clients, one might assume that all inventions resulting from the work of the laboratory, and the corresponding patent rights, would be assigned in full to the clients for whom the work was done. Although this is indeed ordinarily the case, there are many situations where it is not. This is usually a consequence of the fact that inventive individuals are not always working 100 per cent on cases for clients. When not so working, they may make inventions on matters quite unrelated to any client activities. The time not spent on client work should not be idle, however. It is a duty of laboratory management to provide projects on interesting subjects to occupy a portion of the time of some of the staff members. The idea here is not merely to fill idle time, but rather and more particularly to broaden the experience and capabilities of the organization and its staff in new and promising fields of investigation. It is in fact advantageous for the laboratory to set up specific projects, with budgets, and to assign individuals part or full time to those projects. In some instances also the laboratory may be directly engaged in other activities such as the manufacture of specialized equipment or products. These non-client activities are also valuable in improving the professional status and morale of the staff members engaged in them.

It follows that these non-client activities will frequently result in inventions and patents owned outright by the laboratory. These patents may be used as a basis for licensing or to protect any manufacturing activities in which the laboratory is engaged. They may also be used as a basis for entering into professional service work with prospective clients.

These subjects will be discussed in more detail in the following sections.

Classes of Situations

The laboratory's patent policies and procedures may conveniently be considered under four headings:
  (1) Complete ownership by client.
  (2) Complete ownership by laboratory.
  (3) Joint interest by laboratory and client.
  (4) Other situations.

Although it may at first be thought that all patents growing out of the work of the laboratory staff will come under either 1 or 2, there are occasional situations which cannot be so characterized. While the frequency of such other situations may vary greatly from one laboratory to another, they are nevertheless ones which usually require considerable care in working out and administering, in order to avoid conflicts and to assure a fair division of interests between the parties concerned.

These four situations will be discussed separately, in each case outlining the nature of the situation, typical clauses in agreements with clients or other parties, and patent soliciting procedure.

Complete Ownership by Client. The usual professional service work of a laboratory includes the assignment of inventions and patent rights to the client for whom the work is done. While this may appear to require merely a simple statement of purpose, some care should be taken in the wording of the work agreement in order to avoid conflicts of interest, especially between clients.

Defining the Client's Interests. The inventions to which a client is entitled are determined broadly by factors of time, relevance and performance. These factors may be referred to in terms of inventions made respectively *during* the work, *pertaining to* the work, and *resulting from* the work for any particular client. The use of any one of these terms alone can lead to a conflict of interests. Obviously, the laboratory cannot broadly include in its grant to the client all inventions made "during" the work for that client, because "during" is merely a time limitation and has no limitations at all as to client or subject matter. The term "resulting from," on the other hand, has no definite time limitation; neither does the term "pertaining to." In either instance inventions might be made as a result of or pertaining to the work long after the work had been completed. These conclusions may raise the question of the client's right to and interest in inventions which "result from" work done for him, but which occur at a considerably later date than the conclusion of that work. The handling of such inventions is in part a question of ethics of the laboratory and it does indeed happen at times that such inventions are promptly turned over to the client in question. However, it must also be realized that the laboratory cannot be precluded indefinitely from working further on any given subject after its work for a client in that field has ceased. With such a bar, a laboratory would in due time find itself precluded from most lines of endeavor. While this is obviously not in the laboratory's interest, neither is it in the interest of the promotion of the national welfare or that of the clients themselves.

Contract Provisions. The exact wording of any provision regarding patent rights of the client will depend to some extent on the requirements of the particular situation and the wording customarily used by both the laboratory and the client. One suitable form of wording, which takes care of the problems of both time and relevance and which does not need to use all three of the expressions "resulting from," "during," and "pertaining to" is as follows. This is addressed to the client by the laboratory.

"If inventions are made in the performance of this work, and pertaining to it, we will, at your request and expense, take whatever steps are requested by the patent attorney of your selection toward securing patent protection and will assign our right, title, and interest in any patents granted on such inventions to you immediately after issue."

Attorneys. As thus provided, patents are solicited by attorneys selected by the client. These may be the client's own attorneys or may be an independent firm selected by the client. In some instances, the client or its attorneys may suggest that the patent soliciting be handled by attorneys in the neighborhood of the laboratory, as where a large amount of data must be processed and where the client's attorneys are at a considerable distance from the laboratory. The laboratory's patent personnel, if it has any, cooperates with the attorneys in whatever way the latter and the client may request. This often consists of preparation of so-called "patent memoranda" which provide a discussion of the prior art, a description of the invention concerned and the ways in which

the inventor considers the invention to be an improvement over the prior art.

Laboratory Patent Personnel. Whether the laboratory patent personnel may handle patent soliciting on inventions made solely for a client and owned by the client was first decided in the negative in *In re Battelle Memorial Institute,* 127 USPQ 289, 1960 and *Battelle Memorial Institute* v. *Green et al.,* 127 USPQ 547. There was no question of the qualification of the attorneys employed or their admission to the practice of law in the state of Ohio. One issue was the alleged practice by the *corporation* for its sponsors. These cases were heard in the Court of Common Pleas, Franklin County, Ohio. On appeal, however, the judgments were set aside. 133 USPQ 49, 1962. See *Attorneys and Agents.*

Just after the latest Battelle decision, the Florida Supreme Court, in *State of Florida ex rel. The Florida Bar* v. *Sperry* handed down a decision (133 USPQ 157, 1962) holding, among other things, that the preparation and prosecution of patent applications is the practice of law and is consequently forbidden to others than members of the Florida Bar.

The Sperry case was taken to the Supreme Court of the United States (*Sperry* v. *State of Florida, ex rel. The Florida Bar,* 1937 USPQ 578), which vacated the order of the Florida court. Although the U.S. Supreme Court upheld the petitioner's right to practice, it pointed out that because of the breadth of the injunction issued in the case, "we are not called upon to determine what functions are reasonably within the scope of the practice authorized by the Patent Office."

While the Florida decision settles some of the broader issues we may expect subsequent litigation to define "what functions are reasonably within the scope" of authorized practice.

For a further discussion of this case, see *Attorneys and Agents.*

Complete Ownership by Laboratory. In instances were an invention is made by laboratory staff members on matters having nothing to do with work for clients, there is obviously no need for any agreements. Such inventions and the resulting patent rights may be licensed to other parties or may be used in the laboratory's own manufacturing activities.

Licensing by the Laboratory. Although a discussion of licensing activities is outside the scope of this article, it should be pointed out here that the laboratory, if it has any significant number of worthwhile inventions in this category, would do well to set up a division (which may need only one individual) to attend specifically to promoting and consummating license arrangements with prospective licensees, and policing the resulting licenses.

Attorneys. The soliciting of patents on inventions coming under this category will be carried out by the laboratory's patent personnel except in cases where that personnel is insufficient or lacks experience in some specialized fields. It is then appropriate to call in outside attorneys. Such contact with outside attorneys also has the advantage of helping the small patent department in keeping informed on developments in the patent field.

Joint Interest by Client and Laboratory. *Industrial Clients.* Situations occasionally occur in which a patentable invention may be promoted jointly by the client and the laboratory. Sometimes the work for a client, as it progresses, shows indications of involving much broader principles than those in the particular work being carried out for the client. It is of course the client's option how far this work shall be pursued. In many instances the client desires to extend the scope of the undertaking and thus obtain all the benefits from any resulting inventions in the broadened field. In other instances, however, the client may not wish to make any further expenditures on the subject outside his immediate field of interest, but may be willing that such work be done by others. Those others may be a different client or may be the laboratory itself. In either case the work is undertaken only with the full knowledge of the respective interests of all the parties. It is also customary for the first client to retain some form of interest in proceeds from licensing in the broader area outside his field. There is no standard form for making such arrangement; this depends upon the relative efforts by the various par-

ties in the whole development. Matters to consider here include the relative amounts of time and money expended for laboratory work and licensing activities by all the parties concerned.

Patent solicitation and ownership of any resulting patents are likewise not subject to any hard and fast rules, but will depend upon the relative interests of the parties concerned. It may, for example, be most advantageous for the laboratory to have title to the patent and to issue appropriate licenses to the clients concerned as well as to third parties. Details as to field of agreement, royalty rates, etc. will be subject to agreements between the parties.

Government Clients. The patent provisions of Government prime contracts range all the way from licensing to title taking. The Department of Defense generally requires the grant of a royalty-free non-exclusive irrevocable license to the Government, for Government purposes. The laboratory, as contractor, retains title and commercial rights. Other Government agencies, such as the Atomic Energy Commission and the National Aeronautics and Space Administration usually require assignment of all patent rights to them; a license back to the laboratory may be granted under some conditions. Such a license depends largely upon the policies of the agency and on the subject matter of the invention.

When the laboratory is a subcontractor, the prime contractor may seek to require that the laboratory assign to it all rights under inventions made in the performance of the subcontract. Such a requirement may well be necessary under NASA or AEC prime contracts. Under the usual DOD prime contracts, however, where the Government permits the contractor to retain commercial rights, there is rarely any reason why the subcontractor should not be granted the same privilege. However, the subcontractor generally agrees to issue royalty-free licenses to the prime contractor as well as to the Government in such instances.

These differences in regulations have now led to the enunciation of a single overall policy which endeavors to spell out the requirements and conditions in considerable detail. This policy is set forth in a Memorandum from the President dated October 10, 1963 and entitled "Government Patent Policy," 28 FR 10943; 796 OG 3. See *Government Ownership...*

Other Situations. A number of other types of situations may arise but for the purpose of this discussion a description of two will suffice. One of these is the multi-client undertaking; the other is work for clients in fields in which the laboratory already has a proprietary interest.

Multi-client studies are undertaken for members of an industry on a particular subject in which they are all interested. This work may be undertaken for a trade association of the members or for those members of a given industry who are interested in the proposed investigation. Few of these studies result in inventions, and in fact the nature of the work is usually such that inventions would not be expected. If any do arise, however, the resulting patents may be assigned to the trade association or may be owned by the laboratory with a free license to each participant and a royalty-bearing license to any other interested party, the royalties to be divided among the participants.

Another type of situation is that wherein the laboratory carries out an economic survey in a field in which the laboratory has already made a considerable number of technical developments and acquired substantial know-how, at its own expense. These constitute licensed or licensable subject matter. In order to protect the laboratory's interests and those of its licensees, such a survey may be undertaken by the laboratory under the following provisions:

"We are bringing to this study a considerable amount of background acquired by us, either at our expense or through arrangements with others involving royalty-bearing license agreements. It is therefore understood that this undertaking does not convey any patent rights to you under inventions in the general field of _____. Title to all other inventions made in the performance of this work and pertaining to it will be assigned to you at your request. The nature of this particular assignment is such that no new inventions are expected to result."

In such situations it is usually the case that the nature of the work does not contemplate making inventions. However, some provision such as the foregoing is necessary, as there is no predicting when an invention in the field under study may be made.

An especially difficult type of situation is that in which a prospective client wishes to have a new product evaluated for possible end uses. Such possible uses may, and in fact ordinarily will, fall in areas in which the laboratory already has commitments to other clients. Obviously an agreement to assign all inventions to the prospective client would be an invitation to conflict. There are various ways in which this can be resolved, other than by refusing the undertaking altogether. One type of agreement from the laboratory to the prospective client spells out the circumstances in considerable detail:

"Our presently outstanding commitments to clients customarily include the assignment to them of patent rights growing out of the work under those commitments. While we would not offer our services to you if we considered there were a significant possibility of a conflict of interest, it is conceivable that there may be overlapping areas between commitments to other clients and the undertaking proposed for you. In those rare instances where a conflict appears, we shall necessarily have to be the judges of how such patent rights shall be assigned, under the general proposition that we will assign them to you if we are free to do so in light of already existing commitments to other clients.

"Subject to the above, if inventions are made in the performance of this work, and pertaining to it, we will, at your request and expense, take whatever steps are requested by the patent attorney of your selection toward securing patent protection and will assign our right, title, and interest in any patents granted on such inventions to you immediately after issue."

The work done under these arrangements may lead to inventions of interest both to the client with whom the foregoing provision is in effect and to one or more other clients. In such an event, arrangements between clients may resolve the situation, with the laboratory continuing its work for one or more of them under mutually agreeable provisions.

Validity and Infringement Opinions

During the course of its work for clients, the laboratory may run across patents of third parties which appear to conflict with the work being undertaken. In some instances also, the client may ask the laboratory to evaluate the prior art patents from the point of view of validity or infringement.

These situations raise questions of a legal nature, which of course cannot be handled for outside parties by the laboratory. It is nevertheless the duty of the laboratory to call to the client's attention any apparently conflicting patents which the laboratory may run across during the work, with the suggestion that the client have his patent attorney review the situation. The laboratory takes the position that it is ready to cooperate with the client's attorney in such matters as reviewing the technical aspects of conflicting patents and making laboratory runs. If the client has no patent attorney available for the purpose, the laboratory may be in a position to suggest the names of reputable practitioners. The ability to do this is, incidentally, another advantage in the laboratory's keeping in touch with outside patent attorneys, and preferably in various geographical locations convenient to its clients in such areas.

Avoiding and Resolving Conflicts

In the case of any laboratory engaged in a wide variety of undertakings for many different clients, large and small, as well as the Government, the problem of avoiding conflicts between clients in regard to work being undertaken requires the most careful attention. An effective procedure for taking care of this problem is to have all agreements with clients, original as well as modifications, clear through one central office. This office, which may conveniently be known as the contracting office, keeps complete up-to-date records of all undertakings for clients as well as those carried out on the laboratory's own behalf. The latter is of course important for reasons already pointed out. The contract administrator also keeps in close personal touch with the department heads and group leaders so as to be informed as far as reasonably possible on developments under way. Since it is however a physical impossibility for him to be aware of the details of every program, the staff must be trained to keep the contract administrator informed without his being required always to take the initiative in seeking such information.

In order most effectively to use the talents of the laboratory staff it is desirable that they maintain a reasonably close touch with other members of the laboratory staff, except in areas where secrecy is imposed either by the client or by Government regulations. Likewise it frequently becomes advantageous to have staff members work for different divisions at different times depending upon the skills required for any particular project. This interchange promotes the abilities and broadens the horizons of the individuals concerned and consequently enures to the benefit of both client and laboratory.

It is true of course that a development for one client, while originally quite distinct from that for other clients, may expand to the point where a conflict appears possible. In such cases the laboratory would normally confer with the parties concerned in order to avoid conflict; but in many instances this situation may develop into one where a common ground is found to exist between two clients and both will pursue the subject as a joint endeavor. Ownership of any resulting patents will of course be as desired by these clients.

Cross-references: *Attorneys and Agents, Consultant and Patents, Expert Testimony.*

COPYRIGHTS—RELATIONSHIP TO PATENTS

Barbara A. Ringer

In considering whether the same subject matter may be protected by both copyright and patent, and similar questions, it is desirable first to present the general principles of copyright law and practice.

The exclusive rights given by law to the author or proprietor of a literary, musical, or artistic work are known collectively as a copyright. Like patents, copyrights are granted by statute for limited times to encourage and reward creative effort. However, although they are closely related in origin and purpose, and although they actually overlap in the subject matter they cover, patents and copyrights have been given widely divergent legislative and judicial treatment.

Constitutional Origins

In the United States, patents and copyrights stem from the same clause of the Constitution. Article I, section 8 empowers Congress

"...To promote the Progress of Science and useful Arts, by securing for limited Times to Authors and Inventors the exclusive Right to their respective Writings and Discoveries."

The history of the Constitutional Convention does not make clear why the two forms of protection were lumped together in this way, or why patents and copyrights were not mentioned by name. As a result, there has been a good deal of debate as to the scope and construction of the Constitutional language.

James Madison, who, with Charles Pinckney, undoubtedly framed the clause, included the following comments in No. 43 of *The Federalist:*

"The utility of this power will scarcely be questioned. The copyright of authors has been solemnly adjudged, in Great Britain, to be a right of common law. The right to useful inventions seems with equal reason to belong to the inventors. The public good fully coincides in both cases with the claims of individuals. The States cannot separately make effectual provision for either of the cases, and most of them have anticipated the decision of this point, by laws passed at the instance of Congress."

This passage implies that, although the framers recognized patents and copyrights as separate things, they considered them so closely related in nature and purpose that it was natural to deal with them together. It has been suggested that the words "patent" and "copyright" were deliberately omitted from the clause in order to broaden the grant and avoid any technical limitations then attached to the terms. Fenning, 17 Geo. L. J. 116, 1929.

Patents and Copyrights Compared

Despite their common origin and the constant confusion between them in the minds of lawyers as well as laymen, patents and copyrights are essentially different in the subject matter they cover and in the standards, scope, and duration of the protection they offer. See Buckles, "Property Rights in Creative Works," 32 JPOS 414, 1950; Wolff, "Copyright Law and Patent Law: A Comparison," 27 Iowa L. Rev. 250, 1942.

Subject Matter. The "writings" of "authors" covered by the federal copyright statutes are books, periodicals, lectures, dramas, musical compositions, maps, works of art and art reproductions, technical drawings and models, photographs, prints, and motion pictures. 17 U.S.C. Section 5, 1952.

Standards Required. In very general terms, copyrights seek to encourage the creation and dissemination of literary and artistic expression, while patents are aimed at the development of various industrial and scientific fields. Pogue, "Borderland— Where Copyright and Design Patent Meet," 52 Mich. L. Rev. 33, 36, 1953. To carry out this purpose the U.S. patent law requires that an invention meet several basic criteria and that the following be established to the satisfaction of the Patent Office before a patent is granted: originality, novelty, utility, unobviousness to the expert in the art, and, in design patents, ornamentality.

In contrast, the only standard for copyright protection is originality. This means that, if the author has originated his writing independently without copying from the work of another, he is entitled to a copyright even if a similar or identical work is already in existence. See Dworkin, "Originality in the Law of Copyright," 39 B. U. L. Rev. 526, 1959.

Procedural Requirements. The differences between the procedures necessary to secure patents and copyrights are equally striking. Silverman, "The Scope of Protection of Copyrights and Design Patents in the United States," 24 U. Pitt. L. Rev. 21, 1962. The preparation of a patent application is a complex and time-consuming task requiring technical skill and professional knowledge. Its prosecution in the Patent Office usually takes several years and may be quite expensive. The Patent Office, for its part, must give the application a rigorous examination, including a thorough and detailed search of the prior art. A patentee is given no rights until his patent is actually granted; others are free to use his invention with impunity as long as his application is still pending.

On the other hand, copyright is secured by the mere act of publishing a work with a prescribed copyright notice, e.g., "Copyright 1964 by John Author." 17 U.S.C. Section 10, 1952. Registration is, at most, a condition subsequent; copyrights are not granted by the Copyright Office, and it is possible for registration to be deferred for months or even years without affecting the copyright owner's rights. *Washingtonian Publishing Co.* v. *Pearson*, 306 U.S. 30, 1939. The procedure for copyright registration, moreover, is simple, quick, and inexpensive. Pogue, *supra*, pp. 36-38. No search is made by the Copyright Office to establish originality. At the same time, copyrights are much easier to lose than patents; publication of a work without the copyright notice will destroy protection entirely and throw the work into the public domain. *Holmes* v. *Hurst*, 174 U.S. 82, 1899.

Scope of Protection. Both patents and copyrights are monopolies in the sense that they each confer the right to exercise exclusive control over the market for a particular invention or writing. In another sense, however, the monopoly rights of a patentee are much broader than those of a copyright owner. A patent carries with it complete control over "making, using, or selling the invention throughout the United States." 35 U.S.C. Section 154, 1952. During the term of protection, the patent owner may exclude any other person from the manufacture or commercial exploitation of

his patented process or product, even if the other person has developed the same invention independently. Likewise, although the patentee acquires no rights in the general idea or concept of achieving a particular result, he is given a monopoly in the inventive method or means by which this result is accomplished.

In contrast, copyright protects only against those who, having had access to the author's particular literary, artistic, or musical expression, proceed to copy or perform it. The copyright owner has no rights against someone who, without knowledge of his work, creates a similar work independently. *Rochelle Asparagus Co.* v. *Princeville Canning Co.*, 170 F. Supp. 809, DC SIll, 1959; accord, *Fred Fisher, Inc.* v. *Dillingham*, 298 Fed. 145, DC SNY, 1924. Moreover, copyright protection extends only to the author's individual expression in the form of words, music, or art. As soon as his work is published, all of the ideas, plans, methods, systems, information, or concepts underlying the work or contained in it are dedicated to the public domain, and are free for anyone to use. *Baker* v. *Selden*, 101 U.S. 99, 1879; *Continental Casualty Co.* v. *Beardsley*, 253 F.2d 702, CA 2, cert. denied, 358 U.S. 816, 1958.

Duration of Protection. Aside from design patents, which are provided for a term of 3½, 7, or 14 years at the election of the applicant, 35 U.S.C. Section 173, 1952, the patent law provides for a single, unrenewable term of 17 years. 35 U.S.C. Section 154, 1952. Copyright, under U.S. law, lasts for a first term of 28 years and is renewable for a second term of 28 years; its maximum duration is thus 56 years. 17 U.S.C. Section 24, 1952. With certain exceptions and qualifications, ownership of the second 28-year term of copyright reverts to the author or those of his beneficiaries designated in the statute.

Judicial Treatment. One of the most pronounced contrasts between patents and copyrights arises from the distinctly different treatment accorded them by the courts. Seen generally, Fox, "Copyright and Patent Protection: A Study in Contrasts," 12 U. of Toronto L. J. 27, 1957. Despite the stringent examination made by the Patent Office before a patent is issued, the courts have found a large percentage of patents invalid on grounds of lack of novelty or inventiveness. And, despite the very limited examination made by the Copyright Office before issuing a certificate of copyright registration, the courts have generally upheld the validity of copyrights challenged for lack of originality. This liberality of treatment has been referred to by one commentator as "the copyright halo." Silverman, "The Copyright Halo: A Comparison of Judicial Standards for Copyrights and Patents," 23 U. of Pitt. L. Rev. 137, 1961.

In recent years the courts have gone rather far in upholding copyrights in works which contained "a very modest grade of art," *Bleistein* v. *Donaldson Lithographing Co.*, 188 U.S. 239, 250, 1903, or "a modicum of creative work." *Andrews* v. *Guenther Publishing Co.*, 60 F.2d 555, 557, CA 2, 1930. "No matter how poor artistically the 'author's addition, it is enough if it be his own." *Alfred Bell & Co.* v. *Catalda Fine Arts, Inc.*, 191 F.2d 99, CA 2, 1951. Part of this liberal attitude appears to derive from the reluctance of judges to act as critics and from their feeling that no great public harm results from extending limited protection to literary, artistic, and musical works of marginal value. See Herr, "The Patentee v. the Copyrightee," in 5 Copyright Law Symposium (ASCAP) 185, 1954. The imposition of extremely high standards in patent cases may derive from the opposite feeling—that, as a matter of public policy, monopoly over the development of a particular field should be permitted only if the contributions of the inventor have been highly creative and significant. See Michel, "The Standard of Invention and the U.S. Supreme Court," 33 JPOS 297, 1951.

This dichotomy in judicial treatment has attracted a great deal of attention and has been widely criticized. Aside from questions of logic and good jurisprudence, however, the varying attitudes of the courts in copyright and patent cases can have considerable practical importance in those borderline cases where an applicant may choose between the two types of protection.

Overlapping between Patents and Copyrights

Designs. The twilight zone between the patent and copyright laws was once thought to be quite narrow and, aside from the field of ornamental designs for useful articles, there is still relatively little overlapping between the two forms of protection. See Bovard, "Copyright Protection in the Area of Scientific and Technical Works," in 5 Copyright Law Symposium (ASCAP) 68, 1954. Since the 1954 decision of the Supreme Court in *Mazer* v. *Stein*, 347 U.S. 201, however, the area of subject matter eligible for protection under either the design patent or the copyright statute has increased substantially. See Michaelson, "The Nature of the Protection of Artistic and Industrial Designs," 9 Miami L. Q. 148, 1955; Sharpe, "Copyrights and Design Patents—The Common Zone Between," 11 Clev.-Mar. L. Rev. 336, 1962.

In the years since the *Mazer* decision the courts have reinforced the Copyright Office in its practice of accepting for deposit a number of useful articles embodying designs which could also be considered works of art. See, *e.g.*, *Rushton* v. *Vitale*, 218 F.2d 434, CA 2, 1955; *Syracuse China Corp.* v. *Stanley Roberts, Inc.*, 180 F. Supp. 527, DC SNY, 1960; *Peter Pan Fabrics, Inc.* v. *Brenda Fabrics, Inc.*, 169 F. Supp. 142, DC SNY, 1959; *Trifari, Krussman & Fishel, Inc.* v. *Charel Co.*, 134 F. Supp. 551, DC SNY, 1955. Designs for textile fabrics and jewelry, in particular, are registered in large quantities. On the other hand, the Copyright Office will refuse to make registration for designs comprising the external configuration of useful articles and containing no features capable of independent existence as a work of art; designs of automobiles, refrigerators, wearing apparel, and furniture are examples of subject matter that would not be considered copyrightable. This important distinction is expressed in the Copyright Office Regulations, 37 C.F.R. Section 202.10(c) (1959), as follows:

"If the sole intrinsic function of an article is its utility, the fact that the article is unique and attractively shaped will not qualify it as a work of art. However, if the shape of a utilitarian article incorporates features, such as artistic sculpture, carving, or pictorial representation, which can be identified separately and are capable of existing independently as a work of art, such features will be eligible for registration."

Placing Copyrighted Material on Operating Mechanism.

Outside the design area, problems of the borderline between patents and copyrights arise frequently with respect to measuring or computing devices such as slide rules and wheel dials, with respect to printed matter used in the functioning of a machine, and with respect to blank forms and other works designed exclusively for recording information. Material of this sort is not considered subject to copyright. *Baker v. Selden*, 101 U.S. 99, 1879; *Brown Instrument Co.* v. *Warner*, 161 F.2d 910, CA DC, cert. denied, 332 U.S. 801, 1947; *Taylor Instrument Companies* v. *Fawley-Brost Co.*, 139 F.2d 98, CA 7, cert. denied, 321 U.S. 785, 1943; *Aldrich* v. *Remington Rand, Inc.*, 52 F. Supp. 732, DC NTex, 1942. Protection in such cases may be available to the extent that the devices or forms contain copyrightable literary or graphic material such as instructions or illustrations, but copyright would provide no exclusive rights in the device or form itself. *Continental Casualty Co.* v. *Beardsley*, 253 F.2d 702, CA 2, cert. denied, 358 U.S. 816, 1958; *Cash Dividend Check Corp.* v. *Davis*, 247 F.2d 458, CA 9, 1957; *Dorsey* v. *Old Surety Life Ins. Co.*, 98 F.2d 872, CA 10, 1938.

Drawings and Models.

One of the categories of copyrightable matter specified in the copyright statute comprises "drawings or plastic works of a scientific or technical character." 17 U.S.C. Section 5(i), 1952. Sometimes registration for a drawing or model in this category is thought to carry with it exclusive rights in the subject matter illustrated by the copyrighted work, and the same question arises with respect to registration in the other graphic and sculptural arts categories. Can the owner of copyright in a pictorial or sculptural work restrain the manufacture of industrial products embodying the design shown in his picture or model?

Copyright in drawings of cartoon characters and cemetery monuments have been held to protect the owner against the manufacture of toys or headstones based on the drawings. *Fleischer Studios, Inc.* v. *Ralph A. Freundlich, Inc.*, 73 F.2d 276, CA 2, 1934, cert. denied, 294 U.S. 717, 1935; *King Features Syndicate* v. *Fleischer*, 299 Fed. 533, CA 2, 1924; *Jones Bros. Co.* v. *Underkoffler*, 16 F. Supp. 729, DC MPa, 1936. On the other hand, the courts have held that copyright in drawings of furniture, of a dress design, or of the plans for a bridge or a house confer no exclusive rights against manufacture or construction of the articles shown. *De Silva Construction Corp.* v. *Herald*, 213 F. Supp. 184, DC SFla, 1962; *Muller* v. *Triborough Bridge Authority*, 43 F. Supp. 298, DC SNY, 1942; *Jack Adelman, Inc.* v. *Sonners & Gordon, Inc.*, 112 F. Supp. 187, DC SNY, 1934; *Lamb* v. *Grand Rapids School Furniture Co.*, 39 Fed. 474, DC WMich, 1889.

The key to reconciliation between conflicting decisions can be found in *Mazer* v. *Stein*. There the Supreme Court held that, if a copyrighted work of art retains its identity as an artistic work when embodied in a useful article, it will continue to be protected by copyright even if reproduced industrially. Thus, if a copyrighted pictorial, graphic, or sculptural work is merely used as ornamentation for a useful article, and can still be identified as a "work of art," manufacture of the article can be prevented under the statute. If, however, the copyrighted work actully portrays a useful article as such, including its utilitarian function, copyright will not protect it against manufacture of that particular useful article; statutory protection, if available at all, must be sought under the patent law.

Reproduction in Quantity.

Mazer v. *Stein*, supra, involved the protection to be accorded a copyrighted statuette which had been reproduced in quantity by its owner, a manufacturer of lighting appliances, as the base of a table lamp. The Supreme Court held that a copyrightable "work of art" continues to be protected by copyright even after it has been embodied in a useful article, and that the copyrightability of the "work of art" is not affected by its aesthetic qualities or lack of them, by the intention of the artist as to how his work is to be used, by the number of copies reproduced, or by the potential availability of a design patent.

The court in this case did not deal with the question of whether a copyright and a design patent can subsist simultaneously in the same subject matter. Although the question has never been settled, the weight of authority appears to favor requiring the applicant to elect one type of protection or the other. See, *e.g., Korzybski* v. *Underwood & Underwood, Inc.,* 36 F.2d 727, CA 2, 1929; *In re Blood,* 23 F.2d 772, CA DC, 1927. The Copyright Office Regulations provide that "... a copyright claim in a patented design or in the drawings or photographs in a patent application will not be registered after the patent has been issued." 37 C.F.R. Section 202.10(b), 1959.

CORPORATE PATENT DEPARTMENT—FUNCTION AND OPERATION

Worth Wade

When a new company has been incorporated and starts in a business involving inventions, it is advisable to obtain competent outside patent counsel from the start. In this case, the Chief Engineer or Technical Director should act as liaison to coordinate the technical activities of the company with outside counsel. As soon as the number of patent applications becomes large or the company encounters patent litigation, it is advisable to hire staff patent counsel.

In small companies having a "one-man" department, the staff patent counsel reports preferably to the President and relies upon outside patent counsel for assistance in interferences and in litigation started by or against the company.

Position of the Patent Function in the Organization

The Patent Department normally serves other departments. It is a "staff" function instead of a part of the line organization.

In medium and large corporations, the Department may report to General Management, the Technical Executive, Director of Research and Development, General Legal Counsel or the Law Department. Which position is most advantageous for a particular company will depend upon such factors as company size, type and number of products produced, amount of patent work and the nature of the company's inventions.

Patent Counsel Reporting to General Management. Reporting of the Patent Department direct to a top executive provides (a) most efficient control and effective performance of the patent activities, (b) freedom of the patent counsel or department to serve all departments such as production, sales and merchandising as well as the technical departments of the company, (c) equal status of the Patent Department with the general legal counsel or department, and (d) opportunity to render opinions objectively and participate in policy decisions independently of control by other department managers. In most cases, the Patent Department will report to an executive officer, such as the President or Executive Vice President, to whom the Director of Research will also report, and will maintain good relations with the Law Department.

Patent Counsel Reporting to Technical Executive. The second most favorable position for the patent function is that in which the patent counsel or Manager of the Patent Department reports to a Technical Executive, i.e., a vice president to whom the Director of Research and Development and the Chief Engineer also report. When the company's products are of highly technical nature, there is a favorable position for patents because patent counsel has direct contact with the technical staff, can keep constantly abreast of technical advances, and is in a position to influence company policy on new developments. There are, however, some disadvantages in having the patent function in the Technical Department; there may be a loss of objectivity in the patent opinions, due to influence of the Executive, and neglect of production, merchandising, and sales matters.

Patent Counsel Reporting to General Legal Counsel. Many companies place the Patent Department under the company's general legal counsel or Law Department in order to provide better supervision and uniformity in legal policies, decrease overlapping of legal activities of the two types of attorneys, and prevent undue influence of other departments on patent counsel, thereby promoting a more objective approach to patent decisions.

There are also disadvantages in this location. Placing patent counsel in the Law Departments tends to diminish the professional standing of the patent function. Patent counsel may not participate in all policy decisions. Some resentment may arise from the fact that general lawyers make decisions while lacking patent experience. The greatest disadvantage, however, lies in reducing the patent counsel often to the position of rendering intradepartmental decisions without sufficient contact with the technical personnel for advancing original ideas. It should be understood that corporate patent counsel has a very different role to play than outside patent counsel. The corporate patent counsel is required not only to advise what cannot be done but also to suggest *what can be done.*

Proper Use of Outside Patent Counsel. Regardless of the position of the patent function in the organization, it is advisable to retain outside patent counsel for major problems, the best being frequently the least expensive in the long run. It is not advisable for staff counsel to handle litigation on patents or trademarks; but he should be prepared to assist outside counsel in the preparation for trial by obtaining technical data and exhibits, searching and studying the prior art, and recommending and obtaining evidence of prior use. He should consult outside counsel on such complicated problems as patentability of important developments, validity of competitor's patents, infringement, and interferences of complicated or important nature.

Outside counsel should conduct any suits against the Commissioner of Patents as in the Court of Customs and Patent Appeals, answer all letters received by the management alleging infringement, and prepare, sign, and send legal notices to possible infringers.

Management should not rely upon patent counsel, however, for business decisions. After receiving the opinion of counsel, management makes the decision and assumes any calculated business risk.

Patents in a Multi-Product Company. When a company produces a number of different products and has 25 to 50 inventions per year it is advisable to have a separate Patent Department to handle patents and trademarks. One attorney should be assigned to a particular class of product so that he may become expert in its technology and terminology. Outside counsel should still be utilized as stated above. When the company has plants in widely separated locations, it is advisable to make one individual in each plant responsible for reporting patent matters and providing liaison with the Patent Department. See Chart I.

Patents in a Multi-Division Company. In an organization having a number of separate operating divisions, each making a different kind of product, a central patent department of the type shown in Chart I is desirable. The department should assign one or more attorneys to conduct the work of each of the operating divisions and in some cases locate them at the division headquarters. Even if the operating divisions are distinct subsidiary companies but wholly owned, a central patent department is best. A central department is able to formulate and maintain a uniform patent policy and police the use of patents and trademarks by the company and its subsidiaries. If necessary, the services, disbursements and a percentage of the overhead of the Patent Department can be allocated to each subsidiary.

The Patent Function with Partly Owned Subsidiaries. So many conflicts of interest may arise between the parent and jointly owned subsidiary, that it is advisable to have any major subsidiary maintain its own patent counsel or patent department. It is very important that both parents define clearly the date after which all inventions belong to the subsidiary. Otherwise very complicated problems may arise. To avoid antitrust action the parent compa-

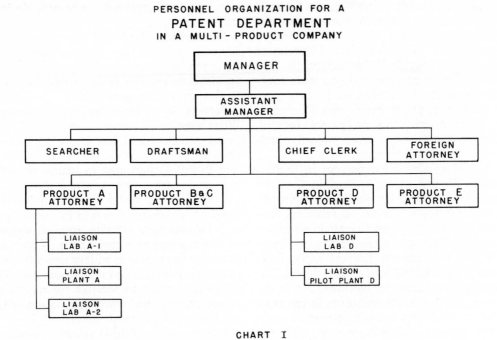

CHART I

Fɪɢ. 1. Organization chart of patent department.

nies should specifically reserve the right to compete with the subsidiary.

Corporate Patent Policies. Patent policies are the responsibility of Management, acting under resolutions of the Board and utilizing the advice of both general legal counsel and patent counsel, the policies being geared to the nature of the company's operations. For example, a patent holding company that is primarily engaged in exploiting inventions will have a policy entirely unsuited to a manufacturing company, and a raw material producer will require a different policy from that of a maker of consumer products.

Some of the more important questions of policy are: (1) Will the company take out patents on all practical inventions resulting from its research effort or only on those that relate to its specific products? (2) What is the primary object in obtaining such patents, e.g., suits for infringement or exploitation of new products? (3) Will customers be charged a royalty to operate under company patents? (4) Will the company acquire inventions from outsiders? (5) What use will be made of foreign patents? (6) Will the company exchange patent rights with

others? (7) How will patents be treated for tax purposes?

The following sections of this guide provide the basis for deciding these and other important policy questions.

Danger of Operating Without a Policy. Operating without a definite patent policy may have serious results. For example, a company owns patents relating to the use of a product. Its salesman "A" offers a royalty-free license to one customer of the product. Unknown to "A," salesman "B" requires a second customer to pay a royalty on the same product. This unequal treatment of customers may constitute a violation of the antitrust law and of the Robinson-Patman Act. To avoid this embarrassing situation, the company patent policy should be administered by a single top executive with the cooperation of staff patent counsel. But the policy should be subject to change as new law and trade situations arise.

Organization and Functions of a Patent Department

The accompanying chart shows the organization of a typical patent department for medium or large size corporations making different products. The personnel of the department comprises a manager, assistant manager, attorneys, draftsmen, searchers, secretaries, and docket and file clerks. The Manager of the Patent Department reports direct to the President and receives policy decisions and instructions through the President. To ascertain company policy on any patent matter inquiry is made to the Patent Department.

The Patent Department utilizes in its work the corporation library which furnishes searches, bibliographies, translations, photostats, and technical information whenever requested.

Functions of the Patent Liaison. The Department may locate a patent liaison representative in each of the large plants, laboratories or technical departments it serves, to initiate and promote patent activities with such groups. He will maintain a supply of invention record forms and, when requested, assist any employee in the preparation of the record, attend to its execution and provide the employee with a copy, maintain a file of such records for the Plant Manager or the Department Head, obtain additional information on any employee's invention and arrange, finally for execution of patent papers. (See *Liaison*)

Five Chief Functions of the Patent Department. The Patent Department serves the Manufacturing, Research, Engineering, Sales and Advertising Departments, in five principal manners.

Searching. The Patent Department employs qualified personnel for making searches on technical developments and patents. (See *Searching*)

Patenting. A major function of the Patent Department is to prepare and prosecute applications for Letters Patents in the United States and various foreign countries. After a novelty search has been made on an invention, a decision is made as to whether or not to file a patent application. If an application is to be filed, the invention is assigned to one of the attorneys in the Department. The attorney may request through patent liaison, or direct from the inventor when no liaison is available, a statement of alternative materials, conditions, propor-

tions, photostats of notebook pages, original sketches, blueprints or drawings. In some cases he may want models, samples, pieces of apparatus, or flow charts of processes. The attorney considers al lthis material and the novelty search in preparing the patent application. He files it in the United States and, in important cases, in foreign countries. (See *Foreign Patents*)

Licensing. Another important function of the Department is to negotiate licenses involving inventions and patent rights or to assist Management in such negotiations. No one has a monopoly on inventive talent. Rights are acquired, when desirable, to inventions and patents owned by others including competitors. Such licenses avoid patent infringement, make use of an improvement not developed by own technical staff, and may permit more efficient operation by combining a development of another with one made by the company. In some cases trading licenses with others avoids the necessity of making cash payments which would otherwise increase the cost of new products and diminish the extent of their use by the public.

Defending. Another important function of the Patent Department is aid in defense of the company's patents and also the company's operations. This aid includes collecting evidence of the infringement, locating witnesses, preparing exhibits, having tests made of prior disclosures and otherwise preparing the case for trial, usually by outside counsel, and frequently seeking a solution of the controversy by negotiation or arbitration. (See *Arbitration* and *Infringement Suits*)

Defending Commercial Operations. The Patent Department cooperates with the management and the technical departments on all new developments which may relate to a patented field. Every reasonable attempt is made to design machines and processes that avoid valid claims of others. If other parties allege infringement of their patent rights, the Patent Department makes a detailed comparison of the operation with the claims of the patent in question and searches the validity of the patent alleged to be infringed. By defending the commercial operations, the Department seeks to protect the capital invested therein, preserve continuity of operation and thus provide job security for personnel employed therein.

Other Functions. The Patent Department files applications to register trademarks used by the company in the United States and certain foreign countries. It protects the trademarks from unauthorized use, opposes the registration or use by others of marks so similar as to cause confusion among consumers of the trademarked goods, and guards against misuse of the mark by the owner, all by working in close cooperation with the Sales, Public Relations, Advertising, and Export Departments in setting up accepted standards of trademark usage.

The Patent Department files applications for patents on new designs, registers copyrights, examines technical articles intended for publication and checks publicity and advertising materials for patent and trademark notices.

Services for Other Departments. The Patent Department also performs a number of services for other departments as follows:

For the Research and Development Department. Provides searches to assist in new product development and patent clauses for research and Government contracts.

For the Production Department. Approves changes in manufacturing specifications. Defends the company against interruption for infringement suits. Prepares opinions on infringement and validity of patents owned by others.

For the Sales Department. Approves patent and trademark notices on invoices and labels. Drafts consumer licenses under patents and trademarks. Prepares special sales contracts and guarantees.

For the Public Relations Department. Approves patent and trademark notices in all publicity releases, lectures, advertising and promotion literature. Checks on compliance with FTC Labeling Act and Food & Drug rules.

For the Purchasing Department. Provides patent clauses in vendor's contracts. Drafts guarantees on patent infringement.

For the Industrial Relations Department. Administers Employee Contract on Inventions. Assists in Management Training Programs.

References

1. This article is largely a condensation of parts of Wade, Worth, "The Corporate Patent Department," Advance House, Ardmore, Pa., 1963.
2. Patent Policies and Practices of Industrial Research Institute Companies. *Research Management*, I, No. 3, 173-176, Autumn 1958.
3. Bakalar, A. B., "The Corporate Patent Department," *Chem. and Eng. News*, **29**, 4583-4586 (1951).

Cross-references: *Attorneys and Agents, Attorneys —Enhancement of Capabilities, Corporate Patent Department—Organization and Management.*

CORPORATE PATENT DEPARTMENT—ORGANIZATION AND MANAGEMENT

John R. Shipman

Certain well established propositions should be kept in mind in considering the organization and management of a corporate patent department.

No one particular type of organization or set of management techniques is suitable for all corporations. Tailoring to fit individual circumstances is required.

The organization must be kept flexible to permit change with varying circumstances, thereby avoiding frequent reorganization which can be highly disturbing.

In an initial organization or a major reorganization of a patent department, it will often be impractical to establish immediately a system which will be satisfactory over an extended period. A succession of changes over a period of time may be necessary and should be planned in advance.

Organization and management, while different things, overlap and are so interdependent that they cannot be considered separately. The first will be a factor in determining certain management techniques and the desire to employ those management procedures may dictate organizational changes.

Some principal factors in determining the best organization and appropriate management for a patent department are first discussed briefly and the discussion is followed by a short review of established types of organizations.

Factors for Consideration

A corporate patent function is a service function. Therefore, not all questions affecting patent organization and management can be settled within the patent department itself. Some are decided in collaboration with other departments and some with only incidental reference to the patent function. For example, the patent function of a laboratory will not normally be a major factor in selecting its location.

But many conditions should be considered in arriving at the patent organization and management techniques to be employed.

Corporate Patent Objectives. The patent organization or management technique or tool should be considered with reference to a clearly defined corporate patent objective. This will be the most important element in determining the types of patent service required, and the relative volume and effort needed for them. These services, in turn, will establish many of the requirements for organization and management actions to accomplish the objective.

A corporate patent objective might be (1) one of a highly protectionist nature, involving vigorous prosecution in obtaining patents and aggressive protection of those patents against infringers, (2) one in which patents, their licensing and associated responsibilities are almost a business in themselves, or (3) one seeking primarily only freedom of action to market the best products the engineers can devise, thereby requiring substantial analysis and evaluation of the corporation's own inventions and the patents of others relative to the products. There are of course many other patent objectives to be found in different corporations.

Nature of the Business. The nature of the business of the corporation will certainly enter into the development of the corporate patent objective just discussed. Regardless of the objective, however, the nature of the business will affect the kind of patent services required and the amount of effort entailed. It is important to consider whether the products are small and simple or large and complex. Are they sold or leased? Who are the customers? Who are the competitors? What are the known policies of others in the business? What scope and variety of technologies are involved? Are the arts old and crowded, highly active and fast-moving, or completely new? What persons or corporations show the most patent activity in the field?

Overall Corporate Organization. The patent organization must be arranged to provide desired patent services to various other parts of the corporate organization. Thus, the over-all corporate and patent organizations must be compatible. Nevertheless, the internal patent organization need not follow the identical pattern of the corporate.

There are many pertinent questions one must ask. Is the corporation centralized, decentralized, or intermediate? If the corporation has divisions, on what basis are they divided (product, function, geography or technology)? What degree of autonomy is given to the divisions? Where are the corporate and divisional managements located? What machinery exists for coordination between divisions?

Research and Engineering Organization. The larger part of the work of a patent department is related to the work of research and engineering. Accordingly, the nature of the R and E organization will strongly influence the choice of patent organization and management.

Many aspects of this factor are of interest, including—How is R and E organized? Is it centralized or decentralized? Where is the work performed? What is the ratio of research to development work and the magnitude of the effort? What is the invention producing record of R and E? What is the invention producing potential? What degree of patent consciousness exists in R and E? What coordination machinery exists?

General Corporate Policies. Obviously the patent department must conform to the general policies of the corporation. However, should good patent organization and management indicate the need for policy changes, variations or exceptions, the matter should certainly be discussed with higher management.

Patent Personnel

A theoretically excellent patent organization and management approach may be planned after due consideration of the corporate patent objective, the nature of the business, the corporate and R and E set-ups, and general corporate policies. In almost every case, however, the ideal plan will promptly fall apart because appropriate personnel are not immediately available to staff the plan.

A compromise is then necessary to best utilize the available individuals and come as close as possible to fulfilling the patent objective. This places on the patent management the burden of (1) providing for improvement of *existing personnel*, so that each person will steadily progress toward his maximum potential capabilities, and (2) employing new people of the right nature and potential to fill the gaps, so that a better organization can be established. Unfortunately, persons having exactly the right combination of capabilities, to fit completely an ideal organizational plan, probably never will be assembled together in a single corporation. If such should by some miracle occur, the condition would promptly disappear as the capabilities of the individuals change with passage of time.

Accordingly, the management of people becomes a most important aspect of the organization and management of a corporate patent department.

Place in Company Organization

This section extends somewhat the discussion of similar subject matter by Dr. Wade in the immediately preceding article, q.v.

As to the problem of determining where the patent department should fit into the over-all corporate organization, several arrangements which have been used with success, together with a few advantages and disadvantages of each, are given below.

Branch of the Legal Department. This has the advantage of bringing the patent department into a desirable legal atmosphere with a degree of common background among the professional people and broad similarity in type of work. It has the disadvantage that the general legal work of many corporations has little relationship to the specific work of the patent department and most general lawyers have little knowledge or understanding of patent or technical matters. As a result the patent effort may be unduly subordinated.

Part of the Engineering Organization. Effective patent work requires close contact and working relationships between the two groups. Their combination seems administratively sound. There is the disadvantage that patent decisions and judgments in the corporate interest frequently must conflict with normal engineering desires and oppose strong engineering pressures. Examples include determining the scope of the patent protection of others which the engineers must avoid or estimating the patent value of an engineering contribution. Some feel that this inherent conflict bars the proper atmosphere for objective patent decisions.

Combined with a Patent Licensing Group. This has the advantage of bringing the patent group in contact with related but broader activities more closely associated with marketing, economic and negotiation problems. Such association is a logical aid in broadening the scope and outlook of the patent attorney. It has the disadvantage that it groups persons of quite different backgrounds and approaches, thereby producing some problems in common administration and management.

Separate Group. This has the advantage of independence for the patent group. It has the disadvantage that the patent department may have difficulty in competing with larger groups for the ear of top management for a sufficient time to obtain adequate consideration of its problems.

Internal Organization

After placing of the patent department in the corporate organization, there remains the problem of the type of organization to be used within the department itself. Some of the more usual arrangements are described. Again, not all characteristics are given and those set forth are not necessarily the most important in all situations.

Centralized. This arrangement has the entire patent department at one physical location with close direct lines of authority and communication. It is used frequently in small corporations and occasionally in large ones. It has the advantage of direct control and the supervision needed for a closely knit operation. It has the disadvantage, in larger corporations where engineering is at different locations, of having the patent professional remote from the inventive sites as well as from other engineering activity and management.

Centralized with Liaison at Remote Engineering Locations. This is a variation of the centralized organization in which one or two patent professionals with liaison functions may be resident at engineering laboratories remote from a central patent group. Such an arrangement is sometimes used in large corporations where it is desired to have both a centralized patent organization and close contact with geographically separated engineering. In the effort to reduce some of the disadvantages of remoteness from engineering, it sacrifices some of the advantages of a regularly centralized patent department.

Decentralized with Complete Local Autonomy. This arrangement has the patent operation divided into a number of independent, geographically separated departments for making all patent decisions with only a very small corporate over-all monitoring staff. It is sometimes used in a large, fully decentralized corporation requiring an extensive patent operation and having several separate, decentralized, engineering laboratories. It has the advantage of quick decisions at the spot where the problems arise; close contact with engineering; and independence for each of the local patent departments, with the associated and desirable sense of responsibility. It has the disadvantages of extremely difficult coordination between geographically separated and independent departments, resulting in severely complicated patent clearance and licensing problems and difficulty in changing the allocation of manpower effort with changing circumstances. It requires more people capable of independent management than a centralized organization and more facilities such as files and libraries.

Decentralized But with Central Control and Coordination. This is a variation of the decentralized organization wherein a little of the independence of the small patent departments is sacrificed in return for some of the natural benefits of a large patent department. This arrangement provides for all decisions on regular operations to be made by the local small department with a central management establishing general policies, minimum general controls and standards, and coordination of manpower and other efforts. It is sometimes used by major, decentralized corporations with large patent departments. It has the advantage of quick local decisions with enforceable over-all coordination and standards for a more uniform corporate patent approach. It also provides close contact with engineering, as well as a very substantial degree of independence for the local patent departments, while permitting shifting of manpower effort as required. Unfortunately, coordination between patent departments, while enforceable, is still more difficult than in a centralized department, and it requires more patent managers and more facilities.

Conclusion

In evaluating any corporate patent organization and management, there should be first a review of the corporate patent objective, nature of the business, over-all corporate organization, research and engineering features, general corporate policies, and patent personnel available. The patent organization and management techniques employed should then be tailored to fit the circumstances with particular care exerted in the handling of people.

An effective and desirable approach to this whole subject is to follow the principle of the "whole patent attorney." To do so is to strive continually to give each patent attorney as much individual responsibility for a complete job as he can carry and then add a little more to cause him to grow. (See *Attorneys—Enhancement of Capabilities*)

Cross-references: *Attorneys and Agents, Corporate Patent Department—Function and Operation.*

CORPORATION PATENTS— STATISTICS OF OWNERSHIP

P. J. Federico

[This article is a condensation, with the author's approval and updating of certain information, of a report made by him in his usual scholarly and thorough manner for the Subcommittee on Patents, Trademarks, and Copyrights, Committee of the Judiciary, United States Senate. The report constitutes Study No. 3 and appears also in 39 JPOS 405-453, 1957.

Even for those of the tabulations that end with data of several years ago, the report is more significant at this time than would be a later, less carefully prepared one. The report analyzes the patent holdings by classes of corporations and concludes with a listing of the numbers of unexpired patents held by more than 600 corporations, the 394 with largest holdings being given herein. The study makes possible comparison of the patent position of a company, numerically at least, with that of others in a given industry. Ed.]

Object of Report

The main object is to present data with respect to the number and distribution of patents, unexpired on December 31, 1955, which were issued to corporations, individuals and government. The data relate primarily to the two questions:

(1) Which companies have taken out the largest numbers of unexpired patents?

(2) How many unexpired patents have been issued to a selected group of the largest corporations?

Reissues, design patents, and plant patents are omitted from this study. Reissues, which averaged 185 a year during the period involved, are revisions of previously issued patents, and their inclusion would amount to counting some patents twice. Design patents are omitted because they relate solely to the ornamental appearance of articles; they averaged 3,749 a year during the period involved. Plant patents issued for new varieties of plants averaged 67 a year. The "regular" patents considered averaged 34,494 per year during the years 1939 to 1955.

Issuance and Ownership of Patents

The present study is substantially limited to ownership by corporations at the time of issuance.

It was estimated that the number of patents acquired by corporations from indi-

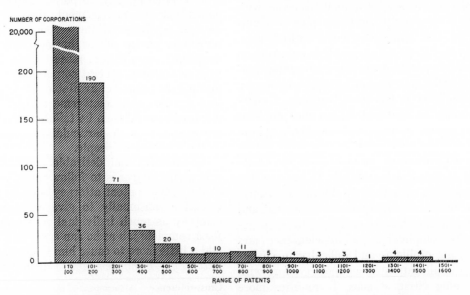

FIG. 1. Number of corporations distributed by ranges in numbers of patents.

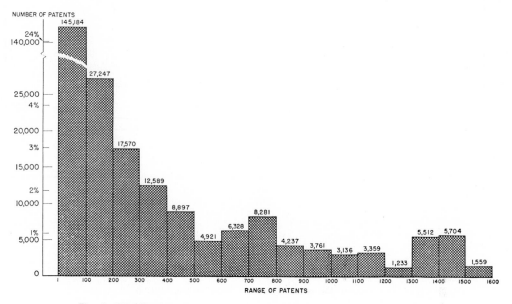

Fig. 2. Distribution of patents to corporations by groups of patents held.

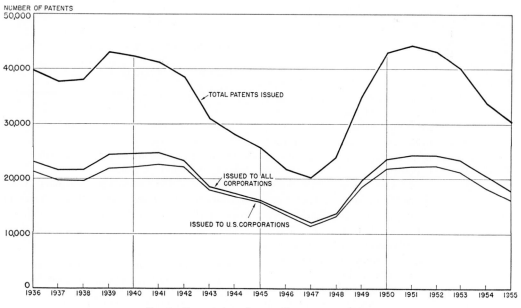

Fig. 3. Patents issued annually to corporations.

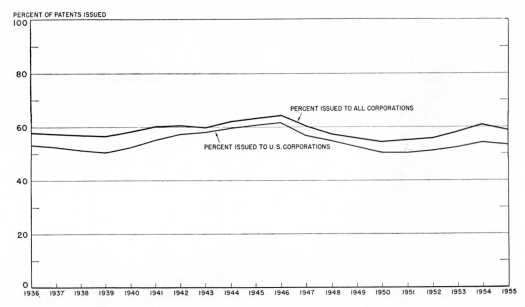

PERCENT OF PATENTS ISSUED

FIG. 4. Per cents of patents issued to corporations.

viduals after issuance was 4 per cent of the total issued during the preceding 17 years and that of this amount one-half per cent was by the selected group of 157 large corporations, 3 per cent by other United States corporations and one-half per cent by foreign corporations.

Since the term of a patent is 17 years, the number of unexpired patents at a given date would normally be the number of patents issued during the preceding 17 years. The total number of patents issued in the 17 years from January 1, 1939, to December 31, 1955 (excluding reissues and design and plant patents), is 586,391. A few patents, which were issued prior to January 1, 1939, 59 in number, were extended under the law relating to extensions of patents of World War II veterans (64 Stat. 316, 66 Stat. 321); a few of these are still unexpired, but they are ignored in the total given. Also, a few patents may have been disclaimed or dedicated by their owners and hence technically would not be in force; no allowance has been made for these. The number of patents issued during the preceding 17 years is taken as the number of unexpired patents or patents in force on December 31, 1955. This total number of patents is divided as shown in Table 1.

TABLE 1. TOTAL PATENTS ISSUED, 1939-55.

Issued to	Number of Patents	Per Cent of Total
1. United States corporations (estimate)	317,726	54.18
2. Foreign corporations (estimate)	25,399	4.33
3. Total to corporations (estimate)	343,125	58.51
4. Individuals (estimate)	234,749	40.03
5. U.S. Government	5,556	.95
6. Alien Property Custodian	2,961	.51
Total	586,391	100.00

Table 2 shows the percentage distributions between various classes of owners for each of the years of issuance of patents in the period 1950 to 1962.

Patents issued to the Alien Property Custodian amounted to 0.04, 0.01 and 0.02 per cent in the years 1950, 1951 and 1952, respectively.

List of Corporations and Numbers of Patents Issued to Them in 1939-55

The following list gives the names of 394 corporations and the number of patents (more than 100) issued to each during the

TABLE 2. DISTRIBUTION OF PATENTS—CALENDAR YEARS.

(*Annual Percentages*)

Year	Total Patents Issued	Issued to Corporations			Issued to Individuals	Issued to U.S. Govt.
		U.S.	Foreign	Total		
1950	43,040	50.61	3.85	54.46	44.05	1.45
1951	44,326	50.32	4.88	55.20	43.30	1.49
1952	43,616	51.22	4.66	55.88	42.50	1.59
1953	40,468	52.46	5.67	58.13	40.24	1.63
1954	33,809	54.18	6.81	60.99	37.06	1.95
1955	30,432	52.85	5.73	58.58	39.15	2.27
1956	46,817	54.47	7.88	62.35	35.55	2.10
1957	42,744	54.41	7.89	62.30	35.45	2.25
1958	48,330	56.11	8.75	64.86	32.50	2.64
1959	52,408	57.03	9.70	66.73	30.56	2.71
1960	47,170	59.76	9.90	69.66	27.70	2.64
1961	48,368	58.62	10.67	69.29	27.67	3.04
1962	55,691	58.47	11.45	69.92	27.78	2.30

TABLE 3. PATENTS ISSUED TO CORPORATIONS, 1955.

Number of Patents	United States Corporations		Foreign Corporations		Total to Corporations	
	Number of Corporations	Number of Patents	Number of Corporations	Number of Patents	Number of Corporations	Number of Patents
1	2,693	2,693	643	643	3,336	3,336
2	702	1,404	134	268	836	1,672
3	315	945	52	156	367	1,101
4	164	656	26	104	190	760
5	100	500	13	65	113	565
6	75	450	7	42	82	492
7	53	371	6	42	59	413
8	32	256	6	48	38	304
9	27	243	5	45	32	288
10	16	160	2	20	18	180
1 to 10	4,177	7,678	894	1,433	5,071	9,111
11 to 20	119	1,693	12	164	131	1,857
21 to 30	36	888	3	70	39	958
31 to 40	26	911	1	40	27	951
41 to 50	11	497	1	41	12	538
51 to 60	7	384	——	——	7	384
61 to 70	6	382	——	——	6	382
71 to 80	5	581	——	——	5	381
81 to 90	2	171	——	——	2	171
91 to 100	0	——	——	——	——	——
101 to 200	10	1,404	——	——	10	1,404
201 to 300	5	1,338	——	——	5	1,338
301 to 400	0	——	——	——	——	——
401 to 500	1	472	——	——	1	472
Total	4,405	16,199	911	1,748	5,316	17,947

17 years, 1939-55. The original report gave the names of other companies—subsidiaries, companies which have merged, and prior names of the same company—if any, which received patents which were added to the patents received by the main company to arrive at the total number here given. It should be understood that the figure given for any individual company does not necessarily represent the actual number of patents owned by that company at the end of 1955, and that the figures have been compiled only for the purpose of statistical summaries.

Corporations of assets above $150,000,000 are designated by (A) and those between that figure and $100,000,000 by (B).

General Electric Co. (A)	10757
American Telephone & Telegraph Co. (A)	8539
Radio Corporation of America (A)	7894
Westinghouse Electric Corp. (A)	7567
du Pont de Nemours, E. I., & Co. (A)	6338
Esso Standard Oil Co. (A)	4899
General Motors Corp. (A)	4041
Eastman Kodak Co. (A)	3784
Bendix Aviation Corp. (A)	3113
American Cyanamid Co. (A)	2872
United Shoe Machinery Corp. (B)	2461
Phillips Petroleum Co. (A)	2424
Shell Oil Co. (A)	2374
The Westinghouse Air Brake Co. (B)	2108
Sperry Rand Corp. (A)	2066
General Aniline & Film Corp. (A)	1919
The Dow Chemical Co. (A)	1884
Minneapolis-Honeywell Regulator Co. (B)	1813
Monsanto Chemical Co. (A)	7747
Socony Mobil Oil Co., Inc. (A)	1697
Universal Oil Products Co.	1665
Union Carbide and Carbon Corp. (A)	1645
B. F. Goodrich Co. (A)	1559
United States Rubber Co. (A)	1469
Hartford National Bank & Trust Co.	1419
International Business Machines Corp. (A)	1410
International Standard Electric Corp.	1406
Standard Oil Co. (Indiana) (A)	1393
International Harvester Co. (A)	1391
United States Steel Corp. (A)	1374
Celanese Corporation of America (A)	1354
Deere & Co. (A)	1233
The Texas Co. (A)	1151
Hercules Powder Co. (B)	1107
International Telephone & Telegraph Corp. (A)	1101
Chrysler Corp. (A)	1089
Imperial Chemical Industries, Ltd. (Great Britain)	1030

Associated Telephone & Telegraph Co.	1017
Curtiss-Wright Corp. (A)	964
Raytheon Manufacturing Co.	948
Allied Chemical & Dye Corp. (A)	935
Allis-Chalmers Manufacturing Co. (A)	914
Wingfoot Corp.	887
American Viscose Corp. (A)	871
American Can Co. (A)	845
United Aircraft Corp. (A)	821
Borg-Warner Corp. (A)	813
Philco Corp. (A)	788
Rohm & Haas Co.	788
Olin Mathieson Chemical Corp. (A)	779
Gulf Oil Corp. (A)	770
The Budd Co. (A)	758
Babcock & Wilcox Co. (A)	746
Joy Manufacturing Co.	745
Pittsburgh Plate Glass Co. (A)	743
The Hoover Co.	737
The Singer Manufacturing Co. (A)	722
Firestone Tire & Rubber Co. (A)	705
Merck & Company, Inc. (B)	700
American Steel Foundries	685
ACF Industries, Inc. (A)	654
Sylvania Electric Products Inc. (A)	632
Petrolite Corp.	621
Pullman Inc. (A)	613
Telefunken Gesellschaft für Drahtlose Telegraphie m. b. h. (Germany)	611
McGraw Electric Co.	607
American Optical Co.	603
Crompton & Knowles Loom Works	602
Food Machinery and Chemical Corp. (A)	588
Standard Oil Company of California (A)	578
Union Oil Company of California (A)	573
Cutler-Hammer, Inc.	565
Sun Oil Co. (A)	536
Stewart-Warner Corp.	530
Libbey-Owens-Ford Glass Co. (B)	523
Norton Co.	515
United-Carr Fastener Corp.	513
Electric & Musical Industries Ltd. (Great Britain)	491
Servel, Inv.	482
Ciba, Ltd. (Switzerland)	480
Air Reduction Co., Inc. (B)	478
Underwood Corp.	476
Ford Motor Co. (A)	467
I. G. Farbenindustrie Aktiengesellschaft (Germany)	467
W. H. Miner, Inc.	461
Thompson Products, Inc. (B)	458
Research Corp.	452
Aluminum Company of America (A)	435
Koppers Co., Inc. (A)	433
Goodman Manufacturing Co.	428
Corning Glass Works (B)	422
The National Cash Register Co. (A)	420

Avco Manufacturing Corp. (A)	416	Bell Aircraft Corp.	273
Studebaker-Packard Corp. (A)	411	Robertshaw-Fulton Controls Co.	273
Polaroid Corp.	408	Tinnerman Products, Inc.	268
General Railway Signal Co.	407	Motorola, Inc.	264
Houdaille-Hershey Corp.	405	J. R. Geigy, A. G. (Switzerland)	263
The Western Union Telegraph Co. (A)	397	Colgate-Palmolive Co. (A)	261
Armstrong Cork Co. (B)	388	Clevite Corp.	259
Sinclair Oil Corp. (A)	387	Armco Steel Corp. (A)	257
Continental Can Co., Inc. (A)	386	J. I. Case Co. (B)	256
Remington Arms Co., Inc.	383	Electrolux Corp.	256
Owens-Illinois Glass Co. (A)	379	Stromberg-Carlson Co.	255
Farnsworth Research Corp.	377	Ciba Pharmaceutical Products, Inc.	254
Owens-Corning Fiberglas Corp.	370	Nopco Chemical Co.	254
The Pure Oil Co. (A)	368	United States Gypsum Co. (A)	254
Hoffmann-LaRoche, Inc.	366	Collins Radio Co.	253
American Motors Corp. (A)	365	Thomas A. Edison, Inc.	253
Interchemical Corp.	363	The Atlantic Refining Co. (A)	251
A. O. Smith Corp. (B)	363	The Carborundum Co.	251
American Radiator & Standard Sanitary		Briggs Manufacturing Co. (B)	248
Corp. (A)	359	Walter Kidde & Co., Inc.	248
Zenith Radio Corp.	359	Northrop Aircraft Inc.	247
Hydraulic Press Manufacturing Co.	354	American Chain & Cable Co., Inc.	246
P. R. Mallory & Co., Ic.	354	Industrial Rayon Corp.	246
Jeffrey Manufacturing Co.	345	Allen B. Du Mont Laboratories, Inc.	244
General Mills, Inc. (A)	344	Illinois Tool Works	243
Ingersoll-Rand Co. (A)	344	General Dynamics (A)	242
The Upjohn Co.	344	I-T-E Circuit Breaker Co.	240
The Standard Oil Co. (Ohio) (A)	343	Industrial Patents Corp.	240
Dresser Industries, Inc.	342	Swift & Co. (A)	239
Houdry Process Corp.	342	Square D Co.	238
Johns-Manville Corp. (A)	341	Harris-Seybold Co.	237
Parke, Davis & Co. (B)	341	Jack & Heintz, Inc.	234
Commercial Solvents Corp.	340	Knapp-Monarch Co.	234
Minnesota Minning & Manufacturing Co.		The Gillette Co.	231
(A)	338	The Timken Roller Bearing Co. (B)	231
Armour & Co. (A)	330	Eli Lilly & Co. (B)	230
Trico Products Corp.	322	The Yale & Towne Manufacturing Co.	230
American Machine & Foundry Co. (B)	319	Cities Service Oil Co. (A)	229
Lockheed Aircraft Corp. (A)	312	Hemphill Co.	228
The General Tire & Rubber Co. (A)	308	The Boeing Airplane Co. (A)	225
Wagner Electric Corp.	308	R. G. Le Tourneau, Inc.	225
Toledo Scale Co.	307	Baker Oil Tools, Inc.	223
National Lead Co. (A)	301	Standard Railway Equipment Manufactur-	
Lorenz, C., Aktiengesellschaft (Germany)	300	ing Co.	220
American Brake Shoe Co.	294	Aktiengesellschaft, Brown, Boveri & Cie	
Clark Equipment Co.	289	(Switzerland)	219
Hazeltine Corp.	287	Ditto, Inc.	218
Baldwin-Lima-Hamilton Corp. (B)	285	Dow Corning Corp.	216
Combustion Engineering, Inc. (B)	284	R. Hoe & Co., Inc.	216
Eaton Manufacturing Co.	284	Republic Steel Corp. (A)	216
Scovill Manufacturing Co.	284	Atlas Powder Co.	215
Bausch & Lomb Optical Co.	283	Niles-Bennett-Pond Co.	215
Crown Cork & Seal Co., Inc.	282	North American Aviation, Inc. (A)	213
Crane Co. (A)	278	Worthington Corp. (B)	211
The Glenn L. Martin Co.	277	Draper Corp.	209
The Cincinnati Milling Machine Co.	274	The Electric Storage Battery Co.	208
Emhart Manufacturing Co.	274	Barber-Colman Co.	207
General Precision Equipment Corp.	274	Union Special Machine Co.	205

Bethlehem Steel Co. (A)	200	Power Jets (research and development), Ltd. (Great Britain)	158
Douglas Aircraft Co., Inc. (A)	200	Weston Electrical Instrument Corp.	158
The International Nickel Co., Inc.	200	General Metals Corp.	157
The Pennsylvania Salt Manufacturing Co.	199	Corn Products Refining Co. (A)	156
Siemens & Halske, Aktiengesellschaft (Germany)	199	Daniel and Florence Guggenheim Foundation	156
Sulzer Frères, Société Anonyme (Switzerland)	199	Manning, Maxwell & Moore, Inc.	155
The Diamond Match Co.	197	Sprague Electric Co.	155
Schering Corp.	197	W. R. Grace & Co. (A)	154
American Enka Corp.	196	Read Standard Corp.	154
Addressograph-Multigraph Corp.	195	Briggs & Stratton Corp.	153
Allmanna Svenska Elektriska Aktiebolaget (Sweden)	195	Sterling Drug, Inc. (B)	153
General Controls Co.	194	Chicago Pneumatic Tool Co.	152
The Ohio Brass Co.	194	Distaquaine Products, Ltd.	152
The Murray Corporation of America	193	Milwaukee Gas Specialty Co.	151
Ex-Cell-O Corp.	189	Alco Products, Inc.	150
Chain Belt Co.	186	Otis Elevator Co.	148
Winthrop Chemical Co., Inc.	186	American Seating Co.	147
Kelsey-Hayes Wheel Co.	185	Container Corporation of America	147
The Lummus Co.	185	The De Laval Separator Co.	147
Pneumatic Scale Corp., Ltd.	184	Foster Wheeler Corp.	147
Reed Roller Bit Co.	184	Rockwell Manufacturing Co.	147
The New York Air Brake Co.	183	Bemis Bros. Bag Co.	146
The Rudolph Wurlitzer Co.	183	The Ohio Crankshaft Co.	145
The Gleason Works	181	Nordberg Manufacturing Co.	145
Rockwell Spring & Axle Co. (B)	181	Sandoz, Ltd. and Sandoz, A. G. (foreign)	145
Roal McBee Corp.	181	Bendix-Westinghouse Automotive Air Brake Co.	144
The Weatherhead Co.	181	Daimler-Benz Aktiengesellschaft (Germany)	144
G. D. Searle & Co.	178	American Smelting & Refining Co. (A)	143
Burroughs Corp. (B)	177	Compagnie Générale de Télégraphie Sans Fil (France)	143
Ethyl Corp.	177	Leeds & Northrup Co.	143
Talon, Inc.	177	The Maytag Co.	143
Dorr-Oliver, Inc.	176	Sperry Products, Inc.	142
The Sherwin-Williams Co.	176	Consolidated Engineering Corp.	141
Tide Water Associated Oil Co. (A)	176	Graflex, Inc.	141
The R. K. LeBlond Machine Tool Co.	175	Mueller Co.	141
The Procter & Gamble Co. (A)	175	Scott & Williams, Inc.	141
Blaw-Knox Co.	174	Sunbeam Corp.	141
Jasco, Inc.	173	Telefonaktiebolaget L. M. Ericsson (Sweden)	141
Carrier Corp. (B)	171	Chicago Bridge & Iron Co.	140
Molins Machine Co. Ltd. (Great Britain)	171	Fairbanks, Morse & Co.	140
Hagan Corp.	170	The National Supply Co. (B)	140
Rolls-Royce Ltd. (Great Britain)	170	Autogiro Company of America	139
The United Gas Improvement Co.	169	National Malleable & Steel Castings Co.	139
Abbott Laboratories	168	Beloit Iron Works	138
International Cigar Machinery Co.	168	The Cleveland Pneumatic Tool Co.	138
National Cylinder Gas Co.	168	Courtaulds Ltd. (Great Britain)	138
The Glidden Co. (B)	167	Infilco, Inc.	138
The Garrett Corp.	165	Link-Belt Co.	138
John B. Pierce Foundation	165	Musher Foundation Inc.	138
Purdue Research Foundation	163	Penn Controls, Inc.	138
The American Laundry Machinery Co.	162	The Commonwealth Engineering Company of Ohio	137
Ilford Ltd. (Great Britain)	159		
The Parker Appliance Co.	159		
American Bosch Arma Corp.	158		
Caterpillar Tractor Co. (A)	158		

For a partial list of corporations owning 1 to 100 patents, reference is made to the original report.

COSTS. See ATTORNEYS AND AGENTS, FEES

COURT DECISIONS ON PATENTS. See AD-JUDICATION(S), INFRINGEMENT SUITS

COURT ROOM PRESENTATIONS. See ADVO-CACY

D

DAMAGES. See ACCOUNTING

DATE OF INVENTION—IMPORTANCE— ESTABLISHING

R. J. Patterson

The following is largely a condensation of the author's article published in 44 JPOS 462, 1962.

Importance of Date of Invention

The main purposes for which dates of invention are important are as follows:

(1) To prove invention before date of prior patents or publications cited as references by the Patent Office. (2) To win in an interference. (3) To prove the date of and facts regarding invention in actual or threatened patent litigation. (4) To establish priority in intra-company conflicts as to inventorship. (5) To establish the name(s) of the correct inventor(s) so that the patent application can be made in the name(s) of the proper individual(s).

Basic Legal Principles

(1) The inventor's testimony and records alone are wholly inadequate to establish inventorship and reduction to practice. He must be corroborated by others.

(2) Conception, being wholly within the inventor's mind, can be proven only by his disclosure to others.

(3) Conception is best proven by a written document disclosing the invention in complete form, dated, signed by the inventor and witnessed by someone else—a witness who *understands* the invention.

(4) Reduction to practice (actual carrying out of the invention) must be proven (corroborated) by someone else, who can swear that he either (a) Watched the inventor carry out the important aspects of the invention, or (b) Carried out the invention on behalf of or at the instance of the inventor.

(5) Neither the witness (of conception) nor the corroborator (of reduction to practice) may be a co-inventor. It follows from this that the inventor(s) should have a witness(s) who is not a co-inventor and who understands the invention.

(6) For credibility, the testimony of a witness or corroborator should be supported by tangible evidence prepared at the time. Such evidence may be in form of writings, sketches, drawings, blueprints, samples, models, etc.

(7) All documents should be dated. Very often, dates of acts and events can be proven, at a later time, by means of orders for material or parts used in the invention, or the like; examples are purchase orders, work plans, analytical test sheets, and job tickets. Even so, it is best to date all records of conception and of reduction to practice.

(8) It is necessary to prove diligence in reducing to practice only in the relatively rare instance where you conceive earlier and reduce to practice later than the other party with whom you are in interference or in a simulated interference. Since you can never know in advance when such a situation will arise, it is important to be diligent in accomplishing reduction to practice and to keep good records of the steps taken towards complete reduction to practice.

Minimum Legal Requirements for Proving Conception and Reduction to Practice

(1) The two elements of a completed invention are:

(a) Conception of the complete invention in mind of inventor(s) and (b) Reduction to practice, the carrying out of the complete invention, including demonstration of usefulness for the intended purpose, by or on behalf of the inventor(s).

(2) Conception, being in the mind of the inventor(s), can be shown only by his communication *in provable form* to someone else who understands it. The best way is for the inventor to make a written description of his idea in his notebook, with sketch or drawing where necessary to portray the invention, date it, get someone else (who it is certain will never be considered as a co-inventor) to read the disclosure, grasp the inventive concept and sign and date the disclosure (and any sketch or drawing). We now have a *provable* conception.

(3) Reduction to practice, being a tangible concrete thing, can be proven by the testimony of persons (not the inventor or a co-inventor) *having actual personal knowledge and understanding of what was done.*

(4) If the inventor reduces to practice by himself with no one observing, he must, in order to get a provable reduction to practice, secure corroboration either by repeating the reduction to practice with someone else observing or by getting someone else to reduce to practice for him.

(5) The corroborator should keep dated, written records (preferably in his notebook) of reductions to practice of inventions of other people which he either observes or performs, to refresh the corroborator's recollection and make his testimony more credible at a later date, often years later, when the reduction to practice must be proved.

(6) The corroborator of the inventor's reduction to practice may best be a fellow worker working in close proximity to him.

(7) Proofs of conception and reduction to practice must be complete, i.e., must include every essential element of the invention. Thus, if the invention involves carrying out a certain process at 80 to 100 psig, the conception must specify 80 to 100 psig and the corroborator(s) of reduction to practice must be able to swear that this pressure was used.

(8) The best primary record of invention is entry in the numbered bound notebook issued to you. It is a permanent record. Other records, such as work plans, analytical test sheets, material orders, and time records can be used to bolster up this primary notebook record.

Content of Records of Work Done

In making records of work actually done, you should be extremely careful to record the following:

(1) What was done. (2) Why it was done (who suggested or requested it to be done and what was the objective of the work). (3) Who did it. (4) When it was done. (5) What were the results and what conclusions were drawn therefrom.

Self-Addressed Letter Disclosure

As a manner of establishing date of invention, there is a time honored custom among certain free lance inventors. They write a description of the invention, execute the description before a notary public or sign before witnesses, send it to themselves by registered mail, and then lock up the document against the evil day when proof of date of invention may be necessary and the document opened.

No case has been found in which the self addressed envelope has been held to be effective in proving date of invention. The Patent Office says: "Letter to yourself will not protect you." See article *Information for the Independent Inventor.*

In an interference proceeding, the Patent Office tribunals found that the appellant "had not established conception prior to his filing date" of August 23, 1932, although he had an "Exhibit 4" concerning which the court said:

"Appellant testified further that on June 6, 1932, he made a written description of the invention and signed it, his wife and daughter witnessing his signature; that he placed it in an envelope, addressed it to himself, and registered it; and that it was opened for the first time when his testimony was taken, on November 2, 1934." *Osterman* v. *Salb,* 37 USPQ 276, 278, CCPA 1938.

Cross-references: *Anticipation, Interferences, Records of Invention.*

DECLARATORY JUDGMENT ACTIONS

Arthur Lewis Whinston

For the procedural steps in Declaratory Judgment suits, reference is made to the section on that subject in the article *Infringement Suits.*

This discussion is adapted from the author's article in 43 JPOS 565, 1961.

The Federal Declaratory Judgment Act of 1934 (28 U.S.C. 2201, 2202) gave a party threatened with an infringement suit by the owner of a patent the right to seek affirmative relief in the form of an adjudication that the patent is invalid or non-infringed.

In order for a declaratory judgment action to lie, the Supreme Court held early in the history of the act, *Aetna Life Insurance Co.* v. *Haworth*, 300 U.S. 227, 1937, that *a justiciable controversy must exist* between the parties. In the early patent cases the courts tended to construe the act narrowly. As the years passed, however, the pendulum swung in the opposite direction. In fact, some recent commentators have suggested that, in correcting the abuses of the past, the courts may have gone so far as actually to hamper the good-faith patentee in proper licensing efforts.

Requirements for Justiciability

In patent cases thus far decided, the courts have generally looked for two elements before finding a justifiable controversy, namely, (1) actual or potential manufacture, use or sale by the plaintiff coupled with (2) threats or charges of infringement, direct or indirect, by the patent owner or his successors in interest. *Technical Tape Corp.* v. *Minnesota Mining & Mfg. Co.*, 200 F.2d 876, CA 2 1952. Only where both conditions are present is the requirement of an "actual controversy" satisfied.

Implied Notice of Infringement. The charge of infringement, however, need not be formally asserted; nor is it necessary that notice be given directly to the plaintiff. *Treemond Co.* v. *Schering Corp.*, 122 F.2d 702, CA 3 1941. The threat may be implied from the conduct of the parties and the situation existing at the time, such as well

publicized litigation against one manufacturer designed to have an *in terrorem* effect on others. *Dewey & Almy Chemical Co.* v. *American Anode, Inc.*, 137 F.2d 68, CA 3 1943; c. d., 320 U.S. 761, 1943.

Hartford National Bank & Trust Co. v. *Henry L. Crowley & Co.*, 219 F.2d 568, CA 3 1955, is an example of a case in which the plaintiff was unable to satisfy one of the required elements necessary for jurisdiction. The plaintiff had originally accused the defendant of infringement. The defendant used this threat as the basis for a declaratory judgment suit in the SNY District Court.

In reply to the plaintiff's accusation of infringement, the defendant's answering letter asserted that his (the defendant's) products did not infringe the plaintiff's patents, but were described and protected by the defendant's own patent. Solely on the basis of this letter the plaintiff then sought a declaratory judgment as to the validity of the defendant's patent in the New Jersey District Court.

The plaintiff's reasoning here was that, since the complaint alleged that the products of the plaintiff's licensees were similar or identical to the defendant's products, the defendant's assertion in his letter that his products were protected by his own patent impliedly charged that the products of the plaintiff's licensees infringed the defendant's patent. This, said the plaintiff, jeopardized its royalty agreements with these licensees and entitled it to a declaratory judgment.

The appellate court, noting that it was the plaintiff who was asserting the similarity of its products to those of the defendant, held that the defendant's answer did not constitute a charge of infringement and affirmed the lower court's dismissal of the New Jersey action. In doing so it cited and thus did not overlook the *Treemond* and the *Dewey & Almy* cases, which were the first to recognize that the charge of infringement may be implied. The court acknowledged that a threat of suit by a patentee may be craftily phrased and need not be given directly, but refused to find that one had been made in this situation.

A similar question arose in *Central Hide & Rendering Co.* v. *B-M-K Corp.*, 19 F.R.D.

290, DC Del 1956. In this case a manufacturer moved to be joined as a party plaintiff in an action by a group of other manufacturers against a patent owner. The defendant had written those already joined demanding that they either take a license or stop the infringing activity. But the court found that there had been no public threat and the patent owner claimed that he had no knowledge as to the movant's allegedly infringing use of the processes in issue. The motion was thus denied, the court holding that, as to the moving party, there was no "actual controversy." This seems to be a definite limitation on *Dewey & Almy* which the Delaware District Court distinguished as having been characterized by "public 'in terrorem' litigation."

Another interesting decision is that in *Research Electronics & Devices Co.* v. *Neptune Meter Co.*, 156 F. Supp. 484, DC SNY, 1957; aff'd, 264 F.2d 246, CA 2 1950. In this case plaintiffs filed suit for patent infringement; defendants' answer sought a declaratory judgment of non-infringement not only as to the three patented devices alleged in the complaint, but also as to "all other devices" owned by plaintiffs. The relief requested was predicated on a letter written by plaintiffs' attorney, in which he mentioned that "other patents and pending patent applications . . . may be infringed by equipment made . . . by you . . .".

The court in its opinion called the reference in the letter to the "other patents" merely tenuous and construed it as nothing more than an attempt to place defendants on notice that at some time in the future a subsequent charge might be lodged as to these patents. Thus, as to the "other patents," it held no justiciable controversy and granted a motion to strike them from the pleadings.

Conditions for Actual Controversy. But in general, the majority of recent decisions have found an "actual controversy" and have permitted the declaratory judgment suit to lie. In *Helene Curtis Industries, Inc.* v. *Sales Affiliates, Inc.*, 105 F. Supp. 886, DC SNY 1952; aff'd, 199 F.2d 732, CA 2 1952, the court sustained a declaratory judgment action that had been filed only 59 minutes after the patent had issued. This was a situation where the defendant patentee, while its application was pending, had informed the trade by advertising in a trade paper that litigation against infringers was a distinct possibility. The defendant had previously sued the plaintiff successfully on a hair-waving patent and had announced that "its active enforcement policy . . . (would) carry over to the cold wave field." The court felt that the plaintiff was not overly apprehensive in regarding this as a clear threat that, when the patent issued, the defendant would sue again. The decision recognized this as a "situation in which a justiciable issue is created at the moment the patent issues," and illustrates that the *Treemond* case is still good law.

In *Millway Knitting Mills, Inc.* v. *Sanson Hosiery Mills, Inc.*, 108 F. Supp. 5, DC EPa 1952, a declaratory judgment suit was sustained even though there had been no direct communication at all between the parties. Defendant, in a prior action involving a third party, had obtained an expression of opinion from the court in that case to the effect that there was at least a strong similarity between its patent and the plaintiff's product. In addition, it was presenting this contention to another court in still another action. The court denied a motion to dismiss, holding that, short of showing actual threats and charges, the plaintiff had made out about as clear a case for relief as could be imagined.

"Area of Conflict" Basis. In the leading case of *Federal Telephone & Radio Corp.* v. *Associated Telephone & Telegraph Co.*, 169 F.2d 1012, CA 3 1948; c. d., 335 U.S. 859, 1948, the court established what has come to be known as the "area of conflict" test. To lay the basis for a declaratory judgment suit, the advertisement must be sufficiently directed at the plaintiff to clearly define an "area of conflict." This test was followed in *Wallace Products, Inc.* v. *Falco Products, Inc.*, 145 F. Supp. 629, DC EPa 1956. There the defendant had advertised its table in a trade paper. The advertisement contained pictures of the table and a listing of the patents which covered it. The court found the photos to be "so like the plaintiff's table that the trade could well believe that the threat of prosecution was specifically directed against the plaintiff and its customers." This, the court held, created an "area of conflict" between the two parties, since a purchaser of the plaintiff's table might think he was participating in an infringement. The court stated that:

"Where a party creates in the trade the impression that he will sue those of the public who buy from a rival manufacturer,...there (is) a real controversy as to the validity or infringement of the patent..."

Even though defendant's counsel agreed to file a judicial admission of non-infringement, the court held that, on the facts, there was a justiciable controversy between the parties.

Cordial Letter Basis. *E. W. Bliss Co.* v. *Cold Metal Products Co.*, 137 F. Supp. 676, DC NOhio 1955, is a case in which a court held that even a cordial letter may constitute a charge of infringement. Defendant in a letter to plaintiff did not threaten infringement litigation in so many words. Indeed, it merely said that the plaintiff's apparatus was "similar" to defendant's. Yet the court found a threat of infringement implicit in the circumspect language of the letter. It followed the test laid down in *Rhodes Pharmacal Co.* v. *Dolcin Corp.*, 91 F. Supp. 87, DC SNY 1950, namely that:

"The test of a justiciable controversy is whether the facts alleged, under all the circumstances, show that there is a substantial controversy, between parties having adverse legal interests, of sufficient immediacy and reality to warrant the issuance of a declaratory judgment."

The court in the *Bliss* case went on to say that:

"If the party bringing the suit is apprehensive that continued use, manufacture or sale of a patented device or method might be cause for suit by the patentee, and said apprehension is fostered by the patentee—either directly or indirectly, then it is for that party that the Declaratory Judgments Act was designed..."

With respect to necessary infringing activity on the part of the plaintiff, the *Bliss* decision held that it is sufficient to come within the pale of the act for the party bringing suit to allege either past or present use, manufacture or sale of the patented device

or method and the intention to continue to do so. Both the *Wallace* and *Bliss* cases indicate that jurisdictional leniency is to be preferred and that doubt will be resolved in favor of a hearing of the case.

Inquiry and Unsatisfactory Reply. Some years ago, in a patent infringement suit, *Clair* v. *Kastar, Inc.*, 148 F.2d 644, 646, CA 2 1945; c. d., 326 U.S. 762, 1945, Judge Learned Hand, while discussing the defense of laches, commented that:

"...[If] a manufacturer fears that he will be charged to infringe, he can always inquire of the patentee, and if the answer is unsatisfactory, he can bring an action for a declaratory judgment."

This broad language, taken literally, might have forced many an unwary patent owner into unwanted and unprovoked litigation. Fortunately, courts have not seen fit to use it to aid plaintiffs in declaratory judgment actions. The courts evidently have felt that if an "unsatisfactory" answer could suffice as a charge of infringement, the act would be extended far beyond legislative intent.

Motion Practice

The procedural aspects of the two motions most commonly used to test jurisdiction in these declaratory judgment actions were discussed at length in *Temp-Resisto Corp.* v. *Glatt*, 18 F.R.D. 148, DC NJ 1955. In this case the plaintiff alleged that it was manufacturing certain fabrics and that the defendant had charged that these fabrics infringed his patent. The plaintiff sought to have the defendant's patent declared invalid or non-infringed.

The defendant moved to dismiss and also for summary judgment. In support of his motions he furnished an affidavit denying that either he or his attorney, during the course of several conversations with the plaintiff's officer, had ever made any direct or implied charge that the plaintiff had infringed the defendant's patent.

In turn, plaintiff's officer submitted a reply affidavit which stated that, at the last of the conferences at which licensing was discussed, the defendant "directly gave me to understand that he considered his patent valid and infringed by our product . . ." The court held that the affidavits raised an issue of fact and denied both motions.

Especially valuable was the court's discussion of the standards to be applied in deciding these motions. With respect to a motion to dismiss, the court said that only the allegations of the complaint should be considered. If the complaint states a cause of action under the Declaratory Judgment Act, affidavits cannot be considered as proof contradictory to the allegations. A motion to dismiss a complaint that states an actual controversy must, therefore, be denied.

As for a motion for summary judgment, affidavits filed in its support may be considered for the purpose of ascertaining whether an issue of fact is presented, but not to determine one which may be raised. Hence, conflicting accounts as to whether conversations between parties amounted to charges of infringement will serve to create an issue of fact and will result in the denial of a motion for summary judgment. Issues of fact as to the adequacy of the plaintiff's infringing activity will likewise cause the motion to be denied. *National Transformer Corp.* v. *Ranney,* 86 F. Supp. 57, DC NOhio 1949. For the motion to be granted, the undisputed facts must show the absence of a justiciable controversy. *Brown* v. *Insurograph, Inc.,* 90 F. Supp. 828, DC Del 1950.

Conclusion

The present attitude of the courts compels a patent owner to proceed cautiously if he would avoid declaratory judgment litigation. Correspondence or even advertising can plunge an unwary patentee into a defense of his patent.

However, there is enough precedent to show that the courts will not tolerate outright harassment of the patent owner and this, of course, is as it should be. The Declaratory Judgment Act is a legislative creation designed to correct patent abuses of the past. It permits a party prejudiced by the wrongful claim of a patentee to initiate action himself and thus remove any cloud or jeopardy created. Properly used, it facilitates an early determination of the validity of a patent and the factual question of infringement. It should not, however, be allowed to become a means of discouraging patent ownership or an impediment to legitimate licensing activity.

Cross-references: *Infringement Suits—Sec. Declaratory Judgments, Infringement, Validity.*

DEDICATION, PRESUMPTIVE—REBUTTAL
Victor G. Trapasso

Presumptive Dedication

We are here concerned not with express dedication by positive commitment, which is irrevocable and uncorrectable, but with dedication by omission and what if anything can be done to rebut alleged dedication.

An approximate balance should exist between (1) that matter which is disclosed in a patent application and is necessarily present for the purpose of enabling those skilled in the art "to make and use the same" and (2) that which is in actuality encompassed by the patent's claim(s). For various reasons, however, this balance does not always exist. Occasionally an inventor may wish to dedicate to the public certain novel concepts. Under such circumstances, the inventor may purposely allow the public to reap the benefits of his toil by allowing a patent to be granted to him containing unclaimed novel disclosure. For less benevolent reasons, the same situation may result; during the pendency of a patent application, an inventor may not realize that certain features of his disclosure are in fact novel and patentable. Accordingly, he may obtain a patent with these features disclosed but not claimed. Also, an inventor may disclose and seek to claim in one patent application a plurality of independent and distinct patentable features, and the Patent Office may require him to restrict what is claimed to only one of these features but not require him to reduce correspondingly his disclosure. This inventor, through design or error, may not file one or more divisional applications claiming the other of these features before a patent has been granted on the application originally disclosing them.

Attempts to Solve the Problem of Unclaimed Patent Disclosures

Some of the ways of attempting to complete patent protection once a patent has issued with unclaimed disclosure therein, are: (1) take advantage of the reissue practice under 35 U.S.C. 251, (2) file another application on the previously disclosed subject matter, or (3) attempt by means of the doctrine of equivalents to have the claims interpreted as being readable in fact on such disclosure.

As will appear from a subsequent analysis of the case law involved, the cases arising under classifications (1) and (2), have become somewhat overlapped in their statements of the law.

Unclaimed Patent Disclosures Are Generally Presumed Dedicated to the Public

As a general proposition, it has been said:

"Nothing is better settled in the law of patents than that the patentee may claim the whole or only a part of his invention and that if he only describe and claim a part, he is presumed to have abandoned the residue to the public. The object of the patent law in requiring the patentee to 'particularly point out and distinctly claim the part, improvement, or combination which he claims as his invention or discovery,' is not only to secure to him all to which he is entitled, but to apprise the public of what is still open to them." *McClain* v. *Ortmayer,* 141 U.S. 419, 1891.

The Presumption of Dedication in Reissue Applications

The extent to which resort may be had to the filing of a reissue application to claim previously disclosed but not claimed matter is definitely limited by statute. It is settled law that a reissue patent may issue only on the same invention as claimed in the original patent. This, in fact, has been the law for over a century. In *Parker* v. *Yale Clock Co.,* 123 U.S. 87, 1887, the petitioner pleaded that he was entitled to claim in a reissue application any matter which was disclosed in the specification or drawing of the patent desired to be reissued, and that this matter constituted "the invention." The Court in interpreting the controlling law,

said that a reissue application could properly be allowed only on the invention which formed the subject of the original patent. Thereupon, the Court invalidated claims in the reissue patent under consideration because they were drawn to a different invention.

Even though the present patent reissue statutes, 35 U.S.C. 251, 252, 1952 for the first time used the word "disclosed" therein, no substantive change apparently was intended, and the case law appears to remain in line with the *Parker* case.

Decisions Holding the Presumption of Dedication Rebuttable

In *Ex parte Mullen* (1890 C.D. 9) a patent was granted to the applicants for improving certain details in the construction of old and well known grain drills. The claims of the patent specifically recited a feed regulating mechanism. Seven days after the issuance of this patent, the same inventor filed a second application for an improvement in grain drill teeth, subject matter which was disclosed but not claimed in the prior patent. The Commissioner had clearly before him the question of whether or not there was a dedication to the public of this previously disclosed but unclaimed subject matter. In deciding the question, the Commissioner divided the cases involved into three different classes of cases:

1. Cases where the claims in the different applications differ nonpatentability. Here, only one patent may be granted.
2. Cases where several dependent inventions are disclosed in one application but only one is claimed. Separate applications may be filed in such cases on the other inventions as long as (a) they are filed in applications which are contemporaneously pending with the parent application, and (b) they are separate and distinct from the invention claimed in the parent application. If neither (a) nor (b) exist, there is a dedication to the public of the unclaimed subject matter in the issued patent.
3. Cases where the invention described and not claimed is absolutely independent of the invention actually claimed in the first patent.

The Commissioner then stated:

"[I]t is obvious from the foregoing that unless the invention sought to be covered by the present application is in a legal sense independent of the invention secured by the earlier patent—that is to say, unless the pending case comes within the third class above, the applicants' right to receive a further patent cannot be sustained. Unless the case comes within the third class, the patent already granted is exhaustive of the right of the applicants to secure whatever was described therein.

"Inasmuch as ... [applicants] ... could not have claimed such improvement either in their first patent or in any lawful reissue thereof it follows that there has been no dedication from failure to make such claims, and it follows, further, that their right to make them in their ... [present] ... application is wholly unimpaired by their previous disclosure.... When, however, the machine is old and well known in the art to which it pertains and the applications profess to cover simply improvements upon such old and well-known machine, the question of dependency or independence depends upon the relation which the improvements bear to each other."

In line with *Ex parte Mullen* is the more recent decision *Ex parte Spence,* 82 USPQ 449, BdApp 1946,

1. On June 29, 1948, an application was filed disclosing and claiming a particular valve and also an independent device. By means of a restriction requirement, the applicant was required to divide out the valve structure.
2. On July 20, 1943, the June 28, 1940 application issued as patent No. 2,324,736 without any claims to the valve structure.
3. On August 8, 1943, a second application was filed including claims to the valve structure disclosed in the first application.

The Board of Appeals cited *Ex parte Mullen* and stated that under the present law, public use or disclosure in a printed publication is not a bar against the issuance of a valid patent provided the patent is applied for within less than a year of the date of said publication or public use. (The same statutory bar exists under the present patent law. See 35 U.S.C. 102(b), 1952.) The Board stated that although the second application could not obtain the benefit of the filing date of the first application because the second application was not copending with the first, i.e., the second application could not be a "divisional" application, the second application was not barred absolutely by the existence of the disclosure in the first application. The disclosure in the

patent was treated as any other publication, and merely as a publication. Since the second application was filed within one year of the "publication" (the patent), applicant was entitled to the second patent.

The Board further said that there is merely a presumption of dedication when a patent issues with unclaimed subject matter disclosed therein. The Board stated, however, that this presumption can be rebutted by the subsequent filing within the statutory period of an application claiming the valve per se.

The guide which the court used in *In re Bersworth,* 189 F.2d 996, CCPA 1951, was the reasoning in *Ex parte Mullen.* The court stated that the claims of the application could not be allowed since they were not for an independent and distinct invention.

The decision rendered in *Ex parte Groll,* 48 USPQ 138, PO BdApp 1940, is an unusual case directly supporting the conclusions of the law set forth in *Ex parte Mullen.* In *Ex parte Groll,* a patent issued *claiming* only the tertiary species of the disclosed invention, of which the primary and secondary species were, however, also disclosed. Nine months later the inventors filed an application specifically claiming the *previously disclosed* primary and secondary species. In the Board's decision rendered April 30, 1940, the claims of the second application were not considered to define a distinct invention because these claims were considered to be broad enough to read on the claims of the patent and vice versa. The Board, on reconsideration, reversed itself on the question of the distinctiveness of the newly claimed but previously disclosed invention and held the claims allowable. Id. 139.

Ex parte Groll, therefore, clearly states that it is permissible to allow claims in an application for patent directed to patentably distinct subject matter disclosed but not claimed in a patent issued prior to the date of filing of the said application.

Decisions Holding the Presumption of Dedication Non-Rebuttable

As previously indicated, all courts are not in agreement with the holdings in cases similar to *Ex parte Mullen.* It is believed that one of the reasons for the contrary holdings of the courts is confusion between reissue and non-reissue circumstances. Thus we sometimes find courts unfortunately relying on decisions and opinions in prior cases which dealt with a reissue situation or with a situation involving double patenting or equivalents. On this basis they may erroneously deny an applicant his right, under United States patent law, to claim in a separate application matter which had been unclaimed in a prior application but which, in such prior application, amounted to matter which was independent and distinct from that which was in fact claimed therein.

Those desiring detailed discussion of such holdings are referred to my article infra, 1961.

Conclusion

Subject matter disclosed and not claimed in an issued patent may properly be claimed in an application filed after the issuance of the patent if the basis for patentability of the application is matter which is independent and distinct from that claimed in the patent and the application is filed within one year after the issuance of the patent.

(The above is largely a condensation of an article written by Victor G. Trapasso, entitled "Unclaimed Patent Disclosures and the Presumption of Dedication," 43 JPOS 140-157, 1961, here reprinted-in-part with his approval. Ed.)

Cross-references: *Abandonment, Disclaimers, Double Patenting.*

DELAY IN CLAIMING

Nelson H. Shapiro

Origin of the Problem

The original claims of a patent application are at best a skilled approximation of the metes and bounds of the protection which may ultimately be granted by the Patent Office. Usually the claims of the issued patent evolve through amendment of original claims, or through the introduction of new claims, while the application is pending. The delays which characterize this evolution may at times determine the validity of the claims.

One Year Bar

The one year statutory bars of 35 U.S.C. 102 are measured from "the date of the application." The statute provides that a person shall be entitled to a patent unless, inter alia,

"the invention was patented or described in a printed publication in this or a foreign country or in public use or on sale in this country, more than one year prior to the date of the application for patent in the United States."

Ordinarily, the date of the application is the filing date of the original application papers, but under some circumstances the effective date for a late claim may be that on which the claim was filed.

In *Muncie Gear Works, Inc. et al.* v. *Outboard Marine and Mfg. Co. et al.*, 315 U.S. 759, 53 USPQ 1, 1942, the application of the patent in suit was filed in 1926, when RS 4886 (the predecessor of 35 U.S.C. 102) provided a two year period for the statutory bar. In 1929 the claims were amended to include limitations to structure not previously claimed. The specification was also amended. Noting that the original application in no way suggested the combination asserted in the amended claims as the invention, the Supreme Court held the claims invalid because of public use which occurred more than two years before the amendment, but less than two years before the filing date of the application. The crux of the decision is that RS 4886 would in terms provide for the invalidity of the claims if they had been offered by application rather than by amendment, and whatever may be the efficacy of an amendment as a substitute for an application, it surely could effect no more than the application itself. Regarding the patent protection encompassed by the late claims, the court viewed the application as if filed when the claims were presented to the Patent Office, and hence subject to statutory bars then applicable.

Unsupported Late Claims

The *Muncie Gear* case is widely cited as authority for invalidating claims which are *not adequately supported by the original application papers* and which are *asserted more than a year after public use, sale, or publication of the invention.* This doctrine is applicable, for example, when the original specification is silent as to the meaning of terminology in a late claim and when the essential character of the description in the claim is pointed out to the Patent Office by amendment more than a year after public use or sale of the invention. *Atlas Specialty Mfg. Co.* v. *Farber Brothers, Inc.*, 130 USPQ 201, DC WTenn 1961. Claims added by amendment more than a year after public use are held invalid under the *Muncie* rule when the application as filed did not disclose the invention of the late claims in "full, clear, concise, and exact terms." *Larsen Products Corp.* v. *Perfect Paint Products, Inc.*, 128 USPQ 326, DC Md 1961.

To avoid the application of the *Muncie* rule it is not enough that the delayed claim is technically readable upon the original disclosure, if in fact the concept defined by the claim is sufficiently different from the invention earlier asserted for patent protection as to constitute a "new invention." In *Shu-Conditioner, Inc.* v. *Bixby Box Toe Co., Inc.*, 126 USPQ 36, DC Mass 1960, aff. 131 USPQ 87, the claims in issue depended upon features which, although shown in the original drawings, were not described or asserted as the invention until the filing of claims by amendment after a statutory bar had risen. The claims were held to be invalid. The same result was reached in *Ful-Vue Sales Co.* v. *American Optical Co.*, 96 USPQ 366, DC SNY 1953, upon similar facts. In *Chicopee Mfg. Corp.* v. *The Kendall Co.*, 129 USPQ 90, CA 4 1961, cert. den. 131 USPQ 498, delayed claims which called for sufficient regularity to obtain an objective were held to be different from original claims calling for strict regularity to produce the same objective, the procedure of the later claims being commercially practical whereas the procedure of the earlier claims was not. The applicant's attempt to broaden the originally disclosed and claimed concept to encompass the practical procedure, at a time when a new application would have been barred, was rebuked under the *Muncie* rule.

Showing of Adequate Support

Application of the doctrine of the *Muncie* case can be avoided, however, by a showing of adequate support for the delayed claims in seasonably filed application papers. The general rule is that an applicant is permitted to add new claims while his application is pending if the new claims are supported by the disclosure of the original application. *Trico Products Corp.* v. *Delman Co. et al.*, 132 USPQ 316, DC SIowa 1961. The *Muncie* doctrine is inapplicable where the original application provides a full disclosure of the invention finally claimed. *Coats Loaders and Stackers, Inc.* v. *Henderson et al.*, 109 USPQ 332, CA 6 1956. The subject matter of the delayed claim may be shown to be adequately supported if it is inherent in the earlier application papers, although not spelled out in precisely the language of the claim. *Binks Manufacturing Co.* v. *Ransburg Electro-Coating Corp.*, 126 USPQ 318, CA 7 1960.

In determining whether a delayed claim is supported by a timely disclosure, the courts look not only to the earlier description of the invention in the specification, but also to *the scope of the invention defined by the earlier claims.* Thus, in *Pursche* v. *Atlas Scraper and Engineering Co.*, 132 USPQ 104, CA 9 1961, the *Muncie* rule was held not to invalidate a claim added by amendment nearly four years after public use of the invention where the scope of the invention stated in original claims extended to and included the matter covered by the claim in issue. Similarly, in *Jones et al.* v. *Sears, Roebuck & Co. et al.*, 127 USPQ 411, DC Colo 1960, aff'd, 135 USPQ 149, 1963, a claim added by amendment was found valid notwithstanding public use more than a year before the addition of the claim, because the claim went no further than to make explicit what was implicit in the original description and claims. As stated in *Engineering Development Laboratories* v. *Radio Corp. of America*, 68 USPQ 238, CA 2 1946, the doctrine of the *Muncie* case "does not prevent amendments which go no further than to make express what would have been regarded as an equivalent of the original; or to incorporate into one claim what was to be gathered from the perusal of all, if read together." Thus, when the final claim merely clarifies the language of an earlier claim without broadening the invention, the *Muncie* doctrine is not applicable. *The Upjohn Co.* v. *Italian Drugs Importing Co., Inc. et al.*, 128 USPQ 236, DC SNY 1961.

Late Claims Filed Within Statutory Period

Under the doctrine of the *Muncie* case a delayed claim defining an invention not suggested by a timely disclosure is made subject to the one year statutory bars of 35 U.S.C. 102. Earlier decisions provide a basis for invalidating such a claim without consideration of the length of the delay. In *The Schriber-Schroth Co.* v. *Cleveland Trust Co.*, 305 U.S. 47, 39 USPQ 242, 1938, the Supreme Court denied a patentee's reliance upon amendatory matter in the claims and the specification, holding that the original disclosure failed to meet the requirements of RS 4888 [now replaced by 35 U.S.C. 112] as to such matter.

In the *Schriber* case the court cited as precedent the decision in *Railway Co.* v. *Sayles*, 97 U.S. 554, 1879, which established the principle that an application for a patent cannot be broadened by amendment so as to embrace an invention not described in the application as filed, at least when adverse rights of the public have intervened. The matter of "intervening rights" (present in the *Schriber* case also) was elucidated in the more recent case of *Benz et al.* v. *Celeste Fur Dyeing and Dressing Corp.*, 70 USPQ 46, CA 2 1946. The court considered the validity of claims asserted by amendment after an intervening successful public use by an independent third person and found the claims invalid because the invention of the claims was not revealed by the original disclosure, even though the period of public use was insufficient to constitute a statutory bar under RS 4886.

Both the *Muncie* and *Schriber* cases are concerned with the failure of the application as filed to suggest the invention ultimately claimed. Under the present patent statutes, the *Schriber* doctrine is based upon lack of compliance with 35 U.S.C. 112, just as the *Muncie* doctrine is predicated upon 35 U.S.C. 102. The definition of the term "application" in Section 102 is derived from Sections 111 and 112 of the statute. Thus, it is not surprising to find a joint *Muncie-Schriber* attack upon delayed claims, as in *Dole Refrigerating Co.* v. *Amerio Freezers, Inc.*, 117 USPQ 87, DC NJ 1958; *National Latex Products Co.* v. *The Sun Rubber Co.*, 123 USPQ 279, CA 6 1959, cert. den. 125 USPQ 668; and *White Machine Co., Inc.* v. *Bon Ton Cleaners and Dyers et al.*, 128 USPQ 228, DC NJ 1961.

Supplemental Oath

As in the *National* and *White* cases, the attack may be bolstered by an assertion that the patentee failed to comply with Section 115 of the statute, in that oath was not made to the subject matter of the delayed claims. Patent Office Rule 67 requires the filing of a supplemental oath to verify matter originally shown or described but not substantially embraced in the statement of invention or claim originally presented. In the *National* and *White* cases new oaths were held to be unnecessary, because the amendments did not enlarge the claims, but in *M & R Dietetic Laboratories, Inc.* v. *Dean Milk Co.*, 132 USPQ 496, DC NIll 1961, claims added by amendment which were broader than anything theretofore disclosed were held invalid in the absence of a supplemental oath. See M.P.E.P. 603.01.

New Matter

Even a supplemental oath will not sustain delayed claims to matter which departs from or adds to the original disclosure. See Rule 118. Moreover, in such cases the claims may also be challenged for violation of 35 U.S.C. 132, which provides that "No amendment shall introduce new matter into the disclosure of the invention." The recent case of *Aetna Steel Products Corp.* v. *Southwest Products Co.*, 127 USPQ 23, CA 9 1960. cert. den. 128 USPQ 557, states that the "new matter" provision of the statute (first introduced in 1952) is no more than a codification of the existing law. Although many of the court decisions involving the *Muncie* and *Schriber* doctrines are concerned with additions to or departures from the disclosure, the issue of new matter, so termed, is seldom considered, even in the cases which come within the present statute. It is much more common to find this issue raised in Patent Office proceedings, which seldom are concerned with the general proposition of delay in claiming. But see *Hartford-Empire* v. *Coe*, 76 F.2d 426, CA DC 1935. As already stated, the courts tend to consider whether the delayed claim defines a different invention from that originally asserted, rather than whether the claim meets the technical definition of new matter.

In Divisional Applications

Delay in claiming by way of a divisional application has posed a special problem for the courts. If the original application did not suggest the invention claimed in the later filed copending application, the late claims are invalid, just as if submitted in the original application. *Coltman* v. *Colgate-Palmolive-Peet Co.*, 41 USPQ 380, CA 7 1939; *Larsen Products Corp.* v. *Perfect Paint Products, Inc.*, supra. Difficulty arises when the invention of the division was fully disclosed in the parent application but was never claimed therein. In *Webster Electric Co.* v. *Splitdorf Electrical Co.*, 264 U.S. 463, 1924, the Supreme Court held that in cases involving laches, equitable estoppel, or intervening private or public rights, a two year time limit prima facie applies to divisional applications and can only be avoided by proof of special circumstances justifying a longer delay. [Acceptable excuses justifying the delay have been conspicuously absent from the cases which apply this rule.] The problem was again considered by the Supreme Court in *Crown Cork and Seal Co., Inc.* v. *Ferdinand Gutmann Co., Inc.*, 304 U.S. 159, 37 USPQ 351, 1938. In a split decision it was held that in the absence of intervening rights, no excuse is required even for a delay of more than two years in presenting a divisional application. Moreover, the court said that where there is no abandonment, the filing of a divisional application less than two years after an intervening patent or publication does not operate to enlarge the patent monopoly beyond that contemplated by the statute. It is interesting to note that in *General Talking Pictures Corp.* v. *Western Electric Co., Inc. et al.*, 304 U.S. 175, 37 USPQ 357, 1938, decided shortly after the *Crown* case, the Supreme Court refused to hold divisional claims invalid in the face of public use by the inventor or his assignee or licensee more than two years before the invention was first claimed. Apparently, such use was not considered to constitute intervening rights, although in the decisions which apply the *Muncie* or *Schriber* rule, public use by the inventor establishes intervening rights of the public. See *Monroe Auto Equipment Co.* v. *Heckethorn Mfg. and Supply Co.*, 133 USPQ 34, DC WTenn 1961.

The present status of delayed claims filed by way of a divisional application appears uncertain. Firstly, Section 120 of the statute provides that a divisional application shall have the same effect as though filed on the date of the parent application. The statute requires that the invention be disclosed in the previous application in accordance with the first paragraph of Section 112 but does not state that the invention must be *claimed* in the previous application in accordance with the second paragraph of Section 112. Secondly, if the invention were fully disclosed in the parent application, the *Muncie* and *Schriber* rules would not be applicable to claims offered by amendment. It is well settled, moreover, that a divisional application is no more than an amendment in the parent application. *Dwight & Lloyd Sintering Co., Inc.* v. *Greenawalt*, 27 F.2d 823, 831, CA 2 1928. Thus, if the claims would not be objectionable if offered by amendment in the parent application, they should not be objectionable merely because they are asserted by division. On the other hand, if the rule of the *Webster* and *Crown* cases were applied to claims added by amendment in an original application, there would be no need to seek support for the claims in the earlier disclosure, as in *Muncie* and *Schriber*, because the matter of disclosure would not be in issue.

The time period which today would be applicable to divisional cases also appears uncertain. The Supreme Court first stated the two year limitation upon divisional applications in a case involving claims copied from a conflicting patent, basing the rule upon an analogy to the court-imposed limitation upon broadening reissues. *Chapman* v. *Wintroath*, 252 U.S. 126, 1920. The reissue limitation was itself based upon a judicial analogy to the two year period of RS 4886. The time limit upon claims copied from a patent is now one year, as provided by 35 U.S.C. 135, while the period for broadening reissues is two years, in accordance with 35 U.S.C. 251. Moreover, as already stated, the two year period of RS 4886 has been superseded by the one year period of 35 U.S.C. 102. It may therefore be questioned whether the one year period of 35 U.S.C. 102 would be applicable to claims asserted by division after intervening rights or whether the two year period of 35 U.S.C. 251 should be applied by analogy to reissue.

Conclusion

Delay in claiming may become fatal to claim validity if the delay is accompanied by other factors, such as inadequate support for the claim in the original application papers. Mere delay, such as the lapse of time permitted in Patent Office prosecution, will not defeat an applicant's rights to claims. *Overland* v. *Packard Co.*, 274 U.S. 417, 1927; cf. *Wirebounds Patents Co. et al.* v. *Saranac Automatic Machine Corp.*, 18 USPQ 171, CA 6 1933.

The principles governing late claiming are "designed to protect the public against abuses, not to deprive inventors of what they plainly never meant to put into the public demesne." *Engineering Development Labs.* v. *Radio Corp. of America*, supra.

Cross-references: *Chemical Applications*—Section *Supplemental Oath, Laches, Reissues.*

DESIGN PATENTS

Barbara A. Ringer and Kelsey Martin Mott

Statutory Background and Provisions

Although Congress, acting under its constitutional power to protect the writings of authors and the discoveries of inventors, passed both copyright and patent laws in 1790, there was no statutory protection for designs in the United States for more than half a century thereafter. The first provisions for the protection of new and original designs for a "manufacture" were included in the Patent Act of 1842, which also set forth specifically the classes of patentable designs. An amendment enacted in 1902 dropped these classes in favor of the general term "article of manufacture" in describing those designs subject to protection; it also substituted the word "ornamental" for the term "useful," which had given rise to some confusion. See *Ex parte Knothe*, 1903 C.D. 42, Comr Pats.

The statutory design provisions now in effect were enacted as part of the Patent Act of 1952, Title 35, U.S.C. The basic design provisions appear in Section 171:

"Whoever invents any new, original and ornamental design for an article of manufacture may obtain a patent therefor, subject to the conditions and requirements of this title.

"The provisions of this title relating to patents for inventions shall apply to patents for designs, except as otherwise provided."

Under Section 173, the term of design patent protection can be three-and-one-half, seven, or fourteen years. The period of protection, which is determinative of the patent fee, must be elected by the applicant before the patent is issued.

The Nature of a Patentable Design

It has been repeatedly stated that the purpose of design patent legislation is to encourage the decorative arts in their relation to manufactured articles: to increase their saleability and to satisfy the aesthetic sense of their purchasers. See *Forestek Plating & Mfg. Co.* v. *Knapp-Monarch Co.*, 106 F.2d 554, 559, CA 6 1939. However, although design patents contemplate the protection of appearance rather than utility, a design that is useful as well as decorative may still be the subject of a valid design patent. *Robert W. Brown & Co.* v. *De Bell,* 243 F.2d 200, CA 9 1957.

Speaking very broadly, a design consists of all the visual characteristics displayed by an object. It may consist of: (1) surface ornamentation applied to an article of manufacture without reference to its general form; (2) the shape or configuration of the article; or (3) both the shape of the article and additional surface ornamentation. *In re Schnell,* 46 F.2d 203, CCPA 1931.

Perhaps the most quoted definition of a design is that of Judge Grosscup in *Pelouze Scale & Mfg. Co.* v. *American Cutlery Co.,* 102 Fed. 916, 918, CA 7 1900:

"...that characteristic of a physical substance which, by means of lines, images, configuration and the like, taken as a whole, makes an impression through the eye, upon the mind of the observer. The essence of a design resides, not in the elements individually, nor in their method of arrangement, but in the tout ensemble—in that indefinable whole that awakens some sensation in the observer's mind."

Thus, the frame of reference both for the validity and for the infringement of a design patent is provided by the design as a whole, and not by the dissected individual elements. *Philco Corp.* v. *Admiral Corp.,* 199 F. Supp. 797, DC Del 1961; *Application of Balmer,* 276 F.2d 405, CCPA 1960. In attacking the validity of a design patent on grounds of lack of novelty, therefore, it is not proper for a defendant to attempt to show piecemeal anticipation of the design. *R-Way Furniture Co.* v. *Duo Bed Corp.,* 216 F. Supp. 862, DC NIll 1962.

For purposes of the patent law, a design does not exist unless it is attached to some tangible object, and protection extends to the design as applied. For example, a two-dimensional picture that has not been applied to an article of manufacture is not a design covered by the statute. *Ex parte France,* 132 USPQ 211, PO BdApp 1961. On the other hand, anything that is the subject of fabrication may generally be considered as coming within the meaning of the term "article of manufacture" as used

in the act. *In re Hadden,* 20 F.2d 275, CA DC 1927.

Standards of Design Patent Protection

In order to be the subject of a valid patent under the statute, a design must fulfill four requirements: it must be new, original, ornamental, and inventive in character. *Spaulding* v. *Guardian Light Co.,* 267 F.2d 111, CA 7, *cert. den.,* 361 U.S. 883, 1959. It has been said that the words "invented" and "new" and "original" must be construed together in applying the rule that there can be no grant of a patent monopoly upon the exercise of the mere skill of an ordinary designer who is chargeable with knowledge of the prior art. *Zangerle & Peterson Co.* v. *Venice Furniture Novelty Mfg. Co.,* 133 F.2d 266, CA 7 1943.

Novelty. An invention of a design is anticipated if it was known or used by others under the same conditions as those set forth with respect to mechanical patents in Section 102 of the patent law. See, e.g., *Lewis E. Hamel Co.* v. *P & K, Inc.,* 185 F. Supp. 278, DC EIll 1960. Novelty must therefore be determined by the state of the art as well as by other factors. However, under Section 172, the time specified with respect to the filing of a foreign application for a patent is six months in the case of designs.

To be "new," a design should create the impression that it is entirely distinct from any previous mental image of an observer; a mere difference from anything an observer may have seen before is not enough. *Blisscraft* v. *Rona Plastic Corp.,* 123 F. Supp. 552, DC SNY 1954, aff. 219 F.2d 238, CA 2 1955. An article may display an artistic advance over the prior art, or may be more pleasing and more likely to tempt a customer, and yet embody nothing "new" if it represents the normal progress resulting from discriminating taste and judgment applied to that already created. *Patriarca Mfg., Inc.* v. *Sosnick,* 278 F.2d 389, CA 9 1960. In other words, it is not enough to show that the design is novel and pleasing enough to catch the trade or that no earlier design is "like" the one in suit. *Amerock Corp.* v. *Aubrey Hardware Mfg., Inc.,* 275 F.2d 346, CA 7 1960.

The standards of novelty and of patentable invention are closely related in the case of designs. It is generally accepted that if, in the eyes of ordinary observers, the overall effect of a design is different from that of others and is not merely a modification of an already existing design, novelty is present. See *Application of Johnson*, 175 F.2d 791, CCPA 1949. However, finding compliance with this test for novelty is not sufficient in itself to determine the existence of a patentable distinction, even though the question of whether a design is unobvious in the inventive sense is necessarily related to the question of novelty. The differences between the design and the prior art, both in degree and in kind, have been said to be the only criteria available to the court in deciding these questions. *Application of Bartlett*, 300 F.2d 942, CCPA 1962.

Originality. Under the copyright law, the fundamental standard of protection is originality: the author must have originated his writing independently, without copying, from the work of another. See Dworkin, "Originality in the Law of Copyright," 39 B.U.L. Rev. 526, 1959. This concept of originality is equally applicable under the design patent law. However, some courts have given the term "original" a broader meaning in the patent context; they have come close to equating it with inventiveness, suggesting that an "original" design must be essentially different from and superior to a design that could be created by a person skilled in the art. Thus, a patent for a textile fabric design consisting of seven stripes gradually increasing in width and density of shade from selvage to selvage was held invalid for lack of originality or invention. *Trojan Textile Corp.* v. *Crown Fabrics Corp.*, 143 F. Supp. 48, DC SNY 1956. It has been said that, to fulfill the requirement for the exercise of the inventive faculty with respect to design patents, creative originality and artistry must be found. *Amerock Corp.* v. *Aubrey Hardware Mfg., Inc.*, 275 F.2d 346, CA 7 1960.

Ornamentality. An ornamental design, within the meaning of the patent law, is generally something that can be considered the product of aesthetic skill and artistic conception. In *Blisscraft of Hollywood* v. *United Plastics Co.*, 294 F.2d 694, CA 2 1961, a pitcher which was held to inspire reactions simply like those inspired by the usual piece of kitchenware, and which was found to have "no particularly aesthetic appeal in line, form, color or otherwise" and "no dominant artistic motif either in detail or in its overall conception," failed to meet the statutory prerequisite of ornamentality. Accord, *Bliss* v. *Gotham Industries, Inc.*, 316 F.2d 848, CA 9 1963.

A neat appearance is not enough; the question is whether the design has any aesthetic appeal. *A. C. Gilbert* v. *Shemitz*, 45 F.2d 98, CA 2 1930. In *E. H. Sheldon & Co.* v. *Miller Office Supply Co.*, 188 F. Supp. 67, DC SOhio 1960, the court stated that the subject of inquiry involved "beauty, ornamentation, something that appeals to the aesthetic sense," and found that a laboratory table unit fulfilled the requirement of ornamentality.

The court in *Kanné & Bessant, Inc.* v. *Eaglelet Metal Spinning Co.*, 54 F.2d 131, DC SNY 1931, a case involving lamps lacking any surface ornamentation or embellishment, indicated that ornamentality implies beauty and that, in the absence of external ornamentation, the patentee must rely on "originality and beauty of outline." In another case involving lamp shades the court rejected "beauty" as the test for ornamentality on the ground that there is no standard for beauty; it said, nevertheless, that what "the designer is striving [for] is not merely ornamentation but beauty," and that "it may lie in form or shape." *Franklin Lamp Mfg. Co.* v. *Albe Lamp and Shade Co.*, 26 F. Supp. 960, 961, DC EPa 1939. In essence, then, the test for ornamentality is the overall aesthetic effect of the design, the appearance of the article as an entirety when judged by the taste and fancy of the average man. *Application of Grigsby*, 5 F.2d 117, CA DC 1925.

Indeed, a patentable design must be primarily ornamental; a design dictated by functional or mechanical requirements is not patentable. *Day-Brite Lighting, Inc.* v. *Compco Corp.*, 311 F.2d 26, CA 7 1962, rev'd on other grounds, 376 U.S. 234, 1964; *Fendall Co.* v. *Welsh Mfg. Co.*, 203 F. Supp.

45, DC RI 1962. Thus, where the only design element of a soap dish not resulting from the article's function was a group of horizontal lines on the side of the dish, the court held the design unpatentable on the ground that it was dictated by functional elements. *Hygienic Specialties Co. v. H. G. Salzman, Inc.*, 302 F.2d 614, CA 2 1962.

To support a valid patent, a design must have an unobvious appearance distinct from that dictated solely by functional considerations. *Application of Garbo*, 287 F.2d 192, CCPA 1961. When the design is wholly or substantially responsive to the utilitarian function of the article embodying it, in the sense that substantially every part of the shape is dictated by the use to which the article is to be put, the design cannot be patented. This does not mean that the design must be purely decorative and non-utilitarian to be viewed as "ornamental." *Ex parte Gibson*, 135 USPQ 128, PO BdApp 1962; *Ex parte Heuck*, 131 USPQ 33, PO BdApp 1961. The design of a thermostatic switch was thus held the proper subject matter of a design patent, even though it had a mechanical function. *Ex parte Levinn*, 136 USPQ 606, PO BdApp 1962.

A design may have movable parts, provided its appearance is not so changed that the design becomes unidentifiable. *In re Koehring*, 37 F.2d 421, CCPA 1930; *Ex parte Dembski*, 130 USPQ 115, PO BdApp 1961. On the other hand, it has been repeatedly held that designs that are concealed or obscured when the articles embodying them are in normal use are not proper subjects for design patents. See, e.g., *Application of Stevens*, 173 F.2d 1015, CCPA 1949.

Patentable Invention. Even though a design is found to be new, original, and ornamental, it must, to be held patentable, also involve inventiveness beyond the skill of the ordinary designer or draftsman. *Day-Brite Lighting, Inc. v. Sandee Mfg. Co.*, 286 F.2d 596, CA 7 1960, *cert. denied*, 366 U.S. 963, 1961. Section 171 of the present statute does not refer to a standard of inventiveness with respect to designs, but it has been held that this section has not changed the settled law as it stood in this respect before the section was enacted. *Hawley Products*

Co. v. U.S. Trunk Co., 259 F.2d 69, CA 1 1958.

Similarity of appearance is always the basic consideration in determining the patentability of designs over the prior art, *Application of Phillips*, 315 F.2d 943, CCPA 1963, although natural similarities resulting from the fact that two articles perform the same function must be taken into consideration. *Application of Crotty*, 272 F.2d 957, CCPA 1959. Even though a design is not actually anticipated by a previous design, it is nevertheless unpatentable if it is no more than an obvious variant. *Application of Levy*, 310 F.2d 751, CCPA 1962. On the other hand, if the later design makes a vastly different impression on the observer, the patent may be upheld despite general similarities to the prior art. See, *Application of McKay*, 316 F.2d 952, CCPA 1963; *Application of Braun*, 275 F.2d 738, CCPA 1960.

A design may be sufficiently attractive and streamlined to achieve commercial success, and yet be within the ability of the ordinary designer in that field. *Jaybee Mfg. Corp. v. Ajax Hardware Mfg. Corp.*, 287 F.2d 228, CA 9 1961. In a close case, commercial success may tip the scales in determining whether a design is patentable; but, where it is impossible to know to what extent sales were induced by promotion, advertising, or functional value, commercial success has been said to carry no weight in support of the validity of a patent. *Day-Brite Lighting, Inc. v. Sandee Mfg. Co.*, 286 F.2d 596, CA 7 1960, *cert. den.*, 366 U.S. 963, 1961.

It is not in itself invention merely to carry forward a known principle, or to do the same thing in the same way by substantially the same means, although with better results. *Lewis E. Hamel Co. v. P. & K., Inc.*, 185 F. Supp. 278, DC EIll 1960; *Application of Lamb*, 286 F.2d 610, CCPA 1961. Similarly, patentability cannot rest solely upon a change in form, size, proportion, degree, material, or color. See, e.g., *Ace Fastener Corp. v. United States*, 276 F.2d 391, Ct. Cl. 1960; *Application of Iknayan*, 274 F.2d 943, CCPA 1960.

All of the elements in a design may be old, as long as they are embodied in such a way that the end result reaches the dignity of patentable invention. *Sel-O-Rak Corp. v. Henry Hanger & Display Fixture Corp.*, 232 F.2d 176, CA 5, cert. den., 352 U.S. 870, 1956. But, where the prior art anticipates a design with "almost photographic similarity," a finding of lack of invention would be compelled. *North American Lace Co., Inc. v. Sterling Laces, Inc.*, 185 F. Supp. 623, DC SNY 1960.

Patent Office Practice

Under the Patent Office Rules of Practice, a thorough examination of the claim stated in the application and of the prior art is made by the design patent examiner, as in the case of applications for mechanical and other patents. 37 C.F.R. Sections 1.101 *et seq.* The rules for design patents, 37 C.F.R. Sections 1.151-1.155, provide: (1) that the rules governing other patent applications are applicable to design applications (Section 1.151); (2) that the representation of the design must conform to the general rules for drawings, that there must be a sufficient number of views to constitute a complete disclosure of the appearance of the article, and that appropriate shading must be used to show the character or contour of the surface represented (Section 1.152); and (3) that no specific description, other than a reference to the drawing, is ordinarily required or permitted, that the claim must refer to the article by name as shown or as shown and described, and that more than one claim is neither required nor permitted (Section 1.153). See *Campbell v. Watson*, 275 F.2d 166, CA DC 1960.

Although Rule 153 limits an applicant to one claim per application, Section 112 of the statute states that "the specification shall conclude with one or more claims." It has been held that there is no conflict between these two provisions, since the latter does not entitle every applicant as a matter of right to present a plurality of claims. *Application of Rubinfield*, 270 F.2d 391, CCPA 1959, cert. den., 362 U.S. 903, 1960. Similarly, Section 121 of the statute provides that, "if two or more independent and distinct inventions are claimed in one application, the Commissioner may require

the application to be restricted to one of the inventions"; this contains no express provision that every applicant is entitled to present more than one claim in an application. On the other hand, it may be permissible in a proper case to illustrate more than one embodiment of a design invention as long as the embodiments all involve a single inventive concept; this concept can be protected by a single claim such as, for example, "The ornamental design for a floor waxer substantially as shown." *Application of Rubinfield*, supra.

To avoid rejection, the design disclosure should depict the configuration and complete appearance of the article of manufacture in which the design is embodied, including the bounds of the configuration of the article. *Ex parte France*, 132 USPQ 211, PO BdApp 1961. Insufficiency of disclosure will also prevent the courts from making an adequate comparison between the drawing in the patent application and the accused design, as, for example, in a case where there had been a failure to disclose fully the contour of the back of a television set, even though the contour was an important part of the design. *Philco Corp. v. Admiral Corp.*, 199 F. Supp. 797, DC Del 1961.

Design patents are based on what the application discloses the appearance of the design as a whole to be. Thus, for purposes of determining anticipation, the thing that must be compared with the prior art is the drawing or print submitted by the applicant, and not the actual design as manufactured and sold. Similarly, in cases of infringement, the comparison must be between the defendant's design and the design as disclosed in the patent. In *Aileen Mills Co. v. Ojay Mills, Inc.*, 188 F. Supp. 138, DC SNY 1960, for example, summary judgment was granted to the defendant because it was found that, although the respective bedspread designs of the two parties as sold to the public were indeed similar, the defendant's bedspread would not make the same total impression on the eye of the ordinary purchaser as that made by plaintiff's design as patented. The court refused to extend the scope of what was actually shown in plaintiff's drawings to encompass the broader "inventive concept embodied

in that design set forth in the drawings."
And, in *Reachi* v. *Edmond*, 277 F.2d 850,
CA 9 1960, the patent application stated
that "the dominant features of my new design are shown in solid lines," and the
lines included a metal sleeve for a table
lamp. Since the defendant's lamp lacked
the metal sleeve and thus created an entirely different effect, the court held that
plaintiff could not recover for infringement
despite the argument that the metal sleeve
depicted was optional and only a minor
feature of the design.

Double Patenting

It is well settled that two patents cannot
properly be granted to the same inventor
on the basis of a single inventive concept,
and that the prohibition against double patenting is equally applicable in design cases.
In *Application of Russell*, 239 F.2d 387,
CCPA 1956, rejection of an application for
a design patent was upheld since the pumps
shown in appellant's application and those
in his earlier design patent were so "strikingly similar in overall appearance" that
one design might be mistaken for the other.
The court held that the differences involved
only "obvious expedients." Similarly, in *Ex
parte Schwartz*, 124 USPQ 8, PO BdApp
1959, the applicant had previously been
granted a design patent on a round box with
decorative features and had applied for another design patent on the box in square
form with an added dispensing mechanism
and spout shown in other references; refusal
of the second application was upheld on
grounds of double patenting.

On the other hand, in *Laskowitz* v. *Marie
Designer, Inc.*, 119 F. Supp. 541, DC SCal
1954, the court found a distinction between
plaintiff's earlier design patent for a reclin-
ing chair and his later design patent for a
chair having a more aesthetic appearance.
And although the Patent Office Board of
Appeals in *Ex parte Blum*, 137 USPQ 377,
1963, rejected one of two applications filed
by appellant as constituting double patenting, it did indicate how he might properly
describe, show, and claim the single patentable design concept represented in the
several figures of the other application.

While it is true that one may have a
mechanical patent and a design patent upon
the same subject matter, there must be a
clear patentable distinction between the two
inventive ideas involved. But, when the two
ideas are indistinguishable and are manifestly the result of the same idea, a second
patent will not be granted. Thus, an application for a design patent on a combined
cap and hanger ring for a flashlight was
held properly rejected for lack of a patentable distinction from the mechanical patent
previously granted to applicant on the same
subject matter. *In re Barber*, 81 F.2d 231,
CCPA 1936. Conversely, a mechanical patent application covering new and useful improvements in a finger ring was held properly rejected because the claims were disclosed in a design patent previously granted
to the same inventor. *Application of Phelan*,
205 F.2d 183, CCPA 1953.

In *Application of DuBois*, 262 F.2d 88,
CCPA 1958, design patent and mechanical
patent applications had been filed on the
same day covering a shoulder cord for a
military uniform. The design patent was
issued, but the application for mechanical
patent was rejected by the Patent Office on
the doctrine of the *Barber* and *Phelan* cases,
supra. The Patent Office's action was reversed on appeal, however, on the ground
that the ornamental design embodied a different inventive concept from the "utilitarian or structural concept defined in the
appealed claims."

Applications for Design Patents

The claim and also the descriptive part
of design applications and patents can be
and ordinarily are identical with other design applications and patents except for (1)
the specific name of the article, (2) the
brief description of the figure(s) of the
drawing and (3) the drawing itself. The
complete application, with blanks to be
filled in, is shown in Form 22 of the Rules
of Practice in Patent Cases and under
Forms herein.

Cross-references: *Copyrights—Relationship to Patents; Trademarks in Relation to Patents*, sections on Design Patents and Trademarks.

DISBARMENT. See ATTORNEYS AND AGENTS

DISCLAIMERS

Hillel Marans

Disclaimers in patent law are either statutory or nonstatutory.

Nonstatutory disclaimers may be *express* disclaimers of claims in a pending application that form the counts of an interference which an applicant desires to terminate, or *implied* disclaimers which result from failing to make claims suggested to the applicant for counts in a proposed interference.

Statutory disclaimers made in issued patents are at present either *subject matter* or *patent term* disclaimers. The first class applies to the part of claimed subject matter of which the patentee is not the inventor or the first inventor. The second class abandons the entire term of the patent or any terminal part of the period of a patent granted or to be granted.

Only statutory disclaimers will be discussed in this chapter.

Few Supreme Court decisions touch upon the disclaimer sections of the Patent Act of 1952, this Court having consistently denied certiorari in such cases. The decisions rendered to date do indicate, however, a trend and serve as a guide to the patent profession, including the examiners of the U.S. Patent Office.

Statutory Provisions

Statutory provisions of 35 U.S.C. relating to disclaimers are:

Section 253. Disclaimer

Whenever, without any deceptive intention, a claim of a patent is invalid the remaining claims shall not thereby be rendered invalid. A patentee, whether of the whole or any sectional interest therein, may, on payment of the fee required by law, make disclaimer of any complete claim, stating therein the extent of his interest in such patent. Such disclaimer shall be in writing and recorded in the Patent Office; and it shall thereafter be considered as part of the original patent to the extent of the interest possessed by the disclaimant and by those claiming under him.

In like manner any patentee or applicant may disclaim or dedicate to the public the entire term, or any terminal part of the term, of the patent granted or to be granted. (R. S. 4917; 35 U.S.C., 1946 ed., 65.)

Section 288. Action for infringement of a patent containing an invalid claim

Whenever, without deceptive intention, a claim of a patent is invalid, an action may be maintained for the infringement of a claim of the patent which may be valid. The patentee shall recover no costs unless a disclaimer of the invalid claim has been entered at the Patent Office before the commencement of the suit.

Subject Matter Disclaimers

Purpose. Subject matter disclaimers are filed to cancel claims known to be invalid in a patent. An example is a claim in an issued patent that has been lost to opponent in interference or held invalid by a court decision holding valid another claim of the same patent.

When a patentee has claimed more than he originally invented or first discovered, he or the owner may disclaim such parts of the thing patented as are not to be held by virtue of the patent or assignment.

The 1952 Act, 35 U.S.C. 253, does not require the cancellation of the invalid claims to render the remaining claims valid, as discussed more fully in the section *Necessity for Disclaiming and Diligence.*

Parts That May Be Disclaimed. Before the Act of 1952, limiting disclaimers were used to some extent, to narrow the scope of a claim without cancelling the claim outright. They were filed when there was a question as to the validity of a claim because of undue breadth and when it was considered that additional limitation would improve the probability of the claim being held valid, without, at the same time, making the claim so narrow as to exclude the infringing device. In many cases, a new element was introduced in the claim instead of merely making the elements already present in the claim more specific. The courts looked with disfavor on such disclaimers, mainly on the ground that the claims so limited were not reexamined in the first instance by the Patent Office, as they would have been in a reissue of the patent. See *Altoona Publix Theaters, Inc. v. American Tri-Ergon Corp.*, 294 U.S. 477, 1935; *Carnegie Steel Co. v. Cambria Iron Co.*, 185 U.S. 403, 1901; and *Otis Elevator Co. v. Pacific Finance Co.*, 68 F.2d 664, 1866.

Although a disclaimer can now be made only of a complete claim, a limiting disclaimer made before Jan. 1, 1953 may still be sued upon. *Diebold Inc. v. Record Files, Inc.*, 98 USPQ 10, DC NOhio 1953. The test of validity of limiting disclaimers is whether they change the character of the claimed invention by extending claims, introducing new elements into them or otherwise altering them in such manner as to seek the benefit of a reissue, without actual reissue.

Necessity for Disclaiming and Diligence. Mr. P. J. Federico in his "Commentary on the New Patent Act" appearing as a supplement to "Title 35 U.S.C. Annotated" 1954 states that:

"The necessity of disclaiming an invalid claim to recover is eliminated by the Statute. One bad claim does not affect other claims. The only thing is that under Section 288 Title 35 U.S.C. the patentee cannot recover costs unless disclaimer of invalid claim has been entered in the Patent Office before the commencement of the suit."

Federico also states that this consideration alone is thought to be sufficient inducement to disclaim seasonably claims known to be invalid, as for example, claims finally lost in interference or finally held invalid by a court of competent jurisdiction.

Effect of Disclaimed Claims on Validity of Retained Claims. In *Hoover Co. v. Mitchel Mfg. Co.*, 122 USPQ 314, CA 7 1959, the court stated:

"Neither will we go as far as defendant would have us do and hold that disclaimer action entirely destroyed the presumption of validity as to the remaining claims. We do think, however, that it materially detracts from the weight to be attached to such presumption and negates plaintiff's argument of an enhanced presumption arising from the careful and meticulous scrutiny exercised by the Patent Office. The presumption of validity, whether it be characterized as ordinary or enhanced, attached with equal force to all of the 38 claims included in the patent at the time of issuance. Some five years later plaintiff by its disclaimer admitted that Babcock was not the inventor of

eleven of the allowed claims. That means that these claims were invalid from the beginning and that they never should have been endowed with any presumption of validity. The most that can be said for the remaining claims is that they carry no more than the ordinary presumption."

Without Any Deceptive Intention. No decisions are found defining explicitly "without any deceptive intention." The decision of *Becton Dickinson and Co. v. Robert P. Scherer Corporation*, 94 USPQ 138, DC EMich 1952, before the 1952 Act took effect, held that there can be no disclaimer under 35 U.S.C. 65 (old) if patentee was guilty of fraud in procuring patent.

Rule 321 and form 43 of the Rules of Practice do not require any recitation beyond the statutory requirement "without any deceptive intention." They require no facts supporting this allegation in the petition for disclaimer. The question of deceptive intention may be raised in a suit for infringement, however, where such facts can be investigated. See *Diebold, Inc. v. Record Files, Inc.*, supra, where it was held that such question must be determined upon proof at trial rather than on motion to dismiss.

How Subject Matter Disclaimers Are Effected. Form 43 reads:

"To the Commissioner of Patents:
"Your petitioner ...., residing at .... in the county of .... and State of .... represents that he is (here state the exact interest of the disclaimant; if assignee, set out liber and page or reel and frame, where assignment is recorded) of letters patent of the United States No. ...., granted to ...., on the .... day of ...., 19.., for .... and that he has reason to believe that without any deceptive intention claims of said letters patent are too broad or invalid. Your petitioner, therefore, hereby disclaims claim .... of said patent.
"Signed at ...., State of .... this .... day of ...., 19...

_____

(Signature)"

Miscellaneous Disclaimer Provisions. Disclaimers may be made in a reissue patent, *Gage v. Herring*, 1883 C.D. 289; 22 O.G. 2119.

Patent Term Disclaimers

Effect of Patent Term Disclaimers on Double Patenting. Before the enactment of 35 U.S.C. 253, supra, an applicant could dedicate to the public the entire term of the patent at the time of the issuance thereof or disclaim all the claims of the patent at any time after its issuance. A number of such dedications and disclaimers are of record in the Official Gazette. However, the provision as to a terminal part of the patent term is new in the statute; Mr. P. J. Federico in his extensive book "Statutory Disclaimers in Patent Law" published in 1935 mentions no case of such disclaimer.

Terminal patent term disclaimer is discussed by Mr. Federico in page 49 of "Commentary on the New Patent Act," supra. He states, in substance, that the proponents of this type of disclaimer contemplated that it might be effective in some instances as combatting a defense of double patenting.

As is usual in cases of this type, the problem first presented itself to the Patent Office soon after the law took effect. The Board of Appeals rendered two opinions on this subject in 1953 in which it held that terminal patent disclaimers are of no avail when the two devices of the patent and the application are not inventively different. Since these decisions have not been published in full, an excerpt of one of the two that appeared in the writer's article "Disclaimer of a Terminal Part of the Patent Term and Double Patenting," 36 JPOS 207, 1954, is here reproduced:

"While appellant contends that filing of this disclaimer will prevent any question of double patenting, 'since there can now be no extension of monopoly, in a patent to be issued on this application expiring on the same date as the prior patent,' we are of the opinion that patentability of the appealed claims is not established by the filing of the disclaimer. The extension of the monopoly of the patent involved, in our opinion, is not the only objection to the patenting of two devices which, as we indicated in our original decision, are not inventively different. It is well settled that under these circumstances only one patent should issue, the power to create a monopoly being exhausted by the first patent. *Miller et al.* v. *Eagle,* 1894 C.D. 147; 66 OG 845; *Underwood et al.* v. *Gerber,* 1893 C.D. 340; 63 OG 1063. An important objection to

double patenting is based upon the complications that can result from split ownership. Conflict between respective owners may occur. The more serious objection is that an infringer might be subject to suit by each of two owners. It is our conclusion, therefore, that the submission of the disclaimer fails to obviate all of the objections to double patenting and does not constitute sufficient basis for reversing the examiner's rejection based on that ground."

The other Board decision is along the same lines as the one copied above. These decisions clearly hold that where a situation of double patenting arises, it may not *ipso facto* be remedied by a disclaimer of a terminal part of the patent. This is the statement now appearing in M.P.E.P. It is the principle stated in *In re Siu,* 105 USPQ 428, CCPA 1955. This *Siu* decision reasons that a terminal disclaimer places patents, which failed to issue concurrently, on the same footing as regards double patenting as patents issued on the same day. Double patenting between the latter is discussed in the article *Double Patenting* and in Sections 10 and 11 of Leon H. Amdur's book "Patent Law and Practice," 1935 and Emerson Stringham's "Double Patenting," 1933, Sections 2856 A, B, C.

Terminal Disclaimers in the Application Stage. Term disclaimers made in pending applications appear not to require the allegation of "without any deceptive intent," since pending applications are in a fluid state. [Such disclaimers of a terminal portion of a patent to be granted may avoid rejection on double patenting. See *In re Kaye,* p. 210.]

Collection of Court Costs in Terminal Disclaimers in Patents

There is no section in Title 35 U.S.C. for terminal disclaimers corresponding to Section 288 for subject matter disclaimers. The question whether costs may be collected if a terminal disclaimer is made after the commencement of suit for infringement seems not yet to have come up for decision. Since the defendant was deprived of the defense of double patenting by the disclaimer filed after the commencement of the suit, it would appear that no costs should be awarded and that plaintiff should be satisfied by the decision of the court of the effectiveness of the disclaimer in the double patenting controversy.

The question of timeliness of a terminal disclaimer does not arise in a pending application.

How Terminal Disclaimers are Effected. In the case of *In re Fahnoe and Shyne*, 123 USPQ 579, 1959, the Commissioner held that the reasonable import of "in like manner" in the second paragraph of Title 35 U.S.C. 253, supra, and Rule 321 (noted above) is that terminal disclaimers should comply with all formal requirements set forth in the first paragraph of the Statute and Rule and all pertinent language thereof. This statement means that the disclaimer should follow, with any necessary modifications, the suggested Form 43 (copied above). This decision also holds that the date of expiration of the patent term should be independently stated and not only as the date of expiration of the older patent. The above decision applies only to terminal disclaimers in patents.

Disclaimers in applications do not require the $10 fee required in patents or the elaborate Form 43.

An example of a terminal disclaimer in a patent already issued appears in the O.G. of May 4, 1954, and reads as follows:

"2,383,080 Frank E. Reilly, Chicago and Chester Holsinger, River Forest, Ill. Method of making curved printing members. Patent dated Aug. 21, 1945. Disclaimer filed April 15, 1954, by the assignee, Electrographic Corporation.

"Hereby enters this disclaimer to that terminal part of its term beyond Oct. 3, 1961, so that said patent No. 2,383,080 may expire simultaneously with the expiration of U.S. Patent No. 2,359,385 granted Oct. 3, 1944."

This notice is attached to each copy of the issued patent.

Terminal disclaimer in an application should be essentially as follows:

"I, John Doe, applicant in the above named application, hereby disclaim the portion of the term of any patent issued on this application which extends beyond (date)."

A notice of such disclaimer appears in the heading of each copy of the patent issued on such application.

Cross-references: *Abandonment, Act of 1952, Dedication, Double Patenting, Validity.*

DISCLOSURES FOR APPLICATIONS— OBTAINING AND PROCESSING

John A. McKinney

Recently we in Johns-Manville made a planned study to develop a program for the disclosure of inventions of value, forwarding them through proper channels to the patent department, and deciding whether or not to file upon them. The procedure finally adopted is given briefly below.

Instructions to Potential Inventors

While periodic lectures are the chief form of instruction, an "Invention Disclosure" form reminds the inventor, at the time of writing his disclosure, of the classes of information required.

We advise our employees to submit, as inventions, what they have done that provides a real (rather than theoretical) advantage to Johns-Manville or for the industry and has never been done before, insofar as the employee knows.

Disclosures that are complete and technical are preferred to attempts to be legalistic.

Invention Disclosure

Utilizing this simple test, J-M employees disclose inventions to the Patent Department in the manner prescribed in the Invention Record Sheet.

This printed form is as follows, space being left on the actual 4-page folder, of letter head size, for typing the information requested.

Sheet 1

JOHNS-MANVILLE CORPORATION

Invention Disclosure

. . . .

Title of Invention _____

Name(s) of Inventor(s) (Give first name(s) in full)

   1. Name _____ Employed at _____

      Citizen of _____

      Residence Address _____
            (Street No., City, County, State)

Field of Invention (Name the broad field as well as the particular application. Indicate the limits of the field wherever possible. Brief example: "This invention relates to production of mineral wool batts and blankets and is particularly concerned with separation of shot from fibre. While primarily applicable to wool formed by spinning, the invention may also be useful with blown wool.")

Purpose of the Invention—Problem to be solved (Describe briefly the problems which gave rise to the invention and the major difficulties which it eliminates).

Sheet 2

Drawing (Draw, paste, or otherwise attach here a sketch or drawing illustrating the invention. Blueprint type sketches are usually not sufficient—pictorial sketches are preferred. With most products and apparatus more than one view is necessary for complete illustration. Processes should be illustrated schematically and compositions should be illustrated graphically where possible).

Sheet 3

Detailed Description of Invention. Describe the invention in such detail that a person moderately skilled in the art may understand its novel features and any unexpected or advantageous results attained. Emphasize particularly and clearly identify those features that produce real advantages over prior practices. Supply any known equivalents or alternative materials, ranges, proportions, etc., that may be used. Attach copies or refer to available pertinent reports or letters, if any. If drawings are supplied, refer to portions of any drawings by numerals.

Sheet 4

Detailed Description of Invention (Cont.).

Sheet 4—at end

Each of the undersigned has been informed regarding the invention, as described in the Invention Disclosure, understands the invention and is witness to the signature(s) of the inventor or inventors as noted.

Date

Signature(s) of the inventor or inventors.

_____　_____　_____

_____　_____　_____

_____　_____　_____

_____　_____　_____

Special Instructions:

This form should be filled out promptly (in duplicate) by the Inventor(s). In order to have the Records accurate and uniform it is recommended they be prepared in collaboration with certain individuals at each location who will assume the responsibility for forwarding the completed duplicate forms to the Patent Department, Manville Research Center, as follows:

    (a)　Research Center—Patent Committee Representative of Department involved.
    (b)　Plants—Industrial Engineer or other person designated by Plant Manager.
    (c)　New York Offices—Division Patent Committee Representative or Patent Attorneys.
    (d)　Sales Offices—Sales Manager in charge.
    (e)　Canadian Products Division—Patent Committee Representative (Production Engineer)

The Patent Department will keep Director of Research Center and Managers of Research Departments informed currently on all Invention Submissions. Retain draft copy for your files if desired.

Docketing and Appraisal for Filing

The disclosure, forwarded as described, is given a docket number and assigned to a particular attorney.

It is then considered by our Patent Committee, a group composed of most of our patent attorneys and representatives from the various Research Departments at our Research Center and from our headquarters for foreign operations. This Committee considers the legal, technical and commercial significance of the invention and determines future action. If a development is of sufficient technical and commercial importance to justify filing a patent application, the Patent Committee usually decides that a novelty search be made before a final decision is made on filing.

Because "an invention," as distinguished from a "development," exists only by virtue of the Patent Statute, we require our attorneys, before preparing a patent application to formulate a complete "theory of the case" under the Statute and pertinent decisions. Except where we are already thoroughly familiar with the prior art, attorneys, in preparing applications, are requested to make a specific review of the prior art. We prefer that this review be as thorough as is practical under the circumstances and include not only patents and publications but also available information on present and past practices of J-M and its competitors.

Our attorneys appraising disclosures during application preparation are instructed to catalog each difference between the development under consideration and the pertinent prior practices and then to determine for each such difference whether or not it produces results which (1) would be advantageous to J-M, (2) would be advantageous to a competitor, or (3) would not have been obvious to one of ordinary skill in the particular art involved. Our attorneys do not rely solely upon the inventor for information and analysis with respect to the significance of the differences over the prior art. They consult engineering, research, production and merchandising functions who may have information bearing on the subject. The attorneys are urged particularly to consult merchandising and production functions, to determine which differences over the prior art the industry would be most likely to adopt, since it is these differences which we wish to emphasize strongly in any patent application.

Prior to the preparation of applications on some important cases, we not only have searched prior patents and publications but also have reviewed every file in J. M.'s possession relating to the broad art in which the invention lies. The purpose of such effort is to collect evidence which supports patentability under Sections 102 and 103 of the Patent Statute. We look primarily for solid evidence of unobviousness.

We also file a few cases, in the category of novel but not economically promising discoveries, partly in recognition of the inventor's work and to maintain morale. These cases, when clearly patentable, are handled in a more routine fashion since they do not justify such substantial investigation.

Recital of Theory of Case

When the investigation of the published and practical art reveals an unobvious advance in the art, we prefer that our attorneys recite the facts briefly in the introductory portion of the patent application. Recital of a concise "theory of the case" not only assists the attorney in formulating his subsequent presentation but also may make more clear to a judge, in case the issued patent is litigated, the nature and merit of the invention.

Cross-references: *Incentives for Inventors, Patentability, Records, Searching.*

DISPUTES. See ARBITRATION, INTERFERENCES

DIVISION. See RESTRICTION

DOUBLE PATENTING
William D. Palmer

Double patenting has always been a problem for the applicant, patentee and attorney, as shown by the numerous decisions in which this issue was present. The Patent Act of 1952 removes some of the problems. It rules out double patenting between parent and divisional applications or patents filed as a result of a requirement for restriction and permits disclaiming the terminal portion of the term of a patent or of a patent to be granted, so as to avoid extension of the monopoly. Such disclaimer also may avoid rejection of an application on that issue. *In re Kaye*, 141 USPQ 829, CCPA 1964. See *In re Robeson*, 141 USPQ 485, CCPA 1964.

The "research team" approach of our modern technology has increased the likelihood of double patenting, since any scientific breakthrough will often result in many associated scientists concentrating their efforts on the theoretical and practical aspects of the same subject. This requires a clear line of patentable distinction between all patent applications which result from such intensified effort. Also, most courts take a stringent view of double patenting.

The Basic Principles Supporting Double Patenting Are Simple—Their Application Sometimes Complex

The basic principles supporting double patenting are simple and clear cut and are set forth in a few representative decisions, as follows:

(1) *Miller* v. *Eagle*, 151 U.S. 186, 1894, the leading case in the field, holds that *one invention can support only one patent.*

(2) *In re Isherwood*, 1917 C.D. 226, CA DC, another leading case, holds that: "The patentability of ... claims may be decided on (applicant's) patent by the same rules which would be applied to test their anticipation by a patent to another." In other words, there exists *only one standard of invention.*

(3) *In re Fischel et al.*, 58 USPQ 80, CCPA 1943, holds that the doctrine of double patenting is applicable to copending applications of different inventors, when owned by the same assignee.

While the foregoing holdings are quite clear, their application to specific situations can take as many twists and deviations as any aspect of patent law. This is primarily due to the fact that the application of the doctrine normally requires a determination of whether one or more patentable inven-

tions are claimed, and the determination of what constitutes a patentable invention often involves factors which weigh heavily in favor of one of the parties concerned.

When the Term "Double Patenting" Should Be Used

The terminology "double patenting" has been loosely used. In some reported decisions, the term has been applied improperly; in other reported decisions, when the principles supporting double patenting should have been applied, either they have been ignored or a specific denial has been made that double patenting was an issue. Before proceeding further, it is advisable, therefore, to set forth the general rules which the weight of authority has established for applying the principles of double patenting.

Briefly, such principles are applicable when *the claims* of an application or a patent and *not the descriptive portion of the specification* are used as prior art against an application or a patent. If the descriptive portion of the specification can be used as prior art against the claims of an application or a patent, then the issue of double patenting need not be raised. Thus the terminology "double patenting" simply means that *the claims* of an application or a patent are not patentable over *the claims* of an application or a patent of the same inventor or of different inventors with the same assignee.

The following are specific situations which can be encountered in the Patent Office:

(1) Inventor A files a basic application. While this is still pending, he files another application *claiming* an improvement which the examiner considers to be unpatentable over the matter *claimed* in the copending basic application. The rejection should be double patenting, since *only the claims* can be used as a part of the prior art.

(2) Inventor B files an application disclosing two inventions which apparently are patentable over each other and also patentable over the prior art. He *claims only one* of the two disclosed inventions. Thereafter, while this application is still pending, Inventor C of the same assignee files an application claiming the invention which is

disclosed but not claimed by Inventor B. The later-filed application of Inventor C can be rejected on the *disclosure* of the copending, prior-filed patent of Inventor B. The condition is not double patenting, since the descriptive portion of the prior-filed patent specification is used to reject the claims of the later-filed application.

(3) Suppose that in example (2), Inventor C swears back of the filing date of Inventor B, under the provisions of Rule 131. Additional art is then cited which is alleged to show that the two inventions disclosed by Inventor B are not sufficiently different to support separate patents. In other words, the matter claimed by Inventor C is not considered to be patentable over the invention claimed by Inventor B. The rejection must now be one of double patenting, since *only the claims* of the prior-filed, copending patent can be used as a part of the prior art.

(4) Inventor D first files a basic application which matures into a patent. Nine months after the patent issues, he files another application which claims matter purporting to constitute a patentable improvement over the invention claimed in his issued patent. The examiner cites additional art which he combines with the claims of the issued patent of Inventor D to show that the later-filed application claims matter which is not patentable over the *claims* of the issued patent. The rejection is one of double patenting, since *only the claims* of the issued patent can be used as a part of the prior art. See *In re Bersworth*, 90 USPQ 83, CCPA 1951.

(5) In example (4), assume the improvement application is not filed until the patent has been issued for more than the one year statutory period. The rejection is not double patenting, since the descriptive portion of the patent specification also forms a part of the prior art.

(6) Inventor E files an improvement or narrow application before he files a copending broader application. The first-filed improvement application is first to issue. The examiner rejects the later-filed broader application on the issued patent. The rejection is double patenting, since the issuance of the last-filed broader application would ex-

tend the monopoly of the invention *claimed* in the first-filed improvement patent. It can be argued that the double patenting rejection would be proper even if the application and the patent claimed inventions which were patentably distinct from each other and from all prior art.

While only the patent claims can be used as prior art in double patenting issues, reference may be made, when evaluating the claims in question, to the specification to define the claims. *In re Greenlee*, 106 USPQ 104, CCPA 1955, and also the entire file wrapper. *Bradford Novelty* v. *Eppy*, 118 USPQ 27, DC ENY, 1958. It is also well settled that other prior art is properly considered in determining whether or not the claims are patentably distinct from those of a patent. *In re Ockert*, 114 USPQ 330, CCPA 1957.

The Three General Classes of Situations Where Double Patenting Is Applicable

It is again stressed that the use of the terminology "double patenting" means simply that *the claims* of an application or patent are not patentable over *the claims* of an application or patent of the same inventor, or of different inventors of the same assignee. The three classes of situations in which the doctrine should be invoked are as follows:

(1) When either (a) two copending applications, or (b) an application and a patent which were copending or (c) two patents that were copending of the same applicant or owned by the same assignee before issuing *do not claim separate and distinct inventions*.

(2) When an application is filed within one year after the issue date of a patent to the same applicant, but *fails to claim* matter patentable over the *claims* of the issued patent.

(3) When two copending applications of the same applicant, or owned by the same assignee, claim a basic invention and a patentable improvement thereover, but the patent or application claiming the basic invention is last filed and last issued, or is last filed and last sought to issue. Decisions

pertinent to this situation are conflicting.

With respect to situation (2), older decisions did not permit the applicant the statutory period in which to claim his disclosed but unclaimed subject matter, but held that such matter was "dedicated." In the case of *In re Bersworth*, supra, claims were rejected on the grounds of dedication to the public, but the holding of "dedication" was based upon the determination that the claims of the application in issue did not define an invention over the matter *claimed* in the applicant's patent reference. Thus the claims were actually rejected for double patenting, as defined herein. For a detailed study of pertinent decisions, see *V. G. Trapasso*, **43** JPOS 140, 1961.

Statutory and Other Considerations Prohibiting Double Patenting

As is concisely set forth in *In re Ockert*, supra, "35 U.S.C. 101, like its predecessor R.S. 4886, provides that an inventor may obtain a [one] patent for his invention. There is no statutory provision for the granting of a plurality of patents on a single invention, and this court has repeatedly held that if two patents are to be granted there must be two inventions." The foregoing decision should be read in conjunction with the dissents in *In re Hession*, **132** USPQ 40, CCPA 1961.

The main objections to double patenting are:

(1) Possible extension of the patent monopoly which would occur if two patents for the same invention did not expire on the same day.

(2) Possible double harassment of infringers. For example, if two patents were to be granted on only one invention, one of these patents could be assigned to another party. The possible infringer would then have to deal with completely different parties for the same invention.

Election and Double Patenting— Different Inventors of the Same Assignee

Applications or patents of different inventive entities but owned by the same assignee, when copending, are subject to the same tests of double patenting as applications or patents of the same inventor. Whenever the inventors in the separate applications are not identical, the inventive entities are different even when one inventor is common to both applications in issue.

Since the term "double patenting" infers two patents granted to one "inventive entity" for only one invention, most current decisions refer to "election" when different inventors are involved. Nevertheless, such decisions apply the tests of double patenting just as if the inventors involved were the same. Thus the difference between "election" and double patenting is merely one of terminology.

The leading case on the subject of election is *In re Fischel et al.*, supra, wherein the court stated:

"We think the true doctrine of election in patent cases is grounded upon one or more of three fundamental propositions. First, the application of the doctrine prevents two patents being issued for the same invention. Second, it prevents an avoidance of the determination of priority. Third, it prevents an extension of the monopoly."

Once the assignee has made his election by allowing a patent to issue on one of the copending applications, this election is irrevocable and cannot be withdrawn even by a disclaimer of all of the claims of the issued patent. *In re Hession*, supra.

Under present Patent Office practices, the examiner can reject copending applications of the same applicant or assignee on the grounds of double patenting, even though no claims are allowed in either of the copending applications. M.P.E.P. 822.01 and 305. The applicant or assignee is thus placed on notice that he must guard against an irrevocable and possibly incorrect election. Since the decision of *In re Hession*, the Patent Office must notify the different inventors, as well as the assignee, of possible conflicts between the copending applications. Office Notice, 776 O.G. 609, 1962.

In a few recent decisions, the courts have indicated that double patenting is not applicable when different inventors are involved, even though the assignee is the same. *University of Illinois* v. *Block*, **107** USPQ 159, DC Ill 1955; *Peelers Co.* v. *Kaakinen*,

126 USPQ 42, DC Wash 1960. The possibility of "election" by the common assignee was not considered. It is submitted that such decisions can be interpreted as contrary to the intent of 35 U.S.C. 101. Certainly, these decisions do not take into account the practical considerations involved. If the principles of double patenting were applicable only when the same inventor was involved, one assignee could obtain many patents supported by only one inventive concept simply by filing plural applications in the names of different inventive entities. CCPA decisions do not support this viewpoint. *In re Borcherdt et al.*, 94 USPQ 175, 1952; also see *Hughes Tool* v. *United Machine*, 47 USPQ 74, DC Tex, 1939; *Brooks* v. *Stoffel Seals Corp.*, 117 USPQ 91, DC SNY, 1958; and *Comm. Solvents Corp.* v. *Watson*, 127 USPQ 353, DC DCol, 1960.

When Different Inventors of the Same Assignee Have Similar Disclosures

In this case the first-filed patent is prior art against the later-filed application—however, this is not the case when the applications are concurrently filed.

When different inventors of the same assignee present an application and a prior-filed patent which was copending with the application, the later-filed application can be rejected on the similar disclosure of the prior-filed patent. *Ex parte Lindeman et al.*, 107 USPQ 331, PO BdApp 1955. The patent can be removed as a reference by swearing back of its filing date under the provisions of Rule 131. Until the patent is so removed as a reference, the rejection is not one of double patenting. After the swearing back, only the claims of the patent can be used as a part of the prior art to reject the claims of the application on the grounds of double patenting.

Concurrently filed applications of different inventors of the same assignee can be cited against each other only on the basis of double patenting. The descriptive portion of either of the applications which first matures into a patent cannot be used as prior art against the other pending application. *Ex parte Clawson*, 1929 C.D. 67, CA

DC; *Ex parte Sparks et al.*, 92 USPQ 233, PO BdApp 1951.

Filing and Issuing Dates—Their Effect on Basic Applications and Patents and Improvements

When Only One Invention is Claimed in Different Applications or Patents, Only Issuing Dates are of Any Consequence. When only one invention is claimed in an application and a patent, or in two patents of the same inventor or owned by the same assignee before issuing, the weight of authority holds that the later-issued patent, or application sought to issue later, is invalid or should be rejected for double patenting. The respective filing dates are of no consequence. *In re Laughlin*, 9 USPQ 126, CCPA 1931; *Ex parte Dean*, 27 USPQ 26, PO BdApp 1934. The same is true even when the earlier application is broader than the later filed patent. *Ex parte Barrick*, 88 USPQ 327, PO BdApp 1949; *Ex parte White*, 3 USPQ 215, Comr. Pat., 1929; also see *Miller* v. *Eagle*, supra.

The foregoing has assumed that only one invention is presented by the basic application or patent and the improvement alleged to be patentable thereover. The applicant or patentee in such a situation frequently has most of the equitable factors in his favor, which in turn can influence the determination of whether one or two inventions are present. Such factors can make double patenting issues as difficult to predict as any encountered in patent law.

Effect of Concurrent Issuing. There exists a split of authority with respect to whether double patenting can be held when patents issue concurrently, but do not claim separate inventions. One line of decisions holds that, since there is no extension of the monopoly, there is no double patenting. *Clark Co. et al.* v. *Jones & Laughlin*, 129 USPQ 97, CA 7 1961; *Shimadzu* v. *El. Storage Bat. Co.*, 31 USPQ 311, DC Pa 1936; *Sanson* v. *Knitting Mills*, 88 USPQ 543, DC NC 1950; *Pursche* v. *Atlas*, 132 USPQ 104, CA 9 1961.

Others hold that concurrent issuing will not preclude double patenting. *Underwood* v. *Gerber*, 149 U.S. 224, 1893. In *Brooks* v. *Stoffel*, 117 USPQ 91, DC SNY 1958, the assignee was permitted to elect on which of concurrently issued patents the monopoly was to rest.

For a full discussion of this subject, particularly as related to the effect of disclaiming the terminal portion of one of the patents, see the article *Disclaimers*.

Basic Application Last-Filed and Last-to-Issue. Where the broad or basic application is filed after the narrow or improvement application, the basic application can be rejected for double patenting. *Ex parte Barnes et al.*, 59 USPQ 309, PO BdApp 1942; *In re Christmann et al.*, 53 USPQ 634, CCPA 1942; *Ex parte Appeal* No. 48,932, 26 JPOS 784, 1944. To hold otherwise would permit the patentee to extend the monopoly of the improvement patent, since the teachings of this first-issuing improvement patent could not be practiced until the basic patent expired.

Basic Application First-Filed and Last-to-Issue. A first-filed broad or basic application can issue after an application which claims an improvement thereof, provided that two inventions are claimed by the respective applications. *In re Calvert*, 38 USPQ 184, CCPA 1938. This will result in some extension of the monopoly for the first-issued improvement patent, but such extension is permitted. Of course if only one invention is claimed by the two applications, only one patent can be obtained.

Some Recent Decisions of the CCPA and the Board of Appeals Are Fairly Stringent

Since 1953, parent and divisional applications or patents, filed as a result of a requirement for restriction, cannot be used as references against one another. 35 U.S.C. 121. In order to be protected under this statute, the divisional application *must* be filed in accordance with an Office requirement. In the recent decision of *In re Ockert*, supra, one applicant had filed six applications, all supported by a common inventive concept. After the first patent issued, the remaining five applications were rejected for double patenting over the issued patent. The applicant contended that had he initially filed all matter in one application,

restriction would have been required and he would have been protected by statute. The CCPA sympathized with the position of the applicant but affirmed the double patenting rejection of the five applications in issue. The CCPA also stated that even if a requirement for restriction would have been proper had all matter been filed in one application, this does not preclude a holding of double patenting when separate applications are filed in the first instance. This decision is to be contrasted with *In re Coleman et al.*, 90 USPQ 100, CCPA 1951 and *Ex parte Coberly*, 56 USPQ 422, PO BdApp 1942. Also see *Ex parte Bloch et al.*, 132 USPQ 207, PO BdApp 1959, which expressly overrules any liberal interpretation of *Ex parte Cohen*, 52 USPQ 189, PO BdApp 1941.

Genus-Species and Separate Species. Separate species claims can be maintained in different applications, provided the species are patentably distinct. *Ex parte Kinzie et al.*, 60 USPQ 462, PO BdApp 1943. The question of patentable distinction between the separate species is properly tested by reference to the prior art, *Ex parte Pyzel*, 128 USPQ 553, PO BdApp 1961, and since the decision of *In re Ruff et al.*, 118 USPQ 340, CCPA 1958, the equivalency of species can only be shown by the prior art. If the separate species are not patentably distinct over one another, then only one patent can be obtained. *In re Borcherdt et al.*, supra.

When separate species are claimed in copending applications, a claim generic to the species can be maintained in either of the applications, provided the species are patentably distinct. See *In re Blattner*, 114 USPQ 299, CCPA 1957, and *In re Muskat et al.*, 89 USPQ 142, CCPA 1951. Of course the separate species must be patentably distinct or only one patent can be obtained, *In re Loiseleur*, 72 USPQ 110, CCPA 1946, and a later-filed, first-issuing species claim can anticipate a generic claim. *In re Dreyfus*, 20 USPQ 301, CCPA 1934. Also, the generic claim can be maintained in only one of two applications. *Ex parte Pearce*, 128 USPQ 122, PO BdApp 1960.

The genus-species situation represents an exception to the general rule that the dominating application must be first filed or first issued. If the separate species claimed in different applications are patentably distinct, a claim generic to the species can be presented in either of the applications at any time before the other application issues. *In re Blattner*, supra; M.P.E.P. 806.04(i). Some decisions have strictly construed this exception, however, for if the generic claim could have been maintained in the parent application but is submitted in a continuation-in-part application, such last-filed generic claim cannot be allowed over the issued parent application. *Ex parte Frey*, 90 USPQ 383, PO BdApp, decided 1946.

When different inventors of the same assignee claim separate species, a claim generic to the species can be presented only in the application of the proper inventor. In such case, if the claimed species are not patentably distinct, a first-issuing species claim can anticipate a claim which is generic to the patented species. *Ex parte Schoeller et al.*, 57 USPQ 174, PO BdApp 1942.

Since the decision of *In re Joyce*, 115 USPQ 412, Comr. Pats., 1957, after election (restriction) is required between species claims, a divisional application claiming the non-elected species cannot be rejected on the patented elected species.

As a related matter, the scope of a Markush claim can be narrowed to avoid double patenting, *Ex parte Ayers et al.*, 89 USPQ 167, PO BdApp 1950, provided that the equivalency of the omitted species and the retained species is not known in the prior art.

Process and Apparatus. If the claimed process can be practiced by another materially different apparatus or by hand, or the claimed apparatus can be used to practice another and materially different process, then the claimed inventions usually are patentably distinct. *In re McKee*, 27 USPQ 353, CCPA 1935 (and decisions cited therein). If only one inventive concept is presented by process and apparatus claims, a broad interpretation may be given to the apparatus claims in order to reject the process for double patenting. *In re Arendt*, 24 USPQ 203, CCPA 1935.

Most of the pertinent decisions antedate the Patent Act of 1952, and some of these decisions were probably influenced by requirements for division. Under present practices, the safest course is initially to file all related matter in one application.

Product and Process. M.P.E.P. 806.05(f) states that restriction is proper (and that two inventions are present) if (1) the process *as claimed* is not an obvious process of making the product *and* the process as claimed can be used to make other and different products, or (2) the product *as claimed* can be made by another and materially different process.

The Manual summarizes the pertinent decisions. If the patented process is the only way of producing the claimed product, the product claims are not allowable, *In re Becker*, 24 USPQ 120, CCPA 1935, but when the product can be manufactured by a process other than the patented process as claimed, the product claims are allowable. *In re Cady*, 25 USPQ 345, CCPA 1935. When a patented process will not necessarily produce the claimed product and the product can be produced by several processes, the product is allowable. *Ex parte Zoss*, 114 USPQ 309, PO BdApp 1956. When process and element claims can be practiced without infringing one another, they represent separate inventions. *In re Coleman et al.*, supra. Product-by-process claims are not patentable over copending patented process claims. *In re Freeman*, 76 USPQ 585, CCPA 1948.

Usually a technological domination is not an important factor in double patenting. For example, even though a patented article has use only in a later-issuing method patent, the domination may be terminated at any time by a further advance in the art. *Jacquard Knitting* v. *Ordnance*, 88 USPQ 348, DC EPa, 1951.

Apparatus and Product. Double patenting is not present when the machine can be used to make articles other than as claimed and the claimed articles can be made by machines other than as claimed. *Hope Basket* v. *Product*, 84 USPQ 342, DC Mich 1950. The tests used to establish double patenting correspond to product and process for making the product, substituting "apparatus" for "process."

Combination and Subcombination or Element. If the combination does not rely on the subcombination for novelty, and if the subcombination can be used apart from the combination, a double patenting rejection is improper. *Ex parte Speier,* 100 USPQ 169, PO BdApp 1952.

When the novelty in an alleged combination resides in an element claimed in a copending patent, claims to the combination are rejectable for double patenting. *In re Land,* 44 USPQ 348 and 352, CCPA 1940. Similarly, if the combination claims derive their patentability from a novel subcombination or element, the last-issuing patent is invalid. *American Communications* v. *Pierce,* 100 USPQ 1, CA 1 1953.

In *Ex parte Douglas,* 51 USPQ 62, PO BdApp 1941, a last-filed application to an element was permitted to issue after the combination which included such element. Two inventions were present, and on this basis, the element claims were allowed. This decision represents an exception to the general rule that the broader application should not be last filed and permitted to issue last. In *Ex parte Roos,* 88 USPQ 469, PO BdApp 1950, a subcombination (or element), which had separate utility, was filed as a divisional application after the combination, and was permitted to issue last.

With respect to combination and subcombination claims in separate applications or patents, the general rule that one invention can support only one patent applies. If only one invention is claimed in separate applications, the last-issued patent or application sought to issue last is either invalid or rejectable for double patenting.

Designs

One Design and One Utility Application or Patent. Two inventions are required to support separate patents. *In re Phelan,* 98 USPQ 156, CCPA 1953; *Columbus* v. *Rona,* 97 USPQ 225, DC SNY 1953. A last-filed but first-issued design patent can be used to reject claims of a first-filed utility application. *Ex parte Schlumbohm,* 94 USPQ 393, PO BdApp 1952.

The weight of authority appears to hold that as between design and utility applications or patents, if the utility claims will read on a device not covered by the design, then there is no double patenting. *Appel* v. *Lilling,* 65 USPQ 281, DC SNY 1945 and

In re DuBois et al., 120 USPQ 198, CCPA 1958.

Miscellaneous Tests for One or Two Inventions

While double patenting issues normally involve a consideration of whether one or two inventions are claimed, there are some miscellaneous tests, particularly relating to double patenting, which have been influential in determining the presence or absence of two inventions.

Tests Which Show Two Inventions. The presence of the following factors has been persuasive in determining that two inventions were presented by claims in issue:

(1) There exists a substantial dissimilarity between the claims. *Technical Tape* v. *Minn. Mining,* 110 USPQ 260, DC SNY 1956.

(2) There is no extension of the monopoly. *In re Davis et al.,* 51 USPQ 458, CCPA 1941.

(3) Different novel features are present in the claims. *Hughes Tool* v. *United Machine,* 47 USPQ 74, DC Texas 1939.

(4) New and different results are obtained by the claimed devices. *Miller* v. *Zaharias,* 72 USPQ 434, DC Wis 1947.

(5) The same examiner handled both patents in issue. *Ruben* v. *Ariston Labs.,* 50 USPQ 279, DC Ill 1941.

(6) Allowed species in different applications is evidence that they are patentably distinct, so that a claim generic to both is allowable. *Ex parte Coss,* 95 USPQ 333, PO BdApp 1952.

Tests Which Show Only One Invention. The following factors have been persuasive in determining that only one invention was presented by claims in issue:

(1) A common essential element supports both patents. *Pierce* v. *Hewlett-Packard,* 105 USPQ 50, CA 1 1955.

(2) The claims in issue cross-read in that the patent cannot be practiced without infringing the application, and the application cannot be practiced without infringing the patent. *In re Hoffberger,* 44 USPQ 306, CCPA 1940. Cross-reading is not essential, however, to a determination that double patenting is present. *In re Ockert,* supra.

(3) The claims in issue merely differ in phraseology. *In re Ward,* 66 USPQ 317, CCPA 1945.

(4) The patent in issue is an obvious variant of an earlier issued patent. *Kress* v. *Aghnides,* 114 USPQ 187, CA 4 1957.

(5) The claims in issue merely differ in scope. *Richmond* v. *Umbach,* 80 USPQ 323, CA 7 1949.

Minimizing the Risks

Many of the most damaging double patenting issues can be avoided by the following soliciting practices:

(1) Whenever possible, include all related matter in one application, in order to be protected under 35 U.S.C. 121.

(2) File the broader or basic application first, and preferably issue it not later than the narrow or improvement application.

(3) Include in the narrow or improvement application a reference to the first-filed basic application.

(4) During the prosecution, make of record all possible double patenting issues, so that these issues will be properly considered by the Patent Office. Double patenting issues normally involve patentability over the available art which includes the claims of the applicant's or assignee's copending application or patent. If the Patent Office has cited and properly applied the prior art, the resulting patent is normally presumed valid over such art.

Cross-references: *Act of 1952—Patents, Claim Drafting, Disclaimers, Restriction, Validity.*

DRAWINGS

Harry C. Hart

When the nature of the case admits, an application for patent must include a drawing. 35 U.S.C. 113. Rule 81. In practice, this includes all applications for design patents, all applications for plant patents, and all applications for "mechanical" patents except those dealing with compositions of matter and chemical processes that can be carried out manually.

Standards

To facilitate examination, reproduction and classification, drawings must meet stringent standards of uniformity and quality. Among them is the requirement of Rule 84(a) that drawings be made on calendered paper of high quality and with India ink. The requirements for design patent drawings are the same. Rule 152. With the exception of drawings for plant patent applications, discussed below, and with the further exception of situations in which a fair representation in pen and ink is physically impossible, it is insisted upon.

Photographs

Where satisfactory pen and ink drawings are impossible, exceptions are made to the foregoing requirements. M.P.E.P. 608.02, which governs, reads in part as follows:

"Clearly, photographs are not drawings. Photographs are not acceptable for a filing date nor for any purpose except as exhibits unless they come within the special categories set forth in the Notice referred to below. Photolithographs of photographs and photographs mounted on proper size Bristol board are never acceptable. See In re Taggart et al., 1957 C.D. 6; 725 O.G. 397 and In re Myers, 1959 C.D. 2; 738 O.G. 947.

"SPECIAL CATEGORIES

"The Patent Office is willing to accept black and white photographs or photomicrographs (not photolithographs or other reproductions of photographs) printed on sensitized paper in lieu of India ink drawings, to illustrate inventions which are incapable of being accurately or adequately depicted by India ink drawings, restricted to the following categories: crystalline structures, metallurgical microstructures, textile fabrics, grain structures and ornamental effects. The photographs or photomicrographs must show the invention more clearly than they can be done by India ink drawings and otherwise comply with the Rules concerning drawings.... (Basis: Notice of October 13, 1959)"

Notice of April 24, 1964, reads in part as follows:

"[The] practice of granting a filing date to an application in which photoprints or other copy of a drawing is presented will be discontinued except upon a showing of circumstances of the kind contemplated by Rule 183." [Rule 183 relates to the requirements for waiver or suspension of the Rules by the Commissioner.]

Plant Patent Drawings

See M.P.E.P. 1606 dealing with drawings for plant patents and article *Plant Patents*.

Design Patent Drawings

M.P.E.P. 1503.02, which deals with drawings for design patents, reads in part as follows:

"*Rule 152. Drawing.* The design must be represented by a drawing made in conformity with the rules laid down for drawings of mechanical inventions and must contain a sufficient number of views to constitute a complete disclosure of the appearance of the article. Appropriate surface shading must be used to show the character or contour of the surfaces represented.

"The necessity for good drawings in a design application cannot be overemphasized. As the drawing constitutes substantially the whole disclosure of the design, it is of utmost importance that it be so well executed both as to clarity of showing and completeness that nothing regarding the shape, configuration and surface ornamentation of the article sought to be patented is left to conjecture. . . ."

A design patent drawing is normally made by a patent draftsman working from an object embodying the new, ornamental design or from a model or mock-up of it. The protection afforded by such a patent is restricted to the ornamental features. No product or object, however, for which a design patent may be sought is wholly devoid of functional features. The drawing, therefore, should emphasize the ornamental features, while the functional features should be played down. It is the attorney's responsibility to see that this is done.

Sample design patent drawings are illustrated in the article *Design Patents*.

Mechanical Patent Drawings

In contrast to the plant patent and the design patent, in which the legal protection is restricted to the thing illustrated, the protection afforded by a mechanical patent is measured by the claims.

While the drawing depicts an illustration of the invention, its purpose is to convey to the reader a notion of something far more general than the specific thing illustrated. To this end, while the drawing should show all of the patentable features, it should reveal them in their broadest aspects, and it should guard against showing features that might later be interpreted as restrictive. Thus, it should show as few as possible of the features which are old and of those which have to do with the setting or context out of which the invention emerges, in contrast to the invention itself. Rule 83. In short, the drawing should be schematic, in contrast to representative.

Just as a good test of the lucidity of the textual description is its ability to conjure up in the mind of the reader a mental image of the apparatus being described so that it can be read and understood without reference to the drawing, so a good test of a patent drawing is its ability to tell its own story without the need for referring to the textual description. As technology becomes more complex, these tests are ever more rarely met.

Legends. In order for a "mechanical" patent drawing to tell its own story in this fashion, it may advantageously contain legends in generous quantity. Krueger and Halpern **2,946,403** contains a schematic drawing, of which a copy is here reproduced (Fig. 1), bearing such legends. From a brief study of this drawing what each apparatus component is, how it is interconnected with the others, the composition of the reagents that take part in the process, and their movements from point to point of the apparatus immediately appear. This drawing goes far toward meeting the foregoing test.

Solicitor's Direction of Emphasis

In the planning of, arranging for, and execution of the drawing in such a case, the patent solicitor can make a great contribution. The inventor may come to him with no drawings at all, in which case the solicitor, with the inventor's assistance, must sketch out the component parts of the apparatus and their interconnections. In so doing he must work merely from a mental image arrived at in the course of conferences, and preferably after the formulation of a tentative claim. On other occasions, the

July 26, 1960   B. O. KRUEGER ET AL   2,946,403

CONCENTRATED FORMALDEHYDE SOLUTION

Filed Aug. 13, 1958

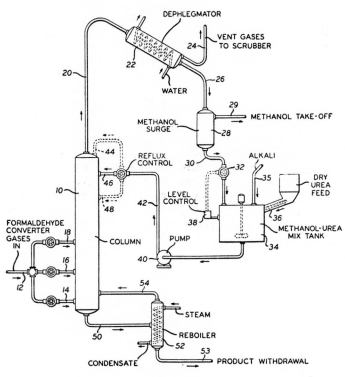

FIG. 1.

inventor comes to his attorney with a full set of manufacturing drawings including a mass of irrelevant detail; i.e., if the invention on which patent protection is sought is a detail of a carburetor, the drawings may well show an entire internal combustion engine in full detail. Nuts and bolts, wholly irrelevant, are shown with the same emphasis as are the patentable features.

It is the attorney's responsibility to boil down such a disclosure, cutting away one irrelevant detail after another, until the patentable features, which together constitute the invention, stand out from their background. This surgical operation is often far more difficult and arduous than building up a drawing showing the patentable features from a mental image alone.

A skillful and experienced patent draftsman can be of immeasurable assistance to the attorney in this part of his work, making suggestions as to what should be drawn in heavy lines, what in light lines, what centered on the page, what left off in a corner, what shown schematically, what in detail, and so on. But to do so, he must be guided by the attorney as to what are the patentable features. Merely to hand the draftsman a complete set of engineering drawings and ask him to proceed is an abdication of the attorney's responsibility.

Having completed this operation of purification and reduction, the skilled attorney then proceeds on a second course of expansion in which he looks upon the element of novelty as a principle or building block which may be applicable in fields and for uses beyond those to which the inventor's original disclosure was specifically directed. He suggests embellishment: if controllable flow of a fluid takes part in the operation, he suggests a valve. If constancy of speed is essential, he suggests a governor. Each step in this course increases the forcefulness of the illustration. The attorney will not actually have added to what may be patented; but he has brought to bear a constructive line of thinking which enables him to pass the inventor's idea along to the public in far better developed and more usable form than that in which it originally came to him.

General Considerations

Good drawings can add enormously to the clarity and cogency of a patent specification; indeed, to any pedagogic exposition.

The following statement, the best known to the writer, is that of Elmer V. Griggs, long a member of the Patent Department of Bell Telephone Laboratories, Inc. It is quoted with Mr. Griggs' permission:

"A drawing to accompany a patent specification is a hybrid of artistic design on the one hand, and of informational composition on the other. A nicely executed circuit drawing will appeal to the esthetic sense of a layman even though he may have little or no technical understanding of what it means. That same drawing presents to the worker in the art, the engineer, or the patent attorney a graphic description of a complex system. The effect of the drawing upon the layman is different from the effect upon the patent attorney but both respond alike to its quality or characteristic of outline. A jumble of weak lines apparently starting nowhere and ending nowhere leaves both the layman and the patent attorney cold. It is quite possible for a drawing sufficiently to comply with the requirements to support a valid patent without attaining that excellence which is desirable for the use of those who must study it over the years and the decades ahead.

"At least three persons cooperate in production of the patent drawing as finally presented to the Patent Office, the inventor, the patent solicitor and the patent draftsman. In many cases, the inventor will present his circuit by a diagram which is logical and informative. In other cases, however, the drawing as it comes from the inventor leaves much to be desired. In many instances, perhaps a majority of cases, it will be found that some recasting of the drawing in more illuminating form is almost essential in order to compare the invention illustrated with the prior art to determine what, if anything, is novel. In such cases, the time spent on revision of the drawing is not a mere artistic overhead but rather a part of the essential analysis which must be done.

"Some general considerations are believed to apply equally to almost all patent drawings. It is generally unwise to have the drawing made up in advance of preparation of any claims. The drawing is one of the vehicles by which the claimed subject-matter is to be brought to the mind of the reader. After the decision is reached as to what is to be claimed, it is soon enough to begin the drawing. Another factor which is sometimes overlooked is that the skilled patent draftsman is not a mere copyist. He should be a collaborator in planning the layout of the drawing to make it as simple and understandable as possible and, also, to enable it most effectively to present that which is to be claimed. If he is to do that sort of job he must know something about the invention; and it is the duty of the attorney to explain the general idea of the invention to him. Even though the draftsman may not be familiar with all the theories involved he can certainly grasp the main purpose of the invention if the attorney understands it well enough to explain it in simple terms.

"Doing what has been suggested will increase the time taken for preparation of a drawing by several hours. It will save, perhaps, as much time for the attorney in the later course of his prosecution of the application and in its consideration during his later career. The time that it later saves in searching is all clear gain. The time it saves the Patent Office Examining Corps and other practitioners will earn their everlasting gratitude."

Guide for Patent Draftsmen

The United States Patent Office has prepared, and has from time to time revised, a "Guide for Patent Draftsmen." Every patent draftsman should have his own copy, for ready reference. It is sold by the Superintendent of Documents, United States Government Printing Office, Washington 25, D.C., currently for fifteen cents.

Cross-references: *Application Writing, Design Patents, Fraud—sec. Inking Drawings, General and Mechanical Applications, Plant Patents.*

E

ECONOMIC VALUE OF PATENTS

Elmer J. Gorn

"It should be made clear at the outset that the value of the patent system cannot be quantitatively measured in the relatively precise manner of such economic variables as national income and its various components."[1] When we confine our attention to certain specific economic aspects of the patent system, however, we can obtain a general idea of the magnitude of its influence upon the level of economic activity in the United States.

For the purposes of this section, the economic value of patents may be defined as: the monetary value of the income, expenditures and development of resources, both public and private, which arises from the ownership of patents or from the expectation of such ownership. The public aspects may be taken as the total monetary values of all goods and services arising from patents. The private aspects may be considered in terms of the increase in profits which the owners of patents derive from such ownership. The latter is the more basic; it is the possibility of such increase which stimulates investment of time, effort and money in research and development, with the hope of producing patentable inventions and perfecting, manufacturing and marketing them.

Nature of the Patent Stimulus

The patent grant gives to its owner a prima facie right to exclude others from the practice of the invention covered by the patent and to collect damages for unauthorized manufacture, use or sale of such invention. Whether or not he can successfully enforce that right, against those who are unwilling to respect it, can be determined only by suit in the Federal courts. Such suits are long and expensive and the patent owner frequently is unsuccessful in sustaining his patent. Thus, the ownership of a patent is in reality only a promise that its owner may be able to exclude others from use of the patented invention.

For the patent owner to obtain increased profits, he must (a) manufacture and sell the goods covered by the patent without competition at higher prices or in larger volume than otherwise would be possible; (b) sell or license his patent in return for a lump sum, royalties, shares in a business, or a combination of these benefits; (c) sell his goods in competition with his royalty-paying licensees and thus obtain an economic advantage resulting from a larger share of the market or a higher percentage profit; (d) relieve his goods from the burden of paying royalties to others, by trading off licenses under his patent for licenses under the patents of others; (e) create multiple sources for the patented goods by licensing others and thus increasing the acceptability of the goods to prospective customers; (f) use the patent as a sales or marketing tool to increase sales of the patented goods; (g) create a new class of customers for his products by licensing others to make patented devices which utilize such products; (h) license a supplier of a patented component, which is purchased both by the licensor and his competitors, thus giving the licensor a competitive advantage, on the goods incorporating the component, equal roughly to twice the royalty on such a component; or (i) otherwise increase the productivity and profitability of his business as, for example, by increasing the morale of his creative engineers and scientists through obtaining patents bearing their names and thus enhancing their general professional reputations. Many combinations and variations of these techniques are used by patent owners, within the limitations imposed by the antitrust law, to make real the promise of increased profits which resides in the patent grant.

The degree of certainty of obtaining an economic reward from a patent decreases as we go back of the date of the grant of the patent, through the pendency of the patent application, to the point at which a potential inventor embarks on an activity which will lead to the invention. The fact that such path, in thousands of instances has led to substantial economic rewards, keeps the patent stimulus alive and sustains the patent system, despite the many attacks which have been made upon it.

The patent incentive, it is recognized, is by no means responsible for all the inventions which flow from the creativity of the human mind. As Victor Abramson,[2] economic advisor to the U.S. Treasury Department has stated:

"A limited number of new inventions is assured to society even without any special stimulus. Accident or observation unrelated to deliberate inventive effort will provide some inventions. Others will be produced by those with an 'instinctive bent' for invention, or who find sufficient reward in the joy of the effort or the satisfaction of accomplishment. Purely economic factors will also support some inventive effort without assured safeguards. Where changes take place in the relative prices or availability of labor, materials, or capital, it may become profitable for business firms to undertake adaptations not requiring costly research, designed to economize the scarce or costly factor or utilize more effectively the plentiful or cheap factor. The obsolescence of existing equipment may spur a search for means to reduce losses. And the competitive advantages which lie in market priority, or the hope of at least temporary secrecy, may lead to a degree of inventive effort."

We must attempt to distinguish between the economic values arising from activities not due to the patent stimulus and those which are generated out of that stimulus.

Expenditures for Obtaining Patents

The Hon. David L. Ladd[3] has stated that the rate at which patent applications are being filed in the U.S. Patent Office "is now nearing 85,000 per year ... approximately 70 per cent of patents issued in 1961

were assigned to companies ... the cost of an average application prosecuted by corporations is in the range of $1,000 to $2,500 ..." From this we see that corporations are spending about $60 million to $150 million each year in their efforts to obtain the issuance of their patents from the United States Patent Office. Mr. Ladd also pointed out that a simple application prosecuted by an attorney on behalf of an independent individual costs about $680. The average case is probably closer to $800, so that such individuals are spending about an additional $20 million in patent prosecution. Thus the annual expenditure by patent applicants for patent prosecution before the U.S. Patent Office lies somewhere between about $80 million and $170 million.

Expenditures for Patent Litigation

An analysis of patent litigation statistics for the years 1949 to 1958[4] shows that an average of 605.7 patent cases were instituted in 86 U.S. District Courts annually during that ten-year period and an average of 555.4 patent cases a year were terminated during the same period. Table 1 presents the statistics of these terminations. Cf. P. J. Federico, 38 JPOS 233, 1956.

The writer interviewed several prominent litigation attorneys and obtained a composite estimate that the average minimum cost of conducting a patent infringement suit to a contested judgment is about $50,000 for each side, or a total of $100,000 for both litigants. However, in some cases the litigants have spent upwards of a million dollars each in major infringement suits, so that the average cost of all such suits must be substantially in excess of $100,000. The 112.2 contested judgment cases a year of Table 42.1 would, therefore, represent an average annual minimum expenditure of perhaps $15 to $20 million. The 26.4 dismissals yearly for want of prosecution and the default judgment cases are probably minimum expense cases. However, they must have involved expenditures of at least $20,000 each, giving an annual minimum average in expense of about $520,000. The remaining average annual dispositions of slightly over 400 cases probably involved

TABLE 1. DISPOSITION OF PATENT SUITS IN DISTRICT COURTS, FISCAL YEARS 1949-58.

	Number of suits	Dismissed for want of prosecution	Default judgment	Consent judgment— Before trial	Consent judgment— During trial	Consent dismissal— Before trial	Consent dismissal— During or after trial	Transfers	Other disposition	Remanded	Contested judgment — Judgment by decision of court before trial	Contested judgment — Judgment after court trial	Contested judgment — Directed verdict	Contested judgment — Other	Contested judgment — Judgment on jury verdict
1949	374	17	6	79	2	142	2	(1)	4	1	30	88	1	0	2
1950	519	36	8	120	6	241	4	(1)	2	1	35	65	0	0	1
1951	549	29	5	121	2	258	9	(1)	13	4	23	79	2	0	4
1952	608	28	2	162	4	262	7	5	13	0	34	87	0	0	4
1953	529	25	5	127	3	249	8	2	5	0	22	79	0	0	4
1954	532	41	2	116	4	240	9	5	4	1	30	77	0	1	2
1955	544	20	5	101	2	274	7	14	10	2	30	78	0	0	1
1956	680	25	5	132	4	394	4	3	1	2	32	74	0	1	3
1957	609	28	7	119	3	298	14	6	10	1	25	95	0	2	1
1958	610	15	1	146	5	297	12	7	16	1	23	86	0	1	0
Total	5,554	264	46	1,223	35	2,655	76	42	78	13	284	808	3	5	22

lower expenditures than in the contested judgment cases. If we assume that an average of about $40,000 was spent on each of these cases, they would represent an average yearly expense of about $16 million. The writer concludes that a conservative estimate of what litigants in patent suits spent for the expenses of conducting the litigation during the years 1949 to 1958 is substantially in excess of $35 million annually.

Total Procedural Cost

From the above, we see that something on the order of at least $150 million is being expended annually merely to carry out the procedure of obtaining patents from the U.S. Patent Office and of litigating them in the U.S. Courts. It is apparent that those who are spending such sums of money must be convinced that the patents themselves have a monetary value greatly in excess of this figure.

Research Expenditures Stimulated by Patents

As stated above, the promise of increased profits from the grant of a patent consti-

tutes a stimulus to the investment of money in research and development which may lead to making patentable inventions. The National Science Foundation [5] reported that $12.4 billion had been expended for research and development in the United States during the fiscal year 1959 to 1960. Of this sum the United States Government supplied $8 billion and nonprofit organizations supplied $0.4 billion. We may assume that the patent incentive played no direct part in inducing the Government and the nonprofit organizations to spend these sums. Private industry supplied the remaining $4 billion. However, as Abramson [2] pointed out, there are various stimuli other than patents which induce private industry to spend money on research and development. S. C. Gilfillan [6] concludes that "All in all it would seem a fair statement, even if regrettably lacking in logical precision and statistical accuracy, to say that patents motivate 15 or 20 per cent of American inventing today." Gilfillan arrived at this conclusion by deducting, from the total sum spent in American organized research, the amounts supplied by the Government and by nonprofit organizations, and then estimating that about one-half of the rest was due to the patent motive. The George Washington University Foundation article [1] suggests that Gilfillan's estimate is too low. Nevertheless, even if we accept it, we find that about $2 billion expended in the year 1959 to 1960 was due to the patent stimulus. The actual figure probably is higher since it does not include money expended on inventive work which was not classified as research or development, or money spent by those who likely would not be reached in the gathering of the basic data by the National Science Foundation.

Patent as a Financing Tool

The promise of a financial reward implicit in the patent grant is a lever for raising the risk capital necessary to convert the invention, from the stage at which a patent can be obtained, to a product on the market available to the public. This conversion usually involves setting up and equipping a manufacturing facility, prototype preproduction and production engineering, advertising, sales effort and the production of a sufficient inventory to fill an anticipated initial sales volume. The more costly this conversion becomes, the greater is the need for patent protection, in order to enable the manufacturer (1) to sell the new product for a sufficient time to recover the investment in making and conversion of the invention and (2) to make a profit at least commensurate with the risks involved.

When an attempt is made to start a new business on the basis of a patented or patentable invention, the problem of raising the necessary capital usually becomes critical. Rarely do those who attempt to start such a business possess enough funds of their own and, therefore, a financial institution must advance the money. In such cases, the possession of a strong patent position is often the determining factor in whether or not the money can be raised. Welfling and Siegel,[7] for example, point out:

"[In] the opinion of the management of High Voltage, the existence and validity of the patents were essential in the establishment of the company. Without the patents, the original capital investment would probably not have been forthcoming from American Research and Development Company and Rosenwald funds. . . . In general, the ownership of patents apparently has often served as the basis for the establishment of new firms."

Even an established business, which seeks to borrow money for the purpose of financing the development and marketing of a new product, often finds a strong patent position effective in obtaining the funds at favorable rates. Sometimes investment advisory services will report a strong patent position which protects the product line of a corporation as a favorable factor, thus tending to raise the price and marketability of the corporation's stock.

In a study on "The Research and Development Factor in Mergers and Acquisitions," Professor M. N. Friedman [8] stated that one of the factors which he has found to be present in the acquisition of one company by another is desire of the "acquiring company . . . to obtain an established patent base in the new field it is entering."

The writer is personally acquainted with a very creative young man who, in a few years, has built a sizeable fortune by making several inventions, patenting them, establishing companies to develop them to points at which their values could be demonstrated, and then selling the companies to larger corporations which desired to market the products involved.

It is clear that the same type of consideration which a financial institution gives to a patent, in deciding whether to lend money to a business for the exploitation of a new product, is often an important factor in the decision of the management of a business to undertake such exploitation. It would be foolhardy for management to invest large sums developing a new product which, after being placed on the market, could be copied within a short time without substantial development expense by a competitor. Ownership of a patent weighs heavily in the decision by management as to whether to develop and market the product.

Up to the present, investigators have been unable to develop statistical data which measure the risk capital which the patent stimulus itself introduces into the American economy. The writer is convinced, however, that the amount is very large.

Patent as a Selling Tool

A product covered by an issued patent may be marked with the number of the patent. This statutory marking under 35 U.S.C. 287, starts tolling damages against an infringer without other notice to him. The seller of the patented product may find that such marking also increases the sales appeal of the product and uses such appeal as part of his sales promotion. Direct reference to the patent in advertising products is also common.

In the highly technical industries, particularly, patents create a public image of the patent owning company as forward moving and creative. References to patents often appear in institutional advertising. Press releases announce the grant of significant patents.

Increasing use is being made of patents as a direct selling tool, especially in obtaining research and development contracts from the Government. These contracts often lead to follow-on procurements of the products developed. The patents which the company has obtained, in the field in which such contracts are sought, are brought to the attention of the Government as proof that the company possesses creative ability which it can bring to bear in carrying out the work involved.

Value from Direct Use in Manufacture in the United States

The Patent, Trademark, and Copyright Foundation of The George Washington University is attempting to obtain an answer to the question of whether the expenditure of money, time and effort, such as described above, is adequately supported by the value which is actually derived from the use of the patent right of exclusion in the manufacture, sale or use of the inventions covered by patents. The Foundation published an interim report by Sanders, Rossman and Harris in September 1958.[9] The following is quoted from the Summary and Conclusions of the report:

"About 75 per cent of patents in our study are reported to have economic value to assignees. Fifty-seven per cent are used or about to be used

in industry. Eleven per cent, though not used, have had or are expected to have other benefits. Seven per cent, not meeting either of the above criteria, are patents that are licensed.

"Of the patents in current use (30 per cent of the total) direct beneficial effects were reported to result from the use in 89 per cent of the cases, most of these being in terms of increased sales and/or reduced production costs. For patents used in the past (19 per cent of the total) beneficial effects were reported for 74 per cent, mostly in terms of increased sales and/or reduced production costs. For the combined group of used patents the percentage with beneficial effects is 84.

"For patents in current use, information was supplied by more than a third of the respondents (34 per cent) in terms of estimated dollar gains or losses. For almost 90 per cent of these, net gain was reported, averaging nearly $600,000 per patent. Since these patents were still being used in industry, and the net gain reported was as of the date on which the questionnaire was answered, the ultimate net gain per patent would be substantially greater than this amount. For the balance in this group a net loss was reported, averaging $88,000. With the passage of time these losses would be reduced and, in most instances, converted into net gains.

"For patents used in the past, specific dollar values are reported for less than a third (27 per cent) of those returning a questionnaire. Of these, nearly two-thirds (63 per cent) reported a net gain, averaging $72,000 per patent. For the balance a net loss is reported, averaging $14,000 per patent.

"For patents about to be used, and for non-used patents losses reported average $12,000 and $4,500 per patent, respectively....

"If the sample of patents for which net gains or losses are shown could be considered a random sample of all the patents in current use, then it can be demonstrated that the present mean gain ($600,000) from these patents collectively would represent less than one-half of the ultimate gain."

Therefore the average gain for each patent used would be $1,200,000 throughout its life. This would represent an average annual gain of about $70,000.

There is a remarkable correlation between this figure and the results of a study by C. D. Tuska, "Independent Inventors and the Patent System." [10] Tuska gleaned his data from reported tax cases dealing largely with patented inventions licensed by independent inventors to corporations. Royalty payments reported for 63 cases show a yearly average royalty payment of

$33,400 for each patent. Fixed sums payments are also reported for 19 cases. It is not possible to compute how much they would increase the average yearly return per patent, but we may assume some increase, for example, to $35,000. A rough rule followed by some patent attorneys in determining an equitable division, between a licensor and a licensee, of the increase in profits due to a patent, is to allot between two-thirds to three-fourths of such profits to the licensee and the rest to the licensor. If we use the two-thirds figure for the cases reported by Tuska, we discover that as an average each manufacturer-licensee made an increased yearly profit of about $70,000 on each licensed patent. Thus the total average yearly gain for each of these patents was about $105,000. Since these figures were taken from tax cases in which the income was sufficiently great to make the tax suit worth-while, it is reasonable to assume that the patents involved were above average of all profitably used patents in their profit production. The fact that the corresponding average figure derived from the Foundation report is two-thirds of that derived from the Tuska study adds credibility to the report figures.

It is difficult to estimate the total annual gain derived from the use of patents. There is a temptation to apply the average gain figures of the Foundation report to all presently unexpired U.S. patents, which at the end of June 1962 numbered about 662 thousand excluding plant and design patents. If we were to apply the Foundation's figures, we would conclude that 27 per cent of these patents were each producing an annual benefit of $70,000 or about $12.5 billion, and that about 14 per cent had been used in the past and had each yielded a benefit of about $72,000 or a total benefit of about $6.7 billion. What increase in the annual benefit figure results from taking into account such patents used in the past cannot be computed on the basis of available figures. The foregoing accounts for only 41 per cent of the patents, leaving an additional 34 per cent which the report indicates were of economic value to assignees. While it would be statistically irresponsible to accept such results as valid, it is not beyond the realm of

possibility that the use of patents is producing a yearly gain of about $15 billion.

Annual Sales of Goods

The average percentage royalty rate derived from thirty cases in the Tuska study,[10] which specify royalty rates and equivalent yearly sales, is about $4\frac{1}{4}$ per cent. Using the same line of reasoning as under the previous heading, we may assume that the total gain by the licensee for each patent in the Tuska study is about three times this royalty percentage or $12\frac{3}{4}$ per cent of the sales of the goods involved. If we assume from The George Washington University Foundation study that the average profitably used patent is about two-thirds as profitable as the average patent in the Tuska study, the average percentage profit due to each profitably used patent is about $8\frac{1}{2}$ per cent. If we were to apply this figure to the $15 billion gain suggested above, we would conclude that patents play a principal role in annual sales in excess of about $175 billion, constituting roughly $\frac{1}{3}$ of the present gross national product. Even if this amount is in error by a factor of three, four, or even five, we see that a very large part of the annual value of the sales of goods and services in the United States are directly affected by patents. The writer will not attempt to estimate what this means in terms of the stimulation of American business to invest its funds in the production of such goods and services, except to point out that it is a major factor.

Value from Foreign Sources

American patent owners are deriving additional gains from inventions made in the United States and patented in foreign countries. To the extent that American patent owners use their foreign patents as they use their United States patents, the nature of the resulting gain is about the same. However, to a much greater extent than in the United States, the American patent owners derive their income by licensing their foreign patents.

The data with respect to gains by United States companies from their foreign patents are quite meagre. However, W. E. Schmidt [11] has reported that in 1957 the American licensing community received royalties of $380 million for the transfer of patents, processes, technology, rental equipment, and other proprietary assets such as copyrights and trademarks.

Summary

The writer estimates that American patent owners are deriving monetary gains of somewhat in excess of $10 billion a year before taxes and that, in order to obtain this gain, they are risking annually between $2 billion and $3 billion in addition to the investment made in producing $100 billion or more of goods and services which involve the profitable use of patents. While the exactness of these estimates is open to question, the data available show the economic value of patents in the United States to be a very significant and important factor in our present day economy.

It is clear also that, while patents are primarily an economic tool, they exert strong psychological force. They motivate inventors to produce, financial people to advance capital, and manufacturers to make and sell goods incorporating the inventions. To the degree that we strengthen such motivations, the material gains will increase and support the continued economic growth of the United States.

References

1. Markham, J. W., Worley, J. S., and Brothers, D. S., 1 *PTC J*, Vol. 1, 20, 1957.
2. Abramson, V., "The Patent System: Its Economic and Social Basis," Study No. 26 of the Patents, Trademarks, and Copyrights Subcommittee of the Senate Judiciary Committee, 6, 1960.
3. Statement of Hon. David Ladd, Commissioner of Patents, before the above Senate Subcommittee on September 4, 1962 re: S.2225. Most of the figures under this heading are taken from that statement.
4. "An Analysis of Patent Litigation Statistics," Staff report of the above Senate Subcommittee, dated Nov. 28, 1960. The statistics represent minimal figures since some patent suits were not reported in the sources used.
5. Testimony of Kathryn Arnow before the above Senate Subcommittee on April 18, 1962 re: S.1084 and S.1176.
6. Gilfillan, S. C., *Rev. of Eco. and Stat.*, Vol. 34, pp. 365-385, 1952.
7. Welfling, W., and Siegel, I. H., "Patent and Other Factors in the Growth of the Electronics Industry in the Boston Area," 1 *PTC J*, 125, 1957.
8. Friedman, M. N., "The Research and Development Factor in Mergers and Acquisitions," Study No. 16 of said Subcommittee, 1958.
9. Sanders, B. S., Rossman, J., and Harris, L. J., "The Economic Impact of Patents," 2 *PTC J*, 340-362, 1958.
10. Tuska, C. D., "Independent Inventors and the Patent System," Study No. 28 of said Subcommittee, 1961.
11. Schmidt, W. E., 5 *PTC J*, 40-51, 1961.

Cross-references: *Accounting and Recoveries from Infringement Suits, Evaluation of Inventions, Foreign Patents, Public Relations and the Patent System, Royalty—Rate and Basis.*

EDUCATION IN PATENT LAW. See TEACHING, EXAMINERS' CAREERS

EMPLOYEE INVENTIONS AND AGREEMENTS

Worth Wade

This article deals with the rights to inventions made under contract by employees and excludes "shop rights," q.v., to inventions made in the absence of a contract.

Recent court decisions and new trends in employee relations are forcing substantial changes in both the form and substance of employee contracts relating to inventions and in the administration of such contracts. More attention is being given to granting the employee additional compensation, above his regular salary, for his inventions.

Trends in Employee Contracts Relating to Inventions

A survey was made by the writer in 1962 of one hundred contracts used by medium and large corporations covering the subject of employee inventions. This survey revealed the following trends:

(1) Shortening the form of these contracts by reducing the number of covenants and expressing them in simple language.

(2) Changing the form of the agreement from traditional legal form with numbered sections to a letter executed in duplicate.

(3) Eliminating "whereas" clauses.

(4) Three basic covenants only: the obligations (a) to disclose; (b) to assign; and (c) to execute papers relating to the employee's inventions.

(5) Limiting the inventions to be assigned to the field of the employer's business or the area of his products.

(6) Relaxing restrictions on employment in a competing industry after termination, by being more specific as to the field and more limited as to period of the restriction.

(7) Providing a monetary consideration for the "hold-over" period.

(8) Additional compensation to the employee-inventor in the form of fixed money awards, especially where the contract requires assignment of "all" inventions.

(9) Employees are better informed and more critical regarding their legal rights and contracts relating to inventions.

Form of the Employment Contract

There is a movement away from the legalistic terminology and formal presentation in the covenants. Experience has shown improved employee acceptance of agreements expressed in simple nonlegalistic language. Further improvement appears to arise from the presentation of the contract in the form of a letter to be executed in duplicate, as in Fig. 1, drafted after a survey of the contracts now in use in the hundred medium and large American corporations and research institutions and considered an average "profile" of such agreements.

Fig. 1. Employee's agreement form.

This letter, in duplicate, will serve as a memorandum between you, as the Employee, and Corporation, as Employer, covering terms of your employment.

The Employer and its affiliated companies are engaged in the manufacture of various products and desire to acquire inventions and improvements relating thereto. The Employee in connection with his duties has or will become familiar with the Employer's business and is expected to utilize the Employer's time, materials, facilities and information in making inventions and improvements relating to such products. As is customary, it is the policy of the Employer to require the Employee to assign to the Employer all right, title and interest in and to all inventions and improvements relating to Employer's products.

Therefore, in consideration of the above and your employment or continued employment by the Employer, and the payment of salary during such employment, it is understood and agreed as follows:

The Employee shall keep, maintain and make available to the Employer complete and up-to-date written records, including photographs and drawings of his inventions and improvements relating to Employer's products, which records shall be the property of the Employer. The Employee shall promptly and fully disclose in writing to the Employer all inventions and improvements whether patentable or not, which relate to Employer's products that the Employee may solely or jointly make during the period of his employment by the Employer including all inventions and improvements made during the period of one year thereafter which relate to any field in which Employee was employed by Employer, and all such inventions and improvements shall be the sole and exclusive property of the Employer. The Employee hereby agrees not to divulge to any unauthorized person any confidential information acquired by reason of his employment by the Employer. The Employee further agrees to assign and does hereby assign and transfer to the Employer all his right, title and interest in and to all such inventions and improvements and in and to any Letters Patent or application for Letters Patent thereon in and for all countries. The Employee further agrees, at the expense of the Employer, to do all things and to execute and deliver all papers necessary therefor whenever so requested by the Employer. In the event of the termination of Employee's employment for any cause, the Employee hereby agrees that he will not, at any time during the year following such termination, accept or continue employment or engage as principal in any field in which Employee was employed by Employer.

This agreement shall inure to the benefit of and be binding upon the heirs, executors, administrators and assigns of the Employee and the successors, and assigns of the Employer.

Kindly sign and return the duplicate to indicate your acceptance.

Very truly yours,

ACCEPTED, Date ___. _____ CORPORATION

EMPLOYEE _____ L. S. by _____

Name and Title

Why Contracts on Inventions Are Justifiable

The confusion which may arise when an employee invents in the absence of a written contract makes an inventions agreement almost a necessity in modern business. The employer hires technical personnel with the understanding that they are to improve the company's operations; provides, at no expense to the employee, technical facilities, materials, assistants and necessary capital; and pays the patent expenses and assumes all the business and legal risks involved. When an employee is new to the business, the employer may train the employee and supply him with specialized and confidential knowledge which he could not acquire in the absence of employment.

What Employees Should Execute Invention Contracts

A survey has shown that inventions in process industries are made by the personnel in various classifications in the following proportions: 60 per cent by Research and Development, 25 per cent by the Executive and Supervisory staff, 10 per cent by Production management and staff, 2 per cent by Sales and 3 per cent by associated non-employees. In general, it is customary in industry to require the invention contract to be signed by all salaried employees, regardless of job classification, when they work under such conditions that there is a good possibility of making inventions. However, it is not customary to have such contracts signed by hourly workers or members of labor unions. In addition, the following types of salaried personnel are usually excluded: secretarial, clerical, guards, cafeteria, accounting, stores and shipping.

Consideration for Contract

The courts have held that "employment" or "continued employment" is adequate consideration for the execution of a contract to assign, to an employer, inventions relating to his business. From recent surveys, it appears that there is a tendency to give the employee, in addition to salary, a fixed money award for each invention. Some companies have found that such awards stimulate invention. However, very few employers are willing to give the employee a share in the income or savings resulting from the use of the invention because such arrangements are difficult to administer and are contrary to the premise that the employee's salary is full consideration for the invention.

Content of Employee Contracts on Inventions

In addition to the basic covenants stated, the following specific features are present in the majority of such contracts: (1) the employer's business is defined so as to limit the scope of the inventions to be assigned; (2) salary is the consideration but the amount of salary is not specified; (3) the contract usually terminates with separation from the payroll; (4) the nature of the inventions to be assigned are specified as all inventions "relating to the business" in 70 per cent of the contracts; "capable of use by the company" in 18 per cent; "relating to the company's products" in 10 per cent; and "relating to the company's investigations" and "suggested by employment" in 6 per cent. The period during which inventions of the employee must be assigned is usually "during the period of his employment" (66 per cent) or "during employment and for one year thereafter" (18 per cent).

Hold-Over Clauses in Contracts on Invention. In the survey of the hundred contracts mentioned above, only 6 per cent contained "hold-over" clauses. Some employee contracts seek to hold the employee responsible for assigning inventions over a period of time after employment ends or to restrain him from working for a competitor of the employer. In general, such "hold-over" clauses do not violate public policy unless the restraints of time, employment and other subject matter are unreasonable. In general, the "hold-over" period should not be more than one year, and the subject matter should be limited to inventions relating to the employer's business. The tendency in industry is to provide some extra compensation for the hold-over period in order to make such clauses enforceable in the courts, the courts having held that the "hold-over" clause must be reasonable and just and strictly construed.

In a recent case, the DeLong Corporation asserted that its former employee, Lucas, violated his covenant "not to disclose trade secrets and confidential information during the restricted period"; it sought "an injunction restraining Lucas from continuing to use trade secrets or confidential information which he obtained during the period of his employment." The court held:

"DeLong is not entitled to such relief. The agreement not to disclose such confidential information for a period of two years plainly relieved Lucas from such restriction when the two years had expired. Thereafter, he was under no such restriction and to impose continuing restraint upon him would not be in accordance with the agreement, nor would the result be equitable." *DeLong Corporation* v. *Lucas*, 122 USPQ 471, DC SNY 1959.

Agreement to Assign Improvements. In the same *DeLong* case, the assignment of improvements was also at issue. A settlement agreement regarding the invention of a slip jack referred to "any and all improvements on the said invention." The court said:

"...[There] is no language which indicates that this was meant to include any future 'improvements' to the assigned slip jack which Lucas might thereafter invent or devise. Moreover, the actual assignments executed by Lucas and accepted by DeLong do not use the word 'improvements' at all.

"A comparison of the language used in the settlement agreement with the language used in the cases cited by DeLong holding assignments applicable to future improvements, indicates plainly the failure of the agreement at bar to accomplish the result for which it contends. The language evinces no more than an intention to cover *improvements in existence at the time of its execution* and does not cover future improvements." (Emphasis added. The case cites numerous decisions.)

Restrictions on Future Employment. It is understood that no contract is valid that withdraws from a man the right to earn a living. This may be expressed in the words that a man's tools cannot be taken for debt or that the operations of his brain may not

be mortgaged. Taking of property necessary for one's livelihood was outlawed in the Magna Charta.

Such limitation as that an engineer may not accept other work in the engineering industries or a chemist in chemistry is obviously improper and void. Restrictions on future employment, if they are to have any chance for enforceability, must define the forbidden field clearly and with severe limitations.

One company is reported to have attempted to modify its research chemists' contracts, so as to require approval by the company of any employment accepted by the chemist for two years after leaving the company. Employment within two of the less industrialized states only was excepted. Fortunately, the attempt was unsuccessful.

Court decisions relating to restrictions on future employment and assignment of inventions to employers have been studied critically by Knoth, 31 JPOS 532, 1949.

Administration of the Employee Contracts Relating to Inventions

The general administration of the contract should be under the jurisdiction of the corporation patent counsel or the corporation patent department. The binding of new employees under such contracts should be the obligation of the Personnel Department or the Industrial Relations Department. The binding of previously employed personnel should be the obligation of the manager of the manufacturing units or the director of the technical department concerned.

Table 1 gives the results of a survey made by the National Association of Manufacturers showing personnel required to execute the agreement to assign inventions as related to the sales volume of the corporation.

Procedure When an Employee-Inventor Refuses Application or Assignment

The employee should be allowed full opportunity to express his reasons for refusal to sign. Explanation and persuasion is the best procedure. In some cases, slight modifications of the terminology and, in rare

TABLE 1. ATTITUDE TOWARD REQUIRING EMPLOYEES TO EXECUTE AN AGREEMENT TO ASSIGN INVENTIONS.

Estimated 1947 Sales	No. Rptg.	Assignment Required		What Employees Are Required to Execute an Agreement[1]									Oral Assignment Required		Scope of Assignment[2]		
		Yes	No	(a)	(b)	(e)	(ab)	(abc)	(abcd)	(abd)	(ac)	Others	Yes	No	(a)	(b)	(c)
$ 50,000 – 100,000	6		6														
100,000 – 250,000	21	7	14	2	2								1	1		1	1
250,000 – 500,000	24	5	19	4			2	3						4	5	6	
500,000 – 750,000	45	9	36	5				1					6	10	4	6	
750,000 – 1,000,000	17	8	9	4	1	1	2	2	4				3	6	4	3	
1,000,000 – 2,500,000	121	45	76	5	1	11	7	13	3	4	1		19	14	13	37	
2,500,000 – 5,000,000	115	62	53	12	1	12	8	7	17	2	2	(acd)1 (bc)1	25	13	20	39	1
5,000,000 – 10,000,000	81	41	40	12		13	1	6	5		2	(acd)1	14	6	16	30	2
10,000,000 – 30,000,000	99	72	27	17		21	8	9	10	1	4	(ad)2	22	14	31	43	
Over 30,000,000	107	75	32	13		12	3	21	19	3	4		6	13	30	50	2
Not Reported	48	26	22	4		7	1	6	4		2		8	8	13	16	1
Total	684	350	334	78	5		32			10	15	5	104	88	136	231	6

[1] (a) Research and engineering staff.
    (b) Executives and supervisory force.
    (c) Other technical operating employees.
    (d) Sales and/or service department.
    (e) All employees.

[2] (a) All inventions of employees resulting from their employment activities.
    (b) Only those in the field of your business.
    (c) Others.

231

cases, of the substance, may be granted where the particular conditions warrant these changes, but no broad exceptions should be permitted, even if it means a choice between signing or losing the prospective employee, the final decision at this point being the responsibility of management.

If an employee, under contract to assign his inventions to the employer, refuses to assign and execute an application for patent, the remedy is for the employer to execute the application, as provided under 35 U.S.C. 118, which reads:

"Whenever an inventor refuses to execute an application for patent, or cannot be found or reached after diligent effort, a person to whom the inventor has assigned or agreed in writing to assign the invention or who otherwise shows sufficient proprietary interest in the matter justifying such action, may make application for patent on behalf of and as agent for the inventor on proof of the pertinent facts and a showing that such action is necessary to preserve the rights of the parties or to prevent irreparable damage; and the Commissioner may grant a patent to such inventor upon such notice to him as the Commissioner deems sufficient, and on compliance with such regulations as he prescribes." See also Rule 47.

Digest of the Law on Employer-Employee Relationship with Respect to Inventions Made by Employee

I.

Right of employer to inventions of employee in the absence of contract to assign:

(1) The title to an invention belongs to the employer when the employee was hired to solve a problem even in the absence of a specific contract to assign, and the Courts will require the employee to make an assignment, under the conditions in the following cases: *Hebbard* v. *American Zinc, Lead & Smelting Co.*, 73 USPQ 312, CA 8 1947; *Marshall* v. *Colgate-Palmolive-Peet Co.*, 77 USPQ 69, DC Del 1948; *National Development Co.* v. *Gray*, 316 Mass. 240, 1944; *Salterini* v. *Schneider*, 45 NYS (2) 645, 1943; and *Control Instrument Co.* v. *Braun*, 72 USPQ 251, N.Y. Sup. Ct. 1947.

(2) There are conditions under which the title to an invention belongs to the employer even if the employee was not hired to solve a problem but was subsequently assigned thereto, and in the absence of a specific contract to assign, and the Courts will require the employee to make an assignment. *Marshall* v. *Colgate-Palmolive-Peet Co.*,

77 USPQ 69, DC Del 1948; *H. J. Heinz Co.* v. *Sefton*, 59 USPQ 77, Pa. Court of Common Pleas, Allegheny Co. 1943; and *State* v. *Neal*, 12 So. Rep. (2) 590, Fla. 1943.

(3) If an employer is entitled to an employee's invention, it is immaterial that the work was done on the invention by the employee outside working hours. *National Development Co.* v. *Gray*, 316 Mass. 240, 1944; and *Crown Cork & Seal Co.* v. *Fankhanel*, 49 F.S. 611, DC Md. 1943.

(4) Employment is consideration between the employer and the employee supporting the assignment and supporting a specific contract requiring the employee to assign inventions. The hiring of an employee is sufficient consideration. *Buckingham Products Co.* v. *McAleer Mfg. Co.*, 108 F.2d 192 CA 6 1940.

(5) Continuation of employment is consideration. *Hebbard* v. *American Zinc, Lead & Smelting Co. et al.*, 68 USPQ 396, DC WMo 1946.

(6) Agreements requiring the employee to assign inventions made by him during his employment are not unconscionable, inequitable, or against public policy. *Crown, Cork & Seal Co.* v. *Fankhanel*, supra.

(7) Agreements have been sustained requiring the employee to assign to the employer *"any and all inventions"* made during the employment. [The cases cited above have sustained agreements where the inventions to be assigned related to the employer's business.] *New Jersey Zinc Co.* v. *Singmaster*, 4 F. Supp. 967 DC S.D. N.Y. 1933; aff. on the point, 71 F.2d 277, CA 2 1934.

(8) A provision included in an employment agreement, requiring the employee to assign to the employer inventions made by employee within a limited time after termination of the employment, provided the inventions relate to a field in which employee was employed by employer, is very strictly construed and must be reasonable and just. Otherwise, it is unenforceable. *Gas Tool Patents Corp.* v. *Mould*, 133 F.2d 815, CA 7 1943.

(9) It is proper to require the employee to keep and make available to employer complete and up to date written records relating to inventions made by employee during employment. The records of the employee-inventor are the property of the employer. *Commonwealth* v. *Kniel*, 150 Pa. Sup. 290, 1942.

(10) The employee may be required by the agreement to disclose inventions made by him to the employer. *H. J. Heinz Co.* v. *Sefton*, 59 USPQ 77, Pa. Ct. Common Pleas, Allegheny Co. 1943.

(11) The employee may be required by the employment agreement to execute and deliver all papers necessary to permit the employer to file applications for patent. *Control Instrument Co.* v. *Braun*, 72 USPQ 251, N.Y. Sup. Ct. 1947.

It is proper to include in an employment agreement a covenant that the employee at the option of the employer will not enter the employment of a competitor of the employer for a stated period of time, provided that such a contract is necessary for the protection of the employer's business and puts no undue hardship on the employee. *Corpus Juris Secundum,* Vol. 17 "Contracts," p. 636, Section 254.

The obligations of the employee with respect to inventions, under an employment contract are binding upon the employee's heirs, administrators, executors, and assigns. *Olds v. Ray-Dio-Ray Corp.,* 294 Pac. 579, Wash. Sup. Ct., 1930.

Cross-references: *Employee-Inventors' Patent Rights Abroad, Incentives, Inventors, Shop Right.*

EMPLOYEE-INVENTORS' PATENT RIGHTS AND COMPENSATION AND EMPLOYERS' RIGHTS IN FOREIGN COUNTRIES

Burton P. Beatty

For assistance in the provision of data reported herein the author thanks his associates in IBM and particularly the Patent Department of IBM Germany, outside counsel for his company, and the late Mr. Richard Spencer of Paris.

The ownership of and compensation for employee inventions in the countries of Western Europe, Canada and Japan are particularly significant to United States companies in view of their extensive research, development activities, or other interests in those areas. It is essential to know and understand the legal requirements of the various countries in respect to the ownership of inventions of employees and what the laws require in the way of compensating employee-inventors.

The laws on this subject are different in each country, it is difficult to systematize them. Therefore, this comparative study covers separately the laws and jurisprudence of Austria, Canada, England, France, Germany, Italy, Japan, Netherlands, Sweden and Switzerland.

Classes of Inventions

Generally speaking, inventions can be classified into three groups:

(1) *Service inventions* are those made by the employee (1) within the scope of his employment; and (2) within the field of business activity of the employer.

(2) *Dependent inventions* include essentially inventions made by an employee (1) outside the scope of the employment; and (2) within the field of business activity of the employer.

(3) *Free inventions* are those made by an employee (1) outside the scope of the employment; and (2) outside the field of business activity of the employer. These belong to the employee.

Country Classification

Countries can also be classified as to ownership of and compensation for employee inventions, into four groups:

(1) Those countries which have no special provisions dealing with the matter. In this group are Canada, Great Britain and France.

(2) The Netherlands, Italy, Austria and Switzerland.

(3) Germany, Japan, and Sweden.

(4) U.S.S.R., for which see *Soviet Patents.*

Western Europe—General

Initially, European inventions belonged to the employee, free and clear of all claims of the employer. However, it came to be recognized that this status could be changed by agreement, express or implied. Presently in common law countries, for the employer to have any right to the inventions of an employee, there must be a written or implied agreement. There remains another method by which the relationship and the right to compensation can be defined, namely, legislation.

Austria was the first country in Western Europe to enact a law covering ownership and compensation of employee inventions. Subsequently, Germany enacted a law on May 5, 1936 that became the most complete and complex European text on the subject. The present German government adopted the essential parts of the earlier legislation on July 25, 1957. Next came Italy where a law less exacting than Germany's was enacted in 1939. It remains in force and effect. Other European nations followed until today most of them, with the exception of France and England, have special laws governing the ownership of and the payment of compensation for employee inventions. In France a draft law has been considered but none has been adopted. Meanwhile, invention compensation clauses are finding their way into French "Conventions Collectives" contracts as but a prelude to possible implementation by law.

The relationship between employee inventors and their employers will be examined herein in connection with private enterprise. No attempt will be made here to analyze this relationship in the public sector where special government regulations may be controlling.

Group I Countries—No Statutory Provisions

Canada. In Canada the rights to employee inventions are determined by the principles of common law in similar manner to Great Britain. By invention agreement the employer can confirm his exclusive right to all service inventions made during the term of employment. Additionally, the employer can obtain by such agreement, in return for employment, the exclusive rights to all service and dependent inventions without special compensation. Free inventions belong to the employee. They can be obtained by negotiation with the employee as from an outside inventor.

Great Britain. By invention agreement the employer can confirm his exclusive right to all service inventions made during term of employment. Additionally, the employer can obtain by such agreement, in return for employment, the exclusive rights to all service and dependent inventions without special compensation. Free inventions belong to the employee. They can be obtained by negotiation with the employee as from an outside inventor. The employer must make a separate compensation agreement for each free invention he wishes to acquire.

Under the British Patents Act of 1949, disputes regarding employee inventions can, on application of either party, be determined by the Comptroller of the Patent Office. If the Comptroller finds that the issue involves complicated points which would be more properly determined by the High Court, he may decline to deal with them. If the Comptroller or the Court comes to the conclusion that there is an express contract determining to whom the rights in the invention belong, the provisions of the contract must be applied.

France. In France the rule is similar to that in Great Britain in that the employer can confirm by invention agreement his exclusive right to all service inventions and acquire dependent inventions of employees without special compensation. Some authorities disagree on this latter point with regard to dependent inventions and maintain that special compensation should be paid for these. However, the weight of authority appears to favor the validity of an agreement which acquires dependent inventions without special compensation. Free inventions belong to the employee. They can be obtained by negotiation with the employee as from an outside inventor. Also, they can be acquired through invention agreement. However, the employer must provide in the agreement for separate compensation for each such invention he wishes to acquire.

In France, employees such as engineers are frequently members of industry groups or "Collectives." These collective groups negotiate with the industry concerned the terms and conditions of their employment and these are subsequently approved by the Government. Referred to as "Convention Collectives," these group contracts override private contracts between employers and employees and may contain patent provisions according to which compensation must in certain cases be paid to employee inventors. The following is a paragraph from the "Convention Collective" of the Chemical Industry:

"If, within a period of five years following the grant of a patent, the invention is exploited commercially, the inventor named in the patent shall be entitled to compensation in proportion to the value of the invention."

Group II Countries

Netherlands. Section 10 of The Netherlands Patents Act of May 8, 1957 is the leading provision with respect to inventions of salaried employees. It reads as follows:

Section 10(1)

"Where the product, process or improvement for which a patent is sought has been invented by a person employed in the service of another person in a position the nature of which entails the application of his special knowledge to the making of inventions of the same kind as that to which the application for patent refers, the employer is entitled to the patent."

Section 10(2)

"Where, in such a case, the inventor cannot be deemed to find in the salary he earned, or in a special payment to be received by him, remuneration for the deprivation of patent, the employer is bound to pay him an equitable sum, having regard to the pecuniary interest of the invention and the circumstances in which it was invented. Should the employer and inventor be unable to agree on the sum, they may approach the Patent Office in writing requesting that the sum be determined by this Office. The Patent Office shall comply with that request, and its decision shall be binding on the parties. Should the employer and inventor not avail themselves of this competence, Section 56 shall apply. All rights of the inventor to claim under this provision shall lapse after the passing of three years from the date of the patent grant."

By Invention Agreement the employer may confirm his exclusive rights in service inventions made during the term of employment but cannot avoid compensating for outstanding inventions. By Invention Agreement the employer may obtain exclusive rights in dependent inventions if the agreement is not contra to Section 10, and does not involve taking undue advantage of the economic dependency of the employee. Accordingly, title to both service and dependent inventions may be acquired by contract. Whether compensation must be paid for any such invention is determined by weighing the salary of the employee against the value of the invention. For important inventions, compensation in addition to salary must be paid. If the employer and employee cannot agree on compensa-

tion, they may ask the Patent Office to settle it. Alternatively, the parties may take the matter to the Hague District Court for decision.

Free inventions belong to the employee. They can be acquired by negotiation with the employee as from an outside inventor. Also, they can be acquired through invention agreement if provision is made for separate compensation for each such invention.

Italy. The question of ownership and compensation for inventions of employees is governed by Articles 23-26 of the Italian Patent Law of June 29, 1939. Articles 23 and 24 are as follows:

Article 23

"Where any patentable invention is made in performance of duties arising out of an employment contract, but no compensation has been expressly provided therefor, all rights to such invention shall be vested in the employer; provided, however, that the inventor shall have the right to be acknowledged as the inventor of such invention; and provided further that said inventor shall receive a fair and equitable reward, to be determined on the basis of the significance of such invention."

Article 24

"Where, notwithstanding the conditions set forth in Section 23 above are not present, any patentable invention is made which pertains to the industry carried out by the firm or governmental department employing the inventor thereof, such firm or governmental department or employer shall have the right to acquire in preference to others, the right exclusively or non-exclusively to use such invention or to obtain any patent thereon, by paying a royalty or price in consideration therefor; provided however, that from such price or royalty there shall be deducted an amount equivalent to any aid that shall have been received from such employer to bring about the invention. Said employer shall exercise his pre-emption right not later than three months after receiving notice of the grant of a patent on such invention. Any right or rights vested in the employer by the exercise of such pre-emption right shall be null and void if consideration therefor shall not be fully paid at maturity."

According to Article 23, service inventions belong to the employer. If an invention is made by an employee whose inventive activity is expressly stated in the Invention Agreement to be the subject of the employment, and whose compensation is expressly arranged to include the assignment of such inventions to the employer, the rights to the invention belong to the employer without the payment to the employee of any compensation beyond salary. In other words, it should be clearly stated in the agreement for these employees that salary is paid in contemplation of making inventions.

Article 24 states that when the contractual conditions of Article 23 do not exist and the invention falls within the field of interest of the employer, the latter has the right of first refusal on an exclusive or non-exclusive license or the purchase of the patent, against the payment of compensation to be fixed after deducting a sum representing the assistance the inventor received from the employer in making the invention.

If the parties cannot agree concerning the premium or other compensation, or the procedures relating thereto, provisions are made for settling the matter by arbitration.

Free inventions belong to the employee. They can be obtained by negotiation with the employee as from an outside inventor.

Austria. The pertinent sections of the Austrian Patent Act of July 1950 are as follows:

Section 5b (1)

"Agreements made between employers and employees, under which any future inventions of the employee are to belong to the employer or the employer is to be granted a right of use under such inventions, are legally valid only if the invention in question is a service invention (Subsection 3). In order to be valid, the agreement must be in written form, which is also satisfied if it is covered by a collective contract."

Section 5c (1) and 5c (2)

"(1) For the cession of an invention made by him to the employer as well as for the granting of a right of use under such an invention, the employee is in any case entitled to an adequate special compensation.

"(2) If, however, the employee has been expressly engaged for inventive work in the employer's enterprise and is actually predominantly doing such work, and if his incumbent work as an

inventor has resulted in the invention, he is entitled to a special compensation only to such an extent as the higher salary to which he is entitled by reason of his employment with a view to his work as an inventor does not already include an adequate compensation for invention."

The term "service invention" according to Austrian Patent Law is broad in scope and includes those inventions which we have classified as dependent inventions. By written Invention Agreement the employer may obtain the exclusive rights in such inventions of employees made during the term of employment. When compensation for such inventions cannot be found in the salary of the employee a special compensation must be paid. This can be interpreted to mean only important inventions need be specially compensated.

Free inventions belong to the employee. Section 5d of the Austrian Patent Act gives the criteria to be considered in assessing compensation. Section 5d reads as follows:

Section 5d

"In assessing the compensation (Section 5c), special consideration should be given under the particular circumstances of the case:

"(a) to the economic importance of the invention to the enterprise;

"(b) to another utilization, if any, of the invention in Austria or in any foreign countries;

"(c) to the share which any suggestions, experiences, previous activities or facilities of the employer's enterprise or instructions by the employer have had in the conception of the invention."

Switzerland. Article 343 of the Swiss Code of Obligations reads as follows:

Article 343

"Inventions made by the employee in the course of his employment belong to the employer if the making of the invention forms part of the employee's work, or if, where such is not the case, the employer reserved this right in the contract of employment.

"In the latter case the employee is entitled to a reasonable remuneration if the invention is of considerable economic importance.

"This remuneration shall be fixed with due regard to the cooperation of the employer and the use made of his organization."

By invention agreement the employer may confirm his exclusive rights in service inventions. Also, by Invention Agreement the employer can secure exclusive rights to dependent inventions in the field of employer's interest made during the term of employment.

Service inventions belong to the employer without payment of compensation beyond salary. Reasonable compensation must be paid for dependent inventions if the right to them is reserved in employment contract. The employee's legal right to compensation for dependent inventions cannot be waived in advance by the terms of the invention agreement.

Free inventions belong to the employee. They can be obtained by negotiation with the employee as from an outside inventor. Also, by invention agreement the employer may obtain exclusive rights to free inventions in specified fields but must provide separate compensation for each such invention.

Group III Countries

Japan. In the absence of an invention agreement with the employee, the employer has a non-exclusive license under any patent obtained on a service invention of the employee. By invention agreement the employer can acquire the exclusive rights in service inventions made during the term of employment but must pay reasonable compensation to the employee for each such invention acquired. The profit which the employer derives from use of the invention is used to determine the compensation amount. However, the contribution of the employer is taken into consideration in the determination. Exclusive rights in inventions other than service inventions cannot be acquired by the employer in advance by agreement with the employee. The same rule applies to exclusive licenses under these employee inventions which belong to the employee. These inventions can be obtained by negotiation with the employee as from an outside inventor.

Article 35 of the new Patents Act of April 13, 1959, which became effective on April 1, 1960, and Article 9(3) of the Utility Model Law are the statutory provisions that govern the questions of ownership and compensation of employee service inventions. They are set forth, as follows, on the basis of translations from volumes 1 and 3, respectively, of "New Industrial Property Code Series of Japan", Trade Bulletin Corporation, Tokyo.

Article 35 reads:

1. The employer, the juridical person, the State, or a local public body (hereinafter referred to as "employer, etc.") shall, in case an employee, an official of the juridical person, a Government public official or a local public official (hereinafter referred to as "employee, etc.") has obtained a patent in respect of an invention the acts leading to such invention belong to the present or past duties of such employee, etc. as well as such invention is, in its nature, within the scope of business of such employer, etc. (hereinafter referred to as "invention in performance of duties"), or in case a person who has succeeded to a right to obtain a patent in respect of the invention in performance of duties has obtained a patent in respect of such invention, shall have a right of ordinary working on such patent right.

2. With respect to the invention which the employee, etc. has initiated, the provisions of a contract, service regulations and any other stipulations which provide in advance that a right to obtain a patent or a patent right be succeeded to by the employer, etc. or a right of exclusive working be created for the employer, etc. shall be invalid, except the invention is the one in performance of duties.

3. In case the employee, etc. has, by a contract or service regulations or any other stipulations, allowed the employer, etc. to succeed a right to obtain a patent or a patent right in respect of the invention in performance of duties or has created a right of exclusive working for the employer, etc., such employee, etc. shall be entitled to reasonable compensation.

4. The amount of compensation mentioned in the preceding paragraph shall be determined in consideration of the amount of profits which the employer, etc. may derive from the invention and of the extent to which the employer, etc. has contributed to the execution of the invention.

Article 9(3) reads as follows:

The provisions of Article 35 (Invention in performance of duties) of the Patent Law shall apply mutatis mutandis to a device initiated by an employee, an officer of a juridical person or a national or local public official.

Sweden. The legal relationships between employers and employees with regard to inventions made by an employee during the course of his employment are governed in Swedish Law by the Act of June 18, 1949 covering the Right to Inventions Made by Employees. The following articles are particularly pertinent.

Article 3

"(1) If research or inventive work constitutes the main task or if invention has been conceived mainly as a result of such activity, or if invention in question implies the solution of a problem presented during employment, the employer is entitled to have the invention assigned to him, provided the invention lies within his field of interest.

"(2) If invention is within the field of interest of employer but has been conceived according to other employment than above, employer has right to work the invention in his field and has priority right to acquire the invention."

Article 6

"(1) The employee is entitled to an adequate compensation; this applies even if something contradictory might have been agreed upon before the conception of the invention.

"(2) For determining the compensation, consideration has to be given to the value of the invention, the extent of the right in the invention which the employer acquired, and the importance the employment may have had in the conception of the invention."

Service inventions belong to the employer who may have to pay reasonable compensation for them if the salary of the employee is out of proportion to the value of the invention. The employer has an option to acquire exclusive or non-exclusive rights to dependent inventions upon payment of reasonable compensation. Free inventions belong to the employee. They can be obtained by negotiation with the employee as from an outside inventor. Also, they can be acquired through invention agreement but the employer must provide for separate compensation for each such invention.

Germany. The German Law of July 25, 1957 requires the employer to compensate the employee for every invention made by him and claimed by the employer. It is applicable to inventions which are subject to protection by patents or by grant of a utility model and to suggestions for technical improvements.

In addition to the law, a set of Directives or regulations issued by the Minister of Labor provides a guide for use in determining the amount of compensation due employee inventors. The regulations are not laws; they serve only as guides and the parties are not bound to follow them.

The law makes a distinction between service inventions and dependent inventions. Service inventions are defined as those inventions made in the course of employment which either: (1) arose out of the activities incumbent upon the employee in the plant or in public administration; or else, (2) depend decisively on the experiences or operations of the plant or the public administration.

Dependent inventions are those which are utilizable in the business of the employer.

Other inventions of the employees are free inventions.

The salaried inventor must report service inventions to the employer in writing. The employer may claim service inventions in whole and become the sole owner of the invention, or in part. In the latter case, the employer has only a license to use the invention. Whether the employer claims the invention in whole or in part, the inventor is entitled to compensation. The amount of the compensation is determined (Section 9) on the basis of (1) commercial applicability of the invention; (2) the duties and position of the employee in the company; and (3) the contribution of the company in the creation of the invention.

Dependent inventions (the German Law includes them with free inventions) which are employable in the business of the enterprise but do not belong to it under the employment relations, must be communicated to the employer who must also be offered a non-exclusive license against the payment of reasonable compensation. (Sections 18 and 19.)

Suggestions for technical improvements must be similarly compensated if they afford the employer a similar advantage. (Section 20.) The employer is also entitled to foreign rights but must release them to the employee if he does not intend to file in foreign countries. (Section 14.) If, however, the employer has agreed to transfer foreign rights to a foreign firm or has obligations abroad, Section 14 does not apply.

The German Law, in Section 12, provides that the kind and amount of the indemnity shall be fixed by agreement between the employer and the employee. In the case of co-inventors, the indemnity shall be fixed separately for each of them. If agreement cannot be reached, the employer fixes the amount of compensation and the employee is given two months within which to oppose it. When the circumstances under which an indemnity was originally fixed become notably changed either the employer or the employee may request a new determination of the amount but sums already paid cannot be demanded back. Provisions are made for arbitrating disputes before the German Patent Office and for judicial proceedings if arbitration fails. When must the compensation be paid? Section 12, paragraph 3 of the law says within 3 months after the issuance of a patent covering the invention. Paragraph 23 of the German Directives states within a period of 3 to 5 years after the patent issues. Therefore, it would seem to indicate that experience had taught that 3 months was not enough and the period was therefore extended to a period of 3 to 5 years while checking for economic feasibility by the employer.

Assessing Compensation of German Employee Inventions

CALCULATION BY FORMULA V = EA

The German Law requires that a suitable compensation be awarded to an employee for his invention which is claimed by the employer. The law does not define what is meant by "suitable." The law does mention three essential criteria to be used as basis of assessment, viz., (1) the commercial use of the invention, (2) the employee's duties and position within the company, (3) the company's share in the conception of the invention.

However, the consideration of these three criteria is not sufficient in itself to determine an adequate compensation. All the circumstances of each individual case should be taken into consideration.

It is realized that it may not be possible to solve all cases occurring in practice by means of a computation by mathematical formula. However, the Directives contain a formula which can be used to compute the compensation for an employee invention. Generally, it may be said that such a formula should have as small a number of factors as possible inasmuch as the value of each factor will have to be assessed. This procedure requires experience in order to achieve satisfactory results in arriving at a suitable compensation.

As set forth in the Directives, the compensation V is calculated as follows:

$$V = EA$$

V being the "compensation to be paid," E being the "value of the invention" and A being the "share factor," indicated as a percentage amount. The application of this formula for determining compensation for employee inventions is explained below.

SHARE FACTOR A

The information used in determining the share factor is obtained by asking the inventor himself. As set forth by the Directives, these questions are included in the "invention disclosure" which can be confirmed in writing by the inventor's superior and checked by the Patent Attorney who knows the situation from personal contact in order to make sure that the questions have been understood and answered in their correct meaning.

VALUE OF INVENTION E

After the granting of a patent or Ge-brauchsmuster, or after the rejection of a German patent application, which, however, has issued into a foreign patent, the Patent Attorney can proceed to determine the value of the invention.

As a rule, the patent right is considered generally from two viewpoints:

SUBJECTIVE VALUE

The patent is reviewed with regard to broad or narrow claims, whether examined or unexamined, and granted with or without opposition. The first alternative in each case increases the value of the invention.

OBJECTIVE VALUE

This is determined by the amount of compensation or other consideration that would be agreed upon with an independent inventor with reference to comparable cases which occurred in the organization or other companies. Also, the amount that the company would pay to obtain a license from an outsider for a six year term in accordance with customary company practice is considered.

WHEN THE INVENTION IS NOT USED.

Empirical values can be established depending upon the industry concerned. *Further,* The following criteria can be considered:
(a) Will there be any use of the invention at a later date?
(b) Could the invention be used as a substitute for the subject matter of a company owned or non-company owned patent already in use?
(c) Might the use of the invention by another company cause any problem to the company?
(d) Might any other party feel the necessity of using the invention?
(Positive answers tend to increase the value of the invention. In the case mentioned under (c), it might be necessary to pay a compensation which exceeds the established empirical figures considerably.)

WHEN THE INVENTION IS USED

(a) Assessment is made by the license analogy method in accordance with licensing practice. A royalty based on the manufacturing costs is considered (comprising labor costs, material costs and factory overhead). The empirically determined and customary license royalty rates for the industry should be applied.

(b) Assessment by the determinable use to the company may sometimes be made when the license analogy method fails. This is the difference between the costs and the proceeds brought about by the application of the invention. This amount is determined by a comparison of costs and returns as established by principles of cost accounting so that interest costs and the elements of risk, necessary operating procedures, and, where it is appropriate, return on the investment may be given due consideration. The amount computed constitutes the value of the invention.

For example, when an invention is made, an investigation is carried out to find the amount of money saved or gained by the invention. The value of the invention is then approximately $16\frac{2}{3}$ per cent of the annual savings realized by the invention multiplied by 6, since the average lifetime of a patent is considered to be 6 years. The result of this computation is the value E of the invention.

This procedure of assessment may be used for checking or changing the result found by the license analogy method. This possibility of determining the compensation by different methods and thereby checking the results is expressly mentioned in the directives. It is believed that this manner of assessment plays an important part in connection with the question of adequacy, because the inventor compensation must be considered a kind of share of the profits and is, therefore, dependent on the profit the employer gets out of the invention.

EVALUATION OF THE SHARE FACTOR A

According to the directives the factors which must be taken into consideration are as follows:

Assignment of the task: How the employee came to make the invention, ranging from a specific assignment with a suggested solution, to complete originality. This factor is to be weighted from 1 to 6.

The extent of employer's aid in developing the invention through technical assistance, know-how and professional knowledge. This factor is also to be weighted from 1 to 6.

Duties and position of the employee: This is the actual position of the employee related to his duties and wages from unskilled worker to manager of the research department. This factor is to be weighted from 1 to 8, viz.:

Employee	Classification Factor
Unskilled workers, laborers, jobtrained workers, apprentices	8
Skilled workers, foreman, laboratory help, mechanics, draftsmen, assistant to master craftsman	7
Master craftsman, senior master craftsman, plant technician, chemical technician	6
Engineers in production departments	5
Designers (in the Technical Engineering Dept.), engineers (in the Testing Lab.)	4.5
Supervisors in the production departments, engineers and designers in development departments	4
Department and plant managers in production departments, supervisors and project managers in development departments, engineers and chemists in research departments, patent engineers	3
Department managers in development departments, supervisors in research departments	2
Research manager, technical manager of entire plant	1

The sum of a + b + c may, therefore, range from a minimum of 3 to a maximum of 20, and is noted along the upper line of the table below. The lower line represents the Share Factor A with a factor A indicated as a percentage amount appearing directly under each possible sum of a + b + c.

For example, in a case where the value of the invention (E) is found to be 10,000 and the sum of a + b + c equals 8 which corresponds to a share factor (A) of 15 per cent, the computation of the compensation amount according to the formula $V = EA$ is as follows:

$$V = 10,000 \times 0.15 = 1,500$$

AREA OF COMMERCIAL USE

It is apparent from the procedures in Germany for determining compensation that the commercial use of a patented invention is a factor which can have an important effect on the compensation amount. One of the factors to be considered in the worldwide operations of a company is the possibility that a German employee invention may be utilized in Germany and in a number of countries foreign to Germany including the U.S., by becoming a part of a machine marketed outside Germany. When such an invention is manufactured, marketed, offered for sale or used in a country foreign to Germany and a patent right has been obtained in that country on the invention, the commercial use of the invention in the foreign country must be considered in determining the compensation for the German employee. The prevailing opinion among German Patent Attorneys, which is based on the Directives, is that where commercial use is made of the invention in a country foreign to Germany but no patent right has been obtained in that country, no compensation is required under German law to be paid to the German employee if the invention has become so widely known that others may work the invention in that country. Accordingly, it is apparent that the compensation amount is based on the existence of a patent right and the extent of use in such foreign country. However, there is a contrary opinion among some German patent professional people that if an employee's invention is utilized in a foreign country, the employer's obligation to pay

a + b + c =	3	4	5	6	7	8	9	10	11	12	13	14	15	16	17	18	19	(20)
A =	2	4	7	10	13	15	18	21	25	32	39	47	55	63	72	81	90	(100)

compensation to the employee and the amount thereof depend, not on the existence of a foreign patent right, but rather on whether the invention is patentable in Germany. This represents the minority thinking. In this view the compensation amount should not be made dependent on the existence of a patent right in the foreign country in cases where the employer actually profits by the utilization of an invention in a foreign country. It contemplates that in such a case the employer should pay an inventor's compensation the amount of which would be computed by the same procedures as if the invention were utilized in Germany.

It is seen that the employee's duties and position within the company, and the company's share in the conception of the invention, in addition to the commercial use of the invention, are used as criteria for assessing the compensation amount for a German employee invention. Accordingly, the criteria for compensation for inventions can vary within a wide range.

Cross-references: *Employee Inventions, Incentives for Inventors, Soviet Patents.*

EMPLOYEES' RESPONSIBILITIES AS TO TRADE SECRETS

Charles E. McTiernan

Statutory Provision and General Principles

The statutory provision respecting liability in the disclosure of trade secrets is:

"One who discloses or uses another's trade secret, without a privilege to do so, is liable to the other if (a) he discovered the secret by improper means, or (b) his disclosure or use constitutes a breach of confidence reposed in him by the other in disclosing the secret to him, or (c) he learned the secret from a third person with notice of the fact that it was a secret and that the third person discovered it by improper means or that the third person's disclosure of it was otherwise a breach of his duty to the other or (d) he learned the secret with notice of the fact that it was a secret and that its disclosure was made to him by mistake." Section 757 of the Restatement of Torts.

In an address before the New York Patent Law Association, printed in 9 The Practical Lawyer 77, 83, 1963, Mr. Granville M. Brumbaugh said:

"The generally accepted theory is that protection of trade secrets is afforded only by a general duty of good faith and that liability rests upon a breach of this duty, for example, a breach of contract or of a confidence, or an impropriety in the method of ascertaining the secret resulting in an unjust enrichment at the expense of the owner of the trade secret."

He also stated, in effect:

(1) The law protects against unauthorized disclosure or use. A disclosure may be made in confidence, or implied. It may not be disclosed in confidence to a person against the disclosee's will, and there must be a reasonable indication that it is actually disclosed in confidence. The circumstances surrounding the disclosure may be such that the disclosee should reasonably understand that the disclosure is made in confidence.

(2) If a person learns of a secret not knowing it to be a secret and then learns that it is a trade secret, he is not liable for his actions before the notice. He is liable for his actions after the notice unless there was consideration or unless he had changed his position to his detriment as a result of the original disclosure.

(3) The remedies include damages arising out of the past transactions, injunctions against future use of the secret, accounting for past damages, and surrender of the goods made.

(4) It is quite impractical for an attorney to advise his client not to deal with trade secrets, dangerous though they may be, since they can be of such great commercial advantage. The client should understand, however, that in dealing with trade secrets he is taking a calculated risk. Cf., 2 Bulletin, N.Y. Pat. Law Association, May 1963.

Increasing Hazard of Trade Secret Disclosures

Disclosure of secret information obtained from employers is a cause of increasing concern and worldwide importance.

The cause is obvious. The annual expenditure for research is now of the order of

20 billion dollars a year. If there were added the extra value created by the research above its cost and the expenses of plant start-ups in utilizing the research results, the total should be expected to approach the market value of the agricultural production in this country, recently running at the annual rate of approximately 36 billion dollars. To make away with any substantial part of that bulky production or even of the produce of a single large farm would be practically impossible, yet the information resulting from a major research may fit into a briefcase.

Under such circumstances, it is not surprising that a termination of employment may lead the ex-employee, facing perhaps a seemingly bleak outlook, to brood on real or fancied unfair treatment, recall that he was paid less for creating the new product, as has been the fact at times, than the salesman for selling it, and seek the seemingly easy road of using the secret information for a fee or the basis for a new position.

There is now appearing a new class of circumstances in which an outside individual having no part in the development obtains information from employees to be disposed of nationally or internationally. One person, charged with such an act, has been pursued from country to country and was reported in 1963 as in a foreign jail. Cf. 41 Chem. Eng. News 19. In another case, an American firm obtained the indictment of three former employees and five others for allegedly transporting stolen antibiotic cultures. 42 *ibid.* 17, 1962. At a recent international technical convention, informal comment among delegates was to the effect that "hundreds" of our secrets were being peddled abroad, a number perhaps not greatly exaggerated if all actual cases could be discovered.

In awareness of the hazard and in spite of the costs involved in litigation, firms with large investments in research are proceeding to protect their property. A representative case involved space-suit testing information. The Goodrich Company warned the terminating employee that he was taking to the new company, a competitor in the line, secret information belonging to Goodrich. The employee is reported to have said that

he was getting a higher salary and better position, that loyalty and ethics have their price and the new employer was paying the price. The Court granted an injunction against disclosure of the trade secrets. *B. F. Goodrich Co.* v. *Fritz Muller "Coroplast" K.g.*, 137 USPQ 568, 1963. In another case, it is alleged, a manufacturer approached the duPont Company for assistance on a project which duPont had developed with an expenditure of $15,000,000 in research. Failing to receive the information, the manufacturer hired a senior member of the research team involved. On the allegation by duPont that he had "peculiarly intimate knowledge" of the trade secrets and information and on the showing made, the court granted a temporary injunction against disclosure of the information. *E. I. duPont de Nemours & Co.* v. *David E. Hirsch*, N.Y. Times, October 13, 1963, Section 3, p. 1.

Legislators are becoming aware of the problem. New York Penal Law 1296(4), by amendment effective July 1, 1964, now makes grand larceny in the second degree, which is punishable by imprisonment for a term not exceeding five years, theft of the following:

"4. Property of any value consisting of a sample, culture, microorganism, specimen, record, recording, document, drawing or any other article, material, device or substance which constitutes, represents, evidences, reflects, or records a secret scientific or technical process, invention or formula or any phase or part thereof. A process, invention or formula is "secret" when it is not, and is not intended to be available to anyone other than the owner thereof or selected persons having access thereto for limited purposes with his consent, and when it accords or may accord the owner an advantage over competitors or other persons who do not have knowledge or the benefit thereof."

Certain parts of the following sections are based on the author's address given before the Practising Law Institute in New York and subsequently published in 41 JPOS 820, 1959.

Employees' agreements relating to protection of confidences and restriction on subsequent employment in competing industry and also protection in the use of information submitted from outside sources are left for discussion in the cross-references listed at the end of this article.

Nature of Information Protectable as Trade Secrets

During his employment, the employee may come into possession of information pertinent to his employer's operation that falls into the following categories:

(1) Technical trade secrets such as secret processes and formulas

(2) Confidential information other than technical such as employer's cost figures and customer lists

(3) General knowledge absorbed by the employee such as known methods of manufacture used by the employer or slight modifications thereof.

A general definition of "trade secrets" is found in the Restatement of Torts, Section 757, Comment (b):

"A trade secret may consist of any formula, patterns, device or compilation of information which is used in one's business and which gives him an opportunity to obtain an advantage over competitors who do not know or use it. It may be a formula for a chemical compound, a process of manufacturing, treating or preserving materials, a pattern for a machine or other device, or a list of customers. It differs from other secret information in a business in that it is not simply information as to single or ephemeral events in the conduct of the business.... A trade secret is a process or device for continuous use in the operation of the business. Generally, it relates to the production of goods as, for example, a machine or formula for the production of an article....

"The subject matter of a trade secret must be secret. Matters of public knowledge or of general knowledge in an industry cannot be appropriated by one as his secret. Matters which are completely disclosed by the goods which one markets cannot be his secret. Substantially, a trade secret is known only in the particular business in which it is used. It is not requisite that only the proprietor of the business know it. He may, without losing his protection, communicate it to employees involved in its use. He may likewise communicate it to others pledged to secrecy. Others may also know of it independently, as, for example, when they have discovered the process or formula by independent invention and are keeping it secret. Nevertheless, a substantial element of secrecy must exist, so that, except by the use of improper means, there would

be difficulty in acquiring the information. An exact definition of a trade secret is not possible. Some factors to be considered in determining whether given information is one's trade secret are: (1) the extent to which the information is known outside of his business; (2) the extent to which it is known by employees and others involved in his business; (3) the extent of measures taken by him to guard the secrecy of the information; (4) the value of the information to him and his competitors; (5) the amount of effort or money expended by him in developing the information; (6) the ease or difficulty with which the information could be properly acquired or duplicated by others." Quoted in *Minnesota Mining & Mfg.* case, infra, p. 101.

To enforce the obligation of nondisclosure, there must be shown the intent to keep the information secret. Representative expedients would be labeling containers for materials used with code numbers only, requiring special permits for access to secret areas of the plant, even for employees, and taking other action described elsewhere herein.

In *Monsanto Chemical Co.* v. *Miller et al.*, 118 USPQ 74, DC Utah 1958, plaintiff alleged that Miller, a former employee, carried away from Monsanto drawings of the electric furnace for making phosphorus and also background information that enabled him to design the furnace for a competitor. In holding the information to be in fact a trade secret, the Court noted that (1) Miller cannot prevail on the ground that he was not furnished a bill of particulars as to what was the trade secret, it being sufficient that he was told an entire operation was secret and not to be divulged, and (2) Monsanto made it a policy not to release to the public information relating to the design of its furnace.

The status of information obtained surreptitiously, although allegedly disclosed in a patent, was the issue in part in a state court case, *Cornale et al.* v. *Stewart Stamping Corp. et al.*, 100 USPQ 361, 364, N.Y. Sup. Ct., Westchester Co. 1954. Here Duarte, a foreman for the employer Stewart, developed a soldering flux which he represented to his employer as the work of one Cornale. It was later found that Cornale actually obtained the information from Duarte and had contracted with Duarte to share profits with him. The profit so divided was $18,094, Cornale and Duarte alleged, in their defense, that certain information disclosed by Duarte to Cornale was of "public record and in the public domain by reason of patents." The Court ordered the return to the employer of the $18,094 that he had paid on the recommendation of his employee Duarte and said the allegation by Cornale and Duarte, of lack of novelty in the information passed, "does not condone their conduct. The information was not obtained through legitimate and fair channels but by furtive means."

Evidence of Disclosure

When there is doubt as to whether an employee has disclosed the information, it is to be expected that a court may rely in part on objective factors.

As pointed out in *Rabinowitz & Co., Inc.* v. *Dasher et al.*, 78 USPQ 163, N.Y. Sup. Ct., N.Y. Co. 1948, an employer does not lose his rights in respect of secret design and operation of machines when he licenses others to use such machines under contracts which expressly require licensees to preserve such secret.

One decision notes that a third party, Universal, after failing to make hydraulic tube supports, went into operation within less than two months of the time of hiring, for after-hours' work, a daytime employee of the plaintiff manufacturer of such supports. The operation followed "exactly the procedure and processes of plaintiff." The Court refused to be so credulous as to believe there had been no disclosure of secret information and said:

"If the defendant can prove that he knew about the information or had the idea prior to its disclosure to him he has a complete defense.... The evidence...shows that Universal did not have the knowledge of how to make the hydraulic tube supports, economically, until Samburn imported the knowledge to it. It could not have produced the supports in so short a period of time without the information gained from Samburn." *Lee* v. *Samburn*, 94 USPQ 153, Calif. Sup. Ct., Los Angeles 1952.

The case of *Carter Products, Inc. et al.* v. *Colgate-Palmolive Co.*, 108 USPQ 383, CA 4 1956, involved both patent infringement and use of secret information. Norman Fine had worked under a secrecy agreement with Foster D. Snell, Inc. Consulting Chemists who, in turn, had done the successful research for Carter on its pressurized shaving cream "Rise," Fine being one of the joint inventors of the cream. When Fine applied for a position with Colgate, that company, knowing of his work with Snell, twice declined to hire him. Finally, Colgate did employ Fine and assigned him within a month to the problem which he had researched with Snell and which he now "solved immediately." Colgate then brought out the competitive pressurized cream "Rapid Shave." While denying the existence of trade secrets, Colgate filed two applications on the subject matter. The Circuit Court noted these points. Also it quoted approvingly the District Judge, 104 USPQ, pp. 326-327, 1955, to the effect that:

"Colgate was obligated to do more than it did towards ascertaining the extent to which Fine was, in fact, restricted [by his agreement with Snell] in what he might disclose to Colgate."

The Court held the patent valid and infringed by Colgate and ordered the applications, filed on the subject by Fine at Colgate's direction, assigned to plaintiff. In approving the special master's award of damages in the amount of $5,283,341, the Court applied the rule that, where trade secrets add to, but do not create, the entire commercial value of the products which embody them, the plaintiff will recover all profits unless the defendant can introduce a method of properly apportioning the value due to each component. The allowance of royalties for patent infringement of up to 10 per cent of defendant's net profit was included in the award. 136 USPQ 348, DC Md 1963.

It is no defense that an employee in a confidential relationship had no express covenant with the employer respecting trade secrets, when it is established that such a relationship and trade secrets are in fact involved. Cf. *Thiberg* v. *Bach*, 95 USPQ 49, DC NJ 1952.

Finally the disclosure of secret information is not excusable on the basis that the information might have been (but was not) discovered independently by a search of patents, court records or other literature, by experimentation or by analysis of a product on the market. See *Minnesota Mining & Mfg. Co.* v. *Technical Tape Corp.*, supra, pp. 102-104.

Employees' Rights

As pointed out in *Continental Car-Na-Var Corp.* v. *Mosely et al.*, 61 USPQ 532, 533, Calif. Sp. Ct. 1944, the ex-employee has the right to pursue any calling, business or profession he may choose, to engage in a competitive business for himself, and enter into competition with his former employer, even for the business of customers of his former employer, providing the competition is fairly and legally conducted.

As to the ex-employee's right to use his knowledge, skill and non-secret information, the Court in *Donahue* v. *Permacil Tape Corp.*, 127 N.E. (2) 235, 240, said:

"They belong to him as an individual for the transaction of any business in which he may engage, just the same as any part of the skill, knowledge, information or education that was received by him before entering the employment. Therefore, on terminating his employment he has a right to take them with him, although he may forget them or abandon them."

There is no hard and fast rule, however, as to what constitutes such knowledge, skill and information. The Continental decision held the defendant entitled "to make use of his general knowledge of chemistry to manufacture floor wax ... so long as he did not transgress upon trade secrets ... of plaintiff."

In *Sarkes Tarzian*, infra, it appears that the ordering, by the ex-employee, of equipment modified by the former employer falls within the "knowledge, skill and information" of the ex-employee.

In one case, the defendant-disclosee had changed greatly the proportions of ingredients of a wood-treating formula which had previously been made public without proportions. The court held that the proportions were material to secrecy and that it was no violation of the secrecy agreement for the defendant to continue to use the new formula without any further payments. *Protexol Corp.* v. *Koppers Co., Inc.* 108 USPQ 238, CA 2 1956; aff. 229 F.2d 635. CA 2 1956. Cf. *Montgomery* v. *Kalak Water Co.*, 131 USPQ 149, DC SNY 1961.

The fact that the ex-employee, on the other hand, was the inventor of the trade secret and did not learn it from the employer or any of its other employees, is not an available defense in those cases where the ex-employee had assigned, during the period of employment, the exclusive right in the trade secret to the employer. In *Pomeroy Ink Co.* v. *Pomeroy*, 78 Atlantic 698, the court found that the employee had assigned his inventions to the company, that such inventions were trade secrets of the company, and that an injunction should be and was granted enjoining the employee from disclosing the secrets.

Precautions and Policing Policies

The Employee's Agreement will ordinarily contain some such provision(s) as the following: (1) nondisclosure outside the company, and nonuse in competition with the company of its confidential information, both during and after the period of employment; and, in some cases, (2) no employment in the same field with a competitor for a fixed number of years after termination of employment or in a limited territory. For forms of such clauses, see Saul Gorden, "Employment and Agency Agreements," New York, Prentice-Hall, Inc., 1940.

No one should be employed whose reliability is in doubt. When employed, he should and usually does receive such treatment as to inspire worthiness of trust. There are certain policing policies that should be followed, however, to establish the fact that the employer does regard his information as secret and because of infrequent but unfortunate infractions that may occur.

Examples of desirable policing steps are:

(1) Clearing all papers or speeches to be presented at a public assembly.

(2) Stamping or applying legends on reports that are distributed, internally or externally, to point out that they contain confidential information.

(3) Keeping the employment agreement clause, obligating employees not to disclose confidential information, within the limits set as permissible, by limiting it to what was learned from the employer. Cf. *Sprague Electric Co.* v. *Cornell Dubilier Corp.*, 66 USPQ 431, DC Del 1945.

(4) Considering whether the employment agreement should set forth what state law controls.

(5) Limiting access to trade secrets by employees and visitors and having a clause in the employee's agreement to the effect that, upon termination, he will not participate in a similar operation for a new employer for a stated period of time. Have visitors, if any, sign a hold-confidential agreement.

(6) Making employees aware periodically of their obligation not to disclose the employer's confidential information and educating them as to obligations respecting it.

(7) Reminding the employee, upon termination, to turn over to the employer all documents containing information pertinent to the employer's business.

(8) Considering, in certain situations, placing the new employer on notice as to the existence of the ex-employee's secrecy agreement.

(9) As the new employer, advising the incoming employee that he is not to disclose confidential information of a former employer.

State Laws Relating to Trade Secrets

Agreements containing clauses not to compete after the period of employment are governed by many state statutes. In Texas, Title 126, Article 7426 is applicable; in Alabama, Sections 6826-6828; in California Business and Professions Code, Sections 16600-16602; in Oklahoma, Title 15, Sections 217-219, and Title 79, Sections 101-103.

In Illinois, as indicated in *Larx Co. et al.* v. *Nicol*, 71 USPQ 115, Minn. Sup. Ct. 1946, it is generally held that an agreement, wherein an employee binds himself for an unlimited time not to engage in a particular business or trade, is valid if such agreement includes a territorial or space limitation; an agreement, unlimited both as to time and territory, is invalid as contrary to public policy.

In Texas, in *Jennings* v. *Shepherd Laundries Co.*, 276 S.W. 726, a contract prohibiting an employee from engaging in the same business as the employer's business for 2 years after leaving employ, was held neither a violation of the antitrust law nor an unreasonable restraint of trade.

The California case of *Sarkes Tarzian Inc.* v. *Auto Devices*, 119 USPQ 20, DC Calif. 1958, considers what state law controls. The employment agreements for some of the ex-employees involved were signed in Indiana. When they quit Sarkes Tarzian, they went to work for Audio Devices in California. The Court, relying on the Restatement, Conflict of Laws Section 377, ruled that since the alleged disclosure of trade secrets was a tort committed in California, then the law of that state prevails. "The place of wrong is in the State where the last event necessary to make an action liable for an alleged tort takes place." However, it is noted that if the validity of the employment agreement had been at issue in this case, then the Court would have applied the law of Indiana. As pointed out in *Sprague Electric Co.* v. *Cornell-Dubilier*, supra, and set forth in Section 332 of the Restatement on Conflict of Laws, the law of the place of contracting is the applicable law in determining the validity of the employment agreement. In any event, an employer, who is relying to a significant extent on trade secrets, should consider setting forth in the employment agreement the state whose law will govern the employer-employee relationships.

California has a statute of significance as to employer-employee relationships. Section 2860 of the California Labor Code reads as follows:

"Everything which an employee acquires by virtue of his employment, except the compensation which is due to him from his employer, belongs to the employer, whether acquired lawfully or unlawfully, or during or after the expiration of the term of his employment."

In New York, Penal Law Sections 553 and 554 pertain to an unauthorized disclosure of secret information by an employee during his period of employment. Section 554 makes guilty of a misdemeanor (1) any person who obtains information belonging to his employer in the course of his employment and who discloses such information without consent of the employer and (2) any person who knows that such information was disclosed without consent of the employer and causes such to be disclosed.

Federal Trade Commission Regulations

With reference to an individual shifting employment, all employers should ascertain whether Federal Trade Commission Trade Practice Conference Rules exist for their industry. Usually these rules include a section dealing with enticing away employees of competitors.

An example of such a section, which was promulgated May 22, 1959 for the Work Glove Industry, is as follows:

"**Section 46.10—Enticing Away Employees of Competitors.** It is unfair trade practice wilfully to entice away employees or sales representatives of competitors with the intent and effect of thereby unduly hampering or injuring competitors in their business and destroying or substantially lessening competition: Provided, that nothing in this section shall be construed as prohibiting employees from seeking more favorable employment, or as prohibiting employers from hiring or offering employment to employees of competitors in good faith and not for the purpose of injuring, destroying or preventing competition."

See Par. 20,046 in 1959CCH Trade Regulation Reporter; *Sugar Creek Creamery Co. v. Momence Milk Cooperative Association,* 75 USPQ 193, DC EIll 1949, which is a case centering around FTC Trade Practice Conference Rules; and "FTC Trade Practice Conference Rules for the Gummed Paper and Sealing Tape Industry," Section 213.15 entitled "Enticing Away Employees of Competitor," Paragraph 20,019, CCH Trade Regulation Reporter, 1959.

General References

Forman, Howard I., "Patents, Research and Management," pp. 401-462, New York, Central Book Co., 1961.

Ellis, Ridsale, "Trade Secrets," New York, Baker Voorhis & Co., 1958.

Cross-references: *Employee Inventions and Agreements; Secret Information—Procedure in Accepting and Protection in Its Use; Shop Right.*

ESTOPPELS IN PATENT CASES
Frederic B. Schramm

An estoppel is a legal barrier which precludes one who has done some act or executed some deed from averring to the contrary. Estoppels may be classified as follows:

(1) Estoppel by record;
(2) Estoppel by deed;
(3) Estoppel by conduct, or estoppel *in pais,* or equitable estoppel;
(4) Estoppel by procedure.

An estoppel by record is an estoppel resulting from the judgment of a court of record, also discussed as *res judicata.* An example of this would be the estoppel of a manufacturer to deny infringement of a patent after the manufacturer had joined in the defense of the law suit brought by the same plaintiff on the same patent and relating to the same accused device which had been held to infringe in the earlier litigation.

An example of estoppel by deed in patent cases is the case of an assignment of a patent wherein the assignor subsequently infringes upon the patent and defends on the ground of prior invention by another.

An example of an estoppel by conduct is a case where a user of a product has supplied samples of the product to the manufacturer and encouraged him to tool up for production of the product for himself and others without limitation or claim of right therein, representing that it may be freely manufactured, and subsequently asserts exclusive rights in the invention thereof.

The fourth type of estoppel is *sui generis* in that it fails to follow in all respects the recognized principles governing the other types of estoppels. It involves the loss of legal rights because of failure to follow some procedural practice within a required time and is in this respect akin to estoppel, and therefore very often referred to as an estoppel. An example is the junior party to an interference losing the right to contest priority to subject matter by allowing the interference to become dissolved without filing a motion under Rule 233 or 234 to amend or to include another application so as to bring the subject matter into the interference. This is sometimes referred to as estoppel by dissolution. Estoppels of this fourth class may not always qualify as equitable estoppels because of a lack of a detrimental reliance upon a representation.

Estoppels must be distinguished from waivers, from laches and from removal of enforceability of rights as by the statute of limitations.

Estoppels may be classified also by the persons entitled to claim them, such as assignees and assignors, and according to who is bound by the estoppel, such as persons participating in patent litigation.

Estoppel by Record

Estoppel by record or *res judicata* rests upon the principle that when a matter has been decided it should not be relitigated between the same parties. The litigants themselves are estopped by the record unless they are victims of fraud and mistake. *American Dirigold Corp.* v. *Dirigold Metals Corp.*, 125 F.2d 446, 455, CA 6 1942.

The general rule is that a judicial estoppel does not arise unless the parties in the two proceedings are the same, and actions which might be a basis for an estoppel will not operate for benefit of persons who are not parties to the former proceedings. *Lawrence* v. *Vail*, 166 F. Supp. 777, DC SDak 1958. Nevertheless, in patent cases certain persons may be held privy to the original parties and therefor affected by the estoppel. Such situations will be discussed in the section "Persons Affected by Estoppel."

Estoppel by record may involve a judicial record or a legislative record. *Ward* v. *Flex-O-Tube Co.*, 194 F.2d 500, CA 6 1952. However, judicial estoppel is what is ordinarily involved in patent cases where estoppel by record occurs.

A logical limitation on estoppel by record is the fact that there has been a final adjudication on the merits. Where a former proceeding was voluntarily dismissed or resulted in a voluntary nonsuit, the party involved is not estopped to deny or contradict allegations made in the former proceeding. *Welch* v. *Lewis*, 184 F. Supp. 806, DC Miss 1960. A bare admission in pleading not transmitted into judgment, cannot work estoppel to assert title. *Sidebotham* v. *Robison*, 216 F.2d 816, CA 9 1955.

Decisions by the Patent Office are not *res judicata* in infringement suits. Participation in a Patent Office interference and losing an award of priority does not estop a defendant in an infringement suit to deny the validity of the patent. The court is not precluded from relieving the alleged infringer and the public from the asserted monopoly where there is no invention. *Mc Elrath* v. *Industrial Rayon Corp.*, 123 F.2d 627, CA 4 1941.

Even a judgment of priority between two inventors in a Patent Office interference is not *res judicata* after both patents are involved in a patent infringement suit and no estoppel is raised. *Chandler* v. *Cutler-Hammer, Inc.*, 31 F. Supp. 451, DC EWis 1940.

The estoppel of a prior judgment extends only to matters litigated, or which might have been litigated, in the former cases. The issues of law and fact must be the same. For example, when a licensee is sued a second time for royalties on manifolds, he is not estopped from again introducing evidence of the prior art, notwithstanding the fact that the breadth of the patent and the license was determined against him in the first action, where the question is whether new and different manifolds came within the license contract. *General Motors Corp.* v. *Swan Carburetor Co.*, 88 F.2d 876, CA 6 1937; C.D., 302 U.S. 691, 1937. Cf. *Paine & Williams Co.* v. *Baldwin Rubber Co.*, 113 F.2d 840, CA 6 1940.

Similarly there must have been an adjudication by a court of competent jurisdiction upon the question of infringement to sustain a plea of estoppel in a suit to determine whether an infringement exists. A judgment of the state court, confirming an arbitration award between the same parties on the question of infringement, does not constitute *res judicata* but may constitute an estoppel. *Cavicchi* v. *Mohawk Mfg. Co., Inc.,* 34 F. Supp. 852, DC SNY 1940.

An adjudication that a patent is valid does not estop defendants from contesting validity in a subsequent action unless there was an adjudication of infringement or the granting of some relief in the former action, particularly when the prior decree was by consent. *Addressograph-Multigraph Corp.* v. *Cooper,* 156 F.2d 483, CA 2 1946; cf. *Pope* v. *Gormully,* 144 U.S. 224, 1892.

The estoppel of a former judgment extends only to matters which were litigated or could have been litigated in the former case. Consequently, a defendant not in privity with the defendant in the former case may obtain an adjudication as to whether his product infringes. *Nash Motors* v. *Swan Carburetor Co.,* 105 F.2d 305, CA 4 1939; *Marcalus Mfg. Co.* v. *Automatic Paper Mach. Co.,* 110 F.2d 304, 306, CA 3 1940. Moreover, the court may also change its position on validity where the alleged infringer is a different party. *Graham* v. *Cockshutt Farm Equipment, Inc.,* 117 USPQ 439, CA 5 1958; *Park-in Theaters* v. *Waters,* 185 F.2d 193, CA 5 1950. Since the claims of a patent are separable, estoppel by judgment does not apply to litigation on claims which were not or could not have been litigated in the previous case. *Ostby & Barton Co.* v. *Jungersen,* 41 F. Supp. 552, 554, DC NJ 1941.

The decision of another circuit court involving the validity of a patent does not have the binding effect of *stare decisis* upon another court passing upon the same patent, *Aeration Processes* v. *Lange,* 196 F.2d 981, CA 8 1952, *Aerated Products* v. *Aeration Processes,* 95 F. Supp. 23, 25, DC SCal 1950, and a decision on the patent is not *res judicata* even in the same circuit where there is no privity between defendants in the two actions. *S. H. Kress & Co.* v. *Aghnides,* 246 F.2d 718, 113 USPQ 395, 114 USPQ 187, CA 4 1957; c.d. 115 USPQ 426, 355 U.S. 889. Nevertheless a decision upon the same patent in a suit by the same plaintiff against a different defendant may have a persuasive effect upon rehearing. *Stoody Co.* v. *Carleton Metals,* 111 F.2d 920, CA 9 1940, c.d., 311 U.S. 671, 1940. Cf. *Bee Mach. Co.,*

Inc. v. *Freeman,* 131 F.2d 190, CA 1 1942; aff. 319 U.S. 448, 1943.

Estoppel by Deed

An estoppel arising from the execution of a written instrument developed from the doctrine of after-acquired title, which stems from the common-law rule of implied warranties. *Robben* v. *Obering,* 279 F.2d 381, CA 7 1960. Estoppel by deed is a distinct kind of estoppel and does not require all the elements of estoppel *in pais. In re Solomon* 40 F. Supp. 62, DC EPa 1941.

The assignment or sale of a patent, the granting of a license under the claims of a patent, and entering into a contract concerning rights in subject matter disclosed in a patent give rise to questions concerning various estoppels, such as estoppel to deny title, estoppel to deny validity, estoppel to deny infringement or estoppel to assert infringement. All of these may be classified as estoppel by matter of deed.

Estoppel to Deny Title. According to 3 Deller's Walker 1994, an assignor or grantor of a patent right who afterwards infringes the right which he has conveyed is estopped by his conveyance from denying the title of the assignee or grantee, citing *Woodward* v. *Lasting Machine Co.,* 60 Fed. 283, 284, CA 1 1894 and numerous other cases. This may be held even where the assignor has been induced to part with his title on fraudulent representation by the assignee, citing *Vacuum Engineering Co.* v. *Dunn,* 209 Fed. 219, CA 2 1913.

Estoppel to Deny Validity. A typical example of estoppel by deed in patent cases arises from a license agreement in which the licensee expressly covenants not to contest the validity of any patents included in the license. Assuming no involvement of questions of public policy or violation of law, particularly the antitrust laws, this is a binding agreement between the parties which effects an estoppel by deed preventing the licensee from contesting the validity of patents. *U.S. Hoffman Machinery Corp.* v. *Richa,* 78 F. Supp. 969, DC WMo 1948; 2 Walker 1492; 3 Walker 1994. The assignor of a patent is likewise estopped to deny validity of a patent assigned. *B. B.*

Chemical Co. v. *Ellis,* 117 F.2d 829, 832, CA 1 1941, aff. 314 U.S. 495, 1942; *United Engineering & Foundry Co.* v. *Cold Metal Process Co.,* 68 F.2d 564, CA 3 1934, c.d. 291 U.S. 675.

An estoppel by deed is ordinarily limited to parties to an instrument. *Ward* v. *Flex-O-Tube Co.,* 194 F.2d 500, CA 6 1952.

Even without an express agreement by a licensee or assignor of a patent not to contest validity of a patent, this is implied, and the licensee or assignor is estopped. While a license is in force, a licensee is estopped to deny validity of the licensed patent. *Tate* v. *B & O,* 229 Fed. 141, 142, CA 4 1915. But an implied obligation not to contest validity is limited to the scope and duration of the license.

A licensee is not estopped to introduce prior art to interpret the claims of the licensed patent or to show that the claims must be construed, in the light of the prior art, too narrowly to cover licensee's construction. In *Westinghouse Co.* v. *Formica Insulation Co.,* 266 U.S. 342, 349, 1924, the court speaking through Mr. Chief Justice Taft said:

"The rule supported by them is that an assignor of a patent right is estopped to attack the utility, novelty, or validity of a patent the invention of which he has assigned or granted as against anyone claiming the right under his assignment or grant. . . .

"The analogy between estoppel in conveyance of land and estoppel in assignments of a patent right is clear. If one lawfully conveys to another a patented right to exclude the public from making, using and vending of an invention, fair dealings should prevent him from derogating from the title he has assigned, just as it estops a grantor of a deed of land from impeaching the effect of his solemn act as against his grantee. The grantor purports to convey the right to exclude others in the one instance, from a defined tract of land, and in the other, from a described and limited field of the useful arts."

A licensee is not estopped to prove that its devices are built wholly according to the teaching of the prior art and that everything necessary to their conception and con-

struction was taught by such art, for such proof merely negatives infringement. *Casco* v. *Sinko,* 116 F.2d 119, 121, CA 7 1940, c.d. 312 U.S. 693, 1941; *Westinghouse* v. *Formica,* supra.

The state of the art may be shown in a suit by the assignee of a patent against the assignor for infringement, to narrow or qualify the construction of the claims and relieve the assignor from the charge of infringement, at least, where the assignor made no specific representation as to the scope of the claims and their construction, on the faith of which the assignee purchased. *Westinghouse Electric Mfg Co.* v. *Formica Insulation Co.,* 266 U.S. 342, 1924; *Kohn* v. *Eimer,* 265 Fed. 900, 904, CA 2 1920; *General Electric Co.* v. *Hygrade Sylvania Corp.,* 61 F. Supp. 476, DC SNY 1944. Cf. *Frank* v. *Columbia,* 33 F. Supp. 279, DC SNY 1940.

An assignee of a patent may not be estopped to assert a failure of consideration due to the worthlessness of the patented device. *Tradick* v. *Emery,* 93 Wash. 648, 161 P. 484.

The New York courts have held, as in *Wicks* v. *Matam,* 75 USPQ 207, S.Ct. NY 1947, that, where considerations for an agreement are certain patents which are later held invalid and void, monies paid and expended pursuant to the agreement may be recovered.

Estoppel to Deny Utility. It has been held that the defendant is estopped to deny utility, his infringement amounting to an admission of utility. *Dunkley Co.* v. *Central California Canneries,* 7 F.2d 972, 976, CA 9, c.d., 270 U.S. 646, 1926; *Seymour* v. *Ford Motor Co.,* 44 F.2d 306, 308, CA 6 1930; *Kansas City Railway So.* v. *Silica Products Co.,* 48 F.2d 503, 505, CA 8 1931, c.d., 284 U.S. 626. Cf. *Kraus* v. *General Motors Corp.,* 120 F.2d 109, CA 2 1941.

Estoppel to Assert Infringement. Circumstances which may estop the patentee to assert infringement are discussed under the heading "Implied License." Circumstances may also arise where a licensee or assignor of a patent is estopped to deny infringement of the patent.

Estoppel to Deny Infringement. When a manufacturer continues to make the devices upon which he has paid royalties under a license agreement it may be estopped to deny infringement. *Miami Cycle* v. *Robinson*, 245 F. 556, CA 6. This conclusion follows from the Rule of Law that the Courts will place upon a contract the interpretation placed upon it by the parties. *Kothe* v. *Taylor*, 280 U.S. 224, 226. It also follows that, where a party continues to make and sell after the termination of the license the same thing that he made and sold under the license, infringement is to be accepted. *Stevens* v. *Schmid*, 73 F.2d 54, CA 2 1934; *National Pigments and Chemical Co.* v. *C. K. Williams & Co.*, 94 F.2d 792, 795, CA 8 1938; Ellis on Patent Assignments and Licenses, 746; *Piaget Novelty Co.* v. *Headley et al.*, 108 Fed. 870, CA 2.

The estoppel to deny infringement is even stronger when the accused party has marked the patent number on the product or has held himself out as manufacturing under the patent. *Piaget* case, supra. Cf. *Lathrop* v. *Rice and Adams*, 17 F. Supp. 622, 626, DC WNY 1936.

In *Dwight* v. *American*, 44 F. Supp. 401, 402, DC SNY 1941, the court said: In Piaget Novelty Co. v. Headley, supra, the defendant was estopped to deny that certain articles, not stamped by it with the plaintiff's patent date, were covered by plaintiff's patent in view of the fact that the defendant had stamped other articles precisely the same with the patent date. Cf. *Cold Metal Process* v. *McLouth Steel Corporation*, 79 USPQ 222, 230, CA 6 1948.

The broad general rules of equitable estoppel or estoppel *in pais* apply equally well in a case of transfers of inventions and patent rights. The Court said in *G.M.C. Process Corp.* v. *Garofano et al.*, 111 USPQ 56, 58; 2 App. Div. 2d 115, N.Y.S.Ct., App. Div. 1956: "[The] dominant equitable rule between assignor and assignee [is] that the patent must be liberally construed to give full value to patent assigned and shut out the assignor from every structure within the fair meaning of the claim."

The assignor of a patent for value with covenant of warranty is estopped when sued by the assignee to claim a narrower construction of the claims than it did to induce the sale. The Court declared in *United* v. *Cross*, 227 Fed. 600, 603, CA 1 1915: "The plaintiff had a right to rely on what the defendant said as to the subject matter that was being sold...." Cf. *Wilson* v. *Byron Jackson Co.*, 93 F.2d 572, 576, CA 9 1937.

Although the estoppel to deny infringement is not as well established as estoppel to deny validity of a patent, the estoppel has been recognized when the assignor is sued for an infringement of a patent which he has assigned or when the licensee is sued for royalties or for infringement taking place after repudiation of the license under certain circumstances. The courts ordinarily do not go into the question of the limiting effect of prior art when the suit is for royalties on an invention defined by the contract. Additional aspects of the question are discussed in an article by Schramm, "Estoppel to Deny Infringement," 42 JPOS 644, 1960.

Incidental Estoppels Arising in Patent Matters

According to 2 Walker on Patents, Deller's Edition, 1404, it has been held that one who signs an assignment in blank is estopped from denying the propriety of the subsequent filling in of the assignment after the filled assignments are invoked by purchasers for value of the patent, who had no notice of any fraud or error in the filling, citing *National Heeling-Mach. Co.* v. *Abbott*, 70 Fed. 54, C.C. Mass. 1895.

2 Walker 1159 declares that where an alteration of a patent has been made by the Commissioner of Patents, at the request of the patentee, and where some party has relied upon the validity of that alteration to the extent of embarking in business because of it, the patentee may be estopped from denying that validity, as against that particular party, citing *Edison Electric Light Co.* v. *Buckeye Electric Co.*, 59 Fed. 691, 699 (Cir. Court Ohio). (See *File Wrapper Estoppel*)

There is an interesting twist in one case which in effect held that the presence of one kind of estoppel precludes another kind from arising. In *Paine & Williams Co.* v. *Baldwin*, 113 F.2d 840, CA 6 1940, the court reasoned that where a patent licensee was unsuccessful in a suit for royalties by his licensor, wherein the licensee pleaded no infringement by reason of the fact that the articles made fell outside the scope of the patent, the decision is not *res judicata* as to the questions of novelty and invalidity over the prior art (even though believed and determined by the court in said suit to be in issue); these questions have a bearing upon patentability and the licensee was estopped to deny validity In a suit for infringement between the same parties, subsequent to the cancellation of the license contract, there is no "estoppel by judgment" and the court can fully consider and determine the question of validity of the claims. *Paine & Williams Co.* v. *Baldwin*, supra.

Circumstances under Which No Estoppel Arises or Estoppel Terminates

We have seen that estoppel to deny validity may be avoided by causing the case to turn on a question of infringement or failure of consideration. There may also be special circumstances which negative estoppel to deny validity.

Where the licensor of the patent repudiates the license by suing the licensee for infringement, he cannot rely upon it as an estoppel. *Tate* v. *B & O*, 229 Fed. 141, 142, 143, CA 4 1915.

Walker also declares that the defendant is not estopped from denying the validity of a patent by the fact that he (1) formerly thought and represented it to be valid, citing *DeLaVergne Refrigerating Mach. Co.* v. *Featherstone*, 49 Fed. 916, 919 C.C. Ill. 1892 and other cases, or (2) once made an application himself for a patent on the same invention, citing *Page* v. *Buckley*, 67 Fed. 142, C.C. Ill. 1895.

Where a licensee effects a valid cancellation of a license pursuant to the terms of the agreement, it is not estopped to deny the validity of the patents involved. *Miehle* v. *Publication Corp.*, 166 F.2d 615, CA 7 1948. The Government would be estopped to assert invalidity of a patent when it had a license under the patent, but after the

license had expired the government has at least a technical right to assert this defense. *Breeze Burners, Inc.* v. *U.S.*, 115 USPQ 179, 180, Ct. Cls. 1957.

When the licensee continues to work under a forfeited license as though it were still in force, the licensor has an option to sue him as an infringer or to sue him for the promised royalties. But if the licensor selects the first of these remedies, this is regarded as a repudiation of the license. The license being at an end and contractual relationship having ceased, the infringer may interpose any defense that he could have set up in the absence of a license. Some of the older cases made an exception where there was an express covenant not to contest validity [*Dunham* v. *Bent*, 72 F. 60, 1895; *Consolidated Rubber Tire Co.* v. *Finley Rubber Tire Co.*, 116 F. 629, 638, 1902].

Estoppel by Conduct

Variously named estoppel *in pais*, equitable estoppel and estoppel by conduct, this type of estoppel involves a detrimental reliance upon a representation. Thus at least three things are required:

(1) A representation to the party asserting the estoppel. (In some cases the representation may be by silence rather than expression, or an act rather than a statement.)

(2) Action in reliance upon the representation.

(3) A detriment to the acting party, or a change of position.

Thus far the elements of equitable estoppel may be determined purely objectively and as viewed primarily from the standpoint of the party estopped. However, three additional elements have been mentioned in some decisions, one of them subjective, as follows:

(1) The party to be estopped must know the facts.

(2) He must intend that his conduct shall be acted on (or must so act that the party asserting estoppel has the right to believe that it is so intended).

(3) The latter must be ignorant of the true facts. *Hampton* v. *Paramount Pictures Corp.*, 279 F.2d 100, CA 9 1960.

Equitable estoppel is intended to prevent a party from denying the truth or accuracy of that which he had previously asserted or from assuming a position which is inconsistent with that he had previously taken. *Friel* v. *National Liberty Insurance Co. of America,* 71 F. Supp. 761, DC Pa 1947.

Elements of Estoppel

Representation. Where the other party is not misled by misrepresentation or put at a disadvantage there is no estoppel. *McIntyre* v. *Double-A Music Corp.,* 179 F. Supp. 160, DC SCalif 1959.

A representation need not be express in order to constitute an element of an estoppel. It may be by silence or acquiescence, especially where the party asserting the estoppel has suffered a legal detriment by making an investment. *Ferroline Corp.* v. *General Aniline & Film Corp.,* 107 F. Supp. 326, 343, DC NIll 1952.

Where owner of alleged secret process for manufacture of iron pentacarbonyl had notice that licensee of process had sold his plant and equipment to defendant, such knowledge was constructive notice that equipment was to be operated with owner's process or one substantially identical, and when plaintiff remained silent for more than three years and permitted defendant to make substantial expenditures and use process, owner was so grossly negligent that he was estopped thereafter to assert claim that defendant had wrongfully appropriated secret process. *Ferroline Corp.* v. *General Aniline & Film Corp.,* supra. This was a case where the defendant's patents allegedly disclosed the alleged secret process prior to knowledge of plaintiff's process.

Where interested parties expressly agreed that a ¾ths majority of directors of a so-called Massachusetts Trust might act on the cancellation of a patent license agreement, and proper action was taken, any and all parties interested were "estopped" after seven years from contending that cancellation did not effectuate what the parties treated it as effectuating. *Activated Sludge, Inc.* v. *Sanitary District of Chicago,* 33 F. Supp. 692; aff. *Guthard* v. *Sanitary District of Chicago,* 118 F.2d 899; c.d., *Sanitary District of Chicago* v. *Guthard,* 313 U.S. 583.

Where the plaintiff knows of the manufacture, use, and sale by defendants, thus causing defendants to incur expense in relying on the acquiescence, the plaintiff may be estopped in equity from enforcing any right in equity. *Better Packages* v. *L. Link & Co.,* 74 F.2d 679, CA 2 1935.

One does not forfeit right under contract by misinterpreting it or by acquiescence in a misinterpretation by the other party unless he thereby misleads the other party to his detriment. *Carey* v. *U.S.,* 276 F.2d 385, 390, Ct. Cls. 1960.

Reliance. A justifiable reliance upon the alleged representations of the other party is one of the requisites of estopping the other party. In *Hampton* v. *Paramount Pictures Corp.,* 279 F.2d 100, 104, CA 9 1960, the court said:

"The doctrine of equitable estoppel does not erase the duty of due care and is not available for the protection of one who has suffered loss solely by reason of his own failure to act or inquire. See *Rex* v. *Warner,* 183 Kan. 763, 332 P. 2d 572. The real cause of Hampton's trouble was not his lack of knowledge of Paramount's interest. Rather, it was his unwarranted reliance on the assertion of a third party and his failure to use the means at hand to ascertain the extent of the interest asserted. See *Marks* v. *Bunker,* 165 Cal. App. 2d 695, 332 P. 2d 340."

Knowledge. Where the evidence showed lack of knowledge on the part of the licensor when the royalties were received, its receipt of the royalties for over a year after suit commenced held neither acquiescence nor estoppel (*res judicata*). *Western Electric Co.* v. *General Talking Pictures Corp.,* 91 F.2d 922, aff. 304 U.S. 175, 1938, reaff. on rehearing, 305 U.S. 124, 1938.

The Court of Appeals for the Second Circuit held in *Bush* v. *Remington Rand,* 213 F.2d 456, 462, 1954, that defendant had burden of proving that inventor was guilty of all elements of fraud before there would be estoppel on ground of inventor's alleged misrepresentations.

"Nor do we find any substance to the defendant's contention that Dysart's silence constituted an estoppel by fraud. The situation in which Dysart acted is clear enough. Although he was Treasurer of the Dalton Co., he had no part in the negotiations with Rand. He was not consulted.

"Since he was not a party to the negotiations, or in any way in a fiduciary relationship with Remington Rand, he had no duty to speak."

Change of Position in Litigation. Although an allegation in pleading of a suit which was never adjudicated on the merits may not give rise to an estoppel, when a party during litigation makes a claim inconsistent with a previous claim, a court may deny the inconsistent claim. Although in some cases the situation is covered by judicial estoppel, all the elements of estoppel by record are not always present, and the whole matter is discussed in connection with equitable estoppel.

A patent holder may not charge that a product infringes his patent and later deny that similar products anticipate the patent. The court below said, in *Georgia Pacific Plywood Co.* v. *U.S. Plywood Corp.*, 148 F. Supp. 846, 856, DC SNY 1956; reversed, as to a different claim, 258 F.2d 124; c.d., 358 U.S. 884:

"The defendant has been caught on the horns of a dilemma. For when it suited its purposes to charge a product to be an infringing product, it did not hesitate to do so, but when it suits its purposes to take a different position it retreats from the other. The Court, of course, will not tolerate such weather-vane arguments which shift with the winds of necessity."

When a patentee has advanced a particular theory of his invention and has obtained a decree of validity based thereon, he may not in a later suit abandon that theory in favor of another when the evidence discloses anticipation as to the first. Dictum of *Bishop & Babcock Mfg. Co.* v. *Sears Roebuck & Co.*, 125 F. Supp. 528, DC NOhio 1954; aff. 232 F.2d 116, CA 6 1956.

The owner of a patent could not resort to the doctrine of equivalency to support charge of patent infringement and, at same time, recapture and withdraw to privacy, as a trade secret, an obvious variant of invention which owner of patent is presumed

to have placed in the public domain in return for patent monopoly. *Dollac Corp.* v. *Margon Corp.*, 164 F. Supp. 41, DC NJ 1958, aff. 275 F.2d 202.

A defendant in an infringement suit was estopped to repudiate affirmation of validity of patent after it had obtained an adjudication of validity of the patent affirming validity both in the Patent Office and in the previous court. *Livesay Industries, Inc.* v. *Livesay Window Co.*, 202 F.2d 378, CA 5 1953; c.d., 346 U.S. 855. The court said on p. 382:

"[Where] one in whose favor a judgment is rendered accepts the benefits, he is estopped from questioning the validity, of the judgment in any subsequent litigation."

In a suit to have patents relied on by a defendant declared invalid and not infringed by plaintiff's machines, a defendant by specifying certain claims as being relied on was estopped from claiming infringement with respect to other claims under its counterclaim, and, upon finding that claims specified were invalid, a general finding that neither patent was infringed was justified, though a finding that either patent was generally invalid was not justified. *U.S. Galvanizing & Plating Equipment Corp.* v. *Hanson-Van Winkle-Munning Co.*, 104 F.2d 856, CA 4 1939.

On the other hand, estoppel does not arise from the mere fact that a defendant is taking a position inconsistent with a former position as to patentability, particularly when the former position was taken (1) in priority proceedings in the Patent Office *Veaux* v. *Southern Oregon Sales, Inc.*, 123 F.2d 455, CA 9 1941; *International Steel Wool Corp.* v. *Williams Co.*, 137, F.2d 342, CA 6 1943) or (2) in a civil action under 35 U.S.C. 146 (*Zalkind* v. *Scheinman*, 80 F. Supp. 299, DC SNY 1948; *Lorenz* v. *Colgate-Palmolive-Peet Co.*, 122 F.2d 875, CA 3 1941; 3 Deller's Walker on Patents 1898, 1626).

Still parties to an interfering patent suit who have urged patentability of their respective patents for many years may be estopped to deny patentability of the subject matter claimed by both patents. The court said:

"[There] is yet good ground for treating

the adversaries, each of whom has received a grant from the government, as estopped by the reception of the grant from avowing want of patentable novelty." *Cutler-Hammer Mfg. Co.* v. *General Electric Co.*, 6 F.2d 376, 377, CA 7 1924.

One is not estopped from maintaining an action for the declaratory judgment of invalidity and non-infringement merely through failure to intervene in a prior infringement suit brought by the patent owner against a customer of the plaintiff. *Ostby* v. *Jungersen*, 41 F. Supp. 552, 554, DC NJ 1941.

An application for patent, made by the defendant prior to the time of an infringement suit covering the same process involved in the patent in suit, constitutes no estoppel against the defendant. *Floridin Co.* v. *Attapulgus Clay Co.*, 125 F.2d 669, CA 3 1942.

A manufacturer seeking declaratory judgment regarding invalidity of patent held by assignee could not claim benefit of estoppel against assignee because of assignee's position taken in interference proceedings between assignee and assignor, where manufacturer was not a party to interference proceedings. *Crowell* v. *Baker Oil Tools*, 153 F.2d 972, CA 9 1946. In this case the assignee of the patent in suit had been involved in an interference with his own patent and had filed a preliminary statement alleging a date earlier than that of the inventor of the patent in suit. The court said on p. 976:

"Consequently, it is claimed that the patent of the Gilstrap method, having been anticipated by Crowell himself, is invalid for want of invention by Gilstrap. There is clearly no basis for a claim of estoppel in favor of the appellee, which was not a party to the interference proceeding."

Implied License. When the patentee permits or encourages infringement or makes infringement of his patent possible by his conduct, he may be estopped to bring an action for infringement, and a license under the patent is implied. An invitation from the patent owner to the defendant to re-establish an infringing structure is evidence from which a license may be inferred, even if the infringer knew of the patent. *Union*

Shipbuilding Co. v. *Boston Iron & Metal Co.*, 93 F.2d 781, CA 4 1938. Selling parts to make the patented article raises an estoppel. *Auto Spring Repairer* v. *Grinberg*, 175 Fed. 799, 1910; *Leitch* v. *Barber*, 302 U.S. 458, 1938. Where the patentee equips a machine to manufacture an article, the owner of the machine acquires an implied licence to use the machine for manufacturing the articles and to employ the methods which were the function of the machine. *St. Joseph Iron Works* v. *Farmers Mfg. Co.*, 106 F.2d 294, CA 4 1939.

On the other hand, sale of an article which constitutes an element of a patented combination has been held not to give an alleged infringer an implied license where the article is capable of other uses. *Nachman Spring-Filled Corp.* v. *Kay Mfg. Corp.*, 78 F.2d 653, 657, CA 2 1935. A mere sale of a patented article does not imply a license unless the circumstances plainly indicate that the grant of a license was intended. *Hunt* v. *Armour*, 185 F.2d 722, CA 7 1950.

Then again the patent owner is not estopped to maintain an action for infringement when the defendant has not relied on the owner's representation concerning the scope of the patent but acted in reliance on its conviction that the patent was not infringed. *Duval Sulfur and Potash Co.* v. *Potash Co. of America*, 13 USPQ 308, CA 10 1957.

2 Walker, on Patents, Deller's Ed. 1469 Section 374 asserts:

"Where the user knew of the patent and the patentee knew of the use, and did not object thereto, it is more reasonable to imply an agreement for a quantum meruit or a royalty, than to imply that the patentee donated the use of his invention to the user, or to imply that the user unlawfully seized upon the invention of the patentee." [citing cases]

Shoprights are analogous to implied licenses but may be confined to a particular plant or otherwise more limited than a general license.

According to Schramm, 44 JPOS 86, 1962:

"The estoppel aspect of the law of shop rights is brought out in Banner v. Lockwood [125 USPQ 29], (California District

Court of Appeal, Los Angeles County, 1960). The defendant had expressly asserted that he was retaining all rights to the invention and refused to relinquish any shop rights and it was held that the doctrine of shop rights did not apply." (See *Shoprights*)

Procedural Estoppel

The fourth type of estoppel with respect to patents which has here been referred to as procedural estoppel, because it is based upon failure to comply with a rule prescribed by an administrative agency, or possibly a statute, arises primarily in interferences. The rules developed in such estoppels may be quite technical and often appear highly arbitrary.

Rule 257, on burden of proof, prescribes that the parties to an interference will be presumed to have made their inventions in the chronological order of the filing date of their applications for patent, that the termination of interference by dissolution shall not disturb this presumption, and that the senior party shall not be deprived of any claim solely on the ground that such claim was not added to the interference by amendment under Rule 233. This has the effect of cutting off the junior party's rights by Rule unless he takes some action to prevent dissolution. Cf. *International Cellucotton Products Co.* v. *Coe*, 85 F.2d 869, CA DistCol 1936; *Avery* v. *Chase*, 40 USPQ 343, CCPA 1939, C.D., 307 U.S. 638.

Estoppel Compared with Waiver and Laches

An equitable estoppel results from a representation intended to be acted upon by a party who acts in reliance thereon to his detriment. The party estopped has no power to terminate the estoppel after it has arisen. On the other hand, a waiver is an intentional relinquishment of a known existing right. *American Locomotive Co.* v. *Gyro Process Co.*, 185 F.2d 316, CA 6 1950; *Yates* v. *American Republics Corp.*, 163 F.2d 178, CA 10 1947; *Cook* v. *Commercial Casualty*, 160 F.2d 490, CA 4 1947.

Since there is no consideration for a waiver it may be withdrawn, but if the con-

sideration is supplied before withdrawal it becomes a binding contract and the waiver can no longer be withdrawn. If another party acts in reliance upon the waiver to his detriment or changes his position, an estoppel may arise. *Coursey* v. *International Harvester Co.*, 109 F.2d 774, 779, CA 10 1940; *McNamara* v. *Miller*, 269 F.2d 511, CA DistCol 1959. Waivers and estoppels are effective basically because someone else has changed his position in reliance upon them. *U.S.* v. *Scott*, 137 F. Supp. 449, DC Wis 1956.

Waiver refers to voluntary or intentional relinquishment of a known right and emphasizes a mental attitude of the actor, while estoppel is any conduct express or implied which reasonably misleads another to his prejudice so that a repudiation of such conduct would be unjust in the eyes of the law. *Matsuo Yoshida* v. *Liberty Mutual Insurance Co.*, 240 F.2d 824, CA 9 1957. Statutes of Limitations are statutes of repose, and that is their end and purpose; and the doctrines developed by human experience and described as laches, stale claims, equitable estoppel, have the same object and purpose. *Fremon* v. *W. A. Sheaffer Pen Co.*, 111 F. Supp. 39, DC Ia 1953, aff. 209 F.2d 627.

It has also been said that estoppel requires consideration but waiver does not. *St. Louis Fire & Marine Insurance Co.* v. *Witney*, 96 F. Supp. 555, DC Pa 1951. A promise, without consideration, not to assert one's patent against defendant is void and does not give rise to any estoppel from asserting infringement of claims. *Leake* v. *N.Y.C.R.R.*, 28 F. Supp. 565, DC NNY 1939.

In equitable estoppel it is the "injury" that is stressed, whereas in laches it is the "injustice" in enforcing a claim after a long delay that is stressed, the plaintiff's "sleeping on his rights." *Caterpillar Tractor* v. *International*, 32 F. Supp. 304, DC NJ 1940, appeal dismissed 120 F.2d 82, CA 3 1941.

Persons Affected by Estoppel

Questions may arise as to whether any persons other than the original or primary actors in a transaction may be affected by an estoppel. The questions arise most frequently with respect to corporations and their officers or stockholders, persons controlling or paying for suit or for defense, and transferees of the original parties. It has been held, in some cases, that others than primary parties may be bound by an estoppel or may be entitled to take advantage of an estoppel.

Ordinarily, to take advantage of an estoppel, a person must be known or identified. In some jurisdictions it is the practice to join fictitious defendants as parties in order that the effective filing date of the complaint against such defendants will be the original filing date rather than the date when such defendants become known and can be added as defendants in their own names. However, it has been held that the naming of fictitious defendants in an infringement action is not binding or conclusive on any actual persons who are not named defendants in their own names. *National Nut Co. of Cal.* v. *Kelling Nut Co.*, 61 F. Supp. 76, DC NIll 1945. It has been said that the defense of an infringement action by a manufacturer not of record must be open and avowed in order for him to have the benefit of a judgment of non-infringement in a suit against a dealer. It does not follow that manufacturer's participation must be known to the plaintiff in order that the non-record manufacturer be bound by a judgment that the patent is valid and infringed. *Caterpillar Tractor Co.* v. *International Harvester Co.*, 120 F.2d 82, 84, CA 3 1941. Privies are not entitled to findings other than those necessary to dispose of a case between the parties in order to avoid giving the record the appearance of an estoppel, and privies are required to prove their right to make use of the judgment. Therefore, the manufacturer of part of apparatus held not to infringe in suit against a dealer is not entitled to a finding that he openly and avowedly conducted the defense with the knowledge of the plaintiff without having entered the case as a party. *Minneapolis Honeywell Regulator Co.* v. *Thermo Co., Inc.*, 116 F.2d 845, 848, CA 2 1941.

Corporations and Officers. Ordinarily corporations are not affected by estoppels relating to their stockholders, directors or officers. But when closely related persons own all the stock of a corporation and one of them controls the corporation, the corporation may be bound by an estoppel affecting the controlling stockholder. The court declared that estoppel by deed to deny validity of a patent assigned by the controlling stockholder extended to the corporation, where all the stock was owned by the assignor, his wife and son. *Automatic Paper Machinery Co.* v. *Marcalus Mfg. Co.*, 147 F.2d 608, 610, aff. *Scott* v. *Marcalus*, 326 U.S. 249, 1945, rehearing denied, 326 U.S. 811, 1945; *Dixie Vortex Co.* v. *Paper Container Mfg. Co.*, 130 F.2d 569, 577, CA 7 1942.

In *Siemens-Halske Electric Co.* v. *Duncan Electric Mfg. Co. et al.*, 142 Fed. 157, CA 7 1905, the court held that a corporation, organized by a patentee who had assigned his patent and by others having full knowledge of the facts and being largely the owners of its stock, is estopped to deny the validity of the patent or to limit the claims by the prior art, to the same extent as the patentee. Where an inventor assigns his patent to his employer and subsequently associates with other former employees of the assignee in managing and controlling the policies of a new corporation, the latter, whether the inventor's alter ego or not, is privy to his infringement and is therefore estopped to deny validity of the patent. *Buckingham* v. *McAleer*, 108 F.2d 192, CA 6 1939.

On the other hand, common stock ownership does not necessarily make two corporations privy to each other, especially when the relationship of parent and subsidiary does not exist. For example, judgment against a selling corporation in patent infringement action was not found *res judicata* against manufacturing corporation although same individuals owned all the voting stock of the two corporations, the officers and directors were substantially the same, the selling corporation did not engage exclusively in selling manufacturing corporation's products, and the books and records of corporation were segregated and parties controlling the corporations treated them separately. *Manville* v. *Columbia Boiler Co.*, 134 USPQ 130, 131 DC EPa 1962.

Participation in Defense or Suit. When a person contributes to the cost of litigation involving two other parties or controls the litigation, he may take advantage of an estoppel or be bound by it. *Doherty Research Co.* v. *Universal Oil Products Co.*, 107 F.2d 548, 550, CA 7 1939.

Res judicata is inapplicable to a previous case with a different defendant in the absence of the existence of privity between the instant controversy and the previous litigation. Privity exists where the manufacturer of the products charged to infringe in both cases furnishes defendants in both actions with indemnity contracts, retains the same counsel to defend alleged infringers, and controls the litigation in both cases. *Switzer Bros., Inc.* v. *Chicago Cardboard Co. et al.*, 116 USPQ 277, CA 7, 1958. See also *Bros., Inc.* v. *W. E. Grace Mfg. Co. et al.*, 117 USPQ 143, DC NTexas 1958. Good faith requires parties participating in and controlling a case, but who are not parties of record, to disclose to the court the fact of such participation, and failing to do so, such parties are not in position to avoid the effect of the judgment as a bar on the ground that there is lack of mutuality of estoppel, if the opposing party subsequently learns of their participation. *Universal Oil Products Co.* v. *Winkler-Koch Engineering Co.*, 27 F. Supp. 161, DC NIll 1939.

Where the assignor of a patent subsequently invents a device which allegedly infringes said patent, licenses a third party to make the device, and agrees with the licensee to bear half the cost of any infringement suit brought against the licensee by reason thereof, and in fact actually does pay such suit costs, the licensee is in privity with the assignor and is estopped to deny the validity of said patent when sued for infringement thereof by the assignee. *Automatic Draft & Stove Co.* v. *Auto. Stove Works*, 34 F. Supp. 472, DC Va 1940.

Nevertheless the fact that two parties were represented by the same attorney or that the expenses of litigation fell more heavily upon one party than the other does not make them privies. In *Manville Boiler Co., Inc.* v. *Columbia Boiler Co.*, 134 USPQ 130, 131, DC EPa 1962, an attorney was engaged to defend infringement action against manufacturer and customer and rendered virtually all his bills to manufacturer, but it was not shown that manufacturer so controlled defense of the action against the customer that the doctrine of *res judicata* should apply.

Transferees. We have seen that the defense of estoppel is personal. *Caterpillar Tractor Co.* v. *International Harvester Co.*, 32 F. Supp. 304, DC NJ 1940. The estoppel running against the assignor of a patent to assert the invalidity is personal to the assignor. *Douglass* v. *U.S. Appliance Corp.*, 177 F.2d 98, CA 9 1949. Transferees of patents, therefore, should not be expected to be subject to estoppels.

Nevertheless, 2 Walker on Patents, Deller's Edition, 1443 Section 360, 1937 declares that the rights acquired by a trustee in bankruptcy include any estoppel which may have existed in the bankrupt's favor against his assignor, citing *Fishel Nessler Co.* v. *Fishel & Co.*, 204 Fed. 790, 1913. Walker asserts that estoppel is involved also in the case of a purchase from a receiver in bankruptcy, particularly if the person against whom the estoppel is invoked is the one who brought about the litigation in which the receiver was appointed, relying on *Schiebel Toy & Novelty Co.* v. *Clark*, 217 Fed. 760, 1914, c.d., 235 U.S. 707.

There may be privity between a manufacturer and his customer. Where the estoppel of a judgment of non-infringement, in a suit by patentee against manufacturer of alleged infringing product, is subsequently invoked by customer of said manufacturer in a suit by the same patentee against it, it makes no difference that the product may have been purchased by the customer prior to the institution of the suit against the manufacturer. The determinative fact is that non-infringement was found with respect to the particular product in a suit between the patentee and the person from whom the product was purchased. *General*

Chemical Co. v. *Standard Wholesale Phosphate & Acid Works, Inc.*, 101 F.2d 178, 179, 180, CA 4 1939; disapproving, *Wenborne-Karpen Dryer Co.* v. *Dort Motor Car Co.*, 14 F.2d 378, CA 6 1926, decided upon the basis of requiring mutuality of estoppels.

Joint Tort Feasors May Be Subject to Estoppel. The rule that an assigner cannot attack the validity of an original patent extends to those who cooperate with the assignor in developing the device under attack and in an infringement suit. *U.S. Appliance Corp.* v. *Beauty Shop Supply Co., Inc.*, 121 F.2d 149, CA 9 1941. See also *Douglass* v. *U.S. Appliance Corp.*, 177 F.2d 98, CA 9 1949.

The rule as to others cooperating in the infringement with the vendor of a patent is discussed by the court in *Continental Wire Fence Co.* v. *Pendergast et al.*, 126 Fed. 381, 384, C.C. Minn. 1903. The court held that where the vendor of a patent who is estopped to question its validity is cooperating with others in its infringement, those who are acting with him are subject to the same estoppel.

Pleading and Proving Estoppel

Walker lists as the twenty-sixth defense to an action for infringement of a patent "that the plaintiff is estopped from enforcing any right of action against the defendant" 3 Walker on Patents; Deller's Ed. Section 683, 1985. The defense may be made in an action at law for damages for infringement or for breach of a contract relating to a patent as well as in an equitable action for an injunction or for an accounting. Estoppel is an equitable defense and may be interposed in an action at law. *Mather* v. *Ford Motor Co.*, 40 F. Supp. 589, DC EMich 1941.

In *Union Shipbuilding Co.* v. *Boston Iron & Metal Co.*, 93 F.2d 781, CA 4 1938, the court held that laches coupled with estoppel may bar not only an accounting for past damages but also an injunction prohibiting use of the patented apparatus by defendant in the future. 3 Walker Section 791, 2109 declares estoppel is also a good defense to a motion for a preliminary injunction, and will prevail against a motion for that relief, upon the same facts that would make it prevail in an action at law.

The court declared in *Montgomery Ward & Co.* v. *Clair*, 123 F.2d 878, CA 8 1941 that although courts of equity will deny the recovery of profits in infringement cases brought after long delay except from the date of commencement of a suit, when the circumstances are such that it would be an injustice to award damages, an injunction applying to future conduct will usually be denied unless the elements of estoppel exist. Cf. *Dreyfuss Dry Goods Co.* v. *Lines*, 18 F.2d 611, 614, DC ELa 1927. The view has been expressed heretofore that equitable estoppel need not be pleaded in patent cases, 4 Walker on Patents; Deller's Ed. 2769, although Walker declares that the defense of estoppel must be fully set up in the answer. 3 Walker 1898, 1899. Formerly where the defense consisted of *res judicata*, the record could be introduced in evidence without being specially pleaded in the answer. *Bradley* v. *Eagle*, 58 Fed. 721, CA 7 1893.

Since the adoption of the Federal Rules of Civil Procedure, however, it would appear that any form of estoppel should be pleaded.

Under FRCP Rule 8 (c) affirmative defenses must be pleaded; the rule specifically mentions "estoppel ... laches ... *res judicata* ...." However, affirmative defenses may also be raised by motion for summary judgment under Rule 56 or by motion to dismiss under Rule 12 (b) (6),2 Moore's Federal Practice 1699, Section 8.28 (2d ed. 1961).

The defense of estoppel requires proof as pleaded according to 3 Walker 2047. Walker declares *in pais* estoppel may be proved by parol or by production of documents. Where the defense depends upon estoppel by deed, the document must be produced or otherwise proved according to the rules of evidence applicable to such cases. Where it depends upon estoppel by record, or *res judicata*, the record must be proved in accordance with the laws governing such evidence. If a record, when proved, stopped short of showing that the point in question was decided in the former case, that fact may be proved by extrinsic evidence, citing

Southern Pacific Co. v. *Earl*, 82 Fed. 690, 693, CA 9 1897; *Russell* v. *Place*, 94 U.S. 606, 608, 1877.

Estoppel to assert a desired scope for a patent claim may be evidenced by pencil notations appearing upon a draft of an unentered amendment to the application presented to the Patent Office after allowance of the claims. In *Glikin* v. *Smith*, 269 F.2d 641, 648, CA 5 1959, the court said:

"The document, however, is a draft of Smith's last amendment prepared by Smith's attorneys and bearing the signature of these attorneys. Presumably it has always been in the possession of the attorneys or the Examiner. The circumstances imposed a burden on Smith or his attorneys to give some sort of explanation for the notations. For what it is worth, and its worth is severely circumscribed by the manifest limitations, we think that the document is admissible."

The burden of proving laches or estoppel is upon the defendant. *Shaffer* v. *Rector*, 155 F.2d 344, 347, CA 5 1946; *Rajah Auto Supply Co.* v. *Belvidere Screw & Mach. Co.*, 275 Fed. 761, CA 7 1921.

Requisites to Enforcement of an Estoppel and Antitrust Public Policy

Estoppels are recognized in order to prevent injury and therefore it is appropriate to consider all the circumstances in an estoppel situation. Estoppels, especially estoppels by conduct, are equitable in nature. Even in actions at law, equitable defenses are admitted. Consequently, the principle of balance of equities may at times provide a reason for refusal to recognize an estoppel which appears to satisfy the definition of an estoppel.

The proper function of equitable estoppel is the prevention of fraud, actual or constructive, and the doctrine should be applied to promote the ends of justice and not turned into an instrument of wrong. *Cook* v. *Ball*, 144 F.2d 423, CA 7 1944; c.d., 65 S.Ct. 93, 2 cases, 323 U.S. 761.

Some of the older cases have ruled on specific phases of the estoppel as follows: In *Peelle Co.* v. *Raskin et al.*, 194 Fed. 440,

DC ENY, the court held that a patentee is estopped to deny the validity of the patent as against an assignee in suit for its infringement, even though facts which render the patent invalid were known to the assignee at the time the assignment was made. This appears to be contrary to present law. In *Vacuum Engineering Co.* v. *Dunn*, 209 Fed. 219, CA 2, the court held that a patentee cannot defend against his suit for infringement brought by his assignee on the ground that he was induced to part with the patent by unfair representations.

The nature of the estoppel and the basis for distinguishing from *Westinghouse* v. *Formica*, supra, is discussed by the Third Circuit Court of Appeals in *Automatic Paper Machinery Co.* v. *Marcalus Mfg. Co.* at 147 F.2d 613:

"Estoppel is an equitable doctrine and its essence lies in mutuality.... He who endeavors to rely on estoppel must himself have acted in good faith and without knowledge that the title to the land was not as represented by the grantor.... If the grantee is not deceived by the representation, he should not be entitled to rely upon it by way of estoppel."

It was held in *Cook Electric Co.* v. *Persons*, 60 F. Supp. 124, DC EMo 1945 that in an action for infringement between the assignee and the assignor, the assignor is estopped to attack the utility, novelty or validity of the patented invention, although, for the rest of the world, the patent may be void or unpatentable. However, an assignee of a patent right who is chargeable with knowledge that the patent property which the assignor sought to convey to him lay in the public domain is not entitled to assert the doctrine of estoppel by deed. *Automatic Paper Machinery Co.* v. *Marcalus Mfg. Co.*, 54 F. Supp. 105, DC NJ 1944; reversed, 147 F.2d 608, CA 3 1945; aff. 326 U.S. 249, 1945.

In *Nachman Spring-filled Corp.* v. *Kay Mfg. Co.*, 139 F.2d 781, the Court of Appeals for the Second Circuit held that where a licensee under a patent has agreed not to infringe B patent under which it is not licensed, licensor and licensee being competitors in the field of B patent, and the licensee is sued for infringement of B patent, an injunction may not be proper and the trial court should hear evidence on the question of violation of the antitrust laws or state laws, an illegal waiver of a public policy defense, or, if the contract is otherwise proper, whether the patent is valid. The court also criticized admission of validity of patents other than those under which licensed. The court said on p. 785:

"[As] the defendant is neither an assignor nor a licensee, the patent-estoppel cases ... may not be protective of the agreement, and, even assuming that the Sola doctrine is limited to price fixing agreements, the agreement here may be illegal under the common law rule as to contracts, not 'ancillary,' in restraint of trade."

Accordingly, it seems unlikely that the courts will enforce an estoppel to deny validity of a patent based on an express covenant to recognize the validity of a patent under which the covenantor is not licensed.

Where the doctrine of estoppel, to the effect that a licensee may not challenge the validity of the patent involved in a suit by his licensor, is in conflict with the Sherman Act's prohibition of price fixing, the Supreme Court may resolve the question even though its conclusion is contrary to that of state court. In such case, where the prohibition of the Federal Statute might be nullified or its benefits denied by the State Statutes or State Common Law Rules, the decision of the Supreme Court is not controlled by *Erie Railroad* v. *Tompkins*, 304 U.S. 64. See *Sola* v. *Jefferson*, 317 U.S. 173, 176, 1942.

It would be difficult to name a facet of the law of estoppel which cannot arise in connection with patents. The possibility of an estoppel is, therefore, of prime importance to those concerned with patents and rights relating to inventions.

Cross-references: *Delay in Claiming, File Wrapper Estoppel, Laches, Shop Rights.*

EUROPEAN PATENT CONVENTION

Leonard J. Robbins

In November 1962 the text of a preliminary draft of a Convention relating to a European Patent Law was officially published by the Commission of the European Common Market.

The protagonists of simplification of international patent protection have followed two related but separate paths. The first, which is more radical, leads towards common patents having automatic and indivisible territorial effect over a number of countries. The second is directed towards harmonization of individual patent laws so that a patent in one country could be extended to cover other countries at the option of the patentee.

Basis for the European Patent Convention in the Treaty of Rome

Patent rights are only inferentially mentioned in Article 36 of the Treaty of Rome, defining certain areas, including industrial property, which may be exempt from the general prohibitions against restrictions on import and export in the six countries. This appears somewhat inconsistent with the provisions of Article 100 authorizing approximation of national laws which may affect the functioning of the Common Market. Even if the six patent laws were completely harmonized, the territorial limitation of the national patent rights might still have a disturbing effect on free import and export. The so-called antitrust provisions of Articles 85 and 86 have not solved the problem: the implementing regulations under these articles indicate that at any rate some legitimate uses of national patents will not be regarded as restrictive business practices.

In effect, the statement of principles by the Council of Ministers recognizes that the special position of industrial property rights, and patents in particular, had not been sufficiently provided for in the Treaty of Rome. Therefore to achieve the broad aims of Article 100, it was necessary to go outside the actual framework of the Treaty and formulate a new and separate Convention creating supra-national patents rights. The solution is clearly not perfect and is a compromise, since national patents could not be suddenly abolished and will remain for an indefinite period in view of the principle of coexistence.

It will therefore be seen that it is difficult to find any mandate in the Treaty of Rome to create an entirely new type of industrial property, unless by virtue of the very broad powers afforded under Article 235 which reads:

"If any action by the Community appears necessary to achieve, in the functioning of the Common Market, one of the aims of the Community in cases where this Treaty has not provided for the requisite powers of action, the Council, acting by means of a unanimous vote on a proposal of the Commission and after the Assembly has been consulted, shall enact the appropriate provisions."

In any event, the fact that the European Patent Convention reached a stage in 1962 where ultimate enactment seems reasonably certain can be regarded as an interesting example of the exercise of new powers through existing legislation in this supranational field.

Preparation of the Preliminary Draft of the Convention

Following the authorization by the Secretaries of State, a Working Group to draft the preliminary text of the Convention was formed early in 1961, comprising representatives of the Six Common Market countries, under the presidency of Dr. Haertel. It is significant that most of these representatives were officials of the Ministries of Justice or Ministries of Economic Affairs of their respective countries, and that industry and the patent profession had no direct representation.

The drafting work proceeded quite rapidly, but under a temporary blanket of official silence. No open hearings were held, although the members of the Working Group consulted periodically with advisors in their respective countries. From the information which gradually became available it was clear that an extremely detailed new supra-national patent law was being prepared, different in many respects from any existing European patent law. It also

became clear that fundamental differences of opinion and viewpoint developed in the Working Group which can only be resolved by the highest authorities of the Common Market.

The text of the draft Convention as released for publication, and which is analyzed and discussed below, comprises 12 chapters and 217 articles. The unsettled issues are indicated by alternative versions of certain articles or by minority dissents.

Procedural Aspects

In preparing the draft Convention, the Working Group endeavored to achieve the following three broad primary objectives: prompt publication of patent applications with provisional grant; a deferred but strict novelty examination system; and final grant of patents of reasonably certain scope.

European Patent Office. An independent European Patent Office will be established. It may have liaison sub-offices associated with the national patent offices. It will comprise the following five main parts:

(1) examining sections dealing with the provisional grant

(2) examining divisions dealing with final or definitive grant

(3) administrative divisions

(4) appeal chambers for hearing appeals from examination and administrative decisions

(5) nullity chambers dealing with nullity suits against final patents.

Applications. A most significant fact is that English has been made an official language and Dutch and Italian have been eliminated. Thus the application can be filed in one of three languages only—French, German or English. All the proceedings will then take place in the selected language.

The application must be accompanied by one or more claims, which are subject to amendment during prosecution, and which will define the scope of the final patent. In the absence of any specific prohibition, it would appear that independent chemical and pharmaceutical claims will be allowable.

The application can be filed directly in

the European Patent Office, or may or must be first filed in a National Patent Office of a contracting state if required by national legislation. Apparently one reason for this is that some states may wish to examine applications for secrecy before transmitting them to the European office. There will be an internal system of priority for one year both ways for European applications and national applications in the contracting states.

Examination. The application first goes to an appropriate examining section which has power to examine for form and all substantive aspects except novelty. The section can require division for non-unity and can finally reject if the application obviously does not describe an invention or has no industrial use. There may be one or more actions, hearings and amendments at this stage. The application if and when in formal order, is then subjected to a novelty search, probably at the International Institute at the Hague. The purpose of this is solely to discover published prior art that may be relevant. The application is then printed with the search report attached and is granted as a provisional patent.

Any third party can then submit comments on the validity of the provisional patent, which are placed in the file and transmitted to the provisional patentee. This is solely for informational purposes.

At any time during the next five years, either the application or any third party can request full novelty examination before an appropriate examining division. When such a request is published it cannot be withdrawn, and any other third party can then intervene.

Such third parties must submit arguments against the scope or validity of the provisional patent and can refer to prior art not mentioned in the search report. All this material is then sent by the examining division to the applicant, who can then file counter arguments on the art, amend or divide. The examination then begins. The Examiner issues an action which may approve or disapprove, partly or wholly the applicant's position. This action is also sent to the various third parties. The applicant

can argue and amend, the others can argue, and the Examiner once again reviews the situation. Until he is satisfied, it appears that any number of actions might be issued, with the same procedure of distributing copies of all documents to everyone involved. Hearings may also be appointed at the request of applicant or the third parties.

Ultimately the application will either be finally rejected or granted as a final or definitive patent for a remaining term of 20 years from the original filing date. The final patent is also printed.

It will be seen that this two-part operation is a new departure as compared with classical European examination and opposition procedure. Every major step will require an official fee. Every final decision of the examining sections and divisions is subject to appeal. Minor inventions are hardly likely to survive the ordeal. However where important inventions are concerned, particularly in highly competitive fields, it would appear inevitable that numerous intervenors would jump in at the full examination stage and that many complications and delays could occur.

European Patent Court. A new European Patent Court will also be established having supra-national jurisdiction over all the contracting states. Its principal function will be to take final appeals from decisions of the European Patent Office Appeal and Nullity Chambers. It is not yet known whether this Court will have an entirely independent existence or will be attached to one of the already existing international courts in Europe.

Infringement and nullity actions will be separated as in present German and Dutch jurisprudence. However, in addition, infringement actions involving European patents will be tried in the national courts according to their own rules so far as they do not conflict with the patent Convention.

It will be possible to start an infringement suit in a national court on the basis of a provisional European patent. However if the defendant raises the issue of validity —which would seem to be almost a conditioned reflex since the provisional patent has not been examined for novelty—then the national court proceedings are suspended. First of all, the provisional patent must be examined for novelty in the examining division of the European Patent Office. If it survives, then a nullity action must be brought before the Nullity Chamber of the European Patent Office. After a possible appeal, it is only then that the infringement suit can proceed.

When a suit is brought under a final, definitive patent, a counter-claim for nullity must likewise first be determined separately.

At any stage of an infringement suit, the national courts can apply to the European Patent Court for rulings on the interpretation of the Patent Convention.

Substantive Aspects

With regard to standards of novelty and patentability, the European Patent Convention is stringent—apparently more severe in some respects than the existing German and Dutch patent laws. Patents will be granted only for novel inventions, resulting from inventive activity and adapted for industrial use. Exceptions are inventions contrary to propriety and the public interest, and also biologically produced plant and animal varieties.

Novelty. An invention is novel if it is not present in the state of the art. The state of the art comprises anything available to the public prior to the effective filing date by written or oral description, use or any other means, and also includes prior European patent applications published on or after the effective filing date; the distinction between prior publication and prior grant of patents is therefore eliminated. Divulgence of the invention up to 6 months prior to the date of application is not a bar if unauthorized or based on an officially recognized exhibition; however the inventor's own prior printed or oral publications are not excused. Inventive activity means that the invention is not obvious from the state of the art. Industrial use means manufacture or utilization in any kind of industry including agriculture.

Contributory Infringement. The doctrine of contributory infringement is codified.

The owner of a European patent can sue a third party who offers or sells an essential element of the invention (a) if the element is exclusively designed for use with the invention, or (b) if the element is clearly intended for such use and the third party knows this or has no valid excuse.

Compulsory Licensing. The exclusive patent rights are circumscribed by compulsory licensing provisions which are decidedly different from those of any present national patent laws in Europe or from those in the International Convention.

At any time after 3 years from the grant of a provisional European patent, or after 4 years from the original filing date, any third party who establishes his bona fides can apply for a compulsory license on reasonable terms on the ground that the invention has not been manufactured or used throughout the whole territory of the contracting states in a manner sufficient to meet the needs of the public therein. The patent owner can submit legitimate excuses: importation is not an excuse. Pharmaceutical patents do not have any special status as regards compulsory licensing.

In addition, if the invention of a subsequent patent cannot be carried out without infringing a prior patent, the subsequent patentee can obtain a compulsory license under the prior patent sufficient for his needs, on request and apparently without any adverse proceedings. However, if the same industrial purpose is involved, the prior patentee can likewise obtain a cross-license under the subsequent patent.

No one can apply for a compulsory license unless he proves that he has first tried to obtain a voluntary license without success. All compulsory licenses are non-exclusive. In general they will be granted only for the whole territory of the contracting States, but in appropriate circumstances they may be limited territorially.

The patent owner can at any time request that the compulsory license should be cancelled on the grounds that the licensee is not fulfilling the requirements of the license, or that the grounds on which the license was originally granted no longer exist. An equitable delay will be allowed before the licensee must cease exploitation if he can prove serious damage.

There is no provision for possible revocation of the patent if the particular compulsory license arrangements prove unsatisfactory.

Finally, national legislation with respect to compulsory licenses in the public interest will apply to European patents.

Miscellaneous Provisions. The territorial scope of a European patent may be restricted by a national patent. It appears that ultimately ownership of both national patents and a European patent for the same invention will only be permitted if emanating from the same inventor. There will be transitional provisions to take care of the existing situation when the Convention goes into effect.

The following other provisions are of significance:

(1) Annual taxes will be payable, beginning the 3rd year from the filing date.

(2) Patents of addition will be granted not subject to taxes.

(3) European patents can only be assigned for the whole territory of the contracting states. Licenses can be granted for part of the territory. Both are only effective as regards the Patent Office and third parties when recorded.

(4) A type of declaratory judgment proceeding is provided before the Patent Office to ascertain if a contemplated activity will infringe a patent.

(5) The Nullity Department of the Patent Office may also act as an arbitration committee in patent disputes.

When the European Patent Office finally opens, only applications in certain technical fields will be examined. These fields will be extended progressively. This will allow gradual recruitment of examiners and the setting up of facilities, but it may be many years later before the full deferred examination system is in operation.

To deal with this situation, it is provided that a European application in an excluded technical field can, at the applicant's request, be transformed into a group of national applications in the contracting states to be dealt with by their own procedures.

If there is partial overlapping of technical fields, division is contemplated.

Access, Adherence and Association

Those procedural and substantive aspects that appear too complex or too radical are in areas where compromise should be possible. The essentially controversial and unsettled aspects of this Convention are deciding who will be able to apply for and obtain European patents and if there will be any nationality restrictions on ownership.

As pointed out originally, because the Common Market machinery was utilized, the original signatories to the Convention must necessarily be only the six Common Market Countries—Germany, France, Italy, Belgium, Holland and Luxembourg. In this economic field, they will be giving up some measure of sovereignty due to the supranational legal organization. Also, since a new patent system of this type is hardly likely to be initially self-supporting from official fees, they will have to foot the bill for deficiencies on a pro-rata basis according to size.

Therefore the European Patent Convention is of an entirely different character from the International Convention which merely establishes certain minimum uniform provisions as applied to otherwise different national patent laws. The European Convention is in fact a club, with use of the club facilities apparently under the permanent control of the original six members.

There are two aspects with respect to applicants which must be clearly distinguished, though they are related. Can anyone else apply for patents under the Convention as finally ratified, apart from nationals of the original six Common Market Countries? What outside countries will be permitted to join the Convention and on what terms so that their nationals can automatically apply?

Nationals of the six Common Market Countries have tended towards the viewpoint that any form of open access would defeat the purpose of the Convention and that new countries could only join on the basis of full membership with all that it implies. Others insist on limitation specifically to other European states. The outsiders very naturally would like completely open access or access available to applicants from any of the International Convention countries.

The open access argument is that the Patent Convention will ultimately become the single patent law of the single European superstate when federation occurs, at which time any foreigner whatever should be able to apply for a patent just as in any other country. A counter-argument is that federation is too distant and speculative and that the European patent office might be swamped with foreign applications even to the detriment of European industry.

As regards the International Convention, the emphasis from the beginning has been that the European Convention must not conflict with the prior commitments of the International Convention. Article 2 of the International Convention provides that applicants from any member country shall enjoy the full benefits of the national patent laws of the other; therefore it has been argued with considerable subtlety and persuasiveness that the European Convention must automatically extend to applicants from all International Convention countries. However opponents insist that the European Convention is entirely different from a national law and that it is in fact a special arrangement between members as permitted under Article 15 of the International Convention. Since there are over 50 members of the International Convention, including most major countries, there would in fact be little difference from completely open access.

It would seem that if there is to be open access, without dues or responsibilities, no other country, even neighboring European countries, would have much incentive to join, since its nationals could in any event apply. On the other hand, the original statement of principles constituting the terms of reference for the drafting of the Convention did envisage both full adherence and some form of partial adherence or association by other states. In particular, when other countries join the Common Market itself as full members, the essential purposes of the Common Market would seem to make it almost necessary for such countries to join the European Patent Convention also and thus submit to the supra-national authority in the field of industrial property.

The Working Group has been unable to solve these problems.

At the beginning of the draft text there is a remark that a preamble ought to be included indicating that the Convention constitutes a special arrangement in the sense of Article 15 of the International Convention. This seems to imply that the Working Group has rejected the argument of open accessibility based on membership of the International Convention.

However Article 5 relating to applicants has two completely opposed variations: (a) unrestricted access for anyone, (b) access limited to legal nationals of the contracting states, and based on one or more prior national patent applications.

As regards outsider countries, Article 211 contemplates permitting countries of the International Convention to apply for full adherence, if necessary with conditions; part of the Working Group wanted this limited to European countries only. Article 212 contemplates offering associate membership to countries of the International Convention on the basis of reciprocal rights and obligations; there is no indication as to the nature of such reciprocity. Both types of admission would require unanimous consent of the original six countries and a special agreement or accord between the new country and the original six.

At the same time, no strings have been attached in the draft text to the assignment of pending applications, provisional patents and final patents to any third party irrespective of national origin.

As regards the position of the United States, owing to the supra-national aspects, it appears that full adherence can hardly be considered even as a possibility, at any rate at the present time. If free access is not permitted by the Europeans, then it will be necessary to study and compare the advan-

tages and drawbacks of some form of association to U.S. interests.

Future Developments. The Committee of
Coordination of the Common Market Commission, on publishing the draft text in November 1962, has thrown the matter open
to limited public discussion.

The exact nature of the further steps is
uncertain. Obviously some revision of the
text will be necessary in the unsettled controversial areas. Will the revision again be
submitted for outside discussion? Possibly
it may not be, since a Diplomatic Conference to adopt a final text has been tenta-
tively set for April 1964. There is a possibility that some provisions may be removed
and placed in a general Industrial Property
Convention relating to common features of
the Patent Convention and of the contemplated future Trademark Convention and
Design Convention.

Development of National Patent Laws

The introductory paragraph of this article
referred to the two related but separate
paths being followed for simplification of
international patent law. The European
patent deals with the more radical solution
—*one patent* for a number of countries. The
less radical approach—*harmonization of individual patent laws*—is also being followed
in Europe.

The active body in the harmonization is
the Council of Europe. This deliberative
body of parliamentarians from about sixteen European states reviews matters of
common interest and, from time to time,
proposes conventions on specific topics. It
produced in 1962 a draft of a new Convention to provide uniformity of patent laws
in the substantive area of patentable subject matter. The draft Convention has had
far less publicity than the proposal for a
European patent, but its progress has been
much more rapid. It was signed in 1963 by
Belgium, Denmark, France, Federal Republic of Western Germany, Italy, Netherlands, Sweden, Switzerland, and the United
Kingdom.

As with many international agreements
of this nature, there are two steps to its
eventual adoption. Each contracting party
first has to sign the Convention and then
deposit an instrument of ratification or acceptance. The Convention enters into force
when eight countries have deposited instruments of ratification or acceptance. From
past experience of similar international
agreements in the field of industrial property this second step may be expected to
take several years.

The provisions of the Harmonization
Convention are similar to certain of those
of the proposed European Patent Convention. However, the new European patent
law contains many features which find no
counterpart in existing patent law of any
European country. The approach of the
Harmonization Convention is quite different, in that it attempts merely to suggest
uniform provisions within the framework
of existing laws, e.g., a common definition of
patentable invention and common novelty
requirements.

What is the significance of this Convention? The differences in national laws sometimes makes, of the task of protecting an
invention in Europe, an undertaking in
which the inventor and his advisor must
proceed country by country and through a
maze of confusing differences. Thus, in Germany prior public use, to be a bar to a valid
patent, must be use in Germany. In Italy
and France, prior public use anywhere in
the world may be a bar. Harmonization of
national patent laws will not remove all
these inconsistencies, but it should simplify
them in large measure.

From a practical viewpoint, the Harmonization proposals will be much easier to
put into practice than the new European
patent. There will be no need to set up a
new Patent Office with all its attendant administrative problems, particularly a new
body of Examiners. Moreover, the general
principle of coexistence of national and
European patents will create many problems if the national patent laws differ from
each other in basic respects and from the
European patent Convention. Such conflicts
of laws have received little intention in the
literature that has rapidly developed on the
European patent, but they do exist and
may be formidable.

Whether (1) a European patent convention or (2) harmonization of individual laws is the better goal for Europe is not easy to say. A partial analogy can be taken from the experience of the United States. Let us assume that each State had developed and retained its own bodies of laws in many fields until well into the twentieth century before the suggestion was made to have Federal laws. Would it have been better then to make the state laws uniform or to enact new Federal laws? For a short-term solution, harmonization to uniformity is probably more acceptable. For a long-term solution, national laws may be expected to serve better the public good.

Cross-references: *Advance Information from Foreign Filings, Foreign Licensing and Antitrust Law, Foreign Patents.*

EVALUATING INVENTIONS FOR FILING

Robert Calvert

The subject matter of this article was presented by the author to the Practising Law Institute, New York, in 1962.

Questions to be answered in evaluating an invention for filing an application include the following: Will it work? Will it sell or find use? Will it be patentable?

Answers by the Inventor

Inventors are generally enthusiastic. They want to file applications. They know the value of publications in their names. As a result, they may submit 2 to 10 disclosures for each one filed.

One large corporation files upon only about 15 per cent of the suggestions received. This low percentage may be due to an award system producing many proposals.

If the inventor is technical and provided with proper facilities and associates, the question of operability will be answered by his experiments. If doubt exists, additional tests to expand the data should give the complete answer. The attorney cannot argue against the facts. After having lived to see two of the three great fundamental laws of science—Conservation of Matter and Conservation of Energy—discarded, the attorney should be prepared to listen to evidence on almost any subject short of Perpetual Motion. The attorney accepts in most cases what he is told about operability and is free to concentrate on the more difficult questions in evaluation.

By the Corporate Attorney

The corporate or house counsel feels that he is expendable. His salary is fixed. The extra cost per case is little in the absence of increase of staff. Many accept this attitude and may file about a fourth to half of the cases proposed. Others believe that patent efforts should be concentrated on a few strong cases.

George S. Hastings, counsel for a corporation having outstanding success with inventions, has listed points to be considered in the evaluation, as follows:

Factor	Weight
Breadth of invention	_____
Degree of development between conception and production	_____
Closeness of relation to proprietary business	_____
Attractiveness of ramifications	_____
Present—sales/profits	_____
Anticipated profits from sales (next 3 years)	_____
Anticipated profits from sales (following 4 to 10 years)	_____
Effect on competition	_____
Licensing possibilities	_____
How inexpensive or expensive to patent and maintain	_____
TOTAL SCORE	_____
SHOULD IT BE FILED ON?	_____

By Outside Counsel

Outside counsel will be generally conservative in filing. He will want the client to understand the uncertainties before initiating expense. He should not be so cautious, however, as to indicate lack of enthusiasm. Neither should he present medals as a reward of genius to proposers of doubtful devices. An attorney did this in Washington some years ago, before the Patent Office interrupted his career as a practitioner. *In re Wedderburn et al.*, 1897 C.D. 77; *Wedderburn* v. *Bliss*, 1898 C.D. 413, Ct. App DC. (See article *Attorneys and Agents*)

Searches

The search as a tool of evaluation needs little discussion. In many cases the art is well known to the inventor or the attorney. Searches are frequently unnecessary, when the invention involves a sequence of individually complicated and unusual elements or steps or when the field is so new that the art can be expected to reside mostly in pending applications. (See *Searching*)

Procedures Clearly Indicated

When the development appears to be unpatentable and commercially unpromising, it is best to do nothing in most cases but preserve the records. When patentable and commercially promising, one should file promptly.

The following classes are the ones requiring exercise of the utmost in judgment.

Patentable But Commercially of No Prospective Value

File in most instances, particularly when the field is significant as in the case of a new class of chemical compounds.

As early as 1935, Enrico Fermi, one of the world's leading scientists, filed an application with associates issued later as U.S. patent 2,206,634 in 1940. It covered the slowing down of neutrons so that they may be absorbed more readily by atoms, in conversion of the latter to radioactive isotopes. It took nearly a decade and a world war to make this discovery more than a research tool. Yet it was ready for use when the need for it arose. That was after Hahn had bombarded uranium with neutrons, to make a heavier element but had found instead two lighter elements. Fermi and the others then noted that the two atomic weights totaled less than the weight of uranium.

A decade ago a leading chemical firm developed a variation of the process of making an important plastic. The cost was higher than the conventional procedure, yet the firm filed upon it. Many years later a patent to a foreign inventor appeared on a linear plastic of superior properties. This linear polymer, it so happens, was the product of the process first mentioned and covered in the earlier application. As a result, the U.S. firm obtained a basic position in the field.

A late sensation is the Telstar radio communication satellite using, among other inventions, a Bell Telephone Laboratories patent of 1937 which had found no use till 1962 (N.Y. Times, Sept. 5, 1962).

Commercially Important But of Doubtful Patentability

Under these circumstances, don't give up! Continue to seek unobvious results. In one case, the art showed the passage of an electric current through a platinum filament in an evacuated glass bulb. Another patent showed a pencil of carbon in the same combination. Then came the proposal of a carbon filament in the evacuated bulb for the same purpose. The commercial possibilities were great. Would you have filed? You may check your answer against the facts. The inventor was Thomas Alva Edison. The invention became his electric light. The patent was upheld. 52 F. 300, CA 2 1892.

Procedure with Seemingly "Frivolous" Inventions

Consider, if you will, two patents that issued years ago. One was a composition dog food in the shape of a bone, actually a flattened dumbbell. It so amused the friends of the able inventor, Carleton Ellis, that a speaker at a chemical meeting presented a take-off application entitled "A Cat Food in the Form of a Mouse." He read a so-called Action, purporting to come from the Patent Office. It recommended the employment, not of a competent attorney as usual, but a competent inventor.

The other "frivolous" patent related to spectacles for hens. A pin inserted through the beak of the hen held in place two discs of sheet lead, cut out at the top, in the shape of a new moon a few days old.

Actually professional egg producers bought millions, no doubt, of the spectacles or blinders. They limited the vision above a certain low level and decreased cannibalism that is very prevalent in white leghorn laying flocks. Ellis licensed his dog food patent to a large company. When the patent expired and the royalties stopped, the company was genuinely sorry. It is said also to be a fact that dogs, thrown the same food in bar and "Dog-Bone" shape, will first eat the latter.

In a recent two-hour TV show there were seven sponsors, all advertising goods that are unnecessary. An invention is not frivolous commercially if it will sell and make employment, without injury to the public.

Research and Development Expenses v. Patent Costs

The almost insignificant expense of seeking patent protection on inventions of major companies, in proportion to the cost of making the inventions, can be seen from a comparison of research and development expenditures and the number of patents issued. A study of the data for three of the world's largest companies in their lines and one of medium size, all U.S. concerns, shows research and development expenditures, exclusive of that on government contracts, of about $100,000 to $150,000 for each *patent issued* to the company. In the case of General Electric Co., for instance, the figures are these: research and development expense, 1950 to 59, average per annum, $137,000,000 excluding advances from government; applications for patents filed in 1961, 1,301. Annual Report for 1961.

Some smaller concerns, in active fields and with little fundamental research, may have a patent a year for 1 to 3 research workers.

Nylon or the transistor was or is worth many times as much to the companies first involved, no doubt, as would have been the case if no patent had been possible. Yet the patent cost must have been negligible compared to the millions invested in such projects before a dollar of profit was made.

The cost in total dollars and time for development of the bowling pin setting machine has been plotted in Fig. 1, prepared

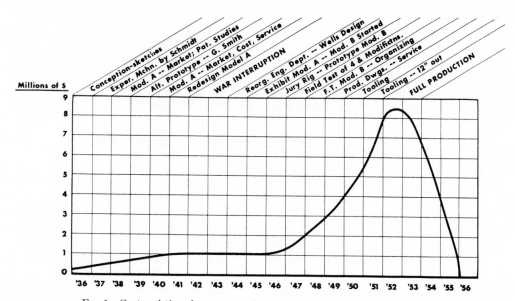

Fig. 1. Cost and time from conception to production of AMF Pinspotter.

by Mr. Hastings for the Practising Law Institute in 1962. No comment is necessary to emphasize the magnitudes as compared to patent costs to be expected, even in a complicated case of this kind.

Morale Factor

One of the prime purposes of the patent system is to encourage the inventor. Periods of greatest patent activity in a laboratory often coincide with those of greatest research advances. A relatively small sum spent on a patent application may stimulate and help to give one who feels "I only work here" the pride and activity of a creative scientist.

Summary

We cannot let encouragement of inventors, honorable, ancient and constitutional as that motive is, control our decisions as to filing applications.

We can, however, recognize that some inventions are "born ahead of their time," as George V. Woodling has said, and should be filed upon even when their economic value is yet to be demonstrated.

We can sometimes establish patentability on the basis of an unobvious result other than the principal object sought by the inventor. The use of sugar to sweeten a vitamin solution, so as to make it more acceptable to a child, is not unobvious or patentable. The use of the sugar to decrease the rate of oxidation of the vitamin, on the other hand, was probably at one time a good invention.

While doing what we can to carry out the Constitutional provision to encourage invention and to help the inventors realize their importance to themselves and the world, we should not clutter up our files or add to the patent office backlog by needlessly filing cases of neither prospective patentability nor commercial value. The Annual Report of the Commissioner of Patents for 1961 has said, "It will take the help of a conscientious, knowledgeable, and cooperative patent profession to reduce the back-

log." To evaluate proposals objectively before filing is a first step to such a cooperation.

Cross-references: *Evaluation of Inventions for License, Incentives for Inventors, Inventors.*

EVALUATING INVENTIONS FOR LICENSE
George S. Hastings

This article has been written following the author's address on the subject before the Practising Law Institute in New York in 1962.

How does a company evaluate the many outside inventions submitted to it for acquisition or license?

The several steps to good evaluation include first those tests that are inexpensive yet adequate for screening out wholly unpromising products, then progressively more exacting tests, and finally the calculation of the expected bearing of the rights to be acquired on the company profits, all as described below.

Initial Screening

Since only a small proportion of the inventions proposed will be suitable, a quick examination by New Products personnel will dispose of the vast majority of license proposals on obvious grounds, such as clear lack of marketability, a field which as a matter of policy the company does not wish to enter, engineering or production impracticability, a patent infringement, or lack of patent protection.

Securing an Option to the New Product

If preliminary screening indicates that the product is worth extensive and often costly study, my own company will often negotiate an option agreement by which it learns the terms on which it can acquire rights to the product if final evaluation is favorable. Should it become clear at this point that the inventor wants far more than a license on his invention is worth to the company, the negotiation stops right there.

Here are the main elements of a good evaluation procedure for proposals deemed worth careful study:

Study the Relationship of the Proposed License to the Company's Business

A good way of doing this is to line up a list of the Company's manufacturing and other facilities, skills, selling ability, research and engineering background, and the like against a list of the requirements of the submitted product. If such a line-up indicates that the company cannot make much of a contribution towards marketing, engineering and manufacturing the product, as compared with many other companies in the field, then this is not likely to be a desirable acquisition unless prospective profits are unusually large.

Determine Marketing Feasibility

Generally the greatest likelihood for mistake in taking a license or assignment of patent rights to a new product is misjudging the market. My company tries to get as many figures with respect to the market and as many customer reactions as practical, particularly regarding customer acceptance, volume, selling price and competition. Is the price going to be too high or the volume too low? Will customers be willing to buy? These questions require interviewing potential customers and distributors.

Determine Its Technical Feasibility

This involves engineering study. Is it operative and practical with the technology and materials available? Can it be made commercially satisfactory without undue complication or cost? Does it accomplish much for the mechanism or material employed, or is the reverse true?

Determine Patent Situation

At this point the prospective licensee should have clearly in mind what he is buy-ing. If the product is not fully developed and on the market, generally he is not buying a new product but certain patent rights which give him, for better or worse, a chance of developing a new product. This chance may take the form of mere freedom from licensor's right to exclude (a non-exclusive license) or this plus the additional right to exclude others (an exclusive license or assignment). Neither of these gives the right to manufacture the product as against other earlier patentees. Hence an infringement search may be called for. However, if the licensor has done considerable research and development work, the licensee may save himself research and development effort by acquiring the R&D, including the detailed, unpublished information often called "know-how," of the licensor. Hence comes the importance of determining breadth of claims, validity of claims, possible infringement of the claims of others, and whether the claims are broad enough to deter copyists?

Test Degree of Completion

Inventions come in all stages of development. The value of the invention depends very greatly on how far along the scale from conception to commercialization the product is located. The risks and costs are very much greater the farther away the invention is from being ready for production and sale. Is the company being asked to do a pioneering job in an unchartered, even if attractive field? If so, remember "the way of the pioneer is hard." See Fig. 1, double or triple all development cost estimates, and divide expected royalty fees by 2 or 3; expect that estimated profits must be higher, to justify taking a license, the more remote the invention is from the marketing stage.

Miscellaneous Considerations Giving Value to a License

There are special reasons which may make a license valuable. If one believes that there is an infringement question, it is often better to acquire a license than risk infringement. A practical alternative which avoids a competitor's patent also has a spe-

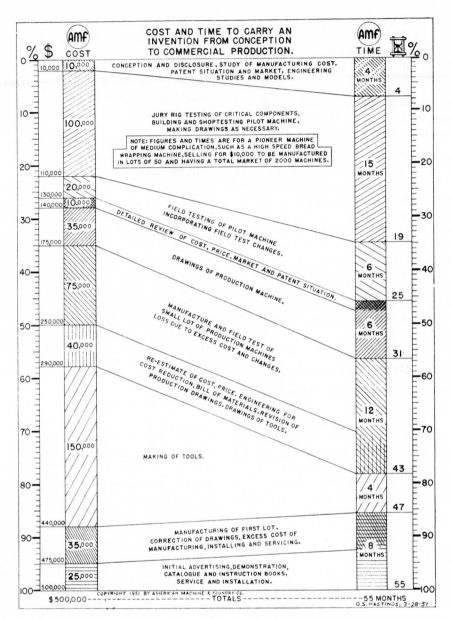

FIG. 1.

cial value. Suppose the patented product renders more effective a product or process already produced by the prospective licensee. This is one of the situations most nearly certain to prove profitable for the licensee. If the licensor can show a company how its present product can be made better, cheaper or more effective, he already has a good start in getting the licensee to sign the agreement.

Profitability

Having found the new invention adequate by the above tests and having obtained a fairly good set of figures, we come to the question of how profitable this product will be to the company. Good volume doesn't help if there is a loss on each item sold.

A simple way of getting at the profitability of a new product proposal is to assume a reasonable volume of sales based on the above-mentioned market studies and to set up a unit profit-and-loss statement for the product in which the profit on each sales unit is determined by subtracting all per unit costs and deductions from the estimated sales price to determine the profit on sales. An illustrative statement follows, in Table 1.

TABLE 1. PROFIT ON SALES.

% of Sales

	% of Sales	$
Sales price	100	$10,000
Manufacturing cost	55	5,500
Gross manufacturing profit	45	$ 4,500

Deductions

Selling	14	$ 1,400
Royalty	5	500
Service	1	100
Contin. engineering	2	200
Installation	1	100
Obsolescence, inventory	0.5	50
Obsolescence, tools	0.5	50
General and administrative	6	600
TOTAL		$ 3,000
Pretax earnings	15.0	1,500
Income tax		750
Net profit on sales	7.5	$ 750

This table approximates the figures on one of the American Machine & Foundry Company's successful products, its high-speed bread-wrapping machine. You will see that despite what seems a very healthy gross profit, by the time all of the necessary deductions are made, only a profit that is quite modest for a new and risky business remains, namely, 7½ per cent after taxes.

This table is valuable in showing how critical each item of deductions is. A change of 2 per cent in pretax costs increases or decreases profits over 13 per cent. Payment of a 10 per cent royalty instead of 5 per cent would have reduced profits almost to the vanishing point. Consideration of these figures will enable the company negotiator to be realistic in negotiating royalties.

While this method gives an indication of prospective profits, it does not take into consideration the company's investment in the new product or the total number of units likely to be sold. How good an investment is this new product for the company? It is obvious that even though profit on unit sales is high, if too much of the company's money is tied up for too long a time considering total sales and profits, the investment in the new product may be a poor one. The general consensus is that a new product should return at least 25 per cent pretax on investment annually if it is to be a good risk.

A formula for determining investment profitability is set forth below:

Is It a Good Investment? Here is one method that AMF uses to figure whether an invention is worth going on with. By applying the formula given below to the approximate figures for one of the company's successful similar products, a useful basis for comparison with the prospective product is developed. This gives the company a rough quantitative measure of the new idea's prospective payoff.

Here is the formula:

$$\frac{\text{Average annual return}}{\text{on average investment}} =$$

$$\frac{\substack{\text{Total of after-tax} \\ \text{receipts during life}} - \substack{\text{Total} \\ \text{investment}} \times \substack{\text{Time-value} \\ \text{of money}}}{\text{Half total investment} \times \text{Life}}$$

Here is how it worked when applied to a typical AMF product:

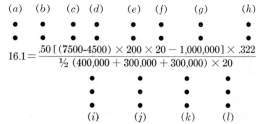

$$16.1 = \frac{.50\,[\,(7500-4500) \times 200 \times 20 - 1,000,000\,] \times .322}{\tfrac{1}{2}\,(400,000 + 300,000 + 300,000) \times 20}$$

(a) average annual return after taxes on average investment; (b) tax rate; (c) selling price; (d) all costs not capitalized, including selling, continuing R&D, G&A, and so on; (e) annual volume; (f) life, in years; (g) total capitalized investment; (h) time-value of money at 15 per cent, average of all yearly discounts because future money is of less value than present money; (i) original R&D, patent, and pre-production costs; (j) initial tooling; (k) other investment: capitalized items such as major redesigns and retooling; (l) life of investment, in years. *This formula has the virtue of being relatively simple to apply, but is only accurate if average annual sales can be estimated. Where annual sales vary greatly, a more accurate method is a year-by-year discount system.*

For a more refined, year by year formula for determining whether the return on investment is adequate, see Roy I. Reul, in *The Harvard Business Review 35*, No. 4 (1957), "Profitability Index for Investment."

Negotiating with Inventors

Inventors tend to put too high a value on their inventions. The less-developed the invention is, the greater is the overvaluation; the inventor has less knowledge of the limitations of the invention. The remedy is a sense of values on the part of the corporate negotiator, based on the kind of study referred to above. Where significant facts are missing, it should be explained to the inventor that allowance must be made for the possibility that the missing facts are adverse. He will argue that the royalty doesn't matter because it can be added to the price. This is not true. Consider again the table on "Profit and Sales." The price is determined by competition, volume desired, what the public will pay, and the cost of manufacture.

How is a fair royalty determined? The negotiator for the corporation should realize that *the inventor must be paid out of the profits of the business, not out of the gross sales price.* Remember our chart on profit on sales: a 2 per cent increase in royalties reduced profits 13 per cent. It is an extra-good manufacturing business which in the long run yields more than 15 per cent pretax (about 7 per cent after taxes) on the sales dollar. *Fortune*'s review of the 500 largest corporations shows that the average profit on the sales dollar in 1960 was 4.4 per cent after taxes. At 5 per cent, the licensee in the long run will be giving the inventor a third of the pretax income of an extra-good business and half that of an average one.

The party that puts up the capital, undergoes the start-up costs, does the manufacturing and selling, and risks its money, should get the major portion of the profits. Thus, 5 per cent is probably about the top royalty for an invention of above-average profitability, developed to a point near the going-business stage. Other factors which may scale the royalty down are the fact that the value added by manufacture is low

compared with material cost, that the product is sold in very high volume at low unit profit (this often calls for scaling down royalties as volume increases), or that the invention is a small part of the whole sales unit on which the royalty is based.

Conclusions

What the licensee seeks is a patented product having a substantial market, moderate costs of manufacture and selling as compared to sales price, and enough patent protection to enable the licensee to recoup something more than his start-up costs.

Hence the value of the invention rests on what the patent rights can add to the owner's or licensee's profits.

However novel, ingenious, broadly claimed, glamorous or useful the invention is, it has value to the licensee or purchaser only as these qualities bear on profits. The final test of value is in the marketplace, and the prospective purchaser or licensee looks only for inventions which will pass this test.

A part of the information herein has been taken from the author's article in "Dun's Review and Modern Industry," June 1958.

Cross-references: *Accounting and Recoveries from Infringement Suits, Economic Value of Patents, Evaluation of Inventions for Filing, Royalty— Rate and Basis.*

EXAMINATION OF APPLICATIONS

Eugene W. Geniesse

The following article is a condensation, with some revision and updating by the author, of his Study 29 for the Subcommittee on Patents, Trademarks, and Copyrights of the Committee on the Judiciary, U.S. Senate, 86th Congress, 2nd Session.

In an examination system for the grant of patents the ideal goals include the following: (1) a complete search of all prior art developments; (2) the citation and intelligent application of such prior art to the claims of the application for patent; (3) a consistent and sustainable determination of the patentable merit of each claim for invention presented; (4) a speedy final disposition of each application for a patent. Each resulting patent should include (a) a clear and adequate description of the asserted invention, and (b) clear and definite claims of determinable scope, defining inventive subject matter.

General Procedure

The Patent Office receives about 85,000 applications for patents annually. The application papers include a specification (description), a claim or claims, an oath, and a drawing if the nature of the invention admits of it (35 U.S.C. secs. 111-115). The Office places these papers in a folder, with identifying data on the face. The back flap serves for the entry of an index of papers as filed. The Application Division prepares duplicate index cards and forwards the application, depending on the subject matter, to one of the following Examining Groups, each with number of subgroups shown:

    Chemical, 8
    Electrical, 7
    Mechanical Engineering, 8
    General Engineering, 9

Prior patents, at a recent date, were classified into 308 distinct classes, which included 53,567 subclasses.

The application goes ultimately to a particular assistant examiner who works on the subject matter of the application.

The assistant examiner receiving the application inspects the application, makes such notes as are necessary to conduct any later "interference" search, and places that application in his file of new pending applications to be examined in the order of filing dates. Each assistant examiner receives an average of about 70 new applications per year.

On reaching the new application for examination in its proper chronological order, which may be from 6 to 18 or more months after filing, it is examined. Since an application is rarely in completely proper form and completely escapes the prior art, the examiner writes a letter, designated an "action," citing pertinent prior patents and other prior art (foreign patents and publications) and detailing his objections to the application and particularly the claims

thereof. The application thereupon becomes a "rejected" application awaiting response by the applicant, usually through his attorney. There are currently approximately 90,000 such pending, rejected applications in the Office.

With some exceptions, an applicant is permitted 6 months in which he may reply to the examiner's action (35 U.S.C. 133). Failure to reply results in abandonment of the application.

A response on the part of the applicant takes up every objection and rejection entered by the examiner, and usually includes an amendment or modification of the claims or description or both and such argument or comments as are appropriate.

The application then becomes an "amended" application, awaiting further action by the examiner. The number of such amended applications currently pending is about 50,000. On reaching the amended application in chronological order, the assistant examiner reexamines the application and takes such "action" as in his judgment, after consulting with the primary examiner, the application requires. This may take the form of a further action on the application, the same or further rejections or objections, a notice of allowance, or a "final" rejection.

A "final" rejection may be entered only if it is in substance a repetition of a former action and may not be entered if a new objection or rejection or new prior art is presented.

A final disposition of the application is attained by an allowance, a final rejection, or abandonment. The latter is usually by failure of the applicant-inventor to file a response. Any of these methods of final disposition relieves the examiner of further direct jurisdiction of the application.

A final rejection may be met by an appeal to the Board of Appeals (35 U.S.C. 7, 134). An unfavorable decision by the Board of Appeals may be met by an appeal to the Court of Customs and Patent Appeals (35 U.S.C. 141, 142, 143, 144) or by civil action in the U.S. District Court for the District of Columbia (35 U.S.C. 145).

The notice of allowance, which may be issued by the examiner at any time during the prosecution, after compliance with the conditions of a final rejection, or on decision of the Board of Appeals, the Court of Customs and Patent Appeals, or a decree of the district court, entitles the applicant to obtain his patent on the payment of the final fee.

Total Task

The first examination and report rarely result in an allowance, only a little over 1 per cent of all applications being allowed on such first examination. This first report, on the other hand, results in abandonment of about 10 per cent of the applications.

DISPOSITION OF APPLICATIONS BY NUMBER OF ACTIONS.

Action	Abandoned	Allowed	Disposed of
	Per Cent	Per Cent	Per Cent
1	10.6	1.4	12.0
2	9.2	9.1	18.3
3	9.9	19.3	29.2
4	6.2	18.8	25.0
5	2.5	8.0	10.5
6	.9	2.3	3.2
7	.7	1.1	1.8
Total	40.0	60.0	100.0

Average number of actions:

Abandoned cases	2.66
Allowed cases	3.57
All cases	3.20

Examination of a New Application

When the assistant examiner to whom an application has been assigned reaches the application in chronological order, he first studies the application itself to determine what is disclosed. He notes any informalities or inadequacies in the papers. He then studies the claims to determine what is sought to be protected.

His study may develop certain preliminary inadequacies or other obstacles to complete examination:

(a) The subject matter may be improperly classified, in which case he seeks to transfer the application to another division.

(b) The specifications and claims may be so completely inadequate that the application cannot be properly examined and the patent must be refused for that reason.

(c) The claims may cover a plurality of distinct inventions, and a requirement for restriction to a single invention is in order (35 U.S.C. 121). In that event the examiner requires restriction of the claims to a single invention, citing patents illustrative of the several classes of inventions involved, prior to consideration of the merits.

Search of Prior Art. After the study of the application, the assistant examiner makes his search of the prior art. This includes the U.S. patents in the subclass or subclasses deemed significant for the claimed subject matter, foreign patents in the same field, which are ordinarily placed in the same subclass as the U.S. patents on the same subject matter, and significant periodicals and treatises. He is expected to familiarize himself with the developments in the restricted field assigned to him and to acquire knowledge of the location of patents and other publications in that art.

The extent and adequacy of search of the prior art is dependent on a number of factors including the following:

(a) *Experience of the examiner.* One familiar with the prior developments can far more quickly uncover pertinent references than can one who has no previous familiarity with the field.

(b) *Competence of the examiner.* This factor involves capability of recognizing relationships between the invention claimed and prior developments.

(c) *Adequacy of classification.* The advantages of adequate classification of all prior patents, both foreign and domestic, are obvious. The difficulties as well as the efforts involved are not so obvious. Some fields of art are more readily classifiable than others. For example, organic compounds (carbon compounds) may be readily classified on the basis of the number of carbon atoms, the presence of functional groups, or the character of the nucleus.

As a different illustration, polishing compositions may include characteristics and functions of cleaning compositions, coating compositions, metal-plating compositions, and abrasive compositions. Such compositions might be classified on the basis of the components thereof, giving precedence to any of the several functions that are present, or on the basis of the type of article to be treated. Classification of such compositions is difficult, and any scheme of classification has its defects.

(d) *Pressure of work.* Confronted with an accumulation of applications awaiting examination and the necessity of disposing of at least a reasonable number of such applications, the examiner necessarily limits his search to the minimum that he considers satisfactory. In the rare instances where he discovers a completely anticipating prior art reference, the search is complete, and more would be a waste of time. The difficulty of determining adequacy of search comes in the usual cases where only art related in some degree to the invention claimed has been found. The examiner's competence and judgment in analyzing the subject matter of the invention, and its possible relationship to prior development, determine the extent and quality of the investigation of the prior art.

Examiner's First Action

After completion of his study of the application and his search of the prior art, the assistant examiner prepares his first "Action" on the application. A copy is sent to the inventor-applicant, usually through the patent attorney or agent, the original remaining in the Office file. The action is signed by the primary examiner. The primary examiner supervises the preparation of the decisions (actions) in each application in his division, and by signing such actions takes responsibility for them. He also supervises the assistant examiner's work in studying the application and making the search. The extent of supervision is dependent on the capability and experience of the particular assistant.

The examiner's decision to refuse a patent may be reviewed by appeal, but such review is sought only in a relatively small number of cases, averaging less than 10 per cent of the total number of applications for patent filed.

In the first action, informalities in the papers are noted, and appropriate correction is required. Any objections as to the language or arrangement of the claims or descriptions are also noted, as are also any deficiencies in the drawings. If the deficiencies of the description or drawing go to the substance and are such as to prevent the issuance of a valid patent, all of the claims presented are refused (rejected) for this reason.

The examiner devotes his principal attention to the claims and their relationship to the prior art references discovered in his search. Here, the examiner may be confronted with up to 20 or even more distinct definitions (claims) of the subject matter, wherein the counsel for the inventor has exercised his highest skill or ingenuity. Each claim must be separately studied, and the examiner must enter a decision, refusing or allowing each such claim. The refusal must take the form of a rejection of the enumerated claim or claims as "anticipated by" or "unpatentable over" particular identified reference patents or publications, and the reason therefor must be given (35 U.S.C. 131, 132). The examiner is guided in this work by the "Manual of Patent Examining Procedure," a looseleaf manual prepared by the Office and kept current by appropriate revisions. A checking and initialing of the typewritten action completes the assistant examiner's work in examination of a "new" application. The primary examiner, having reviewed the action either after typing or while in manuscript form, adds his signature.

Amendment

As already stated, the inventor usually has 6 months to respond to this initial action on the part of the examiner. This may take the form of insistence on allowance in unchanged form, accompanied by appropriate reasons. Or the inventor may modify (amend) the description or claims or both. While the inventor is confined to subject matter present in the application as filed, he may, by way of amendment, so alter or modify the claims as to include more detailed elements or emphasize facets of the invention not previously emphasized. The application thus altered becomes an amended application. It is placed in the examiners' files, awaiting further examination in chronological order. This waiting time may vary from a few months up to 2 years, depending on the condition of work in the division. At the end of fiscal year 1961, the average time was 11 months.

The Commissioner's annual reports present summarized statistical information as to applications filed, actions by the examiners, allowances, abandonments, etc.

Reexamination

When the amended application is reached for reexamination, the assistant examiner must review the application, the first action, and the inventor's response.

On reexamination of the amended application, the examiner is again confronted with the problem of extent of search. The alterations may be such as to necessitate a new search in fields other than those formerly covered. On completion of his study of the file and the references, and of any further search, the assistant examiner prepares a second action, under the primary examiner's supervision, much as in the first examination. Under the practice initiated in 1963, the second action will frequently be a "final rejection" or allowance of the application.

Final Disposition

The process of examination is repeated until the application is finally disposed of as by allowance or by the inventor's failure to file a response. This failure may be for a variety of reasons. The inventor may be confronted with prior art (patents or publications) or other reasons for refusal which convince him of the futility of proceeding further. Practical considerations may prompt him to abandon the application. Deficiencies in the description or subsequent discoveries may cause him to file a substitute or amplified application.

Appeals

Lastly, the final disposition (insofar as the examining division is concerned) may take the form of a "final rejection" which is a final decision on the part of the examiner, refusing, in whole or in part, the claims presented in the application. From this final action by the examiner, the inventor may appeal to the Board of Appeals and obtain a review of the examiner's decision refusing such claims as have been rejected. He may also petition the Commissioner from any final action or requirement relating to form. In the event of appeal or petition, the examiner is required to state his reasons for his action in the form of a written "Examiner's Answer" to the brief filed by the inventor. The Answer must include an adequate explanation of the invention and of the references cited, an exposition of the reasons for refusal of each of the claims on appeal, and appropriate comments as to the contents of the inventor-appellant's briefs.

The inventor is accorded a half-hour oral hearing. The examiner is not present at the hearing.

An unfavorable decision by the Board of Appeals is subject to further review by way of appeal to the Court of Customs and Patent Appeals (35 U.S.C. 141, 142, 143, 144) or of a civil action in the U.S. District Court for the District of Columbia (35 U.S.C. 145).

The inventor may, of course, accept the examiner's final decision. In that event, if there has been a refusal of only a part, but not all of the claims, the inventor may remove the refused claims and obtain allowance of the patent application with the remaining claims. If all claims have been refused, agreement with the examiner's position leaves no other recourse but abandonment of the application.

The examiner's "final" action in theory completes the prosecution of the application before the examiner, but a practice has developed of permitting further attempts to persuade the examiner to adopt a more favorable view, with or without further alteration of the claims and possibly with the presentation of further evidence.

In such further attempts to prosecute after final action, the inventor seeks to improve his position. This may be by significant restriction of the claims so as to escape the rejections, factual evidence in the form of affidavits which purport to establish advantages of the invention or disadvantages of the references, and an oral conference (interview) with the examiner. The substance of the interview, including the contentions advanced and any conclusions reached, must be reported by the inventor (Rule 133). All of these papers (proposed amendments, arguments, affidavits, reports of interviews) become a part of the record without regard to the results.

The "final" action in theory completes the prosecution before the examiner. In the past there was a rather liberal policy of permitting further attempts to persuade the examiner to adopt a more favorable view, accompanied by alteration of claims, presentation of further argument. All such papers are entered in the file regardless of the outcome as is also the required report of any interview had with the examiner (Rule 133). There have been sporadic attempts to restrict such prosecution after final action. A contrary pressure for allowance to get rid of the controversy also exists.

Allowance

At any time during prosecution the examiner may decide to allow the application. He is compelled to take the same step following a favorable decision of the Board of Appeals or of a court.

The allowance is less time consuming than any refusal. The examiner need not explain his decision, and it is not subject to review. He need only determine whether any other inventor has presented an application on the same invention; if none is found, he makes such formal and editorial corrections as seem proper and issues a formal notice of allowance.

On discovering that another application on the same subject matter has been presented, the examiner takes such formal steps as are necessary to institute an "interference" procedure to determine which applicant is the true first inventor and then transfers the application to the jurisdiction of the Interference Division.

Petitions

Petitions may be filed from any unfavorable ruling of the examiner on formal matters (Rules 113, 127, 181, 182, 183). While these petitions are in theory restricted to formal matters, there is an inclination on the part of a small minority of overly contentious attorneys to employ such petitions as a weapon to force the examiner to take a more favorable action in the case. This is a field in which the old axiom that "hard cases make bad law" is applicable. In actual practice most petitions are decided by the supervisory examiner. The latter, confronted with what is to him a harsh ruling in an isolated case, tends to make his interpretation of the rules as liberal as possible in favor of the inventor. The conscientious examiner confronted with such a ruling, perhaps attained by an overly zealous attorney, takes an equally favorable position with respect to all subsequent cases.

The underlying difficulty here is based on the fact that the inventor's interests are at stake, and the Office is reluctant to penalize the inventor by reason of the mistakes made by his attorney. If relief is accorded for one inventor under a particular set of circumstances, other inventors under like circumstances are entitled to the same relief, under the doctrine of *stare decisis*.

Evidence

The examiner may cite and rely on textbooks and treatises to establish facts. The inventor may, of course, also rely on such works, as establishing facts.

The usual factual disputes developed in the processing of a patent application involve questions of the comparative advantages of the asserted invention and prior art developments. These disputes are often resolved by the presentation of evidence or exhibits which must be adequately identified and described in a paper placed in the file. Evidence is usually presented in the form of ex parte affidavits which become a part of the record.

In re McKenna, 97 USPQ 348, 350, CCPA 1953 says:

"Such ex parte affidavits must of course be closely scrutinized and weighed with care it being kept in mind that they may unconsciously and unintentionally be colored as a result of enthusiasm for the subject matter of the application. We think also that an affidavit by an applicant or co-applicant as to the advantages of his invention is less persuasive than one made by a disinterested person."

Cross-references: *Appeals, Examiners, Petitions, Prosecution, Prosecution-Compact.*

EXAMINERS' CAREERS, OPPORTUNITIES AND TRAINING IN PATENT OFFICE

[The first section of this article is a condensation with some revision of the 1960 pamphlet of the Patent Office entitled "A Career for Engineers and Scientists." It gives information for those engineers and scientists who are interested in a career in the patent profession, points out some of the opportunities available to members of the examining corps of the Patent Office, and tells how qualified college graduates may obtain positions as patent examiners. Ed.]

The Patent Office

The Patent Office might be called the Keystone of the American Patent System. It is the responsibility and duty of the Office to receive, examine, and then approve or reject applications for patents and applications for the registration of trademarks.

The Patent Office is responsible for examining and deciding the patentability of claimed inventions. Other units of the Patent Office are responsible for the registration of trademarks, the furnishing of a variety of services to the public, such as the sale of over 6,000,000 printed copies of patents each year and the general administration of the Office.

Work of the Patent Examiner

When an inventor believes he has made a patentable invention, he files, or has a

FIG. 1. Examiners' offices in an examining division of the Patent Office.

registered patent attorney or agent file, an application in the Patent Office. The work of the Office and its examiners is, briefly, as follows: The application is processed and jacketed, fees are collected, etc., and the case is routed to an examiner. Each examiner normally specializes in one field of invention such as "Internal Combustion Engines." The examiner places the case in his "docket" with other pending cases in chronological order as received. When the case is reached for action, the examiner reads the disclosure and examines the drawings, in order to ascertain the nature of the disclosed invention. He studies the "claims" of the application and then searches the "prior art," which encompasses the prior knowledge in the field, including U.S. and foreign patents, periodicals, trade journals, etc., to see whether the claimed invention is novel or whether it has been anticipated by a prior invention. If he can find no equivalent invention in the prior (scientific) art, the examiner decides by the application of legal principles and court decisions, whether the claimed invention is useful and whether it involves patentable invention as distinguished from mere mechanical skill over the most pertinent "prior art." If the application is formally correct, falls within one of the statutory classes of invention, and passes the three tests of patentability, i.e., novelty, utility, and invention, the examiner recommends that a patent be allowed and upon approval by the head of the division the patent is granted. If the claimed invention fails to meet these three tests, it is rejected.

Examiners are expected to work with relative independence after the first few months in the Office. However, they discuss their analyses and decisions with a supervisor. This professional freedom of action is considered to be one of the most valuable rewards of patent examining.

The prosecution of some applications may be complicated by interferences (situations in which two or more inventors claim to have made the same invention at about the same time) and other matters. Rejected applications are subject to appeal to the Board of Appeals in the Patent Office and to the Courts. The validity of patents issued by the Office may be challenged in the Courts during infringement suits. The entire patent examining operation deals therefore with engineering and legal practice. Heavy reliance is placed upon the scientific and legal evaluations made by the examiner.

Professional Development. The widest possible variety of technical publications circulate in the Office, and money to defray the expenses of examiners making professional trips is regularly provided in the budget. Invitations to visit and inspect their operations are received from enterprises of all kinds, and such visits are arranged and normally approved by the Office. Membership in and attendance at the meetings of professional societies are strongly encouraged.

Working Conditions. The Patent Office occupies a major part of the Department of Commerce Building in downtown Washington, D.C. The building is two blocks from the White House and is bounded on the south by the Washington Monument Grounds and on the west by the Ellipse, and the White House. On the east is the District Building and the Labor Department Building. Only two blocks away is the principal shopping district of Washington. The Commerce Building, which was the largest office building in the world until the Pentagon was constructed, is of modern design with all important employee facilities such as health rooms, cafeteria, etc.

The Commerce Building is close to all major lines of transportation. Travel time from many large apartment developments to the Commerce Building is a matter of minutes. Car pools are frequently arranged and are a common form of transportation. Apartments at reasonable rates are plentiful. Rooms are readily available; many of them within walking distance of universities and the Commerce Building. Washington is one of the cleanest and most beautiful of all metropolitan centers and is especially noted for the parks and many points of interest.

Promotional Opportunities. Opportunities for promotion are excellent and probably unexcelled for a similarly large group in or out of the government. Virtually all vacancies are filled by promotion from within the Office. Opportunities for such promotions of meritorious examiners are very good.

Civil Service Benefits. In addition to the outstanding advantages and opportunities described in the foregoing paragraphs, employment in the U.S. Patent Office offers all of the benefits of civil service employment. Employment in the professional corps of the Patent Office has always been outstandingly stable regardless of business booms and depressions. Annual and sick leave benefits are unusually good. Everyone earns 13 workdays sick leave each year, and unused sick leave can be accumulated from year to year. Many federal employees have accumulated over 1,000 hours of sick leave. This would provide full pay checks for approximately six months if a serious illness should strike. For those employees with up to 3 years of service, 13 workdays of annual leave are provided; between 3 and 15 years service, 20 workdays are provided; and those with over 15 years of service receive 26 workdays of annual leave. Military service is counted in computing leave eligibility and also toward retirement which is especially attractive. An examiner with 30 years of service can normally expect to receive from $6,600 to $8,200 per year retired pay. There is also provision for disability retirement. Group life insurance and Health Benefit Program are available at very low cost.

How to Get an Appointment as a Patent Examiner

The Patent Office normally employs a large number of graduating engineers and scientists every year. At the present time, the expanded research and development activities of virtually all companies in the United States have resulted in a gradual but substantial increase in the numbers of patent applications filed. The minimum qualification requirements are a degree in one of the major engineering fields or a degree including or supplemented by 30 semester credit hours in chemistry, 28 semester credit hours in physics or 40 semester credit hours in physics, chemistry and engineering subjects combined of which total 20 hours must be in a pertinent field of engineering; or equivalent experience. [But see 141 USPQ IV, May 11, 1964.]

Information and the necessary forms to use in applying for positions will be furnished promptly upon request by the Personnel Division of the Patent Office, Washington 25, D.C.

This concludes the information from the Patent Office pamphlet.

Fig. 2. A class in the "Academy" for training Examiners.

Salaries of Examiners

The scale of starting salaries for Examiners of various grades, as of July 1964, was as follows:

Grade of Position	Salary ($ per annum)
GS 5	5,990
GS 7	7,050
GS 9	7,465
GS 11	8,945
GS 12	10,250
GS 13	12,075
GS 14	14,170
GS 15	16,460

All basic salaries are subject to a deduction of 6½ per cent for retirement benefits.

Examinations

The Civil Service Commission's Announcements of Examinations for the Position of Patent Examiner give additional information.

Academy for Examiners

[An advanced training course for Examiners, initiated late in 1962 with sixty Examiners in each group, gives a 5-months' training course (See Fig. 2) for Examiners and also for trainees from industry.]

The program is aimed at (1) developing a well-trained Examiner, to be brought to maximum effectiveness in a minimum amount of time; (2) securing a more uniform examining practice throughout the Office; and (3) creating, in cooperation with the new quality control unit, close control of the quality of the work done in the examining operation.

The courses offered in the training program are planned so as to cover all aspects of the Examiner's work. Special emphasis is placed on the heart of the examining job, with nearly 200 hours of study devoted to Preparation for Search and Retrieval of Prior art, Patentability, Response by Applicant, and Practice after Final Rejection. The following is an outline of the curriculum to be offered:

Subject	Approximate Hours
Introduction to the Patent Examining Operation	5
Security Laws and Government-owned Patent Applications, Office Security Requirements	3
Basic Requirements of Patent Application Disclosure	12
Classes of Invention and Types of Claims	27
Preparation for Search and Retrieval of Prior Art	31
Types of Applications	3
Patentability	122
(a) Novelty (d) Formality	
(b) Utility (e) Specialized Situations	
(c) Unobviousness	
Restriction and Double Patenting Practice	16
Formulation of Office Actions	15
Interviews	4
Response by Applicant	7
Affidavit Practice	6
Practice After Final Rejection	13
Aids to Efficient Examining	3
Allowance and Issue Practice	4
Appeal to the Board of Appeals	13
Court Review and Regulatory Matter	13
Reissues	7
Interference Practice	19
Design Patents	1
Trademark and Copyright Law and Practice	2
Comparison of Foreign Patent Systems with the United States Patent System; International Convention and Priority Rights	5
Trends in Public Policy Relating to the Patent System	4
General Review and Guides toward Uniformity in Patent Office Practice	11

Editor's Note

The Editor has previously opened the door to what have proven to be successful careers in patent law, by recommending to more than one science graduate that he become a Patent Office Examiner.

The above information may reveal to others the opportunity for such honorable and worthwhile service. These, it is hoped, will have or be able to acquire the habits of studiousness, eagerness in exploring the literature of science and technology, logic in thinking and writing, some inclination to the law, judgment in making decisions, and working at full mental capacity.

An excellent article in this field is that by Isaac Fleischmann, "The Patent Examiner—Professional Development," 38 JPOS 347, 1956.

Cross-references: *Examination, Information for Independent Inventors.*

EXECUTION OF FORMS. See FORMS

EXPERT TESTIMONY IN PATENT CASES
Foster Dee Snell

It is axiomatic that if a legal case is worth trying at all, it is worth trying right, and this is even more true of patent cases than of other equity cases. For such a trial, the expert is second in importance only to the attorney and frequently serves as "professor" to him.

Selecting the Expert

Finding an appropriate expert is often far from easy. Sometimes the attorney will inquire of attorneys or other experts. The Marquis publication "Who Knows What" can be valuable in gathering a list of names but an expert is rarely selected without one or more third persons giving him a recommendation from their actual experience. It is not at all unusual for an attorney to select an expert for his case based on previous experience with him as an adverse witness.

Generally, and preferably, the expert is not an employee of the client. There is at least a belief that this independence causes the court to give greater weight to his testimony. Spelled out in more detail, the theory is often advanced that the employee's testimony tends to be biased because he wants to retain his position. There is a much better reason. While an employee of the client will initially know much more in detail about the patent or the alleged infringement, he is much less objective in his evaluations than the independent expert. This leads to a statement frequently made that, as a matter of law, an employee's testimony is entitled to less weight than that of an independent consultant, everything else being equal. And while a lawyer may be working on a contingent basis—relatively seldom in patent cases—the expert must never do so. The perversion of his point of view is then unescapable.

Viewed from a distance, the role of the expert may appear to be an easy one. That conclusion is superficial. Court may sit from 10 to 12:30, adjourn to 2:00 P.M. and adjourn for the day at 4:30. There usually follows a conference at the hotel before dinner on "How did we do today" and discussion of specifics in the day's testimony. But after dinner, everyone has some job to do and rarely finishes before midnight. Then after too few hours sleep, there is usually a breakfast conference stretching to nearly 10 A.M. The expert is not under the tension of the trial attorney and doesn't have to work as long hours but he is certainly not apt to spend evenings at leisure.

The expert should be brought into the case early. At times to conserve costs for his client and in the hope of the case being dropped or settled, an attorney will leave the selection of an expert until within a week or two of trial. Rarely is a case so simple that it can then be properly prepared in that time. In one case, the writer was already in a conference with the defendant and his counsel when the Summons and Complaint were served.

Patent litigation can become almost incredibly complex. For the present purpose, the points can be more clearly made by keeping it simple. A suit may be under a single patent or a group of patents. A single patent will be assumed. The suit may be by the patentee or by a licensee or it may be a declaratory judgment case in which the patentee becomes defendant. The suit may have multiple plaintiffs or multiple defendants. The assumption here will be that a single plaintiff is suing a single defendant. In most jurisdictions, either side may have multiple experts if there are issues falling in separate areas of technical expertise. But a single one each for plaintiff and defendant is the usual situation and will be assumed. Usually more than one attorney will be involved on each side but for simplicity, a single one is assumed. Commonly, the "he" referred to means a corporation's officers as well as their patent counsel.

Qualifications. The first step in the trial will be to satisfy the court as to the qualifications of the expert. This consists of a recital not only of his general experience and education, but also of his specific experience in the field covered by the patent-in-suit. This latter can take curious turns. Thus, specific experience with phenol-formaldehyde plastics as a qualification to testify about polyethylene would be inferior to broad experience in polymerization. Similarly, a familiarity with surface chemistry and detergency over a period of years is a more desirable qualification for testimony relating to a soap *product* than years of experience with soap *manufacture*.

Frequently, the problem arises as to whether to use a person who is expert in the technology to which the patent is directed or one who is expert in interpretation of patents but whose knowledge of the technology of the art is somewhat limited. It is rare that one finds both in the same individual. The late Dr. Benjamin T. Brooks combined both talents in the petroleum art. Generally, it is more important that the expert have detailed experience with patents and their interpretations, if only because he understands the language of the attorney and the judge. It is sometimes expressed as the difference between an *expert* witness and an expert *witness*. The latter will often know how to make complex matters simple, the former may bury his pertinent facts in a great mass of non-germane detail.

There is a belief among a limited number of people that the expert testifies to whatever will be to the advantage of his client. It has been known to occur but not too often. The expert is under no obligation to bring out facts or opinions adverse to his client, but he must give an honest answer on cross-examination even if the result is detrimental to his client's case. The trite phrase "If you always tell the truth, you do not have to remember what you said" is applicable here.

Dr. Vannevar Bush has expressed it well in hearings before the Temporary National Economic Committee, 1939, saying that the scientist "should be called upon to be expert not in the particular patents before the court, but in the science which underlies them."

The expert should bear in mind—and this is not always easy—that although he is being paid by the plaintiff or the defendant, he should not be a proponent of one side. This means that his testimony must be free from statements which appear to argue his client's case. Perhaps the dividing line between that and argument in support of his interpretation of facts is a narrow one, even a hazy one, but it exists. Not only does being a proponent make a bad impression on the judge but also, since we are all human, it tends toward the expert's giving half truths. And this is the downward path to trouble on cross-examination.

Claim Analysis

The patent-in-suit is limited to what is claimed. Therefore, a claim analysis is a necessary tool. This takes each claim apart, phrase by phrase and word by word. Then the content of the allowed claims must be contrasted with those given up during the prosecution of the case. These lead to an interpretation of the claim elements which must be met if there is infringement or which must be found in the prior art to prove anticipation. It is usually the expert's first step, whether done formally on paper or mentally.

Then the study of the specification follows to see whether all of the claim elements are in fact included in the specification and are no broader than the specification. The expert's analysis and interpretation of the claims allowed and those abandoned will often be a foundation for the attorney to argue file wrapper estoppel.

Prior Art Study

Prior patents and publications are usually pleaded. These may vary from a half dozen to several dozen. A few decades ago, the citation of a reference in the file history substantially barred it from consideration in subsequent litigation.

It is a usual practice today to plead all

references cited in the file history, no matter how casual their citation, this in spite of the remark attributed to a District Court judge in the past, "You can't make a good omelet from bad eggs, no matter how many you use." So, a plaintiff's expert has the task of studying the file history of the patent-in-suit to determine whether he can find in the cited references any anticipation or other basis for invalidation not detected by the Examiner. Basis for invalidation may be found in the introduction of new matter into the specification during the prosecution. While this is a matter of law, the technical interpretation of it is a matter for the expert. When the patent-in-suit is a continuation-in-part, the problem of the preceding sentence frequently becomes graver and more time-consuming. The defendant's expert has the corresponding problems in order to see what he is apt to meet from the plaintiff. If he does not do so, he may meet with surprises when the plaintiff's case is presented.

Searching. It is meant as no criticism of the Patent Office to say that it is staffed by humans and, therefore, not perfect. On the average, the Examiner has about a day or less to spend on each action on a case. The expert is rarely so limited. Therefore, either the expert or a searcher will make an earnest effort to find additional anticipatory references. The appropriate classifications in the Patent Office are searched. The literature of the particular art involved is first examined through abstracts of which those of Chemical Abstracts are typical. Then the promising technical articles receive individual study.

Books in the specific art often give clues to pertinent publications. Such searching of books should not be confined to those published before the patent was filed as they often refer back to much earlier references. In general, the abstracts and the books are a method of cross-checking and, if the search is thorough, can be expected to turn up many if not all of the same references. Similarly, the Uniterm Index is a cross-check on the patents found in a patent search. This mass of material is then studied, and selections are made as to the references to be pleaded. This phase is often carried out by the attorney prior to the expert entering the case. The technic depends primarily on the magnitude of the case, and the expert often amplifies the prior search by the attorney.

But here we meet some of the more serious complexities of the work of the patent expert. Primarily these arise from the questions as to what is analogous art as distinguished from non-analogous art, often complicated by the application of the doctrine of equivalents.

Art Book. The expert will usually have a loose-leaf art book, sometimes one for patents and one for other publications. In these will be not only the references, suitably marked to call his attention to pertinent passages, but also his abstract of each reference interleaved and often his own experimental data interleaved with the pertinent patent or reference. These are his working books for use on the witness stand.

Ex Parte Experiments

Quite commonly when infringement is suspected, the plaintiff conducts or has others conduct analyses and experimental work. On the basis of the results of such work, decision is made as to whether suit for infringement is to be brought.

When suit is brought, the defendant is behind, timewise. At that point, the defendant will often find it necessary to have such analyses and experimental work as will be persuasive that infringement does or does not exist. The results may determine whether a license should be taken, if available, or the issue contested.

Experiments up to this point are necessarily ex parte, and commonly both sides will proceed thereafter with such experiments. Courts differ in their evaluation of ex parte work. If not contradicted by experimental evidence or highly persuasive oral expert testimony of the other side, such work is usually accepted at its face value.

Evidence based on opinion alone rarely has much place in a patent case, thus making a striking contrast to many negligence cases. Rather, the expert usually has worked in the laboratory on the problem anywhere from a few hours to months or years. Any opinion testimony then is in explanation of tabular data presented, experimental samples shown, and diagrams or models prepared. That not only takes it out of the class of "opinion alone," but, quite commonly, the experts for both sides will concur in their interpretation of a substantial part of the technical evidence. Judges like that, for it simplifies their problem.

Inter Partes Experiments

If one or more experiments become crucial in deciding infringement or validity, it is then desirable to conduct these with experts for both plaintiff and defendant present, viewing the technic and the results critically. In a few jurisdictions, the court may appoint its own expert to conduct the experiments provided both parties consent.

Reports

As a reasonable protection of his client against discovery proceedings, all written matter containing factual or conjectural matter relating to the case should be addressed to the attorney, not to the client. Commonly this will be in the form of reports or memoranda. Insofar as these are intended for presentation as exhibits, they should be complete with statements of experimental conditions, details of construction, etc., often even showing calculations. Where based on the patent-in-suit or a prior art patent, they should indicate where in that patent the experimental conditions are given, any interpretation of those conditions found necessary, and the justification for that interpretation. This latter presents a field where controversy may easily arise.

Preparation For Trial

In many minor cases, not involving patents, the attorney and the expert have a conference of an hour or two and the expert is then examined from limited notes made by the attorney. In patent cases, this is far from the best procedure. The reason is that the attorney rarely knows the technology involved to the extent that the expert does.

Therefore, as a working aid in laying out the ground to be covered, a detailed dictation of questions to bring out the expert's qualifications is desirably followed by an equally detailed series of questions and answers about the experimental work the expert has done and its specific bearing on the patent in suit. The significance of each reference pleaded must be brought out. The question need not be phrased by the expert in the precise legal form that will be used in court, nor is it to be expected that the answers in court will be precisely the same. One thing the dictated material does is to point out the significance of various facts by keeping to relatively short and cogent statements by the witness. The opposite occurred in the case, quite possibly apocryphal, in which the late Dr. Gustav Egloff has been said to have testified for 5 days in answer to a single cross-examination question.

The detailed prepared questions and answers serve to crystallize the thinking of both the attorney and the expert. Revisions in sequence appear desirable. The expert can make clear to the attorney technical details which are important for him to know, not only in presenting his side but in cross-examination of adverse witnesses.

But preparation for testimony is not finished when the direct case is completed. Direct testimony will be followed by cross-examination. For this, the expert needs to have much more information available to him than merely that presented on direct examination. Many relatively simple and clear-cut answers on direct examination will require amplification on cross-examination.

The expert is a privileged character. He cannot be required to answer "yes" or "no" to the equivalent of the Will Rogers example, "Do you still beat your wife?" His reply can be "No but with an explanation," and he can then proceed to explain the limitations on his reply of "No." Likewise, if a cross-examination question is badly worded, intentionally or otherwise, he can say so. If this occurs several times, it can make the expert appear to be fencing with opposing counsel, but that is readily overcome by explaining why the question is not answerable, often by rephrasing it. Such psychological factors are important in any case.

The expert is entitled to be present in court throughout the trial if the attorney judges that to be necessary. Put in another way, opposing counsel cannot "invoke the rule" as is so often done in damage cases. That is important for the function of the expert is not finished when he leaves the stand. Commonly he will sit near the trial attorney when adverse witnesses are testifying on direct testimony or rebuttal. By so doing, he frames questions for cross-examination and by passing them in written form to the attorney supplements the prior technical information he has given him. In addition to this, he usually goes over the day's transcript in the evening to pick up desirable further cross-examination questions or subjects for rebuttal testimony.

Physical Exhibits

Experimental work is usually put in the record as data or other appropriate physical form. Conclusions cannot be shown on such a physical exhibit if there are opinions based on it. Thus, such an exhibit might consist of setting identified phrases from two documents side by side. The court will receive such a chart as an exhibit. Then if the witness concludes from the phrases that they are substantially identical, he must so say on the record and submit to cross-examination.

Similarly, if there are data in the patent with which the expert disagrees, he can set up his own data in the same document with that copied from the patent to make a comparison. This may be evident on the face of it but more often requires interpretation in his testimony.

It is not unusual in a patent case to have the exhibits run into the hundreds for each side. And it is also not unusual for a majority of those exhibits to have been prepared by the expert. Many are prepared in advance but as the case progresses, it is often necessary to prepare additional exhibits to counter some which have been entered by the adversaries. These may be presentation of data already available but in a different form or may represent new data, perhaps obtained by working overnight or over the weekend. The value of such data in tabular form can hardly be overemphasized. It can present matter clearly and succinctly which could not be set forth with reasonable clarity by the witness in question and answer form. It can save hours of testimony. The court reporter, however competent, cannot be expected to know many of the esoteric terms which necessarily are involved. The expert must be prepared to say "yes" to a question by the presiding judge, "Does this present what you would say if questioned about each item by the attorney for your side?" And, of course, opposing counsel can cross-examine him at length about anything which does not appear clear to him and his expert.

As a minor point, it is wise for the expert to prepare before trial a list of the more unusual words which will appear in his testimony and hand it to the court reporter. One can rarely expect his experience to include such words as copper phthalocyanine, not to mention di-*para*-diaminomethoxydiphenyl. Controversies over the meaning of a misspelled word can arise, and at best the preparation and presentation of a long series of corrections to the record is an arduous task.

Devil's Advocate

A few experts take the position that they will only take the "right" side of a case. That is absurd. There are two sides. Each has scientific truths to present. Much law as well as technology enters into the final decision. Just as a known criminal is entitled to be represented by counsel, so both plaintiff and defendant are entitled to have the best possible technological presentation of their case. Likewise, the expert is duty bound to tell the attorney with whom he is working, and often also his client, the weaknesses of their position. If the expert with his somewhat limited point of view—he can't be expected to know the law—could tell who is "right," no judge would be needed; there would be no case.

It follows that one needs to know not only his own case but that of his adversaries. A convenient way to do this is, after his own case is prepared, to dictate a running account of what he would endeavor to bring out if he were expert for the other side. Such a "devil's advocate" memorandum often points up weaknesses in his own presentation which require rectification.

Much beside expert testimony enters into the final decision. As a single example, there may be a decision that there was file wrapper estoppel. So, the expert who boasts that he never lost a case has either a very limited experience or an unusually potent rabbit's foot.

The Neutral Expert

Much paper and ink and many hours of discussion have been spent on the so-called neutral expert. Cf. Role of the Court Expert in Patent Litigation, Study No. 8 of the Subcommittee on Patents, Trademarks, and Copyrights of the Committee on the Judiciary. U.S. Senate, 85th Congress, 1st Session. The writer has had experience with only one case involving a neutral expert. Nevertheless the writer agrees with the broad understanding among typical members of the Federal judiciary that it is not possible to find a neutral expert without some bias. Judge John C. Knox is quoted in said Study, p. 27, as saying that "the appointment by the court of expert witnesses is in a sense unfair to the litigants, inasmuch as the court in most cases, would give more attention or weight to the testimony of its appointed experts than to the evidence offered by the experts of the litigants." It should be noted that the neutral expert referred to above was agreed upon by both sides, but thereafter the criticism of Judge Knox still applied.

Judge John F. Dooling, Jr., in a 1964 discussion of this subject, observed that the "neutral" expert may be disinterested and neutral between the parties as to the *outcome* of the suit but that an expert will rarely be neutral as to the *ideas* involved and that many lawyers would not want an expert to act as aide to the judge and confer with the judge in chambers without the presence of counsel for both parties. Cf. 3 NYPLA Bull. No. 6, 1964.

Settling Cases

The data brought out by the expert's preparation of the case often leads to a settlement negotiated by the attorneys. The defendant may find that he does not have a defense which justifies the expense he would be put to in proceeding with the case. Or, the plaintiff may have his attention called to one or more significant references with which he was unfamiliar. Plaintiffs rarely have made as thorough a search as the defendant does before trial. In one amusing instance, experts for the plaintiff and the defendant had labored for more than a week on inter partes tests prior to trial as ordered by the District Court. At their conclusion, the defendant's expert wrote a memorandum interpreting the experiments in great detail and drawing conclusions. The defendant's attorney showed it to the attorney for the plaintiff. The case was settled the next week and both parties, as well as the taxpayers, saved money.

Cross-references: *Advocacy in Patent Causes, Consultant and Patents, Consulting Laboratories' Patent Policies, Infringement Suits, Patentability.*

F

FEES, CHARGES AND SUBSCRIPTIONS FOR PATENT OFFICE PUBLICATIONS

The major fees are fixed by statute, the minor charges by the Patent Office. The first may be changed by Congress at any time, the latter by the Commissioner of Patents. For this reason it is important to have at hand the latest schedules, all of which can be found in the "Rules of Practice of the U.S. Patent Office in Patent Cases."

Changes in the statutory fees are not imminent at this time. A bill, H.R. 8190, that passed the House of Representatives in 1964, is not expected to pass also the Senate at this session of the Congress. If enacted, the bill would establish maintenance fees of substantial amount, to be paid at three periods during the life of any patent kept in force for its full term. The measure may be revived at a later date.

Statutory Provisions, 35 U.S.C. 41

A. The Commissioner shall charge the following fees:

(1) On filing each application for an original patent, except in design cases, $30, and $1 for each claim in excess of twenty.

(2) On issuing each original patent, except in design cases, $30, and $1 for each claim in excess of twenty.

(3) In design cases: For three years and six months, $10; for seven years, $15; for fourteen years, $30.

(4) On every application for the reissue of a patent, $30 and $1 for each claim in excess of twenty over and above the number of claims of the original patent.

(5) On filing each disclaimer, $10.

(6) On an appeal for the first time from the examiner to the Board of Appeals, $25.

(7) On filing each petition for the re-

vival of an abandoned application for a patent or for the delayed payment of the fee for issuing each patent, $10.

(8) For certificate of correction of applicant's mistake under Section 255 of this title, $10.

(9) For uncertified printed copies of specifications and drawings of patents (except design patents), 25 cents per copy; for design patents, 10 cents per copy; special rate for libraries specified in section 13 of this title, $50 for patents issued in one year.

(10) For recording every assignment, agreement, or other paper not exceeding six pages, $3; for each additional two pages or less, $1; for each additional patent or application included in one writing, where more than one is so included, 50 cents additional.

(11) For each certificate, $1.

B. The Commissioner may establish charges for copies of records, publications, or services furnished by the Patent Office, not specified above.

Additional Fees and Charges

The additional fees and charges that follow are set in Rule 21 and are subject to change by the Commissioner.

(a) For typewritten copies of records, for each page produced (double spaced) or fraction thereof $1.00
(b) For photocopies or other reproductions of records, drawings or printed material, per page of material copied .... .30
(c) [Deleted]
(d) For certified copies of patents if in print:
  For specification and drawing, per copy .... .25
  For the certificate 1.00
  For the grant 1.00
(e) For abstracts of title to each patent or application:

292

For the search, one hour or less, and certificate 3.00

Each additional hour or fraction thereof 1.50

For each brief from the digest of assignments, of 200 words or less 1.00

Each additional 100 words or fraction thereof .... .10

(f) For title reports required for Office use 1.00

(g) For translations from foreign languages into English, made only of references cited in applications or of papers filed in the Patent Office insofar as facilities may be available: Written translations, for every 100 words of the original language, or fraction thereof 3.00

Oral translations (dictation or assistance), for each one-half hour or fraction thereof that service is rendered 4.00

(h) On admission to practice as an attorney or agent 5.00

(i) For certificate of good standing as an attorney or agent 1.00

(j) For making patent drawings when facilities are available, the cost of making the same, minimum charge per sheet 25.00

(k) For correcting patent drawings, the cost of making the correction, minimum charge 3.00

(l) For the mounting of unmounted drawings and photoprints received with patent applications, provided they are of approved permanency 1.00

(m) For photographic prints of patent models, building facilities, etc., if available:

For 5 x 7 photographic print ...... .50

For 8 x 10 photographic print ..... .75

(n) Search of Patent Office records for purposes not otherwise specified in this rule, per hour of search or fraction thereof 3.00

(o) [Deleted.]

(p) Subscription order for printed copies of patents as issued: Annual service charge for entry of order and one subclass, $2.00, and 20 cents for each additional subclass included; amount to be deposited (for price of copies supplied), as determined with respect to each order.

(q) List of U.S. Patents:

All patents in a subclass, per sheet (containing 100 patent numbers or less) .... .30

Patents in a subclass, limited by date or patent number, per sheet (containing 50 numbers or less).. .30

(r) Local delivery box rental, annual 12.00

(s) For publication in the Official Gazette of a notice of the availability of a patent for licensing or sale, each patent 3.00

(t) For special service to expedite furnishing items or services ahead of regular order:

On orders for copies of United States patents and trademark registrations, in addition to the charge for the copies, for each copy ordered .... .25

On all other orders or requests for which special service facilities are available, in addition to the regular charge, a special service charge equal to the amount of regular charge; minimum special service charge per order or request 1.00

(u) For airmail delivery:

On "special service" orders to destinations to which United States domestic airmail postage rates apply, no additional charge.

On regular service orders to any destination and "special service" orders to destinations other than those specified in the preceding subparagraph, an additional charge equal to the amount of airmail postage. (Available only when the ordering party has, with the Patent Office, a deposit account. Rule 25.)

(v) For items and services, that the Commissioner finds may be supplied, for which fees are not specified by statute or by this rule, such charges as may be determined by the Commissioner with respect to each such item or service.

Issuance of Patents without Fees

Filed by Government Employees. Section 266 of 35 U.S.C. reads:

The Commissioner may grant, subject to the provisions of this title, to any officer, enlisted man, or employee of the Government, except officers and employees of the Patent Office, a patent without the payment of fees, when the head of a department or agency certifies the invention is used or likely to be used in the public interest and the applicant in his application states that the invention described therein, if patented, may be manufactured and used by or for the Government for governmental purposes without the payment to him of any royalty thereon, which stipulation shall be included in the patent. Cf. M.P.E.P. 607.01(a).

Filed Under Comptroller General's Opinion. The Comptroller General has ruled (Comptroller General's Opinion's B-111,648 and B-117,353) that fees need not be paid in applications filed by one not a Government employee.

(1) Where there is an assignment of all right, title and interest in the invention and application to the Government or a Government agency; and

(2) Where the invention and application are the result of research sponsored and financed by the Government under contract or agreement requiring that the results thereof be made available to the public, and the application contains a clause dedicating the invention and patent to be granted to the free use of the people in the territory of the United States. M.P.E.P. 607.01.

Miscellaneous Provisions Respecting Fees

Until the filing fee is paid an application will not receive a filing date or be forwarded to an examining division. Rule 22.

Registered attorneys and agents may open in the Patent Office deposit accounts of amounts not less than $25, and can direct the Office to make deductions from them for various charges, even for such major items as file histories or corrections of drawings, but not for filing, issue, petition or appeal fees. Rule 25.

Soft copies of patents may be ordered by means of coupons available in books of either 20 or 100 coupons each, or the patents may be purchased separately.

Charges for Publications

The Rules of Practice of the United States Patent Office in Patent Cases cost 50 cents.

Rule 21 contains the following schedule:

The Official Gazette and other publications in the following list are sold, and the prices therefor established by the Superintendent of Documents, U.S. Government Printing Office, Washington 25, D.C., to whom all communications respecting the same should be addressed (except with respect to items indicated* are supplied by the Patent Office also).

Official Gazette of the United States Patent
Office *:

Annual subscription, domestic	$35.00
Annual subscription, foreign	45.00
Single numbers	1.00

Portions of the Official Gazette supplied separately:

Decision leaflets, domestic $4.50, foreign $7.00, per annum; single numbers	.15
Trademark Section, domestic $10.00, foreign $13.75, per annum; single numbers	.15
Annual index relating to patents; price varies, buckram	6.75
Annual index relating to trademarks; price varies, buckram	2.50
Decisions of the Commissioner of Patents; price varies, buckram	3.75
Classification Bulletins published from time to time (also supplied by the Patent Office), price varies for different numbers, according to size, minimum price 10 cents.	
Patent Attorneys and Agents Available to Represent Inventors before the U.S. Patent Office	.55
Roster of Attorneys and Agents Registered to Practice Before the U.S. Patent Office	.70
Manual of Classification of Patents, dom.	8.50
Foreign	10.50
Manual of Patent Examining Procedure:	
Domestic	4.00
Foreign	5.00
Guide for Patent Draftsmen	.15
Rules of Practice in Patent Cases	.50

Weekly Class Sheets

List showing classification of each patent in the weekly issue. Subscription $5.00 a year.

General References

For discussions of Patent Office fees, with graphs showing totals of receipts of the various kinds and relation to expenditures, reference is made to the excellent studies by the Hon. Robert C. Watson and by Mr. P. J. Federico, 35 JPOS 710 and 725, respectively, 1953.

For changes in fees or subscription rates, consult the latest edition of the Rules.

FILE WRAPPER ESTOPPEL

Granville M. Pine

The doctrine of file wrapper estoppel in patent claim interpretation may be said to correspond generally to the rule of contract interpretation which permits proof of attendant facts constituting the setting of a contract if helpful to interpret the meaning of the written words. *Eustis Mining Co.* v. *Beer, Sondheimer & Co., Inc.*, 239 Fed. 976, DC SNY 1917. The correspondence is not complete, however, as file wrapper estoppel is strongly founded in equity as well as logic, and classifies as a rule of law to limit a patent claim even though the claim language and the specification might authorize a broader interpretation.

The doctrine has its most prominent application when the patent owner attempts to rely upon the doctrine of equivalents in order to prove an infringement of his patent, but it applies also where a patentee claims that his patent is literally infringed. The file wrapper may contain admissions or definitions which negate a holding of "literal" infringement, as well as prevent a holding of infringement based on the doctrine of equivalents.

The doctrine of file wrapper estoppel protects the public from unwarranted expansions of the patent monopoly beyond its legitimate scope. It, in effect, estops the patent owner from interpreting the invention narrowly before the Patent Office and broadly before the Courts.

Effect of Amendment or Cancellation of Claims

As a rule, the correspondence between the applicant and the Patent Office cannot enlarge, diminish, or vary the terms of the patent, but can only confirm the meaning of the issued claims. *Goodyear Dental Vulcanite Co.* v. *Davis*, 102 U.S. 222, 1880.

The purpose of the file wrapper when interpreting the claims of a patent was stated by the Court of Appeals for the Third Circuit to be:

"The claims of a patent must always be explained by and read in connection with the specification and in the light of definitions and admissions made by the applicant in the proceedings in the Patent Office." *Westinghouse Elec. Corp.* v. *Hanovia Chem. & Mfg. Co.*, 179 F.2d 296, CA 3 1949; *Moon* v. *Cabot Shops*, 270 F.2d 539, CA 9 1959, c.d., 361 U.S. 965, 1960.

In general, file wrapper estoppel can arise by reason of an amendment or cancellation of a claim after a rejection by an examiner in the Patent Office based on prior art, arguments presented to the Patent Office, double patenting or formal grounds of a substantive nature. See Rowland, "The Interplay of the Doctrines of Equivalents and File Wrapper Estoppel," 29 Geo. Wash. L. Rev. 917, 925, 1961.

On the other hand, changes made in claims to avoid rejections based on informal matters such as vagueness or indefiniteness generally do not create an estoppel. *Porter-Cable Machine Co.* v. *Knives & Saws*, 204 F.2d 21, CA 7 1953; *Toy Ideas, Inc.* v. *Montgomery Ward & Co., Inc.*, 172 F. Supp. 878, DC Md 1959.

Although, as will be mentioned subsequently, there is some difference of opinion regarding the effect of narrowing a claim in order to obtain its allowance, it is generally agreed that

"the claim as allowed ... be read and interpreted with reference to the rejected claim ... and cannot be so construed as to cover ... what was rejected by the Patent Office...." *Hubbel* v. *United States*, 179 U.S. 77, 80, 1900.

Where claims are amended or rewritten to avoid formal rejections, the doctrine of file wrapper estoppel is applied even where the examiner's rejection is in error. *I.T.S. Rubber Co.* v. *Essex Rubber Co.*, 272 U.S. 429, 1926, because the applicant should appeal from the rejection if he deems it incorrect. See Oldham, "File Wrapper Estoppel," 20 JPOS 115, 132, 1938. In short, an applicant cannot acquiesce in the rejection by the Patent Office in order to secure his patent and later, in a patent infringement action, recover what he gave up by his acquiescence. *Exhibit Supply Co.* v. *Ace Patents Corp.*, 315 U.S. 126, 1942. Nor can an applicant avoid file wrapper estoppel by stating to the Patent Office that the applicant's response is not an acquiescence to the rejection and that he expects to insist on his right to cover the same areas the rejected claim covered. *Parke, Davis & Co.* v. *American Cyanamid Co.*, 207 F.2d 571, CA 6 1953.

Although an estoppel is typically applied after a claim has been narrowed to avoid a rejection, the Supreme Court has applied an estoppel even where the allowed claims were broader than the rejected claims.

"[While] it does not appear why the patent office allowed the broad claims after rejecting the narrower ones...the patentee, having acquiesced in their rejection, is no longer free to gain the supposed advantage of the rejected claims by a construction of the allowed claims as equivalent to them." *Schriber-Schroth Co.* v. *Cleveland Trust Co.*, 311 U.S. 211, 221, 222, 1940.

From the foregoing, it can be seen that an estoppel arises not because of the prior art but because of the patentee's acquiescence in the examiner's position as to what the prior art showed. Thus on the issue of estoppel, the actual teaching of the prior art is generally irrelevant.

There is apparently a difference of opinion between some courts regarding the status of the area between the allowed claims and the cancelled or amended claims.

The Supreme Court has held that a patentee may not recover, by invoking the doctrine of equivalents, anything he has given up to meet the examiner's rejection based upon the prior art. *Exhibit Supply Co.* v. *Ace Patents Corp.*, supra. The Supreme Court holds as material the difference between what the patentee disclaims and what is allowed by the Patent Office, and that difference is strictly construed against him. *Smith* v. *Magic City Kennel Club*, 282 U.S. 784, 1931.

The Second and the Fourth Circuits apparently have applied a more liberal rule than the Supreme Court concerning a narrowing of the claim in order to secure its allowance. Judge Learned Hand wrote for the Second Circuit:

"While the rejection of a claim does of course forbid any interpretation of...[the allowed claims]...which leaves them identical with that rejected, it does not necessarily prevent them being read as equivalent to any species of the rejected claim, which the doctrine of equivalents justifies. It only forbids the patentee from reducing his claim to the rejected claim, simpliciter." *Deitel* v. *Unique Specialty Corp.*, 54 F.2d 359, 360, 361, CA 2 1931.

In *Baker-Cammack Hosiery Mills* v. *Davis Co.*, 181 F.2d 550, 563, CA 4 1950, c.d. 340 U.S. 824, 1950, the court stated:

"When claims are rejected and withdrawn while an invention is pending in the Patent Office the patentee is estopped to contend that the allowed claims should be given the same breadth and interpretation as the abandoned claims."

The strict rule applied by the Supreme Court is justified in that the patentee always has the option of an appeal if he believes the examiner's rejection is in error. Moreover, since amendment or cancellation of the claims is strictly construed against the patentee, the courts generally scrutinize the file wrapper with great care before invoking the file wrapper estoppel doctrine. Thus if the cancelled claims are for a different combination than the allowed claims, then estoppel relates only to the cancelled combinations. *Payne Furnace & Supply Co.* v. *Williams-Wallace Co.*, 117 F.2d 823, CA 9 1941, c.d. 313 U.S. 572, 1941.

In addition, some courts have carefully studied the patent and the invention, and disregarded disclaimers which are a "trivial part of the claims." *United Chromium* v. *International Silver Co.*, 60 F.2d 913, 915, CA 2 1932; cert. denied 288 U.S. 600, 1933.

Also, at least one court has recognized that at the time the patent is being prosecuted, the patentees may not be aware of colorable imitations which utilize the heart of the invention.

"Distinctions are made and limitations are sometimes placed on language of claims by applicant's counsel which are somewhat inaccurate or made to meet a precise prior art citation, and without much thought as to their effect on other structures designed to avoid infringement. We should therefore be careful and avoid such construction of the claims as will defeat the real discovery which the inventor is contributing to the art." *Barrel Fitting & Seal Corp. of America* v. *American Flange & Mfg. Co.*, 74 F.2d 569, 571, CA 7 1935.

Effect of Arguments to the Patent Office

One point of difference that exists between the courts of various circuits relates to the effect of statements which may take the form of admissions or representations made to the Patent Office by the patentee in the course of obtaining the patent. Since the inventor presumably knows more about his invention than anyone else, statements that he has made concerning his invention should be helpful in interpreting the claims.

The Second Circuit stands alone in refusing to consider the arguments presented in the Patent Office in support of applicant's position. *A. G. Spalding & Bros.* v. *John Wanamaker*, 256 Fed. 530, CA 2 1919; *Catalin Corp. of America* v. *Catalazuli Mfg. Co.*, 79 F.2d 593, CA 2 1935. Judge Learned Hand in the *Catalin* case stated the Second Circuit's view in this often-quoted language.

"If the doctrine of the integration of a written instrument has any basis at all surely it should apply to such a document, for if a patent can be construed only by threading one's way through all the verbal ingenuities which casuistical solicitors develop to circumvent the objections of examiners, a labyrinth results from which there is no escape."

The remaining circuits disagree with the Second Circuit for reasons similar to those given in *Cincinnati Milling Mach. Co.* v. *Turchan*, 208 F.2d 222, 227, CA 6 1953.

"While conceding that extrinsic aid to construction may be accepted with caution, yet if within the difficult art of claim draftsmanship terms are employed in an effort to avoid prior art, which are susceptible of construction, there should be no more reluctance to search for precise meaning than in a private contract."

Most courts realize that an inventor's appraisal of his invention as he has explained it to the Patent Office is probably more valuable than his statements at trial and more reliable than the conflicting views of opposing experts.

[We] are bound to notice such statements and admissions as were made by applicant in the course of the proceedings [in the Patent Office] in order to obtain his patent as have (sic) any bearing upon the scope of invention, and on the question of what are the essential features of the patent asked for and granted. Definitions and admissions made by an applicant in order to avoid the state of the art as adduced by the office are always binding on him." *New York Asbestos Mfg. Co.* v. *Ambler Asbestos A. C. C. Co.*, 103 Fed. 316, 320, Cir. Ct. E.D. Pa. 1900, aff'd 112 Fed. 1022, CA 3 1901.

As noted previously, courts hold that if the claims read in the light of the specification and drawings are clear and unambiguous, then declarations to the Patent Office are merged in the issued patent, making remarks to the Patent Office irrelevant. However, a patentee is his lexicographer, and in the course of his arguments to the Patent Office, he may define his terms in a manner which differs from their normally accepted meaning. In short, while the claims on their face may seem to have one meaning when read in the light of the patentee's definition, they may have an entirely different meaning. Thus, proper claim interpretation requires that the claims be carefully read in the light of terms purposely inserted in the claims. *Universal Oil Products Co.* v. *Globe Oil & Refining Co.*, 322 U.S. 471, 1944.

Findings of non-infringement have frequently been based on the representations of the patentee to the Patent Office, which have been held to create material limitations. Thus, a patentee who argued before the Patent Office that his invention was in the use of a one-piece glove was estopped from asserting that his patent was infringed by a two-piece glove. *Sager* v. *Glove Corp.*, 118 F.2d 873, CA 7 1941. Where a patentee argued that his invention was in a prefabricated assembly, an assembly sold in parts to be assembled in the field was not an infringement. *Ric-Wil Co.* v. *E. B. Kaiser Co.*, 187 F.2d 1, CA 7 1951. And where a patentee argued that a particular type of electrode was inoperative in his combination, he could not later claim the inoperative electrode was an infringement even though it fell within the wording of his claims. *Westinghouse Elec. Corp.* v. *Hanovia Chem. & Mfg. Co.*, 179 F.2d 293, CA 3 1949.

The cases mentioned above seem to be clear examples of a patentee taking one position before the Patent Office and an entirely different position before the courts. On the other hand, where the patentee argued that an important feature of his invention was a "unitary motor and casing," the court did not consider this to be a material limitation since the court did not believe that claims were allowed because of this feature. In like manner, clearly erroneous statements to the Patent Office as to the scope of the claims will not estop the patentee or act as a waiver of his rights if the claims are quite clearly not so limited. *Eversharp Inc.* v. *Fisher Pen Co., Inc.*, 204 F. Supp. 649, DC NIll 1961.

Other Events in the Patent Office which May Result in Estoppel

File wrapper estoppel issues may arise as a result of acts in the Patent Office which do not directly concern amendments to the claims or arguments presented to the Patent Office. Thus, statments made in an interference proceeding can be used to create an estoppel. *Cardox Corp.* v. *Armstrong Coalbreak Co.*, 194 F.2d 376, CA 7 1952 c.d. 343 U.S. 979, 1952. The ruling of the Board of Patent Appeals may also place a narrow interpretation upon the claims of a patent. *Kuester* v. *Hoffman*, 152 F.2d 318, CA 7 1945. But no estoppel, as to the scope of a claim, is created by the refusal of a patentee to copy a claim for the purpose of an interference. *Lyon* v. *Boh*, 10 F.2d 30, CA 2 1926.

An applicant for a patent who abandons an application having broad claims in favor of a continuation-in-part application with narrower claims, may be estopped from broadening the narrower claims. *Aeration Processes* v. *Lange*, 196 F.2d 981, CA 8 1952, c.d. 344 U.S. 834, 1952. Similarly, statements or actions of applicant for a reissue patent may be used to create a case of file wrapper estoppel. *Baker-Cammack Hoisery Mills* v. *Davis Co., supra.*

The Effect of File Wrapper Estoppel

It may be seen that although the claims are supposed to define the metes and bounds of the invention, still they cannot be entirely trusted for this purpose. The file wrapper must always be studied to determine whether any admissions or definitions are found therein which narrow the scope or change the meaning of the claims.

The doctrine of file wrapper estoppel introduces factors of patent claim interpretation which are not to be found from an examination of the face of the document itself. However, it seems not to be a violation of the purpose of certainty in the patent statute since the effect is to restrict, and not to broaden, the scope of the claims.

Cross-references: *Claim Interpretation, Delay in Claiming, Estoppels, Laches, Prosecution.*

FOREIGN LICENSING AND ANTITRUST LAW
Sigmund Timberg

General Substantive and Jurisdictional Tests of United States Antitrust Liability

The basic problem in determining the antitrust validity of a patent licensing agreement is to draw a dividing line between legally permissible conditions and covenants, which fall properly within the scope of the patent grant and the reward of the patentee, and illegal conditions and covenants, which attempt to control and regulate industry and commerce in a manner condemned by the Sherman Act. In other words, are the parties to the agreement displaying a legitimate intent to enforce patent monopolies conferred by law or an unlawful intent to restrain or monopolize industry or trade in violation of the Sherman Act?

Simple as this test is to state, it is extraordinarily difficult to apply to specific situations. Only limited guidance can be obtained from the few court decisions applying the Act to license agreements (or assignments) involving non-U.S. patents. The first of these, *United States* v. *National Lead Co.*, 63 F. Supp. 513, DC SNY 1945, aff. 332 U.S. 319, 1947, was decided 55 years after the Sherman Act was adopted. These cases, the litigated residuum of an intensive program of Justice Department patent antitrust cases and Congressional investigations launched during the late 1930's and the 1940's, are so-called classic international cartel cases. They involved dominant U.S. firms in their respective industries (titanium pigments, electrical lamps and machinery, tungsten carbide, chemicals), which were charged with conspiring with similar dominant foreign firms to divide world markets among themselves.

The basic issue posed in these cases was:

Were the agreements of the parties limited to the proper exercise of their legal rights to share their technology and to exclude third parties from access thereto, or did they constitute part of a larger compact or program among competitors for the illicit allocation and division of manufacturing and sales territories? *United States* v. *Imperial Chemical Industries,* 100 F. Supp. 504, 592, DC SNY 1951; *United States* v. *General Electric Co.,* 82 F. Supp. 753, 847, DC NJ 1949 (Lamp case); *United States* v. *General Electric Co.,* 80 F. Supp. 989, 1009, DC SNY 1948 (Carboloy case).

This test of antitrust legality is not all-inclusive. It would not apply to illegal restrictive conditions and covenants in patent license agreements that might unreasonably restrain the import or export trade of the United States without actually making it impossible, or to firms not occupying a dominant market position but nevertheless illegally restraining trade.

The case of *United States* v. *Timken Roller Bearing Co.,* 83 F. Supp. 284, N. D. Ohio 1949, aff. 341 U.S. 593, 1951 dealt with trademark licenses but possesses important implication for international patent licenses. It suggests an alternative test of somewhat broader scope. In this case, the defendant attempted to justify an alleged territorial allocation in the tapered roller bearing field as being reasonably ancillary to (a) the licensing of its foreign trademarks and (b) the making available of unpatented know-how to its foreign licensees. By analogizing a patent licensing arrangement to the sale of technology and drawing upon the classic statement of the "ancillary restraint" doctrine to be found in *United States* v. *Addyston Pipe & Steel Co.,* 85 Fed. 271, CA 6 1898, aff. 175 U.S. 211, 1899, the legality of a patent license under the Sherman Act depends on an affirmative answer to the question:

Are the conditions and restrictions imposed by the licensor (the seller of the technology) restraints which are ancillary to the licensing arrangement, not going beyond what is reasonably necessary for the protection of the parties and not injurious to public?

In the typical international cartel case, patent licensing arrangements are only part of a total complex of business behavior, sometimes involving decades of corporate and industrial history, which must be reviewed by the courts before they can decide which "intent"—the illegal monopolistic or the legal right-enforcing—was predominant. The few litigated cases have involved situations where the "naked division of markets among . . . former competitors" was confirmed by evidence other than the patent licenses themselves. A monopolistic or trade-restraining "intent" is not a simple psychological concept because, under the U.S. antitrust law, persons are presumed to "intend" the natural consequences of their acts. This means that the parties to an agreement, who may in their own minds have "intended" only to disseminate technology among themselves, may be found by the courts to have "intended" to allocate territories and markets. Hence, it is not possible to say that specific restrictions in an international patent license are illegal, apart from the industry context in which they function.

To fill the vacuum left by the incomplete coverage of the international patent cartel cases, recourse must be had to precedents dealing with domestic licenses granted under U.S. patents. In this connection, it is well to bear in mind that the U.S. patent system, while monopoly-oriented, has some positive antitrust features of its own. Even if there were no Sherman Act, certain patent license restrictions would, under the policy of the patent laws, be regarded as invalid, because they are outside the scope of the patent monopoly. Thus, a tying provision conditioning the grant of a license upon the use of the licensor's unpatented materials is a violation not only of antitrust law, but also of the patent law. *Ethyl Gasoline Corp.* v. *United States,* 309 U.S. 436, 1940; *Mercoid Corporation* v. *Minne-*

apolis-Honeywell Regulator Co., 320 U.S. 680, 1944.

Before a restriction held to be invalid in a domestic patent license can be said to be invalid when employed in an international patent license agreement, three major determinations have to be made:

(a) The Sherman Act bans only "unreasonable" restraints of trade. Restraints which might be unreasonable in a domestic United States setting might have a reasonable business justification in the radically different economic circumstances of foreign trade. For example, a factor that serves to differentiate the international from the domestic economic scene is the extent to which governmental trade and currency restrictions make international trade impossible in the first instance. Thus, according to one court: "It is axiomatic that if, over a sufficiently long period, American enterprises, as a result of political or economic barriers, cannot export directly or indirectly from the United States to a particular foreign country at a profit, then any private action taken to secure or interfere solely with business in that area, whatever else it may do, does not restrain foreign commerce in that area in violation of the Sherman Act. For, the very hypothesis is that there is not and could not be any American foreign commerce in that area which could be restrained or monopolized." *United States* v. *Minnesota Mining & Mfg. Co.*, 92 F. Supp. 947, DC Mass 1950. However, another court has pointed out that "... neither the letter of the law nor its purpose 'distinguishes between strangling a commerce which has been born and preventing the birth of a commerce which does not exist.'" *United States* v. *General Dyestuff Corporation*, 57 F. Supp. 642, DC SNY 1944, quoting from *United States* v. *United Shoe Machinery Co.*, 247 U.S. 32, 1917; in accord, *United States* v. *The Bayer Company, Inc.*, 135 F. Supp. 65, DC SNY 1955.

(b) The antitrust laws are concerned only with practices which have a substantial adverse impact on the domestic and foreign commerce of the United States. In this connection, it is well to note that commerce may be adversely affected and illegally restrained even where the physical volume of commerce has increased, or prices have fallen, or the combination has operated beneficially in other respects. "Nor does it necessarily follow that the advance of the art, the rise in production and the decline of prices are attributable to the effects of the combination. *Post hoc, ergo propter hoc* is an invalid argument whether used by the plaintiff or the defendant. Anyone is free to speculate whether, in the absence of the arrangements, the stimulus of competition might not have produced far greater strides in these beneficial directions. The economic theory underlying the Sherman Act is that, in the long run, competition is a more effective prod to production and a more trustworthy regulator of prices than even an enlightened combination." *United States* v. *National Lead Co.*, 63 F. Supp. 513, DC SNY 1945, aff. 332 U.S. 319, 1947. Conversely, restrictions attached by a U.S. licensor to the license of his foreign patents may frequently have no, or only a remote, impact on the foreign or domestic commerce of the United States.

(c) Apart from competitive considerations, the United States courts are concerned with maintaining the integrity of the United States patent system, not that of foreign countries. What is permitted or prohibited to a licensee under a United States patent license is not necessarily a gauge of a licensee's rights under corresponding foreign patents, and may therefore be inapplicable to such license arrangements, which must be evaluated in terms of their effect on United States commerce.

Factors Determinative of U.S. Antitrust Validity

Whether particular patent licensing arrangements are in conformity with the Sherman Act requires the weighing of a number of individual factors. Thus, in the *National Lead* case, 63 F. Supp. 513, at 523-4, the court based its decision that the patent license agreements involved violated the Sherman Act on the following considerations:

"... The agreements applied to patents not yet issued and to inventions not yet imagined. They applied to commerce beyond the scope of any patents. They extended to a time beyond the duration of any then-existent patent.... They embraced acknowledgment of patent validity with respect to patents not yet issued, nor applied for, and concerning inventions not yet conceived.... They extended to countries, such as China, where no system of patent monopolies exists.... They regulated the disposition of the products after sale by the licensees...." (Case citations omitted.)

The rest of this chapter will be devoted to a discussion of the various factors that may enter into the determination of antitrust illegality.

Coverage of Patents; Licensing of "Know-how." At the outset, it is well to recognize the problems created by the fact that, in most current international agreements for the licensing of technology, patents play a minor role. The licensed patents usually do not cover the basic product or methods employed, but are limited to minor improvement features of largely unpatented assemblies, novel combinations of unpatentable features, or minor improvements in manufacturing techniques. Moreover, the most important feature of the licensing arrangement will usually be unpatented technology or "know-how." This may consist of trade secrets, where the licensor renounces patent protection because he wishes to avoid disclosing his invention. Or, more frequently, it will consist of so-called ancillary know-how—the formulae, designs, diagrams, blueprints, manuals and expert personal guidance that is needed to convert a product or process from one which is merely physically operative to one which is commercially successful.

The courts do not look kindly upon efforts to achieve patent protection against imports of a product whose basic patents have expired. See *United States* v. *National Lead Co.*, supra; *United States* v. *Timken Roller Bearing Co.*, supra. Where a firm with a dominant economic position in an industry vigorously asserts improvement patents against would-be entrants into the industry, this is apt to be regarded as an illicit effort on the part of the firm to "fence" itself into control of an industrial field, or to "block" competitors from entering the market. In lieu of relying on patents as an exclusionary device, therefore, the grantors of tech-

nology tend to rely on the rationale that the exclusionary restrictions are reasonably ancillary to their grant of "know-how."

This rationale has thus far been tested in only a few reported international cases, from which it is difficult to speculate in what situations it will be upheld. In two important recent cases, the ancillary restraint defense was rejected. *United States* v. *General Electric Co.* (Lamp case), 82 F. Supp. 753, DC NJ 1949; *United States* v. *Timken Roller Bearing Co.*, supra. In three other cases carrying less weight as precedents (in the first two, antitrust illegality was urged by a party defending a suit on an agreement originally designed for its benefit), the defense was approved. *Thoms* v. *Sutherland*, 52 F.2. 592, CA 3 1931; *Foundry Service, Inc.* v. *Beneflux Corp.*, 110 F. Supp. 857, DC SNY 1953, rev'd on other grounds, 206 F.2d 214, CA 2, 1953; *United States* v. *duPont*, 118 F. Supp. 41, DC Del 1953, aff. 351 U.S. 377, 1956.

One of the matters that the courts are likely to probe is whether the relevant "know-how" has a commercial value substantial enough to justify the ancillary restraint. Thus, the three above-cited cases sustaining territorial exclusions as ancillary to the license of "know-how" have all involved secret processes, as contrasted with the presumably lesser "know-how" incidental to the practice of a patent. There is also indication of a judicial reluctance to give greater protection to unpatented than to patented information. Agreements limiting the use of the licensed "know-how" to the licensee and preventing him from making it available to third parties appear to be a legitimate corollary of the licensor's property rights in the "know-how." (See consent judgment in *United States* v. *United Engineering & Foundry Co.*, 1952-1953 C.C.H. Trade Cases, paragraph 67, 378.) Beyond this, the guide lines as to the circumstances in which "know-how" will or will not justify an ancillary restraint can only be picked out by analogy to the patent and trademark license cases.

Contractual Commitments not to Export or Import. From the standpoint of abstract logic, a patent license containing the negative covenant not to sell for export from the United States does not seem far removed from a patent license to sell limited to the United States; since the latter is legal, it would seem logical to infer the legality of the former. Logic, however, is a deceptive guide in these matters. Despite earlier judicial indications that a licensee's agreement not to export a patented product from the United States is justified as a proper exercise of the licensor's United States patent monopoly (*Dorsey Revolving Harvester Rake Co.* v. *Bradley*, 7 Fed. Cas. 946, No. 4015, DC NNY 1874; *American Optical Co.* v. *New Jersey Optical Co.*, 58 F. Supp. 601, DC EKy 1945;*Brownell* v. *Ketcham Wire & Mfg. Co.*, 211 F.2d 121, CA 9 1954, the current weight of authority is that such a restriction does not fall within the patent grant and is illegal. See *United States* v. *National Lead Co.*, 332 U.S. 319, 1947; Report of the Attorney General's National Committee to Study the Antitrust Laws, p. 237 (1955).

Similarly, it would appear to be risky antitrustwise to include in a patent license agreement a covenant not to import into the United States. The owner of the U.S. patent rights should presumably rely on the exclusionary power inherent in the patent, and on the provisions of the U.S. customs legislation (see 19 U.S.C. 1337, 1337a), which enable the holders of United States patents to prevent the importation of U.S.-patented products or products made under processes patented in the United States.

The Duration of the License Agreement and the Licensing of Future Patents. Even where an international patent license was originally based on basic patents that dominated their respective fields, those patents will, as is clear from the *Timken* and *National Lead* cases, in time expire. Unpatented "know-how" is a transitory phenomenon, which is quickly outmoded and useful only when it is kept current. No licensor of technology can guarantee over the long range that the patent rights and "know-how" which he is currently licensing will continue to constitute a valid basis for the restrictions which he seeks to place on the licensee. Careful licensors, therefore, avoid too long a duration for their patent and know-how license agreements, especially for

the "know-how" communicated by them to competitors. Thus, there might be no objection offhand to a license covering the life of patents presently in being and, let us say, improvement patents thereto (or patents in a defined industrial area) issuing for a term of years thereafter. However, agreements which go further and endeavor to license future inventions or patents for too long a period, or over too broad an area, are subject to critical scrutiny by the courts and by antitrust administrators.

Cross-licensing; Grant-backs; Pooled or "Package" Licenses. The discussion in the preceding sections of this chapter presupposed a one-way patent license, i.e., a United States licensor puts his German patent rights and "know-how" at the disposal of a German licensee and exacts no reciprocal licensing commitment from the licensee. This situation probably rarely obtains for established manufacturing enterprises. If the German licensee is technologically proficient, the United States licensor has an obvious commercial motive for desiring reciprocal access to its patents and "know-how." Even if the German technology is relatively retarded at the time the agreement is entered into, the United States licensor will not wish to run the risk that its license will be the basis for an improved technology on the part of the German firm that will enable it to outstrip its licensor in technical performance and standing in world markets. Thus, significant international patent licensing arrangements will typically involve reciprocal cross-licensing, or a two-way patent interchange.

Whether such a two-way patent interchange involves a violation of the antitrust laws depends, in the final analysis, on the answer to the same fundamental question as governed the legality of the one-way patent grant: Have the parties merely exercised the rights inherent in their patents, or have they used the interchanged patents as the foundation of a structure of illegal competitive restraint and commercial regulation? Before one can answer that large and decisive question, one must take into account the circumstances of the licensor and licensee, the scope of the cross-licensing commitments, and the altered light in which the law views patent pools or aggregates (as contrasted with individual patents).

The United States patent statute endorses the unrestricted assignability of patents, see 35 U.S.C. Sec. 261. Moreover, the courts are cognizant of the interlocking nature of modern inventions. They have long known that the "seamless web" of modern technology renders patent pooling, particularly of competing and improvement patents, desirable both from the legal basis of avoiding patent interferences and litigation and from the functional standpoint of supplying the public with improved products, see *Standard Oil Co. (Ind.) v. United States*, 283 U.S. 163, 1931. They have shown themselves sympathetic to the business convenience and justification for voluntary "package" patent licensing, see *Automatic Radio Mfg. Co., Inc. v. Hazeltine Research, Inc.*, 339 U.S. 827, 1950. Hence, in the normal situation, a United States licensor who requires his foreign licensee to grant back to him the United States patent rights in improvements is not, by that act alone, trespassing beyond the legitimate bounds of the patent monopoly or violating any antitrust canon. *Transparent-Wrap Machinery Co. v. Stokes & Smith Co.*, 329 U.S. 637 1947.

At the same time, under any grant-back arrangement, the U.S. licensor is aggregating under his control not only those patents which originated with him, but those which originated with his German, French, British and other licensees. In this respect, his situation is comparable to that where United States competitors "pool" their respective patents, and legal consequences become relevant other than those which obtain where individual patents are involved. Thus, in the domestic license cases, the courts have taken a critical attitude towards compulsory patent "package" licensing, i.e., requiring a licensee involuntarily to take a license under a group of patents rather than under the patents he specifically desires. They reason that it is as illegitimate to tie one patent monopoly to another, as it is to tie a patent license to the use of unpatented materials. *Ethyl Gasoline Corp. v. United States*, 309 U.S. 436, 1940; *United States v. Paramount Pictures, Inc.*, 334 U.S. 131,

1948 and *United States v. Loew's, Inc.*, 371 U.S. 38, 1962, both of which latter cases deal with the "block booking" of copyrighted films. "Each monopoly must stand on its own footing. Mandatory package licensing is no more than the exercise of the power created by a particular patent upon the acceptance of another patent but that is too much. The protection, or monopoly, which is given to the first patent stops where the monopoly of the second begins." *The American Securit Co. v. Shatterproof Glass Corp.*, 268 F.2d 769, CA 3 1959, cert. denied, 361 U.S. 902, 1959. Similarly, while the acquisition of U.S. patent rights from foreign concerns is legal in ordinary circumstances, it becomes a violation of the antitrust laws to make such acquisitions as part of a combination to exclude Japanese imports of the patented machine, *United States v. Singer Manufacturing Co.*, 374 U.S. 174, 1963.

Where a single U.S. patent is involved, there is legal precedent allowing the licensor of that patent to impose restrictions on the licensee as to the quantities of the patented product which the licensee may produce, the prices he may charge, the territories in which he may sell the patented product, and the industrial fields in which he may exploit the licensed patents. See *United States v. General Electric Co.*, 272 U.S. 476, 1926; *General Talking Pictures Corp. v. Western Electric Co.*, 305 U.S. 124, 1937; *Keeler v. Standard Folding Bedding Co.*, 157 U.S. 659, 1895; 35 U.S. Code Sec. 261, 1952. However, once the U.S. patent rights of others are granted back to the licensor, such restrictions, which might be permissible in the case of the single one-way license, become vulnerable from an antitrust standpoint. Thus, grant-backs were a major determinant of illegality in the international cartel *Lamp* case, supra, and the *Carboloy* case, supra. Cross-licensing may create an irrefutable inference that the licensor and his licensees intended to effectuate an illegal division of territories, markets or fields of industrial operation, or other trade restraints. In such situations, a licensor or group of licensors dominating their respective industrial fields must weigh carefully the antitrust hazards involved if they do not confine themselves to collecting a pecuniary reward for the licensed patent, or if they decline to make patent licenses available to third parties at reasonable royalties.

Another antitrust hazard in the reciprocal licensing situation is that a dominant licensor runs the risk of being charged with "funnelling" the emergent technology in the industry back to itself, and thereby engaging in an illegal "monopolization" in violation of Section 2 of the Sherman Act. See *United States* v. *Aluminum Co. of America*, 91 F. Supp. 333 DC SNY 1950; *United States* v. *General Electric Co.*, supra. If the licensor's patent position was not founded on basic patents covering the product in question, and was thus weak to start out with, his vulnerability to such a charge seems clear. If, on the other hand, his patent position was originally premised on strong basic patents, two somewhat contradictory inferences, both of which have been given expression in the decided cases, are possible:

(a) The United States licensor, by the very act of attempting to buttress his legal patent monopoly, was trying to perpetuate it beyond the duration of his own patents, and was thereby illegally "maintaining" a monopoly, *United States* v. *General Electric Co.* (Carboloy case) and *United States* v. *Imperial Chemical Industries, Ltd.;* also in accord on the domestic front, *United States* v. *Aluminum Co. of America*, 148 F.2d 416, CA 2 1945.

(b) The United States licensor's monopoly was legally fully justified by the patents already held by him, and his prior acquisition of a secret process from a foreign source was an irrelevance that did not affect the general legality of his position. *United States* v. *duPont*, supra.

Since the broad patent coverage assumed in the latter rationale is both rare and bound to deteriorate as basic patents expire, antitrust commentators have recommended that a United States enterprise with dominant status in its field obtain from its foreign confreres only non-exclusive cross-licenses on the latter's United States patents. This makes it legally possible for the foreign manufacturers to import into the United States and to compete for the United States market. But, if the evidence demon-strates that the arrangements between the United States and the foreign manufacturers are intended to, and do, eventuate in the actual exclusion of the foreign manufacturer from the United States market, the foreign manufacturer's abstract legal freedom to import into the United States will not, by itself, save the arrangement from legal condemnation. Similarly, counsels of caution suggest to a dominant United States firm that the technology acquired by it from abroad be licensed or sublicensed without discrimination to other United States manufacturers, lest its patent licensing arrangements with foreign concerns be interpreted as constituting an agreement with those concerns to restrain United States trade to the detriment of domestic competition. See *United States* v. *National Lead Co.*, *United States* v. *Timken Roller Bearing Co.*, *United States* v. *Imperial Chemical Industries, Ltd.*, all above.

Patent Acquisitions and Interference Proceedings. The recent case of *United States* v. *Singer Manufacturing Co.*, 374 U.S. 174, 1963, indicates that patent acquisitions and patent interference settlements may in certain circumstances lead to a finding of antitrust violation. In this case, defendant Singer, the sole U.S. manufacturer of household zig-zag sewing machines, had acquired a conflicting patent held by a Swiss concern —a patent under which Singer prior to the time of acquisition held a non-exclusive license. Singer had also agreed with the Swiss and Italian holders of conflicting patents not to contest, or to try to narrow, each other's claims in patent interference proceedings in any country in the world. There was other evidence of the substantial concern of Singer and its Swiss and Italian co-conspirators with the threat to their market position involved in the importation into the United States of alleged infringing Japanese machines, including the institution of infringement actions and of a proceeding before the Tariff Commission to bar Japanese machines from the country. These factors led the Supreme Court to hold Singer guilty of conspiring with its Swiss and Italian competitors to monopolize the importation, sale and distribution of such machines.

It is indicative of the delicate line dividing antitrust legality from illegality that the Supreme Court's decision involved the acceptance of the very detailed factual findings made by the District Court, see 205 F. Supp. 394, DC SNY 1962, but a reversal of that court's conclusion that no conspiracy existed. Moreover, the Supreme Court's decision states that it is not illegal to acquire a patent for the purpose of excluding competitors or for the owner of such a lawfully acquired patent to exclude infringers. Nor, according to the Court, was it illegal for Singer to acquire full title in the Swiss-owned patent in order better to enforce it on its own account, even though the patent dominated an industry in which Singer occupied the dominant position. The underlying significance of this case is as a cogent reminder that antitrust conspiracy may be implied from the acts and statements of the parties. Cf. *United States* v. *Bausch & Lomb Optical Co.*, 321 U.S. 707, 1944; *United States* v. *Parke, Davis & Co.*, 362 U.S. 29, 1960.

Licensee's Admission of Patent Validity. One of the features invalidating the patent licenses involved in the *National Lead* case was their acknowledgment of patent validity with respect to as yet nonexistent patents and unconceived inventions. This constitutes an exception to the generally prevailing doctrine that, in normal circumstances, a licensee is estopped from challenging the validity of the licensed patents. *United States* v. *Harvey Steel Co.*, 196 U.S. 319, 1905; *Automatic Radio Mfg. Co., Inc.* v. *Hazeltine Research, Inc.*, 339 U.S. 827, 1950.

However, it is not the only such exception. Once there is a basis for inferring that an agreement may violate the antitrust laws, a licensee's covenant not to attack the validity of a patent may lend added weight to the inference. The courts, in the case of domestic price-fixing agreements, have upheld the licensee's right to question the validity of the licensed United States patent since, but for the patent, such an agreement would violate the antitrust laws. *Sola Electric Co.* v. *Jefferson Electric Co.*, 317 U.S. 173, 1942; *Edw. Katzinger Co.* v. *Chicago Metallic Mfg. Co.*, 329 U.S. 394,

1947; *MacGregor* v. *Westinghouse Electric & Mfg. Co.*, 329 U.S. 402, 1947. The probabilities are that a similar result would obtain where the claimed immunity of a United States patent from challenge is based on an international agreement that is questionable from an antitrust standpoint.

Restrictions Not Within the Patent Grant. The District Court in the *National Lead* case noted, as a ground of antitrust objection to the license agreements before it, the fact that they "regulated the disposition of the products after sale by the licensees." This is clearly beyond the scope of the patent monopoly; the accepted rule for 90 years has been that the first authorized sale of a patented article exhausts the patent monopoly. *Adams* v. *Burke,* 17 Wall. 453, 1873; *United States* v. *Univis Lens Co.*, 316 U.S. 241, 1942.

Ordinarily, foreign patentees are primarily concerned with safeguarding from competitive invasion their home territory and other territories marked out by them as their exclusive domain, and do not attempt to control the distribution of the patented product *within the United States* after it leaves the U.S. licensee. However, the *National Lead* case and some Justice Department international cartel complaints serve as a reminder that international patent license agreements may contain restrictions on U.S. manufacture and marketing, such as tying clauses and resale price maintenance, that are not within the patent grant. See *Motion Picture Patents Co.* v. *Universal Film Mfg. Co.*, 243 U.S. 502, 1917; *Carbice Corp. of America* v. *American Patents Development Corp.*, 283 U.S. 27, 1931; *Leitch Mfg. Co.* v. *Barber Co.*, 302 U.S. 458, 1938; *United States* v. *General Electric Co.*, 272 U.S. 476, 489, 1926; *Boston Store of Chicago* v. *American Graphophone Co.*, 246 U.S. 8, 1918. Such restrictions would presumably be unlawful.

Passing to the reverse side of the coin, U.S. parties to international patent license agreements appear to have had the same primary motivation as their foreign counterparts—the desire to protect the United States and other "reserved" territories from competitive intrusion. Hence, the litigated cases generally do not deal with the validity of restrictions imposed on foreign licensees' manufacturing or marketing practices *within the countries* to which their license extends, but cf. *United States* v. *Timken Roller Bearing Co.*, above (price fixing). However, to the extent that such restrictions have a substantially adverse effect on competing U.S. manufacturers and exporters and would not be recognized in the United States as falling within the proper scope of the patent grant, they would appear to raise significant antitrust problems.

Foreign Antitrust Developments

Until the enactment of the German Law against Restraints of Competition in 1957 and the entering into effect, shortly thereafter, of the Rome Treaty establishing the European Economic Community, no jurisdiction outside of the United States and Canada had general antitrust legislation bearing on patent license agreements. Hence, licensors and licensees of non-U.S. patents had no occasion to be concerned with antitrust requirements of a general nature. However, the patent laws of foreign countries contained some specific antitrust provisions.

Compulsory Working and Compulsory Use Laws. The most pervasive of these statutory provisions is the almost universal one providing for the revocation or compulsory licensing of patents not commercially exploited after a certain period of time. This period of time varies; thus, in the case of Brazil it is two years, in the case of Sweden, three years, and in the case of Iceland, five years.

There has been an effort, on the international plane, to standardize the time periods involved, and to mitigate the original severity of the national legislation in this area. That effort, which has consistently had the support of the United States, is embodied in Article 5A of the Paris Union for the Protection of Industrial Property (League of Nations Treaty Series, Volume CXCIII, No. 4459, p. 31, 1938). Article 5A provides that patents may be revoked only if the granting of compulsory licenses does not suffice to prevent unjustified nonuse of the patent, and further provides for a period

of three years from the date of issuance of the patent, or four years from the date of filing the patent application, whichever period expires last, during which no one may demand a compulsory license thereunder. As a result largely of Article 5A, many countries now provide for compulsory licensing of the patent as the only sanction for its nonuse (e.g., Guatemala, Iceland, India, Mexico, Norway, Paraguay, Philippines, Portugal, Sweden, Union of South Africa, Uruguay), and many resort to the revocation or cancellation of patents only in situations where compulsory licensing has failed to achieve the desired purpose or where special conditions apply (e.g., Australia, Austria, Canada, Denmark, Egypt, Finland, Germany, Pakistan, New Zealand, Spain, Switzerland, and United Kingdom).

The 1949 Patent Act of the United Kingdom and the recent patent statutes of some of the British Commonwealth countries contain the most comprehensive provisions of this general type. See *United Kingdom:* An Act to consolidate certain enactments relating to patents 12, 13, 14, Geo. 6, c. 87, 16 December 1949; *Australia:* An Act relating to Patents of Inventions, No. 42 of 1952, Commonwealth Government Printer's Pamphlet F. 4235; *India:* The Indian Patents and Designs Amendment Act, No. 32 of 1950, Gazette of India (Extraordinary), No. 3, New Delhi, 20 April 1950, pp. 29-33; *Union of South Africa:* Act to Consolidate and Amend the Law Relating to Patents, 10 June 1952, Union Gazette Extraordinary, 13 June 1952, pp. 37-45. These statutes require not only the working of patents, but their working to the fullest extent that is reasonably practicable. They also apply sanctions where the demand for an article is not being met on reasonable terms or is being met to a substantial extent by imports, or where there are other situations prejudicial to the development of commercial or industrial activities or the supplying of export markets.

In appraising the antitrust impact of "compulsory working" and "compulsory use" statutes, two reservations are appropriate. In the first place, the indications are that these provisions are rarely applied in practice, and their *in terrorem* effect is, of course, difficult to appraise. See Neumeyer, "Compulsory Licensing of Patents Under Some Non-American Systems," Study No. 19, U.S. Senate Judiciary Subcommittee on Patents, Trademarks and Copyrights, 1959. Second, these provisions are subject to an anti-competitive, as well as a pro-competitive, interpretation. While they are available weapons against the suppression of patents for monopolistic purposes and are designed to assure the public of the benefits of technological advance, they had their origin in a desire to encourage the growth of domestic industries and can be employed as restrictive mechanisms for excluding competitive and cheaper imports of a patented commodity. See Penrose, "The Economics of the International Patent System," 1951. Nevertheless, these provisions have to be taken into account by the United States holders of foreign patents as statutory stimuli to the licensing of local producers and to the local exploitation of such patents.

"Tie-in" Prohibitions. The other antitrust provision specifically embodied in foreign patent legislation appears to be restricted to the United Kingdom and some of the British Commonwealth countries. This is the "tie-in" prohibition against requiring a patent licensee to use, in conjunction with the licensed process or combination or product, only devices or materials supplied by the patentee. See United Kingdom Patents Act, 1949, Sec. 57; Union of South Africa Patents Law, 1952, Sec. 51.

National Antitrust Legislation of General Application. In Canada, the Combines Investigation Act, which has its roots in legislature antedating by one year the enactment of the Sherman Act in 1890 and prohibits combinations which restrain trade or commerce, is applicable to patent license agreements. The statute contains a specific provision that, in any case where the exclusive rights conferred by patents have been used so as to (a) unduly limit the facilities for transporting, producing, supplying, or dealing with an article or commodity which may be the subject of trade or commerce, (b) unduly restrain or injure trade or commerce in such article or commodity, (c) unduly prevent or limit the production of such article or commodity or unreasonably en-

hance its price, or (d) unduly prevent or lessen competition in such article or commodity, the court may issue preventive orders. Such orders may declare any agreement relating to the use of the patent void in whole or in part, restrain the carrying out of the provisions of such agreements, or direct the granting of licenses under the patents involved to such persons and under such terms and conditions as the court may deem proper.

Since World War II, many foreign countries have adopted antitrust legislation of general application which is susceptible of application to patent license agreements. Such legislation represents a radical innovation in the legal traditions of the enacting countries. As regards enforcement, these statutes are to a large extent based on the premise that illegal or undesirable business restrictions will be eliminated by government surveillance and by non-publicized negotiations between the government and the enterprises involved, rather than by the public adjudicatory proceedings that characterize U.S. antitrust enforcement. For these and other reasons, there is very little information available as to the impact of this legislation on patent license agreements and any conclusions in this area are necessarily tentative and speculative.

In the United Kingdom, the Monopolies and Restrictive Practices (Inquiry and Control) Acts of 1948 and 1953, as amended, authorize the Monopolies Commission to investigate and report on restrictive practice matters referred to them by the Board of Trade. The Commissioner's report may, and in most cases must, be laid before each House of Parliament. If the House of Commons by resolution declares that conditions in an industry operate or may be expected to operate against the public interest, an application may be made to the Comptroller-General of Patents under Section 40 of the Patents Act of 1949. If it appears to the Comptroller-General that such conditions in a patent license restrict the use of the invention by licensees or the right of the patentee to grant other licenses under the patent, or if the patentee refuses to grant licenses on reasonable terms, the Comptroller-General may cancel or modify such conditions or order the patent to be endorsed with the words "licenses of right." The effect of such an endorsement is that any person is thereafter entitled to a license on such terms as, failing agreement with the patentee, are determined by the Comptroller-General.

Much of the ground originally covered by the U. K. Monopolies and Restrictive Practices Acts of 1948 and 1953 is now subject to the terms of the Restrictive Trade Practices Act of 1956, which applies to any agreement, between two or more persons carrying on manufacturing, sales or processing activities within the United Kingdom, containing restrictions as to prices to be charged or quoted; terms or conditions of manufacture or sale; quality of goods to be produced, supplied or acquired; types of manufacturing processes to be applied to goods, or the quality or kind of goods to which such processes are to be applied; or the persons to or from whom or the places in which goods are to be bought or sold or manufacturing processes applied. The 1956 Act does not apply to agreements relating only to exports, or to patent licenses or assignments which contain none of the above-enumerated restrictions except in respect of an invention to which the patent relates or of articles made by the use of that invention. The agreements to which the 1956 Act applies are to be registered with a Registrar of Restrictive Trade Agreements, and judicially investigated by a Restrictive Practices Court, which may declare whether or not such restrictions are contrary to the public interest. If any such restriction is declared contrary to the public interest, it is void.

In the Netherlands, the Economic Competition Act of 1958 requires any "regulation of competition," except those exempted by general regulation or special dispensation, to be registered with the Ministry of Economic Affairs. The Minister may issue general orders declaring certain classes and types of restrictive clauses to be invalid, or individual orders invalidating a specific regulation of competition, on the basis that they have a harmful effect on the public interest. Patent license agreements may violate this statute, if they embody practices or clauses extending beyond the exclusive rights of the patentee and not construed as an essential corollary to those rights.

Denmark, Norway, Sweden and Finland possess antitrust legislation that is based on similar broad principles, although their statutory and organizational details vary considerably. In these four Scandinavian countries, enterprises are required to supply to the government information concerning restrictive business practices; a register of such information is maintained; and antitrust enforcement is based to a large extent on the principle that publicity and governmental investigation will, in most cases, provide an effective mechanism for curbing harmful restrictive business practices.

Thus, in Finland, the Law on Restriction of Competition of January 18, 1957, governs agreements which require the contraction or restriction of entrepreneurial activity, which demand the observance of certain prices or practices, which restrict or are intended to restrict the contracting parties' freedom of competition in some other manner; it also governs other restrictions of competition. In addition, it applies to enterprises which have "such a dominating position in some field of entrepreneurial activity that competition must be deemed to be lacking in this sphere or to be essentially restricted." In the case of patents, the law applies only to those competitive restraints which are associated with a patent, but do not belong essentially to the patent grant.

The Swedish Law of 1953 to Counteract Certain Acts in Restraint of Competition, as amended in 1956, forbids resale price agreements; while the Freedom of Commerce Board is authorized to grant exemptions from this prohibition, it has done so in only a few cases, mainly in the books and records industry.

In Finland, under Section 12 of the Law on Restriction of Competition, the Cartel Office can forbid an enterprise from either fixing minimum resale prices or from suggesting prices unless it is expressly stated that the suggested price may be undercut when the Cartel Office considers that such a restraint on competition will be injurious to the consumer.

In Belgium, the recently enacted law of

27 May 1960, which is directed against the abuse of economic power, may apply either to patent owners or patent licensees, if such abuse can be shown. An abuse of economic power exists when one or several persons possessing economic power have harmed the public interest by practices which distort or restrain the normal play of competition or which impair the economic freedom of producers, distributors or consumers, or the development of production or exchange. Economic power is defined as the power which such person or persons have, through industrial, commercial, agricultural or financial activities, to exercise a dominant influence on the supply of goods or capital or on the price and quality of a specific commodity or service.

In Ireland, the Restrictive Trade Practices Acts of 1953 and 1959 provide for inquiries and reports by the Fair Trade Commission, on the basis of which the Commission may make orders which, when confirmed by act of the Parliament, may prohibit restrictive and unfair practices in relation to the supply and distribution of the goods concerned.

In Japan, the Antimonopoly Law, which is patterned after the U.S. model, forbids the unreasonable restraint of competition or unreasonable restriction of business activities on the part of entrepreneurs, where they involve an abuse of the patent right. Article 23 of the Antimonopoly Law provides that this does not apply to acts recognized to be within the execution of rights under the Patent Law. Restrictive provisions limiting the licensee's field of operation, output and geographical area are regarded as within the patentee's power. Likewise, a patentee has the right to designate sales prices for his manufacturing licensees.

Under the Japanese law, the patentee does not, as a rule, have the right to designate the resale price of a patented article. A patentee or licensee desiring to do so must apply to the Fair Trade Commission under Article 24-2 of the Anti-Monopoly Law. The Commission has thus far allowed such resale price restrictions in the case of nine commodities. Also tying clauses are considered illegal, unless the use of the "tied-in" material is indispensable to ensure the technically unobjectionable exploitation of the patent.

The most comprehensive program for applying antitrust standards to patent licenses (outside the United States) has taken place under antitrust laws of Germany and, to a lesser extent, in France and under the antitrust provisions of the European Common Market Treaty. Accordingly, these antitrust measures will be treated separately.

Section 20 of the German Law on Restraints of Competition. With the enactment of general antitrust legislation by Germany and the incorporation of general antitrust provisions in the Rome Treaty establishing the European Common Market, it would appear that the antitrust authorities, both of the Common Market and of its member countries, will, for the first time, have to draw a general boundary line between the proper monopoly functions of the patent and the pro-competitive application of the antitrust laws—a line which the courts of the United States have been drawing for decades—and that patent licensing arrangements will have to conform to that line. It is too early to predict where that line will ultimately be drawn, but the best starting point is Section 20 of the 1957 German Law on Restraints of Competition, which represents the first comprehensive statutory effort to define the scope of the patent monopoly. The following paragraphs will give the broad outlines of this section, together with some incidental comment on the way in which it has been applied and on the comparative United States approach.

The first paragraph of Section 20 commences with a broad statement of principle that most U.S. practitioners dealing with patent license agreements would find familiar and unobjectionable:

"Agreements concerning the acquisition or the use of patents, registered designs (Gebrauchsmuster), or protected brands (Sortenschutzrechte) are invalid if they impose upon the acquirer or licensee any restrictions in his business conduct which go beyond the contents of the said privileges (Schutzrechte)."

Section 20(1) then specifies that restrictions pertaining to the type, scope, quantity, territory, or period of exercise of the patent shall not be deemed to be beyond the contents of the privileges, i.e., the proper scope of the patent monopoly. This duplicates restrictions which under the U.S. patent and antitrust laws, an *individual* patentee may impose on an *individual* licensee. However, such restrictions would raise antitrust questions in the United States where patent aggregates or industry-wide arrangements are involved.

Paragraph (2) of Section 20 authorizes a patentee to obligate his licensee with respect to the price to be charged for the article produced under the patent. This is the prevailing law in the United States where a single patentee licenses his patent to a single licensee. However, Sherman Act problems arise where multiple licensors, multiple licensees, cross-licensing or patent pools are concerned. See *United States* v. *Line Material*, 333 U.S. 287, 1948; *United States* v. *Paramount Pictures, Inc.*, 334 U.S. 131, 1948.

Whether the restrictions permitted under Section 20 are limited to the simple, uncomplicated one-way patent license or are applicable to more complex licensing situations is still unknown.

A licensor may, consistently with Section 20(2), bind his licensee not to challenge the validity of the licensed patent. This is comparable to the United States law, except that in this country such a challenge is permissible where the agreement provides for price-fixing.

Likewise, Section 20(2) permits a licensor to require, as a condition of granting the license, the grant-back of licenses under the patents of the licensee. However, such grant-backs are restricted to "improvements or related inventions if these correspond to reciprocal obligations of the patent owner or licensor." This limitation corresponds to what industry-dominant licensors in the United States might be advised to do as a matter of legal prudence; it probably goes beyond what would be necessary in most U.S. patent licenses.

The power that the German law affords a patentee with respect to patent grant-backs, and challenge of patent validity, and two lesser items that need not be separately discussed, are limited by a statutory proviso that such restrictions cannot remain in force beyond the expiration of the licensed patent privilege. In other words, none of these restrictions can survive the life of the patent, which means that that power of a patentee to impose restrictions on his licensee is limited in point of time.

By way of further complicating an already not too clear picture, Paragraph (3) of Section 20 provides that:

"Upon application, the Cartel Authority may approve an agreement of the nature specified in paragraph (1) if the freedom of economic action of the acquirer or licensee or any other enterprises is not unfairly restricted, and if competition in the market is not substantially restrained through the restrictions involved."

A considerable number of patent license agreements have been submitted for approval under this section. In many cases, restrictive provisions have been either omitted or made less restrictive. Also, in many cases approval of the agreement has been conditioned upon compliance with certain limitations. In some cases, where licensors had made large investments in research involving the use of unpatented materials, tying arrangements requiring the purchase of such unpatented materials have been approved. Some agreements on the part of the licensee not to manufacture other devices competitive with the article for which he holds the license have been sustained. However, an agreement whereby a foreign licensee agreed not to buy unpatented goods from the licensor's competitors has been disapproved.

The concluding paragraph (4) of Section 20 provides that both the general prohibition against restraints of competition in Section 1 of the Act and the various exceptions provided for in Sections 2 to 14, inclusive, "remain unaffected."

In summary, paragraphs (1) and (2) of Section 20 embody probably the first statutory effort to delimit the proper scope of the patent monopoly. And paragraphs (3) and (4) impose on the German Cartel Authority the difficult problem of reconciling the respective areas of antitrust prohibition and patent permission.

It should be noted that Section 21 of the German Act provides that the provisions of Section 20 shall apply, as appropriate, to "agreements concerning the transfer or exploitation of legally unprotected inventions, manufacturing processes, technical designs, and other technological achievements, as well as legally unprotected achievements toward plant cultivation in the field of plant breeding, if such achievements constitute business secrets." What practical effect this provision will have on the licensing and dissemination of know-how is still uncertain.

New French and Italian Antitrust Legislation. No other national statute has tried to sketch the interaction between antitrust and patent policy in as much detail as the German. The official draft of the proposed Italian antitrust law purports to exempt patent license agreements from its scope, but the exemption does not extend to reciprocal licensing contracts of an exclusive nature, or to contracts containing clauses which in themselves have an anti-competitive effect. See Section 3 of Italian "Freedom of Competition" Bill, Parliamentary Paper of the Chamber of Deputies No. 2076, Feb. 24, 1960. Such an exemption would place a host of patent license agreements in antitrust jeopardy, since many customary conditions in patent licenses may be considered anti-competitive.

In France, the validity of patent license restrictions under the prevailing antitrust law, Decree No. 53-704, August 9, 1953, as amended, is not clear. Article 59bis of the French law prohibits every concerted action, convention, combine, express or implied, or trade coalition which has the object or may have the effect of interfering with full competition by hindering the reduction of production costs or selling prices or by encouraging the artificial increase of prices. Article 37 forbids unjustified refusals to sell or to render services, discriminatory sales terms or prices not justified by cost factors, tie-in clauses, and minimum resale price maintenance. It is possible to obtain an administrative exemption from the minimum resale price prohibition, especially in the case of patented or guaranteed articles, but the authorities have been sparing in granting such exemptions. A leading commentator has expressed the view that a patent license imposing an obligation on licensees to buy raw materials from certain sources would exceed the limits of the patent monopoly and would violate Article 59bis of this Decree. Plaisant, "Les Ententes Industrielles sous forme de Sociétés ou d'Associations," paragraph 134, 1955. The Commission Technique des Ententes has decided, in the *Magnesium Cartel* case, that a license to a government-owned firm manufacturing airplane engines used by the French Air Force, which limited the licensee's production of magnesium parts to supplying components for use in its own motors and apparatus, was an abuse of power violating the provisions of Article 59bis of the 1953 Decree and not entitled to an exemption under Article 59ter of the Decree. "Ententes dans l'industrie du magnesium." Annex 3. J. O. No. 1 (Jan. 14, 1960), 10.

Articles 85 and 86 of the Common Market Treaty. The most important foreign antitrust restrictions to which international patent license agreements will in the future have to conform are those contained in Articles 85 and 86 of the Rome Treaty establishing the European Common Market. Article 85(1) and (2) prohibits and declares void—

"...all agreements between enterprises, all decisions of associations of enterprises and all concerted practices which are apt to affect the commerce between Member States and which have as their object or effect the prevention, restriction or adulteration of competition within the Common Market, and especially those which consist in:

(a) fixing directly or indirectly the purchase or sales prices or other conditions of transacting business;

(b) limiting or controlling the production, distribution, technical development or investment;

(c) dividing the markets or sources of supply;

(d) applying unequal conditions for equivalent goods or services vis-à-vis other contracting parties, thereby inflicting upon them a competitive disadvantage;

(e) conditioning the conclusion of contracts upon the acceptance by the other contracting parties of additional goods or services, which, neither by their nature nor by commercial usage, have any connection with the object of these contracts."

Section 3 of Article 85 provides, however, for the exemption of agreements, decisions or concerted practices

"...which contribute to the improvement of the production or distribution of commodities or to the promotion of technological or economic progress, while reserving an appropriate share of the resulting profit to the consumers and without:

(a) imposing on the enterprises involved any restrictions not indispensable for the attainment of these objectives, or

(b) enabling such enterprises to eliminate competition in respect of a substantial portion of the commodities involved."

Article 86 of the Rome Treaty prohibits "the abusive exploitation of a dominant position in the Common Market or a substantial part thereof by one or several enterprises to the extent that it is capable of affecting the commerce between Member States." The same abusive practices are listed in connection with Article 86 as were listed in connection with Article 85(1), with the exception of clause (c).

Putting to one side the problems raised by Article 86 of the Rome Treaty, the validity of a patent license agreement under the Rome Treaty is dependent on the answer to two fundamental questions: Is the agreement prohibited by Article 85(1)? If prohibited by Article 85(1), can it be exempted under the provisions of Article 85(3)?

The Council of the European Economic Community has adopted three comprehensive regulations setting down the requirements for the notification of agreements to the Commission, on the basis of which "negative clearances" may be granted under Article 85(1) and "declarations of exemptions" issued under Article 85(3) (Regulation 17, Official Journal of the European Communities 13/62, p. 204, March 13, 1962; Regulation 27, Official Journal, 35/62, p. 1118, May 3, 1962; Regulation 153, Official Journal, p. 2918, December 24, 1962), but has been slow to make substantive decisions. At one time, the Commission advanced certain proposals for "collective exceptions" covering classes of agreements under Article 85(3), but it subsequently abandoned them, because the comments received, according to the Com-

mission, "have shown that the object of establishing greater certainty as to law cannot be attained at present." European Economic Community Commission Press Release of December 29, 1962. Currently, the Commission is asking the Council for authority to issue exemptions under Article 85(3) for categories of agreements, but it is doubtful whether, if such authority were granted, it would in the near future be exercised with respect to patent license agreements. For the time being, therefore, the extent to which patent licenses will be given exemptions under Article 85(3) will probably be decided on a case-by-case basis.

However, with respect to the prohibitions contained in Article 85(1), the Commission has declared (Official Journal p. 2929, Dec. 24, 1962) that the following provisions appearing in patent license contracts are not subject to the prohibitions of Article 85(1) and hence need not be registered:

"A. Obligations imposed on the licensee which have as their object:

1. Limitation to certain means of exploiting the invention which are contemplated by the law on patents (manufacture, use, distribution);

2. Limitation
   a) of the manufacture of the patented product,
   b) of the application of the patented process, to technically defined areas of application;

3. Limitation of the number of products to be manufactured or of the number of times the right is exercised;

4. Limitation on the exercise of the right:
   a) in time (a license of a shorter duration than the patent),
   b) in space (a regional license for a part of the territory for which the patent was granted, a license limited to exploitation in a given place or to a specified factory),
   c) personal limitations (limitation of the licensee's power to alienate, such as a prohibition against assigning the license or granting sub-licenses);

B. The obligation to affix to the product a notice of the patent;

C. Quality standards or obligations as to supplies of certain products imposed on the licensee to the extent that they are indispensable to assure technically unobjectionable exploitation of the patent;

D. Undertakings concerning the communication of experience acquired in the course of the exploitation of the invention, or concerning the grant of licenses on inventions of improvements or new applications; this however is valid as regards undertakings assumed by the licensee only if these are not exclusive and if the licensor has assumed analogous undertakings;

E. Undertakings of the licensor:
  I. To authorize no other person to exploit the invention;
  II. To refrain from exploiting the invention himself."

Several comments can be made concerning the clearance given by the Commission to the above provisions. In the first place, the clearance does not apply to agreements involving patent pools, reciprocal licenses or multiple parallel licenses. Second, the term of the provisions cannot last beyond the duration of the validity of the licensed patent. Third, the Commission's interpretation, although highly persuasive, can be rejected by the courts and in particular by the High Court of the European Economic Community, which has paramount jurisdiction.

It is instructive to know the rationale underlying the clearance by the Commission of the above-quoted provisions. Those listed under A above are considered not prohibited by Article 85(1), because they are covered by the patent and "imply solely the partial maintenance of the prohibitory rights inherent in the exclusive right of the patentee" in his invention; it is specifically stated that this enumeration of the rights granted by a patent is not exhaustive. The patent marking provision (B above) is cleared, because it has neither the purpose nor the effect of restraining competition but corresponds to the legitimate interest of the patentee. Provision C above, which would appear to give limited authorization to tie-in clauses, comes into play only when quality standards cannot be established by objective criteria but are needed to maintain quality standards for the patented product. In the language of the Commission, it "could not restrain that competition which needs to be protected."

Patent license provisions relating to the cross-licensing of patents and communication of know-how (D above) are deemed permissible, because they can have no re-

strictive effect on competition "when the licensee retains the opportunity of communicating acquired experience or granting licenses to third parties and is enabled to participate in future gains of the licensors in matters of experience and inventions." The Commission pointedly states that it is not passing any legal judgment with respect to possible restrictions on interested parties. The final undertaking held not to be forbidden by Article 85(1), E above, which in effect authorizes the granting of exclusive licenses, is justified on the ground that such exclusive undertakings are not presently capable of affecting commerce among the member states and that it is disputable that they have as their purpose or effect a restriction of competition.

Because of differing national concepts of what is within the proper scope of the patent privilege and what are actionable restrictions of competition, the great number of agreements filed with the secretariat of the European Economic Community, the necessity of conferring with national authorities and the multi-national composition of the Commission, it is estimated that it will be some time before authoritative guidelines are laid down by the Commission. One area that is very much in dispute is whether a patent license agreement may contain prohibitions against exports of the licensed commodity to other countries of the Common Market. The Commission takes the unofficial position in its Practical Guide (see CCH Common Market Report, para. 2717, 1962) that such a prohibition is not within the patent right or the coverage of Article 85(1), while the majority of the German legal writers feel that it does lie within the patent grant. See Deringer, 12 Wirtschaft und Wettbewerb 865, 869, fn. 48 (1962). Thus far the most reliable indicator of the way in which the Common Market will treat patent license agreements is to be found in the decisions of the Federal Cartel Office in Germany, although many other factors have to be taken into account.

National antitrust legislation will continue to apply to the purely "intrastate" commerce of the member states of the European Common Market. It is fair to say, however, that patent license agreements involving France, Western Germany, Belgium, The Netherlands, Italy and Luxembourg (and such other countries as may in time join the Common Market) will be increasingly governed by the provisions of Articles 85 and 86 of the Rome Treaty and the interpretations thereof by the Commission and the courts.

Cross-references: *Antitrust Law . . . , European Patent Convention, Foreign Patents, Licenses, Licenses—Package, Unfair Competition.*

FOREIGN PATENTS

S. Delvalle Goldsmith

The importance of owning patents abroad is illustrated by statistics supplied by the Central Bank at Bonn and reported by the New York Times of May 11, 1964. They show that U.S. owners received from West Germany, for patents and licenses, a total of $51 million for the year 1963.

The report does not show how many employees were added to German payrolls or how much the wealth of the nation was increased by operation under the patent rights. If the royalty rate were 5 to 10 per cent of the gross output, the increased output might be of the order of $500 to $1000 million a year. In addition there would be the benefit to the public in better foods, fibers, medicinal or other products, more economical processes of manufacture or improved machines.

Rationale of Foreign Patents

The subject of "foreign patents," i.e., patents in countries other than our own, involves two complementary sets of questions:

(1) For the inventor: Why should there be any need for foreign patents? Why shouldn't the single patent obtained in his own country protect him in every country where his invention is used?

(2) For the foreign country: Why should an additional patent be granted at all? Hasn't the purpose of patenting been exhausted by the disclosure of the invention to the Patent Office of one country and the granting of a patent there? What advantage is gained by the so-called "underdeveloped" or "developing" countries when they grant patents for foreign inventions?

First, a patent enjoins those within one country only not to infringe upon the rights of the patentee. In general the State cannot control those outside its border and order them not to use the patented invention.

Disclosure of the invention is not the only *quid pro quo* for the patent grant. An important, if not the most important, purpose of the patent grant is to promote economic progress within the jurisdiction, an objective secured not merely by awarding the inventor a "certificate of merit" for disclosure of his invention but by giving him a monopoly of practical value, the use of which will benefit the economy of the country as well as himself.

On this basis, the grant of patents for foreign inventions makes sense. Without such patents there would be little incentive for the inventor (by himself or through licensees) to exploit the invention elsewhere than in his home country. With the protection of foreign patents, however, exploitation of the invention in other countries becomes commercially feasible and desirable, and sufficiently attractive to risk the necessary capital. And receipt by the inventor of the monetary reward stimulates additional invention.

In "undeveloped" countries aiming at "development" and industrialization, the stage of domestic manufacture is nearly always preceded by a period of importation, resulting in the creation of a demand for the goods and establishment of a market. This, too, is "exploitation" and is promoted by patent grants. Moreover, as soon as the "undeveloped" country is ready for any particular type of industry, establishment of it will be aided by existence of capital-attracting patents in the field. The existence of a patent monopoly is generally an *attraction* rather than a deterrent to the business man thinking of setting up an industry. By investing in the manufacture of a *patented* product he has the promise of protection against competitors who have not made the same investment that he has. Moreover, when his activity is based on a successful foreign invention, he usually has the additional assurance of technical assistance, know-how, and possibly advertising and trademark benefits, on the basis of the patentee's manufacturing and sales experience in his home country. If there are conditions to be corrected, it is not necessary to throw out the baby with the bath-water; the advantages of a patent system can be retained and, at the same time, local manufacture can be secured as soon as there is anyone (the patentee or others) who is ready, willing, and able to undertake it.

The term "industrial property," while not commonly used in the United States to mean patents and trademarks, definitely has such meaning in most other countries. Thus, the publication of the International (Paris) Convention is "Propriété Industrielle," now also available in an English version entitled "Industrial Property." The semi-official organization which concerns itself with patent and trademark matters in the international field is "Association Internationale pour la Protection de la Propriété Industrielle" (A.I.P.P.I.).

Selection of Countries for Filing

There are over 130 countries and territories which grant patents, the number varying almost continuously as new laws, country mergers and divisions come into being. Some of these patent-granting countries are of little importance patentwise, and the cost of filing and maintaining patents is often inversely proportional to the size and importance of the country.

While the nature of the patent systems of the various countries and the protection obtainable under the patent laws will naturally have a bearing on the question of "where to file," the answer is usually determined by the following more general factors.

(1) Importance of the invention.
(2) Nature of the invention.
(3) Chances of using the patents, offensively or defensively, in the countries being considered.
(4) Money available for a foreign patenting program.

An invention of minor importance may call for no foreign filing at all or for filing in only a few countries. However, extensive patenting even of a technologically minor invention may be indicated if it is one of a series involved in a business venture or licensing arrangement or if it is the only patentable invention available on which to base such an arrangement.

The nature of the invention will often point to patenting or non-patenting in particular countries. Thus, heavy machinery might be patented in Germany and Sweden, papermaking in the Scandinavian countries, and pharmaceuticals for the treatment of tropical diseases in countries where the diseases are prevalent. An invention that can be practiced easily may require wider protection than a complicated one, and in important consumer countries as well as manufacturing countries. By taking the latter precaution, even if all the manufacturing countries are not covered or if the patents in some of them lapse or are invalidated, export to the chief consumer countries might still be stopped by the patents in those countries.

Potential Use

Where there are existing business or licensing arrangements, it may be required by such arrangements to take out foreign patents in the respective countries. Even where no agreements are in existence, the presence of substantial activity in the field may result in future licensing arrangements based on foreign patents—if there are any such patents to license at the time such arrangements eventuate.

Where markets are supplied by exportation, it may still be advisable to have foreign patents for defensive use, i.e., to ensure that adverse patents will not be obtained that might prevent the sale of the products or to provide a basis for cross-licensing with the holder of an adverse patent. Moreover, for currency control or other reasons, it may not continue to be possible to supply the foreign market by exportation. In the absence of patents it may be difficult to get substantial manufacture profitably started, and the market may be lost to small domestic producers.

Costs

In addition to filing and attorneys' representation fees there will often be substantial translation charges that add to the cost of foreign filing. On the other hand, as the description of the invention has already been prepared for the corresponding application in the home country, this preparation cost is not repeated. Moreover the prosecution of the foreign applications can be (and, indeed, should be) coordinated with the prosecution in the United States Patent Office, which again minimizes repetitive efforts and costs. Even though the form of the foreign applications and the requirements for patentability will be different in the various countries, the technology of the invention and, generally, its relation to the prior art remain the same. The patent attorney who handles the prosecution of the U.S. application preferably should also cooperate in foreign prosecution.

In addition to the fees for filing and issuing patents, a majority of the foreign countries have yearly taxes or annuities which must be paid in order to maintain patents in force; this will be discussed later.

Where expenses must be kept low, at least initially, the provisions of some foreign laws make it possible to delay filing without adverse effect. Thus a program can often be arranged in which one group of foreign applications can be filed initially, another group postponed for nine or ten months, and another group delayed until after the U.S. patent has issued.

Licensing or Filing by a Subsidiary

Should foreign patents be taken out in the name of a foreign subsidiary in order to save or transfer costs? While this may seem attractive, there is danger in having the title to important assets of the parent company held by a foreign subsidiary, even if the subsidiary is wholly owned or controlled.

In the event of nationalization, emergency, or war, patents owned by a local subsidiary would be more susceptible to government control or seizure. Moreover, if the subsidiary is a corporation of a country which is not a party to an international arrangement such as the Paris Convention, the advantages provided by such arrangement will not be obtained for the foreign-owned patent.

Instead of ownership, an exclusive license to the foreign subsidiary will usually accomplish the desired results with less hazard. Transfer and tax problems may also arise where the results of research by a U.S. company are transferred outright to a foreign company.

Under the present U.S. laws, foreign patent applications may not be filed for an invention made in the United States until a license has been granted by the U.S. Patent Office. Such a license is in effect automatically after six months from the filing of the U.S. application unless, of course, the application has been placed under a Secrecy Order in the meantime. Where a Secrecy Order has been issued in the United States application or the subject matter is otherwise classified, special modification or special permission must be obtained before filing abroad. Also, inventions in certain categories require a State Department License, and applications for the Soviet Bloc countries require a Commerce Department License. Obviously, all requirements in these special fields should be carefully taken into account before any foreign filing, especially as the regulations and country and subject matter designations change from time to time.

Incidentally, if the U.S. inventor wishes to file first in a foreign country for any reason and there is no corresponding U.S. application, the foreign filing requires a permit from the U.S. Patent Office if the invention was made in the United States.

Features of Foreign Patent Laws Similar to U.S. Patent Law

(1) The general concept of *invention* is the same throughout the world, viz., an improvement in the art which is something more than the natural expedient of a workman. The degree of "inventiveness" to support a patent varies from country to country (and generally is not defined in the

laws) but in all countries some amount of this essential ingredient must be present.

(2) The need for an *adequate description* of the invention is universal. The description prepared for the U.S. Patent Office will generally be proper for the foreign Patent Offices, except for special requirements in some fields, particularly chemistry and medicine. In some countries a much less detailed description than required in the United States will be satisfactory or even preferable, but, here again, the U.S. description will nearly always constitute at least a proper basis for foreign filing.

(3 The use of *claims* following the description in order to point out the particular features of the invention and scope of the patent is almost universal although there are some countries which either do not use claims at all or do not regard them as defining the scope of the patent.

(4) Filing and issuance *fees* are as universal as death and taxes. In some instances they are complemented by "experts fees" for examination, fees for excess claims or description, printing charges, amendment and other prosecution fees.

(5) Regardless of what examination is made by the Patent Office prior to issuance of the patent, whether sketchy and formal in nature or a complete novelty examination, the final determination of *validity* and scope of the granted patent is left to the courts or, in some instances, to a special section of the Patent Office.

(6) The patent disclosure is generally *available to the public* at least after grant. There are a few exceptions, principally Chile, where the description is not available until one year from grant, and Colombia where, at least theoretically, it is never available. In some countries all or part of the description of a patent is made available to the public even before grant. (See *Advance Information*)

(7) A patent must cover a *single invention*. However the definition of "unity of invention" varies from country to country and, where no examination is made by the Patent Office, patents are often granted including a number of inventions, with some doubt as to what independent protection, if any, has been secured for the various features. In most foreign countries, as in the United States, an issued patent cannot be attacked on the ground that it covers more than one invention, but there are some exceptions to this rule.

(8) On expiration of the patent, the invention covered thereby may be used by anyone. In some foreign countries, however, the original term of the *patent may be extended* in certain circumstances, as stated later.

(9) A patent everywhere grants a *monopoly* to the patentee which he may exercise himself or through licensees. In many countries, where currency controls apply to royalty remittance by a licensee, approval for licenses must be obtained in advance. Protection is afforded by the courts (or in some cases by the patent offices) against infringers of the patented invention, and damages can be obtained for losses resulting from infringement. Damages generally run from the date of grant or publication of the patent but some countries have provisions whereby damages may commence during pendency of the application if the infringer is suitably warned and advised of the contents of the pending application.

(10) The foreign laws, like the United States law, usually provide for the *marking* of patented articles with the patent number or date, with advantages, particularly as regards damages in an infringement action, accruing from such marking. In a few countries marking is required, or essential, before the patent can be enforced. (See *Marking*)

(11) *Government use* of a patented invention is provided for by practically all patent laws, with varying provisions as to procedure, payment, and the proper purposes of such use. Also patent laws generally have special provisions for *defense inventions*, maintaining secrecy and controlling the foreign filing of inventions which may be important to the defense of the country.

(12) Almost all countries prohibit the patenting of inventions of an *immoral nature*, and usually also *ideas*, *financial schemes*, *printed material*, and *principles of science*.

(13) Many foreign countries have special

laws to protect *designs*, similar to U.S. design patents. Some countries also provide special protection for minor inventions, by *"petty patents"* or the like; these will be discussed in a later section.

(14) Finally, nearly every important Patent Office in the world, especially where a substantial examination is carried out, is overloaded, beset by *backlogs*, and unable to meet the burden of searching through the ever-increasing quantity of "prior art." This has led to various proposals for "common patents," or at least "common searching," which will be dealt with subsequently. The immense workloads in the patent offices result in long delays in granting patents, especially where a novelty examination is involved.

Features of Foreign Patent Laws Different from U.S. Patent Law

Priority of Inventorship. Whereas the U.S. law provides that a patent must be granted to the first inventor, the foreign laws (except for Canada and the Philippines) provide for the grant of a patent to the *inventor who first files his patent application*. This theory is deviated from abroad only where there has been fraud (i.e., stealing of the invention), no effort being made ordinarily to determine which of two independent inventors first made the invention. Rather, the first to win the race to the Patent Office with a suitable disclosure gets the patent. While this may seem unfair, and presumably is in some instances, it has the advantage of saving the time and expense of complex proceedings, such as a U.S. interference, to determine who is the "first" of independent inventors. Abroad, it is the filing date or "priority date," if claimed under the International Convention, which makes an instant and inexpensive determination of priority and thus stimulates early disclosure of inventions to the Patent Office.

As indicated above, Canada and the Philippines have procedures for determining the priority of inventions. The Philippines procedure is based on U.S. interference practice. The Canadian procedure is quite different and, even though the parties may be the same as in a corresponding U.S. interference, may result in a different award of priority.

Somewhat related to the above is the fact that, in the United States, only the inventor may apply for a patent (subject to exceptions in very special circumstances); in nearly all of the foreign countries, the inventor's assignee—even a company assignee—may file the patent application in his or its own name. This provides considerable simplification and reduction of expense as compared with filing in the name of the inventor (or, in some cases, a number of joint inventors) and assigning the application later.

About the only foreign countries which require the inventor to appear as an initial applicant are the Philippines, Iraq and Jordan.

It might also be mentioned at this point that, in Great Britain and some of the Dominions and Colonies, an application can still be filed as a "communication from abroad" by a person who has not made the invention but has merely "introduced it into the Realm." Convention priority (discussed below) may not be claimed for such communicated inventions.

Publication and Prior Use. Whereas a U.S. patent is not barred by publication or public use of the invention up to one year before the filing date, patents in most foreign countries may be *invalidated by publication or public use* of the invention *even a day* before the filing (or priority) date. This makes it vital, in most instances where foreign patents are desired, to withhold publication or use of the invention at least until the U.S. application is filed and, preferably, until the foreign applications are filed. In certain countries and under certain conditions (see the discussion below of the International Convention) it is possible for foreign applications to obtain priority from the U.S. filing date. But even this priority will not help if the invention has been published or used *before* the U.S. filing date, and in many countries there is no way of getting back even to the U.S. filing date.

In certain countries, on the other hand, valid patents may be obtained after publication or use of the invention or even after issuance of patents thereon (see "Confirmation or Revalidation Patents" and statutory bars, infra), but it is safest to avoid disclosure of the invention until the desired foreign applications are filed.

In some countries a distinction is made between *"domestic"* publication or use and publication or use *"anywhere."* In other cases a distinction is made between "printed" publication and unprinted publication such as the laying open of a patent to public inspection. Table 1 below summarizes the situation as to the geographic nature of "statutory bars" in the principal foreign countries.

TABLE 1. STATUTORY BARS OF PRIOR PUBLICATION AND USE.

Country	Publication	Use
Argentina	Anywhere	Anywhere
Australia	Domestic	Domestic
Austria	Anywhere	Domestic
Belgium	Anywhere	Domestic
Brazil	Domestic; also anywhere if more than 1 year before the filing (or possibly Convention) date	Domestic
Canada	Anywhere if more than 2 years before filing date	Domestic if more than 2 years before filing date
Chile	Anywhere	Anywhere
Colombia	Anywhere	Anywhere
Denmark	Anywhere	Domestic
France	Anywhere	Anywhere
W. Germany	Anywhere, but publication of invention itself is not a bar if less than 6 months before filing date	Domestic but use of the invention itself is not a bar if less than 6 months before filing date
Great Britain	Domestic	Domestic
India	Domestic	Domestic

TABLE 1. STATUTORY BARS OF PRIOR PUBLICATION AND USE (*Continued*).

Country	Publication	Use
Israel	Domestic	Domestic
Italy	Anywhere	Anywhere
Japan	Anywhere	Domestic
Mexico	Anywhere, but not a bar if less than 6 months before Convention date	Anywhere, but not a bar if less than 6 months before Convention date
Netherlands	Anywhere	Anywhere
New Zealand	Domestic	Domestic
Norway	Anywhere	Domestic
Philippines	Anywhere if more than 2 years before filing date	Domestic if more than 2 years before filing date
South Africa	Anywhere	Domestic
Spain	Anywhere	Anywhere
Sweden	Anywhere	Anywhere
Switzerland	Anywhere	Domestic
U.S.S.R.	Anywhere	Anywhere
Venezuela	Domestic	Domestic, but commercial use or advertising anywhere may be a bar

Further, in connection with statutory bars, it goes without saying that, in any country, the existence of an earlier patent for the same invention is a bar. In some countries, such an earlier patent is a bar for everything it *discloses;* in other countries, it is a bar only for what it *claims.*

In connection with Table 56.1 and the others to follow, it will be understood that tables of this type cannot go into the finer points of the subject under consideration, which in any event would require a review of the facts of a particular situation. The purpose of these tables is to give a comparative general picture of the foreign requirements in question.

The countries included in the tables offer, it is thought, a representative sampling of the principal European, Latin American, and Near and Far Eastern countries. Iron

Curtain countries have been omitted except the U.S.S.R. itself which has been included as an item of possible general interest.

Patentability of Chemical, Food and Pharmaceutical Substances. In the United States new compounds are patentable per se and broad product protection can be obtained. If a new chemical compound having utility is invented, that compound can be protected by a U.S. patent, no matter how the compound was made. This is also true in some foreign countries such as Great Britain, Belgium, Australia, South Africa and France. However in most foreign countries, for one reason or another, new chemical compounds, and particularly new pharmaceutical compounds, cannot be protected per se but only when prepared by a particular process.

Great Britain and France have changed in the direction of the U.S. practice. They now give broad protection for new and useful chemical and pharmaceutical compounds.

Although there is a strong psychological reservation against granting even a limited patent monopoly in a field concerned with human nutrition or medication, adequate safeguards can be obtained for food and medicine patents without giving up the recognized advantages of patents generally.

On the other hand, in some of the commercially less important countries (Turkey, India and Iraq), there have been recent changes in the direction of refusing to grant any patent protection at all for pharmaceutical inventions. Italy has been in the latter class for about ten years and is the only important country where pharmaceutical inventions of other nations can be fully "pirated."

Table 2 summarizes the situation regarding independent product protection (i.e., protection independent of the process of preparation) for chemical compounds and human medicines. In some countries, veterinary medicines are treated in the same way as human medicines; in other countries, differently.

Many countries that do not grant independent *product* protection in these fields, often grant *process* protection of such a broad nature that it approaches product

TABLE 2. PATENTABILITY OF CHEMICAL AND PHARMACEUTICAL PRODUCTS.

Country	Independent Product Claims Obtainable for New Non-pharmaceutical Chemical Compounds	Independent Product Claims Obtainable for New Pharmaceutical Substances
Argentina	Yes	No
Australia	Yes	Yes
Austria	No	No
Belgium	Yes	Yes
Brazil	No (possibly yes if process revealed by product)	No (possibly yes if process revealed by product)
Canada	Yes	Yes (if obtained by non-chemical process)
Chile	Yes	No
Colombia	Yes	Yes
Denmark	No	No
France	Yes	Yes (in a special pharmaceutical patent—"BSM")
W. Germany	No	No
Great Britain	Yes	Yes (if not a mere mixture)
India	No	No
Israel	Yes	Yes
Italy	No	No
Japan	No	No
Mexico	No	No (possibly yes if not a chemical compound)
Netherlands	No	No
New Zealand	Yes	Yes (if not a mere mixture)
Norway	No	No
Philippines	Yes	Yes
South Africa	Yes	Yes
Spain	No	No
Sweden	No	No
Switzerland	No	No
U.S.S.R.	No	No (yes by Author's Certificate, if obtained by non-chemical process)
Venezuela	No	No

protection. Thus in Germany a so-called "analogy process" claim can be obtained where a classic known type of chemical process is used to make the product, i.e., the basis for patentability is provided by the new product with unexpected properties obtained by application of the classic process to a different starting material. Moreover, a large number of different "analogy processes" can be covered in one patent. In Holland a process claim can be obtained which merely calls for bringing the new compound into a therapeutically useful form. Also, in Germany and many other countries, a process claim covers the products of the process. Thus it is not correct to say that most foreign countries deny patent protection for a new chemical or pharmaceutical product; rather they provide such protection in a different way from that under U.S. patent law.

Working Requirements. Theoretically, under U.S. law a patented invention does not have to be "worked" or put into practice in order to continue to enjoy patent protection. This advantage establishes the certainty of the patent right and prevents its extinguishment if, for example, the patentee is financially unable to work the invention or if working is not at the time economically feasible. On the other hand, most foreign laws require working on the theory that the purpose of a patent is not only to give the inventor a monopoly, but also to bring the economic benefits of the invention to the community.

At one time, many foreign laws provided that a patent could be revoked if it were not worked within a few years after grant and at intervals thereafter. This situation has been ameliorated over the years without, however, changing of the basic philosophy of "working." If a patent now is not worked by the patentee or a licensee within a fixed term (usually three years) from grant, a third party ready and able to work the invention may apply for and obtain a compulsory license under the patent, subject to payment of royalty.

In the many years that such compulsory licensing laws have been in force, few cases have arisen thereunder, no doubt for the reason that, when a situation that might involve compulsory licensing comes up, it is usually to the advantage of both the patentee and prospective licensee to negotiate a voluntary, rather than a compulsory, license. The patentee knows that, if he is not reasonable, he may be forced to grant a compulsory license. The licensee knows that, if he can negotiate a voluntary rather than a compulsory license, he will usually be able to secure valuable know-how and other cooperation from the patentee. Due to the paucity of cases, the casual observer may be tempted to regard compulsory licensing as a "dead-letter." Actually it acts behind the scenes to secure exploitation of inventions when economically feasible.

A practice that has arisen over the years in connection with foreign working requirements is that of so-called nominal working. This is a term not mentioned or recognized by the foreign patent laws but which has come to designate the unofficial practice of a patentee, who is unable to or not desirous of working his invention, to advertise or circulate an *offer to license* it. This may have had some value when revocation of the patent was the penalty for non-working, i.e., by permitting, as an argument in defense of non-working, the showing that efforts were made to license and work the invention but that no one was interested (assuming there were no takers to the offer). However such offers are not considered to be of any value when the penalty for non-working is merely compulsory licensing. And, of course, such offers are dangerous where it is *not* desired to grant licenses under the patent.

Unofficial "nominal working," as outlined above, should not be confused with the special *official* steps that may be taken in a few countries in lieu of working, e.g., extensions of time for working and endorsement of a patent for license. These are of substantial value and may be essential to keep a patent in force where actual working is not taking place.

Some interesting sidelights to the working requirement can be mentioned. In Italy this requirement may be met (once only during the life of a patent) by suitably exhibiting the invention at a recognized exhibition. Also, the United States has treaty arrangements with West Germany, Switzerland and Greece excepting U.S.-owned patents of those countries from normal working requirements.

It is also interesting to note that, although U.S. patent law says nothing about working or compulsory licensing, the U.S. Courts have in fact ordered compulsory licensing where they have found abuse of the patent monopoly, particularly in antitrust situations.

The only important countries where the penalty for non-working may still be revocation are Argentina, Brazil and Italy (and also Spain for Importation Patents only). Although these countries (except Argentina) are members of the International Convention which prescribes compulsory licensing rather than revocation as the primary penalty for non-working, domestic enabling laws have not yet been enacted, so that the situation is unclear and revocation is still possible.

Fees after Issuance of Patent. A characteristic of the U.S. patent system (now probably to be changed in an effort to bring in more revenue) has been the absence of additional charges or fees after issuance of a patent. Thus, a U.S. patent remains effective for 17 years without payment of further fees. On the other hand, yearly taxes or annuities must be paid in most foreign countries in order to keep a patent in force. These taxes are generally graduated, being small in the early years of a patent's life and increasing thereafter. In many countries the highest tax may not run to more than $20 to $30 a year but in some, particularly Germany and the U.S.S.R., the taxes may run finally to hundreds of dollars a year. To the government fees, service charges involved in making the payments must be added.

Table 56.3 below gives a general indication of the amount of taxes (Government fees) payable over the life of a patent if the patent is to be maintained in force for its full term. These are usually paid in yearly installments. Some saving, varying from country to country, can ordinarily be achieved by paying all or a number of years' taxes at one time; where the value of a patent is not certain, it may be advis-

TABLE 3. PATENT MAINTENANCE TAXES FOR
LIFE OF PATENT (DOLLARS, APPROXIMATE).

Argentina	2	Italy	325
Australia	300	Japan	200
Austria	1500	Mexico	100
Belgium	600	Netherlands	950
Brazil	25	New Zealand	100
Canada	None	Norway	600
Chile	None	Philippines	450
Colombia	None	South Africa	110
Denmark	650	Spain	80
France	300	Sweden	1100
W. Germany	2600	Switzerland	650
		(if examined)	1500
Great Britain	450	U.S.S.R.	4000
India	250	Venezuela	200
Israel	40		

able, however, to pay the taxes year by year, with the privilege of stopping payment at any time.

An advantage of yearly taxes, apart from the obvious one of bringing more money into the Treasury, is said to be that the patent records are cleared of "deadwood," as less-important patents are allowed to lapse by non-payment of taxes. This aids the manufacturer who must review all patents in force to see what problems of infringement are involved. On the other hand, yearly taxes place upon the patentee the burden of positive action and recurrent expense to keep his patent alive, with possible lapse due to inadvertent non-payment of taxes, or an incorrect decision as to the value of a patent, or just plain lack of money. In most countries there are provisions for late payment of taxes (with fines) and, in some, provisions for reinstatement of a lapsed patent after inadvertent non-payment of taxes, subject to any third party rights that have been acquired since the nonpayment.

Novelty Examination. Even though a U.S. patent may be invalidated by the Courts, it has considerable prima facie strength or validity due to the extensive formal and novelty examination made in the Patent Office. This is true also of patents granted in Germany, Holland, Japan and some other European countries. However in some examinations, as in Great Britain and Australia, the novelty search is not very extensive and is usually confined to earlier patents of the same country. In other countries, such as France, Belgium, and Italy, a patent is granted without any novelty search at all, so that the mere existence of a patent cannot be said to afford any indication that a novel and patentable invention is present. Thus, A could obtain a patent on one day and B could obtain an identical patent the next day.

This is emphasized by the indicia "S.G.D.G." appearing on every French patent, standing for *Sans Garantie du Gouvernement"* (without Government guarantee). It must be remembered however that, even in a strict examination country such as Germany, a patent is issued without government guarantee and may subsequently be held invalid.

Most countries make at least a *formal examination.* Even though an extensive novelty examination may not be made, earlier patents of the same country are sometimes cited, as well as any prior use or publication that may be known to the Examiners or to the experts who are retained to examine the application. Even in a country generally considered a "non-examination" country, objections arise and prior art citations are made in some instances.

Recent developments in the area of examination, in an effort to cope with the difficulties of an increasing mass of prior art and decreasing manpower, have been proposals for a *common examination* or at least a common novelty search, and for a system of *"delayed examination."*

The first of these proposals would make use of an organization such as the "Institut International des Brevets" at The Hague which is already making searches for individuals and some patent offices.

The second proposal, *delayed examination,* is embodied in the recent revision of the Dutch law and also in the recently published draft of a European patent law. Under the delayed examination system, a provisional patent is granted after a more or less formal examination, and this patent

will lapse if a full examination is not requested within a term of years. If the patent does not turn out to be important, the trouble and expense of an examination will thus be avoided.

Oppositions. When a U.S. patent application is allowed (after examination) and the final fee is paid, the patent issues as a matter of course. In many of the foreign countries, however, the application is published after allowance, and third parties may lodge opposition to the grant of the patent thereon. This provides in effect a supplementary examination on an inter partes basis and affords an interested third party the opportunity to limit or eliminate an improper patent by a proceeding before the Patent Office rather than by a Court action later. On the other hand, the opposition practice places another complicated and expensive obstacle in the path of an inventor trying to obtain a patent. In some countries, particularly Germany, the patent departments of the larger companies maintain a close watch on all allowed applications and tend to file oppositions against applications of even remote interest. Thus an allowed application may be faced with multiple oppositions which must be successfully overcome in order to obtain the grant of a patent.

In some of the smaller countries, a patent application is published for opposition even before allowance; any oppositions filed are used to assist the Examiner in his consideration of the application.

Table 4 shows the practice as regards opposition in the principal foreign countries and, where such proceeding is authorized, the stage at which it is permitted.

Form of Claims. It has previously been said that foreign countries almost universally require claims setting forth the scope of protection desired, in addition to a description of the invention. However the form of claims best suited to protect the invention is quite different in the various countries.

In Belgium, Italy and many of the smaller countries, the form of claims is not important. In case of litigation, the Court will look to the specification and the prior art in order to determine the scope of protec-

TABLE 4. PATENT OPPOSITION PROVISIONS.

Argentina	None
Australia	After allowance
Belgium	None
Brazil	After publication of claim during prosecution; also after grant
Canada	None
Chile	After filing
Colombia	After allowance
Denmark	After allowance
France	None
W. Germany	After allowance
Great Britain	After allowance; also belated after grant
India	After allowance
Israel	After allowance
Italy	None
Japan	After allowance
Mexico	None
Netherlands	After allowance
New Zealand	After allowance; also "belated" after grant
Norway	After allowance
Philippines	None
South Africa	After allowance
Spain	None for patents; for Utility Models, after allowance
Sweden	After allowance
Switzerland	None generally; after allowance in special fields where applications are examined
U.S.S.R.	None
Venezuela	After filing

tion afforded by the patent. This is also true in France where there are no claims but only a "résumé" which lists the features described rather than defining the scope of the invention.

In Great Britain, the Commonwealth countries, Canada and most of the European countries, on the other hand, claims are most important in defining the scope of the patent. In contrast with the U.S. system of a series of independent claims, each defining an invention as a complete and operative series of elements or steps, the foreign claims may generally be in a more "narrative" or functional form, setting out the *essential idea* of the invention.

Moreover, in the so-called German-form claims widely used in Europe, the claims are in the form of a *single, independent "main claim"* with the other claims appendant thereto. The main claim is usually divided into two parts: (a) a *preamble* constituting a statement of type or acknowledgment of the features which are common to the invention and the prior art and (b) a *"characterizing clause,"* usually commenced by the words "characterized by the fact that," reciting the novel and patentable features of the invention. In Great Britain and some other countries, the effect provided by the acknowledging preamble of this type of claim is secured by an "acknowledgment of prior art" in the opening part of the specification.

An interesting aspect of German claim practice is that, notwithstanding the many rules regarding formulation of claims and the extensive examination conducted by the Patent Office Examiners, there is a tendency for the Courts to extend the claims to cover *anything novel* and *patentable* described in the specification unless protection for such a concept has been renounced by the patentee during prosecution, an anomaly which defies logical explanation.

Term and Extension of Term. A U.S. patent expires 17 years from grant. There is no possibility of an extension except by special Act of Congress or in the case of certain patents granted to veterans. In some foreign countries, however, particularly in Great Britain and the Commonwealth countries, it is possible to secure an extension of the patent term, up to a maximum extension of 10 years, on a showing of

(1) inadequate remuneration (through no fault of the patentee) for an exceptionally meritorious invention, or

(2) loss of profits due to war.

Obtaining an extension by the first type of showing is difficult and unusual. Obtaining a war-loss extension is much simpler, providing it can be established that it was impossible to exploit the invention, or to exploit it fully, during a war period or a post-war period during which the effects of war persisted. As World War II ended in 1945 and as the normal term of a British patent is 16 years, it is now becoming increasingly difficult to establish a war-connected loss during the term of a patent.

Some of the smaller countries provide for extension of the term of a patent on the payment of a fee and with no showing or only a formal showing, but such extensions are more in the nature of the renewal of a patent by the payment of a tax rather than a special extension to compensate for loss.

There is a wide variation in the foreign countries as to the length of the term and the date from which it commences. Table 5 gives information on these two points for regular patents in the countries in question. In some countries a different term is provided for Confirmation or Revalidation patents. Also in some countries there may still be a few term peculiarities due to extensions following World War II. Where taxes are payable, a patent will lapse before expiration of its normal term in the event of nonpayment.

In many of the foreign countries the term runs from the *filing* date rather than the *grant* date as in the United States. This means that, if there is an examination, the time occupied by examination is in effect subtracted from the patent term. This is very different from the situation in the U.S. where delays in examination in effect lengthen the patent term or at least set ahead its expiration date, and there have been various proposals that a U.S. patent should run, at the most, for a fixed number of years (e.g., 20) from its filing date.

Confirmation or Revalidation Patents. In many foreign countries, particularly in Latin America, so-called Confirmation or Revalidation patents can be obtained after the issuance of other patents and be based thereon, provided the invention is not known or used in the respective country. This fits in with the general theory that a patent should be granted to provide a basis for domestic exploitation of an invention. Even though the invention has been patented elsewhere and has become known as a result of such patenting, there is thus still an opportunity in many countries to secure patent protection and to establish a basis

TABLE 5. PATENT TERMS.

Country	Term in Years	Runs from
Argentina	5, 10 or 15 (shorter terms not extendible)	Grant
Australia	16	Filing
Austria	18	Publication of allowance
Belgium	20	Filing
Brazil	15	Grant
Canada	17	Grant
Chile	5, 10 or 15 (shorter terms extendible)	Grant
Colombia	10 (extendible by 5 or 10 years)	Grant
Denmark	17	Filing
France	20	Filing
W. Germany	18	Day after filing
Great Britain	16	Filing
India	16	Filing or Inter-Dominion priority date
Israel	16	Filing
Italy	15	Filing
Japan	15	Publication of allowance (but not more than 20 years from filing)
Mexico	15 (limited to 12 years if not worked)	Filing
Netherlands	20 from filing or 10 from grant, whichever is longer	
New Zealand	16	Filing
Norway	17	Filing
Philippines	17	Grant
South Africa	16	Filing
Spain	20	Grant
Sweden	17	Filing
Switzerland	18	Filing
U.S.S.R.	15	Filing
Venezuela	5 or 10 (shorter term not extendible)	Grant

for commercial exploitation. Table 6 shows representative countries where such patents can be obtained.

In addition to Confirmation Patents, the mere grant of a foreign patent is not a bar in some countries. Also there are provisions in some territories, principally the British colonies, to provide protection by registration of the granted patent of another country.

TABLE 6. CONFIRMATION OR REVALIDATION
PATENTS GRANTED.

Argentina	Yes
Australia	No
Austria	No
Belgium	Patents of Importation (only remove bars of official publications of other countries)
Brazil	No
Canada	No
Chile	Yes
Colombia	Yes
Denmark	No
France	No
W. Germany	No
Great Britain	No
India	No
Israel	No
Italy	No
Japan	No
Mexico	No
Netherlands	No
New Zealand	No
Norway	No
Philippines	Foreign patent not a bar for 1 year
South Africa	No
Spain	Importation Patent or Utility Model granted if invention is new in Spain
Sweden	No
Switzerland	No
U.S.S.R.	No
Venezuela	Yes

Extent of Geographical Coverage. In some countries, such as Spain and Portugal, a patent automatically extends to the country's colonies. In other countries, such as Great Britain, registration of the Mother country's patent in a colony may be required, or entirely independent protection may be provided. With the breaking-up of colonial empires, the question of protection in colonies becomes of less importance. However, it is interesting to note that in some British colonies which have become independent (e.g., Ghana), registration of the British patent is still the only way of securing protection. In the former French colonies the patent situation remains somewhat unsettled at the moment, but the trend is to grant independent protection under provisions corresponding to those of the French law.

Patents of Addition and Petty Patents. Patents of Addition for improvements in the invention of an earlier patent are obtainable in many foreign countries, but this form of patent is not known in the United States. Patents of Addition are generally granted only to the owner of the principal patent and are not subject to the payment of yearly taxes in addition to those for the principal patents. This is their *raison d'être* which arises only in a system where annuities are payable and where it is desired to provide a less expensive procedure for patenting improvements. The term of a Patent of Addition generally expires with that of the principal patent.

Petty Patents or Utility Models are obtainable in many foreign countries for inventions that do not have the required "inventive height" for a regular patent. They are generally granted for a shorter term and provide a less extensive scope of protection than a regular patent. Only articles having a definite form may be covered, not processes or substances. The principal countries granting petty patents are listed below.

W. Germany—The German "Gebrauchsmuster" is the most famous of petty patents. Its popularity is due to the strict examination and high standards of patentability of the German Patent Office for regular patents. Also, it is granted quickly and without examination or opposition, and is often applied for along with a regular patent. It may even be filed in the form of an "Eventual" (Provisional) Gebrauchsmuster along with a regular application and completed during the pendency of the regular application or if the regular application is rejected.

Japan—The Japanese Utility Model is similar to the German Gebrauchsmuster except that both a Utility Model and regular patent cannot be obtained for the same invention. Also, provisional filing is not possible, but a regular application, if finally rejected, may be converted to a Utility Model, provided its subject matter is proper.

Spain—In this country, Utility Model registrations are frequently applied for, since a regular patent in Spain may not cover an article. Articles can only be covered by a Utility Model. Contrary to the German practice, a Spanish Utility Model is subject to opposition (although a regular Spanish patent is not).

Italy and Brazil—Utility Models are granted, but this form of protection is not used as often as in the other countries in view of the lack of a strict examination for regular patent applications.

Amplified Applications. In the United States, an amplified application can be filed as a continuation-in-part of an earlier application, obtaining the benefit of the filing date of the earlier application for any subject matter disclosed therein. Consequently the original application can be abandoned after the continuation is filed. There is nothing like this abroad except in the Philippines. Elsewhere an application cannot go back of its filing or priority date. If an application is abandoned, its filing date is irretrievably lost.

Disclaimers and Corrections. Reissue patents can be obtained in the United States to correct errors and mistakes. There is no corresponding provision in the foreign laws except in Canada and the Philippines. (In Canada, a reissue must be applied for within four years of grant.) However a number of countries, particularly in the British Commonwealth, have provisions for amending patents at any time after grant by way of "disclaimer, explanation, or correction." New matter may not be introduced, and the claims may not be broadened. Petitions to amend are advertised and are subject to opposition.

International Convention

There is intensive activity at the present time in the direction of a common "European patent" (q.v.). The complicated steps of provisional examination, interventions and final examination requests by third parties, multiple fees and territorial indivisibility may, however, make a European patent less attractive than the individual national patents which, in any event, would be retained for some time.

Proposals have also been made for a common Nordic (Scandinavian) patent and for a European Convention for harmonization of patent laws. The latter has been signed by 9 countries. However the only "common patent" that has come into existence up to now is that of the African-Malagasy Union covering 12 of the former French African colonies.

In contrast with this slow progress toward patents covering more than one country, there has been a consistent record of practical results and progress in the so-called International or Paris Convention of 1883 with its various amendments, the most recent being that of Lisbon in 1958. The International Convention is covered specifically in another article but should be mentioned briefly here as it is of so much importance in foreign patenting activities.

In the first place, the Convention provides a one-year priority period so that, after a first filing in one of the member countries, corresponding applications filed in the other countries within a year can have the benefit of the original filing date. As this is the only means, in most countries, of going back of an actual filing date, the importance of "Convention priority" cannot be overestimated: it is often the difference between a valid and an invalid patent.

In the second place, the Convention provides for "national treatment," i.e., a national of one Convention country must be given the same protection in other Convention countries, regarding industrial property, that their own nationals are given.

In the third place, the Convention includes various rules as to taxes, "working," and other requirements; these assure applicants and patentees of member countries at least a minimum standard of protection for their industrial property rights, including designs and trademarks as well as patents and utility models.

The present members of the International Convention are listed in Table 7. All are members of the Paris Convention of 1883 and have ratified the London Revision of 1934 or the Lisbon Revision of 1958, except those marked as follows: W—bound only by the Washington text of 1911; H—bound only by the Hague text of 1925.

TABLE 7. INTERNATIONAL CONVENTION MEMBERS.

Australia	Haiti	Norway
Austria	Hungary	Poland (H)
Belgium	Iceland	Portugal
Brazil (H)	Indonesia	Rhodesia and
Bulgaria (W)	Iran	Nyasaland
Canada	Ireland	Roumania (W)
Ceylon	Israel	Singapore
Cuba	Italy	S. Africa
Czecho-slovakia (H)	Japan	Spain
	Jugoslavia (H)	Sweden
Denmark	Lebanon	Switzerland
Dominican Republic (H)	Liechtenstein	Syria
Egypt	Luxembourg	Tanganyika
Finland	Mexico	Trinidad (H)
France	Monaco	Tunis
W. Germany	Morocco	Turkey
Great Britain	Netherlands	U.S.A.
Greece	New Zealand	Viet-Nam

Somewhat similar to the International Convention, at least as regards priority, are bilateral treaties between certain members of the British Commonwealth (generally referred to, somewhat inaccurately, as giving "Inter-Dominion" priority); a bilateral arrangement between the United States and the Philippines; and a Buenos Aires Convention between the United States and some of the Latin-American countries.

A number of the former French African colonies have recently joined the Convention, and the Federation of Rhodesia and Nyasaland has been de-federated, bringing the present total to 62 members.

Intangible Benefits of Foreign Patents

It is appropriate, in closing, to emphasize, over and above all practical and commercial considerations, the contribution of foreign patents to better living and improved relations for the peoples of the world.

In the first place, the spread of inventions, from the developed to the developing countries, improves the standard of living in many fields: food, medicine, agriculture, and mining, as well as the more complex mechanical, chemical and electrical arts. The grant of foreign patents plays an important part in spreading out the benefits of technology and invention.

In the second place, cooperation between business and industrial interests in the different countries, brought about by foreign patents, leads to mental and physical contact, interchange of ideas, and working together—all of which are for the good of international relations generally. What we do not know, we do not trust. As we get to know our foreign opposites and they come to understand us, through mutual business ventures often based on patents, we should learn that ideas and aspirations are much alike, the world over. Then ignorance and distrust will give way to understanding and world peace.

Cross-references: *Advance Information from Foreign Filings, European Patent Convention, Foreign Licensing and Antitrust Law, Foreign Patents Utilization, Pharmaceutical Patent Practice, Section on Patentability and Compulsory Licensing Abroad.*

FOREIGN PATENTS—INFORMATION FROM.
See ADVANCE INFORMATION

FOREIGN PATENTS AND KNOW-HOW—
UTILIZATION ABROAD
Worth Wade

Millions of dollars are spent yearly by American inventors and corporations in seeking and maintaining foreign patents. Yet few of these patents ever bring monetary rewards. A better understanding of foreign patent practice, its potentials and pitfalls, should be helpful in converting more foreign patents into profits.

Chief Uses of Foreign Patents

Protecting Export Sales. When the foreign patent covers the product or commercial method of making the product of a United States producer, that producer may use the patent to protect export sales by not licensing foreign competitors. This policy causes no conflict with the antitrust laws because the patent grants the owner the right to exclude all others from making, using or selling the invention. (However, see *Foreign Patents*, "Working")

Protecting Foreign Manufacture. After developing substantial export sales, some American firms find that they can obtain a larger return by manufacture abroad. Since the establishment of the "Common Market" and the "Outer Seven" in Europe, tariff barriers between member nations have been gradually lowered while the duties have been maintained on imports from nonmember nations. If foreign patents of proper scope have been obtained in a foreign country, manufacture in that country is protected from unlicensed competition. The granting of patents by less-industrialized countries also has recently been increased, to encourage American capital investment for manufacture.

Foreign Licensing. In some foreign countries the environment is not favorable to capital investments. This may arise from unstable government, official regulations, high taxes and labor problems. On the other hand trade deficits and currency restrictions may make exports to those countries very difficult. The Middle East, India, Pakistan and China are markets not freely available for many U.S. firms except by licensing of patents or sale of "know-how."

The general rule to follow is to license abroad only inventions that have been commercially developed at home and include usually a technical agreement providing "know-how."

Patent Exchanges. Foreign patents can be used in cross-licensing agreements in which each party gains rights in its home country to patents which the other party may own. When there is little export competition between the parties or the patents relate to different products, such exchanges may not alter the competitive situation between the parties but advance the technical knowledge of both. Where the cross-license is with a foreign competitor, care must be exercised to avoid any restrictive trade practice which might be construed as violation of the antitrust law. Such exchange agreements should not include:

Territorial limitations on export sales of the parties

Price fixing agreements

Quantity restraints or quotas

Tie-in sales of patented or unpatented products.

It is advisable also to avoid:

Automatic licensing of future patents

Access to research and development records

Access to pilot-plant facilities or results.

Ten Steps to Take Before Foreign Licensing

(1) Carefully select the foreign countries with regard to customs, habits and the need for the invention. (2) File only those inventions which are considered essential to make the product. (3) File the foreign patent applications on the most important inventions under the International Convention. (4) Ascertain foreign governmental regulations, duties and currency restrictions. (5) Decide what objective is to be served by the foreign patent. (6) Make market surveys before selecting the foreign prospect. (7) Offer licenses only to inventions that are in commercial use in the U.S. or are more promising abroad than at home. (8) Investigate both the U.S. and foreign taxes that are applicable since many countries have a different tax rate on royalties, know-how fees, stock transfers and agreements calling for personal service. (9) Spell out a separate agreement or a separate consideration for patent rights and know-how, particularly if patentability abroad is beyond reasonable doubt. (10) Send adequate samples and cost data in advance of negotiations.

Selling Know-how with Foreign Patent Rights

Foreign prospects often insist upon inclusion in a patent license of full commercial know-how developed by the American patent owner. In addition to charging a separate fee for know-how, it is advisable to limit the period during which additional know-how will be supplied to 5 to 10 years, even if the patent license runs 16 to 20 years. The services of technical personnel should be charged to the Licensee. He should reimburse the Licensor for such services and for disbursements required to deliver the "know-how." The tax consequences and exchange availability caused by including personal services and know-how should be considered for each country involved. Further, the Licensor should spell out the number of man-hours of technical personnel service to be supplied and the number and frequency of plant inspections which will be allowed. There should be no right of termination of the agreement by the Licensee after receipt of the know-how. The Licensee should not disclose confidential or unpublished "know-how" or trade secrets of the Licensor to third parties.

Restrictions on Export of Know-How. The regulatory restrictions against exporting unpublished technical data to the Sino-Soviet bloc under the Export Control Act were interpreted and applied in a ruling reviewed in *Chem. and Eng. News, 40,* 12 (Dec. 24, 1962). A large domestic engineering company had built in France an oil refinery complex using data developed here. Later it built a like unit in Rumania at a cost of $17,000,000. The Commerce Department's Bureau of International Commerce found no clear proof that the violations of the regulations were wilful. Also, the company stated that the Department had voiced no objection to the project until it was well along to completion. Yet the Bureau barred the company from exporting to said bloc or to Cuba for the next five years and placed the Company's exports to the Free World under surveillance for two years. The Bureau noted that "published" data, free from restriction, is limited to such technology as is available in published form, as in libraries, bookstores, or subscription periodicals or is otherwise provided free to the public.

Fitting the Product to the Foreign Market

It has often been shown that the success of an invention in the U.S. market is no guarantee of success abroad. For selection of the right product and the right prospect for foreign licensing, it is advisable, therefore, to make a thorough survey of the market. A helpful report is "Researching Foreign Markets" published by the National Industrial Conference Board, Inc., New York, which describes sources and method of collecting foreign market information. Also useful are the economic and statistical reports of the World Trade Information Service of the U.S. Bureau of Foreign Commerce. To assist in locating prospective licensees, this Bureau publishes also *Foreign Commerce Weekly,* "World Trade Directory," "A Directory of Foreign Development Organizations and Trade and Investment," and "A Guide to Foreign Business Directories." The Unesco Division of the United Nations published a compilation of the restrictive trade practice laws of member nations in a book entitled "The Organization for European Economic Cooperation." The OEEC publishes a quarterly journal of trade information reporting on the general business climate in the Common Market.

The Foreign Market Survey

The special report "Researching Foreign Markets," supra, describes sources and methods of collecting foreign market information.

The World Trade Information Service publishes economic, operational and statistical reports of which the most useful are the economic. They include basic data, reports of recent economic developments, suggestions about how to establish foreign business, and patent and trademark regulations for various foreign countries.

For certain countries such as Sweden and France, this Service has combined market studies under a single title such as "Doing Business in Sweden." Its Investment Handbook series reports on such subjects as "Investment in Australia" and on more than 17 countries in individual reports.

Other publications of this Service which may be useful are "Foreign Commerce Weekly," "World Trade Directory," "A Directory of Foreign Development Organizations for Trade and Investment," and "A Guide to Foreign Business Directories."

Other informative publications are those of the UNESCO Division of the United Nations and the quarterly publication of OEEC which covers the productivity of the major European countries.

Judging the Competitive Situation

After you know the suitability of your product for the foreign market and its market potential, you determine next whether the product is competitive with similar products in the particular foreign country selected. You may obtain free samples by writing to the principal producers in the country. You may learn names and addresses of competing firms from the "World Trade Directory" published by the Bureau of Foreign Commerce. You can then test the samples against the product to be licensed and estimate production costs from the raw materials and manufacturing methods to be used.

Providing Patent Protection

Foreign patents are not to be filed until six months after the U.S. filing date unless a license is obtained from the Commissioner of Patents. The application may be filed after that period without a license if the Commissioner has issued, during that period, no secrecy order against such filing.

Many countries permit applicants to combine two or more U.S. patent applications if they relate to the same subject matter and if they are filed in this country within one year of each other. This reduces the cost of foreign filing and subsequent maintenance of the decreased number of patents.

Government regulations regarding licensing in any particular foreign country and information as to currency restrictions are available at the consulate of the foreign country and also at the foreign departments of our large commercial banks. In many countries no patent license agreement is effective until it has been approved by one or more government agencies, and the conversion of foreign funds into U.S. dollars, for the payment of "know-how" fees and patent royalties, is subject to approval.

Negotiating with Foreign Prospects

It is difficult to negotiate a foreign license agreement by mail. Personal conferences are more effective. It is advisable for the American patent owner to send an authorized representative abroad, to make a final appraisal of the foreign market and conduct the negotiations. Long before any such visit, however, the prospect should receive samples, general technical and market potential data, cost estimates, patent information and a statement of the commercial progress in the U.S.A. If it is not possible to visit the foreign prospect, then he may send a representative to this country. A third procedure is to engage the services of a foreign agent, at a commission of 5 to 25 per cent, for example. A list of legal and business consultant firms that perform these functions is published by the Commercial Intelligence Division of the Bureau of Foreign Commerce, Department of Commerce.

The following publications are helpful in negotiating foreign licenses: "Licensing Patents and Process to European Manufacturers," by Economic Cooperation Administration of the Office of Small Business, Washington, D.C.; "Foreign License Agreements," 2 Vols., National Industrial Conference Board, New York; and "Check List for Negotiating Licenses on Patents, Know-how, and Trademarks," published by Advance House, Box 334, Ardmore, Pennsylvania.

Effect of Foreign Trade Groups on Patent Policy

In recent years a number of foreign nations have banded together in trade groups such as the European Common Market and the "Outer Seven." Then there are the British Commonwealth nations and loosely connected trade groups in Latin and South America.

After the formation of these groups, it became apparent that licensing policies on foreign patents would have to be revised. Whereas it was possible formerly to issue a separate license for each major nation, many foreign prospects now insist on exclusive licenses within their trade group and the right to sublicense. The customary procedure in this case is to charge the licensee a substantial fee for the exclusive license and know-how and to request one-half of the consideration received from sublicenses. The foreign licensee should, in any event, agree to reimburse the American patent owner for one-half of the cost of maintaining in force the licensed foreign patents; this sharing of expense will discourage the maintenance of any unused patents.

No foreign patent policy can remain static. It should be flexible. It must be subject to frequent review and change as required to adapt it to the trends and fluctuations in the world economic community.

Cross-references: *Foreign Licensing and Antitrust Law, Foreign Patents, Licenses.*

FORMS AND EXECUTIONS THEREOF

Forms for use in filing applications for patents and in other patent office procedures are given in the Appendix to the Rules of Practice. A representative assignment form follows at the end of this article.

It is desirable to use the more common forms, namely those for assignments and filing of applications, in printed format providing adequate blanks for typing the information characteristic of a particular case. The data to be typed would include the inventor's name, citizenship, residence, post office address, and title of invention. Although printed forms can be had from leading stores handling legal documents, patent firms usually have personally printed supplies including the name of the firm or attorney appointed, with the address and registration number. The printing

saves much reading of wholly typed forms that, when used, require checking each time for accuracy of all statements therein.

The order in which the names of joint inventors are typed in the formal paper determines the order in which they will appear in the patent when and if issued.

Executions

When the notarial authorization is not state-wide and the venue recited in the oath does not agree with the county of notarial acknowledgment, then the notary should affix some evidence of authority for said venue (unless the seal shows it), as by stamp or notarial certificate from the county clerk or a court.

"That portion of an oath or affidavit indicating where the oath is taken is known as the venue. Where the county and state in the venue agree with the county and state in the seal, no problem arises. If the venue and seal do not correspond in county and state, the jurisdiction of the notary must be determined from statements by the notary appearing on oath, or from the listing at 604.03 [infra]. Venue and notary jurisdiction must correspond or the oath is improper. The oath should show on its face that it was taken within the jurisdiction of the certifying officer or notary. This may be given either in the venue or in the body of the jurat." M.P.E.P. 604.02.

States in which notarial authorizations are not for the entire state are shown in M.P.E.P. 604.03 (corrected) as follows:

COUNTY ONLY

Alabama	Mississippi
Arizona	Tennessee
California	Texas
Kansas	West Virginia

VARIABLE JURISDICTION

[See explanatory paragraphs (a-f) of M.P.E.P.]

Hawaii (e)	Nebraska (b)
Iowa (a)	Ohio (f)
Kentucky (a)	Virginia (d)
Missouri (a)	

Execution Abroad. Executions of patent papers abroad may be made before a consular or diplomatic officer of the United States or a person authorized by said officer, with a certificate of such authorization to be attached. The oath is to be attested in all cases by the official seal. In the absence of proper authentication of an oath made abroad, the application will nevertheless be given a filing date; the defect in the oath can be subsequently corrected by the applicant.

Correction of Defect in Oath. While an oath may not be amended, omissions such as residence or mailing address of an applicant may be supplied by a letter over the applicant's own signature, without loss of filing date.

For an excellent discussion of these and related points, see M.P.E.P. 603-606.

The following sections are taken verbatim from the Appendix to the Rules, 1960 ed., except for the added comment in brackets.

Forms

The following forms illustrate the manner of preparing various papers to be filed in the Patent Office. Applicants and other parties will find their business facilitated by following them. In special situations such alterations as the circumstances may render necessary may be made, provided they do not depart from the requirements of the rules or of the statute. Before using any form the pertinent rules of practice and sections of the statute should be studied carefully.

List of Forms

1. Petition for patent; by a sole inventor.
2. Petition for patent; by a sole inventor, for himself and assignee.
3. Petition for patent; by a sole inventor, with power of attorney.
4. Petition for patent; by joint inventors.
5. Petition for patent; by an administrator.
6. Petition for patent; by an executor.
7. Petition for patent; by the guardian of an insane person.
11. Oath to accompany application for patent.
12. Oath to accompany application for patent, by an administrator (or executor).
13. Oath not accompanying application.
14. Supplemental oath for amendment presenting claims for matter disclosed but not originally claimed.
16. Combined petition, oath and specification (single signature form), sole inventor.
17. Oath in division or continuing application.
18. Oath in division or continuing application containing additional subject matter.
21. Design patent application; petition.
22. Design patent application; specification.
23. Design patent application; oath.
25. Plant patent application; petition.
26. Plant patent application; oath.
28. Reissue application, petition; by the inventor.
29. Reissue application, petition; by the assignee.
31. Reissue application, oath; by the inventor.
32. Reissue application, oath; by assignee.
33. Oath as to loss of letters patent.
36. Power of attorney or authorization of agent, not accompanying application.
37. Revocation of power of attorney or authorization of agent.
39. Amendment.
41. Appeal from the Principal Examiner to the Board of Appeals.
43. Disclaimer in patent.
44. Interference; preliminary statement of domestic inventor.
45. Interference; preliminary statement of foreign inventor.
46. Interference; disclaimer during interference.
47. Interference; notice of taking testimony.
48. Interference; form of deposition.
49. Interference; certificate of officer.

16. Combined Petition, Oath and Specification (Single Signature Form); Sole Inventor.

Being duly sworn, I, _____, depose and say that I am a citizen of _____, residing at _____; that I have read the foregoing specification and claims and I verily believe I am the original, first, and sole inventor of the invention in _____ described and claimed therein; that I do not know and do not believe that this invention was ever known or used before my invention thereof, or patented or described in any printed publication in any country before my invention thereof, or more than one year prior to this application, or in public use or on sale in the United States more than one year prior to this application; that this invention has not been patented in any country foreign to the United States on an application filed by me or my legal representatives or assigns more than twelve months before this application; and that no application for patent on this invention has been filed by me or my representatives or assigns in any country foreign to the United States, except as follows:

And I hereby appoint _____ Registration No. ____, my attorney (or agent) to prosecute this application and to transact all business in the Patent Office connected therewith.

Wherefore I pray that Letters Patent be granted to me for the invention or discovery described and claimed in the foregoing specification and claims, and I hereby subscribe my name to the foregoing specification and claims, oath, power of attorney, and this petition.

Inventor _____
(First name) (Middle initial) (Last name)

Post office address: _____

_____

State of _____ ⎱
                    ⎰ ss:
County of _____ ⎰

Before me personally appeared _____, to me known to be the person described in the above application for patent, who signed the foregoing instrument in my presence, and made oath before me to the allegations set forth therein as being

under oath, on the _____ day of _____, 19____.

[SEAL]   _____
                (Notary Public or Officer)

NOTE—This form may be executed only when attached to a complete application as the last page thereof.

[When the invention is joint, the form may start:

Being duly sworn, we _____, _____, and _____, depose and say that we are citizens of the United States and residents, respectively, of _____, _____, _____; that we have read _____. Throughout the form, the personal pronouns are changed to plural as are verbs for which the pronouns are the subjects. Notarial acknowledgment forms should be appended separately for each inventor if the inventors are in different locations and are expected to sign before different notaries.]

18. Oath in Division or Continuing Application Containing Additional Subject Matter.

(This form of oath may be used with an application disclosing and claiming subject matter disclosed in a prior copending application of the same inventor and also disclosing additional subject matter.)

_____, the above-named petitioner, being sworn (or affirmed), deposes and says that he is a citizen of the United States and resident of _____, that he verily believes himself to be the original, first and sole inventor of the improvement in _____ described and claimed in the foregoing specification; that this application in part discloses and claims subject matter disclosed in his earlier filed pending application, Serial No. _____, filed _____; that, as to the subject matter of this application which is common to said earlier application he does not know and does not believe that the same was ever known or used before his invention thereof or patented or described in any printed publication in any country before his invention thereof or more than one year prior to said earlier application, or in

public use or on sale in the United States more than one year prior to said earlier application; that said common subject matter has not been patented before the date of said earlier application in any country foreign to the United States on an application filed by him or his legal representatives or assigns more than twelve months prior to said application; and that no application for patent on said invention has been filed by him or his representatives or assigns in any country foreign to the United States, except as follows _____; that, as to the subject matter of this application which is not common to said earlier application, he does not know and does not believe that the same was ever known or used before his invention thereof or patented or described in any printed publication in any country before his invention thereof or more than one year prior to the date of this application, or in public use or on sale in the United States more than one year prior to the date of this application, and that said subject matter has not been patented in any country foreign to the United States on an application filed by him or his legal representatives or assigns more than twelve months prior to the date of this application; and that no application for patent on said invention has been filed by him or his representatives or assigns in any country foreign to the United States, except as follows:

Inventor's full name: _____

_____
(Signature)

_____ ⎱
                          ⎰ ss:
_____ ⎰

Sworn to and subscribed before me this _____ day of _____, 19____.

[SEAL]   _____
                (Signature of notary or officer)

_____
Official character)

21. Design patent application; petition.
To the Commissioner of Patents:

Your petitioner, _____, a citizen of the United States and a resident of _____, State of _____ (or subject, etc.), whose post-office address is _____, prays that letters patent may be granted to him for the term of three and one-half years (or seven years, or fourteen years) for the new and original design for _____, set forth in the following specification.

(The specification and oath follow the petition.)

22. Design patent application; specification.

Be it known that I, _____, have invented a new, original, and ornamental design for

(1) _____, of which the following is a specification, reference being had to the accompanying drawing, forming a part hereof.

Fig. 1 is a (2) _____

Fig. 2 is a (2) _____

I claim:

The ornamental design for a (1) _____ as shown.

_____

(Signature)

NOTES: (1) Insert specific name of article.

(2) Insert brief description of figure or figures of the drawing.

23. Design patent application; oath.

_____,
_____, } ss:

_____, the above-named petitioner__, being sworn (or affirmed), depose__ and say__ that _____ citizen__ of _____ and resident__ of _____, that _____ verily believe__ _____ to be the original, first and _____ inventor__ of the design for _____ described and claimed in the foregoing specification; that _____ do__ not know and do__ not believe that the same was ever known or used before _____ invention thereof, or patented or described in any printed publication in any country before _____ invention thereof, or more than one year prior to this application, or in public use or on sale in the United States more than one year prior to this application; that said design has not been patented in any country foreign to the United States on an application filed by _____ or _____ legal representatives or assigns more than six months prior to this application; and that no application for patent on said design has been filed by _____ or _____ representatives or assigns in any country foreign to the United States, except as follows:

_____

Inventor's full name: _____

_____

(Signature)

_____,
_____, } ss:

Sworn to and subscribed before me this _____ day of _____, 19____.

[SEAL]

_____

(Signature of notary or officer)

_____

Official character)

28. Reissue application, petition; by the inventor.

To the Commissioner of Patents:

Your petitioner, _____, a citizen of the United States and a resident of _____, State of _____ (or subject, etc.), whose post-office address is _____, prays that he may be allowed to surrender the letters patent for an improvement in _____, No. _____ granted to him _____, 19____, whereof he is now sole owner (or whereof _____, on whose behalf and with whose assent this application is made, is now sole owner, by assignment), and that letters patent may be reissued to him (or the said _____) for the same invention upon the following amended specification. With this petition is filed an abstract of title, duly certified (or an order for a title report), as required in such cases.

[Assent of assignee to reissue]

The undersigned, assignee of the entire (or of an undivided) interest in the above-mentioned letters patent, hereby assents to the accompanying application.

_____

(Signature)

31. Reissue application, oath; by the inventor.

_____, the above-named petitioner, being duly sworn (or affirmed), deposes and says that he is a citizen of the United States of America, and a resident of _____, in the State of _____; that he verily believes himself to be the original, first and sole inventor of the invention described and claimed in letters patent No. _____ and in the foregoing specification and for which improvement he solicits a patent; that he does not know and does not believe that said improvement was ever known or used before his invention thereof, that (continue with the allegations and facts required by rule 175) _____

Inventor's full name: _____

_____

(Signature)

_____,
_____, } ss:

Subscribed and sworn to before me this _____ day of _____, 19____.

[SEAL]

_____

(Signature of notary or officer)

_____

(Official character)

A representative assignment of application form follows:

ASSIGNMENT

WHEREAS, We

have invented certain improvements in

for which on   19   ,
We executed an application for United States
Letters Patent; and whereas   COMPANY,
a corporation of the State of   , desires to
purchase the same;

NOW, THEREFORE, in consideration of the
sum of One Dollar and other good and valuable
consideration, the receipt and sufficiency of which
is hereby acknowledged, We hereby sell, assign,
transfer and convey unto the said   COM-
PANY, a corporation organized and existing under
and by virtue of the laws of the State of   ,
and having a principal office at   in the
City of   in the State of   , its
successors and assigns, the entire right, title and
interest for the United States and the territories
thereof, and for foreign countries, in and to the
said application and in and to any invention
therein set forth and in and to any patent which
may issue on said application, or which may issue
on any other application filed in the United States
or elsewhere, aimed to cover any invention disclosed in said above-specified application, or any
reissue, extension or renewal of any such patent
[omit any of these rights not to be assigned]; and
We hereby bind ourselves, our heirs, legal representatives, administrators and assigns properly
to execute without further consideration, any and
all applications, petitions, oaths, assignments or
other papers and instruments which may be necessary in order to carry into full force and effect the
sale, assignment and transfer hereby made, or
intended or agreed to be made.

IN WITNESS WHEREOF, We have executed

this assignment this   day of

19

....
....

STATE OF   ⎫   ....
                  ⎬ ss.:
COUNTY OF   ⎭

On this   day of   19   before
me personally appeared
to me known and known to me to be the person
described in and who executed the foregoing assignment and   duly acknowledged to me
that   executed the same as   own
free act and deed. ....

Notary Public

(Repeat acknowledgment form when assignors
are in different venues.)

Cf. Hineline, H. D., "Forms and Their Uses in Patent and Trademark Practice in the United States
and Canada," 1951. The Michie Co., Charlottesville, Va.

Cross-references: *Assignments, Reissue Patents.*

FRAUD IN PATENT MATTERS

Hobart N. Durham

Fraud and related illegal, unconscionable
or improper activities are to be considered
seriously in the prosecution of a patent application and litigation involving a patent.
There are many restrictions, however,
which may prevent cancellation or invalidation of a patent on such grounds. Although the issue of fraud and related improper activities have often been passed
upon by the courts, only rarely has a patent
been held invalid or unenforceable on such
issue.

There may be many other acts connected
with the preparation, filing and prosecution
of patent applications and litigation of patents which do not amount to fraud, but
which are nonetheless unconscionable and
improper. They may be raised under certain circumstances, against the enforcement
of a patent, and may render the patent invalid or deprive its owner of relief against
an infringer.

In this article, we consider the criminal
or otherwise illegal aspects which constitute
forgery, perjury, or filing of false affidavits
or statements, only as they bear directly on
the validity of a patent, its enforceability
in litigation, or the pendency of an application in the Patent Office.

Actual fraud requires that there be clear
proof of (1) the misrepresentation of some
material fact, (2) knowledge of the falsity
of the misrepresentation by the party and
(3) action by another party induced to act
in ignorance of its falsity. In many patent
cases, charges of fraud have been overruled
for failure to prove some one of these
points. If the defense of fraud is to be asserted in a suit for infringement, the attorney should prepare his defense in the same
manner as though he sought to convict the
patentee-plaintiff of a serious crime, that is,

prove every element of the charge beyond reasonable doubt.

Sanctions

A variety of sanctions may be applied where fraud or improper activity in procurement or enforcement of a patent are proved. These include:

Holding the patent invalid

Holding the patent unenforceable

Holding the patent non-infringed

Award of attorney's fees against the patent owner

Damages and special costs

Disbarment of the attorneys who connived in the fraud

Striking the application from the Patent Office files

Criminal penalties against those involved in the fraud

Destruction of the presumption of validity

Adverse award of priority in an interference

Judicial award of a license to the aggrieved party

Where it has been proved that fraud was practised in an application still pending in the Patent Office, it may be stricken from the files on the petition of a private party or on the initiative of the Commissioner of Patents, either during ex parte prosecution or during an interference.

Statutory Provisions

The Patent Act of 1952 includes several specific provisions dealing with fraud and related matters. Thus the sole basis for the reissue of an inoperative or invalid patent is that the fault arose "through error without any deceptive intention" (35 U.S.C. 251). Absence of "any deceptive intention" is a prerequisite also for a disclaimer (Section 253), for correction of a misjoinder or non-joinder of applicants (Section 256), and for maintaining an infringement suit on a patent containing an invalid claim (Section 288). An applicant's mistake of a minor character in a patent may be corrected only if it is shown that it "occurred in good faith" (Section 255).

The use of the word "patent" in labeling or advertising "for the purpose of deceiving the public" violates the criminal provisions of 35 U.S.C. 292, as does improper marking "with the intent of counterfeiting or imitating the mark of the patentee, or of deceiving the public and inducing them to believe that the thing made or sold was by or with the consent of the patentee."

Development of Doctrine of Fraud

The various patent laws between 1836 and 1952 contained provisions which are generally similar to those of the Patent Act of 1952 (35 U.S.C.), but none of them have provided any positive relief except the *qui tam* actions relative to false marking.

Prior to the Patent Act of 1836, a private litigant within one year of the grant of a patent, could move for its repeal in a United States District Court, upon the basis that the patent "was obtained surreptitiously by, or upon, false suggestion." (Patent Act of 1790, Section 5, and Patent Act of 1793, Section 10.) Since the enactment of the 1836 Patent Act, there has been no corresponding statutory provision with respect to fraudulent acts concerning patents and patent applications.

One of the early cases in which the government was successful in raising the issue of fraud was *U.S.* v. *Gunning et al.*, 18 Fed. 511 (1883), 22 Fed. 653 (1884), 23 Fed. 668 (1885), C.C. S.D. N.Y. The government charged that the patent had been procured by fraud on the ground that the applicant was not the true inventor of the subject matter. The patent was set aside but costs were refused against the defendant, as the defendant might have been a bona fide purchaser of the patent.

Parties Proper to Assertion of Fraud

The party seeking to prove fraud must have a real and substantial interest in the controversy. In *A. B. Dick Co.* v. *Marr*, 197 F.2d 498, 93 USPQ 486, CA 2 1952, the defendant contended that plaintiff had fraudulently suppressed evidence of the prior art. After plaintiff had voluntarily dismissed the action with prejudice, defendant tried to continue the action to prove plaintiff's fraud. The court held:

"A party's minor role as protector of the public interest in these cases does not seem to us enough to prevent this case from being moot."

Except where the government is plaintiff, fraud and related acts are not a ground for attacking the validity of a patent. It is now well established that only the United States government may maintain a suit to cancel or revoke a granted patent. Even the suits brought by the government have *usually* failed to obtain the sought-for revocation by reason of a failure of proof. In one case, *U.S.* v. *Frazer*, 22 Fed. 106, DC NIll, the case was dismissed by reason of the fact that the government had been indemnified by a private party, thus causing the court to hold that it was a private suit, although formally in the name of the government.

While fraud in the procurement of a patent cannot be initially asserted by a private plaintiff in a suit, the private litigant can assert fraud as a defense in defendant's answer to an infringement suit, or in plaintiff's reply to a counterclaim of infringement brought in a declaratory judgment suit. The defense of unclean hands was thus held to be valid when asserted by a declaratory plaintiff in response to the declaratory defendant's counterclaim of infringement in *Wooldridge Mfg. Co.* v. *R. G. La Tourneau*, 79 F.Supp. 908, 76 USPQ 565, DC NCal. 1948.

Fraud in Patent Solicitation

Satisfactory proof of fraud or intolerable conduct on the part of the patent owner can be a defense, but many cases have failed, for lack of adequate proof of one or the other elements of fraud or because the acts were not sufficiently germane to the allowance of the patent application.

For an article on this general subject, see Donald C. Keaveney, "Fraud in the Procurement of a Patent as a Defense to Infringement," 33 JPOS 482, 1951.

There are only a few *reported* Patent Office cases where fraud or other improper activity has caused an application to be stricken from the files. It is not possible to

learn how many unreported cases there may have been involving such a finding. Abandonment of the application, or striking it from the files, closes the file, and it remains secret, unavailable to the public.

In general, there is a heavy burden on the defendant to show that there was actually a fraudulent representation to the Patent Office during the prosecution. *Edward Valves, Inc.* v. *Cameron Iron Works Inc.*, 286 F.2d 933, 128 USPQ 307, 318, CA 5 1961.

Documents and Statements Not Material or Knowingly False—Excused. Affidavits submitted during the prosecution of an application, which later prove to be incorrect, have been excused on the basis that they were not proved to have been *knowingly* false. *Clark et al.* v. *Ace Rubber Products Inc.*, 95 USPQ 24, DC NOhio 1952.

The facts and decision in a 1961 case show the present attitude of the courts on this subject. The applicant Allen, in a sworn statement to the Patent Office, represented that he had made the invention before the effective date of the reference Brown. The Office then withdrew the reference as a basis of rejection. The defendant, in a suit for infringement of the patent later issued to Allen, alleged that the statement of Allen was fraudulent and that it caused the Office, during the subsequent four years of prosecution of the application, to withhold the "Brown patent or any other prior art that had an effective date" later than that set up in said statement. The court said:

"It is not even contended that the Brown patent is pertinent to the present Allen claims. The file wrapper of the Allen patent shows that the withdrawal of the Brown patent played no part in the subsequent allowance of the Allen patent. *A false statement does not destroy the presumption of validity of a patent unless the statement was 'essentially material' to its issuance."* *Edward Valves, Inc.* v. *Cameron Iron Works, Inc.*, supra. Emphasis added

An incorrectly dated, antedating affidavit filed in the Patent Office was held not to constitute sufficient proof of fraud, when the correct date on the drawing would have been prior to the date of the patent on which the rejection was based. *The Foundry Equipment Co.* v. *The Carl-Mayer Corp.*,

104 USPQ 172, DC NOhio 1955; aff. 110 USPQ 169, CA 6 1956.

Without proof of bad faith and fraud, inaccurate statements are not considered as intentional misstatements. *General Metals Powder Co. v. S. K. Wellman Co.*, 57 F.Supp. 220, 62 USPQ 490, DC NOhio, 1944; aff. 157 F.2d 505, 71 USPQ 23, CA 6 1946.

Incorrect statements of commercial success without proof of actual fraud were insufficient. *Haloro, Inc. v. Owens-Corning-Fibreglass Corp.*, 266 F.2d 918, CA DistCol 1959.

Affidavits filed in the Patent Office to secure the allowance of a patent application have often been attacked as fraudulent, but such attacks on the validity of the resultant patent have usually failed, because the affidavits were not proved to have been fraudulent.

In *Marks v. Polaroid Corp.*, 105 USPQ 10, DC Mass 1955, aff. 237 F.2d 428, CA 1 1956, the court held that the factually untrue affidavits were not deliberately false and did not deceive or mislead the Examiner. It went on to hold, contrary to most of the recent cases, that "even if representation was serious ... it would not serve as the basis for action of this Court invalidating the patent as requested by the plaintiffs. Cancellation of patents for misrepresentation in procurement must be initiated by the United States itself."

While holding the patent invalid for lack of invention over the prior art, the Court of Appeals for the 7th Circuit reversed a holding of the lower court that the patent was invalid for fraud on the basis of false and misleading statements furnished to the Patent Office. On appeal, it was held that "To sustain a charge of fraud in this respect would mean there was a conspiracy among several competent and highly respected scientific men." *Armour Co. v. Wilson & Co.*, 168 F.Supp. 353, DC NIll 1958; aff. in part 274 F.2d 143, 124 USPQ 115, Ca 7 1960.

In *Baldwin-Lima-Hamilton Corp. v. Tatnall Measuring Systems Co.*, 169 F.Supp. 1, DC EPenn 1958, aff. 121 USPQ 363, CA 3 1959, it was held by the trial court that reckless false statements made to the Patent Office during the prosecution of the application for the patent in suit would not destroy the presumption of validity unless the statements had been material to the issue of the patent and that, if there were reasonable doubt, the false statements were not a good basis for invalidity. The decision of the trial court that the patent was not infringed was sustained on appeal, not on the basis of anything which transpired in the Patent Office, but because the plaintiff had misused its patents by tie-in sales.

Where the affidavits had been sought by the representative of the patentee and were weasel-worded; there had been no showing that they were knowingly or wilfully false or that they had expedited the grant of the patent; and, where the affiants had been free to change the affidavits, they were held not to be a ground for invalidation of the patent. *Martin et al. v. The Ford Alexander Corp.*, 117 USPQ 378, DC SCalif 1958. The patent was held to be valid and infringed.

Affidavit Asserting No Prior Public Use —Error Excused. An affidavit which alleged that there had been no public use of the invention more than a year prior to the application was held not to be fraudulent, as intent to deceive had not been proved. "... whether or not there has been a public use in varied circumstances is one that for many years has troubled the courts with no unanimity of decisions thereon ... the affiant is not a lawyer." Although the finding of fraud by the trial court was not clearly erroneous, it was reversed as unwarranted. *Huszar v. Cincinnati Chemical Works, Inc.*, 172 F.2d 6, CA 6 1949.

Incorrect Statement as to Commercial Success—Excused. An incorrect affidavit as to commercial success was held to be inadvertent and not fraudulent, where the affiant testified he misunderstood the information given him, and there was no showing that it had been relied on by the Examiner. *Orrison et al. v. C. Hoffberger Co.*, 97 F.Supp. 689, DC Md 1951, aff. 90 USPQ 195, CA 4 1951.

False Laudatory Article—Not Excused. In another case, the subject of more than the usual amount of litigation, *Hazel Atlas Glass Co. v. Hartford-Empire Co.*, 322 U.S. 238, 61 USPQ 241, 1944, the Supreme Court held the patent not to be infringed because it had been procured with the aid of a laudatory article, prepared supposedly by a labor leader represented as hostile but actually by the legal department of Hartford-Empire.

A second case arising from this situation also reached the Supreme Court. It was the action to disbar, from practice in the Patent Office, the patent attorney who submitted the article. Various tribunals below had given diverse decisions. The Supreme Court held for disbarment. *Kingsland* v. *Dorsey*, 338 U.S. 318, 83 USPQ 330, 1949.

Cases on Revival and Reissue. Fraud may also arise in connection with the revival of an abandoned application, and when proved results in a vacation of the revival, restoring the application to its *abandoned* status. In *Peterson et al.* v. *Rosenberger et al.* v. *Peik*, Interference No. 74,841, 170 Mss. 179, 1948, an application had become abandoned April 15, 1934. A petition to revive it was filed March 9, 1935, and was granted May 21, 1935 on the basis of affidavits which were later charged to be fraudulent. In the supporting affidavits, a period of 8 months was represented as "recent," while a 3 months period was set forth as being a period of many months. Although the assignee got its rights by an agreement dated August 1934, which provided for execution of papers for the revival, the revival petition was not filed until March 9, 1935. The Commissioner held that the incorrect allegations were material, especially in the light of the entire more complex circumstances, and he vacated the decision reviving the application.

Where the reissue of a patent is tainted with fraud and has been improvidently and illegally granted, it is void *ab initio*, even as to claims which have been carried over from the original patent. *Staude* v. *Bendix Products Corp.*, 26 F.Supp. 901, DC NInd 1939; aff. 44 USPQ 633, CA 7 1940.

Alteration of Executed Application. Where it is proved that an application has been materially altered (in its specification or claims) after execution, the application will be stricken from the files. When such proof is made during an interference, the interference is dissolved, and in an ex parte proceeding the changed application has been stricken from the files. *Ames* v. *Lindstrom*, 1911 C.D. 68, Comr. Pats., 1910. On appeal, it was further held that the court could not erase the new matter and restore the application to the condition in which the applicant executed it, that the application was not a constructive reduction to practice, and that no valid patent could issue on the application. *Lindstrom* v. *Ames*, 1911 C.D. 384, CA DistCol 1911.

Under modern practice, application papers are not given a filing date if they show suspicion of material alterations which have not been initialled, in the absence of an affidavit from the applicant that the corrections or additions were made before execution of the application.

Judge Arthur M. Smith, while an attorney, discussed the alteration of an application after execution and before filing in part as follows, 41 JPOS 5, 1959:

"There are of course many borderline situations which can be presented and if one wishes to rely upon the dictum in cases such as *Lindstrom* v. *Ames* [supra], one might gamble a bit and make changes in the specification, drawings and claims of the type which could be made properly by the attorney acting under his power-of-attorney after the case is filed in the Patent Office. The safest course, as I see it, is to insist upon a re-execution of the application if any changes are made in it between the time of the execution of the oath and time of filing of the completed application in the Patent Office."

The question whether an application should be stricken because of change subsequent to execution arose in an interference. There were two changes of informalities and also cancellation of "low temperature" before "reaction." The attorney testified that he discussed the cancellation with the inventor who approved it. The Commissioner had held that the change, when considered in the light of the specification, was not "material" in nature. The court held the change to be permissible under the circumstances but warned of the hazards to applications so altered and noted that it was not providing a "standard of propriety for an attorney." *Vandenberg* v. *Reynolds*, 122 USPQ 381, CCPA 1959.

In an interference case, the application

of one of the parties had been altered subsequent to execution and before filing.
"Fluorides" had been expanded to "hal-
ides," and free carbon "as the sole contaminant of the carbide" to "This free carbon,
it will be understood, is a deliberate and
extraneous contaminant when it is present."
The Commissioner noted that such matter
could not have been added by amendment
and ordered the application stricken under
the provisions of Rule 56. *Wainer* v. *Ervin
and Ueltz*, 121 USPQ 144, 1959.

In another case, dates on a sketch had
been changed and false testimony was offered as to when words were added to the
back of an exhibit used to obtain allowance
of claims, later involved in interference.
The applicant did not respond to an order
to show cause why his application should
not be stricken from the files. The Commissioner held: "The fraud committed by this
applicant in the interference proceeding
precludes the issuance of a valid patent on
the application and the application is
hereby stricken from the files." *Ex parte
Mallard*, 1946 C.D. 4, 1946; *Mallard* v.
Kitto, 69 USPQ 568, DC NIll 1946.

*Inking of Drawings after Execution of
Application.* In view of the difficulties involved in making the drawings conform to
the inventor's structure, the final draft of
the application is sometimes forwarded to
the inventor for execution, with the drawings in pencil form. The drawing is occasionally inked after it is approved and after
execution of the application.

The question of propriety of this procedure arose in an interference. One party,
when an adverse judgment of priority was
imminent, raised the issue of alteration subsequent to the execution. The Commissioner
remarked that the inking-in after execution
of the application was not such alteration
as would require that the application be
stricken under Rule 56. *Hopkins* v. *Scott*,
105 O.G. 1263, 1903. See discussion by Harold M. Knoth, 32 JPOS 336, 338, 1950.

This is an area, like many others, where
the attorney or applicant should not deliberately walk near the edge of a ledge although another may have done so and not
fallen into difficulty. Yet the following arguments may be presented for the logic of

allowing the inventor to execute the application before the pencilled drawings are
inked.

The applicant is more apt to make
changes and improve the accuracy and
completeness of the disclosure, if he knows
that the draftsman can include the changes
without substantial additional expense or
effort. It is also noted that the Patent Office
accepts, and at times requires, submission
of whole new sheets of drawings when none
were included originally but where the written specification gives an adequate basis for
all features shown in the drawing. The Office has also consistently accepted photostats of pencil drawings, subject to eventual
submission of properly inked formal sheets
of drawings.

Regardless of these arguments, the safe
practice in view of all possibilities is to ink
the drawings in advance of execution by the
inventors.

Failure to Report Closest Prior Art or Unfavorable Data

It seems strange, in the absence of any
statutory or Patent Office requirement,
that the applicant may be accused of fraud
in not reporting to the Patent Office the
closest art known to him, against an application. Yet there are rare circumstances
under which fraud has been found in not so
reporting. To avoid the possibility of such
circumstances arising, it seems *inadvisable
for the attorney to infer or imply that he
has called attention to the closest art* and
unnecessary to indicate that the Examiner
has cited such art. The decision of the court
in *Admiral Corp.* v. *Zenith Radio Corp.*,
296 F.2d 708, 131 USPQ 456, CA 10 1961,
is so pertinent that it is quoted in full on
the point, except for omission of the cases
cited:

"The courts will deny relief to a patentee who
has behaved unethically in his dealings with the
Patent Office in connection with a patent in suit.
Here the misconduct is based upon the alleged
concealment of the Andrews patent. Difficult as it
is to understand how Zenith could conceal from
the Patent Office the Andrews patent which was a
public record and which had been issued shortly
prior to the Zenith 025 divisional application, we

nevertheless have considered the charge of misconduct. Admiral identifies the Andrews circuit with the 025 circuit on the basis of block diagrams of sufficient generalization to have the systems appear alike. We agree with Zenith that while block diagrams have some utility in the electronic art as a short-hand portrayal of an overall system, they are incapable of disclosing the refinements that distinguish one circuit from another intended for the same general purpose. The significant differences between Andrews and 025 have been pointed out. The solicitors for Zenith testified as to their good faith belief as to the differences. This is not a case of a prior public use of which the Patent Office had no means of gaining information except through the applicant. Here the alleged nondisclosure relates to a significantly different prior patent. If an applicant knows of prior art which plainly describes his claimed invention or comes so close that a reasonable man would say that the invention was not original but had been anticipated, he will not be excused for failure to disclose his knowledge.

"This case falls outside of that rule. The record sustains the findings of the trial court that the Zenith solicitors acted in good faith and were under no professional obligation or moral duty to call the Andrews patent to the attention of the Patent Office while the application which resulted in 025 was pending."

Failure to inform the Patent Examiner of pertinent prior art known to the applicant does not constitute fraud, so long as the prior art known to the applicant is not anticipatory. If it is anticipatory, the patent may be held invalid for lack of novelty, rather than on the ground of fraud. Where the applicant cited a prior patent merely by name after allowance, without giving its patent number, while it was buried in a long list of other citations previously considered, it was held that fraud had not been proved, but the patent in suit was held invalid over the vaguely cited prior patent. *Tipper Tie, Inc.* v. *Hercules Fasteners, Inc.*, 105 USPQ 182, DC NJ 1955.

One of the few reported cases in which a patent has been held to be invalid by reason of the applicant's failure to disclose the best prior art to the Patent Office is *W. E. Pleachaty Co.* v. *Heckett Engineering Inc.*, 145 F.Supp. 805, 111 USPQ 234, DC NOhio 1956. This case held the patent in suit to be anticipated by the applicant's own prior patent which had not been called to the attention of the Patent Office. For this reason, the patent in suit was held to be invalid, on a motion for summary judgment. Here, the patent would appear to have been invalid for anticipation, regardless of any question of fraud.

Defendant's charge of fraud failed, on the other hand, where it was based on the patentee's failure to cite his own prior patent and the court considered the prior patent to have no real pertinency. *Aghnides* v. *Meyer's Co.*, 99 USPQ 488, DC MNC 1954.

In submitting affidavits to the Patent Office, only test results helpful to the applicant were submitted. This was held to have been a misrepresentation to the Patent Office, resulting in a destruction of the presumption of validity, and the patent in suit was held to be invalid and not infringed. *Floridin Co.* v. *Attapulgus Clay Co.*, 35 F.Supp. 810, 47 USPQ 332, DC Del 1940.

Deceptive intention, like fraud, is never presumed. Where there had been many intermediaries between the inventor and the original attorneys, incorrect representations were excused because fraud had not been proved. *Hazeltine Research Inc.* v. *Avco Mfg. Corp.*, 126 F.Supp. 595, DC NIll 1954; aff. 227 F.2d 137, 107 USPQ 187 CA 7 1955.

However, where a patent had been held invalid because the best prior art had not been revealed to the Examiner, and affidavits had been submitted showing superiority over the cited art, but not over the most pertinent art known to the applicant, the trial court held the patent to be invalid for wilful concealment. On appeal, the holding of invalidity was affirmed on another point, but the trial court's holding of fraud was reversed, as the attorney had been precluded from testifying, and the patent was held invalid for lack of invention. *Triumph Hosiery Mills, Inc.* v. *Alamance Industries, Inc.*, 128 USPQ 471, DC MNC 1961, 299 F.2d 793, CA 4 1962.

An applicant need not call the attention of the Examiner to a prior patent which, if pertinent, his search should reveal. *Admiral Corp.* v. *Zenith Radio Corp.*, 296 F.2d 708, 131 USPQ 456, CA 10 1961. In such a case, it would be difficult to prove whether the Examiner had merely overlooked the prior patent or had considered it and decided it was not pertinent.

The charge of fraud on the Patent Office by failure to call the Examiner's attention to prior art, failed in the absence of special circumstances, since the proof of fraud was not clear, unequivocal and convincing. *Becton-Dickinson & Co.* v. *R. P. Scherer Corp.*, 106 F.Supp. 665, DC EMich 1952; aff., 101 USPQ 98, CA 6 1954.

If the prior art has questionable pertinency, the applicant is under no duty to cite it to the Patent Office. In *U.S.* v. *Standard Electric Time Co.*, 116 USPQ 14, DC Mass 1957, the court held that the applicant was not required to set up straw men, if in good faith he believed he could knock them down. Aff., 254 F.2d 598, 116 USPQ 422, CA 1 1958.

Suppression or Omission of Facts

A patentee had settled an interference, suppressing some of the facts, and had listed many licensees to show commercial success in his arguments before the Patent Office. However, he had withheld information that the licenses contained price-fixing provisions. In a suit to recoup royalties which had been paid under such a patent, the charge of fraud was not sustained, as there was no proof that the truth had been deliberately suppressed. However, the patent was held to be invalid for another reason. *American Chain and Cable Co. Inc.* v. *Rochester Ropes, Inc.*, 199 F.2d 325, 95 USPQ 115, CA 4 1952.

In *The Providence Rubber Co.* v. *Goodyear*, 76 U.S. 788, 9 Wall 788, 1870, Goodyear's executor sued on a patent which had been extended. The alleged infringer defended on the ground that the extension had been procured by fraudulent suppressions, concealments and misrepresentations. The Supreme Court ruled that, when the fraud arose on circumstances outside the grant (not on the face of the patent), (1) the decision of the Commissioner of Patents in extending the patent was conclusive until impeached in a proceeding held directly for that purpose, and (2) the court was not at liberty to examine the evidences of fraud in the extension. To the same effect is *Mowry*

v. *Whitney*, 81 U.S. 434, 1872, 20 L.Ed. 858.

Where it is proved that the patent actually contained less than the whole truth as to the invention, and that vital features of a dye to be used had been omitted, the patent was held to be invalid under R. S. 4920 (now repealed). *Electric Boot and Shoe Finishing Co.* v. *Little et al.*, 75 Fed. 276, C.C.D. Mass. 1896; aff., 138 Fed. 732, CA 1 1905.

Connivance between Parties

Connivance between the plaintiff, patent owner, and another to suppress the true facts as to the questions of priority of invention may result in a holding of invalidity or unenforceability. *Keystone Driller Co.* v. *General Excavator Co.*, supra.

Connivance between the litigating parties will result in a dismissal of plaintiff's suit, even where suit is against the other conniving party, if the conduct was not in accordance with the high standards demanded of a plaintiff in equity. The plaintiff and defendant had been involved in patent interference proceedings, the defendant had filed a false preliminary statement, the plaintiff learned of the falsity of these statements and did not inform the Patent Office of their falsity (upon the advice of counsel), but instead negotiated a settlement of the interference by which the defendant abandoned his patent application. Defendant later breached his settlement agreement and was sued for patent infringement. By reason of the fact that the plaintiff had not reported to the Patent Office the defendant's wrongful conduct, the court would not give the plaintiff the relief which was sought, although there was nothing strictly illegal about the plaintiff's conduct in not informing the Patent Office about the falsity of the defendant's preliminary statement. *Precision Instrument Mfg. Co.* v. *Automotive Maintenance Machinery Co.*, 324 U.S. 806, 325 U.S. 843, 893, 65 USPQ 133, 1945.

Unclean Hands

The "Clean Hands Doctrine" is the coming of a party to litigation into court with no record of improper conduct that would prevent his obtaining the relief for which he might otherwise be entitled. (See *Clean Hands*)

A decision on motion held that a defense of "unclean hands" was a good defense and that "fraud being alleged, the defendant should be permitted liberal defensive pleading." The motion to strike portions of the answer was denied. *Radtke Patents Corp.* v. *C. J. Tagliabue Mfg. Co., Inc.*, 31 F.Supp. 226, 44 USPQ 203, DC ENY 1939.

While fraud or acts amounting to unclean hands form an adequate defense, it is a defense which must be properly raised and fully proved if it is to be sustained. Many of the cases in which fraud has been raised as a defense by a private party or by the government, as the basis of a suit for impeachment or repeal of a patent, have failed because fraud has not been adequately proved. If fraud is asserted, none of the elements can be left to conjecture or possible innocent explanation.

A rather different type of unacceptable behavior was involved in *Seismograph Service Co.* v. *Offshore Raydist, Inc.*, 135 F.Supp. 342, DC ELa 1955; 119 USPQ 146, CA 5 1958. Here the plaintiff patentee sued one whose work they had decided to appropriate. The plaintiff had spied on the defendant's work and on his patent counsel, learned that the poor defendant had not filed applications, and then proceeded to file for the patents in suit. The court said "now Seismograph has the effrontery to come into a court of equity to ask that its patents, so obtained, be used to enjoin the very man who gave them life." The District Judge said "The robber baron morality of another day is no longer acceptable...." The court held the patents in suit invalid and ruled that, had the patents been valid, the defendant would have been awarded a royalty-free license.

Not only fraud or illegality, but any really unconscionable conduct by an applicant is sufficient to show his unclean hands, provided the wrongs are directly related to the rights in issue. In an interference, the applicant relied on admittedly forged documents. The applicant expressly abandoned reliance on the forged evidence, but was eventually convicted and sentenced to imprisonment. Judgment of priority was awarded against him and, in his equity interference suit, the suit was dismissed for unclean hands. The applicant then sued at law for damages, but the plaintiff was estopped on the principle of *res judicata* based on the prior Patent Office decision. The suit was dismissed for unclean hands, and the court held the claim was also barred by the statute of limitations. *Mas* v. *U.S.*, 151 F.2d 32, CA DistCol 1945; *Mas* v. *Coca-Cola Co.*, 74 USPQ 275, CA 4 1947; *Mas et al.* v. *Coca-Cola Co.*, 198 F.2d 380, CA 4 1952.

Undue Influence on Court

Fortunately, there have been few cases involving corruption of the courts in patent cases.

Based upon a Master's report, the Circuit Court of Appeals for the Third Circuit in one case vacated its judgment on the ground that it had been corruptly obtained. The Supreme Court granted certiorari to review the taxing of the Master's and attorney's fees and held that, as the *amici* had substantial private interests in the case, their attorney's fees should not be part of the taxable costs. *Universal Oil Products Co.* v. *Root Refining Co.*, 328 U.S. 575, 69 USPQ 454, 1946.

Plaintiff's failure to rebut a previous, corruptly obtained judgment of validity and infringement resulted in it being denied all relief. The subsequent case was remanded to the District Court to determine whether an accounting of costs incurred and damages should be made against plaintiff. The issue of fraud was held to be *res judicata*. *Hartford-Empire Co.* v. *Shawkee Mfg. Co.*, 163 F.2d 474, 74 USPQ 252, CA 3 1947; *Shawkee Mfg. Co.* v. *Hartford-Empire Co.*, 322 U.S. 271, 64 Sup.Ct. 1014, 1944.

Recourse of Government

A private party who sued for damages allegedly flowing from a fraudulently procured patent was non-suited in the Federal court on the ground that only the United States can sue to repeal a patent, and that a suit for damages does not arise under the patent laws. As the suit was by a New York resident against a New York corporation, there was no diversity, and it was further held that the Federal court did not have jurisdiction. *Engler* v. *General Electric Co.*, 42 USPQ 593, DC SNY 1939; aff. 62 USPQ 259 and 64 USPQ 91, 1944.

While only the United States government may sue to repeal a patent, a private defendant in an infringement suit may defend on the ground that the patent was obtained by fraud.

The Court of Appeals for the 7th Circuit, in a case where the plaintiff charged fraud in the procurement of a patent, said "Plaintiff overlooks the well-established rule of law that alleged fraud in the procurement of a patent cannot be raised as a defense in an action for patent infringement. Only the United States can bring a suit charging that a patent was obtained by fraud." *United Mfg. & Service Corp.* v. *Holwin Corp.*, 95 USPQ 176, DC NIll 1952.

In *E. W. Bliss* v. *Cold Metal Process Co.*, 102 F.2d 105, CA 6 1939, plaintiff's allegations of fraud and deception in the securing of the patent were ordered struck from the complaint, on the ground that a private litigant cannot by a bill in equity have a patent declared void on the ground that it had been fraudulently obtained. However, in making this ruling the court went on to hold that an amendment to the complaint could be considered if the defendant sought affirmative relief by way of counterclaim.

The government sued to impeach two separate but related patents in one suit, alleging merely that Bell knew of prior inventions by others while still claiming them as its own. This complaint, although it did not detail the evidence supporting this allegation, was held to state a good cause of action. *U.S.* v. *American Bell Telephone Co.*, 128 U.S. 315, 32 L.Ed. 450, 1888.

In another suit, *U.S.* v. *American Bell Telephone Co.*, 167 U.S. 224, 1897, 17 Sup.Ct. 809, 14 years delay in bringing the suit and the fact that the government had no pecuniary interest in setting aside the patent, subjected the government to the rules governing similar suits between private litigants. The court sustained dismissal of the suit.

In *Dimet Proprietary, Ltd.* v. *Industrial Metal Protectives, Inc.*, 109 F.Supp. 472, 96 USPQ 33, DC Del 1952, the court said "That a proceeding by the United States itself is the sole method whereby a patent can be cancelled or annulled for fraud in the procurement of the patent seems too clear for argument," and struck from the complaint allegations of fraud.

Literature

For certain government cases now of historical importance only, the reader is referred to the following, where they are treated in detail: Deller's Edition of "Walker on Patents," (2nd ed.), Vol. II p. 1186 ff.; Amdur, "Patent Law and Practice," p. 903 ff.; Keaveney, "Fraud in the Procurement of a Patent as a Defense to Infringement," 33 JPOS 482-501, 1951; and Cullen and Vickers, "Fraud in the Procurement of a Patent," 29 George Washington Law Review 110-135, 1960.

Cross-references: *Attorneys and Agents, Clean Hands, Prosecution.*

G

GENERAL AND MECHANICAL APPLICATIONS

George V. Woodling

This article is based upon the author's "Inventions and Their Protection," Matthew Bender & Co., Albany 1, N.Y., 1954.

The Patent Office expects diligence on the part of the inventor in the filing of his application, but undue haste often proves to be as unwise as lack of diligence. Therefore, the effort to get a patent as quickly as possible without due regard to a well-prepared application should be discouraged. A hurriedly prepared application frequently will be found to disclose an inoperative device or can mature into a weak patent giving little or no protection.

Drawing

The applicant for a patent is required by law to furnish a drawing or drawings of his invention whenever the nature of the case admits of it. See article "Drawings" and also Fig. 1 herein.

Specification

The specification shall contain a written description of the invention and of the manner and process of making and using it, in such full, clear, concise and exact terms as to enable any person skilled in the art to which it pertains, or with which it is most nearly connected, to make and use the same; shall set forth the best mode contemplated by the inventor of carrying out his invention; and shall conclude with one or more claims particularly pointing out and distinctly claiming the subject matter which the applicant regards as his invention.

Opening Paragraph Should Be as Broad as the Invention. The opening paragraph is to inform the reader, at the outset of the specification, of the subject matter to which the invention relates so that the remainder of the application may be read with reference to it. Note the opening paragraph "A" of the sample patent 2,342,788, and Fig. 1.

UNITED STATES PATENT OFFICE

2,342,788

WIRE CONNECTING SLEEVE

Leroy H. Burns, Cleveland, Ohio, assignor to The National Telephone Supply Company, a corporation of Ohio

Application July 21, 1942, Serial No. 451,808

2 Claims. (Cl. 16—108)

(The characters **A-F** indicate different sections of the patent but do not appear in the case as sent to the Patent Office.)

A. This invention relates to improvements in wire connecting devices and more particularly to wire connecting devices in the form of a sleeve for making joints in wires which are of high strength and which have a hard surface.

B. A great deal of difficulty has been experienced in making sleeve connecters for hard, high tensile bare steel wires. This difficulty arises from the fact that the wire is so hard that penetration into the surface thereof cannot be successfully attained by known methods used in joining softer wires together by compressing sleeves around the wires to be joined.

C. An object of my invention is to provide for coating the inside wall of a sleeve with a hard material which has the property of penetrating the hard, high tensile bare steel wires.

Another object of my invention is the provision of coating the inside wall of a wire connecting sleeve with fired porcelain, so that when the sleeve is compressed upon the hard steel wire the porcelain is crushed into a multitude of hard, sharp particles which act as an abrasive between the wire and the sleeve to produce a high holding power for joining the wires together.

Other objects and a fuller understanding of my invention may be had by referring to the follow-

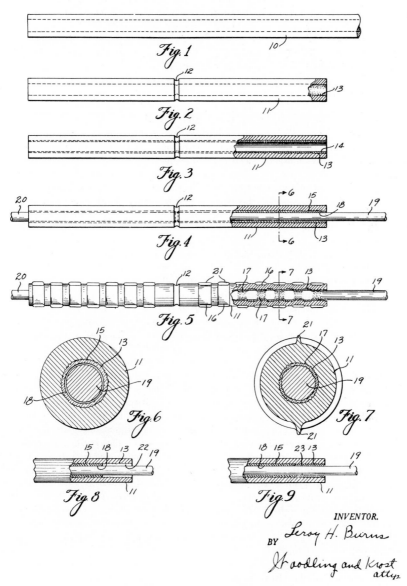

Feb. 29, 1944.   L. H. BURNS   2,342,788

WIRE CONNECTING SLEEVE

Filed July 21, 1942

INVENTOR.

BY Leroy H. Burns

Woodling and Krost
attys.

FIG. 1. Sample of patent drawing.

ing description and claims, taken in conjunction with the accompanying drawing, in which:

D. Figure 1 represents a view of a tube from which my sleeve may be constructed;

Figure 2 is a view of a sleeve cut from the tube in Figure 1 and having the inner wall thereof sand blasted;

Figure 3 is a view of the sleeve in Figure 2 which shows the application of porcelain to the inner wall of the sleeve, the porcelain in Figure 3 being in a liquid or slip state;

Figure 4 is a view of the sleeve in Figure 3 after it has been fired, rendering the porcelain hard for the reception of the wires to be joined;

Figure 5 is a view of the sleeve after it has been compressed about the wire and showing particularly the manner in which the cracked or crushed porcelain penetrates the hard surface of the wires to be joined;

Figure 6 is an enlarged cross-sectional view taken along the line 6—6 on Figure 4, showing particularly the fired porcelain prior to it being compressed about the wire;

Figure 7 is a view similar to Figure 6 taken along the line 7—7 of Figure 5 and showing the disposition of the crushed porcelain after the sleeve has been compressed about the wires to be joined;

Figure 8 is a fragmentary view of the right-hand end of Figure 4 and shows a portion of the porcelain removed so that as the end of the sleeve is compressed about the wire there is an intimate metal to metal contact to provide a good electrical conductivity; and

Figure 9 is a view similar to Figure 8 but shows a metal tube inserted into the end of the wire connected sleeve for making a metal to metal contact between the wire and the sleeve to provide a good electrical conductivity.

E. With reference to the drawing, my finished sleeve is shown in Figure 4 and comprises a metal sleeve 11 having the inner wall thereof coated with a thin layer of fired porcelain 15. In constructing the sleeve 11 I take a long tubular member such, for example, as illustrated in Figure 1 by the reference character 10 and cut it into pieces of suitable length to receive the ends of the wires to be joined. The center portion of the sleeve 11 may be rolled as indicated at 12 in order to provide a restriction in the internal diameter of the sleeve to act as stops for the insertion of the wires from opposite ends of the sleeve. In other words, the internal stops afforded by the external rolling of the sleeve prevents one wire from going beyond the longitudinal center of the sleeve in which event the other wire would not have the full benefit of the engagement by the sleeve. Prior to the application of the porcelain in a liquid state to the inner wall of the sleeve, I preferably provide for sand blasting the internal wall of the sleeve such as indicated by the reference character 13. After the sleeve is sand blasted, the next operation is to dip the sleeve into porcelain in a liquid state, after which the outside surface of the sleeve is wiped clean of the porcelain, thus leaving a thin layer of the liquid porcelain as indicated by the reference character 14 on the inner wall of the sleeve. After the sleeve is dipped and cleaned on the outside, the next operation is to fire the porcelain for making it hard and brittle and for bonding it to the inner wall of the sleeve, as illustrated in Figures 4 and 6. The fired porcelain may be the same as that used commercially as a finish on steel cooking utensils, metal signs, stove parts, etc. It is found that one dipping of the sleeve is sufficient to make a layer of porcelain suitable for joining hard surface wires, although more than one dip or application may be applied depending upon the desired thickness of the lining of porcelain, in which case the sleeve is fired after each dip or application of the porcelain slip.

The sleeve is made of malleable metal and may be pressed about the wires to be joined by any suitable means or other arrangement of dies or rolling tools. In actual practice, I preferably compress the sleeve about the wires to be joined by means of a constant movement toggle clamping tool having clamping dies for engaging the sleeve at spaced intervals. A constant movement toggle type of compression tool is arranged to move the dies inwardly during the compression of the sleeve about the wires a definite amount as determined by the adjustment or setting of the tool. I am not limiting myself to the type of tool for compressing the sleeve about the wires to be joined as a screw or cam actuated press, or a hydraulic ram can be used and are even more desirable on the larger sizes than a constant movement toggle tool. Other tools which can be used are the impact tool and the rolling tool. The Figure 5 shows a sleeve which has been compressed by a constant movement toggle tool and the reference character 16 represents the compressed portions along the sleeve as effected by the dies of the constant movement toggle tool. The flashes or the flow of excess metal between the mating edges of the dies of the tool are indicated by the reference character 21. When the sleeve is compressed, the porcelain is crushed into a multitude of hard, sharp particles which act as an abrasive between the wire and the sleeve to give a good gripping engagement between the sleeve and the wire. The crushed porcelain is indicated by the reference character 17 and has the property of penetrating into the hard surface of the wires to be joined as well as into the inner wall surface of the sleeve, see Figures 5 and 7. Another desirable feature of the porcelain lining is the fact that it is relatively smooth and no difficulty is encountered in inserting the wires into the sleeve. Figure 6 shows the feature that the porcelain makes a smooth wall finish which obviates any difficulty of inserting the wires into the sleeve. The smooth inner wall of the porcelain is indicated by the reference character 18 and the wires to be joined are indicated by the reference characters 19 and 20. In adapting the sleeve for electrical conduction, I preferably use either one of two arrangements as shown in Figures 8 and 9. In Figure 8 I remove a portion of the porcelain lining as indicated by the reference character 22 so that when the right-hand end of the sleeve in Figure 8 is compressed against the wire 19 there is provided a metal to metal contact to give good electrical conductivity. The porcelain may be removed before it is fired. In Figure 9 I show an arrangement of inserting a metal tube 23 which when the sleeve is compressed upon the wires, provides a metal to metal contact between the wires and the sleeve to give good conductivity. The tube 23 takes up the space left vacant as indicated by the reference character 22 in Figure 8.

In my invention the porcelain lining may be considered a sleeve bonded to the inner wall of the malleable outer sleeve 11. The thickness of the porcelain lining is relatively thin compared to the thickness of the wall of the surrounding metal sleeve. Tests show that my invention with the use of porcelain gives a large holding or gripping action between the sleeve and the wire and results from the fact that the porcelain is sufficiently hard to penetrate the hard outer surface of the wires to be joined and the inner wall surface of the sleeve.

The terms "wire" and "tubular body" as used herein are not limited to the showings in the drawing, as obvious variations may be employed. The end-to-end disposition of the joined wires to give a butt connection is not necessarily restricted to the arrangement illustrated in the drawings, as such variations may be made that wall within the scope of the invention as claimed.

Although I have described my invention with a certain degree of particularity, it is understood that the present disclosure has been made only by way of example and that numerous changes in the details of construction and the combination and arrangement of parts may be resorted to without departing from the spirit and the scope of the invention as hereinafter claimed.

F. I claim as my invention:

1. A wire connecting sleeve comprising a tubular body formed of malleable metal whose inner wall is coated with a relatively thin layer of wire engaging material formed of fired porcelain bonded thereto.

2. A wire connecting sleeve comprising an exterior tubular body formed of malleable metal and an interior tubular body of thinner construction than the exterior body and formed of fired porcelain, said fired porcelain being bonded to the inner wall of the exterior body.

LEROY H. BURNS.

In order not to restrict the scope of the patent protection, the opening paragraph "A" should be not only as broad as the invention but also as free of structural features as possible. For example, if an invention relates to the knife C having folding blades and a coacting spring to hold the blades in any one of several selectable positions, as shown in Fig. 2 below, the introductory paragraph of the specification may read:

"My invention relates in general to knives, and more particularly to a knife having *a folding blade.*"

It is best to avoid the practice of stating in the opening paragraph the specification of the several parts of the invention.

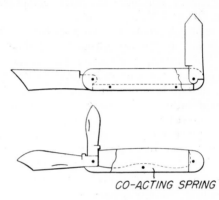

CO-ACTING SPRING

FIG. 2.

The recitation of the *plurality* of folding blades pivotally connected to an end of the handle limits the scope of the invention and, as will be seen later, such a recitation is not so broad in patent law as the recitation of "a" blade.

If a pocket knife has three blades, it has *a* blade plus *two* extra blades, which means that the unauthorized manufacture and sale of a pocket knife with three blades would infringe a patent claiming "a blade." The "two" extra blades are legally insignificant in any attempt to avoid infringement. A fundamental policy in claim drafting to obtain broad protection is to direct the claims to a "minimum structure" (a blade) rather than to a "maximum structure" (a plurality of blades). With a "minimum structure" claim, an unauthorized manufacturer is guilty of infringement whether he makes and sells a device consisting of either the minimum structure or the maximum structure.

Setting Forth Problem Solved Clarifies Objects. Sometimes it is good practice to set forth the general nature of the problem or the deficiencies of prior devices which your invention solves prior to giving a general statement of the objects. This should not amount to a "recital of the history" of the prior art or patents, because such a recital is generally of no assistance in interpreting the scope of the particular invention. Nor is it permissible to make specific derogatory statements as to inventions of others. The inventor, however, may point out within reasonable limits the defects or deficiencies common to prior structures. (See "**B**" and "**C**" of patent)

General Statement of Objects Should Be as Broad as the Invention. The "objects" ("**C**" of patent), such as usually stated in mechanical cases, must be coextensive with the claims, in order to avoid a restricted interpretation of the scope of the invention. They must be as free as possible from structural description of the features of the invention. On the other hand, the objects should not be so broad and general in their terms as to render them meaningless. They should be comprehensive and at the same time as definite as possible. (See *Applications—Electrical and Electronic*)

The purpose of an object is to state the desired result accomplished by the invention. If a structure is recited in an object, it avoids the purpose of the object, because an object with structure no longer states the desired result but the means for producing it. As will be seen later, the means by which a result is accomplished is a function of a claim and not of an object. The recitation of structure in the objects may tend to convert the objects into claims, and produce, in effect, a set of claims in addition to the proper set of claims. This duplication of claims may cause confusion as to the real scope of the patent protection. Consequently, an object which merely paraphrases a claim should be avoided.

Objects Need Not Define Patentable Subject Matter Over Prior Devices. The general statement of the objects, when given at all, need not define patentable subject matter over prior art. This is true because the applicant's invention may consist of a new way of accomplishing an old thing, and thus

the general objects may be the same as the objectives of older devices. Therefore, a statement of the general objects which is commensurate with the prior art is not objectionable.

The inventor may present in his application as many objects as he considers necessary to cover every essential feature of his invention. Accordingly, there is no rule as to the number of objects that may be presented. For a "single thought" invention, one object may be sufficient. If the invention is complicated, it may take a dozen or more objects to state adequately the scope of the complete invention.

In order to focus the attention of the reader upon each object of the invention, it is sometimes a good plan to present each object in a separate paragraph, but it is not necessary. Choice of style generally depends upon the best judgment of the attorney preparing the application. In the sample patent, observe that each object is set forth in separate paragraphs.

General Statement of Objects Should End with an All-inclusive Paragraph. To guard against the possibility of overlooking one or more objects of the invention, it is orthodox practice to end the general statement of objects with a closing all-inclusive paragraph which brings in those features which might have inadvertently been omitted. Note the concluding paragraph of "C," of patent.

Brief Description of Several Views of Drawing Should Not Recite Elements of Invention. As shown in the lines between "**D**" and "**E**" of sample patent, it is not required that the brief description of the several views of the drawing recite the elements of the invention. The main purpose is to introduce generally the several views before going into the detailed description of them. A separate paragraph should be used for each view of the invention shown in the drawing.

The views of the drawing should be numbered consecutively. In laying them out on the drawing paper, it is effective to show each stage of manufacture in separate views leading up to the assembled or complete view of the device, as shown in Fig. 5 of the sample patent drawing. The cross-section or detailed views may be shown in the remaining figures. If a view is a cross-section of a part of another figure, then each end of the section line is designed by the number of the cross-sectional view. Thus, in the patent drawing of Fig. 1, the section for Fig. 6 is designated as on line 6-6 of Fig. 4.

Detailed Description Must Be Clear and Complete. The detailed description immediately follows the brief description of the several views of the drawing. The detailed description begins at "E" on line 14, column 2, of the first page of the sample patent, and ends at "F" on line 40, column 2, page 2. As illustrated in the patent, the description should refer to the different parts of the invention by reference characters. It is required that the reference characters in the description coincide with those in the drawings and that like parts of the invention should be designated by the same characters in all the views.

The purpose of the detailed description is to give a full explanation of the invention on which a patent is sought, and it is the duty of the Patent Office to reject the application if it is inadequately described. If the description is inadequate and there is not sufficient foundation to round out the description by amendment, the applicant may be denied the right to a patent. The description and the drawing must be read in connection with each other. If the description is inadequate but the drawing is sufficient, the description may be rendered adequate by amendment and vice versa. In case of a valid doubt, it is better to over- than under-describe. But over-describing does not mean the duplication of portions previously described. Nor does it mean the inclusion in detail of that which is old or already well known in the field.

The Patent Office is reluctant to admit later discovered knowledge to the patent application and will not permit it if the later discovered knowledge constitutes new matter. However, if the supplemental information is made only to clarify an initial description, then the Patent Office will permit such amendment to the application. To guard against filing an inadequate description or specification, the inventor should explore in advance all possible potentialities of the invention. This may be done by the process of questioning the merits and purposes of the invention with others who are qualified to analyze the disclosure critically.

As a general rule, the inventor should not call different parts by the same name or the same part of the invention by different names. If the part is initially described as a "lever," it would be well to continue to call it a "lever." A departure from this rule is permissible if there is a special reason for establishing a broad range of equivalency of the parts, in which case a "lever" may be variously described as a "pivotally mounted arm" or a "pivoted member."

It is well to give considerable thought to the proper use of words and every effort should be made to use them in their technical and dictionary sense and not in a loose way. Sometimes a review of prior patents in the same general class of inventions may be helpful in selecting and using the right words in preparing the application.

Begin Description by Generally Describing the Complete Machine with Which Improved Part Cooperates. If the invention relates to a mere localized improvement in some part of a machine, the detailed description may begin by describing briefly the complete machine with which the improved localized part cooperates. This method initially sets forth the general environment in which the invention resides and distinguishes what is old from what is new.

Immediately following the brief description of the old parts of the machine with which the newly invented part is to cooperate is a detailed description of the construction and the operation of the newly invented part. It is preferable to keep the detailed description of the construction separate from the description of the operation.

In some patents, the description of the operation is woven into the description of the construction without any separation. The choice between separating the construction and operation or weaving them together in the description depends upon the complexity of the operation of the machine. Regardless of which method is used, the applicant should make certain that the detailed description is sufficient to teach *how to construct* and *how to operate* the device.

If Invention Resides in Entire Machine, Description May Begin by Positively Introducing Essential Elements. If the invention resides more particularly in the entire device than in some improved part, then the patent specification or detailed description may begin by positively introducing the essential elements of the entire device. Suppose that the entire machine relates to a steam engine which consists of five major parts, namely, a cylinder 10, a piston 11, a crankshaft 12, a connecting rod 13 and a flywheel 14. Naturally each of these major parts is made up of a number of subparts. Where the invention resides in the entire device or machine, such as a steam engine, the detailed description may be initiated by drafting a comprehensive first paragraph setting forth a "catalog plus a function" of these essential elements. Such a comprehensive paragraph may conceivably read as follows:

"With reference to the patent drawings, my invention of a steam engine comprises, in general, a cylinder 10, a piston 11 reciprocally mounted in the cylinder 10, a crankshaft 12 mounted for rotational movement, a connecting rod 13 interconnecting the piston 11 and the crankshaft 12, and a flywheel 14 mounted on the crankshaft."

The purpose of a comprehensive paragraph as illustrated above is to give the reader a clear-cut picture of the entire machine at the outset and reduce the difficulty of understanding the invention as the description proceeds.

After the comprehensive first paragraph, the patent specification may then proceed with a separate detailed description of each of the essential parts including their respective subparts to provide a well-rounded explanation. These separate detailed descriptions should point up the inventive features of the machine. The description should conclude with an explanation of the operation of the complete machine.

In the comprehensive first paragraph, avoid the mere cataloging of elements without setting forth their functions or how they cooperate, as illustrated by the following faulty statement: "With reference to the patent drawings, my invention of a steam engine comprises a cylinder 10, a piston 11, a crankshaft 12, a connecting rod 13, and a flywheel 14." Here the reader gains no idea as to how the several parts of the steam engine cooperate, because the function and combinations are omitted.

Dimensions. It is usually unnecessary to describe specifically the kind of material or the dimensions of the parts, because these are matters left to the discretion of those skilled in the art. If these factors, however, go to the essence of the invention, then they must be specifically set forth and frequently are stated in an Example of the invention.

Comprehensive Final Paragraph. See sample patent, page 2, above "F."

Claims And Their Importance

Immediately following the closing paragraph of the detailed description are the claims. (See "F" of the sample patent.) The claims are the most important features of a patent application and are discussed, for general and mechanical cases, under *Claim Drafting* and also under other arts.

Signature

The signature(s) for the patent application will be affixed on the standard "Single Signature Form," No. 16 in the Rules. It provides the Oath, Power of Attorney and Petition. It requires signature by the applicant(s) in person, with the first name in full, middle initial (or name) if any, and last name. It is good practice for an inventor or writer of technical articles to standardize on a single signature, so that he will not be indexed variously but his contributions in a given period will show under the one entry in the Index of Patentees, Chemical Abstracts or elsewhere.

For a discussion of changes in an application after execution, see *Fraud*.

Cross-references: *Applications—Electrical and Electronic, Claim Drafting, Claims—Words and Phrases, Validity—Sec. Functionality of Claims, Chemical, Design, Microbiological, and Pharmaceutical Applications.*

GLOSSARY OF PATENT TERMS

Kurt Kelman

The following abbreviations are used herein: "Section," the indicated section of Title 35, U.S. Code; "R.," rule of no. shown from Rules of Practice of the U.S. Patent Office in Patent Cases; and "M.P.E.P." (followed by the sec. no.) for the Manual of Patent Examining Procedure, 3d ed.

For other subjects and major titles, see the Index.

[As to italic or roman text for Latin and other foreign language terms, the practice here followed generally, with the exception of et al., inter alia (os) and status quo which seem to be anglicized, is that adopted in Merriam's New International Dictionary, Second ed., as explained on page xcvi, note (f). Ed.]

abandonment of contest. In interference cases, the concession of priority or abandonment of the invention by a party, with the written consent of the assignee when an assignment has been made (R. 267).

ab initio. From the start; originally.

abstract of title. Statement of ownership of patent recorded in the Patent Office and obtainable therefrom.

action. See office action.

advancement of application. Examination out of turn, made only upon showing to Commissioner of good and sufficient reason (R. 102).

aggregation. No cooperation between elements of claims, a cause for rejection. An invention need not be aggregative, however, solely because all elements do not function simultaneously (M.P.E.P. 706.03i).

A.I. Series. A separate series of numbers, preceded by A.I., for 1838 to 1861 patents to inventors for improvements on their own patented devices (M.P.E.P. 901.04).

alter ego. Second self.

alternative expression. Alternative expression in claims covering two different elements, such as "alcohol or acetone," objectionable because indefinite. For two *equivalent* parts or alternate words for the *same structure*, such as "rods or bars," the expression is proper (M.P.E.P. 706.03d).

amicus curiae. Friend of the court; one who joins in a court action.

analogous art. References directed to the same necessary function or utility of subject matter, such as brick cutting and dough cutting machines, are analogous art and may be cited, one against the other, by the examiner (M.P.E.P. 904.01c).

annuity. Annual renewal fee to maintain a patent in force; common in foreign patent systems.

antecedent. Positive recital of claimed feature before referring back to it; all terms used in the claims should have antecedents also in the description.

assignor. The transferor (usually seller) of patent rights.

basic patent. See pioneer patent.

Board of Appeals. The Commissioner, Assistant Commissioners and a group of Examiners-in-Chief for review of decisions of examiners on appeals by applicants.

bona fide. In good faith; genuine.

brief. Statement of the facts, reasons, and authorities relied upon to support any action including motions, petitions to the Commissioner, appeals, interference actions, and court proceedings (R. 181, 192, 243, 244).

broader than the invention. Coverage by a claim of more than disclosed in the application or patent.

burden of proof. In interference cases, the burden of proof is on the junior party. In infringement suits, the burden of proving infringement rests upon the plaintiff; of proving invalidity, upon the defendant.

cancellation of claims. Striking claims from an application, by amendment, usually for purpose of complying with the Examiner's holding that the claims are unpatentable.

certificate of correction. Statement of correction issued when, (1) due to fault of the Patent Office, such action is necessary or (2) a mistake of a minor character, made by the applicant, appears in the patent and was made in good faith.

certified copy. A certified copy of the original application, as may be required in priority cases (Sec. 119) or for other purposes.

certiorari denied (abbrev. c.d. or cert. den.) Declination by a court to review the decision of a lower court. An example is the refusal of the Supreme Court to review a case presented to it, ordinarily because of absence of either a constitutional issue or absence of diversity of opinion in Circuit Court decisions on the case.

citation. Prior art listed as anticipatory by examiner; a previous decision relied upon.

citation of authorities. Reference to laws, pertinent court cases or publications to support a position taken.

claims. That part of the specification particularly pointing out and distinctly reciting the subject matter of the invention. (Sec. 112; R. 71, 75).

classification. A subject matter division of patents in the various arts, published in the Manual of Classification and Classification Bulletins.

clean hands. The doctrine that one seeking relief should not be committing a related wrong.

combination. The result or product of interacting elements. All or some of the elements may be new or old but the combination is patentable if it is novel, useful and not obvious in over-all effect.

combination of references. A combination claim may be validly rejected over a combination of references each showing one or more of the claimed features only if the claimed combination as a whole is obvious from the prior art.

Commissioner of Patents. Person designated by the President, with the consent of the Senate, to head the Patent Office.

composition of matter. A new and useful compound or mixture. (Sec. 101.)

"comprising," "consisting essentially of," "consisting of." See *Claims—Words and Phrases*

concealment. Keeping an invention secret and suppressing it, as, for instance, until after another person discovers it and files an application upon it or begins to use it. A concealed and suppressed invention cannot establish a date for priority of inventorship (Sec. 102g).

conception. The mental part of the inventive act which, if relied upon, must be capable of proof, as by drawings or disclosure to another person (M.P.E.P. 715.07). *Mergenthaler* v. *Scudder,* 1897 C.D. 724.

confidential relationship. A fiduciary relationship between client and agent or attorney, or between any two parties.

confirmation patent. Patents granted in some countries on the basis of previously granted patents in other countries.

constructive reduction to practice. Filing application for patents (M.P.E.P. 715.07).

continuation. A second application for the same invention claimed or disclosed in a prior application, filed before the original is abandoned, by the same applicant and introducing no new matter. It may be used to introduce a new set of claims after final rejection for further examination by the Primary Examiner (M.P.E.P. 201.07) and is entitled to the filing date of the original application (M.P.E.P. 210.11).

continuation-in-part application. An application filed during the lifetime of an earlier application by the same applicant, repeating some substantial portion or all of the earlier application and adding matter not disclosed in the earlier case (M.P.E.P. 211.8).

contributory infringement. Infringement arising when anyone induces infringement or sells a component of a patented invention or a material or apparatus used in practising a patented process, knowing the same to be specially made and adapted for use in an infringement of such patent, unless said component is a staple article suitable for substantial noninfringing use (Sec. 271).

copending. Pending, that is, on file and active in the Patent Office at the same time with another application of the same or a different applicant.

copying claim. Amending an application to include a claim from an issued patent for the purpose of an interference (*q.v.*) to determine who is the first inventor of what the copied claim describes.

corroboration of an inventor. Evidence by someone to substantiate statements made by another, as, for example, by one who is not a joint inventor, to confirm an inventor as to date of invention.

count. In interferences, an interfering claim.

Court of Appeals. A court having jurisdiction in its area over appeals from all final decisions of U.S. District Courts.

Court of Claims. A court that hears cases

against U.S. as, in patent causes, for compensation for unauthorized use of a patent.

Court of Customs and Patent Appeals. Full name, United States Court . . . , a court in Washington, D.C. that hears appeals from decisions of the Board of Appeals and the Board of Interference Examiners on the evidence produced before the Patent Office (Sec. 144).

cross-license. The reciprocal grant of patent rights to each other by two or more owners of such rights.

damages for infringement. Award adequate to compensate for the infringement and not less than a reasonable royalty for use, together with interest and court costs (Sec. 284).

declaratory judgment. An action, started by a party threatened with infringement suit, to have validity, infringement or both of the patent determined by a court.

dedication. Making an invention available for free use by any member of the public, by direct statement to that effect or by disclosing in a patent something that is not claimed as a part of the invention.

dedication of term. Making a claimed invention available for free use for a terminal part of the period of the patent (Sec. 253).

deferment of issue. Upon payment of the final fee, deferment by request of issue of the patent up to three months (R. 314).

dependent claims. A claim which refers back to and restricts a single preceding claim. There may be several series of dependent claims in a single application but all claims in each series must be in immediate consecutive order or as close thereto as physically possible (R. 75).

deposit accounts. An amount kept on deposit with the Patent Office by a patent practitioner sufficient to cover services, copies of records, file histories, correction of drawings, and the like ordered by the practitioner. Filing, final, appeal and petition fees are not chargeable against these accounts.

design patent series. Separate series of numbers for design patents preceded by letter D (M.P.E.P. 901.04).

diligence. Continuous activity in reducing an invention to practice.

disclaimer. Abandonment, in writing recorded in the Patent Office, of invalid claim filed without deceptive intent (Sec. 253).

disclosure. Statement of the invention as found in the specification and drawings (if any) or, where sufficiently explicit, in the claims.

dismissal with prejudice. Dismissal of an action, which constitutes an estoppel. See *Estoppel.*

District Courts. Federal courts of original jurisdiction of any civil action relating to patents. Infringement suits may be brought in the district where the defendant resides or has committed acts of infringement and has an established business (28 U.S.C. 1338, 1400).

District Court for District of Columbia. A court having jurisdiction in appeals from all decisions of the Board of Appeals and the Board of Patent Interferences, when adverse parties reside in a plurality of judicial districts not within one state or in a foreign country and when the appeal is not filed with the Court of Customs and Patent Appeals (Sec. 145, 146).

estoppel. A bar to alleging or denying a fact, created by some previous action or statement by the person estopped; a prior act that prevents certain subsequent actions, e.g., publication of an invention for more than one year acts as a bar or estoppel to obtaining a patent for such invention.

et al. And other(s).

examiner. An employee of the Patent Office who examines patent or trademark applications and determines the patentability and scope of inventions, registrability of trademarks, and, with other examiners, questions of priority between rival applicants for the same subject matter.

examiner's amendment. An amendment to correct "obvious errors and omissions" in an application, made by the examiner with notice to the applicant (M.P.E.P. 1302.04).

examiners-in-chief. Senior patent examining personnel who with the Commissioner and Assistant Commissioners constitute the Board of Appeals.

execution of application. Signature before a notary or other authorized person in this country. Some countries require that patent documents of foreigners be legalized by their consulates. An oath for a U.S. patent application executed abroad must be legalized by a U.S. consular or diplomatic officer.

exhausted combination. A combination shown by references to be anticipated. The cooperation and result obtained by the elements in the reference must be the same as in the claim (M.P.E.P. 706.03j).

ex parte proceeding. A proceeding between the Patent Office and the applicant, with no third and opposing party.

fiduciary relationship. See confidential relationship.

file wrapper. Totality of written record in the Patent Office file of an application.

filing date. The date on which the complete or the last part of the application in form acceptable for examination is received (R. 55).

final rejection. Any examination after the first one may result in a "final" rejection. The applicant must then conclude the prosecution within 6 months, appeal to the Board of Appeals, or petition the Commissioner in cases of objections or requirements not involved in the rejection of a claim. Where allowable subject matter is found, the applicant must comply with any requirement or objection as to form (R. 113). At the discretion of the Examiner, an amendment placing the application in condition for allowance or better form for appeal may be entered (R. 116).

force majeure. Irresistible force, e.g., "act of God."

foreign patent application. A foreign patent may not be filed earlier than six months after filing in the U.S. unless authorized by the Commissioner. No license to file may be granted for an application under a secrecy order but may be granted retroactively in other cases where an application has been inadvertently filed abroad without such license (Sec. 184).

forfeited application. One on which the patent has been withheld for failure to pay the final fee (R. 316). If the final fee is not accepted within 1 year after the 6 months period for payment has passed, it is abandoned as of date of forfeiture, i.e., at the end of said 6 months.

generic claim. One which includes within its scope two or more disclosed embodiments, i.e., species. It must cover in a general manner what is comprehended in each of the species (M.P.E.P. 806.04d, e).

genus. A class broader than or including more than one species.

importation patent. See article *Foreign Patents.*

incomplete disclosure. Rejection for incompleteness is based on the omission of an essential element, step or structural cooperative relationship of elements.

index of patents and patentees. Published annually and for sale by the Supt. of Documents, Washington 25, D.C.

inherent disclosure. An inherent property of something originally disclosed; may be explicitly described by amendment without introducing new matter.

injunction. An action in equity prohibiting an act where irreparable damage may otherwise be done, e.g., in patent law, an order to desist from further infringement.

in pais. In the class of matters so triable.

insufficient disclosure. A disclosure lacking such description and details as would enable a person skilled in the art to which the invention pertains to make and use the invention (M.P.E.P. 608.01p).

inter alia (alios). Among others, as applied to persons, things, features, distinctions, reasons.

interference. A proceeding to determine which of two or more applicants for a patent is the first inventor. The interference may involve an application and a patent, provided the claim in the application is made prior to one year from the date on which the patent issued (Sec. 135).

inter partes proceeding. A proceeding, such as an interference, involving two or more opposing applicants or inventors.

International Convention for Protection of Industrial Property. An agreement respecting patent and trademarks giving an applicant in one member country the same effective filing date in other Convention countries for application filed within a year of the first filing date (Sec. 119). See article *Foreign Patents.*

intervening rights. The right created by use or "substantial preparation" for use of an invention (in advance of a reissue) to continue to make, use or sell something claimed in a reissue patent which was described but not claimed in the original patent (Sec. 252).

in terrorem. A warning in, or to create, terror.

ipse dixit. An assertion not proven; mere dictum.

ipso facto. From the act or fact itself.

Jepson claim. A form of claim wherein the known matter is recited in a preamble providing the environment for the improvement set forth in the concluding portion of the claim.

joint inventor. One of two or more inventors who together make an invention.

junior party. In interference, the applicant having the later filing date, without having carried it back (by motion to shift the burden of proof) to an earlier filed application.

laches. Neglect, failure or unreasonable delay in doing something or enforcing a right, which results in injury to the party asserting laches. It is a bar to the enforcement of the right. See article *Laches.*

know-how. Practical information or knowledge for operating with commercial success.

legal representatives. Those who are legally designated to make application for patent, as for deceased or incapacitated inventors (Sec. 117).

letters patent. Grant to an inventor of the right for a limited time to exclude others from using his invention; the certificate of the patent grant.

linking claims. Claims linking otherwise separate species of the invention, such as a generic claim linking up to five species claims embraced thereby; a combination bridging two subcombinations; product-by-process claims linking product and process claims; and a means for practicing a process linking apparatus and process claims (M.P.E.P. 809, 809.2, 809.3a).

machine. Class of patentable subject matter covering a combination of movable parts or one-piece tool adapted to perform useful work.

Manual of Classification. A loose-leaf book listing all classes and sub-classes in the patent classification system, a subject matter index, and related information.

manufacture. One of the classes of patent-able subject matter (Sec. 101); sometimes called "article of manufacture."

marking. Applying patent number. To recover damages for past infringement, patentee must (1) mark any patented article or its package with the word "Patent" (or "Pat.") and the number or (2) prove that the infringer was otherwise notified of the infringement, as by letter, and continued to infringe thereafter (Sec. 287).

means. A force applied, a mode of operation, a specific treatment of specific objects, or a part accomplishing a given mechanical result. See article *"General and Mechanical Applications."*

mental steps. Purely mental steps, such as calculating, comparing, determining, registering, counting, observing, measuring, recording, and computing are not patentable subject matter.

mesne assignment. An assignment by an intermediate party of a right received by said party by assignment.

motion. An application to a competent body or authority to obtain an order directing a particular action. In interferences, motions may be brought to dissolve, to amend, to include another application and to shift the burden of proof (R. 231 to 237).

multiplicity of claims. An undue number of claims. An unreasonable number, in view of the nature and scope of the invention, affords a basis for rejection on the ground of multiplicity. The courts have confirmed, however, applicant's right to restate, by plural claiming, his invention in a number of ways, when there is a difference in scope. (M.P.E.P. 706.03k, l).

new matter. Disclosure not found in either the drawing or specification of the original application, involving a departure from, or an addition to, the original disclosure. It is new matter and is not admissible in amendments or in applications for reissue (R. 118; Sec. 132, 251).

new use. Patentable process based on a new use of a known process, machine, manufacture, composition of matter or material (Sec. 100).

non-exclusive license. A license under a patent which does not prohibit the granting of rights to others.

non-statutory subject matter. New and useful inventions and discoveries not patentable under Sec. 101; examples are the mere arrangement of printed matter, a thing occurring in nature which is substantially unaltered, a method of doing business, and a scientific principle divorced from any tangible structure (M.P.E.P. 706.03a).

notice of infringement. A written communication from a patent owner notifying an infringer of specified claims of a patent and requiring that such infringement cease.

nunc pro tunc. Now as of then, e.g., a step taken now as of an earlier date when the action was due.

oath. Sworn or affirmed statement of the applicant that he believes himself to be the original inventor and that the invention has not been in public use or sale in the U.S. or patented or described in any printed publication in any country more than one year prior to his application.

obiter. In passing; incidental.

obiter dictum (dicta). Words of a court having no direct bearing on the decisive issue in a case.

objection. Criticism raised by examiner as to matters of form rather than substance of claim (M.P.E.P. 706.01); may not be appealed but Commissioner may be petitioned to overrule examiner.

office action. A letter from the examiner stating the results of the examination of the application or of amendment, indicating the Patent Office position on the application. See *Examination*.

Official Gazette. The official weekly publication of the Patent Office which contains at least one selected claim of each patent issued during the week; information on patents, trademarks, and designs; and orders, suits filed and court decisions relating to these fields.

paper patent. A patent whose teaching has not been commercially practiced. Courts tend to construe such patents strictly.

patent agent. Any U.S. citizen, not an attorney at law, who has the qualifications required for, and who has been admitted to, practice before the Patent Office (R. 341). See *Attorneys and Agents*.

parent application. The original application on which a continuation or continuation-in-part application is based.

Paris Convention. See *Foreign Patents—International Convention*.

patent attorney. Any member of a Federal or State bar who has the legal, scientific and technical qualifications required for, and who has been admitted to, practice before the Patent Office (R. 341), or a person not a member of any bar who was admitted as a "registered patent attorney" before 1931.

patent law. (1) The statutes covering patents, principally found in Title 35 of the U.S. Code, and (2) court interpretations thereof.

petition to Commissioner. See *Petitions*.

pioneer patent. First in its field, claiming means or a function never before disclosed. It is liberally interpreted and entitled to broad range of equivalents.

plant patent series. Separate series of numbers for plant patents, preceded by letters P.P. (M.P.E.P. 901.04).

positive inclusion of elements. Positive recital of every feature whereon a claim depends for patentability.

post hoc, ergo propter hoc. After this, therefore, because of this.

preliminary search. An examination of the patents in the Patent Office, made by private searchers at the expense of the inventor, to determine, if possible, whether a subject is patentable.

presumption of validity. Patents are prima facie valid; proof to the contrary rests on the party claiming invalidity (Sec. 282).

prima facie. At first view, e.g., a patent is valid, prima facie, in the absence of proof to the contrary.

primary or principal examiner. The chief of an examining division in the U.S. Patent Office.

prior art. All subject matter bearing on the novelty of a claimed invention under Sec. 102.

priority of invention. In determining priority of invention not only the respective dates of reduction to practice shall be considered but also the date of becoming diligent by the one who was first to conceive but last to reduce to practice (Sec. 102g).

priority right. The right to advance the effective date of filing an application to the filing date of the first corresponding foreign application, provided the foreign country is a "treaty" country and the filing date there is not more than one year prior to the date of the later filing (Sec. 119).

process. The steps involved in changing the physical or chemical characteristics of a material. The steps involved, when they produce unobvious results, are patentable (Sec. 100, 101). Patentable process also includes methods involving the application of some element or power of nature or the utilization of laws of physics, to produce an unobvious and useful result.

prolixity. Reciting in claims unimportant details in manner to hide or obscure the invention (M.P.E.P. 706.03g); ground for rejection as prolix.

protests. Opposition to the grant of a patent by a member of the public; merely acknowledged and filed after referral to the examiner for his information (R. 291).

qui tam. An action in which the plaintiff sues for the state as well as himself.

quid pro quo. Something for something; reciprocal considerations.

references. Prior art relied upon by the examiner in rejecting a claim as non-patentable. The pertinence of each reference, if not obvious, must be clearly explained and each rejected claim specified (R. 106).

reissue. Reissue of a patent, granted when a patent, through error without deceptive intent, is wholly or partly inoperative. See article *"Reissue Patents."*

rejection. Action of the Patent Office denying patentability. Whenever any claim for a patent is rejected, the applicant shall be notified of the reasons together with the information and references on which the rejection was based (Sec. 132). See *Examination.*

res judicata (or *adjudicata*). Requirements for *res judicata* are that the identical issue must have been decided in a previous suit between the same parties as currently involved. *In re Szwarc*, 796 O. G. 597,599, CCPA 1963. Cf. *Comr. Int. Rev.* v. *Sunnen*, 333 U.S. 591. A ground for rejection (M.P.E.P. 706.03w).

restriction of application. Directing claims to a single invention. After a requirement for restriction (formerly called division) because two or more independent inventions are claimed in a single application, a re-

stricted application may be directed solely to one of said inventions. If filed before the patenting, abandonment or termination of the proceedings on the original application, the new case is entitled to the filing date of the original application and neither the original nor the restricted applications or patents may be used as references against each other (Sec. 121, R. 147). See *Restriction* and *Double Patenting.*

revival. Reviving an abandoned application, on the basis of a petition to the Commissioner with a verified showing of unavoidable delay in prosecuting, together with the proposed response and the petition fee of $10 (R. 137).

royalty. Payment for use of an invention, frequently a stated percentage of the sales made under a patent.

Rules of Practice. The regulations established by the Commissioner of Patents governing the conduct of proceedings in the Patent Office and available in pamphlet form (Sec. 6, 11).

scientific principle. Non-statutory subject matter.

secrecy. Prohibition against disclosure; whenever an application for a patent is filed which might affect the national security, the application is made available for inspection by an appropriate agency of the Government. If the agency finds that publication or disclosure of the invention would be detrimental to the national security, the Commissioner shall order the invention kept secret. During this period, prosecution will proceed but no appeal hearing will be set until the secrecy order is removed (Sec. 181).

Series of 1836. Numbers for mechanical, electrical and chemical patents (utility patents) issued since 1836. A citation only by number refers to this series (M.P.E.P. 901.04). See **X**-series.

single signature form. A combined Petition, Oath and Power of Attorney attached to the specification of patent applications as the last page thereof, for execution by inventors.

skilled in the art. The imaginary person familiar with all the teachings in his technical field. An invention is patentable only if it is not obvious to a person having all such knowledge and ordinary skill in the art (Sec. 103).

species claim. A single, specifically different embodiment of an invention (M.P.E.P. 806.04e); up to five species may be claimed in one application (R. 141).

stare decisis. Standing by established principle or precedent, especially in a case on all fours with that at issue.

status letter. Inquiry to the examiner about the present status of an application; usually sent when an unduly long time has elapsed since the examiner last acted on the case.

status quo. State existing; as before.

statutory. Established by act of Congress.

sui generis. Of its (her or his) own class.

supplemental oath. Oath sometimes filed in support of new claims for subject matter originally described but not claimed (R. 67). See *Chemical Applications.*

swearing back. Submitting a sworn statement of facts showing completion of an invention at a date in advance of art cited against an application (R. 131).

term of patent. Period for which patent rights are granted; in the U.S., 17 years from date of grant of "utility" patents and 3½, 7, or 14 years for designs.

traverse. Denial of the propriety of an action, such as requirement of election or restriction.

unobviousness. The new statutory word for the requirement for patentability; the difference between the subject matter sought to be patented and the prior art must be such that it would not be obvious as a whole, at the time the invention was made, to a person knowing all information published and having ordinary skill in the art (Sec. 103).

utility. Lack of utility includes being inoperative, frivolous, fraudulent and against public policy (M.P.E.P. 706.3p). See *Utility.*

utility models. Patents relating to new and useful forms of device inventions; obtainable in comparatively few countries, such as Germany and Japan, but not in the U.S.

utility patents. Patents for new and useful processes, machines, manufactures or compositions of matter, as opposed to plant and design patents.

X-series. Patents issued between 1790 and July 4, 1836, must be ordered by patentee's name and date of issue (M.P.E.P. 901.04).

Cross-references: *Claims—Words and Phrases.*

GOVERNMENT OWNERSHIP AND ADMINISTRATION OF PATENTS

Howard I. Forman

[Dr. Forman has much experience not only in corporation practice but also in connection with administration of federal patent policies. He shows the increasing magnitude of Government ownership of patents; considers the possibility or probability that departure from the principle of exclusivity in grants under the patents, constituting as they will such a large proportion of our total patents, may nullify the cardinal feature and eventually the usefulness of the patent system itself in attracting capital and promoting invention; reviews in detail the history of Government ownership and administration of patents; and at the end draws conclusions that should interest every reader. Ed.]

Introduction

The Federal Government now finances about two-thirds of the nation's entire budget for research and development. It undoubtedly owns more patents than any individual or corporation. Its proportion of the nation's total research and development expenditures and of all patents issued is mounting steadily. Accordingly, its selection of policies with respect to its patents, and its administration of patent rights thereunder, will bear upon one of the most critical issues of our time. The decisions which are to be made by the Congress and the Executive Branch may either preserve the patent system, to which people all over the world have attributed much of our industrial and commercial progress, or destroy the effectiveness of the system, if not the system itself.

The over-all policy should be one that causes full disclosure of non-security inventions to the public, *under conditions which will encourage the investment of whatever capital is required to develop and use them to the fullest possible extent.*

How well the present system has worked is evident in the more than 3,000,000 patents which the United States Government has granted in the almost 175 years since the first patent statute was enacted in 1790. People the world over have attributed a large share of this country's industrial and commercial progress to its inventive productivity, and in turn have credited that inventiveness to the patent system. Whether the patent grant is in any way responsible for the progress of the arts and sciences as the authors of the Constitution hoped it would be, it is indisputable that each of the recipients of the 3,000,000-plus patents has disclosed and added to our published knowledge valuable technical information that otherwise may never have filled our technical libraries.

It is difficult to perceive how such a wealth of technical information, if not itself the direct cause of a new business or industry coming into being, could help but lead to the development of many new articles of manufacture, new processes and new compositions of matter. To be sure, people don't invent with the primary object of obtaining patents any more than people do research with the primary object of filling libraries with technical reports and books. But once an invention is made, if people know that by patenting it they may obtain the right to exclude others from using it for 17 years, there is a powerful compulsion to file for a patent and thus agree to public disclosure of the invention when the patent is issued. This right to exclude brings about at least two important effects: (1) the owner of that right, secure in the knowledge that his invention cannot lawfully be used by a competitor during the term of the patent, may invest money, time and effort to capitalize on it and thereby develop the invention for commercial utilization; (2) competitors affected by the adversely held right may invest money, time and effort to legally circumvent that right and thereby produce a new and improved invention.

In considering the Government's policy, past, present and future, with regard to its ownership and administration of patents, one must not lose sight of the fact that it is the same American patent system which is affected by that policy. Whatever has been or should be done to shape that policy, if the American patent system is to be maintained at all, the same purpose, the same utility, and the same methods of utilization which apply to privately held patent rights must apply to patents in which the Government holds an interest. To do otherwise will inevitably strike at the very heart of the patent system and may eventually bring about its destruction.

Acquisition of Patent Rights by Government

Since World War I, and more particularly since World War II, the Government has acquired a tremendous number of patent rights, an important share of them being the entire right, title and interest therein. In the main, these rights have stemmed from inventions arising out of the research and development work of Government contractors and Government employees. In the former case the nature of those rights has been defined in the contractual instrument itself. In the latter situation, with very little exception, there has been no contractual stipulation, and the nature of the rights which the Government obtained has been determined by statute [1] and executive order.[2] Other sources for the Government's patent portfolio have been outright purchases, gratuitous grants,[3] various statutory and administrative enactments,[4] international agreements,[5] and the operation of Government-owned plants.

Unquestionably, the bulk of the patent rights acquired by the Government stems from research and development work which is to some extent federally financed. As the Government's expenditures for research and development increase so may we expect to see a rise in the number of inventions produced as a by-product of that investment. Although there never is any guarantee that the more money spent in the laboratory the more inventions will result, it is reasonable to expect that the chances of such an outcome are likely. Of course, just as it is true that not all research leads to inventions, so is it true that not all inventions will prove to be patentable. But here, too, one may expect that there will be some proportionate increase of patents as the research budget is elevated.

If there were ever any doubts as to whether the number of patents obtained each year is directly proportioned to the amount of time and effort invested in research and development, they have been dispelled. Objective studies conducted by The Patent, Trademark and Copyright Foundation of The George Washington University, have made it appear rather clear that the number of patents issued actually is a measure of research activity.[6]

Thus, in considering the administration of the Government's patent rights, it be-comes important to compare the magnitude of its investment in research with the total expended by non-governmental interests in the United States. Whereas, the federal research budget was about $25 million in 1930, or about 12 per cent of the total national investment in the exploration for new ideas, it rose to over 70 per cent during World War II and has remained at levels between 50 and 60 per cent in most of the years since then.[7] The trend is still upwards. According to *The Budget, 1962,* federal R & D "spending was expected to reach $10.2 billion in 1962, or approximately *two-thirds* of the national total ($15.3 billion) for research and development."[8] A revised budget estimate has placed this figure for 1962 as approximately $10.8 billion,[9] and other sources estimate that in 1963 it will rise to over $12.3 billion. Figures 1 and 2 and Table 1 which follow,

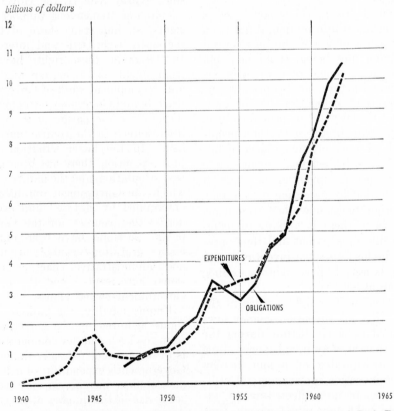

FIG. 1. Trends in federal funds for research and development and R & D plants. Pay and allowances for military personnel in research and development included in fiscal year 1953 and subsequent years. Reprinted from Federal Funds for Science, X, National Science Foundation, NSF 6-82, p. 39 (1962).

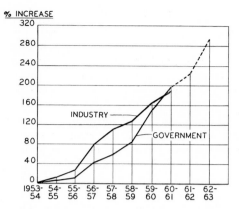

FIG. 2. Growth of research and development expenditures by government and by industry. From the review by Commissioner Ladd, 44 JPOS 363,365, June 1962. Reprinted by permission.

illustrate this trend over the period 1940-1962, and give estimates for 1963:

TABLE 1. RESEARCH & DEVELOPMENT FUNDS, IN MILLIONS

Year	Industrial R & D [1]	Government R & D [2]
1953-54	$ 3,630	$ 3,148
1954-55	4,070	3,268
1955-56	4,640	3,435
1956-57	6,538	4,460
1957-58	7,664	4,985
1958-59	8,218	5,792
1959-60	9,553	7,742
1960-61	10,497	9,297
1961-62	no. est.	10,244 est.
1962-63	no. est.	12,365 est.

From the Review by Commissioner Ladd, 44 JPOS 363, 365, 1962. Reprinted by permission.

[1] Source: Review of Data on Research and Development No. 30 National Science Foundation.
[2] Source: The Budget of the United States, Fiscal Year 1963, p. 358.

Source 1 on page 19 shows that, for the fiscal year 1959-60, the expenditure by Industry of $9,553,000 was from funds supplied to the extent of $4.4 billion by the Department of Defense and 0.7 by other federal agencies, making these amounts 53 per cent of the total. In the 1960-61 year, the proportion of the Industry expense for R & D that was advanced by the Government was 59 per cent of the total.

If the recent past portends the future, one can only expect the Government's share of the country's annual expenditures on research to remain at such levels or possibly continue to grow larger. Without a drastic change in the socio-political trends of the twentieth century, not only in the United States but throughout the world, it does not seem likely that the Government will recede from its tendency to foster more and more of the work carried on in the nation's laboratories. If this is the case, the growth undoubtedly will be accompanied by more inventions and more patent rights will become subject to Government review and possibly Government control. The very number of those patent rights may well dictate what the Government's policy concerning their administration should be.

Magnitude of Patent Portfolio

As of June 1953 the Government owned the full rights to 4,061 unexpired patents.[10] In 1955 this total had risen to 5,203.[11] One authoritative estimate places the number at approximately 12,000 in 1960,[12] and other Government officials have variously placed this figure as high as 14,000 in July 1961.[13]

The foregoing figures bear out the reliability of one writer's estimate made in 1955 that the Government's portfolio of unexpired patents would reach 10,000 by 1960.[14] This doubling in five years' time should lend support to a more recent estimate that by 1970 the Government will acquire title to a total of 15,000 or even 20,000 patented inventions.[15]

In a report entitled "Distribution of Patents Issued to Corporations (1939-55)," [16] the Senate Subcommittee on Patents, Trademarks, and Copyrights disclosed that the largest corporate holder of unexpired patents in 1955 was the General Electric Company which owned a total of 10,757. No figures are publicly available to show the current number owned by that company, but it is doubted that it any longer exceeds the size of the Government's collection. Moreover, if the Government continues its present trend of taking more and more rights to patented inventions arising out of research which it finances at least in part, and if the Government's share of the national research investment continues to outdistance all non-governmental interests, it will without doubt become by far the largest single owner of patents in the entire country.

Source of Inventions

What proportion of the Government's patent rights come from inventions made by its own employees, and what proportion from its contractors? From 1949 to 1952 the Government took title to 2,486 patented inventions of which 850 were originated by its employees and 1,636 by its contractors. In 1953, of the 4,061 patents owned by the Government only 1,807 were products of its employees while 2,254 came from outside sources. In the 26-month period from July 1958 to August 1960 the Government took title to 2,787 patents, an average of approximately 1,200 per year, two-thirds of which were from non-governmental entities.[17]

What proportion of patents added to the Government's portfolio will continue to come from its employees and what share will be contributed by other sources cannot be predicted with certainty. Governmental policies, all subject to variation from year to year, will cause these proportions to change as the policies change. The share of Government-sponsored research to be carried out by its employees, as compared with the share assigned under contract and grants, will have an important bearing on the sources of the patented inventions in which the Government may have an interest. The attitude of the Government regarding administration of the patents on inventions made by its employees, contractors and recipients of research grants will have an even greater bearing on the number and sources of patent rights which the Government will continue to acquire.

Reasons for Acquisition by
Government

⸱ To man, who has been endowed with the ability to think and reason, everything in life must exist in an orderly manner. He generally likes to find a cause or basis for any being or any acts which some being may perform. Presumably, the same should apply to acts of the Government in amassing the largest single collection of titles to patents in the country, and to the Government officials whose policies and practices have made this possible. It is logical, therefore, to inquire as to the reasons for the constantly growing acquisition of patent rights by the Government.

When a statute or an administrative order requires that the Government take title to inventions arising out of research and development work performed by Government employees or contractors, this requirement does not automatically add to the number of the Government's patent rights. The inventions first have to be reported to appropriate federal administrators who must then assess their value to the Government as well as their patentability. Customarily, a determination then is made as to whether the circumstances surrounding their conception and reduction to practice were such as to require assignment thereof to the Government under the terms of the applicable contract or rules governing federal employment. If adjudged affirmatively on these points, the next step is to prepare and prosecute applications for patent. All of these procedures require very large staffs in every Government department which is responsible for carrying on research and development.

For the sake of the present discussion, it will be presumed that the American patent system is still considered, by and large, to be the potent force in the promotion of the progress of science and the useful arts which the authors of our Constitution intended it to be.[18]

As Defense Against Infringement Claims. If patents are of value to inventors and their assignees outside the Government, do they of necessity also have value to the Government? One function of patents is defensive. This certainly applies to the Government which traditionally is a ripe target for claimants seeking damages for alleged unlawful use of their property. Also, every invention conceivably could find some use by or for the Government in this day of far-flung governmental operations, and every holder of a patent right conceivably will become a potential claimant against the Government for patent infringement. If approximately two-thirds of the research and development work in the United States is being at least partially subsidized by federal funds, the Government presumably may have an interest in two-thirds of all the inventions which are being made in this country. It has a clear right and duty to protect itself against the possibility that any of those inventions may, through the procurement of privately held patents thereon, not be available for governmental use without the payment of royalties. The taxpayer should not be obliged to pay twice for the same invention, once through federal subsidization of the research which led to its conception, and a second time through royalty payments.

There frequently are situations in which the use of patent rights owned by non-Government interests is required by the Government either because it will solve important problems sooner, or because in the long run it will be cheaper than to develop another solution. In such cases it is obviously foolish economy for the Government to avoid using and paying for such patent rights. But when the Government can just as readily avoid using inventions covered by patent rights of private interests, without added material expense or loss of valuable time in solving its urgent problems, it is just as logical to do so and eliminate the need to pay royalties unnecessarily. This is particularly the case when the Government, by virtue of its tremendous research and development programs, has access to inventions covered by patent rights which, when properly protected, may forestall the infringement claims of other patent owners.

The Government actually began to patent inventions arising out of research it sponsored during World War I, in order to protect its "shopright" therein. Even so, it took 26 years of litigation to settle all of the patent liability charges against the United States which arose in that war period.[19] World War II and its aftermath left the Government with the job of defending a total of 74 suits as of August 15, 1961, for amounts totalling approximately $1 billion,[20] representing only a fraction of the actual costs involved.[21]

As Government procurement needs have grown, the likelihood of infringement claims against it has increased. When the Government uses an item, particularly one it incorporates into its procurement designs, drawings and specifications, it generally will make or have made large quantities of the item. Frequently, the quantity and cost of the subject of procurement is large enough to make the amounts potentially recoverable in a suit seem worth the financial risk on the part of the patent owner in resorting to litigation. If he is successful in obtaining a judgment in his favor, there will always be money to pay his claim promptly, unlike some cases where the defendant in a suit pleads bankruptcy. Besides, the patent owner will hope that a Government agency will settle the claim out of court.[22]

The Government, under the law, is the only party against whom suit can be maintained when its contractors commit the alleged infractions.[23] This is necessary in order to prevent patent owners from obtaining injunctions which would cause a stoppage of vital work, particularly of a military nature, by the Government's contractors. Of course, in appropriate situations, when the Government is entitled to indemnification by its contractors who performed the allegedly infringing act, the Government may decide to join the contractor in the suit or, upon losing the suit to the claimant, turn about and bring an action against its contractor.

Since the Government currently finances some two-thirds of the nation's budget for research and development, and this figure may grow even larger, it seems reasonable to expect that it can go a long way to defend itself against patent suits by assuring that it gets at least royalty-free rights to the products of its own subsidies. If it is reasonable to assume that inventions now flow in proportion to the amount of dollars (time-effort) spent on research and development, then theoretically only about one-third of the inventions made during any year (i.e. all inventions made entirely by privately funded inventors) will represent potential sources of Government liability. This, however, presumes that the Government will take steps to protect itself as to the patent rights which it may claim by virtue of having subsidized their development. It is for this reason that the Government has an interest in first patenting inventions to whose financing it has contributed and secondly in obtaining a license or an assignment covering the patents.

For Cross-licenses or Exchanges. It is a common occurrence in private industry for workers in closely related fields of research to make inventions which are of interest to their competitors. In many situations licenses for the use of such inventions are arranged, either on a royalty basis or some other suitable *quid pro quo*. When a number of concerns own patent rights which are of interest to others, a common expedient, instead of charging each other royalties, is to cross-license or exchange patent rights with one another.

Such arrangements frequently are more desirable and more readily agreed to than a royalty-based license agreement. It often happens that a cash consideration is not as important to a company as is the opportunity of using another's invention. Frequently, patent pools are worked out whereby several enterprises active in a given industry agree to permit the other members of the pool to use their patented inventions after the original patent owner has had the opportunity to operate under the patent without similar use by the others for a minimum period such as two years.

If such exchanges of patent rights are useful in private industry, it is logical to inquire whether they would be of similar use to the Government. If so, the Government's patent rights have an added value that must be taken into consideration in determining the Government's policies with regard to its acquisition of such rights. If past experience is any criterion, it would seem that the Government can derive the same benefits from cross-licensing and exchanging patent rights as any private concern.

The Navy Department once entered into an extensive program of patent cross-licensing with private industry, shortly after World War I. It had obtained title to 102 patents and applications on radio devices.

After being advised by the Attorney General that it could grant nonexclusive, nontransferable, and revocable licenses in exchange for licenses from private patent owners, it proceeded to grant some 57 cross-licenses. A spokesman for the Navy Department stated that it had "an enormous number of patents from practicaly all of the engineering groups in that field that we could rely on, so that if we were sued by one company or another, we could have so many different alternate ways of making our radio sets that I believe the Government got a real good benefit from it." [24] There is little doubt that the Government benefits from such exchanges, for it gives access to patented inventions owned by nongovernmental interests without having to pay any royalties for the privilege. As long as it is not using its patent rights to prevent others from using the invention covered thereby, it is yielding little or nothing in exchange by permitting its cross-licensees to use its patented inventions.

Just as the Government can exchange patent rights with private parties, so can it barter such rights with foreign governments. It frequently happens that the Government will require the use of inventions in another country, for example in Great Britain. But if the invention is covered by a British patent, the United States will have to obtain a license from the patent owner or possibly suffer a claim of infringement. If the patent is owned by the British government, then it becomes simply a matter of agreement between the countries. If the patent is owned by a private party, the British government must arrange to acquire title to the patent or at least sufficient right in it to grant the United States a license.

In similar fashion, the British government may wish to use a United States patent in America. An example would be the desire of Britain to have an American manufacturer produce certain patented items for it. For a patent privately held, the British must deal directly with the patent owner unless the United States Government wishes to intervene and arrange to obtain the rights needed by the British.

Under mutual assistance pacts [25] which

have been entered into since World War II began, the United States frequently has found it necessary to arrange for an interchange of patent rights and information. In these situations the Government has been called upon by one of the other parties to obtain a license under an American-owned United States patent. The Government can grant the foreign country the rights it seeks and settle with the owners of the patents as best it can. However, all such problems of settlement would be eliminated if the United States owned the patents to begin with. This possible use of patent rights makes their ownership by the Government that much more valuable.

At times the United States needs to practice, in a friendly foreign country, an invention made in this country and possibly covered by an American patent or patent application. If no corresponding patent was applied for or obtained in the foreign country by the owner of the American patent, another party may do so and seek to exclude the United States from practicing the invention or charge royalties for that privilege. Thus, it may be desirable for the Government to seek foreign patents covering the same inventions which are the subject of its domestic patents. A procedure for doing this has been established by executive order.[26] Another use for such American-owned foreign patents is to license them to foreign countries under terms which would be in the public interest.[27] Obviously, this would include cross-licenses, if deemed desirable.

Catalyst for Research and Development.

As great as the country's industrial and technological advancement has been, the need for research and development achievements is greater than ever before. The need for protection against enemies from abroad and economic vicissitudes internally make it mandatory to try every conceivable means for increasing the output of the country's inventive brainpower. If the patent system can help this cause along, it deserves the plaudits of the nation. Informed observers attribute to that system much of the effort that has led to the country's unparalleled research and development activity.

In 1943 the National Patent Planning Commission reported:

"The system has contributed to the growth and greatness of our Nation; it has

(1) Encouraged and rewarded inventiveness and creativeness, producing new products and processes which have placed the United States far ahead of other countries in the field of scientific and technological endeavor;

(2) Stimulated American inventors to originate a major portion of the important and basic inventions of the past 150 years;

(3) Facilitated the rapid development and general application of new discoveries in the United States to an extent exceeding that of any other country;

(4) Contributed to the achievement of the highest standard of living that any nation has ever enjoyed;

(5) Stimulated creation and development of products and processes necessary to arm the Nation and to wage successful war;

(6) Contributed to the improvement of the public health and the public safety.

(7) Operated to protect the individual and small business concerns during the formative period of a new enterprise." [28]

Thirteen years later, the Subcommittee on Patents, Trademarks, and Copyrights of the U.S. Senate's Committee on the Judiciary, concluded in its "Review of the American Patent System," as follows:

"A Government that once contributed little to technological development, other than to enact a patent law and provide a court system to enforce it, has today become a tremendous factor in this area, not only through its own direct research activities and financial assistance to other public and private research institutions, but by increasingly posing the problems that require solution and thereby providing the incentive for their solution." [29]

Only a few theoretical economists have seen fit to challenge the validity of this appraisal, and the basis for their conclusions has been so meagerly documented as to warrant little thoughtful consideration. Circuit Court Judge Evans has said in part:

"The patent system encourages invention, not only in that it rewards the inventor with a patent, but it spurs the competitors to put forth their mightiest effort to produce a product as good, yet different from the patentee's ... It must be admitted that in an effort to avoid infringement of a patent, as much skill is often displayed as is shown in the conception or development of invention itself ... [The] legal monopoly evidenced by a patent excites the competitors to their best to meet or excel the product covered by the existing patent." [30]

A further, more recent and similar view has been expressed by George Frost, a Chicago patent attorney, author and lecturer, as follows:

"Consideration must be given to the role of the system in a specific economic area—the stimulation of competition in research and development. The competition here considered is not of the classical kind between seller of like goods whose attention is primarily directed to the production and sales efforts involved. Rather, we deal with competition in the conception, development, application, and marketing of new products and processes. This competition accepts the differences—and derives its social usefulness from these differences. It is influenced by the patent system in three major respects. First, the patent system provides a protected market with the opportunity for unusual profit necessary to justify the heavy investment in time, effort, and capital necessary to bring the improvement to the public. This same protected market provides an entering wedge by which a business enterprise entering a new field can overcome the obstacles that otherwise discourage entry into an industry already populated. Finally, the ever-present threat of new firms with exclusive rights to new technologies compels existing enterprises to explore avenues of improvement upon pain of sudden obsolescence. All of these effects aid in generating a dynamic progressive environment under which the businessman must compete not only in terms of production and sales technique but must also exert his talents in the direction of technological improvements." [31]

If it be granted that patents *per se* under the American patent system have done all of the worthwhile things attributed by the National Patent Planning Commission, and if they can cause even greater progress through research and development as the Senate Subcommittee on Patents, Judge Evans and Mr. Frost have suggested, does it make any difference if the rights to patents are held by the Government? Does the effective value of patents increase, decrease or suffer no change when the Government owns them as compared with control by private interests? The answer to these ques-

tions might well determine a national policy as to whether the Government should seek to obtain patent rights and, if it acquires them, what it should do with them.

There is no doubt that the technology represented by the patent rights in the Government's control is a great potential spur to national progress that can stimulate a surge of invention. But it must be decided whether such stimulation can best come, as in the views of Judge Evans and Mr. Frost, when the patent rights are held during their lifetime as a legal monopoly while the private patent owner's competitors, of necessity, seek ways and means to avoid or overcome the competitive advantage which the owner possesses thereby. If this is the case, the Government may be obliged to find some means to vest control, over patents in which it may have an interest, in the hands of some private entity which will exercise in commerce the legal monopoly that they represent, in manner to stimulate competitive activity.

The People Pay; The People Should Own

In 1947 the Attorney General of the United States, in a report entitled "Investigation of Government Patent Practices and Policies," stated:

With respect to inventions made by Government employees:

"Inventions financed with public funds should inure to the benefit of the public, and should not become a purely private monopoly under which public-financed technology may be suppressed, used restrictively, or made the basis of an exaction from the public to serve private interests." [32]

With respect to inventions made by Government contractors:

"Where patentable inventions are made in the course of performing a Government-financed contract for research and development, the public interest requires that all rights to such inventions be assigned to the Government and not left to private ownership of the contractor." [33]

The arguments advanced on behalf of these views by the Attorney General and others, which have become known generally as the "title theory," have been aptly summarized as follows:

"[Because] 'the great bulk of inventions made by Federal employees ... result(s) from an operation of Government financed with public appropriations,' their use should not be denied the public which paid for them through taxation, nor should the public be charged a royalty for their use because the royalty charge would in effect be a second tax for use of the inventions." [34]

Presumably, this argument would apply, at least in part, to inventions made under Government contract.

The other side of this question is popularly termed the "license theory." Its protagonists maintain that all the Government pays for is a product and a license to use it for Governmental purposes.

Those who argue in favor of the title theory make reference to industrial practices in which the employer generally acquires all rights to inventions of its employees that are made in the course of or pertaining to their employment. They claim that the Government is in the same position with respect to its employees and contractors, and should also demand title to their inventions for the same reasons. The Government, in this view, is entitled to and could make use of patents on inventions of its employees and contractors in the same way as private individuals and companies are entitled to and can make use of patents on inventions of their employees and contractors.

Roland Anderson, patent counsel for the Atomic Energy Commission and an advocate of the thesis that the "Government should get what it pays for," has urged that the determining criteria as to what is being paid for should be "the programs, objectives, and the over-all requirements of the statutory authority of a particular Government agency or department." [35] This seems to be sound advice. However, he presupposes that the stated requirements and authority of the Government units must necessarily be correct and in the best over-all interests of the people. In this it may be that an incorrect prejudgment is being made.

It sounds logical that "the people" should own what they pay for, in the sense of the law as it applies to private persons. But this does necessarily mean that the maximum good to the maximum number of people will result if patents are owned by the Government, regardless of the fact that public funds paid for the inventions which they cover. Even if the Government has the right to own the patents it paid for, it does not follow that the best interests of the country will be served if the Government holds on to the patents. There may be overriding considerations which merit divesting itself of those rights. This is a question to be resolved when considering Government policy regarding patent ownership and administration and will, therefore, be dealt with in the following sections.

Government Policy re Patents Ownership

In 1883, an act [36] was passed which authorized the various Government departments and agencies to provide free services in preparing, filing and prosecuting applications for patent by Government employees in return for a royalty-free, nonexclusive, irrevocable license for the Government to use the patented invention. Since that date, the Government has been obtaining part or full rights to many thousands of inventions and patents. In 1955 it was reported by Dr. Archie M. Palmer, first chairman of the Government Patents Board, that the Government then had an interest in over 22,000 unexpired patents, of which full title was held in about 5000. As stated previously, the Government in 1960 held title to between 12,000 and 14,000 patents, so it is very likely that its interests in other patents via licenses now exceed 22,000. The trend towards taking title in more and more cases may only have changed the ratio of title-to-license situations, rather than altered the total number of inventions involved. However, the increasing federal expenditures for research and development since 1955 may, and probably have, caused that number to increase tremendously.

The Act of 1883 had for its objective the purely defensive purpose of acquiring for the Government license rights in patents. With such rights, the chances were lessened that someone might obtain patents for the same inventions and assert a claim of infringement against the Government. At that time, relatively few proponents could be found to urge that the Government take title to patents, regardless of how the inventions involved were conceived and reduced to practice. Many persons then, and even today, consider(ed) such taking of title to be unconstitutional and certainly useless.

In the face of these early considerations, it becomes of interest to ascertain what brought about the change which made the United States Government the largest single owner of patents in the country, if not in the entire world. At the same time, it may be desirable to determine the Government's policy—if there is an actual policy—concerning its ownership of the entire right, title and interest in patents.

Historical Development. There is no uniform "title" or "license" policy in the Government today. In a search project report [37] of The Patent, Trademark and Copyright Foundation of The George Washington University, there is described the Government's patent policies in contracts for research and development. Of 12 federal agencies studied, 6 were found to follow the title policy, and 6 were of the opposite view. The former are the Atomic Energy Commission; Department of Agriculture; Department of Health, Education and Welfare; Department of the Interior; Federal Aviation Agency; and National Aeronautics and Space Administration. The six which follow the license approach are the Department of Defense, General Services Administration, Maritime Administration (Department of Commerce), National Science Administration, Office of Civil and Defense Mobilization, and Post Office Department.

The license policy originated with the military departments. Faced with procurement needs in World War I which the Government had never before known, the War and Navy Departments started the first major federal investment in research and development. Because they soon discovered that inventions were being made in the course of that work and frequently were becoming the basis of claims for patent infringement by or for the Government, they sought to obtain patent licenses, royalty-free, from their contractors. Eventually, this policy became a fixture in the defense agencies' procurement procedures and has since appeared in every revision of their administrative rules known as the Armed Services Procurement Regulations. The policy has never been the subject of any Congressional legislation specifically directed thereto. Since the Department of Defense has by far the largest budget for research and development of all federal agencies, its license policy has been applied to most of the patented inventions arising out of the mounting volume of Government-supported research.

The title policy adopted by the various other agencies mentioned in each case resulted from legislation, and in each case it appeared to be as a result of special problems and possibly some special agitation of the day. The Atomic Energy Commission's patent policies stemmed from legislation enacted in 1946 and 1954, following a policy established by its predecessor, the top secret wartime Manhattan Engineer District. The post-World War II period, 1946 to 1962, which brought on much of the concern about profiteering from Government contracts, led to a firming of the policies of the Departments of Agriculture, of Health, Education and Welfare, and of the Interior. The Space Act of 1958, with practically no hearings on the subject, incorporated the AEC-type title policy in the regulations applicable to procurement by the National Aeronautics and Space Administration.

Since 1957 the Subcommittee on Patents, Trademarks, and Copyrights of the U.S. Senate's Committee on the Judiciary has been investigating the Government's patent practices and policies with a view to recommending appropriate legislation. Notwithstanding this exhaustive investigation of Congress, with little reflection, inserted the title policy in the Space Act of 1958. It did the same thing in 1961 when it passed Public Law 87-295 which amended the Saline Water Act of 1952. Similar treatment was given to the helium gas legislation [38] and the Coal Research Act in 1960.[39]

One industrial group, which had been closely studying these developments in Congress for several years, concluded in a November 1961 report: [40]

"1. No firm congressional policy has been established with reference to inventions resulting from government-sponsored research and development.

"2. Despite the lack of an established policy, Congress has continued to write title provisions into new research and development legislation.

"3. In following this course of action Congress appears to be achieving by default what it has thus far refused to accomplish by direct legislative action."

It is strange that Congress should suddenly move with such speed in adopting the title provisions in these new forms of legislation at the very moment when the Senate subcommittee on patents was carefully and methodically evaluating the relative merits of the title v. licensing policies. This is particularly strange when one considers that the tendency towards inaction or inconclusiveness by Congress and the Executive Branch in this field has a history going back well over forty years.

Proposals by Legislative and Executive Branches. In 1919 identical bills were introduced in the Senate and House of the 65th Congress which would have vested the Federal Trade Commission with the responsibility for administering the Government's patent rights by issuing or refusing to issue licenses thereunder, collecting fees and royalties, etc. Although reported favorably by the respective committees which considered them, the bills never came to vote. The House committee report indicated that the purpose of the bill was to place in industrial use the patented inventions of Government employees and of non-Government inventors who donated their iventions to the Government, and to provide a self-sustaining method of administration by means of the fees and royalties collected.[41]

In the 66th Congress, very similar bills were introduced in both houses. The Senate passed its bill, but it was amended in conference with the House. The amended bill, which would have eliminated the Federal Trade Commission's discretionary power to refuse to issue licenses, passed the House but failed to pass the Senate. The Senate report is of interest, particularly if one were to compare it with the debates on the same subject which took place in Congress during the 1960's. It gave nine reasons for enacting its bill, including the following: [42]

"1. There is no fixed or general policy dealing with inventions and patents developed by Government employees in the course or as a result of their official duties, and consequently no governmental administrative machinery for translating such inventions and patents into actual public service.

"2. In cases where patents are developed by the combined efforts of Government employees and others, difficulties at present arise concerning the administration of same because of the conflict between the rights of the inventors and those of the United States.

"3. There is no way at present by which patentees in or outside the Government service can dedicate their patents to the public with the assurance that the public will reap the full benefit therefrom, because an invention covered by a patent so dedicated does not interest capital, and because it may be excluded from public use by patents subsequently taken out by others.

"4. ...the host of inventions developed during the war in many Government bureaus and other organizations, primarily for war purposes, but which have a peace application of inestimable value, should be coordinated, conserved, and translated with industrial use.

"5. ...

"6. It is desirable to have governmental administration of a certain type of patent, not ordinarily attractive to manufacturers, in order to provide production of needed services or materials for governmental or public purposes...."

Another bill [43] was introduced into the 66th Congress, this one relating to "Government owner-ship of radiotelegraphy and cable communication in its military and commercial aspects." It had a provision which would have empowered any Government department to dispose of radio patent rights held by it and to exchange the use of such patents for the use of others of interest to the Government. The bill was not enacted.

In 1922 President Harding, upon the recommendation of a committee established by the Secretary of the Interior, issued Executive Order 3721 establishing a five-man Interdepartmental Patents Board. On this board were one member each from the Agriculture, Commerce, Interior, Justice and War departments. Its objective was to recommend suitable regulations for establishing Government policy with respect to handling inventions and patents evolved by Government employees, and to deal with the matter of licenses thereunder. It recommended that there be established a permanent Interdepartmental Patents Board to control and administer patent rights acquired or owned by the Government, proposing that the Government should own or control all inventions of a secret category in the public interest, and inventions developed in an agency's field of work, "in which inventions the public's interest is paramount, and would be best protected by Government control." [44]

In 1926 a bill [45] was introduced into the House to authorize the President to establish a commission composed of the Secretaries of War, Navy and Commerce. It would have been responsible for issuing licenses under patents owned by the United States on such terms and conditions as the President deemed would be in the public interest. The issuance of both exclusive and nonexclusive licenses was contemplated. This bill was never reported out of the Committee.

The Bureau of the Budget, in January 1928, sought to establish [46] a firm Government policy with respect to invention and patent rights. It coordinated efforts of the Administration to devise proposals which would be acceptable to the Congress, and it arranged to have H.R. 12695 introduced. This bill would have authorized the President to issue regulations governing the issuance of licenses under Government-owned patents and applications on terms and conditions favoring the public interest. Exclusive licenses would have been valid only if approved by the President. The bill passed the House,[47] received favorable action by the Senate Patents Committee, but failed to be called for vote by the Senate. The next Congress saw similar bills introduced, but they also died.

The Chief Coordinator of the Bureau of the Budget tried again, in July 1928. He issued a bulletin to the heads of all departments, stating a need for coordinating policy with respect to the licensing of patents owned by the Government and the cross-licensing of those patents with patents owned by private interests. He asked that all licensing proposals be forwarded to the Chief Coordinator for reference to the Interdepartmental Patents Board. In due course, that Board recommended that the policy which should be adopted should call for the issuance of nonexclusive, nontransferable, revocable licenses, on a royalty or cross-licensing basis, the terms to be established by the head of the department concerned.

In 1930, at the request of the Chief Coordinator, the Board reconsidered its recommendations and, among other things, proposed that public dedication of inventions be the basic policy except when it is determined that the public interest demands that they not be made available for general use. This revised policy included authorization of an infringement suit for unlicensed or unlawful use of any patented invention owned by the Government.[48]

In 1930 and 1932, the Interdepartmental Patents Board made two more legislative proposals which were similar to its preceding proposal except for a requirement that the proceeds from the license or sale of patents be paid into the miscellaneous receipts of the Treasury, and a proposed authorization to grant exclusive as well as nonexclusive licenses.[49]

The Department of Justice canvassed the various departments in 1928-29 and came up with the suggestion that it would institute suit against infringers of Government-owned patents in order to establish that the Government had the legal right to such ownership and that such ownership did not place the patents in the public domain. Nothing ever resulted from this proposal and no infringement suit has ever been filed by the Government.[50]

The Department of Commerce recommended, in 1931, that the President issue an executive order which would establish a uniform policy for the Government, primarily for determining the respective rights in inventions of Government employees. The recommendation specifically proposed that the problem of the Government's patent rights should not be determined at that time.[51]

By Executive order No. 8977, issued in 1941, President Franklin D. Roosevelt established the National Patent Planning Commission, a group composed of some of the country's leading citizens who were familiar with patents and industrial operations. In 1945 it issued its report and recommended:

"... that the Government as a general rule continue to pursue the historic policy of not exercising the right to exclude, conferred by patents which it owns; of not attempting to exclude its own citizens from engaging in any enterprise; of not seeking to derive revenue from patents, and of not undertaking control by means of patents. Inventions covered by patents owned by the Government should be available for commercial and industrial exploitation by anyone, with, however, the recourse open to the Government to take different action in exceptional cases." [52]

The Commission went on to state, however, that

"It often happens, particularly in new fields, that what is available for exploitation by everyone is undertaken by no one. There undoubtedly are Government-owned patents which should be made available to the public in commercial form, but which, because they call for a substantial capital investment, private manufacturers have been unwilling to commercialize under a nonexclusive license. Accordingly, it seems evident that the Government has been handicapped in its effort to further the promotion and development of some of its inventions to the point where they are available to the public in the form of a commercial product." [53]

With this in mind, the Commission further recommended that:

"... legislation be enacted authorizing the several Government agencies ... to issue exclusive licenses in cases where it seems evident that otherwise the inventions in question will not come into general use ... and to sell (assign) patents when it is evident that the offering of an exclusive license will fail to insure satisfactory exploitation." [54]

To accomplish the administrative functions it proposed that there be established a central control body in the Executive Office of the President, preferably within the Bureau of the Budget.

Many more bills were introduced in Congress, and hearings held, after World War II, which only incidentally considered the problem of patent administration by the Government.[55] They proved to be of little consequence. It remained for the Department of Justice to make the most comprehensive study of the problem ever undertaken by the Government. In 1947, after over three years of exhaustive investigation, it issued a three-volume work entitled "Investigation of Government Patent Practices and Policies—Report and Recommendations of the Attorney General to the President." Its recommendations included: [56]

"1. As a basic policy all Government-owned inventions should be made fully, freely and unconditionally available to the public without charge, by public dedication or by royalty-free, nonexclusive licensing.

"2. As soon as an invention is completed under circumstances giving the United States the right to any patents therein, it should be covered by a patent application, unless the head of the agency finds that adequate protection of the public interest may be had by reducing the invention to practice, publishing it, and fully disclosing it to the Patent Office in such form as to make it a part of the prior art.

"3. ...

"4. To the extent that funds are or may be made available for the purpose, projects should be inaugurated by the interested Government agencies under the supervision of the Government Administration, to demonstrate and publicize promising inventions at key industrial and scientific centers, in order to inform and interest business and science, and particularly small business, in their use or development and to eliminate any obstacles to their successful exploitation. Similar publicity should be given to scientific and technical information of an unpatentable nature acquired by the Government.

"5. If the Government Patents Administrator or any other Government agency believes that the commercial use and exploitation of a promising invention would be aided by preliminary experimental, developmental or pilot-plant operations to establish its practicality or effectiveness, the Government Patents Administration may recommend such projects to the appropriate Government agency or to Congress for adoption.

"6. The Government Patents Administrator should prepare and submit to the President for approval, a program to encourage and sponsor the use and practice of Government-owned inventions by small and new business concerns, and should report periodically on the extent of use of Government-owned inventions."

No legislation resulted from the Attorney General's recommendation. Administrative action was, however, taken with respect to inventions made by Government employees when President H. S. Truman signed Executive Order 10096 in 1950. This will be described in detail below.

In the next fifteen years following the Attorney General's report, however, the question of the Government's patent policies commanded more and more attention in Congress. Bill after bill was introduced, and almost every one had as its objective the establishment of a Government-wide, uniform policy. A few, as was pointed out above, were special forms of legislation which only incidentally had included therein provisions concerning the distribution of patent rights arising out of Government contracts. A summary of the more important of these bills appears in Table 2 which follows:

TABLE 2. GOVERNMENT PATENT POLICY LEGISLATION.[57]

Bills	Sponsors	Gov't. Title	Gov't. License	Gov't. Agency	Title in Contractor or Inventor
Across The Board					
S. 1084	McClellan (O'Mahoney)	Yes Note 1		No	No
S. 1176	Long	Yes Note 2		Federal Invention Admin.	Maybe
H.R. 5084	Multer (companion)				
H.R. 6532	Green	Maybe	Royalty-free nonexclusive	Commerce Office of Fed. Inv.	Maybe
H.R. 6548	Toll (identical)	Note 3			Note 4
H.R. 2601	Wiley	Maybe Note 5	See Note 6	No	
Special					
H.R. 1934	Daddario	Maybe Note 7	Royalty-free nonexclusive	NASA	Contractor primarily
H.R. 3239	Brooks	Maybe Note 7	See Note 8	NASA	Contractor primarily
S. 901	Magnuson	Yes Note 9		Defense, HEW, AEC, Commerce, NSF, Treasury	No
Saline Water Conversion Program, P.L. 87-295					
H.R. 7916	Aspenall	Yes		Defense,	No
S. 2156	Anderson	Note 10		HEW, AEC,	
H.R. 8816	Fascell			State	

TABLE 2. GOVERNMENT PATENT POLICY LEGISLATION. (*Cont.*)

Bills	Sponsors	Gov't. Title	Gov't. License	Gov't. Agency	Title in Contractor or Inventor
Arms Control and Disarmament Act, P.L. 87-297					
H.R. 9118	Morgan	Yes Note 11		State, AEC, NASA, Defense	No
Coal Production and Conservation Act, P.L. 86-599					
		Yes Note 12		Interior	No

Notes on Table 2.

(1) U.S. shall have exclusive right and title to any invention made by any person in the performance of any contract or lease executed or grant.

(2) U.S. shall have exclusive right and title to any invention made by any officer or employee of the U.S. (a) in the performance of duties or (b) in development and research for which he was employed; or by any other person (a) under any contract or grant or (b) in performance of services thereunder.

(3) In the event that the Government employee inventor or assignee, or Government contractor, fails to satisfy requirements for commercial exploitation, or if a Government contractor fails to establish an invention award program for those of his employees who make inventions in the performance of the Government contract, title will be vested in the Government.

(4) Title to the invention shall conditionally remain with the inventor or his assignee for a minimum of 5 years after issuance of any U.S. patent thereon or a minimum of 10 years after first actual reduction to practice of the invention. On satisfactory showing that the invention has been commercially exploited, the Administrator shall certify the title as unconditionally vested in the inventor or assignee.

(5) The Government may acquire title to inventions made in the performance of a Government R & D contract in which
 (a) the contract is for the development of a new field of technology in which there is no significant non-Government experience to build upon; or
 (b) the contractor's function is primarily as an administrative agent; or
 (c) the contract is for R & D in fields directly relating to health or safety of the public and the products developed are in a form suitable for commercial use.

(6) The nonexclusive royalty-free license granted to the Government as a minimum shall not convey any right to provide services or supplies to the general public in competition with the contractor or its licensees.

(7) No less than an irrevocable, nonexclusive, royalty-free license in the Government unless the retention or acquisition of a greater right (a) is required by law or (b) is determined by the Administrator of NASA to be required in the interest of national security or the general welfare.

(8) The license to the Government extends also to any foreign government, international organization or group of nations pursuant to any treaty or agreement with the U.S.

(9) All patents and inventions resulting from the federally financed research are to be freely and fully available to the general public. Background rights are specifically excluded. (Floor amendment by Senator R. Long)

(10) "(b) All research within the United States contracted for, sponsored, co-sponsored, or authorized under Authority of this Act, shall be provided for in such manner that all information, uses, products, process, patents and other developments resulting from such research developed by Government expenditures will (with such exceptions and limita-

tions, if any, as the Secretary may find to be necessary in the interest of national defense) be available to the general public. This section shall not be so construed as to deprive the owner of any background patent relating thereto of such rights as he may have thereunder."

(11) Section 32. All research within the United States contracted for, sponsored, co-sponsored, or authorized under authority of this Act, shall be provided for in such manner that all information *as to* uses, products, processes, patents, and other developments resulting from such research developed by Government expenditure will (with such exceptions and limitations, if any, as the Director may find to be necessary in the public interest) be available to the general public. This subsection shall not be so construed as to deprive the owner of any background patent relating thereto of such rights as he may have thereunder.

(12) Section 6. No research shall be carried out, contracted for, sponsored, co-sponsored, or authorized under authority of this Act, unless all information, uses, products, processes, patents, and other developments resulting from such research will (with such exceptions and limitations, if any, as the Secretary may find to be necessary in the interest of national defense) be available to the general public. Whenever in the estimation of the Secretary the purposes of this Act would be furthered through the use of patented processes or equipment, the Secretary is authorized to enter into such agreements as he deems necessary for the acquisition or use of such patents on reasonable terms and conditions.

Employee Inventions and Government Patents Board.

On January 23, 1950 President Truman signed Executive Order 10096 "Providing for a Uniform Policy for the Government With Respect to Inventions Made by Government Employees and for the Administration of Such Policy." Pursuant to that order the Government Patents Board was established. Its first Chairman was Dr. Archie M. Palmer who held that office until he resigned in 1955 to be succeeded by Benjamin B. Dowell, Esq. Dowell died in office, to be succeeded by his deputy, Robb S. McLaughlin, Esq. The Board, as such, passed out of existence on March 24, 1961 when President Kennedy signed Executive Order 10930 which placed its functions in the Department of Commerce. In 1961, the Acting Secretary of Commerce, by a Delegation of Authority (26 F.R. 3118), transferred to the Commissioner of Patents the responsibilities for the work formerly done by the Board.

During the administration of Chairman Palmer, rules were promulgated, and many problems, issues, even terms defined, and thousands of actual cases decided. In a similar way, although to a lesser extent, the administrations of Dowell and McLaughlin saw many more cases decided, generally following the principles laid down by Palmer. The evolution and history of the entire Palmer administration, as well as most of the period of his successor, Benjamin B. Dowell, Esq., with abstracts of their important decisions, have been described in a book by Forman, "Patents—Their Ownership and Administration by the United States Government."[58]

In essence, the administrations under Executive Order 10096 and 10930 have established machinery whereby a determination is first made by the Government agency in which an invention originates and is then reviewed by the Patent Office, as to whether the Government takes full right, title and interest in the invention, or only a nonexclusive, royalty-free license, or no right at all, i.e., leaves full title with the employee. The regulations provide that the Government shall take full title, except in certain instances, to inventions made "(i) during working hours, or (ii) with a contribution by the Government of facilities, equipment, materials, funds or information, or of time or services of other Government employees on official duty, or (iii) which bears a direct relation to or is made in consequence of the official duties of the inventor."[59]

By complicated formulas, through which the contributions and interest of the Government were balanced against those of the employee, decisions have been and are continuing to be reached whereby the Government takes full title in some cases and less then full title in others. The very constitutionality of the whole procedure has been challenged and defended.[60] In contemplation of the possibility that the executive orders establishing first the Government Patents Board and any successor such as the Government Inventions Jurisdiction in the Patent Office) may be ruled unconstitutional, H. J. Res. 454 was introduced by Congressman Celler in 1957. Its object: "To establish a policy for the determination of rights of the Government and its employees in inventions made by such employees and to set forth criteria to be used in making such determinations." An article [61] written by Finnegan and Pogue in support of that bill furnishes an excellent analysis of the pros and cons of the "title" v. "license" theories. The bill itself, as well as the views of Finnegan and Pogue, has been further analyzed in a critique by Forman entitled "Federal Employee Invention Rights—What Kind of Legislation?"[62]

The policies and procedures established by Executive Orders 10096 and 10930, as they have been administratively implemented, have been both praised and criticized from every imaginable source.[63]

Government Policy re Patents Administration

There have been numerous proposals advanced as to what the Government should do with the patent rights it owns. All of these proposals presuppose some policy whereby the Government would be committed to a program which will lead to its acquisition of patent rights. There are many persons, who for one reason or another, strongly recommend against the Government taking more than a royalty-free license to any patent, except perhaps to those patents on inventions of Government employees.

In the main, the controversy as to the disposition of rights to inventions and patents arising incident to Government-sponsored research and development has centered about those rights stemming from work done in the performance of Government contracts. Little is heard or written about the disposition of rights pertaining to inventions made by Government employees. Rarely are the two problems considered together, let alone dealt with as if they were one and the same thing. The reasons are understandable, although not necessarily valid. The Government employees cannot speak with any weight on their own behalf as do the contractors themselves or associations of contractors. Besides, it is generally considered even by many Government employees that they probably should be in no different position with respect to their employer than is the case in private industry, where it is customary for the employees to assign all their inventions to their employer.

Regardless of the source of the patent rights, i.e., from the Government's employees or its contractors, the question of a Government policy for *administration* of those rights remains the same. In considering the establishment of such a policy, it seems only reasonable first to determine *whether* the Government should own any such rights that may require administering. If the answer is in the affirmative, then a firm, well-understood policy of administration would be very much in order, if not essential.

Many supporters of the concept "The Government pays for it, therefore the Government should own it" do not look beyond this point. They care not what happens to the patented inventions after the Government takes title to them, other than that they are placed in the public domain. Ironically, perhaps, many of those who argue strongly in favor of the contractors keeping title to patents on inventions arising out of their Government contracts have, when faced with the possibility of legislation in which the Government would take title to those patent rights, likewise urged that in such event the Government should place those rights in the public domain.

Let us consider what the Government *could* do with such rights, including six principal ways in which those rights could be utilized:

"(1) Dedication to the public for its free and unregulated use

"(2) Nonexclusive, royalty-free license (with or without a revocability provision)

"(3) Nonexclusive, royalty-based license (with or without a revocability provision)

"(4) Either (2) or (3), but on an exclusive basis (with or without geographical or nature-of-use limitations)

"(5) Assignment of a part interest

"(6) Assignment of entire right, title and interest." [64]

The present practice is almost exclusively limited to number (2) with a revocability provision.

There have been presented arguments pro and con as to whether the Government can properly do numbers (4), (5) and (6). Many of these arguments have been reviewed by Forman,[65] who has concluded that the Government can (and, if it decides to acquire patent rights, should) practice (4), (5) and (6). How the Government has and could operate a program for utilizing Government-owned patent property in this manner is described by Palmer [66] in a study specially made for the National Aeronautics and Space Administration.

Which of the six ways for administering its patent rights in the above list should the Government adopt? In recent years the watchword among those who argue that the

Government should always take title to patents arising out of its sponsored research is *the public interest.* They urge adoption of procedures (1) or (2) as being the only ones in the "public interest." What is meant by this term? In the words of Senator Russell B. Long of Louisiana those Government agencies which tend to "give away to the contractor monopolies on Government-financed inventions are injurious to this Nation" whereas those which keep title to the inventions for the Government promote the general welfare. He would make only rare exceptions to this view, and only when the "equities of the situation" so require.[67]

The divergence of opinion comes in interpreting *what* system or policy would best serve the public interest. A spokesman for the largest group of patent lawyers in the United States, the American Patent Law Association, stated the view of its Board of Managers: [68]

"[A] policy permitting a contractor to retain title to inventions made in the performance of Government research and development contracts, in the absence of specific circumstances shown to exist in a particular case, is also shown by the overwhelming weight of experience to be the best way of justly caring for the equities of the contractor, the legitimate needs of Government, *and the long-range public interest*." (Emphasis added.)

Widest Possible Availability. Since "both sides" or the extremists of the controversy as to which form the Government's policy should take agree that it should be in the public interest, it should be only a matter of determining whether the "title" or "license" policy would best meet that goal. Everything that Senator Long has stipulated in his conditions points to a program that would make for the widest possible availability of the inventions in question. If an invention arises out of research or development which is at least in part financed by federal funds, the Government should be concerned with seeing that the invention accelerates scientific achievement, helps the economy, benefits the consumer, promotes competition, gives more opportunities to everyone, and is both fair and just to all the people.

The question is can the objective be best

met by placing the inventions in the public domain, by a program of some Government control over them, or by letting the contractors or others direct their development and utilization?

If the primary object is determined to be that of making the right to use the invention per se available to the maximum number of people, then placing the invention in the public domain or under a system whereby the Government oversees its utilization should be best. To put the invention into private hands will certainly limit the number of people who will get the legal right to practice it and reduce its availability to anyone who may be interested in using it.

Inventions, as such, unlike many other forms of property, are rarely usable in their original state. Further research, development, designing, testing and revising, possibly followed by building a plant and installing machinery and equipment, are frequently required before the invention is put into a commercially suitable state. The investment which must be made between the time of an invention's conception and its conversion to an item acceptable in the marketplace is very large. If someone, whether it be the Government or a private entity, does not see fit to make that further investment, the invention may never move forward on Senator Long's road for furthering the public interest.

In other words, "availability" does not necessarily leads to "utilization," and, if not utilized, thousands of inventions to which the Government has laid and can continue to lay claim may never inure to the public interest. In the words of former Commissioner of Patents, Robert C. Watson,[69]

"Can those patents to which the Government has or will acquire title be used more effectively to promote the public interest than by merely calling attention of the public to their existence and inviting any interested person to exploit the disclosed invention without charge? That method has long been used with conspicuous lack of success. At least it has not generally caused capital to be risked in attempts to commercialize these inventions. The public benefits much more when it receives the patented thing than it does when it is merely given the opportunity to read about it."

Maximum Possible Utilization. It is utilization, then, and not just availability which is in keeping with the public interest. The inventions must become useful. Preferably, they should be useful to every single American citizen, if not every living person, but this is surely to be recognized as possible only in a Utopia. Then to whom must they be useful if they are to pass the public interest test? Perhaps, in a democratic society, it would be satisfactory to hold that they should be potentially useful to a *majority* of the people. This does not necessarily mean that they must be *equally* useful to the majority, but merely that at least a majority should be able to get some benefit out of them. Such a scheme of things would be more than just and fair when compared with hundreds of services and benefits which today are made available by the Government to far less than a majority of the people, and which are considered to be proper governmental functions and responsibilities.

What system or method can provide for the maximum possible utilization of inventions arising out of Government-sponsored research? One would be for the Government to promote the invention, license exclusively as well as nonexclusively, or itself develop the invention for commercial adaptation and acceptance. The British and the Canadian governments have tried this sort of thing with varying views as to their success or failure.[70] It is certainly a procedure which the United States Government *could* adopt, but it would place the Government in direct competition with private enterprise, and as such might alter the entire political-economic philosophy of the country. Accordingly, serious thinking should precede adoption of such a system.

The most widely proposed alternative is to leave the rights to inventions in the hands of the Government contractors who conceived them in the performance of their contract. Many reasons are given by the contractors as to why this is fair, just, and proper both to them and to the Government. Suppose the reasons given as being fair to them are discounted as being self-serving, is there any merit to their view that it is fair to the Government—that is, fair to the people—and thus in the public interest? There may be, if it can be shown that leaving the rights with the contractors will guarantee maximum utilization of the inventions.

One proposal has been advanced [71] whereby such a guarantee will be given by the contractors. Either the inventions, which they would be able to control as their own (subject to a nonexclusive, royalty free right for use by the Government), are acceptably worked on a commercial basis, or they forfeit that control. This gives the contractor a chance to get a return on his own investment in the making of the invention, which he made either before or after receiving the Government contract, and assures that if the invention is not put into the commercial millstream, in a specified period of time, the Government may step in and transfer the exclusive right to the invention to someone else. In this way, the Government can pursue its responsibility of seeing to the development and use of the invention, without departing from the private ownership and management principles under which the country has prospered for almost two centuries.

Two identical bills which would implement this proposal were introduced, in 1961, in the House of Representatives (87th Congress). One was H.R. 6532 by Congressman William J. Green, and the other was H.R. 6548 by Congressman Herman Toll, both of Pennsylvania. When the 88th Congress convened in 1963, Congressman Toll re-introduced his bill as H.R. 4482. In essence, those bills call for the Government contractor to receive a defeasible title to all inventions arising out of their contract. If within five years from the date a patent issues on any such invention, or within ten years from the date the invention is first actually reduced to practice (whichever comes first), the invention is not satisfactorily utilized in commerce, the exclusive right thereto may be taken away and given to another interested applicant therefor. If satisfactorily utilized, the right to the invention becomes complete for the full or remaining term of any patents issued thereon. These bills give recognition to the interest which both the Government and the con-

tractor may have in the invention, but uppermost is the recognition given to the public's interest in it. If the underlying philosophy is accepted as well as a suggested mode of implementation, there is every reason to believe it should be applied to inventions made by Government employees as well as by the contractors. As long as the paramount criterion is to be the utilization of the invention, and if it is decided that such utilization is best done through such Government-chaperoned private activity, then *all* inventions in which the Government has an interest should be made subject to the identical treatment. H.R. 6532 and H.R. 6548 take this into consideration and make provisions for same.

Other proposals which have been advanced fall between the "title" and "license" approaches. Cf. "Statement of Principles for the Evaluation of Federal Government Patent Policy" prepared by the privately supported Government Patent Policy Study Committee.[72] Mainly, the proposals favor leaving the Government contractor with title, but give recognition to the propriety of the Government taking title under some limited circumstances. In those cases, they favor having the Government-owned patents made freely available to any member of the public. While the suggested compromise is logical on a number of points, its disregard for the potential lack of utilization of those patents which are made openly available to all comers may be a serious cause for concern. Those who claim they believe in the unique way in which patents function to foster development and promotion of inventions, by their granting the right to exclude others from infringing for a limited period of time, must find themselves in an illogical position when they rationalize the propriety of making even currently unwanted inventions freely available to all.

A long-awaited "Statement of Government Patent Policy" was released by the White House on October 10, 1963. It provides that all departments and agencies (except those whose patent policy is controlled by statute, as are the Atomic Energy Commission and National Aeronautics and Space Administration) shall take title to inventions when the contract pertains to: (a) matters intended for commercial use by the general public; (b) exploration of fields directly concerning the public health or public welfare; or (c) a field developed almost entirely with Government funds. When the contractor is performing work which builds upon his existing know-how, and the contractor already has an established commercial position in the field in question, he may be permitted to retain title. In certain instances, where it appears that the public interest might be best served if title is permitted to remain with the contractor, even though the contractor is otherwise not eligible by virtue of having no background commercial position, he still may be left with the title.

In all cases the Government would receive at least a royalty free, nonexclusive license. When the contractor is permitted to retain title, he has 3 years from the date of issuance of the patent either (a) to bring the invention to practical use, (b) make it available for license to others on reasonable terms, or (c) show cause why he should have an extension of time to do (a) or (b). The penalty for failure may be a compulsory licensing directive by the Government.

Probably the most important element of this Statement by President John F. Kennedy is its recognition of invention as a valuable national resource and of the need to promote its utilization in the public interest. This represents the first such official pronouncement, from any government source, that gives full recognition to these criteria as essential to government patent policy.

Conclusions

The American patent incentive system is now approximately 175 years old. During almost one-half that period the United States Government has found it expedient to apply for patents on inventions made as a result of research and development work which it paid for, at least in part. At the beginning those inventions were a relatively insignificant portion of all the inventions made in this country each year, and most of them were made by Government em-

ployees. Now those inventions may represent two-thirds to three-fourths of the annual inventive research by Americans, and most of them are being made by Government contractors.

In all this time no single Government policy has been formulated as to what should be done with respect to the rights to those inventions. Should the Government seek to claim all the right, title and interest or should it content itself with obtaining a royalty free, irrevocable right to make and use the inventions for governmental purposes? In the event of electing the former alternative, should the Government attempt to promote the inventions as by granting exclusive licenses or assignments, by setting up Government corporations to make and sell the inventions, or by other such means seek to get the inventions into public use? Or should the Government merely place the inventions in the public domain, or grant nonexclusive licenses to practically all who request them? These and other proposals have been made, and some tried by one or another Government department or agency.

Prior to the President's policy statement of October 10, 1963, everything in the way of Government activity in this area, whether by the legislative or executive branches, has thus far been devoid of sound positive policy.[73] What has been done to date has been largely of a negative character. The practices which have grown up in the various departments and agencies appear to have followed the whims and the views of their early administrators who were first faced with the problem of deciding what to do with rights to inventions arising out of the growing activity of the Government in research and development. A purely provincial attitude was adopted, each department or agency doing what it thought was best for the interests of the people it served or the function it was responsible for carrying out. Little or no thought was given to the effect their actions would have on the other departments or agencies or on the country as a whole. President Kennedy's policy statement should, at long last, end much of this confusion, but only time will tell whether this will be the case after the various departments and agencies come forth with their interpretations and implementations of the new Government-wide policy.

The Congress appeared to follow the same philosophy. Those laws which contain provisions regarding the disposition of rights to inventions arising out of Government-subsidized research always seemed to be based on something the Congress was "against," not "for." Generally, these laws provide for the Government taking full title to all inventions arising out of Government contracts. Congress was evidently opposed to giving a contractor the opportunity to further capitalize on the fruits of a contract for which he had already been paid, whereas the rest of the public would have no similar chance to use the inventive by-products of the contract. But what happened to the inventions themselves never seemed to bother Congress. Whether or not they were developed to a point where they could make useful contributions to the public welfare did not seem to concern the Congress at all. Yet, in the overall picture, the inventions which are thus ignored and fail to provide a full measure of return to the people of America probably represent a greater loss to the people than would the giving of exclusive rights to the contractors.

The Government should, in fact must, develop an affirmative policy regarding the disposition of rights to inventions and patents arising out of the research it sponsors. With its mounting research budgets responsible annually for almost three-fourths of all scientific and technological effort in the United States, the Government must assume responsibility for the proper care of probably three-fourths of all the inventions which will be made each year. As long as research and development were primarily funded by private enterprise, it was the American patent system to which people looked for the proper protection and "nourishment" of inventions.

Now that the Government has become the principal caretaker of the country's inventive productivity, shall it continue to rely on its patent system to perform those functions or should it devise some other system? Will the choice be one which will eventually destroy the American patent system? Or will it be one which, by working through that system, will not only improve it per se but also contribute more than ever before to the betterment of the public welfare?

Let no one deceive himself or others, by asserting that the Government can go on taking title to more and more inventions every year, then make them available to all comers, and give only lip service to a belief in the patent system. When the unique characteristic of exclusivity attached to a patent is separated from it, the patent system tends to atrophy. If some 75 per cent of the inventions which are today being made in the United States are to suffer such a fate because of the Government's elimination of patent exclusivity from them, can the patent system in truth survive? And what if that number reaches 80 to 85 per cent or more?

All other considerations are secondary to the overriding need to develop, promote and utilize the country's inventive productivity. Our survival may indeed depend on how well we meet that need. It can and should be met through the patent system. The inventions in question, when patentable and meritorious, should be patented and held by private interests with the right to exclude all others except the Government.

To assure, however, that the thus privately held patent rights are not forgotten or shelved, the Government should hold an attachment to them: Either the private owners will put those inventions made at Government expense to work or the Government will have the right to find someone else who will. This working should be the Government's prime concern, its principal responsibility and function in this area of inventions for which it has paid. It is a policy which everyone in and out of Government can understand and none can criticize. It would shine as a flashing beacon, pointing in the direction of safety, security and constant improvement to our way of life.

Footnotes

1. Act of March 3, 1883, c. 143, 22 Stat. 603, as amended in 1928, c. 460, 45 Stat. 467 (35 U.S.C. 45). This statute authorized the furnishing of

free patent soliciting services to Government employees, and their exemption from the payment of Patent Office fees.

2. Executive Order 10096, January 23, 1950 which established the Government Patents Board and provided criteria for determining whether the Government should take full title, only a royalty-free license, or make no claim at all under inventions of its employees, generally based upon the circumstances surrounding the making of the invention and the contribution of the Government to its conception and reduction to practice. This order, as well as the Board established thereby, was rescinded by Executive Order 10930 dated March 24, 1961. The functions of the Board were transferred to the Secretary of Commerce and, by delegation, to the Commissioner of Patents. Cf. Federal Register of March 28, 1961, 26 Fed. Reg. 2583; F.R. Doc. 61-3334 filed April 11, 1961. Also, cf. 766 O.G. 291, May 9, 1961.

3. Act of October 3, 1942, P.L. 768, 77th Cong., 35 U.S.C. 89-96, 1946.

4. Act of June 25, 1910 (28 U.S.C. 1498) as amended by P.L. 582, 82nd Cong. (July 1952); Trading With the Enemy Act of 1917, 50 U.S.C.A. (App.) 5(b), 40 Stat. 966 (1918), as amended by the First War Powers Act, 50 U.S.C.A. (App.) 616, 55 Stat. 839 (1941); Tennessee Valley Authority, Act of 1933, 16 U.S.C. 831(d) (i); Atomic Energy Act of 1946, 60 Stat. 768, U.S.C.A. 1811 (Supp. 1946); National Science Foundation Act of 1950 (42 U.S.C. 1871); Executive Order 10096 dated January 23, 1950 as superseded (cf. note 2 above); National Aeronautics and Space Act of 1958, 42 U.S.C. 2457; P.L. 87-295 (1961), amending the Saline Water Act of 1952; the Coal Research Act, P.L. 86-599 (1960); act establishing the Arms Control and Disarmament Agency within the Department of State, P.L. 87-297 (1961).

5. Cf. Agreement of March 27, 1946 amending Agreement of August 24, 1942 between the United States of America and the United Kingdom of Great Britain and Ireland entitled *Interchange of Patent Rights Information, Inventions, Designs and Processes* (Treaties and Other International Acts Series 1510).

6. PTC J., 1, No. 1 (June 1957), pp. 74-75, 89-96; Conference Supplement (1947), pp. 72-73; 2, No. 4 (December 1958), pp. 463, 472-485, 493, 495, 498, 499, 500, 501. See also "Productivity Surprise in Patent Scorecard," Chemical Week, 109 (July 25, 1959).

7. For a breakdown of all research and development expenditures in the United States in most of the years between 1930 and 1952, see Forman, "Patents—Their Ownership and Administration by the United States Government," pp. 11 and 13, New York, Central Book Company, 1957.

8. Federal Funds for Science X, p. 2, 1962.

9. *Ibid.*

10. From records of Index of Inventions maintained by the Government Patents Board pursuant to Executive Order 10096, January 23, 1950.

11. *Ibid.*

12. Palmer, "Administration and Utilization of Government-Owned Property," a report prepared and issued December 23, 1960 under Contract NAS$_w$-177 of the National Aeronautics and Space Administration, p. 11.

13. Daddario, "A Patent Policy for a Free Enterprise Economy," 47 A.B.A.J. 671, 673, 1961.

14. Forman, "Patents—Their Ownership and Administration by the United States Government," p. 17, New York, Central Book Company, 1957.

15. Palmer, cf. footnote 10 above, p. 12.

16. Committee Print, 84th Cong., 2d Sess., 1957, p. 19.

17. Palmer, cf. footnote 10 above, pp. 11, 12.

18. Article I, Section 8, Clause 8.

19. Judge Robert P. Patterson, *Report of Under Secretary of War Patent Conference*, p. 2, December 15-16, 1944, Aberdeen Proving Ground, Md.

20. Westerman, "Patent Provisions in Defense Contracts," 44 J. Pat. Soc'y, 38, January 1962, citing an estimate given by T. Hayward Brown, Esq., Chief, Patent Section, Civil Division, Department of Justice. According to Col. Westerman, who is Chief, Patents Division, Office of The Judge Advocate General, Department of the Army, "this figure does not include the amounts involved in administrative claims of this nature which are pending against the Military Departments," pointing out that they also entail large sums of money. One which he mentioned, in particular, is the claim of the Robert H. Goddard Estate which was settled by payment of $1,000,000. Some 200 patents in the rocket propulsion field were involved. See, also, Forman, "Patents—Their Ownership and Administration by the United States Government," pp. 47 and 49, New York, Central Book Company, 1957.

21. Cf. Westerman, footnote 20, who cites the case of *Autogiro Co. of America* v. *U.S.* (Ct. Cl. No. 50328) which has been pending from 1951 and is expected to be settled in late 1962. Over 183 days of trial have resulted in 16,000 pages of transcript plus 500 pages of exhibits.

22. Authority to do this is covered by such laws as the Act of October 31, 1942 (Section 3), P.L. 768, 77th Cong., 35 U.S.C. 89-96, 1946 ed. Cf., also, Westerman, footnote 20, p. 39.

23. Act of June 25, 1910, 28 U.S.C. 1498, as amended in 1952 by P.L. 582, 82nd Cong.

24. Captain Robert A. Lavender, USN, *Report of Under Secretary of War Patent Conference,* p. 65, December 15-16, 1944, Aberdeen Proving Ground, Md.

25. Major J. Moss, "Lend-Leasing of Patent Rights," *Undersecretary of War Patent Conference, ibid.,* pp. 45-46. Cf., also, "Interchange of Patent Rights, Information, Inventions, Designs of Processes," Executive Agreement Series 268 (1942), pp. 1-6, and Treaties and Other International Acts Series 1510 (1946), pp. 1-10; "Mutual Defense Assistance Agreement Between the United States of America and the United Kingdom of Great Britain and Northern Ireland," Treaties and Other International Acts Series 2017 (1950), p. 9.

26. Executive Order 9865, dated June 16, 1947, 12 Fed. Reg. 3907, as amended by Executive Order 10096, dated January 23, 1950, 15 Fed. Reg. 389.

27. Government Patents Board Administrative Order No. 4, dated March 12, 1951, as amended by Administrative Order No. 6, dated June 24, 1954, 19 Fed. Reg. 3937. Cf., also, Westerman, "International Exchange of Patent Rights and Technical Information for Defense Purposes," 21 Fed. B.J. 152 (Winter, 1961); "Exchange of Patent Rights and Technical Information Under Mutual Aid Programs," Study No. 10 (85th Cong., 2d. Sess., 1958); and "Patent and Technical Information Agreements," Report of the Senate Judiciary Committee's Subcommittee on Patents, Trademarks, and Copyrights (86th Cong., 2d Sess., 1960).

28. First Report of the National Patent Planning Commission, "The American Patent System" (1943), House Doc. No. 239 (78th Cong., 1st Sess.).

29. 84th Cong., 2d Sess., Report No. 1464 (1956).

30. *James P. Marsh Corp.* v. *United States Gauge Co.,* 129 F.2d 161, 165, 7th Cir. 1942.

31. Frost, "The Patent System and the Modern Economy," p. 4, Report of Subcommittee on Patents, Trademarks and Copyrights of the Committee on the Judiciary, U.S. Senate, 84th Congress, 2d Session.

32. Report of Attorney General, "Investigation of Government Patent Practices and Policies," Vol. III, p. 28, 1947.

33. *Ibid.* at 87.

34. Finnegan and Pogue, "Federal Employee Invention Rights—Time to Legislate," 55 Mich. L. Rev. 903, 930, 1957.

35. "If There Is An Invention Under A Government Contract—Who Should Get It?", 21 Fed. B.J. 64,72,73 (Winter, 1961).

36. Act of March 3, 1883, c. 143, 22 Stat. 603, 625, as amended in 1928, c. 460, 45 Stat. 467, 35 U.S.C. 45.

37. Watson, Bright and Burns, "Federal Patent Policies in Contracts for Research and Development," 4 PTC J. 295, 304, 305 (Winter, 1960).

38. P.L. 86-777.

39. P.L. 86-599.

40. "Government Patent Policy By Default?", a publication of the Machinery and Allied Products Institute and Council for Technological Advancement (Washington, D.C., 1962).

41. Rep. Att'y Gen., "Investigation of Government Patent Practices and Policies," Vol. III, pp. 176-179, 1947.

42. *Ibid.,* pp. 181-182.

43. *Ibid.,* p. 184.

44. *Ibid.,* p. 191.

45. H.R. 12412, 69th Cong., 1st Sess.

46. Rep. Att'y Gen., "Investigation of Government Patent Practices and Policies," Vol. III, pp. 193-194, 1947.

47. 69 Cong. Rec. 10388.

48. Rep. Att'y Gen., "Investigation of Government Patent Practices and Policies," Vol. III (1947), p. 201.

49. *Ibid.,* p. 208.

50. *Ibid.,* p. 211.

51. *Ibid.,* p. 212.

52. The Second Report of the National Patent Planning Commission, January 9, 1945, 79th Cong., 1st Sess., House Doc. No. 22, p. 5.

53. *Ibid.,* pp. 5-6.

54. *Ibid.,* pp. 7-8.

55. *Ibid.,* pp. 221-300.

56. Rep. Att'y Gen., "Investigation of Government Patent Practices and Policies," Vol. I, pp. 6-7.

57. From 1962 chart (slightly modified) prepared by the Patent Department of the Automobile Manufacturers' Association, Detroit, Michigan. The bills listed were introduced in the 87th Congress, 1961-62. In the 88th Congress, 1963-64, Senator McClellan substituted a bill, S. 1290, which permitted contractors to retain title in certain situations. Although it has not proved acceptable as such to many industrial groups, it constituted a compromise which was far more suitable than the bill it replaced. Congressman Toll re-introduced his same bill as H.R. 4482. Senator Saltonstall introduced a new bill, S. 1623, which eliminated some of the features in S. 1290 which the bar and industry

had objected to. Even so, neither S. 1623 nor S. 1290 could gain the approval of the American Bar Association's Section on Patent, Trademark and Copyright Law, at its Annual meeting in Chicago, in August 1963.

58. Central Book Company, New York, 1957.

59. "Government Inventions Jurisdiction," 788 O.G. 9 (May 1, 1962), 27 F.R. 3289, April 6, 1962. See, also, Maltby, "Government Patent Policy For Employee Inventions," 21 Fed. B.J. 127 (Winter, 1961).

60. Cf. Forman, "Patents—Their Ownership and Administration by the United States Government," pp. 108 and 117, New York, Central Book Company, 1957.

61. "Federal Employee Invention Rights—Time to Legislate," 55 Mich. L. Rev. 903 (May, 1957), reprinted in JPOS, April and May, 1958.

62. 40 JPOS 468 (July, 1958).

63. Cf. Report on Hearings on H. J. Res. 454, "Rights of Government and Its Employees In Inventions Made by Such Employees," March 3 and April 25, 1958 (House Committee on the Judiciary, 85th Cong., 2d Sess.). Also, Reports on Hearings of Senate Patents Subcommittee, "Government Patent Policy," Parts 1 and 2, April, May and June, 1961.

64. Forman, "Patents—Their Ownership and Administration by the United States Government," p. 165, New York, Central Book Company, 1957.

65. Ibid.

66. Dr. Archie M. Palmer, "Administration and Utilization of Government-Owned Patent Property," December 23, 1960, under Contract NAS$_w$-177 of the National Aeronautics and Space Administration.

67. "Federal Contract Patent Policy and The Public Interest," 21 Fed. B.J. 7 (Winter, 1961).

68. Prepared statement of W. Brown Morton, Jr., Chairman, Committee on Government Patent Policy, American Patent Law Association, presented at Hearings Before the Subcommittee on Patents, Trademarks and Copyrights of the Committee on the Judiciary, U.S. Senate, 87th Cong. (1st Sess.) May 31, June 1 and 2, 1961.

69. "Management of Government-Owned Inventions," 21 Fed. B.J. 121, 123 (Winter, 1961).

70. See Palmer, "Administration and Utilization of Government-Owned Patent Property," Under Contract NAS$_w$-177 of the National Aeronautics and Space Administration (December 23, 1960), pp. 41-45 and pp. 51-70.

71. See Forman, "Wanted: A Definitive Government Patent Policy," 3 PTC J. Res. & Ed. 399, 410 (Winter, 1959); and Forman, "Forgive My Enemies For They Know Not What They Do," 44 JPOS 274 (April, 1962).

72. Organized by the National Council of Patent Law Associations, 802 National Press Bldg., Washington 4, D.C. The statement was published in 1962 and constitutes a summary of many of the recent publications and representations pro and con on the subject here under discussion.

73. Cf. "Patents, Trademarks, and Copyrights," Report No. 1481, 87th Cong., 2d Sess., 1962, a report of the Subcommittee on Patents, Trademarks and Copyrights of the Committee on the Judiciary, United States Senate.

Cross-references: *Economic Value of Patents, Incentives for Inventors, Public Relations and Patents.*

H

HISTORY OF PATENTS ABROAD

Ramon A. Klitzke

We credit one Jacobus Acountius, a citizen of Trent, with providing us with the first written argument, a true petition, for the issuance of the patent grant. The case for the patent as he presented it in 1559 is the case for the preservation of the system today.

"Jacobus Acountius to the Queen. Nothing is more honest than that those who, by searching, have found out things useful to the public should have some fruits of their rights and labors, as meanwhile they abandon all other modes of gain, are at much expense in experiments, and often sustain much loss, as has happened to me. I have discovered most useful things, new kinds of wheel machines, and of furnaces for dyers and brewers which when known, will be used without my consent, except there be a penalty and I poor with expenses and labor, shall have no returns. Therefore, I beg a prohibition against using any wheel machines, either for grinding or bruising, or any furnaces like mine without my consent." Fox, "Monopolies and Patents" 27, 1947.

We record the annals of the patent grant not only to satisfy curiosity as to the genesis of patents but also to interpret better the written law of patents, to profit by the mistakes of others, and, hopefully, to predict something of the future. In so doing, we utilize the results of researches in this area by many scholars, to whom grateful acknowledgment is made.

The patent system begins with the sound concepts of newness and utility, as for a recipe for a new and excellent dish, with protection for the period of one year. Then come recognition of more substantial industrial contributions; concessions and incentives for immigration of artisans with special skills; the requirement for training others in the skills—the forerunner of to-day's publication of the patent disclosure; establishment of industries in the country of the patent grant; the temporary downward trend to granting of monopolies on arts or products that were old even domestically, in order to obtain additional revenue for the sovereign; return to newness and examination for novelty; and, finally, the unobviousness which we call invention.

Nature of Letters Patent

Origin of the Term. The Latin *literae patentes* means "Open Letters." Originally these were documents executed by English sovereigns and intended to be read without the need of breaking their seals, as opposed to "Letters Close," which could not be read without first breaking the seals.

Literae patentes, or Letters Patent, were used for a wide range of purposes. There were patents of appointment of military, judicial and colonial officers and patents of nobility, precedence, land conveyance, monopoly and invention. These patents in England conferred rights, privileges, ranks or titles personally and directly from the sovereign through the exercise of his royal prerogative and were recorded on the Patent Rolls in the Record Office. Letters Patent were intended to be open to the public and traditionally began: "To all to whom these presents shall come." Gomme, Patents of Invention 1, 1946. In this sense, the degree granted by the college or university can be called a Letters Patent, since it begins with the same phrase.

The Monopoly. In the United States the monopoly is:

"...the right to exclude others from making, using, or selling the invention throughout the United States." 35 U.S.C. 154.

In England it is the "sole privilege" to "make, use, exercise and vend" the inven-

384

tion. 16 Halsbury's Statutory Instruments 121, 1953. The United States inventor receives a negative right, the English a positive one.

Early Monopolies

The First Monopolies. Writing in the third century A.D., Athenaeus, in the "Banquet of the Learned," quotes Phylarchus, the historian, as saying that, about 500 B.C., if any confectioner or cook in Sybaris, a Greek colony famous for luxurious living and self-indulgence, invented a peculiar and excellent dish, no other artist was allowed to prepare it for one year. The avowed purpose of this monopoly was to induce others "to labour at excelling in such pursuits." Athenaeus, "The Deipnosophists," 3 Bohn's Classical Library 835, 1854. The Romans were distasteful of monopolies but did see value in rewarding the practical arts. In A.D. 337, the Roman Emperor Constantine decreed that artisans of certain trades who resided in cities were exempt from all civil duties, especially if their leisure hours were employed in perfecting themselves and instructing their sons. Locksmiths, chariot makers, engineers, workers in lead and manufacturers were so privileged. These groups undoubtedly included most of the inventors of that time. No monopolies were granted. In fact, the Emperor Zeno, in A.D. 483, made it clear that there was to be no monopoly of any kind over clothing or food, even if the monopoly was procured under a rescript of an emperor. Code of Justinian: X, LXIV, I and IV, LIX, I; 15 Scott, The Civil Law 155, 1932.

There are no allusions to monopolies in the Dark Ages, but in 1105 the first historical mention of windmills appeared in a diploma to a Norman abbot by Count William of Mortagne, authorizing the abbot to establish them in a certain area. It is also reported that the King of Jerusalem granted annual fees to certain dyers in the 12th century, the art of dyeing consisting wholly of trade secrets at that time. Frumkin, "The Origin of Patents," 27 JPOS 143, 1945. In 1236 King Henry III confirmed a grant by the Mayor of Bordeaux to Bonafusus de Sancta Columba under which he alone was permitted to make cloths of many colors after the manner of the Flemings, French and English for fifteen years. These early grants of privileges were not all for inventions and were not all monopolies.

One of the first real monopolies for invention was granted by the Signoria of Florence to Fillippo Brunelleschi, the great engineer and architect of the magnificent cupola of the cathedral of Florence. The privilege was given in 1421 for three years for a device for transporting heavy loads on the Arno and other rivers. The work of anyone imitating his invention was to be burned.

Venice. The world's first patent law developed in the early Republic of Venice. By 1400, Venice largely monopolized trade between Europe and the rest of the world, and her great power and wealth continued until the discovery of the sea route to the East around the Cape of Good Hope. As early as 1297 a decree was passed which provided that if a physician made a medicine based on his own secret, it had to be kept within the guild and all guild members had to swear not to pry into it. Mandich, "Venetial Origins of Inventors' Rights," 42 JPOS 378, 1960. In 1332 Venice maintained a special privilege fund from which a payment was made to one Bartolomeo Verde, who promised to build a windmill within six months of the payment. Other payments from such funds were reported in the fifteenth century to persons claiming knowledge of mill work and ship design.

The first actual patent of invention or importation was granted in 1443 to Antonius Marini, who offered to build 24 flour mills for each borough of the city of Venice. He did not allege that his devices were new but did request that no one else be permitted to build any mills which operated without water for twenty years. The *Senato* granted the petition, with the provision that a test be made of the mills in one borough and, if the test was successful, Marini was to get his monopoly.

Other similar grants followed, including those in 1460 to a Master Guilemo for dye shop cookstoves and to one Jacobus for a device "to raise standing water, either salt or fresh." John of Speyer, a German printer, received a grant in 1469 for the art of printing which he then introduced into Venice. John's patents state that it was usual to grant such monopolies, and after this time they were granted systematically.

On March 19, 1474, the *Senato* issued an act to regulate the granting and contents of patents in broad and general terms. It provided that any person who built any new device in the city which had not previously been made therein should give notice of it to the General Welfare Board and every other person would be forbidden to make any similar device for ten years. This is clearly the world's first patent act. A considerable number of grants followed this enactment. Mandich, "Venetian Patents (1450-1550)," 30 JPOS 166, 1948.

No account of the Venetian patent system would be complete without reference to Galileo's Patent. From 1592 to 1610 Galileo was Professor of Mathematics at Padua, a part of the Republic of Venice. On September 15, 1594, he received a patent for a device for raising water and irrigating land. He claimed to be able to discharge water through twenty spouts with the motive power of a single horse and successfully operated his machine in a garden. His right extended for twenty years, and the decree provided that infringers would lose their machines and be required to pay a fine of 300 ducats. Federico, "Galileo's Patent," 8 JPOS 576, 1926.

Germany. Until recently, historians have agreed that the English and Venetian patent laws are the oldest existing system in the world today. In 1960 a vehement refutation of this belief was made by Dr. Hansjoerg Pohlmann in a German article now available in English. Pohlmann, "The Inventor's Right in Early German Law," 43 JPOS 121, 1961. Dr. Pohlmann contends that the early German patent law was more advanced than the existing English or Venetian law of the time.

He points out that the Elector of Saxony granted proto-patents as early as 1378 and that numerous patents were granted between 1500 and 1600 for varied inventions. There were frequent German patents for "water works" and "wood saving means," including draining systems, pumps, smelting and refining furnaces, salt pans, stoves, etc.

It is also urged that the German grants were conferred only if the inventor fulfilled special requirements, including a formal examination procedure for novelty, and that they were not arbitrary moments of grace or favor, as were the English grants. A document of 1600 vintage implies that by that time, an extended practice of granting patents existed in Germany under which an inventor had the legal right to expect to receive a patent if he was the first inventor.

Dr. Pohlmann further argues that the ravages of the Thirty Years' War, 1618 to 1648, devastated Germany and destroyed the German patent system so thoroughly that it was forgotten until his researches revealed it. Patent history should be grateful to Dr. Pohlmann for his contributions. Further research may well uncover additional important truths of this relatively important era.

France. French inventors were encouraged in much the same manner as the English and Venetians at this time. In 1536 one Etienne Turquetti received a privilege for the production of silk. Under this he obtained safe conduct of his workers from Genoa and the right to collect royalties from other silk makers who established plants in Lyons after he did. This privilege, however, was nonexclusive.

Another Italian, Theses Mutio, received the first French monopoly patent in 1551, a five-year grant for the art of Venetian glass making. Abel Foullon, a French inventor, received a ten-year grant for a range finder in the same year. He was required to submit what became the first patent disclosure or specification; it was printed in 1557.

Only about one half as many patents were granted in France at this time as in England. Fewer inventors cared to tolerate the kingdom as it then existed. The French monarch actively participated in industry. He was reluctant to grant monopolies to private individuals. While the industrial progress of France surpassed that of England during the Middle Ages, France's political, social and economic progress lagged behind, and guild regulations contrary to a national monopoly system became stronger.

English Grants Before the Sixteenth Century

Sovereign Grants of Monopolies. The English sovereign was early endowed with certain prerogatives which allowed him to bestow various freehold interests, franchises and other liberties upon favored subjects. Such grants were accomplished by the open Letters Patent so that all could see the favor bestowed. The grants were usually given only when the sovereign received consideration in return, inasmuch as monarchs at that time were frequently short of the ready cash needed to operate their respective administrations. Sales of these grants dated from the Conquest onward, and many of them were extremely valuable privileges. For example, towns purchased their privileges from the Crown to hold a fair or market or to take toll for merchandise passing through the town. Such grants were common and do not seem to have been unpopular at all. Maitland, "The Constitutional History of England," 260, 1950.

During the Middle Ages, the merchants and manufacturers in many towns organized guilds for their mutual protection. These Merchant Guilds procured numerous monopolies from sovereigns and frequently monopolized all of the local trade. Craft Guilds also received monopolies from sovereigns. The most powerful early guild was the Hanseatic League, which grew up during the thirteenth and fourteenth centuries. It originated in the "Hanse" towns in Northern Germany but soon expanded throughout Northern Europe. 1 Walker on Patents 4, Deller's Ed. 1937. Henry III encouraged the League to settle in London and granted it many monopolistic trading privileges which were finally rescinded and given to English merchants. Fox, Monopolies and Patents 32 (1947).

Letters of Protection. At this time English industry was far behind the rest of the world. The English sovereigns were eager to induce skilled artisans to journey to England and there establish trades. Edward II and Edward III carefully nurtured English industry and also attracted foreign industry by offering letters of protection to foreign artisans. As early as 1324, Edward II gave his protection to skilled German miners to induce them to come to England.

The English cloth industry more than any other was developed through such early privilege grants. In 1327 Edward III prohibited the wearing of foreign cloth and proclaimed that he would grant franchises to fullers, weavers, dyers and other clothworkers. In 1331 John Kempe of Flanders received the first royal grant having the avowed purpose of instructing the English in a new industry and brought his weavers, dyers and fullers of woolen cloth to England. The king took John under his special protection, and the grant stated that any others who would be willing to cross the sea for the same purpose would be similarly protected. Hulme, "The History of the Patent System Under the Prerogative and at Common Law," 12 L. Q. Rev. 141, 1896, continued at 16 L. Q. Rev. 44, 1900. In 1336, two weavers from Brabant were given such letters to settle at York. Other cloth workers from Brabant settled in London and Bristol with such letters.

These letters of protection granted no monopoly or immunity to authority. They were mere passports to overcome the strict guild regulations against competition, and as the number of these patents increased, the guild power declined. Hamilton, Patents and Free Enterprise 11, T. N. E. C. Monograph No. 31, 1941. In 1337 Edward III's proclamation of 1327 was implemented by an Act of Parliament which provided that all clothworkers of foreign lands would be in the king's protection if they came to England and could dwell and practice their skills where they wished. Edward III extended this policy to other trades. He brought linen weavers from Flanders and clock makers from Delft in 1368.

Legality of the King's Prerogative. The right of the Crown to grant monopolies and privileges had always been recognized. The king, as chief guardian of the common weal, had the power and authority by his prerogative to grant privileges for the sake of the public good although, prima facie, they appeared to be clearly opposed to the rights of others. This right of the English sovereign to grant these privileges was derived from the ancient common law. Hindmarch, "Patent Privileges for the Sole Use of Inventions" 3, 1847.

A *monopoly* right, as distinguished from a mere privilege like a letter of protection, was in derogation of the common right of freedom of trade and could not be granted without some consideration moving to the public. Parliament did not hesitate to insist upon observance of Chapter 41 of the Magna Carta of 1225, which declared that all merchant strangers in the realm should be allowed to buy and sell their goods by the old and rightful customs. Nevertheless, royal grants of trade monopolies were so common that statutes opposing such grants were passed in 1336, 1352 and 1354. In 1373 Edward III granted the right to the sole importation of sweet wine into London to one John Peachie, but Parliament declared this grant void in 1377. In 1378 it was necessary to enact the Statute of Cloths, providing that all merchants could buy and sell without disturbance within the realm, regardless of any statutes, ordinances, charters, judgments, allowances, customs or usages to the contrary. 2 Ric. II, st. 1, c. 1, 1378.

Letters Patent for Inventions. As has been pointed out, the letters of protection were issued merely to induce foreign artisans to migrate to England and to establish their trades there. The immigrants may or may not have included inventors. E. Wyndham Hulme, writing in 1896, claimed that the first patent for a newly invented process was granted to John of Shiedame and his company in 1440. John came to introduce a method of making salt on a scale never before attempted in England. This was, however, probably only a letter of protection similar to that extended to the German miners in 1324. John was not granted a monopoly. There is some slight evidence that Henry VI granted certain monopoly patents in 1456 for the making of a philosopher's stone for medicinal and other purposes, but it is the better view that two successive commissions were merely appointed to look into the matter and that these patents were either warrants for the arrest of the individuals infringing the appointments or dispensations from the penal statute of 5 Henry IV, which made the practice of transmutation a felony.

Allan Gomme, librarian of the British Patent Office until 1944, writes that the first English monopoly patent for invention was granted on April 3, 1449, to John of Utynam, who had returned to England from Flanders at the King's command. No one other than John was permitted to practice his art of making colored glass for twenty years unless he consented thereto. The art had never before been used in England, and John promised to instruct divers lieges of the king in many new arts besides glass making. John may not have been the actual inventor of the process, but this was unnecessary and remains so for a British patent today. A valid English patent can be issued to the first person who introduces an unpublished invention into the realm, unlike the law of the United States, under which only first inventors may apply for patents.

Like earlier patentees, John of Utynam promised to instruct others in his art so that it could be developed in England when the grant expired. Unlike the others, however, John received a monopoly privilege under which he could exclude others from practicing his art for a period of time. This was probably the first time the monopoly privilege extended beyond trade and crafts to a particular process of a particular individual.

The custom of attracting foreigners having special skills was continued. In 1452 a grant was made to three miners and their company, brought over from Bohemia because they possessed "*meliorem scientiam in Mineriis.*" Chancellor Moreton, in a message to Parliament during the reign of Henry VII, noted that the system of inviting and protecting foreign artisans was for the purpose of setting the people to work on various handicrafts, making the realm more self-sufficient, eliminating idleness, and preventing the drawing out of English funds for foreign manufactures. Under this system, English industry advanced from the time of Edward II, when all goods other than articles of everyday use were imported, to a time when cloth making, mining, metal working, coining, ordinance production, glass making, engineering, clock making, sugar manufacturing and paper manufacturing were all well-developed home industries.

The Sixteenth Century Before Elizabeth

The English patent law made greater advances in the Tudor period than in any other. It is true that it was the Statute of Monopolies in the Stuart era that limited monopoly grants, but it is also true that the prerogative under which the sixteenth-century monopolies were granted had existed and been used long before that time. Yet the unprecedented and frequent uses to which Elizabeth put her prerogative were quite unlike any exercise of this sovereign power before. The sixteenth century could well be called the birth years of the English patent system.

The Beginning of the Regular Grants. The use of the patent privilege was fully accepted by the middle of the sixteenth century. On March 20, 1537, Antonio Guidotti, a Venetian who had received papers of denisation from Henry VIII in 1553, wrote from Messina, Italy, to Thomas Cromwell, the King's Principal Secretary, saying that he had persuaded some Italian silk weavers to go to England and practice their craft at Southampton. Cromwell was asked to intercede with the king to grant Guidotti a privilege for fifteen or twenty years to prevent others from making Italian silk. No grant to Guidotti is recorded but the casual manner in which the privilege was mentioned suggests that Guidotti was well acquainted with the Venetian system and he assumed Cromwell would understand what he wanted without much explanation. The English were probably greatly influenced by the earlier Venetian patent system.

In 1552 Edward VI granted a patent of invention to Henry Smyth, a London merchant. The patentee intended to introduce foreign workmen "mete and experte" in the making of Normandy glass. Smyth received a monopoly privilege for twenty years, under which unauthorized persons were pro-

hibited from making such glass. Davies, "Further Light on the Case of Monopolies," 48 L. Q. Rev. 396, 1932.

This was the first of the relatively numerous patent grants of the latter half of the sixteenth century. As had earlier patentees, Smyth promised to instruct others in his art so that the industry could be practiced widely when the grant expired. This patent and the patent to John of Utynam a hundred years earlier gave monopoly privileges for twenty years. Other patent privileges to individuals had not granted monopolies but only privileges to practice the art in England. Before this time the guilds had been the exclusive recipients of monopolies, but now individual inventors and individuals who brought new industries from abroad were to receive monopoly privileges similar to those they had enjoyed.

Although the patent to John of Utynam preceded the Smyth patent by 103 years, there are no known intervening grants. John's patent stands alone in the fifteenth century, and it was not until Henry Smyth that the English system of monopoly patents to inventors for inventions began as a regular custom. The patent to Smyth was followed by a grant by Queen Mary in 1554 to Burchart Cranick of a twenty year sole license to mine, break open ground, melt, divide and search for all manner of metals by a special method.

In the preamble of a statute of 1555, 1 & 2 Phil. & Mary. c. 14, reference is made to certain merchants of Norwich who, having obtained some Italian workmen, so improved the art of making Russels, Sattens, Satten reverses and fustians that they competed successfully with their foreign rivals. They were rewarded with a charter giving practically a monopoly of the industry and other privileges. This is the first historical reference to capitalistic speculative enterprise embarked upon by the newly risen middle class outside of the old merchant and craft guilds. Wealth and political influence were acquired by the middle class in the sixteenth century due to the disappearance of the old nobility during the Wars of the Roses and the redistribution of monastic property under Henry VIII. Joint stock companies having English investors began to appear at this time, and it was no longer necessary for the Crown to finance the entrance of foreign artisans upon English industry because the enterprising merchant class was acquiring resources and seeking investments.

Abuse of the Grants. The early Tudors practiced a perversion of the sovereign prerogative right to an extent unknown before them. Instead of granting open letters for the furtherance of national industry, the Crown began negotiating secretly to attract foreign artisans into its own service. German armorers, Italian shipwrights and glass makers, and French iron founders were brought to England in this manner. The precise relation between the Crown and these people is not known because the grants were not published and were not recorded on the Patent Rolls. The Italian glass makers came to England around 1550 under the protectorate of Somerset but were recalled by the Venetian State. The French iron founders successfully established the art of casting iron ordinance in the Weald district, and soon afterwards the old bronze cannons became obsolete. These practices contributed little to the development of the system of granting patents for inventions, but they were some of the abuses remembered by the Parliaments of the early seventeenth century just before enactment of the Statute of Monopolies.

It is to the customs of Elizabeth, both abusive and otherwise, that the English patent law owes most of its development. Whatever the earlier sovereigns may have done, Elizabeth brought the attention of all England to the Crown's prerogative and did more to cause the development of patent law than all the other sovereigns before her combined. The subject matter of the Elizabethan grants, more than anything else, drew public notice to Elizabeth's patent policies, and it is to this subject matter that we now turn our attention.

Substance of Elizabeth's Grants

Elizabeth's Policies. As the last of the Tudors acceded to the English throne the country was still far behind the Continent in industrial arts. Elizabeth tried desperately to develop industry by importing skilled artisans and encouraging enterprising men to undertake the risks of introducing new industries. She was not without success. For example, following the establishment of the French iron founders in the Weald district through secret negotiations, the pressing need for ordinance at the beginning of Elizabeth's reign was the cause of a number of patents issued at the insistence of William Cecil (Lord Burleigh), and England's ordinance became the best in Europe in 1600. Cecil was greatly desirous of making the realm self sufficient by developing industry of every kind. He accomplished this by granting patents of monopoly after careful inquiry into the novelty of the art and the possible public benefit. An attempt was made to introduce new industry without disturbing the old, and whatever the abuses which resulted, at least the intentions behind the monopoly grants were good.

Had Elizabeth confined her grants to inventors and procurers of novel foreign inventions, the loud cries of Parliaments at the end of her reign may never have been raised. The events of her reign were such that many persons were able to distinguish themselves in civil and military activities, and Elizabeth, being low in funds, rewarded them with monopoly patents for their endeavors. These grants would not have precipitated the intense hatred of monopolies had her patentees not abused their monopoly privileges by raising the prices of commodities and unreasonably restraining and harassing competitors. The most flagrant misuse of Elizabeth's prerogative was in the granting of monopolies in industries which were already established in England. It was such a grant that led up to the Case of the Monopolies, and such grants were attacked most vigorously in the Parliament which passed the Statute of Monopolies.

Jacobus Acountius to the Queen. The Italian patent system, if not greatly influencing the English sovereigns at this time, must be credited at least with strongly suggesting rewarding of inventors by monopolies. Reference has already been made to the letter of Guidotti. In addition to this letter, an undated petition is to be found among the English State Papers of 1559 in which one Jacobus Acountius (or James Acountius, as Hulme calls him), an Italian by birth who had been granted letters of naturalization in England and who received a small Crown pension, prays for a patent for his grinding machine. Guidotti had not thought it necessary to explain the type of privilege he desired, but Acountius presents history with the first recorded reasons for granting Letters Patents for inventions.

The petition of Acountius which has already been quoted, supra, is one of the most important events in history of English patent law. It may not have been the first attempt to convince the Crown that an inventor has a property interest in his invention which should be protected, but it is the first argument to this effect available to us in writing. Here is Jacobus Acountius, a citizen of Trent, "poor with expenses and labor," begging a prohibition against the use of grinding machines without his consent; and, in the centuries to follow, other searching inventors, abandoning "all other modes of gain," and often sustaining "much loss," were to come before their sovereigns like Acountius and receive "some fruits of their rights and labors" to recompense them for their contributions to society. "Nothing is more honest."

The patent grant to Acontius did not issue until 1565, some fifteen grants by Elizabeth being made before his. At least one writer feels it unlikely that six years would have elapsed between the petition and the grant; therefore, the petition may have been placed among the 1559 papers in error and its true date might be 1565.

Subject Matter of the Elizabethan Grants. The best English soap at this time was soft mottled Bristol soap. Hard Spanish soap of Castile was employed for fine laundry work, for which the English soap was unsuitable. On January 3, 1561, Elizabeth's first patent grant was given to Stephen Groyett and Anthony Le Leuryer for the making of "white sope." The grant extended for ten years and stipulated that at least two of the servants of the patentees were to be of native birth (which indicates that the patentees were probably aliens) and that the white hard soap to be made

was to be as good and fine as that made in the "Sope house of Triana or Syvile." The patentees' wares were to be submitted to the municipal authorities for inspection and, on proof of defective manufacture, the privilege was to be void. This was the first of a long line of Elizabethan industrial monopoly licenses granted during the years 1561 to 1600. At least fifty-five such grants were made and possibly more. Many of the patents were reissued up to three times and, counting the reissues, Elizabeth's grants may number seventy-five or eighty. The manufactures monopolized by these grants are astonishing.

It seems fantastic that some commodities, for example salt, were monopolized by one or two individuals, but such was the case. Some of the grants were for inventions and others were for the importation of the article or process into the realm. In Elizabeth's time, the term "invention" covered discovery of inventions and arts of others outside of the realm as well as origination of the invention in the inventor's mind. The terms, "invention," "discovery" and "first finding out" are used indiscriminately on the Patent Rolls and in the literature of the period, and it is difficult to determine which of these early patents were for actual inventions.

Elizabeth's Contributions. The English patent system was not the outgrowth only of the abuse of Elizabeth's monopolies. Once she accepted the policy of Acontius, Elizabeth created the basis of our patent law. What followed was merely inevitable growth and definition of the scope of the basic principles. Neither the Case of Monopolies nor the Statute of Monopolies constitutes the foundation of the English patent system. These were effects, not causes.

It was Elizabeth who first foresaw the value of rewarding inventors. Had she limited her grants to new inventions, the Case of Monopolies and the Statute of Monopolies might never have been a part of history. Unfortunately, however, the Crown's treasuries were low, and Elizabeth too frequently granted patents for purely mercenary reasons, attempting to obtain either a cash payment or a share of the profits from a grant. The grantees often knew little of the particular art, and the monopoly system became a system of plunder. The general public began to suffer and outcries were heard in the Parliament.

Elizabeth was aware of the approaching shackles her power of prerogative was to bear. In the first ten years of her patent grants, twenty-three original grants were made. Only twenty-six grants were made in the next twenty years, and there were only six grants in the years 1591 to 1600. In the last three years of her reign, no original grants were made. As the murmurings increased, her grants decreased, but the damage had already been done and the stage was set for confinement of the monopoly grant to new inventions only. Elizabeth's timidity in making grants at the end of her reign might even have added fuel to the fire of indignation. Among the noteworthy inventions refused patents at this time were Stanley's armor plate, Gainibelli's method of land reclamation, Harrington's water closet, which then had to wait one hundred and fifty years before its introduction and use, and the stocking frame of Lee, which was refused a patent because of the injury it might have done to the hand knitters. Lee subsequently took his stocking frame to France, where it was accepted and patented.

The first public denunciation of monopolies in Parliament came in 1571 when a member named Bell severely criticized monopoly licenses and their abuse. He was reprimanded before the Privy Council, and the Queen advised the House "to spend little time in Motions, and to avoid long Speeches." In 1597 the subject was again brought up in Parliament and again the Queen rebuked its members.

The Cases Leading up to the Statute of Monopolies. In 1599 the *Merchant Tailors' Case, Davenant* v. *Hurdis,* 72 Eng. Rep. 769 (Moore 576), was heard in the Court of the King's Bench. An ordinance of the London Company of Merchant Tailors required every brother of the Company to give at least half of his cloth to be dressed to some other brother of the society, under pain of forfeiture of 10 shillings for failure to do so. The Court held the ordinance void since it was a monopoly. The view of the com-

mon law was that monopolies were void unless for the common good.

In 1601 a declaratory bill was introduced in Parliament which was designed to eliminate the monopoly abuses and restore freedom of trade. After several days of heated debate, the Queen sent a message to the House through the Speaker to the effect that some of the more abusive monopolies would be repealed and that none would be executed until they were tried according to the law for the good of the people. Adams and Stephens, Select Documents of English Constitutional History 325, 1927. Three days later Elizabeth issued a proclamation declaring a number of monopolies to be void and providing that thereafter grants of patents could be tested by any subject under the laws of the realm, notwithstanding anything in a grant to the contrary.

In 1598, Edward Darcy, a Groom of the Queen's Privy Chamber, had been granted a twenty-one-year license for making and importing playing cards. As late as 1603, actions against Darcy were prohibited, but in the Easter Term, 1602 Darcy made the disastrous mistake of bringing an action himself against an infringer, and the common law courts were afforded an opportunity they might not have had for some time. In holding for the defendant and declaring Lord Darcy's grant void, the court pointed out that Darcy had no skill in making cards, and those subjects who had engaged in this trade before the grants were greatly damaged by it. It was definitely against the common law. This is the widely discussed *Case of Monopolies, Darcy* v. *Allen,* 72 Eng. Rep. 830 (Moore 671), 74 Eng. Rep. 1131 (Noy 173), 11 Coke Rep. 86, Abbott's Patent Cases 1 (King's Bench 1602). It was the first complete judicial enunciation of the common law of monopolies. It added, however, nothing to the common law of monopolies, because patents of this type had never been recognized as valid.

In 1603 James I acceded to the English throne, and in 1605 the *Case of Penal Statutes,* 7 Coke Rep. 36, 1605, was decided. In this case it was held that grants of power to dispense with trade penal laws, such as those prohibiting certain types of exports, were void. Those grants which afforded grantees the right to break the law by issuing dispensations from penal laws upon receiving fees were also void. This case was only one more step in the limitation of the Crown's prerogative. These grants had always been in conflict with the laws of Parliament.

In 1607 the *Case of Stannaries*, 12 Coke Rep. 9 (Star Chamber 1607), and the *Case of King's Prerogative in Saltpeter*, 12 Coke Rep. 12 (Parliament 1607), were decided. In the former case, the Star Chamber held that the King's preemption of tin in Cornwall, which James had given to Gilbert Brochouse for twenty-one years, was the King's to give, not by his prerogative but as his own property, being ancient rent and inheritance due the King. In the *Saltpeter* case, Parliament decided the King could grant licenses to certain men to dig for Saltpeter on other men's lands because saltpeter was necessary for the production of gunpowder and this was needed for the defense of the realm. Parliament pointed out, however, that the licenses could not prevent a man from digging for saltpeter on his own land. These cases further defined the power of the Crown. The prerogative was becoming outlined in detail.

James I, unlike Elizabeth, tried to keep the assertion of his prerogative within the common law, at least at the beginning of his reign. In 1603 he issued a proclamation against monopolies. His most famous proclamation was his Book of Bounty of 1610, in which he declared that monopolies were against the laws of the realm and expressly commanded that no suitor should presume to move the King to grant them. Language in the Book was referred to later in the Statute of Monopolies. In 1621 James issued a proclamation revoking certain monopolies, but many were still existent and widespread abuse was common. 11 Coke Rep. 88d.

In 1615 the case of the *Clothworkers of Ipswich*, 78 Eng. Rep. 147 (King's Bench 1615), was decided. Much of the language in the opinion is modeled after that in the Book of Bounty. The Court held an ordinance unlawful which prohibited anyone from being a cloth worker or tailor in the town of Ipswich before he had served an apprenticeship. The Court held that the King could create corporations and give them power to make ordinances governing trade, but they could not thereby monopolize trade in any manner. The Crown's prerogative was thus further defined and limited. The Court spoke favorably of patents for invention, although the case had nothing to do with these.

The Statute of Monopolies

In the spring of 1619 matters came to a crisis. Five silk mercers had been imprisoned by a patentee and there was great public indignation. James released the men but proclaimed a continuance of the monopoly system. Thompson, "Magna Carta —Its Role in the Making of the English Constitution—1300-1629," p. 301, 1943. The following year a great debate was waged in Parliament over a patent for inns, and by 1621, complaints about monopolies were extremely widespread.

On March 27, 1621, James suggested that the House draw up a proclamation against the three most objectionable patents and he "would give Life to it, without alternation." The day before this, however, an act respecting monopolies was reported out of committee to the House and was ultimately passed on May 12th and sent to the Lords. The bill was thrown out by the Lords, and James dissolved Parliament in February of 1622.

Agitation in Parliament continued and on May 25, 1624, the Statute of Monopolies was passed. 21 Jac. I. c. 3. This act was really a declaration of the common law in this area. The only real change the act made was to limit the term of patents to fourteen years. Another important portion of the act declared that patents were to be tested by the common law in the common law courts. Elizabeth, however, had already made this change twenty-three years previously. The Statute of Monopolies is not unimportant, and many of its provisions are in effect today. However, it was certainly not the final word on this subject. Monopoly abuses continued and as late as 1641 the Court of the King's Bench still had to define a valid patent. *Edgeberry* v. *Stephens*, 90 Eng. Rep. 1162 (Holt 475), King's Bench 1691. And it was, of course, not until two hundred years had passed that the system of granting patents lost its clumsiness sufficiently to enable inventors to obtain patents without long drawn out prosecution. Gomme, Patent Practice in the Eighteenth Century. 19 JPOS 256, 1937.

Conclusion

The English patent system owes much of its existence to the reign of Elizabeth. The history that preceded and followed her reign contributed to the development of English patent law, but it was Elizabeth who first recognized the great value of rewarding inventors and it was not until her reign that inventors received patents regularly, as a matter of course.

It is not intended to detract from the importance of the Case of Monopolies and the Statute of Monopolies, but these were only inevitable results following the movement Elizabeth had begun. Once the idea of granting monopolies regularly was accepted by the people and the Crown, it remained only for Parliament and the courts to channel this principle into the proper conduit. Overzealous to please her favorites, Elizabeth extended the theory of Acountius far beyond its reasonable bounds. Finding that her subjects would not tolerate this, she gradually withdrew her policies back within the limits of the common law, which limits had existed long before her reign.

Honest Jacobus Acountius could not have realized the great significance his proposals would ultimately attain. Thousands of inventors since him have been indebted to Elizabeth for her acceptance of the fact that inventors create something of worth which can be protected only by giving them a monopoly for a limited time. While our patent law today may little resemble Elizabeth's, the basic foundations on which she built are those upon which we now build. In many respects we have greatly improved over the ancient systems. The intrinsic truths of those systems, however, remain unchanged.

References

1. Federico, "Origin and Early History of Patents," 11 JPOS 292, 1929.
2. Hulme, "On the Consideration of the Patent Grant," 13 L. Q. Rev. 313, 1898.
3. Hulme, "On the History of Patent Law in the Seventeenth and Eighteenth Centuries," 18 L. Q. Rev. 280, 1902.
4. Janatt, "English Patent System," 26 JPOS 761, 1944.
5. Lipson, "The Economic History of England," Vol. 3, pp. 352-356, 1929.
6. McKechnie, Magna Carta—Commentary on the Great Charter of King John, 384, 1914.
7. Neumeyer, Compulsory Licensing of Patents Under Some Non-American Systems: Study No. 19 of the Subcommittee on Patents, Trademarks and Copyrights of the Committee on the Judiciary, United States Senate, 1959.
8. Octrooiburea Los En Stigter, Manual for the Handling of Applications for Patents, Designs and Trade Marks Throughout the World, Great Britain, 2nd ed., pp. 8-9, 1936.
9. Prager, Frank D., "History of Intellectual Property from 1545 to 1787," 18 JPOS 711, 1936; "Early Growth and Influence of Intellectual Property," 34 JPOS 106, 1952.
10. Ramsey, "The Historical Background of Patents," 18 JPOS 6, 1936.
11. Stephan's Commentaries on the Laws of England, Vol. 1, 21st/ed., 1950.
12. Vojacek, "Back to Queen Elizabeth," 32 JPOS 629, 1950.

Cross-references: *History of Patents—U.S., Invention—Changing Objectives.*

HISTORY OF PATENTS—U.S.

Ramon A. Klitzke

"The Patent System added the fuel of interest to the fire of genius."

Abraham Lincoln

The history of the American patent system is the history of the growth of our country.

Even the colonists recognized the necessity for protecting inventors so that advancement of the useful arts would be encouraged.

Colonial Period

Bounties, premiums and subsidies were used to persuade industrialists to settle in the new world, but such rewards were frequently inadequate inducement. Industrialists, having seen the operation of the monopoly systems of the old world, soon began asking the colonial legislature or governor for monopoly patents to prevent encroachment upon their arts. Being sorely in need of industry, the colonies granted patents, although not freely.

In the year 1641, one Samuel Winslow was granted the very first patent on this continent. He introduced a new method for manufacturing salt into the Colony of Massachusetts, and the General Court granted his monopoly for ten years. The grant prohibited all others "from making this article except in a manner different from his" and was conditioned upon his setting up works within one year.

In 1646 the General Court of the Massachusetts Colony granted Joseph Jenks a fourteen-year patent for his invention of "engines of mills to go by water." He was the first founder to work in iron and brass in the new world and many of the early colonial records refer to his activities. His may have been the first patent for a true invention and was certainly the first patent granted for machinery in this country. He also made dies for the early Massachusetts coinage, including the famous pinetree shilling, and built the first fire engine used in this country.

These early colonial patents were issued by the special acts of the legislatures, there being no general delegation of power to issue patents. The "Body of Liberties" adopted by the General Court of Massachusetts in 1641 expressly prohibited the granting of monopolies but excepted "such new inventions as are profitable to the country, and that for a short time." Connecticut had a similar law in 1672 to which it added, in 1715, a provision for "due encouragement" to any person who discovered "commodities that may be of use for the country." South Carolina encouraged petition for monopolies in a 1691 act.

Massachusetts granted the greatest number of patents of any single colony. Connecticut was second, and the colonies of Virginia, South Carolina, New York and Rhode Island also issued patents. Many of these grants were for the introduction of new industries into a colony, and some of them were merchant trading monopolies. Few mechanical inventions drew the interest of the early colonists since known industries were much more sorely needed. Protection sometimes extended to unsuccessful efforts to introduce new industries and, on the other hand, many industries sprang up without any legislative protection whatever. Many of the colonies gave no patent protection until after the Revolution. Even Pennsylvania, the principal manufacturing colony in the 18th century, was without protection for inventors (although Walker lists two 1717 patents to a Thomas Masters for 14-year terms). In any event, it does not appear that colonial patents had any permanent or general influence on industry.

State Patents

After almost nine years of revolutionary war, the people of America realized their ideal of a loose association of sovereign states, rid of the Crown that had tried to rule them from a distant shore. It was natural that these states should continue to guard the privilege of granting monopolies to inventors, a practice which had been copied from the English Crown, and it is not surprising that few monopolies were granted.

Special acts of the legislatures were still needed for a patent grant but now the idea of the inventor's right in his property began to replace the ancient concept of the patent as a special favor from the Sovereign.

Only South Carolina made a serious attempt at general patent legislation. A 1784 Act provided for the copyright of books and had a short section which extended the fourteen-year monopoly right to inventors of useful machines. In actual practice it was still necessary to obtain a special act from the legislature, however. Two patents were granted by the state of South Carolina in 1786.

After the Revolution, Pennsylvania led the other states in the number of patents granted. A 1780 patent was issued for a currier's oil and many other grants followed. Pennsylvania granted its own patents even after the adoption of the Federal Constitution, but this practice was common at that time among the states. Federico suggests that the states probably still have the power to grant patents, although never exercised.

The State of Connecticut continued its colonial practice of granting monopolies for the introduction of new industries, as for periods of seven to twenty-five years for the manufacture of glass, cloth, snuff and refined sugar. The snuff protection failed.

New Hampshire was active in granting patents at this time. Oliver Evans, the first typical American inventor, received many grants from New Hampshire, as well as from Pennsylvania and Maryland. Evans not only completely revolutionized the manufacture of flour but was also the first steam engine manufacturer.

In 1785 John Fitch completed a model of a steamboat and in 1786 he moved a small steamboat on the Schuylkill River in Pennsylvania. The patent history of the steamboat is replete with the problems created by the separate patent systems of the various states at this time. Fitch, James Rumsey, Arthur Donaldson, Robert R. Livingston and Robert Fulton were all experimenting with the steamboat and beset the legislatures of Pennsylvania, Virginia, Maryland, New Jersey, and New York with varying degrees of success. In 1807 Fulton operated the "Clermont" on the Hudson River, and with the aid of a New York act granting the exclusive privilege of navigating steamboats in that state, he soon monopolized the public steamboat carrier business. Fulton and Livingston even monopolized the Mississippi River steamboat traffic by means of a special act passed by the Orleans Territory legislature in 1811. In the celebrated case of *Gibbons* v. *Ogden*, the U.S. Supreme Court, speaking through Chief Justice John Marshall in 1824, declared the New York Livingston and Fulton monopoly unconstitutional since it interfered with interstate commerce. The Court expressly refused to decide whether the states could grant patents for inventors generally, however. 9 Wheat. 1, 6 L. ed. 23, 1824.

These state patents were mere transitions between colonial days and the time when the federal government would take over the granting of patents under the new Constitution. The system of rewarding inventors never lapsed; the Constitutional provisions for inventors were really only continuances of principles well engrained in American culture.

The Constitutional Provision

On May 14, 1787, the Constitutional Convention began to meet daily in Philadelphia. The men present were well aware of abuses the English Crown had practiced with respect to grants of monopoly, were decidedly against the initiation of any similar system in their young government, but knew also the value of a system of protection of authors and inventors, as the history of the Convention bears out.

In a pamphlet published later, Charles Pinckney of South Carolina claimed to have been the proposer of the constitutional clause securing to authors and inventors the exclusive rights to their performances and discoveries. But no such clause was present when the Pinckney Plan was first submitted to the Convention, and the draft Constitution reported out by the Committee of detail, on August 6, 1787, had no predecessor to our present author and inventor clause. It was on August 18 that James Madison and Pinckney both submitted proposals for additional powers to be granted to the Federal Government, and among these were powers to secure rights to authors and inventors.

It does not appear that much opposition to these proposals arose. The delegates felt that protection of inventions and literary works by the several states could not adequately preserve the common law rights in intellectual property and that this could be done far more effectively by a single mode of protection. The delegates were probably aware of the troubles some inventors had experienced in obtaining protection from the various states, as exemplified by some of the steamboat inventors. On August 22 the Convention adjourned in the afternoon to witness the trial of one of John Fitch's steamboats on the Delaware River and some of the delegates rode on its first trip.

On September 5, 1787, the Committee of detail reported out to the floor of the Convention, and our present author and inventor clause was there approved, becoming Article I, Section 8, Clause 8 of the Constitution:

"Section 8. The Congress shall have Power ... To promote the Progress of Science and useful Arts, by securing for limited Times to Authors and Inventors the exclusive Right to their respective Writings and Discoveries ..."

For the first time in the history of the world a constitutional instrument had recognized that man has property rights in the products of his intellect and that it is in the interest of progress to protect these rights for a limited time. Note that neither the word "patent" nor "copyright" is to be found in the clause finally reported out of the Committee, although both of these terms were present in the original Madison and Pinckney proposals. Note also that trademarks are not protected under this clause. It was not until many years later that the Supreme Court of the United States decided that trademarks could be granted by the Federal Government under its power to regulate interstate commerce.

On September 17, 1787, the delegates signed the Constitution, to become effective later upon ratification. The constitutional provision was only the first of many steps needed to protect inventors and authors. Following the ratification of the Constitution, an implementing law had to be passed, and long and difficult administrative and judicial roads had to be traversed before intellectual property was to reach its contemporary status.

The First Patent Act

Legislative Action. The First Session of the First Congress of the United States opened on March 4, 1789. A little over a month later, one David Ramsay of South Carolina petitioned the House, through Thomas Tucker, Representative from South Carolina, for the sole and exclusive right of vending and disposing of two books he had written on history of the revolution. On the same day, one John Churchman presented a petition in which he alleged that he had invented several different methods for explaining the principles of magnetism. He desired the patronage of Congress for a voyage to Baffin's Bay to make "magnetical experiments." These two petitions were referred to a committee of three, and a few days later this committee reported back to the House that the petitions for the right to vend the book and to protect the invention of Churchman should be granted but that the petition for the voyage should be denied because of "the present deranged state of our finances."

Before action could be taken on bills for these two individuals, other petitions began to come in. John Fitch petitioned for a steamboat patent, Englehart Cruse for a steam engine patent and Jedidiah Morse for a copyright on the first American Geography. These three were referred to another committee. During the session about eighteen individual petitions were received, most of them for patents, and it became apparent to the Congress that it would be impossible to consider each petition individually and that an act would be necessary under which the responsibility for examining these requests could be delegated.

On the day that the Churchman and Ramsay petitions were reported out of committee, another committee was appointed to bring in a bill or bills making general provisions for securing to authors and inventors the exclusive right to their writings and discoveries. The new committee, consisting of Benjamin Huntington, Connecticut, Lambert Cadwalader, New Jersey, and Benjamin Contee, Maryland, was destined to be the first informal board of patent examiners since all requests for patents or copyrights were thereafter referred to them. On June 23, 1789, Huntington presented a bill that the committee had drafted. This bill provided for both copyrights and patents and might well have been passed except that this first session of Congress was ended on September 29, 1789, before any action could be taken.

The Second Session of the First Congress convened on January 4, 1790; four days later, it was addressed by President Washington in his first annual speech to the Congress. He urged the "expediency of giving effectual encouragement" to the introduction of new and useful inventions from abroad, and "to the exertions of skill and genius in producing them at home." The Senate, in its answer to this address, promised "early attention" to this matter, and the House proceeded to move with comparative swiftness in the matter. A patent bill was soon reported out of committee to the House and was then passed by both houses of Congress. On April 10, 1790, President Washington affixed his signature to the first patent act. A separate copyright act soon followed, receiving presidential approval on May 31, 1790.

While the patent bill was being discussed, an inventor almost succeeded in persuading Congress to grant him a patent by special act. A bill granting Francis Bailey the "exclusive privilege of making and vending certain punches for stamping the matrices of types, etc.," was passed by the House but held over by the Senate until after consideration of the general patent bill. Congress still has the power to grant an individual patent itself if necessary, but it never does. Congress has removed legal obstacles from the paths of inventors and granted extensions of patent terms, but it has been many years since it has seen fit to take such action in an individual case.

Provisions of the First Patent Act. Prager feels that the Patent Act of 1790 marked the end of mere common law in the regulation of patents and that a new departure occurred at that time. Important provisions were made by the statute for (1) examination for novelty, (2) written specifications, and (3) a board of patent examiners. For the first time in history, the intrinsic right of an inventor to the fruit of his intellectual labor was recognized by a statute. The English Statute of Monopolies had not gone this far.

The subject matter for a patent was defined as "any useful art, manufacture, engine, machine, or device, or any improvement therein not before known or used." A patent specification, drawing, and, if possible, a model had to be submitted in support of the petition for a patent. A board

of patent examiners was created which was comprised of the Secretary of State, the Secretary of War and the Attorney General. The Board had the power to issue a patent if they deemed the invention to be "sufficiently useful and important." The term of the patent was to be fixed by the Board but was not to exceed 14 years, a term which was taken from the Statute of Monopolies. There was no appeal provided from the Board's absolute authority to grant patents. The Department of State had the responsibility for administering the patent law. 1 Statutes at Large 109-112.

This first patent act, while short by today's standards, represented considerable effort on the part of the First Congress and was average in length compared to other laws passed at that time. We would consider the act unduly simple and quite inadequate to cope with anything as complicated as invention but it nevertheless constituted a major step in the progress of patent law at that time and it appeared to serve its purpose well during its short duration.

Operation of the First Patent Law. The first "Patent Board," or "Patent Commission" was comprised of Thomas Jefferson, Secretary of State, Henry Knox, Secretary of War, and Edmund Randolph, Attorney General. The Board did the best it could with respect to the examination of inventions before granting patents but, with each member having considerable other duties, little time could be found to devote to inventors, and relatively few patents were granted. Jefferson was a man of substantial scientific attainment, and although he never applied for a patent, he invented a number of useful devices, including a mould board for the plough, a revolving chair, a chair which could be folded into a walking stick, a pedometer for counting steps, and a machine for treating hemp. After some initial skepticism, he became an avid supporter of the patent system and was an enthusiastic first administrator of it. The Board frequently required models of inventions and often held hearings.

The Act of 1790 had overlooked the possibility of conflicting claims by inventors, so the Board was quite disturbed when four inventors applied for patents covering the steamboat. Hearings were held in April of 1791 and the four claimants, John Fitch, James Rumsey, John Stevens and Nathan Read, were allowed to state their cases. It was eventually decided to grant patents to each of the applicants, but it is unlikely that duplicate grants were made to any of them. The titles of the patents suggest that each inventor received grants covering differing aspects of the steamboat, but copies of the patents themselves have not been found so there is no way of knowing whether overlapping grants were made.

The Patent Board did not grant patents as freely as some inventors desired. Three patents were issued in 1790, 33 in 1791, 11 in 1792, and 10 in 1793 prior to the new patent act passed in that year. The chief reason for the relative failure of the 1790 Act is that the members of the Board could not devote sufficient time to its administration. Jefferson wrote that the investigation of applications required a great deal of time to understand and treat them with justice and that the Board did not have this time to contribute. Because of these difficulties it was probably Jefferson who wrote a patent bill which would have completely relieved the Board of any judicial responsibility in the grant of patents and this bill was introduced in 1791, less than a year after the adoption of the first act.

The Period of Registration without Examination

Regression. The Act of 1790 constituted an innovation that the world had long needed, including provision for the examination of patent applications for novelty and utility.

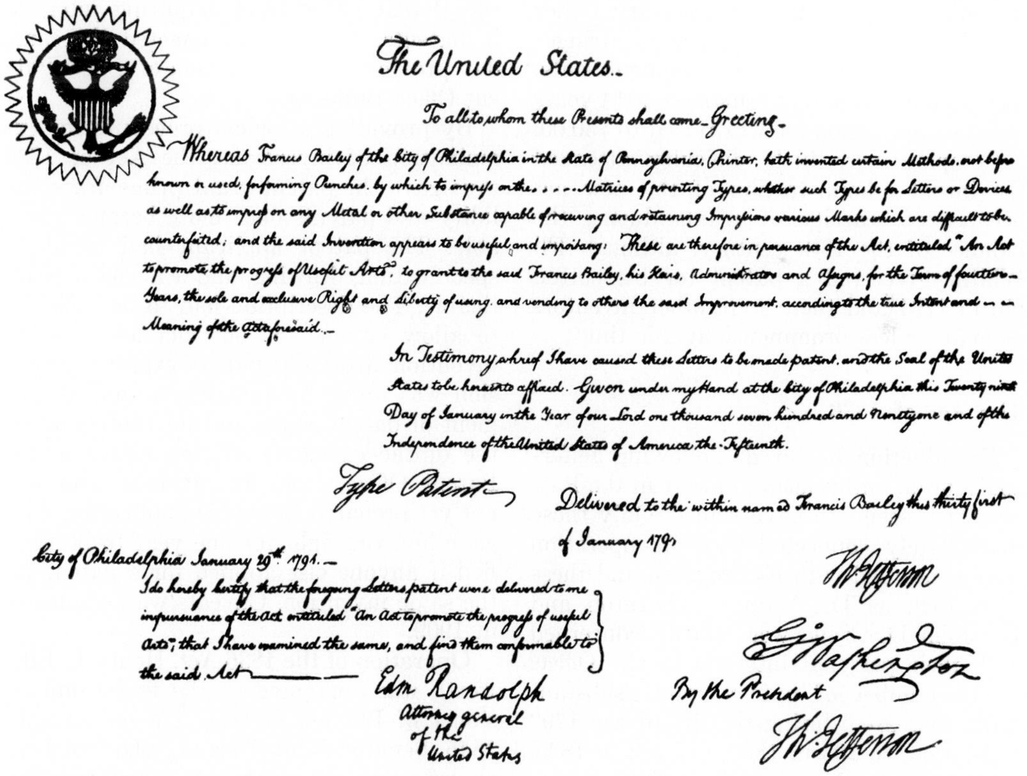
The United States.

To all to whom these Presents shall come_Greeting.

Whereas Francis Bailey of the City of Philadelphia in the State of Pennsylvania, Printer, hath invented certain Methods not before known or used, for forming Punches, by which to impress on the . . . . Matrices of printing Types, whether such Types be for Letters or Devices as well as to impress on any Metal or other Substance capable of receiving and retaining Impressions various Marks which are difficult to be counterfeited; and the said Invention appears to be useful and important: These are therefore in pursuance of the Act, entituled "An Act to promote the progress of Useful Arts", to grant to the said Francis Bailey, his Heirs, Administrators and Assigns, for the Term of fourteen Years, the sole and exclusive Right and Liberty of using and vending to others the said Improvement, according to the true Intent and Meaning of the Act aforesaid.

In Testimony whereof I have caused these Letters to be made patent, and the Seal of the United States to be hereunto affixed. Given under my Hand at the City of Philadelphia this Twenty ninth Day of January in the Year of our Lord one thousand seven hundred and Ninety one and of the Independence of the United States of America the Fifteenth.

Type Patent

Delivered to the within named Francis Bailey this thirty first of January 1791

Th: Jefferson

City of Philadelphia January 29th 1791.

I do hereby certify that the foregoing Letters patent were delivered to me in pursuance of the Act entituled "An Act to promote the progress of useful Arts"; that I have examined the same, and find them conformable to the said Act

Edm Randolph
Attorney general of the United States

G Washington

By the President

Th: Jefferson

FIG. 1. This fourth United States Patent, signed by George Washington, Thomas Jefferson and Edmund Randolph in 1791, is the earliest patent of which a copy is available in the Patent Office. The patent states in part that Francis Bailey of Philadelphia "hath invented certain Methods not before known or used, for forming Punches, by which to impress on Matrices of Printing Types... and that said invention appears to be useful and important."

Bills to replace the 1790 Act, however, were introduced in Congress in February 1791 and March 1792, and a bill introduced in December 1792 was eventually passed. It was approved by the President on February 21, 1793, and remained in force until 1836. It proved troublesome and inadequate in administration.

The most important change made in the 1793 Act was the cancellation of the requirement, "if they shall deem the invention or discovery sufficiently useful and important." This eliminated the examination and made the patent grant a simple clerical procedure. A second section provided that the inventor of an improvement in a patented device could not use the original invention and the original inventor could not use the improvement. A third section required the inventor to swear that he was the true inventor and to furnish an exact description of the invention, a drawing and a model, if deemed necessary. Other sections provided for assignments, infringements and defenses in infringement suits. The term of the patent remained at 14 years but the application fee was raised to $30.00.

Comparatively little difficulty attended the initial administration of the new act because of scarcity of grants during the balance of the 18th century, although Eli Whitney received a patent for his cotton gin in 1794 and there were other inventors of more or less prominence at this time.

The Act of 1836

Examination Restored. Following Jefferson's initial enthusiasm, interest in the Patent Office seems to have waned. Only those immediately connected with its operation were concerned with its progress, and these men, such as Dr. William Thornton and Dr. John D. Craig, were chiefly concerned with their personal interests in the Office.

The number of patent grants substantially increased during the life of the 1793 legislation, to 203 in 1809 and 752 in 1835. In 1834 Cyrus McCormick received a patent for his reaper, and in 1836 Samuel Colt obtained one for a revolving gun, the first of the famous "six-shooters."

However, discontent with the patent law continued to grow. Senator John Ruggles from Maine complained that many of the patents granted were worthless and void, and frauds had developed. Patents had become of little value, and the object of the patent law had been defeated. The reason for this, of course, was that patents were being granted without any examination for novelty.

Following Senator Ruggles' recommendations, the Congress passed the bill that accompanied his report, and the patent law of the United States was once more dramatically changed. The 1836 Act provided for a systematic examination method of granting patents, established the Patent Office as a separate bureau with a Commissioner of Patents, kept the patent duration at 14 years but subject to an extension of 7 years, provided for appeals from refusals to grant patents, established a register of all patents issued, and prohibited employees of the Patent Office from acquiring interests in patents. Another law enacted the same day provided for the erection of a new Patent Office Building.

By providing a logical procedure for examination of inventions, the Act of 1836 thus gave the patent grant prima facie validity and patents once more became valuable. The patent applicant had to file a specification, drawing, and a model if practicable. The description had to be sufficient to allow anyone to construct and use the invention after the patent expired. Provision was made for inheritance and assignment of patent rights and for protection by use of the caveat, a written notice to the Patent Office, from an inventor who was not yet prepared to file his application, that gave him the right for one year to be notified if anyone else applied for a patent for the same invention. Caveats were abolished in 1909.

Operation of the 1836 Act. Henry L. Ellsworth was appointed as the first Commissioner of Patents in 1836. He served until 1845. Senator John Ruggles, who had been chairman of the committee which was appointed to consider the patent laws and who submitted the report and bill which precipitated the 1836 Act, received the first patent under the new act, the subject mat-

Fig. 2. Blodgett's Hotel—home of the Patent Office, 1810-1836. (This and other illustrations in this article are by courtesy of the Journal of the Patent Office Society.)

Fig. 3. United States Patent Office building, 1836-1932.

Fig. 4. Department of Commerce Building, present home of most officials and divisions of the Patent Office.

ter being a traction wheel for locomotive steam engines.

On December 15, 1836, the Patent Office was completely destroyed by fire, the loss being estimated at 7,000 models, 9,000 drawings and 230 books. The next year the Congress appropriated $100,000 to replace the records, as well as the most valuable and interesting models destroyed.

The 1836 Act served its function extremely well. Investigations into the novelty and utility of inventions began to take on an orderly form, and the American public regained its respect for the American patents. Other countries in subsequent years followed some of the aspects of the United States law in formulating their own patent laws.

No one will ever know the extent to which the patent law contributed to the technological advance of this country during the 19th and 20th centuries, but epoch-making inventions appeared and inventors received patents of great value for their discoveries: Samuel Morse for his magnetic telegraph; Charles Brush, Peter Cooper Hewitt, Charles P. Steinmetz and Thomas Edison, electricity; George Pullman, sleeping car construction; George Westinghouse, the air brake; George B. Selden, Charles E. Duryea, R. E. Olds and Elwood Haynes, automobiles; James Oliver, the chilled plow; Samuel P. Langley, Glen H. Curtiss and the Wright brothers, aeronautics; Ottmar Mergenthaler, William Bullock, the Hoes, Tolbert Lanston and Henry A. Wise Wood, typesetting and printing; Christopher Latham Sholes, typewriting machines; Alexander Graham Bell, the telephone; Hannibal Goodwin and George Eastman, photography; and Edward Muybridge and C. Francis Jenkins, motion picture production; all of these men were leaders in the rise of American technology to a new level.

The Period Up to 1951

Legislative Changes. In 1837 Congress provided for the submission of a duplicate set of drawings so that one could be attached to the grant itself. The fire of 1836, of course, was the moving factor in this legislation. Later, when patents began to be printed, there was no longer a need for duplicate drawings. This act of 1837 also allowed an inventor to disclaim part of his invention where he had inadvertently claimed more than was rightfully his.

In 1839 the Congres authorized the employment of two assistant examiners since the work of the Office had greatly increased. This act also required the Commissioner to publish a classified list of patents and authorized the purchase of a thousand dollars' worth of books for the scientific library.

An amendment of 1842 made designs patentable for seven years and also required that a patentee mark his patented article. In 1848 the Commissioner alone was given the power to extend a patent, and in 1849 the Patent Office was placed under the newly created Department of the Interior. An 1852 act allowed appeals from the Patent Office to justices of the United States Court for the District of Columbia.

In 1861 the Congress passed a bill which allowed the taking of testimony by deposition for interference cases in the Patent Office and also created a Board of Appeals consisting of three examiners-in-chief.

Because of the numerous amendments which had been made to the 1836 Act, the Act of 1870 was passed to consolidate all of these laws into one entity. This act also conferred power on the Commissioner to establish regulations consistent with law for the administration of his office. The patent term was increased to a maximum of 17 years at this time. This was by far the most important patent act since 1836.

Plants became patentable under the Act of May 23, 1930. In 1935, Patent 2,000,000 was issued and in 1961, No. 3,000,000.

The Act of 1952 is discussed in the article under that title and throughout this work.

Standard of Invention. In 1850 the United States Supreme Court established the standard of patentable invention, *Hotchkiss* v. *Greenwood*, 52 U.S. 248, 1850. The Act of 1952, 35 U.S.C. 103, first defined invention in the statute. If the differences between the invention and the prior art are such that they would have been obvious as a whole to a person having ordinary skill in the art, then a patent should not issue.

A considerable number of the patent claims brought before the courts are declared invalid. This may suggest a conflict of views between the Patent Office and the courts as to what constitutes patentability, but as any patent attorney will testify, the Patent Office diligently strives to maintain a proper standard of invention.

The Patent Office of today, in all its ramifications, could not have been conceived of during the time of Thomas Jefferson when all patents were examined by the Attorney General and two members of the president's cabinet. Yet the seeds sown in that first Patent Act of 1790 have brought forth bountiful and rich fruit.

General References

Abramson, Victor, "The Patent System: Its Economic and Social Basis," Study No. 26 of the Subcommittee on Patents, Trademarks and Copyrights, Committee on the Judiciary, U.S. Senate, 1960.*

Allen, Julius W., "Economic Aspects of Patents and the American Patent System: A Bibliography," Study No. 14 of the Subcommittee on Patents, Trademarks and Copyrights, Committee on the Judiciary, U.S. Senate, 1958.*

Allyn, Robert Starr, "Supreme Court Patent Cases, 1875 to 1881 v. 1935 to 1941," 25 JPOS 27, 1943.

Anonymous, "John Fitch, Inventor of the Steamboat," 8 JPOS 439, 1926.

Anonymous, "The Patent Profession and the New Deal," 16 JPOS 595, 679, 1934.

Beard, Charles A., and Beard, Mary R., "The Rise of American Civilization," London, Macmillan & Co., 1946.

Bush, Vannevar, "Proposals for Improving the Patent System," Study No. 1 of the Subcommittee on Patents, Trademarks and Copyrights, Committee on the Judiciary, U.S. Senate, 1956.*

Calvert, Robert, "The New Patent Law," 31 Chem. and Eng. News 4186, 1953.

Deller, Anthony William, "America is Ideas," International Nickel Co., Inc., 1960.

Edwards, Victor L., "Efforts to Establish a Statutory Standard of Invention," Study No. 7 of the Subcommittee on Patents, Trademarks and Copyrights, Commitee on the Judiciary, U.S. Senate, 1958.*

Ewing, Thomas, "The American Patent System," 19 JPOS 33, 1937.

Faarand, Max, ed., "The Records of the Federal Convention of 1787," 4 vols., 1937.

Federico, P. J., "Colonial Monopolies and Patents," 11 JPOS 358, 1929.

Federico, P. J., "State Patents," 13 JPOS 166, 1931.

Federico, P. J., "The First Patent Act," 14 JPOS 237, 1932.

Federico, P. J., Ed., "Outline of the History of the United States Patent Office," 18 JPOS No. 7, 1936.

Federico, P. J., "The Patent Office Fire of 1836," 19 JPOS 804, 1937.

Federico, P. J., "The Patent Office in 1837," 19 JPOS 954, 1937.

Federico, P. J., "The Patent Trials of Oliver Evans," 27 JPOS 586, 657, 1945.

Fenning, Karl, "Growth of American Patents," 8 JPOS 52, 1925.

Fenning, Karl, "The Origin of the Patent and Copyrights Clause of the Constitution," 17 Georgetown L. J. 109, 1929, 11 JPOS 438, 1929.

Fenning, Karl, "N. R. A. Codes," 16 JPOS 189, 1934.

Fenning, Karl, "Patents and National Defense," 22 JPOS 869, 1940.

Frost, George E., "The Patent System and the Modern Economy, Study No. 2 of the Subcommittee on Patents, Trademarks and Copyrights, Committee on the Judiciary, U.S. Senate, 1957.*

Goldsmith, Harry, "Abraham Lincoln—Invention and Patents," 20 JPOS 5, 1938.

Gottschalk, Robert, "Some Recent Patent Decisions and Current Trends," 25 JPOS 80, 1943.

Gottschalk, Robert, "Further Comments on Recent Patent Decisions and Current Trends," 26 JPOS 151, 1944.

Harlow, Ralph Volney, "The Growth of the United States," Vol. II, p. 105, 1943.

Hofstadter, Richard, William Miller, and Daniel Asron, "The United States—The History of a Republic," New York, Prentice-Hall, Inc., 1957.

Hunt, Clinton N., "Walter Hunt—American Inventor," Clinton N. West, 1935.

Kintner, Earl W., "1961-62 Management Survey of the U.S. Patent Office," Study of the Subcommittee on Patents, Trademarks and Copyrights, Committee on the Judiciary, U.S. Senate, 1962.*

Ladd, David L., "Annual Report of the Commissioner of Patents Fiscal Year 1962," U.S. Dept. of Commerce, Patent Office, 1962.

Lutz, Karl B., "A Clarification of the Patent Clause of the U.S. Constitution," 18 George Washington L. R. 50, 1949.

Lutz, Karl B., "The Constitution v. The Supreme Court, Re: Patents for Inventions," 13 U. of Pitt. L.R. 449, 1952.

Machlup, Fritz, "An Economic Review of the Patent System," Study No. 15 of the Subcommittee on Patents, Trademarks and Copyrights, Committee on the Judiciary, U.S. Senate, 1958.*

Marans, Hillel, "Forty Years of U.S. Patent Office (1917-56)," 39 JPOS 737, 818, 851, 1957.

* Articles available from U.S. Gov't. Printing Office, Washington 25, D.C.

Muir, Andrew Forest, "Patents and Copyrights in the Republic of Texas," 12 J. of Southern History 204-222, 1946.

O'Mahoney, Joseph C., "Patents, Trademarks and Copyrights," Report No. 72 of the Subcommittee on Patents, Trademarks and Copyrights, Committee on the Judiciary, U.S. Senate, 1957.

O'Mahoney, Joseph C., "Review of the American Patent System," Report No. 1464 of the Subcommittee on Patents, Trademarks and Copyrights, Committee on the Judiciary, U.S. Senate, 1956."

Penrose, Edith Tilton, "The Economics of the International Patent System," Baltimore, The Johns Hopkins Press, 1951.

Prager, Frank D., "Standards of Patentable Invention from 1474 to 1952," 20 U. of Chi. L.R. 69, 1952.

Prager, Frank D., "The Changing Views of Justice Story on the Construction of Patents," 4 Amer. J. Legal History 1, 1960.

Prager, Frank D., "The Influence of Mr. Justice Story on American Patent Law," 5 Am. J. of Legal History 254, 1961.

Prager, Frank D., "Historic Background of and Foundation of American Patent Law," 5 Am. J. of Legal History 309, 1961.

Prager, Frank D., "Trends and Developments in American Patent Law from Jefferson to Clifford (1790-1870)," 6 Am. J. Legal History 45, 1962.

"Proceedings in Congress during the Years 1789 and 1790, Relating to the First Patent and Copyright Laws," 22 JPOS 243 and 352, 1940.

Ramsey, George, "The Historical Background of Patents," 18 JPOS 6, 1936.

Rich, Giles S., "The Principles of Patentability," 42 JPOS 75, 1960.

Roeming, George C., "Court Decisions as Guides to Patent Office," Study No. 25 of the Subcommittee on Patents, Trademarks and Copyrights, Committee on the Judiciary, U.S. Senate, 1960.*

Senate Committee Report, 1836, 18 JPOS 853, 1936.

Stein, Philip Van Doren, ed., "The Life and Writings of Abraham Lincoln," Random House, 1940.

United States Department of Commerce, "The Story of the United States Patent Office, 1790-1956," 1956.*

Wade, Worth, "History of the American Patent Incentive System," 44 JPOS 67, 1962.

Walker on Patents, Vol. 1 (Deller's Edition), 1931.

Webb, John M., "Patents—The Changing Standard of Patentable Invention: Confusion Compounded," 39 JPOS 777, 1957.

Willner, Warren H., "Origin and Development of the Doctrine of Constructive Reduction to Practice," 36 JPOS 618, 1954.

Wyman, Wm. I., "The Scientific Genesis of Basic Inventions," 18 JPOS 22, 1936.

Cross-references: *Act of 1952—Patents, History of Patents Abroad, Invention—Changing Objectives, State Laws Relating to Patents.*

IMPORTATION OF PATENTED GOODS

Anthony P. DeLio and Daniel P. Worth

This article is in part a condensation by the authors of their publication in 25 Geo. Wash. L. Rev. 341, 1957, reprinted in 39 JPOS 282, 1957. A later section considers recent cases before the U.S. Tariff Commission.

An importer of articles or products into the United States infringes any patent that covers them, by selling or using them. The same result follows as to sales or use by those who take under the importer. *Thomson-Houston Elec. Co. v. Ohio Brass Co.,* 80 Fed. 712, 721, CA 6 1957; *Columbia and N. R. R. Co. v. Chandler,* 241 Fed. 261, CA 9 1947.

However, in most cases the patent owner does not discover that his patent is being infringed until the goods have been sold by the importer and are in the hands of numerous outlets. He then may seek out each of the infringing outlets and bring a multiplicity of suits. A partial solution to the problem is found in Section 337 of the Tariff Act, under which disputed goods may be denied entry at the border. The Tariff Act thus operates as a supplement to the remedies a patent owner has available to protect his property, 35 U.S.C. Section 261 stating that "... patents shall have the attributes of personal property."

Under the patent laws, the owner of a *process* patent finds himself in an even more difficult predicament. He is entitled only to protection against those who infringe his process by making, using or selling his *process* within the United States. The patent has no extraterritorial operation. Importation and domestic sale of *goods* made by his process abroad is not an actionable wrong because he does not have a patent on these goods and the patent laws offer him

no redress against the importer or seller. Thus, if entry into this country cannot be prevented, the owner of a process patent is helpless if forced to rely on the patent laws. Exclusion under Section 337 of the Tariff Act is the only remedy he may invoke. See *In re Amtorg Trading Corp.,* 75 F.2d 826, 831-832, CCPA 1935; *The Wood Paper Patent,* 90 U.S. (23 Wall.) 566, 1893; *Cochrane v. Badische Anilin und Soda Fabrik,* 111 U.S. 293, 1884; *General Electric Co. v. Wabash Appliance Corp.,* 304 U.S. 364, 1938; Geo. Wash. L. Rev. 224, 230, 1935.

One solution that has been attempted is to draft patent claims to define a product in terms of the process. Protection on the product is not afforded the patent owner, however, where an old product is produced by a new process, a situation which is frequently the case. See the *Wood Paper* and *Amtorg* cases, supra.

Protection under the Tariff Act

In 1922, Congress, recognizing the impossibility of foreseeing and legislating against all variations of harm arising from importation, directed the President to exclude goods whenever he found certain unlawful activities existing. 42 Stat. 943. Section 337(a) of the Tariff Act presently describes these unlawful activities as:

"... unfair methods of competition and unfair acts in the importation of articles into the United States, or in their sale ... the effect or tendency of which is to destroy or substantially injure an industry efficiently and economically operated, in the United States ..." 46 Stat. 703, 1930, 19 U.S.C. Section 1337 (later amended by 54 Stat. 724, 19 U.S.C. Section 1337a, 1940.

Section 1337.—Unfair Practices in Import Trade—
(a) Unfair Methods of Competition Declared Unlawful. Unfair methods of competition and unfair acts in the importation of articles into the

405

United States, or in their sale by the owner, importer, consignee, or agent of either, the effect or tendency of which is to destroy or substantially injure an industry, efficiently and economically operated, in the United States, or to prevent the establishment of such an industry, or to restrain or monopolize trade and commerce in the United States, are declared unlawful, and when found by the President to exist shall be dealt with, in addition to any other provisions of law, as hereinafter provided.

(b) *Investigations of Violations by Commission.* To assist the President in making any decisions under this section the commission is hereby authorized to investigate any alleged violation hereof on complaint under oath or upon its initiative.

(c) *Hearings and Review.* The commission shall make such investigation under and in accordance with such rules as it may promulgate and give such notice and afford such hearing, and when deemed proper by the commission such rehearing, with opportunity to offer evidence, oral or written, as it may deem sufficient for a full presentation of the facts involved in such investigation. The testimony in every such investigation shall be reduced to writing, and a transcript thereof with the findings and recommendation of the commission shall be the official record of the proceedings and findings in the case, and in any case where the findings in such investigation show a violation of this section, a copy of the findings shall be promptly mailed or delivered to the importer or consignee of such articles. Such findings, if supported by evidence, shall be conclusive, except that a rehearing may be granted by the commission and except that, within such time after said findings are made and in such manner as appeals may be taken from decisions of the United States Customs Court, an appeal may be taken from said findings upon a question or questions of law only to the United States Court of Customs and Patent Appeals by the importer or consignee of such articles. If it shall be shown to the satisfaction of said court that further evidence should be taken, and that there were reasonable grounds for the failure to adduce such evidence in the proceedings before the commission, said court may order such additional evidence to be taken before the commission in such manner and upon such terms and conditions as to the court may seem proper. The commission may modify its findings as to the facts or make new findings by reason of additional evidence, which, if supported by evidence, shall be conclusive as to the facts except that within such time and in such manner an appeal may be taken as aforesaid upon a question or question of law only. The judgment of said court shall be final.

...

(e) *Exclusion of Articles from Entry.* Whenever the existence of any such unfair method or act shall be established to the satisfaction of the President he shall direct that the articles concerned in such unfair methods or acts, imported by any person violating the provisions of this chapter, shall be excluded from entry into the United States, and upon information of such action by the President, the Secretary of the Treasury shall, through the proper officers, refuse such entry. The decision of the President shall be conclusive.

(f) *Entry under Bond.* Whenever the President has reason to believe that any article is offered or sought to be offered for entry into the United States in violation of this section but has not information sufficient to satisfy him thereof, the Secretary of the Treasury shall, upon his request in writing, forbid entry thereof until such investigation as the President may deem necessary shall be completed; except that such articles shall be entitled to entry under bond prescribed by the Secretary of the Treasury.

(g) *Continuance of Exclusion.* Any refusal of entry under this section shall continue in effect until the President shall find and instruct the Secretary of the Treasury that the conditions which led to such refusal of entry no longer exist.

The Tariff Commission is authorized to assist the President in determining when violations of Section 337(a) exist. This is only an advisory jurisdiction, since the existence of these unlawful practices must "be established to the satisfaction of the President."

Other portions of Section 337 provide for initiation of proceedings by the Commission (complaint under oath or on its own initiation), procedure (notice, hearing, establishment of a record), and appeal (to the CCPA). It should be noted that these proceedings are not governed by the Administrative Procedure Act, since no final order can be issued by the Commission. A novel feature of the appeal is that only one party—the importer or consignee—has the privilege of appealing. This point was utilized in *In re Orion*, 71 F.2d 458, CCPA 1934, when the appellee moved to dismiss on the ground that the appellant was neither an importer nor an assignee and therefore had no standing to appeal.

Since these proceedings are lengthy and tedious, as well as expensive, the domestic manufacturer is faced with the problem of obtaining some form of interim remedy prior to the completion of the administrative investigation. While the courts can offer no relief, the President may alleviate the problem by directing exclusion, subject to entry under bond, of the articles in question until investigation is completed.

The 1940 Amendment

In 1940 Congress amended the Tariff Act. 54 Stat. 724, 19 U.S.C. Section 1337a. The language of the amendment is as follows:

"The importation for use, sale, or exchange of a product made, produced, processed, or mined under or by means of a process covered by the claims of any unexpired valid United States letters patent, shall have the same status for the purposes of Section 1337 of this title as the importation of any product or article covered by the claims of any unexpired valid United States letters patent."

This amendment was designed to afford the same protection to process patent owners as was afforded theretofore to product patent owners. 86 Cong. Rec. 8969, 1940. The amendment does not relieve the process patentee from proving the required elements for relief under Section 337(a) of the Tariff Act.

Von Clemm Case

In re Von Clemm, 229 F.2d 441, 1955, represents a late decision by the CCPA concerning protection of patent owners under Section 337 of the Tariff Act. Plaintiff, assignee of U.S. Letters Patent 2,488,507, filed a petition with the U.S. Tariff Commission alleging unfair methods of competition and unfair acts of importation by the defendant. The patent held by the plaintiff covered a method of making synthetic star sapphires and star rubies and the resulting product.

In proceedings before the Commission, the defendant admitted that the product claim met the description of the stones he was importing, but denied any unfair methods of competition because he claimed there was no "palming-off."

The Tariff Commission found that the imported stones met both process and product claims in the plaintiff's patent and that this constituted unfair acts of importation and unfair methods of competition. A rec-

ommendation for an exclusion order was made. The defendant appealed the decision of the Commission to the CCPA.

On appeal, as stated in the Briefs, the defendant-appellant raised, inter alia, the following issues: (1) no finding of "palming-off" having been made, Section 337 was not violated; (2) the patent had to be considered as a whole and infringement of *all* the claims must be proved; and (3) no substantial injury to a domestic industry was proved to warrant an exclusion order. Plaintiff answered these contentions by (1) citing previous cases as controlling in deciding whether Section 337 was violated by defendant's conduct; (2) pointing to expert testimony plus defendant's admission as proof of process infringement; and (3) stating that the importations hurt the domestic manufacture, who in this case constituted the "industry." As *amicus curiae*, the Department of Justice denied that a finding of "palming-off" was essential to a finding that Section 337 was violated.

The court answered the question of whether the traditional concept of unfair competition (that is, "palming-off") defined the boundaries of "unfair *methods* of competition" in accordance with its previous decisions. It pointed out that not only did the latter phrase cover acts which are not technical torts, but that importation inherently involved questions of a different nature than those arising in internal commerce.

Avoiding the argument on "infringement," the court applied the readability test, stating that defendant's admission as to readability of the claims and the expert testimony of the plaintiff as to the process employed in making the stones were controlling. These factors, coupled with defendant's failure to explain how the stones were made, provided substantial evidence to support a finding of "unfair methods of competition and unfair acts in importation." Having found "unfair methods of competition," the court held that the record contained substantial evidence to prove the remaining statutory requirements, i.e., "tendency to injure" (from sales at prices below plaintiff's); that plaintiff, a single manufacturer, constituted an "industry";

and that said industry was "efficiently and economically operated."

Validity of Patent Not Questioned

Unless a patent has been held invalid by a court of competent jurisdiction, the validity may not be questioned by the Tariff Commission or the Court of Customs and Patent Appeals. In the *Von Clemm* case, the CCPA said:

"We have repeatedly held that in cases of this character involving alleged unfair acts in connection with a patented article or process, the validity of the patent or patents involved may not be questioned by the Tariff Commission nor by this court on appeal therefrom, but that a regularly issued patent must be considered valid until a court of competent jurisdiction has held otherwise." 108 USPQ 371, 383, decided 1955.

Enforcement of the Exclusion Order

Convincing the Tariff Commission is not the end of the road for those who seek the exclusion order. The existence of the proscribed conduct must be ". . . established to the satisfaction of the President . . . ," who then issues the exclusion order to the enforcement agency.

Once the exclusion order has been issued, it has in the past operated prospectively to exclude *all* articles of the nature described in the order. *S. J. Charia and Co.* v. *United States*, 135 F. Supp. 727, Customs Court 1954; *Emery Holcombe and Blair* v. *United States*, 89 USPQ 343, Customs Court 1951. This appears to be in derogation of the statute, which requires that excluded goods meet two tests: (1) the articles themselves must be the specific ones concerned in the unlawful activities, and (2) the importation of said articles must be by a person violating the Tariff Act. Section 1337(f), supra. The controversy in the "patent exclusion" cases has raged about the "readability" of the order (patent) as determined by the Customs authorities, ignoring—or perhaps assuming—the statutory requirement that the importer himself be a violator. *Ibid.* The result of this theory seems to be that if the readability test applies, the importer is automatically a wrongdoer, and hence the goods should be excluded.

The importer has no judicial remedy against exclusion of goods under the Tariff Act. *Frischer & Co.* v. *Elting*, 60 F.2d 711, CA 2 1932. The courts can only give indirect relief by holding a patent invalid, and in such instance any modification of the exclusion order is within the discretion of the President. *In re Orion Co.*, 71 F.2d 458, CCPA 1934.

Most of the exclusion orders issued by the President have expressly provided for entry of excluded goods under license or similar authorization of the patent owner. TD 47028, 65 Treas. Dec. 733.

Because the Tariff Commission and the CCPA are unable to pass on any question dealing with the validity of a patent, the parties may be subjected to a multiplicity of suits hence required to incur inordinate expenses. Further, it is quite possible for a conflict to occur as to the validity of a particular patent, since two constitutional courts could disagree on the issue, with one court finding a specific patent valid, another invalid. In this situation the parties involved are faced with uncertainty as to which decision is binding upon the Tariff Commission and the CCPA. No definite policy has yet been enunciated by either tribunal. In the *Orion* case, where there was an even division, the CCPA assumed the patent to be valid. It could easily have held the other way. See *In re Orion*, supra, at 92 (Canadian decision disregarded); cf. *Badische Anilin & Soda Fabrik* v. *Kalle*, 94 Fed. 163, C. C. N. Y. 1899 (decisions of foreign court not controlling as to patentable invention, but entitled to weight); *Brown Mfg. Co.* v. *Mast*, 53 Fed. 578, C. C. Ohio 1892 (comity requires a court to follow decisions in another circuit, unless new evidence appears or the decision was clearly wrong; in case of conflicting decisions, the latest one is followed).

Uncertainty also exists as to the effect of a patent being held invalid subsequent to the order of exclusion. Revocation of the exclusion order is not automatic, but is within the President's discretion. See concurring opinion, *In re Orion*, supra; Section 1337(g) of 1930 Tariff Act, supra.

It must also be concluded that the question of what constitutes an "industry" has not been satisfactorily answered. Since multiple licensing exists, is injury to one licensee sufficient to warrant a finding of substantial injury to an industry, or must all licensees be harmed? Can domestic licensees claim injury to the industry when the importer is also a licensee?

Also, the cases present a paucity of information as to what constitutes "... an ... efficiently and economically operated ..." industry. Does this mean that a bankrupt business has no remedy, or does it mean that proof of profits is sufficient to meet this requirement?

Finally, there is actually no specific mention of protection afforded a process patentee in the Tariff Act. Since Section 1337(a) states that the same protection afforded a product patentee is given to a process patentee, it is possible through judicial interpretation to give protection to neither. If the patentee seeks protection under the patent laws, he finds no remedy against importation. It seems unfair to have such uncertainty as to protection afforded a patent owner, in view of the fact that specific legislative protection is afforded the owners of trademarks and copyrights.

The strictness of application of the statute in restraining imports may be expected to depend at times not only upon the specific facts in a given case but also in part upon political attitudes and diplomatic considerations.

Proceedings before the Tariff Commission

This section is a verbatim quotation from pp. 218-219 of the article by Richard R. Wolfe, 39 JPOS 214-219, 1957.

Initiating A Proceeding Before the Commission.
Proceedings are started before the Tariff Commission by filing a complaint with supporting exhibits and affidavits.

As a next step, the Commission sends out its investigators to look into the facts and report back confidentially to the Commission.

It is fully within the discretion of the Commission as to whether there shall be a public hearing or any other proceeding on the complaint. Unless the Commission itself acts to set the matter down for public hearing it will simply die there.

Conduct of the Public Hearing. When the complaint is set down for a public hearing, all of the importers named in the complaint are notified. They may file answer and appear if they wish to do so. They are not compelled to do either.

The complainant offers such evidence as he has to sustain the allegations of his complaint. His witnesses are cross-examined not only by counsel for the importer or importers but also by counsel for the Commission and often by the Commissioners themselves.

One peculiarity of the proceeding is that the Commission has before it two records—the public one made by the evidence tendered at the public hearing, and the confidential record made up of the reports of the Commission's own investigators and auditors. It is, indeed, a criminal offense for any official to reveal the content of the confidential record. Before the public hearing, the Commission will have had its auditors review the complainant's financial records, particularly because of the statutory requirement that it be shown that the acts complained of will tend to substantially injure or destroy an efficiently operated American industry. Likewise the Commission will have a confidential report from the Custom's office of all shipments made of the accused goods.

Consequently, the importers have access to only so much of the complainant's financial records as the complainant puts in the public record. The complainant, on the other hand, can ascertain from Customs the names of importers and the dates of import but not the quantities or valuation.

At the conclusion of the hearing, the case is briefed, Counsel for the Commission advises it on any disputed questions of law, and the Commission makes its findings of fact.

Those findings are forwarded to the President, and, if favorable to the complainant, are accompanied by a recommended form of exclusion order.

Review by the CCPA. The CCPA has jurisdiction, upon the application of an importer, to review questions of law.

On the fact side, the findings of the Commission are treated much as the findings of a District Court under Rule 52(a).

The record before the Court is the public record. So in testing the sufficiency of the evidence to support the findings they can look only to the public record. No one has yet had to test out the interesting question of what would happen to a finding based expressly upon the confidential record alone.

At least there is a warning there for the complainant to be conservative in making out a full case on the public record if he can do so.

The Government may appear—but again peculiarly enough—only by leave of court. In our case the Solicitor General sought, and was given, leave to brief and argue the appeal which he did in opposition to the importer. So it is one proceeding, at least, in which the Department of Justice acts on behalf of a patentee. They did so wholeheartedly and very ably.

Recent Decisions by Tariff Commission

Through the courtesy of Mr. Donn N. Bent, Secretary of the U.S. Tariff Commission, Washington 25, D.C., the following literature has been made available:

TC Publication 55, April 1962. This gives an 81-page transcript that should be helpful in understanding the proceeding in a complaint of unfair competition and plea for exclusion of a product infringing a patent claim. This is the *Coin-Purse* case in which a majority of the Commission held for the complainant but the President rejected the recommendation. See below.

TC Public Information Releases. These show, in some cases, the guide lines that are currently followed by the Commission in deciding cases on exclusion under Section 337.

The following passages (to the end of this article) are taken from parts of those releases that state the reasons for the holdings.

Injury to Domestic Industry Not Proven. *Coin Purse Case.* The President (October 16, 1962) rejected the majority recommendation of the Tariff Commission that certain self-closing coin purses be prohibited from importation into the United States. Chairman Dorfman had dissented from the majority opinion.

In a complaint filed under Section 337 of the Tariff Act of 1930, Quikey Manufacturing Company of Akron, Ohio, had alleged that certain self-closing coin purses were being imported into the United States and sold in the domestic market without license from Quikey, which holds a patent on such purses, and that as a result of this unfair method of competition substantial injury was being caused to Quikey. In a 5 to 1 decision, the Tariff Commission decided in favor of this contention. See citation, supra.

To warrant issuance of an exclusion order under the statute, it must be shown to the satisfaction of the President that the alleged unfair methods of competition have the effect or tendency of destroying or substantially injuring an efficiently and economically operated domestic industry. Chairman Dorfman dissented on the ground that the proper domestic "industry" had not been identified so that adequate data could be developed, and that the evidence did not show any effect or tendency to destroy or substantially injure what the complainant identified as the "industry."

Woven Mat Case—Chicago Weaving Corporation—1960. The preliminary inquiry did not disclose to the Commission a *prima facie* case of substantial injury to a domestic industry resulting from the importations or sales in question. A substantial decline in sales, by domestic producers, of woven mats of the kind or class to which complainant's patent relates, began before there were any imports of such mats, and their sales of such mats in 1959 were less than in 1958 by a quantity equal to approximately three times the quantity of imports in 1959. 25 Federal Register 5008, June 7, 1960.

Phonograph Pickup Cartridges, Elements, and Needles. Complaints leading to the institution of the investigation were filed by the Brush Electronics Company (a division of the Clevite Corporation) of Cleveland, Ohio, and The Astatic Corporation of Conneaut, Ohio.

The charges originally related to 12 patents. In the course of the investigation complainants withdrew 4 of the patents, and one of the patents was eliminated from consideration by the Commission. Of the 7 remaining patents, 2 related to cartridges, 2 to elements, and 3 to needles and holders therefor. One of these 7 patents is the subject of a patent suit in the Federal courts.

The Commission found that the evidence regarding the complained of imports does not establish that any industry in the United States is being, or is likely to be, destroyed or substantially injured by reason of such imports; and that there is therefore no occasion for making findings regarding "infringement" or the existence of other unfair methods of competition or unfair acts. TC Release of May 4, 1959.

Product Made under Claim of U.S. Patent—Complaint of H. & A. Manufacturing Company—Badminton Rackets. The allegation of unfair methods of competition and unfair acts was based on the contention that the imported rackets are made in accordance with the claims of a United States patent owned by the complainant.

The statute involved declares unlawful unfair methods of competition and unfair acts in the importation or sale of an article having the effect or tendency of substantially injuring or destroying an industry efficiently and economically operated in the United States. If, after a formal investigation, the Tariff Commission finds such facts to exist, it submits a report to the President with a recommendation for the exclusion from entry into the United States of the offending article.

After a full investigation, including a public hearing, the Commission unanimously found no violation of Section 337. The full Commission agreed that if unfair methods of competition or unfair acts are present, it has not been established that their effect or tendency is to substantially injure or destroy a domestic industry. The majority of the Commission (Commissioners Talbot, Sutton, Jones, and Dowling) did not rule on the question of whether or not the imported article was made in conformity with the claims of the patent. However, Commissioners Brossard and Schreiber were of the view that the imported articles are made in accordance with the claims of the patent in question and that therefore unfair methods of competition and unfair acts were present. TC Release April 22, 1957. For complaint, see 21 F.R. 4695, August 18, 1956.

Suspending Action because of Related Proceeding. The United States Tariff Commission (in January 1960) decided to hold in abeyance its decision on the merits in the investigation instigated by the Singer Manufacturing Company under Section 337 of the Tariff Act of 1930, pending the outcome of an antitrust action filed by the Department of Justice against Singer on December 22, 1959 in the United States District Court for the Southern District of New York.

In the antitrust action against Singer, the Department of Justice charges, among other things, that Singer entered into arrangements with Gegauf and an Italian sewing-machine manufacturer whereby Gegauf would assign his patent rights to Singer for the purpose of enabling Singer to prevent Japanese imports; that Singer would use the Gegauf patent rights along with its own to exclude imports, and the parties would determine which European manufacturer would be permitted to export household automatic zigzag sewing machines to the United States; and that Singer, in carrying out the attempt to monopolize, obtained and used patent rights for these exclusionary purposes. 28 F.R. 6845, July 3, 1963.

Involvement of Patent Licenses or Agreements. *Push-button Puppets.* The complaint alleged that certain push-button puppets that are infringements of a United States patent owned by a Swiss citizen, and under which Kohner Brothers are exclusive licensees in the United States with the right to sublicense, are being imported and sold in the United States by unauthorized persons, and that the imports of the infringing articles are substantially injuring the domestic industry producing the patented puppets.

The preliminary inquiry disclosed that Kohner's licensees have imported substantial quantities of the patented push-button puppets, and that Kohner has also imported such puppets. The purpose of Section 337 is to protect American industries and to further and promote the production of domestic products. *Frischer Co.* v. *Bakelite Corporation*, 39 F.2d 247. Where Section 337 is sought to be invoked on the ground that a domestic industry established under the protection of a United States patent is being injured by imports that are covered by the claims of the patent, the Commission cannot accept the proposition that if the importer pays the owner of the patent a royalty, the industry is not being injured, but if no royalty is paid by the importer, there is injury to the industry. To invoke the statute in order to protect the rights of patent owners arising out of the naked monopoly of a patent would be to employ the statute for the protection of patent rights as such. This the Commission has repeatedly held not to be the purpose of the statute. The protection of patent rights must be sought in the appropriate courts having jurisdiction over such matters. 23 F.R. 8642, November 5, 1958.

Expansion Bracelets and Parts. After preliminary inquiry in accordance with Section 203.3 of its Rules of Practice and Procedure (19 C.F.R. 203.3), the United States Tariff Commission, on the 18th day of June 1958 dismissed the two complaints filed under Section 337 of the Tariff Act of 1930 (19 U.S.C. 1337) by Speidel Corporation, 70 Ship Street, Providence, Rhode Island, alleging unfair methods of competition and unfair acts in the importation and sale in the United States of certain *expansion bracelets and parts thereof.* Notice of the receipt of these complaints was published in 21 F.R. 8473.

The principal reason for the dismissal of the complaints is that while the prayer in the complaints was for the total exclusion from entry into the United States of foreign articles made in accordance with United States patents because the effect or tendency of such imports is to destroy, substantially injure, or prevent the establishment of, domestic industries producing expansible bracelets of construction and design covered by the claims of such United States patents, Speidel, since the filing of the complaints, has entered into extensive licensing arrangements with major importers of allegedly offending bracelets.

Section 337 is not an extension of the patent laws and its purpose is not to protect patent rights as such. The complaints set forth that the domestic-manufacturer licensees are not granted licenses to import, and pray for the exclusion from entry of all bracelets which infringe complainant's patents in order that the public will not "lose an important domestic industry developed by private capital" whose economic justification was based on the protection of the patents. Complainant's action in granting import privileges to several of the large importers charged in the complaints as violating Section 337 indicates that complainant is not so much concerned with the protection from injurious import competition of domestic industries that owe their existence to the patents involved as he is with royalties, whether the royalties come from domestic producers or from importers. For

dismissal of the complaint, see 23 F.R. 4715, June 26, 1958.

No Action against Infringing Domestic Importer. The United States Tariff Commission, on June 7, 1963, dismissed without prejudice the complaint filed under Section 337 of the Tariff Act of 1930, as amended (19 U.S.C. 1337), by the Clopay Corporation of Cincinnati, Ohio.

The preliminary inquiry disclosed the following facts: Only one domestic concern has imported the folding doors in question; the complainant has not instituted an infringement action in a Federal court against the importer or any other person; and the complainant has not notified the importer of the alleged infringements and demanded that they be terminated.

[*Summary.* An unofficial summary of recent decisions on complaints seeking to bar imports under Section 337 shows the following significant, even if only approximate, data: Exclusion recommended by the Commission but rejected by the President, 1 case; complaints dismissed, 14; discontinued or withdrawn, 3. Ed.]

INCENTIVES FOR INVENTORS AND STIMULATION OF INVENTION AND DISCLOSURE

Donald L. Brown

This article discusses incentives for inventors under the patent system. It considers monetary, status recognition and other rewards beyond the statutory provisions, summarizes the special incentives programs of representative companies, and reveals the results of experimentation with several plans. It emphasizes encouraging disclosure of inventions and ideas. It then shows the changing attitude towards special awards for inventions by comparing surveys reported at various times between 1930 and 1962 and concludes with a discussion of the relevant policies of government, university and other non-profit organizations.

Varying Incentives for Different Classes of Inventors

The effectiveness of any invention-incentive plan will, obviously, depend largely upon the desires and aims of the prospective inventors under the plan. Money awards may have less appeal to financially independent, scientifically trained, job-secure researchers, for instance, than some form of status recognition. An incentive-award system adapted to the diverse aims of inventors in all levels of the economy will presumptively be the most effective and, unfortunately, the most difficult to administer successfully.

Any incentive plan should, moreover, stimulate not only inventors and the inventive act itself but also prompt disclosure of new inventive concepts and suggestions and their use. An invention which is made but never disclosed is of no value to the economy.

We may classify potential "inventors" as (a) independent or self-employed, (b) employed by an industrial organization engaged in business for profit, (c) employed by a government agency, or (d) employed by a non-profit organization such as a university or research institute. Each of the last three classifications should properly be understood as comprising only those employees who are obligated to disclose and assign inventions to their employers. In the absence of such an obligation, the employee stands substantially in the position of an independent inventor.

The Independent Inventor. The patent system today provides, for all practical purposes, the only incentive in any way effective in reaching such independent, self-employed inventor. It offers hope of financial reward through exploitation, sale or license of the exclusive rights granted to him. There is no alternative, such as a cash award invention-incentive plan, which contemplates any payment to an independent inventor. True, he may sell an idea to some industrial corporation even when it is not patented; if he has had any experience in such negotiations, however, he will appreciate that in the absence of patent protection, he must accept substantially only what the corporate purchaser thinks his idea may be worth. Most corporations today will entertain and consider a suggestion from an outsider only if it is protected by a patent or patent application or is submitted with

what amounts to a release to the corporation of any liability for its use, beyond what the corporation may set as the value. But, under the stimulus of the patent system, the independent self-employed inventor remains numerous, active and productive.

A recent study dealing with incentives and deterrents to invention was conducted by J. N. Mosel, B. S. Sanders and I. H. Siegel for The Patent Trademark and Copyright Foundation of the George Washington University, at the instigation of The National Inventors Council which had become concerned over the lag in the number of unsolicited defense ideas being presented to the Council. The report, 1 PTC J 185, 1957, considers reasons for the failure to invent, or more accurately, to disclose inventions and examines incentives which may be effective to stimulate invention and disclosure by individual, independent inventors.

One question was "What is the most important thing you (the inventor) want in return for an invention of yours?" The replies indicated importance in the following order:

(1) Financial benefits
(2) Status recognition by the inventor's employer, e.g., job advancement
(3) Satisfaction derived from use of the invention
(4) Satisfaction of accomplishment
(5) Recognition by others of the inventor's contribution

The survey also indicated that inventors responding to the questionnaire overwhelmingly preferred to deal with industry rather than with the defense agencies because of greater chance of financial reward, greater interest shown in the invention, less red tape, and fewer restrictions.

The survey suggests that the lag or decline in the number of new ideas submitted to the defense agencies is due primarily to a failure to disclose rather than failure to invent, and hence that remedial action might most effectively be directed to the provision of incentives or the elimination of deterrents to disclosure.

Company Incentive Plans

Let us first consider plans of a few representative corporations with excellent records of technological progress and achievement.

Westinghouse Electric Corporation. In 1956, Westinghouse Electric Corporation adopted a "Voluntary Invention Award Plan" which provides for four different kinds of invention awards. A so-called "disclosure award" of $50 is paid to each inventor of a meritorious disclosure irrespective of whether a patent application is or is not filed thereon. An additional "most meritorious disclosure award" of $200 is paid to the inventor of that disclosure which is judged the most meritorious in each group of fifty disclosures processed by a disclosure committee. If the disclosure should be of a joint invention, then an award of $300 is divided equally among the joint inventors. A further award of $50 is paid to each inventor at the time an application for patent covering his invention is filed in the United States Patent Office, and a special award of varying amount but never more than $5000 may be made to an inventor where the invention has, in the judgment of management, proved of outstanding commercial value to the corporation.

All these awards are voluntarily made by the corporation, which reserves the right to amend or terminate the plan at any time. Disclosures of new inventions or suggestions are first sent to the corporate patent department which records, classifies and acknowledges them. They are then referred, through patent committee attorneys, to committees who decide on awards and who determine whether applications for patent shall or shall not be filed. The basic disclosure award is granted for a relatively high percentage, about 60 per cent of the submitted suggestions. Only a few special awards are made each year and these are usually in connection with an invention covered by an issued patent which has been demonstrated to be of commercial value. These special awards are initiated by the various operating divisions of the corporation with the help of the patent department and the patent disclosure committee.

The basic disclosure award has been given for thirty years. Initially it was $25 but several years ago it was increased to the present $50 award. Publicity is given to all awards in the corporation house publication and the awards are usually made in connection with some formal presentation before a group of the inventor's associates. Special awards are made formally at the plant of the operating division involved and usually by the Vice President of Engineering in connection with the division or plant manager. Every effort is made to give publicity to the awards and to place them upon a basis such that they will be considered as a recognition by the corporation of the contribution made by the employee.

The corporation believes that the award system provides stimulation and incentive to inventive activity, while recognizing that such incentive is hard to measure. It feels also that even the relatively nominal disclosure award is effective as an inducement to the inventor to expend the extra effort which may be required to prepare an adequate and complete disclosure of his invention.

Raytheon Company. The Raytheon Company has for the past five years made cash awards to employee inventors submitting patentable invention disclosures. When a disclosure is approved for patent filing the inventor receives a $50 award, if the invention is sole. If the invention is joint, each inventor receives $35. When the patent application is actually filed a second award equal to the initial award is made to the inventor or inventors.

In some instances prolific inventors, recognized as important and productive personnel because of the quality and number of their suggestions, have received additional rewards in the form of salary increases and promotions. The company gives some weight to the number and character of patents obtained by an employee in assessing and evaluating his creative productivity. It has found no difficulty in administering a system of fixed cash awards and considers such a system preferable to one employing varying cash awards depending upon the importance of the invention. This is because of the great difficulty in assessing, on a comparative basis, the value of any invention at the time the disclosure is made and is being considered for patent filing, which is the time the company feels the award should be made.

Not only does the company believe that its award system constitutes an incentive to invention, but it is even more confident that it constitutes an incentive to prompt and full disclosure of new ideas and suggestions by its employees.

A survey of 27 companies made by Beckman Instruments, Inc. indicated that most of them gave cash employee invention awards, usually varying from $10 to $100. Some of these companies suuplemented the awards with gifts of corporate shares, salary increases or other inducements. Few believed that the awards acted as important stimulants to invention although most felt that they did stimulate the disclosure of inventions by corporate personnel. Whether or not cash incentive awards stimulate invention activity or simply the disclosure of such activity by the inventor, the result would seem to be the same.

Eastman Kodak Company. Eastman Kodak Company takes the position that its research and technical employees and others of its employees who are expected to invent should be rewarded not by specific cash awards but by recognition through salary increases and promotions. This policy has been followed with little or no difficulty. It is, of course, recognized that not all good inventors are supervisory material, but they can be given a satisfactory status. They can, for example, be classified as senior research associates with salary and status adequately recognizing their contribution to the corporation. It is felt that a system of cash awards to technically qualified personnel is unnecessary and difficult to administer. With respect to employees who are not employed as technical people and who ordinarily would not be expected to make inventions, an award is made which is based upon the value of the suggestion or the estimated saving to the company therefrom. Suggestions from this group are referred to a committee which meets periodically to assess the value of the suggestion and make the award.

Polaroid Corporation—Experimentation. Polaroid Corporation has experimented with several different plans for rewarding employees for suggestions, whether or not patentable.

Contests. It first tried employee contests in which awards were given for meritorious suggestions for cost reduction techniques, improved product handling or improvements in product, process, or apparatus. The contests had definite termination dates. The suggestions submitted were processed by committees including production, sales, patent, research and engineering personnel. Many awards in varying amounts were given for meritorious suggestions. This "contest plan" was not particularly satisfactory. Many duplicate suggestions were made, old ideas were revived and jealousies created among personnel in connection with awards. The amounts of the awards became the subject of considerable discussion and argument. As a result such system of awards was abandoned many years ago.

Fixed Awards. The corporation also tried briefly a system of fixed money awards for ideas and suggestions of merit. This also proved somewhat unsatisfactory, although relatively easy to administer and less conducive to employee dissatisfaction than was the contest plan.

Profit Sharing. For the past several years Polaroid has effectively stimulated new inventions and suggestions and the disclosure thereof through a profit-sharing plan in which all employees participate. This plan, supplemented by a retirement benefit plan, has resulted in an unexpectedly large number of valuable suggestions from corporate employees at all levels of employment. These suggestions have not only embodied novel and patentable product, process and apparatus improvements but have resulted in appreciable cost savings, in expediting the flow of materials through the plant, and in other non-patentable but valuable contributions to company profits. The introduction of the profit-sharing and retirement benefit plans was accompanied by comprehensive explanation to all company employees that every new suggestion of value, whether important or minor, contributed to corporate profits and, through the profit-sharing and retirement plan, to employee financial rewards.

Status Recognition. In addition, the company provides recognition to those who make valuable suggestions through promotion and salary increases and other status awards. In this connection, it is the expressed policy of the company, so far as its scientific and technical personnel are concerned, that the employee's status will in part at least depend upon the character and number of the scientific publications accredited to him. Patents are considered as scientific publications. The urge of the research scientist to publish in scientific journals seems much greater than that of the engineer, so that while many non-patentable suggestions are disclosed in publications emanating from research personnel, it is much less common for engineering personnel to publish except through patents. In fact publications, exclusive of patents, which originate with the research group outnumber those originating with engineering personnel by more than 100 to 1.

Patent Activity. As a further stimulus to invention and to the disclosure of novel ideas and improvements, the corporation maintains a large and active patent department. Each attorney is expected periodically to contact certain research or engineering personnel to obtain disclosures of such new inventions or suggestions for improvements as have been made. He is expected to summarize each of these suggestions and then place it upon his docket. He is expected further to confer with the inventor and to discuss with him ways of broadening the concept of the invention, and such additional research as will permit adequate scoping of the invention if an application is to be filed. As a result of such activity, it is believed that technical personnel are acutely aware of the desirability of both disclosing all new concepts and patenting such of these concepts as may have any value to the corporation.

Patent Releases. The corporation, furthermore, has adopted the policy of releasing to the inventor all rights in inventions falling outside the corporation's present or contemplated business, even though these inventions may have been made on company time and with company equipment and under certain circumstances, in consideration of the assignment to it of a per-

centage interest in the employee's invention, usually of the order of 25 per cent, and the company has assumed the expense of the preparation and prosecution of applications for patents on the invention.

Suggestions. A new idea or suggestion may be submitted by any employee to his supervisor, who forwards it to the department head with his recommendation as to value and novelty, and the department head then forwards the suggestion to the patent department where a search is made for novelty. If clearance is requested by the employee, i.e., release of company interest so that he may himself exploit the invention, this question is referred to a management committee. By such procedure every employee is assured that his suggestion will reach not only his supervisor and his department head, but also the patent department and, frequently, top management.

Results at Polaroid. This rather complicated plan, one which includes not only a profit-sharing plan and a retirement fund, in which all corporate employees share, but which involves a recognition of serendipity through salary increases, promotions and other status awards, is probably unsuited to the average corporation. Polaroid Corporation is, however, a new product company, substantially its entire product line is covered by patents on inventions made by its own employees, and it shows no indication of departing from its expressed policy of marketing only such novel products and devices. Under these circumstances the incentive plans outlined above are considered to have been highly successful and to have resulted in the disclosure of many improvements and suggestions which more than justify the trouble and cost of administration. There is every indication also that employee morale has been maintained at a high level because of the realization that each employee has an opportunity of contributing substantially to the welfare of the entire group, and that each such contribution will be recognized and acknowledged by management.

du Pont Company. E. I. du Pont de Nemours & Co. has employed a bonus plan which provides for bonuses in the form of common stock of the company, or cash to be invested in such stock, or cash, as grants to employees who have contributed in an unusual degree to the success of the company by their inventions, ability, industry, and loyalty, and whom it is deemed desirable to have interested in the business as stockholders or to reward by additional cash compensation.

The plan provides for two classes of bonus awards. The Class A bonus awards are granted for conspicuous service of any nature, for example, for an invention or improvement which results in a profit or saving or in a reduction of risk of personal injury or damage, or an unusual and ingenious solution of a business or technical problem. The Class B bonus awards are granted to those who have contributed most in a general way to the company's success. The Class A bonus awards, which include those given for inventive suggestions, may be granted irrespective of the company's earnings. They are granted without regard to departmental lines or limitation as to length of service. Each case is considered on its merits. Recommendations for bonuses are made either by the president or the department head and are acted upon by the executive committee which may authorize the award of Class A bonuses not exceeding $1,000 for any part of a three part bonus award. Ordinarily a bonus award comprising shares of stock in the company is paid one-fourth at the time the award is made and one-fourth at the end of the year in which the award is made and each of the next succeeding two years. Where a Class A bonus award has been recommended for service which it is believed will result in a continuing money saving to the company, the bonus may take the form of a three-part award based upon savings over a five-year period. The first of these awards is made at the close of the year in which the improvement has been in regular operation for six months on a reasonably representative commercial basis. The second award is made at the end of the third year and the third award at the end of the fifth year of the period of commercial exploitation, provided continued savings result. Where no further savings will result after the third year's exploitation, the award is treated as

a two-part award and final payment then made.

In the administration of this plan, as well as in most of the other successful incentive award plans, the awards are made only after relatively formal consideration by a committee of top management and under conditions of widespread publicity. The contribution made by the employee is formally acknowledged and the appreciation of the corporate management made clearly apparent. Consideration and recognition by management and by the employee's supervisor or other superior is believed to be at least as important, if not more important, than the actual cash value of the award.

Results—Summary. All of the corporations to which we have referred, du Pont, Raytheon, Polaroid, Westinghouse and Eastman Kodak, have large patent portfolios. There can be no question but that the patent grant serves as an incentive, at least to the corporation to urge its employees to invent.

Dr. Land, president of Polaroid Corporation, an outstanding inventor, scientist and industrialist and the holder of more than 200 patents, has said that it is impossible, without the protection of patents, for a new company working on a major advance in science or technology to be properly financed, to go through the extremely difficult periods of study, invention, development, engineering and production, and to advertise and distribute its products and services. And he has suggested that without the protection and incentive of the patent system industry would be faced with what he has described as "a cesspool of secrecy," which could lead to disastrous retardation of the general progress of science. (Land—"Thinking Ahead," *Harvard Business Review*, Sept., Oct., 1959, *37*, No. 5).

Changing Attitude of Industry to Incentives

Proposals for bonuses or cash awards to inventors, usually as alternatives to patent grants, are being constantly made and have been made since prior to the enactment of our first patent law. Madison, for example, proposed a system of premium payments to inventors in the discussions leading up to the adoption of the Federal Constitution, and similar proposals were made not only in this country, but in England, Russia, Holland and most of the European countries at various times during the 19th century. Russia established a commission to determine awards for inventors in lieu of patent grants more than 125 years ago. These suggestions have been reviewed and discussed by Professor Machlup in "An Economic Review of the Patent System," Study No. 15 of the Subcommittee on Patents, Trademarks and Copyrights of the Committee on the Judiciary, U.S. Senate, 85th Congress, 2nd Session. Cf. separate article herein on *Employee-Inventors Patent Rights in Europe.*

Attitude in 1930. Dr. Joseph Rossman made a survey in 1930 of policies to stimulate invention and disclosure of suggestions by company employees. *Ind. and Eng. Chem., 27,* 1380, 1510. He also reviewed a prior related survey by Dickinson.

Rossman found that, of the 230 companies responding to requests for information, 89 made no active attempt of any kind to stimulate invention or disclosure by any employees; 66 made cash awards; 31 granted increases or promotions; and a very few companies, less than 10, gave the employee-inventor either royalties if his invention became the subject of a patent and was commercially used, or a share in profits directly attributable to the adoption and use of a suggested improvement. Such royalty or profit-sharing plans frequently involved the payment of a royalty of the order of 5 per cent for a relatively short period, for example, three to five years. Where single, lump cash awards were made, these were usually in no way dependent on the ultimate value of the suggestion, i.e., an award of $25 or $50 might be made for every suggestion which was found to qualify for the award. Occasionally, the award systems were scaled to the estimated value of the contribution, from a minimum of $5 for a suggestion of intangible value to a maximum of $100 or more for the best suggestion in each yearly period, for example.

Rossman reported that 32 of the companies covered by his survey employed some sort of suggestion system for stimulating ideas and inventions. Suggestion reward systems were originally introduced for the purpose of stimulating patentable inventions and in this respect they may be said to have been failures, for few patentable ideas resulted from such systems. However, suggestion reward systems have in many cases been effective as stimuli to the disclosure by employees of nonpatentable suggestions of value. Both Rossman and Dickinson reported that a very few suggestions made by employees in companies utilizing a suggestion reward system are patentable but Dickinson found that, of 300 suggestions made by the employees of one company, 80 per cent were adopted. Both Rossman and Dickinson found that the suggestion reward plan, to be effective, should be formalized, widely explained to employees and easy for employees to use; that suggestions should be acknowledged, submitted to regularly established committees so that the employee is confident that his suggestion is routed through established channels and not suppressed by his supervisor or disregarded by the committee to which it is submitted; and that the employee should be advised as to the action taken and the reasons therefor. Rossman suggested that the greatest stimulus is to be found in the intimate, daily contact between company officials and technical and research personnel.

Government Survey of Industry Attitudes in 1952. In 1952 a committee appointed by the Chairman of The Government Patents Board, to study a government program of incentives, awards and rewards, reported that a minority of the companies investigated took no positive measures whatever to stimulate inventions or their disclosure. This attitude seemed to be characteristic of those well established industries where process and equipment were standardized.

The committee found that most companies, however, encouraged invention on the part of all employees although many concentrated their major efforts on their engineering and research staffs. These companies stated that the important discoveries almost invariably were made by those employed to invent, i.e., by research and technical personnel. In most instances, the incentive took the form of a cash award, although in many cases such awards were substituted or supplemented by salary increases, either with or without promotion. In many cases, a fixed payment was made, irrespective of the value of the suggestion at the time of disclosure. Where the awards were made only in the event that the suggestion was considered patentable, the usual practice was to make the award at the time the patent application was filed. In many cases a supplementary award was made at the time the patent was granted.

The committee found that many companies had award systems which provided for a basic and rather nominal, fixed award with supplementary variable cash awards or bonuses. These might take the form either of a percentage of royalties collected under a patent license or a supplementary payment based upon a determination of the value of the invention, either as measured by savings to the corporation or by profits realized from the use of the invention or both.

In a very few cases the committee found that awards were made to groups or teams which had been working on the problem. Where this was the case and where the award was not a fixed award divided among the members of the team but was based upon profits or savings resulting from the invention, the practice commonly was to pay into a fund a percentage of the royalties derived from the use of the invention or a percentage of the profits or savings derived from its use. Such funds were usually distributed annually, in pursuance of some previously established apportionment among the members of the group or team. The apportionment was frequently based upon the salary earned by the individual employee, weighted, in some cases, by his years of service.

The award system, it was found, resulted in prompt disclosure and report of new suggestions, better cooperation between inventors and patent attorneys with more efficient operation of corporate patent departments, increased patent consciousness on the part of management and, where the plan was seriously and conscientiously administered, a substantial improvement in management-employee relations. (Costa, Law of Inventing in Employment, pp. 213 et seq.)

Attitude in 1962. Recent surveys, one conducted by Rossman, the results of which were publicly reported at the annual public conference of The Patent, Trademark and Copyright Foundation in June 1962, indicate a somewhat greater use by industry of awards and incentives for invention than either Rossman or Dickinson reported thirty years ago. About 40 per cent of the companies covered by Rossman's most recent survey now provide cash incentive rewards for inventive suggestions. Some, however, still make no further effort apparently to stimulate invention than to make clear that salary and position within the company are determined in part by the frequency and importance of the employee's inventive contribution.

Many companies now use a system of multiple awards, the first being given when the suggestion is received and approved for award, a second when a patent application is filed and still another when the patent issues. Usually the initial award is the smallest, for example, $25 or $50, and the payment at the time the patent issues the largest, for example, $100 to $500.

Several of the companies reporting, grant one or more special annual rewards. These are relatively large, of the order of $1000 to $5000. The award is formally made and given wide publicity. Such rewards are not only of monetary value to the recipient, they also enhance his professional status and reputation—something of perhaps greater importance to him and hence a greater stimulus to future inventive activity.

All companies making cash incentive awards and covered by the survey regard these awards as fringe benefits which bear little or no direct relationship to the value of the inventive contribution. Half the reporting companies make no attempt to evaluate the contribution beyond qualifying it for an award; the rest attempt merely a gross evaluation which might form the basis for an increase in salary or a promotion.

Few of the reporting companies feel that

the cash incentive award system results in any substantial increase in the output of inventive ideas.

There seems to be no doubt, on the other hand, that these awards serve as effective stimuli to prompt disclosure of the novel idea and improve employee morale and employee-management relations.

Rossman finds, as might be expected, that many of the patentee-inventors covered by the survey believe that increased cash rewards for inventive disclosures would be the most effective stimulus, while others suggest better facilities, greater freedom to do undirected research, more recognition by management and improved dissemination of information with respect to corporate needs for development of new products.

For a 1963 Survey by the National Industrial Conference Board of the practice of industrial firms in giving monetary incentives to inventors, see Carl G. Baumes and G. Clark Thompson, Business Management Record, August 1963, pp. 12-20.

Government Incentives Legislation

In December 1959, the Subcommittee on Patents, Trademarks and Copyrights of the Committee on the Judiciary of the United States Senate published an exhaustive Study No. 22, by Jibrin and Corry of the Legislative Reference Service, on the legislative history of government assistance to invention and research.

Government employees incentive awards are now covered by the provisions of Chapter 25 of Title 5, USCA (68 Stat. 1112). Departmental awards programs are now carried out under such regulations and instructions as are issued by the United States Civil Service Commission. All executive departments and independent agencies of the executive branch of the government with the exception of the Tennessee Valley Authority and the Central Bank for Cooperatives are included within the scope of the regulations.

The head of each department is authorized to pay cash awards to civilian officers and employees of the government who by their suggestions, inventions or superior accomplishments contribute to the efficiency,

economy or other improvement of government operations. The President is also authorized to pay cash awards to such civilian officers and employees of the government. Such cash awards are to be in addition to the regular compensation of the recipient of the award and its acceptance shall constitute an agreement that the Government of the United States may use the idea, method or device for which the award is made without further claim for compensation by the recipient, his heirs and assigns. Awards granted under the Act are limited to $5,000 except that an award in excess of such amount but not in excess of $25,000 may be granted with the approval of the United States Civil Service Commission cases and for highly exceptional and unusually outstanding suggestions.

In addition to these cash awards, provision is made by Executive Order No. 10717 of June 28, 1957 for a special honorary award to be known as the President's Award for Distinguished Federal Civilian Service in special cases. This shall consist of a gold medal and an appropriate citation and may be presented by the President to civilian officers or employees of the federal government for exceptionally meritorious or outstanding civilian service and for such contributions to the government or the public interest as require, in the opinion of The Distinguished Civilian Service Awards Board, greater public commendation and official recognition than that which can be accorded by the head of the government department. Presumably such awards are not limited to those who make suggestions or inventions for which the cash awards provided by the Act are granted.

Other Government Activity. In 1947, the Department of Justice published the result of an investigation covering a three-year span and entitled "Investigation of Government Patent Practices and Policies —Report and Recommendations of the Attorney General to the President." The Attorney General recommended against the adoption of any system of special financial rewards, promotions or salary increases to government employees because of a patentable invention or discovery. He suggested that the offer of a premium to the employee who produced the invention might induce secrecy and lack of cooperativeness on the part of research and technical employees, involve administrative difficulties in the selection of the person to whom the reward should be made (especially where the invention was the result of group endeavor) and cause dissatisfaction among unrewarded members of a research group as well as among personnel assigned to functions not likely to produce patentable inventions. He suggested that any system of cash bonuses, promotions or salary increases which might be adopted should provide for awards for meritorious suggestions or ideas regardless of whether or not they were patentable, that such a system would be free of the objections to an award system limited to patentable suggestions and that it might remedy in part inadequacies in the salary structure. He further suggested public and official recognition of meritorious contributions as an additional effective incentive to invention. The present system of government incentive awards follows closely the recommendations made by the Attorney General.

The publication entitled "Inventors Awards—Hearing before the Sub-Committee on Patents etc. of the Committee on the Judiciary, United States Senate," June 7, 1956, reports testimony received in connection with the consideration of a then pending bill relating to government invention-incentive awards.

Both the Secretary of Commerce and the Director of Legislative Programs for the Department of Defense emphasized that the government departments were unable to provide any award to an inventor not employed by the government whose invention might be utilized by the government, unless the inventor had a valid patent covering his invention, since to do so would require an expenditure of funds not authorized by law.

Those testifying before the Sub-Committee were generally in agreement that some government-authorized award system was desirable as an incentive to invention. Senator O'Mahoney, the chairman of the Sub-committee, suggested that incentives "be primarily directed toward the development of inventions and discoveries which would be helpful in the maintenance of peace and making the standard of living better than it is," rather than limiting incentives to inventions applicable to national defense.

Ray M. Harris, Patent Adviser to the Office of the Assistant Secretary of Defense for Supply and Logistics urged that incentives directed to the *disclosure* of the invention were of greater importance than those directed to *making* it.

There was general agreement as to the desirability of some incentive cash award system which would provide for the payment of deserved awards not only to government employees, but to others as well, and would include unpatentable as well as patentable suggestions. There was also general recognition of the extreme difficulty, if not impossibility of establishing any "fair value" award system.

The National Inventors Council was created in August 1940 by the Secretary of Commerce to receive, evaluate and pass on to appropriate branches of the armed services all ideas, inventions, new products and processes which might be submitted by any members of the public as contributions to the war effort. The Council provided a much needed screening of submitted ideas as well as an established impartial, sympathetic body in which the independent inventor might with confidence submit a suggestion for consideration by the armed services. In the first six years of its existence the Council received more than 360,000 suggestions, evaluated more than 200,000 of them, conducted many thousands of interviews, and recommended approximately 8000 suggestions to the army and navy.

Non-Profit Organization Incentives

In recent years research and related programs carried forward in colleges, universities and technical schools and supported by extramural sources have assumed rapidly increasing importance in the over-all picture of scientific progress and research budgets. New York University, for example, which is actively engaged in many research programs sponsored by government and by private industry, had a budget in

1961 for research costing about $17,000,000. More than 3000 persons associated with the university, largely faculty and graduate students, were actively engaged in such research.

Much research conducted by non-profit organizations (and, for that matter, much industrial research) is government-sponsored, and may be paid for either by a research grant or pursuant to a research contract. In the latter case, as Connor has pointed out (6 PTC J 139, 1962), the Government initiates the research, seeks out a contractor, buys the research, and usually requires the assignment of all or part of the patent rights on inventions made or reduced to practice in the performance of the contract. In the case of a governmental research grant, the organization and its scientist-employee have work they wish to do, and seek financial aid from government. If their proposal is found to merit support they receive a grant, giving freedom to pursue such leads as they may find attractive and to publish when they please. At least until recently, patent rights to inventions made under a government research grant were not ordinarily assigned to the government, nor was there any obligation to report them. Now the Public Health Service requires disclosure of inventions made under research grants, and may require them to be patented and assigned to the government. Connor estimates that in 1961 the National Institutes of Health supported some 14,000 research projects with government grants totalling $273,000,000 and that this represented about 30 per cent of the total expenditures for medical research in the nation.

National Science Foundation. In 1950, the National Science Foundation was created for the purpose of developing and encouraging a national policy for (1) promoting basic research and education in the sciences, (2) initiating basic scientific research by making contracts or arrangements including grants, loans and other forms of assistance, (3) appraising the impact of research upon industrial development and the general welfare, (4) conducting research in national defense, and (5) awarding scholarships and fellowships in the sciences. The Foundation comprises a director and a board of members eminent in scientific fields. The Foundation is provided by the Treasury with such sums as "may be necessary" to enable the Foundation to carry out its functions.

National Research Council. In 1916, President Wilson accepted an offer by the National Academy of Sciences to create the National Research Council for the purpose of encouraging the investigation of scientific phenomena, increasing scientific research directed to the development of American industries, the employment of scientific methods in strengthening the national defense, and such other applications of science as will promote the national security and welfare.

When patentable discoveries are made in the course of work carried on under the auspices of the Council, patents obtained thereon are assigned to the Council and the results of such discoveries are dedicated to the public in such manner as the Council deems most effective.

University Incentives

Many universities have established independent, but closely affiliated, non-profit foundations or institutions to serve primarily as patent-management agents and to relieve the university and its scientific personnel of the burden of obtaining patents and exploiting patentable inventions. Some of these foundations, notably the Wisconsin Alumni Research Foundation and the Rutgers Research and Endowment Foundation, have obtained large patent-royalty incomes, but these are not common.

In many cases the foundations enter into patent-management agreements with Research Corporation, a non-profit organization which acts as patent-management agent not only for universities and university-affiliated foundations, but also for other non-profit research organizations.

Generally, where the exploitation of the patented invention is by a patent-management corporation or by some other non-profit organization, the inventor receives a percentage, usually not more than 15 per cent and often less, of the royalties received from licensing the invention, the remainder going for scientific investigation and experimentation.

The inventor thus receives a financial reward only if his invention is patentable and only after a patent thereon has been successfully and profitably exploited. Much research conducted by non-profit organizations is government-sponsored and most of this is directed to activities where the government asserts an overriding interest such that there is little or no opportunity for commercial exploitation. Moreover, much research conducted by non-profit organizations is basic or pure research, which may not lend itself readily to patenting.

In any event, a comparatively small number of patents have been obtained by universities and other non-profit organizations and, while many significant and valuable discoveries have been made by their research personnel, the chance that any individual researcher will receive a financial reward from an invention made by him while in the employ of a university or other non-profit organization is so slight as to be practically nonexistent.

In lieu of special money awards, non-profit organizations are now able to offer scientific and technically trained personnel advantages which in many cases more than compensate for lack of such financial incentives as industry is prepared to make for inventive contributions.

Dr. Charles S. Draper, chairman of The National Inventors Council and head of The Department of Aeronautics and Astronautics at Massachusetts Institute of Technology, an outstanding inventor-scientist, has suggested (5 PTC J 71, 1961) that so far as the university-affiliated inventor-scientist is concerned, the patent system provides at best only a weak incentive to invent. In his own case, he suggests that the patent-inspired motivation to invent is very nearly zero, primarily because the financial reward to the university-affiliated inventor from patents is so slight. Dr. Draper suggests that in a suitable atmosphere, such as that provided by the university, the interest of the work itself gives such a strong motivation to solve difficult problems that the addition of special financial rewards would probably not cause any

project to be pursued with greater vigor than it now receives. He recognizes, however, that the provision of suitable financial awards for outstanding innovative contributions would probably pay worthwhile dividends to the public interest, and he suggests that some system of financial award be established to supplement the patent system and provide recognition and financial benefits for inventors.

There is some basis for questioning the effectiveness of the non-financial inducements offered by non-profit organizations as incentives to invent. Palmer, Patents and Non-profit Research, comments on the "comparatively small number of discoveries and inventions patented by educational institutions." While many universities have established independently incorporated, affiliated research institutes or foundations which provide patent management and exploitation services, very few of these foundations have derived appreciable income from patents or acquired any substantial patent portfolio.

Summary

It is in the best interests of the public that effective incentives to invent be provided and that novel inventions and suggested improvements be promptly disclosed.

The patent system and the financial rewards potentially arising from proprietary rights in commercially valuable patented inventions provide effective incentives at least to industrial corporations and to such independent and self-employed inventors as have the facilities and the ability to exploit commercially their patentable ideas. The inventor who does not have the means available for commercial exploitation and the scientist who is employed by an industrial organization, the government, or a non-profit organization may be expected more promptly to disclose new inventive concepts and perhaps also to be more productive thereof if incentives to invent and to disclose are provided beyond those inherent in the patent system.

These incentives take many forms. The widespread use of cash incentive awards throughout industry has undoubtedly proven of some incentive value, if not as a stimulus to invent then at least to prompt disclosures of novel concepts. Such awards may also provide status recognition, wholly independent of monetary value, particularly when the cash award is granted in such formal manner as to become known to the recipient's associates and fellow workers, accepted as a status symbol and considered valuable as such. The award of a citation would probably have much the same incentive value.

It is suggested that, if cash awards are employed as incentives, they be numerous, not limited to patentable inventions but also given for any suggestion which is considered meritorious whether it relates to an improvement in product, process or equipment, better sales technique, a cost-saving practice, handling of personnel problems, or, in fact, anything of value to the employer.

Effective incentives to invent and to disclose, other than cash awards, are widely employed, not only in non-profit organizations but in private industry as well. These are of many kinds. The employee may receive promotion or some other improved status such as a superior rank or title, either with or without corresponding salary increase, clearly dependent upon competence in research and the production of novel and valuable new developments.

Other incentives to effective research activity are pleasant conditions for the researcher, association with more congenial fellow workers, greater freedom in the selection and carrying forward of research projects, or opportunity to relinquish other and less agreeable responsibilities. Such incentives are apparently as effective in industrial organizatios as they are in non-profit organizations, although it is believed that they are less frequently employed in the former.

In many industrial organizations profit-sharing plans have been successfully employed and found highly effective in the stimulation of suggestions of all kinds, both patentable and unpatentable, from all groups of employees, technical and non-technical, skilled and unskilled. Where such profit-sharing plans are coupled with effective employee suggestion programs and where management seriously and conscientiously administers the latter, the results would seem to be almost invariably effective. The volume of valuable suggestions is high, internal disputes, jealousies and rivalries between employees are at a minimum, and management-employee relations become generally excellent.

An incentive plan which is effective in one industry may be ineffective in another. Even in the same industry, a plan highly satisfactory in one corporate organization may, when adopted by another, prove unsatisfactory. The character of management, the personal desires and aims of the employee groups, the willingness effectively to implement and administer complex plans —all these are factors which weigh heavily in the success or failure of any incentive plan.

Generally speaking, a simple plan of relatively nominal cash awards is the easiest to administer. The more complex plans, however, have proved most effective and produced the greatest number of valuable suggestions and inventions.

Cross-references: *Employee Inventions and Agreements to Assign, Employee-Inventors Patent Rights and Compensation in Foreign Countries, Inventor's Psychology, Taxation,* Section on Payments to Employees for Assignments.

INFORMATION FOR INDEPENDENT INVENTOR—ABSTRACT OF ELEMENTS OF THE PATENT SYSTEM

This presentation is dedicated specifically to the interests of the solo inventor lacking both experience with patents and contact with others with whom to confer. Reading this title first, he will acquire an over-all view of patent procedures, rights, and utilization before turning to the index for more detailed information on selected subjects of immediate interest to him.

This is one of the best brief articles of its scope ever written on our patent system as a whole. Although Mr. Maurice A. Crews, when Assistant Commissioner of Patents, first presented the circular for discussion (41 JPOS 159, 1959), he disclaims credit with the comment that the article represents the collective thought or work of hundreds of associates and attorneys. The public appeal of it is evident from the fact that more copies of it were sold (at 15¢ each) during 1961 than of any other government publication.

The article follows. Ed.

Patents and Inventions
An Information Aid for Inventors

U.S. Department of Commerce

What Is a Patent?

A patent is a grant by the United States to an inventor of the right to exclude others for a limited time from making, using, or selling his invention in this country. It is a printed document in which the invention is fully disclosed and the rights of the inventor are defined. When an inventor secures a patent he has the opportunity to profit by manufacture, sale, or use of the invention in a protected market or by charging others for making or using it. In patents granted for invention of new processes, machines, manufactures, compositions of matter or plants, the patent rights run for 17 years from the date when the patent is granted. A patent for an ornamental design for an article of manufacture may run for 3½, 7, or 14 years, as desired by the patentee.

The Importance of Patents

It is natural to ask why the Government makes this offer of protection under the patent law. The answer is in the Constitution itself, which provides that Congress may secure this right to inventors *in order to promote the progress of the useful arts*. The public benefits from this system for three reasons:

First, by offering patent protection, *it induces the inventor to make the invention*.

Second, if the inventor succeeds with the help of the patent in developing and marketing the invention, *this gives the public the opportunity to use it*.

Third, since the inventor must describe the invention in the patent, and copies of the patent may be purchased by the public for 25 cents each, *the knowledge of the invention is made available to everyone*.

If it were not for the patent law many inventors would be unable to develop their inventions and would abandon their ideas instead of going forward with them, and many others would keep them secret as long as they could, *instead of publishing them in patents which stimulate others to make still further inventions*.

The Independent Inventor

A great deal of the progress of the United States has resulted from inventions made by inventors working independently of any large organization. It is believed that such people will make many important inventions in the future, just as they have in the past. These inventors are often puzzled by such problems as whether to seek patent protection and what steps to take to obtain the benefit of the patent law. In the following discussion we will therefore assume that you have made an invention and that you need a practical guide to help you in solving these problems.

You should seek professional advice at a very early stage in connection with any invention, and this pamphlet is provided as an outline of the basic facts you should know in cooperating with your patent practitioner.[1] It cannot possibly serve as a substitute for the detailed professional advice you will need in relation to your particular problems.

Summary of Basic Steps

The questions uppermost in the minds of most inventors are these: (1) Should I try to obtain a patent? (2) If I decide to try to obtain a patent, what steps can I take to secure the best possible patent protection? (3) What steps can I take to improve my chances of developing and marketing my invention successfully?

It is important that you realize that there is no way in which you can get assurance in advance that you will be granted a patent, or that you will be able to profit if you obtain one. However, you may improve your chances greatly by following the suggestions made in this pamphlet if your invention is useful and new. If on the other hand the features you consider important are not new or are not useful, these suggestions will help you to discover this early enough to avoid useless expense. The steps you should take are these:

(1) Study your invention in relation to other available ways of doing the job, and decide whether the invention provides advantages that make it salable.

(2) Get a trustworthy friend to sign his name as witness on a dated drawing or description of the invention, and keep careful records of the steps you take and their dates.

(3) Make a search to find the most closely related prior patents. This can be done for you by any patent practitioner.

(4) Compare the patents found in the search

[1] The word "Practitioner" is used in this pamphlet to refer to persons who are registered to practice in the Patent Office by preparing and prosecuting patent applications, regardless of whether these persons are patent attorneys (all except a few of whom are lawyers) or patent agents (nonlawyers).

with your invention. Your decision whether to seek patent protection should be based on your own comparison of these patents with the features of your invention which you believe to be new and valuable, and on the advice of your practitioner.

(5) If you find that your invention includes valuable features not shown in the patents found in the search, instruct your practitioner to prepare for you an application for patent and to file it in the Patent Office. Help him prepare a good application by giving him all the useful information you can provide.

(6) Keep in close personal touch with the progress of your application in the Patent Office. Tell your practitioner promptly of any changes you may make in your invention and of the steps you take to develop and market it. Study the patents which the Patent Office may cite against your application. Help your practitioner to overcome rejections by pointing out in what ways your invention is better than those described in earlier patents.

Each of these points is explained in some detail in the following sections.

First Step

Make Certain It Is Practical. Many persons believe they can profit from their inventions merely by patenting them. This is a mistake. No one can profit from a patent unless it covers some feature which provides an improvement for which people are willing to pay. You should therefore try to make sure that your invention will provide this kind of advantage before you spend money in trying to patent it.

Second Step

Witnesses, Records and Diligence. *Importance of Witnesses.* It may become important for you later to be able to prove the date when you first conceived the idea of your invention. If you made a written description or drawings or built and tested it, you may also need to prove these facts and dates, and your diligence in completing and testing it. You will not be able to prove any of these things to the satisfaction of the Patent Office or a United States court unless your own testimony is supported by one or more other persons who have knowledge of these facts from first-hand observation, so that at least one other person can testify in your behalf as your corroborating witness.

Make and Keep Good Records. You should prepare a record in the form of a sketch or drawing or written description promptly after you first get the idea of your invention, and ask one or more of your trustworthy friends to read and understand and sign and date this record as witnesses. You should also keep a carefully dated record of other steps you take in working on the invention, and get one or more friends to witness these steps and sign their names as witnesses to your records. You should keep correspondence about the invention, sales slips of materials you buy for use in working on it, and any models or drawings, so that these will be on hand if needed to help you prove the facts and dates of the steps you have taken.

Letter to Yourself Will Not Protect You. Many persons believe that they can protect their inventions against later inventors merely by mailing to themselves a registered letter describing the invention. This is not true. Your priority right against anyone else who makes the same invention independently cannot be sustained except by testimony of someone else who corroborates your own testimony as to all important facts, such as conception of the invention, diligence, and the success of any tests you may have made. It is therefore important that some trustworthy friend witness these things. The invention will not be fully protected until patented.

Third Step

The Search. *Why the Search Is Important.* You cannot obtain a valid patent if your invention is anticipated by any earlier printed publication or patent in any country, or by commercial use in the United States. If you decide that your invention is valuable enough to patent, your next step should be to make a careful search through patents already issued to find out if it is new as compared to these patents. This is important for a number of reasons:

First, it involves less expense to make a search than to try to obtain a patent. If you learn through the search that the invention cannot be patented you will save money.

Second, even if none of the earlier patents shows all the details of your invention, they may show the only *important* features or they may show other ways of doing the job that are as good or better than yours. If this is the case, you will not want to try to get patent protection on an invention that cannot be commercialized.

Third, even if nothing is found in the search which comes very close to your invention, you will still find it helpful to consider the closest patents of others in taking steps to obtain a strong patent on your own invention.

Search in Patent Office Search Room. The search should be made in the Search Room of the Patent Office in Washington. You may come to Washington and make this search for yourself if you wish; the staff of the Patent Office Search Room will assist you in deciding which patent classes and subclasses should be searched. Many inventors have done this and have found it to be helpful and stimulating. However, making a proper search requires both skill and experience. Most inventors hire experts to make their searches, both for this reason and in order to save the time and expense of a trip to Washington. Patent practitioners having offices in any part of the country can make the searches, either personally on one of their trips to Washington, or through an associate located in Washington.

Get Help From Patent Office Roster. The Patent Office has a roster of all registered practitioners who are available to prepare and prosecute patent applications for inventors and you may choose someone from this roster to make your search. You can buy a copy of this roster from the Superintendent of Documents, U.S. Government Printing Office, Washington 25, D.C. [1964 price 70¢], or see one at any of the field offices of the U.S. Department of Commerce or the Small Business Administration, at your State Department of Commerce and Industry, or at a public library designated as a depository for Government publications. If you would like to have a list of those practitioners with offices in your own region, the Patent Office will send you this without charge. Address your request to Commissioner of Patents, Patent Office, U.S. Department of Commerce, Washington 25, D.C.

Your Searcher Will Furnish Estimate. The search to determine whether your invention is new is called a *Preliminary Search,* as it is preliminary to the possible preparation and filing of a patent application. You may ask the practitioner you have chosen to furnish an advance estimate of the cost of making such a search for you, and also an estimate of his further fees in case you should later decide to file a patent application. The search fee will depend somewhat on whether you decide to have the search cover both the United States patents and readily available foreign patents, or only the United States patents. Most inventors prefer to save expense by omitting the search of the foreign patents.

Explain Invention to Searcher. You should explain to your searcher the features which you believe are new and important, and how they work to provide improved results. This explanation may be made through drawings or sketches, models, written description, oral discussion, or a combination of all of these.

Keep Correspondence for Evidence. Correspondence about the search should be kept in a safe place, as it may be needed later to prove dates and other facts about the invention.

Fourth Step

Studying Patents Found in the Search. *Study Search Results.* Your decision whether to try to get a patent is primarily a business decision. It should be based on your own consideration of the practical advantages of your invention over the closest patents found in the search. Your searcher will send you copies of these patents. If any of them is exactly like your invention you will have no chance to obtain a patent. On the other hand one or more patents may describe inventions which are intended for the same purpose as yours, but are different in various ways. You should study these and decide whether it is worthwhile to go ahead.

Are Your Important Features New? If the features which make your invention different from prior inventions provide important advantages, you should discuss the situation with your practitioner to determine whether, in his judgment, there is a fair chance for you to obtain a patent covering these features.

No Patent Can Cover Old Features. There is one point which you should especially bear in mind. You cannot obtain a patent which will prevent others from using inventions shown in prior patents, *and any patent which you may be able to obtain will cover at best only features which make your invention different from these prior patents.*

Fifth Step

Preparing the Patent Application. *Patent Application Includes Written Description.* If you decide to try to get a patent, it will be necessary for you to send to the Patent Office a formal written application describing your invention and petitioning the Commissioner of Patents to grant you a patent. This is called *Filing the patent application.*

Employ Registered Attorney or Agent. Every inventor has the right to prepare his own patent application and *Prosecute* [2] it in the Patent Office without the help of any attorney or agent. However, the task of prosecuting a patent application to obtain strong protection requires a great deal of professional knowledge, and skill based on training and experience. An inventor who prepares and prosecutes his own application is therefore almost certain to endanger his chances of obtaining a good patent, unless he has a great deal of experience in these matters. The following discussion of Patent Office procedure is therefore provided to help you cooperate with a registered patent practitioner whom you choose from the Patent Office roster, and not with the thought that you should prepare and prosecute your own application.

Only Registered Persons May Legally Represent You. If your search has been made by a registered

---

[2] The word "Prosecute" means the writing of letters and legal amendments to the Patent Office to convince the Patent Office examiner that a patent should be granted, and to fix the legal scope of the patent protection.

patent attorney or agent, you will probably want to have this same person prepare and prosecute your patent application. In any case, in selecting someone for this purpose you should realize that only registered persons are permitted to represent you. It is illegal for anyone to hold himself out as a practitioner qualified to prepare and prosecute patent applications unless he is so registered. All of the attorneys and agents available to represent private clients and who have been examined by the Patent Office and found qualified are listed in the roster. This roster is for your protection against unqualified or unscrupulous persons claiming competence to represent you.

An Application Consists of These Parts. The patent application will include a petition, a power of attorney, and an oath. Since these are very much the same in every application they are called the *Formal Papers.* Attached to these formal papers will be a description of the invention, called the *Specification,* which ends with definitions of the invention called *Claims.* There will also be a drawing if the invention is one that can be illustrated.

Importance of Care. A great deal depends upon the care and skill with which the specification and claims are written. If you fail to supply your practitioner with enough information to help him write a good specification and claims, the patent which you obtain may be so restricted that it has little value, or you may even lose your right to obtain a patent. While your practitioner will doubtless ask you questions to bring out the important points, it should be helpful to you in answering these questions to understand some of the basic priciples of patent law and Patent Office practice.

Patent Specification Must Describe Invention. The patent law requires that the patent specification must provide a description of the invention which is sufficiently full and clear to teach a person skilled in the field of the invention to make and use it. The patent must also contain claims that distinguish your invention from others and your most important problem will be to secure the grant of claims which cover your invention fully and give your patent the best chance for commercial success. You should read the application carefully before signing it.

Do Not Limit Patent Unnecessarily. If the claims of your patent are limited to unimportant incidental features, other persons may be able to use the important features without paying you anything merely by making simple changes. If your invention can be carried out in different ways, your practitioner will try to make this clear in the patent specification. He will try to claim the invention in language broad enough to include

these different ways if this is necessary for your protection. You should therefore be careful to explain to him any other ways you may have in mind for obtaining the principal advantages of your invention, and not merely the best way.

Critical Importance of Breadth of Claims. The claims are the most important part of the patent application. They define the boundaries of your patent rights and fix the amount of protection granted to you by the patent. Even though you may have made a broad invention, it will not be protected unless your claims are also broad.

Claims Must Distinguish Invention. You will understand from the previous discussion that your claims cannot properly be allowed if their language is so broad that they describe earlier inventions. On the other hand, one or more of your claims should be written in language which is general enough to provide the proper legal protection. The difficult job that your practitioner has to accomplish is first to find the features which distinguish your invention from earlier ones, and then to prepare claims which define it in language which is broad enough to provide proper protection while still including one or another of the features which distinguish the invention from earlier ones.

Ask Practitioner to Send You Office Actions. As discussed in the next section, your patent application will be studied by a Patent Office examiner. There will usually be an exchange of letters between your practitioner and the Patent Office to determine whether a patent shall be granted, and the claims it shall contain. In order to make sure that you are informed about these developments, you should establish an understanding with your practitioner that he will furnish you promptly a copy of each letter he receives from the Patent Office and of each patent discussed by the Patent Office in these letters. Ask him also to send you a copy of each letter of amendment or argument which he may file in response to these Patent Office letters. The Patent Office furnishes two copies of each of its letters called, *Office Actions,* to the practitioner, so that he may send you one if you want it. Your practitioner can obtain for you copies of the United States patents cited by the examiner at a cost of 25 cents each. You can be helpful to your practitioner by reading these patents and discussing them with him.

Sixth Step

Patent Office Prosecution. *The Patent Office Examiner's Task.* Every application is examined by a Patent Office examiner who will first read your application to satisfy himself that the invention has been properly described and will then read the claims and make a search among prior patents and printed publications to find those most closely related to the features covered in these claims. This search by the examiner is similar to the preliminary search already made for you, but the examiner's search will be more far-reaching in most cases.

Patent Office Letter of Rejection. In presenting claims broad enough to protect you fully, your practitioner may write some of them in a form so broad that the examiner will hold them to be unpatentable. The examiner will make an *Office Action* in the form of a letter in which he will reject your claims if he finds earlier patents or publications which show the features you are claiming. He will also reject them even though they include some new feature, if he decides that the new feature would be obvious to a person having skill in the field of the invention. The examiner almost always finds one or more earlier patents or publications close enough to some of your claims to cause him to reject them; some claims may be rejected while others may be held to be allowable. The action of the Patent Office in rejecting claims that cannot be validly patented serves as a guide to practitioners in their efforts to secure for their clients strong and valid patents.

Avoiding or Overcoming Rejection. Every Patent Office action must be answered within six months of the date it is mailed, or within a shorter time period if required by the examiner. This answer is in the form of a letter addressed to the Commissioner of Patents. This letter may direct him to cancel some of the original claims, and to change the language of other claims. In any case the letter must point out the reasons for believing that a patent should be granted. Such a letter is called an *Amendment.* In submitting such an amendment, your practitioner will try to avoid adding limitations which will restrict your patent unreasonably.

Help Your Practitioner in Prosecution. While your practitioner will make a careful study of patents cited in the office action in preparing your amendment, it will be helpful to him if you also study these patents. The information you will obtain in this way will help you to decide whether you should abandon your patent application or whether you should continue with your efforts. If you decide to continue you may, by your own study and knowledge of the practical details, be able to point out features and advantages which will help your practitioner in preparing the amendment.

Tell Practitioner Promptly About Changes. It is important that you tell your practitioner promptly of any changes in your invention which you have made or plan to make. The Patent Office rules do not permit an application to be changed by describing new matter such as improvements, after it has been filed in the Patent Office. However, it is important that you keep your practitioner informed so that he can do everything possible to secure full coverage and properly protect your interests. If he finds he cannot fully protect your improvements in the application already on file in the Patent Office, he may recommend that you file a new application to obtain the full protection you may need.

Reconsideration by Examiner. After the examiner receives your amendment, he will again study the application and make a second office action. This may be a notice of allowance, telling you that you will be granted a patent, a rejection of all claims, or a rejection of some claims while allowing others. This exchange of office actions and amendments may be repeated until the application is allowed by the examiner, or until the examiner states that the rejection is *final.*

Where To Get Further Information. The prosecution of your application may include an appeal from the decision of the examiner to the Board of Appeals of the Patent Office, or other procedures not discussed in this pamphlet. *You may obtain information on these procedures from the other Patent Office publications.* The Patent Office cannot act as your individual counsellor; you should seek detailed counsel from your own legal adviser. If you have any question of a general nature regarding patents, however, you may write to the Patent Office, Washington 25, D.C. If your question relates to commercial promotion of your invention or patent, you may write to Business and Defense Services Administration, U.S. Department of Commerce, Washington 25, D.C., or get in touch with one of the other offices mentioned in the answers to questions 42, 43 and 45 [, infra.]

Marketing and Developing the Invention

Importance of Development Effort. Let us assume now that you have obtained your patent and that you want to know what you may do to profit from it. You were told at the beginning of this pamphlet that you could not hope to profit unless your invention provided some result or feature having an advantage which would enable you to sell it. It is equally true that you are very unlikely to profit, even after you have received a patent, unless you either use the invention yourself or persuade others to use it by pointing out to them the advantages which it provides. Patents seldom promote themselves. It is unlikely that other people, merely by reading the patent, will recognize the advantages and come to you with an offer to purchase the patent or license rights under it.

Help from Answers to Questions 41-45. Neither the Patent Office nor any other Government agency can help you to the extent of acting as a salesman on your behalf to encourage others to adopt the features of your patent and pay you for their use. However, the Patent Office and other Government agencies provide services which may help in your own activities. Services which may be helpful are discussed in the answers to questions 41 to 45 in the question and answer section at the end of this pamphlet.

When May Invention Be Revealed? Many inventors ask when they may safely reveal their inventions to others in their efforts to obtain financial backing or to induce some person or business organization to buy their patent rights. No answer can be given to this question which may be safely applied to every individual situation; you should seek competent legal advice in regard to your own particular problem. However, the following general statements may be helpful.

Precaution After Patent Issuance. After the patent is issued it is safe to reveal to others everything that is actually described or illustrated in the patent. These details are then no longer secret, for they are published in the printed copies of your patent which are available to anyone for 25 cents each. A precautionary word should be given, however, in connection with later inventions or improvements which are related to the patent. You should be guided by legal counsel in deciding what to say to a prospective purchaser or licensee.

Added Precaution Before Patent Issuance. If you decide to try to sell the invention or license rights under it while your application is still pending in the Patent Office you will need to consider another point. Your patent application serial number and filing date are maintained in confidence by the Patent Office, and these and other dates may be important if any question arises as to who is the first inventor. You should avoid revealing this information prematurely or carelessly, and get legal advice on this point in connection with any negotiation.

Further Precaution Before Applying for Patent. It is also possible to negotiate with a purchaser for sale of rights in your invention even before you have applied for a patent, but such a procedure involves other problems. Many people submit their inventions to prospective manufacturers, after having them witnessed, without having first applied for patent protection. The inventor may feel that this is the only course available if he has no way of determining whether his invention has merit, or if he is unable to afford the cost of a patent application. If you contemplate taking such a course, you are strongly urged to seek legal advice before doing so.

Answers to Questions Frequently Asked

Meaning of Words "Patent Pending":

(1) *Q. What do the terms "patent pending" and "patent applied for" mean?* A. They are used by a manufacturer or seller of an article to inform the public that an application for patent on that article is on file in the Patent Office. The law imposes a fine on those who use these terms falsely to deceive the public.

Patent Applications:

(2) *Q. I have made some changes and improvements in my invention after my patent application was filed in the Patent Office. May I amend my patent application by adding a description or illustration of these features?* A. No. The law specifically provides that new matter shall not be introduced into the disclosure of a patent application. However, you should call the attention of your attorney or agent promptly to any such changes you may make or plan to make, so that he may take or recommend any steps that may be necessary for your protection.

(3) *Q. How does one apply for a patent?* A. By making the proper application to the Commissioner of Patents, Washington 25, D.C.

(4) *Q. Of what does a patent application consist?* A. An application fee, a petition, a specification and claims describing and defining the invention, an oath, and a drawing if the invention can be illustrated.

(5) *Q. What are the Patent Office fees in connection with filing of an application for patent and issuance of the patent?* A. A filing fee of $30 plus $1 for each claim in excess of 20 is required when the application is filed. A final fee of $30 plus $1 for each claim allowed in excess of 20 is also required if the patent is to be granted. This final fee is not required until your application is allowed by the Patent Office.

(6) *Q. Are models required as part of the application?* A. Only in the most exceptional cases. The Patent Office has the power to require that a model be furnished, but rarely exercises it.

(7) *Q. Is it necessary to go to the Patent Office in Washington to transact business concerning patent matters?* A. No; most business with the Patent Office is conducted by correspondence. Interviews regarding pending applications can be arranged with examiners if necessary, however, and are often helpful.

(8) *Q. Can the Patent Office give advice as to whether an inventor should apply for a patent?* A. No. It can only consider the patenta-

bility of an invention when this question comes regularly before it in the form of a patent application.

(9) *Q. Is there any danger that the Patent Office will give others information contained in my application while it is pending?* A. No. All patent applications are maintained in the strictest secrecy until the patent is issued. After the patent is issued, however, the Patent Office file containing the application and all correspondence leading up to issuance of the patent is made available in the Patent Office Search Room for inspection by anyone, and copies of these files may be purchased from the Patent Office.

(10) *Q. May I write to the Patent Office directly about my application after it is filed?* A. The Patent Office will answer an applicant's inquiries as to the status of the application, and inform him whether his application has been rejected, allowed, or is awaiting action by the Patent Office. However, if you have a patent attorney or agent the Patent Office cannot correspond with both you and the attorney concerning the merits of your application. All comments concerning your invention should be forwarded through your patent attorney or agent.

(11) *Q. What happens when two inventors apply separately for a patent for the same invention?* A. An "interference" is declared and testimony may be submitted to the Patent Office to determine which inventor is entitled to the patent. Your attorney or agent can give you further information about this if it becomes necessary.

(12) *Q. Can the 6-month period allowed by the Patent Office for response to an office action in a pending application be extended?* A. No. This time is fixed by law and cannot be extended by the Patent Office. The application will become abandoned unless proper response is received in the Patent Office within this time limit.

When to Apply for Patent:

(13) *Q. I have been making and selling my invention for the past 13 months and have not filed any patent application. Is it too late for me to apply for patent?* A. Yes. A valid patent may not be obtained if the invention was in public use or on sale in this country for more than one year prior to the filing of your patent application. Your own use and sale of the invention for more than a year before your application is filed will bar your right to a patent just as effectively as though this use and sale had been done by someone else.

(14) *Q. I published an article describing my invention in a magazine 13 months ago. Is it too late to apply for patent?* A. Yes. The fact that you are the author of the article will not save your patent application. The law provides that the inventor is not entitled to a patent if the invention has been described in a printed publication anywhere in the world more than a year before his patent application is filed.

Who May Obtain a Patent:

(15) *Q. Is there any restriction as to persons who may obtain a United States patent?* A. No. Any inventor may obtain a patent regardless of age or sex, by complying with the provisions of the law. A foreign citizen may obtain a patent under exactly the same conditions as a United States citizen.

(16) *Q. If two or more persons work together to make an invention, to whom will the patent be granted?* A. If each had a share in the ideas forming the invention, they are joint inventors and a patent will be issued to them jointly on the basis of a proper patent application filed by them jointly. If on the other hand one of these persons has provided all of the ideas of the invention, and the other has only followed instructions in making it, the person who contributed the ideas is the sole inventor and the patent application and patent should be in his name alone.

(17) *Q. If one person furnishes all of the ideas to make an invention and another employs him or furnishes the money for building and testing the invention, should the patent application be filed by them jointly?* A. No. The application must be signed, sworn to, and filed in the Patent Office, in the name of the true inventor. This is the person who furnishes the ideas, not the employer or the person who furnishes the money.

(18) *Q. May a patent be granted if an inventor dies before filing his application?* A. Yes; the application may be filed by the inventor's executor or administrator.

(19) *Q. While in England this summer, I found an article on sale which was very ingenious and has not been introduced into the United States or patented or described. May I obtain a United States patent on this invention?* A. No. A United States patent may be obtained only by the true inventor, not by someone who learns of an invention of another.

Ownership and Sale of Patent Rights:

(20) *Q. May the inventor sell or otherwise transfer his right to his patent or patent applica-*

tion to someone else? A. Yes. He may sell all or any part of his interest in the patent application or patent to anyone by a properly worded assignment. The application must be filed in the Patent Office as the invention of the true inventor, however, and not as the invention of the person who has purchased the invention from him.

(21) *Q. If two persons own a patent jointly, what can they do to grant a license to some third person or company to make, use or sell the invention?* A. They may grant the license jointly, or either one of them may grant such a license without obtaining the consent of the other. A joint owner does not need to get the consent of his co-owner either to make, use, or sell the invention of the patent independently, or to grant licenses to others. This is true even though the joint owner who grants the license owns only a very small part of the patent. Unless you want to grant this power to a person to whom you assign a part interest, you should ask your lawyer to include special language in the assignment to prevent this result.

(22) *Q. As joint inventor, I wish to protect myself against the possibility that my co-inventor may, without my approval, license some third party under our joint patent. How can I accomplish this?* A. Consult your lawyer and ask him to prepare an agreement for execution by you and your co-inventor to protect each of you against this possibility.

Duration of Patents:

(23) *Q. For how long a term of years is a patent granted?* A. Seventeen years from the date on which it is issued; except for patents on ornamental designs, which are granted for terms of $3\frac{1}{2}$, 7, or 14 years.

(24) *Q. May the term of a patent be extended?* A. Only by special act of Congress, and this occurs very rarely and only in most exceptional circumstances.

(25) *Q. Does the patentee continue to have any control over use of the invention after his patent expires?* A. No. Anyone has the free right to use an invention covered in an expired patent, so long as he does not use features covered in other unexpired patents in doing so.

Patent Searching:

(26) *Q. Where can a search be conducted?* A. In the Search Room of the Patent Office in the Department of Commerce Building at 14th and E. Streets Northwest, Washington, D.C. Classified and numerically arranged sets of

United States and foreign patents are kept there for public use.

(27) *Q. Will the Patent Office make searches for individuals to help them decide whether to file patent applications?* A. No. But it will assist inventors who come to Washington by helping them to find the proper patent classes in which to make their searches. In response to mail inquiries it will also advise inventors as to what patent classes and subclasses to search. For a reasonable fee it will furnish lists of patents in any class and subclass, and copies of these patents may be purchased for 25 cents each.

Attorneys and Agents:

(28) *Q. Does the Patent Office control the fees charged by patent attorneys and agents for their services?* A. No. This is a matter between you and your patent attorney or agent in which the Patent Office takes no part. In order to avoid possible misunderstanding you may wish to ask him for estimates in advance as to his approximate charges for: (a) the search, described previously in steps three and four; (b) preparation of the patent application, step five, and (c) Patent Office prosecution, step six.

(29) *Q. Will the Patent Office inform me whether the patent attorney or agent I have selected is reliable or trustworthy?* A. All patent attorneys and agents registered to practice before the Patent Office are expected to be reliable and trustworthy. The Patent Office can report only that a particular individual is, or is not, in good standing on the register.

(30) *Q. If I am dissatisfied with my patent attorney or agent may I change to another?* A. Yes. There are forms for appointing attorneys and revoking their powers of attorney in the pamphlet entitled "General Information Concerning Patents."...

(31) *Q. Will the Patent Office help me to select a patent attorney or agent to make my patent search or to prepare and prosecute my patent application?* A. No. The Patent Office cannot make this choice for you, as it would be unfair for it to select some of its practitioners for recommendation as against others. However, your own friends or general attorney may help you in making a selection from among those listed as registered practitioners on the Patent Office roster.

(32) *Q. How can I be sure that my patent attorney or agent will not reveal to others the secrets of my invention?* A. Patent attorneys and agents earn their livelihood by the confidential services they perform for their clients, and if any attorney or agent im-

properly reveals an invention disclosed to him by a client, that attorney or agent is subject to disbarment from further practice before the Patent Office and loss of his livelihood. Persons who withhold information about their inventions from their attorneys and agents make a serious mistake, for the attorney or agent cannot do a fully effective job unless he is fully informed of every important detail.

Plant and Design Patents:

(33) *Q. Does the law provide patent protection for invention of new and ornamental designs for articles of manufacture, or for new varieties of plants?* A. Yes. If you have made an invention in one of these fields, you should read the Patent Office pamphlet "General Information Concerning Patents."

Technical Knowledge Available from Patents:

(34) *Q. I have not made an invention but have encountered a problem. Can I obtain knowledge through patents of what has been done by others to solve the problem?* A. The patents in the Patent Office Search Room in Washington contains a vast wealth of technical information and suggestions, organized in a manner which will enable you to review those most closely related to your field of interest. You may come to Washington and review these patents, or engage a patent practitioner to do this for you and to send you copies of the patents most closely related to your problem.

Infringement of Others' Patents:

(35) *Q. If I obtain a patent on my invention will that protect me against the claims of others who assert that I am infringing their patents when I make, use, or sell my own invention?* A. No. There may be a patent of a more basic nature on which your invention is an improvement. If your invention is a detailed refinement or feature of such a basically protected invention, you may not use it without the consent of the patentee, just as no one will have the right to use your patented improvement without your consent. You should seek competent legal advice before starting to make or sell or use your invention commercially, even though it is protected by a patent granted to you.

Enforcement of Patent Rights:

(36) *Q. Will the Patent Office help me to prosecute others if they infringe the rights granted to me by my patent?* A. No. The Patent Office has no jurisdiction over questions relating to the infringement of patent rights. If your patent is infringed you may sue the infringer in the appropriate United States court at your own expense.

Patent Protection in Foreign Countries:

(37) *Q. Does a United States patent give protection in foreign countries?* A. No. The United States patent protects your invention only in this country. If you wish to protect your invention in foreign countries, you must file an application in the Patent Office of each such country within the time permitted by law. This may be quite expensive, both because of the cost of filing and prosecuting the individual patent applications, and because of the fact that most foreign countries require payment of taxes to maintain the patents in force. You should inquire of your practitioner about these costs before you decide to file in foreign countries.

National Defense Inventions:

(38) *Q. I have made an invention which may be of interest to the Armed Forces or other Government agencies. How shall I bring it to their attention?* A. The National Inventors Council was established for the specific purpose of helping inventors bring new and promising ideas to the attention of U.S. Government agencies. For information on the Council's policies and procedures, send for a free copy of "Facts About the National Inventors Council" from the National Inventors Council, U.S. Department of Commerce, Washington 25, D.C.

(39) *Q. Is there any method by which I can find out what types of inventions the Government needs?* A. The National Inventors Council publishes a booklet, "Inventions Wanted by the Armed Forces," describing unclassified problems confronting the military agencies. You may obtain a copy of this publication without cost from the nearest U.S. Department of Commerce Field Office or from the National Inventors Council, U.S. Department of Commerce, Washington 25, D.C.

(40) *Q. I believe that the publication of a granted patent on my invention would be detrimental to the national defense. For this reason, I am reluctant to file a patent application unless there is a special method of handling cases of this nature. What should I do?* A. You need have no qualms about filing an application in the U.S. Patent Office. If it is determined that publication of the invention by the granting of a patent would be detrimental to the national defense, the Commissioner of Patents will order that the invention be kept

secret and will withhold the grant of a patent until such time as a decision is made that disclosure of the invention is no longer deemed detrimental to the national security. If an order is issued that the invention of your patent application be kept secret, you will be entitled to apply for compensation for any use of the invention by the Government, if and when the application is held to be allowable.

Developing and Marketing Inventions and Patents:

(41) *Q. Will the Patent Office advise me as to whether a certain patent promotion organization is reliable and trustworthy?* A. No. The Patent Office has no control over such organizations and cannot supply information about them. It is suggested that you obtain this information by inquiring of the Better Business Bureau of the city in which the organization is located, or of the Bureau of Commerce and Industry of the State in which the organization has its place of business. You may also undertake to make sure that you are dealing with reliable people by asking your own patent attorney or agent whether he has knowledge of them, or by inquiry of others who may know them.

(42) *Q. Are there any organizations in my area which can tell me how and where I may be able to obtain assistance in developing and marketing my invention?* A. Yes. In your own or neighboring communities you may inquire of such organizations as chambers of commerce, banks and area departments of power companies and railroads. Many communities have locally financed industrial development organizations which can help you locate manufacturers and individuals who might be interested in promoting your idea. You can also obtain assistance from one of the field offices of the U.S. Department of Commerce or of the Small Business Administration located near you. The addresses of these offices are listed in the answer to question 45.

(43) *Q. Are there any State government agencies that can help me in developing and marketing of my invention?* A. Yes. In nearly all states there are State planning and development agencies or departments of commerce and industry that are seeking new product and new process ideas to assist manufacturers and communities in the State. If you do not know the names or addresses of your State organizations you can obtain this information by writing to the Governor of your State.

(44) *Q. Can the Patent Office assist me in the developing and marketing of my patent?* A. Only to a very limited extent. The Patent Office cannot act or advise concerning the business transactions or arrangements that are involved in the development and marketing of an invention. However, the Patent Office will publish, at the request of a patent owner, a notice in the "Official Gazette" that the patent is available for licensing or sale. The fee for this service is $3.

(45) *Q. Can any U.S. Government agency other than the Patent Office assist me in the development and marketing of my invention?* A. The Business and Defense Services Administration of the U.S. Department of Commerce, Washington 25, D.C., may be able to help you with information and advice, as its various industry divisions maintain close contact with all branches of American industry, or you may get in touch with one of the Department of Commerce field offices.

The Small Business Administration publishes monthly a products list circular containing brief descriptions of issued patents believed to be likely to interest prospective manufacturers, and these circulars are distributed to many business organizations. You may write a letter to the Small Business Administration, Washington 25, D.C., requesting that your invention be listed in this publication, and your request will be honored if the Small Business Administration decides that publication is desirable. The Small Business Administration has over 50 offices at various cities in the United States, and it offers through its products assistance program information and counsel to small concerns who are interested in new products. You may wish to get in touch with one of these offices of the Small Business Administration....

Cross-references: *Act of 1952, Attorneys and Agents, Disclosures, Profiting from Patents.*

INFORMATION FOR PATENT APPLICATION. See DISCLOSURES

INFORMATION FROM FOREIGN PATENTS. See ADVANCE INFORMATION

INFORMATION FROM THE U.S. PATENT OFFICE—UTILIZATION

Isaac Fleischmann

[This article is a condensation with the author's approval of a contribution by him in R/D Research/Development, Vol. 15, page 26, 1964. Ed.]

Importance of Information Available

The U.S. Patent Office, a Bureau of the Department of Commerce, has the largest reservoir of applied technology in the world. At present, there are more than three million U.S. patents and seven million foreign patents on file. From about 85,000 patent applications received, about 50,000 new patents issue annually.

By a thorough search of patents in the particular area of interest, valuable research dollars can be and have been saved in reduced R & D costs; repetition of research already done by other companies has been avoided; solutions have been provided for many problems encountered by companies in the process of developing products; and ideas have been generated for potentially profitable new products.

A good example demonstrating progress as a direct result of R & D programs under a patent system is the tremendous expansion in this century in the uses of nickel in industry, because of the inventions and discoveries yielded by research programs which have advanced knowledge in the art. Thus, the International Nickel Company is careful to consider the knowledge disclosed in prior patents when planning its R & D programs and, consequently, has been very successful in developing patentable inventions in this field.

Unfortunately, however, some companies waste vast sums because they use the important patent search technique not at all in their research, not effectively or not nearly enough. One such disaster involved a large electronics firm. It spent eight million dollars for two inventions and then executed extensive development programs on them, only to find out that both ideas had been conceived earlier and the results were on file at the Patent Office.

Waste of time, money and energy, such as illustrated above, is really unnecessary. It could have been prevented by a thorough search of all related patents before investment had been made or research performed.

As already indicated, R & D programs are aided not only by patents showing a company what it can't do, but also by competitors' patents creating a challenge to research personnel to produce something better.

Often neither engineers nor management have enough knowledge about patents and the Patent Office. If they could only realize the staggering amount of scientific knowledge that is available and how it can be used, they could avoid costly mistakes such as duplicating research, they could use the vast storehouse of patented knowledge as an effective stimulant for new ideas, and thereby open the door to further use of ideas never properly developed. Perhaps there was no market for the product when it was patented; possibly certain products could not previously have been manufactured profitably.

Accessibility of Patent Information

Once a company realizes the advantages offered by the patent resources, it usually wants to know how it can gain access to the particular patents that will be useful for its special purposes. To operate at maximum efficiency, the patent system must rely heavily on speed and precision in its retrieval of information. What with the tremendous repository of data stored in the Patent Office, there is a great strain on its operations. Despite this and a limited budget, the Office continues to aid companies to obtain the patent material they need and is ever striving to do so more rapidly and accurately.

The classification system used by the Patent Office allows a company to examine all existing patents in the particular field of technology in which it has interest. The U.S. patents are divided, to facilitate orderly reference, into some 300 main classes and redivided into 62,000 narrower subclasses. In addition to these and the foreign patents, the Patent Office has hundreds of thousands of technical articles, both domestic and foreign. While the patents are strictly nothing more than pictures and descriptions of inventions, they represent billions of dollars and many years of research, often difficult, frustrating at times and costly.

Searches

Ordinarily, a state-of-the-art search should go back to the earliest developments in the particular field of interest. Sometimes this will be many years, but in the case of such recent innovations as silicones and transistors, it will not be. The state-of-the-art search consists of gathering and examining all of the existing patents on the subject of interest. Its intention is to save R & D from wasteful research and to suggest possible solutions to various technological problems.

There are other types of patent searches also. The novelty search is made to help determine if the idea is new enough to justify making a patent application. This is probably the easiest search to make and usually takes only a day or two to complete. A company makes an infringement search in order to determine whether or not it is likely to infringe patents of others. The search should be very thorough. Finally, there is the validity search, which is made to find out if the validity of an existing patent should be challenged in court; the cost is comparatively high, but it is often justified because more than half the patents so challenged are ruled invalid.

The expense involved cannot be stated accurately, even in general terms. The cost is governed by such factors as the type of invention and its complexity. An unofficial source has estimated that a state-of-the-art search usually costs between $150 and $300; the novelty search, $65 to $150; the infringement search from $250 to $1000, and the validity search as high as $5000. Nevertheless searches are usually worth more to a company than they cost.

It is generally more effective to make an intensive search in a narrow field than a superficial search in a wide field.

The Patent Office, located in the Department of Commerce, Washington, D.C., is the only place in the country where a stack of patents may be pulled from their specific subclass and examined to see how previous inventors have tried to achieve a certain objective. The Public Search Room at the Patent Office and the Scientific Library are open to the general public, patent attorneys and agents representing or working for companies or individual inventors.

Within its financial limitations, the Office is gradually moving toward the eventual mechanization of its entire information system. With the growing vastness of an already tremendous operation, the need for electronic storage and retrieval of data is great. Mechanization has already begun, but its completion is still years away. Such mechanization will help the Patent Office and industry by speeding up the retrieval of information and also by allowing much faster processing of applications.

Companies around the country can go to nearby libraries to do their searching, but such searching is likely to prove much slower and less satisfactory than searching in the Patent Office. However, the Office offers two ways in which a company may keep up with patent progress. The first is by subscribing to the Official Gazette, better known as the "OG," at the rate of $35 per year. It lists all of the approximately 1000 patents issued weekly and, since it is published on the same day the patents issue, it is the quickest way of finding them. The second is for the company to place a standing order for new patents in any subclass of interest. The charge for this is slight, and the patents themselves cost only twenty-five cents each. The Patent Office even employs a deposit account system for regular customers. The company maintains a minimum monthly balance from which the charges are deducted. This system also speeds up orders.

Private firms can help themselves make the most of Patent Office facilities by emphasizing teamwork between its R & D and its patent departments.

It should be obvious to all types of companies that the U.S. Patent Office can greatly aid their R & D endeavors, in saving time, effort and money. However, use of the patent resources cannot be any more effective than company managements make it. In any case, the potential is at hand for virtually all research and development units to use for benefit to themselves.

Appendix
Partial List of Patent Office Publications

This list may be helpful to a researcher of patent information:

General Information Concerning Patents—This pamphlet contains a vast amount of general information concerning the granting of patents expressed in non-technical language for the layman. Available from the Superintendent of Documents at 15¢ each.

General Information Concerning Trademarks—Contains information concerning the granting of trademarks. Available from the Superintendent of Documents at 15¢ each.

How to Obtain Information from U.S. Patents—Explains how U.S. Patents can be used to keep up to date in any field of technology. It provides "how to do it" information for making novelty or state-of-the-art searches in or outside of Washington. Available from the Superintendent of Documents at 20¢ per copy.

Patents and Inventions—An aid for inventors in deciding whether or not to apply for a patent, in obtaining patent protection and in promoting their inventions. Available from the Superintendent of Documents at 15¢ each.

Official Gazette—Contains the weekly issue of patents issued each Tuesday. It consists of a selected figure of the drawings and one claim of each patent granted, an illustration of each trademark published for opposition, a list of trademarks registered, and other trademark information; decisions in patent and trademark cases rendered by the courts and the Patent Office; notices of suits; index of patentees; disclaimers filed; and other information. Available from the Superintendent of Documents at $1.00 each single copy, $35.00 domestic annual subscription, and $45.00 foreign.

A listing of all Patent publications can be obtained from the Commissioner of Patents, Washington, D.C., 20231.

Patent Copy Libraries

Libraries not otherwise identified are Public Libraries. All of them have U.S. patents in numerical order.

Los Angeles, Sunnyvale, Atlanta—Georgia Tech. Library, Chicago, Boston, Detroit, Kansas City—Linda Hall Library, St. Louis, Newark, Albany—University of State of New York, Buffalo—Buffalo and Erie County Public Library, New York City, Cincinnati, Cleveland, Columbus—Ohio State University Library, Toledo, Stillwater—Oklahoma State University Library, Philadelphia—Franklin Institute, Pittsburgh, Providence, Madison—State Historical Society of Wisconsin, and Milwaukee.

Cross-references: *Searching in Washington, Searching Patent Literature outside Washington.*

INFRINGEMENT

John R. Janes

Constitutional and Statutory Rights of Patentees against Infringers

The rights of the patentee against those who would infringe or encroach upon his patent closely follow the constitutional provision that the Congress shall have the power to promote the progress of useful arts by securing to inventors the exclusive right to their discoveries:

"Every patent shall contain a short title of the invention and a grant to the patentee, his heirs or assigns, for the term of seventeen years, *of the right to exclude others from making, using, or selling the invention throughout the United States,* referring to the specification for the particulars thereof." 35 USC 154. (Emphasis added.)

Since a patent is granted for a term of seventeen years from the date of grant, after which the patent becomes available for the free use of the public, a patentee's rights can be encroached upon only during the seventeen-year term of the patent.

The right granted the patentee is *to exclude others from making, using or selling the invention throughout the United States.* The patent does not give the patentee the right to make, use or sell the invention. This latter right is subject to any rights existing at the time the patent was granted, such as prior patents owned by others. *Herman v. Youngstown Car Mfg. Co.*, 191 Fed. 579, 1911. The patent secures to the inventor the *exclusive* right to make, use and vend the thing patented, and consequently to prevent others from exercising like privileges without the consent of the patentee. *Bloomer v. McQuewan*, 14 How. 539, 549; *Continental Paper Bag Co.* v. *Eastern Paper Bag Co.*, 210 U.S. 405, 425.

The right to make can scarcely be made plainer by definition. It embraces the construction of the thing invented. *The right to use* is a comprehensive term that embraces the right to put into service any given invention. Recognizing that many inventions would be valuable to the inventor because of sales of the patented machine or device to others, Congress granted also the exclusive *right to sell* the invention covered by the letters patent. To sell is also a term readily understood. Its use in the statute secured to the inventor the exclusive right to transfer the title for a consideration to others. *Bloomer* v. *McQuewan*, **549**. Each of these rights can be encroached upon separately, or together, in any combination.

The territory within which the patent right extends is limited to the United States, defined in 35 U.S.C. 100(c) as including the States and territories and possessions of the United States of America. While the U.S. patent right does not extend to foreign countries, a U.S. patentee may avail himself of the patent laws of those countries.

The present patent statute defines infringement as any violation of the patentee's exclusive rights. 35 U.S.C. 271(a):

"Except as otherwise provided in this title, whoever without authority makes, uses or sells any patented invention, within the United States during the term of the patent therefor, *infringes the patent*." (Emphasis added.)

A person who wishes to make use or sell the patented invention without liability for infringement to the patentee can acquire from him an assignment grant or license to make and/or use and/or sell whole or in part, and either exclusively or nonexclusively, for all or part of the territory.

It is presumed that a person who purchases the invention from the patentee or the owner or assignee of the patent has an implied license to use the invention and to sell the invention to others, in the absence of any contrary statement by the patentee, and accordingly is not an infringer.

All persons who without authorization of the patentee make, use or sell an invention are infringers under the patent law.

A patentee has recourse to the Federal Courts against those who infringe his patent. 35 U.S.C. 281.

An important limitation is placed on the recovery of damages in such an action, however. No damages can be recovered under 35 U.S.C. 287 by a patent owner who, subsequent to issuance of the patent, has manufactured or sold devices covered by the patent, except on proof that the infringer was notified of the infringement and that

he continued to infringe thereafter, in which event damages may be recovered for infringement occurring after such notice. The filing of an action for infringement under Section 281 constitutes such notice. So does marking of the patented article with the patent number. In any case, no recovery of damages can be had for any infringement committed more than six years prior to the filing of the complaint or counterclaim for infringement in civil rights.

Notice of infringement was not required to start tolling of damages when the patent owner, subsequent to issuance of patent, had not manufactured or sold products coming under any claim of the patent. *Cameron Iron Works, Inc.* v. *Edward Valves, Inc. et al.*, 122 USPQ 497, DC STex 1959; *Wing Railway Appliances Co.* v. *Enterprise Railway Equipment Co.*, 297 U.S. 387, 1936. See also article *Marking with Patent Notice —U.S.*

Determination of Infringement: The Test of Identity or Correspondence

A patent is made up of a specification, drawing, if needed, and claims (35 U.S.C. 154). The *claims* define the enforceable limits of the patentee's exclusive rights. Their language and scope is therefore most important. The meaning of the claims is interpreted *in the light of the description* of the invention in the specification; the scope of the claims is determined not only by their language but also *in the light of the history of prosecution* of the patent application in the Patent Office. See *File Wrapper Estoppel.*

It is important to note that the specification can explain the nature of the invention as defined in the claims, but cannot ordinarily limit the claims further than their express language permits.

The patentee is (absolutely) bound by the language that he has chosen to adopt in formulating his claims. The courts do not usually modify the claims, either by way of extension or limitation:

"If the patentees have not claimed the whole of their invention, and the omission has been the result of inadvertence, they should have sought to correct the error by a surrender of their patent and an application for a reissue. They cannot expect the courts to wade through the history of the art, and spell out what they might have claimed, but have not claimed ... *When the terms of a claim in a patent are clear and distinct* (as they always should be), *the patentee in a suit brought upon the patent, is bound by it.* Merrill v. Yeomans, 94 U.S. 568. *He can claim nothing beyond it.* But the defendant may at all times, under proper pleadings, resort to prior use and the general history of the art to assail the validity of a patent or to restrain its construction. The door is then opened to the plaintiff to resort to the same kind of evidence in rebuttal; *but he can never go beyond his claim.* As patents are procured *ex parte,* the public is not bound by them, but the patentees are. *And the latter cannot show that their invention is broader than the terms of their claim; or, if broader, they must be held to have surrendered the surplus to the public."* (Emphasis added.) *Keystone Bridge Co. v. Phoenix Iron Co.,* 95 U.S. 274, 278, 1877.

Accordingly, when the meaning of the claims is clear, the scope of a patent can be determined precisely and accurately. The test of infringement is whether there is correspondence between the claimed subject matter, and the questioned subject matter. The patentee is furthermore bound by any changes made in the claims to overcome art cited by the Examiner during his prosecution of the patent application. See *Royer* v. *Coupe,* 146 U.S. 524, 532, 1892.

"Where a patentee inserts in his specification, limitations and restrictions for the purpose of obtaining his patent, he cannot, after he has obtained it, claim that it shall be construed as it would have been construed if such limitations and restrictions were not contained in it. (Phoenix Caster Co. v. Spiegel, 133 U.S. 360, 368; Yale Lock Co. v. Berkshire Bank, 135 U.S. 342, 379; Dobson v. Lees, 137 U.S. 258, 265.)"

Accordingly, in determining infringement, the usual procedure is to determine the scope of the claims, taking into account the description of the invention in the specification and the prosecution history of the claimer and then to compare this carefully and in detail with the questioned subject matter.

A claim is composed of the recited elements, and if all of the recited elements are present, infringement exists. A machine to infringe must have the claimed construction or means by which the invention is carried out. A process to infringe, must include each of the claimed steps. An article of manufacture or composition, must include each recited element of the article or composition.

Although each element of the invention covered by the patent claim must be present for infringement, it is not necessary that they be exact counterparts. The patented invention can, for example, be employed as an element in a later invention. It can be an equivalent thereof. It is not even essential that the function, effect, or intended purpose, be the same, so long as the basic essentials of the claimed invention are present. Indeed, if the basic essentials of the invention are present, there may be variations in other particulars of relatively minor importance.

Difficulties arise when there is not identity, but merely substantial correspondence. It is impossible in the scope of this article to do more than merely indicate the nature of the problem by referring to examples in each of four statutory classes of inventions, i.e, machine, process, article of manufacture, and composition of a matter. Designs and plant patents are left for separate articles.

It is important to note the language of the claims introducing the specified machine, process, article of manufacture, or composition of matter. The terms used in the claims to introduce the structure, process, article, or components of the composition, may have a particular significance; the terms "comprising," "consisting of," and "consisting essentially of," are defined in *Claims—Words and Phrases.*

Test of Infringement by a Machine. If the invention of the patentee is a machine, it is infringed by a machine which incorporates in its structure and operation the substance of the invention, that is, by an arrangement of mechanism which performs the same service or produces the same effect in the same way, or substantially the same way. If the device differs from that of the patentee only in form, or in a rearrangement of the same elements of a combination, the device is an infringement even if in certain particulars it is an improvement upon that of the patentee. In *Westinghouse* v. *Boyden Power Brake Co.*, 170 U.S. 537, 569, 1898, the Court said:

"Mere variations of form may be disregarded, but the substance of the invention must be there."

However, if the device so far departs from the principle of the invention that the substance of the invention is not there, there is not likely to be infringement. In *Westinghouse*, the Supreme Court compared the patented device and the device in suit, and concluded that the functions of the two were practically the same, but that the means used were so different that it was impossible to say that they were mechanical equivalents. In the *Paper Bag* case, 210 U.S. 405, 1908, the Supreme Court noted that the issue was whether the machines used by the alleged infringer involved an equivalent of the invention as claimed, and concluded that they did:

"But abstractions need not engage us. The claim is not for a function, but for mechanical means to bring into working relation the folding plate and the cylinder. This relation is the very essence of the invention, and marks the advance upon the prior art. It is the thing that never had been done before, and both the lower courts found that the machines of the Continental Company were infringements of it." p. 422.

If the alleged infringement employs the principle of the invention, minor variations or lack of correspondence in certain details will not avoid infringement. Ordinarily a change in form, addition of a part, omission of a part, division of one element into two parts, a combination of several parts into one element, a transposition or reversal of the parts or a substitution of an equivalent part will not avoid infringement if the principle of the invention is employed. Even an improvement will not suffice if the improved device incorporates all of the inventive features recited for the patented device. If, on the other hand, the change or modification results in an avoidance of the very part or parts which constitute the essentials of the machine, and the basis on which the patent was granted, then there can be no infringement.

The Supreme Court pointed out in *Water-Meter Co.* v. *Desper*, 101 U.S. 332, 335, 1879:

"It is a well-known doctrine of patent law, that the claim of a combination is not infringed if any one of the material parts of the combination are omitted. It is equally well known that if any one of the parts is only formally omitted, and is supplied by a mechanical equivalent, performing the same office and producing the same result, the patent is infringed."

The statement of use in a claim, i.e., a radio, or a drill press, is not necessarily a limitation. The transfer or adaptation of the patented device to a similar sphere of action where it performs substantially the same function is not sufficient to avoid infringement. The Court noted in *Western Electric Co.* v. *LaRue*, 139 U.S. 601, 606, that:

"...the application of the patented device to another use, where such new application does not involve the exercise of the inventive faculty, is as much an infringement as though the new machine were an exact copy of the old." Citing cases.

Test of Infringement by a Process. A patent for a machine is directed to a mechanical device or combination of mechanical powers and devices to perform some function or to produce a certain effect or result. The mechanical device is accordingly defined in the claims in terms of the structure of which it is composed to produce this effect or result or function.

Where the obtention of the result or effect is expressed in terms of steps in the operation, as when produced by chemical action, the operation or application of some machine, element or power of nature, interaction of one substance with another, the resulting claim is called a process claim. Obviously, the two may overlap, because a machine can be invented particularly designed to carry out the operation or process based on a certain structure or combination of parts. Nonetheless, separate patents can be granted, one for the process and one for the apparatus, and each will to some extent be subject to the other.

Just as a mechanical patent is not granted for a principle and is definable in claims only in terms of the structure by which a principle is put into operation, so also a process patent is not granted for a principle, but is defined in claims only in terms of the steps which are employed to carry out a principle or apply it to effect a useful result.

Tilghman v. *Proctor*, 102 U.S. 707, 728, 1880, dealt with the infringement of a patent for a process for producing free fatty acids and a solution of glycerine from those fatty and oily bodies of animal and vegetable origin which contain glycerine as their base. The claim defined the invention in these terms:

"The manufacturing of fatty acids and glycerine from fatty bodies by the action of water at a high temperature and pressure."

The defendants advanced several reasons to show that their process did not conflict with the patented one. They asserted they did not use the apparatus described in the patent, but the Court found that they used apparatus strong enough to sustain the pressure necessary to prevent water from being converted into steam, and accordingly did practice the process defined. They asserted also that they used a different method for maintaining a mixture of water and fat, but the Court found that this variation was of no consequence. The method or apparatus for effecting the continued mixture used by the defendants, the Court thought, might be patentable in itself, but that did not avoid infringement. The defendants argued that they used not water alone in admixture with fat but also added lime in amounts ranging from 4 to 7 per cent. On this point, the Court said:

"...the process of Tilghman, modified or unmodified by the supposed improvement, underlies the operation performed in the defendants' boilers." p. 732.

The defendants urged that they heated the vessel, not by an outside application of heat, as described in the patent, but by the introduction of superheated steam. The Court answered this as follows:

"But we think that this does not alter the essential character of the process. The heating by steam is clearly an equivalent method to that of heating by an external fire."

The defendants also argued that they used only a low temperature, 310° F, as compared to 612° F in the patent. The Court held as follows:

"The precise degree of heat, as we have seen, is not of the essence of the patent. The specification only claims that a high degree of heat, such as would be sufficient to melt lead, is most effective and rapid in producing the desired result, . . . It is probably true, as contended for by the defendants, that by the use of a small portion of lime, the process can be performed with less heat than if none is used. It may be an improvement to use the lime for that purpose; but the process remains substantially the same. The patent cannot be evaded in that way." (pp. 732-733)

In short, the defendants employed the basic essentials of the patented invention, and were therefore held to infringe the claims.

Test of Infringement by Article of Manufacture or Composition of Matter. It is customary to claim a chemical product in terms of its formula, physical and chemical properties, or the process by which it is prepared. The claim can also define the product by reciting the steps of the process by which it was prepared. If the latter, to infringe the claim, the process set forth in the claims must be carried out, and thus the infringement of this type of claim is determined by the principles of infringement of process claims, as set forth in the preceding section. If the claimed definition is in terms of structure or chemical and physical properties, then to infringe the compound must correspond to the structure or properties set forth. Absent any express limitation in the claim to the contrary, the compound or product will infringe the claim if it meets the requirements set out in the claim, unless the compound has additional properties or structural features which so change the compound or product that it no longer has the essential characteristics of the invented compound. A substituent might render the compound patentably distinct from the compounds disclosed in the patent, due to additional properties it conferred, but this would have no bearing upon the question of infringement, if the compound otherwise had the properties of the claimed compounds.

Infringement of claims to chemical compositions or mixtures composed of two or more ingredients is determined by application of the same principles. For infringement, each of the ingredients must conform to the definition in the claim. If so, it is not important that it is there allegedly for a different purpose.

Omission of one or more of the material ingredients of the composition avoids infringement, but omission of an immaterial ingredient does not, just as in the case of a patent for a machine. Thus, in *Samson Granite Co.* v. *Crozier-Straub, Inc.*, 41 F.2d 628, 632, 1930, the claims were for a building block composed of cement, coarse and fine coal, and cinder and ash retaining all of their original mass. The gist of the invention was the use of furnace ash, without sifting or selection, in the manufacture of cement building blocks from an aqueous mix of the components. The defendant carefully screened the cinder and ash to remove all particles smaller than $3/16$ inch in diameter and more than $3/4$ inch. He then crushed the latter to about $1/2$-inch diameter for recombination with the over $3/16$-inch material. The exact proportion of the fines was controversial, but apparently ranged from 8 to 10 per cent. The Court held:

"...if after removal of a part of the mass the remainder functions substantially as the original mass would function before any of it was withdrawn, the composition is substantially that of the patent. The mere discarding of some of the mass without changing the functional alignment of its elements will not avoid the patent.

In *Lampus* v. *Crozier-Straub*, 41 F.2d 746, CA 3 1930, the defendant added slag to the mixture. The Court found that the commercial block had all the characteristics of the patented blocks and held that the addition of slag to the mix did not avoid infringement.

Determination of Infringement: Test of Non-Identity but Substantial Equivalency

The courts have clearly recognized that there are many situations in which to per-

mit an imitation of a patented invention which does not copy every literal detail would be to convert the protection of the patent grant into a hollow and useless thing.

"The essence of the doctrine is that one may not practice a fraud on a patent. Originating almost a century ago in the case of Winans v. Denmead, 15 How. 330, it has been consistently applied by this Court and the lower federal courts, and continues today ready and available for utilization when the proper circumstances for its application arise. 'To temper unsparing logic and prevent an infringer from stealing the benefit of an invention' a patentee may invoke this doctrine to proceed against the producer of a device 'if it performs substantially the same function in substantially the same way to obtain the same result.' " *Graver Tank & Mfg. Co.* v. *Linde Air Products Co.*, 339 U.S. 605, 607, 1950.

The Court noted that the doctrine is applied in cases involving mechanical or chemical equivalents, in devices or compositions. What constitutes equivalency is determined against the context of the patent, the prior art, and the particular circumstances of the case. Complete identity for every purpose and in every respect is not required, consideration being given to the purpose of the invention, the qualities of the ingredients which it has combined with the other ingredients, the function which it is intended to perform, and whether persons skilled in the art would have known of the equivalency.

In the *Graver* case the claims called for electric welding fluxes composed of alkaline earth metal silicates and calcium fluoride. The allegedly infringing composition contained silicates of calcium and manganese and calcium fluoride. Manganese silicate is not an alkaline earth metal silicate, and the alleged infringer argued no infringement on this basis. The Court held:

"It is difficult to conceive of a case more appropriate for application of the doctrine of equivalents. The disclosures of the prior art made clear that manganese silicate was a useful ingredient in welding compositions. Specialists familiar with the problems of welding compositions understood that manganese was equivalent to and could be substituted for magnesium in the composition of the patented flux and their observations were confirmed by the literature of chemistry. Without some explanation or indication that Lincolnweld (the manganese silicate flux) was developed by independent research, the trial court could properly infer that the accused flux is the result of imitation rather than experimentation or invention. Though infringement was not literal, the changes which avoid literal infringement are colorable only. We conclude that the trial court's judgment of infringement respecting the four flux claims was proper, and we adhere to our prior decision on this aspect of the case."

In *University of Illinois Foundation* v. *Block Drug Co. et al.*, 112 USPQ 204, 241 F.2d 6 CA 7 1957, the Court found that a dentifrice composition containing thirteen per cent urea infringed a claim calling for from one to ten per cent of urea together with other ingredients. The Court noted that, even with such changes in percentage, the result was the same, arrived at in the same manner, and thus held the composition was the equivalent of the patentee's composition.

The range of equivalents to which a patent may be entitled may depend upon several factors: If the patent is for a limited improvement in a crowded art, the patent may be entitled only to an extremely limited range of equivalents. *Graham* v. *Cockshutt Farm Equipment, Inc.*, 117 USPQ 439, 441, CA 5 1958.

"As the principle is commonly put, the inventor is entitled to a range of equivalents commensurate with the scope of his invention: broad if his invention is broad; narrow if his advance is a small one in a crowded field." *Nelson* v. *Batson*, 138 U.S.P.Q. 552, 554, CA 9, 1963.

Thus, in the case of a combination patent using known elements, the construction of the claims, to avoid invalidity, must be restricted so as to exclude all which was disclosed by prior patents or in public use or known to the public. *Computing Scale Co.* v. *Automatic Scale Co.*, 204 U.S. 609, 1907.

No permissible range of equivalents can expand a claim to cover the use of that which was not new. *International Harvester Co.* v. *Killeser Mfg. Co.*, 67 F.2d 54, 61 CA 9 1933.

Moreover, it is well settled that the doctrine of equivalents cannot be used to expand claims to cover elements or equivalents of an element that have been specifically eliminated from the claims and which the patentee is precluded from claiming by the doctrine of file wrapper estoppel.

"It is a rule of patent construction consistently observed that a claim in a patent as allowed must be read and interpreted with reference to claims that have been cancelled or rejected, and the claims allowed cannot by construction be read to cover what was thus eliminated from the patent..." *Schriber-Schroth Co.* v. *Cleveland Trust Co.*, 311 U.S. 211, 220, 221, 1940.

This doctrine of estoppel was applied to a claim directed to a material selected from the group consisting of cellulose acetate and cellulose nitrate, which was inserted in lieu of broader claims in order to obtain an allowance. *Parmelee Pharmaceutical Co.* v. *Zink*, 126 USPQ 467, DC WMo 1956. The District Court held that what the patentee had disclaimed before the Patent Office, he could not regain by recourse to the doctrine of equivalents. The Court of Appeals, Eighth Circuit, 128 USPQ 271, 277, 1961, held that the defendant's film of shellac performed the same function in retarding salt formation as the claimed film of cellulose acetate or cellulose nitrate. The Court noted, however, that the prior art, as disclosed by the record and the file wrapper, was crowded, so that the patent in question was not a pioneer patent and the doctrine of equivalents was inapplicable to the defendant's use of shellac.

Contributory Infringement

The doctrine of contributory infringement has been a part of our law for about eighty years. The doctrine has been characterized as an expression of both law and morals, because it seeks to prevent the appropriation of another's patented invention. It seeks also to enjoin those who assist infringement by supplying someone else with the means and directions for infringing a patent. A person who makes a special part that is the heart of a patented invention and supplies it to others with directions to complete the invention is obviously appropriating benefit of the patented invention.

Giles S. Rich has pointed out that, historically, the doctrine of contributory infringement developed to prevent the evasion of patents by using only a part of the invention as claimed, to counteract the undue restriction upon the patentee from his having to accept claims that define not only what was invented but also the scope of the patent monopoly, and to soften the effect of the rule that a claim is not infringed unless the defendant uses every feature recited in the claim.

The first reported case of contributory infringement is believed to be *Wallace* v. *Holmes,* 29 Fed. cases 74, No. 17, 100, 1871. The claims there called for a complete kerosene lamp, including the chimney, the invention being the burner. The defendant sold the lamp of the invention minus its chimney, and asserted noninfringement on the ground that the chimney was an element specified in the claims. The court granted recovery.

On the other hand, where the element sold was capable of use not only in the patented invention but also for other purposes, the alleged infringer was absolved from infringement. The first reported case in this category is *Saxe* v. *Hammond,* 21 Fed. cases 593, No. 12, 411, 1875. This became the principle of *Carbice Corp. of America* v. *American Patents Development Corp. et al.,* 283 U.S. 27, 30, 31, 1931, that an inventor cannot use his patent to control the manufacture, use or sale of an unpatented material:

"The invention claimed is for a particular kind of package employing solid carbon dioxide in a new combination. If the patent is valid the owner can, of course, prohibit entirely the manufacture, sale, or use of such packages ... But it may not exact as the condition of a license that unpatented materials used in connection with the invention shall be purchased only from the licensor; and if it does so, relief against one who supplies such unpatented materials will be denied. The limited monopoly to make, use, and vend an article may not be 'expanded by limitations as to materials and supplies necessary to the operation of it.'"

The doctrine of contributory infringement was written into the patent statute for the first time in the Patent Act of 1952, to codify in statutory form the principles of contributory infringement established by the courts up to that time and, at the same time, eliminate the doubt and confusion as to the scope of contributory infringement. The doctrine is set out in three separate paragraphs of Section 271:

"(b) Whoever actively induces infringement of a patent shall be liable as an infringer.

"(c) Whoever sells a component of a patented machine, manufacture, combination or composition, or material or apparatus for use in practicing a patented process, constituting a material part of the invention, knowing the same to be especially made or especially adapted for use in an infringement of such patent, and not a staple article or commodity of commerce suitable for substantial noninfringing use, shall be liable as a contributory infringer.

"(d) No patent owner otherwise entitled to relief for infringement or contributory infringement of a patent shall be denied relief or deemed guilty of misuse or illegal extension of the patent right by reason of his having done one or more of the following: (1) derived revenue from acts which if performed by another without his consent would constitute contributory infringement of the patent; (2) licensed or authorized another to perform acts which if performed without his consent would constitute contributory infringement of the patent; (3) sought to enforce his patent rights against infringement or contributory infringement."

Paragraph (c) recites the principle of contributory infringement and is concerned with the usual situation in which contributory infringement arises. The component of a patented machine, manufacture, combination or composition, or material or apparatus sold for use in practicing a patented process must constitute a material part of the invention, and must be known to be especially made or especially adapted for use in the infringement, before there can be contributory infringement. Likewise, the sale of staple articles of commerce suitable for noninfringing use does not constitute contributory infringement.

Section 271 (b) recites in broad terms that one who induces infringement is likewise an infringer. Report of the Committee on the Judiciary Revision of Title 35 U.S.C. May 12, 1952. It is important to note that the word "induces" connotes an act that is effective and results in direct infringement. A mere attempt to induce infringement is insufficient, as for example, a solicitation of orders which are not filled, advertising, and the like. *Hautau et al.* v. *Kearney & Trecker Corp.*, 124 USPQ 28, DCE Mich 1959. The term "actively induces infringement" therefore is intended to cover only situations in which actual infringement results.

Section 271(d) represents an effort to restrict the application of the misuse doctrine to contributory infringement. The section says in effect that a patentee who merely does what he is authorized to do by Section 271 paragraph (c) of the patent statute is not guilty of misuse of the patent. The first clause of Section (d) states that the patent owner shall not be denied relief for infringement or contributory infringement or deemed guilty of misuse simply because he derived revenue from acts which would constitute contributory infringement. The second clause states that he is not guilty of misuse if he licensed or authorized another to perform such acts, and the third states that he is not guilty of misuse if he seeks to enforce his patent rights against infringement or contributory infringement. In short, a patentee is not deemed to have misused his patent simply by reason of doing anything authorized by Section 271.

As an illustration of Section 271(b), a defendant was held to be guilty of inducing infringement by selling a component part of a patented device and demonstrating how that part could be used to recreate the original patented device. *Fromberg, Inc.* v. *Thornhill et al.*, 137 USPQ 84, CA 5 1963.

As an illustration of Section 271(c) we may consider *Dr. Salisbury's Laboratories* v. *I. D. Russell Co. Laboratories*, 101 USPQ 212 WMo 1953, aff. 101 USPQ 137, 212 F.2d 414, CA 8 1954. The patent in question called for a composition of two substances, water and the compound 3-nitro-4-hydroxyphenyl arsenic acid, for controlling and preventing coccidiosis, a disease common in fowl. The compound was neither a patented nor a patentable compound, and it was sold generally as a chemical. It was sold by the defendants in both powder and tablet form, for mixing with water by the user. The Court held that Section 271(c) did not effect a change in the law, and that the sale

of a nonpatentable component of a patented combination under 271(c) does not give rise to a cause of action for infringement. Though subsection (c) defines a contributory infringer to be anyone who sells a component of a patented machine or composition knowing it to be especially adapted for infringing use, it specifically provides that said components not be a staple commodity of commerce suitable for substantial noninfringing use. The Court held that the unpatented 3-nitro-4-hydroxyphenyl arsenic acid was a staple commodity which did not lose its identity as a common raw material merely because of its sale by the defendant.

On the other hand, it was held that the sale of components especially designed for use in patented staplers constituted contributory infringement. *Sasser* v. *Senco Products, Inc.*, 242 F.2d 565, CA 6 1957.

Repair, Replacement or Reconstruction

To what extent can the owner of a patented machine, article of manufacture, or composition, operating under authority from the patentee, repair, replace or reconstruct parts of the patented invention in order to keep it in use? It is quite clear that repairs or reconstruction or replacement can, in the course of time, lead to a complete replacement of every part of the original embodiment of the invention.

In *Wilson* v. *Rousseau*, 4 How. 646, the Supreme Court held that a complete reconstruction or renewal of the patented invention is not permitted. If, however, the repair is less than reconstruction, and is to maintain the patented invention in operating condition, then it is recognized as repair or restoration and is permitted. Here the machine in question was a planing machine which, properly made, would last in use for several years, but its cutting knives wore out and had to be replaced every sixty to ninety days. Obviously, the use of the machine depended on the replacement of the knives, and hence the Court held that frequent replacing of the knives, according to the intention of the inventor, was not a reconstruction of the invention, but only repair or restoration of as much of it as was absolutely necessary to restore the machine to what it was in the beginning of its use, or before that part of it had been worn out. Unless the knives were replaced, the invention would have been of little use both to the inventor and to others. Indeed, the Court noted that the replacement of parts that wear out did not alter the identity of the machine but preserved it, though every part of its original material might not be in it.

In *United States* v. *Aluminum Company of America*, 148 F.2d 416, 425, CA 2 1945, the Court pointed out that the patentee cannot prevent those to whom he sells his invention from reconditioning parts worn by use, unless they in fact make a new article.

The principle was reemphasized by the Supreme Court in *Aro Mfg. Co., Inc.* v. *Convertible Top Replacement Co.*, 128 USPQ 354, 1961, 365 U.S. 336, 1961. The Court held that a license to use a patented combination included the right to preserve its fitness for use, so far as it may be affected by wear or breakage. Maintenance and use as a whole of the patented combination through replacement of a spent unpatented element does not constitute reconstruction. Reconstruction of a patented entity constitutes such a complete reconstruction of the entity as to in fact make a new article. Replacement of individual unpatented parts, one at a time, whether of the same part repeatedly or different parts successively, was no more than the lawful right of the owner to repair his property. Accordingly, the Court held that replacement of a fabric top, an unpatented element of the combination patent covering a convertible automobile top construction, including the fabric top, did not constitute either direct or contributory infringement.

On the other hand, if the original use was unlicensed and thus an infringement, then repair is equally without authority and constitutes infringement. *Aro Mfg. Co., Inc.* v. *Convertible Top Replacement Co.*, 141 USPQ 681, 685, 1964.

The complete replacement of the essential features of the invention has been held in the Fifth Circuit to be reconstruction and, accordingly, contributory infringement. *Fromberg, Inc.* v. *Thornhill et al.*, 137 USPQ 84, CA 5 1963. The patented combination in this case was a hollow metal tube and a compressed, expansible rubber cylindrical plug inserted in the hollow tube for its whole length, for insertion in a tubeless tire to repair a puncture. By a special tool, the assembly was inserted into the hole in the body of the tire, the rubber plug was pushed out of the metal tube, and the tube withdrawn from the tire. The hole was thus filled with the rubber plug, which, being released from the compression of the tube, expanded considerably to seal the hole.

The defendant in this case sold what was called a "miracle plug," a single piece of compressible rubber, designed for insertion into the empty tube resulting from use of the patented invention. By first inserting the tail into the empty tube, the "miracle plug" could be forcibly drawn into the tube for its full length, after which a device identical with the original patented combination was created.

The Court noted that the issue of infringement turned on the question of whether the new article constituted repair or reconstruction, and held it to be reconstruction.

However, the Ninth Circuit, in *Fromberg, Inc.* v. *Gross Mfg. Co., Inc.*, 140 USPQ 641, 1964, held that it was not contributory infringement to sell a Fromberg package of metal tube and plug plus a supply of plugs to be inserted in the empty Fromberg tube. The Court indicated its disagreement with the earlier case and pointed out that, in its view, the tube was not intended to have and did not have a "single shot function." It thus treated the case as one of permissible repair.

In *Wilbur-Ellis Co.* v. *Kuther*, 141 USPQ 703, 1964, the Supreme Court held that the modification of a machine, originally designed to pack fish into cans of one-pound size, so as to make it possible to pack in five-ounce cans, was insufficient to constitute reconstruction and, therefore, within the patent rights purchased, since size was not the invention and there was no restriction on size in the license.

Cross-references: *Accounting after Infringement, Act of 1952—Patents, Infringement Suits, Claim Interpretation and Patent Construction, Plant Patents.*

INFRINGEMENT CLAIMS AGAINST U.S. GOVERNMENT—SETTLEMENTS

Harry M. Saragovitz

For details of procedure in infringement suits against the Government in the Court of Claims, see the succeeding article "Infringement Suits."

Administrative Claim or Suit?

At the present time only the three military departments (Army, Navy, and Air Force), Defense Supply Agency, National Aeronautics and Space Administration (NASA), and the Atomic Energy Commission have the authority to negotiate and settle patent infringement claims before suit is filed against the Government in the U.S. Court of Claims.

Where a Government agency infringes a patent and the law does not specifically provide that agency with authority to negotiate and settle such a claim, it may be possible to bring such a claim before the General Accounting Office of the Government. Saragovitz, 42 JPOS 111, 1960. The other alternative, which is available in all situations of this type, is the filing of a suit for patent infringement against the Government in the Court of Claims under 28 U.S.C. 1498. Here too, it is possible to negotiate a settlement with the Government through the Department of Justice at any time after suit is filed.

Where it is possible for the patent owner to bring an "administrative claim" against an Executive branch of the Government, a decision must be made as to whether it is more advantageous to the patent owner to bring such claim and attempt a negotiated settlement or to file the suit. Most lawyers will agree that a negotiated settlement is more advantageous to both parties because it is far less expensive to file and maintain than a suit in the U.S. Court of Claims. Even if the administrative claim is unsuccessful, suit may still be filed in the Court of Claims, taking advantage of the "Tolling Statute," 35 U.S.C. 286, which tolls the 6 year statute of limitations contained in 28 U.S.C. 1498. Another advantage of filing an administrative claim rather than a suit in the Court of Claims is that the patent is not placed in jeopardy, with the danger of the patent being declared invalid as a result of the litigation. In addition, a claimant is not required to exhaust his administrative remedies before filing suit. Thus the claimant may file suit during the pendency of an administrative claim, if for any reason he believes that his interests would best be served by breaking off negotiations and filing suit.

What Constitutes a Patent Infringement Claim Against the Government?

The law is vague as to what actually constitutes an "administrative claim." 10 U.S.C. 2386 states merely that the military departments are authorized to use current procurement funds to buy releases from patent infringement claims and to purchase licenses for the future etc. but does not define or set forth how such a claim is to be lodged. The Atomic Energy Act and the statute establishing the National Aeronautics and Space Administration (NASA) are also silent as to the definition of an "administrative" patent infringement claim. 35 U.S.C. 286 tolls the 6 year statute of limitations in the Court of Claims if a claim has been received by a government agency but does not define "claim" other than to state that it must be "in writing."

The three military departments have agreed that a charge of patent infringement, in order to be considered as a claim, and operative to place the "Tolling" Statute (35 U.S.C. 286) in effect, must include the following essential elements:

(1) An allegation in writing that claimant's patent has been infringed by the manufacture, use, or disposition by the Government agency

(2) A statement of the patent or patents alleged to be infringed.

(3) A request for compensation for the rights alleged to be infringed

(4) A showing as to how at least one claim of the patent covers the alleged infringing device

(5) Designation of the alleged infringing equipment together with technical data thereon

If the possible infringing equipment is classified information and not available to the public, then the information requested in item 5 cannot be given. Instead, a statement by claimant is required as to the basis for his belief that his patent is being infringed.

Administrative claim procedure is unlike court procedure in that there is no burden of proof upon the patent owner to prove his case. He merely submits a communication containing the required elements to the agency or agencies involved and waits to hear from them. The receipt of a claim by a Government agency authorized to handle such claims starts an expensive and time consuming procedure including: (1) Title search, (2) Extent-of-use investigation, and (3) Validity investigation (if extent-of-use investigation is positive).

The claimant may be asked for further information such as: (1) Licenses existing under the patent and copies thereof, (2) Litigation in which the patent is or was involved, (3) Others (including government agencies) charged with infringement, (4) Other information pertinent to the claim.

Indemnity Situations

Let us assume that the "X" Company has lodged an administrative claim for patent infringement with the Department of the Army, alleging that certain radio receivers manufactured for the Government by the "A" Company infringe a patent owned by the X Company. After acknowledgment of receipt of the communication (assuming all the elements of a claim were present), the claim is taken up in the order of receipt. Let us say that investigation reveals that the patent was actually infringed and appears to be valid. Then Department of the Army patent personnel will contact the claimant and request a conference to determine whether a settlement may be negotiated. Such a settlement could include a release for past infringement coupled with a future license on a running royalty basis. If it appears that no more of this item will

be purchased again, then a release for past infringement is all that is necessary. Should terms agreeable to both sides be worked out at a negotiation session (or by correspondence) then a contract of settlement is drawn up and executed by both parties. The matter is thus ended.

The foregoing is an example of the least complicated of situations. Let us go further and assume that the radio receivers were manufactured for the Department of the Army by the A Company, under a contract in which the A Company has agreed to indemnify the Government for liability arising from patent infringement in carrying out the contract. We now have a complicating factor because the Government should not settle such a claim without the consent and payment by the indemnifier. In other words, if the Government agency, after a careful and thorough investigation, believes it would be to the best interest of the Government to settle and the A Company, for any reason at all refuses to consent and pay for such settlement, the Government agency has no alternative other than to deny the claim, thus forcing the X Company to file suit in the U.S. Court of Claims. However, if the A Company (the Government contractor and indemnifier) is bankrupt or his share of the over-all infringing procurement is very small, it is possible for the Government agency to release the indemnifier and settle the entire claim. Release of an indemnifier is permitted infrequently and only when such an action is in the best interest of the Government.

Let us look at another situation, one where there is no patent indemnity article in the prime contract with the Government but the subcontractor who manufactures the allegedly infringing material for the prime contractor (to be incorporated into equipment supplied to the Government) agrees to indemnify the prime contractor and its vendee against any liability arising from patent infringement. A third party beneficiary situation results which may prove quite puzzling. Although there is no privity of contract between the subcontractor and the Government, there appears to be no reason why the subcontractor indemnifier could not be joined as a party in a suit against the Government in the U.S. Court of Claims for patent infringement. The Government should not enter into any settlement agreement with the patent owner unless the subcontractor-indemnifier agrees to the settlement and is willing to pay his proportionate share. In both cases the Government may be prevented from settling a claim on very reasonable terms if the indemnifier for any reason does not agree to the settlement and pay his proportionate share.

The patent indemnity clause can be a very annoying thorn in the side of the Government. If an indemnifier were to set aside a certain amount (3 or 5 per cent, etc.) of the contract price to take care of the contingency against which he has agreed to indemnify, and no patent infringement takes place, then this contingency fund inures to the benefit of the contractor resulting in a higher price paid by the Government. If an infringement arises out of the contract and the Government believes that a settlement should be negotiated and the claimant's price appears fair, the indemnifier can wreck this whole proceeding by merely refusing to enter into the agreement and pay his share. This forces the Government to deny the claim, whereupon the claimant must sue the Government in the Court of Claims. During such a suit the Government cannot maneuver in any manner detrimental to the indemnifier; otherwise the indemnifier will be released.

Factors Entering into Negotiations for Settlement

It is considered that Government patent personnel who enter into negotiations for settlement of an administrative patent infringement claim should approach the problem as attorneys for an adversary. In other words, it is their duty to protect their client (the U.S. Government) from unwarranted or baseless claims and to attempt settlement of meritorious claims only, and those on terms favorable to the Government. The Government attorneys should proceed on the basis that they will not settle a claim merely to buy peace from a lawsuit when, in their honest judgment, there is no basis

on which to pay. The Government attorney, like his colleague in private or corporate practice, must size up the situation as to how the patent would fare in court.

In addition to the factors which enter into every negotiated settlement of this type commercially, i.e., validity, extent of use, the art or field involved, and other existing licenses under the same patent, the Government patent attorney will also point out that, as a user of large quantities, the Government would expect a lower royalty rate and that the law provides the patent owner a "reasonable compensation" for the unauthorized use of his patent but no punitive damages or injunction. It will also be pointed out that previous settlements in the same field will influence the royalty rate. In addition, for the payment of a lump sum for release of past infringement a lower rate is expected than for future procurement, unless no future license is to be purchased by the Government.

Many claimants who are unsuccessful as low bidders on Government contracts feel that they should be compensated for the loss of such business in addition to the "reasonable compensation" to be received for the patent infringement. Some firms do not realize that in those situations where invitations for bid are used, the contract must be awarded to the lowest responsible bidder even though one of the higher bidders owns a patent covering the equipment bid upon. This is the will of Congress, reiterated by the Comptroller General, in opinions reported in 122 USPQ 222, 1959; 125 USPQ 477, 1960; 127 USPQ 471, 1960; and 133 USPQ 496, 1962. Under such circumstances the only recompense the unsuccessful bidder who owns the patent can obtain is a "reasonable compensation," with no injunction against the Government.

Information Available to Patent Owners Concerning Extent of Use

If the patent owner happens to be an unsuccessful bidder on a contract, he will then have a definite idea as to the equipment involved and the amount to be manufactured. Even this information may be inaccurate because the contract may either be terminated or revised upwardly or downwardly. The Department of Commerce periodically publishes information regarding unclassified contracts entered into by various Government agencies. These periodic reports are revealing. They aid the patent owner in deciding whether or not a claim or a suit should be filed against the U.S. Government. If the equipment or subject matter happens to be security classified, this source is of no help and the claim or suit must be filed on a strong belief, based on other knowledge, that the patent is being or will be infringed.

One area in which there is difficulty in tracking down possible infringement by the Government is in the field of components supplied by a subcontractor to a prime contractor. Let us assume that the Government prime contractor is also manufacturing for commercial use and will use the same component in his commercial apparatus as in the Government equipment If the subcontractor supplies a number of the alleged infringing components to the Government prime contractor, there is no assurance that all or even 50 per cent of them will be used in manufacturing the Government equipment. If the patent owner happens to be an unsuccessful bidder to supply the components to the prime contractor, the patent owner will almost always assume that 100 per cent of the alleged infringing components will go into the Government equipment and none in the prime contractor's commercial equipment. The final end-use of such components is not always simple to determine.

At the Negotiation Table

When, during the course of an administrative claim for patent infringement, the time is ready for a conference, the Government's attorney will have had completed (a) a title search, (b) an extent-of-use investigation and, if necessary, (c) a validity investigation. If the situation is one where the Government did not copy exactly the patented equipment, process, or compound, there may be room for discussion as to why the patent claims do not cover the alleged infringing device, process, or compound. If the Government has uncovered a strong defense, the Government attorneys should be free to discuss all possible defenses including prior patents, prior publications, prior knowledge and use, file wrapper estoppel, and readability of the claims on the alleged infringing device, process, or compound. Revealing the strong defenses may convince the claimant that it would be useless for him to bring suit in the U.S. Court of Claims and that his claim is without merit.

If the Government has no adequate defenses as to validity of the patent, the conference should proceed directly to a determination as to what type of settlement and what terms would be to the best interests of both parties.

The claimant's attorney should come to the negotiation conference with a well conceived plan of settlement and not consider the session as just an opportunity to rail at the Government's alleged infringement. He should seek to settle the entire patent problem, not to approach it piecemeal. For example, if the claimant is the owner of a large group of patents but has alleged infringement of only one or two of this group, the claimant should investigate the possibility of infringement of the remainder of his patents. This approach will benefit both sides. It will permit a package deal on the entire group of patents, represent a saving to the Government so far as price is concerned, and aid the claimant in clearing up the entire matter in one settlement agreement.

The Settlement Contract

The contract of settlement negotiated between the Government and a claimant will resemble its commercial counterpart in many respects. There will also be some marked differences. All Government contracts are required by statute to include certain clauses, such as

(a) Gratuities
(b) Officials Not to Benefit
(c) Covenant Against Contingent Fees
(d) Disputes
(e) Successors and Assigns
(f) Assignment of Claim

Because of policy considerations the settlement contract will not contain

(a) A guaranteed minimum payment
(b) A guarantee to use or exploit the invention
(c) Exclusive right to make, use, or sell.

One clause which is always present in such negotiated contracts of settlement relates to the payment of sums of money by the Government. It states that such payment "shall be subject to the availability of funds." This gives pause to the claimant until it is explained that the money for such payment is taken from the yearly appropriation for the purchase of equipment and supplies. In effect the clause warns the Government contracting officer that the funds must be available when he executes the contract; otherwise he may be penalized or held criminally liable.

Denial of Claim

If after thorough investigation and consideration the Government attorneys are of the opinion that the claim is without merit, then a short letter is written to the claimant denying the claim and giving reasons for the denial. Such letters may reveal less as to the reasons for the denial than the information exchanged with the claimant during the negotiation or bargaining sessions. The receipt by the claimant of a letter of denial of a claim acts to terminate the tolling provisions of 35 U.S.C. 286 so that the claimant must make up his mind as to whether he should drop the matter or file suit in the U.S. Court of Claims.

Once suit is filed, the entire matter comes within the purview of the Department of Justice. The government agency before which the claim was originally lodged loses jurisdiction completely. As stated previously, negotiation and settlement of the suit through the Department of Justice is still possible at any time after suit has been filed in the Court of Claims. In most cases where settlement is to be achieved in a Court of Claims action the Department of Justice will obtain the opinion of the interested government agencies as to the desirability of the proposed settlement.

In any case in which an administrative claim for patent infringement has been denied and a suit has been filed in the Court of Claims, the Department of Justice is supplied with all of the material and information developed during the investigation of the claim, plus additional material and information requested by the Department.

Cf. Louis H. Le Mieux, Patent Jurisdiction of the Court of Claims, 41 JPOS 112-150, 1959, with list of cases decided.

Cross-references: *Infringement Suits, Accounting and Recoveries from Infringement Suits, Royalty-Rate and Basis.*

INFRINGEMENT SUITS

Walter H. Free

Jurisdiction and Venue

As in the case of other civil litigation, a patent infringement action must be instituted in a court having jurisdiction over both the subject matter and the entity being sued. As to subject matter, Federal District Courts have original and exclusive jurisdiction (28 U.S.C. Section 1338). *United States* v. *American Bell Telephone Co.,* 159 U.S. 548, 1895. As to jurisdiction over the entity being sued, the action must be brought in the Federal district (1) where defendant resides or (2) where defendant has committed acts of infringement *and* has a regular and established place of business. 28 U.S.C. Section 1400(b). *Fourco Glass Co.* v. *Transmirra Corp.,* 353 U.S. 222, 1957; *Blaski* v. *Hoffman,* 260 F.2d 317, CA 7 1958, aff. 363 U.S. 335, 1960. The word "resides," in the case of a corporate defendant in a patent infringement suit, means the state of incorporation. *Fourco Glass Co.* v. *Transmirra Corp.,* supra, p. 226. Thus, patent actions differ from other civil actions, wherein the defendant may be sued in any Federal judicial district where he can be served with process and, in the case of a corporate defendant, the Federal district in which it is incorporated or licensed to do business or is doing business.

To have "a regular and established place of business" within a particular Federal district, defendant must be engaged in carrying on in a continuous manner a substantial part of its ordinary business within that district and must have a place of business therein, and such place of business must be "regular and established." *Phillips* v. *Baker,* 121 F.2d 752, CA 9 1941, cert. denied, 314 U.S. 688, 1941.

In many states it is provided by statute that if a foreign corporation does not have a regular and established place of business therein, the Secretary of (that) State may accept service on behalf of the corporation. These state statutes, however, are not applicable in patent infringement actions. *Holup Industries, Inc.* v. *Wyche,* 290 F.2d 852, CA 4 1961.

Pleadings

The Complaint. A patent infringement action is begun by filing a complaint. The complaint must allege jurisdiction over the defendant, the identity of the patent in suit, plaintiff's title to the patent (or plaintiff's right to bring suit), and infringement by the defendant. Certain allegations are not necessary but are preferable if they have occurred. For example, if it is the case, the fact that defendant was given notice that it was infringing plaintiff's patent should be alleged.

The plaintiff need not allege facts which negative the defenses raised by the defendant. The grant of the patent is enough to show, until the contrary appears, that all the conditions under which an invention is patentable, in accordance with the statutes, have been met. 35 U.S.C. Section 282; *Mumm* v. *Jacob E. Decker & Sons,* 301 U.S. 168, 171, 1937.

The Answer. The defendant in his answer can plead non-infringement, invalidity or unenforceability of the patent in suit. The defendant as alleged infringer must give notice in the pleadings or otherwise in writing to the plaintiff as adverse party at least thirty days before the trial, of the country, number, date and name of the patentee of any patent and the title, date and page numbers of any publication relied upon as anticipation of a patent in suit or, as showing the state of prior knowledge in the art to which the patent pertains; and the name and address of any person who may be relied upon as the prior inventor or as having prior knowledge of, or having previously used or offered for sale, the invention of the patent in suit. 35 U.S.C. Section 282; *Edward Valves, Inc.* v. *Cameron Iron Works, Inc.,* 286 F.2d 933, CA 5 1961, mod. on other grounds, 289 F.2d 355, CA 5 1961, cert. denied, 368 U.S. 833, 1961. In the absence of such notice, proof of said matters may not be made at the trial except on such terms as the court requires. *Fairchild* v. *Poe,* 259 F.2d 329, CA 5 1958. But the plaintiff can waive the requirement of notice by failing to object to the introduction of such evidence. *Monroe* v. *Bresee,* 239 Fed. 727, CA 7 1917.

The defendant may plead alternative and inconsistent defenses in his answer. *Electric Storage Battery Co.* v. *Shimadzu,* 307 U.S. 5, 16, 1939. For example, he may plead that he is the original inventor rather than patentee and may also assert lack of invention.

Counterclaim. The issue of validity of the patent in suit may be raised by a counterclaim in an infringement suit. *Altvater* v. *Freeman,* 319 U.S. 359, 1943. The principal purpose of a counterclaim attacking the validity of a patent is to require the court to adjudicate the issue of validity even though the complaint, alleging infringement, has been dismissed by the court or voluntarily withdrawn. *Altvater* v. *Freeman,* supra; *Van Alen* v. *Aluminum Co. of America,* 43 F. Supp. 833, DC SNY 1942. A defendant may also counterclaim for infringement by the plaintiff of defendant's patent, even if the patent which is the subject of the counterclaim is not related to the patent which is the subject of the complaint. *Foundry Equipment Co.* v. *Carl-Mayer Corp.,* 10 FRD 200, DC NOhio 1950. Finally, counterclaims in a patent infringement action which raise the issue of plaintiff's monopolistic practices are permissible. *Mercoid Corp.* v. *Mid-Continent Inv. Co.,* 320 U.S. 661, 1944.

Persons Joined. Persons having a joint interest in the subject matter of the litigation and indispensable to its ultimate determination must be joined on the same side as plaintiffs or defendants. Federal

Rules of Civil Procedure, 19. Thus, a co-owner of a patent must be joined as a plaintiff in an infringement suit by the other co-owner. *Rainbow Rubber Co.* v. *Holtite Mfg. Co.*, 20 F. Supp. 913, DC Md 1937. Cf. *Aberdeen Hosiery Mills Co., Inc.* v. *Kaufman*, 18 FR Serv. 19a. 1, Case 5, DC SNY 1952. When a person who should join as a plaintiff refuses to do so, he may be made a defendant, or, in the proper case, an involuntary plaintiff. Federal Rules of Civil Procedure, 20; cf. *Gibbs* v. *Emerson Electric Mfg. Co.*, 29 F. Supp. 810, DC WMo 1939.

Because an infringement of a patent is a tort, plaintiff may sue any or all of the infringers jointly liable to him. *Conmar Products Corp.* v. *Tibony*, 63 F. Supp. 372, DC ENY 1945.

All persons may join in one action as plaintiffs or defendants whenever there is a question of law or fact common to all of the plaintiffs or defendants and the claims involved arise out of a single transaction or occurrence or series of transactions or occurrences. Federal Rules of Civil Procedure, 20. For example, joint infringers of a patent may join as defendants in one action. *Looper* v. *Colonial Coverlet Co., Inc.*, 29 F. Supp. 121, DC ETenn 1939.

Intervenors. Certain parties may be allowed to intervene in a pending patent infringement suit. Intervention is allowed either as of right or within the discretion of the court. Federal Rules of Civil Procedure, 24. Generally, when intervention is merely permissible, it must rest upon independent jurisdictional grounds. It may not depend upon the jurisdiction of the original suit. But where intervention is a matter of right, the intervenor may depend upon jurisdiction of the original suit, where ancillary to it. *Hartley Pen Co.* v. *Lindy Pen Co.*, 16 Federal Rules Decisions 141, DC SCalif 1954. A party may intervene in an action as a matter of right when the protection of his interest by the existing parties to the action is or may be inadequate and the intervenor is or may be bound by the judgment of the action. A patent owner having an interest in keeping the reputation of his patent from stain of a judgment of invalid-

ity would have such an interest. *A. L. Smith Iron Co.* v. *Dickson*, 141 F.2d 3, CA 2 1944. On the other hand, permissive intervention is permitted when applicant's claim or defense and the original action have a question of law or fact in common. *Hartley Pen Co.* v. *Lindy Pen Co.*, supra. Accordingly, a manufacturer is usually permitted to intervene in an action against his customer. *Chandler Co.* v. *Brandtjen, Inc.*, 296 U.S. 53, 1935. But see *Demulso Corporation* v. *Tretolite Co.*, 74 F.2d 805, CA 10 1934. When intervention has been granted, intervenor becomes a party to the action and is entitled to litigate fully on the merits.

Discovery

To aid the court in bringing to light all pertinent facts, define and narrow the issues, and allow the parties adequately to develop their own cases, the parties are permitted to "discover" evidence that may be helpful to their own case or weaken their adversary's case. *Foundry Equipment Co.* v. *Carl-Mayer Corp.*, 11 FRD 302, DC NOhio 1951.

There are several methods of discovery: (1) written interrogatories, Federal Rules of Civil Procedure, 33; (2) production of documents, *ibid.* 34; (3) oral or written examinations, *ibid.* 26-31; and (4) requests for admissions, *ibid.*, 36.

Interrogatories. Interrogatories are written questions relevant to the controversy served on the adverse party who must answer them in writing unless there is a valid ground for not answering them. *Babcock & Wilcox Co.* v. *North Carolina Pulp Co.*, 25 F. Supp. 596, DC Del 1938.

The party served with the interrogatories may refuse to answer them because they are not relevant to the action, *Hercules Powder Co.* v. *Rohm & Haas Co.*, 3 FRD 328, DC Del 1944; because they call for opinions, conclusions or contentions, *Stanley Works* v. *C. S. Mersick & Co.*, 1 FRD 43, DC Conn 1939; or because the subject matter of a particular interrogatory is privileged, *Zenith Radio Corp.* v. *Radio Corp. of America*, 106 F. Supp. 561, DC Del 1952. However, courts are very liberal in patent cases in requiring interrogatories to be answered in order to narrow the issues and advise each party of the exact claims made by his opponent. *Tinker & Rasor* v. *Pipeline Inspection Co., Inc.*, 16 FRD 465, DC WMo 1954.

The interrogatories should be specific and definite and not of a "fishing" character. *Pierce* v. *Submarine Signal Co.*, 25 F. Supp. 862, DC Mass 1939. Plaintiff may be required to answer defendant's interrogatories regarding dealings between him and a third party concerning the patent in suit, *V. D. Anderson Co.* v. *Helena Cotton Oil Co.*, 117 F. Supp. 932, DC EArk 1953; or regarding an alleged infringing product, *E. I. du Pont de Nemours & Co.* v. *Byrnes*, 1 FRD 34, DC SNY 1939. Plaintiff may also be required to answer interrogatories regarding the dates of his invention, the places and dates of first disclosure, the dates and places of first reduction to practice, *Chandler* v. *Cutler-Hammer, Inc.*, 31 F. Supp. 453, DC EWis 1940. Defendant may be required by interrogatories to disclose information pertaining to his alleged infringing acts, *Claude Neon Lights* v. *Rainbow Light, Inc.*, 31 F.2d 988, DC SNY 1927; or to disclose the names of those who are conducting the defense of the action, *Chenault* v. *Nebraska Farm Products*, 9 FRD 529, DC Neb 1949. Interrogatories may also inquire into the existence, description and location of documents, books or other tangible items.

Production of Documents. Having ascertained the existence, description and/or location of documents, books or other tangible items, a party may request the production of these tangible items for inspection and copying. However, production of these items may be refused if they are privileged or not relevant. *Lever Bros. Co.* v. *Procter & Gamble Mfg. Co.*, 38 F. Supp. 680, DC Md 1941.

Parties have been required to produce license agreements, *Activated Sludge, Inc.* v. *Sanitary District of Chicago*, 6 FR Serv. 34.62, Case 2, DC NIll 1942; drawings and descriptions of the invention, *Prosperity Co.* v. *St. Joe Machines*, 2 FRD 299, DC WMich 1942; product studies, *E. I. du Pont de Nemours & Co.* v. *Phillips Petroleum Co.*, 24 FRD 416, DC Del 1959; and documents bearing on the validity of the patent

in suit, *Technical Tape Corp.* v. *Minnesota Mining & Mfg. Corp.*, 18 FRD 318, DC SNY 1955.

Oral or Written Examination. Any party may take the testimony of any person including a party by oral examination. The person being examined may be examined regarding any matter, not privileged, which is relevant to the subject matter involved in the pending action. The taking of depositions of another is usually deferred until after the answer has been served. However, in an unusual or exceptional case, a deposition will be permitted to be taken before the answer is served. *Seman* v. *Leibovitz*, 1 FRD 280, DC EPa 1940. Generally, oral examinations take place in the order in which they are noticed. *Unlandherm* v. *Park Contracting Corporation*, 26 F. Supp. 743, DC SNY 1938.

Examination of a witness may also be effected by written questions similar to interrogatories. *Spaeth* v. *Warner Bros. Pictures, Inc.*, 1 FRD 729, DC SNY 1941. This method of examination is not as effective as oral examination and a party concerned that this method will harm his case may demand an oral examination. The party served with such interrogatories may utilize cross-interrogatories to attempt to insure a thorough exploration of the issues. The use of written examination is frequently reserved for examining witnesses in foreign countries when the parties are unable to examine such witnesses orally.

Requests for Admissions. The parties may request in writing admissions by each other as to the truth of relevant documents or facts within each other's knowledge. By this method the genuineness of documents may be investigated, *Booth Fisheries Corporation* v. *General Foods Corporation*, 27 F. Supp. 268, DC Del 1939, as may the truth or falsity of facts be inquired into, *Hise* v. *Lockwood Grader Corporation*, 153 F. Supp. 276, DC Neb 1957.

Summary Judgment

As in other civil actions, a summary judgment may be granted in a patent infringement action if there is no disputed issue of material fact and the moving party is entitled to a judgment as a matter of law. Federal Rules of Civil Procedure, 56; *American Securit Company* v. *Hamilton Glass Company*, 254 F.2d 889, CA 7 1958.

Since summary judgment is granted prior to a trial of the controverted issues, the judgment sought summarily can only be rendered on the pleadings, depositions, admissions and affidavits of the parties. *Allen* v. *Radio Corporation of America*, 47 F. Supp. 244, 246, DC Del 1942. After reviewing the above documents the court must be convinced that no genuine issue of fact exists before it will grant the motion for summary judgment. *Chiplets, Inc.* v. *June Dairy Products Company*, 89 F. Supp. 814, 816, DC NJ 1950. Moreover, many courts have adhered to the proposition that summary judgment may not be granted where there is the slightest doubt as to the facts. See, *Servaas & Co.* v. *Dritz*, 185 F. Supp. 61, 63, DC SNY 1960. This general policy has been particularly emphasized in patent infringement cases. *Rankin* v. *King,* 272 F.2d 254, 258, CA 9 1959. This stems from the fact that in patent cases many courts do not want to preclude the use of expert testimony from those skilled in the relevant art. *International Silver Co.* v. *Pomerantz,* 271 F.2d 69, 71, CA 2 1959. However, a court will grant summary judgment in determining the validity or infringement of a patent where the issues, without expert aid, are easily understandable by anyone of ordinary intelligence. *George P. Converse & Co.* v. *Polaroid Corp.,* 242 F.2d 116, 121, CA 1 1957.

Summary judgment has been granted on the issues of validity, *Alco Kar Kurb, Inc.* v. *Ager,* 286 F.2d 931, CA 3 1961, and infringement, *Steigleder* v. *Eberhard Faber Pencil Co.,* 176 F.2d 604, CA 1 1949, cert. denied, 338 U.S. 893, 1949. Summary judgment has also been granted dismissing an infringement suit because the patent owner was guilty of misuse of his patent. *Morton Salt Co.* v. *Suppiger Co.,* 314 U.S. 488, 1942.

Pretrial Procedure

Under the Federal Rules of Civil Procedure (Rule 16), the parties may have a pretrial conference, which has the effect of simplifying the issues, determining the necessity or desirability of amendments to the pleadings, obtaining admissions of facts and documents which will avoid unnecessary proof, limiting the number of expert witnesses to be used, and generally accelerating the disposition of the action. The nature of patent actions invites pretrial conference so as to eliminate the morass of extraneous material that might otherwise protract the length of the trial.

A Federal court can implement the Federal Rules of Civil Procedure. For example, in the Northern District of California a pretrial conference is mandatory. In that district the parties must request or respond to a request for a pretrial conference within fifteen days after the case has been transferred to the Civil Action Calendar. Each party is required to serve and file with the court a very extensive pretrial statement. On the other hand, in the Federal Eastern District of Illinois a pretrial conference is permissive and the court may on its own motion or on the motion of any party to a pending action direct the parties to appear for a pretrial conference as provided by the Federal pretrial rules. The failure of the parties to adhere to the rules governing the pretrial conference can result in the dismissal of the action. *Link* v. *Wabash Railroad Co.,* 370 U.S. 626, 1962.

In order to alleviate court congestion, a party may, and in many district courts must, give notice to the court when he is ready for trial. The case is then placed on a trial calendar after those cases for which notice has already been filed, and advances on the calendar as each case ahead of it is disposed of until it is taken for trial.

To insure compliance with the calendar rules, many courts penalize noncompliance. For example, in the Federal Southern District of New York, cases which have been pending for more than one year and are not on the trial calendar may be called for review and, in the court's discretion, dismissed for want of prosecution.

Trial by Judge or Jury

After the case proceeds to trial, its ultimate determination can be made by either a jury or a judge. The validity of the patent, infringement of it, and the amount of damages to be awarded can be made by a jury under proper instructions by the court as to the law, including a definition of the scope and meaning of the patent. Generally, a jury trial may be had in a patent infringement action only when the plaintiff seeks damages rather than an injunction or an accounting to determine defendant's liability resulting from the infringement. *Beaunit Mills, Inc.* v. *Eday Fabric Sales Corporation*, 124 F.2d 563, CA 2 1942. However, doubt has been cast upon this view by the case of *Dairy Queen* v. *Wood*, 369 U.S. 469, 1962, wherein the Supreme Court held that the right to trial by jury is not lost as to legal issues where these issues are characterized as "incidental" to equitable issues.

The plaintiff, in a patent infringement suit, can control the right to trial by jury by attention to the way in which his complaint is framed. *Shaffer* v. *Coty, Inc.*, 183 F. Supp. 662, 668, DC SCalif 1960. For example, where the patentee's complaint is equitable and the alleged infringer's counterclaim is legal, the issues of validity and infringement will be triable by a court and not a jury. *Reliable Machine Works* v. *Unger*, 144 F. Supp. 726, DC SNY 1956. If legal issues remain after the conclusion of the trial on plaintiff's complaint, a demand for a jury trial on the counterclaim may then be made and considered in the light of the status of the case at that time. *Reliable Machine Works* v. *Unger,* supra. On the other hand, if the patent owner seeks legal relief, a defendant counterclaiming for equitable relief cannot deprive the plaintiff of a jury trial. *Van Alen* v. *Aluminum Company of America*, 43 F. Supp. 833, DC SNY 1942. Similarly, the patentee's counterclaim in a declaratory judgment action will determine whether or not a jury trial can be had. If the counterclaim is equitable in nature, a jury trial will be precluded. *Telechron, Inc.* v. *Parissi*, 108 F. Supp. 897, 898, DC NNY 1953. Even though a patentee seeks legal relief and is therefore entitled to a jury trial, the court may first determine the equitable defenses raised by the defendant and dispose of the case, thereby

eliminating the need for a jury trial. *Mather* v. *Ford Motor Co.*, 40 F. Supp. 589, 592, DC EMich 1941.

Because of the technical nature of a patent infringement suit a jury trial is usually undesirable and is rarely had, even where one of the parties has a right to have the case tried by jury.

Prima Facie Proof. Once the case goes to trial it is imperative that the plaintiff make out a prima facie or complete case as to the issues raised by the pleadings in order not to have his action dismissed by the court prior to the presentation of defendant's evidence.

The plaintiff by introducing evidence of the grant of and right to sue under the patent in suit and of infringement thereof presents a prima facie case. It is not part of the plaintiff's case to negate prior publication, prior use, or other affirmative defenses that may be raised by the defendant, because the grant of letters patent is prima facie evidence that the patentee is the first inventor of the device claimed in the letters patent and of its novelty. *Mumm* v. *Jacob E. Decker & Sons*, 301 U.S. 168, 1937.

The defendant has the burden of proving the invalidity of the patent, *Mumm* v. *Jacob E. Decker & Sons*, supra. The burden of proof shifts to the defendant as to the question of infringement after the plaintiff has made out his prima facie case, and the defendant must overcome plaintiff's evidence of infringement. *Bennet* v. *Fowler*, 8 Wall. 445, 448, 1869.

The defendant can overcome the plaintiff's prima facie case by presenting evidence that the patent in suit is invalid or unenforceable against defendant or that the defendant is not guilty of infringement.

Defenses. There are basically three types of defenses, i.e. statutory (35 U.S.C. Sections 101-103, 112), non-statutory technical, and non-statutory equitable.

Several of the statutory defenses are: (a) the claimed invention is not the type of subject matter for which a patent may be obtained, *Hotel Security Checking Co.* v. *Lorraine Co.*, 160 Fed. 467, CA 2 1908; (b) the claimed invention was in public use, *Egbert* v. *Lippmann*, 104 U.S. 333, 1881, or on sale in this country longer than the permissible statutory one-year period prior to filing the patent application, *Consolidated Fruit-Jar Co.* v. *Wright*, 94 U.S. 92, 1876; (c) the claimed invention was known or used by others in this country before the invention by the applicant for patent, *Smith* v. *Hall*, 301 U.S. 216, 1937; (d) the claimed invention was abandoned, *Consolidated Fruit-Jar Co.* v. *Wright*, supra; (e) the patent does not particularly point out, and its claims do not distinctly define, the claimed invention, *United Carbon Co.* v. *Binney & Smith Co.*, 317 U.S. 228, 1942; (f) the claimed invention was previously patented or described in a printed publication in this or any foreign country, prior to the invention or discovery of the applicant, *Electric Storage Battery Co.* v. *Shimadzu*, supra; (g) the claimed invention would have been obvious to one skilled in the art, *Sinclair & Carroll Co.* v. *Interchemical Corp.*, 325 U.S. 327, 1945.

Two examples of technical non-statutory defenses are (a) the patentee attempted to enlarge the scope of his patent claim to define the allegedly infringing subject matter after it had been previously narrowed expressly or by conduct of the patentee in the Patent Office, *Schriber-Schroth Co.* v. *Cleveland Trust Co.*, 311 U.S. 211, 1940 (this is known as the doctrine of "file wrapper estoppel"); (b) the patented subject matter did not rise to the dignity of invention, *Great A. & P. Tea Co.* v. *Supermarket Equipment Corp.*, 340 U.S. 147, 1950.

Equitable defenses usually result from the prior conduct of the plaintiff directly connected to the subject matter of the controversy. Examples of equitable defenses are: (a) misuse of the patent, *Mercoid Corp.* v. *Mid-Continent Co.*, 320 U.S. 661, 1944; (b) "unclean hands" by reason of plaintiff's inequitable conduct, *Keystone Co.* v. *Excavator Co.*, 290 U.S. 240, 1933; (c) the patent owner is guilty of an inexcusable delay in instituting an infringement suit, which delay is prejudicial to the defendant, *Rome Grader & M. Corp.* v. *J. D. Adams Mfg. Co.*, 135 F.2d 617, CA 7 1943; this defense is known as "laches."

After the defendant presents his case, the plaintiff may then rebut (if he deems it necessary) the defenses interposed by evidence of the defendant. The plaintiff may also rebut any evidence offered by the defendant on the question of infringement.

Briefs. After conclusion of the trial the court will usually require each party to sum up by final argument or supply briefs, or both, stating that party's position on each facet of the controversy. Briefs and final argument should be augmented with legal support, e.g., relevant cases, statutes, etc.

Generally, briefs are filed after trial. However, a court may require the parties to submit briefs prior to the trial. *Zenith Radio Corp.* v. *Radio Corporation of America*, 16 FRD 356, DC Del 1954.

Judgment

While there has been a tendency in the past to dispose of patent cases on the ground of noninfringement, it has come to be recognized that of the two questions, validity has the greater public importance and should be fully adjudicated. *Sinclair & Carroll Co.* v. *Interchemical Corp.*, 325 U.S. 327, 1945.

When an adjudication is made regarding the validity and infringement of a patent, a judgment is entered to this effect and is binding upon the parties to the suit and those in privity with them. *Minneapolis-Honeywell Regulator Co.* v. *Thermoco, Inc.*, 116 F.2d 845, CA 2 1941.

Damages. Upon finding for the plaintiff, the court awards damages adequate to compensate for the infringement but in no event less than a reasonable royalty. 35 U.S.C. Section 284. Generally, an accounting is had to determine the liability of the defendant. Though the recovery of profits is not statutorily provided for, it has been held that the profits of an infringer are a proper factor in considering damages where other measures are not totally adequate. *Graham* v. *Jeoffroy Mfg., Inc.*, 253 F.2d 72, CA 5 1958, cert. denied, 358 U.S. 817, 1958; *Hartford National Bank and Trust Co.* v. *E. F. Drew & Co.*, 188 F. Supp. 353, DC Del 1960, aff. 290 F.2d 589, CA 3 1961, cert. denied, 368 U.S. 825, 1961.

There are two statutory limitations on the recovery of damages. First, no monetary recovery can be had for any infringement committed more than six years prior to the filing of the complaint. 35 U.S.C.

Section 286; *United States Air Conditioning Corp.* v. *Governair Corp.*, 216 F.2d 430, CA 10 1954. Secondly, the patented article must be marked with the number of the patent and the word "patent" or the abbreviation "pat." When the article does not lend itself to such marking, the requisite notice can be placed on a label affixed to the patented article, or such notice may be placed on the package containing the article. Lack of such patent marking notice results in denial of damages to the patent owner, unless the infringer is directly notified of the infringement (as by letter) and continues to infringe thereafter, in which event damages may be recovered only for infringement occurring after such direct notice. 35 U.S.C. Section 287; *General Electric Co.* v. *George J. Hagan Co.*, 40 F.2d 505, DC WPa 1929. Cf., *Allied Stamping Co., Inc.* v. *Standard Electric Equipment Corp.*, 57 F.2d 296, DC ENY 1932.

Injunction. In an infringement suit the plaintiff generally asks the Court to enjoin the defendant from further infringement.

There are two types of injunction: preliminary and permanent. The preliminary injunction may be granted before the trial of the issues and is granted to maintain the status quo between the parties. The purpose of a preliminary injunction in a patent infringement suit is not finally to determine the ultimate rights of the parties, but rather to protect their respective rights pending the final disposition of the litigation. Relief of this character is extraordinary in its nature, but available within the sound discretion of the court. Whether it should be granted or withheld depends upon the peculiar circumstances of the case. Unless the facts set forth in affidavits filed in support of the motion for a preliminary injunction disclose that the moving party will be irreparably damaged unless the injunction is granted and that the party seeking injunctive relief will likely prevail, such preliminary relief should be withheld. *Meccano, Ltd.* v. *John Wanamaker*, 253 U.S. 136, 141, 1920; *Joseph Bancroft & Sons Co.* v. *Shelley Knitting Mills, Inc.*, 268 F.2d 569, CA 3 1957.

Because granting or denying of a preliminary injunction is in the sound discretion of the trial court, it will not be disturbed upon appeal unless contrary to some rule of equity or the result of an improvident exercise of judicial discretion. *Meccano, Ltd.* v. *John Wanamaker*, supra. The party seeking a preliminary injunction bears the burden of establishing his right to such injunctive relief and the fact that irrevocable harm will result to him if it is not granted. *Joseph Bancroft & Sons Co.* v. *Shelley Knitting Mills*, supra. Courts are reluctant to grant a preliminary injunction to a patent owner unless the patent has been previously held valid in other litigation and is clearly infringed and unless the defendant's defenses have no merit. *Pacific Cage & Screen Co.* v. *Continental Cage Corp.*, 259 F.2d 87, CA 9 1958.

A preliminary injunction also may issue against a patentee as in the case where the patentee, in bad faith, circulates information regarding the alleged infringer, for the purpose of causing irrevocable injury and permanent damage to his reputation and to deprive him of customers. *Solex Laboratories, Inc.* v. *Plastic Contact Lens Co.*, 268 F.2d 637, CA 7 1959.

Generally, a plaintiff whose patent has been adjudicated as valid and infringed is entitled to a permanent injunction against further infringement by the alleged infringer and those controlled by or otherwise in privity with him. *Hazeltine Research* v. *Admiral Corp.*, 87 F. Supp. 72, DC NIll 1949, aff. 183 F.2d 953, CA 7 1950, cert. denied, 340 U.S. 896, 1950. Similarly, the patentee may be permanently enjoined from interfering with the business of the successful defendant and harassing his customers. *Kessler* v. *Eldred*, 206 U.S. 285, 1907. If a preliminary injunction has already been issued, it will be made final and perpetual by the final decree if so adjudged by the trial court.

A permanent injunction, as in the case of the preliminary injunction, can be issued against the plaintiff, restraining the plaintiff and its privies from directly or indirectly asserting the patent in any way against the defendant or his customers. *Larsen Products Corp.* v. *Perfect Paint Products, Inc.*, 191 F. Supp. 303, DC Md 1961.

A permanent injunction against one who infringes a patent can only exist during the life of the patent and expires when the patent expires. *Hughes Tool Co. v. A. F. Spengler Co.*, 73 F. Supp. 156, DC WOkla 1947, app. dism., 169 F.2d 166, CA 10 1948. Similarly, an injunction will not be granted when the patent in suit has expired. *Caterpillar Tractor Co. v. International Harvester Co.*, 120 F.2d 82, CA 3 1941.

Contempt. If, after entry of a judgment that the defendant was guilty of infringement and after enjoining him from further infringement, the defendant continues to infringe, he is guilty of contempt of court and subject to penalty. *Kiwi Coders Corp. v. Acro Tool & Die Works*, 250 F.2d 562, CA 7 1957.

Appeal

From an unfavorable final decision, the unsuccessful litigant may appeal to the Federal Court of Appeals of the circuit wherein the judgment was entered. 28 U.S.C. Section 1291. The unsuccessful litigant may also appeal from interlocutory decisions such as a judgment which is final except for an accounting, or an order of the district court granting an injunction. 28 U.S.C. Section 1292. The appeal is governed by the procedural rules which set forth when and how the appeal is taken, the evidence of the trial, its mode of compilation, etc., e.g., Federal Rules of Civil Procedure, 73.

Certiorari to Supreme Court

The unsuccessful litigant in the Court of Appeals cannot appeal to the Supreme Court, which is not an appellate court in the usual sense. Review by the Supreme Court of patent cases is discretionary.

The unsuccessful party may petition for a writ of certiorari to review the decision of the Court of Appeals. 28 U.S.C. Section 1254. The writ of certiorari may be granted before or after rendition of the judgment or decree. Generally, a writ of certiorari will not be granted by the Supreme Court in a patent infringement suit unless there is a conflict of decisions between Courts of Appeal. *General Talking Pictures Corp. v. Western Electric Co.*, 304 U.S. 175, 1938;

cf., *Muncie Gear Works, Inc. v. Outboard Marine & Mfg. Co.*, 315 U.S. 759, 1942. However, the Supreme Court has, in the absence of conflict of decisions, reviewed decisions which involve important "public interest" patent questions. See, for example, *Aro Mfg. Co. v. Convertible Top Replacement Co.*, 365 U.S. 336, 1961; *Sinclair & Carroll Co. v. Interchemical Corp.*, 325 U.S. 327, 1945. The petition to the Supreme Court is also governed by procedural rules which set forth the time for taking the petition, how the petition is taken, etc. Rules of Sup. Ct.

The Court of Appeals may also certify any question of law as to which instructions are desired, and upon such certification, the Supreme Court may give binding instructions or require the entire record to be sent up to it for a decision of the entire matter in controversy. 28 U.S.C. Section 1254.

Declaratory Judgment

Distinguished procedurally from the traditional patent infringement action, where the owner of a patent or one otherwise entitled to sue thereunder institutes the action, is a declaratory judgment proceeding where one accused of infringement may sue the accusing patent owner.

Notwithstanding the procedural differences, the Federal district courts have jurisdiction over a declaratory judgment action to adjudicate questions of patent invalidity and noninfringement, since it is an action arising under the patent laws of the United States. 28 U.S.C. Section 1338(a); *Grip Nut Co. v. Sharp*, 124 F.2d 814, CA 7 1941.

Jurisdiction and Venue. Although jurisdictional requirements are the same as in patent infringement actions, the same venue provisions do not apply to a declaratory judgment action involving a patent, although the general venue provision still applies, i.e., the defendant-respondent may be sued in virtually any Federal Judicial District wherein he can be served with summons (28 U.S.C. Section 1391). *De Luxe Game Corp. v. Wonder Products Co.*, 157 F. Supp. 696, DC SNY 1957. Therefore, in a declaratory judgment action, even a corporation may be sued in any Federal district wherein it is doing business, whether or not it has a regular and established place of business within that district. *Metlon Corp.* v. *Dow Chemical Co.*, 182 F. Supp. 546, DC SNY 1959.

Justiciable Controversy. The existence of an actual controversy which is judicially determinable is a necessary prerequisite to the court's jurisdiction over an action for declaratory judgment.

Pleadings and Pretrial Procedure. The general rules of pleading are applicable to an action for declaratory relief. However, the pleadings must show that an actual controversy is presented. *Federal Tel. & Radio Corp.* v. *Associated Tel. & Tel. Co.*, 169 F.2d 1012, CA 3 1948, cert. denied, 355 U.S. 859, 1948.

Instead of instituting the action, the alleged infringer may await suit and seek declaratory relief in a counterclaim. *Altvater* v. *Freeman*, 319 U.S. 359, 1943.

Cross-claims, third-party claims, joinder of parties, intervention of parties, pretrial procedure including discovery, are governed by the same Federal Rules of Civil Procedure that are applicable to patent infringement suits.

Summary judgment procedure is also applicable in a declaratory judgment action. *Miller* v. *Stiffel Company*, 158 F. Supp. 762, DC SNY 1958.

Trial by Jury or Judge. The Declaratory Judgment Act preserved the right of jury trial for both parties. Federal Rules of Civil Procedure, 57; *Beacon Theatres, Inc.* v. *Westover*, 359 U.S. 500, 504, 1959. Determining whether or not a defendant in a declaratory judgment action is entitled to a trial by jury depends upon whether he would have been entitled to a jury trial had he brought the action. Thus, where the patent owner counterclaims for relief legal in nature and demands a jury trial, he will be entitled to a jury trial though the complaint seeks equitable relief. *General Motors Corp.* v. *California Research Corp.*, 9 FRD 565, DC Del 1949. As noted above, it is the patent owner's complaint in a patent infringement suit that determines the method of trial and not the accused infringer's counterclaim for declaratory relief. *Van Alen* v.

Aluminum Co. of America, 43 F. Supp. 833, DC SNY 1942.

Though the parties are reversed in a declaratory judgment action the burden of proof does not shift. The defendant patent owner still has the burden of proving infringement (*Philip A. Hunt Co.* v. *Mallinckrodt Chemical Works*, 72 F. Supp. 865, DC SNY 1947, aff., 177 F.2d 583, CA 2 1949) while the defendant has the burden of proving the invalidity of the patent (*Cummings* v. *Moore*, 202 F.2d 145, CA 10 1953) by introducing into evidence the statutory and non-statutory defenses referred to previously.

Judgment. Upon the determination of noninfringement or invalidity, the declaratory judgment plaintiff is entitled to injunctive relief restraining the defendant from harassing its customers and itself with suits and notices of infringement, providing a proper basis is laid in the pleadings and proof for the granting of such relief. *Vermont Structural Slate Co.* v. *Tatko Bros. Slate Co.*, 253 F.2d 29, CA 2 1958. A patent owner who continues to harass the manufacturer or its customers after he has been enjoined from doing so will be in contempt of court. In addition, damages, accounting, or other relief may be sought and obtained in the same petition for declaratory relief (29 U.S.C. Section 2202). *E. Edelman & Co.* v. *Triple-A Specialty Co.*, 88 F.2d 852, CA 7 1937, cert. denied, 300 U.S. 680, 1937. See also, Borchard, Declaratory Judgments, p. 817, 2nd Ed., 1941.

Appeal and Certiorari. Review of a decision in a declaratory judgment action by the Supreme Court is governed by the same general statute and rules as govern the granting of certiorari in suits for patent infringement actions. Appeals to Courts of Appeal are governed by the same statutes and rules as are applicable in patent infringement suits.

Suits Against the Government for Patent Infringement

Jurisdiction and Venue. Exclusive jurisdiction of infringement claims against the Government has been conferred upon the

Court of Claims by Act of Congress. 28 U.S.C. Section 1491. Whenever an invention, covered by a United States patent, is used or manufactured by or for the United States without license of the owner or other lawful right to use or manufacture the same, the patent owner's sole remedy shall be by action against the United States in the Court of Claims for the recovery of his reasonable and entire compensation for such use and manufacture. 28 U.S.C. Section 1498(a).

If a suit against the Government is improperly brought in a Federal district court, the district court will usually on its own motion transfer the case to the Court of Claims where the case will proceed as if it had been filed initially in the Court of Claims on the date it was filed in the district court. 28 U.S.C. Section 1406(c). The power of the district court to transfer cases precludes inequitable dismissal of cases that could no longer be brought in the Court of Claims because of the Statute of Limitations.

The converse is also true. Thus, a case erroneously filed in the Court of Claims can be transferred to a proper Federal district court where the case proceeds as if it had been filed initially in the district court on the date it was filed in the Court of Claims. 28 U.S.C. Section 1506.

The patent owner cannot sue a manufacturer who sells to the Government. His sole remedy is against the Government. *Western Electric Co.* v. *Hammond*, 135 F.2d 283, CA 1 1943. Therefore, a contractor who manufactured something for the Government is relieved of liability for infringement. *Bereslavsky* v. *Esso Standard Oil Co.*, 175 F.2d 148, CA 4 1949. See, *Identification Devices* v. *United States*, 121 F.2d 895, CA DC 1941, cert. denied, 314 U.S. 615, 1941.

Pleadings. There are no technical forms of pleadings required by the Court of Claims. The petition need only set forth a statement of the facts on which each claim is based, including the facts upon which the Court's jurisdiction depends, and the claim or claims of the patent or patents alleged to be infringed by the Government. Ct. Cls. Rule 12.

The Government must set forth its defenses in its answer, except that the defenses of lack of jurisdiction and failure to state a proper claim may be made by motion. Failure to assert defenses constitutes a waiver of such defenses with the exception of the aforementioned defenses. Ct. Cls. Rule 16.

Discovery. The parties can "discover" evidence in a manner similar to a litigant in a civil action for patent infringement. Upon motion of any party showing good cause therefor and upon notice to all other parties, the Court of Claims can order any party to produce and permit the inspection and copying or photographing of any designated documents, papers, books or other tangible things that are relevant. Ct. Cls. Rule 26.

If the plaintiff proceeds under the above motion for discovery, the Government can contend that the document sought is privileged. But this privilege is not an absolute privilege. *Kaiser Aluminum & Chemical Corp.* v. *United States*, 157, F. Supp. 939, Ct. Cls. 1958. On its own motion the Court of Claims may at any time "call" upon any department or agency of the United States for any information or papers it deems necessary. 28 U.S.C. Section 2507(a). And upon motion by any party for call, the Court of Claims may order the adverse party to deliver up to the moving party for purposes of discovery or for use as evidence at the trial any non-privileged documents, papers, books, or other tangible things that are relevant to the issues of the case. Ct. Cls. Rule 27(b).

The plaintiff's motion for call may be denied if the head of the Governmental department or agency deems compliance injurious to the public interest. *Kaiser Aluminum & Chemical Corp.* v. *United States*, supra. The denial of a motion for call can be disastrous to the plaintiff, since it may result in preventing him from proving infringement and consequently result in dismissal of his petition or complaint, *Pollen* v. *United States*, 58 F. Supp. 653, Ct. Cls. 1943.

Pretrial Procedure. An extensive pretrial procedure is provided for in the Court of

Claims for the purpose of simplifying the issues, determining the necessity or desirability of amending the pleadings, avoiding unnecessary proof, limiting the number of expert witnesses, etc. Ct. Cls. Rule 28. The trial Commissioner, to whom the case is referred, may direct the attorneys for the parties to appear before him to consider those matters and direct each party to submit to the other documents or statements of fact for the purpose of obtaining the other party's admission as to their genuineness.

Trial by Commissioner. The Commissioner at the trial of the action ascertains the disputed facts from the evidence presented and embodies his findings of fact in a report. 28 U.S.C. Section 2503. The Court of Claims may direct the Commissioner also to include his recommendation for conclusions of law in his report. The plaintiff may file his brief on the law in cases where the Commissioner has been directed to recommend conclusions of law. After the receipt of evidence has closed, the plaintiff can request that findings of fact be made by the Commissioner. Ct. Cls. Rule 45(b).

If the Commissioner's report includes his recommendations for conclusions of law, the Court of Claims may, upon motion by any party, adopt the Commissioner's report as the basis of its judgment in the case, unless notice in writing of intentions to except to the Commissioner's findings or recommendations are filed by one of the parties within fifteen days after filing such report. Ct. Cls. Rule 46. The party who excepts to the report may file a brief on the facts and law, and the adverse party may file an answering brief.

Exceptions to the Commissioner's report are filed before the court and not the Commissioner. They are considered by the court, and jurisdiction over the report and the entire record are reserved by the court. The findings of fact and conclusions of law are not final and conclusive until officially made by the court. In all instances the court reserves the right to pass on the case as an entirety. 28 U.S.C. Section 2503(b); *Pratt v. United States*, Ct. Cls. 1, 85, 1937, cert. denied, 302 U.S. 750, 1937.

Court of Claims. After the time for filing briefs has expired, the case is argued before the Court of Claims, unless there is a motion made for summary judgment or the Commissioner's report has been accepted as the basis for judgment. Ct. Cls. Rule 47(a). The argument may be waived by the parties. Ct. Cls. Rule 47(d).

The court can determine, on its own option, the facts and conclusions of law. The court may adopt the Commissioner's report, may modify it or reject it in whole or in part, may direct the Commissioner to receive further evidence, or may refer the case back to him with instructions. Ct. Cls. Rule 48. The losing party before the Commissioner is hampered by a presumption that the findings of fact made by the Commissioner are correct. Ct. Cls. Rule 48.

Judgment. The Court of Claims after reaching its decision on a motion for summary judgment or in a non-summary judgment case directs the entry of an appropriate judgment. Ct. Cls. Rule 52. The Court of Claims is specifically authorized to award reasonable and entire compensation for the unlicensed use by the Government of a patented product, 28 U.S.C. Section 1498(a), but is not authorized to award specific damages or attorney fees. *Regent Jack Mfg. Co., Inc.* v. *United States*, 292 F.2d 868, Ct. Cls. 1961. As is the case in actions against nongovernmental defendants, the patent owner cannot recover damages for infringements committed more than six years prior to filing the complaint or counterclaim for infringement. 35 U.S.C. Section 286. However, if the patent owner notifies the applicable Governmental department or agency of his claim after the infringement has taken place, the six year limitation period is "tolled," i.e., it ceases to run against the patent owner and does not resume until the Government mails a notice to the patent owner that his claim has been denied. 35 U.S.C. Section 286. For example, if the patent owner notifies the applicable Governmental department three years after the infringement has taken place and does not receive a denial of his claim until four years thereafter, he is not barred from bringing suit by the six-year statute of limitation. See, *Fairchild Engine*

& Airplane Corp. v. *United States,* 285 F.2d 131, Ct. Cls. 1961.

Notwithstanding the Supreme Court admonition in *Sinclair & Carroll Co.* v. *Interchemical Corp.,* supra, that a court should fully inquire into the patent's validity in the public interest, the Court of Claims need not pass upon its validity if it finds the patent not infringed. *Radio Patents Corp.* v. *United States,* 169 F. Supp. 489, Ct. Cls. 1959. Conversely, the Court of Claims has refused to pass upon the question of infringement after finding the patent in suit invalid. *Paley* v. *United States,* 140 F. Supp. 552, Ct. Cls. 1956.

Certiorari, The Supreme Court. The judgment of the Court of Claims may be reviewed by the Supreme Court by writ of certiorari granted on petition of the United States or of the claimant, or by certification of any question of law by the Court of Claims as to which instructions are desired (28 U.S.C. Section 1255). On writ of certiorari to the Court of Claims, the record to the Supreme Court is required to include the pleadings, findings of fact and the judgment. The opinion, if any, is also included. *United States* v. *Esnault-Pelterie,* 299 U.S. 201, 205, 1936. The ultimate facts are set forth by the Court of Claims and are included in the record, but the evidence is not. *United States* v. *Esnault-Pelterie,* supra. However, the Supreme Court, in the exercise of its review power, is not precluded from looking at any evidence of record, which, whether or not called to the attention of the Court of Claims, is relevant to and may affect the correctness of the Court of Claims decision. *Marconi Wireless Co.* v. *United States,* 320 U.S. 1, 44, 1943.

Review by the Supreme Court is limited to questions of law. *United States* v. *Esnault-Pelterie,* 303 U.S. 26, 29, 1938. However, the Supreme Court can send the case back to the Court of Claims to consider evidence, not previously considered, which would be determinative of questions of fact. *Marconi Wireless Co.* v. *United States,* supra. Questions of invention and infringement of patents may not be determined by the Supreme Court as questions of law where the Supreme Court is unable to examine testimony heard by the Court of Claims or its Commissioner and cannot determine its value in the light of the disputes revealed. *United States* v. *Esnault-Pelterie,* supra, p. 31. There is one exception to this rule. If it appears that no substantial dispute of fact is presented, and the case may be determined by a mere comparison of structures and extrinsic evidence is not needed for purposes of explanation, or evaluation of prior art, or to resolve questions of the application of descriptions to subject matter, the questions of invention and infringement may be determined by the Supreme Court as questions of law. *United States* v. *Esnault-Pelterie,* supra, p. 30.

Eastland Bill. The granting of certiorari by the Supreme Court in Court of Claims cases is very rare, thus leaving the Court of Claims in the position of ultimate arbiter of the controversy. In the effort to remedy this situation, Senator Eastland in 1961 introduced a bill in the Senate which in part provided for the establishment of two tribunals within the Court of Claims, i.e., a trial division and an appellate division. The bill called for a chief judge and four associate judges to constitute the appellate division, while the trial division would consist of eighteen judges.

Pursuant to this bill, a case filed in the Court of Claims would be heard and determined by a judge in the trial division, who would be the counterpart of a district court judge. The judgment of the trial division judge will be the final judgment of the Court of Claims, unless it is appealed. The appellate division, in its review, would conform to the review principles of the Federal Courts of Appeal. Cases in the appellate division of the Court of Claims may then be reviewed by the Supreme Court by writ of certiorari granted on petition of the United States or the claimant or by certification of any question of law.

Cross-references: *Accounting and Recoveries from Infringement Suits, Adjudication of Patents under 1952 Act, Adjudications by Circuits and Arts Involved, Advocacy in Patent Causes, Appeals, Briefs—Planning and Writing, Declaratory Judgment Actions, Infringement Claims against the U.S. Government—Settlements.*

INJUNCTIONS IN PATENT CASES

Alan B. Bagley

General Principles

The general principles of equity relative to injunctive relief apply to patent suits. The granting or withholding of an injunction is a matter addressed to the sound discretion of the court which must balance the equities of the parties. *Gordon Johnson Co.* v. *Hunt*, 109 F. Supp. 571, 96 USPQ 92, DC NOhio 1952.

Specifically, statutory authority for injunctions against patent infringement is found in the Patent Act of 1952, 35 U.S.C. 283, which reads:

"The several courts having jurisdiction of cases under this title may grant injunctions in accordance with the principles of equity to prevent the violation of any right secured by patent, on such terms as the court deems reasonable."

This section, like the first portion of R.S. 4921, the previous statute, incorporates the thought "on such terms as the court deems reasonable." This phrase is in accord with the principles of equity applied in all types of litigation. It emphasizes the fact that an injunction is not a matter of right but comes from the sound exercise of the court's legal discretion to adjust the relief to the facts and law in the particular case.

Preliminary Injunction

Against Infringement. A motion for preliminary injunction against patent infringement, as in other civil actions, involves the exercise of the court's sound discretion.

The purpose of such an injunction is to preserve the existing state of things between the litigants. It should not be granted unless it appears likely that the patent owner will prevail at the trial and unless denial of the preliminary injunction will cause him irreparable injury pending trial. *Superior Electric Co.* v. *General Radio Corp.*, 194 F. Supp. 339, 129 USPQ 248, DC NJ 1961. Validity and infringement of the patent must be clear and, generally, beyond question. *Zandelin* v. *Maxwell Bentley Mfg.*

Co., Inc., 197 F. Supp. 608, 131 USPQ 69, DC SNY 1961. Usually, it is not sufficient that the patent previously had been adjudicated to be valid, provided the alleged infringer, against whom a preliminary injunction is sought, is not bound by the prior judgment and provided his defense of invalidity or noninfringement is not a sham. *Heyman Mfg. Co.* v. *Electrix Corp.*, 131 USPQ 387, DC RI 1961; *Pacific Cage & Screen Co.* v. *Continental Cage Corp.*, 259 F.2d 87, 119 USPQ 338, CA 9 1958; *Leavitt* v. *McBee Co.*, 124 F.2d 938, 52 USPQ 193, CA 1 1942.

In cases decided years ago, prior to the present more stringent attitude taken by the courts concerning the validity of patents, it was more important than it is today that the patent is presumed to be valid and/or that its validity has been adjudicated by a court. It is very doubtful that a present-day court would award a preliminary injunction on an unadjudicated patent unless other factors (e.g., admission of validity) were also present. Even an adjudication, especially if it be by a court in another circuit, has less weight than formerly. It is clear that the patent owner has a greater burden than he would have had some 30 or more years ago.

In addition to the factors mentioned above which the court will consider on a motion for a preliminary injunction, the court also finds pertinent the financial responsibility of the alleged infringer (*Sinko Tool* v. *Casco Products*, 89 F.2d 916, 32 USPQ 618, CA 7 1937) and the relative convenience and inconvenience to the parties. In these matters, the court follows the general rules applied on the hearing of motions for preliminary injunction in other types of civil actions. The court necessarily takes into account any defenses, in addition to invalidity or noninfringement, which the alleged infringer may raise. For example, a substantial defense based on laches, estoppel, license, or patent misuse will avert an injunction unless, of course, the defense is so presented that the court can rule thereon at the hearing on the motion without the necessity of awaiting the trial for its determination.

As in other types of civil actions, a bond

is required upon the granting of a preliminary injunction. Thus, a patent owner who is successful in obtaining such an injunction takes the risk that he will be required to make the alleged infringer whole if it be determined at a later stage in the litigation that the injunction was improvidently granted because the patent was invalid or not infringed or because there existed some other reasons why the injunction should not have been granted.

Against Prosecution of Actions. It frequently happens in patent litigation that a patent owner will file an infringement action against a manufacturer or the latter's customer in one federal district court and that the manufacturer or customer will sue the patent owner in another district court, seeking a declaratory judgment of invalidity or noninfringement of the involved patent. Under these circumstances, it is the usual practice for one or the other of the parties to ask one of the involved courts to stay the prosecution of the action before it or to enjoin the opposing party from prosecuting the action in the other court. While disposition of this matter rests in the court's sound discretion (*Kerotest Mfg. Co. v. C-O-Two Fire Equipment Co.*, 342 U.S. 10, 92 USPQ 1, 1952, certain guide lines have developed in the adjudicated cases. Before the court will act, it should appear that the parties and the issues are the same. In determining whether the parties are the same, the court may consider the fact that intervention in one or the other of the actions can be had. *Telephonics Corp.* v. *Lindly & Co., Inc.*, 291 F.2d 445, 130 USPQ 3, CA 2 1961. The next important factor is timing. The earlier filed action, in the absence of very unusual circumstances, is permitted to proceed in preference to the later filed suit, provided, of course, that venue was properly laid in the first action. *Harris-Intertype Corp.* v. *Photon, Inc.*, 185 F. Supp. 525, 127 USPQ 188, DC SNY 1960; *Crosley Corp.* v. *Westinghouse Electric & Mfg. Co.*, 130 F.2d 474, 54 USPQ 291, CA 3 1942; *Firestone Tire & Rubber Co.* v. *General Tire & Rubber Co.*, 130 USPQ 138, DC Md 1961. Important also are the convenience of the parties, counsel, and witnesses, residence of the parties, and locale of the alleged in-

fringement. *Telephonics Corp.* v. *Lindly & Co., Inc.*, 291 F.2d 445, 130 USPQ 3, CA 2 1961.

A patent owner may be enjoined from threatening suit or prosecuting pending infringement actions against a manufacturer's customers where there is pending an infringement action against the manufacturer who is financially responsible. This rule has special application where a considerable number of suits against customers is involved. *Andreadis* v. *Rolley Co.*, 128 USPQ 75, DC Nev 1960. However, the courts recognize that a patent owner has a statutory right to sue one who uses alleged infringements purchased from the manufacturer and that this right ought not to be interfered with except for compelling reasons. *American Chemical Paint Co.* v. *Thompson Chemical Corp.*, 244 F.2d 64, 113 USPQ 103, CA 9 1957.

Likewise, where it has been adjudicated between a patent owner and a manufacturer that the former's patent is invalid, the court will enjoin the patent owner from suing, or threatening to sue, the manufacturer's customers. *Vermont Structural Slate Co., Inc.* v. *Tatko Bros. Slate Co., Inc.*, 253 F.2d 29, 116 USPQ 479, CA 2 1958; *Zoomar, Inc.* v. *Paillard Products, Inc.*, 258 F.2d 527, 118 USPQ 392, CA 2 1958. This rule was held to apply, and an injunction was granted, in *Helene Curtis Industries, Inc.* v. *Sales Affiliates, Inc.*, 247 F.2d 940, 114 USPQ 469, CA 2 1957, where the patent owner was suing customers under the cloak of another corporate shell in another circuit for infringement of a later-issued continuation-in-part patent, which was invalid for substantially the same reasons as the earlier invalid patent. Moreover, an injunction may be granted against suing customers where it has been held that the manufacturer does not infringe the patent. *Plymouth Rubber Co., Inc.* v. *Minnesota Mining & Mfg. Co.*, 203 F. Supp. 595, 133 USPQ 173, DC Mass 1962.

Laches and Estoppel

Mere delay constituting laches does not bar an injunction against patent infringement, although it may forfeit the patent owner's right to damages. However, an injunction may be barred under the general equitable doctrine of estoppel if there be more than mere delay. This "added something" must be based upon the patent owner's action or inaction under circumstances which made it reasonable for the alleged infringer to rely thereon in such a way (e.g., expenditures for machines to manufacture alleged infringements) that the grant of an injunction against him would be inequitable. *Menendez* v. *Holt*, 128 U.S. 514, 1888. The mere fact that the alleged infringer changed his position in some particular is not necessarily sufficient to warrant denial of an injunction. Thus, in *Royal McBee Corp.* v. *Smith-Corona Marchant, Inc.*, 295 F.2d 1, 130 USPQ 377, CA 2 1961, it was held that an injunction was proper where the change in position consisted solely of advertising expense and increased publicity so that the damage which would have been caused by an injunction would have primarily affected the alleged infringer's prestige. There is authority to support the position that mere delay will bar an injunction if sufficiently prolonged, it having been held, for example, in *General Electric Co.* v. *Sciaky Bros., Inc.*, 134 USPQ 55, CA 6 1962, that injury will be presumed and an injunction refused where unexplained delay exceeds the applicable statute of limitations (six years, 35 U.S.C. 286).

Injunction Against Patent Owner or Licensor

In infringement actions wherein the defendant counterclaims for injunctive relief, the court, upon dismissal of the complaint, may award an injunction to the defendant. Thus, in *Larsen Products Corp.* v. *Perfect Paint Products, Inc.*, 191 F. Supp. 303, 128 USPQ 417, DC Md 1961, after holding the patent invalid but not passing on infringement, the court permanently enjoined the plaintiff from asserting the patent against the defendant or its customers with respect to defendant's allegedly infringing product.

Licensors, who act contrary to the terms of the license, may be enjoined upon the licensee's suit. For example, in *Brumley*

Metals, Inc. v. *Bargen*, 275 F.2d 46, 124 USPQ 348, CA 7 1960, a licensor was preliminarily enjoined from disposing of molds which, contrary to the license, it had used to make articles for licensee's competitors.

Injunctions Against Disclosures

An employer, who alleges that his employee developed an invention (for which he applied for patent) on the employer's time, premises, and expense, was granted a temporary injunction restraining the employee from processing, disclosing, licensing, or transferring the application. *Action Bag & Envelope Co., Inc.* v. *Lerner*, 130 USPQ 480, NY SupCt KingsCty 1961.

Courts will enjoin the disclosure or use of trade secrets, which are recognized as a species of property (*In re Bettinger Corp.*, 197 F. Supp. 273, 130 USPQ 443, DC Mass 1961), but it must appear that the alleged trade secret is in fact secret, that its nature is such as to make it is subject to treatment as a trade secret, that it was disclosed to defendant under an express or implied obligation to preserve secrecy, and that defendant either proposes to use or reveal it or has already done so. *Ferroline Corp.* v. *General Aniline & Film Corp.*, 207 F.2d 912, 99 USPQ 240, CA 7 1953; *Colgate-Palmolive Co.* v. *Carter Products, Inc.*, 230 F.2d 855, 108 USPQ 383, CA 4 1956; *Simplex Wire & Cable Co.* v. *Dulon, Inc.*, 196 F. Supp. 437, 130 USPQ 143, DC ENY 1961.

In *Filler Products, Inc.* v. *Hale*, 129 USPQ 247, DC NGa 1961, the court temporarily enjoined an inventor, who had assigned his patent application to his former employer, from disclosing information concerning the application and also from disclosing confidential information and trade secrets.

Miscellaneous Issues

A patent owner's right to an injunction is not affected by the fact that he has made no use of his patented invention. *Continental Paper Bag Co.* v. *Eastern Paper Bag Co.*, 210 U.S. 405, 1908; *Hartford-Empire* v. *Obear-Nester*, 71 F.2d 539, 22 USPQ 270, CA 8 1934.

His right to an injunction against infringement is coextensive with the life of his patent, not arising until the issuance of the patent and terminating with its expiration. *Freedman* v. *Friedman*, 242 F.2d 364, 113 USPQ 1, CA 4 1957; *Smith, Kline & French Laboratories* v. *Clark & Clark*, 157 F.2d 725, 70 USPQ 382, CA 3 1946. Thus, an injunction was granted, in *Otis Elevator Co.* v. *John W. Kiesling & Son, Inc.*, 87 F. Supp. 408, 83 USPQ 289, DC ENY 1949, where the patent was to expire in six months, although in one case it was refused when the patent expired on the next day. *Clair* v. *Kastar, Inc.*, 51 F. Supp. 207, 58 USPQ 313, DC SNY 1943.

Although in some cases injunctions have been refused where infringement has ceased and the circumstances indicate that the infringer does not contemplate its resumption (*LeClair* v. *Shell Oil Co.*, 183 F. Supp. 255, 126 USPQ 115, DC SIll 1960), other courts have indicated that they have no discretion to refuse an injunction against an infringer (*J. R. Clark Co.* v. *Jones & Laughlin Steel Corp.*, 186 F. Supp. 22, 125 USPQ 433, DC SInd 1960) or have considered cessation of infringement and a statement of an intent not to infringe in the future to be insufficient where the infringer stands ready to resume infringement at any time. *Eversharp, Inc.* v. *Fisher Pen Co., Inc.*, 132 USPQ 423, DC NIll 1961. However, it has been held that a trifling infringement is of insufficient importance to warrant a court's grant of an injunction. *Condenser Corp. of America* v. *Micamold Radio Corp.*, 145 F.2d 878, 63 USPQ 244, CA 2 1944.

Where a patent has reissued, an injunction should not restrain infringement of the original patent which was surrendered on the grant of the reissue patent. *Metallizing Engineering Co., Inc.* v. *Metallizing Co. of America*, 62 F. Supp. 274, 66 USPQ 286, DC SNY 1945.

Irrespective of whether a judgment of patent validity and infringement will be *res judicata*, as against a manufacturer who controls the defense of an infringement action against its customer, but does not become a party to such action, venue jurisdiction sufficient to warrant an injunction against such a manufacturer is lacking. *Brock* v. *Brown*, 138 F. Supp. 628, 108 USPQ 363, DC Md 1956; *Keiser* v. *High Point Hardware Co.*, 199 F. Supp. 623, 131 USPQ 368, DC MNC 1961, reversed on other grounds, 311 F.2d 850, 136 USPQ 612, 1963. This result necessarily follows from the holding of the Supreme Court in *Schnell* v. *Peter Eckrich & Sons, Inc.*, 365 U.S. 260, 128 USPQ 305 (1961), that a nonresident manufacturer does not subject itself to the court's jurisdiction by openly assuming and controlling the defense of an infringement action against its customer.

Cross-reference: *Infringement Suits.*

INTERFERENCES

W. P. Epperson

An interference is a quasi-judicial and litigative proceeding instituted by the U.S. Patent Office to determine priority of invention between rival claimants of the same patentable subject matter. The major part of all interference proceedings is under the jurisdiction of the Patent Office and most are concluded therein; but appeals to the Court of Customs and Patent Appeals (35 USC 141) or to a Federal District Court (35 USC 146) are available to a losing party. An interference involves two or more pending U.S. patent applications, or one or more pending applications and an issued U.S. patent.

Statutory Provisions and Patent Office Rules

The statutory authority for an interference is 35 U.S.C., Sections 135(a), 102(g), 23 on taking testimony, and 24 on subpoena of witnesses.

Pursuant to this statutory authority, the Commissioner of Patents has established Rules 201 to 286. The U.S. Patent Office has also issued instructions to the Examiners in Chapter 1100, Sections 1100 to 1112 of the *Manual of Patent Examining Procedure*, 3d ed. These instructions are of assistance to applicants or patentees involved in interference and to their attorneys.

Literature

An authoritative textbook is Charles W. Rivise and A. D. Caesar's *Interference Law and Practice*, 4 Vols., 1940-48, Michie Co., Charlottesville, Va. Although published more than a decade ago, there have been relatively few major changes in interference practice resulting from the codification of the patent statutes in 35 U.S.C., 1952 and other more recent amendments. This textbook is therefore useful in studying the intricate details of interference procedure and the earlier cited cases, when supplemented by search of more recent court decisions, particularly those of the CCPA.

A number of useful and interesting articles on this subject are found in the *Journal of the Patent Office Society*, such as the article of Charles W. Rivise and A. D. Caesar, "Interferences between Pending Applications," 21 JPOS 887, 1939; Louis F. Kreek, "Proof of Priority of Invention in Interferences," 35 JPOS 551, 1953; and Benton Baker, "Outline of Patent Office Interference Practice," 36 JPOS 30, 122, 185, 1954.

Complexity of Interference Practice

Interference procedure is complex. It demands close adherence to procedural rules, and the applicable law requires interpretation on the basis of the diverse facts involved. Consequently, an applicant or patentee involved in interference is well advised to have the services of a patent attorney skilled in this field. It is a highly specialized proceeding which is encountered in less than 1 per cent of the patent applications filed; statistics for a recent ten-year period show only one interference for each 110 applications. See the very comprehensive statistical study of interferences by Daniel v. De Simone, James B. Gambrell, and Charles F. Gareau, "Characteristics of Interference Practice," 45 JPOS 503-591, 1963.

This proceeding can be expensive and time-consuming. Because of delays which have been involved in the issuance of a patent on an application prevailing in interference, particularly where a patentee is the losing party with resultant prolongation of the patent monopoly, there have been criticisms of this system which is unlike that of nearly all of the other patent-granting countries throughout the world. To partially counteract this delay, 35 U.S.C. 135 has been worded to enable the Commissioner of Patents to issue a patent to an applicant who is adjudged the prior inventor by decision of the Board of Patent Interferences (consisting of three Examiners of Interferences), even though a losing party takes an appeal to the court. This is done where a losing party files suit in a Federal District Court under 35 U.S.C. 146, but not where an appeal is taken to the CCPA under 35 U.S.C. 141. *Ugo Monaco and Montecatini* v. *Watson*, 122 USPQ 564, CA DC 1959. But note the provision in 35 U.S.C. 141 whereby any adverse party to the interference can force the appellant to the CCPA into a 35 U.S.C. 146 suit by notice within twenty days after such appeal is filed.

It is possible that what is published here may within several years become of only historical significance; the U.S. patent laws may be changed to bring them into harmony with those of the Common Market countries and to enable a U.S. citizen to become eligible for a Common Market patent. (The latter is now under active consideration and estimated to become available about 1965 or shortly thereafter for citizens of the Common Market countries.) In that event, the earlier or earliest filing date or Convention date (35 U.S.C. 119) of a U.S. application would determine priority, and our present interference practice would be abolished. On the other hand, there are proposals, as in the 1963 Committee Reports of the Section of Patent, Trademark and Copyright Law, American Bar Association, pp. 25-33, for simplifying and expediting interferences which could result in changes of the present laws and material modification of the interference practice as it now exists.

This review is based on the interference practice which has grown up over many years, since the act of July 4, 1836, Chapter 357, Section 8, 5 Stat. 117, and is the practice in existence at the present time.

Initiation of Interference between Applications

Since pending applications are preserved in secrecy (Rule 14), the responsibility for determining whether an interference exists between them devolves on the Examiner except under special circumstances, as where an applicant or assignee has had access to another's pending application by reason of a previously declared interference. Rule 226. The possibility of interference is kept in mind by the Examiner; when an application is otherwise ready for allowance, he first makes his interference search to determine if an interference should be declared instead of then issuing a notice of allowance. M.P.E.P. 1101. It should be noted that there is no duty on the part of the Examiner to declare an interference merely because there is a supporting disclosure in another application unless the latter applicant is also claiming the same or substantially the same invention, or has shown an intention to claim the subject matter found allowable, as by the prosecution of claims to a genus along with other elected species. M.P.E.P 1101.01.

A special situation arises where a later filed (junior) application is ready for allowance, and an earlier filed (senior) application discloses, but does not claim, allowable subject matter of claims of the junior application; then the Examiner is instructed to discuss this matter with a Supervisory Examiner, to determine the action to be taken. Where conflicting applications owned by a common assignee are involved, the common assignee will be required to elect the application in which the conflicting claims are to be retained. Rule 78(b) and M.P.E.P. 1101.01 (b).

Counts. It is considered desirable that any count (claim) of an interference be made in identical language in the applications of all parties involved. For this purpose, the Examiner may select an allowed claim (or claims) from an application ready for allowance and propose that claim (or claims) to any other prospectively interfering applicant. Or the Examiner may formulate a count (or counts) for proposal to all prospective parties; and each such formulated claim should be allowable, in good form, and free from indefiniteness, ambiguity and other defect.

By amendment of January 27, 1962, there is now an exception to the requirement for claims in the same language in all applications involved in the interference. This is in the special situation where it is not possible for all applicants, because of their respective disclosures, to make a claim in identical phraseology. In such case, the interference may be declared on a count which differs from the corresponding claim of one or more of the conflicting applications by an "immaterial limitation or variation." Rule 203(a). Whether a limitation or variation is immaterial or material may be an issue inviting more litigation between the parties by way of motions; and this issue is found more often in the decisions relating to copying a claim from an issued patent where it has had a longer history. Where an applicant fails to make a claim proposed for interference within the time limit allowed, this constitutes a disclaimer of the subject matter covered by the claim. Rule 203(b).

Informal Statement of Date of Conception of Invention. To avoid the declaration of needless interferences, a junior applicant, whose effective U.S. filing date is from about six months to two years subsequent to the filing date of a senior applicant, can be called upon by correspondence from a Patent Office Law Examiner to state in writing under oath the date and character of the earliest fact or act, susceptible of proof, which the junior applicant can rely on to establish conception of a particular claim (Rule 202). If this statement under Rule 202 fails to antedate a senior applicant's filing date, the interference is ordinarily not declared.

Initiation of Interference Involving Issued Patent

The responsibility for determining whether a claim should be copied in a pending application from an issued patent is generally that of the applicant. In certain circumstances, where the Examiner has cited the patent as a reference and the applicant has attempted to swear back of the effective filing date of the patent by an affidavit under Rule 131, the Examiner may make a requirement that the applicant copy from the patent a claim or a suitably modified claim (omitting an immaterial limitation or variation), for purposes of interference on the ground that the applicant's disclosure supports such a claim. The Rule 131 affidavit may be refused, with the Examiner holding that the patent can only be overcome through interference proceedings. See 29 Fed. Reg., 9398, 964.

Because the Examiner purposely may not declare an interference between pending applications which have conflicting disclosures but do not claim substantially the same invention, and because the Patent Office is not infallible in locating every situation where an interference should be declared, it is a common practice particularly in corporate patent departments to follow currently issuing U.S. patents. In addition to checking on possible situations justifying the copying of a patent claim or claims for purposes of interference, this follow-up system is important with respect to possible infringement problems as well as for informational purposes.

Factors Affecting Decision on Seeking Interference. The question of whether a claim should be copied from a patent is a matter deserving careful consideration. First, 35 U.S.C. 135(b) requires that such a claim must be made in the application prior to one year from the date on which the patent was granted. But this requirement is satisfied and the claim of the patent can be copied where the applicant had claims to substantially the same invention in his case at any time prior to the expiration of the critical period, even though such claims had been cancelled. *Cryns* v. *Musher*, 73 USPQ 290, CCPA 1947. Note that a different rule applies where the copied claim contains a material limitation (such as a temperature limitation which had been held critical in securing the patent), which the applicant had not previously claimed. *Andrews* v. *Wickenden*, 93 USPQ 27, CCPA 1952.

While it is a general rule that all limitations in a count of a declared interference are material on the issues of right to make and priority of invention, this rule does not

apply to an estoppel under 35 U.S.C. 135(b); where the applicant was claiming the inventive substance of the patent claim less than one year after the patent issued, immaterial limitations in the patent claim were disregarded in holding that no estoppel existed and the interference was properly declared. *Rieser* v. *Williams*, 118 USPQ 96, CCPA 1958.

Secondly, an important consideration is the matter of the respective filing dates of the patentee and the applicant; if the applicant will be senior party in the interference, this gives him a substantial advantage usually justifying his attempt to provoke the interference apart from the question of the applicant's actual invention dates. If the applicant will be junior party, then the matter of his actual invention dates with reference to the filing date of the patentee is material. Where the effective filing date of an applicant is subsequent to the filing date of a patentee, Rule 204(b) requires that the applicant must file an affidavit antedating the patentee's filing date. By notice of April 30, 1963, 790 O.G. 577, this affidavit must set forth sufficient facts to establish a prima facie case of priority for the applicant relative to the filing date of the patentee.

Unusual care should be exercised with respect to filing an application after the issuance of a patent for the purpose of provoking an interference with that patent, since the burden of proof on the applicant in such case is beyond a reasonable doubt. *Conner* v. *Joris*, 113 USPQ 56, CCPA 1957. This is distinguished from the usual case involving copending applications or a patent whose application was copending (*Creamer* v. *Kirkwood et al.*, 134 USPQ 330, CCPA 1962), and where the burden of proof is by a mere preponderance of the evidence. *Alpert* v. *Slatin*, 134 USPQ 296, CCPA 1962. An interesting sidelight is that this last-mentioned case holds that the Federal shopbook rule of 28 U.S.C. 1732 does not apply to reports of scientific research and tests.

The prior art cited against the application of the patentee during its pendency, see Rule 235(d), and the interpretation placed on the language of the patentee's claim to distinguish from this art, are matters which must be considered in connection with an applicant's right to make a patented claim on the basis of the applicant's disclosure. For this purpose, the file wrapper of the patentee is inspected; or generally a file history of the patent is ordered, either directly from the Patent Office or from a firm or individual located in Washington who will, on request, obtain access to the file in the Patent Office and make a copy thereof.

Another rule which requires consideration, in deciding whether to seek interference, is that, where the terms of a claim copied from a patent are ambiguous, the one copying the claim is bound by the meaning intended by the patentee, as shown by his disclosure. Just what is an "ambiguity" within the meaning of this rule has been the subject of much litigation in interference proceedings. But when the term was used by the patentee to mean one thing, and where it is necessary to give the term a different meaning for an applicant copying the claim to support the same on the basis of his disclosure, then the interference will be dissolved on the basis of this ambiguity rule. *Smith* v. *Wehn*, 138 USPQ 52, 54, CCPA 1963. Testimony may be taken in the absence of express limitation otherwise to properly resolve this issue. *Chedaker et al.* v. *Lo*, 318 F.2d 333, CCPA 1963.

Where the situation involves a prima facie case of priority over the filing date of the patentee, then all of the claims of the patent which the applicant believes he can make should be copied by amendment with a request for interference, said amendment also pointing out how all the terms of the copied claims are supported by his disclosure (Rule 205).

Right to Make Claim

It has been recognized for some time (*Ex parte Card & Card*, 1904 C.D. 383) that an interference in fact may exist, but because of an immaterial limitation or variation in the patent claim, the exact language of the patent claim cannot be made by the applicant. In such case, a determination of priority is properly required; and this is now specifically provided for in Rule 205, and the procedure to follow is set forth in detail in M.P.E.P. 1101.02. From the latter, the "immaterial" limitations or variations include (1) some differences in ranges of temperature, pressure, or concentration, etc., between a claim or claims of the patent and the disclosure of the applicant but with substantial overlapping of such ranges; and (2) some differences in the subgroups or species of a Markush chemical grouping (see *Chemical Applications, Claim Drafting*, or 1925 C.D. 126) again with substantial overlapping. Note that in such case, the applicant should copy the identical patent claim when the applicant's disclosure is broader, and he should copy the patent claim modified in accordance with his disclosure with respect to range or Markush grouping when his disclosure is narrower. Then provision is made during the motion period of the interference to substitute in certain circumstances a still broader count on which the issue of priority is determined.

Where there is doubt on the question of applicant's right to make a patented claim in its identical language, it is considered good practice to copy the patented claim in identical language and also to copy the claim in modified form as an alternative for purposes of the interference. It has been held that a belated motion to make a modified claim of a patent should be dismissed, where filed after a motion to make the identical claim of the patent was denied on the ground of no right to make; the original motion also should have proposed the modified claim in the alternative. *Landauer* v. *Knol et al* v. *Lindenblad*, 108 USPQ 296, Comr. Pats. 1955.

Reissuing Patent for Interference Purpose

An interference will not be declared between issued patents. 35 U.S.C. 291 provides for relief for interfering patents only by civil suit in a federal district court.

However, under certain circumstances, a patentee may file an application for reissue of his patent for the purpose of provoking an interference with a claim or claims of another issued patent. Here again the one-year rule applies within which the reissue applicant must be claiming the same or substantially the same invention. Also note that, in the case where the patent of the prospective reissue applicant has been granted more than two years at the time he decides that an interference would have been proper, then the last paragraph of 35 U.S.C. 251 applies. This states that no reissued patent should be granted enlarging the scope of the original patent unless the reissue application was filed within two years from the grant of the original patent. A claim is broader for purposes of a broadened reissue if it is enlarged in scope in any respect, namely, in any part or clause of the claim; and the fact that the claim may be more limited in other respects or clauses is immaterial. *In re Freedlander*, 62 USPQ 309, CCPA 1944; *In re Ruth*, 126 USPQ 155, CCPA 1960. Some of the special problems in this field are discussed by Herbert H. Thompson, in "Reissues In Interference," 33 JPOS 163, 1951.

Setting Up the Interference

Notices of an interference are prepared by the Examiner to supply each party with the name, address, assignee if any, and attorney of each other party, but no information as to serial numbers and filing dates of pending applications, or the relative order of filing dates, is given at this stage. The notices also set forth in a table the relation of the counts in interference to the claims of the respective parties. Each interference includes only counts that all parties involved therein can make. If there is patentably distinct interfering subject matter between less than all of the parties, which may also involve another party, a separate interference is declared.

An attempt is made to select the broadest claim defining the conflicting subject matter which is patentable in each of the pending applications as the interference count. Additional counts will not be included unless each additional count is considered to be patentably distinct from the main count, and from each other, such as to support separate patents in the event of a split award of priority. M.P.E.P. 1105.03.

While Rule 201(b) provides that a claim must be patentable to all parties before an interference is declared, and this is the law (*In re Chromy and Allen*, 137 USPQ 884, 887, CCPA 1963), note that if an interference has otherwise been declared and it reaches the CCPA on appeal, then the sole issue in that Court is priority of invention, and patentability to one or more of the parties will not be considered. *Loukomsky v. Gerlich*, 121 USPQ 213, CCPA 1959. But the doctrine of this last case does not apply in an ex parte appeal where the issue is patentability. *In re Gemassmer*, 138 USPQ 229, 230, CCPA 1963.

The Examiner forwards the notices of the interference to an Examiner of Interferences who assigns an interference number thereto and sets a time limit of generally about forty-five days for the filing of preliminary statements by each of the parties. If the notices are in proper form, the Examiner of Interferences then declares the interference by mailing a copy to each of the parties in care of their attorneys. If one of the parties is a patentee, a copy is also sent directly to the patentee, and a copy is also sent to the assignee where the patent has been assigned. The applications of the parties are now under the jurisdiction of the Examiner of Interferences (Rule 211), and ex parte prosecution is suspended except as to possible question of another interference or with respect to special matters on order from the Commissioner (Rule 212).

Preliminary Statement

The preliminary statement that the Examiner of Interferences now requests is so important that Rule 216 respecting it is copied in full below.

"**216. Contents of the preliminary statement.** The preliminary statement must state that the applicant made the invention set forth by each count of the interference, and whether the invention was made in the United States or abroad.

"(a) When the invention was made in the United States the preliminary statement must set forth as to the invention defined by each count the following facts relating to conception of the invention, and reduction of the invention to practice:

"(1) The date upon which the first drawing of the invention was made; if a drawing of the invention has not been made prior to the filling date of the application, it must be so stated.

"(2) The date upon which the first written description of the invention was made; if a written description of the invention has not been made prior to the filing date of the application, it must be so stated.

"(3) The date upon which the invention was first disclosed to another person; if the invention was not disclosed to another person prior to the filing date of the application, it must be so stated.

"(4) The date of the first act or acts susceptible of proof (other than acts of the character specified in subparagraphs (1), (2), and (3) of this paragraph) which if proven, would establish conception of the invention, and a brief description of such act or acts; if there have been no such acts, it must be so stated.

"(5) The date of the actual reduction to practice of the invention; if the invention has not been actually reduced to practice before the filing date of the application, it must be so stated.

"(6) The date after conception of the invention when active exercise of reasonable diligence toward reducing the invention to practice began.

"(b) The preliminary statement in every case must also set forth:

"(1) The serial number and filing date of any prior copending application in the United States by the same applicant, not specified by the examiner in the notice of interference, disclosing the invention set forth by the counts of the interference, the benefit of the filing date of which application may be claimed as the effective filing date of the application or patent involved.

"(2) The filing date and country (and number, if known) of any application for the same invention in a foreign country, the filing date of which may be claimed under 35 U.S.C. 119.

"(c) If a party intends to rely solely on a prior application, domestic or foreign, and on no other evidence, the preliminary statement may so state and may then consist only of the identification of the prior application and need not be signed or sworn to by the inventor." (End of Rule 216.)

This preliminary statement which each party is required to file under oath is a pleading, which cannot be used as evidence, setting forth facts as to invention dates.

This should be prepared with care and after a thorough investigation; no earlier date than that alleged in the statement will be awarded to a party, except where an amended preliminary statement is timely filed by motion under Rule 243. Such motion may seek to correct a material error

arising through inadvertence or mistake. It requires satisfactory showing that the correction is essential to the ends of justice. Rule 222.

Since only inventive acts in the U.S. are considered on the issue of priority (35 U.S.C. 104), except for civil or military personnel serving abroad in a governmental capacity for the U.S., Rule 216(a) provides for the allegations in the preliminary statement of different facts where the invention was made in the U.S. from those provided in Rule 217 for an invention made abroad. The allegations of Rule 216(b) are common to both. In addition to specifying in the preliminary statement any earlier filed U.S. application on which the party intends to rely, 35 U.S.C. 120 requires the later application to contain, or be amended to contain, a specific reference to the earlier filed application.

Convention Date. The party may claim in his preliminary statement an earlier effective filing date, under the Convention by virtue of 35 U.S.C. 119, on the basis of a U.S. application filed within twelve months of the earliest filing of a pending application or patent for the same invention in a foreign country. Note particularly the second paragraph of this statute. It prescribes certain procedure which must be followed to obtain this right. By amendment of September 18, 1961, third paragraph of 35 U.S.C. 119 was added. This provides that the foreign application can be a subsequently filed application and not the first filed application in that country, provided the said earlier or first filed application in that country has been abandoned without having been laid open to public inspection and without serving as a basis for claiming a right of priority.

Reduction to Practice. While the allegations in the preliminary statement are generally spoken of as "facts," there are certain ones which are mixed questions of law and fact requiring interpretation. For example, the date of the "actual reduction to practice" may require interpretation as to whether the experiments which have been performed would be held to constitute an actual reduction to practice as that expression has been construed by Court decisions.

Thus it has been held that, in the absence of either actual service tests or positive correlation between them and simulated tests, there is no way of knowing the extent to which laboratory tests can be said to be predictive of performance expected under actual conditions of use; and such laboratory tests are not sufficient to establish an actual reduction to practice. *Harding* v. *Steingiser and Salyer*, 138 USPQ 32, 35, CCPA 1963.

Utility. This same case holds that, although no specific limitation with respect to utility or purpose appears in the count, it nevertheless must be considered in determining whether laboratory tests were sufficient on this issue; and the first question is what was the practical use to which the applicant intended to put his invention. This appears to be a harsh rule; and the dissent of Judge Rich in that case to the effect that proof of substantial utility for any purpose should be sufficient is of interest, albeit not the law of the majority. In this connection, see Baylor G. Riddell, "Laboratory Tests as a Reduction to Practice," 44 JPOS 91, 1962 and cases cited therein.

While late decisions may cast a shadow on the doctrine established in the *Sinko Tool* decision by Judge Learned Hand, it is well to remember his statement to the effect that reduction to practice requires a satisfactory test under service conditions only in those cases when a person "qualified in the art [would not be] willing to manufacture and sell the invention as is." *Sinko Tool & Mfg. Co.* v. *Automatic Devices Corp.*, 71 USPQ 199, CA 2 1946.

Diligence. The date when "active exercise of reasonable diligence toward reducing the invention to practice" began, also, may not be just a simple allegation of fact; it can require interpretation of the law and what constitutes "substantially continuous diligence" on the basis of the facts involved. This can be an important allegation. While a party who is the first to conceive and also the first to reduce to practice is entitled to the award of priority without any requirement for diligence (*Diamond* v. *Woodyard et al.*, 88 USPQ 372, CCPA 1951), a party who is the first to conceive but is later in his reduction to practice must prove substantially continuous diligence from just

prior to the time the other party entered the field down to his later reduction to practice, in order to prevail. *Morway et al.* v. *Bondi*, 97 USPQ 318, CCPA 1953. So, if a party alleges that his active diligence began on a date which is subsequent to the filing date of another party, the former can be placed under order to show cause why judgment should not be rendered against him at that time. Rule 225.

Showing of Earliest Dates. Consequently, it will be seen that the allegations of the preliminary statement are frequently not free from doubt. Under these circumstances, it is recommended as good practice to allege in the preliminary statement the earliest dates which a party can hope to prove on the basis of the facts involved, since no earlier date will be accorded to that party even though his subsequent proofs would establish an earlier date. For further information, see Anthony S. Zummer, "Pitfalls in Preliminary Statements," 41 JPOS 668, 1959.

Adding or Subtracting Inventor. When investigating the facts of invention for the preliminary statement, it may be found that fewer than those executing the application as joint inventors may actually have been responsible for making the invention of the count and entitled to earlier invention dates than would otherwise be permissible. *Perkins et al.* v. *Engs et al.*, 49 USPQ 247, CCPA 1941. Or it may be found that another person or persons should be added as joint inventor or inventors. 35 U.S.C. 116 and Rule 45(b) and (c) now provide for either subtracting from or adding to the originally filed inventorship, and this is preferably done by amendment prior to the time the preliminary statements are approved. M.P.E.P. 1111.07. This is discussed in *Inventors* and also in *McGavack* v. *Strube*, 50 USPQ 513, PO BdApp 1938.

Motions

When the preliminary statements have been filed in accordance with Rule 219 and have been approved, or the time for filing same has expired, the Examiner of Interferences provides each party with the serial number and filing date of each adverse party and notice of any applications in addition to those directly involved in the interference which the parties are entitled to inspect. Rule 226. The preliminary statements and any affidavits under Rules 131, 202 and 204 are not open for inspection at this time. The notice also generally includes the setting of a time, not less than thirty days and usually about sixty days, for the bringing of any motions (Rule 231) as specified in Rules 232 to 235 inclusive. Note, however, that any junior party, failing in his preliminary statement to make out a prima facie case with respect to the filing date of a senior party, is placed under order to show cause (Rule 225), and special procedure then applies to him which frequently results in judgment on the record against him.

This motion period is the time to attempt either to get the interference dissolved or to amend the counts so that the issues remaining for the determination of priority are settled in better form from the standpoint of the party's proofs. It is also the time to determine whether an effort should be made to have any other interference declared. This is a critical period which should be assessed carefully in the light of the file histories of the parties and in view of their relative filing dates. The senior party is in the most favorable position, since ordinarily no estoppel for failure to bring a motion will subsequently apply against him in the event the interference is dissolved without an actual award of priority against him. *Myers* v. *Denke et al.*, 21 USPQ 125, Comr. Pats. 1934 and Rule 257(b).

It is noted that Rule 234 and M.P.E.P. 1105.03 construe and overrule decisions in that the former specifically relieve any party to an interference from the doctrine of estoppel for failure to bring a motion to include an application (same inventor or co-owner) as to subject matter not disclosed both in his application or patent already in the interference and also in an opposing party's application or patent. However, in view of such earlier decisions as *Ex parte Geyer*, 56 USPQ 69, PO BdApp 1942, it is still believed good practice for a party to move in one interference to set up any new interference between other applications (or

any one of them) involved in that interference and any application owned by the common assignee of said party, where said party has a prima facie case on dates with respect to said new interference. In an interference declared as a result of a decision on motions in another interference, however, a new motion period will not be set. Rule 233(e).

To Dissolve. In the case of a junior party whose alleged dates are sufficient to keep him in the interference but who feels quite doubtful about prevailing, this is the time to consider seriously a motion to dissolve, preferably on the ground of non-patentability to all parties. Rule 232(a) and (c). This is particularly true where the common subject matter is commercial or potentially commercial. For this purepose a rather comprehensive search of the prior art is justified since, if successful, this will save the cost of subsequent infringement proceedings or of a license. In this connection, not only the interference count or counts should be considered in this art search, but also any claim to common subject matter that might be made, since another party has a right to bring a motion to amend within thirty days of the filing of the motion to dissolve. Rule 233(b).

However, where one of the parties is a patentee, a motion to dissolve for non-patentability may not be brought, except for a motion by an applicant that the count is unpatentable to the patentee but is patentable to said applicant and this is an issue ancillary to priority. Rule 232(b) and Rule 258.

Further, a party may wish to move to dissolve on the ground that any other party cannot make any one or more of the counts of the interference by reason of lack of disclosure, Rule 232(a)(3), or on the ground that there is no interference in fact where a claim of a patent has been made in modified form on the basis that the omitted limitation or variation is actually material. Rule 232(a)(4). Note the distinction between "interference in fact" and "right to make," where a claim is copied from a patent in modified form omitting a limitation which is held material. *Brailsford* v. *Lavet et al.*, 138 USPQ 28, 31, CCPA 1963.

Also, the Examiner can dissolve an interference under Rule 237 on his own motion and on a ground, such as double patenting, which need not be ancillary to priority. *Eckert* v. *Reiling*, 138 USPQ 315, Comr. Pats. 1962.

Miscellaneous Motion Procedures. Of course, a junior party should not overlook an opportunity to move to shift the burden of proof under Rule 235.

Also, a junior party with relatively good dates should consider a motion to amend under Rule 233(a) and (d), as well as to substitute any co-owned application or to propose any new interference involving a co-owned application or patent. Rule 234. This is for the purpose not only of avoiding any question of estoppel with respect to subject matter disclosed in his application or patent involved in the interference, but also of attempting to capture subject matter disclosed in any opposing party's case which may not be disclosed in his own application or patent involved in the interference, thus showing his intention to claim that subject matter. The net result is frequently a superabundance of proposed counts, only a relatively few of which may be approved in any event for interference proceedings; but this is a course of action designed to preserve the party's rights.

Note the requirement for service upon opposing parties of papers filed in an interference in accordance with Rule 248, with certain exceptions as enumerated in Rule 247.

Any motions under Rules 232 to 235 found by the Examiner of Interference to be in proper form are set for hearing before the Examiner for oral argument, Rules 236(b) and 244(b), the date of hearing determining the time for filing briefs under Rules 236(a) and 244(a). The decision of the Examiner on motions is final, except for petition for reconsideration, Rule 244(c) and M.P.E.P. 1105.07, and there is no appeal. Rule 244(d). However, any losing or aggrieved party, whose motion under Rule 232 for dissolution has been denied, can request that the interference be set down for final hearing before the Board of Patent Interferences under Rule 258, for reconsideration by the latter of any issue of said motion

under Rule 232 which is ancillary to the question of priority of invention, such as the lack of right of a party to make the count for failure to disclose. It has been held that the following matters are not ancillary to priority: (1) whether the count is broader than a party's disclosure; (2) the question of inoperativeness when not raised before the Examiner; and (3) whether a party discloses the "best mode" or a "specific embodiment" under Rule 71. *Moler et al* v. *Purdy*, 131 USPQ 276, Bd. Pat. Intfs. 1960. This last case should be noted in connection with the question of a party's right to correct or amend his preliminary statement under Rule 222.

Relatively prompt action by the Examiner in issuing his decision on motions has now been implemented. Cases in which the practice requires that the Examiner act within sixty days, such as decisions on motions, M.P.E.P. 1105.06, take priority over special cases without specific time limits. By notice of April 17, 1963, 790 O.G. 578, the Examiner is instructed to take up such cases at least thirty days before the sixty-day period expires, to insure compliance.

Testimony

After the interference survives the motion period, the Examiner of Interferences sends notices to the parties remaining therein, assigning times for the taking of testimony (Rule 251), the service and filing of copies of the record (Rule 253), and the filing of briefs (Rule 254). Final hearing before the Board of Patent Interferences (Rule 256) is usually not set at this time. The junior-most party is assigned a time of about sixty days within which his testimony-in-chief is to be taken first, followed at stated intervals of about thirty days each for the taking of testimony-in-chief of the next junior party in inverse order of filing dates, and so on to that of the senior party. This schedule is then followed, at stated intervals of about fifteen days each, for the junior parties to take any rebuttal testimony in the order of their filing dates. This affords the senior party a substantial advantage since, if junior parties do not take any testimony-in-chief, the senior party automatically wins; and even if they do, the senior party may decide he can stand on his filing date without taking testimony.

The dates as set forth above, as well as those previously mentioned for the filing of preliminary statements and motions, can initially be extended, usually by about 30 to 60 days, upon mere stipulation of the parties or their attorneys. Rule 245. For good cause, further extensions of time are granted on motion or stipulation supported by a verified showing. Note that the stipulation should specify the actual new dates, which should not fall on a Saturday, Sunday or holiday in the District of Columbia.

After the interference is in condition for the taking of testimony, which is evidenced by receipt of the above notice, the preliminary statements and any affidavits under Rules 131, 202 and 204 are then opened for inspection by the opposing parties. Rules 227 and 226.

The details of this testimony period and subsequent proceedings are beyond the scope of this paper, except to note the rigorous requirement for corroboration of the inventor's testimony and self-serving documents with respect to both conception and actual reduction to practice. *Senkus* v. *Johnston*, 77 USPQ 113, CCPA 1948; *Jex* v. *Wiese et al.*, 124 USPQ 457, Bd Pat Intfs. 1959. In this connection, note that an operator (not an inventor) who repeats an inventor's experiment and understands what he is doing is a competent corroborating witness as of the date of the operator's work.

Settlements

Now that the issues for determination of priority are clarified and settled, and the dates of invention alleged by the parties in their preliminary statements are known by each other, this is the time to consider again the matter of settlement. Where it is evident that the satisfactory taking of testimony by a junior party can also force the senior party to take testimony in an effort to prevail, then the fundamental basis for a settlement is present.

The purpose of such settlement is to avoid the time and expense of (1) the preparation for and the taking of testimony, (2) the preparation and filing of the record and briefs, (3) the attendance and argument at final hearing, provided by Rules 251 to 258, with all the uncertainties of the outcome, and (4) the possibility of the losing party being unable to operate under the patent of the winner.

While it has been stated in some quarters that the Justice Department looks askance at interference settlements, this statement is too broad and it is only the abuses which are condemned, such as an agreement unsupported by the evidence and which may extend a patent monopoly. See in this connection the article by Nathan M. Briskin, "An Area of Confusion; Patents, Monopolies and the Anti-Trust Laws," American Bar Association Journal, p. 661 (July 1963). Particularly since Public Law No. 87-831, approved October 15, 1962, added part (c) to 35 USC 135, which requires that a copy of any such interference settlement agreement must be filed in the Patent Office, the Justice Department or any other Government agency will have access thereto on written request and this should mitigate against improper settlements.

Where the settlement agreement involves a mutual exchange of free nonexclusive licenses or operating rights, or the same plus licensing rights without obligation to account to any other party, it is customary to limit these rights to the interference counts and/or claims to common subject matter disclosed in the applications or patent involved and granted to the respective parties on the basis of said applications or patent, or any divisions, continuations, continuations-in-part or reissues thereof. Where there are more than two parties, such as a 3-party interference involving A, B and C, and the common subject matter is different between A and B and between A and C for example, there can be three separate settlement agreements between A and B, A and C, and B and C. The settlement specifically provides that no rights are granted by the said agreement under any other claim now or hereafter owned or controlled by any of the parties except as set forth. This restricts the agreement to the overlapping patentable subject matter involved or which could be involved in the said interference. Thus, the settlement does not include rights under any dominating protection which any party might have previously obtained on the basis of another application not involved in the interference; and this is thereby excluded from the scope of the agreement even though it would require a separate license with royalty to permit practice of subject matter covered by claims falling within the grant.

As evidence that a bona fide attempt is made to find the first and true inventor on the basis of the evidence, the agreement provides for exchange on an agreed date of the evidence with explanation thereof between the attorneys for the respective parties, who will then attempt within a fixed time period to reach mutual agreement on priority in accordance with the applicable law and rules of the Patent Office. The agreement further provides that, where the attorneys cannot so agree, the issue of priority is to be submitted for determination to the Board of Patent Interferences of the U.S. Patent Office, preferably on the basis of a stipulated record (to the extent that the parties can agree by stipulation to thereby reduce and simplify the issues), supplemented as need be by affidavits or the taking of testimony on other points. Care should be exercised in respect to the form and content of the stipulation, and also with respect to any alleged factual matter in an affidavit which may be filed, so that the right to contest the legal effect thereof is properly preserved for brief and argument at final hearing. *Pines* v. *McAllister*, 89 USPQ 312, CCPA 1951; *Crawford* v. *Howald et al.*, 124 USPQ 425, Bd. Intf. Exrs. 1950. The agreement usually provides that the decision of the Board of Patent Interferences shall be final.

The agreement also provides that the parties will file such papers in accordance with Rule 262 as will terminate the interference in accordance with any mutual agreement on priority. While certain attorneys have preferred an abandonment of the contest for this purpose, which can be filed upon a showing of sufficient cause by an assignee of the entire interest, Rule 262(c), this has the same effect under Rule 262(d) as a concession of priority signed by the inventor with the written consent of the assignee. *In re Fenn*, 137 USPQ 367, CCPA 1963.

Where a losing party is a patentee, a formal disclaimer under 35 U.S.C. 253 should also be filed, noting the definition of "patentee" in 35 USC 100(d) as including successors in title to the patentee.

Abandonment or Continuation of Contest

If settlement on a satisfactory basis cannot be agreed upon, or is thought not feasible, then careful consideration should be given, particularly by junior parties, as to whether the time and expense of further prosecution of the interference by the taking of testimony, etc., is justified. This should be weighed on the basis of the potential commercial importance of the subject matter in issue, together with the prospects of success of the party in view of information then available, including a comparison of his own case with the dates alleged in the preliminary statements of opposing parties as supplemented by any testimony already taken.

While a decision to carry a hard fought interference through to the bitter end can involve financial risks many times greater than the original cost of filing the application, the fact that at least one other party is working in the same identical area is an indication that the invention is thought to have commercial potential. Also, there is the matter of prestige, which at times may be mostly pride or downright stubbornness.

There is the possibility that, by the time a patent is finally issued as a result of winning a fully contested interference which was of commercial importance when initially declared, the art may have passed the invention by and gone on to noninfringing practices, perchance as the result of research work of opposing parties who were deliberately spurred into this activity by knowledge gained in the interference. Conversely, mere potential of an interference issue may never ripen into commercial use; and although one party eventually wins on priority, all parties lose financially.

But where the invention of the interference issue is of a dominating or relatively broad nature in a commercially developing art or active licensing field, a hard interference fight can result in merited reward.

Cross-references: *Clean Hands Doctrine,* Section on Interference Settlements, *Date of Invention, Inventors, Patentability,* Section on Concealment and Suppression, *Prosecution of Patent Applications, Records of Invention.*

INTERNATIONAL LICENSES AND ANTITRUST LAW. See FOREIGN LICENSES AND ANTITRUST LAW

INTERVENING RIGHTS. See REISSUE

INTERVIEWS WITH EXAMINERS

John L. Sigalos

Timing

Prosecution of an application is carried out by correspondence supplemented in many instances by interviews with the Examiner. It seems to some to be unwise to exhaust both procedures simultaneously. They hold that the two should be used to complement each other and that interviews should be delayed until after the correspondence possibilities have been exhausted. At that stage, the issues will have become crystallized and reduced in number and the claims amended to distinguish them, literally at least, from the closest art. The sole question then remaining should be the patentable significance of the distinctions. Finally, the fact that a case under interview is at a late stage makes both the attorney and the Examiner fully aware of the need of utmost care by each, in the presentation and judgment, respectively.

While such reasoning seems sound, it may not apply with full force, if at all, under the accelerated prosecution now being tried by the Patent Office, in an effort to reduce period of pendency of applications in the Office. At this time, it seems desirable to learn, before making even the first amendment, either from the Examiner's Action or by interview in person or by telephone with him, about what he can be expected

to hold allowable. *See Prosecution—Compact* and *Prosecution of Patent Applications,* first main section.

Preparation for Interview

Suitable preparation involves, first, arrival at the proper mental attitude. All theories aside, it must be admitted that the attorney wants to obtain allowance or an indication that it will follow. Secondly, careful advance preparation of the case is essential. The attorney should know the art, have determined what he will ask for, and probably have at hand an amendment written with the precision and realism that the thought of facing the Examiner inspires. An amendment prepared in advance also aids in directing the course of the interview to specifics of claim language and pertinency of the references rather than to generalities.

The Interview

The technique here as elsewhere will vary with the attorney. All attorneys, however, will probably seek to avoid long conversational diversions that waste time and delay getting to the point. Accuracy in all statements made and of all data relied upon is imperative. The attorneys will emphasize only matters of patentable significance and base no arguments for patentability on features that are not recited in the claims, have no basis in the specification, or are too limiting to be acceptable to the client. They may admit, at the outset, certain contentions of the Examiner such as showings of the art, point out the distinctions in applicant's case, note that the issue is patentability of those distinctions, and call attention to the unobvious results.

The attorneys will or should keep in mind the truisms that (1) the pleader should know the opposite side of the case well enough to be able to state it in the words of the opposition and (2) the way to win an argument is to avoid the argument or at least the image of being argumentative. The object of the interview is to present the inventor's case in a persuasive manner and not to engage in a debate.

Confirmation

The amendment filed after the interview will confirm the principal reasons presented at the interview for allowance and can, it is to be hoped, submit claims that seemed at the interview to describe the invention properly (or that have received favorable attention). Since the Examiner may wish to change his opinion on further consideration or after conferring with the head of his unit, there is doubted the appropriateness of stating that the Examiner has agreed to allow the claims, the nearness of approach to such statement varying with the definiteness of the result of the interview.

When the interview has ended favorably, it seems to be good practice to submit the confirming amendment promptly, in order to aid in disposing of the case.

INVENTION

Richard J. Dearborn and R. Bradlee Boal

The intent and effect of Section 103, relating to invention, has been interpreted by the Honorable Giles S. Rich, one of the chief architects of the 1952 Act, in part as follows:

"1. [The 1952 Act introduced the requirement of "invention"] into the statutes for the first time, in section 103. . . . Though one may call section 103 'codification' it took a case law doctrine, expressed in hundreds of different ways, and put it into statutory language in a single form approved by Congress. In such form it became law superior to that which may be derived from any prior court opinion.

"2. The Patent Act of 1952 expressed this prerequisite to patentability without any reference to 'invention' as a legal requirement. Nowhere in the entire act is there any reference to a requirement of 'invention' and the drafters did this deliberately in an effort to free the law and lawyers from bondage to that old and meaningless term. The word 'invention' is used in the statute only to refer to the thing invented. That is why the requirement of 'invention' should be referred to, if at all, only with respect due to that which is dead.

"3. The act sets as the standard of patentability the unobviousness of the invention, at the time it was made, to a person having ordinary skill in the art. Therefore, what we have today, and have had since January 1, 1953, is a requirement of *unobviousness*, rather than a requirement of 'invention.'" 42 JPOS 89, 1960.

The directness of "unobviousness" and its advantages over "invention," the latter being a derived term with a meaning clouded by many varying and often conflicting decisions, are recognized. Yet the latter term is so much a part of the judicial history of patent law that it is not likely to disappear from the language of patents in the near future. Even though the terminology may change, the connotations of "unobviousness" and "invention" overlap, and many of the theories and concepts associated with the development of the requirement of "invention" are certain to shape the development of the requirement of "unobviousness."

Robinson defined the process of invention as follows:

"The mental faculties employed in the inventive act are the *creative* not the *imitative* faculties. An invention is the product of original thought. It involves the spontaneous conception of some idea not previously present to the mind of the inventor. Industry in exploring the discoveries and acquiring the ideas of others; wise judgment in selecting and combining them; mechanical skill in applying them to practical results; none of these are creation, none of these enter into the inventive act. Only when the mind of the inventor originates an idea new to himself if not to all the world, does he call into exercise his own inventive skill, and perform the mental portion of the inventive act." I Robinson, The Law of Patents, p. 116, 1890.

Section 103 states that "Patentability shall not be negatived by the manner in which the invention was made." However, it is interesting to note that long before this provision was incorporated into the statute, Robinson made the following statement:

"The law draws no distinction between those operations of the creative faculties which manifest themselves in long-continued study and experiment, and those which reach their end by sudden intuition or apparent accident." Supra, p. 126.

Another eminent authority offers the following commentary:

"An invention is the result of an inventive act; it consists in (1) a mental operation involving the conception of an idea and (2) a physical operation involving the reduction to practice of the inventive concept. An invention is the product of original thought; it is a concept, a thing evolved from the mind. It involves the spontaneous conception or 'happy thought' of some idea not previously present to the mind of the inventor; it is the creation of something which did not exist before ..." I Walker, Deller's Ed., pp. 110-11, 1937.

Judicial History of the Standard of Invention

Since Section 103 is generally considered to be a codification of existing law on the "standard of invention," it is useful to review the history of judicial interpretation of the standard of invention.

In *Hotchkiss* v. *Greenwood*, 11 How. (52 U.S. 248, 267, 1850), the Supreme Court held for the first time that the test of invention is whether or not the advance required more ingenuity and skill than that possessed by a mechanic of ordinary skill in the art. In *Hotchkiss*, the invention in question consisted of the substitution of clay for wood or metal in a door knob. The court held that this advance did not meet the standard of invention.

In *Atlantic Works* v. *Brady*, 107 U.S. 192, 199, 1882, Mr. Justice Bradley clearly pointed out why the standard of invention requires more than that the advance merely be new and useful. He stated:

"It was never the object of those [patent] laws to grant a monopoly for every trifling device, every shadow of a shade of an idea, which would naturally and spontaneously occur to any skilled mechanic or operator in the ordinary progress of manufactures. Such an indiscriminate creation of exclusive privileges tends rather to obstruct than to stimulate invention. It creates a class of speculative schemers who make it their business to watch the advancing wave of improvement, and gather its foam in the form of patented monopolies, which enable men to lay a heavy tax upon the industry of the country, without contributing anything to the real advancement of the arts. It embarrasses the honest pursuit of business with fears and apprehensions of concealed liens and unknown liabilities to lawsuits and vexatious accountings for profits made in good faith."

Despite the fact that the Constitution does not use the word "invention" at all,

judicial sentiment as expressed by Justice Bradley seems so ingrained, in the judicial interpretation of the law, that novelty and utility may never be the sole criteria for patentability.

One of the most significant cases in recent years is that of *Cuno Engineering Corp.* v. *Automatic Devices Corp.*, 314 U.S. 84, 1941. The advance made by the patentee Mead in that case was to employ a bimetallic thermostat to automatically return an automobile cigarette lighter to the "off" position when the lighter plug reached the proper temperature. The prior art showed various "cordless" car lighters, but all of them had to be held in place until the operator estimated that the proper temperature had been reached. The prior art also showed that the use of bimetallic thermostatic elements was common in flat irons, coffee percolators, and electric toasters. In concluding that in view of the prior art the Mead combination did not rise to the dignity of "invention," Mr. Justice Douglas said:

"We may concede that the functions performed by Mead's combination were new and useful. But that does not necessarily make the device patentable. Under the statute ... the device must not only be 'new and useful,' it must also be an 'invention' or 'discovery.' ... It has been recognized that if an improvement is to obtain the privileged position of a patent more ingenuity must be involved than the work of a mechanic skilled in the art. ... That is to say, the new device, *however useful it may be, must reveal the flash of creative genius, not merely the skill of the calling.* If it fails, it has not established its right to a private grant on the public domain." Supra, p. 90. Emphasis added. Case citations omitted.

The Cuno case was of particular importance in creating what has sometimes been termed an "elevated" standard of invention. This standard demands that the invention exhibit a "flash of creative genius."

The reaction to the Cuno decision was prompt and widespread. Generally the cases subsequent to Cuno fell into the following three categories.

Acknowledging New Standard of Invention. In the first category is Judge Learned Hand's decision in *Picard* v. *United Aircraft Corporation*, 128 F.2d 632, 636, CA 2 1942, where he stated as follows:

"We cannot, moreover, ignore the fact that the Supreme Court, whose word is final, has for a decade or more shown an increasing disposition to raise the standard of originality necessary for a patent. In this we recognize 'a pronounced new doctrinal trend' which it is our 'duty, cautiously to be sure, to follow not to resist.'"

Not long after the *Cuno* case Mr. Justice Jackson commented on the "strong passion in this Court for striking [patents] down so that the only patent that is valid is one which this Court has not been able to get its hands on." *Jungersen* v. *Ostby and Barton Co.*, 335 U.S. 560, 572, 1949.

Applying Old Standard. In category (2) is the case of *In re Shortell*, 142 F.2d 292, 296, CCPA 1944, where, although recognizing and acknowledging the view taken by the Second Circuit in the Picard case, Judge Lenroot said:

"While recognizing, of course, that it is the duty of this court to follow the law as declared by the Supreme Court, we do not conceive it to be our duty to change our basis of decision merely because some courts assume that there is a 'new doctrinal trend' with regard to the standards required for invention.

"In our opinion it is not within the province of the courts to establish new standards by which invention is to be determined. It seems clear to us that the creation of new standards for the determination of what constitutes invention would be judicial legislation and not judicial interpretation.

"It follows, from the foregoing, that *until* Congress shall otherwise legislate, or *the Supreme Court shall otherwise specifically hold*, this court will continue to hold that if a process or thing constitutes patentable subject matter, is new and useful, and the process performed or thing produced would not be obvious to one skilled in the art, invention should be presumed and a patent may properly issue therefor." Emphasis added.

Refusing to Follow Cuno Case. In category (3) is the case of *Chicago Steel Foundry Co.* v. *Burnside Steel Foundry Co.*, 132 F.2d, 812 CA 7 1943, where Judge Evans wrote:

"Approaching the specific question in this case— the patentable novelty of the apparatus described in the two claims of plaintiff's patent here involved—we are rejecting the flash of genius test. We are adhering to the view which we believe all scientific knowledge and advance in knowledge is built on—the step by step advance—the test and error method. Also we are following the view that invention lies in, and must be determined by, the product, not in the mental activities or contortions that brought it forth." pp. 817-818.

Statutory Provision Bearing on Flash of Genius Doctrine

The "flash of creative genius" test imposed by the Supreme Court in the *Cuno* case, supra, created such a storm of protest from inventors, research scientists and patent counsel that a revision of the law was proposed and, after long discussion, the Act of July 19, 1952, was enacted.

Now an invention may result from a "flash of creative genius" or equally from the combined efforts of several scientists engaged for long years in working to solve a problem which has baffled an industry.

Combination of Old Elements

The standard by which to judge cases involving a "new combination of old elements" was laid down in the now famous case of the *Great Atlantic and Pacific Tea Co.* v. *Supermarket Equipment Corp.*, 340 U.S. 147, 1950, where the court had before it a patent on the familiar supermarket check-out counter, Mr. Justice Jackson in the majority opinion stated as follows:

"The conjunction or concert of known elements must contribute something; only when the whole in some way exceeds the sum of its parts is the accumulation of old devices patentable. Elements may, of course, especially in the chemistry of electronics, take on some new quality or function from being brought into concert, but this is not a usual result of uniting elements old in mechanics....

"This counter does what a store counter always has done—it supports merchandise at a convenient height while the customer makes his purchases and the merchant his sales. The three-sided rack will draw or push goods put within it from one place to another—just what any such a rack would do on any smooth surface—and the guide rails keep it from falling or sliding off from the counter, as guide rails have ever done. Two and two have been added together, and still they make only four....

"This patentee has added nothing to the total stock of knowledge, but has merely brought together segments of prior art and claims them in congregation as a monopoly." pp. 152-153.

The *A & P* case is of particular importance in view of the high proportion of inventions involving "new combination of old elements." Indeed Judge Learned Hand has said:

"...It is idle to say that combinations of old elements cannot be inventions; substantially every invention is for such a 'combination': that is to say, it consists of former elements in a new assemblage." *Reiner v. I. Leon Co.,* 285 F.2d 501, 503, CA 2 1960.

As noted above, there was confusion in the courts following the *Cuno* case as to whether the old Hotchkiss standard or a newer, more elevated standard was law. This confusion was largely dispelled with the advent of the 1952 Patent Act and present Section 103. Although Section 103 has not yet been interpreted by the Supreme Court, in *Lyon* v. *Bausch & Lomb Optical Co.,* 224 F.2d 530, CA 2 1955, Judge Hand made it clear that he considered that the statute restored the standard of invention established in the *Hotchkiss* case. Later he said, in *Reiner* v. *I. Leon Co.,* 285 F.2d 501, 503, CA 2 1960:

"We still cannot escape the conclusion—as we could not when Lyon v. Bausch & Lomb Optical Co., supra, was decided in 1955—that Congress deliberately meant to restore the old definition, and to raise it from a judicial gloss to a statutory command." p. 503.

It seems probable that the courts in the future generally will follow *Lyon* v. *Bausch & Lomb* at least until the Supreme Court has occasion to interpret Section 103.

Guides for Determining Whether Invention Is Involved

While guides are of limited value in applying the "standard of invention," courts generaly attempt to use some guides or at least give lip service to them in measuring a particular advance.

In *Reiner* v. *I. Leon Co.,* supra, Judge Learned Hand acknowledged the difficulty in measuring "invention," in these words:

"To judge on our own that this or that new assemblage of old factors was, or was not, 'obvious' is to substitute our ignorance for the acquaintance with the subject of those who were familiar with it. There are indeed some sign posts: e.g., how long did the need exist; how many tried to find the way; how long did the surrounding and accessory arts disclose the means; how immediately was the invention recognized as an answer by those who used the new variant?...Great commercial success, when properly scrutinized, may be a telling circumstance."

The circumstances and facts surrounding the invention seem at times to outweigh, quite properly, abstract principles and definitions set forth under different sets of facts. Judge O'Connell has said:

"A fertile source of error in the patent law is the misapplication of a sound legal principle established by a court of competent jurisdiction in one case to a subsequent situation in another case wherein the facts are essentially different and the principle has no application whatsoever." *In re Newton,* 88 USPQ 554, 556, CCPA 1951.

Conclusion: A Subjective Decision

In view of the subjectiveness of the interpretation of Section 103 by the courts, many have argued that novelty and utility should be the sole criteria of patentability. In this context Mr. Justice Brown's statement in *McClain* v. *Ortmayer,* 141 U.S. 419, 426, 1891 seems particularly apposite:

"To say that the act of invention is the production of something new and useful does not solve the difficulty of giving an accurate definition, since the question of what is new as distinguished from that which is a colorable variation of what is old, is usually the very question in issue....

"In a given case we may be able to say that there is present invention of a very high order. In another we can see that there is lacking that impalpable something which distinguishes invention from simple mechanical skill. Courts, adopting fixed principles as a guide, have by a process of exclusion determined that certain variations in old devices do or do not involve invention; but whether the variation relied upon in a particular case is anything more than ordinary mechanical skill is a question which cannot be answered by applying the test of any general definition."

Novelty and utility, as the sole criteria of patentability, have much in their favor. The late Drury W. Cooper, an eminent patent counsel with long years of experience in trying patent cases, advocated that patentability be determined simply by answering the questions: Is it *new?* Is it *useful?* 23 JPOS 319, 1941. From the standpoint of the public welfare and the promotion of commerce and industry, it is hard to conceive of a better yardstick for measuring patentability or one more definite and more easily determined. The Hon. Giles S. Rich, speaking as a private citizen, supports such a standard in **28** Geo. Wash. L. R. **393.**

Cross-references: *Act of 1952, Anticipation, Invention—Changing Objectives, Monopolies . . . ,* Section on Unobviousness . . . , *Patentability, Validity.*

INVENTION—CHANGING OBJECTIVES

Judge Florence E. Allen

This is a reprint, with some revision, of my address before the Cincinnati Patent Law Association, 40 JPOS 312, 1958.

Invention is as old as the human race. The development of the alphabet from picture-writing is a high instance of invention. There is no recorded history of the making of the basic inventions such as the wheel and axle, the inclined plane and wedge, and the lever and pulley. Perhaps the wheel was developed through men's experience of rolling rocks or trees, but, however it came, it was one of the primary inventions. How the Egyptians raised the pyramids and the Mayans of Yucatan raised their colossal structures we cannot explain. At some point these tremendous achievements must have depended for their accomplishment on highly efficient mechanical devices.

Early Handmaid of the Military

The Greeks who manifested the highest intellect of ancient times were interested in pure mathematics rather than in mechanical adaptation of scientific principle. Archimedes, whose war machines held the Romans at bay in Syracuse for several years, scornfully dismissed his devices as not worthy of description. He discovered specific gravity and invented hydrostatics. He invented a screw which pulled up water from the hold of a ship, and this screw was used down through the centuries for the lifting or lowering of water. Plutarch says that by a triple pulley, Archimedes could move a three-masted sea-going galley, that he pulled the Roman ships up in the air, shook them and let them fall, destroying themselves and everything in the ship. His ballista dropped stones that weighed tons upon the Sambuca, the great moving bridge built by the Romans to reach over the walls of Syracuse, and broke it up. Also, Archimedes is said to have transmitted fire to the Roman ships by means of burning lenses. But he did all these things under order of the tyrant of Syracuse. Invention *per se* he considered so relatively unimportant that not one of his treatises deals with the mechanical structures that he devised and used so successfully. And yet, as to mathematical genius, Whitehead says, "When the Roman soldier stabbed Archimedes, the world knew as much mathematics as was known at any time until, say, the fourteenth century, when its advance was resumed." Whitehead also says, "We might just as well have had the industrial age in the time of Archimedes; everything necessary was known . . . apparently all that was lacking was that in Sicily or Magna Graecia people did not sit by their fires and watch the lids of their kettles lift from the steam of the boiling water." So the surpassing intellect of ancient times, having devoted some inventive thought to the colossal machines of war under the orders of a tyrant, passed on to consider the construction of the sphere, the relation of the sphere to the cylinder in terms of proportion, and kindred abstract subjects, but did not create devices useful in ordinary living.

Leonardo da Vinci, too, who has been called the most gifted of all the sons of men, was chief military engineer of Milan, and military engineer to Cesare Borgia, directing huge works in the canals and harbors of central Italy. Leonardo, in his notebooks, spends many pages on the problem of flight. One of the chapters is on a "flying machine." An article by a distinguished scholar says that experts concede that all Leonardo needed for flight was "petrol"; but he was compelled to use his mechanical and mathematical genius on works of war.

His magnificent studies of flight and motion, wind and water, were considered foolish by his contemporaries.

The Romans were more practical. Perhaps the necessity of securing water for the growing city and their vastly expanding empire made them acquainted with the use of power. Sheer necessity forced them to devise methods of transporting water, of controlling it and of employing its power in daily life, and through that, other devices useful and inventive were developed.

Roman Empire

I once drove along the Roman wall, built under Hadrian, in the 72-mile stretch that separates Scotland from England. Ruins show not only that the wall was wide enough for four chariots to drive abreast along its top, but that in the living quarters, Rome had already progressed to modern ideas of sanitation. There were baths and toilets apparently flushed by water. The sanitary conception of the Romans was so much higher and further advanced mechanically than that of the British people through centuries of living, that Churchill in his "History of the English Speaking People" says,

"...for nearly three hundred years Britain, reconciled to the Roman system, enjoyed in many respects the happiest, most comfortable, and most enlightened times its inhabitants had had. In this period, almost equal to that which separates us from the reign of Queen Elizabeth I, well-to-do persons in Britain lived better than they ever did until the late Victorian times. From the year 400 until the year 1900 no one had central heating and very few hot baths. A wealthy British-Roman citizen building a country house regarded the hypocaust which warmed it as indispensable. For fifteen hundred years, his descendants lived in the cold of unheated dwellings, mitigated by occasional roastings at gigantic wasteful fires. Even now a smaller proportion of the whole population dwells in centrally heated houses than in those ancient days. As for baths, they were completely lost till the middle of the nineteenth century. In this long, bleak intervening gap cold and dirt clung to the most fortunate and highest in the land."

It seems to be established that in the realm of sanitation, for which Rome had done so much, the Christians, reating from the luxury of the Roman baths, refused to recognize virtue in anything sponsored on so extravagant a scale by infidels and pagans. As a result, not only the plain people, but the nobles and kings, were not clean. The perfumes sought in the search for the eastern sea passage were partly because Britain had forsaken the cleanliness of the Romans and, with it, had abandoned the mechanical devices that made cleanliness possible.

Middle Ages

Of course, the stunting of mechanical initiative was inevitable during the Dark and Middle Ages, 450 A.D. to 1550 A.D. In the destruction which ensued upon the fall of Rome, 475 A.D., the devices and apparatus known to the Roman Empire were completely lost. Such a simple article as the comfortable and beautiful Greek chair, developed by the fifth century B.C., was revived by France in the eighteenth century. For centuries men sat on the ground, on cushions, on benches without backs. A print of 1468 shows the nobility of France sitting on benches without backs as judges in a trial of the Duke d'Alençon for high treason. The trial lasted three months. The judges had no chair; only the king himself was accorded a kingly seat. In those days, because of the instability of the times, persons who traveled, including kings, traveled with their furniture. They had to take it with them (1) to have any furniture to use; (2) to have any furniture when they ended the trip. All of their furniture was what could be contained in chests. The prints of the time show rooms and palaces containing no furniture but chests. It took centuries to develop movable tables, comfortable chairs, settees or sofas, and when developed, these things for long periods of time were for the comfort of only the wealthy people.

As Europe recovered from the seventh century night, invention was also to some degree held back by the organization of the Guilds. Before a man could be an artisan, or indeed a merchant, or a shopkeeper, he had to be a citizen of the town. Typical of the restrictions which hampered initiative was an English Act of 1389, the first of a series of similar provisions forbidding tanners to be shoemakers or shoemakers to be tanners. In Strasbourg, in 1474, an ordinance prohibited weavers from selling the cloth they made.

Necessarily these meager comments touch only a few high spots of this backward period. There were exceptions in the general picture. For instance division of labor had been used for centuries as in the loading of galleys on the canals of Venice.

England

In England, invention on an important scale gradually entered the field of spinning. Arkwright, around 1767, set up a successful cotton mill. He used a spinning frame that spun a vast number of threads of varying degrees of firmness. The spinning jenny of Hargreaves had been unable to spin threads of the hardness required for the warp. The Encyclopaedia Britannica calls the Arkwright spinning frame the foundation of British industrial supremacy. But the inventions that especially held the public eye were those calculated to amuse and astonish the ruling classes. The inventions of automatons showed that mechanical facility existed. In the 17th and 18th centuries, the automatons were miraculously perfected. Around 1738, Vaucanson had three which were exhibited in Paris, described by Diderot—The Flutist, The Drummer, The Duck. The flutist had movable lips, a movable tongue and movable fingers, all of which played the flute. The drummer beat the drum and also played a shepherd's pipe. The mechanical duck had wings that beat the air; it waddled and swam, quacked, and picked up grain. These were real mechanical achievements, but they were not made for production or for any useful purpose, except the very limited one of diversion. Vaucanson was made Inspector of Silk Manufacturing under Louis XV and planned a silk factory in which he wound the threads from the cocoons as they lay in the bath. It was not adopted in general. France at that time was not greatly interested in commercial inventions. This was two decades before Arkwright's spinning factory.

American Style—Servant of All

When the United States of America was founded, the inhibitions and traditions of the Old World were abolished to a large degree. Men who came to America no longer worked for kings or lords. They were no longer members of crafts which controlled their wages, their occupations and their employment. Here, they were free and initiative was released. It was released in a country which, as part of its basic doctrine, announced a belief in the dignity and rights of the individual. Inevitably, it followed that men worked as never before for themselves, for their families, and for the comfort and convenience of their individual surroundings.

The immensity of the country and the lack of labor made it necessary to invent. And so, here not only did the substitution of the machine for the hand proceed apace, but the assembly line method was early foreshadowed. In 1836, Haskell and Moore, two farmers in the middle west, patented a reaper with an endless belt which carried the grain to a thresher and a winnowing means, fan and sac-filling apparatus. This combine sprung up in a wilderness.

In 1783, the idea was applied in Pennsylvania by Oliver Evans to a mill operated in a continuous production line. Evans had the Archimedian screw and bucket conveyor for transporting the grain. The screw moved the grain horizontally; the line of buckets raised the grain to the top story of the mill, from which it was set in motion by gravity, and carried by a moderately inclined strip of leather. The grain was carried to the millstones and back to the upper story in one continuous operation. The millers in Congress attacked Evans' patent because they did not wish to pay the royalties. Thomas Jefferson supported the millers. He stated that every part of Evans' device was old. The elevator was the Persian wheel of Egypt, and the conveyor was the screw of Archimedes. This was true. But it was a true combination—a new and useful result obtained in a new way. It opened a new door in the history of invention.

The reaper and binder of Haskell and Moore and the mill of Oliver Evans were the forerunners of the assembly line of Ford (1913) in which the parts of the automobile are placed on elevated platforms, carried past successive groups of workmen and affixed to the machine. Ford, of course, bound together hundreds of operations to create one complicated machine in the beginning of the use of the assembly line as we now know it.

The era required rapid production and production *for all*. The assembly line made this possible. It also made possible the ownership of cars and other inventions by the middle-class and working people.

In America, the patent system has been, in the terms of the statute, "useful" not for a limited class, the rich, or, as in Europe, the nobles, but for the generality of men without exception. It has been developed in this country as nowhere else for the protection, beautification, and simplification of ordinary peacetime life. While it has been used in the wars which have been forced upon us (witness the Monitor-Merrimac incident), it primarily recognizes the dignity and importance of the American citizen.

The significance of the American attitude that mechanical ingenuity should be applied to simple problems of living is illustrated by the careers of two of our greatest men, Franklin and Jefferson. Franklin invented a heat-radiating stove at a time when all England was shivering before grates. Having pulled down lightning and being conscious of the havoc that lightning could work, Benjamin Franklin invented a lightning rod to protect human beings, the home, the family, the barn in which the harvest was stored, and the livestock, from the dangers of lightning. Certain churches objected to Franklin's lightning rod upon the ground that lightning was an evidence of the wrath of God which no mortal should endeavor to avert, but the lightning rod still proved its value and became an accepted device. Franklin also invented bifocal lenses. Although not a mechanical genius like Archimedes, he still was a remarkable man who by the breadth of his interest in every human problem not only greatly advanced the movement for freedom in the Colonies but made outstanding contributions to the solution of practical living problems. This

was, and still is an outstandingly American trait. It is invention American Style. If the American was confronted with a problem, he did not say, as the English, that questioning of a problem "isn't done," nor did he accept the existence of hardship or inconvenience with a shrug as certain continentals; he applied his ingenuity to disposing of the problem. In this sense Benjamin Franklin and the devices on which he worked, were a typical example of invention American Style.

Thomas Jefferson was another outstanding example. Jefferson's inventions were mainly improvements or adaptations—remarkable for the fields they covered as well as for showing Jefferson's creative qualities of mind.

Jefferson continually thought of accommodating machines "to the small and more numerous callings of life." He favored cheap, ingenious, small mechanical devices applicable to "our daily concerns." So, although Jefferson, constantly occupied with great affairs, realized the problems of the mighty French canal system to the extent that he actually designed an improved gate for the locks, he was repeatedly designing intimate domestic improvements. His dumbwaiter was the first in the form of a lift or elevator. He copied a beautiful European clock for Monticello and had the face inside the house as well as fronting on the porch. He made a three-piece walking stick which could be transformed into a stool. He had a four-membered music stand which could be used by a quartet and then folded back, leaving one rack for a soloist. He was constantly pointing out the advantage of mechanics in the home, for instance, that a small steam engine could pump water to a tank from which all rooms could be supplied with running water.

He invented a moldboard for the plow. The problem was to receive the sod, raise it gradually, and reverse it. Jefferson arranged the movements of the board from horizontal to perpendicular so that with a lighter implement he plowed a deeper furrow with less expense of power and money than was secured by former devices. A French agricultural society gave him a gold medal for this achievement. Thus, the man who wrote the Declaration of Independence was also an inventor American Style.

All of us know, from our own experience, the vast development of invention in America which has concerned itself with peace-time living. I myself have lived through the time of the student lamp, the carbide light, and the gas light. The rapid development of electronics came about since that time. As a child of seven or eight, there then being no boys in the family, I chopped the kindling and made the fire every morning in three stoves. Now in my simple home I turn a switch and in a few moments a gentle uniform heat is established throughout the whole house. Archimedes would have dismissed the pop-up toaster, the pressure cooker, the thermostat frying pan, the electric range, the power mower, and the infra-red light, as being unworthy of high intellect; but they have enormously eased the pressure upon many a mother or father of a family. The very theory of mass production arises from the belief, peculiarly American, that the benefits of life, including the fruits of invention, should be available to the nation as a whole. And so the ordinary person has a fountain pen, an inexpensive watch, considers it not impossible to buy a typewriter, and fully intends to own a car.

As I come of the generation born before there ever had been an automobile, I have some measuring rod by which to estimate the revolution wrought by the automobile and made available to the entire people through assembly line production. The Wright brothers, unlike Leonardo da Vinci, had petrol so they could keep their wonderful machine in the air. While both the automobile and the airplane are used for war purposes, they are used for many beneficial purposes, even as atomic power may be.

I am aware as I say this of the huge and wonderful achievements of American invention, such as the development of new and enormously important processes in the chemistry of metals. The actual inventive thinking expended in the laying out of our great industrial plants is a monument to the ingenuity and creative invention of the American people. Also, I know that American invention has been used for defense, as the Manhattan project. I stress the homely achievements of American creative thought because they seem to me to carry out the American tradition. Many another country at the time that Bell invented the telephone would have used it to enhance the convenience and comfort of the ruling classes and no one else. Here the telephone is the servant of the entire people. Automation is being developed and we find it not merely in the Pentagon, if, indeed, it is there, but in the hotels which serve our court so courteously here in Cincinnati and in the office buildings to which the entire people resort. I venture to say that the triumphant course of the Explorer in its orbit will turn out to be for the benefit of the entire nation and not, as with some other machines, for the destruction of all.

As we stand on the threshold of American achievements in the development of power and the mastery of outer space, the American viewpoint on invention is still all-important—the viewpoint that the nation's inventive ingenuity should be used to help in all phases of life. It is the American doctrine that invention should be employed not only for governmental purposes, but to make life healthful, comfortable and less burdensome to the entire people, to the ordinary men and women, as well as to the officials and high brass of any class or profession.

These propositions were substantiated during the Second World War. We repeatedly heard from returning soldiers how on islands in the Pacific, with pieces salvaged from destroyed tanks and autos, men made ice machines, washing machines. In the Battle of the Bulge one boy crossed a river to a source of electric power and strung a line which electrified his hospital unit. If the story of these enterprises had been gathered from the armed forces in general, it would have made an overwhelming record demonstrating that American ingenuity still exists and still naturally applies itself to the solution of the problem in hand not for the benefit of a lord or king but for the common good.

If we permit the despotisms of the Old World to be reestablished here, American inventive power will inevitably be destroyed. Invention American Style is the indispensable servant of Freedom American Style. But Invention American Style cannot exist without Freedom American Style.

Cross-references: *History of Patents—Abroad, also in the United States, Invention, Public Relations and the Patent System.*

INVENTORS

Thomas B. Graham

Every person is an inventor.

Inventors of record include, for instance, presidents, cabinet officers, scientists, athletes, musicians, and farmers. There is no restriction as to sex, citizenship, nationality, age, position, or mental condition. Patents have issued alike to Abraham Lincoln; the foreign discoverer of the Peace Rose; estates of the deceased; and Robert W. Patch, probably our youngest inventor, who, at an age of 6 years, filed for a toy truck and obtained patent 3,091,888, issued on June 4, 1963. While most patents are in the name of one or two inventors, U.S. patent 3,112,394 on a computer was issued to Patrick B. Close and 20 co-inventors. 796 O.G. 1078, 1963. The total of 21 inventors is reported to be probably the record number and could be justified only by an invention of the utmost complexity.

Selection of the Inventor

Since the patent Statute requires that the application for patent be in the name of the inventor, it is of prime importance that the proper inventor be designated.

The inventor must be a natural person, not a corporation. He is the one responsible for the feature that makes the new process or article, the ornamental design or plant patentable.

While it is usual to accept the experimenter as the inventor, because this is the normal condition, the inventor in organized research is often a person in a supervisory capacity. The controlling factor is: who supplied the inventive concept in form that

worked without the need of further invention.

Sole and Joint Inventors

Research frequently is not a solo operation. Hence, it is common to see two, three or more people recognized as joint inventors. The Statute provides for this condition (35 U.S.C. 116, 256), and case law is liberal in recognition of joint invention.

Statistically, it is perhaps unlikely that two people, even if working together, will have the identical new concept at exactly the same point in time. Neither the Statute nor the Courts require such coincidence. It is enough that separate contributions result in a patentable combination. *Moler and Adams* v. *Purdy,* 131 USPQ 276, PO BdApp 1961.

It is not necessary to identify and allocate the individual concepts utilized.

The present Statute is relatively broad also in its requirements for identification of inventor when more than one person is involved. If there is a sound basis for question about the addition of a name to an application, the doubt should be resolved in favor of adding the name. The Statute requires that the application be signed by the inventor. If one of the group is the true inventor, the application meets the need. If it is later found that a joint inventor has been omitted or a name included improperly, the error is subject to correction.

Adding or Subtracting Inventors

Inventors' names may be added to (or subtracted from) a joint application or patent when an error arose in naming or not naming an inventor, "and such error arose without any deceptive intention on his part." 35 U.S.C. 116.

If the application or patent, with incorrect statement of inventorship, is involved in interference and if diligence is not shown in correcting the inventorship, such correction may not be allowed. In a case on this point, the attorney for the party V. raised the question in 1956, but made no move to add the name of the joint inventor until the testimony was completed in 1958. His motion to add was denied on the ground of lack of diligence in converting to a joint application. *Van Otteren* v. *Hafner and Cork,* 126 USPQ 151, 153, CCPA 1960.

Rule 45 gives the procedure for such conversion:

"If an application for patent has been made through error and without any deceptive intention by less than all the actual joint inventors, the application may be amended to include all the joint inventors upon filing a statement of the facts verified by, and an oath as required by rule 65 executed by, all the actual joint inventors, provided the amendment is diligently made. Such amendment must have the written consent of any assignee."

"The 'required statement of the facts' must include, at the least, a recital of the circumstances, including the relevant dates, of (1) the misjoinder and (2) the discovery of the misjoinder." M.P.E.P. 201.03.

Reissuing the patent is not permitted for correcting the inventorship. *Ex parte Johnson* and allied cases, 117 USPQ 412, 416, PO BdApp 1956.

In a case before the District Court of Nebraska in 1958, an application for the John Blue Co. had been prepared in the name of Blue and Johnson. The general manager of the company had Johnson's name removed and the application filed by Blue alone. Later the name of Johnson was added, the court said by "reissue" (obviously an error since the patent in suit was an original, 2,771,846). The court noted that the removal of Johnson's name from the application, as initially drawn, was intentional. The court said regarding this removal:

"...It was not the result of inadvertence, accident or mistake and is not a correctable error, being one of judgment only. For this reason if no other the patent is invalid."

These words may be regarded as *obiter*, since the patent was held invalid on the basis of claiming a mere aggregation. In any event, it is uncertain whether other courts will adopt such reasoning regarding deliberate omission of a name. The Statute provides for addition when the error has arisen without deceptive intention on *the part of the person* omitted or joined improperly.

The provisions of the Patent Act of 1952, for adding or subtracting a name apply also to patents issued in advance of the date of that act. *Van Otteren* case, supra, 153.

Application by Other than the Inventor

The Patent Act of 1952, 35 U.S.C. 116, provides for filing applications by others, but in the name of the inventor(s), under the following circumstances:

The Inventor	Application May Be Made for Him by
Is deceased or under legal incapacity	Legal representative
Joint inventor refuses to sign or cannot be reached	Other joint inventor
Refuses to sign or cannot be reached	Person showing sufficient proprietary interest in invention

The showing of "sufficient proprietary interest in the matter" when the inventor refuses to sign the application or "cannot be found or reached after diligent effort," all as required under Section 118, is made most directly by filing a copy of the employee's contract or other agreement in writing for assignment of the invention.

The matter of adequacy of proof of sufficient proprietary interest is discussed by Assistant Commissioner Crocker. *In re Application Papers of Gray,* 115 USPQ 80, 1956. The written assignment of an application and any " 'reissue, division, or continuation of said application' is not interpreted as establishing petitioner's ownership of a 'continuation-*in-part*' of the original application." (Emphasis added.) Inadequate also as proof was the affidavit of the petitioner's general manager "asserting a 'general understanding' that petitioner's employees were under an obligation to assign their inventions to petitioner." The applicant, however, had filed an affidavit, in connection with the original application, in which affidavit he had described his "specific work assignments" including "experimentation, research and development in the field in which the present invention resides." This and other evidence in the case led to the decision that sufficient proprietary interest existed for the filing of the application by the employer, in accordance with other cases cited.

Rule 47 says in part:

"(b) Whenever an inventor refuses to execute an application for patent, or cannot be found or reached after diligent effort, a person to whom the inventor has assigned or agreed in writing to assign the invention or who otherwise shows sufficient proprietary interest in the matter justifying such action may make application for patent on behalf of and as agent for the inventor. Such application must be accompanied by proof of the pertinent facts and a showing that such action is necessary to preserve the rights of the parties or to prevent irreparable damage, and must state the last known address of the inventor."

Refusal to Sign Application Because of Alleged Lack of Invention

In a case under the old law, refusal to sign an application was based upon the allegation that the process and product of the proposed application had been learned from a visit to the factory of the maker of the machine utilized. The employer, it was held, "failed to meet the burden which lay upon it of showing applicants refusal [to sign] to be capricious or without merit." *Guth* v. *Minnesota Mining and Mfg. Co.*, 22 USPQ 89, CA 7 1934.

The court under such circumstances will not require the applicant to make what might be a false oath. The new law, under the circumstances described in Section 118, permits the employer to file the application in behalf of the inventor.

General Observations

It is important to note that the Statute is completely silent as to correction of names on an application or patent where the entire list of inventors is wrong, i.e., where the names include no actual inventor. This silence is taken to mean that no correction can be made because the elementary requirement of an application signed by an inventor has not been met; a sheaf of paper has been filed in the Patent Office.

However, if a patent names one true inventor and also a non-inventor, with no deceptive intention, the error may be corrected. Conversely, omission of a true joint inventor can be corrected. The misjoinder or non-joinder of inventors with the true inventor will not invalidate a patent, if the error is corrected as provided for in 35 U.S.C. 116 and 256.

However, an application for patent carrying the name of no correct inventor does not meet the basic requirement of the Statute. On this point, Mr. P. J. Federico, now a member of the Board of Appeals, has made the following observation:

"Patent Office practice permits the simultaneous omission of an erroneously joined person and addition of an erroneously omitted inventor in an application; thus an application filed by A and B as joint inventors can under the appropriate circumstances be amended to become an application of A and C as joint inventors, but an application filed by A as inventor, or by A and B as joint inventors cannot be amended to become an application of C as inventor either by one or two steps." 35 U.S.C.A. 28, 1954.

As a working formula in an organization, it is imperative in filing any application, therefore, to make sure that a true inventor signs. Also, a careful investigation should be made to identify all joint inventors, if any.

To make certain of including at least one true inventor, doubts should be resolved in favor of adding rather than omitting a name on the border-line between inventor and non-inventor.

Nothing perhaps is more damaging to laboratory morale than preemption of credit for inventions by those having more direct connection than the actual inventor with reporting the experimental work. A patent is looked upon as something a bit more exciting than an ordinary journal publication and perhaps properly so. The subject matter of a patent, by law, must have utility. It has been subjected, before allowance, to scrutiny usually considerably more detailed than the preview for a journal. Allowance of the patent amounts to an expression of belief by the Patent Office that the inventor has made a significant contribution worthy of a patent. For this as well as other reasons, assignment of credit for invention should be carefully made.

Cross-references: *Act of 1952, Incentives for Inventors, Information for Independent Inventors, Inventors' Psychology, Taxation,* Section on Payments to Employees for Assigments.

INVENTORS' PSYCHOLOGY

Robert Calvert

The inventor works mostly for financial reward, recognition of status in his profession or circle of friends, and satisfaction and pride in making a contribution.

Appraisal of Inventors

Dr. Joseph Rossman,[1] who early showed the soundness of judgment and keenness of analysis that have marked his later work as a patent lawyer, learned from 710 inventors, 78 research directors, and 176 patent attorneys what they considered to be the characteristics of inventors. His data in simplified form appears below. Where the Table shows "Perseverance 71%," for example, it means that 503 of the 710 or 71 per cent of the inventors who replied to the

TABLE 1.

| | Listed in Replies, % of Total, from | | |
Characteristic	710 Inventors	78 Research Directors	176 Patent Attorneys
Perseverance	71%	53%	11%
Imagination	29	45	19
Knowledge and memory	26	—	—
Business ability	23	—	—
Lack of business ability	—	—	15
Originality	21	48	36
Common sense	19	—	—
Analytical ability	16	62	25
Confidence	15	20	—
Keen observation	9	15	10
Mechanical ability	6	—	3
Training and education	—	26	—
Reasoning and intelligence	—	26	—
Optimism	—	—	7

questionnaire considered they had that quality, presumably to a degree substantially above normal.

The first column of figures shows the large proportion of inventors who give credit to perseverance.

The next column shows the recognition by their associates, the research directors, of this same hard road to invention and emphasis also on imagination, originality and analytical ability.

The attorneys' percentages, it will be noted, are much lower because the reply from the individual attorney listed fewer items on the average.

Patent-Mindedness

The 1,039 patents issued to Edison indicate that he was patent-minded and no doubt able to recognize an invention when he had made it.

Most research men in a company having a positive patent policy soon become patent-conscious.

An example of this and of its importance is the following case. A chemist in a then small industrial laboratory made a water solution of a water-insoluble therapeutic agent. Although in daily use in millions of homes, it could previously be administered only in solid form or as an oil dispersion of unpleasant taste. His patent attorney advised against filing an application on the ground of non-patentability. The chemist was patent-minded and he was himself a student in an evening course in patent law. He did not accept this decision but persisted until the case was filed. The patent was allowed, was licensed to a score of companies, and is still used around the world.

Those who work alone or in small groups are apt to overlook potentially important inventions. This is unfortunate because the small company, or individual, has most need of patent protection. It, or he, suffers more from competition in an open field than the large corporation.

Fortunately most inventors have a middle-ground psychology. They direct their research to the company's problems and objectives, not primarily to making inventions. When a by-product invention does appear, however, they recognize it, appraise it realistically, and consider filing upon it, particularly if it is of commercial promise.

Imagination

The imagination of youth is no doubt one of the reasons for the predominance of young inventors over older ones in making outstanding inventions. Lehman [2] and Schmookler [3] show the ages of (a) those making the greatest inventions and (b) those who are most prolific in numbers of patents taken currently. The following Table, summarizing the significant data, points heavily to youth for the greatest inventions and the 30 to 50 year age as the most prolific.

TABLE 2. INDEX OF RATE OF INVENTIONS PER MEMBER OF SPECIFIED AGE GROUPS—MODAL GROUP = 100.

Age Group	40 Greatest Modern Inventions	554 Important Modern Inventions	84 Contemporary Inventions Selected at Random
15-19	12	12	0
20-29	67	71	15
30-39	100	100	95
40-49	40	56	100
50-54	13	25	75
55-84	0	4	13

The importance of stimulating exercise of the imagination is recognized. The stimulation on a practical basis is attempted in the so-called "brain-storming" sessions regularly held by many organizations. Cf. Alex F. Osborn, "Applied Imagination. Principles and Procedures of Creative Thinking," New York, Charles Scribner's Sons, 1953.

Enthusiasm

If imagination is the self-starter for the inventor, enthusiasm is a driving force that propels him continuously forward. Enthusiasm leads to optimism. Both inspire the inventor to unexpected achievement and ultimate success. And both are contagious. They penetrate to the assistants and give them that feeling of importance in themselves which leads to the best work.

Curiosity

Many inventors have a strong sense of curiosity. Benjamin Franklin no doubt had it when he flew his kite into the area of lightning, to test the theory that lightning is electricity. He was overly curious when he sent an electric charge through four or five men holding hands, in series, to test the effect on humans. They fell to the floor, he reported, got up and said they felt nothing!

The electronics engineer demonstrates his curiosity when he designs a home-invented, though unsuccessful, device for automatically cutting off the spoken commercials in a musical program. The research chemist is curious and, for that reason, more interested in his work when he wonders what the distillation temperature of a compound with a new substituent, the solvent power, and other properties of his new compound will be.

Urge to Make Contribution

In the days before the world was ready to pay for scientific results, the chief motives for activating experimenters must have been curiosity, the satisfaction of making a contribution to science, and an inborn liking for knowledge. It is doubtful that Faraday, for example, had any personal monetary incentive in mind when he moved a conductor in a closed circuit through a magnetic field and discovered the generation of electric current which became the basis for the world's dynamos. When asked by a politician what good there was in the discovery, Faraday replied in effect: Of what use is a new born baby? Some day you can tax it.

Priestley with a powerful lens was able to focus so much of the sun's rays on oxide of mercury that he liberated oxygen. He had no use for this amazing discovery. He noted, however, that mice placed in a bottle of gas were enlivened and he forecast that his "antiphlogiston" might at a later date serve as a breathing luxury for the rich.

These gentlemen, like their modern successors, attended early meetings of other experimenters, wrote papers, corresponded with scientists throughout the world and must have found great satisfaction and, for them, adequate reward in their mutual approbation and in opening, just a little more, the then almost closed door to nature's secrets.

These same motives activate inventors today.

Desire for Recognition of Contributions

When an inventor says to his attorney, "It is wholly immaterial to me whether you put my name on the application (for patent) or not," the attorney should assume that there is not a word of truth in the statement. He should accept it only as evidence of a desire to be agreeable, cooperative and self-sacrificing, all perhaps being a net advantage to the considerate inventor in the long run.

Actually inventors have in their inventions the pride of a parent for a child. They abhor separation from the offspring of their brain. They may in a whole lifetime make only a few such contributions, or even no others. One invention every 2½ to 4 years seems to be about the average for scientists in the oil, chemical and electrical industries.[4] The inventors want the profession to know where the credit is due.

"A United States patent," says Barnes,[5] "is issued in the inventor's name . . . [His] name will be forever attached to that patent. . . . Issued patents are tangible evidence of his worth as an inventor, and they are perfectly salable in a quest for a job wherever he goes. They will have an effect on his salary." For many industrial workers, patents are about the only type of publication available to them. Those who make the inventions deserve to appear in the publications.

Creativeness

Creativeness is perhaps the resultant of the forces and psychological factors motivating the active inventor. Brown [6] characterizes creative scientists essentially as follows:

(1) Intellectually curious and inquisitive;

(2) Flexible, open-minded, and receptive to new information;

(3) Able to recognize problems, sensitive to needs, and adept in defining problems clearly and accurately;

(4) Compulsive or almost so in seeking recognition and praise from colleagues in their own groups and professions;

(5) Mentally restless, intense, wrapped up in what they are doing, persistent, goal- not method-oriented, impatient with anything that gets in their way, anti-authoritarian, boldly critical of established concepts, and unhampered by restrictions.

Cf. John W. Haefele, "Creativity and Innovation," New York, Reinhold Publishing Corporation, 1962.

Desire for Financial Rewards

Many of our greatest inventors worked in part for noble reasons. They worked also for financial rewards. Edison, when he had left the economic exigencies of youth far behind and reached the pinnacle of fame, still kept the dollar sign in his formulas and equations. When, as a manufacturer he was negotiating for a supply of plastic for a use not requiring highest quality, he once said to the author, "Make it cheap. Load it with fillers."

Although the employee-inventor receives pay for his inventions in the form of salary, he may long for direct compensation for inventions and services beyond the expected, such as bonuses initiated about fifty years ago by a few companies that are now amazingly large and prosperous. It is to be remembered, however, that the teamwork of many cooperating persons goes into the development, manufacture and launching of a new product. It is true that the employee-inventor sparks such a team. Yet he cannot claim all the credit for the commercial outcome. New products stimulate company growth and brings benefits in which the inventor shares in the long run, with his associates.

Education

The requirement of ability is axiomatic. In these days of complicated arts and inventions, formal education is becoming more and more important. The study by Schmookler [3] of the occupations of patentees shows heavy preponderance of technically trained inventors.

TABLE 3. INVENTORS SURVEYED—CLASSIFIED BY OCCUPATION.

Age Group	Technologists	Executives	Others
20-29	5	0	0
30-39	24	2	5
40-49	14	5	9
50-59	10	7	0
60 and up	2	1	0
Total	55	15	14

Outstanding scientists and professors have obtained patents on many important discoveries.

Business Judgment

Inventors are traditionally dreamers. To dream a little or much is helpful and perhaps even a necessity. Dreaming, however, suggests the impractical. Actually the inventors of today, if the facts could be gathered, might be found to be second in business judgment only to executives selected primarily because of previously demonstrated qualities of leadership. Scientifically trained or oriented minds, a mathematical approach to problems, judicious selection at an early age of a difficult science major, and subsequent years of first-hand experience in the factories or laboratories of the country are unsurpassed as bases for business ability.

Inventors' names frequently suggest, in fact, a bluebook of business achievement. The following are a few of the many names of inventors, identified in some way with New York state alone, that remain a part of industrial lore.

Robert Fulton	Steamship
George Westinghouse	Air brake
Thomas A. Edison	Lighting lower N.Y., etc.
Gail Borden	Condensed milk
John W. Hyatt	Celluloid plastic
George M. Pullman	Sleeping car
Peter Cooper	Mercury vapor lamp
George Eastman	Photographic devices
Charles H. Otis	Elevator
L. E. Waterman	Fountain pen
Isaac M. Singer	Sewing machine
Elmer A. Sperry	Gyrocompass

Receptiveness for New Ideas

Pride is common to many inventors and is desirable within limits. Excessive pride, on the other hand, often causes resentment at seemingly unnecessary intrusions of ideas from others. It raises road blocks against the outside inventor approaching a corporation having its own research program.

At the Cleveland Seminar of the National Association of Manufacturers, in 1948, Norman N. Holland said:

"My experience generally has been that people in a corporation hate to admit that somebody outside or a competing concern can do something better than they can. It's a matter of pride. And they always feel if they burn enough midnight oil that they can produce something better."

The President of the Western Union Telegraph Company in 1876 was asked his opinion of the Bell Telephone patent by Chauncey M. DePew, a friend who had been offered one-sixth interest in it for ten thousand dollars. The answer was:

"There is nothing in this patent whatever, nor is there anything in the scheme itself, except as a toy." [7]

This was the opinion of a great electrical "expert" on a patent generally considered now to have proven the most profitable financially of any ever issued.

Receptiveness to new ideas is a quality to be cultivated.

References

1. Rossman, Joseph, "Industrial Creativity; the Psychology of the Inventor," New Hyde Park, N.Y., University Books, 1964.
2. Lehman, H. C., "Memoirs of the American Philosophical Society," Vol. 33, Princeton, 1953.
3. Schmookler, Jacob, 38 JPOS 223, 1956.
4. Howard, F. A., 4 PTCJ 57-66.
5. Barnes, C. E., 5 PTCJ 70.
6. Brown, A. E., *The Indicator*, 9 (Dec. 1961).
7. Dodds, L. B., and Crotty, F. W., 30 JPOS 83, 1948.

Cross-references: *Incentives for Inventors, Inventors, Research Laboratory Directors Patent Responsibilities.*

K

KNOW-HOW. See FOREIGN PATENTS AND KNOW-HOW AND FOLLOWING ARTICLE

KNOW-HOW—LEGAL PROTECTION INTERNATIONALLY

Stephen P. Ladas

This article is printed in somewhat condensed form with permission from The Patent, Trademark and Copyright Journal of Research and Education. It has also been published in French and Spanish language reviews.

Increasing Importance of Know-How

Know-how is increasingly important in international agreements and international investment, the handmaid of progress and core of industrial competition. Also, it has assumed an aura of fascination particularly for newly developing countries which see in it a mystical factor to resolve or bridge over the difficult initial steps of technical and economic development.

In international trade, know-how may be involved in various forms. It may be part of an agreement relating to patents, designs or trademarks. It may be secondary to those rights. On the contrary, patent rights may be mere appendages to the principal grant of know-how. Or know-how may be the sole subject matter of a license agreement. Finally, know-how may be in a package deal of a construction or engineering contract, under which a firm undertakes to erect a plant and supply the know-how for its construction and operation. Know-how agreements may even replace patent agreements in underdeveloped countries where foreign inventors do not generally take out patents in view of the lack of local industry using the inventions covered by the patents.

Legal Problems

In connection with all these types of agreements involving know-how, several legal problems arise, such as: the propriety and adequacy of clauses seeking to protect the licensor's know-how; their legal enforceability and the kind of remedies available not only against licensees but also against third parties; tax problems on the royalties or other compensation payable by the licensee in the country of the payee and in the receiving country; and finally, antitrust law problems with respect to restrictive clauses included in the agreement. These problems depend largely on the question of the legal nature of the right in know-how.

Definition of Know-How. Some of the difficulties in dealing with this basic question stem from the absence of precise definition of the expression "know-how." While this is a convenient term to denote a variety of different matters, it does not define protectable subject matter. Indeed, in ordinary use know-how may include tangible materials: recipes, formulas, designs, drawings, patterns, blueprints, technical records, specifications, lists of materials, technical product and process manuals, written instructions for operating the process and analytical means for checking and controlling the product and the process and the like; and intangible information consisting in practical procedures, details of workshop practice, technical training, and personal visitation and inspection. It also may include singly or in combination:

Information relating to a patented invention not included in a patent specification

Inventions capable of being patented but not patented

Inventions incapable of being patented in

a particular country because of the subject matter being excluded in the patent law

Inventions incapable of being patented by reason of lack of inventive height

Industrial designs capable of being registered but not registered

Industrial designs having functional characteristics

Skill, experience and craftsmanship of technicians.

Secrecy Factor. The element of secrecy may not be indispensable as to all of the subject matter involved, yet the possessor of the know-how, the subject of a grant, must want to preserve it against unauthorized publication. Nor is the element of "exclusiveness" indispensable since more than one person may develop the same know-how, and if each of them preserves it from publication, each of them may have a right to his creation.

Because of these differences and the indefiniteness of the term "know-how," agreements often avoid the use of such term or use it subsidiarily and instead employ terms describing and defining the subject matter of the grant more specifically, such as secret or technical information, manufacturing processes, or knowledge relative to the use and application of the industrial technique required for the establishment and operation of a particular plant or the production of the subject matter of the agreement.

Variability in Recognition as Property Right

The question of the legal nature of the right in know-how usualy proceeds with the query whether in the particular country this is recognized as a property right or not. In countries with a codified civil law, there is a definite classification of "property" rights and the only class available for know-how would be that of "intangible rights." Roubier, "Le Droit de la Propriété Industrielle," p. 372. But there has been no thoroughgoing legal analysis of this right in know-how so as to distinguish the various types of relationships involved and give it an orderly pattern. There is a recognition that know-how can be sold, licensed, assigned, taxed,

subjected to levy, exchanged for stock in a corporation, etc., but no conscious attempt on the part of writers or the Courts to resolve all problems created by dealings with know-how. Nash, "The Concept of Property in Know-How," 6 PTC J. 289, 294, 295, 1962.

There has been a tendency to dodge the issue by pointing out that there is always the contract which is law between the parties and that any violation of undertakings under the contract with respect to know-how may be reached by an action under the contract. This, however, leaves out the whole aspect of protection against third parties, e.g., employees and competitors who may obtain unauthorized disclosure of know-how and use it without the owner's consent, and does not dispose of the necessity to supplement the absence of a contract by reference to other law.

Common Law Countries. In common law countries, the concept of property is somewhat more flexible, and the Courts have granted protection by reference to rules of law or equity in all cases of inequitable or unfair conduct. As Justice Holmes was able to say in *DuPont Powder Co.* v. *Masland*, 244 U.S. 100, 1917:

"The word 'property' as applied to trade secrets is an unanalyzed expression of certain secondary consequences of the primary fact that the law makes some rudimentary requirements of good faith."

The British Courts also have avoided the question of definition. The Master of the Rolls, Lord Greene, in *Saltman Engineering Co.* v. *Campbell Engineering Company*, 65 R.P.C. 203, 213, 1948, held that:

"Even if Mr. Ransom did not make a contract with the defendants, it does not alter the fact that the confidential drawings handed to the defendants for the purpose of executing the order placed with them were the property of Saltman Engineering Co., and the defendants knew that."

He stated the general principle as follows:

"If a defendant is proven to have used confidential information, directly or indirectly obtained from the plaintiff, without the consent, expressed or implied, of the plaintiff, he will be guilty of an infringement of the plaintiff's rights."

Most interesting in connection with the nature of know-how are the statements of Lord Radcliffe in *Rolls-Royce Ltd.* v. *Jeffrey*, 1 All England Reports 801, 805, 1962. He said that the case involved first "the nature of this asset of the appellants which is conveniently comprehended in the word 'know-how,'" and continued:

"I see no objection to describing this as an asset. It is intangible, but then so is goodwill.... It is a reality when associated with production and development as that of Rolls-Royce, and a large part, though not the whole of it, finds its material record in all those lists, drawings, and manufacturing and engineering data that are specified in the various license agreements.... An asset of this kind is, I am afraid, that I must use the phrase, sui generis. It is not easily compared with factory or office buildings, warehouses, plant and machinery, or such independent legal rights as patents, copyrights or trademarks, or even with goodwill. 'Know-how' is an ambience that pervades a highly specialized production organization and, although I think it correct to describe it as fixed capital so long as the manufacturer retains it for his own productive purposes and expresses its value in his products, one must realize that in so describing it, one is proceeding by an analogy which can easily break down owing to the inherent differences that separate 'know-how' from the more straightforward elements of fixed capital.... Know-how has the peculiar quality that it can be communicated to or shared with others outside the manufacturer's own business, without in any sense destroying its value to him."

Rationale of Know-How

It is submitted that it may be advisable to look closely into the genesis of know-how and its development, in the most usual cases. We have really two situations:

(a) An invention is made and application is filed for a patent. This necessarily must be filed as quickly as it is completed so that it may not be anticipated by another inventor working in the same field. So far as the requirements of the patent law are concerned, the disclosure may be complete. The public is advised as to what the invention is, and the process or method of manufacture is fully disclosed. But after the application is filed, the inventor must still work out practical details of workshop technique so that the invented process or product may be manufactured at the least possible cost. There is no holding back of information which should have been disclosed in the patent application, because these details are both not patentable and not even known to the inventor at the time of filing the application.

(b) Research is a continuous process of improvement of technology step by step. The improvement may consist in adjusting machinery or tooling, in using a certain type of metal rather than another, the laying out of a plant, the siting of the various types of equipment, the layout of the valve system, and the use of one known chemical rather than another. It may take research of many years and considerable investment to work out all these improvements one by one, but no patent can be obtained on them, because they are not patentable inventions. If they were patentable, the manufacturer would prefer to take a patent and be protected under the patent law rather than rely on the uncertainties of know-how protection, or take the risk that the same know-how may be developed by others or may be published. While a competing manufacturer doing similar research and spending time and money might eventually work out the same technological improvements, it is economically advantageous to him to acquire such know-how at once from the one who developed it rather than remain behind in the technology.

Applicable Law

With respect to know-how, there is generally no specific all-embracing Statute which attempts to define and regulate the competitive relationship, analogous to patent, design or trademark legislation. Such detailed Statute may be considered unnecessary if other general legislation applicable to know-how does in fact recognize, reconcile or satisfy the competitor relationship involved and if the Courts have in fact defined and circumscribed the right by the remedies granted. We have in most countries in the world the analogous condition in a law of unfair competition which generally is not a full statutory law. Most often this law has been fashioned as a full-bodied law by the Courts on the basis of a single provision in the Civil Code or of a general principle formulated by a succession of Court decisions. Yet it stands now as a quite clearly established legal ordering of the conflicting interests, claims and demands of competitors in the market place through this type of unfair competition law.

Precisely the same appears to be the case in respect to the right in know-how, as a review for a number of countries reveals.

First, we have the German Law of 1909 against Unfair Competition. This outlaws generally, in its first section, competitive conduct contrary to honest practices. It specifies and prohibits in subsequent sections various acts of unfair competition, such as acts causing confusion of the public, deceptive and unfair advertising, discrediting of competitors, and interference with contracts. Then in Sections 17 to 19, it prohibits unauthorized disclosure and misuse of business or manufacturing secrets. These Sections read as follows:

"Section 17

"(1) An employee, worker or apprentice of a firm who unlawfully imparts a business or manufacturing secret entrusted or made accessible to him by reason of his employment relationship to anyone during the term of service for the purpose of competition or for personal gain or with the intention of damaging the owner of the firm, will be liable to imprisonment of up to three years and to a fine, or to either.

"(2) Anyone making use for purposes of competition or personal gain of a trade or manufacturing secret or imparting the same to third parties, knowledge of which he obtained through the means described in paragraph (1) or through conduct of his own contrary to the law or contra bonos mores, will be punished in the same manner.

"(3) If, when imparting the said information, the perpetrator knows that use is to be made of the secret in foreign countries, or if he himself makes use of it in foreign countries, he may render himself liable to imprisonment up to five years.

"(4) The provisions of paragraphs (1) to (3) also apply in cases where the person receiving the information is already familiar with the secret or is entitled to know it, without the perpetrator being aware of this fact."

"Section 18

"Anyone unlawfully making use of or imparting to third parties for the purpose of competition or personal gain any designs or instructions of a tech-

nical nature confided to him in the course of his business dealings, particularly drawings, models, stencils, cuttings and formulae, is punishable with imprisonment up to two years and with a fine, or one of these two measures. Section 17, par. 4, applies equally."

"Section 19

"Acts contrary to the provisions contained in Sections 17 and 18 entail liability for the resulting damages. Where several persons are involved in such an infringement, there is a joint liability."

In all these cases, the owner has a right to sue for damages under Section 19 and may also file criminal complaint under Sections 17 and 18. He may also obtain an injunction against such unauthorized use or threatened misuse of his know-how under the general provisions of the German law. It is highly significant that Germany had dealt with the relationships involved in know-how under the general provisions of the Unfair Competition Act. Indeed, the German Supreme Court (Bundesgericht) in a decision in 1951, 17 B.G.H. 2 p. 42, has placed the whole subject of know-how squarely under the general principles of unfair competition. It stated:

"With respect to so-called secret processes and other commercial or manufacturing secrets, the protection involved is in accordance with the general provisions of the Civil Code and the law against unfair competition. Secrecy is protected by the right to unrestricted exercise of commercial activity (Section 823, par. 1, and Section 826 of the Civil Code, and Articles 1, 17 and 18 of the Act against Unfair Competition). Under these articles a petition, by application of Section 1004 BGB for injunction of unauthorized use is available against the person to whom the licensor has entrusted a commercial secret in business relationship. If, under manufacturing arrangements, the licensor communicates to the licensee process instructions based on commercial secrets, this constitutes entrusting of technical instructions in the meaing of Article 18 of the Act against Unfair Competition."

Next, it should be noted that similar legislative treatment of the competitive relationships in know-how is made in other countries. Indeed, provisions analogous to those of the German Unfair Competition Act exist in the Austrian Act against Unfair Competition of 1923, Sections 11 and 12; the Norwegian Law of July 7, 1922, Section

11; the Danish Law of March 29, 1924, Section 11; and the Swedish Law of May 29, 1951, Sections 3 to 5.

Belgium has a special Arrêté Royal of December 23, 1934 which provides in Article 2 for a summary remedy by the President of the Tribunal, akin to an injunction, in certain cases of unfair competition, and these cases specifically include "the unauthorized use of models, specimens, technical combinations and formulae of a competitor and generally of all information or documents entrusted to another." Here again, misuse or unauthorized use of know-how is dealt with by analogy to other acts of unfair competition. This is in addition to the action for damages available under the broad provision of Article 1382 of the Civil Code which is the foundation of all law of unfair competition.

In other civil law countries, such as France, Italy and the Netherlands, the basis of protection of know-how is also unfair competition law, as the foundation of all law of industrial property to which know-how is generally assimilated. Know-how is deemed a combination of things organized toward an industrial purpose which constitutes a new value that the law protects against interference, and such protection is the proper function of the law of unfair competition. See Bouvier, "Le Droit de la Propriété Industrielle," Vol. II, pp. 368 *et seq.;* Mario Rotondi, "Unfair Competition in Europe," 7 Amer. Jour. of Comparative Law, 327, 333, 1958.

Articles 1382 to 1383 of the French and Belgian Civil Codes, which are the basis of the unfair competition law in these two countries, find their counterpart in Article 2598 of the Italian Code, and Articles 1401 to 1402 of the Dutch. In Italy, there is also a special provision in Article 2105 which affords protection against the divulging of "information relating to the organization or methods of production of an enterprise, or the making use thereof in a manner that may prejudice it." Thus, for the purposes of this action, it is quite immaterial whether the secret information which is abused is directly misappropriated by someone concerned with it or has been acquired through third parties. In the Netherlands, injunction may be issued by the Courts against the unauthorized use of know-how.

Penalties and Recoveries

All four countries last mentioned also contain specific provisions in their Penal Codes. Article 309 of the Belgian and Article 418 of the French Codes provide for criminal punishment of anyone who fraudulently, or with intention to cause harm, communicates manufacturing secrets to third parties. In Italy, Article 623 of the Penal Code subjects to criminal punishment anyone who, having had access by reason of his status or profession to information intended to remain secret, communicates such information to others or exploits the same for his own benefit. In the Netherlands, Articles 272 and 273 of the Penal Code contain penal provisions against intentional divulgation of secret information which should be kept confidential because of the actual or previous professional position of the person who divulges, or because a commercial or industrial enterprise had ordered that such information be kept secret.

Cases of dealing with know-how which are not reached by these penal provisions are covered by the law of unfair competition.

Common Law Countries. In common law countries, the position is somewhat different. Wrongful appropriation, misuse or unauthorized divulgation of know-how, are essentially an equitable wrong against which the Courts will grant a remedy. The Courts will do so under the rules of law and equity of the common law, rather than in application of any statutory law. Thus, the law for the protection of know-how has developed entirely through case law, by the Courts administering relief in cases where they considered that inequitable conduct was involved. Heretofore, there has been no effort to classify and distinguish the various cases, examine the relationships involved and suggest a possible general theory of the nature of the right in know-how. The first such attempt is made in the excellent book by Amédée Turner, "The Law of Trade Secrets," London, 1962. The law in the United States of America and Great Britain is now remarkably similar in essence, although the reasoning, emphasis and legal theory, may not be alike.

In Great Britain and generally in British law countries throughout the world, the notion of a law of unfair competition as such has not found acceptance as yet. In the absence of explicit contractual provisions relating to know-how, in which case the position is defined by the contract, the English Courts look to the relationship and give relief on the basis of a theory of implied contract or breach of confidence or trust. Turner, p. 235.

In the United States, on the other hand, in addition to these theories, there is also applied a doctrine of unjust enrichment concurrently, complementarily or in the alternative. Turner, p. 265.

But while the legal jargon used may be different from that in civil law countries, what the Courts really do is to find a relationship between the parties which makes it unfair for the defendant to appropriate, misuse or make an unauthorized disclosure of know-how communicated by the owner thereof, and in essence they apply the basic principles of the unfair competition law. Indeed, the conduct prohibited involves not so much the revelation, wrongful appropriation, or misuse of know-how as such, but the economic implication of interference with an advantageous competitive position represented by the value of the know-how to the owner thereof.

This appears in a particularly clear light in the cases involving an unrelated third person who obtains disclosure of the know-how innocently and the question is whether such person may be restrained. *Stevenson, Jordan & Harrison Ltd.* v. *MacDonald & Evans,* 68 Reports of Patents, Designs, Trademarks and Other Cases 190. On appeal, 69 R.P.C. 10, the judgment was reversed on the ground that the confidential nature of the subject matter was not substantial enough to warrant protection. Lloyd-Jacob J. remarked:

"Counsel for the plaintiff expressly disclaimed any suggestion that . . . the defendants were aware that . . . Mr. Hemming was acting in breach of his duty to the plaintiff. Does this circumstance frank their avowed intention to consummate Mr. Hemming's wrongdoing? The original and independent jurisdiction of this Court to prevent, by the grant of an injunction, any person availing himself of a title which arises out of a violation of a right or a breach of confidence, is so well established as a cardinal principle that only a binding authority to the contrary should prevent its application by this Court."

In the United States, the decisions of the Courts have established the position which the Restatement of Torts [Section 758(b) comment (e)] summarizes to the effect that the answer depends upon weighing the loss to the innocent party against the benefit of the plaintiff. It would be wrong to charge the defendant with damages or profits for the period after he knew the facts of the disclosure in the case when he has changed substantially his position by exploiting the disclosures beforehand.

Taxation of Income from Know-How

For a discussion of United States policy, as now defined only incompletely, see *Taxation* Section on Know-How.

Two decisions of the House of Lords are of particular interest. In the first case, *Moriarty (Inspector of Taxes)* v. *Evans Medical Supplies Ltd.,* 3 All E. R. 718, 1957, a British company, manufacturers of pharmaceutical products and wholesale druggists, made an agreement with the Government of Burma to supply information as to certain secret processes relating to the manufacture of pharmaceutical products and technical data, drawings, designs and plans for the erection of a factory and the installation of machinery therein. The consideration to be received in return was £100,000. The question arose as to whether this sum was ordinary income or a capital gain. The Court of Appeal held that, insofar as the consideration was in respect of the imparting of information as to secret processes, the receipt was a capital receipt, such secret processes and formulas being in this respect akin to patents. On the other hand, insofar as the consideration related to the drawings, designs and plans and information relating to the supply of prototype machinery, laying out and installation of such machinery, etc., it was a payment for services and therefore ordinary income.

The House of Lords held that there was no case for apportioning the sum in the manner directed by the Court of Appeal, and held that the whole sum was a capital profit and therefore not taxable. Viscount Simonds and Lord Tucker pointed out that the ownership by this company of these secret processes and know-how had enabled the company to acquire a substantial share of the market for pharmaceutical products in Burma. Even though the whole value of these secret processes and know-how might not be lost at once to the company as the result of the agreement, their value would be greatly diminished and it was doubtful whether they would, within a measurable period of time, have any value at all remaining to the company.

In the more recent decision in *Rolls Royce Ltd.* v. *Inland Revenue Commissioners*, the House of Lords upheld the decision of the Court of Appeal that lump sum payments made by certain foreign governments and companies to Rolls Royce in return for technical knowledge, plans and a license for an interchange of staffs to enable them to manufacture specified types of aircraft engines did not represent the value of a capital asset and was assessable for income tax. 1 All E. R. 801, 1962. See similar holding by the Court of Appeal in *Musker (Inspector of Taxes)* v. *English Electric Co., Inc.*, a 1963 case. The taxpayer's position was that its know-how was part of its fixed capital. The House of Lords, particularly Lord Radcliffe, looked into the nature of know-how and admitted that this was a capital asset so long as the manufacturer retains it for his own productive purposes. It is the kind of intangible entity that can very easily change its category according to the use to which its owner himself decides to put it. Rolls Royce turned the know-how to account by undertaking for reward to impart it to the others in order to bring about an alternative way of deriving profit in lieu of manufacture and sale of their own engines to the governments of companies with whom they entered into license agreements. The case was distinguished from the *Moriarty* v. *Evans* case

in that in the latter the company had sold to the Burmese Government a secret process on which the success of its business in Burma had to depend, and it had, in effect, disposed altogether of its Burmese trade.

Indeed, the reconciliation of the two decisions is possible on the facts of each case: more or less total loss of the asset in the first case, and a more or less limited dilution of the asset in the second case, particularly since the information disclosed was only that bearing on the production of a single type of engine.

Know-How Provisions of International Convention

The general conclusion resulting from an analysis of legislation and Court decisions being that the competitive relationships involved in know-how are governed by the broad principles of the law on unfair competition, it should then follow that in the international field the stipulations of Article 10bis of the International Convention are applicable. This Article reads as follows:

"(1) The countries of the Union are bound to assure to persons entitled to the benefits of the Union effective protection agaist unfair competition.

"(2) An act of competition contrary to honest practices in industrial or commercial matters constitutes an act of unfair competition.

"(3) The following in particular shall be prohibited:

1. all acts of such a nature as to create confusion by any means whatever with the establishment, the goods, or the industrial or commercial activities of a competitor;

2. false allegations in the course of trade which are of such a nature as to discredit the establishment, the goods, or the industrial or commercial activities of a competitor;

3. indications or allegations the use of which in the course of trade is liable to mislead the public as to the nature, the manufacturing process, the characteristics, the suitability for their purpose or the quantity of the goods."

Resolution of International Chamber of Commerce. The general principle announced by this Article is that any act of competition contrary to honest practices in industrial and commercial matters is prohibited, and this would apply to unauthorized disclosure or misuse of know-how.

The International Chamber of Commerce in 1955 undertook to study the problem of protection of know-how on an international basis. After long investigation of the law and practice of the various countries, it adopted a Resolution in 1961 setting forth rules for the protection of know-how. International Chamber of Commerce, Statements and Resolutions 1959-1961, pp. 98 and 99. This Resolution reads as follows:

"Technological improvements developed by business enterprises whether patentable or not, commonly referred to as know-how, have become in recent times tremendously valuable subjects of industrial property supplementing patents and other rights, have assumed a great economic importance, and are the subject matter of an increasing number of very important agreements between business enterprises.

"The protection of know-how on an international basis is therefore a keenly felt need if the communication of know-how between enterprises to promote economic and technical progress is to be encouraged.

"Hardly any country so far has dealt in an adequate and comprehensive way with the protection of industrial know-how, although existing national laws on contract, breach of trust and unfair competition are sometimes applicable to the subject.

"Accordingly, the International Chamber of Commerce has set out hereunder in a summary form provisions which are highly recommended for incorporation in national legislation:

"1. Industrial know-how means applied technical knowledge, methods and data necessary for realizing or carrying out in practice techniques which serve industrial purposes.

"2. Where such know-how is of a secret character it constitutes a valuable business asset and should be protected in law.

"3. Know-how should be regarded as secret in character if it has not been published in a form available to the public and the undertaking which has developed it or lawfully acquired it takes all reasonable steps to prevent its unauthorized disclosure. Such know-how is hereinafter referred to as 'secret know-how.'

"4. It should be unlawful for an undertaking to use industrial know-how which it knows or ought to have known to be the secret know-how of another undertaking, without the consent of that undertaking.

"5. It should also be unlawful to divulge the secret know-how of an undertaking, or to transfer it to others, without the consent of that undertaking.

"6. Nothing in these provisions should affect the right of an undertaking to use, divulge or transfer any industrial know-how which it has itself originated and developed by its own independent means or to use any such know-how which has been published in a form available to the public.

"7. A injunction or an order to pay damages or both should be available in respect of the unlawful use, divulgence, or transfer of secret know-how.

"8. In addition to the above provisions, it should be possible, even in the case of a bona fide use of the secret know-how of another, to order the user to compensate that other, if the circumstances make it equitable to do so."

The following comment is suggested on this Resolution. See Document No. 450/198 dated December 27, 1960 of the International Chamber of Commerce. It will be noted that it is limited to industrial know-how. It does not deal with commercial, financial or other know-how. It was felt that the need for protecting other types of know-how may not be as great as that for protecting industrial know-how, and attention should primarily be directed to the latter. Then the resolution is limited to know-how of a secret character, know-how which has not been published in a form available to the public and which the owner thereof has taken all reasonable steps to prevent from being published. This means:

(a) that the owner thereof ensures that non-licensed third parties do not use, publish or transfer it to others;

(b) that know-how which has been divulged or transferred to others without the authorization of the owner may still be considered "secret" if the owner has taken all adequate measures to prevent its disclosure;

(c) if the know-how has been published in such a way that not only an unauthorized third party has obtained knowledge of it but it has become available to the public generally, the know-how is no longer revocable and the only remedy may be damages chargeable to the person who published the know-how.

Ex contrario, paragraph 6 of this Resolution states that secrecy does not imply exclusivity. Therefore, if another party should develop or possess similar know-how or acquire such from another owner or come to know of it from a publication available to the public, the other party is free to use, divulge, or transfer it without regard to the fact that another enterprise has a secret know-how of its own.

The Resolution then proceeds to suggest a system of protection of know-how. Paragraph 4 deals with unlawful use of know-how and the protection is deemed to exist in all cases of bad faith. If the user knows or ought to know that the know-how is the secret know-how of another, and uses it without the consent of the owner, the use is unlawful.

Paragraph 5 deals with unauthorized divulgation or transfer of secret know-how. Both are deemed unlawful when there is no consent by the owner of the know-how. No requirement of bad faith is included in this provision. The transferee may have received the know-how in good faith, for instance, as a licensee or sublicensee or employee thereof, or may be an independent third party who paid value for the same. The act of transfer by such person and particularly the act of publication constitutes a serious damage to the owner. If the latter asserts his rights before such transfer or divulgation, the act by the transferer is unlawful.

Paragraph 7 of the Resolution recommends that the remedies against unlawful use, transfer or divulgation should be an injunction or an order for payment of damages, or both. The International Chamber of Commerce would have recommended the remedy of injunction generally but it had to take note of the fact that this is not known in the legal system of a number of civil law countries.

Because of the basic need of preserving the secrecy of know-how, the Courts may adopt procedures to prevent publication as a result of litigation. Thus, in *Amber Size & Chemical Co. Ltd.* v. *Menzel*, 2 Ch. 239, 1913; 30 R.P.C. 433, where it was obvious that the question of the aspects of plaintiff's processes which were claimed to be secret had to be disclosed to someone on behalf of the Court, the Court's solution was for the parties to agree on an expert

or experts to whom disclosures could be made on behalf of the Court, or to a small list of experts from whom the Court could make a selection.

Finally, paragraph 8 provides that even in the case of a bona fide use of secret know-how by an independent third party distinguished in paragraph 4, the law should provide for an equitable compensation of the owner of the know-how. In other words, no unjust enrichment action should be allowed in the case where one in good faith obtains knowledge of secret know-how and uses it for this purpose.

Regulations of European Economic Community

It is as a result of this Resolution that the International Chamber of Commerce insisted on the Commission of the European Economic Community for the inclusion of know-how, together with the other rights of industrial property, in the special dispensation from notification of agreements relating to industrial property.

It will be recalled that the first draft of the Regulations submitted by the Commission to the Council of Ministers of the European Economic Community provided for compulsory registration of all agreements containing restrictions prohibited under Article 85(1) of the Treaty. As an exception to this rule, no registration was required in respect of agreements imposing on the transferee or licensee of patents, designs and trademarks, limitations in the exercise of these rights. Thus, the exception was limited to patent, design and trademark agreements. As a result of strong representations on the part of the International Chamber of Commerce, the final text of Regulation No. 17 extended this particular exception to know-how agreements as well.

Indeed, this Regulation which now requires notification of agreements for the purpose of obtaining the benefits of Article 85(3) of the Treaty dispenses from such notification, under Article 4(2)(ii)(b) of Regulation No. 17:

"agreements to which two enterprises only participate and which have the sole effect

to impose upon the purchaser or the user of

rights of industrial property—namely, patents, utility models, designs or trademarks—or upon the beneficiary of contracts involving the transfer or licensing of manufacturing processes or knowledge relative to the use and application of industrial techniques, limitation in the exercise of these rights."

This is a recognition, by what constitutes a legislative act of the European Economic Community, of know-how as a right equivalent to industrial property. The Regulation recognizes the *right* in know-how, since it speaks of limitations which may be imposed in the exercise of the right in know-how as they may be imposed in the exercise of the patent right, the design right or the trademark right.

The terms used in this provision are:

"manufacturing processes or knowledge relative to the use or application of industrial techniques"

Comparison of Regulations with German. It is interesting in this connection to compare these terms with those used in the German Act of 1957 Against Restrictions of Competition. Section 20 of this act deals with permissible restrictions in agreements relating to patents, utility models and rights relating to varieties of plants. Section 21 applies, so far as applicable, the provisions of Section 20 to agreements involving the transfer or exploitation of:

"legally unprotected inventions, manufacturing processes, technical designs and other technological achievements...if such achievements constitute business secrets"

The terms describing know-how in Regulation No. 17 are broader than those in the German Act of 1957 and do not even include the requirement of secrecy contained in the latter.

Thus, the German law not only recognizes and protects, under the law of unfair competition, business and manufacturing secrets, but it also permits, so far as applicable, the same restrictions in agreements relating to such secrets as in the case of agreements relating to patents.

Since both Section 21 of the German Act of 1957 against Restriction of Competition and Article 4(2)(ii)(b) of Regulation No. 17 of the Common Market deal with limitations in agreements relating to know-how, it is of interest to first consider the effect of the German antitrust law, before proceeding to consider the provisions of the Common Market antitrust law.

To understand the scope of the exemption of restrictions in know-how license agreements under Section 21 of the German law, we must relate them to the restrictions permitted in patent license agreements under Section 20 of the German law.

First is the restriction relating to the character, extent, quantity, area or time of use of a patent. Certainly, this is applicable to know-how. The owner of the know-how may dispose of his right by transfer or license for a limited purpose or application only for a limited area or for a limited time.

Second are the restrictions imposed on the acquirer or licensee of a patent justified by the interest of the owner or licensor in the technically unobjectionable exploitation of the object protected by the patent. It is difficult to conceive how this restriction may be generally applicable to the grant of know-how, except in two cases. The first is where the licensee of the know-how uses a marking on his goods referring to the name of the licensor. In such case the interest of the licensor and the reputation of his name justifies his right to technically unobjectionable exploitation of the know-how. Another case is where the licensor of the know-how also licenses the use of his trademark. In such case the validity of his trademark as well as the interest in its reputation and goodwill may justify the same restriction.

Third is the obligation assumed by the acquirer or licensee regarding the pricing of the patented article. The object of the restriction is to prevent the licensee from underselling the patentee and competing unfairly with him. It does not seem possible to permit such a restriction in the case of the licensing of know-how.

Fourth is the obligation imposed on the acquirer or licensee for the granting back of information or of a license for the use of inventions relating to improvements on condition of a reciprocal obligation by the seller or licensor. It is not seen why this obligation would be objectionable with respect to grant of know-how. Subject to the condition of reciprocity and to the condition that the license back to the licensor should not be exclusive to the latter, this tends to encourage the sharing of knowledge and promotes rather than restricts competition.

Fifth is the obligation on the acquirer or licensee not to challenge the licensed patent. It is not seen why this obligation on the communicatee of know-how would be objectionable when it is not on the patent licensee. Contesting the right of the licensor in his know-how is violation of the basic foundation of the contract. However, it must be understood that the licensee should have the right to show that the know-how furnished by the licensor has become public property without the fault of the licensee.

Finally, there is the obligation imposed on the acquirer or licensee relating to regulation of competition outside the area of applicability of the law. This provision in the German law meant that the licensee might be restricted with respect to competition outside Germany. The same restriction could apply in Germany with respect to the grant of know-how. However, this provision is no longer applicable insofar as interstate trade in the Common Market countries are concerned, and the same would be true with respect to know-how.

Know-How under Common Market Antitrust Law

Coming now to the Common Market Antitrust Law, we have before us Article 4(2)(ii)(b) of Regulation No. 17 that dispenses from notification agreements relating to know-how and containing "limitations in the exercise of the right" in know-how. What are these limitations which are presumably outside the prohibition of Article 85(1) of the Treaty?

The Commission of the EEC in its "Communication" on patent license agreements published December 24, 1962 has specified certain restrictions which it deems as not included within the scope of the prohibitions of Article 85(1) of the Rome Treaty. In this "Communication," the Commission ex-

plains why it has not attempted to specify restrictions in agreements relating to know-how which may also be deemed outside the scope of prohibitions of Article 85(1), and states:

"The question of application of Article 85(1) of the Treaty ... to agreements relating to the exploitation ... of creations not protected by law which represent technical improvements ... must be the subject of a further decision."

The words in this statement "not protected by law" are unfortunate since it is obvious from the above exposition that know-how is protected by law. Obviously the Commission refers only to the fact that there is no full statutory law governing the relationships involved in know-how, and indicates its uncertainty as to how far it may consider applicable to know-how agreements, restrictions analogous to those in patent license agreements deemed outside the scope of prohibitions of Article 85(1). But whether or not the Commission determines to issue a statement of interpretation with respect to restrictions in know-how license agreements, it is undeniable that restrictions "within the exercise of the right" in know-how are permissible. Not only is this true because of the inclusion of know-how in Article 4(2)(ii)(b) of Regulation No. 17, but also because of the saving clause of Article 222 of the Rome Treaty which provides that "the Treaty shall in no way prejudice existing systems and incidents of property." Certainly the right in know-how is an existing system and incident of property.

Indeed, precisely because the right in know-how is not fully defined by statutory law and is broadly covered by the protection of the law of unfair competition, it becomes essential for the parties concerned to at least define their respective rights and duties in the license agreement. This fixes the limits for which the use and application of the furnished know-how is granted or authorized.

It follows that a know-how license agreement may contain the following restrictions as outside the scope of prohibitions of Article 85(1) of the Treaty:

(a) Restrictions calculated to protect the

know-how against unauthorized disclosure or transfer to third parties. This is necessary to preserve the secrecy of the know-how and the right of the owner in the know-how.

(b) Restrictions against the use of the licensed know-how beyond the use or application for which it is being licensed. This is a limitation within the scope of the right in the know-how.

(c) Limitations on the use of the know-how with respect to time. This means that the license to use the know-how may be limited for a certain term only, and therefore the licensee may be required not to use such know-how after termination or cancellation of the agreement. This is, of course, subject to the qualification that the know-how has not become available to the public.

(d) Limitations with regard to area. This refers to the *use* of the know-how and not the marketing of merchandise made by the use of such know-how. It is not possible, with respect to know-how, to conceive of separate rights in know-how granted by separate States as independent rights. The right in know-how is a single right and it may be enforced under the law of any country. But once this right has been licensed and products have been made by the use of such know-how, it is not possible to limit the sale of such products to a particular country.

(e) Limitations with respect to person.

The owner of the know-how may provide that the licensee shall not assign the license or grant a sublicense to another. This is both a limitation inherent in the right in the know-how and a means of protecting the secrecy of the know-how.

(f) An obligation on the licensee to affix on the product a legend referring to the owner of the know-how. This is a means of promoting the reputation of the licensor of the know-how and involves no restriction on competition.

(g) The license of the know-how may be granted on an exclusive or nonexclusive basis. The former means that the owner of the know-how undertakes not to furnish such know-how to any other party. This involves no more of a restriction than an exclusive license under a patent does. Indeed, it is of lesser importance, since the exclusivity under a patent may endure for 15 to 20 years, whereas ordinarily the value of the know-how has a commercial value of a much more limited time.

Finally, the restrictions discussed above as permissible under the German Antitrust Law in know-how license agreements should be deemed proper "limitations in the exercise of the right" under Article 4(2) (ii) (b) of Regulation No. 17.

Cross-references: *Employee Inventions and Agreements, Foreign Patents, Foreign Patents and Know-How Utilization, Taxation of Income from Patents and Know-How, Secrets of Trade and Employees' Responsibilities.*

L

LACHES

Frederic B. Schramm

Laches has been defined as a doctrine of equity whereby lapse of time bars relief. Ballentine's Law Dictionary. However, a mere lapse of time before institution of an action is not sufficient to constitute laches. Equity concerns itself not merely with a lapse of time but with the inequity of permitting a claim to be enforced after such a time. *Preston* v. *Kaw Pipe Line Co.*, 113 F.2d 311, 10th Cir. 1940; c.d. 311 U.S. 712.

Elements of Laches

Various courts have listed two or more elements as being necessary to constitute the defense of laches in patent infringement cases. These include delay, change of position, that plaintiff's claim was known to the defendant and that there was an opportunity to sue. Associated with delay are inaction, lack of diligence, negligence and actual representations by plaintiff. Associated with change of position are change in the conditions, prejudice or injury to defendant, defendant's reliance on inactivity of plaintiff or that plaintiff induced the prejudice.

In order to constitute laches in a suit to enjoin infringement of patents and for an accounting, there must have been inexcusable delay in instituting the suit and prejudice resulting to the defendant from such delay. *Potash Company of America* v. *International Minerals and Chemical Corp.*, 213 F.2d 153 (10th Cir. 1954).

It has been said that to establish a defense of laches in patent infringement cases, the claiming party must show that there has been either (1) unreasonable delay on part of complainant in bringing suit without valid and sufficient excuse or (2) delay on part of complainant with ensuing detriment or change of position of the other party. *Webster* v. *Speed Corp.*, 158 F. Supp. 472, DC Ore 1957, aff. in part, remanded in part 262 F.2d 482. Another court has described the requirements for the defense of laches as lack of diligence on plaintiff's part and injury to complaining party due to such lack. *Salem Engineering Co.* v. *National Supply Co.*, 75 F. Supp. 993, 999, DC WPa 1948.

The Court in *Armstrong* v. *Avco Mfg. Corp.*, 137 F. Supp. 680, 108 USPQ 76, 77, DC Del 1955 included as elements: (1) knowledge by patent owner of the infringement, (2) length of the alleged delay and reasons therefor and (3) the activities of the parties during the period. Injustice to the party sued has been held an essential element in laches. *Caterpillar Tractor Corp.* v. *International Harvester Co.*, 32 F. Supp. 304, DC NJ 1940; appeal dismissed 120 F.2d 82, 3rd Cir. 1941.

The Court said in *Shaffer* v. *Rector Well Equipment Co.*, 155 F.2d 344, 345, 5th Cir. 1946:

"The elements necessary to constitute laches have been uniformly held to be: (1) an alleged invasion by the defendant of the complainant's right, of which the complainant has had knowledge and an ample opportunity to establish the same in the proper forum; (2) a delay of the plaintiff in the assertion of such rights, by reason of which the defendant has good reason to believe that the alleged rights are worthless or have been abandoned; and (3) changes in the condition or relation of the parties during the period of delay making it unjust to the defendant to permit the plaintiff thereafter to recover."

Delay to Constitute Laches. The Court held in *General Electric Co.* v. *Sciaky Bros., Inc.*, 187 F. Supp. 667, 675, DC EMich 1960:

"There is no fixed period, except as provided in the statute placing time limitation on damages recoverable for patent infringement, limiting time within which patent infringement action must be brought, but diligence must be observed to escape a charge of laches, and whether the complaining party had been diligent under all the circumstances, decides the question of laches; mere lapse of time is not conclusive."

Accord *Whitman* v. *Walt Disney Productions, Inc.*, 148 F. Supp. 37, 39, DC SCalif 1957, aff. 263 F.2d 229, 9th Cir.

Negligence of patent owner in enforcing its rights may be held to destroy the right of prevention of further infringement. *Remington Rand* v. *Acme Card System Co.*, 29 F. Supp. 192, 199, DC SOhio 1939; appeal dismissed 106 F.2d 1014; *Pennington Engineering Co.* v. *Houde Engineering Corp.*, 43 F. Supp. 698, 705, DC WNY 1941, aff. 136 F.2d 210; c.d. 320 U.S. 771.

The need for diligence on the part of the plaintiff was pointed out in *Cubbison* v. *Delco Products Corp.*, 29 F. Supp. 202, 206, DC SOhio W.D. 1939, aff. 126 F.2d 466, 6th Cir.

The negligence or lack of diligence of the plaintiff which will give rise to the defense of laches is often characterized as "sleeping on one's rights." *Potash Co. of America* v. *International Minerals and Chemical Corp.*, supra.

A mere delay however in bringing the patent infringement action does not bar the plaintiff from relief on the ground of laches. *Mercoid Corp.* v. *Minneapolis Honeywell Regulator Co.*, 133 F.2d 811, 7th Cir. 1943; reversed as to a different point 320 U.S. 680; rehearing denied, 321 U.S. 802; motion denied, 2 cases, 323 U.S. 672, 7th Cir. 1943. *Whitman* v. *Walt Disney Productions, Inc.*, 263 F.2d 229, 231, 232, 120 USPQ 253, 255, 256, 9th Cir. 1958.

Persistence in unauthorized use of patented invention is continuing trespass; a mere delay in seeking redress cannot destroy the right of patentee to compensatory damages. *Middleton* v. *Wiley*, 195 F.2d 844, 8th Cir. 1952.

Plaintiff Spurred into Activity. Where the plaintiff delays in bringing suit for infringement of his own patent until after there is a threat of suit against him on another patent, or an actual suit is brought against him, or delays investigation of apparatus made by competitors and actually covered by plaintiff's patent until suit against plaintiff is threatened, the infringement suit is barred. *Dallas Machine and Locomotive Works* v. *Willamette-Hyster Co.*, 28 F. Supp. 207, DC Ore 1939, aff. 112 F.2d 623, c.d. 311 U.S. 702; *Aerovox Corp.* v. *Dubilier Condenser Corp.*, 25 F. Supp. 299, DC SNY 1938, aff. *Aerovox Corp.* v. *Cornell Dubilier Corp.*, 108 F.2d 749, 2d Cir. 1940.

Length of Delay. The Court said in *Hartford-Empire Co.* v. *Swindell Bros.*, 96 F.2d 227, 233, 4th Cir. 1938:

"In the recent case of Denominational Envelope Co. v. Duplex Envelope Co., 4 Cir., 80 F.2d 186, 194, Judge Soper, speaking for this court, said: 'The length of time during which a party may rest upon his rights, without being guilty of laches, varies with the circumstances of each case, and in order to constitute the defense, the lapse of time must be so great and the relations of the defendants to the rights claimed must be such that it would be inequitable to permit the plaintiff to assert them.' And generally that 'laches . . . is not mere delay, but *delay which works a disadvantage to another,*' see Leonard v. Gage, 4 Cir., 94 F.2d 19, 25; Schmelz Liquidating Corp. v. Williams, 4 Cir., 86 F.2d 167, 169; 1 Pomeroy, Equitable Remedies, 21." (Emphasis added.)

Although there is no fixed period of delay requisite to the defense of laches, the courts have, in some cases, used the six-year statutory period of limitations for actions at law as a basis of reference. Delay for more than such a period has been presumed to have injured defendant unless the contrary could be shown by the plaintiff. *Whitman* v. *Walt Disney Production, Inc.*, supra. Relief may be denied despite the fact that the delay is short of the period of the statute of limitations, where circumstances render it inequitable to grant relief because of the delay in instituting suit. *France Mfg. Co.* v. *Jefferson Electric Co.*, 106 F.2d 605, 6th Cir. 1939, c.d. 309 U.S. 657, rehearing denied, 309 U.S. 696.

Where patentee informed Aluminum Company in March, 1931 of patentee's contention that company was infringing patent, the patentee's delay in bringing infringement suit and an action for conversion of patentee's drawing until 1940 was a sufficiently long duration to constitute laches if other elements of defense were present. *Van Alen* v. *Aluminum Co. of America*, 43 F. Supp. 833, 836, DC SNY 1942.

On the other hand, the defense of laches has been denied in various cases from periods as short as one month and three days to twenty years. A patent infringement suit commenced one month and three days after entry of interlocutory decree in previous suit brought by plaintiff against another party less than two months after issuance of patent, for contributory infringement thereof, was not barred by laches. *Philad* v. *Vanatta*, 28 F. Supp. 539, 543, DC SCalif 1939, appeal dismissed 109 F.2d 1022 (9th Cir.). A suit brought 15 months after earliest date on which defendant might have infringed patent was held not unreasonably long in *Pierce* v. *American Communications Co.*, 111 F. Supp. 181, DC Mass 1953, vacated with respect to a different issue 208 F.2d 763 (1st Cir. 1953). A four year delay was allowed in *Bruen* v. *Huff*, 100 F. Supp. 713, 717, DC WPa 1950. A delay of 13 years after issuance of patent before bringing a suit for infringement, although it might not amount to laches absolutely precluding recovery, was a factor for consideration. *Keller* v. *American Sales Book Co.*, 26 F. Supp. 835, 839 (DC WNY 1939), aff. 113 F.2d 113, 2d Cir.

In a case where the defendant was partially responsible for the delay, a suit for accounting for royalties in a patent license contract was not barred although not brought to trial for 20 years. *St. Louis Car Co.* v. *J. G. Brill Co.*, 25 F. Supp. 244, 247, DC EPa 1937, aff. *J. G. Brill Co.* v. *Meissner*, 99 F.2d 999, 3d Cir. 1939.

Excuses for Delay. In an equity action for patent infringement the facts may show such a long delay in bringing suit that the plaintiff must give sufficient reason for the delay. *Pennington* v. *Houde*, supra.

There was an adequate excuse for overcoming a defense of laches after a period of seven years when there had been an honest endeavor to effect an amicable settlement of dispute and avoid litigation over the period of the delay. *Holland Co.* v. *American Steel Foundries*, 95 F. Supp. 273, DC NIll 1951, reversed as to a different point 190 F.2d 37, c.d. 342 U.S. 859, opinion supplemented 101 F. Supp. 388, aff. 196 F.2d 749; c.d. 344 U.S. 855.

Negotiation for a cross-license did not excuse delay where the negotiations had ceased 7 years before suit and the unexplained delay exceeded the applicable period of statute of limitations. *General Electric Co.* v. *Sciaky Bros., Inc.*, 134 USPQ 55, 6th Cir. 1962.

Excuses for failure to make timely claim were declared inadequate however where there was an alleged lack of funds in bringing patent infringement action, *Whitman* v. *Walt Disney Productions, Inc.*, 148 F. Supp. 37, 40, DC SCalif 1957, aff. 263 F.2d 229, 9th Cir. 1958; where patentee died, his estate became bankrupt, and trustee in bankruptcy failed to make timely claim of infringement, *Delaney Patents Corp.* v. *Johns-Manville*, 29 F. Supp. 431, 435, DC SCalif 1939; and where patentee was unable to pay patent attorneys, *Arrowood* v. *Symington-Gould Corp.*, 71 F. Supp. 693, DC SNY 1946. However, laches was not imputed to a patent owner because of his failure to prosecute to judgment a suit against an infringer, after the latter had become totally insolvent and had disappeared. *Huntington Dry Pulverizer Co.* v. *Newall Universal Mill Co.*, 91 Fed. 661, C.C.N.Y. 1899.

Suing Other Infringers

In *Salem Engineering Co.* v. *National Supply Co.*, supra, the Court declared that a patentee in getting his patent sustained is not bound to assert his claims to their fullest scope by suing every conceivable infringer. In numerous cases delay has been excused and subsequent suits have been held not barred by laches where the plaintiff was already engaged in litigation upon the patent. *Clair* v. *Kastar, Inc.*, 148 F.2d 644, 2d Cir. 1945; c.d. 326 U.S. 762; *General Electric Co.* v. *Sciaky Bros., Inc.*, supra. The same applies to litigating title to patents in a State Court. *Taylor Engines* v. *All-Steel Engines*, 192 F.2d 171, 9th Cir. 1951.

Change of Position

The Court said in *Craftint Mfg. Co.* v. *Baker,* 94 F.2d 369, 374, 9th Cir.:

"There must be reliance on the delay resulting in a change of position by the party asserting laches."

In many cases the change of position which has justified a defense of laches has been the expenditure of money for the construction of plant or advertising. *Brennan* v. *Hawley Products Co.,* 182 F.2d 945, 7th Cir. 1950, c.d. 340 U.S. 865; *Lukens Steel Co.* v. *American Locomotive Co.,* 197 F.2d 939, 2d Cir. 1952; *Potash Co. of America* v. *International Minerals and Chemical Corp.,* 213 F.2d 153, 10th Cir. 1954.

The fact that two of the most important witnesses for the defendant were dead when the action was brought without legally adequate excuse for the delay in bringing the action was also considered in barring the action for laches in *Brennan* v. *Hawley Products Co.,* 182 F.2d 945, 7th Cir. 1950, c.d. 340 U.S. 865; cf. *Boris* v. *Hamilton Mfg. Co.,* 253 F.2d 526, 7th Cir. 1958.

The fact that the defendant could have changed over to a noninfringing production if infringement had been promptly asserted was considered also as a bar to laches in *Rome Grader & Machinery Corp.* v. *J. D. Adams Mfg. Co.,* 135 F.2d 617, 7th Cir. 1943.

It is the inequity or injustice of plaintiff's assertion of rights after a delay which gives rise to a bar of laches. *Arnold Bernstein Shipping Co.* v. *Tidewater Commercial Co.,* 84 F. Supp. 948, DC Md 1949; *Preston* v. *Kaw Pipe Line Co.,* 113 F.2d 311, 10th Cir. 1940, c.d. 311 U.S. 712.

The defense of laches is not sustained unless the prejudice or change of position of the defendant was induced by the plaintiff by deceitful acts or by silence and acquiescence by plaintiffs or intentional or reckless inducement by plaintiff. *Shaffer* v. *Rector Well Equipment Co.,* supra; *Wisconsin Alumni Research Foundation* v. *Vitamin Technologists,* 41 F. Supp. 857, 866, DC SCalif 1941, aff. in part and reversed in part 146 F.2d 941, c.d. 325 U.S. 876, rehearing denied, 326 U.S. 804.

The Court said in *Shaffer* v. *Rector Well Equipment Co.,* supra:

"The expansion of a business from the profits reaped by infringement is not a prejudicial change of conditions so as to authorize the defending infringer to invoke the defense of laches against a patent owner who has forborne to hail him into Court, meanwhile attempting to settle his claims amicably."

Clear Proof of Changed Position Required. However, a defense of laches cannot be upheld in the absence of clear proof of changed position. *Harries* v. *Air King Products Co.,* 87 F. Supp. 572, 588, DC ENY 1949, aff. 183 F.2d 158. The defendant must show conclusively that he has been prejudiced as a result of plaintiff's delay in order to sustain defense of laches. *Bishop and Babcock Mfg Co.* v. *Sears Roebuck and Co.,* 125 F. Supp. 528, 529, DC NOhio 1954, aff. 232 F.2d 116, 6th Cir.

Where a defendant suffered no damage because of the delay and continued in the same business after cancellation of the license, laches did not lie against the plaintiff. *Kennedy et al.* v. *Trimble Nursery Land Furniture, Inc.,* 22 F. Supp. 8, 9, 37 USPQ 256, DC WNY 1938. The Court said in *Rudenberg* v. *Clark,* 72 F. Supp. 381, 389, DC Mass 1947:

"...the bar of laches [would not apply] in a case where both the equitable owner and the holder of the legal title regarded it as to their mutual interest to leave their respective interests in a vague but friendly posture rather than to sharpen those rights by presenting them in adversary fashion either by formal claims or by litigation."

Where a charge of infringement was not made until 10 years after allegedly infringing product was announced to the trade, and where that product during the period was in wide commercial use on a national scale by one who could not have been said to have drawn upon the patent in suit for his device, the suit for infringement was barred by laches. *Delaney Patents Corp.* v. *Johns-Manville,* supra.

Infringement Known to Plaintiff. After the patentee becomes aware of the existence and general nature of the defendant's alleged infringing device, unreasonable delay in bringing suit will give rise to defense of laches. *Young* v. *General Electric Co.*, 96 F. Supp. 109, 139, DC NIll 1951. In this case a delay of six years was involved before the patentee gave notice of infringement. Laches barred both accounting and injunction where the plaintiff knew for over 4½ years that defendant intended to manufacture frames according to a patented design. *Lukens Steel Co.* v. *American Locomotive Co.*, 197 F.2d 939, 2d Cir. 1952. Plaintiff's knowledge was a factor in upholding the defense of laches to a suit for assessment of damages for an entire period of three years also in *Middleton* v. *Wiley*, 99 F. Supp. 513, 514, DC WMo 1951, reversed in part 195 F.2d 844, although further use was enjoined and the patent owner was allowed $1.00 damages.

However, the defense of laches was unavailing in the case where the plaintiff knew of the infringing sale for only three years before bringing suit. *Clair* v. *Montgomery Ward & Co.*, 36 F. Supp. 664, DC WMo 1940, modified *Montgomery Ward & Co.* v. *Clair*, 123 F.2d 878. Even when the infringement went on for a considerable period of time, the defense of laches was not sustained when the suit was brought promptly after the plaintiff first learned of infringement. *Hamilton Beach Mfg. Co.* v. *P. A. Geier Co.*, 74 F.2d 992, 24 USPQ 98, 7th Cir. 1934; *Hampton* v. *Paramount Pictures Corp.*, 279 F.2d 100, 105, 9th Cir. 1960.

Although acquiescence and laches, however long on the part of the patentee, may be excused by satisfactory proof that he had no knowledge or means of knowledge that his patent was being infringed, it has been held that one alleging want of knowledge must have used reasonable diligence to have informed himself of the facts. *Van Alen* v. *Aluminum Co. of America*, supra; *Pearson* v. *Central Ill. Light Co.*, 210 F.2d 352, 7th Cir. 1954. This is analogous to an alleged concealment relied upon to toll the statute of limitations, in that it is not necessary that the plaintiff know all the facts or that all the evidence needed to prove his case should be in his hands to start the period of laches or start the statute of limitations running, particularly when the plaintiff has a means of discovering the facts under circumstances which should have put him on inquiry. *Tracerlab, Inc.* v. *Industrial Nucleonics Corporation*, 133 USPQ 306, 307, DC Mass 1962.

On the other hand, where the defendant knew that he was an infringer, laches is not a bar to testing the validity of a patent or to an accounting. *Shaffer* v. *Rector Well Equipment Co.*, supra. See also *Wisconsin Alumni Research Foundation* v. *Vitamin Technologists*, supra; *Foxboro Co.* v. *Taylor Instrument Companies*, 58 F. Supp. 313, 323, DC WNY 1944, reversed 157 F.2d 226, c.d. 329 U.S. 800; *Middleton* v. *Wiley*, 195 F.2d 844, 847, 8th Cir. 1952; *Salem Engineering Co.* v. *National Supply*, supra.

A person cannot make a defense of laches available to himself by changing his position with notice of rights of persons against whom the defense is asserted. *United States ex rel Givens* v. *Work*, 13 F.2d 302, 56 Appeals DC 330, c.d. 273 U.S. 711, 1926. Moreover the fact that the infringer has been trespassing on the patent owner's rights for years with impunity does not raise the bar of laches in a suit for injunction and accounting when the infringer has admitted knowledge of the patent and notice of his wrongdoing. *France Mfg.* v. *Jefferson Electric Co.*, supra. See also *Shaffer* v. *Rector Well Equipment Co.*, supra.

Cases where laches were found are tabulated in 3 Walker, Deller's ed., p. 1877 and 4 Walker 2659. Cases where no laches were found are tabulated in 3 Walker 1877 and 4 Walker 2661.

Effect of Declaratory Judgment Act

The Courts have reached different conclusions as to the result of enactment of the Declaratory Judgment Act, 28 U.S.C. 2201-2202, on the defense of laches. In *Brennan* v. *Hawley Products Co.*, 182 F.2d 945, 7th Cir. 1950, c.d. 340 U.S. 65, the court held that a corporation charged with infringement could still interpose the defense of laches although it had not resorted to the federal declaratory judgment action for relief, there being no burden on the defendant to pursue the remedy afforded by the Federal Declaratory Judgment Act.

On the other hand, in *Pierce* v. *International Telephone & Telegraph Corp.*, supra, the court asserted that in order to sustain defense of laches in patent infringement suits, it takes more to prove prejudice to alleged infringer by delay since enactment in 1934 of the statute, giving an alleged infringer the right to declaratory judgment, than it did before. Defendant's counterclaim for patent infringement was not barred for laches in a declaratory judgment suit for invalidity and noninfringement of a patent. *Gordon Johnson* v. *Hunt*, 109 F. Supp. 571, DC NOhio 1952.

Pleading and Proving Laches

It was considered at one time that a special pleading of laches as a defense was not necessary. *Nagy* v. *L. Mundet & Son, Inc.*, 23 F. Supp. 543, 545, 38 USPQ 54, DC ENY 1938; *United* v. *Ireland*, 51 F.2d 226, 232, 8th Cir. 1931, c.d. 284 U.S. 683, 1932.

However, under the Federal Rules of Civil Procedure (effective September 16, 1938), Rule 8(c), affirmative defenses must be pleaded, the rule specifically mentioning laches; and if affirmative defenses are not pleaded, they are waived under Rule 12(h). Nevertheless, Professor Moore asserts that affirmative defenses may also be raised by Motion for Summary Judgment under Rule 56 or by Motion to Dismiss under Rule 12(b)(6). 2 Moore's Federal Practice 1699, Section 8.28, 2d ed., 1961.

It was held that a defense of laches, which was neither pleaded by the patent infringer in its answer in patent infringement suit nor urged at original trial as defense to injunction or accounting and which was made for the first time before a special master before whom accounting proceeded, was not timely. *Victory Fireworks and Specialty Co.* v. *Commercial Novelty Co.*, 26 F. Supp. 126, DC Md 1939.

The Court held in *Bergeron* v. *Mansour*, 152 F.2d 27, 31, 9 F.R.S. 8 c. 33, Case 1, 1st Cir. 1945, that the defense of laches must be pleaded affirmatively in the answer under F.R.C.P. Rule 8(c) and cannot be raised on appeal where it was not pleaded or otherwise brought before the trial court.

2 Moore's Federal Practice, 2d ed., 1962, Section 8.27 [3] declares:

"Any matter that does not tend to controvert the opposing party's prima facie case as determined by applicable substantive law should be pleaded, and is not put in issue by a denial made pursuant to Rule 8(b)." p. 1851.

"Failure to plead matter which constitutes an affirmative defense does not, however, preclude a party from taking advantage of the opposing party's proof, if such proof establishes the defense. Thus, although illegality is normally an affirmative defense, if the illegality appears on the face of the contract, or from the opening statement of plaintiff's counsel, or from plaintiff's proof, the defendant may take advantage of it by proper motion, and if necessary the court will raise the objection itself." p. 1853.

"Under the 1946 amendment to Rule 12(b), it is also made clear that a defendant may raise an affirmative defense by a motion to dismiss for failure to state a claim; and that the court may treat such a motion as a motion for summary judgment." p. 1863, section 8.28.

Federal Rules of Civil Procedure Rule 12(h) asserts:

"A party waives all defenses and objections which he does not present either by motion as hereinbefore provided or, if he has made no motion, in his answer or reply…" Cf. *Riley* v. *Titus*, 190 F.2d 653, 656, 15 FRS 56 c. 43, Case 2, CA Dist Col 1951, c.d. 342 U.S. 855; *United States* v. *A-1 Meat Company*, 146 F. Supp. 590, 594, 23 FRS 56 c. 432, Case 1, DC SNY 1956.

The burden of proof to establish the defense of laches is on the defendant. *National Nut Co.* v. *Sontag Chain Store Co.*, 107 F.2d 318, 323, 9th Cir. 1939; *United Drug Co.* v. *Ireland*, 51 F.2d 226, 8th Cir. In *Shaffer* v. *Rector Well Equipment Co.*, supra, the Court said:

"The failure of defendant to prove injury or damage to itself—a vital element in the establishment of laches—would be fatal to such a defense, even if it had maintained that defense in other respects."

An intervenor is not entitled to raise the defense of laches if it was not open to the defendant in the action between the original parties. *Salem Engineering Co.* v. *National Supply Co. et al.*, supra; *Pierce* v. *American Communications Co.*, supra.

In an infringement suit, the Court, in its discretion, may grant a separate trial on the issue of laches, as an equitable defense, which should be disposed of first by the Court sitting as a court of equity. *Skinner v. Aluminum Co.*, 95 F. Supp. 183, 184, DC WPa 1951. Laches is a question of fact. *Frank Adam Electric Co.* v. *Federal Electric Products Co.*, 200 F.2d 210, 212.

Nature of the Defense of Laches

No hard and fast rules can be made as to the requirements for establishing a defense of laches in patent infringement cases as each case must stand on its own facts. *B & M Corp.* v. *Miller*, 150 F. Supp. 942, 947, DC WKy 1957. Laches in a patent infringement suit is a defense which should be applied on equitable principles and cannot be urged by defendant failing to follow such principles. *Huntman Stabilizer Corp.* v. *General Motors Corp.*, 53 F. Supp. 43, DC NJ 1943, aff. in part and reversed in part 144 F.2d 963, c.d. 65 S. Ct. 271, 2 cases 323 U.S 782. As an equitable defense it may be interposed in an action at law. *Mather* v. *Ford Motor Co.*, 40 F. Supp. 589, DC EMich 1941.

Laches is a personal defense which flows from the relationship of the parties. *Salem Engineering Co.* v. *National Supply Co.*, 75 F. Supp. 993, DC Wpa 1948; *B & M Corp.* v. *Miller*, 150 F. Supp. 942, DC WKy 1957; *Pierce* v. *International Telephone & Telegraph Corp.*, supra. Like estoppel, laches is an equitable defense, but whereas "an injury" to the defendant is necessary in estoppel, in laches the court looks for "injustice." *Caterpillar Tractor Co.* v. *International Harvester Co.*, 32 F. Supp. 304, 308, DC NJ 1940, appeal dismissed 120 F.2d 82, 3d Cir. 1941.

Effect of Laches

The nature of the circumstances determines just what relief will be barred by laches. In many cases, damages and the right to an accounting may be barred although injunction as to future infringement may be granted. *Van Alen* v. *Aluminum Co. of America*, supra.

4 Deller's Walker 2659 (1937 Section 880 C) asserts that laches will bar a preliminary injunction, but a permanent injunction will sometimes be granted in spite of laches. However, a permanent injunction will not be granted when the circumstances create an estoppel.

The Court declared, in *Whitman* v. *Walt Disney Productions, Inc.*, 148 F. Supp. 37, DC SCalif 1958, aff. 263 F.2d 229, 9th Cir. 1957, that a plaintiff who is chargeable with laches cannot recover the damages suffered or the profits defendant has gained. Laches will continue to constitute a bar to recovery of profits and damages even though the patent in suit has expired during litigation and injunctive relief is no longer in question.

But generally an equity court will not refuse an injunction in a patent infringement suit on account of delay in seeking relief where the proof of infringement is clear, even if delay is such as to preclude party of any right to accounting for past profits. *Shaffer* v. *Rector Well Equipment Co.*, supra. See also *Rajah Auto Supply Co.* v. *Belveder Screw & Machine Co.*, 275 Fed. 761, 7th Cir.; *Imperial Brass Mfg. Co.* v. *Hackney*, 75 F.2d 689, 7th Cir.; *Montgomery Ward & Co.* v. *Clair*, 123 F.2d 878, 8th Cir. 1941; *Hampton* v. *Paramount Pictures Corp.*, 279 F.2d 100, 105, 9th Cir. 1960.

Where plaintiff knew of infringement, assessment of damages for the entire period was held inequitable, but further use was enjoined in *Middleton* v. *Wiley*, 99 F. Supp. 513, DC WMo 1951, reversed in part 195 F.2d 844.

The Court declared that a delay of some years in bringing infringement suit was no defense to action to stop infringement from time of suit, where the claim for relief for the period prior to suit had been abandoned. *Royal Typewriter Co.* v. *L. C. Smith & Corona Typewriter*, 76 F. Supp. 190, DC Conn 1948.

An injunction applying to future conduct will usually not be denied unless the elements of estoppel exist. *Montgomery Ward & Co.* v. *Clair*, 123 F.2d 878, 8th Cir. 1941. In *Union Shipbuilding* v. *Boston Iron & Metal Co.*, 93 F.2d 781, 783, 4th Cir. 1938, the court held that laches coupled with estoppel may bar not only accounting for past damages but also an injunction prohibiting use of the patented apparatus by defendant in the future. The Court said:

"[The] facts warrant the legal conclusion of the court that the defense of laches and estoppel had been made out and that the owner of the patent had thereby forfeited any right it might otherwise have had not only to an accounting for past infringement, but also to an injunction prohibiting the use of the patented apparatus by the defendant in the future."

Laches By or Against Others

Although the circumstances giving rise to a bar of laches against a patentee may be binding upon his successor in interest, the successor in interest of the alleged infringer is not necessarily entitled to avail himself of the bar of laches when sued by the owner of the patent. Where the owner of infringing machines went out of business and his tools were purchased by another who then began alleged infringing operations, the failure of the owner of the patent infringed to sue for the prior infringing acts did not constitute laches. *DeSimone* v. *R. H. Macy & Co., Inc.*, 57 F.2d 179, 13 USPQ 217, 2d Cir. 1932.

Likewise a lessee cannot take advantage of his lessor's rights to set up laches. The Court said in *Pierce* v. *American Communications Co.*, supra:

"Defendant here as lessee of infringing equipment cannot assert laches as to its lessor, the manufacturer of the equipment (if indeed plaintiff is guilty of laches), as a defense to its own violation of plaintiff's rights." [Cases cited.]

Whether one infringer can take advantage of the fact that the patentee has not sued other infringers depends upon the circumstances. Although the violation of plaintiff's patent by several parties does not give an unabridged license to all to invade the plaintiff's patent rights, a patent owner may abandon any rights to enforce a valid patent by permitting, without protest, a large scale infringement by the industry generally. *Eastman Kodak Co.* v. *McAuley*, 41 F. Supp. 873, DC SNY 1941; *Veaux* v. *Southern Oregon Sales*, 33 F. Supp. 605,

607, DC Ore 1940, aff. 123 F.2d 455, 9th Cir.

The laches of an assignor of a patent may be imputed to his assignee. *Booth Fisheries Corp.* v. *General Foods Corp.*, 27 F. Supp. 268, 271, DC Del 1939; *Skinner* v. *Aluminum Co. of America*, 105 F. Supp. 635, 637, DC WPa 1952. The same bar may be encountered by the licensee of a patentee whose conduct had given rise to laches. *Boyle Leather Goods Co.* v. *Feldman*, 30 F. Supp. 914, DC SNY 1940, reversed as to another patent 113 F.2d 261.

Whether the purchaser of an alleged infringing machine has a defense of laches which might have been set up by the vendor depends on the circumstances. Where the notice of alleged infringement was not given to the purchaser until the suit was instituted, the defense of laches was not available. *Greenhouse* v. *Plaza Beverages*, 55 F. Supp. 891, 895, DC ENY 1944. See also *Caterpillar Tractor Co.* v. *International Harvester Co.*, supra. On the other hand, where the plaintiff had the means of knowledge and reasonable diligence would have brought home to him the extensive sales by both the manufacturer and the purchaser from the manufacturer, the purchaser is covered by the protection which laches affords the manufacturer. *Van Alen* v. *Aluminum Co. of America*, supra.

Other Aspects of Laches

Questions of laches sometimes arise with respect to pleading or conduct of litigation after the litigation has commenced.

An eight-month delay before filing a motion to amend the answer by setting up prior invention of another is not laches precluding such an amendment where interrogatories have been interposed by each party and answered; lengthy depositions have been taken; and other proceedings had, even where a defendant had in its possession for some considerable time copies of certain of the papers upon which the motion is based. *Utah Radio Products Co.* v. *Delco Appliance Corp.*, 19 F. Supp. 143, 145, 32 USPQ 115, DC WNY 1937.

On the other hand, a motion by defendant for a new trial for allegedly newly discovered evidence to show anticipation was properly denied for lack of diligence and for failure to show that a different result would be obtained if a new trial were granted. *Jamco, Inc.* v. *Carlson*, 274 F.2d 338, 10th Cir. 1959. The same applies to newly discovered evidence bearing on the issue of priority. *General Electric Co.* v. *Minneapolis Honeywell Regulator Co.*, 35 F. Supp. 35, 36, DC ENY 1940, reversed on a different issue 118 F.2d 278, 2d Cir. 1941.

Various other aspects of laches are covered in other articles in this handbook. Laches in presenting claims is discussed in *Delay in Claiming.* (See also *Abandonment of Invention, Disclaimers*, and *Reissues*)

The meaning of the defense of laches was well summarized by the Court in *Galliher* v. *Cadwell*, 145 U.S. 368, 372, 1892, thus:

"The cases are many in which this defense has been invoked and considered. It is true, that by reason of their differences of fact, no one case becomes an exact precedent for another, yet a uniform principle pervades them all. They proceed on the assumption that the party to whom laches is imputed, has knowledge of his rights, and an ample opportunity to establish them in the proper forum; that by reason of his delay, the adverse party has good reason to believe that the alleged rights are worthless, or have been abandoned; and that because of the changing condition or relations during this period of delay, it would be an injustice to the latter to permit him to now assert them."

Cross-references: *Abandonment, Delay in Claiming, Disclaimers, Reissues.*

LIAISON BETWEEN INVENTOR AND ATTORNEY

Roy A. Kinckiner

Major factors causing loss of valuable patent rights are often the lack of understanding and difficulties in communication between the inventor and his attorney. These circumstances may make the provision of special liaison desirable to secure prompt and adequate patent protection.

This article defines the problem of liaison, describes the uses of an intermediary to supply it, points out the place of liaison in the company organization, and considers the advantages and disadvantages. For the sake of balanced presentation and comparison, the article discusses also the more usual practice in which the inventor works directly with the patent attorney.

Problem

The problem involves the resolution of and decisions on various technical and economic matters; transmission of the necessary information to the patent attorney; delineation of fine technical differences between the invention and prior art that must be distinguished in the most effective patent application; and establishment of adequate communication between the inventor and attorney.

Organization

Many organizational arrangements are used to improve the effectiveness of patent procurement. Most of these are variants of two basic procedures distinguished as follows:

(1) *The inventor works directly with the patent attorney or the patent agent.* The attorney handles the inventor's problems from preparing and prosecuting the patent application through licensing, infringements, contracts and suits. The attorney may be expected to have (a) at least four years of technical training leading to a Bachelor of Science degree or equivalent, (b) a three-year general law training leading to a law degree, (c) admission to the bar, and (d) Patent Office registration proving knowledge of patent law.

Patent agents, as discussed in this article, desirably have (a) at least a four-year technical training with the B.S. degree, (b) five or more years' experience in some technical field, and (c) Patent Office registration.

(2) *An intermediary provides liaison between the inventor and the patent attorney.* The intermediary develops with the inventor the information necessary for the preparation of the patent application and communicates this information in writing to the attorney. The intermediary should have (a) at least a four-year technical course

leading to the B.S. (or similar) degree, preferably graduate work also, (b) five or more years' technical experience, and (c) a working knowledge of U.S. Patent Office procedures and patent law practically equivalent to that required to pass the examination for registration. Because of his predominantly technical qualifications, the intermediary is usually given a title such as "patent engineer," "patent chemist," "patent physicist," or the like. In this article we shall designate him generally as a "patent scientist."

Both of these types of organization can produce satisfactory results if persons having the proper qualifications are selected and directed effectively by management. In fact, both alternatives are being used successfully in some form by the Du Pont Company. Each system, however, presents its own particular problems that require the understanding and attention of management.

The size of the company dictates the type of organization to an important degree. Only where a number of patent scientists and attorneys are required to handle the business of patent protection can such persons be organized under one or more common heads as specialized groups. Otherwise, those handling patents will probably be assigned to research, development, design and manufacturing groups. However, the functions, duties and responsibilities for effective patent prosecution do not change with the size of the organization; only the grouping of the personnel and the individual assignments vary.

When the company is sufficiently large to have a legal or patent department, the patent attorney is logically a member of such a department; we will assume that this is the situation for the purposes of this article. There are other organizational positions that the attorney can occupy, the practices of some 250 manufacturing companies in this respect being set forth in a survey entitled "The Patent Counsel in Company Organization" in the August 1960 issue of *Business Records*.

The two basic arrangements or systems are now examined in more detail and compared.

Inventor Works with the Patent Attorney. When the inventor works with the patent attorney, there are the important advantages of directness in communication and avoidance of insertion of additional persons in the line of communication. Those who favor this direct contact claim that it provides more effective and efficient use of manpower.

The attorney in this system normally takes the initiative in developing the information required for a patent application. Given a thorough understanding of the technical area of the invention, the experienced patent attorney can eliminate the deficiencies in the inventor's knowledge of patent art, procedure and law.

Under this system, the supervision of the inventor must take the responsibility for detecting invention, notifying the attorney properly, and meeting schedules, particularly if the location of the attorney differs from that of the inventor. Management of the inventor's department also must place appropriate emphasis on patents, since procurement of patents will be maintained to just about the degree management desires. Thus direct responsibility for patent procurement will rest upon a laboratory or division head whose primary duties lie in some other area, e.g., research, development, design or manufacture. Under these circumstances, patents may tend to suffer; the remotely located attorney can do little about the uncovering of invention unless his assistance is invited.

Where the company or its subdivisions are small and compact, and its technical interests are not too wide, direct contact between the inventor and the patent attorney is the preferred and perhaps the most logical method of operation.

Use of a Patent Agent. Where it is not possible to acquire attorneys with the requisite technical training, it may be desirable to substitute a patent agent for work with the inventors and Patent Office. Patent agents can be developed from scientists having the desired technical background and experience.

The organizational arrangements may differ in several ways when a patent agent is used. Since the agent cannot perform the legal services in licensing, infringements, and various aspects of negotiations and contracts, it is necessary to employ a patent attorney also or to engage outside legal counsel as occasion demands.

It is probably preferable to assign the patent agent to the inventor's organizational grouping because the agent is basically a scientist. If this is done, it unifies and simplifies the responsibility for patent prosecution under one head.

If the patent agent is assigned to the patent or legal department, on the other hand, the administrative situation is the same as that for a patent attorney except, as noted previously, the patent agent must refer all legal matters outside Patent Office procedures to an attorney.

The exigencies of the situation frequently dictate the decision as to whether to use a patent attorney or agent, working directly with the inventor, to prepare and prosecute patent applications. Some of the questions that may be faced are:

Are the technical complexities of the patent situation beyond the reasonable understanding of available attorneys? Which are the greater, the legal or technical complexities and which will have the greater influence on patent applications? If no adequate person is available, is it easier to train the available attorneys in the technical aspects of the work or to train a scientist in patent procedures?

Patent Scientist as Liaison between Inventor and Attorney

When the patent scientist is used as an intermediary between the inventor and the patent attorney, a threefold advantage may result: (1) release of the attorney to handle a greater number of patent applications and legal situations; (2) relief of the inventor to a significant degree from work on patents; (3) increased emphasis on patent procurement.

Where patent attorneys are not available to handle the volume of applications and legal problems, the use of a patent scientist can release a significant amount of the attorney's time for concentration on the legal aspects of patents, by relieving the attorney of much work in defining the invention and establishing experimental support.

The greatest advantage claimed by those who favor the liaison system is the ease with which the patent scientist communicates with both the inventor and attorney. If properly selected and trained, the patent scientist speaks the language of both. Being a scientist, he understands the technical complexities. Because of his repeated experience, he may detect patentable differences that would escape the inventor. Further, the patent scientist saves the inventor the work of collecting and organizing the detailed information required for a patent application, work that the inventor frequently dislikes and seldom takes the time to understand.

Similarly, the patent scientist soon learns what the attorney needs in order to prepare an application and the scientist can meet the need with little excess. Thus, he saves the attorney not only time that would otherwise be consumed in extracting the information from the inventor, but also time spent in sifting an unnecessarily large mass of data.

The use of a patent scientist may increase the emphasis placed on patents; this is his principal function and the measure of his attainment.

Members of operating or research management can delegate some of the duties and responsibilities in regard to patents (e.g., promotion, scheduling, and evaluation of cases and education of the staff) to the patent scientist. However, final responsibility for adequate patent protection rests with management, and it must lend wholehearted support to the effort.

It is important, in the author's opinion, to make the patent scientist readily available to the inventor for personal contact. When the patent scientist is a member of the inventor's organization and the volume of patent work permits, the patent scientist can well be located on the site of the inventor. Where the volume of patent work is not sufficient at one location, the patent scientist may cover a number of locations and schedule periodic visits to each of them. In this latter situation, he may be located advantageously at one site, under a common supervisor. Even when the patent scientist is a member of the legal or patent department, the foregoing considerations also apply. With the patent scientist readily available to the inventor, easy access to the attorney is of lesser importance. Frequent communication between the patent scientist and attorney is less necessary than between the patent scientist and inventor, and the use of written communication can further reduce the frequency of personal contact between the patent scientist and the attorney.

Those who do not favor the use of a patent scientist claim that it is an inefficient form of organization because it introduces an unnecessary third person and thereby increases the cost of patent procurement. The introduction of any additional person in a line of communication tends to produce complications and duplication of effort. The use of a patent scientist is no exception to this general rule. However, if the patent scientist and the patent attorney use care in division of work, the scientist can save at least an equivalent amount of the inventor's and attorney's time in compensation for his own. Vigilance is required, however, to prevent inefficient operation.

Although this system places the ultimate responsibility for the progress and administration of patent work with a laboratory, division or department head, there is an organizational arrangement which can take much of the administrative load from him. This arrangement, described in a following section headed "The Patent Manager," unifies responsibility for patent work.

Duties of the Patent Scientist

The duties of the patent scientist are not peculiar to his use. If adequate patent protection is to be acquired promptly and at reasonable cost, the duties must be performed in any system of organization by either the inventor, his supervision and management, the patent attorney, patent agent or patent scientist. The more common duties of the patent scientist are:

(1) The patent scientist prepares the plan for the research or development workers to search prior patent art. He encourages searching at an early stage of the investigation in order to reduce duplication of the work of others and guide selection of investigational paths likely to be productive.

(2) He assists the research or development worker in interpreting the prior art and defining the invention, a duty particularly important because the inexperienced inventor may miss some of the finer points in distinguishing invention.

(3) He takes the initiative in securing economic appraisal of potential patents, calls on informed individuals for their opinion, and consolidates the results.

(4) From data supplied him by the inventor, the patent scientist prepares a final "patent memorandum" for transmission to the attorney. It is a written communication giving a description of the invention, the difference between it and prior art, the preferred embodiment, any necessary technical background and sketches of suggested drawings, all in such form that the inventor and his supervision can check the accuracy of the statement of the case.

(5) He reviews, together with the inventor, the patent application before filing, to determine the completeness of the claims and correctness of the specifications.

(6) He conducts a study of the records concerning inventorship and supplies the necessary copy to the attorney for final determination of inventorship.

(7) Since he frequently reviews research records, he helps to improve the quality of such records.

(8) He schedules cases so that applications can be prosecuted in sequence according to their value and the commercial needs of the company.

(9) Where research, development or design of large volume and variety are conducted in a given area, he correlates technically the many patent applications that may result and assists in planning the strategy and timing. This aid is of special value when several attorneys are engaged in preparing the applications.

(10) He acts as consultant to management in the many business decisions that are part of filing, refiling and licensing.

This may involve assembly of the many facets of the situation into a comprehensive report to management.

In general, all these duties should be accomplished, of course, in close cooperation with the inventor, the inventor's supervision, and the attorney. No blocks should be imposed. Communication lines between the inventor and the attorney should be kept open at all times, and each party should keep the other properly informed.

Qualifications of the Patent Scientist

Since the liaison patent scientist is the key to the successful operation of the intermediary system, he must be carefully selected for successful operation of the system. Desirable qualifications for a patent scientist are:

(1) A broad and fundamental training and background in the technical area in which he will operate. As he cannot be expected to have intimate acquaintance with all technology he must handle patent-wise, he must be willing and able to apply his knowledge of scientific fundamentals adeptly to new situations and compare them analytically with the prior art.

(2) A working knowledge of the United States Patent Office practices and the preparation of patent applications, so that he can aid both the inventor and attorney and minimize their time requirements. This knowledge may be developed to some extent on the job, although considerable outside study will be required.

(3) Good business judgment.

(4) The ability to get along with persons in all levels of an organization and to retain the confidence of the research worker despite the less-specialized technical knowledge of the patent scientist. He must of necessity be in a staff position and accomplish his aims by persuasion coupled with respect for his opinion.

(5) The ability to administer his work effectively. With the output of 25 to 50 scientists to handle (the number will depend on the prolificacy of ideas and the length of time between steps), good records and effective procedures are essential.

The Patent Manager

When the volume of patent and associated work warrants it, and when a number of separate research, development or other functional organizations need coordination, it is at times desirable to group the patent scientists under a manager. Although he may have some other title, such as director or head, he has responsibility for administration of work involved in the promotion of patents and associated activities.

The patent scientists can still be located convenient to the inventors. Under this arrangement, the patent scientists usually have responsibility to two men: first, the patent manager, and, second, the head of the company group they serve directly. They look to the patent manager for guidance, training and necessary decisions on patent policy, procedure in working with the inventors, and order of priority for potential patents.

The principles of management usually call for a man to be responsible to one supervisor only; hence, the responsibility of the patent scientist to two men in separate groups may be questioned. However, the situation described above works well in the Du Pont Company, although not used in all departments. It requires that the management of the area being served and the patent manager be reasonable persons, and that they cooperate closely in the handling of patent work.

The use of a patent manager tends to avoid relegation of patent work to a secondary position, as may occur when the responsibility is placed on a laboratory director or a design, plant, or department manager. With patents as his sole responsibility, the patent manager should bring to this activity a dedication and singleness of purpose that is otherwise less probable.

Creation of such a separate patent group under a manager can weld the patent scientists into a cohesive group that permits better coordination and scheduling of the work, it can promote their education and progress, achieve increased status for the group, and thereby raise morale. The patent manager coordinates the work of his organization with that of the patent attorney in preparing applications and obtaining legal advice from him as needed.

The patent manager should combine experienced leadership, administrative abilities and well-developed business acumen. He should also be thoroughly grounded in the scientific and engineering areas in which the patent work falls. Further, he must know the elements of patents and patent office procedures. A patent manager with these qualifications can render valuable assistance to management in all phases of the patent business and especially in the exploration of new products and processes where a proprietary patent position is of paramount importance. To enable the patent manager best to fulfill this function, it is desirable that he report directly to the level of management charged with responsibility for the direction of research and development, manufacture, or engineering in the several functional organizations served by the patent section.

Procedures

Certain procedures have been found helpful in promoting the effectiveness of the patent scientist.

Notice of Invention. The prospective inventor should not only recognize invention early, but also notify his supervision and the patent scientist. To this end, use of a "Notice of Invention" form is recommended. See form below. A letter of notice will do equally well, but a form of 1 to 2 pages insures that the necessary information is not overlooked.

Case #_____

Date _____

Engineering Department

NOTICE OF INVENTION.

To:

From: _____

(Prospective Inventor)

Description of Invention (to cover essential features of patentable matter only)

Value of Invention (brief outline of potential commercial value in qualitative terms if no dollar figures have been obtained, and statement of how

potential is to be realized; i.e., by new product, improved product, improved process, proprietary position, licensing, manufacturing, etc.)

Prior Patent Art (extent to which reviewed and references to significant patents that might be anticipatory)

Approved (signature of supervision)

Originated by (inventor)

The Notice of Invention form, properly filled in, is forwarded by the inventor through his supervision to the patent scientist. It serves as a record of the invention and the possible inventor, permits the patent scientist to schedule his effort and determine his workload, shows the patent scientist and the inventor's supervisors the desirability of early assistance and direction toward perfecting the invention, and accelerates the preparation of the patent application.

Appraisal of Patent Proposal. A second form also proves useful in early appraisal of commercial value of an invention, one of the most difficult decisions concerning a potential patent. Most well-staffed laboratories will have a large backlog of work and more inventions available than personnel can handle. An early decision as to the commercial value of an invention is, therefore, necessary so that the more promising ones can be given precedence. A thorough economic study, involving marketing surveys, manufacturing costs, estimates of investment costs and manufacture of prototypes, is many times more costly than can be justified at an early stage. While no preliminary appraisal can provide such quantitative information, the appraisal can supply a surprising amount of information that will aid in decision making. (See *Appraisal of Patent Proposal*)

Case #_____

Date _____

Engineering Department

APPRAISAL OF PATENT PROPOSAL.

Subject

Inventor

1. List references concerning any published matter related to this development.

2. Give source and date of information that would indicate public use (product, process, or equipment) of this or any significantly related development.
3. What additional commercial uses can you visualize for this development?
4. How do you rate the commercial value of this development?
   a. High _____ Medium _____ Low_____
   b. Why?
5. How do you rate the technical novelty of this development?
   a. High _____ Medium _____ Low_____
   b. Why?
6. Do you think that we should apply for a patent?
   a. Yes _____ No _____
   b. What reasons in addition to those shown above affected your decision?

Signature __

The patent scientist can play an important part in gathering and interpreting this information. He can initiate action by forwarding the forms to the knowledgeable persons. He can study the returned forms, collate the information, transmit a summary with his conclusions and recommendations to those in management whose decision is required or who are to be kept informed, and, when necessary, augment or arrange for augmenting the information through further literature or economic studies.

Patent Review Committee. In many cases, decisions can be made readily as to the desirability of filing a patent application and as to the strategy and the timing. In other more complex cases, however, the facts may not be clearly delineated, and business judgment or acumen (perhaps intuitive) will be the basis for any immediate decision. For these cases group discussion proves beneficial, as by a patent review committee.

The review committee may be composed of the patent scientist, the inventor, the inventor's supervision, and the members of management who will ultimately make the necessary business decisions. The patent scientist here again takes the initiative in arranging for the meeting, preparing pertinent information, and placing it in the hands of the committee members prior to the meeting. The information should consist of a brief description of the invention; a summary of the pertinent facts and nature of the decision required; and also the patent scientist's recommendation. It is good practice to make him the chairman of the meeting and responsible for such follow-up as may be necessary.

An advantage of a formal group or committee for such discussions lies in the experience gained by its members through repeated considerations of the difficult cases.

Summary

In industrial companies, patent organizations may differ widely in structure and form, yet most are variants of two basic forms. In one, patent attorneys communicate directly with the inventors in supplying all the patent services, from defining the invention and preparing the patent applications through prosecution, contracts, licenses, infringements and suits. This form is especially effective with closely knit technical organizations in which communication lines are short and contacts easily made. Difficulty may be experienced in finding patent attorneys with the requisite technical knowledge; without such knowledge, technical communication is often difficult and understanding incomplete.

The second form uses a patent scientist as an intermediary between the inventor and the patent attorney. Suited to larger, more loose, and more technically diverse industrial organizations, it can be effective of saving time and thus extending the talents of the patent attorneys over a much broader area than they might cover otherwise. The intermediary should be closely associated with the inventor both by location and organization, to facilitate close cooperation. The potential disadvantage of the extra link in the communication chain can be offset by close rapport between the inventor, the patent scientist and the patent attorney. Where it is difficult to obtain patent attorneys with broad technical knowledge and understanding, the use of patent scientists can extend the attorneys' output of patent applications.

In larger companies using a number of

patent scientists, a separate functional organizational grouping of the patent scientists, headed by a patent manager, can be useful in relieving line organization of many duties and responsibilities in promoting and protecting invention through patents and in increasing the emphasis on such protection.

With any type of patent organization, ultimate responsibility for effective patent procurement rests with line management, no matter how it distributes the duties, and patent protection will be obtained in direct proportion to management's desire and emphasis.

Cross-references: *Attorneys and Agents, Corporate Patent Department, Disclosures, Records, Research Directors' Patent Responsibilities.*

LICENSES—INDEMNITY (HOLD HARMLESS) CLAUSES

William E. Currie

The prospective licensee, in negotiating for patent rights, may seek to be held harmless for infringement of the patent rights of others and also to be relieved of payments due under the agreement if the licensed patent is infringed by competitors.

The licensor may be willing to accept some responsibility for infringement by the licensee in operating under the license. The obligation may be (1) only to defend against infringement suits, (2) to defend and hold harmless against the consequences of such suits up to a certain amount, or (3) to defend and hold harmless without limit. Any such obligation, particularly the last, may involve the licensor in very large expenditures and would be reasonable only where the assured profits from the license are correspondingly great.

The licensor may also agree if and when his patent is infringed by others,

(a) To forego royalty payments from his licensee so long as the infringement continues unabated, or

(b) To impound the payments during a suit that he may conduct against the infringer and return them if the outcome of the suit does not stop the infringement.

Notwithstanding the foregoing situations,

the licensor is entitled to receive royalties from the licensee so long as the license is in force, in the absence of provisions to the contrary.

There is no warranty implied in a license agreement with respect to indemnity or remission of payments; whatever protection the licensee is to receive in these matters must be stated.

The licensor will prefer either to omit all reference to such protection or to limit his liability carefully. He needs, however, to draw a contract that the licensee will accept and, having accepted, will not be seeking to cancel, as unfair or unfavorable, at some early opportunity which other clauses may provide. A good license should please both parties.

In seeking to reduce his liability to an acceptable minimum or to omit the liability altogether, as seems to be done in a large proportion of patent licenses, the licensor can honestly urge that his share of the profit will be much less than that of the manufacturer working under the license. Under such circumstances, it would be manifestly imprudent for the licensor to hold the licensee harmless, on say, a million dollars of sales a year, when the licensee may have received only fifty thousand dollars of royalty. The licensor may suggest, if disagreement persists, that the licensee make an infringement search, to supplement the patentability search made by the Examiner before issuance of the patent.

The licensee's potent argument for better terms is his opportunity to decline the license. It is probably rare, however, when both parties wish to see the agreement consummated, that the negotiations will fail over the hold harmless clause. This is true, particularly, when the license is liberal, as some agreements are, in provision for termination by the licensee.

Provisions of Indemnity Clauses

When the licensor accepts protective provisions for the licensee, the license agreement will contain clauses relating to one or more of the following situations, although not necessarily with the terms stated as illustrations.

(1) The licensor's liability to the licensee for patent infringement in operating under the licensed patent shall not exceed (1) a fixed percentage, never more than all, of the total royalties that licensee has paid or (2) a fixed minimum.

(2) In case of continuing infringement of the licensed patent rights by others, all payments of royalty otherwise required will be suspended (or reduced to a stated level) until the patent owner abates the infringement (or takes certain steps such as filing suit for infringement within a certain period of time after the licensee brings the infringement to the attention of the licensor).

(3) All license payments shall cease if the patent is held invalid by a court of last resort or in a decision from which no appeal is taken.

(4) The licensor may agree to waive royalties, in whole or in part, or may give the licensee the right to terminate the agreement, if its business is adversely affected by infringement by others or by unlicensed competition.

(5) If what happens amounts to an eviction of the license from all benefits under the license, the licensee may be entitled to terminate the license, as noted under "Termination" in the *Licenses under U.S. Patent Rights.*

(6) The licensee, if he is to be held harmless, to the extent stated or in fact at all, for the infringement of patent rights of others, must operate according to designs and instructions provided or approved by the licensor, this to avoid adding infringing features from the patents of others. Such designs and instructions may be recited in part at least in the agreement.

(7) The licensee, when sued or threatened with an action for infringement, will promptly notify the licensor in writing and, in case of suit, will cooperate with the licensor, this cooperation including supplying available information and assistance from technical and other employees, as requested, either free or for a charge as specified in the agreement.

(8) Licensor's liability to licensee does not extend beyond the manufacture, use and sale of what is patented, i.e., not to infringement due to use of the invention as an element of a patented composition or process. It does not extend, for example, to the licensed product when sold in a patented rubber composition or as part of a patented radio circuit.

(9) The license should state who, as between licensor and licensee, is to institute, conduct and pay for the suit (or share the responsibilities or costs of both) and who receives the recoveries that may result from the suit. If an exclusive licensee declines to initiate or join in a suit against an infringer of the licensed patent, the licensor may proceed with the suit and join the exclusive licensee as a party to it.

(10) The licensor shall not remove the possibility of a suit against the infringer of the patent, under exclusive license, by giving the infringer a release or license.

(11) The licensor should seek to list the specific patent(s) about which the other party has expressed concern and limit the indemnity provision to it or them.

Failure to bring suit against infringers of the licensed patent rights does not amount to granting them a release from infringement or a license without royalty. The licensee is not entitled to invoke a provision assuring him of a license on as favorable terms as any other licensee, merely because the licensor does not sue infringers.

It should be noted again that in the absence of express agreement, the licensor is under no obligation to prosecute infringers or contribute to the cost of infringement suits brought by the licensee. Moreover, general undertakings to give such "assistance, cooperation and scientific advice as will contribute to the perpetuation, publication and furtherance in all respects of the licenses" or the like, cannot be construed as an agreement to protect the licensee from the effects of infringement of the licensed patent rights. *Photochart* v. *Del Riccio*, 83 USPQ 401, Cal DC of Appeal 1949.

Defense and Hold Harmless Provisions in Sale of Goods

Where a sale of goods is involved, the seller gives an implied license to the buyer. From the standpoint of liability for infringement, this license is different from the license under which a licensee manufactures. One who sells an article or composition has had an opportunity to determine whether infringement is likely and should have done so. Therefore, an agreement to hold the buyer harmless, in case he is sued for infringement on account of his purchase, may include some such clause as the following:

"Licensor, in consideration of the purchase by Licensee, hereby agrees to hold Licensee safe and harmless against any and all suits for patent infringement brought against Licensee, the alleged act of infringement consisting of the use or sale of said product heretofore purchased from Licensor...."

The Uniform Commercial Code, adopted in many states, shows the general acceptance of the duty of the seller to guarantee the buyer against charges of infringement in use of the product purchased. The following is the general nature of one of the provisions of the Code:

"Unless otherwise agreed a seller who is a merchant regularly dealing in goods of the kind warrants that the goods shall be delivered free of the rightful claim of any third person by way of infringement or the like but a buyer who furnishes specifications to the seller must hold the seller harmless against such claim which arises out of compliance with the specifications."

Hold Harmless Agreements in Government Contracts

"(a) Whenever an invention described in and covered by a patent of the United States is used or manufactured by or for the United States without a license of the owner thereof or lawful right to use or manufacture the same, the owner's remedy shall be by action against the United States in the Court of Claims for the recovery of his reasonable and *entire compensation* for such use and manufacture..." (Emphasis added.)

The purpose of this statutory provision (28 U.S.C. 1948) is to make certain that no manufacturer, for fear of patent infringement, will hesitate to make whatever the Government needs. Now, however, many purchasing agencies of the Government return this liability to the manufacturer (or contractor) by means of some such clause as the following in purchase orders or contracts.

"Patents.—The contractor shall hold and save the Government, its officers, agents, servants, and employees, harmless from liability of any nature or kind, including costs and expenses, for or on account of any patent or invention, article, or appliance manufactured or used in the performance of the contract, including their use by the Government."

In a case involving this provision, the Government's invitation to bid and the specifications of the contract described articles to be furnished to the Government in general terms and made no reference to trade name or name of any patented device. If fulfillment of the contract required use of a patented process, this should have been ascertained by the contractor before he made his bid. Since he agreed by contract to save the Government harmless from liability on account of any patent, the contractor is obligated to supply devices even if they are covered by a patent owned by a third party. Opinion of the Comptroller General of the United States, 104 USPQ 189, 1951.

Hold Harmless Agreements with Cities

In a case involving a contractor who has agreed to hold a city harmless for patent infringement in completing his contract, it was held that he must either obtain for the city the rights from the patent owner, when continuing use of the structure is enjoined, to continue to use it; remove it at the contractor's expense and refund all payments made to him; or modify it to a noninfringing structure. *Nau* v. *Vulcan Rail and Construction Co.*, 50 USPQ 484, N.Y. Ct. Appeals 1941.

Cross-references: *Licenses—Package, Licenses under U.S. Patents, Licensing Experience of U.S. Corporations.*

LICENSES—PACKAGE
Joseph W. Burns

The practice of licensing several patents in a "package" or "group" in one license agreement for a single royalty has been subject to attack in recent court decisions.

No question has been raised as to the legality of such agreements entered into voluntarily by a licensee. But where the patent owner refuses to license patents individually or to fix a separate royalty rate for each patent, the authorities are in conflict as to whether such a policy constitutes patent misuse or a violation of the antitrust law.

Business Reasons for Package Licenses

The practice of including several patents in a single license agreement is so common that appropriate clauses are included in standard contract forms in many books on patent licenses.[1] Very often the licensor has developed a group of patents which relate to a single process, method, or technology. There may be a basic patent and several improvement patents. Sometimes the license covers two groups of patents covering alternative processes. In many cases the licensee desires the licensor's know-how and technical information, including whatever patents he may own.

Although court decisions discussing misuse look at a patent as a single grant of monopoly by the government which stands alone, licensees consider patents in terms of competing technologies. A single competitive technology may encompass any number of patents. Whether the several claims of a single patent, or the various claims of a group of patents, are involved is immaterial. In some instances the Patent Office itself may be responsible for the issuance of several patents rather than one; Section 121 of the Patent Code makes this matter largely discretionary with the Office.

An important reason for package licenses is the desire of the licensee to receive the future improvements developed by the licensor. Since only one product is created, regardless of the number of patents used, a single royalty for the use of any or all of the patents or know-how is the most practical and desirable method of compensation for both parties. It is very difficult to evaluate each patent individually or to divide a royalty between patents and know-how, as recognized by the official groups which have studied the problem.[2]

Authorities Holding Compulsory Package Licenses Constitute Patent Misuse

The first successful attacks on compulsory package licenses were made in *The American Securit Co.* v. *Hamilton Glass Co.* (summary judgment granted, District of Indiana), reversed 254 F.2d 889, CA 7 1958, and *The American Securit Co.* v. *Shatterproof Glass Corp.*, 154 F. Supp. 890, DC Del 1957, aff. 268 F.2d 769, CA 3 1959, cert. denied, 361 U.S. 902, 1959. Although the Supreme Court denied certiorari, the Third Circuit decision appears to be in conflict with decisions of the Second, Fourth and Seventh Circuits in *E. R. Squibb & Sons* v. *Chemical Foundation, Inc.*, 93 F.2d 475, CA 2 1937; *Baker-Cammack Hosiery Mills* v. *Davis Co.*, 181 F.2d 550, CA 4 1950; *Hazeltine Research, Inc.* v. *Avco Manufacturing Co.*, 227 F.2d 137, CA 7 1955; *Apex Electrical Mfg. Co.* v. *Altorfer Bros. Co.*, 238 F.2d 867, 872 CA 7 1956; and *Hazeltine Research, Inc.* v. *Admiral Corp.*, 183 F.2d 953, CA 7 1950.

For discussion of this case see *Harvard Law Review*, Vol. 73, pp. 1630-1632, 1960; *Law Forum*, pp. 180-184 (Spring 1960); *Villanova Law Review*, Vol. 3, pp. 398-399 (April 1958).

The Patent Section of the American Bar Association at the annual meeting in Washington in 1960 passed a resolution stating in part as follows:

"WHEREAS, the decision of the U.S. Court of Appeals for the Third Circuit in *American Securit Co.* v. *Shatterproof Glass Co.*, 122 USPQ 167, 268 F.2d 769 (cert. denied) has cast a shadow on the practice of package licensing . . .

"NOW, THEREFORE, be it resolved that the section approves in principle the good faith licensing of a plurality of related patents in the same patents."

The Third Circuit decision in *Shatterproof Glass* is in direct conflict with *United States* v. *Libbey-Owens-Ford Glass Co. et al.*, 119 USPQ 86 DC NOhio 1958, CCH Trade Regulation Reports Section 69,147, on the same facts and appears to be contrary to the principles of *Transparent-Wrap Machine Corp.* v. *Stokes & Smith*, 329 U.S. 637, 1947 and *Automatic Radio Mfg. Co.*

v. *Hazeltine Research, Inc.,* 339 U.S. 827, 1950.

The Third Circuit held that even though Securit granted licenses to seven licensees for a flat royalty of 2¢ per square foot of tempered glass made by the use of any, some or all of its tempering patents, its refusal to grant Shatterproof a license to use only some of those patents at a lower royalty, was a patent misuse depriving Securit of its right to sue for infringement. It also held this refusal was a violation of the compulsory licensing provisions of the consent decree in *United States* v. *Libbey-Owens-Ford,* although Shatterproof had an absolute right to petition the Ohio Court to fix the lower royalty rate it desired.

The Ohio Court held directly to the contrary, stating:

"After petitioner (Securit) had granted licenses to the first applicants on all the patents for a royalty of 2¢ per square foot, it would have been very difficult, if not impossible, for it to fix a royalty on each patent at the request of a later applicant in view of the provisions of the Consent Decree prohibiting discrimination among licensees."

The importance of the Third Circuit's decision is its holding that compulsory licensing of two or more patents is per se a patent misuse regardless of (1) the nature of their disclosures; (2) whether one is a basic invention and another a minor improvement; (3) whether they are product, apparatus, or process patents; or (4) whether the package of patents are dominant in the art.

A contrary result was reached in *Apex Electrical Mfg. Co.* v. *Altorfer Bros. Co.,* supra, where the Court reversed a judgment holding that there was a misuse of patent under the antitrust laws. It held valid a practice under which applicants could obtain a license under one, two, or three patents for the same royalty, stating that this did not constitute requiring licensees to take unwanted patents.

In *Baker-Cammack Hosiery Mills* v. *Davis Co.,* supra, the defendants alleged misuse in an infringement suit on several grounds, including one: "that the licensee is required to take a license for all fifteen patents at 2¢ per dozen pairs, and may not

obtain a license under a smaller number of patents at a smaller royalty." The Court stated (p. 570):

"...nowhere in this case does it appear that free competition has beeen stifled or that any attempt has been made to control the producers as to prices or quantities or areas of production. Furthermore, the patent privileges have been offered freely to all maufacturers, and it is to their obvious advantage to possess the right to incorporate in their output all the modern improvements in the manufacture of hosiery."

The Third Circuit decision also raises a serious question with respect to the validity of expiration provisions common to many patent licenses. It ruled that standing alone "Paragraph 8(a) of Securit's Standard Licensing Agreement, which provides that that agreement shall continue 'in full force and effect to the expiration of the last to expire of any' of Securit's patents set out in 'Schedule A,' constitutes a patent misuse for it extends the payment of royalties under patents which may expire to the expiration date of that patent most recently granted to Securit."

The Second Circuit held in *E. R. Squibb & Sons* v. *Chemical Foundation, Inc.,* 93 F.2d 475 (1937), that there is a presumption that royalties are not to be paid after the expiration of a patent and that if the intention is to have them continue longer, the parties should phrase the contract in language from which such an intention may fairly be inferred. The holding of the Third Circuit appears to be contrary to the decision in the *Squibb* case.

Authorities Supporting Validity of Compulsory Package Licenses

Until the Supreme Court settles the conflict, there is authority for continuing the practice of compulsory package licenses. The Third Circuit's basis for finding a misuse was that "tying" together two patents was a restraint of competition. However, the Supreme Court has not yet held that tying together two patents is a misuse. In *Transparent-Wrap Machine Corp.* v. *Stokes & Smith,* supra, the Supreme Court held that tying improvement patents to the basic patent did not constitute an unlawful monopoly. It stated that while in Clayton Act, Section 3, "Congress made it unlawful to condition the sale or lease of one article on an agreement not to use or buy a competitor's article (whether either or both are patented), where the effect is 'to substantially lessen competition or tend to create a monopoly.'" Congress has not applied this to two patents. *Morton Salt* v. *Suppiger*, 314 U.S. 488, 1942, involved an allegation of violation of Section 3 by tying-in an unpatented product.

In *Automatic Radio Mfg. Co.* v. *Hazeltine Research, Inc.*, 339 U.S. 827, 1950, the Supreme Court held there was no patent misuse where a licensor of a group of patents required the licensee to pay royalties on a percentage of sales, even though none of the patents was used. The Court cited as an example of an unlawful tie-in "conditioning the granting of a license under one patent upon the acceptance of another and different license." The only case cited was *United States* v. *Paramount*, 334 U.S. 131, 1948.

In *United States* v. *Loew's, Inc.*, 371 U.S. 38, 1962, the Supreme Court, while applying the *Paramount* decision to block-booking of films for television, cited only those patent cases which had involved tying-in a product.

Due to the nature of a patent right, phrases such as "restraint," "monopoly," "tying," and "block-booking" are not applicable.

The first determination in relation to any patent misuse or antitrust question must be directed to the nature and character of the patent rights involved. The fact that an agreement or practice reaches outside the area of a single patent does not render it automatically illegal. The legality of the agreement or practice must be determined as a matter of general law. This principle was established by the Supreme Court in *Transparent Wrap*.

There are several important distinctions between a patent package license and the "block-booking" of copyrighted motion pictures. In block-booking two different products are involved, each of which produces a separate royalty, and each of which is in competition with similar products (motion

pictures). With package licensing, the two patents tied together are part of a single technology or process, for which a single royalty is paid, and both are used together to produce a single product. There is no competition involved with respect to the two patents.

When an exhibitor is required to accept a second picture as a condition of obtaining a first, competitors of the producer of the two block-booked pictures are deprived of the opportunity to license one of their pictures in place of the second. Pictures of other producers, even though copyrighted, can and do compete for the same income from admissions. A motion picture is a product and the practice constituted tying different products together. The Supreme Court considered the requirement of accepting a second picture as constituting "another and different license."

In patent package-licensing, there is no requirement that the licensee use all the patents. He can use the one he wants, and use a third party's patent which is competitive with the second patent, instead of the second patent. Unlike block-booking, the patent package license does not require the use of unwanted patents or deprive owners of competitive patents of the opportunity to license their patents.

Since package licensing of process patents has no effect on competition or the sale of products in trade or commerce, it would appear that no public policy is involved which could be considered as resulting in a misuse. Where a group of patents relate to a single process, method or technology, a package license of those patents does not cause any injury to the public or injury to competition. Where a process involved a great many patents, it is impractical if not impossible to accurately apportion the royalty among the patents. The value to a licensee of the right to use patented inventions is purely a question of business economics, not of antitrust law or public policy. In many cases, if not in most, it is an advantage to a licensee to have the privilege of using whichever of the inventor's patents he finds useful. In addition, many licenses grant rights to future inventions, whose value is unascertainable at the time a license is executed. Where an owner of a patented process grants licenses freely to all competitors, each licensee wants to have the same rights as his competitors. The privilege of having rights to future inventions without increase in royalty is generally considered very valuable. The licensee loses nothing, since he does not pay unless he uses the patent. Far from constituting a misuse, the Supreme Court said in *Hazeltine* (p. 834) "What it [the licensee] acquired by the agreement into which it entered was the privilege to use any or all of the patents and developments as it desired to use them."

The practice of declining to license one patent for less than the royalty charged for a group should not be held unlawful per se without consideration of what the patent is, its relation to the group of patents, its value, or the value of the others in the group. For example, if two patents are complementary and one cannot be used without the other, the real benefit to a licensee is the ability to use the machine or process, and that has a single value to him, regardless of the number of patents involved. The patentee has a right to measure his reward by the value of the invention to the licensee. If a potential licensee believed one patent was invalid and wished a license only under the other, the benefit to him would be exactly the same as if he were licensed under both, since he could not achieve the result without using the licensed patent. A patentee should be entitled to the same royalty, even though only one patent is licensed. It may be very difficult to determine which of the two patents has a greater value.

The only lawful objection a licensee could have for not wanting a package license, which includes a patent he does want, is that it might deprive him of the opportunity to assert invalidity against patents he did not want. Where a licensee may cancel at any time, he has not assumed any unreasonable obligation.

Even in the *Paramount* case (1948) and the *Loew's* case (1962) the Supreme Court did not outlaw block-booking of motion pictures where the purchaser acted voluntarily. In view of the different nature of patents, the courts should recognize that

when a licensor has granted a package license at the request of the licensee, the "most-favored customer" clause in most license agreements would make it practically impossible for the licensor to set a lower royalty for less than the package.

Footnotes

1. Hineline, Harris, "Forms and Their Use in Patent and Trade Mark Practice in the United States and Canada," Charlotte, Va., The Michie Co., pp. 140-141, 1951.
   Gordon, Saul, "Gordon's Modern Annotated Forms of Agreement," New York, Prentice-Hall, pp. 728, 731, 1940.
   Deller, "Walker on Patents," pp. 1515, 1517, New York, Baker, Voorhis & Co., 1937.
   Belsheim, "Modern Legal Forms," Section 6602, pp. 255, 256, West Publishing Co., 1958.
2. The Report of the Attorney General's National Committee to Study The Antitrust Laws, p. 239.
   "A package license may include more than one or all of the licensor's patents. Packaging is frequently used to avoid troublesome questions of infringement, complex bookkeeping, the difficulty of determining which patents cover the present and future needs of the licensee, cost differences, and similar practical considerations.
   "The practice of licensing all or a number of an owner's patents in a package has become widespread. It avoids questions of infringement, bookkeeping and the like. More frequently it has been necessitated by the complexity to which technology has progressed in a particular area." (Antitrust Problems in the Exploitation of Patents, a Staff Report to Subcommittee No. 5, Committee on the Judiciary, H. R. 84th Congress 2nd Session, December 31, 1956, page 14.)
   "When a group of patents is licensed as a package, it is usually easy to arrive at a royalty rate for the entire package, but major difficulties present themselves when a licensee, wishing to pick and choose among the patents in the package demands an adjustment in the royalty." (*ibid*, p. 15).

Cross-references: *Antitrust Law, Licenses Under U.S. Patents.*

LICENSES UNDER U.S. PATENT RIGHTS
William E. Currie

Introduction

A license under United States patent rights is a contract dealing with a particular kind of intangible property—issued patents or pending patent applications and those inventions which have been reduced to practice by actual use. The subject matter of the licenses is unique but the drafting of them is part of the general law of contracts.

An oral license is valid unless it is within the area of contracts which, under various state or other laws, must be in writing to be valid. A letter agreement from licensor to licensee is adequate for a complete license where the letter contains all essential provisions, notwithstanding such statements as "formal license agreements may be drafted in the near future by your attorney and submitted to us for consideration." *Pleatmaster, Inc. et al.* v. *Consolidated Trimming Corp.*, 117 USPQ 60, CA 6 1958. Informal arrangements of these types are generally undesirable and are to be avoided.

Licensing in advance of filing an application is unusual but may sometimes be desirable as, for example, when the licensee wishes to obtain technical information from the licensor as early as possible.

Licensing under future inventions, as part of a license dealing with existing patent rights, is valid if the inventions are limited to a field of reasonable scope or to a time of reasonable duration. Unlimited agreements to assign or license are regarded as placing an undue burden on inventive work and void as against public policy. Questions of this kind most frequently arise in connection with contracts made by employees who assign their inventions to their employers.

Scope of License

The licensor of a single U.S. patent has the right to restrict the grant with respect to class of activity (making, using or selling), time, geographical area, volume of production, and sizes of articles to be produced. Cf. *United States* v. *General Electric Co.*, 272 U.S. 476, 1926; *General Talking Pictures Corp.* v. *Western Electric Co.*, 305 U.S. 124, 1937; *Keeler* v. *Standard Folding Bed Co.*, 157 U.S. 659, 1895; 35 U.S.C. 261.

If nothing is said in the agreement about the scope of any of these rights, the agreement will generally be construed to include all rights which the patent can convey. The right to make implies the right to use what the licensee makes but not necessarily the right to sell it unless the licensee has no other use for the thing made.

Protection Against Loss of Rights or Secrecy of Information

Licenses should contain a provision for termination if the patent rights licensed are held to be invalid or not infringed by what the licensee does.

When a license provides for secret information, either with or without accompanying rights under a patent, it is important to state what adjustment is to be made in the rate of payments if the secret information becomes public knowledge.

Otherwise the licensee may find himself paying for patent rights that others are infringing openly or for information long after it has become available to the public. The *Listerine* case tested the necessity of continuing annual payments, currently at the rate of $1,500,000 a year, on a purchased formula after it became generally known and open to free use by others. The decision holding that the payments must be continued shows what serious obligations can arise from failure to provide for terminating payments for information. *Warner-Lambert Co., Inc.* v. *John J. Reynolds, Inc.*, 123 USPQ 431, DC SNY 1959; aff. 126 USPQ 3, CA 2 1960.

Price Control

A patent license may control the price of first sale of a patented product, in the absence of exceptional circumstances, but not the price on resale. *United States* v. *General Electric Co.*, 272 U.S. 476, 1926. This rule remained undisturbed in *United States* v. *Line Material Co. et al.*, 333 U.S. 287, 76 USPQ 399, 1948.

Price control has been held to be improper:

(a) When the patent licensed was later held to be invalid. *Niash Refining Co., Inc.*

v. *Avedon Manufacturing Corp.*, 120 USPQ 130, NY Sup. Ct. 1959.

(b) When the license grants rights under patents of *two or more owners. Consolidated Packaging Machinery Corp.* v. *Kelly et al.*, 116 USPQ 276, CA 7 1958.

(c) When licenses with price-fixing clauses are granted to a plurality of licensees under a patent. The "Third Circuit at least [considers that] such licenses constitute a violation of the antitrust laws and a misuse of the patent which renders the patent unenforceable by the patentee." *Tinnerman Products, Inc.* v. *George K. Garrett Co., Inc.*, 126 USPQ 130, DC EPa 1960.

(d) When price control is effected through cross licensing. *United States* v. *New Wrinkle, Inc. et al.*, 342 U.S. 371; 92 USPQ 158, 1952.

While a number of the issues above can be argued pro and con, provisions for price control are probably not to be found in many licenses, if any, being drawn at this time. Their omission avoids uncertainties that might arise.

Right of Licensee to Deny Infringement

While the licensee is ordinarily estopped to challenge validity, it can deny infringement. In a leading case,

"The court also concluded that even though the appellee (licensee) is denied, under the circumstances of this case, the right to challenge validity, this does not bar it from questioning the scope of the patents in connection with its defense of non-infringement . . . this estoppel for manifest reasons does not prevent him from denying infringement . . . it is admissible to show the state of the art involved." *Midland Steel Products Co.* v. *Clark Equipment Co.*, 82 USPQ 87, CA 6 1949.

In holding a patent valid over the art, a court may so restrict the claims by interpretation as to save the licensee from infringement.

Contest of Validity

So long as the license is in force, the licensee under the usual circumstances cannot challenge the validity of the patent.

Cf. *Midland Steel Products* case above. The situation is modified when the license contains a price fixing clause. *Sola Electric Co.* v. *Jefferson Electric & Manufacturing Co.*, 317 U.S. 173, 1942.

Basic Forms of Licenses

In the simplest form, a license may be granted as follows:

In consideration of the sum of   dollars ($), receipt of which is hereby acknowledged, Licensor hereby grants to Licensee an unlimited, nonexclusive, paid-up license under United States Patent No.   , granted   . This license is personal to Licensee and is not assignable or transferable without the consent of Licensor, except as part of the sale of Licensee's entire business.

An agreement of this kind is excellent from the standpoint of the licensor if he can obtain a sum which he is sure is satisfactory. He has no further obligation to the licensee nor the licensee to him. In general, the prospective licensee will not want to pay any large sum before he has had an opportunity to operate under the license. Therefore, the usual form of patent license is on an exclusive or nonexclusive basis with royalties paid at suitable intervals.

The following form of license is applicable when the patent rights deal with a product. If a process or mechanical device is to be licensed, the same principles apply, with the changes required by the difference in subject matter. Reference should be made to "Rights Granted" in this article. If an exclusive license is to be drafted, suggestions are available below.

License Agreement

MEMORANDUM OF AGREEMENT, effective as of the   day of   , 19   , made between   , a corporation of   , hereinafter designed "Licensor" and   , a corporation of   , hereinafter designated "Licensee," whereby, in consideration of the rights and obligations hereinafter recited, it is agreed:

1. Licensor, the owner of United States Patent No.   granted   , for

hereby grants to Licensee a nonexclusive license under said patent, and under any other United States patents acquired by Licensor during the term of this Agreement, to the extent but only to the extent that said patents are dominated by the claims of said Patent No.   . Licensee shall have the right to make and use within the United States of America, its territories and possessions, the inventions covered by said patents, hereinafter designated the "Product," and the right to sell the same throughout the world.

2. Licensee agrees to pay to Licensor a royalty of five per cent (5%) of the sales price of said Product, after trade discounts but before cash discounts and with allowance for goods returned and goods subject to customer's credits, and a royalty of five per cent (5%) of the established sales price of said Product used by Licensee but not sold. Goods shall be considered as sold hereunder on the date of invoice or date of shipment, whichever shall be the earlier. (Note: The amount and method of computing royalty is of course to be determined by negotiation. The provisions suggested are often adopted.)

3. Licensee agrees to keep true and accurate books of account in which shall be entered all its sales and uses hereunder. On or before the last day of January, April, July and October of each year during the term of this Agreement, Licensee agrees to furnish to Licensor a statement of said sales and uses during the preceding calendar quarter, certified by an executive officer of Licensee, showing the royalty due Licensor hereunder. Licensee agrees to accompany such statements with the royalty so shown to be due.

Licensee agrees that Licensor, or its duly accredited representative shall have the right, at all reasonable times during business hours, to inspect Licensee's books of account and records for the purpose of verifying such statements.

4. Licensee agrees to pay to Licensor, as a minimum royalty,   Dollars ($), beginning with the   calendar quarter of 19   , for operations hereunder during each calendar quarter, or part thereof, during the term of the Agreement. In the event that earned royalties for which accounting is made during any quarter shall fail to equal said minimum, Licensee agrees to remit the difference to Licensor with its statement for that quarter.

5. Licensee agrees to apply suitable patent notice, including "Licensed under U.S. Patent No.   ," on labels affixed to all of its shipments of said Product.

6. In case of default by Licensee for any reason under this Agreement, Licensor may give Licensee written notice thereof, by registered mail, and Licensee shall have the right, within thirty (30) days after receipt of said notice, to correct such default. If the default is not so corrected, Licensor shall have the right to terminate this Agreement by notifying Licensee to that effect.

7. This Agreement shall continue until the expiration of said patents, unless sooner terminated as provided in Article 6. No such termination shall relieve Licensee from making any payments which may have accrued prior to the effective date thereof.

8. This Agreement shall inure to the benefit of and be binding upon the parties, their successors and legal representatives. It shall not be assignable by either party without the consent of the other in writing.

9. The addresses of the parties for the receipt of notices and payments are as follows:

Licensor:

Licensee:

Executed by the duly authorized officers of the Licensor and the Licensee as of the date hereinabove first stated.

Licensor:

Attest: By _____

_____
Secretary   Licensee:

                                          By _____
Attest:

_____
Secretary

Optional Provisions. As stated above, the forms and general information in this introduction are minimum requirements that must at least be considered in drawing license contracts.

The following features may be desired.

From Licensor's Standpoint. Protection against the licensee failing to be diligent in effectuating the license, that is, using the invention, particularly when there is no requirement for minimum royalty payment.

Acknowledgment of validity of patents licensed and agreement not to contest them.

Patent marking and patent expense.

Agreements involving secret information usually should provide that any inventions, made by the licensee during the term of the agreement and based upon such information, is to be made available royalty-free to the licensor. This prevents a possible patent build-up by the licensee operating as a detriment to the licensor.

From Licensee's Standpoint. Protection against infringement of patents of others arising from operation under the license (a "hold harmless" clause) and from unlicensed competition.

Protection against discrimination by the licensor in favor of other licensees, i.e., a "favored nations" clause.

Personal services in making the invention work if not involving tax complication.

Supplying of technical information by the licensor if required.

Release from claims for past infringement.

Termination of payment for know-how, if any in contract, when the originally confidential information becomes public knowledge through no fault of licensee.

From Standpoint of Licensor and Licensee. Cross licensing. See Currie, "Survey of Fields in Patent Agreements," 38 JPOS 250, 1956.

Status of affiliates and subsidiaries.

Arbitration.

Force majeure.

What law governs.

The royalty payments may be decreased as volume of royalty-paying business increases. Minimum royalty payments in excess of earned royalties may be carried over as credits against royalties in future years, and payments in excess of minimum royalties in any year may be carried over as credits against minimum royalties in future years, or not, as the parties prefer.

Sometimes in a nonexclusive license, and usually in an exclusive license, the licensee should seek to obtain a license under the licensor's future patent rights which relate to the subject matter of the license. Otherwise, the licensor may obtain a patent on an improvement which he can license to another. The original licensee is then at a competitive disadvantage.

An exclusive licensee cannot divest himself of the license, when there is no provision to that effect, except in some special cases, such as the invalidity of the patents licensed. Termination is usually optional with the licensor if there is default in payments or reporting. The licensor may prefer to let the agreement stand and proceed against the licensee as an infringer if he continues to practice the invention. Therefore, a provision for termination by the ex-

clusive licensee, at some reasonable time after the license becomes effective, should be considered.

Rights Granted

Nonexclusive Licenses. These are, in principal legal effect, agreements by the licensor not to sue the licensee under the patent rights licensed. Grants which emphasize this effect are immunity from suit or covenant not to sue. These two terms are substantially synonymous. They convey rights which would probably be construed as strictly personal to the one who receives them; that is, there is no implication that he has the right to assign the immunity from suit or the covenant not to sue. Even when the immunity is as to a specific object, the grantor usually has no implied obligation to assist the grantee in carrying out that object. Such implications may be held to exist under special circumstances. *Farmland Irrigation Co. v. Dopplmaier*, 113 USPQ 88, 91, Cal. Sup. Ct. 1957.

Exclusive Licenses. An exclusive license is not necessarily a sole license. The courts have usually passed on this question when it was necessary to determine whether a so-called exclusive licensee (one or more prior licensees being in existence) had the right to bring a suit for infringement in his own name, or whether, as a non-exclusive licensee, he had no such right. The prior licenses do not prevent maintaining the suit in the "exclusive" licensee's name, with joinder of the patent owner as voluntary plaintiff. *Paul E. Hawkinson Co. et al. v. Carnell et al.*, 45 USPQ 536, CA 3 1940.

A licensor who purports to grant an exclusive license is bound not to enlarge thereafter the number of nonexclusive licenses. *Mechanical Ice Tray Corp. et al. v. General Motors Corp.*, 62 USPQ 397, CA 2 1944.

Licensor's Status under Exclusive License. The grant of an exclusive license bars the licensor from practicing the invention, unless he has specifically reserved the right to do so. *Cutter Laboratories, Inc. v. Lyophile-Cryochem Corp. et al.*, 84 USPQ 54, CA 9 1949.

Sublicenses. The mere grant of a license to make, use or sell a patented article does not confer upon the licensee the right to transfer his license, unless the patentee has consented thereto. Sublicenses can be granted only where the license expressly authorizes it. *Rock-Ola Manufacturing Corp. v. Filben Mfg. Co., Inc.*, 78 USPQ 175, CA 8 1948; *Federal Laboratories, Inc. v. Commissioner of Internal Revenue*, 73 USPQ 453, TC 1947.

Sublicenses may be restricted as to scope and as to royalty to be paid by the sublicensees to the licensee, in his capacity as licensor. The licensees should be made responsible for collection of royalties and fulfillment of other requirements of the main license.

Cross-licensing. The simple case is a licensor having patent rights desired by the licensee and the licensee having patent rights desired by the licensor. Cross-licensing will permit each to operate without being charged with infringement of the patent rights of the other. No legal difficulty is involved in this. The licensor may grant a license and receive in return a corresponding cross-license, with or without payment of royalty, depending on the value of the licensee's patent rights.

Arrangements which result in avoidance of patent litigation are in general regarded as beneficial to the public, where they permit freedom of action to the licensor and the licensee and enable them to place a better product on the market. Without the cross-licensing agreement, the operations of one or both of the patent owners might be blocked. Aggregation of patents in the same field, but not overlapping or mutually infringing, would in general be likely to be questioned as to legality.

Form for Cross-licensing

A form follows:

Licensee agrees to grant to Licensor, insofar as Licensee is not precluded from so doing by agreements with others, a nonexclusive, royalty-free license under Licensee's Patent Rights, as defined herein, coextensive with the license granted by Licensor to Licensee hereunder. Licensee further agrees that, as to any of its Patent Rights which, during the term of this Agreement, can be exercised by Licensee only upon payment of royalty to others, Licensee will offer to grant to Licensor a license on terms as favorable as Licensee offers to any of its licensees.

Rights for Affiliates and Subsidiaries. The above provisions may be modified to include subsidiaries and affiliates.

Reciprocal Rights from Licensees of Licensor. Licensor may grant to Licensee a nonexclusive, royalty-free license under Licensor's Patent Rights, with the right of Licensee to grant sublicenses to others without accounting to Licensor; provided, however, that Licensee shall have no right to license Licensor's Patent Rights without first obtaining from its sublicensees the right to license Licensor under their patent rights on a basis fully reciprocal as to scope and duration.

Similarly, if a licensor grants the right to a licensee to pass on technical information to sublicensees, provision should be made that this applies only where the sublicensee makes a reciprocal grant in favor of the original licensor.

It is desirable that the licensor keep the licensee informed as to what licensor does with the licensing right granted to it by the licensee; also that the licensee have the right to disapprove if it does not want the license granted.

Improvement Patents. The licensor may agree to notify the licensee of any inventions constituting improvements on the process claimed in the patent rights specifically included in the agreement, and to include the patent rights on those inventions in the agreement at the request of the licensee. In a case involving an agreement of this sort, a patent issuing on a continuation-in-part application, although that application was not listed in the agreement, was held to be under it, since the two applications in question contained common subject matter. *Mall Tool Co. v. The Sterling Varnish Co. et al.*, 94 USPQ 340, DC WPa 1952.

Duration of Agreement. This may be expressed as a definite time, either by stated date or by duration of patent rights in existence. It is left indeterminate where the license runs for the life of licensed patents and future improvements on them. This in theory could run indefinitely, with improvement patents issuing just before the parent patents expire, and other improvement patents issuing on these improvement patents. It is usual to limit the patents licensed at least to those which are based on inventions made before a fixed date.

There are two situations in which the licensed patents become ineffective: (a) their terms expire, (b) they are held to be invalid or so limited as not to be infringed by what the licensee does.

A clearly expressed requirement for payment of royalty, although the patent licensed has expired, has been held an unreasonable restraint of trade, by in effect extending patents beyond their legal term. *Ar-Tik Systems, Inc.* v. *Dairy Queen, Inc.*, 133 USPQ 109, CA 3 1962. The problem arises usually in "package licensing" where the licensor takes a license under a number of patents and the agreement extends to the expiration date of the latest patent.

Licensed patents which are held invalid by a court of last resort or by a lower court, from whose decree no appeal is taken, usually are held not to require payment of royalty. If the patents are not litigated, this does not help the licensee. Although he may have good reason to believe that the licensed patents are not valid, he is estopped to contest their validity.

Term of Foreign Patents. There may be doubt as to what should be considered the term of a foreign patent, for example, where it has been allowed to lapse for nonpayment of a required fee. It has been held that the provision "to the full end of the terms for which said Letters Patent are or may be granted" required that the term of a Belgian patent under the agreement be treated as if it extended to the end of that period to which it could have been prolonged if the licensor had paid all taxes due upon it and had caused it to be worked as required by the law of Belgium. *Chicago Pneumatic Tool Co.* v. *Ziegler,* 66 USPQ 377, CA 3 1945.

Limitations of Extent of License. Since the owner of a patent has the right to exclude others from using his invention for 17 years, he exercises less than his total privilege under the patent law when, on

terms agreeable to him, he gives up part or all of that right to another. In so doing, he must, however, avoid violating other law.

The owner may limit the license under his patent to a part only of the United States. *Waterman* v. *Mackenzie*, 138 U.S. 252, 1891. Such territorial restriction, it has been held, cannot operate to prevent the purchaser of a patented article, from a maker licensed within the territory, from using the article outside that area. *Adams* v. *Burke*, 17 Wall. 453.

He may limit a license for making diesel engines to those of small size only (*Lanova Corp.* v. *Atlas Imperial Diesel Engine Co.*, 75 USPQ 225, Sup. Ct. Del 1947) ; the right to make a patented clothes washer to machines of capacity 4.06 cu ft or larger (*Bendix Home Appliances, Inc.* v. *Bassett et al.*, 90 USPQ 345, DC NInd 1951) ; the number of units that may be manufactured under the license; the term of the license; or the rights under certain claims only.

The right to sue for infringement in such a defined field arose in a case in which the plaintiff had an exclusive license limited to a device for use with aircraft and guided missiles. The Court of Claims said:

"The patentee granted to plaintiff's predecessor an exclusive license to use the patent for certain specified purposes. . . . It would seem, therefore, since the licensor had exclusive rights in the patent for this use, it should have the right to maintain an action for its unlawful use for this purpose." *Pratt and Whitney Co., Inc., et al.* v. *United States,* 114 USPQ 246, Ct. Cls. 1957.

An agreement granted the licensee the right to make, use and sell rolling mills under the patent. In the absence of an express provision to the contrary, the right thus granted by the contract must be construed to have had the same territorial limitation in its scope as in the case of the patent, that is, the right did not extend beyond the territorial limits of the United States. *Cold Metal Process Co.* v. *United Engineering Co.*, 110 USPQ 332, CA 3 1956.

Competitive Sales and Quantity Limitations. Public policy is involved with respect to commitments by the licensee to restrict its activity. This restriction is of advantage to the licensor by protecting his royalty receipts and is permissible within narrow limits. The licensee may insist that the licensor not compete with his exclusive licensee by selling unpatented articles competitive with those covered by the patent.

Agreement Not to Sell Competing Articles. At least to the extent that the licensee agrees not to infringe the licensed patent rights, as by purchasing infringing products and selling them without paying royalty to the licensor, or the like, there is nothing illegal involved. *United Lens Corp.* v. *Doray Lamp Co., Inc.,* 36 USPQ 118, CA 7 1937.

The implied obligation by the licensee to refrain from competition with the licensor is subject to the condition that it is economically feasible and does not require the licensee to perform where he has no reasonable chance of success. In the last analysis, the right to be vindicated is that of exploitation in good faith of the licensed patents, unfettered by voluntary competition on the part of the licensee. *Guardino Tank Processing Corp.* v. *Olsson,* 81 USPQ 318, N.Y. Sup. Ct. 1949.

If the competition with which an exclusive licensee is faced comes from something that is not commercially better than that which he is licensed to make, he must meet the competition with the licensed device. The licensee cannot legally overcome competition by purchasing the right to make the competing article and substituting it for the licensed article without violating the implied covenant to use his best efforts to further the purposes of the license. But if the competition comes from a better article, the licensee need not try to meet it with the licensed device, but may obtain and exercise the right to make or use the competing article. *Mechanical Ice Tray Corp.* v. *General Motors Corp.,* 62 USPQ 397, CA 2 1944.

A covenant to use due business diligence in the manufacture and sale of the devices embodied in the licensed patent rights, and push the sale by all proper and legitimate enterprise, does not bar the party so covenanting from using a later invention superseding that of the contract. *Eclipse Bicycle Co.* v. *Farrow,* 199 U.S. 581, 588, 590, 1905.

Quantity Restrictions on the Licensee. The license may restrict the licensee as to quantities to be produced under the license, in order to retain a share of the market for the licensor or to distribute the production equitably among several licensees. Unless there is an express agreement to the contrary, the licensee may produce to as great an extent as he pleases under the license granted, if he pays royalty in corresponding amount.

Restrictions of the quantity or sizes the licensee may produce are usually held valid as being within the powers of the patentee, who may exclude others entirely if he wishes to do so.

Agreements Not to Impair the Rights of the Licensor. The licensor may not obtain the expected royalty income if his exclusive licensee retains the license, pays the required minimum royalty, but sells a device which is competitive with that licensed, thereby reducing the sales of the licensed product. Even in a nonexclusive license, the licensor may be adversely affected by the licensee's sale of competing products.

Therefore, it is desirable to provide that the licensee will not impair the rights of the licensor by actions of this kind. The desired result may be obtained by securing the licensee's agreement not to manufacture or sell competing devices during the term of the agreement, nor to assist in setting up a competing business. Such agreements should not attempt to restrict the licensee with respect to sale of products serving the same purpose as those licensed but different from them in kind.

The competing product may be a substitute for the licensed device, not infringing the patent rights licensed; or it may infringe them. The licensee may agree merely to use his best efforts to commercialize the licensed device, leaving it to judicial interpretation, if necessary, to interpret what that means, or the licensee may agree not to compete with the licensed device.

Agreement by Licensee to Use Best Efforts to Effectuate the License. The amount of damages suffered by the licensor on account of the licensee's breach of his obligation to use his best efforts to make and sell the patented device, is dependent upon whether such efforts would be feasible and profitable. *Rogers* v. *Engelhard Industries, Inc.*, 125 USPQ 439, DC NJ 1960.

A provision that the licensee will use best efforts to supply the demand for windows does not require the licensee to use best efforts to create a demand for the patented windows, but merely to use best efforts to supply the demand. The licensee is not required to sell any patented windows. *Krantz* v. *Van Dette et al.*, 119 USPQ 380, DC NOhio 1958.

Where an exclusive license to use process patents contains a provision that the licensor be paid substantially the same for each pound of article produced in excess of a stated amount, there is an implied obligation on licensee's part to use reasonable efforts to exploit the patents. Whether or not the licensee made reasonable efforts to exploit is a factual issue. *Caron* v. *Nickel Processing Corp.*, 106 USPQ 124, N.Y. Sup. Ct. 1955.

Sales Restriction on the Licensor. Where the licensor had agreed not to manufacture or sell articles covered by the patent rights exclusively licensed to the licensee, the Court held that the licensor was precluded from manufacturing or selling patented items substantially similar to the patented items. The licensor is prohibited from making or selling unpatented articles which are competitive with, and used for the same purpose as, the patented articles. *Touchett* v. *E Z Paintr Corp.*, 113 USPQ 16, DC EWis 1957.

Oral Licenses—Statue of Frauds

Oral licenses are not necessarily invalid but they may be so if they are contrary to the provisions of the Statute of Frauds in the State in which the contract is made, as where the license is not to be completed within the term of one year. The fact that the license may be completed within one year is sometimes not sufficient, as where a parol license to sell patented articles for four years was held void as within the California Statute of Frauds, even though a contemporaneous written agreement contained an option to terminate the license on the licensee's breach of contract, bank-

ruptcy, insolvency or receivership. *Gate-Way, Inc.* v. *Hillgren et al.*, 81 USPQ 178, DC SCal 1949

On the other hand, an oral agreement is not made unenforceable under the Statute of Frauds merely because royalty payments would be due more than one year after the date of the agreement. *Hazen* v. *Gary*, 84 USPQ 99, Sup. Ct. Kans 1949.

Implied Licenses

Implied licenses arise from acts of the parties, without a written agreement. These acts include selling a patented product; the sale carries with it the right of the buyer to do something with the product, either to use it or sell it. License under a patent gives the licensee rights under another patent of the licensor that would otherwise be infringed by working under the first patent.

The situations involving no written agreement are very diverse. One illustration is as follows:

"Any language by the owner of a patent or any conduct on his part exhibited to another from which that other may properly infer that the owner consents to his use of the patent in making or using it, or selling it, upon which that other acts, constitutes a license and is a defense to an action for tort.... [M]utual confidence and mutual effort in which each party hoped to profit created [in another case cited] an atmosphere in which silence was misleading. *B & M Corp.* v. *Miller*, 114 USPQ 217, DC WKy 1957.

A clear case of implied license comes into existence when a patent owner accepts money as royalty, even though there has been no formal agreement for license.

Care in handling negotiations with respect to licensing and in embodying the conclusions in formal agreements will avoid implied licenses.

Implied by Law. A licensor cannot exact a second royalty. If the licensee would be adversely affected by having to infringe another patent owned by the licensor, in order to use the licensed patent, the licensee has an implied license under that other patent. *De Forest Radio Tel. and Tel. Co.* v. *Radio Corp.*, 20 F.2d 598, CA 3 1937. This is so, even though the licensee could practice the licensed invention without trespassing on other patents of the licensor, under special conditions. *Cold Metal Process Co. et al.* v. *Republic Steel Corp.*, 109 USPQ 185, CA 6 1956.

A party purchased a device covered by one group of claims drawn to a subcombination. The Court held that he did not automatically obtain a license under another group of claims covering the general combination when it was not necessary to use the subcombination in the particular combination covered by the second group of claims. *Hunt* v. *Armour & Co.*, 88 USPQ 53, CA 7 1950.

By Purchase of Article. Defendant argued that in purchasing radio tubes in the open market from the plaintiff's licensee, he acquired an implied license to assemble and test the complete superheterodyne receiver. The court held that there was no implied license. Although the tubes were primarily designed for the use complained of, there were other uses and the notice accompanying the sale of each tube negatived the grant of any license.

A mere sale imports no license except where the circumstances plainly indicate that the grant of a license is to be inferred. It was not sufficient that the tubes were primarily designed for the use to which objection is made. The tubes could be used to replace others which had been sold by the licensee. The notices that the "tubes are to be used in systems already licensed for use" were explicit and clear. *Radio Corp.* v. *Andrea*, 34 USPQ 312, CA 2 1937.

Agency. There is an implied license to have others do for the licensee that which he would have the right to do for himself under the license. This does not mean that the licensee has the implied right to grant sublicenses, but only that the licensee can empower an agent to manufacture articles conforming to the license. The licensee must account to the licensor for all royalties whether accruing from its own manufacture or from that of its agent. *Heywood-Wakefield Co.* v. *Small et al.*, 37 USPQ 363, 369, CA 1 1938.

A licensee may lease part of the plant of one of its subsidiaries and manufacture

there solely for licensee's purposes and under its supervision. *I. F. Laucks, Inc.* v. *Balfour-Guthrie & Co.*, 35 USPQ 206, DC WWash 1937.

Resale. When equipment is sold with a license to operate a patented process in it, there may be an implied right to sell the equipment with a license to use it, so that the purchaser has the right to use the equipment. To prevent argument on this point provision should be made for transfer of the license with the sale of the equipment if so desired.

Sale of Licensed Equipment as Part of Sale of Plant. A license to make and use equipment, with no right to sell it, should provide that the licensee may sell the equipment along with the plant in which it is used.

Sale of Composition. A licensor is estopped to bring suit against one who buys from him a material which the licensor knows is to be used in the practice of the process which he has licensed to the buyer. *Leitch Manufacturing Co.* v. *Barber Corp.*, 302 U.S. 458, 36 USPQ 35, 1938.

It makes no difference whether the article or composition in question is covered by a patent or not, so far as extinction of the patent monopoly is concerned. An incident to the purchase of any article, whether patented or unpatented, is the right to use and sell it and the authorized sale of an article which is capable of use only in practicing the patent is a relinquishment of the patent monopoly with respect to the article sold. *United States* v. *Univis Lens Co., Inc.*, 316 U.S. 241, 53 USPQ 404, 1942. The fact that the only use is under the patent distinguishes this case from *Radio Corporation* v. *Andrea*, supra.

The general rule is that the purpose of the patent law is fulfilled with respect to any particular article when the patentee has received his reward for the use of his invention by the sale of the article. Once that purpose is realized, the patent law affords no basis for restraining the use and enjoyment of the thing sold.

Composition Containing Patented Chemical. Where the patent licensed covers a composition containing a chemical made by a process covered by licensor's patents but obtainable from the licensor or elsewhere, the possible implication that the licensee has the right to make the chemical, for use in the composition licensed, should be rebutted. A suitable provision is as follows:

The license herein granted to manufacture, use and sell the licensed composition, does not include the right to manufacture, use or sell, as such, any compound covered separately by Licensor's patents.

Sale of "Know-how" does not Amount to License.
Sale of information, although covering the same or substantially the same subject matter as that in a later acquired patent, did not amount to a paid-up license under the patent when the license agreement indicated that the parties used license and "know-how" with different meanings. *Henry J. Kaiser Co. et al.* v. *McLouth Steel Corp.,* 122 USPQ 225, DC EMich 1959.

Termination

Rights of Licensor and Licensee. A suitable general clause as to termination may provide that

No failure on the part of Licensor to exercise its right of cancellation for any one or more defaults shall be construed to prejudice its right of cancellation for any subsequent default.

The licensor has the right to provide for termination of the agreement *on notice by him,* not by default of the licensee. It may be to the advantage of the licensor to refrain from giving notice of termination, keep the agreement in force and proceed against the licensee as an infringer. The following case illustrates the disadvantage of not retaining the positive right of the licensor to terminate the agreement. The agreement provided that

All rights, privileges and benefits of the respective parties under this license agreement and the license hereby granted to Licensee shall be terminated and cancelled for all purposes without notice in the event that Licensee shall fail to pay to Licensor within sixty (60) days after the expiration of any quarterly period of any year after the calendar year 1940, the amount of all royalties to which Licensor is entitled for such quarterly period

in accordance with the provisions of this License Agreement.

The licensee urged that its failure to pay royalties for sixty days automatically terminated the agreement, under the language quoted. The appellate court sustained this contention. *Mason* v. *Electrol, Inc.,* 62 USPQ 319, N.Y. Ct. Appeals 1944.

Date Based on Beginning of Operations. If the plant in which the licensed process will be operated requires a long time in construction, it may be desirable to fix the duration of the license as a certain time after the start of operations.

Termination for Default—Form

"Upon failure of Licensee to fulfill any of the provisions of this Agreement, Licensor may terminate the Agreement by notice in writing addressed to the Licensee and transmitted by registered mail, provided, however, that the Licensee shall have thirty (30) days from the date of receipt of such notice to fulfill the provisions of this Agreement and thus maintain it in full force and effect." The provision may be made applicable to both parties.

Unless the language is inescapable, a party will not be permitted to profit under an agreement by his own wrong. In a case where a licensee refused to pay minimum royalties for the life of the patents licensed, as he had agreed to do, a reference to nonperformance in the agreement did not free him from the licensee. *Miller* v. *O. B. McClintock Co.,* 49 USPQ 458, Minn. Sup. Ct. 1941.

Acceptance of or Demand for Past Due Royalties. Termination is not affected by subsequent acceptance of royalties, if the licensor at all times informed the licensee that it had no existing license and that royalties were accepted only pending negotiation of a new license. *Hayslip et al.* v. *Textag Co. et al.,* 86 USPQ 470, DC NGa 1950.

Repudiation of the License Agreement. The licensee, on the other hand, should seek the right to terminate the agreement on reasonable notice, if the circumstances justify it. In general, the licensor will not be willing to permit termination at the option of the licensee. The licensor may have imparted technical information of value to the licensee or have incurred other obligations based on the continuance of the license. A right to terminate, at some date reasonably distant, may be acceptable to both parties. Otherwise the licensee cannot in most cases escape from the agreement, even though he may have good reason to believe that the patent rights are invalid. *Muth* v. *J. W. Speaker Corp.*, 114 USPQ 327, DC EWis 1957.

Repudiation of the license agreement, if effective at all, cannot affect liability for royalties prior to it. Unilateral notice of repudiation is in itself ineffective. *Automatic Radio Manufacturing Co., Inc.* v. *Hazeltine Research, Inc.*, 82 USPQ 324, CA 1 1949.

Impossibility of Performance. The decision here, in the absence of a *force majeure* clause, will depend on the facts of the particular case and the attitude of the Court considering the agreement. Cf. *The Ohio Citizens Trust Co.* v. *Air-Way Electric Appliance Corp. et al.*, 62 USPQ 493, DC NOhio 1944.

One view is that, when a party voluntarily undertakes without qualification to do a thing, performance is not excused because, by inevitable accident or other contingency not foreseen, it becomes impossible for him to do the act or thing which he has agreed to do. This doctrine protects the integrity of contracts. *Nichols* v. *Nichols*, Ct. App. NY, 132 N.Y. Law J., No. 28, August 10, 1954.

Trivial Defaults. Trivial defaults will not usually justify termination of the agreement, especially where there has been considerable delay by the offended party in calling attention to the defaults and seeking termination of the agreement. *Edward G. Carr* v. *Jaeger Machine Co.*, 21 USPQ 191, CA 7 1934.

Survival of Executory Provisions. Where a license provided for payment of minimum royalty within six months and, before the expiration of the six months, the licensee had terminated the license in accordance with power granted in the license, he need not pay royalty. If a party cancels a contract according to its provisions, the remaining executory obligations are termi-

nated. If the right to terminate is valid, all undertakings then unperformed by the licensor and licensee are ended. If the contract specifically preserves two rights on cancellation of the contract, rights not specifically preserved terminate with cancellation. *Blain* v. *Sullivan-Waldron Products Co.*, 78 USPQ 191, DC Del 1948.

End of Useful Life of Leased Equipment. The generally accepted rule is that end of useful life of the licensed subject matter terminates the agreement. In a case on this point, the Court held that it is a lawful limitation as to time where a lease of patented drilling bits merely provides for termination of right to use on the happening of a future event, namely, termination of useful life of the original cutter teeth and/or bearings. *Cole* v. *Hughes Tool Co.*, 103 USPQ 1, CA 10 1954.

Trademarks as Affecting Termination. Assuming that the parties do not contract otherwise, the licensee is not liable for royalties after expiration of the licensed patent rights. However, the licensee is liable for royalties until termination of the license, even after expiration of the most important patent, where licensed trademarks and other licensed patents are still in force, inasmuch as the license was permissive in that the licensee could use any or all of the licensed patents and trademarks, but need not use any of them. *Zajicek et al.* v. *Kool Vent Metal Awning Corp. of America*, 127 USPQ 227, CA 9 1960. This case is illustrative of the bearing of trademarks as termination.

Insolvency of the Licensee. A stipulation in a licensing agreement providing that all rights therein would be cancelled and revert to the licensor upon insolvency of the licensed corporation is valid and enforceable. *In re Michigan Motor Specialties Co.*, 288 F. 377.

Right to Rescind for Fraud. Where the applicant for a patent was notified that his application would not become a patent, he is not entitled to performance of a license. The applicant had induced the agreement by his statement that the patent was coming through shortly. The license was induced by fraud. *Hooks* v. *Dowless et al.*, 97 USPQ 530, DC ED NGa 1953.

Arbitration Form. Upon failure of either party to fulfill any of the provisions of this Agreement the other party may terminate the Agreement by notice in writing addressed to the delinquent party and transmitted by registered mail, provided, however, that the delinquent party shall have thirty (30) days from the date of receipt of such notice to fulfill the provisions of this Agreement and thus maintain it in full force and effect, or to request arbitration of the dispute, in which latter event the delinquent party shall have thirty (30) days from an adverse decision in the arbitration within which to fulfill said provisions of this Agreement. It is understood that such notice will state, in full, the reasons for any such termination.

Foreign Licenses—Withholding Tax. If there is likelihood that the withholding tax required from a licensee in a foreign country by his Government may reach a point so high as to make licensing unattractive, provision should be made for terminating the license if the return to the licensor falls below an agreed point.

Invalidity or Restriction of Licensed Patent Rights. A licensee may learn by search of the prior art or by a court decree that the licensed patent rights are invalid. Since the licensee is estopped to contest the validity of the licensed patent rights, so long as the license remains in force, the licensee's problem, if it wishes to escape further payments of royalty, is to secure a release from the licensor.

Properly drawn provisions for regulating conduct under a license, in the event of holdings of invalidity or noninfringement, will in general avoid the need for litigation on the point. The following form may be used:

If and when, before the normal termination thereof, the licensed patent has been so judicially interpreted that the licensed device, as made under this Agreement, would not under such interpretation, be a infringement, Licensee shall be relieved from further royalty liability hereunder to Licensor for devices made and sold by Licensee to parties within the jurisdiction of the court rendering the adverse decision, until such judicial interpretation has been so modified as to bring again the licensed device within the purview of the patent.

Cf. *Harley C. Loney Co.* v. *Perfect Equipment Corp.*, 84 USPQ 12, CA 7 1949.

Cross-references: *Antitrust Law, Assignments, Foreign Licensing and Antitrust Law, Licenses— Indemnity Clauses, Licenses—Package, Licensing Experience of U.S. Corporations, Managing and Marketing Patents, Royalty Rate and Basis, Taxation of Patent Transfers.*

LICENSING EXPERIENCE OF U.S. CORPORATIONS

Robert B. Bangs and John F. Creed

This article is a reprint, with revision by the authors and subsequent abbreviation, of parts of a study made by them for The Patent, Trademark, and Copyright Foundation of George Washington University and published in the *Patent, Trademark, and Copyright Journal of Research and Education* (PTC J), Vol. 5, pp. 191-215, 1961.

Universe of Study and Responses Received

This article gives results of a questionnaire survey addressed to 252 American corporations that, in 1955, each owned 150 or more patents. Replies were received from 62 corporations that owned more than 50,000 U.S. patents and more than 43,000 foreign patents at the end of 1959. The results are not necessarily typical for all corporations or representative of those that own only a few patents.

Licenses for Own Use

TABLE 1. NUMBER OF U.S. PATENTS LICENSED FOR OWN USE BY THE REPORTING CORPORATIONS (DEC. 31, 1959).

Number of Licenses	Number of Reporting Corporations
None	2
1-9	11
10-49	15
50-99	9
100-249	4
250-999	5
1000 and over	3
No report	13
Total	62

Among the sixty companies reporting, twenty said they obtained no licenses whatever from foreign corporations. Those that did obtain licenses from abroad frequently obtained a relatively high proportion of their licenses from this source. Thus seven companies stated that fifty per cent or more of their licensed patents were from foreign corporations, and three additional companies put the proportion at from thirty to fifty per cent. In chemicals and drugs foreign technology is quite advanced; American corporations license many foreign product and process patents for use in this country. In automobiles and heavy machinery, on the other hand, few if any licenses are obtained from foreign companies.

TABLE 2. NUMBER OF FOREIGN PATENTS LICENSED FOR OWN USE BY THE REPORTING CORPORATIONS (DEC. 31, 1959).

Number of Licenses	Number of Reporting Corporations
None	16
1-9	10
10-49	5
50-99	5
100-249	4
250-999	2
1000 and over	2
No report	18
Total	62

TABLE 3. SOURCES [1] FROM WHICH U.S. PATENTS LICENSED FOR OWN USE BY THE REPORTING CORPORATIONS WERE DERIVED.

Source of Licenses	Number of Reporting Corporations
Solely from other U.S. corporations	10
90-99% from other U.S. corporations	15
50-89% from other U.S. corporations	22
10-49% from foreign corporations	8
10-49% from individuals	23
Over 50% from individuals	2
No report	7
Total	87

[1] As the source categories in Table 3 are not mutually exclusive, the total is greater than the number of reporting corporations.

Form of Payment

For a corporation, the tax advantages in a patent sale or exclusive license by running royalty route are less obvious than for an individual inventor. Nevertheless exclusive licenses may still be advantageous to a corporation—if only in postponing tax liability. By giving exclusive license, instead of outright assignment, the seller retains basic legal title and can provide for termination of the license in case royalty payments are defaulted. Also, when a patent is sold there is often considerable uncertainty about its commercial value in the minds of both buyer and seller. The fairest arrangement to both parties may well be the running royalty. It is also in a sense the least speculative form of payment, since it is directly related to the value of the patent in actual use.

Licensing Practice and Tax Considerations Involved

Although corporations do not sell patents frequently, they do an extensive business in nonexclusive licensing, both in this country and abroad.

TABLE 4. FORM IN WHICH PAYMENT WAS TAKEN WHEN PATENTS WERE SOLD OR LICENSED EXCLUSIVELY BY REPORTING CORPORATIONS.

Form of Payment	Per Cent of Companies Reporting	
	U.S. Patents	Foreign Patents
Running royalty exclusively	35	59
Running royalty in 51-99% of cases	31	22
Lump sum payment exclusively	10	4
Lump sum payment in 51-99% of cases	7	0
Fixed installments exclusively	7	4
Fixed installments in 51-99% of cases	10	11
Totals	100	100

To determine the part played by tax considerations in company decisions whether to license its own patents to others on an exclusive or nonexclusive basis, a question was included on this point. We simply asked whether tax considerations *sometimes* influenced these decisions, not whether taxation was the sole or the determining consideration. As already noted, only the proceeds from exclusive licensing arrangements are eligible for capital-gains treatment.

TABLE 5. FORM IN WHICH PAYMENT IS RECEIVED
FOR PATENTS LICENSED TO OTHERS.

Type of Payment	Number of Companies Reporting		
	Chem. Pats.	Mech. Pats.	Elec. Pats.
Lump-sum payment	9	8	4
Flat rate royalty	25	36	19
Flat rate royalty with minimum	14	16	10
Sliding scale royalty	12	11	7
Totals	60	71	40

No customary practice, varies with each license   2
Take all types of royalty and non-royalty
    payments   4
Cross-licenses only—no royalties paid or
    received   4

The replies to this question were distributed as follows. With regard to U.S. patents, 12 companies reported tax considerations did influence their decisions concerning the form of licensing for patents they owned; 44 companies reported tax considerations did *not* influence their decisions. With regard to foreign patents, the results were broadly similar—12 companies were influenced by tax considerations, while 24 were not.

A U.S. company may be willing to give an exclusive license on a foreign patent when it has determined not to operate directly in the foreign country, whereas the grant of an exclusive license to the corresponding domestic patent would foreclose the U.S. company from its use in this country. These and other factors of economic advantage generally outweigh the tax factors in determining license policy.

Package Licenses and Know-How

When a license is given to other producers it very often carries with it considerably more than the unadorned right to use the patent rights in production. Among our reporting companies, forty-four (71 per cent) stated that they customarily licensed some combination of patents, know-how, and trademarks—the most usual combination being patents and know-how. Only twelve companies (19 per cent) said they regularly licensed patents only, not in combination with either know-how or trademarks.

Four companies said they had no customary policy but made decisions on a case-by-case basis. Only two companies failed to reply to this question.

In foreign licensing, it is apparently more usual to include know-how in the package than to license only the patent, as is sometimes done with U.S. patents.

The use of package licenses raises an interesting tax question. Proceeds from exclusive patent licenses can normally be reported as capital gains. It is less well established that proceeds from exclusive licenses to know-how may be so reported. (See " 'Know-How' Licensing and Capital Gains," PTC J, Vol. 4, No. 2, pp. 93-108, 1960)

When package licenses including know-how were employed, eight corporations said they allocated some portion of the proceeds to the know how; thirty-six did not. Among the eight companies who did allocate the licensing proceeds, only four had claimed capital gains treatment for the proceeds attributable to the know-how. In no case had these claims been denied by the International Revenue Service up to 1960, although two corporations reported that audits for certain taxable years, in which sales of know-how were reported as capital gains, had not been completed.

[It is understood, from a source outside this study, that one corporation refers to know-how in its agreements as "confidential technical information" and takes in payment, particularly from foreign licensees, stock of the other company. Should this stock be sold later, the income is reported as capital gain. When the license agreement provides for technical services, the payments are called "reimbursements" for such services. In any case the amounts to be paid under the various categories are spelled out separately, so that royalties or other payments for patent rights cannot be confused with other income. Ed.]

Volume of Income from Patent Licensing

To get some picture of the income earned from patent licensing activities, questions were included that called both for the number of patents licensed to others and for the income resulting therefrom. In all, forty-two corporations, with **19,197** patents licensed (both U.S. and foreign), responded to these questions. The income reported by the forty-two corporations was (**$38.5** million or) just over **$2,000** annually per license. There was considerable dispersion about this average in the earnings per license reported by the different companies.

The basic data on number of patents licensed to others and earnings from these licenses are given in Table 6.

The income figures in Table 6 represent company averages for the five-year period ending with 1959. The number of patents licensed is for the single year 1959. This may differ considerably from the average number of patents licensed during the five-year period and thus may help to explain some of the variation in average income per patent licensed from company to company.

This variation in income per license is readily apparent from Table 6 and may be summarized as follows:

2450 patents produced only $909,000 or less than $400 per patent licensed;

14,141 patents produced $20.2 million or nearly $1500 per patent licensed;

1149 patents produced $7.1 million or nearly $6200 per patent licensed;

261 patents produced $6.2 million or nearly $24,000 per patent licensed.

By company, license income ranged from zero to $9.5 million.

On the basis of our reported information, it is possible to extrapolate rough estimates of the aggregate amount of patent license income earned by U.S. corporations. The calculation is as follows. In our reporting group we have 8,713 U.S. patents licensed, out of a total of 44,495 owned by those corporations that reported on their licensing arrangements, a licensing rate of just over eighteen per cent. (This compares with a licensing rate of twenty-three per cent obtained in the patent utilization studies of the Foundation. These studies cover all corporations on a sample basis and the reporting period is different.) For foreign patents the rate of licensing is considerably higher,

TABLE 6. NUMBER OF PATENTS LICENSED TO OTHERS AND INCOME FROM LICENSING.

Company Number	Number of Patents Licensed	Annual Income per License, Average ($ thousands)
3	112	10
4	193	800
7	45	500
8	131	42
9	21	85
10	799	1660
11	15	110
12	442	125
13	575	2500
14	46	50
16	326	2400
18	25	2
19	1056	0
20	1000	1752
22	102	378
23	133	500
25	248	183
26	219	227
27	15	15
28	15	2
29	140	4000
33	58	42
34	56	21
36	11	17
37	123	50
38	140	4000
40	38	5
42	57	390
43	11	60
44	11	1
46	245	495
47	18	200
48	30	24
51	1688	2250
52	218	2
54	511	350
55	6	12
56	9080	9500
57	58	1502
58	432	50
60	740	4200
62	8	12
Totals	19,197	38,524

namely 13,420 out of 32,207 patents owned, or nearly forty-two per cent. This higher rate probably is attributable, in part at least, to the fact that foreign patenting is more selective; only those inventions which have a likely valuable use are protected by patents abroad.

If the corporations in our reporting group

that did not report licensing activity had roughly the same rates of licensing as the corporations who did report, we can raise our figures of number of patents licensed to a full group coverage of about 9,200 U.S. and 18,200 foreign—or a total of 27,400 for all the corporations in our universe.

It will be recalled that our reporting group included about sixteen per cent of all patents owned by U.S. corporations; on this basis the estimated total number of patents licensed by corporations may be projected at in excess of 171,000. It is probable that this figure is too high, since it is doubtful whether the licensing rate runs as high for small corporations owning only a few patents as for larger corporations owning numerous patents. Discounting for this lower rate of licensing among unsurveyed corporations, it is still probable that the number of patents licensed by all U.S. corporations falls somewhere in the range of 100,000 to 150,000.

We also know from our reporting group that licenses to 19,197 patents produced $38.5 million of income on the average during the five-year period 1955 to 1959. Applying the same method used to extrapolate number of patents licensed, if the ratio of income per licensed patent in our group is applied to the estimated total of all patents licensed by corporations, the projected average annual income of all U.S. corporations from licensing works out to $200 to $300 million. It is probable that the lower figure is somewhat nearer the truth since the patents owned by smaller corporations may be somewhat less valuable on the average than those owned by larger corporations. It should be emphasized again that the $200 to $300 million is a five-year average, not an estimate for any single year. A current estimate would in all probability be considerably higher.

The extrapolations made above should, of course, be treated with every caution. They may well be fairly wide of the mark. Nevertheless, for what they are worth, they do indicate that patent licensing is a large and important activity and that substantial sums are paid each year for the industrial property represented by patents and related know-how.

Cross-references: *Economic Aspects, Foreign Patents, Licenses, Profiting from Patents, Taxation of Income from Patents and Secret Information.*

M

MANAGING AND MARKETING PATENTS—PATENT DEVELOPMENT

Worth Wade

After a patent has been obtained, the most difficult task remains, namely, converting it into profits. This section considers the problems of the private inventor, the new small company, and the established corporation in making patents pay.

The Private Inventor

Many private inventors fail to profit from their inventions due to lack of business experience or the inability to delegate the major functions of a business to experienced associates.

One pattern for the private inventor is to mortgage his home, borrow money from his friends, incorporate a small company, and assume the title of President and Technical Director. When the initial money is spent, the inventor often sells shares for funds to continue the business, the inventor's equity being proportionately reduced. In many cases, this procedure ends in bankruptcy or loss of control of the company or of the invention to others.

Establishing a New Company Based on Inventions. The inventor should first obtain an answer to the all-important question: Will the patent protect the capital investment? He should submit the patent to the screening of a patent audit for answers to the additional questions: Is there a need for the invention? Is it practical? Will it compete?

If the patent meets all these tests, then the inventor is justified in licensing or establishing his own company.

It is very important that the inventor obtain the expert assistance of associates experienced in production, merchandising, selling, and accounting and taxes. In many cases, it would be advisable for the inventor to confine himself to the role of Technical Director and leave the business management of the company to others.

The first step is to select a single article that can be sold profitably to meet a current need. The income from such sales should be reinvested in the business on sound principles and not dissipated entirely in further experimentation and development of new problems. An excellent handbook on this subject is Lasser's "How to Establish a New Business" (Simon and Schuster).

As soon as the business has grown sufficiently to justify more capital, application may be made with the Securities and Exchange Commission to register stock for public sale, for expansion and working capital.

In the merchandising and selling of the patented product, care should be used to avoid violation of the trade practice and antitrust laws.

In many cases, funds may be obtained, without sale of stock, by licensing the invention in foreign countries after commercial success has been attained in the United States.

Patent Development

Patent Development is a business procedure for converting patent rights into profits, either by manufacture or licensing. Although Patent Development, as a corporate function under that name, is only about 10 years old, it has already proved a real benefit to industry. Arthur D. Little, Inc., now offers such a service to industry. It functions in the border area between new product development and patent licensing. It uses a new combination of technical, patent, economic and market procedures by which an untried and unused idea is converted from a "paper patent" into profits.

The primary objects of Patent Development are:

(1) To provide new sources of income
(2) To diversify sales
(3) To improve methods and products
(4) To create more favorable public relations
(5) To increase the morale and productivity of technical employees.

Ordinary "new product development" is concerned primarily with improving existing products and creating new products for the company to manufacture. There are many by-products of the research effort which do not fit into the business field of the company. Frequently these are patented but are not commercially developed. This results in expense and loss of potential income from licensing, a lowering of the morale of the inventors and possible criticism from management and the stockholders.

Patent Development requires some preparation. These are initial steps:

Improve Communication Between the Inventor and Management. The Patent Attorney or Patent Department should provide all technical employees with a standard form of "Invention Record" together with instructions on how to fill it out and where to send copies.

When an invention record is received by the Patent Department, the inventor should receive a prompt acknowledgment; the subject should be docketed and a preliminary novelty search made. The inventor should receive a copy of the novelty report with the prior patents and a request for his comments. If a patent application is filed, the inventor should retain a copy. An abstract of the application should go to Management.

Teach Employees How to Make Good Legal Records. The Patent Department should work out, with the Director of Research and Development, the Chief Engineer and the Plant Manager, the following: (1) a standard form of laboratory notebook, (2) a standard method of keeping the notebooks and abstracting them, (3) a system for abstracting the subject matter of the notebooks by the company librarian, and (4) a standard form of invention contract for all technical employees in the laboratory plants and sales department to sign. The Manager of the Patent Department and the Manager of the Patent Development should receive copies of all technical reports and screen them for possible patentable developments.

Provide Technical Employees with a Handbook on Patents. The management should distribute a patent handbook or make a suitable book available to all technical employees who are required to execute the contract on inventions. Such a one is "Patents for Technical Personnel," Advance House, Ardmore, Pa.

How to Establish a Patent Development Department

An adequate Patent Development program requires an individual or a small group definitely assigned to this function. Experience has shown that this program should not be left to the Patent Department or to an existing New Product Development group in the Research and Development Department.

Patent Development in a Small or Single Product Company. In an organization classifiable as a "small" business or having a single product, the Patent Development program can be carried out by a single technically trained employee, whose title should be Manager of Patent Development and who should report either to the President or the Vice President in charge of Research and Development.

Patent Development in a Medium-sized or Multi-product Company. In a company which has well-organized departments for Patents, Engineering, New Product Development and Market Research, the ideal position for Patent Development is a small separate department or section with the "Manager" reporting to the Vice President or Director of Research and Development.

Selecting a Patent Development Manager. The success or failure of a Patent Development program will depend largely upon the qualifications of the Manager. He should have technical training, as well as a degree in science, preferably in the primary field of the business of the company. The broader his education is, the better. In addition the Manager should have at least five years of close association with research and development, preferably in the field of new product development, and some experience in patent soliciting or licensing. A lively imagination, inquisitive mind, and positive attitude toward new things are essential. He must be persuasive but tactful, aggressive but not offensive.

How to Make a Patent Audit

How do we find that particular patent which can be converted into profits? To do this, the patent rights are subjected to a selective screening which includes:

(1) A survey of existing records and patents owned by the Company,

(2) A classification of unused ideas and patent rights,

(3) An abstract of the ideas and inventions,

PRELIMINARY COST SURVEY

Short Title:

File No.:
Date:

1. Annual production recommended:
2. Estimated total cost of plant (not including working capital):
3. Working capital required:
4. Production cost estimate:

Prepared by _____

Item	Unit	Unit Cost	Units Required	Annual Cost Dollars	Cost per Pound or Article
RAW MATERIALS:					
Total materials cost:					
DIRECT COSTS:					
Supervision (man/year)					
Operating labor (man/hour)					
Maintenance (5% plant cost)					
Supplies (20% maint. cost)					
Overhead					
Electrical power					
Water					
Total direct costs:					
INDIRECT COSTS:					
Depreciation @ 7%					
Taxes @ 1.5%					
Insurance @ 1%					
Total indirect costs:					
Total production costs:					

5. Estimated selling, administrative and research costs:
6. Estimated selling price:
7. Indicated profit per unit:
8. Annual profit before taxes:
9. Estimated taxes on income:
10. Indicated net profit:
11. Period to pay off total plant cost:
12. Should this product be manufactured by our company or licensed?
13. Name of licensee recommended:
14. Royalty which could be expected (based on profits indicated):
15. Annual minimum royalty which could be expected:
16. Total cost of this project to date:

Should this project be terminated or continued? _____

(4) An audit of the unused inventions.

The "Patent Audit Sheet." A printed or mimeographed Patent Audit Sheet is filled out for each invention, patented or unpatented. An abstract should indicate the general character of the invention as well as the specific use fields. In no case should the abstract consist only of a copy of a broad claim. The abstract for a patent should indicate the nature of the claims, for example, by stating "Claims are drawn for process, composition, article, apparatus," etc., as the case may be. The form should have headings and space to be filled in on such subjects as utility or operability, market need to be supplied by it, possible volume of use, competitive price aspects, and decision to be reached at a Patent Audit Conference as to steps to be taken to market or otherwise use the patent, know-how, or product of the invention.

The Figures that follow are from the booklet "Selecting and Negotiating with Licensees," Practising Law Institute, New York, copyrighted by the author and here published with his consent and cooperation. Other information prepared by him on this subject can be found in his article in "Patents, Research and Management," Howard I. Forman, Ed., New York, Central Book Co., 1961.

MARKET RESEARCH: INDUSTRY
SURVEY

File No.

Date:

1. Company Name and Address:
2. Personnel interviewed:
3. Check relation of Company to proposed product of this invention:
   _____ producer of raw material needed
   _____ manufacturer of competitive product
   _____ converter of competitive product
   _____ distributor of competitive product
   _____ retailer of competitive product
   _____ user of competitive product
4. Description of competitive product:
5. Unit price and annual quantity sold or used by this company of competitive product:
6. Annual quantity of all competing products sold by the entire industry:
7. Rank of this company in the industry:
8. Advantages of our proposed product over competitive product:
9. Would these advantages enable our product to command a premium price:
10. What changes will be necessary in our product to meet the demands of the trade:
11. Will this company test our proposed product:
12. What new products, if any, have been introduced by this company within last five years:
13. What city, state or Federal regulations apply to the competitive products:
14. Is there a real need for our proposed product in this trade: Opinion of personnel interviewed:

MARKETING RESEARCH: PRODUCT
SURVEY

File No.

Date:

1. Company Name and Address:
2. Personnel interviewed:
3. Description of the proposed product:
4. Check relation of Company to proposed product:

   _____ manufacturer   _____ retailer
   _____ converter   _____ user
   _____ distributor   _____ other:
   _____ dealer

5. What is the sales trend of competing devices or products?
6. What annual sales could be expected for the proposed product?
   domestic market   export market
7. What selling price could be expected for the proposed product?
8. What changes will be necessary to meet the demands of the trade?
9. What city, state or Federal regulations apply to the sale and use of the product?
10. Can distributors and dealers obtain insurance on the product?
11. Will this company test our product?
    If so, state specifications and conditions to be met:
12. Is there a real need for the product in this trade, in the opinion of the person interviewed?
13. Would you recommend this Company:
    to manufacture the product _____
    to distribute the product   _____
    to sell the product   _____

How to License Patent Developments

If the decision is to license, the Manager of Patent Development must find the licensee. The Industry Survey will have revealed which company is the leader in the field and which is most aggressive in development. New developments should not always be offered to the leader of the field. The leader already enjoys the most sales, has the best products and quality, and is usually least in need of outside ideas. Experience shows that often the second or third factor in the industry is more receptive and therefore more satisfactory as a licensee.

Before the prospect is selected, the basic patent claims are analyzed. Do they cover the process or the product produced? Will they be infringed by the raw material producer, the manufacturer, or the user? The best prospect is the company which will require the use of the claims. Failure to select the right segment of industry as licensee can result in disappointment.

The various prospects should be analyzed carefully as to: (a) financial standing; (b) research activity; (c) contribution of new products to their income within the last five years; (d) percentage of the market; (e) reputation for quality and service.

Great care should be used in making the contact. The initial license proposal should be made to the President or to the Vice President in charge of Sales or Production, with emphasis on the contribution the invention can make to sales and profits. In some cases, the manager of purchasing can be approached, in place of the Vice President in charge of Production, if the invention will result in lower cost of production.

When making an initial proposal, the Manager of Patent Development should submit the following:

(1) Samples which are proper for the intended use,

(2) Specifications of properties of the product or process,

(3) Cost analysis which shows that the licensee can make a profit on the invention,

(4) Market survey showing the depth and size of the market,

(5) The patent estate, its scope and strength.

The Patent Development Manager should expect that his proposal will be submitted to at least the following groups within the prospect company:

(a) The Patent Department, to pass upon the scope of the claims,

(b) The marketing group, to pass upon expected sales,

(c) The engineering and accounting departments, to pass upon costs,

(d) The production and research departments, to pass upon the technical aspects.

The Manager of Patent Development must be prepared to answer satisfactorily the questions of all these groups and to defer actual license negotiations until the prospect has tested the invention.

During license negotiations a "Check List for Negotiating Patent Licenses" should be used. A suitable check list is published by Advance House, P.O. Box 334, Ardmore, Pa. This list, when used, will reduce the chance that some important factor may be overlooked.

Licensing Know-How

Special care should be exercised in granting rights to "know-how." To some persons "know-how" includes only operating specifications of a commercial plant, but to others it may mean all information from the plant back to the notebook in the research laboratory. Therefore, it is advisable to specify in detail the exact nature of the "know-how" to be licensed. If the transferor expects to claim "capital gains" treatment for the income, under the tax law, the grant must convey "all substantial rights," with no personal service included. Also there should be no retained right of the transferor to permit unauthorized disclosure of the know-how; otherwise the transfer has the same status as a nonexclusive license under a patent. *Du Pont* v. *U.S.*, 203 F.2d 1, 129 USPQ 473, 479, Ct. Cls. 1961.

In view of the uncertainty of tax treatment of income from know-how in the future, some may wish to exchange it for stock in the company to which the know-how is supplied, in the hope that sale of the stock, if later made, should be capital gain.

Adjusting the Product to Fit the Market

The preliminary Industry Survey of the market may indicate that the product should be redesigned. In this case the product should be sent back to the laboratory or engineering department and be carefully redesigned, with the price and the type of expected consumer in mind.

Samples of a prototype machine should be developed for use in demonstrating and promoting the new product. Finally, before the new product is placed on the market, the redesigned or improved product should be reexamined carefully by the Patent Department to ascertain if any additional patent protection is possible.

Promoting the New Product

In many cases sales interest can be stimulated by announcing a new product while it is still in the pilot stage, but this should be done only if the technical problems of producing the commercial product appear to be soluble. When patent application on the product has been filed, the reference "patent pending" or "patent applied for" may be used. No such notice should ever be used if there is no application actually filed.

Licensing a Customer

There is nothing improper in charging a customer a royalty to use a patented product or a patented process using an unpatented component sold by the patent owner but purchasable elsewhere. When the producer has spent much time and money in research and development and the product or process is covered by a patent, it is strictly a question of trade policy whether or not the purchaser should be charged a royalty.

Two commonly accepted methods of licensing a customer are: (1) making an agreement with the customer or (2) adding a royalty to the price of the component and then granting the license by label notice. Typical label notices granting licenses under both patented and unpatented products are shown below.

Label License for a Patented Product

"The product invoiced herewith and processes for making such products are claimed in U.S. Pat-

ent No. _____. The price of the product includes a prepaid royalty at the rate of _____ cents per pound (or per cent of price) of said product, for which royalty the purchaser hereby acquires a nonexclusive license to use and sell said product."

Label License for an Unpatented Product Sold for Use in a Patented Process or Apparatus

"Process for use of the product invoiced herewith and (apparatus for use of the product) are claimed in U.S. Patent No. _____. The price of the product includes a prepaid royalty at the rate of _____ cents per pound (or per cent of price) of said product, for which royalty purchaser hereby acquires a nonexclusive license to use the product in said patented process (or apparatus). Anyone may obtain such a license from the seller on royalty terms then currently offered, whatever the source of the product used."

It should be noted that the licenses do not require the purchaser to use only materials made by the patent owners. He may use unpatented material purchased from others upon payment of the same royalty to the licensor. It is good practice in such label notices to indicate the exact amount of the royalty.

Cross-references: *Accounting and Recoveries from Infringement Suits, Economic Aspects, Liaison between Inventor and Attorney, Licensing, Profiting from Patents, Records, Royalty Rate and Basis, Taxation,* Section on Know-How.

MARKET SURVEYS AND PATENTS
Walter E. Scheer

The building of a strong patent position is a goal to be sought in marketing, but not strictly for its own sake. The financial return is determined largely by the marketing of the product covered by the patent. An exquisite chemical reaction protected by an impregnable patent position may be economically worthless if the resulting product cannot be sold at a profit. Conversely, a marketing opportunity with enormous potential profits is not viable if the product involved is covered by patents held by others and not available for licensing or purchase.

The relationship between marketing and

patents is, therefore, of extreme importance to marketing people as well as to those concerned primarily with patents. This relationship is somewhat more complicated for chemical patents than for other arts, but the underlying factors are doubtless similar in all industries.

There are three phases of chemical marketing in which patent considerations are important: Market research, market development, and final sales.

Market Research and Patents

Market research comprises a study of the existing or potential markets for a product whose manufacture is being considered. The resulting market survey guides management in deciding whether or not manufacture of the new product is advisable. Along with other important information such as existing production of competitors, present and future size of the market at various price levels, customers and end use pattern, a market research study should also consider patent problems. Some aspects normally covered are the following:

(1) A survey to determine whether the new product infringes any existing patents not available for licensing. While composition of matter and process patents are of obvious importance, a use patent in the wrong hands can also severely restrict sales.

(2) Effort to obtain as good a patent position as possible by both internal research and acquisition of key patents held by others.

(3) Analysis of the patent situation to show whether it is strong, weak, or unimportant. The patent analysis is to be weighed along with other marketing data uncovered in the survey, to determine the feasibility of a new project.

(4) Effect of the patent situation on future marketing policies, so that strategy for future marketing can be recommended.

Market Development and Patents

Market development as used here means finding new uses for chemicals, rather than developing increased sales for existing uses

with new customers. In the chemical field, it can mean new uses for existing products as well as uses for new materials for which commercial applications do not yet exist. Market development is necessary not only in the early stages of a new project, but normally even after the project has reached commercial maturity. Finding new uses for existing products increases sales and gives competitive advantages. In fact, finding uses for new products is at times essential before they can even be manufactured.

Patents can be important here, either as an aid or as a deterrent to success. When this market development work is done by or for the supplier himself and a new patentable use is discovered, he gains a favored position. Even though it is not permissible to use a patent to enforce the sale of an unpatented product, there are nevertheless other means, such as outright licensing of customers and non-customers or even of competitors, of obtaining both prestige and financial return from a patent.

When the new use is discovered and patented by a customer, on the other hand, it is sometimes possible to convince the customer that it is to his best interest to license the raw material supplier and allow him to sublicense other customers, so as to increase the sales of the supplier and give added royalty income from competitors to the customer finding the new use.

When an important new raw material is developed, it is frequently desirable for the company developing it to explore its uses thoroughly before releasing sample quantities to outside potential customers. This enables the developer of the new raw material to patent as many uses as possible before the new product becomes available to others. This reduces the risk that an important use for the new product may be patented by a consumer or a competitor, thereby severely restricting the market or making necessary the payment of substantial royalties.

Sales and Patents

Undoubtedly the most important effect of patents on marketing occurs in the area of actual sales. A good sales executive attempts to use the patent position of his company to gain maximum advantage and reasonable profit. The antitrust law, the patent law, and the moral obligations of a corporation to the public provide controls, when observed. There are indications that restrictions may be enlarged by future legislation, especially in fields closely related to the public health and welfare.

In general, there are two areas where patents can be used to influence sales, namely, relationships with customers and relationships with competitors.

Relationships with Customers. In the case of a strong composition of matter patent, the patent can be used to reduce destructive competition. Such a position confers a greater responsibility on the holder not to abuse his rights, while balancing the obligation to the stockholders with the obligation to the consuming public. Consideration must also be given to the effect of lowered sales prices in increasing sales and, therefore, in lowering production costs; in many cases, a lower sales price may actually increase total profits due to a larger market and lower unit production costs.

Relationships with Competitors. The decision as to whether or not to license competitors is basic and should be faced as early as possible. In the chemical industry the practice of licensing competitors has increased recently, probably because of greater penetration of the field by the petroleum industry, where licensing has always been a preferred method of operation.

Responsibility of Management. Problems of pricing, licensing and other patent matters concerning relationships with customers and competitors in the marketing area are usually best handled by top management in cooperation with development, marketing and patent executives, all working closely together. This assures consideration of all phases of the marketing-patent relationship in reaching decisions on company policy.

Cross-references: *Licenses, Profiting from Patents, Use Patents and Their Utilization.*

MARKETING PATENTS. See MANAGING

MARKING WITH PATENT NOTICE IN FOREIGN COUNTRIES
David Toren

Purpose of Marking

Marking of patented products serves two distinct and very different objectives. It gives notice to the public of the existence of an industrial property right and at the same time warns potential infringers. It also promotes sale of the product, as the purchasing public regards patent legends as suggesting improved quality or originality.

This article deals with the first mentioned, legal aspect only of marking. It summarizes the marking provisions of some of the important industrial countries. It highlights the issues involved by hypothetical situations. It concludes with a recommendation that *patented products moving in international commerce should be marked with the abbreviation of the name of the granting country as well as the patent number*, e.g., U.S. Patent (or U.S. Pat.) 3,000,000.

Marking Problems

Let us assume that an American manufacturer enters the foreign markets after having obtained foreign patent protection. He has previously marked his product pursuant to the U.S. marking provisions, 35 U.S.C. 287. How, if at all, should he supplement the marking legend in order to comply with the respective foreign provisions and prevent loss of substantive or remedial rights?

The problems are numerous and, unfortunately, in many instances, little comfort can be offered to the harassed exporter. Although the patent laws of a few foreign countries contain express statutory provisions for marking articles covered by patents and provide sanctions in case of noncompliance, the provisions often are sketchy, leave a great deal unsaid, and lack interpretation, while foreign case law on marking problems is generally nonexistent.

Scope of Investigation

In addition to searching the respective foreign laws, this investigation had the helpful cooperation of reputable patent practitioners in the various countries concerned. Their viewpoints on the specific problems posed, incidentally, were far from unanimous.

The result of this investigation is presented first in Tables of general interest and then as related to six definite problems which frequently confront American exporters. The views expressed reflect the majority opinion of the foreign patent practitioners consulted.

Compulsory Marking

In every country in which marking is said, in the following tables, to be not compulsory, it is reported to be advisable, except for patent marking in Argentina and design marking in Sweden, in each of which no comment is offered.

TABLE 1. PATENT MARKING.

Country	Compulsory	Suggested Wording
Argentina	No	—
Austria	No	Patent No. ...
Australia	No	Patented No. ...
Belgium	No	Brevet Belge No. ...
Bulgaria	No	Patent No. ...
Brazil	No	Patentado No. ...
Canada	Yes	Patented, 19—
Chile	Yes	Patent No. ... plus date of issue
Denmark	No	Dansk Patent No. ...
Finland	No	Patent No. ...
France	No	Breveté S.G.D.G.
Great Britain	No	Patent No. ...
Holland	Yes	Ned. Octrooi No. ...
Hungary	No	Szab. (Pat.)
India	No	Pat. No. and yr.
Israel	No	Patent No. ...
Italy	No	Brevettato
Japan	No	Patent No. ...
Luxembourg	No	Breveté No. ..
Mexico	Yes	Patente plus No. and filing date
Norway	No	Norsk Patent No. ...
Pakistan	No	Patented, plus number and year
S. Africa	No	Patent No. ...
Sweden	No	Patenterad
Switzerland	No	Swiss Federal Cross plus number
Venezuela	Yes	Patentado No. ...
W. Germany	No	DBP plus number

TABLE 2. DESIGN MARKING.

Country	Compulsory	Suggested Wording
Austria	No	Muster No. ...
Australia	Yes	Reg. Des. No. ...
Belgium	No	Modèle déposé
Brazil	Yes	D.I. No. ... or M. I. No. ...
Canada	Yes	Rd plus year of registration
Denmark	No	D.M. and number
France	No	Modèle déposé
Great Britain	No	Regd. Design No. ...
India	Yes	Registered and number
Israel	No	Regd. Design No. ...
Italy	No	Modello Depositato
Japan	No	Design No. ...
Mexico	Yes	Pat. Mod. No. ... plus filing date
Norway	No	N.M. and number
Pakistan	Yes	Registered and number
S. Africa	Yes	Registered and number
Sweden	No	—
Switzerland	No	Modellschutz
Venezuela	Yes	Patentado
W. Germany	No	DBGM plus number or Geschmacksmuster plus number, respectively

Design protection does not exist in Bulgaria, Holland, Finland and Luxembourg. In Chile, designs are not covered by the Industrial Property Law.

Problem 1. Are There Any General Penalties if the Marking Provisions are not Complied with?

AUSTRALIA—*Patents:* No. *Designs:* Registrant who fails to mark the articles may be fined £20; provision not usually enforced.

CANADA—*Patents:* Patentee who, in contravention of the [compulsory] marking requirements, sells or offers for sale a patented article, is liable to a fine not exceeding $100 and, in default of the payment, to imprisonment not exceeding two months. No reported case enforcing this section.

Designs: Failure to mark the articles may result in an adjudication that the registration is invalid. In *Allaire* v. *Hobbs Glass Ltd.*, plaintiff, who sued for infringement, had marked his designs by pasting a label on the article bearing the legend "Patents pending Canada and U.S.A. 1939 " The Court declared plaintiff's design registration null and void as the label did not conform with the marking provisions.

The Court relied heavily on decisions interpreting Section 51 of the previous British Patents, Designs and Trademarks Act of 1883 which provided that "the design shall cease" unless a prescribed mark has been applied to the protected article. British decisions interpreting this section are *Wooley* v. *Broad* (1892), 9 R. P. C. 429; *Wedekind* v. *General Electric Co.* (1897), 14 R. P. C. 190; In the *Matter of Rollason's Registered Design* (1897), 14 R. P. C. 893, 909.

CHILE—*Patents:* Same as Mexico.

HOLLAND—*Patents:* Patentee is liable to a fine not exceeding 300 guilders. Section not enforced in practice. *Designs:* Design protection does not exist in Holland.

MEXICO—*Patents:* No damages could otherwise be recovered in an infringement suit. In fact, the bringing of an infringement suit is dependent on proper marking. *Designs:* Same.

FRANCE, SWEDEN, WEST GERMANY, SWITZERLAND, GREAT BRITAIN, AUSTRIA, BELGIUM, ITALY, JAPAN, BRAZIL, VENEZUELA, FINLAND, LUXEMBOURG, ARGENTINA, PAKISTAN, INDIA, BULGARIA, NORWAY, DENMARK, HUNGARY, ISRAEL, SOUTH AFRICA—*Patents:* No. *Designs:* No.

Problem 2. If the Patentee or Registrant does not Comply with the Marking Provisions, would that have any Bearing on an Infringement Suit Brought by Him, i.e., may he, for example, Recover Damages from an Infringer Although he did not Act in Accordance with the Marking Provisions?

AUSTRALIA—*Patents:* Damages would not be recoverable, if the defendant satisfies the Court that he was not aware of the existence of the patent. Onus of proof is on the defendant. (Section 124-(1) (2) of the Australian Patents Act.) *Designs:* Without marking, very difficult, if not impossible, to recover damages.

BRAZIL—*Patents:* Marking may have some evidentiary value but is not conclusive. *Designs:* Same.

CANADA—*Patents:* Not decided. Believed plaintiff may more readily succeed in his suit if he can prove marking. *Designs:* Since the registration

may be declared invalid if the marking provisions are not complied with, Plaintiff will probably not be able to recover damages.

CHILE—*Patents:* Same as Mexico.

FINLAND—*Patents:* Marking has no bearing on the issue. *Designs:* Design protection does not exist.

GREAT BRITAIN—*Patents:* Section 59-(1) of the British Patents Act of 1949 reads:

"In proceedings for the infringement of a patent damages shall not be awarded against a defendant who proves that at the date of the infringement he was not aware, and had no reasonable ground for supposing that the patent existed; and a person shall not be deemed to have been aware or to have had reasonable grounds for supposing as aforesaid by reason only of the application to an article of the word 'patent,' 'patented,' or any word or words expressing or implying that a patent has been obtained for the article, unless the number of the patent accompanied the word or words in question."

However, proper marking alone is perhaps not conclusive as to the infringer's liability for damages since the infringer may still be able to show that he was not aware of the marked articles. *Designs:* Section 9-(1) of the Registered Designs Act contains corresponding provisions.

HOLLAND—*Patents:* Plaintiff may recover damages irrespective of marking. *Designs:* Design protection does not exist in Holland.

INDIA—*Patents:* Same as Pakistan. *Designs:* Same.

ITALY—*Patents:* Marking has evidentiary value to show that the infringer must have known of the patent. Thus, it facilitates plaintiff's case. *Designs:* Same.

JAPAN—*Patents:* Recovery of damages facilitated by showing compliance with marking provisions. According to the new law of 1960, the patentee shall "endeavor" to mark. No interpretation available. *Designs:* Same.

MEXICO—*Patents:* The bringing of an infringement suit is dependent on proper marking. *Designs:* Same.

PAKISTAN—*Patents:* Section 30 of the Patent Law is similar to British. *Designs:* Section 48(1)(b) provides for no recovery in absence of marking or other notice.

SOUTH AFRICA—*Patents:* Section 52 of the South African Patents Act of 1952 is very similar to the British. *Designs:* Section 89(1) b of the Designs, Trade Marks and Copyright Act, No. 9 of 1916, is similar to British. Yet the provisions in said section/or in Section 67 of the Designs Rules of 1917 do not prevent the owner of a registered design from obtaining an interdict (injunction) on infringement.

VENEZUELA—*Patents:* Recovery of damages facilitated by showing compliance with marking provisions. *Designs:* Same.

WEST GERMANY—*Patents:* Marking might have some evidentiary value in an infringement suit as damages are only recoverable for deliberate or negligent infringement. *Designs:* Same.

FRANCE, SWEDEN, SWITZERLAND, AUSTRIA, BELGIUM, LUXEMBOURG, ARGENTINA, BULGARIA, HUNGARY, NORWAY, DENMARK, ISRAEL—*Patents:* Marking has no bearing on the issue. *Designs:* Same.

Problem 3. May a Patentee or Registrant who has not Marked his Articles Remedy the Situation by giving Actual Notice to a Potential Infringer?

AUSTRALIA—*Patents:* Yes. *Designs:* Yes.

BRAZIL—*Patents:* Yes. *Designs:* Yes.

CANADA—*Patents:* No. *Designs:* No.

CHILE—*Patents:* No.

FINLAND—*Patents:* Marking has no bearing on an infringement suit. The problem does not arise. *Designs:* Design protection does not exist.

FRANCE—*Patents:* Recoverable damages are not retroactive. However, retroactive damages may be allowed under certain circumstances, provided the patentee, before the "délivré" date, has given actual notice to the potential infringer by sending him a certified copy of the patent application. In these instances, the Court may grant damages from the day of such actual notice. *Designs:* Same.

GREAT BRITAIN—*Patents:* The prevailing view of the British practitioners may be summarized as follows: If a person has specifically had his attention drawn to a patent so that he knows it relates to or bears on what he (the defendant) is doing, then it is difficult to see how the defendant could subsequently establish innocence. *Designs:* Same.

HOLLAND—*Patents:* Marking has no bearing on an infringement suit. The problem does not arise. *Designs:* Design protection does not exist.

INDIA—Patents: Same as Great Britain. *Designs:* Same.

JAPAN—*Patents:* Actual notice will remedy the situation. *Designs:* Yes.

MEXICO—*Patents:* No. However, it is the opinion of some Mexican lawyers that if the patentee's articles were originally sold without markings and upon discovering infringement, markings are applied to the articles, the patentee may then bring an infringement suit. *Designs:* Same.

PAKISTAN—*Patents:* The prevailing view is that by giving actual notice, the patent owner may hold the infringer liable for damages. *Designs:* No.

SOUTH AFRICA—*Patents:* Once the defendant has been given specific notice of the existence of the patent he cannot plead ignorance, and damages would run from at least the date of receipt by him of such notice. *Designs:* The section provides specifically for the giving of such notice.

VENEZUELA—*Patents:* Yes. *Designs:* Yes.

WEST GERMANY—*Patents:* Since marking has no direct bearing on an infringement suit, the problem does not arise. However, where the patentee marks his articles to indicate the existence of a patent without giving the number, he must inform an interested third person of the patent number upon request. This provision (Section 55 of the Patent Law and Section 22 of the Utility Design law) has resulted in a tendency to omit any kind of marking. *Designs:* Same.

BELGIUM, AUSTRIA, ITALY, SWITZERLAND, LUXEMBOURG, ARGENTINA, BULGARIA, HUNGARY, NORWAY, DENMARK, ISRAEL—*Patents:* Since marking has no bearing on an infringement suit, the problem does not arise. *Designs:* Same.

Problem 4. Generally, Would it be Sufficient to Mark the Cartons or Containers for the Patented Article or Design, or is it Absolutely Necessary to Mark the Article or Design Proper?

AUSTRALIA—*Patents:* Carton marking would appear to be sufficient, although some patent attorneys advise article marking. *Designs:* The articles should be marked, if possible.

BRAZIL—*Patents:* Carton marking is ordinarily deemed sufficient. *Designs:* The article should be marked.

CANADA—*Patents:* If at all possible the articles should be marked. But see Sections 24-(2) and (3) of the Canadian Patent Act. *Designs:* If at all possible, the articles should be marked. Section 14-(2) of the Industrial Design and Union Label Act: "The mark may be put upon the manufacture by marking it on the material itself or by attaching thereto a label with the proper marks thereon."

FRANCE—*Patents:* Since marking is not compulsory, carton marking is certainly sufficient. *Designs:* Same.

GREAT BRITAIN—*Patents:* Carton marking would appear to be sufficient. *Designs:* Same.

HOLLAND—*Patents:* Section 36 of the Dutch Patent Act provides that "where the nature of the product precludes the marking from being affixed to the product itself, the marking shall be distinctly displayed on the package." *Designs:* Design protection does not exist.

INDIA—*Patents:* See Great Britain. *Designs:* The article should be marked, if possible.

JAPAN—*Patents:* Article marking is preferred. *Designs:* Same.

MEXICO—*Patents:* If at all possible, the articles should be marked. *Designs:* Same.

PAKISTAN—*Patents:* See Great Britain. *Designs:* Article should be marked, if possible.

SOUTH AFRICA—*Patents:* Article marking preferred. *Designs:* Article marking prescribed.

SWEDEN—*Patents:* Marking is not compulsory. *Designs:* Same.

SWITZERLAND—*Patents:* Marking is not compulsory. *Designs:* Same.

VENEZUELA—*Patents:* Article marking preferred. *Designs:* Same.

WEST GERMANY—Patents: Marking not compulsory. Some patent practitioners advise article marking. *Designs:* Same.

AUSTRIA, BELGIUM, ITALY, FINLAND, LUXEMBOURG, ARGENTINA, BULGARIA, NORWAY, HUNGARY, DENMARK, ISRAEL—*Patents:* Since marking is not compulsory, the patentee may proceed as he deems fit. *Designs:* Same, except design protection does not exist in Finland.

Problem 5. Is it Required that the Marking be *Permanently* Attached to the Article or Design, for example, by Embossing or Engraving, or is it Sufficient to Mark by a Removable Label, Tag or the Like?

AUSTRALIA, BRAZIL, CHILE, GREAT BRITAIN AND JAPAN—*Patents:* Prevailing view is that label marking is ordinarily sufficient. *Designs:* Same.

CANADA—*Patents:* If possible, the marking should be permanent. However, see Section 24 (2) (3), (Problem 4). *Designs:* Section 14(2) of the Industrial Design and Union Label Act cited in Problem 4 permits label marking.

INDIA—*Patents:* Permanent marking is preferred. *Designs:* Same.

MEXICO—*Patents:* Permanent marking appears preferable. *Designs:* Same.

PAKISTAN—*Patents:* Permanent marking is preferred. *Designs:* Same.

SOUTH AFRICA—*Patents:* If at all possible, marking should be permanent. *Designs:* Same.

FINLAND, FRANCE, SWEDEN, WEST GERMANY, SWITZERLAND, AUSTRIA, ITALY, LUXEMBOURG, ARGENTINA, BULGARIA, HUNGARY, NORWAY, DENMARK, ISRAEL—*Patents:* Since marking is not compulsory, the patentee may proceed as he deems fit. *Designs:* Same, except that in Finland there is no design protection.

Problem 6. If the Patented Article or Registered Design relates, for example, to a Ceiling Light Installation Comprising a Large Number of Similar Lighting Elements and Lenses, Would it be Required to Mark every such Element and Lens, or Would it be Sufficient to Mark the Crates or the Like Containers in which the Installation is Shipped?

AUSTRALIA—*Patents:* Marking at least some of the elements is advised. *Designs:* Same.

BRAZIL—*Patents:* Mark carton and some of the elements. *Designs:* Same.

CANADA—*Patents:* Crate marking would probably not be sufficient. After the installation has been assembled and installed, sufficient markings should be visible so as to make it clear that the patent refers to the installation proper. *Designs:* Those parts of the installation which are protected by the design registration, e.g., the lenses, should be marked.

CHILE—*Patents:* Similar to Canada.

FINLAND—*Patents:* Marking not compulsory. *Designs:* Design protection does not exist.

GREAT BRITAIN—*Patents:* Either carton marking or marking of individual elements would satisfy Section 59-(1), Problem 2. *Designs:* Same.

HOLLAND—*Patents:* As many as possible of the elements constituting the installation should be marked. Crate marking would probably not be deemed sufficient. *Designs:* Design protection does not exist.

INDIA—*Patents:* See Great Britain. *Designs:* Same.

JAPAN—*Patents:* The major elements and the cartons should be marked. *Designs:* Same.

MEXICO—*Patents:* Preferred to mark the crates and as many of the elements possible. *Designs:* Same.

PAKISTAN—*Patents:* See Great Britain. *Designs:* Same.

SOUTH AFRICA—*Patents:* Care should be taken to mark no part as patented, if that particular part is not covered by the patent. Since the patent would relate, presumably, to the combination of the elements, once installed, markings should be placed so as to be visible after installation and as to make it clear that the patent refers to the installation proper. The marking of the crate may be adequate if the defendant is the recipient of the crate and it can be shown that he could reasonably be expected to have seen the marking before the crate was unpacked. *Designs:* Those parts of the installations which are protected by the design registration should be marked. If it is the installation as a whole which is protected, the marking should be placed in such a position as to make this clear.

VENEZUELA—*Patents:* The carton and some of the elements should be marked. *Designs:* Same.

FRANCE, SWEDEN, WEST GERMANY, SWITZERLAND, AUSTRIA, BELGIUM, ITALY, LUXEMBOURG, ARGENTINA, BULGARIA, HUNGARY, NORWAY, DENMARK, ISRAEL—*Patents:* The patentee may proceed as he deems fit.

The data above was published in part by the author in **43 JPOS 274, 1961.**

Summary

Statutory marking provisions are aimed exclusively at giving the public adequate notice of the existence of an industrial property right. As the consequences of violations of industrial property rights may be serious, patent markings serve a very useful purpose. Many infringement suits could no doubt be avoided if the infringer knows that his competitor's product is patented. Marking before the grant of the patent with "Patent Pending" or equivalent legend, while having no legal effect, may deter entrance into the field by one who might thus avoid infringing a later issued patent.

In our present era of extensive international trade, the producer of patented goods, which may reach far-away countries, should inform the consumer or potential infringer of the producer's patent rights; it is obviously more equitable to compel the producer to place a notice on his goods than to require the competitor to find out the patent situation for himself.

Unless the law of a country prescribes a particular mode of marking, it is believed that the manufacturer should be free to choose the method which best suits the purpose.

The six problems presented have not dealt with the question of multiple marking of a product patented in several countries. Most of the foreign patent practitioners consulted advise prefixing the name or abbreviation of the granting country to the patent number, so as to avoid misunderstandings and violations of false marking provisions which exist in many countries.

From an international point of view, very little purpose is served by a marking legend unless the granting country is included. Americans traveling abroad, upon return, frequently present their U.S. patent attorneys with a foreign-made product bearing no further indication than a five- or six-digit number, presumably a patent number. It is then a most time consuming, frustrating and expensive endeavor to ascertain with certainty the country or countries in which the product is patented.

It is believed that unifying patent marking statutes would fulfill a long-felt need, particularly in view of the advent of the European Patent.

Cross-references: *Accounting and Recoveries from Infringement Suits; Marking With Patent Notice—U.S.*

MARKING WITH PATENT NOTICE—U.S.

(Editorial Comment)

General Observations

When patented articles do not carry the patent marking, the penalty for failure to mark is that there shall be no recovery for infringement in advance of the date of notice thereof. *Zenith Radio Corp.* v. *Radio Corp. of America,* **78** USPQ 186, DC Del 1948.

In most cases, there are advantages for the patent owner in patent marking. These include:

(1) Start of the tolling of liability for infringement without the need of direct notice to infringers.

(2) Warning to prospective entrants into the field covered by the patent.

(3) Sales advantage from an exclusive position with a product identified as new.

(4) Improved image of patentee as progressive.

The mark "Patent Pending" or "Patent Applied for," having the same meaning under the statute, may provide the last three of these advantages.

A disadvantage at times is the key supplied by the patent number to the exact protection relied upon, the composition used or process of manufacture. This disclosure may be significant when the protection is weak, and knowledge of the patent number would for that reason aid an infringer in learning what is required to design around the patent claims. Also, estoppels may arise when a licensee affixes the patent notice and then alleges that the product falls outside the license or that the license has been terminated.

Intentional false marking, in an effort to obtain unfair advantages or deceive the public, is punishable by a cash penalty. Also it may lead to a holding of misuse or unclean hands in a court action.

When there is nothing to which the patent number can be applied, as in the case of (1) a process or (2) a product never manufactured by the patent owner subsequent to issuance of the patent, then he is not remiss in failing to mark, and marking is not required under such circumstances to start the tolling of damages. *Cameron Iron Works, Inc.* v. *Edward Valves, Inc. et al.,* 122 USPQ 497, 507, DC STex 1959. Cf. *Wine Railway Appliance Co.* v. *Enterprise Railway Equipment Co.,* 297 U.S. 387, 1936.

Statutory Provision

The Patent Act of 1952, 35 U.S.C. Section 287, reads:

"Patentees, and persons making or selling any patented article for or under them, may give notice to the public that the same is patented, either by fixing thereon the word 'patent' or the abbreviation 'pat.', together with the number of the patent, or when, from the character of the article, this can not be done, by fixing to it, or to the package wherein one or more of them is contained, a label containing a like notice. In the event of failure so to mark, no damages shall be recovered by the patentee in any action for infringement, except on proof that the infringer was notified of the infringement and continued to infringe thereafter, in which event damages may be recovered only for infringement occurring after such notice. Filing of an action for infringement shall constitute such notice."

Nature and Need of Mark

The law is liberal in recognizing and making allowances for the problems that may confront the patent owner or licensee in marking articles.

Under the former statute, the court held, however, that notice is required for initiation of liability when a nonproductive patent owner did not require licensee to affix patent notice to machines made by licensee and no patent marking was applied. *Gordon* v. *Easy Washing Machine Corp.,* 49 USPQ 321, DC NY 1941.

In a plant patent case, the patent owner "informed" the buyer of trees that the trees were patented and that buyer "could not asexually reproduce or sell the trees without the plaintiff's [seller's] permission." This was held sufficient notice at least as to a plant patent. The plaintiff in one document had admitted that the trees carried no patent marking but subsequently sought to correct this statement. The defendant had not clearly denied the sufficiency of the notice. *Nicholson* v. *Bailey,* 125 USPQ 157, DC SFla 1960.

Act Ineffective as Notice

Marking that is illegible without magnification is ineffective in giving notice to infringers. *Trussel Mfg. Co.* v. *Wilson-Jones Co.,* 10 USPQ 47, CA 2 1931. So also would be a patent number under an obscuring label, as was the case with a lipstick a few years ago, the patent having expired but the impression being cultivated in the trade that there was a patent on the article.

During the pendency of an application for patent, a manufacturer affixed to his machine a brass plate reading "Patent Pending." After the patent issued, he changed the plate to read: "Patent Pending 2,215-010." Although the number was that of the issued patent, the Court held the notice ineffective and that the defendant did not know of the patent until the date of filing of the infringement suit. *Maescher* v. *Reliance Mfg. Co.*, 110 USPQ 113, DC SInd 1956.

In a case involving marking by a licensee, for a non-productive patent owner, applying the patent notice to only about 65 per cent of the devices manufactured under the license was held not to entitle the owner to an accounting for infringement from the date of such marking. *Hazeltine Corp.* v. *Radio Corp. of America*, 35 USPQ 438, DC NY 1937. But see *Bruen* v. *Huff et al.*, 91 USPQ 334, 338, DC WPa 1950. Here the defense alleged that the exclusive licensee did not mark "at least some" of the articles and thus showed "bad faith and malice." The Court said the failure to mark was probably due to inadvertence, did not attach much weight to it, and, while holding the claims of the patent invalid on other grounds and assessing costs on that issue against the plaintiff, said "the costs accruing under the charge of unfair competition will be taxed against the defendants" who raised that charge.

Friendly conversation between officers of plaintiff and defendant corporations, when patent was not shown or any suggestion made that defendant's devices infringed the patent, is not notice. *Hazeltine Corp.* v. *Radio Corp. of America*, 16 USPQ 275, DC NY 1933.

Effect of Patent Marking

The importance of proper patent marking is shown in *International Nickel Co.* v. *Ford Motor Co.*, 119 USPQ 72, 85, DC SNY 1958, as follows:

"...INCO has not shown that it gave the notice required.... Evidence of Ford's state of mind, i.e., that Ford knew of the patent and had the soundest possible reason to believe that INCO would regard quantity production of nodular iron as an infringement, is irrelevant.... There can be no recovery for the period before the defendant is expressly notified by the patentee that it is infringing a particular patent."

Estoppels Created by Application of Patent Notice. A licensee, alleging that a license has been terminated or for other reason

does not exist, cannot ordinarily support such position if the licensee at the time is applying the patent number to its product. In *Kennedy* v. *Engelhard Industries, Inc.*, 129 USPQ 85, 88, CA 3 1961, the Court said:

"... [Licensee, Hanovia,] cannot be heard to deny its license at the very moment it was claiming its protection by affixing notices to some of its products.... the notice is adequate to show that Hanovia claimed that its contract rights were still in being."

When the scope of a patent has been restricted by a court case, the continuing application of the patent number to the article by the licensee will be a factor in determining whether it is still obligated under the license.

"Another factor to be considered is the defendant's [Hanovia's] persistence in asserting its rights under the patent, subsequent to the finding in the Westinghouse case.... Under the circumstances, Hanovia, by its affixment of the patent notices, has placed itself in the unenviable position of having supported the very contention which now it would deny, namely, that the protection of the patent persisted after the Westinghouse decision." *Rogers* v. *Engelhard Industries, Inc.*, 125 USPQ 439, 441, DC NJ 1960.

Multiple Patent Marking

In a leading case involving the effectiveness, as notice to infringers, of multiple patent marking, the Court said:

"The relevant testimony was that on the containers in which the bits were marketed there was a marking that the devices were patented by 'one or more of the following patents,' followed by the numbers of the patents in suit, and others not presently in controversy. Marking in that manner was sufficient to meet the exactions of the statute. Chicago Pneumatic Tool Co. v. Hughes Tool Co., 97 F.2d 945, certiorari denied, 305 U.S. 643, petition for rehearing denied, 305 U.S. 673." *Chicago Pneumatic Tool Co.* v. *Hughes Tool Co.*, 91 USPQ 227, CA 10 1951.

In a patent on flaw-detecting devices known as Reflectoscopes, the defendant in a suit for infringement alleged misuse because the tag on the devices had the notice "Manufactured under one or more of the following patents" followed by the numbers. The District Court said: "[The defendant suggested] 'that anyone reading the list of 50 patents obviously would be frightened at the cost of investigating and would very likely go no further.' Cline, who was in charge of standardizing equipment purchases for Alcoa, said he never looked at the name plates." The Court noted also that Sperry had as many as 50 patents in the field and that Sperry was currently using one-third of its patents, the particular set used varying for different detectors sold. The Court dismissed the counter claim based on alleged misuse and also held claims valid and infringed. 120 USPQ 363, 384. The Circuit Court, in the appeal case, pointed out that "the patents in suit were properly listed on the patent tag" and ruled that there was no misuse or antitrust violation, but held the claims invalid on other grounds. *Aluminum Co. of America* v. *Sperry Products, Inc.*, 127 USPQ 394, 407, CA 6 1960.

False Marking

The statute, 35 U.S.C. 292, reads:

"(a) Whoever, without the consent of the patentee, marks upon, or affixes to, or uses in advertising in connection with anything made, used or sold by him, the name or any imitation of the name of the patentee, the patent number, or the words 'patent,' 'patentee,' or the like, with the intent of counterfeiting or imitating the mark of the patentee, or of deceiving the public and inducing them to believe that the thing was made or sold by or without the consent of the patentee; or

"Whoever marks upon, or affixes to, or uses in advertising in connection with any unpatented article, the word 'patent' or any word or number importing that the same is patented, for the purpose of deceiving the public; or

"Whoever marks upon, or affixes to, or uses in advertising in connection with any article, the words 'patent applied for,' 'patent pending,' or any word importing that an application for patent has been made, when no application for patent has been made, or if made, is not pending, for the purpose of deceiving the public—

"Shall be fined not more than $500 for every such offense.

"(b) Any person may sue for the penalty, in which event one-half shall go to the person suing and the other to the use of the United States."

Cf. *Smith Welding Equipment Co.* v. *Pearl et al.*, 115 USPQ 127, DC WPa 1957.

In *Piece Control Tag Co.* v. *Stry-Lenkoff Co. et al.*, the Court said:

"Lenkoff and his corporation, in an effort to deceive the public, had printed upon his tags 'PTD U.S.A.' This, the Court finds was a deliberate effort on the part of the defendants to imply and create the general impression that the tags were patented in the United States."

The Court imposed a fine of $500 on the defendant and dismissed its counterclaim as well as plaintiff's complaint. 107 USPQ 207, 210, DC WKy 1955.

Misuse of Patent. In the *Surgitude* case, the Court said:

"[The bandage] is formed when the tubular fabric is stretched over the part of the body to be bandaged and then is twisted at one end and returned. ...[A] tubular fabric is not new.... [The] plaintiff has sought to create the impression, by this marking on the boxes that this patent covers the unpatented gauze. The Court finds this to have been done with intent to deceive the public and to restrain trade in the unpatented tubular gauze. This ... constitutes a misuse of the patent, and warrants denial of recovery to a plaintiff in an infringement action." *Surgitude Products Corp. et al.* v. *Scholl Mfg. Co., Inc.*, 116 USPQ 253, 1958, DS SNY 1958.

Unclean Hands. False patent marking was responsible for a holding of unclean hands and dismissal of a trademark suit in *Magic Foam Sales Corp.* v. *Mystic Foam Corp.*, 89 USPQ 190, Ohio Ct. Com. Pleas 1950. Here the plaintiff, since the inception of the "Magic Foam" business in 1932, had used labels bearing the words "Patent Pending" when no patent was ever applied for.

A trademark case on this point involved the following circumstances. After a patent had expired in 1944, the product still carried the mark "Patented U.S.A." In an earlier patent suit, a defendant had brought the error, in continuing the patent marking, to plaintiff's attention. The plaintiff then removed the patent marking before the beginning of the trademark suit. In the latter suit, the attorney for the plaintiff testified that he had been in government service overseas during the war at the time the patent expired and was unaware that the marking should have been removed in 1944. The Court observed:

"Here the misrepresentation was apparently inadvertent, without intent to deceive. It would not appear that prospective rivals were deterred from entering the cotton tipped applicator field. As soon as plaintiff became aware of its error, it ceased making the misrepresentation." The Court held against the charge of unclean hands. *Q-Tips, Inc. v. Johnson and Johnson*, 95 USPQ 264, DC NNJ 1952.

Wrongful intent, such as would make the patent owner chargeable with unclean hands, is not shown when a patent number was inadvertently applied to a product not coming within the scope of the claims and the application of the number was discontinued when the error was discovered. *Freeman Mfg. Co. v. Federal Dept. Stores, Inc.*, 130 USPQ 67, DC EMich 1961. Cf. *Guide v. Desperak et al.*, 111 USPQ 32, DC SNY 1956.

In an Eighth Circuit case, the issue was misuse through false marking. Salsbury's Laboratories sold, in dry form, a chicken medicine with instructions on the label for mixing with water or food. The final mixture was the subject of patent 2,450,866, but the label on the unpatented, active but dry component carried the patent number. The Court held this to constitute misuse and reversed the District Court which had held the patent infringed. *I. D. Russell Co. et al. v. Dr. Salsbury's Laboratories*, 94 USPQ 199, CA 8 1952. (For an acceptable form of label license, see *Managing and Marketing Patents*)

Cash Penalties. The plaintiff-informer, who brings the *qui tam* action to collect the fine of $500 for "every" offense in false marking, half for the government and half for himself, is not required to show any injury to himself from the defendant's mismarking. *Fear v. Horner Sales Corp.*, 84 USPQ 267, DC WPa 1950.

A lawyer's acting as the informer and bringing suit in his own name, to collect the penalty under Section 292, was questioned in *Zuckerman v. Pilot et al.*, 46 USPQ 473, DC SNY 1940. The Court said *obiter:*

"...Although the statute does not include any ban against a lawyer becoming an informer and bringing a suit such as this, I do not believe that Congress ever expected that the legal profession would indulge in these practices.... In my opinion no lawyer should permit himself to be used as a 'dummy' plaintiff, while the real plaintiffs, competitors of the defendants, hide their identity."

A corporation has been held, in a brief decision, not to be a "person" within the meaning of Section 292 and therefore not to qualify as the informer-plaintiff in an action thereunder. *Forest R. Etling., Inc. v. Weather Seal, Inc.*, 58 F. Supp. 269, 63 USPQ 182, DC NOhio 1944. A later decision notes the *Etling* case but arrives, after more detailed discussion, at the contrary holding that the corporation is a "person" under Section 292 and does qualify for instituting and conducting the *qui tam* proceeding. *Victoria-Vogue, Inc. v. Valcourt, Inc.*, 113 USPQ 41, 50 DC SNY 1956. The diversity of opinion seems not yet to have been resolved.

These conflicting decisions are, no doubt, examples of fitting the law to justice based on all facts in the cases.

The question of what constitutes "every such offense," for which the fine is now $500, arose in *Krieger v. Colby et al.*, 95 USPQ 4, 9, 10, DC SCalif 1952. Here the plaintiff sought to collect the fine for false marking. The patent at issue was for the design of a cap which, to a considerable extent, resembled a rabbit's head and face and was called a "Hep Cap." While the suit was tried under the old statute 35 U.S.C. 50, this contained the present wording "every such offense" but specified the amount of the fine as $100. The Court said in part:

"Plaintiff originally contended that she would be entitled to a penalty upon each sale.... However, this is not the law.... According to Roberts' testimony, eight separate shipments were received on different days.... It appears from the testimony of Roberts himself that there were at least...eight different offenses for which a penalty of $100 each could be assessed, making a total liability of $800 for false marking—$400 of which must go to the United States of America."

It is noted that the fines under the present Patent Act for eight offenses would have been $4,000. The Court also awarded $1,000 to one of the parties for use of the patent rights, or a total $1,800 for all parties. The lawyer's fees, for the plaintiff alone, although set at a seemingly very low daily rate, were $3,000.

The by-products of false marking, such as loss of patent rights through misuse or unclean hands and costs of suits, are likely to outweigh heavily the cash fines, as in the *Krieger* case.

Cross-references: *Accounting ..., Clean Hands Doctrine, Unfair Competition.*

MEDICAL ASSOCIATIONS AND PHYSICIANS' PATENT POLICIES

William H. Edgerton

Medicine, the oldest active science known to man, has evolved from the crude trepanning of the cave man to the complex tools and techniques of medicine developed during the present century. A large number of physicians must now engage in clinical trials or enter into full-time medical research. The physician, even in his individual practice, evaluates new drugs and improved techniques.

As the physician becomes creative, he needs answers at times to such questions as these: Have I made an invention? What does the code of ethics of the profession dictate as to the development of it? How may I use it to benefit the public most? Will patenting it facilitate raising capital necessary to manufacture it, make the expensive clinical tests required before marketing, and increase the distribution of it?

Historical Arguments on the Ethics of Medical Patents

The origin of the controversy over whether medical inventions should or should not be patented is commonly attributed to the unscrupulous traveling "patent medicine man" selling cure-alls of unknown composition of the "rub-on or take it" variety. While the patent medicine era, without a doubt, aggravated the situation, the basic philosophical question had been debated on

and off for many years both in the United States and overseas.

In the first session of the House of Representatives, William Hoy petitioned that "... an adequate compensation may be made him for his labour and assiduity in the discovery, which in that case he will make public ... an infallible cure for the bite of a mad dog." [1]

The famous chemist Gay-Lussac, in a speech in the French Parliament in 1843, stated:

"I admit that the quacks are a plague to society. But they pursue their fraudulent operations whether they have patents or not, and in all imaginable forms. If we should in this act exclude all trades in which quackery exists, the statute would be quite useless. There exist then no reasons for distinguishing the pharmaceutical preparations from the other inventions which can be protected by patent."

An article, published in the Journal of the American Medical Association on September 18, 1897 and entitled "Is It Ethical for Medical Men to Patent Medical Inventions?", concluded that "patent medicines" should be eliminated altogether with all secrecy in medicine. One prominent physician who eloquently endorsed this conclusion was Dr. E. R. Squibb, founder of the now prominent pharmaceutical house. He publicly stated: "I do not myself think that anything should be patented by either physician or pharmacist."

The first quarrel between the authority of the state and national medical associations came when the State Medical Society of Ohio violated one of the articles of the national code of ethics by adopting in 1855 the resolution "That it is not derogatory to medical dignity, or inconsistent with medical honor, for medical gentlemen to take out a patent right for surgical or medical instruments." The State Medical Society of Ohio was requested either to rescind the resolution or to leave the national association.

In 1916, the American Medical Association voted to accept and administer medical patents, particularly that of Dr. E. C. Kendall of the Mayo Clinic who had just discovered thyroxin. Later the Association returned the patents in a reversal of policy. In 1918, The Judicial Council of the Association also declared it unethical for the University of Minnesota and the Mayo brothers to consider patenting a medical discovery and using the commercial proceeds to finance a research fund.

Nevertheless, more and more people in medical research came to realize that patenting medical inventions offered a solution to the problems of commercial development, positive control of quality and, not the least, finances for the growing medical research effort. Many independent or university-related foundations were set up to administer the growing list of important medical patents, often after violent arguments for and against such arrangements.

Insulin was controlled by the University of Toronto; the Doisy patents on theelin, by the St. Louis University School of Medicine; the Dick scarlet fever antitoxin, by the Scarlet Fever Committee, Inc.; various Vitamin D patents, by the Wisconsin Alumni Research Foundation; and cyclopropane anesthetic, by the Purdue Research Foundation.

The ethics of medical patent policy was thoroughly discussed in a symposium at the 94th Meeting of the American Chemical Society in 1937 and in an excellent historical review by Dr. Archie Palmer in 1948.[2] In the chemical symposium, the eminent Dr. Morris Fishbein of the *Journal of the American Medical Association* reiterated his opinion that the A.M.A. should sponsor the development of a corporation for the nonprofit administration of patents in the medical and health fields. However, the Board of Trustees of the A.M.A. in 1952 formally adopted a committee report recommending that an A.M.A. sponsored corporation for patent development should *not* be formed because of the serious legal and ethical implications.

Professional Associations

The physicians in the United States usually belong not only to general medical associations, such as the American Medical Association together with its affiliated state societies, but often as well to associations emphasizing a medical specialty. The latter organizations seldom have a statement of ethics in the patent area but often endorse the position of the A.M.A. as does the American College of Physicians. The American Academy of Pediatrics is understood to have worked with the Wisconsin Alumni Research Foundation in formulating the latter's policy of handling medical patents.[3]

The A.M.A. which traditionally discouraged its members from holding medical patents adopted the following resolution in 1949:

"The ethical physician will not receive remuneration from patents on or in the sale of surgical instruments, appliances and medicines, nor profit from a copyright on methods or procedures. The receipt of remuneration from patents or copyrights tempts the owners thereof to retard or inhibit research or to restrict the benefits derivable therefrom to patients, the public or the medical profession."

The statement was revised in 1955 to read:

"A physician may patent surgical instruments, appliances, and medicines or copyright publications, methods and procedures. The use of such patents or copyrights or the receipt of remuneration from them which retards or inhibits research or restricts the benefits derivable therefrom is unethical."

In 1957, the A.M.A. Principles of Medical Ethics were again revised. The Judicial Council has stated that the spirit and intent of the 1955 statement is reflected in the Principle appearing in Section 2:

"Physicians should strive continually to improve medical knowledge and skill, and should make available to their patients and colleagues the benefits of their professional attainments."

The Council simultaneously amplified this position by publishing an opinion on the subject in the *Journal of the American Medical Association* on March 30, 1957:

"*Question:* May I patent a surgical or diagnostic instrument that I have developed?

"*Answer:* Yes. It is not unethical for a physician to patent a surgical or diagnostic instrument he has discovered or developed. Our laws governing patents are based on the sound doctrine that one is entitled to protect his discovery. Medicine, recognizing the validity of our patent law system, accepts it, but in the interest of the public welfare and the dignity of the profession insists that once a patent is obtained by a physician for his own protection, the physician may not ethically use his patent right to retard or inhibit research or to restrict the benefits derivable from the patented article. Any physician who obtains a patent and uses it for his own aggrandizement or financial interest, to the detriment of the profession or the public, is acting unethically."

Clearly, from the viewpoint of the A.M.A., it is ethical for a physician to patent his medical inventions and even to profit thereby as long as his action does not suppress the benefit of the patented invention to the public.

Other Obligations

The physician must also recognize that if he is a full- or part-time employee of an organization, such as a university, clinic or hospital, the organization might have rights to his invention ranging from a shopright to exclusive rights depending on the conditions of his employment. Most public-supported institutions are dedicated to providing benefits of their research to the public freely.

The United States Government is now the largest source of funds supporting medical research in the United States, mostly through Public Health Service grants. The National Institutes of Health are the principal grantees of such funds. Present patent policies of the N.I.H. require that all inventions developed or reduced to practice under its grants must be reported and assigned to the Government.

The physician not solely in private practice should, therefore, investigate carefully the patent policies of his employer and the source of funds which in any way supported his research, when he contemplates patenting his invention.

The Physician's Invention

The invention may take any form which, necessarily, is novel under the patent law, unobvious over the prior art and useful in the medical field. Exemplary are new sur-

gical devices, diagnostic tools, new organic compounds, synergistic combinations of old drugs, the process of using such combinations, or the use itself, with unobvious results, of either a new compound or even an old substance if compounded or modified in significant manner adapting it to the new use.

The bulk of patentees of medical inventions are physicians, organic chemists, biochemists, pharmacists or pharmacologists who are actively engaged, full-time, in medical research in a pharmaceutical house, a university or a foundation-sponsored laboratory. Over the past decade, however, the policies of the Patent Office have kept pace with the advance of medical research. In the early 1950's, precedent for medical composition patents, i.e., old compounds in dosage unit form having a new medical utility, was established with the issuance of the isoniazid (U.S. 2,596,069) and disulfiram (U.S. 2,567,814) patents, together with medical method patents which cover new therapeutic uses of old compounds (e.g., U.S. 2,997,422 and U.S. 2,987,442) as provided for in the 1952 recodification of the patent act, 35 U.S.C. 100.

Since the Patent Office and the courts have adopted a progressive attitude toward patenting new medical discoveries, the physician should be ever alert to novel medical advances in his practice which might be best developed fully for the benefit of mankind by patenting and full commercial exploitation.

Development of the Invention

The age old polemics over the ethics of medical patents have been largely decided by the increasing economic and sociologic complexities of our society. The toxicological, pharmacological and clinical evaluation of new medicinals is tremendously expensive. The distribution system in its present form must also be complex, to insure uniformity and availability of a new drug to the patient as rapidly as possible. The time-recognized benefits of using medical patents as a means of positive quality control over a drug are more important than ever.

Simple medical devices can be manufactured and sold at times with relatively small capital investments. On the contrary, estimates of the average cost of developing a new ethical medicinal from test tube to market currently range around one million dollars. As the requirements of the Food and Drug Administration regarding toxicity and efficacy of the new drug become more stringent, development costs increase proportionately.

Pharmaceutical companies are reluctant to invest the necessary capital and the time of their development experts in an invention unless patent protection is available to insure at least an opportunity to recoup the investment.

The medical profession now recognizes and endorses the use of the patent system to develop medical inventions for the common good, as reflected in the quoted policy statements of the American Medical Association.

Procedure for the Physician-Inventor

The physician has two courses of action available to him if he decides to patent his invention.

First, he can proceed to contact a patent attorney who will investigate patent prospects and file a patent application. Then, if the physician so decides, he can contact a pharmaceutical house for possible commercial development of the invention. While it is best to file the application first, it is not advisable to wait for the patent to issue since this may take from one to four years. This is the universally recommended procedure endorsed by attorneys and pharmaceutical companies alike. The physician may estimate his costs of filing an application as $300 to $1000. A complicated prosecution of an application might amount to more than the initial charges. With the obvious complexities of medical patent law, contacting an attorney with some experience in this specialized field is desirable.

Second, he can contact a pharmaceutical company directly, either through its Director of Research and Development or through his detailman, after or even prior to taking steps for patent protection. Most pharmaceutical companies have efficient systems

for appraising product suggestions, such as checking patent prospects, evaluating the market, and, finally, determining whether the invention submitted is being studied in its own research department or has been previously suggested either in the literature or from internal sources. If the invention is accepted, the company then will often file and prosecute the patent application for the submitting physician while further tests and development proceed.

Product suggestions, particularly if the doctor has some clinical experience with the product, are universally respected and the doctor's proprietary rights are fully recognized. Royalties depend on the expected market, cost of development and scope of patent protection, but often range from 1 to 5 per cent of the market sales.

Summary

The practice of heating the head in an oven for insanity, opening the skull of a Pharaoh on what would surely prove his death bed, and bleeding the patient by application of leaches represent the level to which the healing art had risen in the more "advanced" civilizations of antiquity or the more recent past, after practice of some crude form of healing for perhaps a million years. The aid from other sciences in the 20th century and the incentives afforded by our patent system, to undertake the extensive research required to develop anesthetics, vaccines, antibiotics, analgetics and other therapeutic agents of today, has now given birth to the precise science of medicine.

The medical profession in the United States recognizes and generally endorses the use of the patent system as a tool for bringing the inventions of its members promptly into the general use for benefit of the public, provided the invention is not willfully repressed, is made widely available and is exploited with dignity.

Working under this code of ethics, the medical profession has cooperated with federal agencies, the drug industry and the other groups, in manner to lengthen the life expectancy of a baby born in this country from about 45 years to 70.2 years, this within the lifetime of some men and women now living!

References

1. Journal of the House of Representatives of the United States Congress, page 143, September 18, 1789.
2. *J.A.M.A.*, **137**, 497 (1948).
3. *Ind. & Eng. Chem.*, **29**, 1324 (1937).

Cross-references: *Microbiological Patents, Pharmaceutical Patent Practice, Utility.*

MEDICINAL PATENTS. See PHARMACEUTICAL

MICROBIOLOGICAL APPLICATIONS AND PATENTS

Harvey W. Edelblute

Science of Microorganisms and Microbiological Processes—Patentability of Microbiological Processes and Products—Non-Patentability of Bacteria—Patent Specification—Claiming the Product—Claiming the Process.

Microbiological processes are among the most widely used and least understood procedures, even though they have been employed since the beginning of life. Man could not live without them. They digest his food. They promote synthesis of essential materials within his body. It was, in fact, a major scientific breakthrough when researchers at the University of Notre Dame, not many years ago, succeeded in maintaining several generations of laboratory animals under strictly germ-free conditions.

Microbiological processes have been used for years to make beer, wine, cheese, bread, pickles and sauerkraut, rett flax, age tobacco, bate leather, produce silage and digest sewage. Now they produce a vast variety of chemicals and drugs such as alcohols, ketones, fatty acids, amino acids, vitamins, antibiotics, steroids and enzymes.

This article will consider the preparation of patent applications in which microorganisms are involved as principal elements of the invention; requirements of the Patent Office with regard to disclosing the invention and claiming it; and various means of describing the processes and products. For those not familiar with microbiology, the article starts with a review of that science.

Science of Microorganisms and Microbiological Processes

Individual species of microorganisms are distinguishable from one another by morphological characteristics and biochemical behavior. They transform one chemical substance to another, in the microbiological process, by means of enzymes, often with the aid of coenzymes and other obscure metabolic products of the growing microorganism.

Complexity of Fermentation Process. The fermentation process involves several distinct stages or steps. Included among these are growth, assimilation, biosynthesis and dissimilation. Growth involves increase in cell size and numbers by such methods of reproduction as budding, splitting or through development of spores or conida. Assimilation involves transfer of the various components of the fermentation medium into cell substance. Biosynthesis is the formation of complex compounds within the cell. Dissimilation is destructive metabolism which involves release of energy and results in true excretion products or new substances. The production of even relatively simple chemical compounds from other simple compounds in the microbiological process is extremely complex.

Various Chemical Reaction of Microorganisms. Microorganisms can carry out many different types of chemical reactions. Among these are the following:

Chemical Reaction	Organism
Oxidation	Many organisms
Reduction	Yeasts
Condensation	Yeasts
Esterification	Yeasts
Amination	Yeasts
Phosphorylation	Yeasts
Amidation	*Pseudomonas chlororaphis*
Deamination	*Aspergillus oryzae*
Hydrolysis	*Streptomyces griseus*
Decarboxylation	*Escherichia coli*
Methylation	*Scopulariopsis brevicaule*
Dismutation	*Bacterium ascendens*
Acylation	*Streptomyces venezuelae*
Dehydration	*Bacillus polymyxa*

The above list, far from complete, illustrates the vast potentialities of the microbiological process.

Many fermentation processes result in the production of a plurality of products of which only one is desired. Sometimes the fermentation process produces the desired product first, but the fermentation continues until that product is attacked and converted to other, undesirable substances. It is, therefore, important to know how to stop the fermentation process when the desired product is obtained in the highest yield. In other fermentation processes, some metabolic product may be toxic to the microorganism, and the fermentation becomes self-limiting. Removal or inactivation of the toxic substance may result in continuation of the fermentation and an increase in yield. Many other techniques are known to be useful in influencing the course of the fermentation so as to obtain the optimum results. These often form the subject matter of inventions. This paper deals with the patentability of microbiological processes, not their mechanism or other important but obscure details.

Distinguishing New from Old Organism and Process. One of the principal difficulties faced by both patent attorney and Patent Examiner, in considering the novelty of a microbiological process, is the determination of whether or not the microorganism used is the same as one described in a prior art process. Prior art writings as found in text books, patents and scientific journals are often of little help. Differences in nomenclature and classification present formidable obstacles, due to the rapid and haphazard growth of the science of microbiology. The mycologists, who are chiefly concerned with the study of that branch of botany dealing with fungi, established systems of nomenclature and classification particularly suited to their study. The bacteriologists, who are principally concerned with the disease-producing organisms, developed their own systems. Pioneering investigators and writers, being dissatisfied with what was already available, or finding it inadequate, often set up other classification systems. As a result, a single microorganism may be referred to in the literature by several different family, tribe or genus names. A citric acid-producing organism which one investigator describes as a *Citromyces* might, for instance, be referred to by another as being of the genus *Aspergillus*. It is exceedingly difficult, therefore, and impossible in many cases, for the Patent Examiner to determine whether a microorganism described in the prior art for performing some useful function is the same as the one described in a patent application before him. It is often equally difficult for the attorney to demonstrate that the organisms are, in fact, different.

Classification of Microbiological Organisms. If the classification of a microorganism being used in a new process or distinguishing it over a prior art organism is important, the attorney should be careful to secure the advice of one who is competent in the particular art involved. The inventor may not be trained in taxonomy or qualified to give advice on this important matter.

Viruses. The very tiniest of microorganisms, the viruses, are not able to synthesize their own food requirements and must depend upon living tissue for growth. Processes involving viruses must, therefore, be carried out in the living tissue of laboratory animals or in incubating chick embryos. Recently it has been found possible to propagate viruses in living tissue growing *in vitro*. The discovery, by Dr. J. F. Enders of Harvard University, of suitable methods of propagation of the poliomyelitis virus in isolated animal tissue growing in glass laboratory vessels made possible the commercial development of the Salk polio vaccine. Soon, a measles vaccine will be made available in the same way.

Although the viruses have a diameter of less than 0.2 micron, they are responsible for some of the most deadly and terrifying of diseases, such as rabies and poliomyelitis. They are also the causative agent of virus pneumonia, trachoma, smallpox, encephalitis, measles, mumps, yellow fever, distemper, hog cholera, and many others.

Since viruses are microorganisms, processes of utilizing them for useful purposes would seem to come within the scope of this chapter. The principal use of viruses, insofar as patentable processes are concerned, is in the production of vaccines, and patents have been granted on such processes which will be discussed later.

Rickettsia. The rickettsia are also a group of microorganisms which propagate only in the presence of living matter. They are somewhat larger in particle size than the viruses but are generally less than half a micron in diameter. They can usually be resolved microscopically by visible light. They are responsible for many important diseases of the typhus and spotted fever group. Microbiological processes employing these organisms are the subject matter of patents which describe and claim processes of attenuating the microorganism, propagating it in living tissue, preparing vaccines and diagnostic antigens from the product, and stabilizing the vaccines.

Bacteria and Fungi. The most important of the microbiological processes from a commercial point of view are those which employ bacteria and fungi. The bacteria, called Schizomycetes by the bacteriologist, are divided into a number of Orders, the most important of which are the *Actinomycetales* and *Eubacteriales*. These Orders are divided into Families which are divided into Tribes and then into Genera. The Genus may have innumerable Species which are subdivided into strains, groups, phases, forms, variants and stages. The fungi, which include yeasts and mushrooms are similarly subdivided.

To illustrate schematically how bacteriologists classify microorganisms, a system which is abbreviated and simplified for purposes of this article, follows.

A. Organisms which are photosynthetic with the evolution of oxygen and possess green plant chlorophyll.
B. Organisms not so characterized.
 Schizomycetes—lack chlorophyll.
Order:
1. *Myxobacteriales.* Rod-shaped. Slime-producing. Form motile, plasmodium-like aggregations.
2. *Thiobacteriales.* Various shapes. Contain sulphur. Rarely form endospores.
3. *Chlamydobacteriales.* Non-motile, filamentous alga-like; occurring chiefly in stagnant water. Have shell sheath often impregnated with iron.
4. *Actinomycetales.* Filamentous or rod-shaped

bacteria or fission fungi; tend strongly to the development of branches and lacking bacteriopurpurin.
5. *Eubacteriales.* Simple non-filamentous, unbranched, having no sulphur or iron. Includes spherical, spiral and rod-shaped forms.
6. Others not included above.

To illustrate further this classification system, the *Actinomycetales* order is, for instance, broken down to a single genus as follows:

Order: *Actinomycetales*
Family: *Streptomycetaceae.* Vegetative mycelium does not fragment into bacillary or coccoid forms. Conidia born on sporophores. Primarily soil forms.
Genus: *Streptomyces.* Growth in the form of a much branched mycelium with a typical aerial mycelium. Spores are formed in chains. Aerobic. Saprophytic soil forms.

There are numerous species of *Streptomyces* which may be subclassified in strains, groups, phases, forms, variants and stages. It will be understood that there are a number of different families of the *Actinomycetales* and also several genera. Bergey's "Manual of Determinative Bacteriology," 7th ed., is an authoritative reference book on nomenclature and taxonomy in this field.

If each species of a given microorganism carried out only a single chemical transformation, the problems of patenting microbiological processes would be greatly simplified. Such is not the case. Over a hundred species of yeasts, bacteria, and molds are known to produce alcohol, and many produce citric acid.

The first of the commercially available antibiotics, penicillin, is produced by *P. notatum*, *P. chrysogenum*, *A. flavus*, *A. giganticus*, and several other organisms. Streptomycin is produced by *S. griseus* and *S. bikiniensis*. A number of other antibiotics may be produced by two or more different species of microorganisms. Alpha-aminoadipic acid can be converted to L-lysine by numerous species of the genus *Saccharomyces* as well as by species of the genera *Torulopsis*, *Candida*, *Nematospora*, *Kloeckera*, and many others. In fact, this seems to be a common ability of the enzymes of all yeast cells. So many different fungi were found to have the ability to oxygenate certain steroids that U.S. Patent 2,602,769 claims this function for the whole order of Mucorales.

The attorney should be particularly careful, therefore, when drafting the specification, to determine whether or not the microbiological transformation he is attempting to describe is one peculiar to a particular strain of a single species, a characteristic of an entire order, or somewhere in between.

While some particular biochemical products and microbiological transformations can be brought about by several distinct species, it has also been found that strains of a single species often have the ability to produce two or more entirely different substances sometimes concomitantly and sometimes without producing any appreciable amount of the other. For instance, strains of *Bacillus brevis* will produce the antibiotics gramicidin and tyrocidine, *B. subtilis* will produce bacillomycin, eumycin, bacitracin and subtilin, and *Streptomyces griseus* will produce streptomycin, grisein, and cycloheximide.

Training Microorganisms. Microorganisms of a given species can be "trained" to produce large amounts of a given substance. By selecting strains of species or by treating them with mutating or attenuating agents, which include a wide variety of physical and chemical forces, strains are developed which are far superior to their parents in performing a desired biological function. Patents have issued on such mutation processes as, for instance, U.S. 2,938,835, according to which a griseofulvin-producing organism of the genus *Penicillium* is treated with the radioactive sulfur isotope of mass No. 35 to produce mutant strains having enhanced griseofulvin productivity.

Patentability of Microbiological Processes and Products

Microbiological processes and products are patentable on the same basis as other processes and products. Neither the statutes nor the decisions of the courts make any distinction. If the product or process is new and useful and unobvious to one having ordinary skill in the art, it is patentable, provided the applicant can describe the invention and the process of making and using it in such terms as to enable any person skilled in the art to make and use the same. But he must also particularly point out and distinctly claim the subject matter, and this sometimes proves to be very difficult.

Early Decisions. There are relatively few court decisions dealing extensively with the patentability of microbiological processes and products. Although several defendants have argued that bacteriological processes and products are not patentable because they are the result of forces of nature, the courts have paid little or no attention to these defenses.

One of the earliest decisions in which doubts as to the patentability of fermentation processes was raised was *Cameron Septic Tank Co.* v. *Saratoga*, 159 Fed. 453, CA 2 1908, in which Patent 634,423 of 1899 was involved. This patent claimed a process of digesting sewage with anaerobic bacteria. The action of anaerobic bacteria in sewage decomposition processes was known at the time of the application of Cameron *et al.*, but they were the first to instruct the art of digesting sewage without forming solid sludge. The defendant contended that the process claims were void because they covered "a process of nature, and one which cannot be covered by anyone."

The court noted "use of one of the agencies of nature for a practical purpose." However, it held the claims valid and infringed.

In *Dick et al.* v. *Lederle Anti-toxin Labs.*, 43 F.2d 628, DC SNY 1960, the patent 1,547,369 had claims to a process of isolating hemolytic streptococci specific to scarlet fever and product claims such as "A sterile toxin specific to scarlet fever." Despite the contention that the subject matter was not proper for a patent, the court held the claims of the patent to "embrace only processes or methods or means, each of which is the proper subject of a patent," and the patent was declared valid and infringed.

Weizmann Patent. A decision of considerable importance to the microbiological field is *Guaranty Trust Company of New York et al.* v. *Union Solvents Corp.*, 54 F.2d 400, DC Del 1931. The patent involved was

1,315,585 to Charles Weizmann for a process of producing acetone and butyl alcohol, claim 1 reading as follows:

"1. The process of producing acetone and butyl alcohol by the fermentation of liquids containing natural substances rich in starch by means of the herein described bacteria which are capable unaided of converting sterile fermentable grain starch substantially into acetone and butyl alcohol, and also liquefying gelatin."

It was admitted that Weizmann was not the first to produce acetone and butyl alcohol by a fermentation process. Limited quantities of these substances had been previously obtained by other fermentation processes. Weizmann, however, solved the problem of producing butyl alcohol and acetone in commercial quantities better than with any other known bacteria. He did this by discovering a particular species of bacteria unknown to bacteriologists and invented the process of successfully employing them. It was evident that the process was operable and useful. Millions of pounds of acetone and butyl alcohol had been produced by the Weizmann process and an important and extensive new industry had been established.

The defendant contended that the Weizmann patent failed to disclose adequate identifying characteristics of the bacteria and that the bacteria could not be isolated by following the directions of the patent. The court pointed out, however, that the certainty of the disclosure required by law [*Minerals Separation Ltd.* v. *Hyde,* 242 U.S. 261, 1916] is not greater than is reasonable having regard to the subject matter. It was observed that the specification of Weizmann was such as to require those skilled in the art to resort to their skill, in order to practice the invention, but not to require use of inventive faculties.

As to the characteristics of the bacteria set forth in the Weizmann patent, the court held that the evidence sustained the view that one with ordinary skill in the art would be able to recognize and distinguish them. [Actually, the number of characteristics used in designating the bacteria of Weizmann were very few in comparison to what is now required by the Patent Office.] An expert on bacteriology freely admitted that any one of the tests alone might not be characteristic, but pointed out that the combination of characteristics set forth designated an organism corresponding to no other known bacteria.

Plaintiff introduced testimony of experts who were able to isolate the Weizmann bacteria following the general procedures described in the patent. Certain deviations from these procedures were attacked by the defendant, but it was noted by the court that the techniques used were well known and it was wholly immaterial whether or not the procedure was followed exactly as described. On the other hand, the defendant produced witnesses who testified that they had followed the Weizmann isolation procedure exactly as described, but had failed to obtain the desired bacteria. The court said "Their testimony is not convincing. They failed, it is true. What the results would have been had they repeated their tests is not known." The court then quoted from a British patent case in which it was observed that "the specification is intended for the guidance of those who are desirous of obtaining [the microorganism] and not for people who wish to avoid getting it," and:

"If anyone followed instructions with the intention of obtaining a bacillus having the qualities mentioned in the specification, I am convinced that he will succeed. I do not say that he will succeed every time, for it is possible that the particular piece of soil or the particular specimen of cereal being worked upon may not contain BY (Weizmann's bacteria) or may only contain it in negligible quantities. But these are the risks attendant on every attempt to isolate a particular bacillus and Dr. Weizmann does not attempt to guarantee the searchers after his bacillus from such risks."

Finally, after deciding that the defendant employed a bacterium of the same kind described in the Weizmann patent and that this particular bacillus had not been described in the prior art, the court took up the contention of the defendant that the invention of the Weizmann patent was unpatentable since it is for the life process of a living organism.

"...Were the patent for bacteria per se, a different situation would be presented. As before stated, the patent is not for bacteria per se. It is for a fermentation process employing bacteria discovered by Weizmann under conditions set forth in the specification and claims. Undoubtedly there is patentable subject-matter in the invention." [Citing cases.]

This decision was sustained on appeal.

Later Cases. Although the current practice of the Patent Office is not nearly as liberal as was the court in the *Weizmann* case, the Board of Appeals has recognized the principles set forth in this case. In *Ex parte Prescott et al.*, 19 USPQ 178, 1933, the Board had before it a rejection of claims to a process of manufacturing butyl and isopropyl alcohol by aerobic fermentation. In considering the Examiner's views that the bacteria are only doing that "what by nature they are capable of doing and therefore there is no invention involved," the Board said that if these views were to be accepted it would hardly be possible to grant a patent on any chemical process. The Board further observed:

"...the appellant has not only discovered a new reagent, the bacillus technicus, but he has also discovered that when applied to a suitable mash it will produce butyl and isopropyl alcohols without ethyl alcohol, a result which is valuable and hitherto unknown to anyone. Such substitutions of elements in old processes are uniformly recognized as inventions."

Patent Office Classification of Microbiological Patents

Patents involving fermentation processes are found throughout the Patent Office, but principally in Class 195, Chemistry, Fermentation. This class contains approximately 2400 patents covering various fermentation processes, products, and apparatus for conducting fermentation processes.

Patents on antibiotics, medicinal substances, vaccines, and other microbiological products are found in Class 260, Organic Chemistry, Carbon Compounds, or Class 167, Medicines, Poisons and Cosmetics, according to what is claimed.

Class 99, Foods and Beverages, has a substantial number of patents on fermentation processes, particularly those concerned with the making of beer, wine, bread, pickles, cheese, yogurt, and other foods and beverages.

Class 71, Chemistry, Fertilizers, has many patents concerned with processes for fixing nitrogen and preparing compost with the aid of microorganisms.

Patents are also to be found in Class 47, Plant Husbandry; Class 127, Sugars, Starches and Carbohydrates; Class 131, Tobacco, and still others.

Subject Matter of Representative Patents

Among the patentable processes and products involving the use of viral agents will be found vaccines, antigens, tissue culture methods, attenuation procedures, stabilizing agents, and others. U.S. Patent 2,768,114 claims, for instance, a rabies vaccine and a method of preparing the vaccine; 2,518,978 claims a method of attenuating virulent hog cholera virus and the resulting vaccine; 2,798,835 claims a Newcastle disease vaccine; 3,014,834 claims a method of establishing the non-virulence of an attenuated strain of hog cholera virus; 3,019,168 claims a process of treating polio virus with heat and ultraviolet light to reduce its infectivity. Still other processes in which viral bodies are involved are found in 2,946,724 which is directed to the stabilization of live poliomyelitis vaccines with gelatin and 2,879,202 in which virus vaccines are stabilized with hexahydric alcohols. U.S. 2,705,696 is directed to the production of antigens from viral and other microbiological bodies. Patent 3,000,788 describes a process of growing canine hepatitis virus in tissue cultures. Many other issued United States patents which involve the use of viruses could be mentioned, but the foregoing are believed to indicate the wide variety of microbiological processes which may be the subject of patent applications with this group of microorganisms.

Processes involving the use of bacteria and fungi cover an amazing range of subjects. Many specific patents will be referred to in other sections of this article.

Non-Patentability of Bacteria

Since bacteria can be regarded as asexually reproduced plants, it is not surprising that someone applied for a patent under the plant statutes for an asexually reproduced and distinct new variety. In one such case, *In re Arzberger*, 46 USPQ 32, 1940, the applicant claimed a species of bacteria which he discovered and called *Clostridium saccharo-butyl-butyl-acetonicum-liquefacies.* After getting off to a shaky start in the Patent Office as to whether or not bacteria were plants or animals, the case reached the Court of Customs and Patent Appeals. The Court held that for purpose of the decision, bacteria of the application were asexually reproduced plants. It also held, however, that R.S. 4886 was intended to aid agriculture and that the word "plant" was used in the statute "in the common language of the people" and not in its strict scientific sense. It was noted that in the Congressional hearings on the bill, which resulted in the plant statute, not one word was said about patents for bacteria and the like. It seems almost certain that the Patent Office will not allow plant patents on induced strains of bacteria and other low forms of vegetative life even though they may be regarded in the scientific sense as asexually reproducible plants.

Patent Specification

There is nothing in Title 35 of the United States Code or in the decided cases which indicates that a specification describing a microbiological process or product must satisfy requirements other than those which have been laid down for inventions in other arts. While the description of the invention should be directed to those in the art, microbiological processes are not fully understood even by experts in the field. For this reason, the patent examiner, the courts and others called upon to study the disclosure may have great difficulty in fully comprehending it. The attorney, therefore, should put forth every effort to make sure that the disclosure is adequate under any standards that might conceivably be applied.

Although it is entirely proper to rely upon the disclosure of a patent or scientific publication to complete a description, because such disclosure is already in the prior art, the attorney should not follow this practice too liberally or literally. The specification should be complete in itself insofar as is reasonably possible. Neither the Examiner nor the public should be required to search elsewhere for extraneous matters to understand the invention.

Describing the Process. Many of the patentable inventions involving microbiological processes are directed to improvements in some previously described process. These may cover a multitude of subjects. They may involve control of such physical conditions as temperature, aeration, agitation, and foaming or addition of special nutrients, precursors, inhibitors, antiseptics, and other substances applicable to a specific fermentation or to fermentation processes in general.

The discovery that antibiotics could be produced by fermentation processes led to the filing of a great many patent applications. Many attorneys faced, for the first time, the problem of preparing adequate descriptions of such processes. It was known that the microorganism needed water, a source of assimilable carbon and nitrogen, and mineral elements, some in trace amounts; that most of the processes were aerobic and the fermentation required aeration; that some needed additional agitation; and that the processes needed had to be carried out within very narrow temperature and pH ranges. The permissible derivations from these requirements were not known with certainty to the early workers in the art. With the lapse of time, however, it has become generally recognized that these conditions are about the same for most antibiotic fermentation processes. Now they can be described in the specification in almost routine fashion. A typical description found in a recently issued patent is as follows:

"...Such processes involve cultivating the bacterium in a suitable nutritive medium, preferably at about 22 to 32° C under aerobic conditions and with agitation. The standard culture media contain a source of carbohydrate, such as sugars, starch, and glycerol; a source of organic nitrogen, such as bean meals and particularly soybean meal, wheat gluten, cotton seed meal, lactalbumin, and enzymatic digests of proteins; and a growth-promoting substance, such as distillers solubles and yeast extracts. Mineral salts like sodium chloride, sodium nitrate, and potassium phosphate, a buffering agent like calcium carbonate and a vegetable or mineral oil are usually also incorporated therein. After growth for a suitable time until an appreciable antibiotic potency has been imparted to the medium, generally a period of about one to five days, the mycelium which is formed is usually separated from the broth containing the elaborated (antibiotic), and the latter is then recovered by various procedures."

This same paragraph could be included in almost any antibiotic patent application without being seriously in error or objectionable to the Patent Office. Additional descriptive matter peculiar to the process being described is usually necessary, however. Since there are so many different possible improvements in various fermentation processes, some of a general nature and some specific to a given microorganism, no effort will be made to discuss these in detail. The general rules of specification writing apply.

Describing the Microorganism. Since the microorganism is an essential part of the microbiological process, it is necessary to include in the specification sufficient information about it to enable one skilled in the art to obtain and use it. If the microorganism is one that is commonly available, there is no problem in obtaining suitable cultures. In such cases mere mention of the species, genus, or family and an allegation that any of these are suitable for use in the process may be all that is needed, in addition to a disclosure of a specific embodiment of the process and the best mode of carrying out the invention. Rule 71(b).

The description of a microorganism such as might be used in the production of an antibiotic is not a simple matter. When the microorganism is one that has not been previously described in the literature and given a name by which it can be identified, the specification must give distinguishing characteristics sufficient to enable the art to recognize the microorganism. Although microbiologists are often in disagreement

as to what tests are sufficient to identify and classify a microorganism, there are a number of fairly well-standardized test procedures which are generally acceptable and most of the patents on the production of new antibiotics contain adequate descriptions. A typical one is found in the Davisson *et al.*, U.S. Patent 2,895,876. In Patent 3,018,220 three strains of a species of *Streptomyces hygroscopices* are described which have the ability to produce hygromycin B, the descriptions occupying approximately three full pages of text.

Although some microorganisms can be adequately identified by merely mentioning their name, these are mutants which possess some particular unique ability to carry out a desired function and which cannot be distinguished from their parent strain except by the result they produce. The difficulty in describing these microorganisms in nonfunctional terms is sometimes insurmountable; this obstacle has been overcome in many instances by depositing cultures of the strain in a place where it can be maintained and made available to the public when the patent issues. This requirement has led to a controversial and unsettled problem.

Deposit of Cultures. With the development of mutant strains by the employment of specific techniques and the difficulty of reproducing some of these mutants, it became apparent that in some cases no amount of descriptive matter in the specification would make it possible for those in the art to reproduce the mutant as described with certainty. Obviously, if the specification writer could not describe the invention so that its teachings could be followed with a reasonable degree of certainty, a patent could not be obtained. One solution to this problem that occurred to several was to deposit cultures of the new microorganisms in some public place and then refer to the fact in the specification. This meant depositing the culture of the microorganism before the patent application was filed. Although only the Patent Office, the applicant, and the culture collector knew that there was such a culture on deposit, there was always the serious possibility of losing control of the culture before patent protection was obtained.

Several schemes were developed to comply with the requirements of the Patent Office without this loss of control of the cultures. Some applicants deposited their new microorganisms with culture collections on the understanding that they would not be released to anyone without permission of the donor. Some irrevocably authorized the culture collection to make the culture available immediately, or in other cases upon issuance of the patent. Others deposited cultures in their own private collections. Some cultures were deposited in more or less obscure culture collections in universities, agricultural experimental stations, and institutions of various kinds where they were not likely to be found before the patent issued. Some cultures were deposited in culture collections in foreign countries. Many applicants insisted, however, that the culture need not be deposited at all if the description of the invention contained in the specification was legally adequate. It was pointed out, for instance, that in the Weizmann Patent 1,315,585, discussed earlier in this article, cultures of the new microorganism had not been deposited, and the defense that the disclosure of the organism was inadequate was brushed aside by the court for the reasons given above. Many other patents have been issued since that time without the critical microorganism having first been made available to the public.

Although not now available for publication, it seems that there are decisions by the Board of Appeals holding that certain applications claiming microbiological processes were fatally defective, *ab initio*, because the microorganism described therein could not be reproduced with certainty and the public might not be able to practice the invention. Depositing the culture after the filing date did not cure the defect, said the Patent Office, and attempts to introduce the culture collection identification number in the specification were refused as constituting new matter. The writer is unaware of the nature of those disclosures that were held to be fatally defective, and perhaps

they were inadequate to enable those skilled in the art to practice the invention in the circumstances of those particular cases. As noted above, some microorganisms are easily described and can be found almost everywhere, and no reason is seen why the applicant cannot adequately describe his invention as a matter of fact and in accordance with law without first making available his culture to the world at large. On the other hand, there are specific mutant strains which cannot be distinguished from other strains of the same species except in terms of the novel result that they are capable of producing.

In considering the wisdom of depositing cultures in public places, prior to the time the application was filed, so that it can be said that the microorganism is generally available to the public, a number of things must be taken into account which have not been settled by the Patent Office and courts.

Depositing the microorganism in a culture collection does not necessarily insure the fact that the organism will be alive or available to the public at the time the patent issues. The Department of Agriculture laboratory at Peoria, Illinois, for instance, is under no legal obligation to receive cultures, maintain them, or give them out on request. Some culture collections do not want certain kinds of microorganisms. None want to be burdened with cultures of a great many strains that they may already have. Maintenance of a large collection of cultures can be very expensive. Some collections are privately controlled and while they may receive cultures and give out subcultures from time to time, on request and for a small fee, they may also refuse to do this. The cultures may die or change characteristics on storage. There is no certainty that subcultures would be available to the public if deposited either before or after the application was filed.

There is also the matter of location. Would, for example, availability of the microorganism in a foreign country fulfill the requirements of 35 U.S.C. as interpreted by the Patent Office? The Centraalbureau voor Schimmelculture, Boarn, Holland is considered to be an international repository. However, there is some doubt as to the continued availability of its cultures to United States citizens. Also, would an inventor in England who filed an application in England, first depositing a culture in a recognized collection in that country, and who within a year filed the same application in the United States, be accorded full rights under the International Convention by the United States Patent Office?

As will be apparent from the foregoing, the inventor is faced with a dilemma for which there is no present solution. It is the opinion of this writer that too much emphasis has been placed upon the description of the microorganism used in the process by the Patent Office. It seems to be forgotten that this is only a part of the disclosure. The manner in which one skilled in the art would set about to reproduce the invention from the written disclosure seems to be misunderstood. The skilled worker does not ordinarily try to find a particular organism having all of the characteristics set forth in the specification when attempting to reproduce the invention described. The taxonomy of the microorganism is very helpful and would indicate to the skilled worker that this general type of microorganism would be the most likely one to look for, but a partial description is all that is ordinarily needed. The antibiotic is the important thing that is sought.

Unfortunately, the matter of depositing cultures of microorganisms in connection with the filing of patent applications has not been settled at the present time, and may not be settled until the Patent Office takes a definite stand supported by law and approved by the courts. The attorney preparing a patent application involving the use of a new microorganism will have to make his own decision as to what is proper under the circumstances.

Requirements for Disclosure. Although the United States Patent Office has not publicly set forth the requirements of disclosure of microorganisms employed in the invention, the Swedish Patent Office, in February, 1962, issued rules for patent applications relating to microbiological processes which may prove useful to the patent attorney in drawing up the disclosure for United States specifications. Some of the most important of these rules are summarized as follows:

"Known organisms are characterized sufficiently by their scientific names or other scientific designations, if necessary accompanied by a reference to some publication describing the technique employed for their systematic determination.

"Organisms that have been hitherto unknown must be described so fully and elaborately that confusion with other organisms is avoided.

"If it is not possible to draft a description such as to exclude confusion with other organisms, or if due to the organism being very rare there is reason to assume that it will be difficult to find it in free nature, or if, finally, its production is not reproducible with certainty, then it is suitable and desirable that the organism be deposited at a scientific internationally known Swedish or foreign Institution which is independent of the inventor (applicant). In that case the name (depository designation) attributed to the organism at the Institution should be stated.

"Statements about the conditions or circumstances under which an organism was found, or about the methods by which it was isolated, cannot as a rule be accepted as defining the organism in a satisfactory manner.

"In cases where an organism is novel and the steps taken for isolating it may be considered to be reproducible, these steps have to be described. The cultivating conditions (substrates, nutrients, any chemical or other agent used for stimulation and influencing the development in a desired direction, pH, temperature, irradiation, etc.) have to be described in clear and definite terms, with a statement also about the limit values and optimum values."

The following statements would be required where the new microorganism was an Actinomycetes of the Genus Streptomyces, for instance.

"1. Name of organism, or possibly its reference number in a public cultivation deposit and where possible (desirable) date and place of isolation.

"2. Description of growth on or in a specific substrate, with a detailed description of the microscopic properties and characteristics and of the microscopic morphology (including shape and size of spores, morphology of sporulation, branching characteristics of mycelium, and width of hyphae).

"3. Growth properties (morphology of colonies, statement about colors and also about secreted pigments if any) with respect to at least 10 standard substrates.

"4. Physiological properties of the organism

when grown in substrates containing milk, nitrate, gelatine, starch, tyrosine and if desirable cellulose.

"5. Capacity of the organism to produce hydrogen sulfide on inorganic and organic substrates.

"6. Statement about its ability to utilize a number of carbon sources.

"7. Reference should be made to the most closely related strain or strains mentioned in Bergey's Manual of Determinative Bacteriology (1957) accompanied by a statement as to how the organism may be distinguished from these known organisms.

"8. Supplemental statements, where possible or desirable, as regards individual properties such as for instance production of antibiotics.

"9. The description of the physical and chemical properties of the antibiotic should be accompanied by a Table setting forth the quantitative special effects of the substance. Furthermore, there should be a Table indicating by merely plus (+) and minus (−) signs whether or not the substance is active against Gram-positive and Gram-negative bacteria, fungi and yeasts, and possibly moreover against protozoans, virus and Rickettsiae if this is known to applicant."

Microorganisms of other genera may require descriptive matter other than illustrated above.

The Swedish Patent Office does not require a prior deposit of the microorganism in all cases. It is recognized that it may be possible to describe a new microorganism in such manner that it can be located, or reproduced, with reasonable certainty. The rules do not indicate whether or not the microorganism must be placed on deposit in a culture collection before the patent application is filed.

The Patent Offices of most countries are much more liberal in allowing ancillary matter to be introduced into the application without having it refused as constituting "new matter" than is the United States Patent Office. It is also significant that the Swedish Patent Office will accept deposit of the microorganism in foreign institutions as long as they are internationally known and independent of the inventor.

Depositories. Among the various culture collections that have been mentioned in United States patents as having cultures of the microorganisms forming the subject matter of the patent are the following:

(1) Northern Regional Research Labo-

ratories, Culture Collection Section, Fermentation Division, Peoria, Ill.

(2) American Type Culture Collection, Washington, D.C.

(3) Rutgers Institute of Microbiology, New Brunswick, N.J.

(4) Centraalbureau voor Schimmelculture, Boarn, Holland.

Describing the Product. Because microbiological products are often extremely complex, it is difficult to characterize them in the same way that a chemist would describe a simple organic compound. They are usually first obtained in minute amounts with other complex organic material, sometimes with other closely related antibiotics. Very seldom is it possible to precipitate the antibiotic from its fermentation liquor, crystallize the material, and determine the melting point and empirical formula as in the case of a chemical reaction product. Several years may elapse before the structure of the antibiotic is known. Lack of these facts does not make the new antibiotic without utility. Because of the intense competition in the search for new and better antibiotics and other microbiological products, the inventor cannot afford to take the chance of losing his potential patent rights by waiting until he has all of the information concerning the new product that he would like to have. Fortunately, it is possible to describe and claim these new products in terms of their physical, biological, and chemical properties without knowing the structure of the molecule.

There are many physical, chemical, and biological properties that can be determined with relatively minute amounts of complex organic substances and these can be used to distinguish the substance from all other previously known materials. Among the most important of these are the R_f values. Since this is one of the most common techniques used to detect and distinguish antibiotic activity, a brief description of the technique will be given.

R_f *Values.* R_f values are usually determined by paper chromatography. There are a number of variations in the procedure. Most commonly, a long, thin strip of paper is used. Although special grades of paper are usually employed, other materials which are inert to the solvent and which tend to absorb the antibiotics could be used. In carrying out the procedure, a minute amount of the substance is placed on the strip of paper near one end and the spot is marked. The amount of the unknown substance so placed may vary considerably. As little as 0.002 milliliter of a solution of 15 gammas per milliliter of tetracycline is sufficient for determination of its R_f values. Some antibiotics require more, others less. The paper is then dried, and one end (that closest to the point on which the unknown antibiotic has been applied) is placed in a buffered solution of a solvent or a mixture of solvents. The strip of paper may be suspended vertically with one end dipping in the solution so that the solution rises up the strip of paper by capillary action; or it may be placed with the upper end in a small cup containing the solvent so that the solution descends. The whole is enclosed so that the atmosphere around the paper strip is maintained saturated with solvent vapor. As the solvent moves along the length of the paper, it carries with it the antibiotic which is successively absorbed on and desorbed from the cellulose fibers. The antibiotic moves along slower than the solvent. When the solvent front has reached a desired point along the length of the paper strip, the paper is removed and the front of the solvent is marked. This strip of paper is then examined to determine the location of the antibiotic. The ratio of the distance that the antibiotic has moved from its original position to the distance that the solvent has moved from that same position is called the R_f value.

The position of the antibiotic on the strip of paper may be determined in a number of ways. In some cases it can be observed with visual light, when the antibiotic is a colored substance. If the antibiotic fluoresces, it can be observed with ultraviolet light. If it gives a color with organic reagents, the strip of paper is sprayed with a solution of such a reagent and the position of the antibiotic determined. In some cases it is possible to prepare antibiotics with radioactive isotope moieties, and the position may be determined with a Geiger counter or some similar device. Most frequently, the position of the antibiotic is determined by bioautographic methods. In this latter method an agar plate seeded with a desired bacterium, fungus, or other microorganism is prepared and the strip of paper is laid upon the surface of the agar. It is then incubated and, if the antibiotic is active against the microorganisms in the agar plate, no growth will occur near the antibiotic, thus marking the location of the antibiotic.

A related technique is paper strip electrophoresis. In this technique electrodes are placed at selected points along a paper strip having an antibiotic between them, and the movement of the antibiotic under the influence of the applied electric potential is noted.

As will be inferred from the foregoing brief description, an antibiotic should be soluble to some extent in the solvent system employed. A large variety of solvent systems may be selected and used, and the R_f values thus obtained will be different with each solvent system. This makes it possible to obtain a large number of R_f values for any one antibiotic. This paper strip chromatography technique has been developed to such an extent that it has been said that it will distinguish antibiotics related so closely that infrared, ultraviolet, and various color reaction tests will not detect any difference.

U.S. Patent 2,878,289 gives the R_f values for a number of tetracycline antibiotics and shows how members of this closely related family of antibiotics can be distinguished from each other by the technique described. See Fig. 1, infra.

The lower part of Fig. 1 is a reproduction of Fig. 1 of the patent and illustrates the different R_f values exhibited by a mixture of demethyltetracycline, tetracycline, chlorodemethyltetracycline, and chlorotetracycline in a solvent system consisting of 0.3 M NaH_2PO_4 and butanol at a pH of 3.0. Point 2, marked on the paper strip, was the place where the mixture of antibiotics was placed. Point 3 represented the solvent front when the paper strip was removed from the solvent. Points 4, 5, 6, and 7 represent, respectively, the positions of the four antibiotics at that time.

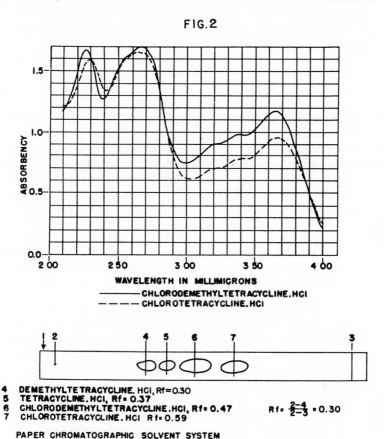

March 17, 1959   J. R. D. McCORMICK ET AL   **2,878,289**

6-DEMETHYLTETRACYCLINES AND METHODS FOR PREPARING THE SAME

Filed May 28, 1956   5 Sheets–Sheet 1

FIG. 2

WAVELENGTH IN MILLIMICRONS
——— CHLORODEMETHYLTETRACYCLINE.HCl
– – – – CHLOROTETRACYCLINE.HCl

4   DEMETHYLTETRACYCLINE.HCl, Rf=0.30
5   TETRACYCLINE.HCl, Rf = 0.37
6   CHLORODEMETHYLTETRACYCLINE.HCl, Rf = 0.47
7   CHLOROTETRACYCLINE.HCl Rf = 0.59

$$Rf = \frac{2-4}{2-3} = 0.30$$

PAPER CHROMATOGRAPHIC SOLVENT SYSTEM
0.3 M NaH$_2$PO$_4$
pH 3.0/BUTANOL

FIG. 1

INVENTORS.
JERRY ROBERT DANIEL McCORMICK
URSULA HIRSCH
ELMER RAYMOND JENSEN
NEWELL OSCAR SJOLANDER
BY *Harvey W. Eslethete*
ATTORNEY

Fig. 1.

R_f values have been used in characterizing antibiotics in many other patents. Among those that present this data in ways other than that illustrated above include the patents to H. Brockman *et al.*, No. 2,953,495; J. E. Phillips *et al.*, No. 3,006,813; and H. C. Murray *et al.*, No. 2,602,769. In some cases the R_f values are simply set forth in a table, no pictorial representation being included in the drawings. Among these may be mentioned the patent to Gaeumann *et al.*, No. 3,033,760.

Ultraviolet Absorption Spectra. Ultraviolet absorption spectra are very commonly used in characterizing antibiotics. This is a valuable tool in most cases. Fig. 2, shown on the next page is copied from U.S. Patent 2,878,289 and illustrates the ultraviolet absorption spectra of chlorotetracycline and chlorodemethyltetracycline. As will be observed, the maximum absorptions and the intensity of the absorptions differ considerably. Ultraviolet absorption curves such as this are found in many antibiotic patents.

Infrared Absorption Spectra. The infrared absorption of chemical compounds is also a very important and commonly used means of characterizing antibiotics and of distinguishing them from others. This was first used in the patent to B. M. Duggar, No. 2,482,055, issued September 13, 1949. Use of these infrared curves met with favor in the Patent Office and has been continued, with improvements, whenever possible. The infrared curves are the result of absorption of infrared light when it passes through a sample of the antibiotic which may be mixed in a simple hydrocarbon oil, mixed with crystals of potassium bromide and pressed into a thin disk, or incorporated with some other substance whose infrared absorption characteristics are relatively simple. Since the resulting infrared curve is the result of vibration of individual atoms and groups of atoms in the molecule, the curve can reveal a great deal of information, if interpreted by someone with experience. Although the infrared technique is very effective in distinguishing one molecule from another, it is not easy to explain the meaning of the individual absorption bands until after the structure of the molecule is known. When the antibiotic is of a highly complex structure containing many vibrating groups, or if the sample is contaminated with appreciable amounts of impurities or consists of a mixture of closely related antibiotics, the value of the infrared curve, as the sole means of distinguishing the product under examination, is considerably lessened. It remains, however, one of the most important characterizing means available.

Fig. 2 is a reproduction of Fig. 4 of U.S. Patent 2,878,289 and shows, superimposed, the infrared absorption spectrum of tetracycline and demethyltetracycline. Although these two large, complex molecules differ only in a methyl group, the differences in the infrared absorption curves are obvious, even to the unskilled observer.

Other Physical Characterizing Data. Melting points of organic compounds, one of the oldest and most commonly used means of partial identification, are usually not suitable for antibiotics and other substances of high molecular weight particularly when they are mixed with closely related substances.

Solubility in solvents, a very useful means of characterizing new organic materials, is often used in describing and claiming new antibiotics.

Crystallography can be a highly critical characterizing means if the antibiotic can be obtained in crystalline form, which is sometimes exceedingly difficult. The patent to J. E. Phillips *et al.,* 2,990,329, uses crystalline structure to a considerable extent. One of its drawings is a photomicrograph of uniaxial positive hexagonal prismatic rods of ristocetin A. The alpha, beta, and gamma indexes of refraction, if measured and considered together, provide a highly satisfactory means of distinguishing crystalline materials; this was done in the Duggar patent, 2,482,055, covering aureomycin.

X-ray diffraction patterns on crystalline material are occasionally used in characterizing antibiotics. Patent 2,990,329 mentioned above has a table giving the X-ray diffraction pattern under the conditions specified. Patent 2,602,769 also mentioned above, illustrates an X-ray diffraction pattern in its Fig. 2.

Optical rotation of dilute solutions of the antibiotic are very easily measured and are of considerable value in characterizing the antibiotic. This technique was used, for example, in U.S. Patents 2,482,055 and 3,018,-220.

Still other physical properties have been mentioned in the patent literature. The pK values are sometimes given, molecular weight is sometimes estimated, and electrophoretic movement can be described. Obviously there are many more physical characteristics which can be determined and which may prove of particular value in special instances, but the foregoing characteristics are those most used.

Chemical Properties. Elemental analysis

March 17, 1959   J. R. D. McCORMICK ET AL   **2,878,289**

6–DEMETHYLTETRACYCLINES AND METHODS FOR PREPARING THE SAME

Filed May 28, 1956   5 Sheets–Sheet 3

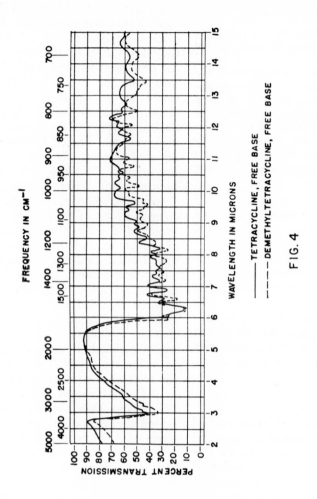

FIG. 2.

is one of the techniques most commonly used in characterizing new compounds. The empirical formula may be calculated from this data, but this is considered a risky practice by many chemists when dealing with antibiotics.

There are also many qualitative tests of great value. United States Patent 3,032,470 issued to J. Ziffer *et al.* contains, for instance, the following paragraphs:

"Phytostreptin gives positive permanganate and biuret tests and negative anthrone, ferric chloride,

Molisch, ninhydrin, Millon Liebermann Buchard, maltol, Pauly, Ehrlich (dimethylaminobenzaldehyde), Sakaguchi and Fehling tests. It gives no color with cold concentrated sulfuric acid. It is precipitated from aqueous solution by ammonium sulfate, calcium chloride, barium chloride, cupric chloride, sodium chloride, zinc chloride, picric acid, phosphotungstic acid, trichloroacetic acid, methyl orange and Reineck salt.

"The polypeptide nature of this antibiotic was revealed by hydrolysis with 6 N HCl. The hydrolysate, now ninhydrin positive, was analyzed using two dimensional paper chromatographic techniques. The presence of at least eight ninhydrin-positive components was detected, of which the amino acids valine, alpha-alanine, proline, leucine (or isoleucine), arginine, glycine and serine were identified."

The relatively simple colorimetric tests are highly significant in revealing functional groups in the complex molecule.

Biological Characteristics. The antibiotic activity against various microorganisms is usually included in the description and is highly significant in characterizing the antibiotic, as well as indicating its utility. As noted above, the Swedish Patent Office considers these biological properties to be a necessary part of the disclosure.

Claiming the Product

A product may be claimed by its method of production, when it cannot be described otherwise in adequate manner, as by formula, name or tests. A good discussion of the ground rules for claiming chemical products of uncertain composition is found in *Ex parte Fox*, 128 USPQ 157, PO BdApp 1961. In the *Fox* case, the specification disclosed the preparation of a product identified as 1,1″-methylene bis-(2-isonicotinyl-hydrazine) which was said to be a white microcrystalline precipitate melting at 167.5 to 171.5° C and having antitubercular properties. Sometime after the application was filed, it was discovered that the product was actually hexahydro-1,3,5-triisonicotin-amido-s-triazine monohydrate. Nearly three years after the application was filed, the applicant inserted a new name and formula for the compound and added a product claim as follows:

"45. A compound selected from the group consisting of hexahydro-1,3,5-triisonicotinamido-s-triazine and acid addition salts thereof."

The Examiner contended that the amendment introduced new matter and that the original application did not contain a factual description of the product except by the process of making it and that the only way that the product could be claimed would be by "product by process type claim." The applicant cited *Ex parte Geiger*, 92 USPQ 382, PO BdApp 1951, and other decisions, and argued that the formula or name of a compound could be corrected if the original disclosure fully teaches how to secure and recognize the product. The Board held, however, that the melting point, color and form of the product were not sufficient to identify it apart from its method of production and that the decisions relied upon by the applicant were not controlling. They further held that reference to the product as being an antitubercular agent was not regarded as a physical characteristic for identification. The Examiner's view that the disclosure was inadequate to warrant the change in name of the product or to define the product in terms other than the method of production was sustained.

In *Ex parte Brian et al.*, 118 USPQ 242, PO BdApp 1958, the applicants had presented claims which defined the product in terms of its physical and chemical characteristics and also by its method of production. It was argued that both types of claims were necessary because the Examiner had criticized those claims in which the product was defined by its physical and chemical characteristics. The Board, however, did not consider this sufficient to warrant both types of claims. They further observed that "to warrant the claiming of a product by its method of production it must appear that such product cannot be otherwise defined." They also went on to observe that it is necessary to recite all critical process limitations in such claims.

Although microbiological products may be claimed in various ways, according to the circumstances, a given applicant may not use several types of product claims or take his choice. He should use the most conventional method available to him, the chemical formula, if it is known. If the formula is not known, but enough physical and chemical properties are known for identification, these should be liberally used. Not all would seem to be necessary, but usually the Examiner will try to get as many in the claim as possible. If there are not enough of these properties to satisfy the Examiner, the applicant may be forced to define the product in terms of the process by which it is made.

By Common Name. The simplest way of claiming a new biological product is by its common, trivial or generic name as in U.S. 2,449,866 wherein the sole product claim is: "Streptomycin." Waksman and Schatz were able to obtain such a claim because streptomycin had been described in printed publications before the application was filed. This, of course, is not usually the case, since publication before filing does not often occur.

In *Ex parte Brian et al.*, supra, a claim to "An alkali metal salt of gibberellic acid" was refused since it identified the product only by applicants' coined name which was not art recognized.

A claim of U.S. 2,699,054 to Lloyd H. Conover is simply: "Tetracycline." Conover was able to claim this antibiotic by its common name in this patent because it was a continuation-in-part of an earlier filed application and the term "tetracycline" and means of identifying the material were known to the public before the continuation-in-part was filed. It would seem preferable to use "tetracycline" in the claims rather than the cumbersome full chemical name which is, "4-dimethylamino-1,4,4a,5,5a,6,11,12a-octahydro-3,6,10,12,12a-pentahydroxy-1,11-dioxo-2-naphthacenecarboxamide."

An example of using the common name in modified form in claiming new antibiotic products is found in U.S. 2,878,289 to McCormick *et al.* in which Claim 2, for instance, is simply "6-Demethyltetracycline." The relatively simple product claims of this patent were accepted by the Patent Office in view of the fact that at the time of filing the application, the structure of tetracycline had been determined and it had further been determined by the applicants that the new compound of Claim 2 differed from tetracycline in having no methyl group at the 6 position.

Generally speaking, the Patent Office has not been very liberal in allowing the applicant to claim his new antibiotic by its common name, even though the specification clearly defines the substance and there would be no doubt in the minds of those in the art as to what was intended to be covered by the claims. The position of the Patent Office in allowing use of common names of antibiotics in the claims has been confusing at times, however. In U.S. 2,516,080 to Sobin *et al.*, the process claims are directed to "A process for producing Terramycin . . ." etc., but the antibiotic is defined in the product claims only by its various biological, physical and chemical characteristics, without reference to the term "Terramycin."

Another example of this seemingly inconsistent practice is found in U.S. Patent 2,953,495 to Brockmann *et al.* wherein the applicant was allowed to use the term "Actinomycin C" in the single product claim, but this was followed by 43 lines of descriptive physical and chemical data and a section commencing with the phrase "produced by cultivating a strain of *Streptomyces chrysomallus* . . ." under certain specified conditions. It would seem that the material in 40 or more lines of this claim, which is found in the specification, could well have been omitted from the claim without making it any less definite. In the Brockmann *et al.* decision cited above, the Board held that the term "Actinomycin C" was indefinite in defining the product but *when used in a method claim "it is relatively immaterial what the appellants call the product as long as it is not misleading or misdescriptive."* (Emphasis added.) Recently issued patents indicate that the Patent Office is more realistic than formerly as to what is required in the product claims.

By Chemical Name. There are several patents in which a new microbiological product is claimed by its chemical name. In one of these, U.S. Patent 2,965,633 issued to A. M. Moore *et al.*, one of the claims is as follows:

"1. 6-diazo-5-oxonorleucine."

Of course, it is necessary to know the correct chemical name before filing the application if claims of this type are to be obtained, a situation that does not arise very often. Claims of this kind are really of the structural formula type since they actually define the structure in terms of particularly placed organic groups rather than by bonded molecules.

By Chemical or Structural Formula. New microbiological products may often be claimed in terms of their chemical structure, just as in the case of any other organic chemical compound. This was done, for instance, in Patent 2,998,438 issued to Charney *et al.* wherein the sole claim is as follows:

"The fungicidal agent, eulicin, having the structure:

$$H_2N-\overset{\overset{\text{C}}{\|}}{C}-NH-(CH_2)_5-\\ \qquad CH-CH-(CH_2)_3-NH_2\\ \qquad \overset{|}{OH}\ \ \overset{|}{NH}-C-(CH_2)_5-NH-C-NH_2\\ \qquad \qquad \overset{\|}{O} \qquad \qquad \overset{\|}{NH} \qquad ."$$

Patent 3,014,922 issued to Gaeumann *et al.* defines the new antibiotic halothin in Claim 1 as follows:

"A compound of the formula

$$\begin{array}{c}S-\!\!\!-\!\!\!-C=\!\!=C-NH-R\\ |\qquad |\qquad |\\ S\qquad C\qquad C=O\\ \diagdown\ \diagup\ \ \diagdown\ \diagup\\ CH\qquad N\\ \qquad H\end{array}$$

in which R represents a member selected from the group consisting of hydrogen, lower alkanoyl and phenyl lower alkanoyl."

By Physical and Chemical Properties. As noted earlier, there are many different types and kinds of physical and chemical properties which may be readily obtained. The manner in which these are used in the claims can be illustrated by Claim 1 of Patent 3,023,145 issued February 27, 1962 to Hata *et al.*

"1. Protomycin, said antibiotic being characterized as a pale yellow viscous liquid, soluble in methanol, ethanol, acetone, chloroform, ethyl acetate, butylacetate, dioxane, ether, and benzene, insoluble in carbon tetrachloride, carbon disulphide and petroleum ether, having a molecular weight of about 274 by the Rast method, having

shown upon analysis 64.71% carbon, 8.59% hydrogen, 4.27% nitrogen, and by difference 22.40% oxygen, having absorption maxima in the ultraviolet region at about 209 mμ ($E_{1\ cm}$ 1% 649) and 233 mμ ($E_{1\ cm}$ 1% 533) and 280-285 mμ ($E_{1\ cm}$ 1% 27), having a rotation of $[\alpha]_D$ 27° C = 126° (c. = 1.08 CHCl$_3$), having characteristic infrared absorption peaks at about 2.90, 3.05, 3.19, 3.30, 3.40, 5.85, 5.91, 6.20, 6.50, 6.70, 6.90, 7.08, 7.29, 7.82, 7.94, 8.71, 8.95, 9.25, 9.42, 10.10, 10.32, 11.09, 11.45, 11.52, 12.00, 12.12, 13.38 and 14.25 microns, absorbing bromine, discoloring potassium permanganate, giving positive Diazo, Nessler's and Molish color reactions, giving negative Millon's, biuret, Sakaguchi, ferrichloride, Tollen's, nitro-prusside, silver mirror, Liebermann's, Meyer, Wagner and ninhydrin reactions, and forming an acetyl derivative melting at about 110-111° C."

For another example, see Patent 3,032,470, to Ziffer *et al.* They name microorganisms which are resistant to and affected by the antibiotic. Hata *et al.* do not indicate in their claim what organisms are affected by protomycin although the specification discloses them. Hata *et al.* rely upon a number of colorimetric tests whereas Ziffer *et al.* do not.

Although three or four carefully selected physical or chemical properties may adequately identify and distinguish one organic compound from all others, the Patent Office usually insists on having all of the characterizing properties found in the specification in the claims. Since a new compound defined by ten or twelve properties is no different than when defined by only three or four, the Examiner's wishes are usually complied with by the attorney, to expedite prosecution of the application.

Product by Process. A substantial number of microbiological patents have issued in which the product is claimed with reference to the process by which it is made. In one of these, U.S. 2,895,876, Davisson *et al.*, one such claim appears as follows:

"5. A new biologically active substance identified as catenulin, which is prepared by the process of Claim 1, and the acid salts of said substance."

Formerly, the Patent Office required the applicant to put all physical and chemical characterizing data into the claim, in addition to reference to the process. In some instances, this additional characterizing data was considerable as in the case of Brockmann *et al.*, 2,953,495 mentioned above, More recent practice seems to favor claims of the type allowed to Davisson *et al.*

Certain types of microbiological products cannot be defined by physical or chemical properties. For instance, vaccines defy description except in functional language. In Patent 2,518,978, issued to Cox *et al.*, a new hog cholera vaccine was claimed as follows:

"5. A hog cholera vaccine capable of stimulating the production of protective hog cholera antibodies when injected into normal non-immune hogs, without producing the usual pathological symptoms of hog cholera, said vaccine containing a live, non-pathogenic strain of hog cholera virus, developed by the process of Claim 1."

The functional limitations appearing in this claim exclude many other hog cholera vaccines from its scope.

When considering defining a new product in terms of the process by which it is made, the attorney should also consider the scope of the resulting claim. If the process is defined too narrowly, the product, even though entirely new, may not be adequately protected. If the same product can be produced by another process, the value of the patent is substantially decreased. In *Purdue Research Foundation* v. *Watson*, 122 USPQ 445, DC DistCol 1958, the following statement is made:

"Where one has produced a composition of matter in which invention rests over prior art compositions, and where it is not possible to define the characteristics which make it inventive except by referring to the process by which the composition is produced, one is permitted to so claim his composition, but his *protection is limited to compositions produced by his process referred to in the claims*. When the composition is thus claimed in terms of the process of preparation, the product cannot be defined in such a manner as to assert a monopoly on the product by whatever means produced." (Emphasis added.)

In many of the product claims in which reference is made to a process, certain strains of species of the microorganism are named in the claims. For instance, in 2,992,162, mentioned above, Candicidin is defined, in part, as a product "produced by the process of growing a culture of *Streptomyces*

griseus, No. 3570, in a nutrient medium."

There seems to be no case interpreting the breadth of such a claim in an infringement suit. *Purdue Research Foundation* v. *Watson*, cited above, implies that the product would not be covered if produced by a streptomyces of another species. However, it would seem unfair to permit someone who contributed nothing to the development of the new product to use another strain of the species, even though it may have been isolated from another source. Such a person would unquestionably be taking advantage of the teachings of the patent without making any contribution of his own to the useful arts. In the opinion of the writer, the Patent Office is in error in insisting that the particular culture collection number of the organism producing the product be set forth in the product claims when it is necessary to define the product in terms of the process by which it is produced. This is particularly true where the nature of the disclosure is such that it is obvious that several strains will produce the same product.

In U.S. 3,018,220, for instance, the broad method claim calls for cultivating a "hygromycin B-producing strain of *Streptomyces hygroscopicus*" to produce hygromycin B. Other specific claims call for the use of the same species of *Streptomyces*, but refer to collection numbers NRRL-2387, 2388, and 2389. In this particular patent, the product was defined in terms of its physical and chemical properties, but at times the applicant is not able to provide enough of these to satisfy the Patent Office and reference to the process is required.

A preferred manner of claiming the new product seems to be illustrated in the Davisson *et al.* patent mentioned above. The process of Claim 1, which is referred to by the product claim, includes the step of "cultivating *Streptomyces catenulae*." This microorganism was said to be a previously unknown one which had been isolated from soil. A full description of *S. catenulae* was given in the specification and the organism was said to have been deposited with the American Type Culture Collection at Washington, D.C. as collection No. ATCC 12,476. This writer feels that the inventor should be entitled to claims covering catenulin no matter how produced.

A comprehensive article on the subject, "Product by Process Claims and Their Current Status in Chemical Patent Office Practice," by Jon S. Saxe and Julian S. Levitt, appears in 42 JPOS 528, 1960.

Claiming the Process

Some of the problems connected with the claiming of microbiological processes can be studied by referring to specific claims which have been granted by the Patent Office in recent years. The claims to be discussed are not necessarily in the best form, and some of them might not have been allowed under current practices in the Patent Office.

The patent covering streptomycin, 2,449,-866, was issued in 1948. Many of the claims call for fermenting *Actinomyces griseus* in a medium containing meat extract. While meat extract might have been considered an essential requirement of the process at that time, subsequent events have shown that streptomycin can readily be produced in a medium free of meat extract. Other claims require corn steep liquor as an essential component of the fermentation medium. This is a more difficult limitation to avoid as corn steep liquor has been found to be a very important ingredient of most antibiotic liquors. Unless the invention is dependent upon some particular nutrient elements, these should not be recited in the claims. More general phraseology is desirable.

One of the broader claims of the Waksman *et al.* patent is as follows:

"10. A process for the production of streptomycin that comprises growing a culture of a streptomycin-producing strain of *Actinomyces griseus* in a medium containing corn steep liquor, at a suitable incubation temperature and for a suitable period of cultivation, to form streptomycin in the culture broth, separating the culture broth from the organism growth, and recovering streptomycin from the broth."

The Duggar patent covering Aureomycin, U.S. Patent No. 2,482,055 issued September 13, 1949 contains the following claim:

"7. A process which comprises the steps of aerobically fermenting an aqueous nutrient liquor at a temperature within the range 20° to 35° C at a pH between about 4 and 7 with the fungus *Streptomyces aureofaciens*, whereby aureomycin is produced."

When drawing claims to processes such as these, the attorney should keep in mind at all times that conditions which seem essential in the early stages of the development may be found to be unnecessary with further development.

For an example of a more recently issued patent on preparing antibiotics, reference is made to 2,972,569, 1961, to Oliver *et al.* on a process of preparing hortesin. Claim 1 follows:

"1. A process of producing a composition of matter having antifungal activity which comprises cultivating the microorganism *Streptomyces versipellis* NRRL 2528 in an aqueous nutrient medium containing an assimilable source of carbon, nitrogen, and essential trace minerals under submerged aerobic conditions until antifungal activity is imparted to the said solution."

It will be noted that this process claim is not much different from some of the others mentioned above except that it recites "*Streptomyces versipellis* NRRL 2528." Many more recently issued patents could be mentioned in which the culture collection number is specifically named. Whether or not this claim would give protection against the use of another strain of *S. versipellis* is not known to the writer. Apparently some attorneys felt that they could safely limit the claims to specific strains of the microorganism where there was a product claim to give protection.

As might be expected, many process claims deal with improvements which give better yields or the like. In Patent No. 2,828,245, 1958, to Freaney, the invention was based upon the discovery that certain conditions of aeration give better yields of viomycin. The claims of this patent are devoted to this improvement. An example is Claim 1.

"1. A process for the production of viomycin which comprises culturing the organism *Actinomyces vinaceus* on a liquid nutrient medium aerated at a superficial air velocity of from about

0.7 to about 1.0 until the pH of the medium reaches 8.0, then increasing the superficial air velocity to from about 1.5 to about 2.0 until the fermentation is completed, and recovering the viomycin produced."

Not all microbiological process patents deal with antibiotics. U.S. 2,500,825, issued 1950, to Hutchings is directed to the production of pteroyldiglutamylglutamic acid. Claim 1 is as follows:

"1. A process of producing the physiologically active substance, pteroyldiglutamylglutamic acid, which comprises the steps of inoculating a growth medium with a non-pathogenic microorganism of the genus Corynebacterium, allowing fermentation to take place, and separating pteroyldiglutamylglutamic acid from the fermented medium."

While this limitation as to separation of the acid was not a serious one in this particular case, it should be kept in mind that many antibiotic products are used in animal feeds, for which it is not always necessary to separate the antibiotic from the fermented medium. Such limitations should not, therefore, be used unless necessary or unless the attorney is certain that they would do not harm.

Claim 1 of U.S. 2,602,769 issued July 8, 1952 to Murray *et al.* is as follows:

"1. A process for the production of an eleven oxgenated steroid comprising the step of aerobically subjecting a steroid containing an eleven methylene group to the action of oxygenating enzymes produced by a growth of an oxygenating species of fungus of the order Mucorales."

This claim is not limited to any particular steroid except those that have an 11-methylene group, and it is not restricted to any particular species of fungus. It covers all oxygenating species of the order Mucorales, which is large. As might be expected, this claim is based upon a tremendous amount of experimental data and the Examiner was apparently convinced that the applicants were entitled to a claim of such scope.

Similarly, in Patent 2,980,590, 1961, to Broquist *et al.* for the production of lysine, the broad process claims were not limited to any particular microorganism. In fact, the claims merely call for subjecting the intermediate raw material to the action of the enzymes of yeast. It was shown in the specification that these enzymes could be extracted from the yeast cells and perform their function in the absence of the living propagating cells. Claim 1 of the patent is as follows:

"1. A method of preparing free L-lysine which comprises the step of subjecting alpha-aminoadipic acid in amounts from 1 to 10 mg./ml. to the action of the enzymes of yeast at a pH from 3.0 to 5.0 and a temperature from 5° C to 50° C."

Sometimes the amount of work available will not support such broad claims as just discussed. Claim 1 of U.S. Patent No. 2,-789,940, 1957, to Feldman *et al.* is as follows:

"1. A process which comprises the step of subjecting a member of the group consisting of Reichstein's Substance S and esters thereof to the oxidative fermentative action of *Botrytis cinera* and recovering therefrom hydrocortisone."

In this process claim the applicants covered only the one species, *Botrytis cinera,* and a small group of related steroids.

The particular facts of each case will govern the scope of claims sought and granted.

Cross-references: *Medical Associations and Physicians' Patent Policies, Pharmaceutical Patent Practice, Plant Patents, Utility.*

MISUSE. See USE PATENTS

MISUSE OF PATENTS
J. Philip Anderegg

General Principles

A patentee may be denied relief against an infringer or contributory infringer of his patent, or against a licensee thereunder in a suit for royalties, if the patentee has employed the patent in an effort to secure for himself or for someone else a complete or partial monopoly, or even merely a preferred position, in the sale of something other than the invention claimed in the patent, or if he has employed the patent in any of various anti-competitive ways such as an effort to hinder trade in goods competitive with the invention. In such a case, the patentee is said to have "misused" his patent, and he will not be allowed successfully to assert it in court against anyone until he has discontinued his misuse thereof and until the consequences of his misuse have been dissipated. It is in general immaterial that such conduct of the patentee may not have injured the infringer or licensee against whom the patentee seeks relief. Indeed, that infringer or licensee may be a stranger to the actions of the patentee which constitute misuse.

Rationale of the Patent Misuse Rule. A United States patent confers upon its owner the right to exclude others from making, using or selling the invention claimed therein. How then shall the owner of the patent best exploit it? One view (a dissenting one) is that all he may do is to exclude all others, be himself the sole maker or seller, and sell the patented invention for all that the traffic will bear, or else sell licenses (presumably nondiscriminatory, unrestricted, and nonexclusive in type) for all that the traffic in licenses will bear. See "Report of the Attorney General's National Committee to Study the Anti-Trust Laws," U.S. Government Printing Office, p. 235, 1955.

It has also been suggested, in another dissenting view, that, since the patentee is entitled to keep the public from enjoying the invention at all until the expiration of the patent, he should be entitled not only to forbid to the public access to the invention unconditionally, but also on any condition which does not tend "to bring about a state of things that there is a predominant public interest to prevent." Holmes, J. dissenting, in *Motion Picture Patents Co. v. Universal Film Mfg. Co.*, 243 U.S. 502 at p. 520, 1917. Thus the grant of a patent license only on the condition that the licensee commit an act in itself tortious or criminal would certainly render the patent unenforceable even under this standard. On the other hand, the grant of a license on the condition that the licensee purchase from the patentee unpatented components or materials to be used by the licensee in making the patented article under the license would

not have had that result, if Mr. Justice Holmes's view had prevailed because, as he thought, the patentee was entitled to suppress the invention entirely for any reason whatever, or for no reason at all. By such a license the patentee would be enabled to dominate the market for the unpatented components or materials only to the extent of the public's desire to obtain the patented article, to which it had no right anyway without the patentee's consent.

As Mr. Justice Holmes himself had said, however, the life of the law has not been logic, but experience, and we must live with another standard, perhaps less definite than either of the last two suggested, and which represents the accommodation made by the Federal courts between the policy of the patent laws and the policy of the antitrust laws. In recent years, it has been the policy of the antitrust laws which has been given the benefit of the doubt in cases of apparent conflict between the two.

Certainly the present law is clear that the power of the patentee to refuse a license does not include the lesser power to license arbitrarily on his own conditions. *U.S. v. Masonite Corp.*, 316 U.S. 265, 1942.

In 1926 the Supreme Court said, in *U.S. v. General Electric Co.*, 272 U.S. 476, that a patentee might grant a license to make and sell, limiting however the licensee's right to sell by limiting the method of sale and the price, "provided the conditions of sale are normally and reasonably adapted to secure pecuniary reward for the patentee's monopoly," at page 491. In that case, a license from G.E., a manufacturer of incandescent lamps, to Westinghouse to make incandescent lamps under G.E.'s lamp patents and to sell them at prices fixed by G.E. from time to time, was held not to constitute a violation of the antitrust laws, and the validity of the license was sustained.

The Department of Justice has urged the Supreme Court to overrule the 1926 G.E. case, and in *U.S. v. Line Material Co.*, 333 U.S. 287, 1948 four out of the eight justices participating voted to do so. The 1926 G.E. case thus continues as a precedent, perhaps a weakened one and restricted by subsequent holdings to its particular facts. At least one of the Federal Courts of Appeals has held that plural licenses of the type sustained in the G.E. case constitute patent misuse. *Newburgh Moire Co., Inc.* v. *Superior Moire Co., Inc.*, 237 F.2d 283, 111 USPQ 126, CA 3 1956.

The phrase of the G.E. opinion, sanctioning a license to make, use and sell on conditions "provided the conditions of sale are normally and reasonably adapted to secure pecuniary reward for the patentee's monopoly" has been much quoted. It is however for the Federal courts to decide which "conditions" fit this rule. They have decided that the power of the patentee to refuse a license does not include the lesser power to grant a license on condition that the licensee purchase from the patentee, for use in practicing the patent, components or materials which the patentee cannot exclude others from making, using or selling by means of the patent licensed. Specifically, it has been held by the Supreme Court that, if the patentee does grant such licenses, he may not enforce his patent against an infringer, *B. B. Chemical Co.* v. *Ellis*, 314 U.S. 495, 1942, or against a contributory infringer, *Mercoid Corp.* v. *Mid-Continent Co.*, 320 U.S. 661, 1944.

Likewise, if he leases machines made by or for him under his patent on condition that unpatented materials handled or dispensed by the machines be purchased from him, he may not obtain relief against a direct infringer making machines which infringe the patent. *Morton Salt Co.* v. *G. S. Suppiger Co.*, 314 U.S. 488, 1942. The grant of such a license, or of such a lease, constitutes "misuse" of the patent.

More generally, the Supreme Court and the lower federal courts have denied relief to patentees in a variety of circumstances, the common feature of which has been an attempt by the patentee to use the leverage of his patent to advance his commercial interest in something other and different from the invention claimed in his patent.

The denial of relief has been grounded on an application or extension of the equitable maximum that

"He who comes into court must come with clean hands"

and that courts may appropriately withhold their aid where the plaintiff is using the right asserted by him contrary to the public interest. *Morton Salt Co.* v. *Suppiger Co.*, supra. It is said that the privilege to exclude which is conferred by the patent is conditioned by a public purpose. *Mercoid Corporation* v. *Mid-Continent Co.*, supra. It is said also that patents, though based upon express constitutional authority, constitute an exception to a pervasive philosophy of competition expressed in the antitrust laws, and that the exception will be narrowly restricted to the precise terms of the grant, i.e., to the power to exclude from making, using or selling the invention defined by the claims of the patent as interpreted in the light of the descriptive specification. *Ethyl Gasoline Corp.* v. *U.S.*, 309 U.S. 436, 1940.

It is further said that the advancement of science and the useful arts to the benefit of the public is the dominant purpose of the patent system and that reward to the inventor is subordinate. *U.S.* v. *Masonite Corp.*, 316 U.S. 265, 1942. Hence, it is concluded, the injury to the public, as, for example, in the loss of competition for supply to the public of unpatented materials even as to the incorporation thereof into the patented article, which loss would tend to flow from successful prosecution of infringement suits on misused patents, takes the place of and makes unnecessary any showing that the misuse complained of has injured the infringer. *Morton Salt Co.* v. *Suppiger Co.*, supra.

Misuse of Patents Through Use Thereof as the Effective Means of Restraining Competition with the Patentee in the Sale of Unpatented Materials

The *B. B. Chemical, Morton Salt* and *Mercoid* cases already cited held that a patentee may not grant a license to practice a patent or lease a patented machine on condition that the licensee obtain from the patentee, or from a source selected by him, unpatented materials for use in practicing the patent or in using the leased machine. The rule holds as to both article and process patents and for suits against both direct and contributory infringers. It has been applied notwithstanding the patentee's undertaking to meet the market price for the material, *International Salt Co.* v. *U.S.*, 332 U.S. 392, 1947, and even where the inducement to buy supplies from the patentee is less than a refusal of a lease or license except upon the buyer's agreement to do so. Thus in *White Cap Co.* v. *Owens Illinois Glass Co.*, 203 F.2d 694, 97 USPQ 192, CA 6 1953, it was recognized to be misuse for the holder of a patent on a machine to lease machines built thereunder on terms which indemnified the lessee against claims of third parties for patent infringement, but only as to use of the machines with materials supplied by the lessor.

Indeed, the holder of a patent on a process or compound who derives revenue from sales of an ingredient used in the process or compound may be well advised in selling the ingredient, at least if it is a staple article or commodity of commerce having substantial non-infringing use, to state separately on his sales one price for the ingredient and another price for the license to use the ingredient in the process or compound of his patent, and to declare his willingness to sell at the same price licenses for practice of the patent with the ingredient as purchased from any source.

Neither may the patentee use his patent in other ways to sell something which is not protected and claimed in the patent.

Thus it has also been held to be misuse for the patentee to refuse to lease or sell the patented article except in combination with other apparatus not covered by the patent, where the article and apparatus were physically and functionally separate. *Cardox Corp.* v. *Armstrong Coalbreak*, 194 F.2d 376, 92 USPQ 296, CA 7 1952; *Stearns* v. *Tinker & Rasor*, 252 F.2d 589, 116 USPQ 222, CA 9 1957. Even if so physically and functionally severable, however, when the patented product is to be used as part of a larger system and when the patentee has assumed or in the trade will be held to have assumed responsibility for the whole, then he may be justified in refusing to sell the patented product except with the other components of the system. *Electric Pipe Line* v.

Fluid System, 231 F.2d 370, 109 USPQ 24, CA 2 1956; *Dehydrating Process Co.* v. *A. O. Smith Corp.*, 292 F.2d 653, CA 1 1961. As to the requirement of physical and functional severability, this last case observes, that a one-legged man is not entitled to demand that a shoe seller sell him a left shoe. When such severability exists however, and when the art has matured to the point where components of a system from separate manufacturers can be expected to work satisfactorily together, the charge of misuse might be better avoided by establishing specifications for the performance of the other components of the system, rather than by insisting that they be purchased from the patentee.

Other Types of Patent Misuse

Patents have been held to be misused in a wide variety of ways other than those already discussed. A few examples will be given here.

(1) The threat or prosecution of actions for patent infringement, when carried out as part of a plan to effectuate or perpetuate a monopoly different from that of the patents sued upon, as, for example, where all of the patents in a field are combined into common ownership, especially if the patents are non-interfering so that one patent can be practiced without a license under the other. *Kobe, Inc.* v. *Dempsey Pump Co.*, 198 F.2d 416, 94 USPQ 43, CA 10 1952.

(2) Grant of a license on condition that the licensee (or licensor) shall abstain from making or dealing in goods competitive with those covered by the licensed patent. *National Lock Washer Co.* v. *Geo. K. Garrett Co.*, 137 F.2d 255, 58 USPQ 460, CA 3 1943; *McCullough* v. *Kammerer Corp.*, 166 F.2d 759, 76 USPQ 503, CA 9 1948.

As to nonexclusive licenses, this principle seems to be well-established law. An exclusive licensee, on the other hand, is usually said to be under an implied obligation to exploit the patent in good faith, since the patentee has usually disabled himself from doing so and has at least promised to grant no further nonexclusive licenses. At least prior to *Mercoid Corp.* v. *Mid-Continent Co.*, 320 U.S. 661, this obligation was thought to require the exclusive licensee to refrain from dealing in goods competitive with the invention of the licensed patent. Yet the Third Circuit Court of Appeals has concluded that the rule of the *National Lock Washer* case applies even in the case of an exclusive license. *Park-in Theatres, Inc.* v. *Paramount-Richards Theatres, Inc.*, 185 F.2d 407, 88 USPQ 165 CA 3 1950.

(3) Refusal of the patentee to distribute the patented product to dealers except on conditions that the dealers agree not to sell other goods competitive with the patented product, or on condition that the dealers agree to accept from the patentee other goods not covered by the patent. *Russell* v. *Consumers Insulation Co.*, 226 F.2d 373, 107 USPQ 131, CA 3 1955; *Preformed Line Products* v. *Fanner*, 328 F.2d 265, 140 USPQ 500, CA 6 1964.

(4) Grant of a patent license withholding from the licensee the right to practice the patent insofar as such practice would fall within the claims of an expired patent. *Prestole Corporation* v. *Tinnerman Products, Inc.*, 271 F.2d 146, 123 USPQ 242, CA 6 1959. This was held to be misuse of the unexpired patent in extending the monopoly of the expired patent.

(5) Grant of a license under plural patents with royalties, based upon a product definition not coextensive with the claims of unexpired patents, to continue until the expiration of the last licensed patent. *American Securit Co.* v. *Shatterproof Glass Co.*, 268 F.2d 769, 122 USPQ 167, CA 3 1959. And see *Ar-Tik System, Inc.* v. *Dairy Queen, Inc.*, 302 F.2d 496, 133 USPQ 109, CA 3 1962. The question whether a patent license calling for the payment of royalties after expiration of the patent is a misuse is however not fully settled. *Thys Co.* v. *Brulotte*, 138 USPQ 411, Wash. S.Ct. 1963, held that it was not. Certiorari has been granted by the Supreme Court. And it should be noted here that, in *Automatic Radio Mfg. Co.* v. *Hazeltine Research Co.*, 339 U.S. 827, 1950, the Supreme Court sustained, in a suit for royalties, a nonexclusive license under which the licensee had acquired for ten years the privilege of using, in the manufacture of the licensee's "home" products, any or all of the licensor's present or future patents related

to radio broadcasting apparatus, in return for a royalty payment consisting of a small percentage of the licensee's sales of complete radio broadcasting receivers (with a $10,000 a year minimum) whether any of the licensed patents and applications were embodied in those receivers or not.

(6) Grant of a license under one patent on condition that the licensee accept a license under another patent, at least where large numbers of patents are involved. *American Securit Co.* v. *Shatterproof Glass Co.*, 268 F.2d 769, 122 USPQ 167, CA 3 1959, cert. den. 361 U.S. 902, 1959.

(7) Grant of plural nonexclusive licenses limited as to field, with a separate field for each licensee, where the effect of such licenses is to insulate the licensees from competition with each other in the sale of apparatus embodying the patented invention. *Baldwin-Lima Hamilton Corp.* v. *Tatnall Measuring Systems Co.*, 169 F. Supp. 1, 120 USPQ 34, DC EPa 1958, affirmed per curiam 268 F.2d 395, 121 USPQ 363, CA 3 1959, cert. den. 361 U.S. 894.

Conclusion

Like other branches of the law, that concerning misuse of patents is in a condition of continued change. As recently as 1955, the Attorney General's Committee to Study the Antitrust Laws expressed the opinion (at page 251 of its Report) that the misuse doctrine should extend only to those cases where a realistic analysis shows that the patent itself significantly contributes to the practice under attack. It cannot as yet be said, however, that this expression of opinion has restricted the type of conduct held to constitute misuse.

A recent development which may become important is the increasing interest of the Federal Trade Commission in misuse or abuse of patents as constituting unfair methods of competition and unfair practices in interstate commerce, in violation of Section 5 of the Federal Trade Commission Act. An example of this is the Federal Trade Commission Order issued December 17, 1963 (F.T.C. Docket No. 7211) to Charles Pfizer and Co., Inc., requiring Pfizer to grant non-discriminatory licenses, with know-how, under its tetracyclene patent. This order was based on findings by the Federal Trade Commission that Pfizer had obtained its patent through misrepresentations to and withholding of information from the Patent Office in the prosecution of the application on which the patent issued. Another example is the Federal Trade Commission order to a maker of patented shrimp processing machinery to lease the machinery on non-discriminatory terms and to sell it to U.S. as well as to foreign shrimp canners. The order was based upon a finding that discrimination in leasing terms has been imposed in order to protect the manufacturer's interest in shrimp canning, and that the machinery had become a necessity in the shrimp processing industry. *Grand Caillou Packing Co., Inc. et al.*, F.T.C. Docket No. 7887, June 4, 1964.

Cross-references: *Act of 1952—Patents, Antitrust Law and Patents, Clean Hands Doctrine, Copyrights in Relation to Patents, Infringement, Managing and Marketing Patents, Section on Label Licenses, Monopolies..., Package Licenses, Trademarks in Relation to Patents.*

MONOPOLIES, "INVENTION" AND SECTION 103

Judge Giles S. Rich

[The following is a reproduction approved by the author of his Kettering Award Acceptance address delivered under a different title and published in the 1964 Conference Number of the Patent, Trademark, and Copyright Journal of Research and Education of the Patent, Trademark and Copyright Research Institute of The George Washington University. Certain headings have been added. Ed.]

I believe in incentive systems. Over 20 years ago a prize competition lured me into some intense study and writing[1] which, through a traceable chain of events, has led to the opportunity for this address.

I did not win the prize. Neither did the other contestants, save one.[2] But they all contributed something. That is the way incentive systems work. They bring out all kinds of efforts, excellent, good, mediocre,

indifferent, and bad. But the *system* brings forth the effort. Society benefits from the good and mediocre, as well as the excellent, efforts. The bad efforts don't hurt it any. They may even prevent others from making mistakes if they are made known.

The patent and copyright laws create such incentive systems. The copyright laws provide an incentive which brings out the greatest works of literature and art as well as a lot of trash. The patent system works in a similar way. But you can't get cream without producing milk and, anyway, it is the milk that society lives on.

I don't suppose you will be surprised if I talk about the patent system. The aspect of it I will talk about is the one I think causes the most trouble, the clarification of which I therefore believe would do the most good.

Monopolies—Bad and Good

A monopoly merely gives rise to *power* which can be put to either good or bad uses. Hence, in the case of monopolies created by government grant, which all patents are so far as the rights they create are concerned,[3] we have to distinguish between good and bad monopolies.

I will take two well-known examples from history. First, the bad monopoly. Queen Elizabeth granted to one Darcy, a member of her court, a monopoly of playing cards for 21 years so that he could make some money. But playing cards were old and well-known and others were earning a living from making and selling them in England. This monopoly, which was by Royal Letters Patent, therefore took from the public a freedom in business which it had long enjoyed before the patent; therefore, it was bad.[4]

In Venice in 1594 the Doge, on behalf of the government, granted to the great Galileo a "privilege," which was the Venetian name for a patent, on a machine which he had *invented* "for raising water and irrigating land with small expense and great convenience," on the condition that it had never before been thought of or made by others. Galileo made a couple of significant remarks in his petition for the privilege. He said, "it not being fit that this invention, which is my own, discovered by me with great labor and expense, be made the common property of everyone . . ."; he also stated that if he were granted the privilege, "I shall the more attentively apply myself to new inventions for universal benefit." In short, he was not inclined to divulge his invention only to have it copied; but if the government would give him some reasonable protection he would not only divulge it and build it but might even apply himself to making some more inventions. Deeming this to be a *good* use to which to put a limited monopoly, the Council voted to grant him a "privilege" or patent of monopoly for 21 years.[5]

The Venetians were accustomed to doing this, having granted about 1600 "privileges" in the 15th and 16th centuries.[6]

The English in 1624 enacted a statute [7] abolishing and prohibiting future monopolies of the bad Darcy sort and authorizing the continuing grant of Letters Patent for new inventions within the realm, which has continued to this day.

The founding fathers came to America from the mother country, bringing with them knowledge of this practice of granting monopolies. In the nearly 150 years of the colonial period preceding the Federal Constitution, the colonies and then the States granted numerous patents for new inventions as well as monopolies to encourage the founding of new industries, including, as the English did, encouragement of setting up in America industries already practiced abroad.[8]

It is not surprising that, when it came to the writing of a Constitution, provision should be incorporated, with no controversy at all, for Congress to make laws for the granting of patents to inventors, or that George Washington should urge its speedy enactment, or that the very first Congress should enact our first Patent Act of 1790.[9]

Then began our patent system. One might describe it as a great experiment which goes on continuously, getting more complex all the time, in which this Institute is playing, for the first time, a vital role in finding out how the system actually works, as an aid to preserving its basic principles and saving the obvious good that is in it.

In this experiment, which involves a mixture of economics, law, technology, and psychology, we still have the centuries-old problem of monopoly power being utilized for socially good and socially bad ends and of deciding which is which.

The greedy nature of some men is such that there are always pressures toward the creation of bad monopolies. Undue preoccupation with countering this pressure, however, has quite blurred the vision of many well-intentioned but not too well-informed people to the good uses monopoly can be put to and to the good that monopoly power can do, properly channeled and not so proscribed as to lose its effective power.

Paradoxically, in the working of the patent system, monopoly often promotes competition. Numerous instances are all around us, wherever two products serving the same general purpose have achieved, with the aid of patent protection, commercial production. And only after such production is there any possibility of market competition.

To this point I have taken note that the *primary* distinction between good and bad patent monopolies is that the good patent does not monopolize something the public *already has*, so as to take something away from the public. The invention covered by the good patent must be *new*, and so our statutes have always provided, though the provision was not always enforced.[10]

Patentability

But beyond bare novelty one must go one further and troublesome step to have a sound system and keep the monopoly on the good side.

As we refrain from granting patents on inventions that are not new, we must also refrain from granting patents on those inventions which would arise *spontaneously*, given the need or the desire for them, as the yelp of the dog surely follows from stepping on his tail, or with *only a nominal expenditure of time, effort, money or wit*— especially if the invention is one of real utility likely to meet with popular demand.

It was not long after the Patent Act of

1836—in 1850 in fact—that the United States Supreme Court made this clear in the "doorknob case," *Hotchkiss* v. *Greenwood*.[11] What was involved was the trial judge's charge to a jury that if *no more ingenuity or skill was required* to construct the patented doorknob *than was possessed by an ordinary mechanic acquainted with the business*, then the patent was invalid.

The Supreme Court approved the charge. The opinion said: "In other words, the improvement is *the work of the skilled mechanic, not that of the inventor*." (My emphasis.) The decision made clear that patents are not to be granted on inventions which are no more than what the ordinary mechanic acquainted with the business would produce as a matter of course in the pursuit of his calling. Such mechanics are expected to produce *new* things, such as were involved in that case, which was the attaching of an old clay doorknob to an old metal shank in precisely the same manner that metal doorknobs had been attached to such shanks before. Technically the assembly was *new*, but the court found novelty was not enough.

In referring to "mechanics" in this matter we can take them to be representative of a class—all those with ordinary skill in the various callings, ordinary shoemakers, ordinary chemists, electronic technicians of ordinary skill, etc.

Due to the reasoning of the case, that the new doorknob "was the work of the skillful mechanic, not that of the inventor," what came out of it after 1850, and is still with us, was an injection into the law of what has ever since been called the "requirement for invention."

As is usual with a "doctrine" derived from a court opinion, the doctrine persists while the facts out of which it arose are forgotten. The opinion in the first case is quoted to the judge in a second and he does an opinion embroidering on it, his words being quoted in turn and reembroidered and so on.

I think the resulting situation with respect to the law on the "requirement for invention" was well summed up by Judge Learned Hand, who knew as much patent law as any judge ever has, at a Senate hearing in which your then Dean Colclough and I both participated in 1955, as follows:

"You could find nearly anything you liked if you went to the opinions. It was a subject on which judges loved to be rhetorical.... patent lawyers ... like to quote all those things. There are lots of them." [12]

This proliferation of views on what did and did not amount to "invention" went on for 100 years. We were enlightened with the view that "invention" resulted from the exercise of the "inventive faculties" and other circular reasoning. Our present standard text, Walker, now in its seventh edition, says "An invention is the result of an inventive act." [13] Whole books on the patent law were written around such concepts. People collected the statements pro and con in volumes equally divided about in the middle—"invention" on one side, lack of it on the other. Negative and positive tests for detecting its presence evolved. So did exceptions to each test. And patent lawyers selectively quoted all of this mass of material as though it proved something. Judges like Learned Hand found, in his words, that "They never seemed to tend toward enlightenment." [14]

This requirement finally evolved into a *"standard* of invention" which the courts pretended was being raised and lowered like an elevator as though it were something tangible. They also proclaimed in all seriousness—and are doing so this very summer—that this "standard" was to be found in the Constitution, where there are only two words on which it could possibly be predicated, the word "inventors" and the word "discoveries." [14a] You really have to be on the Supreme Court to find a "standard" there because the only way it works is this: if you think the lower court was wrong in sustaining the patent, you proclaim that it applied too low a standard and reverse its decision.[15]

Some judges got it fixed in their minds that if a thing is an "invention" then it is patentable and if it is not patentable then it is not an "invention," not realizing that the same things are invented over and over —by the use of the inventive faculties or by inventive acts or what have you—and although clearly "inventions," their originators being as firmly convinced of it as was Galileo, they are not patentable for want of novelty. So it is customary for judges to approach all inventions gingerly in their opinions by referring to them as "alleged" or "supposed" inventions.

All an invention is, however, is something which has been found out, or devised, or discovered. The question today is not what to call it but whether under the statute it is patentable. Hundreds of "real" or "true" inventions, all resulting from "inventive acts" and the exercise of the "inventive faculties," are held unpatentable every day for lack of novelty.

The Patent Office, of course, proceeded on the same basis, and still does so to a dwindling extent, rejecting applications for want of "invention" and granting them when it could be persuaded that "invention" was present. And through it all the patent lawyers and the judges persisted in telling all concerned that "invention" was something which could not be defined, like God! Patent validity came as a matter of grace, from on high. This was a messy state of affairs. The surprising thing is it worked so well. But not well enough.

In 1941 a Commission, appointed by President Roosevelt, and headed by Charles F. Kettering,[16] came out with a report which said:

"One of the greatest technical weaknesses of the patent system is the lack of a definitive yardstick as to *what is invention*. To provide such a yardstick and to assure that the various courts of law and the Patent Office *shall use the same standards,* several changes are suggested. It is proposed that Congress shall declare a national standard whereby [mark these words] *patentability* of *an* invention shall be determined by the objective test as to its advancement of the arts and sciences." (My emphasis.) [17]

One apparent thought there was to stop talking about whether a thing is or is not an "invention," to take anything presented as *an* invention, and then to determine its *patentability* according to a standard which Congress was to declare, Congress never having said anything about it up to that time.

For some years nothing came of the Kettering Commission proposal but in the 79th, 80th, and 81st Congresses, from 1945 through 1949, identical bills were pending entitled, unfortunately but almost inevitably, "A bill to declare a national policy for determining invention." Now I have just said that the problem was not really to determine "invention," but to determine the *patentability of* inventions and this matter of language is one of major concern. Kettering got a hold on the distinction, but it keeps fading away like Alice's cat.

People don't think so much as they talk; and when they do think, they tend to think in words, at least about legal abstractions. Words are used to describe things, concepts, and experiences we have in common so that we can communicate. This thing, this concept, this experience every patent examiner, lawyer, and judge had come up against in practice was called the "requirement of invention" or just "invention"—the undefinable something or other that has to be there. This proves to be a cliché, meaningless though it is, that is hard to break away from. I taught for many years, and presumably my students learned, that the prerequisites to patentability were novelty, utility, and invention. There was nothing else to teach. Thinking and its concomitant words had not progressed beyond that point in the '30s and '40s. But today they have. Any current textbook and most cases, you will find, use the old terminology. But it isn't true any more and hasn't been for eleven and a half years—in my opinion, that is.

My not believing in ghosts or angels doesn't mean, *in law,* that there are no ghosts or angels, because if you think there are, and are frightened or informed by them, then they exist. As long as judges say there is a requirement for "invention," and many still do, then there is one. If you take a patent into court and the judge invalidates it for want of "invention" you *know* there is one. But why am I saying there is none? Am I talking theory or law; if law, then what kind of law? Or am I talking nonsense?

Section 103 of 1952 Act. The outcome of those bills to determine invention, and one or two other bills, was that Congress got interested in revising and codifying the patent law and did so.[17a] In the new law (Title 35 U.S.C.) is a section, 103, described at the time by those who wrote it, at least in one place, as "incorporating a requirement for invention."[18] It was also described more carefully and accurately elsewhere[19] as providing a *"condition which exists in our law and has existed for more than 100 years ... by reason of decisions of the courts."* (My emphasis.) And that "condition" is described in the title of this new Section 103 as one for the existence of "non-obvious subject matter." The addition of Section 103 was stated in the House Report on the bill[20] to be *one of the two major changes or innovations in the statute.*

What Section 103 itself says is that what is patented must *not* have been *obvious* to one of *ordinary* skill *in the art involved,* at the *time* the invention was made. The parallel with what would be expected of the "ordinary mechanic acquainted with the business" in the "doorknob case" should be clear.

This is not a "standard of invention," and it is not called a "requirement of invention." The presence or absence of "invention" is not mentioned. The use of the term "invention" was, in fact, carefully avoided with a view to making a fresh start, free of all the divergent court opinions and rhetorical pronouncements about "invention."[21] And in doing that it was contemplated, as the House Report states,[22] that "This section should have a stabilizing effect and minimize great departures which have appeared in some cases."

As has been pointed out by one of the drafters of that section, Mr. Federico, in his Commentary,[23] what Section 103 was gunning for was

"... some modification ... in the direction of moderating the extreme degrees of strictness exhibited in a number of judicial opinions over the past dozen or so years; that is, that some change of attitude more favorable to patents is hoped for. This is indicated by the language used in Section 103 as well as by the general tenor of remarks of the Committees in the reports and particular comments."

The real vice or inadequacy of the judge-made requirement for "invention" was in the truism Mr. Federico also restated, "the so-called standard of invention ... is an unmeasurable quantity having different meanings for different persons." It left every judge practically scott-free to decide this often controlling factor according to his personal philosophy of what inventions should be patented, whether or not he had any competence to do so or any knowledge of the patent system as an operative socio-economic force. This was too great a freedom because it involves national policy which should be declared by Congress, not by individual judges or even groups of judges on multiple-judge courts. In Section 103 Congress made such a policy declaration. It did not there declare what should constitute "invention." It was a statement of something to take the place of this vague concept. And it was made in the face of judicial declarations, made in the *absence* of a statute, which Congress expressly desired to modify.

Unobviousness versus Standard of Invention. I would like to inject a new term into the language so we can discuss the matter rationally. I would like to call it the *third requirement* of patentability. The statute sets out all the requirements in the clearest possible form. Section 101 says inventions must be *new* and *useful,* requirements one and two; Section 102 defines novelty; and Section 103 lays down the *third requirement.* I repeat its clear-cut title:

"Conditions for patentability; non-obvious subject matter."

Upon examination in the Patent Office or upon adjudication in court, under the statute, when novelty, utility, and unobviousness as defined in Section 103 are found to exist, there is *patentability* and *that is the end of the matter.* An examination for the presence or absence of "invention," or of precedents on that muddy issue, is not called for and is not proper. It is a work of supererogation. It illustrates, furthermore, a failure to grasp the meaning of the statutory provisions. There is no such prerequisite in the statutory law.

When, as is the case with the "requirement for invention," the century's accumulation of judicial precedents ranges from A to Z and when Congress, looking at the situation under the guiding light of Kettering's statement that *this is no yardstick and is the greatest technical weakness of the patent system,* determines to make a yardstick and says the measure shall be "M," right in the middle of the alphabet, it behooves everyone concerned with administering that law to follow the measure "M" and to stop flitting about arbitrarily from A to Z, lighting upon that letter which seems most appealing.

But what do we have today? A host of lawyers, examiners and judges all doing their level best to follow the law as Congress wrote it? Anything but that! What we have today is a mish-mash, and that is a nice old English term, older than the 1624 Statute of Monopolies. Why do we have a mish-mash?

First, a century of thinking and writing about a phenomenon in one set of nomenclature is a hard thing to overcome. Also a lot of people go on administering the patent laws and practicing under them without bothering to read the revision of them, so they are not aware that there has been a change.

Second, by hindsight it is apparent that those most intimately concerned with the writing and expounding of the new patent act in 1952, themselves brought up in the "requirement for invention" tradition (and I speak as one of them), did a very poor job of informing the public what it was they had done. One reason for this was that, on the average, their own comprehension of what they had done was not too clear. Remember, they were all of the school that "invention" *could not* be defined and there they were, trying to put a provision on that very subject into the statute. In going as far as seemed to be possible in that direction, they knew they were not making a *definition* but rather a *statement of policy,* a *specific required approach* to a difficult problem, which approach they thought would stop some of the nonsense, derogatory of the patent system, that had been going on. In pursuit of that objective, the drafters and Congress did one thing, by way of a statement of policy to counteract

a judicial trend, which has had a clear-cut effect. Following a phrase casually dropped by the Supreme Court in *Cuno* v. *Automatic,*[24] in 1941, that "the new device, however useful it may be, must reveal the flash of creative genius," some courts took off on a quest for such a flash and, not finding it, invalidated patents. The last sentence of Section 103 stopped this abruptly with the legislative command: "Patentability shall not be negatived by the manner in which the invention was made." But the judicial reaction to the first sentence,[25] in contrast, got to be all fouled up.

Third, the members of the bar have a lot to answer for in creating and perpetuating the mish-mash because it is they who, desiring to make use of some of the extreme cases antedating the patent act to invalidate patents in litigation, played down Section 103 and early in its life persuaded a number of courts that it made no change whatever but was "mere codification."[25a] They are now paying more attention to Section 103 as they learn that it can help them when they are on the other side, but they are learning slowly and my generation of lawyers, at least, is still talking, out of habit, in terms of "invention." Just listen to them!

Find me a trial lawyer for an infringer who will not urge on the court, as the existing test for "invention," the views expressed by the Justices of the Supreme Court in *A & P* v. *Supermarket,* in 1950,[26] two years before the effective date of Section 103, and I will joyfully transfer my Kettering Award to him. He would deserve it more than I do. I have no clients. Herein lies a grave defect in the development of sound law through adversary proceedings.

Fourth, in the legislature the mish-mash has been described in detail, up to 1957 (the first 5 years of the act), in Senate Committee Study No. 7. What is its title? "Efforts to Establish a Statutory Standard of Invention."[27] The Senate Patent Subcommittee is still striving to bring about a higher degree of uniformity in the courts, in the various groups of the Patent Office, and between the two organizations, but in what terms does it do its own thinking? The subcommittee's annual Report (No.

107), April 3, 1963, is concerned about the "Patent Office 'standard of invention' " and refers to the development by that office of a "policy statement pertaining to standards of invention." The report for the next year (No. 1018), May 1, 1964, again refers to the need to eliminate differences within the Patent Office and between it and the courts "concerning the standard of invention." Meanwhile, apparently without the committee's knowledge, the Patent Office Academy has been teaching that there is no "standard of invention," that "invention" is meaningless, and that the prerequisite is as stated in Section 103. Might it not do some good and help to achieve the uniformity the subcommittee so much desires if its own members, and staff, could convince themselves, in spite of what uninformed judges have said, that the 1952 Patent Act was intended by their fellow legislators to *replace* the "standard of invention," which never was a standard, with a requirement of unobviousness to a particular kind of person at a particular time?

Amid the confusion, there are some encouraging signs in the courts. During the first few years after the 1952 act, many courts took the position that Congress really had done *nothing* in enacting Section 103 and went about their old business of looking for "invention." Then in 1955 came Judge Learned Hand's *Lyon* v. *Bausch & Lomb* [28] opinion and in 1960 his *Reiner* v. *I. Leon* [29] opinion, both of which realistically appraised and appreciated what Section 103 had done, namely, to restore the law to what it had been 20 or 30 years earlier, as he said, "to change the slow but steady drift of judicial decision that had been hostile to patents. . . ." In the former opinion he remarked that " 'invention' became perhaps the most baffling concept in the whole catalogue of judicial efforts to provide postulates for indefinitely varying occasions." In the latter he said "It is not for us [the judiciary] to decide what 'discoveries' shall 'promote the progress of science and the useful arts' sufficiently to grant any 'exclusive right' of [to?] inventors. Nor may we approach the interpretation of Section 103 . . . with a predetermined bias." While saying "The test laid down [in Sec-

tion 103] is indeed misty enough," he was able, with the evidence provided, to follow it. Certiorari was denied in both of these cases. In both cases the patents were sustained. The Supreme Court could easily have upset him had it wanted to. In fact, Judge Hand remarked to me and others at that Senate hearing in 1955 [30], "Oh, they must take it," referring to *Bausch & Lomb*. Later during the hearing he testified,[31] "whether we were right in construing it [Section 103] as meaning that the old rules were to apply, remains to be seen. I hope the case will go up." From the viewpoint of the writers of the law, he was very right!

Last April (1964) in *Marvel* v. *Bell*,[32] the Fourth Circuit Court of Appeals, which in 1954 said Section 103 merely codified the law, came to the conclusion, after reading a number of cases which "have undertaken to comprehensively set forth the standard of invention to be used as a test," that

"When the mass of verbiage has been distilled, however, we have little more to guide us than the test which is incorporated in Section 103. . . ."

The Court then went in search of the "objective criteria of [un]obviousness." Perhaps, next time, that court will take the final step and *start* with the statute, ignoring the "mass of verbiage" it replaces. It seems a logical place to start, especially since it was intended to displace some of those cases in which the verbiage appears.

Last May (1964) the Sixth Circuit Court of Appeals, in *Monroe Auto Equipment Co.* v. *Heckethorn Mfg. Co.*,[33] said, "It is virtually a practical impossibility to define adequately that abstraction which we call invention,"[34] and then, in spite of that difficulty, said "we must have objective references and a place from which to start. For this we turn to the statute . . . Section 103." A very good place to start! But then the court came to a very unnecessary conclusion "that invention is synonymous with unobviousness. Thus to say that a device lacks invention and that it is obvious is to state the same legal proposition in two ways."[35] It concluded that while obviousness "does not begin to solve the problem," it "gives us a touchstone for the contextual meaning of invention." It also concluded that in a patent case decision is arrived at by three steps: a determination of what the prior art was, what the patentee has made, and whether it would have been obvious, viewing the prior art from the time just prior to when the patented device was made. That is just what Section 103 says! It is beginning to take hold and the next step will be to realize, what should be so clear, that when the unobviousness question has been determined, there is nothing more to do and the question of "invention" can be forgotten.[36]

I cite these as straws in the wind. A study in the Columbia Law Review in 1963 [37] concludes that "nothing indicates that the courts are moving toward a common interpretation of the statute." I am not so sure. I say give them time. They are stirring like live cocoons. We have only had this statute for a dozen years and the judges who have been there that long, as many of them have, are still indoctrinated with the old "standard of invention" terminology they learned from the old patent lawyers and the old textbooks. There will be new editions of all three in due course.

I might mention the Court of Customs and Patent Appeals which has been turning out a consistent stream of opinions, for at least the eight consecutive years of which I have personal knowledge, strictly applying the obviousness formula of Section 103 to determine *patentability*, not the presence of invention, and slowly but surely warping the Patent Office into basing its actions on the statute. The results are beginning to show in the actions and board opinions we review. I believe we have invaded the Patent Office Academy. The Solicitor's office writes its briefs in the language of the statute.

Assistant Secretary of Commerce Hollomon made a speech in New York in March, 1964, in which he is reported to have said that he "believes that the courts and the Patent Office should both follow the same standard *of patentability*." This would be nice but is obviously impossible until one or the other of them decides to standardize. A good place to begin would be the Patent Office, a lot easier than in the courts. Dr. Hollomon further said "that a standard of

patentability should be more definitely set forth." He is to be complimented on his terminology, in not talking about a "standard of invention," but I think we should experiment with *using* the Section 103 standard before we try to create another one. I find it very workable. It was a harder job to get it than he may imagine and in twelve years no better one has been proposed. The "criteria which may be worked out," referred to in the Revision Note to Section 103, have never materialized. I doubt they ever will.

I have had two practical suggestions in the back of my mind for some time. One is to have a sort of wallpaper border printed up to run around all the patent examiner's rooms on which the words *New Useful Unobvious Patentable* are repeated endlessly. This could be designed into the new Patent Office building. Most inscriptions on the present Patent Office are not very useful. They might put on the Constitutional clause so people could see it contains no *standard* for determining patentability.

The other suggestion—and this one is more serious—is based on the discovery that lecture courses are given for new and other Federal judges from time to time on how to be a judge, printed in books and given to the judges, compliments of the West Publishing Company. This Institute or some other disinterested party or organization should prepare a lecture on the basic elements of patent law in up-to-date terminology as used in Title 35 U.S.C. and see to it that the Federal judges get it. Even a glossary would help, in which it would appear that the "requirement for invention" became obsolete in 1953 by an act of Congress, along with many prior court opinions discussing it, being replaced by unobviousness as defined in Section 103 as the *third requirement* for patentability. By limiting the lecture to the terms of the statute and their clear meanings I do not see how the bar could object and many judges would be grateful.

I was recently discussing this subject with a young patent lawyer, urging that we should all stop talking about the "standard of invention." She said, "What difference does it make?" That is a fair question which has to be answered, and with my present answers I will end:

The differences it will make—the reasons why we *must* learn to make this change—are these, among others:

Until we stop talking about a "requirement for invention," it will never be clear that *the third requirement* is that stated in Section 103 *and no other;* that when Section 103 has been complied with, there is no further and different requirement called "invention"; that compliance with Section 103 is the policy judgment of Congress on how to bring the invention within the Constitutional purpose.

Because looking for the presence of "invention" in addition to compliance with Section 103 defeats the legislative purpose.

Because talking about both unobviousness and "invention" as different things leads to weird and confused thinking.

Because testing patentability by the presence of "invention" gives judges and the Patent Office too much freedom to decide patentability of new and useful inventions on the basis of a personal view as to what *should* be patentable, instead of accepting the view of the legislature on that question of national policy.

Because it will get all those concerned with the administration of the patent system—Patent Office, Courts, and the bar—speaking the same language, a sine qua non to the communication of intelligence.

Because you cannot use "invention" as both an abstract noun and a concrete noun in the same statute or opinion without confusion. The invention is the thing that has been produced by the "inventor." There will be muddy thought as long as one has to say: this invention (in the concrete sense) is unpatentable because it is not an invention (in the abstract sense).

Because it will do more than anything else I can think of to bring about that long-sought-for greater uniformity of opinion on patentability.

Because it makes the prerequisite to patentability intelligible—as I hope I have been.

To quote Learned Hand—that well-named judge—once more, maybe I am only "shovelling smoke." Time alone will tell.

References

1. The Linthicum Foundation Competition, 1941, Dean John H. Wigmore, Northwestern University Law School, Chairman. The writer's contribution was published in five installments in the 24 JPOS 85, 159, 241, 328, and 422, commencing Feb. 1942.

2. The winner was Laurence I. Wood whose paper was published in book form, 1942, by Commerce Clearing House, Inc., under the title "Patents and Antitrust Law."

3. Dean Wigmore,[1] in his foreword to the Wood book,[2] said:

   "...I take the opportunity to intrude my personal opinion, that neither Courts nor treatise-writers have been radical enough in defending the legitimacy of the 'monopoly' in a patent, as distinguished from the ordinary trade-monopoly. Is it not a fact that every property-right we have is a 'monopoly'? The right to our house or our automobile is simply a right to keep anyone else from entering or using it without our consent; and is that not a monopoly?

   * * *

   "Of course patent-rights can be so *used* as to merit the distrust attaching to a monopoly, by contracts fixing prices, by tying agreements, by pools and the like. But so can gold mines and all the necessities of life by bargains be used monopolistically; yet no one blames the mine-owning right itself or the food-ownership right itself; the blame is directed to the use of it.

   "And so I for one regard it as unfortunate that courts and treatise-writers have not stood up more boldly for the fundamental right-ness of the patent right itself. I say 'for one,' because I do not recall reading anywhere an adequate defence of the theory of the patent-right."

4. *Darcy* v. *Allin,* 11 Co. Rep. 846; 1 W.P.C. 1. See "Monopolies and Patents" by Harold G. Fox, University of Toronto Press, 1947, p. 318. The case also has the popular title "The Case of Monopolies."

5. Journal of the Patent Office Society, Centennial Number, "History of the Patent Office," Vol. 18, p. 23, July 1936.

6. *Ibid.* Most of the privileges were for copyrights but a small percentage were for inventions.

7. The Statute of Monopolies, May 25, 1624, 21 Jac. I, c. 3. For its history see Fox,[4] supra, Chap. IX, pp. 113-126.

8. See JPOS,[5] supra, pp. 35-58.

9. *Ibid.,* pp. 55-62.

10. *Ibid.*, pp. 77-82, 230. Under the 1793 Act, for example, there was no examination for novelty over a period of 43 years. About 10,000 patents issued under that act for terms of 14 years, less than the number issued today in 3 months.

11. 52 U.S. 248.

12. Hearings pursuant to S. Res. 92, 84th Cong., 1st Sess., on the American Patent System, Oct. 10-12, 1955, p. 113.

13. Walker on Patents, Deller Ed., Vol. 1, p. 110.

14. Hearings,[12] supra, p. 113.

14a. I am not unaware of the statement of the *objective* in Article I, Section 8, Clause 8, "To promote the progress of . . . useful arts." See "Principles of Patentability," 28 Geo. Wash. L. Rev. 393. When Congress exercised its power under that clause and set up a patent system, so long as the *system as a whole* functions to further the Constitutional objective, it would not seem that the statement of the objective could set any "standard" for patentability of any single invention.

15. See *Great Atlantic & Pacific Tea Co.* v. *Supermarket Equipment Corp.*, 340 U.S. 147, 87 USPQ 303 (1950), where the two concurring opinions below were held to have applied a "standard of invention . . . that is less exacting than that required. . . ."

16. For a note on who Kettering was and his prolific accomplishments in the fields of business, research and inventing, see "The Kettering Archives" by Eugene B. Jackson, 44 JPOS 331, May 1964.

17. Report of National Patent Planning Comm., June 18, 1943, H. Doc. 239, 78th Cong., pp. 6, 10.

17a. See Giles S. Rich, "Congressional Intent—Or, Who Wrote the Patent Act of 1952?," in *Patent Procurement and Exploitation,* BNA 1963, pp. 61-78.

18. House Report No. 1923, 82nd Cong., 2nd Sess., to accompany H.R. 7794, p. 5.

19. *Ibid.*, p. 7.

20. *Ibid.*, p. 5.

21. The writer speaks from personal knowledge as one of the drafters.

22. Footnote 18, at p. 7.

23. "Commentary on the New Patent Act," by P. J. Federico, 1954, published in Vol. 1 of 35 U.S.C.A.

24. *The Cuno Engineering Corp.* v. *The Automatic Devices Corp.,* 314 U.S. 84, 51 USPQ 272 (1941).

25. Section 103. *Conditions for patentability; nonobvious subject matter*

"A patent may not be obtained though the invention is not identically disclosed or described as set forth in section 102 of this title, if the differences between the subject matter sought to be patented and the prior art are such that the subject matter as a whole would have been obvious at the time the invention was made to a person having ordinary skill in the art to which said subject matter pertains. Patentability shall not be negatived by the manner in which the invention was made."

25a. A little reflection should show that when judicial precedents constituting the "law" range from the very liberal to the most strict, it is a patent absurdity to speak of a statute taking a middle ground as a "codification" of existing law. See Footnote 17a, supra.

26. Footnote 15, supra, 340 U.S. 147. This was a case preeminently in the minds of the drafters of the 1952 Patent Act, having been decided during the writing of the first drafts. See Footnote 17a.

27. Study of the Subcommittee on Patents, Trademarks and Copyrights of the Committee on the Judiciary, U.S. Senate, 85th Cong., 1st Sess., pursuant to S. Res. 95, Study No. 7 (1958).

28. *Lyon* v. *Bausch & Lomb Optical Co.,* 224 F.2d 530, 106 USPQ 1 (2d Cir. 1955).

29. *Reiner et al.* v. *I. Leon Co.,* 285 F.2d 501, 128 USPQ 25 (2d Cir. 1960).

30. Footnote 12, supra.

31. *Ibid.*, p. 120.

32. 330 F.2d 164, 141 USPQ 269.

33. 141 USPQ 553.

34. The full quotation is (141 USPQ at 553):

"It is virtually a practical impossibility to define adequately that abstraction which we call invention. Long ago the Supreme Court said: 'The truth is the word cannot be defined in such a manner as to afford any substantial aid in determining whether a particular device involves an exercise of the inventive faculty or not. In a given case we may be able to say that there is invention of a very high order. In another we can see that there is lacking that impalpable something which distinguishes invention from simple mechanical skill.' McClain v. Ortmayer, 141 U.S. 419, 427 [Nov. 2, 1891]. This court consistently has echoed this view." [Cases cited.]

35. A case was cited for this proposition, *In re Jacoby, Jr.,* 309 F.2d 513, 135 USPQ 317, 50 CCPA 734, in which the opinion was written by the present author. The Patent Office Board of Appeals had said the claimed invention "must be unobvious and involve invention." In a footnote to a reluctant but needed quotation of that statement the writer said:

"To add to the statement that it must be unobvious, as required by 35 U.S.C. 103, the further statement that it must 'involve invention' is merely to state the same legal proposi-

602

tion in two different ways. It would seem to
suffice to state it once, and that, preferably, in
the words of the statute."

It should be clear that this was intended to
put the proposition, developed more forcefully
in the present paper, as gently as possible and
that it was *not* intended to suggest that "invention" and "unobviousness" as provided in
Section 103 are alternative *equivalents* for
determining patentability, which they are not.

36. Along with it can be forgotten the "complexities" of another issue wrestled with by the
court in deciding whether "unobviousness" is
a question of law or fact. Compare *Armour &
Co. v. Wilson & Co.,* 274 F.2d 143, 124 USPQ
115 (7th Cir. 1960). The presence or absence of
"invention" before 1953 was always, in my
judgment, the determination of an issue of

public policy—what inventions *should* be patented. As such it is a "question of law." This
policy has now been legislatively expressed in
Section 103. In that section (Footnote 25,
supra) the following potential issues of fact
appear: (1) What are the *differences* between
"the invention" and "the prior art"? (2) What
is disclosed by the prior art presumed to have
been available to the inventor? (3) What was
the level of ordinary skill in the art at the
time the invention was made? (4) Other fact
issues relating to *circumstances* indicative of
the presence or absence of obviousness, traditionally taken into account.

Cross-references: *Act of 1952—Patents; Antitrust
Law and Patents; Clean Hands Doctrine; Invention; Patentability.*

N

NUMERICAL TREATMENT OF SCOPE OF CLAIMS

Donald Babcock Keyes

While Professor of Chemical Engineering at the University of Illinois, I asked the Dean of the Law School if he would not create a course in Patent Law for our chemical and chemical engineering students. He smiled at me and said, "I will not!" He explained that, in his opinion, if my students became patent attorneys, they would be primarily technical men and only secondarily lawyers. He had no qualified person on his staff and for obvious reasons could not and should not hire one. Referring to my previous experience as a director of research in industry and my continuous contact with practising patent attorneys, he suggested that I teach such a course myself. So, I tried.

Though the class may have learned little, I learned much.

The students were highly intelligent. They could and did ask the most embarrassing questions. "Professor, just how do you determine the number and scope of claims to cover specific inventions?"

Let us suppose that you were a patent attorney and were asked this question. Wouldn't you have turned slightly pink? You might have said that you were paid extra to answer such questions and that the answer would vary from invention to invention, no two cases being exactly alike. You might have added that no great artist has ever told how to create a masterpiece.

Unfortunately, I as a "layman" was in no such position. I had to give some kind of a plausible answer. I recalled the old story of the rabbit that climbed the tree. Now of course rabbits don't climb trees but this one had to—a dog was after him. There was nothing else that he could do.

That was exactly my predicament. I had to invent an answer. Unlike most inventors, I could explain the basis of my invention. The class understood it and seemed to enjoy operating under a system having an optical and pseudomathematical appeal.

Briefly it might be considered as a "chart system" in which the broadest categories of materials or conditions, constituting the broadest claim, appear at the top. Then come specific limitations represented in the claims that are of more narrow scope and least apt to be anticipated by the prior art. An example will illustrate the chart.

A friend of mine once "invented" a drink which consisted of water, alcohol, juniper juice, and a *blue* dye. He called it, very appropriately, "Swillko." Let us assume he wished to patent it. What claims might he draft?

The horizontal lines of Table 1 indicate the content of three possible claims. The limitations increase as we go down in the vertical columns, in the search for a patentable combination.

Note that the sum of the numbers associated with the constituents in the first claim is 10, second claim 26, and third claim 42. Thus the greater the limitation of the scope of the claim, the greater the sum. It is also obvious from mathematics that $4^2 - 2$ or 14 intermediate combinations can be made and corresponding claims written between claims 1 and 2 and that the resulting sums of these arbitrary units of limitations will lie between 10 and 26. What is most interesting is that the relative breadth or value of each combination is known.

A similar chart can be created for a process invention in which each new step can be modified by such factors as temperature, pressure, and concentration ranges.

From the claim writer's viewpoint, he now has a method by which he can quickly

TABLE 1.

Scope of Claim No.	Content of Composition Claims			
1	(1) Water	(2) + Alcohol	(3) + Blue Dye	(4) + Juice
2	(5) Distilled Water	(6) + Ethyl Alc.	(7) + Light Blue Dye	(8) + Juniper Juice
3	(9) 55 parts of D.W.	(10) + 45 parts of E.A.	(11) + 0.1 part of L.B.D.	(12) + 5 parts of J.J.

and easily chart the content of numerous claims in their descending order of breadth. He then can select the few that he wishes to use in the application. Also he has substitutes available when he wishes to present new claims during the prosecution of the application.

Most young scientists and engineering students are mathematically minded. Though this scheme of claim generation uses only arithmetic, it did appeal to engineering college students years ago. There is no valid reason why it should not appeal to others today.

Cross-references: *Application Writing, Claim Drafting.*

O

OPERABILITY

Norbert Ederer

This article relates to operability of a device as disclosed and, to a lesser extent, as claimed.

Importance of Workability of the Device

An inoperative device is not useful,[1] but the operative devices are not inherently useful in the patent sense.[2] Inoperativeness is a ground for rejection of an application.[3] In an interference proceeding, an inoperative device is neither a reduction to practice nor proof even of conception.[4,5] Inoperativeness of a patent in suit is a basis for invalidity.[2] Conversely, inoperativeness of a reference makes it ineffective for purposes of anticipation.[1]

The basis for these principles is obvious. The consideration for the patent monopoly is the free use of the invention after the expiration of the patent. If the patentee has given nothing useful to the public, he should have no patent monopoly. As a corollary, the patentee should not be permitted, by patent on an inoperative device, to hamper production of useful devices. Also an inoperative device should not anticipate an operative one, as the former does not confer benefit on the public while the latter does.

The above principles are well recognized. The difficulty in their application lies in the determination of whether or not the device under consideration is operative.

Perfection of Operation Ordinarily Not Required

Is operability a "yes" or "no" proposition or is it a matter of degree? What de- gree of perfection is required of an inventor? The answer usually given is: The device is operative if it performs its intended function. As we shall see, some devices are adjudged as to operability on the yes or no basis, others as a matter of degree.

In the *Telephone* cases,[6] Alexander Graham Bell's famous telephone patents were before the Supreme Court. On the question of operability, the following facts were undisputed: Bell had not and could not construct a telephone in accordance with his own teaching prior to the issuance of his patent. Others constructed the first Bell type telephone in accordance with the patent disclosure. Its speech reproduction was poor but intelligible. The defendants had superior telephones not disclosed by Bell.

The Supreme Court sustained the patent. On the issue of operability the Court stated [6a]:

"The law does not require that a discoverer or inventor, in order to get a patent for a process, must have succeeded in bringing his art to the highest degree of perfection; it is enough if he describes his method with sufficient clearness and precision to enable those skilled in the matter to understand what the process is, and if he points out some practicable way of putting it into operation."

In *Hildreth* v. *Mastoras*,[7] an infringement proceeding, the Supreme Court was confronted with the question of operability of a candy pulling machine. Previously this operation had been performed manually. The application leading to the patent in suit had been involved in several interferences,[8] in each of which its operability was sustained over the attack of the adverse parties. It also had withstood successfully an attack on its operability in another infringement proceeding.[9] Admittedly neither the plaintiff nor the defendant used the device exactly as disclosed. It was undisputed that the changeover from manual to machine candy pulling had revolutionized the art.

The Court, in sustaining the patent, stated [10]:

> It is not necessary, in order to sustain a generic patent to show that the device is a commercial success. The machine patented may be imperfect in its operation; but if it embodies the generic principle and works, that is, if it actually and mechanically performs, though only in a crude way, the important function by which it makes the substantial change claimed for in the art, it is enough."

The law of these cases is followed in numerous other decisions.

Degree of Imperfection Permitted

The general rule is that the deficiency in the operability will not defeat an otherwise meritorious invention, or an otherwise valid anticipation, if the deficiency can be remedied with the exercise of merely the skill of the art and without further invention. This rule applies in ex parte,[12] interference [13] and infringement proceedings.[14] A whole gamut of devices benefit from this rule.[15] With respect to these devices, operability is decided on a "matter of degree" basis.

Failure Nondetectable. On the other hand, there are devices whose operability is considered strictly. An early case was *McKenzie* v. *Cummings*,[16] decided by the Court of Appeals for the District of Columbia. The issue at bar was whether Cummings' construction of a vote-registering machine constituted an actual reduction to practice. It was proved that the machine failed to register correctly about once in a hundred times. It registered correctly the remaining ninety-nine times. The machine was held inoperative and worthless, since no electorate could afford to commit the registration of its electoral will to such a machine.[16a]

In *Carlin* v. *Crumpton,* in an interference appeal decided by the Court of Appeals for the District of Columbia,[17] the isue was a modification of the register or totalizer used in the construction of cash registers,

adding machines, etc. The improvement was directed to indicating negative numbers resulting from the subtraction of a number greater than the minuend. Carlin sought to establish a reduction to practice of a machine which failed to give consistently correct results, unless in certain circumstances adjustments were made by the operator in accordance with specified rules. *"A machine which fails to give with absolute certainty the correct result is so impractical and inoperative as to be worthless."* [18] (Emphasis added.)

The *McKenzie* v. *Cummings* and *Carlin* v. *Crumpton* cases are authority for the rule of law applicable to digital computers or more generally dicretely operable devices amongst others.

Among the discretely operable devices held to fall within the doctrine of *McKenzie* v. *Cummings* are typewriters,[19] telephone dial digital wheels [20] and cômputing scales.[21] A computing scale is used to weigh a parcel and imprint thereon the correct postage automatically. There are contrary decisions respecting typewriters,[22] and linotype machines.[23] In the Mergenthaler linotype case,[23] the defect of the machine was not in its insertion of wrong characters, but in its inability to maintain uniform line lengths. The line length occasionally varied by $\frac{1}{64}$ inch, a defect that was recognized immediately, first by an outsider, then by the patentee,[23a] and later by others. The theory of the defense was not invalidity of the patent in suit but rather a narrow construction of the patent which would avoid infringement. The Court held that the patent disclosed an important advance in the art, should be given liberal construction, and was therefore infringed.

In U.S.C. 146 interference proceeding, *Sperry Rand Corporation* v. *Bell Telephone Laboratories,* the issue of operability was at most of secondary moment only in the final disposition of the case.[24] The interference involved the ENIAC computer and a contemporaneous Bell Laboratories electronic digital computer.

Failure Detectable and Correctable. Cummings cited *Coffee* v. *Guerrant* [25] as authority for the proposition that, when a machine accomplishes its purpose in a man-

ner reasonably satisfactory to practical men
and fairly promising good results, although
not then constructed with thorough mechanical skill in all its parts, it may be regarded
as a successful reduction to practice. The
machine in the *Coffee* v. *Guerrant* case was
a tobacco-stemming machine, which did
fairly good work but occasionally permitted
as many as 30 per cent of the tobacco leaves
to pass the blades without having the stems
properly removed. The Court thought that
this inaccuracy or imperfection would not
necessarily have prevented the machine
from coming into commercial use, even
though it had never been perfected so as to
permit no leaf to pass unstemmed. The
escaping leaves might well be gathered and
thrown back; and the machine might have
been found remarkably useful notwithstanding the imperfection.

Failures Creating Hazards to Life. The
strict "yes-no" rule is invoked for devices
that are inherently dangerous to life and
limb. In *Badowski* v. *United States* [26] a
patent for a parachute that would not open
was held not to anticipate the patent in
suit which was directed to a good parachute.

In *Kuhn* v. *Jennings* [27] the construction of
an electrical circuit breaker was held not
to constitute a reduction to practice because
it was held that the device did not have the
utility required by the counts and was not
subject to the severe overload, endurance
and breakdown tests accepted as standard
for devices of its kind. A circuit breaker
case to contrary effect is *Andrew* v. *Nil-
son*. [28]

In *Katz* v. *Horni Signal Manufacturing
Corp.*, [29] the patent in suit involved a traffic
detector. It utilized as an essential element
an air core inductor. As such it did not
operate every time under given traffic conditions. The defendant used an iron core
which rendered the detector operative at
all times. It was held that the patent was
limited to a construction of a traffic detector with an air core and therefore not
infringed. In the words of the Court:

"That the traffic detector might operate a few
times is insufficient; unless it operates every time
under given conditions, it is a menace to traffic
and the patent lacks practical utility."

Construction of a railroad knuckle that
broke under actual test conditions, solely
by reason of the fact that an inferior metal
was used, was held not to be a successful
reduction to practice. [4] The knowledge of
the superior metal was within the skill of
the art. The invention was not in the composition of the metal but in the structure
of the knuckle.

The rule of hazardous devices has exception. An automobile brake that occasionally would not be effective was held to be
a valid reduction to practice. [30] A patent
for a dangerous electrical aerial advertising
sign was held to be a good anticipation of
a hazard-free sign. [31]

"Negative" Results. The rule of hazardous devices does not cover the discretely
operable or digital devices, as they are not
inherently dangerous to life and limb. In
order to embrace the digital devices, the
rule is extended to include devices which
produce incorrect and therefore "negative"
results with no warning to the interpreter
that the results are incorrect. Such devices
are deemed inoperable in the patent sense,
although upon occasion or even most of the
time they produce correct or "positive" results, because the operator has no way of
distinguishing the "positive" from the "negative."

In *Curtiss-Wright Corporation et al.* v.
Link Aviation, [32] the subject matter of the
patents in suit was electromechanical flight
trainers or simulators. Such a flight trainer
includes dummy flight instruments similar
to those found in an actual aircraft. Operation of the controls actuates the instruments via electromechanical computing systems. The object is to match the trainer
control actuation-instrument response to
that of an actual aircraft. Thus the student
may be given flight training before he is
permitted to operate the controls of an
actual aircraft. This type of training is especially useful for "blind flying," that is,
reliance on instruments alone under conditions of darkness or fog.

One of the theories of the defense was
that the devices as disclosed in the patent
were inoperative in the patent sense because they provided "negative training." In
other words, the devices disclosed in the

patents operated correctly in some situations so as to simulate actual flight conditions. In other situations, the operation of the controls resulted in instrument response that had no counter-part in an actual airplane. It was further argued that an airplane trainer based on the disclosures of the patents would instill dangerous habits in a trainee that he would have to unlearn in the actual aircraft. Reliance was placed on psychological experience that a person, in a moment of emergency, tends to do that which he has learned first. The trainee, in an emergency, might operate the controls so as to obtain the inherently incorrect instrument readings and, relying on them, meet sudden death.

The Court was asked to invoke the rule of *McKenzie* v. *Cummings* and *Carlin* v. *Crumpton*. Although there was some force in the argument, the Court found the disclosed airplane trainers operable on a "matter of degree" basis appraising them as of the date of their invention (1941) rather than on the basis of modern standards.

There are still further devices subject to the "yes-no" rule because of some latent actual or possible "danger," and others even though not inherently "negative," or "dangerous." These devices, because giving rise to some peculiar substantive and procedural problems, will be considered following the sections on these problems.

Substantive and Procedural Aspects

This section deals with substantive and procedural aspects of the law on operability that may arise at any stage beginning with the ex parte prosecution and terminating with an infringement proceeding.

In *Coffin* v. *Ogden* [33] and *Dashiel* v. *Grosvenor*,[34] the Supreme Court held (with respect to an anticipatory patent) that a patent is presumptively for an operative device. It is unlikely that the patentee sought to obtain a patent for something worthless. The rule of presumption of operability is followed in many cases. It produces some interesting and at times surprising results.

Ex Parte Prosecution. In the ex parte prosecution, in the normal case, operability is not questioned unless the disclosed device is clearly inoperative on its face.[35] This follows from the Patent Office policy that any doubts are resolved in favor of the applicant. Once the patent issues, the *Coffin* v. *Ogden* and *Dashiel* v. *Grosvenor* presumption attaches to it. The presumptive validity of an issued patent also extends to the aspect of operability. It would appear that the presumption of operability should be a weak one, as the Patent Office has no laboratory facilities to test the disclosed device,[35] but, on the contrary, the presumption has great weight.

In the normal ex parte prosecution, the Examiner may not question operability without convincing argument to support his position.[35a] Should he have good grounds, the applicant can overcome the Examiner's rejection by affidavit attesting to operability.[35b] Similarly, an inoperative anticipating reference may be overcome, but this is more difficult especially where the reference is a United States patent. The difficulty is great even by affidavit [36] to say nothing of mere argument,[37] thanks to the *Coffin* v. *Ogden* and *Dashiel* v. *Grosvenor* presumption.

There are some exceptions to the rule of resolving doubts in favor of the applicant. In *In re Chilowsky*,[38] the Court of Customs and Patent Appeals evolved the following set of rules: In the usual case where the mode of operation alleged can be readily understood and conforms to known laws of physics and chemistry, operativeness is not questioned, and no further evidence is required. On the other hand, if the alleged operation seems clearly to conflict with a recognized scientific principle, as for example where an applicant purports to have discovered a machine to produce perpetual motion,[38a] the presumption of inoperativeness is so strong that very clear evidence is required to overcome it.[38b] A third type of situation involves devices that are of such nature that they could not be tested by any known scientific principles. In such a case, it is incumbent on the applicant to demonstrate the workability and utility of the device and make clear the principles on which it operates.

In re Chilowsky was before the Court of

Customs and Patent Appeals for a second time [39] on the issue of sufficiency, as distinguished from operability, of the disclosure.

Interference Proceedings. In interference proceedings, the question of operability arises in several ways.

There may be an attack on the operability of the disclosure of the application or patent involved in the interference. This rarely meets with success in view of the *Coffin* v. *Ogden* and *Dashiel* v. *Grosvenor* presumption. Before an interference is declared, some claims must have been found allowable, and the presumption attaches that the Examiner has reviewed the disclosure and found it to be operative.

The presumption is so strong as to lead to an apparent anomaly under the following set of facts. Party A unsuccessfully attacks the operability of the party B disclosure. B attempts to establish an actual reduction to practice of a device that is identical with that in the B disclosure, but fails to prove its operability. It was held that this would not destroy the presumption of the operability of the B disclosure.[40] The rationale is based on the burden of proof. B's disclosure is presumptively operative and A has the burden of proving inoperability. Argument alone is not sufficient [41] nor are ex parte tests, or even inter partes tests, unless A shows that the defect could not have been cured by the exercise of merely the skill of the art.[42] In establishing his own prior actual reduction to practice, B has a heavy burden of proof.[40] He must show affirmatively that the device has been successfully reduced to practice, or that any imperfection may be corrected by the exercise of merely the skill of the art.[40, 42]

Infringement Proceedings. In infringement proceedings, it appears that the presumption of operability of the patent disclosure is given even greater weight. Mere draftsman's errors will not defeat an otherwise meritorious invention.[43] It has been held that an infringer is estopped to deny the operability of the disclosure.[44] This proposition seems to be too sweeping; a correct statement of the proposition is, he who infringes by utilizing the device as disclosed in the patent rather than merely as claimed, is estopped to deny its operability.[45] The rationale is that it is always easy to render the adversary's device inoperative, so that attacks on operability are considered with suspicion.[46]

Operativeness of References

The great weight accorded to the presumption of operability attaches not only to the patent in suit, but also to patents cited as anticipations.[47] In either case, it is not sufficient to show that the device is inoperative, but affirmative proof is required that it could not be rendered operative with the exercise of merely the skill of the art.[48]

There is a conflict of authority as to whether or not a claim directed to an operative device must distinguish from an inoperative structure advanced as an anticipation. Most cases are silent on this question. The Court of Claims has held [26] that a valid claim may read even on a prior inoperative device. The Court of Customs and Patent Appeals has held to the contrary.[49]

A related interesting proposition of law is this. Where a claim for a manufacture or composition of matter is disclosed by a prior reference, the claim must be rejected or invalidated, even though the prior reference discloses an inoperative process for making the manufacture or composition.[50] This is because the claimant can stand in no better position than if no process whatsoever had been disclosed by the prior art.[51]

Speculative Inventions. Following the rule of barring patents on speculative devices,[38a, 38b] patents have been refused for a system for regenerating air, useful in planetary and interplanetary stations and ships,[3] and a method of fog precipitation.[52] Medical inventions fall into the class of speculative devices; the applicant must produce proof of therapeutic qualities.[53]

The rule of law with respect to speculative devices at times is a harsh one. It is well-settled law that the inventor need not actually reduce his invention to practice before applying for a patent, and yet it appears that he is compelled to do so under the rule. In the *Chilowsky* case,[38] the subject matter of the application was atomic decomposition of uranium and its components. The application was filed on December 20, 1944. It was rejected by the Examiner and the Board of Appeals because speculative and not obeying any known physical laws and scientific principles. The Examiner required proof that the reactor disclosed could be constructed and operated by following the disclosure, or that the reactor had been constructed and had been operated.

The prosecution was protracted for a sufficiently long time to permit support of the physical theories by scientific papers written at a much later time. The Court was thus in a position to state that "the basic laws governing atomic fission are known" (at the time of appeal before the Board of Appeals) and had no difficulty in classifying the case as within the group of "usual cases."

A somewhat similar factual situation is found in a recently decided case, *Commissariat à L'Energie Atomique et al. v. Watson, Comr. Pats., et al.*[54] Here the French inventors applied for a patent covering processes for the production of nuclear energy on April 5, 1940. The application was rejected by the Examiner and by the Board of Appeals for failure to prove operability. During the pendency of the application, a secrecy order was placed on the application and other scientific papers, rendering the required proof impossible. Also the Alien Property Custodian seized title and continued the prosecution. Apparently his prosecution was rather half-hearted because the application was abandoned. At the time of the decision of the Board of Appeals on November 17, 1950, the proof of operability still could not be furnished. In 1954, the application was returned to the applicants by the Alien Property Custodian. The applicants contended that they could not produce sufficient data to prove operability until August 1955, when a number of scientific papers pertaining to atomic energy were declassified. They petitioned the Commissioner of Patents to revive the abandoned application. The petition and repeated requests for reconsideration were summarily denied.

A 35 USC 145 suit was filed, which was dismissed by the District Court for lack of jurisdiction. On appeal, it was held that although the District Court's holding was technically correct, the complaint should have been treated as one for mandamus directing the Commissioner to exercise his discretion to determine whether the abandonment was due to unavoidable circumstances and, upon so finding, grant the petition to revive.

Testing Medical and Insecticide Inventions. The policy is stated in *Isenstead v. Watson, Comr. Pats.:*[55]

"Great care should be taken with applications for medical patents; while granting of a patent is not a certificate that the medicine is a good medicine, it gives kind of official imprimatur on which some members of the public are likely to rely. Therefore, the Patent Office should be careful and perhaps even reluctant to grant a patent on a new medical formula until it has been thoroughly tested and successfully tried by more than one physician."

The strict rule applicable to medical patents is also invoked in infringement proceedings. *Hoover v. Eckerd's Cut Rate Medicine Co.*[56] The defendant attacked the operability of the patents in suit which were directed to calcifying dentifrices. The plaintiff offered to prove operability by performing tests on dead teeth. This proof was found to be insufficient because of testimonies to the effect that live teeth would react differently. The patents were found to be for inoperative devices.

In the interference *Smith v. Bousquet*,[57] it was held that indoor testing of an insecticide used on codling moth larvae was insufficient to prove reduction to practice for the reason chiefly that the tests, though successful, were not made under the natural surrounding conditions where the codling moth larvae are found. The outdoor test was considered necessary because of the possible negative result of damaging foliage or parts of plants. By way of contrast, in *Smith v. Swaine*,[58] another interference proceding, an indoor laboratory test of an insecticide on mosquito larvae was held to be a satisfactory test for reduction to practice since water is a natural habitat of mosquito larvae, distinguishing from *Smith* v. *Bousquet*.

In *ex parte Tiger*,[59] it was held that a temporary reaction product could support a patent over the Examiner's rejection on the ground of inoperability.

Operative Devices Which Are Not Useful

There is some case law which accepts the doctrine of the *Bell Telephone* cases and *Hildreth* v. *Mastoras* in principle, but holds that devices even though operative are nevertheless not useful with the meaning of the patent statute. One such situation is where the invention is an improvement invention and its purpose is to make large scale commercial use practical. It turns out, however, that the device is suitable only for laboratory use. Under such circumstances, a finding of no patentable utility has been made with respect to a sheet metal drawing press,[60] a method and apparatus for feeding molten glass for blowing into bottles or similar hollow ware,[61] and a refrigerator.[40] To contrary effect is a case [62] whose subject matter is storage batteries.

A similar rule of law applies with respect to devices that require experimentation and inventions of others, not to make the device in question operative, but to make devices in conjunction with which the operative device is to be used. The doctrine has been applied to inventions of airplane torpedoes which were ultimately used, but not until airplanes were invented capable of carrying the torpedoes.[63] This doctrine is somewhat similar to that relating to speculative devices (see the atomic energy cases above) and is for this reason considered harsh.

Operability as Claimed

Claims Incomplete or Description Incorrect. The question of operability of the device as claimed arises in connection with rejection or invalidation of claims on the grounds that they:

(a) are directed to a device which as disclosed is inoperative.

(b) are incomplete, omitting an essential element and are therefore directed to inoperative structures [64] or, alternatively, conceding that they (the claims) cover subcombinations of an operative full combination, are nevertheless unpatentable because the claimed structure has no utility apart from the full combination.[65]

(c) cover inoperative structures in addition to operative structures.[66]

(d) are broader than any invention disclosed or contemplated by the inventor.[67]

A further ground related to the first ground is to the effect that the claim is misdescriptive of the invention.[32] In other words, the claimed structure is not in accord with the disclosed structure; one of the two structures is inoperative, and no matter which, the claim is invalid. Otherwise, the first ground is actually trivial in the sense that it is but a restatement of the proposition that no valid patent can be granted on an inoperative device (as disclosed).

The remaining three grounds will be considered at greater length with reference to *Special Equipment Co.* v. *Coe, Comr. Pats.*,[68] below. The third ground, as a general proposition, is not considered valid with respect to mechanical (including electrical) inventions, unless the fourth ground comes into play, as will be seen below. With respect to chemical cases, the third and fourth grounds are considered to be essentially the same.

The invention in issue in *Special Equipment Co.* v. *Coe*, supra, is directed to successively and automatically bobbing (cutting off stems), splitting, paring, and coring pears, in preparation for canning or other processing. One of the issues raised and decided adversely to the applicant in the Patent Office, and later by the Court of Customs and Patent Appeals,[69] was the alleged inoperability (as disclosed) of an anticipating prior patent.

A second, continuing or renewal application was filed which claimed the structures of the first application, but omitted the splitting knife. Apparently the second application contained no disclosure of operation of machine without splitting knife and of the concomitant requirement of presplitting the pears. The claims of the second application were rejected by the Patent

Office as incomplete, broader than the invention disclosed, and as covering constructions not contemplated by the inventor.

The case finally reached the Supreme Court.[70] A film demonstration was presented before the Court, to show that the machine was indeed operative, even without the splitting knife. The Court reversed, in a 5 to 4 decision, and remanded the case to the Court of Appeals. The majority held that the statutes permit, and it is the settled practice of the Patent Office, many times sustained by the Supreme Court,[71] to allow claims to a combination and also its *subcombinations*.

The machine, less splitting knife, was thus considered a subcombination of the full combination comprised of the machine including the splitting knife. This points up to countering the above ground (b) of incompleteness, inoperability or lack of utility of the claimed structure. The subcombination may be inoperative in the sense that it cannot perform the function of the full combination. The subcombination is, however, operative in the full combination, and in the further sense that with the passage of time the subcombination may or will acquire separate or independent status.

The Patent Office or the Court in the ex parte prosecution may be persuaded that a claim, far from being an incomplete full combination claim, is in fact a complete subcombination claim.

On remand, the Court of Appeals [72] held against allowance on a different basis, namely, that the claims were broader than any invention disclosed or contemplated by the inventor and therefore properly refused. There was no disclosure that the pears had to be presplit for the machine to process them properly without the splitting knife. The claims called for "pears" and this was construed to mean "whole pears" and not "half pears," contrary to the required mode of operation. The Court considered that the claimed inventions were not those of the original inventor, but rather those of an astute patent attorney.

Inoperativeness of Certain Members of Chemical Claim. In a chemical case, a claim that covers both operative and inoperative compositions, may be held invalid and also broader than any invention disclosed or contemplated by the inventor.[66] While the details of circumstances for this holding are properly features of Validity (q.v.), it may be said here that a decision of the Supreme Court illustrates the need of directing the selection within a general class if all members of the class are to be claimed. In the *Rubber Accelerator* case,[73] involving Weiss' patent covering the use of diphenylguanidine and in fact of any disubstituted guanidine, Chief Justice Taft said:

"We come then to the question of the validity of claims 1, 5 and 9 of the patent, which seek to appropriate to the patentee the process of treating rubber by combining with the rubber compound "a disubstituted guanidine." Now the class of disubstituted guanidine includes not only D.P.G. but all other derivatives of guanidine in which two of the hydrogen atoms of guanidine nucleus have been substituted by other groups.

"... The experts show that there are between 50 and 100 substances which answer this description, of which there is quite a number that are not accelerators at all. Weiss could certainly not claim the entire group of such compounds. He makes no *showing that there is any general quality common to disubstituted guanidines which made them all effective as accelerators*. Claims for their exclusive use cannot therefore be sustained." (Emphasis added.)

References

1. *Western Electric Co.* v. *La Rue,* 139 U.S. 601, 1891.
2. *Hartford Empire Co.* v. *Obear-Nester Glass Co.,* 22 USPQ 270, CA 8 1934.
3. *In re Martini,* 123 USPQ 220, Bd. App. 1959.
4. *Gilman* v. *Hinson,* 1906 C.D. 634.
5. *Rowe* v. *Holtz,* 12 USPQ 234, CCPA 1932.
6. 126 U.S. 1, 526.
6a. 126 U.S. 536.
7. 257 U.S. 27.
8. *Thibodeau* v. *Hildreth,* 1905 C.D. 675, 677; see also related interferences *Jenner* v. *Dickinson, Thibodeau* v. *Dickinson,* 1905 C.D. 672.
9. *Hildreth* v. *Lauter,* 208 F. 1005, DC Md 1914; aff. 219 F. 753, CA 4 1915.
10. 257 U.S. 34.
11. *Baldwin-Lima Hamilton Corp.* v. *Tatnall Measuring Systems Co.,* 120 USPQ 34, DC Pa 1958; aff. 121 USPQ 363, rehearing denied 122 USPQ 357, CA 3 1959.
    Freedman v. *Overseas Scientific Corp.,* 248 F.2d 274, 115 USPQ 42, CA 2 1957.
    Hunt Tool Co. v. *Lawrence,* 242 F.2d 347, 113

USPQ 7, CA 5 1957, modifying 111 USPQ 37, cert. den. 113 USPQ 594.

12. *In re Spence,* 120 USPQ 82, CCPA 1958, 1959—pipe coupling.

13. *Field* v. *Knowles,* 183 F.2d 457, 108 USPQ 322, CCPA 1956—ice making apparatus.

14. *International Nickel Co.* v. *Ford Motor Co.,* 166 F. Supp. 551, 119 USPQ 72, DC SNY 1958 —cast ferrous alloy.

15. See References 12, 13, 14.

16. 1904 C.D. 683.

16a. 1904 C.D. 686.

17. 45 App. D.C. 166, 1916 C.D. 211.

18. 1916 C.D. 213.

19. *Paul* v. *Hess,* 24 App. DC 467, 1905 C.D. 610.

20. *O'Donnell* v. *Schmidt,* 1906 C.D. 662.

21. *Computing Scale Co.* v. *Standard Computing Scale Co.,* 195 F. 508, CA 6 1912.

22. *Remington Cash Register Co.* v. *National Cash Register Co.,* 6 F.2d 585, DC Conn. 1925.

23. *Mergenthaler Linotype Co.* v. *Press Publishing Co.,* 57 F. 502, 1893 C.D. 685, DC SNY.

23a. 57 F. 505.

24. 171 F. Supp. 343, 121 USPQ 39, DC SNY 1959; 122 USPQ 602, DC SNY 1959; 135 USPQ 254, DC SNY 1962; aff. 137 USPQ 497, CA 2 1963.

25. *Coffee* v. *Guerrant,* 3 App. D.C. 497, 1894 C.D. 384.

26. 140 F. Supp. 544, 109 USPQ 293, Ct. Cl. 1956; on reargument 118 USPQ 358, 1959.

27. 142 F.2d 67, 61 USPQ 414, CCPA 1944.

28. 27 App. D.C. 451, 1906 C.D. 717.

29. 52 F. Supp. 453, 59 USPQ 196, DC SNY 1943.

30. *Leichsenring* v. *Freeman,* 41 USPQ 478, CCPA 1939.

31. *In re Rohlfs,* 5 USPQ 469, CCPA 1930.

32. 124 USPQ 266, DC SNY 1959, 1960.

33. 18 Wall, 85 U.S., 120, 1873.

34. 162 U.S. 425, 1896 C.D. 329. See also *Metropolitan Engineering* v. *Coe,* 25 USPQ 216, CA D.C. 1935.

35. *In re Quattlebaum,* 84 USPQ 383, Pat. Off. Supv. Exr. 1947, 1950.

35a. *Ex Parte Ogorzaly,* 68 USPQ 156, 1945, 1946.

35b. *Ex Parte Valenzi,* 65 USPQ 524, PO Bd App 1943, 1945.
Ex Parte Ruskin, 95 USPQ 96, PO Bd App 1952; here the affidavit was found insufficient, but also unnecessary, as the sworn to specification stated that the device (a therapeutic compound) was stable.

36. *Douglas Aircraft Co.* v. *Watson, Comr. Pats.,* 12 USPQ 602, DC DistCol.
See also *In re Pio,* 42 CCPA 746, 104 USPQ 177, 1955, where even the affidavit of the prior patentee proved of no value.
See also *In re Wagner,* 41 USPQ 504, 1939—here the anticipating patent was inoperative

in part, but to the extent operative, it was a valid reference.

37. *Ex Parte Kuzmitz,* 113 USPQ 255, PO Bd App 1956, 1957.

38. 108 USPQ 231, 1956.

38a. *See Buck* v. *Ooms, Comr. Pats.,* 72 USPQ 211, CA DC 1947.

38b. See *In re Perrigo,* 48 F.2d 965, 9 USPQ 152, 1931—production of electrical energy from the ether.

39. 134 USPQ 515, CCPA 1962.

40. *Field* v. *Knowles,* 86 USPQ 373, CCPA 1950. See also *Farrington* v. *Mikeska,* 155 F.2d 412, 69 USPQ 509, CCPA 1946.

41. See *Garrett* v. *Cox,* 110 USPQ 52, CCPA 1956.

42. See also *Tanset* v. *Higgonet et al.,* 215 F.2d 457, 103, USPQ 457, CCPA 1954.

43. *Western States Machine Co.* v. *S. S. Hepworth Co.,* 64 USPQ 141, CA 2 1945. See also *In re Japikse,* 86 USPQ 70, CCPA 1950.

44. *Balaban* v. *Polyfoto Corp.,* 55 USPQ 141, DC Del 1942.

45. *Condenser Corp.* v. *Micamold Corp.,* 60 USPQ 286, DC ENY 1944.

46. *Webster Loom Co.* v. *Higgins,* 105 U.S. 580, 1882.

47. *Simmons Co.* v. *A. Brandwein & Co.,* 115 USPQ 307, CA 7 1957.

48. *International Nickel Co.* v. *Ford Motor Co.*[14] *Robertshaw Fulton Co.* v. *Patrol Valve Co.,* 93 USPQ 414, DC NOhio 1952.

49. *In re Hollingsworth,* 100 USPQ 386, CCPA 1954.

50. *In re Attwood,* 117 USPQ 184, CCPA 1958.

51. *In re von Bramer et al.,* 127 F.2d 149, 53 USPQ 345, CCPA 1942.

52. *Ex Parte Vang,* 72 USPQ 18, BdApp 1946, 1947.

53. *Ex Parte Ruskin.*[35b]

54. 124 USPQ 126, CA DC 1960.

55. 115 USPQ 408, DC 1957.

56. 16 USPQ 327, CA 3 1933. See also *Friedman* v. *Scientific Corporation,* 15 USPQ 42, CA 2 1957.

57. 45 USPQ 347, CCPA 1940.

58. 53 USPQ 385, CCPA 1942. See also *Bluestone* v. *Schmerling,* 121 USPQ 417, CCPA 1959.

59. 69 USPQ 181, PO Bd App 1945, 1946. See also *Ex Parte Ruskin.*[35b]

60. *Cleveland Punch & Shearworks* v. *E. W. Bliss Co.,* 145 F.2d 991, 64 USPQ 77, CA 6 1944.

61. *Hartford Empire Co.* v. *Obear-Nester Glass Co.*[2]

62. *Electrodynamics Co.* v. *U.S. Light and Heat Co.,* 278 F. 80, CA 2 1922.

63. *Moffett* v. *Fiske,* 50 F.2d 868, 10 USPQ 12, CA DistCol 1931.

64. Ellis, "Patent Claims," Chapter 32, New York, Baker Voorhis & Co., 1949.

65. Ellis, *ibid.,* Chapter 15, authorities cited.
66. *Ellis, ibid.,* Chapter 28, authorities cited.
67. Ellis, *ibid.,* Chapters 5, 6, 16, authorities cited.
68. 324 U.S. 370, 64 USPQ 525, 1945.
69. *In re Ewald,* 129 F.2d 340, 54 USPQ 82, CCPA 1942—pear coring machine.
70. 323 U.S. 697, 63 USPQ 358, 1944.
71. *Deering* v. *Winona Harvester Works,* 155 U.S. 286, 302.

    Leeds & Catlin v. *Victor Talking Mach. Co.,* 213 U.S. 301, 318.

    Altoona Publix Theatres v. *American Tri-Ergon Corp.,* 294 U.S. 477, 487, 24 USPQ 308, 313, 1935.

    Mercoid Corp. v. *Mid-Continent Investment Co.,* 320 U.S. 61, 667, 60 USPQ 21, 25, 1944.

    Also cited for proposition that contrary to what the Court of Appeals had thought, allowance of the full combination claims without allowance of the subcombination claims would not prevent the free use of the subcombination; *The Corn-Planter Patent* (*Brown* v. *Guild, Brown* v. *Selby*), 23 Wall., 90 U.S. 181, 1874.
72. Now styled *Special Equipment Co.* v. *Ooms, Comr. Pats.,* 153 F.2d 121, 68 USPQ 64, 1945.
73. *Corona Cord Tire Co.* v. *Dovan Chemical Corp.,* 276 U.S. 358, 1928.

Cross-references: *Anticipation, Interferences, Utility.*

ORGANIZATION. See CORPORATE PATENT DEPARTMENT

P

PATENT ATTORNEYS. See ATTORNEYS AND AGENTS, ASSOCIATIONS

PATENT DEPARTMENT. See CORPORATE

PATENT NOTICE BY MARKING AT HOME AND ABROAD. See MARKING

PATENT POLICIES. See CONSULTANT, CONSULTING LABORATORIES, MEDICAL ASSOCIATIONS AND PHYSICIANS, RESEARCH CORPORATION, RESEARCH DIRECTOR

PATENT PROCEDURES OF THE UNITED STATES—APPRAISAL FROM ABROAD

James G. Fife

It has often been said that the onlooker sees most of the game and certainly one viewing the United States Patent system across the Atlantic Ocean sees many features in it which may be regarded as unique.

Advantages

Thorough Examination of Applications. The United States Patent system undoubtedly has many excellent features and in particular the thorough search and examination which usually results in a Patent which has a reasonable chance of being respected by competitors and being held valid.

Continuations-in-part. The possibility of filing Continuation-in-part Application as the invention is developed is also a feature which is very useful to the inventor although it may prove something of a pitfall to the U.S. inventor when he endeavours to file abroad under the International Convention. If the Continuation-in-part Application is filed more than a year after the filing of the parent Application, the application abroad can claim priority under the International Convention only for the additional matter.

Claiming Product in Chemical Case. In chemical cases, the United States system has the advantage that claims to the product can be made although this feature is no longer unique since it is now to be found in the law of Great Britain and a number of countries of the Commonwealth.

No Compulsory License. From the point of view of the inventor there is also an advantage in the absence of compulsory license provisions from the United States Act which is of particular importance in the pharmaceutical field since many countries, including the United Kingdom, have provisions which render it easy to obtain a compulsory license, particularly in respect of pharmaceutical inventions.

Contributory Infringement. The possibility of bringing an action for infringement against a contributory infringer is also an advantage to the Patentee which is absent from the systems of many other countries.

Disadvantages

The United States system has, however, a number of disadvantages, some of which are connected with formalities and some of which are more fundamental.

Formal Requirements. It seems that, when the United States Act is next revised, consideration might be given at any rate to dispensing with some of the irritating formal requirements which do not seem to serve any useful purpose. Examples of these are the requirement for drawings in very simple cases such as inventions relating to laminates which obviously should require no illustration.

Costs. The thorough examination and the high cost of all goods and services in the United States render the prosecution rather expensive by European standards, but this is in part compensated for by the fact that there are no renewal fees.

Requirement of Oath Unusual. The necessity for an Oath might also be reviewed because the United States is now the only important country which requires an Oath by the inventor. If it were possible to dispense with the Oath, it might also be possible to have the Application filed direct in the name of the Assignee, with mention of the inventor, which would save a good deal of trouble and expense.

Rigid Claim Drafting Rules. Consideration might also be given to the somewhat rigid rules with regard to the drafting of claims. While it is true that it is now possible in the United States to have dependent claims in suitable circumstances, the somewhat artificial rules relating to the drafting of claims are liable to render the claims difficult to understand and also to increase the number of claims which are necessary. It is usually possible to overcome the difficulties by using artificial language to avoid alternatives and in chemical cases to resort to the Markush type of claim. Although the writer is naturally prejudiced in favour of the British system of claim drafting, there is something to be said in favour of a system which allows the claims to be drafted in any way which the Applicant desires provided that it is clear that the claims as a whole are succinct.

Difficulty in Proving Patentability. A more serious disadvantage of the United States Patent system is the great difficulty often experienced in convincing the Examiner of patentability even in the case of an outstanding invention. This difficulty arises partly from the Examiner's practice of making a mosaic of documents after having read the Applicant's specification and, to a lesser extent, from the legal requirement of treating a prior grant as though it were a prior publication.

Proof of Utility in Pharmaceutical Cases. In pharmaceutical cases, the Examiner often raises very serious objections based on lack of utility. It is hoped that this practice will improve in view of some recent decisions such as those of the Court of Customs and Patent Appeals in the cases of *In re Bergel & Stock*, 130 USPQ 205, 1961 and *In re Krimmel*, 130 USPQ 215, 1961.

Interference Proceedings. The expense of litigation is not peculiar to the United States Patent system, but the Interference procedure seems to be very expensive and complicated. Consideration might well be given to replacing this by an Opposition procedure such as to be found in the laws of the United Kingdom, Germany, Holland and the Scandinavian countries. In this connection, the practice of proving dates in advance of filing is a cause of uncertainty, and consideration might be given to adopting the practice of most of the important countries of allowing the Applicant to rely for priority only on his date of application or priority under the International Convention. This at any rate has the advantage of certainty because it can be determined as a matter of fact what was the disclosure in the application as originally filed.

Appeals to Courts. Appeals from the decisions of the Patent Office also tend to be expensive and complicated, particularly when it is necessary to take an Appeal to the Court of Customs and Patent Appeals or to a federal district court.

The System Works Well

From the above, it will be seen that the observer from abroad sees many difficulties and defects in the United States Patent system, but in spite of these a United States Patent is very well worth having as is evidenced by the large number of applications which are filed from abroad as well as by U.S. nationals.

Since the above was written by Dr. Fife, the results have been compared from a questionnaire sent abroad by a group of American patent attorneys engaged in foreign practice and reported by V. Alexander Scher, 34 JPOS 544, 1962. A brief summary of the 31 answers received follows.

Unfavorable features noted most frequently: Need of execution and ribboning of papers before U.S. consular official; initialing before him of all minor as well as major changes made by applicant; preparing and executing assignments when applications are filed in names of assignees; supplying names of inventors when the foreign case is filed without inventors' names; having drawing in provisional application, to establish date of complete disclosure even though specification is understandable without reference to drawing; specification too complete, detailed and exhaustive; claims too much a catalog of innumerable parts, or steps when a process, without sufficient reliance on functional statements; complication of prosecution by election and restriction requirements and occasional citation of unrelated art; more expensive drawings because of higher standards and also unavailability of Bristol board in some countries and of qualified draftsmen; high government fees on filing and issuance; and more rapid turnover of examining personnel.

Favorable features: Patience of the Examiners in processing applications poorly prepared because of inadequate technical, translating or other facilities abroad; efficiency of Patent Office examinations; acceptance of informal drawings and permission to replace them later; and a patent system that is well established and the "most efficacious in its application."

Cross-references: *Act of 1952—Patents, Examination, Forms for Patent Procedures and Executions Thereof, Information for Independent Inventor.*

PATENT SEARCHING. See SEARCHING

PATENT STATUTE. See ACT OF 1952

PATENTABILITY

Richard J. Dearborn and R. Bradlee Boal

A patent is not a gift or award to the inventor, but in many respects is more in the nature of a contract between the inventor and his government.

The inventor must, in his application for patent, describe and illustrate his invention and the best way known to him of using it.

The United States, on its part, grants to the inventor the right to prevent others, except with his consent, from manufacturing, using or selling the invention for a limited period of time, usually seventeen years.

At the end of the seventeen years the patent expires, and the invention is *then* open to the public and may be used freely. The public welfare is thus served by the complete and accurate disclosure required of the inventor when he files his application for patent. Thus the present system contrasts greatly and favorably with the system of protecting advances which prevailed only a few centuries ago.

The public benefits in two ways from our patent system: (1) The public has immediate access to the teaching of the invention since copies of the patents are freely available to the public from the date of issue of the patent. This teaching adds to the knowledge of a particular art and enables others to build on it and develop new inventions while the patent monopoly is still effective. (2) After expiration of the seventeen years of life of the patent grant, the public is completely free to use or practice the invention in any way.

Conditions for Patentability—General

Pursuant to the enabling clause in the Constitution,* Congress has prescribed the conditions for patentability of an invention in Sections 101 to 103 of 35 U.S.C. These provisions constitute the statutory guide lines both for the Patent Office in determining whether a patent is to be issued and to the federal courts in considering the validity of an issued patent challenged by an accused infringer.

The conditions prescribed in these sections are relatively simple and few in number. Section 101 defines the type of invention which may be the subject of the patent. Section 102 prescribes the requirements commonly referred to as public use, abandonment and anticipation. Section 103 provides the standard for measuring "invention."

Together these three sections provide the conditions which, broadly speaking, are called novelty, utility and invention and which, if satisfied, warrant the issuance of a patent or an adjudication of validity.

* U.S. Constitution, Article I, Section 8. "The Congress shall have power ... to promote the progress of science and useful arts, by securing for limited times to authors and inventors the exclusive right to their respective writings and discoveries."

Section 101—Inventions Patentable

Section 101 defines the kinds of discovery or invention which may be protected by a patent as follows:

"Whoever invents or discovers any new and useful process, machine, manufacture, or composition of matter, or any new and useful improvement thereof, may obtain a patent therefor, subject to the conditions and requirements of this title."

For Design Patents (authorized by Section 171) and Plant Patents (Section 161), see articles on those subjects.

Section 101 excludes mere ideas or concepts from patent protection. Thus, for example, a new theory of the relationship between mass and energy or a new theory of the composition of the moon's surface could not be the subject of a patent.

Furthermore, unless the process, machine, manufacture, or composition of matter is useful, it cannot be the subject of a patent. On this basis, a perpetual motion machine which would serve no useful purpose cannot be the subject of a patent.

Since most inventions of the type on which applications are filed are useful, this particular provision usually presents no obstacle to the prospective patentee. However, in chemical cases it sometimes has proved to be a stumbling block. For example, a particular composition of matter may by itself be of no use to man, but may be useful as an intermediate in the production of an end product or composition of matter which is itself useful. At one time such a composition of matter was considered unpatentable for lack of utility. However, today, in an appropriate case, the Patent Office will allow a patent on such composition of matter. *In re Nelson and Shabica,* 280 F.2d 172, 126 USPQ 242, CCPA 1960.

Statutory Bars

Anticipation and Abandonment of Invention. These statutory bars to patenting are discussed in *Anticipation* and *Abandonment.*

Not Invention of Applicant. The statute, 35 U.S.C. 102, provides:

"A person shall be entitled to a patent unless he did not himself invent the subject matter sought to be patented...."

Except in the case where the inventor is dead or under legal incapacity, the actual inventor generally must apply for the patent. Rule 41. In addition, the applicant must make an oath that he believes himself to be the original and first inventor or discoverer of the invention. Rule 65. He must also state under oath that

"[He] does not know and does not believe that the same was ever known or used before his invention or discovery thereof, ... that to the best of his knowledge and belief the invention has not been in public use or on sale in the United States more than one year prior to his application, or patented or described in any printed publication in any country before his invention or more than one year prior to his application, or patented in any foreign country prior to the date of his application on an application filed by himself or his legal representatives or assigns more than twelve months prior to his application in this country." Rule 65.

In the case of death or legal incapacity, 35 U.S.C. 117 provides that legal representatives of the inventor may make application in lieu of the actual inventor. Rules 42 and 43.

In certain other special cases, someone other than the actual inventor who has a proprietary interest in the invention may make application in place of the inventor. 35 U.S.C. 118 and Rule 47 prescribe the procedure which must be followed in the case of the recalcitrant inventor. (See *Inventors*)

Concealment and Suppression. Section 102(g) provides that

"A person shall be entitled to a patent unless

"(g) before the applicant's invention thereof the invention was made in this country by another who had not abandoned, suppressed, or concealed it. In determining priority of invention there shall be considered not only the respective dates of conception and reduction to practice of the invention, but also the reasonable diligence of one who was first to conceive and last to reduce to practice, from a time prior to conception by the other."

The first sentence of this Section concerns concealment and suppression. The second sentence deals with determining priority of invention and is more fully covered in *Interferences.*

While the first inventor, as a general rule, is entitled to the protection afforded by the patent law, situations do arise where such person may be denied the right to a patent and in some cases the right may be awarded to another. Robinson states the rationale behind this exception to the general rule as follows:

"Upon principle,... the first inventor who discloses the invention is entitled to the patent, unless a prior conceiver of the same idea, who is on that account more meritorious than the later, is in good faith endeavoring to bestow the same invention on the public. Out of this principle grows the rule that such a first conceiver must use reasonable diligence in reducing his idea to practice, in order to entitle him to a patent as against a subsequent conceiver who has first produced the concrete art or instrument. And the same reason exists for requiring an inventor who has first completed the invention to proceed with reasonable diligence to disclose it by applying for a patent, if he desires to claim it as against a subsequent inventor.... [This rule] may on equitable grounds be regarded as the more correct, since an inventor who, having perfected his invention, voluntarily conceals it and unreasonably delays his application for a patent, thereby wilfully misleads subsequent and innocent inventors into the belief that the field covered by the invention is still open, and he therefore ought to be estopped from patenting the invention and appropriating its exclusive enjoyment to himself after their honest efforts in the same direction have succeeded." I Robinson, Law of Patents, p. 553, 1890.

For this reason, the statute requires that an inventor try to bestow the fruits of his invention or at least the teaching of the invention on the public with reasonable promptness in order to be entitled to a patent.

The leading case dealing with suppression and concealment of invention is *Mason* v. *Hepburn,* 1898 C.D. 510, 517, D.C. Cir. 1898. This case involved an appeal from a decision by the Commissioner of Patents in an interference proceeding. The Court of Appeals agreed that Mason had reduced the invention to practice first. However, Mason neither marketed the gun (the invention was for a magazine clip to be used

on a gun) nor in any other way made his invention available to the public. In fact, he made no application for patent until three months after the patent to Hepburn had issued (approximately seven years after Mason's alleged reduction to practice). Mason's alleged reduction to practice). The court noted these facts and then went on to say:

"Considering, then, this paramount interest of the public in its bearing upon the question as presented here, we think it imperatively demands that a subsequent inventor of a new and useful manufacture or improvement who had diligently pursued his labors to the procurement of a patent in good faith and without any knowledge of the preceding discoveries of another shall, as against that other, who has deliberately concealed the knowledge of his invention from the public, be regarded as the real inventor and as such entitled to his reward.

"The true ground of the doctrine, we apprehend, lies in the spirit and policy of the patent laws and in the nature of the equity that arises in favor of him who gives the public the benefit of the knowledge of his invention, who expends his time, labor, and money in discovering, perfecting, and patenting in perfect good faith that which he and all others have been led to believe has never been discovered by reason of the indifference, supineness or willful act of one who may, in fact, have discovered it long before."

This privilege of the subsequent inventor is sometimes called a case of "intervening private rights." Similarly, there are also instances where there may be "intervening public rights." Amdur, Patent Office Rules and Practice, p. 1303. See also *Kendall et al.* v. *Winsor,* 21 How. 322, 328, 1858.

Standard of Invention: Unobvious to One Skilled in the Art

Section 103. Conditions for patentability; non-obvious subject matter.

"A patent may not be obtained though the invention is not identically disclosed or described as set forth in section 102 of this title, if the differences between the subject matter sought to be patented and the prior art are such that the subject matter as a whole would have been obvious at the time the invention was made to a person having ordinary skill in the art to which said subject matter pertains. Patentability shall not be negatived by the manner in which the invention was made."

Section 103 is new with the 1952 Patent Act and codifies what has frequently been called the "standard of invention." (See *Invention*)

Statistics indicate that in the last decade, a stricter standard of invention has been applied than in the Patent Office. In addition to the considerations expressed above, this deduction may be partially explained by the fact that when a patent is litigated, the party asserting invalidity has an opportunity to go far more deeply into the question of validity than the Patent Office. For one thing, he has the benefit of all the material which came to light in the course of the patent prosecution. In addition, he can himself make an independent search for new anticipatory material. Furthermore, expert testimony against patentability may be presented at trial, whereas no such testimony was presented in the Patent Office. Still further, at the time the application is being prosecuted, the Patent Office has no way of assessing the practical value of the invention. On the other hand, when a patent reaches litigation, it has already been tested in the market place and it is easier at that stage to assess its utility and value to the industry concerned.

The above considerations not only partially explain the seeming difference in attitude of the Patent Office and the courts to an invention but to a large extent justify such a difference. It makes sense for the Patent Office to resolve doubt in favor of the inventor, as the Office does, in a doubtful case where it is in no position to assess the practical value of an invention. On the other hand, for the reasons outlined above, the court is in a better position to assess the merit of an invention, and it can more surely make a final decision with respect to the patent's validity.

A second deduction which one may draw from statistics is that a patentee in the past decade has been given more liberal treatment in the Fourth and Fifth Circuits than in the First, Second and Third. This apparent difference in standard of patentability is more difficult to explain. However, because application of Section 103 calls, to a large extent, for a subjective judgment by the court, it is logical that different courts will apply different subjective standards.

A third observation which one may make from certain tables given in *Adjudications* is that the ground of invalidity most frequently relied on by the Courts of Appeals in the past decade has been lack of invention, i.e., failure to meet the standard of Section 103. This reliance on Section 103 may be partially explained by the fact that where a court is doubtful about the validity of a patent and, after weighing all the equities involved, concludes that the invention does not merit a patent monopoly, the court's conclusion is more easily based on Section 103 than on any other section of the statute. Furthermore, because it is more difficult to show error in interpretation of Section 103 than any other section, a court is less likely to be reversed where it relies on Section 103 than on a more technical ground. In other words, lack of invention has become a convenient, catchall ground for an adjudication of invalidity.

Cross-references: *Abandonment, Adjudications, Anticipation, Interferences, Invention, Monopolies* ... section on Unobviousness, *Validity*.

PETITIONS IN PATENT SOLICITATION

Edward C. Vandenburgh

Most of the controversies arising between applicants and examiners involve the question of "invention" of the claimed subject matter over the prior art. To the extent that an applicant believes that any such rejections of claims are improper or unfounded, the correct procedure for obtaining review of the examiner's decision is by way of appeal to the Board of Appeals in the first instance, and subsequently to the courts. This subject is discussed under *Appeals in Patent Solicitation*.

In contrast, objections or requirements of an examiner as to most matters of form, compliance with the rules, etc., are reviewed by way of petition to the Commissioner of Patents. Basically the latter procedure is one in which the Commissioner is requested to exercise his overall supervisory authority as head of the Patent Office to direct the

Patent Office employee, who is believed to be acting improperly, to correct his action.

In many instances, an applicant would prefer to obtain review by way of petition, rather than by way of appeal. This not only avoids the requirement of paying a fee in most instances, but also leads to a decision more promptly, since a heavy backlog of work faces the Board of Appeals. However, any matter that is appealable ordinarily will not be reviewed by the Commissioner on petition. Rule 181(a). This is not to say that the Commissioner cannot do so, since his supervisory authority extends over the Board as well as the examining corps. If the Commissioner deems it appropriate, he can act with respect to decisions of the Board and has done so in some instances. See for example, *The Kroger Co.* v. *Country Club Ice Cream Co.,* 130 USPQ 34, Comr. Pats. 1961 (a trademark case). The generalization may be made that rejections of claims are appealable while objections that do not result in the disallowance of claims are petitionable. However, exceptions have been made, at least in part occasioned by individual Commissioners believing that there is a necessity to act in a particular instance to prevent injustice.

Characteristics of a Petition

One important facet of a petition is that it is not responsive to an office action and will not stay the running of time for a response. Rule 181(f). Thus if the time for a response to an office action is coming to an end, the applicant must take other appropriate action to prevent the application from becoming abandoned. In cases not under final rejection, this appropriate action would be to file a communication that is responsive to the outstanding office action. If the outstanding office action constitutes a final rejection, an appeal to the Board of Appeals (on the appealable matters, usually present) would be filed to prevent abandonment.

The petition should identify the application involved. It would be addressed to the Commissioner of Patents. An appropriate title of course would be, "Petition To The Commissioner" or the like. It should set forth: (a) a recitation of the facts giving rise to the controversy; (b) the specific points to be reviewed; and (c) the action requested of the Commissioner. The reasons and arguments justifying and supporting the propriety of the action requested should be embodied in the petition or accompany it in the form of a brief. As in the case of other legal arguments, authorities, i.e., statutes, rules or prior decisions should be cited where appropriate. Normally the facts involved in the controversy will already be of record in the Patent Office and no further evidence is required. However, if further evidence is necessary, as is often the case with respect to a petition for the institution of a public use proceeding, additional facts may be supplied in the form of affidavits and exhibits accompanying the petition.

Processing of Petition in Patent Office

There is no hard and fast procedure followed by the Patent Office in the processing of a petition and in deciding the issues thereby raised. This is due to the varied character of the questions that may occur. However, in the usual case of review of an objection made by an examiner in the course of ex parte prosecution of an application, the petition is submitted to the examiner involved for a statement of his position. A copy of this statement then is supplied to the petitioner. In other instances, the matter may be handled more informally. An opportunity for an oral hearing normally is not provided.

In the usual instance, the decision is made by another on behalf of the Commissioner. See *In re Schuyler,* 117 USPQ 229, Comr. Pats. 1957. Rule 181(g). In reaching a decision, the Commissioner is not limited by the requirements of the rules but may take action contrary thereto when appropriate. See 35 U.S.C. 6, Rule 183 and *Kingsland* v. *Carter Carburetor Corp.,* 77 USPQ 499, 168 F.2d 565, CA DC 1948. Normally the courts will not interfere in the Patent Office matters of the type that are reviewed by way of petition to the Commissioner. However, if the Commissioner's decision is arbitrary or capricious, review may be obtained by way of mandamus in federal district court despite the fact that a matter of discretion is involved in the decision. See *Commissariat à L'Energie Atomique et al.* v. *Watson Comr. Pats.*, 124 USPQ 126, 274 F.2d 594, CA DC 1960, and "Remedies Against the United States and Its Officials," 70 Harv. L. R., 829, 846-849.

Matters Petitionable

While Rule 181(a) gives three general categories of matters passed on by the Commissioner by way of petition, these can be grouped as to matters (a) in which the decision is rendered by the Commissioner in the first instance and (b) in which the Commissioner acts to review a prior decision or action of a member of the Patent Office staff.

The petitionable matters upon which the Commissioner acts to render a decision in the first instance are:

(1) To make an application "special" to expedite its prosecution. Rule 102.

(2) To review an abandoned application. Rule 137. A fee is required in this instance.

(3) To permit the delayed payment of the final fee for the grant of a patent where the time therefor has expired. Rule 317. The payment of a fee is required in this instance.

(4) To obtain access to an existing or abandoned application of another. *In re Application Filed April 28, 1951*, 122 USPQ 280, Comr. Pats. 1959. *In re Application for Trimless Cabinets*, 128 USPQ 95, Comr. Pats. 1960.

(5) To request institution of public use proceeding. Rule 292.

(6) To rescind, remove or modify a secrecy order. Rules 5.4 and 5.5.

(7) To obtain a license for foreign filing. Rules 5.11-5.14.

The following are typical of the actions, objections or requirements of an examiner that are reviewed by the Commissioner upon petition:

(1) The premature entry of a final rejection. 706.07(c) Manual of Patent Examining Procedure. *Ex parte Pearce*, 128 USPQ 122, PO BdApp 1959.

(2) A requirement for restriction. Rule 144. *Ex parte Auer*, 104 USPQ 149, PO BdApp 1954.

(3) A holding that an application is abandoned, as for example on the basis that a response allegedly was insufficient. 711.03(c) Manual. *Ex parte Mygatt*, 1912 C.D. 354, 184 O.G. 801, Comr. Pats. 1912.

(4) A requirement to correct the drawings, add or delete figures, etc. *Ex parte Saunders*, 119 USPQ 258, PO BdApp 1957.

(5) The refusal to grant a filing date. 1002.02 Manual.

(6) The refusal to enter an amendment. Rule 127.

(7) A holding that an amendment constitutes "new matter," provided that a rejection of a claim is not predicated thereon. *Ex parte Baril et al.*, 124 USPQ 509, PO BdApp 1958.

(8) A holding that an appeal to the Board is not in proper form or does not relate to an appealable question. Rule 193.

(9) The refusal of the examiner to follow prior decision of the Board of Appeals with respect to the same, or a parent, application. *Ex parte Barley*, 116 USPQ 592, PO BdApp 1957.

(10) The issuance of a rejection which is unclear, as for example, by reason of multifariousness. *In re Leflar*, 85 USPQ 377, Supervisory Exmr. 1947.

As a general rule any rejection of a claim, whether on the basis of lack of invention, form, terminology, etc., is a matter for appeal rather than petition. *Ex parte Martin*, 104 USPQ 124, Supervisory Exmr. 1952. However, such rejections of claims have been reviewed on petition in some instances, e.g., *Ex parte Dahlen*, 21 USPQ 397, Comr. Pats. 1934.

Cross-references: *Appeals in Patent Solicitation, Prosecution of Patent Applications.*

PHARMACEUTICAL PATENT PRACTICE

I. Louis Wolk

Many aspects of pharmaceutical application and patents are unique and involve problems that exist in no other branch of patent practice.

The special patent problems date from the development of chemotherapy. They arise partly from the diverse nature of pharmaceutical products and partly from the special scrutiny given by the Patent Office and the courts to products intended for human therapy. It is not surprising, therefore, that practice relating to pharmaceuticals is perhaps the most complex and most controversial in the entire field of patents or that it varies greatly in foreign countries, as tabulated later herein.

History

The modern age of chemotherapy may be said to have begun with Paul Ehrlich's discovery of Salvarsan in 1909, as a treatment for syphilis. This was the first proof that substances could be discovered or synthesized which could be given internally, to attack disease-producing bacteria in the body, without injury to the patient. Salvarsan was not patented.

Despite this promising beginning, the fulfilment of the promise in any substantial degree was delayed until 1935. Then Domagk of I. G. Farben published the results of his historic experiments with a red dye, Prontosil (see Table 1), and demonstrated that this dye could kill streptococci in animals without damage to the animals themselves. Shortly thereafter Fourneaux, in Paris, discovered that the active structural component was sulfanilamide—itself an old compound.

From this time on, development came swiftly. The state of knowledge of synthetic organic chemistry, especially in Europe, was such that related compounds could be synthesized and tested and the biological rationale for the exploitation of "leads" developed. Newer sulfonamides having special effectiveness against certain organisms, fewer side effects, or lower toxicity followed quickly, among them sulfapyridine, sulfadiazine, sulfamerazine and sulfamethazine.

The discovery of the effectiveness of penicillin in 1941 opened the door to the new field of antibiotics leading to the discovery of streptomycin in 1943, chloromycetin in 1948, and tetracyclines—chlorotetracycline in 1948, oxytetracycline in 1950, and tetra-

cycline in 1952. Numerous other developments in the field of microbiology led to the discovery of other antibiotics from microorganisms.

The synthesis of sex hormones, such as testosterone in 1935 and estrone in 1936, and of cortisone in 1946 opened the way to further advances in steroids. The synthesis of the vitamins, beginning in the 1920's, revolutionized the treatment of dietary deficiencies.

In the 40 years following 1923, each of several of the listed inventions of Table 1 may separately have saved more human lives than were lost on the battlefields of the two world wars plus the wars of Napoleon. For the United States, where new drugs can be patented, it can not be said to be mere coincidences that over 70 per cent of the inventions selected for the Table, as important, are assigned to domestic corporations. Since the breakthrough with Insulin in 1923, our life expectancy at birth has lengthened by more than 12 years. With this record, we can hope that government policies will preserve a climate favorable to continuing improvement in such vital statistics.

The U.S. patent numbers and other information regarding patented drugs may be found in Table 1 which lists representative, but not all important pharmaceutical inventions since 1923. This Table is based upon information developed during Hearings before the Subcommittee on Antitrust and Monopoly of the Committee on the Judiciary of the U.S. Senate, on S. 1552, December 7-9, 1961, pp. 2144-2149, and other information believed to be reliable.

The superscripts show, in abbreviated form, the name of the assignee thus: [ab]Abbott Labs.; [al]Allied Labs.; [ah]American Home Products; [am]American Cyanamid; [b]Burroughs Wellcome; [c]Ciba Pharmaceutical Products; [ca]Carter Products; [e]Eaton Labs.; [el]Eli Lilly; [en]Endo Products; [g]Geigy; [h]Hoffman-LaRoche; [i]I.C.I. England; [l]Lakeside Labs.; [m]Merck; [me]Merrell; [n]National Research Development; [ol]Olin Mathieson; [os]Osterreichische Stickstoff W.; [p]Parke, Davis; [pf]Pfizer; [re]Research Corp.; [ro]Roche-Organon; [ru]Rutgers Research; [s]Schering; [se]Searle; [sm]Smith, Kline and French; [soc]Soc. Usine Chimique Rhone-Poulenc; [sp]Spojene Farmaceutike; [sy]Syntex; [u]Upjohn; [un]University Zavodny, Narodni Podnik; [sy]Syntex; [u]Upjohn;

unUniversity of Toronto; ucUnion Chimique Belge; usvU.S. Vitamin and Pharmaceutical; wWinthrop Chem.; usU.S.A.

Table 1 illustrates how cooperation among various disciplines in the fields of chemistry, physics, and biology has resulted in contributions of revolutionary scope. Even greater progress is anticipated in the years to come.

Patent Disclosure

In general, the patent disclosure embodies principles applicable to chemical patent specifications in general, but with modifications as discussed below.

Special scrutiny and the higher standards required of pharmaceutical patent disclosures inevitably create problems with respect to their nature and adequacy. Certain of these problems stem from the difficulty in defining some of the inventions in terms of chemical structure, as in products of fermentation, complex mixtures and the like; defining the scope of the invention where predictability of activity of equivalents is sometimes questionable; and satisfying higher standards of utility or efficacy frequently raised by the Patent Office.

Utility. The critical scrutiny which is characteristically applied to pharmaceutical applications by the Patent Office, and to a certain extent by the courts, stems to a large extent from an extreme sensitivity generated by a few incidents in the past. A number of patents issued on remedies found to be ineffective received a certain amount of publicity. The grant of a patent—to some, a badge of approval by the government—brought criticism of the Patent Office when the remedy failed. Under present-day conditions, with the effective and complex machinery of the FDA and the FTC, the marketing of products with false claims is not a practical possibility. Nevertheless, the Patent Office practice developed to the point where mere compliance with 35 U.S.C. 101, namely, that an indication of utility be given, was not enough. Proof of utility in the form of clinical data was required. After *Isenstead* v. *Watson*, 115 USPQ 408, DC Dist Col 1957, the Patent Office began to require evidence of safety as well as

efficacy in human therapy whenever the specification or claims indicated either expressly or by implication that the product was intended for human use. In other words, the product had to be demonstrated as "safe, effective, and reliable," the Court in this case having said:

"It is right and proper that the Patent Office should be very careful and perhaps even reluctant to grant a patent on a new medical formula until it has been thoroughly tested and successfully tried by more than one physician."

This approach, followed with particular rigidity in applications which related directly or even by implication to cancer remedies, began to be modified in 1961, after a series of decisions by the Court of Customs and Patent Appeals, one of which specially stated that:

"The fact remains that Congress has not charged the Patent Office with the task of protecting the public against possible misuse of Chemical Patents." *In re Krimmel,* 130 USPQ 215, 1961. *In re Bergel et al.,* 130 USPQ 205, 1961 and *In re Dodson,* 130 USPQ 224, 1961.

This philosophy was emphatically reiterated by the CCPA, under the "factual situation" in *In re Hartrop et al.,* 135 USPQ 419, 1962, which said:

"Bearing in mind that absolute proof of such a proposition as 'safety' of a drug or medicament is impossible and that 'proof' of 'safety' is relative with the degere of 'proof' dependent on the quantity and quality of the available evidence, bearing in mind what evidence of 'safety' has been submitted in the case at bar, and bearing in mind that inherent in the concept of the 'standard experimental animal' is the ability of one skilled in the art to make the appropriate correlations between the results actually observed with the animal experiments and the probable results in human therapy, we hold that appellants' claimed solutions have been shown to be useful within the meaning of 35 U.S.C. 101. In holding as we do, we realize that no clinical evidence has been submitted as to the 'safety' of these solutions. Therefore there is lacking that degree of 'proof' which such evidence would provide. However, we do not believe that such a degree of 'proof' is necessary in view of the factual situation in the case at bar. We think that a sufficient probability of safety in human therapy

TABLE 1. PHARMACEUTICAL INVENTIONS.

Products Classified	Patent Number/Year	Inventor(s)
Antihistamines		
Tripellenamine (Pyribenzamine)	2,406,594/46	Djerassi Huttrer Scholz [c]
Diphenhydramine	2,421,714/47	Rieveschl [p]
Pyrathiazine	2,483,999/49	Hunter Reid [u]
Chlorpheniramine maleate	2,567,245/51	Sperber Papa Schwenk [s]
Chlorcyclizine	2,630,435/53	Baltzly Castillo [b]
Anesthetics		
Thiamylal sodium	2,153,729/39	Volwiler Tabern [ab]
Hexylcaine HCl	2,486,374/49	Cope [m]
Hydroxydione	2,708,651/55	Laubach [pf]
Dyclonine	2,771,391/56	Bockstahler [al]
Halothane	2,849,502/58	Suckling Raventos [i]
Pramoxine HCl	2,870,151/59	Wright Moore [ab]
Antibacterials—Synthetic		
Sulfaguanidine	2,218,490/40	Winnek [am]
Chloroquin phosphate	2,233,970/41	Andersag Breitner Jung [w]
Phthallyl sulfathiazole	2,324,015/43	Moore [m]
Sulfisomidine	2,351,333/44	Gysin [g]
Sulfamethazine	2,407,966/46	Sprague [m]
Sulfamerazine	2,407,966/46	Sprague [m]
Sulfadiazine	2,410,793/46	Winnek Roblin [am]
Nitrofurazone	2,416,234/47	Stillman Scott [e]
Sulfisoxazole	2,430,094/47	Wuest Hoffer [h]
Chloroguanide	2,467,371/49	Curd Rose [i]
Isoniazid	2,596,069/52	Fox [h]
Primaquin phosphate	2,604,474/52	Elderfield Werble [usa]
Nitrofurantoin	2,610,181/52	Hayes [e]
Sulfadimethoxine	2,703,800/55	Bretschneider Klötzer [os]
Sulfamethoxypyridazine	2,712,012/55	Clark [am]
Antibiotics		
Streptomycin	2,449,866/48	Waksman Schatz [ru]
Chlortetracycline	2,482,055/49	Duggar [am]
Chloramphenicol	2,483,885/49	Crooks Rebstock Bartz [p]
Bacitracin	2,498,165/50	Johnson Meleny [usa]
Dihydrostreptomycin	2,498,574/50	Peck [m]
Oxytetracycline	2,516,080/50	Sobin Finlay Kane [pf]
Penicillin V	2,562,410/51	Behrens Soper Corse [el]
Erythromycin	2,653,899/53	Bunch McGuire [el]
Tetracycline	2,699,054/55	Conover [pf]
Oleadomycin	2,757,123/56	Sobin Routien Lees [pf]
Cycloserine	2,773,878/56	Shull Routien Finlay [pf]
Nystatin	2,797,183/57	Hazen Brown [re]
Neomycin	2,799,620/57	Waksman Lechevalier [ru]
Demethylchlortetracycline	2,878,289/59	McCormick Hirsch Jensen Sjolander [am]
Kanamycin	2,931,798/60	Umezawa Maeda Ueda
Spiramycin	3,000,785/61	Ninet Binnert Preud'homme [soc]
Novobiocin	3,049,534/62	Wallick [m]
6-Aminopenicillanic Acid (Process)	3,121,667/64	Rott [ol] Walzinski
Anti-inflammatory Agents—Nonsteroid		
Phenylbutazone	2,562,830/51	Stenze [g]
Probenecid	2,608,507/52	Miller [m]
Antiparasitics		
Diethylcarbamazine citrate	2,467,895/49	Kushner Brancone [am]
Pyrvinium pamoate	2,925,417/60	Eislager Worth [p]
Biologicals		
Streptokinase-streptodornase	2,701,227/55	Ablondi Adams [am]

TABLE 1. PHARMACEUTICAL INVENTIONS. (*Continued*)

Products Classified	Patent Number/Year	Inventor(s)	Products Classified	Patent Number/Year	Inventor(s)
Cancer			*Diuretics*		
4-Amino-10-methylfolic acid	2,512,572/50	Smith Cosulich [am]	Acetazoleamide	2,554,816/51	Clapp Roblin [am]
			Chlorothiazide	2,809,194/57	Novello [m]
Triethylene-melamine	2,520,619/50	Wystrach Kaiser [am]	*Nervous System—Mental Health*		
Triethylenethio-phosphoramide	2,670,347/54	Kuh Seeger [am]	Chlorpromazine HCl	2,645,640/53	Charpentier [soc]
Mercaptopurine	2,697,709/54	Hitchings Robbins [b]	Meprobamate	2,724,720/55	Berger Ludwig [ca]
Busulfan	2,917,432/59	Timmis [b]	Promazine	2,799,619/57	Seifter
Chlorambucil	2,944,079/60	Ross Everett Roberts [n]	(formulation of compound in unit dosage form)		Monaco Hoover [ah]
Cardiovascular			Azacyclonol HCl	2,804,422/57	Schumann VanCampen Pogge [me]
Naphazoline	2,161,938/39	Sonn [c]			
Ethyl biscou-macetate	2,482,510/49	Rosicky [sp]	Perphenazine	2,838,507/58	Cusic Hamilton [se]
Hydralazine	2,484,029/49	Hartmann Druey [c]	Chlordiazepoxide	2,893,992/59	Sternbach [h]
Phenoxyben-zamine hydrochloride	2,599,000/52	Kerwin Ullyot [sm]	Hydroxyzine	2,899,436/59	Morren [uc]
			Prochlorperazine	2,902,484/59	Horclois [soc]
Diphenadione	2,672,483/54	Thomas [u]	Trifluproma-zine HCl	2,921,069/60	Ullyot [sm]
Mecamylamine	2,831,027/58	Pfister Stein [m]			
Chlorisondamine chloride	2,846,382/58	Allen [c]	*Nervous System—Other*		
Methyldopa	2,868,818/59	Pfister Stein [m]	Phenobarbital	1,025,872/12	Hoerlein
			Phenylephrine	1,932,347/33 1,954,389/34	Tegerlotz
Guanethidine sulfate	2,928,829/60	Mull [c]	Meperidine	2,167,351/39	Eisleb [w]
Diabetes			Alphaprodine HCl	2,498,433/50	Lee Ziering [h]
Insulin	1,469,994/23	Banting Best Collip [un]	Dimenhydrinate	2,499,058/50	Cusic [se]
			Racemorphan	2,524,855/50	Schnider Grüssner [h]
Protamine zinc insulin	2,232,641/41	Scott Fisher [un]	Cyclizine	2,630,435/53	Baltzly Castillo [b]
Acetazolamide	2,554,816/51	Clapp Roblin [am]	Methsuximide	2,643,257/53	Miller Long [p]
Chlormerodrin	2,635,982/53	Rowland [l]			
Aminometradine	2,650,922/53	Papesch Schroeder [se]	Ethoheptazine citrate	2,666,050/54	Diamond Bruce [ah]
Mercumatilin	2,667,442/54	Schlesinger Weiner Gordon [en]	Glutethimide	2,673,205/54	Hoffmann [c] Tagmann
			Nalorphine	2,364,833/54	Weijlard Erickson [m]
Phenformin	2,961,377/60	Shapiro Freedman [usv]	Meclizine	2,709,169/55	Morren [uc]
Tolbutamide	2,968,158/61	Ruschig Aumüller Horger Wagner Scholz Bander [u]	Dextropropoxy-phene	2,728,779/55	Pohland [el]
			Trimeprazine	2,837,518/58	Jacob Robert [soc]
			Anileridine phosphate	2,966,490/60	Weijlard Pfister [m]

TABLE 1. PHARMACEUTICAL INVENTIONS.
(*Continued*)

Products Classified	Patent Number/Year	Inventor(s)
Steroid Hormones—Corticoids		
Cortisone acetate	2,183,589/39	Reichstein Schlittler [ro]
Hydrocortisone acetate	2,183,589/39	Reichstein Schlittler [ro]
Hydrocortisone *t*-butyl acetate	2,736,733/56	Rogers [m] Conbere
Prednisolone *t*-butyl acetate	2,736,734/56	Sarett [m]
Prednisolone phosphate	2,789,117/57	Sarett [m]
Triamcinolone	2,789,118/57	Bernstein Renhard Allen [am]
Fluprednisolone	2,841,600/58	Hogg Spero [u]
Fludrocortisone acetate	2,852,511/58	Fried [ol]
Methylprednisolone	2,897,218/59	Sebek Spero [u]
Prednisone and Prednisolone	3,134,718/64	Nobile [s]
Steroid Hormones—Other		
Norethandrolone	2,721,871/55	Colton [se]
Norethynodrel	2,725,389/55	Colton [se]
Norethindrone	2,744,122/56	Djerassi Miramontes Rosenkranz [sy]
Testosterone propionate	2,311,067/43	Ciba [c]
Vitamins and Related Substances		
Vitamin B_{12}	2,563,794/51	Rickes Wood [m]

has been demonstrated in the case at bar to satisfy the requirement of 35 U.S.C. 101 that appellants' invention be useful."

"...[The] public must be protected absolutely against the advertising and sale and other distribution of harmful drugs, medicines and the like in all situations, including this one if such be the case. We believe that Congress has recognized this problem and has clearly expressed its intent to give statutory authority and responsibility in this area to Federal agencies different than that given to the Patent Office This is so because the standards established by statute for the advertisement, use, sale or distribution of drugs are quite different than the requirements under the Patent Act for the issuance of a patent."

These decisions and others also clearly establish that animal tests may provide adequate proof of utility even where ultimate human use is indicated and whether or not efficacy in humans is presently or ultimately demonstrated. It may be noted that the Bergel case disclosed, but did not claim, anti-tumor activity. Animal tests, even where ultimate intended use was for humans, had previously been accepted as adequate utility for reduction to practice, in *Archer* v. *Papa*, 121 USPQ 413, CCPA 1959. Where the claims recite or depend for patentability upon a specific use, the nature of proofs required must be commensurate.

This careful approach to the question of utility in such cases is illustrated by the Board of Appeals decision in *Ex parte Adolf Gashler*, published in the U.S. Official Gazette for June 2, 1964, although the case was decided on December 20, 1961. The decision holds claims to an injection fluid unpatentable for lack of proof of operativeness where the specification indicated cancer-curing utility for humans. The Patent Office interpretation of the *Krimmel* and *Bergel* decisions may be understood from the following language in the *Gashler* case:

"While appellant urges the claims not to be drawn to a cancer-curing agent, the first paragraph of page 9 of the specification specifically stated that solutions prepared from the claimed compositions are to be injected into human beings for combating cancer and to achieve a result not hereto achieved. The Examiner therefore was justified in requiring proof of such utility as compliance with the provisions of 35 U.S.C. 101. *Commonwealth Engineering Co.* v. *Ladd,* 131 USPQ 255. As stated in said decision, great care is required in the consideration of patent applications directed toward inventions intended for medical use. The court therein differentiated from the situation presented in *In re Krimmel,* 48 CCPA 1116; 130 USPQ 215, where persuasive tests indicating operativeness were presented. Similarly, the situation at bar differs from the factual situation presented in *In re Krimmel* supra, as well as that in *In re Franz Bergel et al.,* 48 CCPA 1101 and 1102; 292 F.2d 958 and 955; 130 USPQ 205 and 206, where utility directed toward the treatment of cancer in human beings was not expressed and tests evidencing operability in test animals were accepted.

"The only evidence presented herein is set forth in the Wolfe affidavit of November 20, 1958, which is deficient for the reasons set forth by the Examiner. This affidavit expresses an opinion and conclusions resulting from tests, the data of which have not been presented in this record."

(See *Utility*)

It may be noted that the Patent Office has so far been reluctant to accept these decisions except upon fact situations closely related to those previously decided so that each case, at least insofar as the Office is concerned, must stand on its own feet.

Affidavits. While proof of utility, when required, need not be included in the specification and may be supplied by affidavit, the material referred to in the affidavit must generally be based upon a statement or allegation in the specification. *Ex parte Pennell et al.,* 99 USPQ 56, PO BdApp 1952.

The affidavits themselves must be accurate, convincing, and soundly based, the data should be statistically significant, and reasonable controls should be included. The data may be accumulated outside the United States. *Ex parte Gonzalez-Barcena et al.,* 102 USPQ 365, PO BdApp 1954. The affidavit must relate to allegations made in the specification. If the showing is unrelated to matter originally disclosed, it may not be convincing. *Ex parte Dole,* 119 USPQ 260, PO BdApp 1957; also *In re Herr,* 134 USPQ 176, CCPA 1962.

The Patent Office has, in a few cases so far, implemented the specific authorization to transmit questions relating to drugs to the Secretary of the Department of Health, Education and Welfare, as provided in the Drug Industry Act of 1962 amending— among others—Section 702 of the Federal Food, Drug and Cosmetic Acid (21 USC 372). These questions have related mainly to adequacy of clinical data in affidavits and the like.

Unknown Structure. One aspect of pharmaceutical inventions not frequently encountered in other fields of chemistry is uncertainty as to the chemical structure of the product, as with products obtained from natural sources, by fermentation or from complex chemical reactions. In such circumstances, the product may be defined in terms of its chemical and physical properties provided that it can be so identified apart from the process by which it was produced. *Cochrane et al.* v. *Badische et al.,* 111 U.S. 293; 1884 C.D. 230. But see *Graham* v. *Montevier,* 103 USPQ 24, DC NIll 1954; *Ex parte Fox,* 128, USPQ 157, PO BdApp 1957; *Ex parte Brockman et al.,* 127 USPQ 57, 1959; and *Benger Labs. Ltd.* v. *R. K. Laros Co.,* 135 USPQ 11, 1962, the latter saying:

"The precise chemical structure of the claimed product is not known to either the plaintiff or the defendants, nor to any of the impressive array of experts whom they called and, being unknown, it is not nor can it be described or claimed by chemical structural formula. However, nothing in the law requires the courts to deny a patent to the inventor of a new and useful product merely because laboratory technique has not advanced to a point where the chemical structure can be recognized and described. All that is necessary is that the patentee make as full disclosure as he reasonably can and that he describe the product with sufficient particularity that it can be identified and that those who are interested in its manufacture are enabled to determine what will and what will not infringe."

An interesting decision which illustrates the problems which may arise in attempting to define a new product in terms of its properties is *In re Fisher,* 135 USPQ 22, 1962, rehearing denied 137 USPQ 150, CCPA, 1963. The claims at issue were directed to a hormone which was defined in terms of certain properties including potency. The claims were denied by the majority of the court both times primarily on the ground that "potency" was a result rather than a physical characteristic. Particularly noteworthy are the strong dissents by Judges Rich and Smith in dissenting from the denial of the petition for rehearing.

Support for Generic Claims. A problem, which occurs frequently in chemical cases, is especially common in pharmaceutical cases. This is the difficulty in supporting generic or broad claims that cover numerous compounds, every one of which cannot be subjected to animal or clinical tests. Generally, a reasonable number of examples will support a generic claim, but this is a matter which depends on the facts in each case. In *Ex parte Burtner*, 115 USPQ 297, 1957, the Board of Appeals stated:

"We are of the opinion that the showing of the vast superiority of two members of the group of six compounds covered by the claims over the nearest compound of the prior art may be considered sufficient to show the superiority of the entire group."

On the other hand, in *Schering Corp.* v. *Gilbert et al.*, 68 USPQ 84, CA 2 1946, Patent No. 2,345,384, the Court, in holding the generic claim 4 invalid, said:

"The claim is for an enormous number of as yet nonexistent compounds and is far broader than any disclosure in the patent."

The Board of Appeals has held that where acceptable clinical evidence is adduced for certain members of a class of compounds, clinically untested members are patentable if their relationship to those tested, plus successful animal tests for both, provide a rational basis for concluding that they have sufficient utility to be of commercial value for treating humans or possibly animals. *Ex parte Murphy*, 134 USPQ 134, 1962 (Patent No. 3,040,025).

In a microbiological case the disclosure of a single strain was held adequate to support a claim to a process for the use of a species of microorganisms to produce an antibiotic. *Ex parte Benedict et al.*, 111 USPQ 354, PO BdApp 1956.

The law on this point is believed well expressed in *In re Cavallito et al.*, 127 USPQ 206, 209, CCPA 1960, where the Court stated:

"In the final analysis the board's holding appears to be that as a matter of law nineteen examples are not enough to support a claim embracing many thousands of compounds. We are unable to agree to that proposition. The sufficiency of a disclosure depends not on the number but rather on the nature of the claimed compounds per se and the nature of the supporting disclosures. If a claim covers compounds which are closely related, a comparatively limited disclosure may be sufficient

to support it. If, however, the claim covers compounds which are related only in some structural respects, a more extensive supporting disclosure may be necessary to support it. Moreover, the selection of the examples and other exemplary material used as the disclosure to support a claim must be adequately representative of the area covered by it. In some instances a limited disclosure which is typical of various areas covered by a claim may be of greater value in determining the patentable characteristics of the claimed compounds than a more extensive disclosure would be if related only to a limited portion of the area."

On the other hand, the greater scrutiny given to the disclosure in pharmaceutical cases is emphasized by the language of the court in *In re Henri Riat et al.*, 140 USPQ 471, CCPA 1964. This case involved an azo dyestuff invention, and the CCPA stated:

"Whether a disclosure gives reasonable assurance that all of the compounds embraced by the claims would be useful for the purposes intended must be determined by the particular circumstances of each case, including the nature of the compounds per se and the supporting disclosure. Here, in contrast to Cavallito which involved pharmaceutical compounds where unpredictability is particularly notorious, we are concerned with azo dyestuffs which constitute an art-recognized genus."

An important related proposition involves the question of prophetic disclosures. This is clearly discussed in the case of *Lawson et al.* v. *Bruce et al.*, 105 USPQ 440, 42 CCPA 893, 1955 and in *Herr* v. *Wettstein et al.*, 140 USPQ 190 PO Bd of Interferences, December 14, 1962. In the *Lawson* case no specific working example was disclosed, the compound was only named, and the appellees merely asserted that the compound could be made by procedures analogous to those disclosed in the examples with respect to other compounds. There were given no independently identifying properties or qualitative physical constants. The principal starting material was undisclosed and had to be deduced, as distinct from the *Herr* case where the starting material was fully named.

In the *Herr* case, the Board stated:

"As it is clear from the *Lawson et al.* case, it is not required in an application disclosure that identification by analysis, physical properties, etc., be set forth. These are matters relating to proof of actual reduction to practice. For constructive reduction to practice it is sufficient if the compound be accurately named and a method of preparation is disclosed, as in the case here, and there is no requirement that an applicant actually reduce the invention to practice."

Manner of Use. Unless inherent or obvious, the disclosure should contain an indication of the manner of use of the pharmaceutical product. This may be a discussion of the mode of administration and a recommended size or range of dosage, even though the claims are not necessarily so limited.

Antibiotics and Microbiological Products

To the extent that antibiotic agents are produced by chemical syntheses, their patent disclosure and claims correspond to those utilized in connection with organic chemical compounds, whether protected as such or as chemotherapeutic agents. When these are produced by microbiological methods, special problems exist. A complete discussion of this aspect occurs elsewhere in this work. Production is carried out by the fermentation of nutrient media by microorganisms which are themselves generally previously unknown, and which have been discovered in soil samples or developed by mutation of other organisms. Thus, the organism itself must be adequately described and disclosed as well as the conditions under which the fermentation is carried out. The products of fermentation must be isolated and identified. Where the structure of the product can be defined, the problem of claiming may be simplified, but where the structure is unknown or has not yet been determined the matter of defining the product may be complicated.

Under present practice, the Patent Office requires that a culture of the microorganism be deposited with a recognized culture collection prior to filing of the application in the Patent Office. This is on the theory that merely describing the morphology of the organism is not adequate disclosure since there is no assurance that the organism will be readily available to others upon issuance of a patent, and that the disclosure

is incomplete unless there is evidence of the existence of the organism at the time of filing. Recognized culture collections include the following: American Type Culture Collection (ATCC), 12301 Parklawn Drive, Rockville, Maryland; Institute of Microbiology, Rutgers University, New Brunswick, New Jersey; and Northern Regional Research Laboratories (NRRL), U.S. Department of Agriculture, Peoria Illinois. A typical manner of identifying a new microorganism by reference to its deposit and by its morphological description may be found in U.S. Patent No. 3,102,076. (Cf. *Microbiological Applications and Patents*)

New Use

The invention of a new chemical compound which may have a therapeutic or other use, if it be clearly new by patent standards and not complicated by questions of obviousness, equivalency, homology, and the like, involves comparatively few problems. This is in contrast to the difficulty encountered in obtaining adequate patent protection for a discovery based on the new use of an old compound.

The problem was dramatically illustrated in the celebrated case of *Morton* v. *N. Y. Eye Infirmary*, 6 Blatch 116, 2 Fisher 320. Morton, the inventor of the use of ether as an anesthetic, attempted to enforce his patent claims to its use. The Court held the patent invalid on grounds of unpatentability and said that if the claims were to be construed as for a process or an art, it was outside the scope of the patent laws. Numerous subsequent decisions reaffirmed the principle of the Morton case, at least to the extent that the new use was claimed as a product.

The modern line of cases, prior to the Patent Act of 1952, may be said to rely on *In re Thuau*, 57 USPQ 324, 326 CCPA 1943, in which the Court considered claims to a therapeutic agent which was an old compound for tanning and held that a new use of an old compound without modification, was not patentable. (See *Chemical Applications*) On the other hand, the Patent Office recognized the patentability, as a process, of a new use of an old material, notably in *Ex parte Wagner*, 99 USPQ 207, PO BdApp 1950, and in *Ex parte Muller*, 81 USPQ 261, PO BdApp 1947, which related to a process of killing insects by the use of an old chemical.

The question of patentability of new uses and the propriety of process claims to new uses of old products, a continuously controversial subject, was clarified in the Patent Act of 1952, 35 U.S.C. Section 100(b) reading:

"The term 'process' means process, art or method, and includes a new issue of a known process, machine, manufacture, composition of matter, or material."

Thus the stamp of statutory approval was placed upon a new use in terms of a process.

As to pharmaceutical inventions, the statute was applied in *Ex parte Zbornik et al.*, 109 USPQ 508, PO BdApp 1956, and numerous other cases. These decisions allowed claims directed to processes for the treatment of disease based upon the new use of old materials.

In an interesting 1963 case, *In re Caldwell*, 138 USPQ 243, the CCPA allowed claims to the use of aspirin for feeding ruminants, poultry, and swine on a showing that its action as a growth promoter was new and unobvious. One of the allowed claims reads as follows:

"The method of stimulating growth of ruminants, poultry and swine which comprises feeding animals rations supplying an effective amount of aspirin for growth stimulation."

The importance of this practice to the industry is well stated by Fellner, 41 JPOS 56, 1959.

"[The] point of novelty lay in the application of a chemical compound to a new object or environment whereby a new process was evolved. Recognition of the concept that a specific disease or pathological environment alone may be 'material acted upon' and thus constitute a tangible and evaluative criterium in passing on the patentability of methods involving old operational steps and instrumentalities is a gratifying advance in patent jurisprudence and provides the pharmaceutical industry with new opportunities to protect its valuable discoveries by process claims in cases where composition claims would be barred under the In re Thuau rule."

Enforcement of Use Claims. Fellner also stated: "The major problem with this type of claim lies in the difficulty of enforcing it against infringement." The old compound may be sold in commerce and the patentee, to enforce his patent, might have to sue a small distributor or ultimate consumer, despite the increased protection offered by Sections 271(b) and (c). However, the problem of enforcement in the case of prescription drugs, is greatly minimized by the fact that the manufacturer or seller of the product is required to include with it under Federal Food and Drug Regulations, a complete written description of the drug and its manner and purpose of use. This may clearly establish infringement, under these sections, of a process claim based on a new use of an old material, if this was the purpose or function for which the drug was being sold.

Old Compounds with Therapeutic Uses As New Products. While the doctrine of *In re Thuau* lives on, the patentability of old products *in product claim form* has been upheld where such products are combined with other materials or exist in a novel physical form or relationship. Numerous patents have been allowed to issue in which the old compound is claimed as associated with a carrier, or in "unit dosage form." Such claims may be invalid unless there is something unobvious in this association. In *In re Rosicky*, 125 USPQ 341, 1960, the CCPA held, with respect to claims to an old compound plus a pharmaceutical carrier:

"Appellant, to overcome this ground of rejection relies primarily upon a number of prior art patents which include claims to compounds in the environment of carriers of various types, presumably to establish that the utilization of a carrier in admixture with a compound can make an old compound patentable. We know of no authority which compels such a conclusion."

However, specific proportions having at least some degree of criticality may impart patentability.

On the other hand, in *In re Craige*, 90 USPQ 33, 1951, the CCPA held, under the former statute:

"While it is true that in certain cases invention might be present in a very slight alteration, and the Thuau doctrine avoided, such alteration must always amount to more than mechanical or professional skill."

A change in form or state may permit patentability of an old compound, e.g., penicillin in a new crystalline form, *Ex parte Conn et al.*, 119 USPQ BdApp 1955.

Recovery of Purified Materials. Recovery of a purified material may or may not be patentable depending on such factors as set forth in an old case, *Kuehmsted v. Farbenfabriken*, 172 F. 701, CA 2. A pure isomer-free addition salt was allowed in *Ex parte Yale et al.*, 119 USPQ 256, PO BdApp 1958.

In the case of *In re Doyle et al.*, 140 USPQ 421, CCPA 1964, a claim to solid 6-amino-penicillanic acid, used as an intermediate in the preparation of synthetic penicillins, was allowed where limited to a purity defined by a narrow melting point range over prior art disclosing solutions containing the same compound in lower purity. This was on a showing that the impure compound when used as an intermediate would not produce practical yields of final product—citing *In re Williams*, 80 USPQ 150, CCPA 1949.

New Combinations. Old compounds may be patentable in new combinations, even with other old materials provided the results are unobvious and not merely additive. In this connection the term "synergism" has been frequently applied to define the more than additive effect or result of new combinations. In *Ex parte Abramson*, 72 USPQ 239, 1947, the Board of Appeals allowed a therapeutic combination of epinephrine in an aqueous glycerin solution on a showing that the specific claimed proportion of 10 per cent of glycerin represented the difference between success and failure in nebulization therapy over the 8.3 per cent of the prior art. Claims to an ointment of an old drug in a particular carrier were held valid and infringed in *Rystan v. Warren-Teed*, 92 USPQ 419, DC NTex 1952, but claims to an ointment were refused by the District Court of D.C. in *Rudd v. Kingsland*, 88 USPQ 418, 1951,

where there was no showing of a greater than additive effect.

Methods of Treating the Body and Administering Drugs

The *Morton* case, supra, which appeared to hold that methods involving treatment of the body were unpatentable and not within the statutory class of inventive processes, was later followed in a number of cases both within and without the Patent Office. However, an augmented Board of Appeals (made up of ten members and Commissioner Watson) in *Ex parte Scherer*, 103 USPQ 107, 1954, with one dissent, carefully distinguished over the *Morton* case and other cases, in holding a method of injecting fluids into the human body to be patentable, saying

"It cannot be categorically stated that all such methods are unpatentable subject matter merely because they involve some treatment of the human body."

The majority decision ignored *In re Saunders et al.*, 69 USPQ 340, CCPA 1946, as well as *Martin v. Wyeth*, 89 USPQ 238, DC Md 1951.

However, the *Saunders* case was distinguished by the Board in *Ex parte Campbell et al.*, 99 USPQ 51, 1954, in allowing a claim to a process for combatting clotting of blood in a human being by the administration of a specific anticoagulant, based upon the new use of the compound. The Board pointed out that the *Saunders* decision relied upon an analogy between the material used and the prior art. This policy has now become uniform as indicated by *Ex parte DeBeer et al.*, 129 USPQ 127, PO BdApp 1960, involving a method for administering muscle relaxant drugs; *Ex parte Lewis*, 123 USPQ 84, PO BdApp 1959, directed to a method of feeding animals; and *Ex parte Timmis*, 123 USPQ 581, PO BdApp 1959 (U.S. Patent No. 2,917,432), directed to a process for producing remission in patients suffering from chronic myeloid leukemia.

Processes for Making New Products. The novelty of the product will not support the patentability of the claims to processes for making it even though it is patentable per se. *In re Albertson*, 141 USPQ 730, CCPA 1964; *In re Hoeksema*, 141 USPQ 733, CCPA 1964; and *In re Ross et al.*, 134 USPQ 320, CCPA 1962, citing *In re Larsen*, 130 USPQ 209, CCPA 1961.

The CCPA has held that a process may be patentable if it produces a product even if the product is not shown to be useful. This was on the theory that under 35 U.S.C. 101 a process is a separate category of invention and its utility is satisfied by disclosure of its ability to produce a known product even where such product is not itself useful. *In re Manson*, 142 USPQ 35, CCPA 1964. It is not clear whether the decision would be the same where the product is also new, but the same reasoning should apply.

Inventions Derived from Natural Products

Mere discovery of a natural phenomenon, or isolation or purification of a product known to exist in nature cannot make the product itself patentable, although the process of preparing the product may be patented. This principle has been followed by the Patent Office and Courts in numerous cases. *Ex parte Snell*, 86 USPQ 496, PO BdApp 1950 (pyridoxine derivatives); *Ex parte Reed et al.*, 135 USPQ 34, 1961— U.S. Patent No. 3,049,549. In the latter case, the Board of Appeals, in an excellent review of prior decisions pro and con on this subject, stated that a patent should not issue where the claimed product occurred naturally in liver and other products, is merely extracted therefrom, and its growth stimulating properties are, and have been, recognized in the parent material. A substance merely extracted from its parent material even in purer form is devoid of invention; however, the substance may be patentable if it possesses a utility not possessed by the parent material and not evident from the art, or if it is recovered in a form which did not exist before.

The Board distinguished from other situations where products obtained from natural products or found therein were held to be patentable. The law is clearly defined in such decisions as *Sterling Drug* v. *Watson*, 108 USPQ 37, DC Dist Col 1955 (pure *d*- or *l*-orterenol); *Ex parte Hickman*, 46 USPQ 235, PO BdApp 1940 (vitamin A concentrate); *Ex parte Parke et al.*, 74 USPQ 335, PO BdApp 1944 (new crystalline form of vitamin); *Merck* v. *Olin Mathiesen*, 253 F.2d 156, 116 USPQ 484, CA 3 1957 (vitamin B_{12} concentrate); *Kuehmsted* v. *Farbenfabriken*, 179 F. 701, CA 7 (pure aspirin); *Parke-Davis* v. *H. K. Mulford*, 196 Fed. 496, CA 2 1912 (pure adrenalin) and others.

The principles stated in the *Merck* case, reviewing the important decisions in this field, are:

"The compositions of the patent here have all of the novelty and utility required by the Act for patentability. They never existed before; there was nothing comparable to them. If we regard them as a purification of the active principle in natural fermentates, the natural fermentates are quite useless, while the patented compositions are of great medicinal and commercial value. The step from complete uselessness to great and perfected utility is a long one. That step is no mere advance in the degree of purity of a known product. From the natural fermentates, which, for this purpose, were wholly useless and were not known to contain the desired activity in even the slightest degree, products of great therapeutic and commercial worth have been developed. The new products are not the same as the old, but new and useful compositions entitled to the protection of the patent.

"...The patentees have given us for the first time a medicine which can be used successfully in the treatment of pernicious anemia, a medicine which avoids the dangers and disadvantages of the liver extracts, the only remedies available prior to this invention, a medicine subject to accurate standardization and which can be produced in large quantities and inexpensively, a medicine which is valuable for other purposes, as well as for the treatment of pernicious anemia. It did not exist in nature in the form in which the patentees produced it and was produced by them only after lengthy experiments. Nothing in the prior art either anticipated or suggested it.—"

Similar considerations apply to process claims. *Vitamin Technologist* v. *Wisconsin Alumni Research Foundation et al.*, 58 USPQ 293, CA 9 1943, with respect to claims covering irradiation of foods, etc. with ultraviolet rays, states:

"Dr. Steenbock's great contribution to science and human needs was his more exact recognition of what had transpired in all these prior practical uses of the ultraviolet rays in producing the unnamed Vitamin D in food substances.... However our Congress as yet has provided no system of reward to the pure scientist."

The claims were broad enough to include rays of the sun. If they had been limited to a specific type of artificial radiation the claims might have been valid.

The FTC Tetracycline Case

In a proceeding before the Federal Trade Commission (Docket No. 7211, before the FTC in the matter of American Cyanamid Co. *et al.,* decision dated August 8, 1963), the patent on tetracycline was held by the Commission in 1963 to have been obtained on the basis of misrepresentation of facts and suppressed information during prosecution before the Examiner, and under the doctrine of *Hazel Atlas* v. *Hartford Empire Co.,* 322 U.S. 238, 1934, and *Precision Instrument Mfg. Co. et al.* v. *Automotive Maintenance Machinery Co.,* 324 U.S. 806, 1945, the patent had become unenforceable. (See *Fraud* and *Clean Hands Doctrine*)

During prosecution the claims were rejected by the Primary Examiner on disclosures in the earlier patents on chlortetracycline (aureomycin) because of later discovered information that tetracycline was co-produced with aureomycin, the rejection being on the ground that no invention was involved in the identification of tetracycline as one of the products of the earlier reaction, citing *In re Lieser,* 74 USPQ 104, CCPA 1947; *Allen et al.* v. *Coe,* 57 USPQ 130, CA DC 1943; *Parke-Davis* v. *Mulford,* supra, and *In re Krebrich,* 96 USPQ 411, CCPA 1953. In his rejection in the tetracycline case, supra, the Primary Examiner was quoted by the FTC as stating:

"While neither Duggar and Niedercorn may have realized that tetracycline was produced, they did appreciate, and disclose, that the product was an antibiotic.... It has long been held that the purer form of an old product is not inventive and the (apparent) mixture of the prior art meets the claim."

In referring to the Parke-Davis case, the Federal Trade Commission said:

"The Parke Davis case decided in 1911 by Judged Learned Hand announced the general rule that a purer form of an old product is not inventive, but found an exception to that rule in the case where extraction and purification created a product which has a new utility that is different in kind rather than merely in degree."

However, the application was allowed after a showing by affidavit that the amount of tetracycline produced previously, as the by-product, was too small to be recoverable in any practical quantity. Much of the argument in the FTC holding relates to the alleged inequitable conduct and centers around the adequacy and good faith of the material presented in the affidavit filed in the Patent Office prosecution. The decision of the Commission has been appealed to the Court of Appeals for the Sixth Circuit.

Biologicals—Serums and Vaccines

Patentable subject matter in the pharmaceutical field comprises also biologic products and processes relating to serums and vaccines and related products. These include any virus, therapeutic serum, toxin, antitoxin, or analogous materials such as vaccines of rickettsial, viral, or bacterial origin, immune serums, human blood and derivatives from blood, diagnostic products and the like. They are generally obtained by the processing of organisms such as bacteria, viruses and the like, by attenuation, mutation, growth under varying conditions or on different media, extraction from killed materials and various other procedures developed in the field of immunology.

The principles of patent disclosure and claims discussed herein with respect to pharmaceuticals apply as well to this important and growing field of therapy. The types of patent coverage obtainable extend from compositions and combinations of products useful in immunology to processes of preparing or administering them.

The general requirements for disclosure in the area are described in *Ex parte Szabo,* 136 USPQ 305, 1963, in which the Board of Appeals stated, with respect to a process for preparing an anticancer vaccine:

"The examiner has pointed out many ambiguities and generalities in the specification which fails to set forth the specific conditions, proportions, and expedients required to obtain a hitherto unavailable anti-cancer vaccine. Not only are the details of the injection to produce the tumor, the amount of formaldehyde used in producing the vaccine, and the precise amount and kind of tumor tissue produced and employed, not specifically defined but the number of serial passages, the isolation and identification of malign tumor, and complete details of conversion into the vaccine are lacking. Since the specific tumor is not defined, it cannot be determined what type of tumor the vaccine is to protect against. This rejection will, therefore, be sustained.

"Similarly, in view of the absence of knowledge in the art of the preparation of a successful anti-cancer vaccine and of sufficient evidence in the record before us of the operativeness of the claimed vaccine for its intended purpose the examiner's rejection based upon lack of utility will be sustained."

On the other hand, where the techniques of preparation are better known in the art, the disclosure requirements are not as stringent. See *In re Bankowski*, 138 USPQ 75, 1963. Here the CCPA stated:

"Inasmuch as only a limited number of tissue-culturing techniques is used in the art, it would be within the expected skill of the art to apply one of these known techniques to a different virus."

Combinations of antigens which are known to be separately effective, in the absence of demonstrated synergism, are not patentable. *In re Davis et al.*, 134 USPQ 257, CCPA 1962. This decision contains a definition of "synergism" taken from Webster's New International Dictionary, 1954 ed., as follows:

"synergism—1. Physiol. Co-operative action of discrete agencies such that the total effect is greater than the sum of the two effects taken independently."

A vaccine derived from a new tissue source, that is, one not previously used for culturing a specific virus, may be patentable as set forth in *Ex parte Beard*, 45 USPQ 711, PO BdApp 1940. Also methods of treatment involving the use of serums or vaccines may be patented.

Interference Problems in Pharmaceutical Patent Cases

As in other areas of practice, the problems in pharmaceutical interferences conform to those in chemical cases generally. There are some aspects, however, which deserve special consideration. The nature of certain types of inventions in this field may create problems in determining inventorship. This is based upon the general principle that "conception of the invention consists in the complete performance of the inventive act." *Mergenthaler* v. *Scudder*, 11 App. D.C. 264, 1897 C.D. 724, as restated in *In re Tansel*, 117 USPQ 188, 45 CCPA (Patents) 834, and other cases. Where novel compounds are discovered by a party who submits them for screening or for testing to determine utility and actual utility is determined by another party, questions of conception and inventorship may arise. It appears clear that, if a product is submitted for testing for a particular purpose or a particular screening, the submitter would generally be the inventor. Note particularly *Applegate et al.* v. *Scherer et al.*, 141 USPQ 796, 51 CCPA, where submission of a chemical for test as a lampricide was held to constitute conception, and the reduction to practice through testing by the submittee was held to inure to the benefit of the submitter. The submittee claimed to be the inventor here. Where an assistant carries out his functions under the supervision and direction of a supervisor, the presumption is that his work inures to the benefit of the supervisor and the assistant is a proper corroborating witness. *Damaskus* v. *Homan et al.*, 141 USPQ 923, Patent Office Board of Interference Examiners, decided March 26, 1964. The same decision held that actual reduction to practice of a drug is not proven by one successful test since this is not sufficient to establish reproducibility of results—citing earlier decisions.

Pharmaceutical Patent Claims

Representative claims in U.S. pharmaceutical patents, shown below, illustrate various approaches to claiming specialized types of subject matter as used in the recent past. These claims must be considered in the light of existing practice in each case to keep pace with the trend of Patent Office policies and CCPA decisions.

New Chemical Compounds

7. A compound of the group consisting of (1) benzenesulphonylureas of the formula

wherein R is a member of the group consisting of hydrogen and methoxy, and (2) pharmaceutically acceptable basic salts thereof.

8. N-benzenesulphonyl-N'-cyclohexylurea. Patent 2,968,158.

1. p-Bis-(2-chloroethyl)-aminophenylalanine. [An anti-tumor compound.] Patent 3,032,584.

Old Chemical Compounds

(a) Dosage Form

3. A therapeutic composition in dosage form comprising an orally administrable liquid pharmaceutical carrier bland to the gastric mucosa, and a member of the class consisting of 1-monoacetylerythromycin and 1-monopropionylerythromycin. 3,013,942.

(b) Old Compound Plus Carrier

1. A therapeutic composition comprising an orally administrable pharmaceutical carrier and a compound selected from the class consisting of 1-monocetylerythromycin and 1-monopropionylerythromycin. 3,013,942.

(c) New Form or Environment

1. An inhalable, substantially dry, live virus vaccine comprising substantially dry particles containing at least one species of a substantially dry, avirulent, live virus selected from the group consisting of Newcastle disease virus, infectious bronchitis virus and mixtures of the same dispersed in a substantially dry, inert, noninflammable, nonexplosive, nontoxic, nonirritating, substantially static free, flowable, nonhygroscopic, solid diluent, said particles which contain said virus being obtained from the propagation medium in which said virus is prepared and having an average particle size in the range of between about 10 to 50 microns with the majority of the particles having a size not less than 10 microns and the particles effecting immunization having a size not exceeding approximately 50 microns. 2,798,835.

1. An anthelmintic composition comprising a liquid suspension of about one part by weight of phenothiazine and at least about one part by weight of an inert, nontoxic, palatable, liquid, viscous stable agent having adhering characteristics and substantially enveloping said phenothiazine, said stable agent being selected from the group of animal-edible syrups and oils consisting of lecithin, olive oil, corn syrup, mineral oil and cod liver oil, said composition possessing sufficient consistency to preclude its flowing freely through legumes and the like. 2,840,504.

1. A parenterally administrable preparation of nystatin which comprises nystatin and a soluble saccharin, said preparation being such that, when provided in the form of an aqeous solution, the nystatin is present in a concentration greater than 3,000 units per ml of solution. 3,011,946.

(d) Specific Formulations, Synergism, etc.

2. A composition for administration to bovine animals for the treatment of ketosis, consisting essentially of from about 15 to about 30% calcium lactobionate and from about 85 to about 70% calcium lactate, said composition having a pH in a 10% aqueous solution at 25°C within the range from about 5 to about 6. 2,856,327.

2. A medicinal preparation comprising a muscle relaxing drug selected from the group consisting of tris-(d1-ethylamino-ethyl-hydroxy)-1,2,3-benzene ethylaminotriiodethylate and 3-o-methoxy-phenoxy-2-hydroxypropyl-carbamate, and their derivatives, and the tertiary alcohol of α-[(p-chlorophenyl)-α-phenyl]-4-pryidyl carbinol which is a normally inactive compound capable of substantially increasing the myorelaxing effectiveness of said muscle-relaxing drugs. 3,010,873.

1. An anti-fungal product comprising, in synergistic combination, boric acid and an organic compound, in an amount of from about 0.2 to about 5.0 mols per mol of boric acid, selected from the group consisting of lactic acid, salicylic acid and propylene glycol; combined with water and sufficient base to provide a pH of between about 9 and 11. 2,968,590.

A pharmaceutical which comprises aspirin and sorbitol in approximately equal proportions by weight. 3,039,927.

Products Related to Products of Nature

1. The compound vitamin B_{12}, an organic substance containing cobalt, together with carbon, nitrogen, hydrogen, oxygen, and phosphorus, said compound being a red crystalline substance soluble in water, methyl and ethyl alcohol and phenol, and insoluble in acetone, ether and chloroform and ex-

hibiting strong absorption maxima at about 2780Å., 3610Å. and 5500Å., and an L.L.D. activity of about 11,000,000 L.L.D. units per milligram. 2,563,794.

1. A vitamin B_{12}-active composition comprising recovered elaboration products of the fermentation of a vitamin B_{12}-activity producing strain of fungi selected from the class consisting of Schizomycetes, Torula, and Eremothecium, the L.L.D. activity of said composition being at least 440 L.L.D. units per milligram and less than 11 million L.L.D. units per milligram. 2,703,302.

1. A crystalline product of manufacture consisting of a member selected from the group consisting of reserpine and the therapeutically active acid addition salts thereof. 2,752,351.

Serums and Vaccines

1. A trivalent live poliomyelitis vaccine suitable for oral administration comprising a mixture of Type I virus attenuated to avirulence to man by successive passages through the nervous tissue of rodents, Type II virus adapted to chick embryo propagation by successive passages through the nervous tissue of suckling rodents and then attenuated through chick embryos until avirulent to man and Type III virus avirulent to man, the trivalent vaccine being in dosage unit form containing at least log 6 of each virus, the Type II virus of the mixture not inhibiting infection by the other two. 2,966,443.

5. A respiratory virus vaccine product for poultry comprising a chorioallantoic menstruum of embryonated chicken egg origin and live virus ATCC No. 87101 attenuated by consecutive serial passages through said embryonated chicken eggs, said vaccine being capable of immunizing fowl against said virus infection, having an ELD_{50} titer of at least 103.8, and being produced in accordance with claim 1. 2,998,349.

Antibiotics

(a) Defined by Physical and Chemical Properties

2. A substance effective in inhibiting the growth of gram-positive bacteria, selected from the group consisting of thiostrepton and the salts thereof, said thiostrepton being a weakly basic substance having the following elementary analysis: C = 51.75%, H = 5.30%, S = 9.22%, N = 15.84%, O = 17.89%; has an antibacterial spectrum including the following bacteria: Micrococcus pyogenes var. aureus, Streptococcus pyogenes C203, Bacillus subtilis, Streptococcus faecalis, Lactobacillus acidophilus, Clostridium septicus, Dyplococcus pneumoniae type 3, Corynebacterium diphtheriae and Mycobacterium tuberculosis var. bovix (BCG); possesses a crystalline structure in the pure state; is substantially soluble in dioxane, chloroform, N,N-dimethylformamide, N,N-dimethylacetamide and benzyl alcohol, and relatively insoluble in water and the lower alkanols; darkens at about 235° C and melts at about 246-256° C with decomposition; has an absorption spectrum measured in methanolic HCl with shoulders at the following wave lengths: 240, 280, and 305 millimicrons; and an infrared spectrum when suspended in hydrocarbon oil in solid form substantially as shown in the drawing. 2,982,689.

1. A novel composition of matter active against Pasteurella multocida, Salmonella pullorum, Salmonella schottmuelleri, Staphylococcus aureus, and Proteus vulgaris which in its pure crystalline form has an infrared spectrum which exhibits characteristic absorption bands expressed in reciprocal centimeters at the following frequencies: 3400, 3230, 17-1710, 1498, 1415-1420, 1325, 1290-1295, 1250-1255, 1040-1042, 1227-1230, 1170-1173, 1140, 995, 917-918, 872, 865, 800, 780, 725, 690; has a characteristic papergram pattern as shown in Figure 3: has a maximum in the ultraviolet spectrum at 228 millimicrons; consists of the elements carbon, hydrogen, nitrogen, and oxygen in the molecular proportions of $C_{14}H_{27}N_5O_{12}$; is optically active; and is soluble in water, lower alkanones and lower alkanols. 3,027,300.

(b) Defined by chemical structure

1. A compound of the formula

in which R represents a member selected from the group consisting of hydrogen, lower alkanoyl and phenyl lower alkanoyl. 3,014,922.

(c) Product by Name

A compound chosen from the group consisting of tetracycline, the mineral acid salts of tetracycline, the alkali metal salts of tetracycline and the alkaline earth metal salts of tetracycline. 2,699,054.

Methods of Treatment or Use

3. Process of preserving matter against attack by members of the class consisting of molds and bacteria which comprises treating said matter with di-bromo-penta-chlorocyclohexane. 2,799,613.

1. A process for the treatment of warm blooded animals exposed to metal poisoning which consists in administering to a living warm blooded animal which has acquired a toxic amount of a metal, a composition comprising an organic compound of molecular weight not more than 500 and of the

formula R—R′—COR″ wherein R is a monovalent radical of the class consisting of

$$CH_2-CH_2-CH-, \quad CH_2-CH_2-CH-$$
$$\underset{S}{\big|}\text{—————}\underset{S}{\big|} \quad \underset{SH}{\big|} \qquad \underset{SH}{\big|}$$

$$CH_2-CH-CH-, \quad CH_2-CH-CH-$$
$$\underset{\underset{O}{\overset{\|}{S}}}{\big|}\text{————}\underset{S}{\big|} \quad \underset{S}{\big|}\text{————}\underset{\underset{O}{\overset{\|}{S}}}{\big|}$$

and the C-alkyl derivatives of these radicals wherein the alkyl radical has not more than 4 carbons, R′ is an alkylene radical of not more than 8 carbon atoms and R″ is selected from the class consisting of hydroxyl and groups hydrolyzable thereto, in the amount of from 0.05 mg/kg animal body weight/day to about 100 mg/kg body weight/day. 2,840,505.

6. A process for the treatment of ketosis in bovine animals which comprises administering orally a composition consisting essentially of a lactobionate salt in an amount within the range from 15 to 30%, said lactobionate salt consisting of an amount within the range from 15 to 100% calcium lactobionate and an amount within the range from 85 to 0% of a member selected from the group consisting of sodium lactobionate and ammonium lactobionate, and from 85 to 70% of a lactate salt consisting of an amount within the range from about 15 to 85% calcium lactate and an amount within the range from about 85 to 15% of a member selected from the group consisting of sodium lactate and ammonium lactate, said composition having a pH in a 10% aqueous solution at 25° C within the range from about 5 to about 6. 2,856,327.

1. The method of stimulating meat-source animal growth which comprises adding to the animal's feed ration in a quantity sufficient to provide an amount of about one to about fifty milligrams daily per 100 pounds of animal weight, a member of the group consisting of a penilloic acid, a penicilloic acid and nontoxic salts. 2,860,049.

15. A process for the lowering of blood sugar in the treatment of diabetes which comprises orally administering an effective amount of a composition having as the essential active ingredient N-4-methyl-benzene-sulphonyl-N′-n-butyl-urea. 2,968,158.

6. The method of combating an infection caused by an organism susceptible to erythromycin, which comprises orally administering to the infected subject a member of the group consisting of 1-monoacetylerythromycin and 1-monopropionylerythromycin, in a total daily dose amount of about 200 mg to about 2000 mg. 3,013,942.

A method of temporarily alleviating the symptoms of chronic and acute myelocytic leukemias which comprises the administration to the patient

of the compound 2,5-bismethanesulphonoxyhexane. 3,041,231. See *Ex parte Timmis*, 123 USPQ 581.

A method of treating animals and humans in need of an analgesic and sympathomimetic which comprises administering to such animals and humans a composition the essential active constituent of which is a compound selected from the group consisting of 4-methyl-2-aminopyridine and its pharmaceutically acceptable acid addition salts, said composition being free from cocaine-like effects and administered in an amount to provide a dosage of about 100 to 200 milligrams of the compound and the composition containing, in addition to the compound a pharmaceutical vehicle therefor. 2,937,118.

1. A method of immunizing a person against measles comprising administering an effective dose of a measles virus to said person at one situs substantially simultaneously with the administration of an effective dose of gamma globulin to said person at another situs. 3,106,514.

Methods of Manufacture

(a) Fermentation

2. A process which comprises growing an oxygenating strain of Aspergillus ochraceus in an aqueous nutrient medium containing sources of assimilable carbon and nitrogen under aerobic submerged conditions in intimate contact with a steroid having an eleven methylene group to produce an 11α-hydroxy steroid. 2,802,775.

7. A process for producing Actinomycin C, which comprises cultivating a strain of Streptomyces chrysomallus in an aqueous nutrient-containing, carbohydrate medium under submerged areobic conditions until substantial antibacterial activity is imparted to said solution, and then recovering Actinomycin C from the fermentation broth. 2,953,495.

1. A process for producing the antibiotic substances PA1033A and PA1033B which process comprises cultivating the microorganism S. griseofaciens ATCC13180 in an aqueous nutrient medium containing a source of carbohydrate, a source of organic nitrogen and inorganic salts, under submerged aerobic conditions until substantial antimicrobial activity is imparted to said medium. 3,021,259.

(b) Vaccines

1. A process of preparing a vaccine for immunizing poultry against respiratory infection comprising the steps of isolating live virus ATCC No. 87101 from viruliferous tissues of the diseased birds, sterilizing the isolate against bacterial contaminations, injecting the isolate into the chorioallantoic system of embryonated eggs, incubating the eggs for at least three days, harvesting the inoculum

from the chorioallantoic menstruum of said eggs and serially passing it in the same manner through the chorioallantoic system of other embryonated eggs for not less than five consecutive passages. 2,998,349.

Foreign Patent Problems with Pharmaceuticals

The American patent system is advanced in the scope of patent protection available for new and inventive chemical products. It makes no distinctions between pharmaceutical and other chemicals in scope of available patent protection. Outside the United States, there are few countries in the world that do not have special provisions with respect to the patentability of foods and medicines, their licensing and working, diversity in the practice, and complexity of procedure that should be recognized by the patent practitioner.

It is recommended, therefore, that foreign patent cases be handled with firms or agents specializing in foreign practice and knowing matters which vary so greatly from one country to another.

In many foreign countries articles of food or medicine may not be patented, although processes for their production may be protected, as shown in Table 2 and notes referring thereto.

TABLE 2. PATENTABILITY OF CHEMICAL AND PHARMACEUTICAL PRODUCT CLAIMS THROUGHOUT THE WORLD.

	Chemical?	Pharmaceutical?
Argentina	yes	no
Australia	yes	yes
Belgium	yes	yes
Bolivia	no	no
Brazil	no	no
Canada	yes	yes [1]
Ceylon	yes	yes
Chile	no	no
Colombia	yes	yes
Congo	yes	yes
Costa Rica	yes	yes
Cuba	yes	yes
Denmark	no	no
Dominican Republic	yes	yes
Ecuador	no	no
France	yes	yes
Guatemala	yes	yes
Germany, Western	no [2]	no [2]
Great Britain	yes	yes
Greece	no	no
Haiti	yes	yes
Honduras	yes	yes
Iceland	yes	no
India	no	no
Indonesia	yes	yes
Hong Kong	yes	yes
Ireland	no	no
Israel	yes	yes
Italy	yes	no
Japan	no	no
Jordan	yes	yes
Liberia	yes	yes
Malaya	yes	yes
Mexico	no	no
Netherlands	no	no
New Zealand	yes	yes
Nicaragua	yes	yes
Norway	no	no
Panama	yes	yes
Paraguay	yes	no
Peru	yes	no
Philippines	yes	yes
Rhodesia-Nyasaland	yes	yes
Salvador	yes	yes
Spain	no	no
Sweden	no	no
Turkey	yes	no
Union of South Africa	yes	yes
U.S.A.	yes	yes
Uruguay	no	no
Venezuela	no	no

[1] Product by process and composition claims, also products if made by other than chemical processes.

[2] Claim to process covers the product if it represents a technological advance. See p. 320.

The French law permitting pharmaceutical product claims is new.

All of the countries listed permit patenting process claims for pharmaceuticals except Italy and Sweden— Sweden allowing them when the process involved is chemical and Italy considering a new law.

In applying the above chart, it must be remembered that any "yes" or "no" answer may be qualified by the variable interpretation of the laws and practice in each country.

In summary, foreign practice with respect to pharmaceutical patents generally follows practice with respect to other types of chemical cases, with an important difference in those countries where medicinal product patents are not granted and in Italy where neither the products nor processes may be patented as yet.

Also several countries have special compulsory licensing provisions for pharmaceutical products which permit arbitrary license grants, without considering such factors as working. Table 3 illustrates the pattern of compulsory licensing in most countries. Here again special statutory provisions and practical factors are involved which require expert advice.

TABLE 3. COMPULSORY LICENSING IN FOREIGN COUNTRIES.

A. Countries having some form of compulsory licensing.
B. Countries having no provision for compulsory licensing.
C. Countries which have special compulsory licensing provisions for pharmaceutical patents.

Argen.	B	Ger., W.	A	Nicar.	B
Austl.	A	Ger., E.	A	Norway	A
Austria	A	Gr. Brit.	C	Pakis.	A
Belgium	A	Greece	A	Par.	A
Bolivia	A	Guat.	B	Peru	B
Brazil	A	Hung.	A	Phil.	A
Bul.	A	India	C**	Poland	A
Canada	C	Iran	B	Port.	A
Chile	B	Iraq	B	Russia	A
China, Tai.	A	Ire.	A	Spain	A
Colom.	B*	Israel	A	Sweden	A
Congo	B	Italy	B*	Switz.	A
Cuba	B	Japan	A	Syria	B
Denmark	A	Jugosl.	A	Turkey	A
Dom. Rep.	B	Luxem.	A	U. S. Afr.	A
Ecuador	A	Mexico	A	Un. Arab R.	A
Egypt	A	Neth.	A	Ur.	A
Finland	A	N. Z.	A	Ven.	B
France	C				

* New law pending which would impose compulsory licensing upon drug patents.
**New law under consideration which would curtail drug patents.

At the present time, interesting and complex cross-currents are at work which involve compulsory licensing and patentability aspects of pharmaceuticals. In more sophisticated nations, there is an increased tendency to extend product patent protection to pharmaceutical products. For example, recent legislation in Great Britain and France and pending legislation in Italy. In addition, the proposed Common Market patent system does not distinguish between pharmaceutical products and other products with respect to patentability. In other areas such as Canada, India, Colombia, and the Philippines, attempts are being made to restrict severely or abolish drug patents altogether. In the long run, there can be no question that the fundamental purpose of patent protection in providing incentives to research must be recognized by all forward-looking nations, as borne out clearly by the discovery record in the strong patent countries. (See Table 1.)

Conclusion

An impartial study of the modern pharmaceutical industry will reveal three important characteristics: rapid rate of growth, strongly competitive nature, and active creativeness resulting in a high level of invention. Obviously, these results are interrelated. Accelerating or retarding any one should affect the others. At this time, the drug industry spends on research a high proportion of its sales, almost three times the average for industry as a whole, much of it on fundamental research. Competition through new product development is intense. The rapid rate of invention speeds obsolescence. The market life of new products is often short. Patent activity and expense is necessarily great, both here and abroad.

In the United States all human prescription drugs must be approved by the Food and Drug Administration before marketing. Even production facilities and clinical testing activities are rigidly scrutinized and controlled. Wholly apart from government controls, the safety precautions by ethical drug manufacturers are frequently more stringent than required. Similar, but less rigid controls, exist in some other countries. For such reasons, the problems encountered in marketing new drugs in the United States should be obvious.

Attacks on the drug industry have been primarily based on allegations of high cost to consumers and high profits. These are no higher than in other high-risk, research-oriented industries, taking into account the obstacles which must be overcome in developing and marketing new products. The obstacles wholly aside from those set up for political purposes are formidable. These include among others such problems as a recognition of need and conceiving of a possible solution to the problem, synthesis of new chemicals, screening of new chemicals through *in vitro* and animal tests, animal safety tests, exploratory clinical trials, chronic toxicity tests, market survey, human clinical testing, approval by Food and Drug Administration and education of physicians in properties and uses of new drugs.

Quantitatively stated, the drug industry each year tests many thousands of compounds which may yield only a few marketable compounds. In 1962, for example, almost 170,000 compounds were tested pharmacologically in the United States, and 1,300 of these clinically, but only 28 new chemotherapeutic agents were marketed during that year.

The outstanding achievements in the creation of new drugs in recent years, with its effect on the span of human life, have come in those advanced countries having patent systems affording maximum protection for pharmaceuticals, either product, processes, or both. In the United States, where the strongest coverage of drug products is obtainable under our system, the achievements are especially noteworthy. Of 540 new drugs introduced into the United States during the twenty-year period, 1941 to 1961, 333 were discoveries from the United States; 44, Switzerland; 31, Germany; 23, United Kingdom; 55, from eleven other countries, and the remaining 54, unidentified as to national origin. Such results are not a mere coincidence.

An unprecedented tribute was given to the research accomplishments of the American pharmaceutical industry in a statement transmitted to the Senate Subcommittee during the Hearings on S. 1552, supra, pp. 2212-2216, by fourteen Nobel Prize winners in the fields of medicine, physiology, and chemistry. The statement reads in part as follows:

"We have in this country seen remarkable progress in man's effort to conquer disease. The research laboratories of the American pharmaceutical industry have played an important role in this progress. In addition to offering most helpful cooperation to the research conducted in universities, hospitals, private institutes, and elsewhere, they have themselves made many valued and important contributions to advances in such fields as the treatment of infectious disease, hormonal disease, atherosclerosis, cardiovascular disease, nutritional disease, and mental illness.

"The scientists in the laboratories of the pharmaceutical industry have in fact become partners in today's total research effort, frequently initiating fundamental research, still more frequently associating with scientists in universities and elsewhere in a joint endeavor. We find in these men true collaborators.

"The industry laboratories also bring unique skills and facilities to the essential task of developing a new discovery into an effective drug available to the physician. Their contributions are a necessary and irreplaceable part of today's medical research. . . .

"We believe it is important to record publicly our recognition of the many significant contributions made by the research laboratories and scientists of this industry to the progress of medicine."

Cross-references: *Chemical Applications, Medical Associations and Physicians' Patent Policies, Microbiological Applications and Patents, Prosecution of Patent Applications, Utility.*

PHYSICIANS' PATENT POLICIES. See MEDICAL ASSOCIATIONS

PLANT PATENTS
Harry C. Robb, Jr. *

At the present time, the nursery industry is estimated to be a multimillion dollar industry—probably in excess of three-quarters of a billion dollars annually. According to figures published by the Department of Agriculture and also gathered from other reliable sources, the sales of rose plants alone in 1959 amounted to over 15 million dollars at their value in the field. This represents an increase of about 40 per cent over the average annual rate for the decade from 1949 and embraces some 47¾ million plants. Adding to these totals those sales of potted and packaged plants, but excluding cut roses, the total value rises to something like 50 million dollars total wholesale value. The trade estimated the retail sales of roses in 1961 at roughly 150 million dol-

* Copyright © 1962 by Harry C. Robb, Jr. Written for this Encyclopedia and published with his consent.

lars, which is conservatively considered as being approximately 15 to 20 per cent of the total sales of all nursery stock.

According to the U.S. Census Bureau figures, over one thousand growers with sales amounting to over 2 thousand dollars each were counted as selling approximately 48 million rose plants in the year 1959.

In considering the fact that it is conservatively estimated that it takes from 7 to 10 years to develop a new rose to the marketing point, at a cost estimated to run from 50 to 100 thousand dollars for breeding, testing and promotion expenses, the importance of plant patents covering new rose varieties, as well as plants of other types, immediately becomes obvious. Much of the progress which has been made in the past quarter of a century, at least, can be largely attributed to the incentive and the protection afforded by plant patents. These patents, which are a special type, have admittedly become the very backbone or heart of the nursery industry.

Historical Background

Prior to the year 1930, no protection under the patent laws was obtainable by the breeder or discoverer of a new variety of plant. This in itself greatly limited the quantity and scope of plant breeding, yet there were some breeders who devoted their lives to research and development in horticulture which greatly benefited mankind. One outstanding example of this, which is well known to the public, is the work done by the eminent horticulturist Luther Burbank. Mr. Burbank observed that "A man can patent a mouse trap or copyright a nasty song, but if he gives to the world a new fruit, he will be fortunate if he is rewarded by so much as having his name connected with the result."

Mr. Burbank succeeded in carrying on his work largely through remuneration received from writings, lectures, and, in some instances, through licensing of the use of his own name. He failed to live to see the important step that was taken in the year 1930 to afford protection to originators and discoverers of new varieties of plants through the grant of plant patents. In that

year, Congress saw fit to "remove the existing discrimination between plant developers and industrial inventors" by enacting what is commonly called the Plant Patent Act.

Prior to this enactment, practically the only way the originator of a new plant variety could realize direct financial benefits from his work was to withhold the plants from the market until a substantial stock could be carefully produced, and then begin to sell the plants at as high a price as could be obtained for them. This usually resulted in progressive diminishing of sales and financial returns each year following the first year or two of sales, and, ultimately, the originator of the new plant would completely lose all control over that which he himself had created.

It was not the purpose of plant patents to make fortunes for individuals or vast profits for businesses by creating monopolies. As a matter of fact, a patent is not a monopoly at all in the strict sense of the term, because monopolies fundamentally take away from the public something, or some right or benefit, which the public already had. In the case of a patent, including a plant patent, the patent gives to the public something new and beneficial which it did not have before and which the public may freely enjoy after the patent term expires at the end of a period of 17 years. Thus, the patentee is given the exclusive control over the invention or discovery for only a limited and relatively short period of time.

As originally enacted by Congress in the Act of May 29, 1930 (46 Statutes at Large, 376), another class of inventions capable of being patented was established. This new class of invention or discovery was incorporated in the then-existing patent statutes, and thus was founded upon the same cornerstone, so to speak, as all other patentable inventions, this cornerstone being the Constitution of the United States. Article 1, Section 8 of the Constitution provides that "The Congress shall have power . . . to promote the progress of science and useful arts, by securing for limited times to authors and inventors the exclusive right to their respective writings and discoveries."

By purposely incorporating the provisions for plant patents in the patent statutes formerly in effect and providing for the patenting of regular industrial inventions, plant patents became subject to the benefits of the precedents previously laid down for over a century with respect to patents, which had their beginning as such in the United States about the year 1790, based largely on English law which was adopted about the year 1624 to provide protection for inventors. However, the patent system as it is now generally known in the United States, was originally established in 1836, and the essential features thereof still remain in effect today and are generally applicable to plant patents.

The Original Plant Patent Act. As originally enacted, the Plant Patent Act was in the form of amendments to appropriate sections of the revised statutes, the basic provisions being found in Section 4886 R.S. As thus amended, the statute read as follows:

"Any person ... *who has invented or discovered and asexually reproduced any distinct and new variety of plant other than a tuber-propagated plant,* ... may, upon payment of the fees required by law, and other due proceeding had, obtain a patent therefor." (Amendments in italics.)

It will be observed from this language that the patent is to be directed to the distinct and new *plant*, rather than to its flowers, fruit, seed, or other products. Also, it should be emphasized that the statutory provisions expressly require asexual reproduction of the plant *before* obtaining a patent.

As pointed out by the legislative history of the original Plant Patent Act, the new and distinct varieties referred to by the Act were intended to fall into three classes, namely, sports, mutants and hybrids. In the first class, the sports, the new and distinct variety results from bud variation and not seed variation, as when a plant, or a portion of a plant, may suddenly assume an appearance or character distinct from that which normally characterizes the variety or species.

In the second class, the mutants, the new and distinct variety results from seedling

variation by self-pollenization of species, while in the case of the third class, the hybrids, the new and distinct variety results from seedlings of cross pollenization of two species, two varieties, or of a species and a variety. In the third class, the term "hybrid" is used in its broadest sense.

It is additionally important to understand that it was the Congressional intent of the original Plant Patent Act to cover *cultivated* sports, mutants, and hybrids, but not wild varieties such as those constituting chance finds of the plant explorer. Such deliberate omission of the wildings, or so-called chance finds, was not considered in any sense to be a limitation on the usefulness of the statutes to those who follow agriculture or horticulture as a livelihood and who were permitted under the Act to patent their discoveries.

It is still further significant that in order to qualify for a plant patent, the variety must be "distinct," as well as new. It therefore must have characteristics that are clearly distinguishable from those of existing varieties, and it is immaterial whether the new characteristics are inferior or superior to those of existing varieties. The Patent Office was therefore not required to pass judgment on the question of superiority or inferiority of new plants on which patents are sought, because experience has shown that matters of superiority are not always appreciated at the time new varieties are created, and as the result, some views that may initially be arrived at are subsequently found to be somewhat absurd.

Among the many characteristics which may be referred to as establishing novelty and distinctiveness of a new plant variety are the following: habit; immunity from disease; resistance to cold, drought, heat, wind or soil conditions; color of flower, leaf, fruit, or stems; flavor; productivity, including ever-bearing qualities in the case of fruits; storage qualities; perfume; form; and ease of asexual reproduction. Any one or more of the foregoing, or a new combination of characteristics, may suffice to make the variety a new and distinct variety, with due regard for minor differences of degree which may not be sufficient to support a patent on the new variety.

The Plant Patent Act expressly excepts tuber-propagated plants. This exception was made because plants of this type are usually propagated by the same part of the plant that is customarily sold as food. However, the term "tuber" was used in its narrow horticultural sense, as meaning a short thickened portion of an underground branch. It was not intended to embrace in this exclusion such things as bulbs, corms, stolons or rhizomes, and substantially the only plants intended to be excluded from the Act as "tuber-propagated" were the Irish Potato and the Jerusalem Artichoke.

The prerequisite of asexual reproduction of a new and distinct plant variety was predicated on the fact that a plant patent covers only the exclusive right of asexual reproduction, and obviously it would be futile to grant a patent for a new and distinct variety unless the variety had been demonstrated to be susceptible of asexual reproduction. Asexual reproduction includes vegetative propagation by any of the conventional methods such as budding, grafting, layering, division, own-rooting, and the like, or by use of cuttings or vegetative portions of the plant other than seeds.

Subsequent Changes in the Plant Patent Act. The statutory provisions pertaining to plant patents remained unchanged from May 1930 until January 1953 when the new codification of the entire body of U.S. patent laws became effective. Even then, the provisions remained basically the same, as provided in 35 U.S.C., Sections 161 to 164, inclusive. Shortly thereafter, in 1954, Section 161 of Title 35 was amended to clarify the language, as the result of a question raised by the Patent Office for the first time after nearly twenty years of established practice with respect to the scope of the language of the statute so far as newly found seedlings were concerned. Despite the fact that the Patent Office had previously granted many patents on varieties which had originated as newly found seedlings, it abruptly began to refuse patents where the plant originated as a newly found seedling, even though the origination occurred in a cultivated area. See *Ex parte Foster*, 90 USPQ 16, PO BdApp 1951. As the result of this situation, the nursery industry took appropriate steps to remove any further questions of this kind by having Congress enact amendatory legislation of a clarifying nature, while leaving the plant patent provisions basically the same. As amended September 3, 1954, Section 161 was changed to read as follows and stands in this amended form at the present time:

"Sec. 161. PATENTS FOR PLANTS—Whoever invents or discovers and asexually reproduces any distinct and new variety of plant, including cultivated sports, mutants, hybrids, and newly found seedlings, other than a tuber-propagated plant, or a plant found in an uncultivated state, may obtain a patent therefor, subject to the conditions and requirements of this title.

"The provisions of this title relating to patents for inventions shall apply to patents for plants, except as otherwise provided."

Preparation and Filing of a Plant Patent Application

The rules of the Patent Office relating to applications for patent on other inventions or discoveries are also applicable for the most part to applications for patents on plants, except as otherwise provided. (See Rule 161 of the Rules of Practice of the United States Patent Office in Patent Cases.)

Although the patent statutes expressly provide that "No plant patent shall be declared invalid for noncompliance with Section 112 of this title, if the description is as complete as is reasonably possible" (35 U.S.C. 162), every reasonable effort should be made to make a complete disclosure of the new plant in the patent application therefor, since identification of the new plant variety and its differences from other varieties must be established from information appearing within the patent itself, and not from extraneous sources. Such disclosure should therefore include a complete botanical description of the new variety, as well as appropriate illustrations showing as clearly as possible all of the tangible features of novelty which are capable of being visually illustrated.

Typical examples of plant patents for several types of new plant varieties will be found in the appendix annexed to this article.

In applying for a plant patent, the applicant must be the person who has invented or discovered and asexually reproduced the new and distinct variety for which a patent is sought, and in the oath of the application, the applicant must state that he has asexually reproduced the plant, in addition to the usual averments required for other ordinary patent applications, and including the usual statements pertaining to the absence of any statutory bars, all as provided in Form 26 of the Rules.

Thus, as in the case of ordinary patents, a valid plant patent cannot be obtained if the new variety has been in public use or on sale in the United States more than one year prior to the filing of the U.S. plant patent application, or if the new variety has been described in a printed publication which was published anywhere in the world more than one year prior to the filing of the U.S. plant patent application, or if the new variety has been previously patented in a foreign country more than one year prior to the filing of the U.S. plant patent application. See *Cole Nursery Co.* v. *Youdath Perennial Gardens, Inc.*, 31 USPQ 95, DC NOhio 1936; *Bourne* v. *Jones*, 98 USPQ 205, 206, CA 5 1953, cert. denied 98 USPQ 490, 1953.

Also, where the plant is a newly found plant, the oath must state that it was found in a cultivated area. Rule 162.

A complete plant patent application should include a specification, claim, oath and a drawing as the essential elements thereof. In the case of the specification, the new plant variety should be distinguished over related known varieties and its antecedents, and the specification should particularly point out where and in what manner the new plant variety has been asexually reproduced. Also, in the case of a newly found plant, the specification should particularly point out the location and character of the area where the plant was discovered. Rule 163.

The claim of the application is required to be in formal terms to the new and distinct variety of the specified plant as de-scribed and illustrated, but the claim may also recite the principal distinguishing characteristics. More than one claim is not permitted in plant patent applications. Rule 164.

The drawings required for plant patent applications are not considered as mechanical drawings and should be artistically and competently executed. Figure numbers and reference characters need not be used in the drawings unless required by the Examiner under special circumstances. The drawing should disclose all the distinctive characteristics of the plant capable of visual representation. The drawings *may* be executed in color, and when color is a distinguishing characteristic of the new variety, the drawings *must* be in color. Otherwise, the drawings may be executed in black and white, in the nature of a line drawing, a halftone black and white reproduction, or other appropriate black and white photographic or photolithographic reproduction. In some cases, it may be desirable to make certain views of the drawing in color, and other views in black and white, but this is largely governed by the circumstances of each individual case, and should be determined principally from the standpoint of providing a reasonably complete visual disclosure of the new plant variety and its distinguishing characteristics.

In the case of color drawings, two copies must be filed in the Patent Office in each application, and such color drawings must be made either in permanent water color or oil, or in lieu thereof, they may be photographs made by color photography or otherwise properly colored on sensitized paper. In each instance, the paper must correspond in size, weight and quality to the paper required for drawings of other regular patent applications, with the usual blank spaces for headings and signatures, as well as the usual 1-inch margin line as required for the drawings of ordinary patent applications. Rule 165.

As noted in the foregoing, all color illustrations or drawings must be filed in duplicate in plant patent applications. This also applies to the specifications and claim of every plant patent application which likewise must be filed in duplicate. The reason for this is that all plant patent applications are normally referred to the U.S. Department of Agriculture for an advisory opinion on the alleged novelty and distinctiveness of the variety which is the subject of each application, and it accordingly becomes necessary to have a duplicate copy of the specification, claim and drawing for reference to the Department of Agriculture without risking loss of the "original" application papers as the result of this extra handling thereof and, in particular, to avoid the risk of loss, mutilation or destruction of the official drawings which are usually rather expensive when they are executed in color. The Patent Office accordingly maintains a complete original copy of each plant patent application in its own files at all times, and the required duplicate copies are referred to the Department of Agriculture. All amendments must also be filed in duplicate for the same reasons.

Prosecution

The applicant for a plant patent may be required to furnish specimens of the plant or of its flower or fruit, in a quantity and at a time in its stage of growth as may be designated, for purposes of study and inspection of such specimens. When specimens are required, they must be properly packed and forwarded in conformity with instructions furnished to the applicant. Rule 166. When it is not possible to furnish such specimens, they must be made available for official inspection where grown.

Plant patent applications are customarily examined and prosecuted in the same manner as other ordinary patent applications, subject to the same general rules as may be applicable thereto, with certain special exceptions which are not sufficiently important to justify discussion herein.

The Grant

In the case of a plant patent, the grant covers the right to exclude others from asexually reproducing the plant or selling or using the plant so reproduced. 35 U.S.C. 163. Accordingly, unauthorized reproduction of a patented plant, even without sale of the plants so reproduced, constitutes infringement of the patent rights. By the same token, mere sale of plants asexually reproduced, without authorization of the patent owner, also constitutes infringement of the patent rights.

Actions for infringement in the case of plant patents are normally handled in the same general manner, and involve the same general procedures, as customarily followed in the case of infringements of other patents of the ordinary industrial type. For this reason, it should not be necessary to cover this aspect herein, and for a more comprehensive explanation and discussion of the subject of patent infringements, reference can be made to other associated topics relating to ordinary patents.

Since the Plant Patent Act has been in effect for only a little over thirty years, there have been comparatively few plant patents adjudicated by the courts. This speaks well for the nursery industry as a whole, since it is rather evident from the limited number of litigated cases that the various members of the industry are inclined to respect the rights inuring from plant patents to the owners thereof. Of course, many controversies have been settled without resort to litigation.

Licenses Under Plant Patents

Perhaps one of the principal reasons why there has been so little litigation involving plant patents is the liberal licensing policies which have been observed by most owners of such patents. While there has never been any compulsory licensing requirement in the United States patent system, contrary to what has been the practice for many years in a great many foreign countries, most plant patent owners in the United States have freely shared with others the benefits of their new varieties by permitting other nurserymen to propagate and sell the new varieties subject to payment to the patent owner of a modest royalty. This has been a definite advantage, not only to the members of the nursery industry themselves who frequently derive substantial profits from the new varieties, but also an important advantage to the public at large by virtue of the fact that it encourages and promotes wide distribution of the new varieties. At the same time, it has resulted in maintenance of better and more uniform plant qualities.

One of the outstanding examples of successful marketing of a patented plant, which resulted in substantial benefits to the general public, the owner of the U.S. patent rights and the licensees of said owner, is the case of the new rose which is commonly known in the United States by the varietal name "Peace," this rose having been originally bred and developed by one of the leading European breeders who sold the U.S. patent rights to one of the leading American rose growers. A copy of the patent on this rose, which is identified as Plant Patent No. 591, is found in the annexed appendix. Throughout the life of this patent, which has now expired, the rose variety enjoyed exceptionally wide popularity in the United States and was available throughout the country from the owner of the U.S. patent rights and from many licensees who were licensed to propagate and sell this variety under license arrangements with the owner. The exceptional popularity of the variety resulted in an unusually large volume of sales from which the owner of the patent rights and the licensees derived substantial profits. In addition, it has been conservatively estimated that the original breeder of this new rose received in excess of $500,000 in royalties for the U.S. patent rights.

Litigated Patents

The patent on the rose "Peace" (Plant Patent No. 591), as well as the patents covering such other outstanding new rose varieties as "New Yorker" (Plant Patent No. 823) and "Charlotte Armstrong" (Plant Patent No. 455), were all sustained as valid and infringed in the course of infringement litigation instituted by the respective patent owners in the Eastern District of Texas. *Armstrong Nurseries, Inc.* v. *Smith et al.; The Conard-Pyle Company* v. *Smith et al.;*

and *Jackson & Perkins Company* v. *Smith et al.,* 120 USPQ 220, DC ETex 1959.

Other Typical Plant Patents

It is rather curious to note that of all of the leading apple varieties that are commercially available today, most of them originated as sports. The Plant Patent Act was purposely designed to encourage the discovery of new sports and to encourage preservation of the same by asexual reproduction, so that mankind would gain the benefits therefrom which would otherwise be lost by virtue of the inability of nature alone to reproduce true to form.

One of the more recent and valuable discoveries made in the horticultural field is a new apple variety commonly known as the Bisbee Apple and on which Plant Patent No. 1565 (see appendix) was granted to one of the leading fruit tree nurseries. It is reported that the patent owner paid about $25,000 for the original tree and the patent rights covering this new variety which is characterized by bearing bigger apples of a much deeper red color and ripening approximately two weeks earlier than any other so-called Delicious type of apple. While the tree is normally only about two-thirds the size of standard trees, it is so compact, and the fruiting spurs are so full and close together that the trees bear practically twice as many apples as the standard Delicious-type trees. Obviously, the good productivity, handsome appearance and good flavor of the fruit are highly important characteristics from a commercial standpoint, with the result that it has been estimated that well over 300,000 trees of this new apple variety were planted in one year in yards, on farms and in commercial orchards. Without the incentive resulting from the ability to patent this new apple variety, it is highly improbable that the new Bisbee Apple would have been discovered and preserved.

Another plant patent of general interest is one covering a new variety of Honey Locust Tree, which is the subject of Plant Patent No. 836. Prior to the breeding of this new variety, it was well known that most all Honey Locusts were fast growing and deep rooted trees, and thus were very advantageous from these standpoints. However, they usually bore very long, sharp thorns and an abundance of seed pods, which made such trees both dangerous and untidy. With this background, one of the outstanding growers and distributors of shade trees began a careful program of breeding and selection, and after fifteen years of work, the breeder succeeded in producing five trees which bore no seeds and no thorns. In due course, a final selection was made, and after some twenty-two years of hard work and the investment of tremendous sums of money to produce a thornless and seedless Honey Locust Tree of attractive shape, these objectives were achieved, and the variety was patented and has been extensively distributed by the patent owner and by licensees who pay only a small royalty to the patent owner.

Many other interesting and important examples could be given, but the foregoing will suffice to illustrate the principle and advantages of plant patents, without exceeding the limits which are inherent in an article of this kind. The history of plant patents conclusively shows that it has enjoyed definite and remarkable success in the United States, even in the comparatively short period of time which has elapsed since the Plant Patent Act was first enacted in the year 1930. However, the surface has been hardly scratched, so to speak, and there is ample opportunity for new developments and discoveries in this field which will be highly beneficial to all concerned in the years to come.

Plant Patent Cases on Anticipation, Validity and Infringement

Brief Catalog Publication as Anticipation. In a 1962 case, the issue was whether a brief catalog description of a new rose met the statutory requirement for prior publication such as would, if sufficiently early, anticipate the discovery by another. The court held that the description did not.

"...[D]escriptions in printed publications of new plant varieties, before they may be used as statutory bars under 35 U.S.C. 102(b), must meet the same standards which must be met before a description in a printed publication becomes a bar in non-plant patent cases. 35 U.S.C. 161 does not contain any limitation on this interpretation of the clause 'described in a printed publication,' and Congress has not 'otherwise provided.' When so considered, the descriptions in the printed publications here in issue (which pictured the rose in color and briefly described its color, sheen, blooms, fragrance and foliage) do not meet the requirement of an 'enabling' description, as the statute has been interpreted in numerous cases." *In re LeGrice,* 133 USPQ 365, CCPA 1962.

Anticipation by Prior Knowledge or Use. The importance of being the first to *recognize* and *reproduce asexually* the new variety of plant is shown by the Board of Appeals case *Ex parte Moore,* 115 USPQ 145, 1957.

Miller observed in his yard a peach tree that bore annual crops of large, luscious peaches. After the tree had borne seven crops, Moore, a friend of Miller, saw the tree, requested and obtained with Miller's consent ten scions, and grafted them on native root stock. Moore repeated the grafting until he had several generations before he applied for his patent, thus demonstrating that the tree was in fact a new variety. The Board reversed the Examiner and held that Moore, having first recognized the tree as a new variety and met the statutory requirement of asexual reproduction of it, was the inventor and entitled to a patent.

A different conclusion, on a different set of facts, was reached on the issue of prior public use in *Bourne* v. *Jones,* 98 USPQ 206, DC SFla 1951; aff. 98 USPQ 205, CA 5 1951; cert. denied 99 USPQ 490.

Here the party Bourne reproduced asexually the varieties of sugar cane claimed in his three patents before the court. Referring to the work of Stevens, an employee of the University of Florida, as agronomist in the sugar cane investigation for which the patentee Bourne was the cane breeder, the court said:

"Stevens distributed F-31-436 and F-31-962 [eyes for budding, to cane growers] more than two years prior to Bourne's applications for patents covering these varieties. . . . It is very important to note that Bourne had no authority whatsoever to direct the work of Stevens, nor did he have any measure of control over the distribution made by Stevens."

The court noted that Bourne, the patentee, first reproduced the plants, concluded that Stevens should have been named as a joint inventor, rejected the plaintiff's [Bourne's] contention that the distribution by Stevens represented only experimental use, and held such use public.

On the basis of prior public use, the court held the patents invalid. The decision implies that the class of use might have been different if Bourne had directed the field tests and obtained the results as a part of his experimentation.

Validity. In another case, in which validity of a plant patent was an issue, the facts were the following:

The patentee had discovered a new and distinct variety of seedless navel orange tree in a small grove of about fifteen other navel orange trees. The tree was about twenty-five or thirty years of age. He had some budwood cut from this parent tree and used the cuttings to reproduce the trees which are the subject of his patent. A question before the court, in a motion by the defendant for a summary judgment in defendant's favor on the ground of invalidity of the patent, lack of patent infringement and unfair competition, was whether the existence [and fruiting] of the tree, for the many years before its discovery by the patentee-plaintiff, constituted "knowledge or use by others" or such "public use" as to make his Plant Patent 625 upon the tree invalid.

Noting that there had been submitted no evidence that the distinctive character and value of the tree had been "appreciated" by any one prior to the patentee-plaintiff or that anyone had any knowledge of the "existence" or use of the parent tree, the court held that its mere existence did not overcome the presumption of validity of the patent. The court, however, refused the summary judgment on other grounds. *Nicholson* v. *Bailey,* 125 USPQ 157, DC SFla 1960.

Infringement. For cases on infringement, see *Armstrong Nurseries, Inc.* v. *Smith et al.* and joined cases, 120 USPQ 220, DC ETexas 1958; *Kim Bros.* v. *Hagler,* 120 USPQ 210, DC SCal 1958, aff. 125 USPQ 44, CA 9 1960.

Cross-references: *Adjudications, Anticipation, Infringement, Microbiological Applications and Patents, Profiting from Patents.*

APPENDIX

June 15, 1943.   F. MEILLAND   Plant Pat. 591
ROSE PLANT
Filed July 15, 1942

Inventor
FRANCIS MEILLAND
BY ROBB & ROBB
Attorneys

FIG. 1. Drawing of Plant Patent 591. Shown in four colors in original and soft copies of patent. The famous "Peace" Rose.

UNITED STATES PATENT OFFICE

591

ROSE PLANT

Francis Meilland, Tassin-les-Lyon, France, assignor to The Conrad-Pyle Company, West Grove, Pa.

Application July 15, 1942, Serial No. 451,039

1 Claim. (Cl. 47—61)

The present invention relates to a new and distinct variety of hybrid tea rose plant, a seedling resulting from a definite effort to produce an improvement in this class of roses.

The primary features of this new variety which connote its distinctive advance over existing types are the exceptional vigor and enduring quality of its foliage and the character of its bloom, first in respect to its size; second, its perfection of form; and third, with respect to its exquisite blend of coloring, more particularly apparent in the accompanying illustration of a specimen thereof.

The following is a detail description of the new variety, color terminology being in accord with Ridgway's Color Standard:

Type: Hardy; bush; outdoor; seedling; for cut flowers and garden decoration.
Class: Hybrid tea.
Propagation: Holds its distinguishing characteristics through succeeding propagations by budding.

Flower

Locality where grown: West Grove, Pennsylvania.
Flowers borne: Singly to stem on strong, medium long stems.
Quantity of bloom: Abundant outdoors.
Continuity: Intermittent, almost continuous.
Fragrance: Moderate; tea.
Bud:
   Peduncle.—Medium long; heavy; erect; stiff; Dark Citrine, Plate IV; rough. Prickles—moderately few, Garnet-Brown, Plate I.
   Before calyx breaks.—Size—large. Form—globular with an inconspicuous neck; with foliaceous appendages on the surface of the bud; with bristle-like foliaceous parts extending beyond the tip of the bud equal to about one-fourth of its length.
   As calyx breaks.—Pale Lemon Yellow, Plate IV, flushed with Nopal Red, Plate I.
   As first petal opens.—Size—large. Form—ovoid. Color—Outside—Lemon Yellow base to Martius Yellow edge, Plate IV. Inside—Lemon Yellow base to Martius Yellow edge, Plate IV, and tipped Shrimp Pink, Plate I. Opening—opens up well.
Bloom:
   Size when fully open.—Large; five to five and one-half inches.
   Petalage.—Very double; from fifty to fifty-five petals arranged regularly.
   Form.—Cupped; high centers; globular at first; becoming cupped and high centered; petals remaining at first tightly rolled inward; becoming later, at maturity, loosely rolled outward.

Petals: Leathery; inside and outside satiny.
   Shape.—Outside—oval; scalloped with apex flat with one notch. Intermediate—ovate; scalloped with one notch. Inside—ovate; scalloped with one notch.
   This description of a newly opened flower was made from a rose grown outdoors during the month of November, 1941, at West Grove, Pennsylvania.
   Color.—*Outside petal*—Outside surface—Lemon Yellow base to Martius Yellow, Plate IV, edged Rose Pink, Plate XII. Inside surface—Lemon Yellow base to Martius Yellow, Plate IV, edged Rose Pink, Plate XII. *Intermediate petal*—Outside surface—Lemon Yellow base to Martius Yellow, Plate IV, edged Rose Pink, Plate XII. Inside surface—Lemon Yellow base to Martius Yellow, Plate IV, edged Rose Pink, Plate XII. *Inner petal*—Outside surface—Lemon Yellow base to Martius Yellow, Plate IV, edged Rose Pink, Plate XII. Inside surface—Lemon Yellow base to Martius Yellow, Plate IV, edged Rose Pink, Plate XII.
   This description was made from a rose that was open for three days outdoors, in November, 1941, at West Grove, Pennsylvania:
   Color.—*Outside petal*—Outside surface—Lemon Yellow base to Martius Yellow, Plate IV, edged Rose Pink, Plate XII. Inside surface—Lemon Yellow base to Martius Yellow, Plate IV, edged Rose Pink, Plate XII. *Inside petal*—Outside surface—Lemon Yellow base to Martius Yellow, Plate IV, edged Rose Pink, Plate XII. Inside surface—Lemon Yellow base to Martius Yellow, Plate IV, edged Rose Pink, Plate XII.
   General color effect.—Newly opened flower—Martius Yellow, Plate IV. Three days open—Martius Yellow, Plate IV.
   Behavior.—Drop off cleanly; do not fade.
   Flower longevity.—On bush in garden four to five days in November. Cut roses grown outdoors kept at living room temperatures four to six days in November.

Reproductive organs

Stamens: Many; arranged irregularly.
Filaments: Short and long; Nopal Red, Plate I; most with anthers.
Anthers: Medium size; Light Orange Yellow, Plate III; open at various times.
Pollen: Abundant; Capucine Yellow.
Pistils: Many.
Styles: Medium length; thin; bunched.
Stigma: Straw Yellow, Plate XVI.
Ovaries: All enclosed in calyx.

2
591

Hips: Short; pointed; with inconspicuous neck; pear-shaped; Bice Green, Plate XVII; smooth; walls thick, fleshy.

Sepals: Falling soon; moderately long; spear-shaped; recurved. 5

Seeds: Few; medium large.

Plant

Foliage:

Leaves.—Compound of five leaflets; normal; large; leathery; glossy. 10

Leaflets.—Ovoid with apex acute; base round; margin serrate.

Color.—Mature—Upper surface—Dark Varleys Green, Plate XVIII. Under surface—Light Elm Green, Plate XVII. Young— 15 Upper surface—Roman Green, Plate XVI, veiled with Claret-Brown, Plate I. Under surface—Varleys Green, Plate XVIII, shaded Claret-Brown, Plate I.

Rachis.—Medium heavy; upper side, smooth, 20 grooved; under side, sparsely thorny.

Stipules.—Medium long; medium wide; moderately long points, turning out at an angle of less than 45°, recurved toward the stem. 25

Disease.—Resistant to mildew and blackspot.

Growth:

Habit.—Upright; much branched.

Growth.—Vigorous.

Canes.—Moderately heavy.

Main stems.—Dull Cedar Green, Plate VI. Thorns—several; medium long; straight; hooked downward; with narrow base. Prickles—none. Hairs—none.

Branches.—Dull Cedar Green, Plate VI. Thorns—several; medium long; hooked downward; with narrow base. Prickles—none. Hairs—none.

New shoots.—Bright Victoria-Lake, Plate I. Thorns—many; medium long; hooked downward; with narrow base. Prickles—none. Hairs—none.

I claim:

A new and distinct variety of rose plant of the hybrid tea class, characterized as to novelty by its exceptionally vigorous growing habit and enduring quality of its foliage, size and perfection of form of the bloom, and their unusual blend of coloring, substantially as shown and described.

FRANCIS MEILLAND.

CERTIFICATE OF CORRECTION.

Plant Patent No. 591.   June 15, 1943.

FRANCIS MEILLAND.

It is hereby certified that the name of the assignee in the above numbered patent was erroneously described and specified as "The Conrad-Pyle Company" whereas said name should have been described and specified as --The Conard-Pyle Company--; and that the said Letters Patent should be read with this correction therein that the same may conform to the record of the case in the Patent Office.

Signed and sealed this 23rd day of May, A. D. 1944.

Leslie Frazer

(Seal)   Acting Commissioner of Patents.

Feb. 12, 1957   R. A. BISBEE   *Plant Pat. 1,565*

APPLE TREE

Filed May 3, 1956

Inventor
R. A. BISBEE
BY ROBB & ROBB
Attorneys

FIG. 2. Drawing of Plant Patent 1,565. Shown in four colors in original and soft copies of patent. ("Starkrimson" T.M. Reg.)

Plant Pat. 1,565
Patented Feb. 12, 1957

1,565

APPLE TREE

Roy A. Bisbee, Hood River, Oreg., assignor to Stark Bro's Nurseries and Orchards Company, Louisiana, Mo., a corporation of Missouri

Application May 3, 1956, Serial No. 582,613

1 Claim. (Cl. 47—62)

The present invention relates to a new and distinct variety of apple tree which was discovered by me as a bud sport of the variety which has long been sold in commerce under the trademark "Starking Delicious" (unpattented), the discovery having been made in my cultivated orchard which is located approximately four miles south of Hood River, Oregon.

At the time of my discovery, my attention was attracted to a particular tree in my orchard which appeared to be bearing fruit that was quite different from the normal fruit of the parent variety, such differences being evidenced by an earlier coloring of the fruit, as well as a color pattern in the form of a uniform over-all red blush that was quite different from the normal striped color pattern of the parent variety. Further and continued observations of the sport showed that its tree size was somewhat smaller than that of the trees of the parent variety of the same age, but more upright in growth, and the trees of the sport showed the development of considerably more fruit spurs than are normally found on trees of the parent variety. In addition, the new sport has proved to be earlier-bearing and highly productive at an earlier age than trees of the parent variety.

After my initial discovery of the sport, I promptly took steps to preserve and propagate the same, and asexual reproduction by grafting, as performed by me in my orchard near Hood River, Oregon, accompanied by continued observations and testing of the new sport, have fully established that the distinctive characteristics aforementioned come true to form and are established and transmissible through succeeding propagations.

While my new variety more nearly resembles its parent than any other variety, it is definitely distinguished therefrom, as well as from all other varieties of which I am aware, and the distinctive features thereof constitute substantial improvements over the parent variety and represent exceedingly desirable characteristics from both a commercial and home orchard stand-point.

The accompanying drawing shows typical specimens of the foliage and fruit of my new variety, as well as the fruiting spur growth of a typical tree thereof, all as depicted in color as nearly true as it is reasonably possible to make the same in a color illustration of this character, with one of the views of the drawing showing a cross-section of a typical fruit specimen.

The following is a detailed description of my new variety, with color terminology in accordance with Ridgway's Color Standards and Nomenclature, and with the Horticultural Color Guide, as indicated, except where general color terms of ordinary dictionary significance are obvious:

Observations made from specimens grown near Hood River, Oregon.

Dates first and last pickings: From about September 25th to about October 10th; usually ripens simultaneously with the trademarked variety "Starking Delicious."

Tree: Medium size; medium vigorous; upright; dense; vase-formed; hardy; very productive; regular bearing.

Trunk.—Medium stocky; medium smoothness.

Branches.—Medium thickness; smooth; with many spurs. Twigs—color — Diamine Brown, Plate XIII, Color No. 3', Tone M (Ridgway). Lenticels—medium number; medium size.

Leaves.—Medium size; medium width (about 2⅛ inches); medium length (about 3½ inches); ovate; taper-pointed; thick; rugose. Color—Ivy Green, Plate 0960, p. 187, vol. 2 (Horticultural Color Guide). Margin—coarsely serrate. Petiole—medium length (about 1 inch); thick.

Flowers: Medium early; large.

Color.—White, with tinge of Carmine, Plate 21/3, p. 21, vol. 1 (Horticultural Color Guide).

Date of first bloom.—May 11th.

Date of full bloom.—May 15th.

Fruit:

Maturity when described.—Eating ripe.

Size.—Uniform. Axial diameter—about 3½ inches. Transverse diameter—about 3⅛ inches.

Shape.—Conical; ribbed.

Cavity.—Symmetrical; rounded toward apex; acute; undulate; pubescent toward apex. Depth—about ½ inch. Breadth—about 1¼ inches.

Markings.—Some present near apex. Color—Wood Brown, Plate XL, Color No. 17''' (Ridgway).

Basin.—Symmetrical; flaring base; wide; furrowed; mammiform. Depth—about ⅜ inch. Breadth—about 1$\frac{1}{16}$ inches.

Stem.—Clubbed; stout; pubescent; about ⅞ inch long.

Calyx.—Closed; segments persistent; broadly lanceolate; acute; about $\frac{5}{16}$ inch long; approximate at base; prostrate; reflexed from base at apex. Outer surface—pubescent. Inner surface—pubescent.

Eye.—Small; partially closed.

Skin.—Thick; tough; smooth; waxed. Dots—obscure; few; small; even; ruptured; angular; color—Chinese Yellow, Plate 606/3, p. 68, vol. 1 (Horticultural Color Guide); distribution—uniform. Ground color—Straw Yellow, Plate 604/1, p. 67, vol. 1 (Horticultural Color Guide). Color markings—blushed; self-colored; bright; color—Chrysanthemum Crimson, Plate 842/2, p. 169, Vol. 2 (Horticultural Color Guide).

Bloom.—Wanting.

Scarfskin.—Wanting.

General color effect.—Deep red all over.

Flesh.—Rather juicy. Color—Satiny White, with Yellowish tint and tinged with Carmine, Plate 21, p. 21, vol. 1 (Horticultural Color Guide) in vascular bundles. Texture—firm; fine; crisp. Flavor—mild; rich. Aroma—distinct. Quality—best.

Core.—Median; distinct in cross-section; indistinct carpellary area. Bundle area—medium size; cordate; symmetrical at base; acute at base; in bundles opposite and alternate with cell. Halves of core—unequal. Bundles—inconspicuous; in one whorl; color—Chartreuse Green, Plate 663/3, p. 90, vol. 1 (Horticultural Color Guide). Core lines—clasping. Calyx tube—glabrous toward base; broadly obconic; urn-shaped; depth of tube to shoulder about $\frac{3}{16}$ inch; entire depth about $\frac{9}{16}$ inch. Styles—present; distinct toward base; pubescent toward base. Stamens—in one distinct whorl; marginal. Axillary cavity—present. Seed cells—axile; open. Cell walls—distant; thick; tough; length—about ⅝ inch; breadth—about $\frac{5}{16}$ inch. Longitudinal section—broadly oval; acute at apex. Cross section—broad. Surface—fissured.

1,565

3

Seeds:
  Number.—5 perfect; 3 imperfect; 2 per cell.
    Length—about 5⁄16 inch. Breadth—about 5⁄32 inch.
  Form.—Obtuse.
  Color.—Chestnut, Plate II, Color No. 9, Tone *m*
    (Ridgway).
Use: Market; dessert.
Keeping quality: Good; about 110 days in ordinary storage.

  I claim:
  A new and distinct variety of apple tree, substantially

4

as herein shown and described, characterized particularly
as to novelty by its general similarity to the trademarked
variety "Starking Delicious" (unpatented), but being distinguished therefrom by its somewhat smaller tree size
but more upright growth, its development of more fruit
spurs, its earlier-bearing habit and greater productivity,
the earlier coloring of its fruit, and the more uniform
over-all red blush of its fruit.

No references cited.

PROFITING FROM PATENTS BY MANUFACTURE, LICENSE OR SALE

Alfred E. Wilson

Alternative Procedures

In the commercialization of a patent, the inventor or owner of the patent can manufacture and sell the device covered by the patent; license others, the licenses being either exclusive or nonexclusive in nature; or sell the patent or any fractional portion thereof outright for a lump sum consideration, for specified annual payments over a period of years, or for payments dependent on production or extent of use.

The type of business relation that is best suited for a particular situation is dependent on a number of factors. These include the initial capital requirement, the sales potential for the device under consideration, the cost of sales, and the approximate profit that can be made on the device at a suitable price.

This sales price should be set at a level to insure a sufficient volume of sales to meet the commercial demand adequately and not so high as to encourage competitors to copy the device or to design modifications or substitutes not covered by the patents. The scope of the patent coverage that can be procured with respect to a particular development thus has a substantial bearing on the manner in which the device should be commercialized.

Manufacture by Inventor

Where the inventor himself manufactures and sells the device, he relies on his patent to exclude others from commercializing competitive devices and receives his remuneration, for the use of his invention and patent, from the profits made on the sale of devices covered by the patent.

In such situations, the inventor may operate (1) individually, (2) as a partnership with others, or (3) through a corporation. Where manufacture and sale are handled by an individual or through a partnership, the only Federal taxes that are involved are the Federal income taxes paid by the individuals on their individual incomes. Where the commercialization of the patent is handled through a corporation, a 30 per cent Federal income tax is imposed on the first $25,000 per year of profits after operating expenses including salaries are met. Thereafter the current Federal income tax is 52 per cent on all such profits. When money is paid by the corporation to the individual, in the form of dividends, he then pays additionally his normal income tax on the dividends received from the corporation.

There is understandably an inclination to operate either as an individual or through a partnership to avoid the double taxation so involved.

Licensing

Where the device is commercialized by the granting of a license to others to manufacture and sell, the owner may collect a royalty, frequently a percentage of the manufacturer's selling price.

The royalty percentage that can be procured varies with the scope of the patent and the competitive situation with respect to the device under consideration. In the majority of instances where good patent coverage is available, a royalty of 5 per cent of the selling price of the device covered by the patent is justified. In certain industries where the volume of production is low and costs are high, such as aircraft and certain chemical fields, higher royalties are justified, ranging up to 7 or 8 per cent or even more. In industries where production is high and competition very severe, like the automobile industry, royalties are very much less, often of the order of a few cents a car or a fraction of one per cent of the sales price of the component covered by the patent. In many industries such royalties would be considered low indeed, but where production is high the net return to the owners of important patents is indeed very gratifying.

In instances where it is decided that the invention will be commercialized on a licensing basis, consideration must be given to whether a single exclusive license or several nonexclusive licenses will best meet the needs in the particular situation.

Tax considerations have an important bearing on the manner in which the device should be commercialized. If an exclusive license is granted which is effective to transfer to the licensee all substantial rights to the patent, the transaction may qualify under Section 1235 of the Tax Statute as the sale of a capital asset held for more than six months and may entitle the inventor or patentee to long-term capital gains treatment. This means that the Federal income tax imposed is not more than 25 per cent regardless of the amount of the income or profit and the period of time over which the income is paid. Under Section 1235 the payment may be (1) made as a lump sum paid on execution of the agreement, (2) based on the payment of specified amounts annually over the life of the patent, or (3) dependent on the extent of use of the invention. A royalty based on a percentage of the sales price or a specified amount per unit can thus qualify for capital gains treatment under the tax laws regardless of the extent of use of the invention or variations in the annual royalty income because of

fluctuation in the extent of use of the invention from year to year.

Sale of All or Fractional Interest

The inventor may sell all, undivided portions, or fractional interests in his patent application or patent issued thereon, in the same manner as for other personal property.

The purchaser from the inventor can qualify for long-term capital gains when he sells or grants an exclusive license under his rights, provided he meets the requirements of Section 1235 of the Tax Statute, as stated in the *Taxation of Patent Transfers*. When these qualifications are met, he will qualify as the owner of a "holder's interest" and be entitled to long-term capital gains treatment.

Care must be exercised where a fractional interest in an invention or patent is sold because, in the absence of an agreement to the contrary, all owners of any fractional interests can independently grant licenses and collect royalties and there is no obligation to account to the co-owners of the remainder of the invention or patent.

Selection of Best Procedure

A determination as to how to make money with patents is thus dependent on a number of factors.

In the majority of instances where individuals are involved, a licensing program, exclusive or nonexclusive, probably best serves the needs of the parties who do not make a business of inventing, but who may have an occasional idea of sufficient importance to be commercialized profitably. The licensing relieves the inventor of the complex problems involved with the manufacture and sale of the device and makes available to him the experience of successful manufacturers and merchandisers, on a basis whereby his income will be in the form of royalties collected proportionately to the use made of his invention.

Licensing minimizes danger of loss since his obligation is generally limited to the procurement of patent coverage and construction of specimens to demonstrate his device. It is ordinarily of great importance to build a good model, so that the operation of the invention can be demonstrated readily and interested parties can appreciate the advantages of the device.

There is a natural tendency for inventors to reach for the larger profits that may result from the commercialization of the invention individually or through a partnership to manufacture and sell the patented device. As a general rule, such operations are not recommended; the risk involved in such operations far outweighs the advantages to be expected therefrom unless the parties involved are experienced at merchandising devices of the same class.

Immunity from personal liability is achieved, when operating as a corporation, in connection with debts or liabilities resulting directly from the business. In such instances, many experienced parties justifiably feel that they would prefer to pay the increased taxes resulting from operations as a corporation in exchange for the freedom from personal liability in connection with operations connected with the business.

Cross-references: *Accounting and Recovery from Infringement Suits, Licensing Experience of U.S. Corporations, Managing and Marketing Patents, Royalty—Rate and Basis.*

PROSECUTION—COMPACT

Harold B. Whitmore

This article is a condensation by the author of an address on the new and accelerated prosecution of applications, delivered by him before the New Jersey Patent Law Association and printed in 44 JPOS 719-729, 1962.

Complete First Action

Compact prosecution as former Commissioner Ladd explained it in 44 JPOS 635-644, 1962, involves a complete action by the Examiner, followed by a very complete response by the applicant, followed in turn by what may be, in a majority of cases, a concluding second action by the Office.

This very complete first action by the Office involves these concepts. First, the Examiner handling the case makes as complete a search as practicable, and puts into the record the art which meets both the concept and the wording of the claims, as well as further art which is cited and adequately explained as pertinent to significant though unclaimed features. When his search has been completed, if he is not the most expert man in the art involved, he will have his field of search and his broadest claim checked by the Examiner who is the most expert in that field.

A second requirement of this first action is that it must explain clearly the Office attitude on every essential factor in the case. And the third requirement is that before the letter leaves his desk for the typist, the Examiner must be satisfied that, so far as feasible, in the absence of some new factor, the case will be ready for concluding action after applicant's next response.

Complete Response by Applicant

After this complete first action by the Examiner comes the complete response by the applicant. Most attorneys automatically give this thorough and complete response to such a complete first action. It saves their time, gives them a quick and total knowledge of how they stand. The fact that, where this procedure has been used, the proportion of completed appeals to final disposals has dropped 60 per cent suggests the attorney's satisfaction.

This type of prosecution will deprive no applicant of anything. By receiving a total picture of our attitude on the very first action, with two opportunities to submit claims of any desired wording and scope (first, upon filing, and second, in the first response), a high proportion of applicants find their cases equitably concluded on the second action.

In one sentence, compact prosecution means changing afterthoughts into forethoughts. It means that all of the searching which was inefficiently spread out over two or three actions previously will be concentrated, wherever possible, into the first action; and it means that your first response will, in the words of the notice, consolidate the planning and prosecution of all claims of any desired wording or scope which were not already in the original application into the first response.

The statutes entitle you to claim one invention. If you claim an invention, have it rejected, and then go off in a new direction, you are claiming a new invention. After the second action, Rule 112 indicates that your reply is not a proper response. Such matter, being nonresponsive, will have to be canceled.

If you are merely perfecting a claim along lines already followed, this may be proper; but if your amendment includes adding new limitations which would require a new search, you are now claiming something basically different, even though more limited. This would tend to indicate that you are claiming a new invention, not merely responding to a second action on the invention formerly claimed; so again your amendment would not be properly responsive to the Office action. Enforcement of Rule 112 is a relatively new field in which we shall have to feel our way.

Interviews

Another question—How about interviews?

Some divisions have found it very effective, after this type of initial action by the Office and a complete first response by the applicant, to encourage an interview after the first response. If the first action and the first response are such that a final concluding action seems feasible, Office rules make the case special and permit the Examiner to act on it immediately. Try to make an appointment with the Examiner, prearranged to give him time to review what you have proposed, and at the interview, try to agree on what is allowable. If you succeed, the Examiner waits for a supplemental amendment embodying the agreement to be filed, and allows the case. This has been effective and is a great time saver.

After final rejection, however, interviews will not be encouraged.

Modifications in 1964

Among several 1964 modifications of examining procedure are two which require (1) that essentially *all* second actions be *final*, but (2) that interview and amendment practice after final rejection be liberalized. See Address of Commissioner Edward J. Brenner, 803 O.G. 893, June 23, 1964; Optimum Examining Procedure Memorandum #4, 804 O.G., July 7, 1964. Essential features of the address are quoted in *Prosecution of Patent Applications*, q.v. See also the author's review in 801 O.G. 887, April 28, 1964.

Amendments after Final Rejection

In Commissioner Ladd's talk to the Examining Corps, he said, "In 60 to 80 per cent of the cases, the second action can be made final. It may be an allowance, or an outright final rejection, or a final rejection with suggestions for amendment under the provisions of Rule 116." Where an attorney does not conform to this equitable pattern of equal treatment for all, the Office has, in a firm application of Rules 112 and 116(b), an effective tool to ensure compliance. After the final rejection, to avoid the dribble-type of afterthought prosecution, which in the past has wasted so much of the Examiners' time, Rule 116(b) will be rigorously enforced, and at no time after final rejection will substantial amendments in substance be approved, whether before, during or after appeal, or after allowance, except upon a showing of good and sufficient reasons why they are necessary—really necessary—and were not presented earlier.

Other Innovations

Enough as to what constitutes compact prosecution. May I re-emphasize that it is only one of the several simultaneous measures by which we hope to improve the quality and promptness of our service to you. The new "Guidelines of Patentability," reorganization of the Examining Corps for better control over quality and examiner performance, needed long-term planning and better information retrieval systems;

all will help. These are vital parts of our improvement program.

Other questions merit brief comment.

"Can all cases reach a clear and equitable issue by the second action?" No. Requirements for restriction, new references in active arts, highly complex systems, other circumstances, will require added actions in many cases. For example, until compact prosecution is fully understood and practiced, one "other circumstance" may be the failure of an Examiner to deliver that first action, complete in all essentials, which is the bedrock upon which compact prosecution stands. Any action by the Examiner which falls significantly short of that may make a final next action inappropriate and premature. Your bringing such actions to our attention, combined with the better control of quality which reorganization will provide, should soon eliminate them. Experience shows that, in the majority of applications, two good actions are enough.

"Will not compact prosecution so increase the number of continuing applications and the number of appeals as to offset any benefits?" Two years experience in a pilot division shows no perceptible increase in continuation applications; and in appeals, relative to cases concluded, an actual decrease of more than 60 per cent.

Instruction of Examiners and Others

One more question. "Because the success of this program depends so much upon a thoughtful, knowledgeable and complete explanation of his application of the references in the first action, are steps being taken to increase the quality of the Examiner's work?"

For new Examiners, we now have the intensive and thorough training of the new Academy. For all Examiners, we are formulating guidelines to clarify both practice and patentability where confusion and conflict now exist. Where greater uniformity is required, reorganization will provide better supervision. Where greater freedom and responsibility are needed, our goal is to qualify each Examiner for that responsibility.

He must develop the confidence and, shall

I say, the courage, to allow claims when appropriate on the first action; the humility, where opinions differ, to respect the judgment of others; yet the courage too, when clear error or new art would invalidate any presumption of validity, to reject a previously allowed claim.

He must develop the understanding that the main purpose of the Patent Statutes is to grant patents, not to deny them; the strength to resist pressures for patents which, although disclosures may be new, would violate 35 USC 103; the knowledge and wisdom to seek the proper balance under the Patent Statutes between the rights of the inventor and the public rights.

For the first time, the Patent Office has a planned thorough quality control program under way. This is a topic by itself; so, to the question, "Are steps being taken?," I say simply, but emphatically, "Yes."

Pilot Division Results

Compact prosecution was tried experimentally, first, in a division concerning which there had been some question as to effectiveness of its examinations and allowances. A new Primary Examiner was put in charge, with directions to re-examine every claim, rejected or allowed.

Statistics, such as actions per week and disposals per week, measures of production which had long been relied upon in rating examiners for promotion, inevitably dropped. However, the new Primary was convinced that a different type of measure offered a better solution to the old backlog problem. The division adopted a new procedure based on the following principles.

First, adequate proper quality was the prime essential in every case—better no patent at all, than an issued patent with no honest basis for the statutory presumption of validity.

Second, to make the most progress in the least time, each examiner was instructed to make the next action in each application, new or old, so thorough that the case could be concluded on the following action. Inevitably, the statistical figures, such as actions and disposals per week, dropped off for the next few months; but a little later, as responses came in, the production figures returned to former levels.

Then came the big surprise. The disposals continued to rise. From an earlier figure of 55 disposals per month, they rose above 70, above 80, above 90. In the 13th month, the total crossed 100; and for more than a year, now they have averaged above 110 disposals per month. Double the level of two years before.

To determine whether the results obtained in a single division could be extended to a larger group, this practice was extended to a group of nine divisions during the last 6 months of Fiscal 1962. The results were so encouraging that on July 24, Commissioner Ladd authorized the extension of the same practice to the entire examining corps.

Explanation of Increased Efficiency

Research showed this almost phenomenal rise was due to a combination of several factors. First, the freedom from quotas seemed to have freed the examiners from strain and frustration. Their work pattern was more relaxed and more effective. Morale was higher.

Second, to cut personnel turnover, the Commissioner has gone all out to make working conditions more efficient and attractive and to obtain so far as possible salary levels which would stop outside employers from luring away the experienced men who are our most productive and valuable asset. Two young examiners who had planned to resign were so pleased with the new conditions and new procedure that they decided to stay. These two examiners alone accounted for an average rise, because of their increasing experience, of about 8 disposals per month.

But in addition, this very complete action in almost all cases had evoked either a correspondingly complete response, or abandonment. Nearly all cases, if not abandoned, were ready for final action, and therefore under the rules were "special." The same examiner who had made the preceding action could himself wind up the case, and do it immediately. The loss of time due to transfer of dockets and re-studying forgotten subject matter was wiped out. Attorneys had the advantage of dealing throughout these two stages with a single examiner.

It was the multiplied effect of these three things, better morale, compact prosecution, higher retention of experienced examiners, as well as other factors, which had brought this surprising result.

It should be remembered that other factors are working with compact prosecution toward the desired improvements.

For example, the proposed reorganization will help. Another help will be establishing "Guidelines of Patentability," through a series of memoranda outlining what principles shall be followed by Examiners in areas where conflict and confusion now exist. The content of these will be available also to you. The efforts to reduce turnover seem promising; resignations in the last 5 months have been 25 per cent lower than in the corresponding period last year. Finally, through the cooperation of First Assistant Commissioner Reynolds with Chairman McCann and other members of the Board of Appeals, a great deal of progress was made last year in bringing the Board's docket more nearly up to date, further increasing final disposals.

The total of what was accomplished by the entire Patent Office in Fiscal 1962 is significant.

The Patent Office in Fiscal 1961 concluded prosecution of 78,000 patent applications. In Fiscal 1962, with approximately the same personnel, the total was 89,000, 11,000 more than in the preceding year. This is an average increase, in the entire operation, of 14 per cent.

Besides all factors already mentioned, this was due in part to the accelerated effect of making all third action cases special, an effect perhaps now exhausted. But toward the end of the year, compact prosecution made an increasing contribution.

All of the measures discussed are part of a dedicated effort by Commissioner Ladd and his entire staff to solve the problems of the past. I understand that Secretary Hodges' comment to Commissioner Ladd was simply, in effect, "Find everything that's wrong, and fix it."

This is not too "simple," but we are trying. Compact prosecution is a most promising part of our effort. It is an act of faith, faith that our Examiners, given the chance and the time to learn new ways, will give you that kind of first action you've always wanted. Faith that you, given this kind of action, will join us in this effort to make patents and the Patent System mean more to America.

Cross-references: *Examination, Examiners, Prosecution of Patent Applications.*

PROSECUTION OF PATENT APPLICATIONS

Robert Calvert

The objections and rejections by the Examiner in cases before him are usually a cause of temporary disappointment to the applicant or attorney or both. Such "Actions" call attention, however, to changes which, if necessary and made, improve the prospects not only for allowance but also for the patent, should it be issued and come before a court for adjudication.

The requirements to be met during this prosecution are presented in detail in the "Rules of Practice of the U.S. Patent Office in Patent Cases," pp. 101-138, and in the excellent commentary, the "Manual of Patent Examining Procedure," edited by Mr. Ernest A. Faller, largely in Sections 700-822.01.

The attached Patent Application Flow Diagram (Fig. 1) shows the course of a patent application from filing to issuance or abandonment. The Diagram is based largely on that submitted by Commissioner Ladd in his "Statement" of September 4, 1962 to the Subcommittee on Patents of the Senate Committee on the Judiciary.

The late Mr. Ernest F. Klinge, at one time Assistant Commissioner of Patents, is reported to have said that an applicant for a patent should come riding on "three white horses": clear disclosure, innovation transcending the skill of the art, and utility. S. Wolffe, 41 JPOS 61, 1959.

As supports for effective prosecution, such needs would be sound invention, complete and favorable presentation in the application, and good subsequent solicitation. We are here concerned with the last step.

Accelerated Prosecution

In an address delivered to the Professional Staff of the Patent Office and published in 803 O.G. 893, 1964, Commissioner Edward J. Brenner noted that the Patent

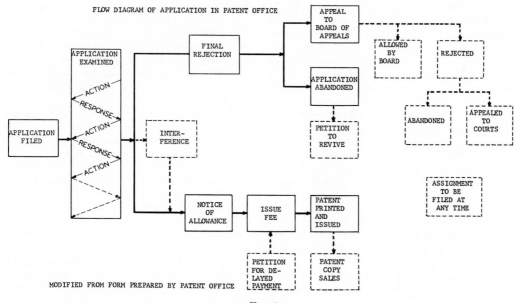

FLOW DIAGRAM OF APPLICATION IN PATENT OFFICE

MODIFIED FROM FORM PREPARED BY PATENT OFFICE

Fig. 1.

Office, over the past three years, has been able to dispose of only 75,000 new applications a year whereas it has received an average of about 85,000. In view of this condition, the prospective increase in the number of applications to be filed in the foreseeable future, and the results of thorough reviews of the critical situation within the Office and with others of experience in the patent profession, he announced new procedures effective July 1, 1964.

Single copies of the address may be obtained by writing to the Commissioner of Patents. The new system might well be named "Cooperative Prosecution." It requires the cooperation of the practitioner, in placing his application in form for disposal at an early stage of the prosecution, and of the Examiner when he finds allowable subject matter disclosed but not properly claimed, in suggesting claim changes that would make for allowability. The new system further implements *Prosecution— Compact*, q.v.

The remainder of this section is a verbatim reproduction of those paragraphs of the Commissioner's address that are selected as being of most direct bearing on the new procedures.

The main features of the new examining program are as follows: (1) Priority of examination will be assigned to the patent applications having the oldest filing dates; (2) the examiners should, wherever possible, assist the applicant or his attorney or agent by indicating allowable claims or suggesting ways in which claims may be made allowable; (3) shortened periods will be set for response to most Office actions; (4) in essentially all cases, second actions on the merits will be final and (5) the examiner will be authorized to permit an interview in each case after final rejection. . . .

As a part of the first Office action on the merits, the examiner in all cases in the future should identify any claims which he judges, as presently advised, to be allowable and/or should suggest *any way* in which he considers that rejected claims may be amended to make them allowable. If the examiner does not do this, then by implication it will be understood by the applicant or his attorney or agent that in the examiner's opinion, as presently advised, there appears to be no allowable claims nor anything patentable in the subject matter to which the claims are directed. It is hoped that the Office will be able to indicate the existence of

allowable claims or suggest amendments to claims to make them allowable in *at least fifty per cent* of the applications in the first Office action on the merits. I believe that in doing this, we will be taking a big step forward in making for effective and successful compact prosecution. Incidentally, the requirements of Rule 111, requiring that amendments, regardless of source, should be supported by approximate remarks, shall be waived with respect to specific amendments suggested by the examiner.

The period for response will be set to expire four months from the date of the first Office action on the merits. Any extension of time for reply must comply with the provisions of Rule 136(b).

In the event the examiner suggests in the first Office action on the merits ways in which he considers that rejected claims may be amended to make them allowable, the examiner may also suggest that a personal interview or telephone interview would appear advisable to reach an early agreement on the allowable claims in the application prior to the applicant's filing a first response.

With respect to the second Office action on the merits, the examiner should not ordinarily make a second search of the prior art unless necessitated by amendments to the claims by the applicant in the first response, except to check to determine whether any reference which would appear to be substantially more pertinent than the prior art cited in the first Office action has become available subsequent to the initial prior art search. As in the case of the first Office action on the merits, the examiner in the second Office action should identify any claims which he judges, as presently advised, to be allowable and/or should suggest *any way* in which rejected claims may be amended to make them allowable.

All second actions on the merits should be made final. However, the Group Supervisors have the right in exceptional circumstances to authorize the issuance of a non-final second Office action on the merits.

The period for response to a second Office action on the merits shall be set to expire four months from the date of the action with the following exception. In any case where a new reference is cited as a ground of rejection in the second Office action on the merits, except as necessitated by an amendment to the claims in applicant's first response, the applicant shall be permitted the full period of six months from the date of the Office action for his response. Also, in such a case, an amendment touching the merits of the application may be submitted after final rejection without the showing required by Rule 116(b). Again, in the case of second Office actions on the merits where a shortened period of four months is set, any extension of time for reply shall be in accordance with the provisions of Rule 136(b)....

We are also planning to make the following changes in interference practice. First, effective July 1, 1964, interferences will not be declared *between pending applications* if there is a difference of more than three months in the effective filing dates of the applications in the case of inventions of a simple character, or a difference of more than six months in the effective filing dates of the applications in other cases. Second, an affidavit showing filed in accordance with Rule 204(b), which we plan to amend, shall be considered by the Board of Patent Interferences to determine whether it is of a character that would be sufficient to establish an award of priority upon final hearing for the junior party with respect to the filing date of the senior party. This change is necessitated by a recent court decision stating that such affidavits are a matter for the Board of Patent Interferences to consider rather than the Primary Examiner. We plan to publish in the *Federal Register* and the *Official Gazette* in the near future, the changes proposed in the rules to accomplish this change in interference practice. Third, the Office will be somewhat more liberal in setting up interferences *between patents and patent applications* and establishing the interference counts therefor where it is apparent that both parties are claiming the same invention.

Advancement of Examination— Making Case "Special"

The accelerated prosecution and examination, described above, may decrease the need or cause omission eventually of the procedure for having applications examined out of turn. A Patent Office circular of January 2, 1962 states the current requirements, as follows:

While applications ordinarily are taken up for action by the Patent Office in the chronological order in which they are filed or amended, certain exceptions are made, under the conditions set forth below.

I. MANUFACTURE

An application may be made "Special" on the ground of prospective manufacture upon the filing of a petition by the prospective manufacturer alleging under oath:

1. The possession by the petitioning manufacturer of sufficient presently available capital (stating approximately the amount) and facilities (stating briefly the nature thereof)

to manufacture the invention in quantity. If the prospective manufacturer is an individual, there must be a corroborating affidavit from some responsible party, as for example, an officer of a bank, showing that said individual has the required available capital to manufacture;

2. That the petitioning manufacturer will not manufacture, or will not increase present manufacture, unless certain that the patent will be granted;

3. That affiant obligates himself or the petitioning company, to manufacture the invention, in the United States or its possessions, in quantity immediately upon the allowance of claims which will protect the investment.

If the prospective manufacturer is a corporation, the affidavit must be made by an officer of the corporation, who must swear also that the Board of Directors has authorized him to make the affidavit and thereby to obligate the corporation to manufacture the invention in quantity immediately upon the allowance of claims that will protect the investment.

4. As a pledge in evidence of good faith, that if the application is allowed, the person making the affidavit will furnish a statement under oath (not to be made of record in the case), within three months of such allowance, showing (a) how much money has been expended in the manufacture of the device; (b) the number of devices manufactured; and (c) the extent to which manufacture has affected the employment of labor.

An attorney of record in the application (or applicant, if not represented by an attorney of record) must file an affidavit to show:

1. That he has made or caused to be made a careful and thorough search of the prior art; and

2. That he believes all of the claims in the application are allowable.

Also, the attorney will be expected to see that the sworn statement is filed in compliance with the pledge, if the application is allowed, and may be called upon for an explanation if a satisfactory statement is not filed.

II. INFRINGEMENT

Subject to a requirement for a further showing as may be necessitated by the facts of a particular case, an application may be made "Special" because of actual infringement (but not for prospective infringement) upon the filing of a petition alleging facts under oath to show (1) that there is an infringing device actually on the market and (2) when the device, product or method alleged to infringe was first discovered to exist; supplemented by an affidavit of the applicant's attorney to show (3) that he has made a rigid comparison of the alleged infringing device with the claims of the application, (4) that, in his opinion, some of the claims are unquestionably infringed, (5) that he has made or caused to be made a careful and thorough search of the prior art and (6) that he believes all of the claims in the application are allowable.

Models or specimens of the infringing product or that of the application should not be submitted unless requested.

III. APPLICANT'S HEALTH

An application may be made "Special" upon a showing as by a doctor's certificate, that the state of health of the applicant is such that he might not be available to assist in the prosecution of the application if it were to run its normal course.

IV. APPLICANT'S AGE

An application may be made "Special" upon a showing, as by a birth certificate or the applicant's affidavit, that the applicant is 65 years of age, or more.

V. CONTINUING APPLICATION

Upon petition, a continuing application will be made "Special" if it contains only claims which have been held allowable in an earlier application to the same applicant or presents claims differing therefrom only in matters of form or by immaterial terminology.

An application will not be made "Special" where the petitioner has not been diligent in filing the petition or in responding to an Office action, after the development of the circumstances qualifying the case for special action, since it is not fair to other applicants who are diligently prosecuting their applications to have them further delayed in order to give precedence to an application in which response has been delayed.

Attitude of the Attorney

Years ago a prominent attorney answered the first Action, which rejected the claims on art, with a single sentence amendment: "What the applicant wants is consideration, not reconsideration."

The next Action was an almost equally short "document": "The courtesy of the attorney is appreciated. The application is again rejected on the references and for the reasons of record."

The next amendment appointed a new attorney. The case eventually went to allowance.

The words, quoted from memory, are essentially correct and complete.

The attitude and manner that will bring the best results over the years, for most attorneys, is not that of the eager combatant ready to argue every issue, whether material or immaterial, but that of the open-minded, realistic, earnest but friendly advocate. He will comply with the Examiner's suggestions whenever it is possible to do so without undue harm to his case or unjustified hardship to his client; he will reduce the issues as early as possible to those that are important; and he will lay the foundation for recognition in future work before the same division as one who insists on all to which he is entitled but knows when the limit has been reached.

It is inadvisable, however, for the attorney to extend courtesy to the point of saying that the references cited represent the closest art. Fraud may be alleged if it should later be shown that the attorney knew much closer art. See *Fraud*, Failure to Report Closest Art.

The Patent Office may request the applicant, through his attorney, to cite the art pertinent to his application. Compliance with the request will be voluntary, at least during an experimental period in which the effect of the order is observed. 780 O.G. 3, 1964.

It is required that business with the Patent Office be conducted "with decorum and courtesy." Complaints if any against personnel are to be made "in communications separate from other papers." Rule 3.

It has been said that the inventor or attorney who writes to the Patent Office should visualize a corps of about a thousand Examiners—mostly engineers, chemists, physicists, biologists, geologists, and mathematicians, scientists by training or nature and usually both, frequently graduates also in law—set in the midst of the most extensive and best classified and indexed patent literature in the world where they studiously compare the claims in the applications with the disclosures of the literature.

Not visible in the picture, but constituting in reality the guiding spirit, is the unchanging purpose of these Examiners to determine to the very best of their abilities whether each application claims an invention and to grant the patent only in that event. The Examiners are expert in analyzing argument. As one has said informally, they come to know in many cases what type of argument to expect when they first turn to the attorney's name.

Like scientists in general, they are above political or other undue influence. To attempt the use of influence is to damage the prospects for an application. A member of Congress or other official of the United States who receives a fee for services rendered an inventor in the Patent Office is subject to fine or imprisonment. 18 U.S.C. 281; Rule 341(f). As to voluntary service from members of Congress, the Patent Office at one time advised applicants "not to impose upon Senators and Representatives labor which will consume their time without any advantageous results."

The Examiners are human too. They admire an attorney who fights for his rights and protects his client. They appreciate, at the same time, fair and understanding treatment of the arguments which the Examiners present. There is no point in the attorney's implying that "any one of grade school intelligence should see" what the

Examiner has failed to see. Such statement shows lack of appreciation of the highly skilled, sincere, yet human official to whom the remark is addressed.

Visualizing the earnestness and fairness of the Examiner and understanding his argument are the first steps in an effective answer to his argument. R. Calvert, "Patent Practice and Management," p. 123, New York, Reinhold Publishing Corp., 1950.

Amendment—General

An order applying to Rule 112, 781 O.G. 1, August 7, 1962, now requires that amendments after the second action upon patentability should contain no additional limitations that would necessitate further searching. If this Rule is maintained, it means that all limitations that might later be desired in the claims should be introduced, in one claim at least, in answer to the first action. In comment on this regulation First Assistant Commissioner Edwin L. Reynolds has said in part:

"Petition will lie from denial of entry of an amendment under the aforementioned condition and will be governed by all the requirements of Rule 181.

"An applicant may ordinarily avoid nonentry of an amendment on this ground by including in his application at the time of filing, or after the first complete action, the most detailed claim that he would be willing to accept as well as the broadest claim to which he considers himself entitled.

"Inasmuch as this practice presupposes an essentially complete first action, its application will ordinarily be deferred in any case where a new reference is cited in a subsequent action for any purpose other than to meet newly added limitations." 791 O.G. 2, 1963.

An amendment, if it is to save the case from abandonment, must request reexamination or reconsideration; respond to every ground of objection or rejection in the prior Office action unless requesting that certain matters of form be held in abeyance until a claim is allowed; make a bona fide attempt to advance the case to final action; and point out specifically how the language of the claims, new or old, distinguishes them patentably from the references cited. Rules 111 and 119. If there is still time in which

FIG. 2. An examiner at work on an application.

to act or if the period is extended, the Office frequently will advise the attorney when his amendment is not fully responsive and thus provide an opportunity to correct the default.

While attorneys seek to cooperate with the Patent Office, it is important to avoid cancellations or limitations of claims that are not absolutely necessary for distinction from the art or for other impelling reason. Otherwise there will occur not only unjustified narrowing of scope but also file wrapper estoppel against broadening the claims by court interpretation to include, as equivalents, what the applicant has in effect disclaimed deliberately by reducing the breadth of the claims.

It is natural and desirable that the attorney in his amendments should exhibit knowledge of his subject. This he can do best by careful selection of points of significance, weighing each argument, and omitting or improving any that does not pass the test for correctness and conviction.

In view of the burden on the Examiner, it is doubtful that an amendment twenty pages long, in a simple case where five or six pages would do, will receive the concentrated attention of the shorter amendment, particularly on the important issues. Then there may be a feeling that the better the proof, the fewer the words required to give it. It will be recognized, however, that amendments in certain electronic, machine or other complicated cases may of necessity be extremely long.

The best language is sincere, direct, brief, and free from circumlocutory expressions. Such "fine" phrases as "not an iota of evidence" or "a single scintilla of proof" may fit into the vocabulary of some writers but are of doubtful value to any.

Selection of Valid Issues Only

When there is a strong issue to be argued, it is frequently a question whether to supplement it with weak ones. In a proceeding some years ago, an able attorney argued, among other points, that a claim was not a part of the disclosure of a patent for purposes of anticipation. When questioned on the point, as the brief was in preparation, he cited a decision from the very court before which he was to appear. When the case had been heard, the court was so earnest in correcting the ambiguity of its previous decision that it all but overlooked the other stronger issues which the attorney had also presented. What the court intended in the old decision was that the disclosure of a patent is not to be judged by the claims alone.

Period for Responses

To save an application from abandonment, the applicant's answer to a Patent Office action is due within four months of most actions by an Examiner or within a shortened period set by the Office. Extension of a shortened period may be obtained for good and sufficient cause if requested within the shortened period. Rule 136(b).

Payment of the final or issue fee is due within 6 months of the date of allowance. If the fee is not paid in that period, the application is forfeited, with the right of the applicant, however, to pay the fee within an additional 12 months when he submits a sufficient and verified showing (as, for example, that the delay was unavoidable) and a petition fee of ten dollars. Rule 317. If the case is not so reinstated, the application has the status of an abandoned case as of the date of 6 months after the allowance. A response due within six months of January 3d, for instance, in a given year is timely if received by midnight July 3d. Henry Kolin, 44 JPOS 426, 1962.

Abandonment of Application

An application becomes abandoned by failure to respond to a Patent Office action or expressly by a letter of abandonment signed by the applicant himself and the assignee, if any, of record.

Petition to Revive Abandoned Application

"An application abandoned for failure to prosecute may be revived as a pending application if it is shown to the satisfaction of the Commissioner that the delay was unavoidable. A petition to revive an abandoned application must be accompanied by a verified showing of the causes of the delay, by the proposed response unless it has been previously filed, and by the petition fee" ($10). Rule 137.

The need for such revival arises when no response has been made to a Patent Office action within the period set. For effectiveness of the Petition, it is important to show absence of intent to abandon, a docket system adequate ordinarily to avoid oversights, and the special circumstance that caused failure of the system in the particular case.

The fee is necessary also to revive an application which became abandoned through an insufficient response. If the basis of the petition, however, is that the response actually was sufficient and if this is finally shown to be the case, then the application was never abandoned and no fee is required.

Filing of Assignment

Despite the reasons for prompt filing of assignments, it is not uncommon for attorneys to delay filing an assignment to the time of paying the issue fee, unless the applicant changes his employment or becomes hostile in the meantime. Assignment records, being open to the public, may if filed early disclose to a competitor a field of research or to an opponent in interference the approximate date of filing.

Responses to Technical Objections

It is difficult to formulate an answer in advance of the study of all related facts. Stereotyped language that fits any set of facts is generally worthless. Yet the attempt is here made to consider a few of the various kinds of objections. The responses are simplified in many instances by noting the bases for such objections, as given in the Rules beginning with 106 and M.P.E.P. 706.

The obvious response to technical objections is compliance when there is no reason for contrary action. This is the usual condition. At other times the objection is traversed, that is, the need or propriety of it is denied. Occasionally it is desirable or necessary to refile the case.

Defect in Oath or Other Papers. Oaths are reported as defective if there is: unreasonable delay between the time of execution and filing, 5 weeks delay having been held in one case to be reasonable (M.P.E.P. 602.05); inconsistency in typing and signing of name of an inventor; absence of statement of residence; and other less frequent omissions or errors. The response in most cases should be a new oath.

Lack of signature to an amendment or the like is to be corrected by supplying a properly signed amendment.

Absence of power of attorney is met by a new power dated as of the earliest time at which the attorney has made a submission in the case.

Absence of mailing address for the applicant can usually be corrected by noting it in an amendment, *without* seeking to amend the oath—an act not permitted.

Amendment Not Fully Responsive. File new amendment to correct the omission of a response to any ground of rejection, within the original time limit or a new one that may be set by the Examiner.

Amendment Telegraphic. Send mail confirmation promptly.

New Matter. Objection is made on the ground that an amendment introduces new matter, i.e., "matter not found in either [the specification or drawing], involving a departure from or an addition to the original disclosure." Rule 118.

Consider the case in which an applicant was allowed to insert the word "nonporous," on the basis of cross-hatching of the pertinent part in his drawing; such cross-hatching was said to show metal and the application expressly referred to a patent showing metal in the part in question. *National Latex Products Co. v. The Sun Rubber Co. et al.,* 123 USPQ 279, CA 6 1959.

Types of subject matter that can usually be inserted are published properties of a material disclosed, information from a previously filed and copending application of the same applicant, and details of a test or method that has been set up as used and is described in a publication of date as early as the filing of the application.

Claim is Functional. Either recite the necessary structure or traverse on the ground that (1) the functionality, if any, does not arise at the point of novelty or (2) the claim recites a combination of two or more functional means, which distinguish it from the "single means" type of claim. In any event, introduce at least one claim, on the same feature, that is free beyond doubt from being merely functional.

Non-statutory Subject Matter. An example would be claiming a system of doing business.

If the disclosure provides a basis, change the claims and presentation to a statutory class—article of manufacture, composition, process, machine, design or plant. Otherwise traverse the objection or abandon or refile the case.

Utility Solely as Nuclear Material or as Atomic Energy in an Atomic Weapon. Determine the latest regulations and possibilities, e.g., by discussion with the Patent Office; it may be necessary to refile, with a showing of different utility.

Single Means Claim. A claim distinguishes from the prior art solely in a single element (or step) defined as a "means" (or "step") serving a certain function.

Recite the structure of the means or step, or combine it with other means or steps. Claims to a combination of two or more mechanical means for functions stated, for example, are free from this objection.

Alternative Expression. An example of an alternative expression that makes a claim indefinite is "a ketone or an ether." In such a case, resort to separate species claims if there is a generic claim, to the Markush form in a chemical application when there is sufficient similarity of chemical nature or function to make the two materials permissible in the Markush group, or, in a mechanical case, to the argument that the parts are equivalent, as in the instance of "rods or bars." MPEP 706.03d.

Negative Limitations. Such statements as "metal, excepting nickel" are not permitted.

Consider use of a Markush group listing the metals that work, or examine the specification for disclosure of a property common only to all operable metals and recite metals of that property. Consider also, in objections to negative limitations, whether it is only the wording that is negative in form, for a positive feature; terms of the class "anhydrous," "colorless," and "nonpoisonous" are satisfactory.

Incompleteness of Claim. Complete it or traverse the objection.

Claims are Prolix. Correct the wordiness so that unimportant details do not obscure the invention.

Multiplicity of Claims. Select claims of number not larger ordinarily than that which the Examiner indicates as adequate. Cancel the others, or retain them, if it is desired to have the multiplicity reviewed by the Board of Appeals.

Aggregation. Seek to show that there is a combination in which two or more elements coact to produce a single and patentably significant result, not simply an aggregation of independent, non-coacting parts. Make certain that the claims recite the coaction of the parts or their cooperation. Otherwise the claims are only a catalog of the several members.

Old Combination. The elements, it is alleged, serve only the functions of like elements in a former combination. Traverse or claim the new part separately, e.g., a new and different catalyst per se although a combination in which other catalysts have been used is old.

Restriction and Election. Restriction is proper when two or more inventions are claimed that are independent and distinct, as shown by separateness of classification, having obtained separate status in the art, or requiring a separate search. The response to the initial requirement of restriction is ordinarily election of species, traverse of the requirement and request for reconsideration of the requirement.

Election of species is required also when the number of species claims (sufficiently distinguished to support separate patents) exceeds five or there is no patentable claim at the time that is generic to all species. The reply is an election pending the determination of the patentability of a generic claim. Factors in the election are the relative prospects of the several species for commercial success and for patentability in case the generic claim is never allowed.

Inconsistency of Claims and Disclosre. Correct the part having the less solid support in the case as filed or being the less important.

No Utility. Traverse. If the utility cannot be proven in the case as filed, refiling is in order provided there is actually utility for a purpose not injurious to the public welfare.

Foreign Patenting before U.S. Filing. A patent abroad, based on an application filed by the applicant more than 12 months in advance of his U.S. filing date and issued in advance of the U.S. filing date, is a bar to the U.S. case. There is no effective answer unless the U.S. application is directed to a patentable improvement not shown in the foreign case.

Foreign Filing Without License. If an invention made in the United States is inadvertently filed abroad by the applicant less than 6 months after his U.S. filing date, without a license from the U.S. Patent Office, try first to get a retroactive license for the filing. Such retroactivity is frequently given. Note, however, that

"A license (for foreign filing) does not apply to acts done before the license was granted unless the petition specifically requests and describes the particular acts and the license is worded to apply to such acts." Secrecy Orders 5.15(c), Rules of Practice.

When an application has not been filed in this country, no application is to be filed abroad without first obtaining the permit. Rule 5.11. (See *Foreign Patents—Permit to File*)

Adjudication Previously or Res Judicata. Traverse on the ground that the invention is different from that previously at issue or that the earlier decision is not yet final because an appeal is still pending or the time limit for filing an appeal has not passed.

Improper Markush Group. (1) The members of the Markush group do not belong to a recognizable chemical or physical class. Submit that they possess at least the common property mainly responsible for their *function* in the claimed relationship.

(2) The Markush groups to the same

chemical function are of varying scope, e.g., two elements in one claim and three in another. Make both scopes the same.

Undue Breadth of Claims. In a chemical case, show if possible that there are enough examples disclosed, perhaps with a statement of the general properties required for each class of material claimed, to illustrate the class and guide the expert in the selection of operable materials only. In a mechanical case, note that broad claims may be supported by disclosing a single form of an apparatus or structure. *In re Vickers et al.,* 1944 C.D. 324, CCPA.

Operativeness of Application Questioned. Choose manner satisfactory to the applicant for showing operativeness. Manual 608.03. In a leading case in which the issue was inoperativeness, it was said

"Under such circumstances, we do not consider that a broad allegation that the application disclosure is speculative, coupled with a recitation of various difficulties which might be encountered in attempting to put it into practice, and a further assertion that there might be still other difficulties which could not be foreseen, constitutes a sufficiently definite statement of a basis for rejection." *In re Chilowsky,* 108 USPQ 321, CCPA 1956.

Non-patentability

The most common and ordinarily the most difficult to meet of all rejections is that based on non-patentability of claims over the references cited by the Examiner. For this reason, in part, there are entire articles herein devoted to the subjects *Invention* and *Patentability,* q.v.

A common form of traversing rejection on a reference is to prove that it does not disclose the structure or produce the result claimed in the application in issue. The simplest proof of this may be something which the reference itself says regarding solubility, stability, or effectiveness under conditions which the applicant claims, but the reference does not provide. When such proof of difference in result is not available in the record but the difference is suspected, then the applicant or other qualified person may prove as much by experiment.

It is required to show also that the difference is significant in the patent sense.

In making tests to show the distinction between the application and the reference, the applicant will frequently utilize knowledge which he has gained from his own work and thus "improve" upon the disclosure of the reference. Knowing, for instance, that a specific type of catalyst is necessary, he may unwisely add it to the reference composition that uses no catalyst of any kind. While the experimenter is expected to supply reasonable mechanical skill in testing a reference (M.P.E.P. 716), supplying experience beyond that level may penalize the applicant by making the reference better than it is and, at the same time, laying himself open to the charge of not having followed strictly the teaching of the reference.

As to art which shows an element that is set up by the applicant, in his own application as equivalent to an element that he claims, the leading case is *In re Ruff and Dukeshire*, 118 USPQ 340, CCPA 1958. It holds that the equivalence, to anticipate an application, must have been known in advance of the discovery of the equivalence by the applicant. In other words, the application at issue will not be used to defeat itself on that point.

Product "Inherently Produced" in Earlier Process. In 1964 the patentability of a chemical element and the process of making it was recognized, even though a previous process of Fermi *et al.* was accepted as inherently giving a trace proportion of the element. The CCPA, in reversing the rejection by the Patent Office, said:

"If the statements in Fermi *et al.* are accepted as factual on the basis of the Smyth Report, appellant asserts (and the solicitor does not deny) the maximum amount of curium 242 that could have been produced in the Fermi *et al.* reactor operated for 100 days at 500 kilowatts power can be calculated to be 6.15×10^{13} [10^{-13}] gram. Thus appellant asserts that the reactor could have produced no more than one-thousand-billionth of a gram of curium 242, and this one one-thousand-billionth of a gram would have been distributed throughout forty tons of intensely radioactive uranium reactor fuel. This amount, of an unknown, unconcentrated isotope, if present, would have been undetectable." *In re Seaborg*, 140 USPQ 659. Cf. *Atomic Energy Patents*,

Selection from Numerous Alternatives in Art "Would Give" Product. Patentability for a narrow range of proportions or conditions has frequently been argued on the basis that operating on either side of that range, but within much broader limits shown by the art, would not give the kind of results obtained by the applicant.

Now there has been decided a case in which the applicants selected, for each of four positions in a chemical compound, a specific unit from among an almost or quite infinite number of combinations possible from the disclosure of a reference.

The application claimed tetracyanoethylene of the formula

$$NC-C-CN$$
$$\|$$
$$NC-C-CN$$

A reference patent 2,264,354 to Alder *et al.* showed the structure

$$R_1-C-R_2$$
$$\|$$
$$R_4-C-R_3$$

in which "R_1 and R_2 stand for a member of the group consisting of CN, acyl, and an esterified carboxylic acid group, R_3 stands for a member of the group consisting of hydrogen, CN, acyl, and an esterified carboxylic acid group, and R_4 stands for a member of the group consisting of alkyl, oxyalkyl, aryl, CN, acyl and an esterified carboxylic acid group."

The Patent Office rejected the application on said patent. The applicant proceeded under 35 U.S.C. 145 in an appeal, finally to the Court of Appeals for the District of Columbia.

Experts are reported to have said in effect that: The general formula shown in the Alder patent gives rise to an "infinite number of possible compounds." The acyl, alkyl, aryl, oxyalkyl, and esterified carboxylic acid groups mentioned in the patent, they held, "represent *classes* or *groups* of substituents, within each of which are an infinite (or indefinite) number of specific elements." Dr. Cope said in his testimony:

"I would say that this is so broad that for a chemist to be led to any specific compound by this formula would be just about the same as being led to a specific Chinese baby being born at this moment."

The Appeals Court held that "the disclosures in the Alder patent would not have taught one skilled in the art the subject matter of claim 1." *E. I. duPont de Nemours & Co.* v. *Ladd*, 328 F.2d 547, 1964.

Effective Dates and Qualifications of References

See *Anticipation*.

Swearing Back of Reference

There are circumstances under which the applicant can remove a reference by proof of reduction to practice of his invention in this country or diligence under specified conditions in advance of the date of a publication or of filing of the application for a patent cited against him. Rule 131 on this point reads in part as follows:

"(b) The showing of facts shall be such, in character and weight, as to establish reduction to practice prior to the effective date of the reference, or conception of the invention prior to the effective date of the reference coupled with due diligence from said date to a subsequent reduction to practice or to the filing of the application. Original exhibits of drawings or records, or photocopies thereof, must accompany and form part of the affidavit or their absence satisfactorily explained."

As to the nature of the evidence required, it has been said:

"...the function of an affidavit under Rule 131 is primarily directed to establish in sufficient detail what structure, article or composition was made or what acts were performed at or prior to the date specified, rather than to a positive showing of who performed the acts, since the appellant's affidavit that he conceived the invention and he performed the acts or that the acts were performed under his direction are normally sufficient for that purpose..." *Ex parte Blair*, 114 USPQ 557, PO BdApp 1957.

Should it be established that the portion of the patent disclosure relied on as the reference was introduced into the patent application by amendment and as such was new matter, the date to be overcome by the affidavit is the date of the amendment. M.P.E.P. 715.

A Rule 131 affidavit can be used to overcome a reference published more than a year prior to a patent applicant's filing date if the reference was secondary rather than anticipatory. *In re Palmquist and Erwin*, 319 F.2d 547, CCPA 1963, 138 USPQ 234. Rejection on the grounds of obviousness must be based on the state of the art at the time of invention, rather than at the time of filing.

When a cited U.S. patent has a Convention date based on previous foreign filing, the date that is to be sworn back of is the U.S. filing date, not the Convention date. Commissioner's Order, O.G. for June 9, 1964. (See *Anticipation*)

Conditions for Removal of Reference. The reduction to practice relied upon to overcome a reference, under Rule 131, must relate directly to the subject matter claimed by the applicant. In *Ex parte Mayfield* the invention claimed was a growth promoter in *feed* for chickens. The Examiner refused to remove a reference when the affidavit under Rule 131 showed, at a sufficiently early date, use of the promoter in the *drinking water*. Another affidavit, submitted later and considered by the Board of Appeals, showed a promoter in the feed. The later affidavit was held to be insufficient, however, because it related to the promoter in the form of the acid whereas the claimed compound was the sodium salt. 123 USPQ, PO BdApp 1959.

When the applicant can make a claim of the reference patent, he cannot remove the reference by swearing back of it.

"[If] a patent, sought to be overcome as a reference, claims as well as discloses the invention in issue, Rule 131 does not apply and the reference can only be overcome by way of an interference proceeding." *Ex parte Beeber et al.*, 123 USPQ 221, PO BdApp 1959.

In discussing the trend towards requiring a showing of utility for "completion of the invention" under Rule 131, Pirri (44 JPOS 730, 1962) urges that such showing should not be required under the statutes as they now stand. The fact that question exists indicates the desirability of including evidence on utility in the affidavit under the Rule.

Diligence and Date of Reduction to Practice. The attempt was made in a representative case to establish reduction to practice, in a Rule 131 affidavit, as of the date from which the applicant was diligent in making and perfecting the invention. The Board held the showing unavailing when the applicant could not show also that he was the first to conceive of the invention. For the latter there is required not "a mental concept alone but a definite concept reduced to record or disclosed to others." *Ex parte Kantnor and Wilson,* 117 USPQ 455, PO BdApp 1958.

Inoperativeness of Reference

To prove a reference inoperative, by affidavit, and remove it as a reference, the affidavit must be to facts, not opinions. It should show the willingness to apply reasonable mechanical skill by the expert in trying to make the invention work, without supplying inventive ingenuity, it seems, from the application in issue. When the applicant claims a chemical compound and the reference in question discloses it, it is not necessary for anticipation that the process of the reference for making the compound should be operative. Conditions under which affidavits are unavailing are set forth in M.P.E.P. 716.

Affidavits to Distinguish from References

Affidavits under Rule 132, to distinguish what is claimed in an application from a reference, have been rejected as unavailing in many cases and accepted as adequate in others. For effectiveness the affidavit should report demonstrated facts, not mere opinions; relate if possible to an advantage disclosed in brief at least in the application; and show that comparative tests on the prior art, if any are relied upon, were made according to directions in that art.

Opinions Not Enough

"In an affidavit ... the affiant states that he could not predict what the physiological activity would be of a compound formed by substituting a β-car-

boethoxyethyl group for the 3-carbomethoxyethyl group of the reference. It does not appear to us that this affidavit meets the issue, which is whether the compound formed by such substitution did in fact have different physiological activity from the reference compound." *Ex parte Nathan and Hogg,* 121 USPQ 349, PO BdApp 1957.

An affiant stated that the disclosure in the art "of using minute amounts of various metals to improve the characteristics of the welding arc would never suggest to me that such metals would act as deoxidants if added to the arc in welding titanium." The Board of Appeals said: "This statement merely amounts to an expression of opinion ... it can, therefore, be given no weight." *Ex parte Johnston,* 118 USPQ 238, 1957.

Directions of Art to be Followed. To "determine whether prior art disclosures would lead to the same results ... the experiments should have been conducted in a manner precisely following the prior art disclosures, detailed notes should have been taken, and the person who performed the experiments should have been produced as a witness." *Commonwealth Engineering Co. v. Watson, Comr. Pats.,* 127 USPQ 355, DC Dist Col 1960.

Use of 5 minutes' treatment when the reference used only 5 seconds was considered improper in *In re Eisenhut,* 114 USPQ 287, PO BdApp 1957.

Joint and Sole Inventors or Authors. When joint inventors seek to remove a reference in the form of a patent issued to one of them as sole inventor, but not sufficiently early to constitute a statutory bar, the procedure is a Rule 131 affidavit unless the patent claims the subject matter of the application. In the latter event, the patent can be removed only by interference. When the patent at the time of its issuance and the application are owned by a common assignee, "then the assignee, by taking out the patent, must be considered to have made an election and to have waived the right to receive a second patent on the appellants' application." *In re Ward and Switzer,* 111 USPQ 101, CCPA 1956.

An application of Hirschler was rejected on a publication of an article on the subject by him and Amon. A filed "an affidavit which pointed out that affiant took no part in writing the article and was not the inventor of the subject matter described in the article, but was merely listed as co-author of the article in order to receive credit for having collaborated on the research program under the direction of the present appellant (H)." The affidavit was accepted as removing the joint article as a reference, it being noted that the publication was of date too late to be a statutory bar. *Ex parte Hirschler*, 110 USPQ 384, CCPA 1956.

Evidence of Commercial Success

Evidence of commercial success may tip the scales in favor of patentability when the question is otherwise in doubt. M.P.E.P. 716.

Standard of Invention

Occasionally an inventor will insist that the granting of a patent on the subject matter of his invention to another, perhaps a few years before, shows that his application also should be allowed. He overlooks the fact that the patent is a reference against him whereas it was not a reference against the patentee.

The inventor has perhaps an unformulated concept of the standard of invention required. The standard of invention can be used effectively as an argument for patentability in rare cases only. In most instances it is one of the weakest arguments that can be presented. The Patent Office decides a case on its merits, not by accepting as a controlling precedent an action that may have been originally in error.

A circumstance in which the standard of invention may positively control is that in which a patent is issued on a certain subject and an applicant can and does swear back of that patent. He can thus remove the reference when he does not have in his application the specific disclosure required for interference with the issued patent. Under these circumstances it seems that what the applicant claims, if sufficiently close to what is patented, should meet the standard required for invention. The situation is

complicated, however, if there is rejection also on a reference not cited against the application that has issued.

Amendment after Final Rejection

During the six months after a Final Rejection, in which period the case remains before the examining division, the applicant may offer amendment.

The amendment will be entered if it makes the application allowable without further searching and introduces no new issues, cancels claims, complies with any formal requirement that has been made, or presents rejected claims in better form for consideration on appeal. Amendments touching the merits of the application may be made upon a showing of good and sufficient reasons why they are necessary and were not earlier presented. *Ex parte Tino*, 125 USPQ 27, Supervisory Examiner 1958; also Rule 116(b).

Amendments which increase the total number of claims in the application will not be considered, by some divisions at least, as placing the case in better form for appeal.

In one case, the applicant sought to swear back of a reference under Rule 131, after his application was under Final Rejection. Noting that the need for such affidavit should have been obvious to the applicant after the first office action, the Board of Appeals affirmed the Examiner in refusing to accept the affidavit. *Ex parte McGrath*, 109 USPQ 70, 1955.

Continuing Prosecution after Appeal

Conductance of appeals is the subject of other articles herein. It is necessary to point out here, however, the importance of doing all that is possible to dispose of the case before the Examiner.

The Brief. The brief that is filed should comply with Rule 192 and should contain a concise explanation of the invention, a copy of the claims, and a request for oral hearing, if desired. The brief should be complete in itself except for references to affidavits or exhibits which are part of the file. In presenting his reasons why the Examiner should be reversed, the attorney should present the problem his client was trying to solve, discuss the prior art, describe his client's solution of the problem and point out the new and improved results obtained through the client's solution.

The brief should be clear, complete and concise. All pertinent portions of the references should be analyzed, including any pertinent portions not specifically relied on by the Examiner. The claims on appeal should be analyzed pointing out the structure not shown in the references and pointing out how this claimed structure contributes to the new and improved result. It is not sufficient merely to point out differences between the claimed structure and the references. The broad claims should be analyzed as well as the specific claims.

Many times, applications which disclose patentable subject matter are lost before the Board for failure to distinguish materially over the art, i.e., often the appellant's argument is more specific than his claims.

Amendment after Allowance

As to amendment under Rule 312 subsequent to allowance, the Manual at 714.16 says in part:

"Consideration of an amendment under Rule 312 cannot be demanded as a matter of right. Prosecution of a case should be conducted before, and thus be complete *including editorial revision of the specification and claims* at the time of the Notice of Allowance. However, where amendments of the type noted are shown (1) to be needed for proper disclosure or protection of the invention, and (2) to require no substantial amount of additional work on the part of the Office, they may be considered and, if proper, entry may be recommended by the Primary Examiner. . . .

"[The] remarks accompanying the amendment must fully and clearly state the reasons on which reliance is placed to show: (1) why the amendment is needed; (2) why the proposed amendment or new claims require no additional search or examination; (3) why the claims are patentable and, (4) why they were not earlier presented."

Supplemental Oath

Supplemental oaths supporting claims enlarged beyond their original scope or di-

rected to a feature not claimed initially are not common today; whether a court decision may at some time change the practice cannot be forecast. It may be a safeguard in extreme cases to file the supplemental oath, after allowance, when counsel has reason to believe the oath is necessary, regardless of a recent helpful decision which says:

"Since the material features were all described in the original application, even though not claimed, there was no necessity for the supplemental oath . . . adequate disclosure in the *'statement of invention'* (i.e., the specifications) alone is sufficient to avoid the necessity of a supplemental oath." *American Safety Table Co., Inc.* v. *Schreiber et al.,* 122 USPQ 29, CA 2 1959. Emphasis added. See also *National Latex Products* case, supra.

On this point the Manual at 603.01 says only:

"Since the decision in Cutter Co. v. Metropolitan Electric Mfg. Co., 275 Fed. 158, [CA 2 1921] many supplemental oaths covering the claims in the case have been filed after the case is allowed. Such oaths may be filed as a matter of right and when received they will be placed in the file by the Issue Branch, but their receipt will not be acknowledged to the party filing them. They should not be filed or considered as amendments under Rule 312, since they make no change in the wording of the papers on file."

There were exceptional circumstances in this *Cutter* case. The question arose as to whether the new claims in issue were based on the drawing or adequate supporting words in the specification. Original claims had been cancelled as a result of rejections or the outcome of interference proceedings. The Court held in effect that the new claims were for a different invention and not for "mere changes in detail" from subject matter originally claimed.

An excellent review of numerous cases on the effect of supplemental oaths appears in *M & R Dietetic Labs., Inc.* v. *Dean Milk Co.,* 132 USPQ 496, 507, 508, DC NIll 1961. The Court says in part (case citations omitted):

"A supplemental oath is not necessary when the amended claims 'may fairly be derived from the original specification.' Nor is a supplemental oath necessary where the amendments 'presented claims

for matter substantially embraced in the statements of invention or claims originally presented,'
or 'the material features were all described in the
original application.' A supplemental oath has been
held to be required 'only when an applicant claims
some phase of the invention quite different from
what was originally claimed.' It has been held that
where no 'new structural element was inserted, but
it was merely an insertion of an added advantage
of the structure originally described in the claim'
no supporting affidavit was required for such an
amendment. . . .

"The amendment adding [the product] claims
26 and 27 is broader than anything theretofore
disclosed in the specifications. It makes no reference to process and covers any product by whatsoever method achieved. Certainly such an amendment unsupported by a supplemental oath is invalid."

In the *M & R Dietetic* case, the claims
which originally covered a *process* were
"licked into shape," as another court has
said, to cover the *product* which a competitor had brought to the market, "without
the support of a supplemental oath of the
inventors, and without their approval."

Cases such as this point up the need, in
the specification, of a statement of the invention as broad as any claim that might
be ultimately allowable over the art. Effective prosecution of an application starts
with the preparation of a good application.

Cross-references: *Anticipation, Delay in Claiming,
Double Patenting, Examination, Fraud, Interviews, Patentability, Petitions and Appeals, Restriction, Utility, Validity.*

PUBLIC RELATIONS AND THE
PATENT SYSTEM

Virgil E. Woodcock

Specialists entitled to practice before the
United States Patent Office have, or soon
acquire, a broad knowledge of technology
and a considerable enthusiasm for the part
the American patent system has played in
making the United States the strongest industrial nation. Yet, a careful evaluation of
the attitude of the public toward the patent
system reveals a neutral position, certainly
a lack of enthusiasm. Severely critical attitudes have been taken by an outspoken
vigorous minority.

Objectives

The trend by the government in increasing each year the amount spent on research
and the increasing number of companies
dependent upon government contracts for
their healthy existence make imperative a
contribution by every patent specialist to
a public relations program for the patent
system.

Those who believe in the system concur
that the best public relations program will
be one which provides facts and reliable
information on the purpose of the system
and how it functions. They believe that
each of the caustic criticisms against the
patent system has been based on misunderstanding.

A patent provides the inventor and his
business enterprise with the right to exclude
all others from practicing the invention defined in the claims for a period of seventeen years. It provides the independent inventor and the new business enterprise with
a protected market for the development
and sale of the invention. It has in the past
brought to the inventor a feeling of safety
in disclosing his invention after the filing
of a patent application. It has given him a
business asset on which the initial business
efforts may be financed, at least in part. It
has given him royalties with which he has
been able to continue his research to produce new and better products. It has provided, for the successful, a royal road from
little business to big business, the Polaroid
Company and the inventions of Dr. Land
being the most recent of many classic examples.

Those who have criticized the patent
system blame it for the high prices of pharmaceutical products, the antitrust violations
as exemplified by the *Hartford Empire*
case, and the price fixing of the electrical
manufacturers. Professors allege that since
a patent establishes ownership of an invention in the inventor or his assignee, it retards dissemination of knowledge about the
invention, whereas in fact, the very creation
of the property and the invention makes
the inventor feel safe in disclosing his ideas
to the Patent Office and to the public as
soon as the patent issues. Because of the

increasing sums spent by the government in research, it is urged that the research field, as a whole, be taken over by the government—a philosophy quite repugnant to our free enterprise system.

Source Material

The American Patent Law Association has available a Public Relations Manual which outlines not only its programs but summarizes those of many Patent Law Associations. It includes a section on the Office of Information Services of the United States Patent Office. There is a section from The Patent, Trademark and Copyright Research Institute of The George Washington University. So far, most public relations programs for the patent system have centered in the foregoing organizations.

Additional material, such as in the following Studies of the Subcommittee on Patents, Trademarks and Copyrights of the Committee on the Judiciary, United States Senate, are readily available for all to use:

(1) Study No. 2, 84th Congress, 2d Session, "The Patent System and the Modern Economy" by George E. Frost

(2) Study No. 28, 86th Congress, 2d Session, "Independent Inventors and the Patent System" by Clarence D. Tuska

For a scholarly discussion of the weaknesses of the patent system, see Study No. 15, 85th Congress, 2d Session, by Fritz Machlup. This study is to be contrasted with a less temperate one, No. 11, *ibid.*, by Prof. Seymour Melman.

The Field Service of the Department of Commerce arranges for the display of Information Panels. They are decorative, informative and useful for the education of the public on the patent system. The Panels, as well as free literature, are available from the Office of Information Services. Informative leaflets are also provided by The P.T.C. Research Institute.

From all three organizations, motion pictures, slide-sound programs, and speakers are available on a wide range of subjects for widely different audiences.

The "Journal of the Patent Office Society" and the "Journal of the Patent, Trademark and Copyright Research Institute" present relatively up-to-date viewpoints concerning the patent system. These, in conjunction with investigations of the Congressional Committees, afford ample material for new and informed approaches in interesting the lay audience in the patent system and the constructive part it has played in making it possible for a new business to meet the growing costs of labor, the constant competition of the market place, and the continued stream of improvements which add up to a continual rise in the standard of living in the United States.

Since it is the purpose of the patent system to promote the progress of the useful arts, it is essential that all who profit from it, the public, the inventors and the patent specialists, should know its strength as well as its weaknesses. They should have available reliable information on which to judge the attacks and the alternative proposals, some of which are copied from the Soviet system, such as awards and upgrading of living standards for the successful inventors.

The Patent Law Association

The principal objects of every patent law association are essentially the ultimate purposes of the public relations program. For example:

(1) to advocate steadfastly our Constitutional provision for the promotion of science and the useful arts;

(2) to further high standards of professional ethics;

(3) to promote the development and administration of the patent trademark and copyright laws; and

(4) to increase knowledge of patent law and related subjects.

For the foregoing reasons, some associations provide that the public relations committee shall have the duty of recommending to the governing body of the association ways and means for increasing the prestige and influence of the association in its relations with the public and with other organizations. This means that the program of the association as a whole in attaining the objectives of its constitution essentially is a part of the public relations program. As such, its impact on the public should be of concern to the public relations commit-tee. To illustrate, a committee on unauthor-ized practice and legislative committees may take positions which association members may conclude are in the public interest, but as viewed by the layman, such actions may appear only of benefit to the patent practitioner. To many laymen, the prohibi-tion against advertising of personal serv-ices is not well understood. The historical background and the reasons why doctors and lawyers and members of other profes-sions do not advertise need to be constantly set forth. Resolutions limiting practice to special classes, members of the Bar, and those who pass Patent Office examinations, represent further examples, and so do the current debates involving the premise that any invention having to do with the health, welfare and defense of the country ought to be freely available without regard to property rights of the inventors who have created inventions in these fields.

With the abundance of informed and un-informed attacks on the patent system, every public relations committee has ade-quate challenge, so much so that the mag-nitude of the program may itself be enough to defeat, for any one year, any substantial accomplishment by a given committee. Ac-cordingly, there have been outlined minimal suggested programs. If during the next year and each succeeding year every one of twenty or thirty committees on public re-lations could move forward and mark down at the end of the year three or four com-plete programs, there would be accom-plished much more than has ever been done thus far.

A Suggested Program

First Year

1. Panel on Plant Patents at Flower Show
2. Two 2-hour talks—Patents for Engineers—to the seniors at the Engineering Schools
3. Organize Speakers Bureau—plan speeches from APLA Slide Collection
   a. General Public
   b. Mechanical and Electrical Engineers
   c. Chemists
4. Cooperate with local Lawyer Reference Serv-ice.

Second Year

1. Find audiences for the three prepared speeches. Have them rated: delivery, content, questions asked
2. Repeat talks at Engineering Schools
3. Promote newspaper releases when local inven-tor receives patent
4. Plan article for House Organ.

Third Year

1. Cooperative program with Engineers' Club
   a. Patent course, or
   b. Joint meeting with panelists: Patents, Trademarks and Coprights
2. Continue earlier programs.

The above programs are short, conserva-tive and well within the capacity of accom-plishment by a relatively small committee. They follow the philosophy that it is better to plan on the conservative side and mark down accomplishments than to plan a pro-gram in such broad outlines of all-encom-passing character that at the end of the year nothing but hope is passed along to the successor committee.

The Individual Inventor

Those who practice patent law know that the day of the independent inventor is not at an end. They know that invention con-tinues to be the product of the unusual, the imaginative and perceptive mind. But case histories and actual narratives of how these inventions come into being need to be disseminated everywhere. There can never be too many of these human-interest stories. They may even include some failures, since every invention is scarcely a successful one. Why does one invention succeed where an-other falls by the wayside?

A continual flow of anti-patent view-points affects men in high places. For ex-ample, President Eisenhower, in his farewell address, seemed to adopt this philosophy of the lessening importance of the individ-ual inventor. After pointing out that this country today is spending annually on mili-tary security more than the net income of all United States corporations, he said:

"Today, the solitary inventor, tinkering in his shop, has been overshadowed by task forces of scientists in laboratories and testing fields,

"In the same fashion, the free university, historically the fountain head of free ideas and scientific discovery, has experienced a revolution in the conduct of research. Partly because of the huge costs involved, a government contract becomes virtually a substitute for intellectual curiosity. For every old blackboard, there are now hundreds of new electronic computers."

Would President Eisenhower have made the foregoing statements, had he had before him the following from one of the speeches of Dr. Edwin H. Land?

"I do believe wholeheartedly in the individual capacity for greatness, in one way or another, in almost any healthy human being under the *right* circumstances, but being part of a group is, in my opinion, generally the *wrong* circumstances. Profundity and originality are attributes of single, if not singular, minds. Two minds may sometimes be better than one, provided that each of the two minds is working separately while the two are working together; yet three tend to become a crowd."

Dr. Land recognizes that the inventor is an extraordinary man; that the insight and imagination from which these new discoveries come are present in some inexplicable way in some of our clients. We are baffled by their absence in other equally trained men. As Dr. Land puts it:

"Science is an awkward, disorganized, inefficient activity; it is simply more efficient than any other human activity!"

Dr. Land says that our vast investment in science and engineering is not overwhelmingly inefficient because:

"It is that, spontaneously and unpredictably, individuals arise here and there in the world, here and there in time, who introduce great clarifications, new words, new language, and fresh statements which cause the race to jump ahead by 10, 20, or 100 years."

As to the importance of the patent system, Dr. Land, in speaking of small companies, new companies, said:

"It is impossible—without the protection of patents—for a new company working on a major advance in science or technology to (1) be properly financed; (2) go through the extremely difficult periods of study, invention, development, engineer-ing, and production; or (3) afford to advertise and distribute its products and services."

Procedures in Public Relations

The majority of patent specialists are patent lawyers duly admitted to practice before the State and Federal courts. But the agents, whose practice is restricted before the United States Patent Office, are equally bound to the same high standard of ethical conduct, that is, the "professional conduct generally applicable to attorneys before the courts of the United States." The use of advertising, circulars, cards and similar material to solicit patent business is now forbidden to all.

As a general policy, the patent specialists should promote a better understanding of the patent system through the duly organized patent law associations. They may then participate as members of speaker bureaus. Their activities will be subject to committee approval. Only the name and the fact that he is a lawyer or agent should be stated in the introductions on radio programs. One should be careful not to answer questions of specific character. Within the foregoing limits, there is much room for constructive efforts.

Reference has been made above to the abundance of material included in the Public Relations Manual available from the American Patent Law Association. Every public relations committee could well utilize a copy of that Manual as the basis of a corresponding one for the local association. If in loose leaf form, it could include the names and addresses of the men and women contacted in order to promote particular programs, as at universities and engineers' clubs. There would be included copies of the more successful speeches, slides and films having to do with inventions of local interest, names of newspaper reporters and free-lance writers who wish information on the patent system. There would then be greater continuity between the work of one committee and its successor in this important field.

As various committees create new approaches, new materials and discussions of real educational value, such new approaches should be made available to all interested in the public relations program to the end that, with many modest approaches, there will be developed a body of facts, a body of literature, and educational tools which can be brought to bear on any problem at any given time to the great benefit of the patent system.

An effort has been made to illustrate the need of prepared discussion on how best to bring to our audiences the importance of the patent system, its What, Why and How.

Crash Programs and the Patent System

On other matters too, we must be candid. The crash program which brought the atomic bomb into existence was remarkably successful. The crash program "to catch up with Russia" has been successful in getting satellites into orbit.

Russia's continued crash programs, its national policy of government control of the people, particularly of the scientists for government purposes, have been successful. After all, survival may be a greater incentive than the patent system, and in Russia survival even for the individual is *not* taken for granted.

In our country, the crash programs and the cold war itself have been used to support all kinds of plans to change the American way of doing things. Any student of political science, certainly every Constitutional lawyer, will say we are in the midst of a social change, indeed, a social revolution.

The patent provisions of the Space Act are evidence of the successful efforts of their authors to diminish the importance of the patent grant. The disciples of false prophets continue to undermine in this country the proper conclusion on the part of an inventor that a patent means something; that a patent will protect him in his right to exploit his invention. If the incentive to advance the arts be dismissed to a point where we engender dependence upon the State for research funds, and if we move away from the individualistic competition which characterizes our free enterprise system, those who have endeavored to emas-

culate the patent system will have done the greatest possible injury to this country.

History demonstrates that from the free-lance inventors come ideas representing great breakthroughs in all fields of technology. It is to the continuance and the maintenance of a national attitude in this country favorable to the production of invention that our public relations program should be dedicated—not for the sake of obtaining patents, but because through patents the incentive for the production of new things has been proven by time. It is through patents that new concerns do arise and then grow into big businesses.

The Patent, Trademark and Copyright Research Institute has documented the fact that from 46 to 64 per cent of the issued patents are used, that is, the inventions have been manufactured and sold. As a result of this one research product by the Research Institute, Dr. Sanders, of the Research Institute, provides an excellent example of how to straighten out facts about the patent system. He referred to the first Committee Report, from Senator O'Mahoney's staff, and said:

"This is a chapter heading: 'The Effect Upon the Patent System and the Economy of the Issuance of Vast Numbers of Unused Patents.' Then follows:

" 'The accumulation of vast numbers of unused patents by some companies and the effects of such accumulation (1) as a deterrent to newcomers attempting to enter these industries and (2) on the conduct of research by others is a matter of real concern. Related to this problem is the number of patents issued to corporations as against those issued to independent inventors. Indeed, the fate of the independent inventor, heretofore a prolific source of new inventions, is a cause for alarm.'

"Now, I do not mean to say at all that this was misrepresenting the facts. There were no facts. These were legitimate inferences from what was presumed to be known. I'm sure if the subcommittee were writing its report today it would write it differently.

"Our findings to date indicate that every one of these assertions on which we have been able to shed some light appear to be almost the opposite from what has been commonly assumed to have been the facts.

"On the score of 'vast numbers of unused patents,' our findings to date indicate that as far as the assigned patents are concerned—and the subcommittee was addressing itself to that group primarily—55 to 65 per cent of the patents by the time they are ready to expire are being used, or have been used, in industry.

"Our earlier study indicated that assignees, owning 75 per cent of the patents sampled, retrospectively, considered the patent of value to them."

The more numerous the facts which are marshaled together in answer to non-factual criticism of the patent system, the more effective will be any public relations program. Every inventor, patent practitioner and assignee can contribute facts through the P.T.C. Research Institute. If the factual summaries are sent to the Institute, the Office of Information Services of the United States Patent Office, and the American Patent Law Association, they can be made widely available to all.

Cross-references: *Attorneys' Professional Ethics, Economic Aspects, Invention—Changing Objectives.*

PUBLICATION OF INVENTIONS

Warren T. Jessup

Publication of an invention, in the absence of protective steps, constitutes a surrender of the invention to the public.

Motives for Publication

Intangible Motives. A major intangible motive for publishing is the inventor's struggle to obtain recognition—to establish status in the intellectual community. Another is the common desire of creative thinkers to have their ideas accepted and used, wholly apart from any personal credit to the author.

While such intangibles often dominate, they provide little if any substance for use in assessing legal consequences of the publication.

Publication to Establish Conception. Proving the date of conception of an invention is one of the steps in establishing priority of invention. Any writing adequately disclosing an invention can, with proper corroboration, serve to establish conception of an invention.

Publication does not constitute a reduction to practice of one's own invention. *Kear v. Roder,* 47 USPQ 458, CCPA 1940. Ironically, a publication by another party is as effective as reduction to practice when used to preclude a later applicant from patenting the disclosed invention. 35 U.S.C. 102.

Publication to Preclude Later Patenting by Someone Else. A valuable attribute of publication, from a defensive standpoint, is the fact that one year after the publication date it becomes an absolute bar to a patent application by anyone on the subject matter published, irrespective of when the applicant may have actually made his invention. 35 U.S.C. 102(b).

For this reason, a company may occasionally encourage research and development personnel to publish inventions or designs in technical periodicals, sometimes relatively obscure ones, as a purely defensive measure; as of the date of publication, the company will have a "defensive" disclosure and, one year thereafter, a safeguard against a competitor's filing an application and obtaining an enforceable patent on the same subject matter.

Several agencies of the United States Government, particularly in the Department of Defense, would welcome some means for easily and effectively making such defensive publications.

The patent bar has debated the question of "publication patents." American Bar Assoc., Sec. of Pat. Tr. Mk. and Copyr. Law, Summ. of Proc. 1959 p. 66, 1962 p. 54, 68. Same, Committee Reports 1958 p. 26, 1959 p. 77, 1961 p. 60. Any such "patent" would of course have no force and effect as a monopoly, would be purely defensive, and at the present time, is without any immediate prospect of initiation or recognition.

Publication of Marginal Merit Inventions

In 45 JPOS 733, 1963, Gunther A. Hauptman compares the merits of publication with attempts to patent marginal inventions in so-called defensive patents. He notes that the latter places an unnecessary burden on the Patent Office but is effective in preventing later patenting, by another, of the thing disclosed and also in providing at times an offensive value for trading or other purposes. Publication, on the other hand, avoids filing expense, decreases the load of work for the Patent Office and affords the desired defensive protection. It possesses, however, no offensive or trading opportunities. Also, publication in the standard professional and scientific journals with the promptness desired is not feasible, he concludes, because of their specialized standards and processing delays. He then says:

"As part of its invention protection policy, the International Business Machines Corporation has for five years published the 'IBM Technical Disclosure Bulletin.' Increasing corporate research and engineering activity caused the problem of properly protecting inventions to grow. It was recognized that even if patent applications could be filed on all inventions, the value of the issued patents would not always justify the expense—to say nothing of the imposition on the Patent Office —of preparation and prosecution. Therefore, the novelty and commercial value of every IBM invention is carefully examined to decide whether publication or filing is the desirable route for obtaining protection."

Methods and Effects of Publication

Patenting the Invention. Publishing an invention by obtaining a patent thereon has the effect of establishing constructive reduction to practice of all that is fully disclosed in the patent, as of the date when the application was filed. 35 U.S.C. 102(e).

On the other hand, if the application is abandoned prior to issuance as a patent, it is unavailable as part of the prior art, either as a publication or otherwise, unless accompanied by a published abstract or other reference which opens the abandoned file to the public. *Ex parte Lipkin*, 129 USPQ 427, PO BdApp 1960. Furthermore, to be evidence of prior invention or reduction to practice, a disclosed invention must be contained in the patent as issued; if the subject matter is dropped from the application, it loses its effect as a bar. *Fessenden* v. *Wilson et al.*, 9 USPQ 274, CCPA 1931.

Publication in Magazines, Books or the Like. Publication of an invention in a magazine or book has much the same effect, as a disclosure, as the issuance of a United States patent. The effective date, however, is that on which the publication becomes available to the public. Unlike the filing of a United States patent application, the deposition of a manuscript with the editor is not the effective date. *In re Schlittler et al.*, 110 USPQ 304, CCPA 1956.

A publication made to deceive the Patent Office on the merits of an invention, will, if discovered, lead to disciplinary action. *Kingsland* v. *Dorsey*, 338 US 318, 1949. (See *Attorneys and Agents*)

Intracompany Publications. It is not unusual in modern industry for inventions and designs to be disclosed first in publications having limited dissemination, such as intracompany circulars and reports among contractors and subcontractors. The weight of authority is that such disseminations are not publications within the meaning of the patent law, although they may serve as persuasive evidence of conception and, under some circumstances, of reduction to practice. *Ex parte Suozzi*, 125 USPQ 445, PO BdApp 1959.

Similarly, publications which are kept secret, either through law or by company policy, are not publications within the meaning of the patent law. For example, a classified Government or industry report is not a publication under the patent laws until such time as the classification is removed. M.P.E.P. 707.05(f). This is in contrast to establishing a "public use" under 35 U.S.C. 102(b); the sale of production equipment under a confidential Government contract has been held to be a public sale which starts the one-year statutory bar. *Piet et al.* v. *United States*, 123 USPQ 21, DC SCal 1959.

"Printed" Publication. Title 35 U.S. 102, uses the term "publication" twice, preceded in both instances by the adjective "printed." This was originally considered to rule out any means except a printing press. *Keene* v. *Wheatley*, 14 Fed. Cases 1764. In recent years other means of making an almost indefinitely large number of copies have come into being, so that the strict printing press rule is no longer followed. While a paper read before a meeting is not a "printed publication" within the meaning of the patent law (*Corona Cord Tire Co. v. Dovan Chemical Corp.*, 276 U.S. 358, 1927), it has been held that a typewritten thesis deposited in a university library and made freely available to the public for inspection, constitutes a "printed publication" within the meaning of the law. *Ex parte De Grunigen*, 132 USPQ 152, PO BdApp 1958.

Foreign Publications and Rights. A foreign publication has, by statute, substantially the same force and effect in this country, as anticipation, as a domestic publication. 35 U.S.C. 102(b). As to the dates on which the disclosures of patents of the various countries become effective as anticipating disclosures, see M.P.E.P. 901.05-(a, b); *Anticipation* herein; and *In re Ekenstam*, 118 USPQ 349, CCPA 1958.

Content of Publication

Irrespective of the motive for publishing an invention, that motive will not be achieved unless the invention is properly disclosed in the publication. Many articles in highly specialized technical publications, while speaking to the "man skilled in the art," at times assume more skill and background than is justified. While colleagues may understand what the writer intends to convey, the technical author who publishes with one of the patent law objectives in mind should not take too much for granted. He should accompany his article with sketches if necessary to a clear disclosure of all critical features. *Preformed Line Products Co. v. Fanner Mfg. Co.*, 124 USPQ 288, DC Ohio 1960.

Furthermore, the inventor-author should neither depreciate his own contribution nor overly credit forerunners in the field. Undue modesty may otherwise be seized upon later by an opponent to establish lack of unobviousness and thus lead to invalidation of the patent.

Review of Manuscript

Prior to dispatching a technical paper to the publisher, it is desirable to have it reviewed from a number of standpoints and perhaps by different individuals or departments if a corporation or other large organization is involved.

For Invention Aspects. A technical paper may at times be published wisely for the purpose of placing some of the material in the public domain, but only after steps have been taken to secure such patent rights at home and abroad as company policy dictates. The paper, prior to publication, should be reviewed by those in the management who decide patent policies, e.g., the patent department, a liaison agent or a specially constituted committee which makes the management decision.

For Contract Obligations. There are instances, particularly in large organizations, where a review of the manuscript is necessary to correlate it with possible contract obligations. This applies, for instance, where development work has been done under a Government contract or subcontract requiring that the contracting Government agency be given opportunity to file patent application(s) prior to public disclosure. There may be situations where a license, under either patent rights or know-how, inhibits the licensee from making public any improvements or other information without the approval of the licensor or other party. Here also approval before publication is imperative.

Cross-references: *Abandonment, Anticipation, Date of Invention, Interferences, Research Directors' Patent Responsibilities.*

R

RECORDS OF INVENTION
Jerome N. Field

The system of making and keeping records should be as simple as consistent with effectiveness in describing the work done and establishing the necessary dates. It should not be so complicated as to discourage continuing use of it or perhaps so legalistic and involved as to encourage in the researcher the idea that his chief function is to get his name on as many patents as possible. For most purposes it is sufficient to make the record on consecutive pages of a permanently bound notebook, have the experimenter date each page at the top and also date and sign at the end of each experiment, have the record and also occasional physical embodiments of the invention witnessed by someone who can understand what he has read and seen and who will not be a joint inventor, and make frequent progress reports on the work to the laboratory head or other qualified executive.

When an invention record is written, it is impossible to know whether it will later become important in a patent controversy. Frequently, a seemingly unimportant entry becomes critical in a patent dispute involving significant sums of money and professional and business prestige.

Procedures

The following points summarize the established procedures employed by U.S. corporations in maximizing the value of notebooks in interparty patent disputes.

Completeness of Disclosure. Notebook entries must be sufficiently clear, concise and complete to enable anyone skilled in the art to understand and repeat the experiment performed. They should include the observations, calculations, diagrams, plans and sketches, concentration and proportions of reagents, reaction conditions and apparatus employed. They should identify reactants by name, formulas and source if rare and, if new, by method of preparation. They should record the chemical or other structure of trademark or tradename goods, describe the work in detail, and conclude with a statement of the significance of the work recorded. Most important, they should clearly describe any unusual or unexpected results. For the purpose of clarity, each laboratory notebook page should state specifically the subject matter under investigation, e.g.: Quinonimine—Preparation of Dichloride Derivatives, project number (if any), date, and reference by book and page number to the last previous entry on the subject.

Execution by Inventor and Corroboration by Witnesses. Most large industrial research establishments require all researchers to sign their entries at the end of each work-day. If the invention was conceived at a date prior to the notebook entry, the inventor should state the date of conception. Under no circumstances should he back-date the record to create the impression that the entry was made at an earlier time. In the case of important entries, a few laboratories provide for the notarization of notebook signatures.

Most research establishments require each day's entries to be initialled or countersigned by at least one corroborating witness, i.e., someone who observed the recorded experiment but did not participate in the experiment itself and who is not a joint inventor. Other laboratories require notebook entries to be witnessed at weekly intervals by at least two persons not directly involved in the work performed. The signing of notebook entries by corroborating witnesses is particularly important in the case of final work or data demonstrating the successful completion of an investigation. The corroborating witnesses' signatures and observations are critical since the inventor's records and signature alone are of no value in proof of dates.

The witnesses should satisfy themselves that there are no blank spaces on the pages witnessed, that all tables and data are complete, and that the entry witnessed is a full and faithful record of the work observed.

Corrections and interlineations on the witnessed page should be initialled and dated by the inventor, erasures being avoided. If such corrections or interlineations are made after the notebook has been witnessed, these changes should be signed and dated by the entrant and the witness to the original entry. The witness must fully understand the subject matter observed before he signs and dates the entry. To ensure that the corroborating witness' testimony will be adequate to prove reduction to practice, some corporations require important experiments to be repeated by a non-inventor. This procedure is unquestionably the safest means of complete corroboration.

A form, as on a rubber stamp, which may be used for signature of the experimenter and the corroborating witness follows:

Signed _____ Date _____

Pages _____ read by me and fully understood.

Witness _____ Date _____

_____   _____

Statements Concerning Worthless Experiments. Categoric statements concerning the worthlessness or lack of utility of the product or process described are to be avoided. Such comment as "n.g." can prove embarrassing at a later date as evidence of failure or of the inventor's lack of appreciation of the work performed. The notebook entry should be a precise, factual statement of what was done and the results observed.

Use of Ink. Ink entries are preferable to pencil entries because they are more nearly permanent and less suspect from the standpoint of tampering. If pencil entries are made they should not alternate with ink on the same page since such alteration creates the impression that the entries were made at different times. In litigation the record must then be fortified with testimony showing that the pencil or pen entries were not an afterthought on the part of the entrant. At best this is a thankless task, to be avoided by legible, neatly kept ink entries. Some research organizations even go so far as to require permanent ink.

Erasures. Under no circumstances should an entry be erased or a page removed. Corrections should be made by crossing out the entry with a single line, all crossed out entries should remain legible. The new entry should be initialed and dated by the entrant and should be inserted directly above or following the deleted material. These changes should be made before the witnessing of the entry. If changes are made after the original entry has been witnessed, the change should be cosigned and dated by the witness. Even in the absence of initialing and dating by the entrant, review of the page in later years should show the striking out of the incorrect entry and the addition of the correct one. Only in this way can suspicious and, in later years, unexplainable erasures be avoided.

Added Material. Charts, standardized data sheets and the like may be made part of the notebook by permanent attachment. Alternatively, this data may be completely copied into the notebook. Copied data, however, should be accompanied by a specific reference to the original record and the original record should be filed for future reference. For greatest safety the original record should also be dated, signed and witnessed.

In the course of employment it is often impractical to attach analytical sheets, special charts, and the like, permanently to the notebook or to copy them completely. In these cases, the written material should be signed, dated and witnessed and the essential information transcribed into the notebook with a cross reference in the notebook to the original material. The loose reference material should then be collected, indexed and filed in a readily accessible location. Because of the danger of research personnel collecting data on loose sheets, some research organizations insist that loose sheets may not be kept without patent counsel's explicit approval.

Empty Pages. Pages should not be skipped. Generally speaking, it is not necessary to use a new page each day if the experiment is a continuing one. However, some research establishments do require research personnel to employ a new page for each daily entry, with a line drawn across the unused portion of the previous page. This procedure avoids embarrassment at a later date when, in litigation, it might be maintained that a researcher could have made an entry on an earlier blank page.

Duplicate Pages. Many research laboratories provide tear-out pages and carbon paper so that research personnal may keep duplicate copies of their notebook entries. These copies are customarily sent to the supervisor or central filing office at designated intervals after the original notebook is collected. All copies are then filed for future reference. Frequently original entries are microfilmed to provide duplicate copies in case of loss or destruction. From a practical standpoint, it is generally felt that the microfilming procedure and central filing system for the preservation of original notebooks are more than justified by the better prospect of prevailing in a contested case that might otherwise be lost.

Security Precautions. When not in use, notebooks should be stored in locked files. When notebooks are completed or a particular notebook has been terminated for some other reason, it should be filed and the date of its terminal use noted.

Most industrial research organizations have established security provisions for research personnel. For example, it is customarily required that the employee's notebook be delivered to central filing upon termination of employment.

Employees are also required to report the loss of a notebook promptly to appropriate supervisory personnel.

New Ideas. Distinct from recording work actually performed is the entry into the notebook of new ideas, i.e., inventive concepts. Though some research institutions prefer new ideas to be recorded in separate

notebooks or on invention forms, the majority desire the original entry to be entered into the laboratory notebook. When recorded in the laboratory notebook, the basic inventive concept should be stated broadly. The entrant should then elaborate upon specific details, preferred conditions and equivalents, stating specific examples if possible. If new ideas are also described in a memorandum to patent counsel, the laboratory notebook should preferably make reference to the preparation of this memorandum. If a concept appears useful, it should be duly recorded, even if the entrant does not consider it patentable.

The foregoing points cover the procedure for protecting patentable inventions through proper maintenance of laboratory notebooks. The overriding requirements are completeness, accuracy, and permanency of the notebook, all to be expected in any well-ordered research organization, and adequate corroboration.

Cross-references: *Date of Invention, Disclosures,* Section on Invention Disclosure Form, *Interferences, Research Directors' Patent Responsibilities.*

RECOVERIES FROM INFRINGEMENT. See ACCOUNTING.

REISSUE PATENTS
Leonard F. Stoll

It has been stated that in each year in recent times the number of patents reissued amounts to approximately one-third of one per cent of the number of patents granted. P. J. Federico, Intervening Rights in Patent Reissues, 30 Geo. Wash. L. Rev. 603, 1962. From a purely numerical standpoint, it would seem that reissued patents do not play a major role in protecting inventors' rights. It should be recognized, however, that in most cases a patent is reissued by the patent owner only if he feels it to be an important one. In addition, the reissue application is not filed until several years after the first blush of inventive zeal has dissipated; the expenses of reissue are incurred as a result of cool business logic. Thus, reissued patents may represent a very substantial percentage of commercially valuable patents. Actual practical experience indicates that almost every infringed patent of demonstrated value is at least considered at one time or another for reissue.

35 U.S.C. Sections 251 and 252 provides for reissued patents, not as new patents but simply as corrected forms terminating on the same date as the originals. The underlying reason for the reissue grant was summed up by the Supreme Court over a century ago, in *Grant* v. *Raymond*, 6 Peters 218, 8 L. Ed. 376, 1832, as follows:

"...The great object and intention of the [patent] Act is to secure to the public the advantages to be derived from the discoveries of individuals, and the means it employs is the compensation made to those individuals for the time and labor devoted to these discoveries, by the exclusive right to make, use and sell the things discovered for a limited time. That which gives complete effect to this object and intention, by employing the same means for the correction of inadvertent error which are directed in the first instance, cannot, we think be a departure from the spirit and character of the Act...The communication of the discovery has been made in pursuance of law, with the intent to exercise a privilege which is the consideration paid by the public for the future use of the machine. If, by an innocent mistake, the instrument introduced to secure this privilege fails in its object, the public ought not to avail itself of this mistake, and to appropriate the discovery without paying the stipulated consideration. The attempt would be disreputable in an individual, and a court of equity might interpose to restrain him."

The law of reissue prior to passage of the 1952 Act was largely a hodgepodge of disagreements and confusion varying from year to year and from court to court. The 1952 Act not only codified but also changed much of the reissue law, and court decisions under the old law are to be relied upon only in the light of the new statute and subsequent decisions.

Basis for Reissue

The only errors properly correctable by reissue are substantial errors made by the patentee that render the original patent wholly or partially inoperative or invalid.

Minor errors in an issued patent are correctable by a certificate of correction under 35 U.S.C. 255, mistakes made by the Patent Office are correctable under Section 254, and claims are cancellable by disclaimers under Section 253. While cancellation of one or more complete claims could conceivably be effected under the reissue provisions of the statute, this at best would ordinarily be inadvisable; the filing of a reissue application subjects the entire application (including any of the original claims which are resubmitted) to a complete examination by the Patent Office and permits the citation of additional references. *Ex parte Dikeman*, 93 USPQ 133, Supervisory Examiner 1952.

Circumstances justifying reissue of a defective patent are stated in 35 U.S.C. 251 as follows:

"Whenever any patent is, through error without any deceptive intention, deemed wholly or partly inoperative or invalid, by reason of a defective specification or drawing, or by reason of a patentee claiming more or less than he had a right to claim in the patent, the Commissioner shall, on the surrender of such patent and the payment of the fee required by law, reissue the patent for the invention disclosed in the original patent, and in accordance with a new and amended application, for the unexpired part of the term of the original patent. No new matter shall be introduced into the application for reissue.

"The Commissioner may issue several reissued patents for distinct and separate parts of the thing patented, upon demand of the applicant, and upon payment of the required fee for a reissue for each of such reissued patents.

"The provisions of this title relating to applications for patent shall be applicable to applications for reissue of a patent, except that application for reissue may be made and sworn to by the assignee of the entire interest if the application does not seek to enlarge the scope of the claims of the original patent.

"No reissued patent shall be granted enlarging the scope of the claims of the original patent unless applied for within two years from the grant of the original patent."

The language of the statute which recites the defect in the patent as occurring through "error without any deceptive intention" replaces the previous wording "through inadvertence, accident, or mistake" but has been held to have the same meaning as the earlier wording. *Riley* v. *Broadway-Hale Stores, Inc.*, 98 USPQ 433, DC SCalif 1952; *In re Beyers*, 109 USPQ 53, CCPA 1956; *In re Handle*, 136 USPQ 460, CCPA 1963; *Nickerson* v. *Barefoot Sole Co.*, 136 USPQ 96, CA 6 1963. As a result, prior case law as to what may or may not constitute inadvertence, accident, or mistake under the old law should be considered in determining what constitutes an error without any deceptive intention under the new law.

At least one case subsequent to the 1952 Act has indicated that failure to claim priority under the International Convention is not an error to be recognized under the reissue law. *Ex parte Arkless*, 116 USPQ 214, PO BdApp 1955. But see *Benger Labs., Ltd.* v. *R. K. Laros Co.*, 135 USPQ 11, DC EPa 1962, which permitted the correction of a claim for priority by way of reissue. Another case held that inventorship cannot be corrected by reissue. *Ex parte Johnson*, 117 USPQ 412, PO BdApp 1958. Another case denied that an alleged mistake of the Examiner meets the requirements of the reissue statute as to "inadvertence, accident, or mistake." *Ex parte Ziherl and Kish*, 116 USPQ 162, PO BdApp 1958. In holding that claims deliberately cancelled during the prosecution of the original patent cannot be recaptured by reissue, recent decisions have probed whether the claims sought by reissue were substantially the same as previously cancelled. The answer is affirmative if the same references as defeated the earlier claims now defeat the newly presented reissue claims.

It has frequently been held, that to be entitled to reissue, the "same invention" sought to be protected by reissue must be not only amply supported by the original disclosure but also indicated originally as a part of the invention to be protected. This test, while undoubtedly legally correct, is difficult to apply; the best evidence of the applicant's intention to claim certain subject matter in the original patent would have been, of course, his actually claiming it. However, as pointed out above, these cases also hold that claims originally given

up cannot be recaptured by reissue. In view of these somewhat inconsistent propositions, it would seem more correct to say that the reissue claims are limited not to that subject matter which it was intended to claim but rather that which should have been but was not claimed in the original patent. The problem may be simplified if the original specification includes as one of its objects the provision of the invention in terms somewhat broader than the broadest claim presented and as broadly at least as the applicant may ever wish to claim the invention by reissue.

Circumstances Not Voiding the Right to Reissue

In *Ex parte Allwein*, 99 USPQ 177, 1953, the examiner had held insufficient the basis for reissue, on the ground of inadvertence, when the applicant had filed for reissue only after his attention had been called to another's patent in the field. The Board of Appeals reversed, saying in part: "It has been many times held that failure to present claims of sufficient breadth may be regarded as inadvertence."

Public Use by Inventor before Filing for Reissue. The effective filing date of the reissued patent, insofar as it is barred by public use under 35 U.S.C. 102(b), was at issue in *Crane Packing Co.* v. *Spitfire Tool and Machine Co.*, 125 USPQ 89, CA 7 1960; cert. den., *ibid.*, 667. In this *Spitfire* case, the original patent issued on August 28, 1951 and the reissued patent on February 8, 1955, the latter on an application filed June 25, 1953, within the two-year period for filing a broadened reissue under the statute.

The reissue added claims 11 through 14. The Court held these claims were invalid because of the statutory bar, under 35 U.S.C. 102(b) relating to public use for more than a year before filing the application. Plaintiff conceded such sale and public use in the United States of plaintiff's commercial device covered by the added claims but contended that the reissued patent had the effective filing date of the originally filed application for the purposes of Section 102(b).

The Court held against plaintiff's contention on the basis that, although an application for a broadened reissue can be filed under Section 252 within two years after the original patent issued, Section 251 of the act incorporates by reference Section 102(b) which is therefore applicable to reissues. The Court held claims 11 to 14 invalid because of plaintiff's own sale and public use more than one year prior to the filing date of the reissue application.

The *Spitfire* case in effect was nullified as to Patent Office practice. The Board of Appeals, in *Ex parte Strassburger*, 127 USPQ 417, 1960, considered especially the *Spitfire* case because of its unusual holding. P. J. Federico, speaking for the Board, noted an estimate that the *Spitfire* decision, if followed, might invalidate claims in as much as ninety per cent of the reissued patents. He noted also the long-established rule that Section 102(b) applies not against the filing date of a reissue application but against the filing date of the application of the original patent for which reissue is sought. The Board held specifically that the new claims, appearing in the reissue application but not in the original patent, had the effective filing date of the application for the original patent insofar as Section 102(b) is concerned. It would appear that, by the same reasoning, this holding should apply to all statutory bars under Section 102 of the Act. Mr. Federico pointed out that the Court in the *Spitfire* case failed to distinguish between (1) a statutory bar against new reissue claims and (2) estoppel against enforcement of the new reissue claims by virtue of intervening rights.

In the case of *Union Asbestos and Rubber Co.* v. *Paltier Corp.*, 132 USPQ 219, 1962, the same 7th Circuit Court of Appeals that had rendered the *Spitfire* decision sat, with the seven judges *en banc*, to consider again some of the issues involved in the case. The Court recognized that, under Section 102(b), the original patent could be prior art against the reissue application filed more than one year after the original patent if the "apparent holding" of *Crane* v. *Spitfire* were carried forward to its logical conclusion. The Court then said that it had not intended any such revolutionary change in the patent law as to reissued patents.

There were three contrary opinions differing with the majority opinion rejecting *Crane* v. *Spitfire*. These minority opinions were based on the ground that *Crane* v. *Spitfire* involved new claims directed to an inventive concept differing from that which was encompassed by the original claims. They urged that, in the *Asbestos* case, supra, there was only a modification of the original claims so that the principle of the *Muncie Gear* case (*Muncie Gear Works, Inc.* v. *Outboard Marine and Mfg Co.*, 315 U.S. 759, 1942) was not applicable to the *Asbestos* facts and that it was not necessary to overrule *Spitfire*, as did the majority of the Court. These differing opinions in *Crane* v. *Spitfire* are probably reconcilable on the basis of the "same invention" requirement of Section 251.

In the case of *Hartzell Industries, Inc.* v. *McCauley Industrial Corp.*, 134 USPQ 278, CA 6 1962, the Court dealt with a similar question. It held, in reversing the District Court, that the latter's decision was repudiated by the majority of the 7th Circuit Court of Appeals sitting in the *Asbestos* v. *Paltier* case and also noted that the Patent Office refused to follow the *Spitfire* case in the *Strassburger* decision. Accordingly, the Court of Appeals for the 6th Circuit held that the new claims of a reissued patent are not invalid because of sale under Section 102(b) more than one year prior to the application for the reissued patent if the newly issued claims are based not on new matter but on the invention disclosed in the original patent applied for not later than a year after such sale.

Time for Filing Reissue Applications

Broadened reissue claims, to be filed within two years from the grant of the original patent, have been defined as claims which would be infringed by a procedure not infringing an original claim.

The Statute makes no requirement as to the time in which narrowed reissue applications may be filed. In *Baltz* v. *Botto,* 111 USPQ 376, DC WTenn 1956, it was held that more than six years is not too long.

In *Rohm and Haas Co.* v. *Roberts Chemical Co.*, the Court held more than nine years delay in filing for the reissue permissible under the patent statute. 113 USPQ 423, CA 4 1957. Eleven years delay in refiling, on the other hand, was held too long in *A. O. Smith Corp.* v. *Affiliated Gas Equipment Co.*, 98 USPQ 169, 172 CA 5 1953.

With respect to broadened reissue applications Arthur M. (now Judge Smith has said:

"While Section 251 expressly prohibits granting broader claims in a reissue applied for more than two years after issue of the original patent, it does not mean that a patentee may wait two years to apply for such a patent. The cases still require the patentee to act with diligence when the error is discovered. Despite the enactment of the two-year rule in Section 251, it would seem that intervening rights may still be acquired and the defense of 'laches' still is applicable." Smith, A. M., Patent Law, Vol. 1, p. 576, Overbeck Co., Ann Arbor, Mich., 1954.

Reissue Applications

A reissue application is physically quite different from the standard application. Section 1401.06 of the Manual of Patent Examining Procedure provides that the specification of the reissue application may consist of cut-up soft copies of the original patent, with each column mounted on a separate sheet of paper. Original drawings may be used if they are to be unchanged.

The following is a convenient quick checklist for the contents of a reissue application:

(1) *Petition for reissue* should include an offer to surrender the original Letters Patent, the Rule reading as follows:

"Rule 178. Original patent. The application for a reissue must be accompanied by an offer to surrender the original patent. The application should also be accompanied by the original patent, or if the original is lost or inaccessible, by an affidavit to that effect. The application may be accepted for examination in the absence of the original patent or the affidavit, but one or the other must be supplied before the case is allowed. If a reissue be refused, the original patent will be returned to applicant upon his request."

(2) *Specification* (*including claims*) should be identical with the original with the exception that matter to be omitted should be enclosed in brackets and any added material should be underlined.

(3) *Reissue oath* should contain sufficient facts to show that the inoperativeness or invalidity of the original patent resulted through error and without deceptive intent and preferably should be sufficiently specific with respect to dates to show promptness in filing the reissue application once the error was discovered. The reissue oath customarily repeats any new claims sought to be added by reissue. See Rule 175, Form 32.

(4) *Consent* by the assignee, if any. Rule 172.

(5) *Letter* requesting an abstract of title. Rule 171.

(6) *Request* for transfer of the original drawings (which may be used if unchanged).

(7) *Filing fee.*

The notice of allowance of the reissue application gives the date on which the reissue application will issue as a patent. No final fee is required.

The most frequent situation in which reissue is refused is that in which the patentee finds that one or more elements of his claim are not necessary to the result and seeks to obtain reissue claims omitting that element or elements. It is almost universally held that unless the broadened claim is clearly defined in the original patent as constituting a part of the invention, reissue of a claim of this type is improper. *Southern Saw Service, Inc.* v. *Pittsburgh-Erie Saw Corp.*, 111 USPQ 362, CA 5 1956; *Hazeltine Research, Inc.* v. *Avco Mfg. Corp.*, 107 USPQ 187, CA 7 1955. One Board of Appeals decision has stated, however, that equivalents described in the original patent may be claimed by reissue since they are a part of the original invention under the doctrine of equivalents. *Ex parte Heacock*, 134 USPQ 446, 1962.

Effect of Reissue

35 U.S.C. 252 on the effect of reissue reads as follows:

"The surrender of the original patent shall take effect upon the issue of the reissued patent, and every reissued patent shall have the same effect in operation of law, on the trial of actions for causes thereafter arising, as if the same had been originally granted in such amended form, but insofar as the claims of the original and reissued patents are identical, such surrender shall not affect any action then pending nor abate any cause of action then existing, and the reissued patent, to the extent that its claims are identical with the original patent, shall constitute a continuation thereof and have effect continuously from the date of the original patent.

"No reissued patent shall abridge or affect the right of any person or his successors in business who made, purchased or used prior to the grant of a reissue anything patented by the reissued patent, to continue the use of, or to sell to others to be used, the specific thing so made, purchased or used, unless the making, using or selling of such thing infringes a valid claim of the reissued patent which was in the original patent. The court before which such matter is in question may provide for the continued manufacture, use or sale of the thing made, purchased or used as specified, or for the manufacture, use or sale of which substantial preparation was made before the grant of the reissue, and it may also provide for the continued practice of any process patented by the reissue, practiced, or for the practice of which a substantial preparation was made, prior to the grant of the reissue, to the extent and under such terms as the court deems equitable for the protection of investments made or business commenced before the grant of the reissue."

Intervening Rights

The intervening rights doctrine went through several stages of development prior to the 1952 Patent Act.

At one time a Circuit Court held in effect that intervening rights under a reissue patent do not arise unless the one who seeks to establish the intervening rights can show that he had knowledge of the dedication to the public by means of the original patent disclosing but not claiming the subject matter in issue. *National Nut Co. of Calif.* v. *Sontag Chain Stores Co.*, 43 USPQ 302, CA 9 1939. The Supreme Court reversed this decision. It held that the constructive notice of the dedication, implied by the recording of an issued patent, is sufficient for the creation of intervening rights by one having no other knowledge of the patent. 45 USPQ 448, 1940.

Judge Learned Hand once held, under the old statute, that intervening rights acquired by a party, where the delay in filing the application for a broadened reissue was longer than two years, extended to the public in general. In *Otis Elevator Co.* v. *Atlantic Elevator Co.*, 8 USPQ 356, CA 2 1931, he wrote:

"Intervening rights are only another aspect of the policy which makes laches (inexcusable delay) alone enough, and it is not legitimate to turn it into an independent ground of denial. So it does not seem proper to limit it to those cases in which a personal estoppel can be proved, not only, as we have said, because this would involve a radical recasting of the law, if it is to be consistent; but because it is not agreeable to its origin. So far as we can find, *no court has yet actually held that a reissue may be good at large, but bad as to one who has acquired vested rights after the original issue.*" (Emphasis added.)

This doctrine was restated, also under the old law, in *Schenk et al.* v. *United Aircraft Corporation*, 51 USPQ 519, DC Conn 1941. Here the Court said:

"...the intervening use by this defendant is not personal to this defendant. It can be availed of by any other defendant whom the plaintiff might sue elsewhere upon these claims."

Now we consider that the statute, with its two-year rule, makes the intervening right personal and leaves to the discretion of the court the question of extent of continuing operation permitted, after the reissue appears, to even the creator of the right.

Section 252 eliminates much of the confusion by establishing two classes of intervening rights. These are (a) those applying to things actually made prior to the grant date of the reissued patent, which intervening rights are made absolute under the statute, and (b) all other continuing rights of the intervenor which are at the discretion of the Court and to be governed by the rules of equity.

This division into two classes is confirmed in the *Southern Saw Service* case, supra. Here the Court held that, where the defendant bought a machine which infringed only new reissue claims and no original patent claims before the issuance of the reissued patent, then the defendant has an absolute right to continue the use of the machine without payment. Under the provisions of Section 252, intervening rights for such use of the machine bought before the grant of a broadened reissue patent are absolute.

Circumstances Bearing on Creation of Intervening Rights. In one case the defendant, asserting intervening rights, had acquired a "purely experimental, noncommercial machine for the purpose of approaching the plaintiff looking toward an 'arrangement,' with only limited experimental and no commercial use of that machine." The Court held this "not sufficient in law to create an intervening right." *Pittsburg-Erie Saw Corp.* v. *Southern Saw Service, Inc.*, 107 USPQ 203, DC NGa 1955.

In the case of *Weller Mfg. Co.* v. *Wen Products, Inc.*, 109 USPQ 73, CA 7 1956, at least one original unchanged claim of the original patent, carried forward into the reissued patent was infringed by the defendant. The Court ruled that there was no intervening rights under Section 252. Cf. *England* v. *Deere and Co.*, 125 USPQ 103, DC SI 1960.

The plaintiff, in a declaratory judgment proceeding, had acquired confidential information relating to defendant's patented machine through a trusted employee of defendant. The Court would not consider the alleged intervening rights of the plaintiff, because the plaintiff was not in a position to invoke the aid of equity to protect himself against his own wrong. *Funchion* v. *Somerset Knitting Corp.*, 116 USPQ 519, DC ND NC 1958.

In *General Plastic Corp.* v. *Finklestein*, 110 USPQ 192, DC EPa, 1956, the reissue had two claims. Claim 1 of the reissued patent was identical with the original claim 1 except that the original claim 1 called for an "inverted V-shape strap" while the new claim 1 recited a "generally U-shaped strap." The latter language conformed to the drawing of the original patent. The defendant claimed intervening rights on the basis of his acts in advance of the reissue and the allegation that the reissue claim was not a repetition of a claim in the original patent. The Court held that reference to the specification including the drawings showed the change in claim 1 to be merely a correction of a misdescription which did not change the scope of the claim and that claim 1 of the reissue therefore was identical with claim 1 of the original patent. The defense of intervening rights was denied.

Scope of Intervenor's Rights. In the leading *Southern Saw Service* case, above, the defendant-appellant had purchased the accused machine long before the filing for reissue of the patent in suit. "The only original claim which appellee has urged was infringed [in the original patent] is claim 19, but that claim was abandoned without appeal in the prosecution of the reissue application, and cannot be considered here as a claim carried over into the reissue." The Court of Appeals reversed the court below which had denied the right of appellant to continue using the accused machine.

A sound basis for intervening right and continuing the right appears in *Gerhardt* v. *Kinnaird*, 117 USPQ 474, DC EKy 1958. The Court noted that:

"After the issue of the original patent, and with knowledge and appreciation of its limited character ... the defendants built a non-infringing item ... employed additional workmen ... spent money and time to put the truck and trailer body for transporting stacked articles into commercial use on a large scale ... [and] sold this product extensively."

The Court held this "to support a private intervening right in the nature of a license as against a valid reissue."

It is important to note that Section 252 refers to the reissued patent as having the same effect as to identical claims as the original patent. While the author knows of no cases in point, the commentary on the 1952 Patent Act (U.S.C.A.) indicates the possibility of intervening rights arising not only to broader but also to narrower reissue claims which are not repeated from the original patent.

While the earlier confusion involving reissued patents has been resolved in large measure by the Patent Act of 1952, much remains to be determined as to the exact extent of the continuing rights of an intervenor. It is considered that, as the law now stands, it is within the discretion of the court to grant to him whatever relief it deems just and equitable as to new things made after the reissue. Presumably, the metes and bounds of intervening rights will be established case by case with application of the basic rules of equity and in view of the extent of practice or preparation therefor by the intervenor in advance of reissue of the patent.

Cross-references: *Delay in Claiming, Laches.*

RESEARCH CORPORATION PATENT POLICIES

Albert S. Davis, Jr.

Research Corporation is a foundation whose principal office is in New York City and whose net income, by law, is distributed in unconditioned grants to universities, colleges, and learned societies and institutions for the support of academic research, investigation, and experimentation, primarily in the natural sciences. In form a stock corporation, it cannot pay dividends, and it owns all its own stock. See P.L.N.Y. 1932, c. 523. It was formed in 1912 at the instance of the late Frederick G. Cottrell, who made to it a territorial grant of patent rights under his then just-discovered electrostatic precipitation processes for the separation and collection of dusts, mists, and fumes from industrial gases and air. It pioneered in that field of electrical equipment. This activity has, since 1954, been carried on world-wide by an industrial subsidiary, Research-Cottrell, Inc., located in New Jersey.

Purpose. During the thirties, universities and colleges increasingly recognized that inventions made in the course of on-campus research, even to some extent when sponsored by commercial firms taking over all patent rights, brought with them problems of inventorship, patentability, patenting, and licensing which these institutions were not equipped by interest, ability, or personnel to solve. Research Corporation, because of its experience with the Cottrell patents, did have such resources. Beginning about 1935, it tendered to the academic, scientific

and technological institutions of the country its good offices for these purposes. These problems and the use of Research Corporation's services intensified sharply with the entry of the Federal government into the financing of academic scientific research, during World War II and thereafter. At the present time, well over 125 such institutions have contracts or understandings with the Corporation.

Provisions of Agreements. While each agreement is "tailor-made" to the needs of the particular institution, they generally follow a standard pattern.

The institution may, but need not, offer to Research Corporation any invention made by its faculty. The Corporation's staff, with the advice of independent patent counsel, weighs the invention for sound patentability and probable industrial interest. If it is accepted for action, the counsel prepare and prosecute a patent application; the invention, patent application and any patents are assigned to Research Corporation by the inventor. The Corporation then attempts to interest industry in accepting a patent license or licenses. The Corporation itself does not carry on pilot-scale or commercial reduction to practice or evolution of know-how. Its licenses are commonly nonexclusive, though exclusivity is granted for limited periods where the licensee faces heavy expenditure in reduction to commercial practice and introduction upon the market. Royalty rates and bases are consonant with those charged in private industry. Substantial attention is given to enforcing due diligence by the licensee, through suitable minimum royalty and research and development performance clauses and otherwise.

When the inventor is to be paid a share (decided by the institution, but not exceeding 15 per cent) of the gross royalties, the remainder of the royalties (after subtraction only of any out-of-pocket litigative expenses and the cost of any foreign patents) is divided 50-50 with the institution. In cases where the inventor is to receive more than 15 per cent, or the institution wishes to keep his payment in its hands, the royalty distribution pattern shifts to one of 42½ per cent to Research

Corporation and 57½ per cent to the institution.

Cooperation with Individual Inventors.
In the absence of such an overall agreement with an institution, particularly where a college or university claims no equity in a particular invention or campus inventions generally, the Corporation cooperates with individual academic inventors to much the same result.

Occasionally philanthropic scientists having no primary academic affiliation have turned to Research Corporation to assist them in their invention patent problems and in the development of their inventions in the public interest. Notable among these is Dr. Robert R. Williams, who with his co-workers assigned to the Corporation the patent rights on the synthesis of vitamin B_1. The great part of the royalties on its manufacture have gone to the Corporation, to help support its grants programs in the natural sciences, and to its Williams-Waterman Fund for the Combat of Dietary Diseases. This Fund has distributed some $4,500,000 for research in nutrition and diseases attributable to dietary deficiencies, such as beri-beri, pellagra and kwashiorkor. There are other such special-use funds, notably the Brown-Hazen Fund, which is financed by royalties from Nystatin.

Evaluation of Proposals for Patenting.
The review by the Corporation's staff and its counsel of inventions so submitted to it yields some rough data on "useful patentability" of inventions from these sources. At present about 375 submissions are received per year. Of these, some 55 are filed upon. Currently, out of 450 groups of related patents, the top 6 yielded 93 per cent of the overall royalty income, and about 25 more have produced some royalties.

Representative Patents. Illustrative among the more significant patents so obtained and licensed by Research Corporation are those on vitamin B_1, pantothenic acid, vitamin K, vitamin A, Nystatin, cortisone, reserpine, the van de Graaff generator, the cyclotron, the Barrow microwave horn, cottage cheese, gas turbines, Merthiolate, and high-pressure presses.

From the royalties so derived and from the earnings of its industrial subsidiary, the Corporation has made grants of over $18,000,000 to hundreds of colleges, universities and scientific institutions, the only condition imposed being that the results be published for the benefit of the scientific community.

Bibliography

Research Corporation, Annual Reports
Palmer, A., Studies on university and research institutions invention and patent management (National Research Council).

Cross-references: *Incentives for Inventors, Medical Associations and Physicians' Patent Policies.*

RESEARCH DIRECTOR'S PATENT RESPONSIBILITIES

Eugene H. Leslie and Robert Calvert

The Chemical Director of one of the world's largest and most progressive companies, when asked the subject to which he gave most attention, replied "Patents." Guidance of associates in the patent field may be more profitable, in proportion to the time required, than almost any other of the research director's activities.

In a broad sense, the research director should make every effort to ensure such personnel relations and work environment as to stimulate and encourage original thought, initiative and a desire for accomplishment. Under such creative conditions, he can expect that new or improved products and processes will appear as a continuous flow of potential material for patents of commercial value.

Development of Patent-Mindedness

Patent consciousness in an organization does not come automatically or by accident. Most scientists entering industry have had no formal education in the field of patents.

The director, to meet the need, may have an occasional meeting of his group on the subject of patents, with a presentation by himself, an associate, his attorney or an outside attorney, almost any attorney being expected to be pleased with this opportunity of promoting the patent system.

Once patent activity is initiated, periodic

reports on it to management should prove catalytic in spreading interest and enthusiasm within the company.

The scientists will quickly adopt the idea. Receiving patents will raise morale, often from the level of compounders or sample matchers to that of scientists from whom creative achievement is expected and will come. Patents provide an opportunity for publication, to which the scientists turn as a means of recognition of professional status in their own organization as well as nationally or internationally.

Moderation in Patent Activity

The research director and his division heads may eventually have to moderate the enthusiasm of certain employees for patenting. Otherwise some ambitious laboratory or staff members may come to regard patents as an end in themselves. They may prefer to rush from invention to invention, without following through, completing and making commercially successful a previous promising development. Firm policy in recommending cases for filing is a means of control to be continuously exercised, although not to such an extreme as to suppress initiative and originality.

Knowledge of Patent Law

The director will gradually learn the basic principles of patent law particularly applicable to his responsibilities. Among his obviously valuable reading matter will be correspondence from his attorney, applications prepared or being prepared, Patent Office actions on applications, the attorney's amendments and occasionally at least the Official Gazette. There are also discussions between the attorney and inventors which the director may attend. He will wish to do some reading of articles and books on patent law. Evening courses in patent law or the five-month "Academy" now conducted in the Patent Office may prove very valuable to the young director or to someone being groomed for sharing or accepting the patent responsibilities.

It is not necessary or desirable that the director convert himself into a patent attorney or one who places his opinion on patent matters and law above that of the attorney. A speaking acquaintance with the subject, however, frequently has led to the rescue of an important invention about to be laid aside. In some instances, most profitable patents have been obtained after attorneys had advised against filing, as not patentable, and the research director or his inventor had then supplied additional data or disclosure providing a new basis for patentability.

Designation of Inventors and Effect on Morale

The legal aspects of choice of inventors are discussed in the article "Inventors." Since a joint inventor's name may now be added to or subtracted from an application or patent when an "error arose without any deceptive intention on his part," the legal hazard in either misjoinder or nonjoinder of a joint inventor has been decreased under the 1952 Patent Act. It is considered necessary, however, that the application as filed carry the name of at least one true inventor.

The problem of effect on organization morale of improper naming of inventors remains. Such improper designation lowers the morale of an organization, particularly when such choice is recognized within the organization as intentionally improper.

Inventors are a zealous lot. They are enthusiastic particularly over a child of their own imagination and ingenuity. They experience a real psychological wrench when such a child is taken from them and assigned publicly to another.

The research director, no less than the experimenter, has his scientific pride. His associates should not take advantage of his generosity or of his solicitude for the organization as a whole. They should not accept allocation to them of inventions that belong properly to the director.

The contributions of the director and the experimenter are recognized and, at the same time, the validity of the patent is best protected, when the inventors are named in accordance with the law. After all, laws are codified rules of conduct of man towards man that have been formulated on the basis of centuries of experience.

Checklist of Responsibilities

In suggesting responsibilities to be accepted by the research director personally or delegated in whole or in part, it is recognized that there are different techniques best adopted for use by different directors and that the following concepts are to be modified to suit varying circumstances.

(1) Establish patent consciousness to the extent that research workers who obtain unobvious results of commercial promise will recognize the patent possibilities and report them.

(2) Avoid such overenthusiasm on the part of any worker as would lead him to neglect the full development of earlier research in favor of always seeking a new invention.

(3) Keep the current Official Gazette available to all in the library or elsewhere. Make it assigned reading for about an hour a week by someone interested in patents, when the research organization is as large as ten or more and there is no other service in the company that reports on patents of interest as issued.

(4) Check the keeping of laboratory records at intervals and note whether they meet the requirements stated in *Records of Invention,* or are of other good form, with witnessing signature by a qualified person who is not a joint inventor.

(5) Forward, or have the inventor forward, reports of commercially promising new developments, and leave to the attorney the decision, with your advice, as to whether or not patentability exists.

(6) Endeavor, without offending or becoming too skeptical, to have the true inventor(s) receive the credit for the invention or shift the burden of decision to the attorney.

(7) Answer promptly patent correspondence that requires a response.

(8) Support the attorney with additional experiments as required. A day or so of work in the laboratory may prove such points as failure of a reference to give a certain result, a surprising property of the new product, or other information to save an application from becoming abandoned.

(9) Check applications, claims as amended and claims again as allowed.

(10) Note whether claims, as allowance approaches or at all times, cover the commercial operations being practiced or anticipated.

(11) Inform management as to whether the expenses of foreign filing and subsequent payment of taxes, to obtain and maintain patents in force abroad, are justified.

(12) Advise management of suspected infringement, whether by you of another's patent or by others of your patent.

(13) Remember that research workers long for increased professional status and that patents, being publications, contribute to the feeling of importance that lifts the morale of the workers.

(14) Delay publication of research results of patentable nature until after an application for patent is filed in this or some other country adhering to the International Convention (q.v.). Then, if publication has been made, complete any foreign filing within the year allowed under the Convention for claiming the benefit of the first filing date, it being remembered that not all countries adhere to the Convention and that, for some of them, actual filing must precede the first publication.

(15) Consider the example of a very large and active corporation that notes, from the Official Gazette, the initial upsurge of patent activity in any part of its field and then decides whether to start research on subjects shown by its competitors to be of new interest.

Cross-references: *Disclosures for Applications, Foreign Patents, Incentives for Inventors, Inventors, Inventors' Psychology, Records of Inventions, Patentability, Publication of Inventions.*

RESTRICTION OF APPLICATIONS

William D. Palmer

Restriction practice in one form or another is followed in every major country where patent applications are subject to examination. Under our patent system, restriction is frequently required, and the possibility of such requirement should be considered when drafting the application.

Changes in practice in recent years include the following: (1) Restriction to five species should not be required unless the examiner considers that nonelected species will support a divisional application. (2) An application should not be rejected on the basis of double patenting over a patent to a species elected in response to a Patent Office requirement. (3) Provisions are made for filing divisional cases without new signatures of inventors, but under narrowly prescribed conditions which will be detailed later in this article.

Purpose of Restriction

As an oversimplified explanation of restriction practice, it can be stated that the claims of one patent application must relate to only one patentable invention. In some foreign countries, this is expressed by stating that there must be "unity of invention" between the claims. In the United States, if more than one invention is presented in different claims, the examiner may require the applicant to "restrict" or limit the scope of his claimed subject matter. Restriction practice sometimes goes beyond requiring an applicant to prosecute in one application only those claims which relate to one broad inventive concept; it may require an applicant to restrict or limit his claims to one of two or more claim groupings which are closely related in concept, because of the Office classification system and its relation to restriction practice. *In re Moss et al.*, 40 USPQ 479. A related reason for requiring restriction is that the applicant, having paid only one filing fee, is entitled to have only one invention searched and examined for patentability. *In re Hirschhorn*, 74 USPQ 183.

To base a requirement for restriction solely on a different field of search would not always be fair to an applicant, particularly since the Office classification system is set up for the convenience of examination and does not necessarily follow a scientific classification of the subject matter involved.

Ex parte Milas, 71 USPQ 212. In the usual case, factors other than a different field of search normally must also be present before the examiner can require restriction.

Division Practice (Prior to the Patent Act of 1952)

Prior to the Patent Act of 1952, restriction was termed division. There did not exist any express statutory authority for the Commissioner to require division, although some courts stated that the Commissioner's authorization to do so was to be found in R.S. 4886. The case law and the procedures in the Office varied considerably as the practice developed. For example, before 1904, division was a matter to be reviewed by the Commissioner on petition. This practice was overruled in *Steinmetz* v. *Allen*, 192 U.S. 543, 1904, which held that requirements for division should be appealable. The *Steinmetz* decision was controlling on the Office until it was overruled by the Patent Act of 1952.

Patent Act of 1952— Section on Restriction

35 U.S.C. Section 121 reads:

"Divisional applications. If two or more independent and distinct inventions are claimed in one application, the Commissioner may require the application to be restricted to one of the inventions. If the other invention is made the subject of a divisional application which complies with the requirements of section 120 of this title it shall be entitled to the benefit of the filing date of the original application. A patent issuing on an application with respect to which a requirement for restriction under this section has been made, or on an application filed as a result of such a requirement, shall not be used as a reference either in the Patent Office or in the courts against a divisional application or against the original application or any patent issued on either of them, if the divisional application is filed before the issuance of the patent on the other application. If a divisional application is directed solely to subject matter described and claimed in the original application as filed, the Commissioner may dispense with signing and execution by the inventor. The validity of a patent shall not be questioned for failure of the Commissioner to require the application to be restricted to one invention."

Effect of Section 121 and its Interpretation. The most important aspect of Section 121 is that parent and divisional applications or patents, filed as a result of a requirement for restriction, cannot be used as reference against one another. To be protected under this statute against an allegation of double patenting, the divisional application *must* have been filed in compliance with an Office requirement for restriction.

The wording of Section 121 is inconsistent with the Revisor's Notes. It is stated that "If two or more *independent and distinct* inventions are claimed in one application, the Commissioner *may* require the application to be restricted to one of the inventions." [Emphasis supplied.] The Commissioner interpreted the wording *independent and distinct* to mean *independent or distinct*, as explained in MPEP 802.01. Such an interpretation is necessary to avoid abolishing much of the previous division practice. The Revisor's Notes state that Section 121 "... enacts as law existing practice with respect to division, at the same time introducing a number of changes."

The word *may*, as it appears in the above-quoted sentence of this Section, makes the requirement of restriction not mandatory, but discretional with the Commissioner. See P. J. Federico, "Commentary on the New Patent Act," 35 U.S.C.A. 1, 34.

For arguments that the term "independent and distinct" does not mean "independent or distinct," see Philip M. Dunston, 41 JPOS 46, 1959 and Robert K. Sharp, 36 *ibid.* 527, 1954. (See also *Act of 1952—Patents*)

Independent Inventions, Species and Genus-Species. The Office practice in genus-species situations was changed by two decisions, *In re Joyce, Comr. Dec.,* 115 USPQ 412 and *In re Herrick et al., Comr. Dec.,* 115 USPQ 412. In accordance with these decisions, after election (restriction) is required with respect to species in excess of five, a divisional application claiming the non-elected species cannot be rejected on the basis of double patenting over the patented elected species. Nor should restriction to five species be required unless the examiner "after considering the matter" is of the opinion that the nonelected species will

support a divisional application. These decisions have had a great effect on patent soliciting practices, particularly in some chemical arts where many species are apt to be claimed in one application.

To avoid any question of double patenting, all possibly *related inventive concepts should be combined in one application* as originally filed, whether these concepts are expressed as independent inventions, such as separate species, or related but distinct inventions. *In re Ockert*, 114 USPQ 330. Under prior Office procedures, the practices differed considerably with respect to *independent* inventions and *related but distinct* inventions; under present Office procedures, the practices with respect to such claimed inventions are more similar.

Relation between Restriction and Double Patenting

MPEP 800 considers under one heading the subjects of restriction and double patenting. While these aspects of patent law were separately evolved, they are related by virtue of their "mutual exclusion." As concisely set forth in *In re Coleman et al.,* 90 USPQ 100:

"If division would have been necessarily required in the first instance, then double patenting cannot be urged if the copending claims issue in separate patents. If, conversely, a rejection on the ground of double patenting is proper, it is a necessary corollary that a requirement for division would have been improper."

This principle, essentially restated in MPEP 804, places a heavy burden on the Patent Office to guard against erroneous requirements. There is no fixed rule, however, which precludes a holding of double patenting against matter originally filed in separate applications, even though a requirement for restriction would have been proper had the matter initially been filed in one application. *In re Ockert*, supra.

Under present practices, almost no current decisions on petitions from restriction are reported. As a result, most of the controlling cases applicable to this subject antedate the Patent Act of 1952. As between related but distinct inventions, the controlling decisions are summarized in MPEP 806.05(a) to (g). It is virtually impossible to establish set rules which apply to all situations. Even though the requirement for restriction might be entirely proper as tested by Section 806.05(a) to (g), the requirement should be tempered by Section 804. Because of the related nature of restriction and double patenting, any current decisions on double patenting may indirectly influence restriction practice. The converse is equally true.

Initial Classification and the Examiner's Requirement for Restriction between Related but Distinct Inventions

When the patent application is filed, the most comprehensive claim normally determines the division to which the application is initially assigned for examination. For example, if the novelty resides in a modified chemical composition (A), which has particular utility in conjunction with a known element (B), the applicant will normally claim the composition (A), the combination (AB); perhaps a process claim to the use of the composition (A) will also be submitted. The comprehensive claim (AB) will normally govern the assignment of the application in the Office. If the examiner rejects the combination claim (AB) on the basis of "old or exhausted combination," he cannot require restriction between combination claim (AB) and composition claim (A). MPEP 806.05(b).

Most requirements for restriction will normally be made on the first action of the examiner, although they can be made at any time up to final action. MPEP 811.01. In making the requirement between *related but distinct* inventions, the examiner must show that they are "distinct" in addition to showing one or more of the following, see MPEP 808.02:

(1) a "separate classification" in that examination of the claims for patentability requires a separate field of search and that the claims also set forth separate subjects for inventive effort;

(2) the claims set forth separate sub-

jects for inventive effort even though classified together; or

(3) a separate field of search is required for one of the distinct subjects.

Usually the examiner will show that there exists a "separate classification," as by a representative examiner's letter outlined in MPEP 817.

In making the requirement, the examiner normally will not examine any of the claims for patentability. One exception to this arises when the applicant has presented linking claims which serve to bridge the different claim groupings. Such claims, if allowable, justify claiming in one application the different claim groupings. Accordingly, the linking claims must be examined for patentability and rejected before any requirement for restriction can be made. When a linking claim is presented, no divisional application should be filed until the examination of such claim is completed, to avoid possible double patenting. MPEP 804.01.

While the requirement for restriction is petitionable and not appealable, appeal can be taken from the examiner's designation of claims as falling within a nonelected claim grouping, provided the applicant traverses such grouping of the claims. MPEP 821.

Applicant's Necessary Response to a Requirement for Restriction

In response to the requirement for restriction, the applicant *must* provisionally elect to prosecute one of the claim groupings which the examiner has designated, MPEP 818.03(a) and Rule 143, even though the applicant traverses the requirement. To preserve also the right to petition for review of the requirement, the applicant must traverse the requirement. Rule 144.

A representative response to a requirement for restriction between related but distinct inventions is as follows: "In response to the requirement for restriction, the applicant provisionally elects to prosecute claims 1-8, inclusive, designated 'Group I' by the examiner." This election is only provisional since the restriction requirement may be withdrawn, in which case the applicant's previous election is also withdrawn.

Claims which the applicant does not elect to prosecute in the application desirably are retained until a divisional application is filed. On the next Office Action, if the requirement is not withdrawn, the examiner will withdraw the nonelected claims from further consideration, in accordance with Rule 142(b).

If the requirement is to elect to prosecute one or five species, in accordance with Rule 146, the applicant *must* provisionally do so and designate the elected species, in order to complete the response. In the following sections, the prerequisites to showing "distinctness" between different classes of inventions are considered in greater detail. The abbreviated holdings of the case decisions should be compared to MPEP 806.05(a) to (g).

Method and Apparatus

Restriction Properly Required. Assuming a different classification, restriction is proper if the method as claimed can be practiced by apparatus materially different from that claimed or by hand, *In re Moss et al.*, supra, and/or when the apparatus as claimed can be used in methods other than as claimed. *Ex parte Luaces*, 68 USPQ 154; *Ex parte Romanelli et al.*, 64 USPQ 433. When the method and apparatus represent independent subjects of invention, restriction is proper. *Ex parte Jones et al.*, 50 USPQ 479.

Restriction Not Properly Required. If a distinct status in the art is not shown, the search being the same, restriction is not properly required. *Ex parte Leguillon*, 38 USPQ 552. A showing that it is common to claim both method and apparatus in the same patent has been used to overcome such requirement. *Ex parte Davis et al.*, 18 USPQ 276. But see, *In re Young et al.*, 81 USPQ 139. Motivated by the possibility of double patenting, some older decisions reversed a requirement for division when only one inventive concept was presented. *Ex parte Noling*, 50 USPQ 31; also see MPEP 804.

As a practical matter, a restriction requirement between method and apparatus claims should be traversed with caution, since in the usual case, if restriction is not proper, the method can be classed as the mere function of the apparatus. See *In re Washburn*, 86 USPQ 108.

Product and Method of Making

Restriction Properly Required. If a separate status in the art is shown, restriction is proper when the claimed product can be made by other than the claimed method, *In re Shoemaker*, 29 USPQ 209; or by hand, *In re Burns*, 29 USPQ 423; even when the claimed method can make only the claimed product, *In re Ferenci*, 20 USPQ 242. Different claimed methods for making the claimed product justify restriction, *Ex parte MacArthur et al.*, 72 USPQ 329. When the examiner states that the product can be made by a method other than as claimed, more than a mere denial on the part of the applicant is needed to overcome the requirement. *Ex parte Liebowitz*, 77 USPQ 59.

Restriction is proper when the claimed method does not necessarily make the claimed product (i.e., the method can be used to make other products). *Ex parte Reid*, 1901 C.D. 123. In such a situation, MPEP 806.05(f) also specifies that the claimed method should not be an obvious method of making the claimed product, since if it were, the method should be rejected as an obvious method of making the product. MPEP 706.03(q).

To summarize, the claimed inventions are distinct when the product can be made by other methods or the method can be used to make other products, provided the method is not an obvious method of making the product.

As a related matter, a claimed method for making all claimed product species cannot be generic to such species since it is not in the same statutory class. *Ex parte Schmerling*, 82 USPQ 457. Also, product-by-process claims normally cannot link product and process claims since product-by-process claims are not allowable when the product can be otherwise defined. *Ex parte Hurd,* 72 USPQ 383. But see MPEP 809.03(a).

Restriction Not Properly Required. Restriction is not proper when method limitations are included in product claims, *Ex parte Bannerman et al.,* 72 USPQ 36, or there is doubt that the product as claimed can be produced by any other method and the method as claimed will not produce any other product. *Ex parte Cowper-Coles,* 1902 C.D. 257.

Combination and Subcombination or Element

Restriction Properly Required. Restriction is proper when the combination as claimed does not include the details of the subcombination as claimed and a separate search is shown. *In re Coulter,* 69 USPQ 531. If the subcombination is shown to have separate utility, restriction is proper even when all the details of the subcombination are included in the combination. *In re Goerke et al.,* 29 USPQ 421. But see, MPEP 806.05(c). Restriction cannot be avoided by limiting the subcombination in its preamble to use in the combination. *Ex parte Hopkins,* 79 USPQ 191.

Separate and related subcombinations or elements which would otherwise be divisible from one another can sometimes be linked together by a combination claim or claims which set forth the related effects of the separate subcombinations or elements. These linking claims must be examined for patentability and rejected before restriction can be required between the separate combinations. As a general rule, subcombinations which have separate utility cannot be linked by a claimed combination. *In re Feight,* 85 USPQ 274.

Restriction Not Properly Required. Restriction is not proper if the subcombination has no utility apart from the combination and the combination claim includes all the details of the subcombination. *Ex parte Goldsmith,* 55 USPQ 156. Nor is restriction proper if the subcombination is essential to the combination, *Ex parte Roop,* 102 USPQ 355, or if the subcombination and combination are closely related. *In re Ferenci,* 29

USPQ 162. If the element has not attained a distinct status in the art, or there is doubt as to a distinct status in the art, restriction is improper. *Ex parte Pratt,* 46 USPQ 560; *Ex parte Romanelli et al.,* 64 USPQ 433. Restriction is not proper when the combination is not patentable over the subcombination. *Ex parte Van Zandt,* 21 USPQ 26. A subcombination process which makes possible a continuous process is not divisible therefrom. *Ex parte Mason,* 32 USPQ 406.

An allowable combination claim can link subcombination claims which have no use other than in the combination. *Ex parte Newhall,* 97 USPQ 454. Even though a separate classification is shown, a common essential element can link claims. *Ex parte Ledin,* 43 USPQ 194. A combination claim which incorporates different compositions as indispensable elements can link such compositions. *Ex parte Hawkins,* 13 USPQ 36.

In accordance with MPEP 806.05(c), "distinctness" to support restriction can be shown when the subcombination as claimed has utility apart from the combination *and* the combination as claimed does not depend on the subcombination as claimed for its patentability. Also, 35 U.S.C. 121 has placed an additional burden on the Office to guard against erroneous requirements for restriction, MPEP 804. This can influence the point in the prosecution where restriction can properly be required. For example, if the combination claim includes all details of the subcombination or element, it would appear that restrictions cannot properly be required until the combination claim is examined and determined *not* to depend on the subcombination or element for patentability. And this reasoning should prevail even though the subcombination has utility apart from the combination. But see, *In re Goerke et al.,* supra.

Composition and Method of Using

Restriction Properly Required. Restriction is proper when the classification is shown to be different, *Ex parte Guest et al.,* 88 USPQ 505, even when the primary novelty is alleged to reside in the composition and not in its use. *Ex parte Ruthruff*, 64 USPQ 130. A composition and its use are often regarded as separate and independent subjects matter of invention, *Ex parte Borglin*, 57 USPQ 465, and when a composition might have uses other than as claimed, though none is shown, restriction is proper. *In re Young et al.*, 81 USPQ 139. Restriction is sustained when the composition and use claims are separately classified and differ in scope. *Ex parte Proctor*, 48 USPQ 706.

Restriction Not Properly Required. Some of the foregoing pre-1953 decisions may not be found to be supported by the Patent Act of 1952. In explanation, claims to the use of a composition will frequently include all details of the claimed composition. These composition claims and use claims may or may not be separately patentable over one another.

Genus-Species and Species

Under previous Office practices, an applicant who presented independent inventions in the form of different species was required to elect to prosecute not more than five species. If no generic claim was presented, or if no generic claim was found to be allowable, the applicant was required to elect to prosecute only one of the presented species.

In accordance with 35 U.S.C. 121, and as previously pointed out, after election (restriction) is required with respect to species in excess of five, a divisional application claiming the nonelected species cannot be rejected on the basis of double patenting over the patented elected species. *In re Joyce*, supra. Nor should restriction to five species be required unless the examiner is of the opinion that the nonelected species will support a divisional application. *In re Herrick et al.*, supra.

Under present practices, it does not appear that the Patent Office can require an applicant to elect to prosecute only one species when the claimed species are not sufficiently distinct to support separate patents. To illustrate this point, if an applicant claims similar processes for producing a

nitrile, using either hydrogen cyanide or sodium cyanide, with the equivalency of these compounds being known with respect to their functioning in the claimed processes, it would be contrary to the policy set forth in MPEP 804 to require election of one species. Also see, *Ex parte Crigler*, 125 USPQ 448.

Summarizing the logical extension of the *Herrick* and *Joyce* decisions, when different claimed species are not sufficiently distinct to support separate patents, it would appear that *any* requirement to elect (restrict to) one or five species is improper. See MPEP 806.04(h). This reasoning should also apply when no claim generic to the claimed species is even presented. See MPEP 808.01(a).

Particularly in chemical practice, an applicant may submit a large number of species claims in one application. Such claims will often be rejected on the grounds of multiplicity. MPEP 706.03(l). In such case, the examiner should require the applicant to select (*not elect*) a specified number of species claims to prosecute. In response, the applicant must select species claims not to exceed the number specified, even though the rejection on multiplicity is traversed. If this rejection is not withdrawn, the applicant will have thus preserved his right to appeal from such rejection. On its face, this practice does not involve restriction, but it is similar in that the claimed subject matter is being limited. If the rejection on multiplicity is sustained, it appears that additional applications drawn to the nonselected species will not be protected from double patenting under Section 121.

Designs

There appears to be little doubt but that 35 U.S.C. 121 is applicable to designs, in accordance with the extensions of the *Herrick* and *Joyce* decisions.

In order to take advantage of the benefits of 35 U.S.C. 121 and avoid possible double patenting, all design embodiments relating to one inventive concept should be included in one application. *In re Russell*, 112 USPQ 58. It is quite proper to include more than one design embodiment in one application, *In re Rubinfield*, 123 USPQ 210, even though only one claim is permitted. *Campbell* v. *Watson*, 124 USPQ 164.

Traversing a Requirement for Restriction

Certainly there are some Office requirements for restriction which are improper. Whether such improper requirements can be successfully traversed depends on the soliciting attorney. Even though 35 U.S.C. 121 protects an applicant against an erroneous requirement, it would appear to be in the applicant's best interests to traverse with all possible vigor those restriction requirements which are considered to be erroneous.

Traverse of Restriction between Related but Distinct Inventions. Representative case law is set forth in previous sections. Special caution should be taken when traversing any requirement between "method and apparatus" to avoid admitting in the record that the claimed method only sets forth "the mere function" of the claimed apparatus. Also, it is advisable to consider the possible improper or premature nature of any requirement between "combination and subcombination or element" where all of the details of the subcombination or element are included in the combination. The same applies to "composition and method of using."

Traverse of Restriction between Separate Species. Any requirement for election of species which are not sufficiently distinct from one another to support separate patents can be traversed on the grounds that such requirement for election is contrary to *In re Herrick et al.*, supra. Such a traverse has its dangers, however, for if a subsequent search shows that one of the species is known in the art, the applicant will have at least inferred in the record the equivalency of the other claimed species.

Petition from Restriction

It has been stated that in order to preserve the right to petition from a requirement for restriction, it is necessary to trav-

erse the requirement. Rule 144. Such petition can be made at any time after the requirement is made final, but not later than appeal.

In the usual case, if the traverse of the requirement is not successful, the examiner will make the requirement for restriction *final* and withdraw the nonelected claims from further consideration. A petition is then proper.

Under present practices, a petition from a requirement for restriction will usually be reviewed by the Director having authority over the examining division involved. If the requirement is affirmed and the applicant still feels that the requirement is not proper, further petitions can be filed. If an issue is reached on what constitutes a proper discretion on the part of the Commissioner to require restriction, the applicant can petition to the Commissioner (in person) for a further review. A restriction requirement will be reviewed under 35 U.S.C. 145. *Torok* v. *Watson*, 103 USPQ 78.

Shift of Election by Applicant

Having once elected to prosecute one of the designated claim groupings, the applicant cannot shift his position and elect to prosecute nonelected claims. MPEP 819. To permit such a shift might necessitate additional work or expense to the Office. When no additional work or expense is involved, however, the applicant may be permitted to shift his election. MPEP 819.01.

When an applicant has claimed his invention in different classes, e.g., product and process or combination and subcombination, and the examiner holds that the invention resides in the product rather than the process, for example, the applicant is permitted to prosecute such previously nonelected claims, and this is not regarded as a shift. MPEP 820.

Filing a Divisional Application

To be entitled to the benefit of the filing date of the original or parent application, a divisional application must be filed while the parent application is still pending and must also contain a specific reference to the parent application.

Most attorneys prefer not to file a divisional application until the prosecution of the claims in the parent application is substantially completed. There are advantages in such a procedure, since in many cases, similar issues will be present in both the parent and divisional applications. This may influence the form of the claims in the divisional application. Also, the parent application may contain linking claims which should be examined for patentability before a divisional application is filed, in order to avoid possible double patenting. MPEP 804.01. As another possibility, the examiner may withdraw his requirement of restriction while the parent application is still pending; a new case filed at such time might meet objection on the ground of double patenting. Delayed filing of the divisional application may be desirable also if the invention is not in commercial use.

In some situations, on the other hand, it is of benefit to file a divisional application as soon as possible, as in a potential infringement situation. As another possibility, the applicant or assignee may have pending other applications which constitute improvements over the basic, parent application. In such case, it is normally desirable to have the parent and divisional applications both issue before the improvements thereover.

If the restriction requirement was traversed, a divisional application can be filed with reasonable safety at any time after the examiner has considered the traverse and adhered to the original requirement. If the restriction requirement was not traversed, a divisional application can be filed at any time after the requirement is made.

The proper form of an Oath for a divisional application is outlined in the Rules. The divisional application must contain a specific reference to the parent application, in order to claim priority thereunder. 35 U.S.C. 120, 121.

In accordance with 35 U.S.C. 121 and Rule 147, a divisional application can be filed without new signatures by the applicants on request to the Office to prepare and certify a copy of the original application as filed. A proposed amendment cancelling the irrelevant claims and other matter should be submitted with the application papers under the provisions of Rule 147. This rule is strictly construed, and no new claims should be added by the proposed amendment, or a filing date may be refused in the absence of the signatures. *In re Perret*, 131 USPQ 122. If there are two or more nonelected claim groupings, all of these previously nonelected groupings can be filed in one divisional application under the provisions of Rule 147. *In re Appln. Papers of Egbert*, 132 USPQ 65. The application cannot be filed under Rule 147 if the restriction requirement was made with respect to claims which were added after the original application was filed. *In re Appln. Papers of Kopf et al.*, 779 O.G. 290.

If new claims are added when the divisional application is filed under Rule 147, and the Office does give the application a filing date, a Supplemental Oath should be filed before the divisional application issues.

In conclusion, restriction practice has been greatly affected both in adjective and substantive law by the Patent Act of 1952, even though very few recent decisions relating to restriction have been reported. They have, however, proved to be very important. Since additional changes in restriction practice can be expected, new decisions in this field should be studied with interest.

Cross-references: *Act of 1952—Patents, Double Patenting, Prosecution.*

ROYALTY—RATE AND BASIS

Albert S. Davis, Jr.

The manner of establishing the royalty rate for patent rights and the basis for calculation varies with the circumstances. In an ideal case, the parties bargain at arms' length but seek a meeting of the minds, rather than failure. The licensor will be pleased with the fact of licensing, if it can get its price. So will the licensee, at the right price. Not all licenses, royalty rates and royalty bases, unfortunately, are bargained out in such a climate. When they are not, something must be allowed, by way of bonus or discount, for the unwillingness characterizing one or both of the parties.

Factors to Consider

It is possible to list the usual factors to be considered in royalty setting. The schedule will read (patent-by-patent, if there is more than one) on such questions as (1) the probable degree of validity in the event of determined resistance to voluntary license, (2) the forums in which a case could be tried and their comparative records in holdings for or against the patent owner, (3) breadth of claim and ease of particular or even general avoidance of it, and (4) the prospective profitability—not only direct benefits, but also fringe benefits such as ease of sale or use of the to-be-licensed product or process v. competitive alternatives.

Such detailed lists, when made, are usually for private calculation, not for exchange in bargaining. Any general checklist, moreover, may fail to reflect the unusual conditions in a particular case and the relative degrees of importance of the several factors.

As a result, the evaluation almost always comes back to the test of the marketplace, a result to be estimated largely on the basis of: (a) royalty patterns in the industry or the most nearly related industry; (b) experience with the product or closely related products; and (c) calculations of a reasonable share of anticipated profits. None of these guides is infallible but together they are the best available. Both expert opinion presented in a suit and court decrees, whether litigated or consent, will usually rest upon them.

Royalty Rate Patterns

All industry experience had a beginning somewhere. In the pharmaceutical field, for instance, the establishment of royalties at a range of 5 to $7\frac{1}{2}$ per cent of net sales for rights to synthesize Vitamin B_1, at a relatively early point in the modern expansion of the industry, led others to follow that pattern. In this, and in a great many other industries, a standard has been so set that it is often accepted without much questioning. When a rate becomes thus more or less traditional, an unusual circumstance or determined bargaining is ordinarily required to change it. Typical causes of a change are: (a) the invention is the key to a major industrial breakthrough; (b) the royalty sought is out of proportion to the contribution of the invention as compared to the development work required on the part of the licensee; (c) the royalty is excessive in relation to the anticipated profit; and (d) the pressure which one party to the bargaining can exert upon the other, whether directly, indirectly or not related at all to the patent and the technical and legal contribution it makes. On occasion, e.g., where the industry is controlled by one or a few corporations which have developed a peculiar pattern inequitable to the outsider, the pattern is not a proper guide. All these circumstances can distort the usual royalty scale. Since they vary so much from case to case, generalizations are hazardous.

Bargaining on an industrial article usually hinges largely on the profit to be expected. This is especially noticeable with patents or applications on "gadget" and "quick sales impact" items; the scope of protection against competition, i.e., infringement is deemphasized in such circumstances.

Analysis of a great number of cases, both bargained-out and imposed as damages by the courts, makes it clear that a royalty rate of 25 to $33\frac{1}{3}$ per cent of the anticipated profit is about the average, with many exceptions outside this range. In the automobile industry, because of the enormous volume of business, and for other reasons, a royalty of a fraction of 1 per cent of the value of the patented part is not uncommon.

Royalty Base

A royalty rate is meaningless unless it is applied to a solid royalty base. Here, a problem arises. Is the royalty to be charged for the right to use patents? Or is it to be proportioned to and based on actual operation under patent claims?

Where a complex patent body or, even

more, "know-how" is licensed, the tendency is to apply the royalty without respect to extent of operation that would otherwise constitute infringement. This type of arrangement provides (a) relief of the licensor from proving infringement, case by case, when it receives royalties seemingly too low and (b) freedom of the licensee to proceed with production, secure in the knowledge of a fixed burden and able to design plant or plan production without concern as to impact of the license on any given course of action.

Where the licensed subject matter is not complex and know-how is not involved, the tendency, on the other hand, is to hold the licensee more rigorously to an accounting for royalties on a product or process covered by one or more claims of the licensed patent. Even with a license for the right to use patents to make a product, where there is no accounting, claim-by-claim, it is obvious that there must be agreement on just what the license covers. This is usually specified in licenses by reference to a fairly broad field of activity, such as "synchronous electric motors." Here, as in the claim-by-claim case, it is also usual to state that certain areas of income from a licensed product either are or are not included in the royalty base.

Sales Basis. By far the most common royalty base is the sales volume. It is the easiest to determine; the disclosure does the least violence to the licensee's business secrets such as costing and estimating methods and mark-up factors; the sales basis forces the licensee to pay only when it has marketed the product or the product of the licensed process and should have the needed cash in hand or in sight; and it, of all the methods related generally to profitability, is the least capable of manipulation to the hazard of the licensor's interests.

Deductions from Sales. It is usual to employ some such phrase as "net sales" and base the accrual of the royalty on the licensee's billings less such peripheral deductions as sales and use taxes, discounts and allowances (but not commissions, unless they are normal in lieu of discounts), packing and crating, outbound transportation or freight, returns, and special services.

Special Services. For a large machine which must be erected in the field, is royalty to be paid on receipts from separately billed preliminary engineering studies, prototypes or pilot plants, erection services, instruction in operation, testing, and guaranteed first-year servicing? The tendency is to include them in the base for calculation of royalty, because their existence is directly traceable to and tied with the product.

With a smaller machine, and a fairly narrow patent, such as a radio transmitter, a question arises as to what may or may not be considered "auxiliaries." The prospective licensee usually insists stoutly that they are not to be included in the royalty base. An excellent example here is the power source. A power pack expressly designed for a transmitter, particularly where the claims include the phrase "a source of power," is apt to be subject to payment of royalty; a shelf power unit, even though its other sales possibilities are relatively limited, is less likely to be so subject.

Cost as Basis. A royalty based on "cost," however the definition of that word is phrased, is in the long run detrimental to the licensor. The licensee will be expected to exert every effort to bring the cost down without reducing its price by the same amount. The net result is that the more profitable the invention becomes to the licensee, the less is the income to the licensor, unless increased volume offsets the decreased cost per unit. Even that is cold comfort, since the licensor would still be better off with a percentage of sales unless competition forced a disproportionate reduction of the price.

Profit or Savings Basis. A royalty based on "profit" or "savings" is an open invitation to a continuing dispute. Even where "cost," overhead," and "net sales price" are carefully defined, there is a clear area for manipulation of items to be fed into these phrases. Obvious examples are the effect on the "profit" or "savings" of plow-back for research and development and overhead for administration, sales, advertising and marketing. The licensee will consider these vital to the continued success of his operation. The licensor will consider each of them, beyond a point upon which it cannot agree with the licensee because their short-term and sometimes their long-term interests diverge, as deliberate inroads upon its income. The licensor will see itself as being asked to pay for the licensee's normal expenses of doing business and its royalties being plowed back into the licensee's R and D expenses. Even where a relatively simple product is involved and there is a considerable area of agreement as to what constitutes "cost," the verification of "cost" alone may involve the licensee in unwanted disclosure of its affairs, particularly when the licensor is a direct or indirect competitor in the same or allied lines. While a neutral report-verifying auditor should be a complete answer to this objection, actual experiences show it often is not.

Summary

A negotiator or "decider" (judge, arbitrator, expert, or executive) charged with setting a royalty figure should consider the following points:

(1) Is the license to be for operation under specific claims or for the right to use patents as, and if, wanted?

(2) Is there a standard level of royalties, determinable from trade experiences, actual licenses, or court decrees?

(3) What is the anticipated increase from operation under the license?

(4) Is 25 to $33\frac{1}{3}$ per cent of that antici-

pated profit consonant with the established pattern for royalty?

(5) What is the royalty base to be used and is it broad or narrow?

(6) What peripheral deductibles affect the royalty base?

(7) Is there reason to depart from the preferred sales volume royalty base?

(8) How should the royalty base be specifically defined?

General References

Ball, W. B., ed., "Dynamics of the Patent System," pp. 207 et seq., New York, Central Book Co., 1960.

Behrman, J. N., and W. E. Schmidt, "Royalty Provisions in Foreign Licensing Contracts," 3 PTC J 272, 1959.

Davis, A. S., Jr., ed., "Patent Licensing," New York, Practising Law Institute, 1958.

Forman, H. I., ed., "Patents, Research and Management," New York, Central Book Co., 1961.

Hoar, R. S., "Patent Tactics and Law," 3d ed., pp. 2 et seq., New York, Ronald Press, 1950.

McFadden, J. A., Jr., and C. D. Tuska, "Accounting and Tax Aspects of Patents and Research," p. 6, Princeton, N.J., D. Van Nostrand Co., 1960.

"Royalty Rates for Chemical Process," Chemical Week, p. 70 (Feb. 18, 1956).

Cross-references: *Accounting after Infringement Suits,* particularly the tabulation of royalty rates set in numerous court decisions, *Arbitration, Economic Aspects, Evaluating Inventions for License, Licensing, Licensing Experience of U.S. Corporations.*

RUSSIAN PATENTS. See SOVIET

S

SEARCHING AND RETRIEVING INFORMATION ELECTRONICALLY

Martin Kalikow

Any information classifying and retrieving system must employ one or more appropriate media of communication such as language, code or signals. Most information today is stored and expressed in the form of language. The language of a document may be analyzed as follows:

Meaningful

Level 9. Subject—Document
Level 8. Theme—Several Paragraphs
Level 7. Complex Idea—Single Paragraph or Several Sentences
Level 6. Basic Idea—Single Sentence
Level 5. Complex Concept—Phrase or Complex Word
Level 4. Basic Concept—Single Simple Word
Level 3. Complex Character—Syllable

Unmeaningful (Code)

Level 2. Basic Character—Single Letter
Level 1. Bit—Single Dot

In retrieving any document the number of possible choices increases geometrically as we move from lower to higher levels. At the "bit" level (1) we have a single choice; at the basic character level (2) we have 26 choices corresponding to the letters of the alphabet, etc. Most of our present library-type indexing and abstracting services are operating at the "complex concept" level (5) in which there may be as many as fifty thousand (words and phrases) choices for a given field.

Requirements

Any efficient mechanized classification and retrieval system must, however, in order to meet present and future needs, be able to function at the "idea" level (6) rather than at the "word" (complex concept) level (5).

The searcher must be able to search for the "idea" directly and obtain results which tell him how close each document searched comes to the "idea" being searched. In other words, all of the concepts (and their relations) which make up the idea being searched must be able to be searched simultaneously and as a single entity. Where they are all (or substantially all) found in a given document, he can be fairly certain that a similar or related idea is involved. This is the principle underlying "coordinate indexing" systems of classification and retrieval, and substantially all systems which are currently being proposed by documentation experts for meeting our future information handling needs are based upon some variation of this "coordinate indexing" principle.

One other important principle which follows from the above is that the classification must be at a level no higher than the "complex idea" level. If a document contains several complex ideas, someone must segregate and abstract these ideas separately. If several complex ideas are combined in a single abstract, the retrieval will be unreliable.

Systems in Use

There are several classification and retrieval mechanisms currently being used which are based upon this coordinate indexing principle and which range from simple "descriptor cards" to "peek-a-boo" cards to programmed general purpose computers. The mechanism selected depends upon many factors such as size and content of file, speed of searching desired, and the like.

In the "Marked Descriptor Card" system, the identification number of the document classified is marked in a particular digit column of each card representing a respective "descriptor" (code term) under which the document is indexed. In retrieval, the searcher selects certain descriptor cards which he deems essential to the idea being searched and retrieves all document identification numbers which appear on all (or most) of the cards.

In the "Punched Hole Descriptor Card" (Peek-a-boo) system, the identification number of the document is indicated by a hole punched in a particular location on each card representing a respective descriptor or term under which the document is indexed. In retrieval, all of the cards representing essential concepts of the idea being searched are superimposed in front of a light source. Points of light pass through the selected cards only at those locations where the holes in each card are aligned to one another. The locations of these registering holes indicate the document identification in accord with the original classification.

In the "Punched Hole Document Card" system, the card represents the document and each term by which the document is indexed is punched into a respective assigned location on the card. In retrieval, a master card is prepared in which all of the terms representing the idea being searched are punched into corresponding locations. The pattern of holes in each document card is then compared against that of the master. The comparison can be made by a card sorting machine (McBee, Zatocoding, Punched Card Sorter) or by superimposing the cards over a light source.

In most current mechanized searching systems, a computer is programmed to simulate the operation of the "Punched Hole Descriptor Card" coordinate indexing system. Each punched hole descriptor card record is read into tape, and the retrieval is done by collating in computer storage all matching (document) numbers in all of the selected descriptor card records. In a separate step the matched numbers are typed out together with the abstract of the corresponding document. The utility and speed of the system is further increased by the fact that a considerable number of simul-taneous searches may be conducted during one run of the tape. The reasonable capacity of a large system at the present time is therefore several million document abstracts (complex ideas).

Encoding

In each of the above systems, except the very large computerized system, it is essential that the language and ideas of the document be translated into some type of normalized language or code (descriptors). Such translation may be done either by human minds or by a computer program based upon a "thesaurus" stored within the computer.

In general, the difficulty and expense involved in human translation depend upon how many levels are skipped. As mentioned above, no more than a single complex idea can be reliably classified and retrieved at a time. Therefore, each document must first be abstracted at least down to the complex idea level. This is the first encoding step. If conventional language is used, we have skipped from level 9 to level 7. This is, for example, the encoding problem which confronts an abstracting service. If we wish to use selected distinct complex concepts (descriptors) the translation problem becomes more difficult since we are skipping down to level 5. Likewise, the translating difficulty increases as we skip to the basic concept level (4) and further increases as we skip down to the syllable level (3). With expert classifiers the "idea" (abstracting) and "language" coding steps can be combined, i.e., the classifier can read the document and directly select the code "words" which define each of the complex ideas to be classified. However, the more levels to be skipped in the translation, the more "expert" the translator must be.

In some very large computerized document retrieval systems, the full text of the document is read into storage preferably by electronic optical scanners. The precise location of each word in the document is also stored in the computer and retrieval is on the basis of selected combinations of words set forth in particular word orders by the searcher in a plurality of "search questions" supplied to the computer. Such a system has been applied to legal searching of State Statutes and holds promise for application to patent searching.

Techniques for Computer Searching

In such large computer searching systems, it is possible to make searches at several different levels of "idea complexity." In one case, for example, a search may be conducted for all *documents* in which a given *single word* (representing a single concept) appears. In another case, it may be more logical to search for all *sentences* in which a certain *phrase* (representing a complex concept) occurs. In yet another case, a search for all *paragraphs* containing a selected combination of descriptive words or phrases (complex idea) may be indicated.

There are often procedures within the computer for relating words and phrases of similar meaning to one another (thesaurus) as well as for relating complex-concept words to combinations of more rudimentary concept words which express similar meanings (semantic factoring). This enables the computer to search for a given idea regardless of the many ways the idea may be expressed in any document so long as the idea to be searched is submitted to the computer in accord with one of the possible modes of expression.

There are usually also procedures for determining and adjusting retrieval on the basis of the pertinency of the ideas as expressed in the various documents being searched to the idea as expressed in the search question. By permitting an adjustable degree of leeway in the pertinency of the document to the question being asked, a predetermined amount of "overpull" can be achieved. As the degree of required pertinency is relaxed, a greater volume of documents is retrieved, but the number of non-pertinent documents (false drops) also correspondingly increases.

In the more sophisticated systems, there are also procedures for determining the order of and relationship between words (syntax, role-indicators, etc.) as well as for "weighting" the various concepts (words or phrases) of the search question in accord with the relative importance of these concepts to the content of the search.

At the present time, the greatest impediment to the introduction of electronic document searching systems lies in the high total cost of preparing and reading the information contained in the documents whether in the form of abstracts or full text into computer storage. It is anticipated, however, that the advent of more efficient optical scanners and of computers with greater rapid access storage capacity will eventually reduce these costs sufficiently to make such systems practical for a wide field of uses including patent searching.

In an article on this subject, Arthur Schwartz, 44 JPOS 803, 1962 says:

"To date the [Patent] Office has about 18,000 patents on various forms of mechanized search systems. In the electrical arts there are about 1,500 dealing with miscellaneous transistor circuits, and 800 on electrical switch contact materials. The greatest progress has been made in the chemical areas where there are about 15,000 references being searched, dealing with resin, phosphates, steroids, pesticides and organometallics. About 10,000 alloy patents are in the process of being coded, and work is being conducted on the respirator, transmission and carburetor arts....

"First, Examiners working in the art that is to be coded, together with full-time members of the Patent Office Research and Development staff, make up a dictionary of terms. This is a list of art terms, elements, circuits, etc. that they feel should be included, i.e., that the Examiner in his search will be looking for. Each term has a specific definition and each is given a number. The numbers may run into the thousands depending on the subject matter....

"The numbers corresponding to a particular term, element, location in a carbon chain, etc. are then coded onto a punch card or into a computer.

"The next problem comes in asking the machine questions—the right questions. Here the Examiner working in the art must put together the numbers corresponding to the terms he is looking for in such a manner as to get the best art available...."

See also B. E. Lanham and J. Leibowitz, 40 JPOS 86, 1958; Joseph Stitleman, 46 JPOS 390, 1964.

Bibliography

The National Science Foundation publishes frequent comprehensive reports on information storage and retrieval. The 440-page issue for 1962,

"Current Research and Development in Scientific Documentation," No. 11, and certain others are available from the Superintendent of Public Documents, Washington 25, D.C. The reports discuss the progress with conventional as well as electronic systems by many companies, societies and agencies.

Cross-references: *Examination, Searching in Washington, Searching the Patent Literature outside Washington.*

SEARCHING IN WASHINGTON, D.C.

Philip E. Siggers

Categories of Searches

There are six categories of searches made in the Patent Office by non-employees. Because the time requirement and cost vary enormously for the different kinds of searches, it is important for those who request them to know the differences and to specify the type wanted.

Preliminary Search. By far the most frequently made is the preliminary search or examination (often termed a "pre ex") which seeks to locate the United States patents most pertinent to an inventive concept, prior to filing an application for patent. Hundreds of such searches are made every business day.

State of the Art Search. Often a preliminary search is elaborated to include many subclasses and the citation of many patents; it is then known as a "state of the art" or "collection" search, its purpose being to give the interested party a much broader view of the condition of the prior art (patents and publications).

Infringement Search. A person, firm or corporation, considering the investment of a substantial sum in the commercialization of an invention but seeking to avoid the risk of being sued for infringement, may authorize an infringement search. This studies the claims of unexpired patents in the field of the invention. Such a search will usually consume several days or weeks and is necessarily fairly expensive, but is often well worthwhile. The results are negative if they reveal no claims likely to be held infringed.

Sometimes an infringement search is expanded to include expired patents whose disclosures limit the scope of apparently infringed claims of later patents, so that they would not be considered infringed. Such search is termed a "justification" search.

Validity Search. If a patent is considered infringed, a search is undertaken to determine whether the claims define a new invention or whether the claimed invention lacks novelty. This validity search is far broader than any other as it may require examination of foreign as well as domestic patents and reading of technical books, magazine articles, and other literature available at libraries.

Index Search. Frequently one is informed that a patent has issued to a party on a particular subject matter. The annual indexes (with their listings of names in alphabetical order) and the indexes in the weekly Official Gazettes subsequent to the bound volumes are then examined. The Search Room card indexes of patents, arranged in alphabetical order, may also be examined. While they may yield quickly the information desired, they are not fully reliable or up-to-date.

Assignment Search. Then there are assignment record searches. These seek to determine who owns a particular patent or who has a recorded license under the patent. They may reveal present ownership of patent applications and sometimes disclose, by the date and title of the invention, the approximate time of filing of an application of particular interest. Often assignment and index searches are made together as checks against each other. The assignment records are never up-to-date, while the indexes appear each Tuesday in the Official Gazette. However, an index search may not reveal the present title to a patent, as an assignment of an application may be submitted for recording after the final fee has been paid, in which case the index will be misleading or incomplete as it will show the title of record only at the time of payment of said fee.

Facilities, Procedures and Miscellaneous Information

Search Rooms. In the present Department of Commerce Building, on the ground

Search Room, U.S. Patent Office

floor, is a large hall comprising the Patent Search Room and the Attorneys Room.

In a large area adjacent to the Search Room are loose copies of the more than three million United States patents issued since July 1, 1836, conveniently arranged in classes and subclasses. As most of the patents are cross-referenced into other subclasses, there are probably over ten million total copies immediately available to any searcher, and this total number grows at the rate of several thousand a week.

Chemical, electrical and mechanical patents are being reclassified constantly; this process has been going on since 1898 and will continue, no doubt, as long as there is a Patent Office. Sometimes an entire class or subclass is removed from the Search Room area for reclassification, and the copies of patents in it may then be searched only in the examining group or in one of the classification divisions.

Conferring with Associate Examiners. Of major importance at times in searching is the privilege of briefly interviewing associate examiners to ascertain whether the most pertinent subclasses have been searched or get a suggestion as to the proper field of search. Sometimes days of work are saved by a ten-minute interview with a well-informed examiner.

Using Patent Collections. There are important advantages and some drawbacks to searching in one of the Patent Office groups.

The advantages are: (1) The complete art is searchable including the examiner's unofficial cross-references and foreign as well as domestic patents, often noting other fields of search. (2) A searcher has the opportunity of asking questions. The disadvantages are: (1) Searches in the examining groups are permitted only during office hours, 8:30 a.m. to 5:00 p.m., Monday through Friday. (2) The space in which an outsider may search is usually cramped; sometimes no chairs are available, and no surface on which to spread out a drawing; there is frequently considerable movement of examiners past the spot of searching. Some of the examiners' copies may be withdrawn and temporarily placed in files of cases under examination, and there is no way of ascertaining whether the boxes of copies being searched are complete.

Résumés of Unpatented Applications. Scattered through the bundles of patent copies in the Search Room are sheets bearing clippings from Official Gazettes of résumés of unpatented applications. These résumés were published for only a brief period and are effective as publications only. The files of the abandoned applications on which the résumés were based may be inspected by filing in the Attorneys Room a petition to the Commissioner and must not be removed from that room.

Issued Patent Stacks. Arranged in metal stacks along corridors in the Search Room are bound volumes of copies of patents from No. 597,703 (January 1, 1898) up to well above No. 3,000,000. In the Scientific Library Annex, bound volumes of all copies from No. 1 (dated July 13, 1836) to No. 597,702 are arranged on shelves, so that any searcher during office hours may inspect copies of the more than three million United States patents without resorting to the loose bundles of classified patents. Also the annual indexes, patent card indexes, and late copies of the Official Gazette are in the Attorneys Room and Search Room. Earlier Official Gazettes (back to January, 1921) are in the Scientific Library; still older Gazettes are in the Library Annex.

Microfilms and Reading Machine. Because of the vast space taken up by the patent copies bound in volumes, the Patent Office has recently made a radical change. Beginning July 10, 1962 with No. 3,042,924, microfilm copies of patents have been made; these microfilms are stored in a metal cabinet in the Search Room. A Recordak Lodestar Reader machine stands adjacent to this cabinet and anyone, during the hours the Search Room is open, may operate this machine and read from the microfilm the copies of patents of interest.

Index in Classification Manual

The 308 classes of invention presently existing are constantly being changed. On the other hand, the 93 classes of designs are scarcely ever modified, as the Patent Office seems to think it is more important to reclassify mechanical, electrical and chemical patents. Design patents arranged in subclasses can be searched only in a separate location, now at 1406 G Street, N.W.

The Manual of Classification listing the 308 classes, 93 design classes and scores of thousands of subclasses is in almost constant use by searchers. An index to this Manual is revised and republished about every five years. The Superintendent of Documents in Washington sells these publications at a reasonable price and mails revision sheets four times a year at no extra cost. Classification bulletins, containing definitions of most of the classes and subclasses and giving valuable search notes,

are available in the Search Room or by purchase from the Superintendent at low cost.

There is also a Classification Index of Patents in the Search Room. This is a card index, each card bearing 100 numbers, with a class number and a subclass number opposite each. Thus a searcher, encountering a cross-referenced patent of interest, may consult this classification index and learn where the patent is classified, thereby perhaps being guided to a better field of search.

Knowing the availability of the facilities and services such as those detailed herein, the untutored searcher at a later date may learn the then current arrangements and locations by conferring with the head of the Search Room.

Inspection of Files of Patents and Applications

To inspect files of patents and pending and abandoned applications, inspection of the applications requiring special permission, one must go to the Attorneys Room and deposit an order slip. Patent files from No. 2,275,000, presently stored in the Patent Office, may be obtained in an hour or less. They can not be removed from the Attorneys Room by anyone except employees of the Office. To make room for newly patented files which are being received at the rate of about 1,000 per week, the older files are transported from time to time to, and stored in, a Government warehouse, now in Franconia, Virginia. At present, all files between No. 664,001 and No. 2,274,999 are in Franconia; to have such a file brought to the Attorneys Room, on written order, requires 1 to 3 days.

Patent files prior to 1836 (which are not numbered) and patent No. 1 of 1836 to No. 664,000 are in the National Archives Building, Pennsylvania Avenue and 7th Street, N.W. By depositing a written order in the Attorneys Room, one can usually inspect these Archives files within 24 hours.

Abandoned files may be inspected only by parties in interest or on petition to the Commissioner of Patents. The vast majority of abandoned files have been destroyed. Files of pending cases may be inspected by showing power of attorney or facts, in a petition, to justify access.

Mechanized Searching

Presently located in Room 4612 of the Commerce Building is the Mechanized Examining Division. Here the disclosures of certain patents relating to carbon chemistry have been reduced to cards which may be run through machines when a search is made. At this time, patents relating to steroids, phosphates, phosphoric acid esters, and some resin chemistry are included in this Division. The same patents are searchable in the usual way in the Search Room.

Translations

When making a validity search or a search in the examining group, sometimes a foreign patent is found which seems to be of interest, but often the pertinence of the patent can only be determined by having a few words or paragraphs translated. By going to the Translation Section of the Scientific Library, one may obtain a verbal translation without cost and usually without waiting.

The Scientific Library

The Patent Office's Scientific Library, referred to above, houses over 7,000,000 copies of foreign patents (mostly in 285,000 bound volumes), 110,000 books and 73,000 volumes of scientific periodicals.

British patent copies are available for inspection and reproduction from A.D. 1617; French (with indexes), from 1791; German, from 1877, all to the latest copy received. Other well-represented countries are: Australia, Austria, Belgium, Canada, Czechoslovakia, Denmark, Italy, Japan, the Netherlands, Norway, Pakistan, Sweden and Switzerland, altogether about 27 countries, mostly with incomplete sets of copies.

Reproductions of any foreign patent or publication in this library may be obtained by paying in advance or by charging the cost to an account established with the Patent Office. The cost is now thirty cents a sheet. About three weeks will elapse before delivery is made. Copies so ordered will be mailed anywhere at no additional cost.

Other Libraries in the Washington, D.C. Area

The libraries of outstanding importance are: the Library of Congress, facing the Capitol building; the Commerce Department library on the seventh floor; the Department of Agriculture library on Independence Avenue between 12th and 14th Streets, S.W.; the National Bureau of Standards library on Connecticut Avenue at Van Ness Street, N.W., with a large collection of scientific material; and the Atomic Energy Commission library at Germantown, Md. (not open to the general public). The same restriction applies to the National Library of Medicine, incorporating the old Army Medical Library and other libraries. These facilities would be made available to scholars on request.

Other libraries that are more or less restricted include those of the National Aeronautics and Space Administration, the Federal Aviation Agency, the National Academy of Sciences, the Armed Forces Institute of Pathology, and the National Archives.

The American Chemical Society, at 1155 Sixteenth Street, N.W., offers splendid library facilities to its members.

Finally, the Superintendent of Documents, at the Government Printing Office on North Capitol Street, has scores of thousands of Government publications for sale at incredibly low prices.

Cross-references: *Anticipation, Searching and Retrieving Information Electronically, Searching Patent Literature Outside Washington.*

SEARCHING PATENT LITERATURE OUTSIDE WASHINGTON

David F. Gould

[This article is written from the viewpoint of one who, after service as a research laboratory director, has specialized in recent years in reports of information from patents, bibliographies and literature studies in special fields, for corporation researchers and executives. Ed.]

Introduction

The most common objective of patent searches is still the information needed in connection with problems of patentability, validity, or infringement. Yet accelerated growth in industry has increased the communicative property of patents and consequently the requirements of a widening group of people for up-to-date patent searches for other purposes.

Patents become more and more the major storehouses of the latest technical information. Von Wimmersperg [1] estimates the creative thinking that is frozen in patents as "about twenty times larger than represented by market products." The breadth of interest in patents is illustrated in Table 1.

TABLE 1.

For the Attorney
(a) Patentability of an invention
(b) Infringement by self or others
(c) Defensive use in contesting validity of another's patent

For Management

(a) Information on:
    Activities of competitors
    Geographical variation in business
    Trend of commercial activity
(b) An aid in selecting foreign markets
(c) An aid in forming a basis for licensing patents

For the Researcher and the Engineer

(a) Information on new materials, equipment, processes, products, and applications
(b) Technical history of a material, process, or product that will help avoid repetition of work and assist in planning new work
(c) Source of ideas for new attacks on technical problems (consistent with property rights of patent owners)

For the Sales Department
Information on:
    Activities of competitors
    Uses of potential value in sales promotion
    Possible outlets for products

The classified files of all domestic and many foreign patents that are available in the Patent Office make that the outstanding source of patent information. A great deal of patent searching, however, is done outside of Washington, particularly searches

that are less concerned with legalities than with technical information. Frequently, abstracts and technical indexes lead the technical man to the desired information without traveling and with a minimum of searching, mainly because their type of indexing and style of composition are in line with his thought processes. When a comprehensive search is needed, those abstracts and indexes may supply the numbers of important patent subclasses to be searched. As one example, sixteen of a series of patents located through technical journals and abstracts, as being pertinent to a study on a certain type of resin, were found to be divided among fourteen patent subclasses.

Search Material—Copies of Patents

The following Depository Libraries for United States patents maintain files of them ("inc." means incomplete). Individual libraries in the list may also hold foreign patents, either on specific subjects or from selected countries.

Albany, N. Y., University of State of N.Y.
Atlanta, Ga., Georgia Technical Library (inc.)
Boston, Mass., Public Library
Buffalo, N.Y., Buffalo and Erie Co. Public Library
Chicago, Ill., Public Library
Cleveland, O., Public Library
Columbus, O., Ohio State Univ. Library
Detroit, Mich., Public Library
Kansas City, Mo., Linda Hall Library (inc.)
Los Angeles, Cal., Public Library
Madison, Wis., State Historical Soc. of Wis.
Milwaukee, Wis., Public Library
Newark, N.J., Public Library
New York, N.Y., Public Library
Philadelphia, Pa., Franklin Institute
Pittsburgh, Pa., Carnegie Library
Providence, R.I., Public Library
St. Louis, Mo., Public Library
Stillwater, Okla., Oklahoma A. & M. College
Toledo, O., Public Library

The New York Public Library, at the new location of its Patent Section at 521 West 43rd Street, ranks next to the Patent Office for patent searching but does not have classified files. Its stacks hold patents of 39 countries including the following complete files: United States, Belgian (since 1950), British, Danish, French, German (with an early gap), Japanese (minus a war year), and Swedish.

Copies of foreign patents may be purchased from the originating patent offices, and photocopies may be obtained from our Patent Office or from some city, technical and college libraries, government laboratories, trade associations, and technical associations.

Status of Foreign Patents

In contrast to current United States practice, foreign patents sometimes lapse before the end of their normal term, because of nonpayment of the taxes required at stipulated periods or of nonworking. If a foreign patent becomes of particular interest, from licensing or other standpoints, the status may usually be determined by request directed to the originating patent office or through a patent attorney practicing in the country in question. A few patent journals, such as the Australian, carry lists of patents voided for nonpayment of taxes or fees.

Search Material—Official Patent Journals

U.S. Official Gazette. The Official Gazette issued by the United States Patent Office is at present second only to numerical and classified files of copies of patents, as a source of information on domestic patents. Over 500 libraries throughout the country and many corporations and patent attorneys maintain files of it. Among the advantages offered by the Official Gazette are the following:

(a) Since July 1, 1952, patent entries in the Official Gazette have been arranged not only numerically but also *in order by class and subclass numbers*. Then, beginning in 1955, the annual Index of Patents lists all patents issued during the year in each subclass. A limited search covering subsequent years may now be made without recourse to other subclass lists, and those subclass lists already at hand may be brought up to date.

(b) Patents disclosed in the Official Gazette are indexed by the name of the inventor and the assignee, if any. These in-

dexes supply information on the activities of individuals or corporations that may be of considerable help in planning patent searches or in posting the Management or Sales Department on new developments.

(c) The Official Gazette serves as an index of technical developments, from which the researcher or the development engineer may select items to be studied further from the complete patents.

As a source of complete technical information, the Official Gazette is lacking in at least two respects. It prints usually only one important claim, occasionally two. The claim printed gives little indication of the fund of information that may appear in the body of the patent and that may be highly important to the reader, e.g., points of superiority over other products or processes, performance data, or uses. Furthermore, the claims are written by necessity in a condensed legal style which is often difficult for the nonlegal reader to comprehend fully. Miller has questioned whether this style, convenient principally to the attorney, is acceptable today in view of the communicative properties required in a patent.[12] He has suggested improvements which, it is to be hoped, may lead to further study of the subject.

Patent Journals of Foreign Countries. Patent journals issued by foreign countries are not as readily available to us as is our Official Gazette. Also, these journals vary in content and usefulness.

A list of representative journals and a brief statement of contents appear in Table 2. The publication *Chemical Abstracts*, in its list of periodicals abstracted, gives the names and locations of libraries holding the individual patent journals.

The importance of many foreign patents, the lack of ready accessibility of the official journals, language difficulties for most readers, and the fact that in some countries, patents are open to inspection for a considerable period before complete information about them appears in journals or printed copies become available have led to the establishment of private abstracting and translating services. These services perform such an important function that they are considered further in another section.

Some journals of foreign countries list only the title of the invention, the name of inventor or assignee, and related data. These lists are available in some technical libraries. The New York Public Library, for example, has such lists from Cuba, Italy, Mexico, Netherlands, Spain, Switzerland, and Venezuela.

TABLE 2. REPRESENTATIVE FOREIGN PATENT JOURNALS.

Australia—The Australian Official Journal of Patents, Trade Marks and Designs carries abridged titles of new applications and the principal claim of accepted complete specifications. (Department of Patents, Canberra, A.C.T., Australia)

Belgium—Recueil des Brevets d'Invention has abridged descriptions of patents, classified according to the International Classification, and an annual name index. (Service de la Propriété industrielle et commerciale, Bruxelles, Belg.)

Canada—The Canadian Patent Office Record is similar to the United States Official Gazette. (Queen's Printer, Ottawa, Ontario, Canada)

Czechoslovakia—The journal Vynálezy has long-title, classed lists of applications laid open to inspection and of patents granted but has no abstracts. (Urad pro patenty a vynálezy, Prague, Czech.)

Denmark—Dansk Patenttidende has long-title, classed lists of applications laid open to inspection and of patents granted but has no abstracts. (Directoratet for Patent—og Varemaerkevaesenet, Copenhagen, Den.)

France—Bulletin Officiel de la Propriété Industrielle carries abridged descriptions of patents. Medicament patents are handled separately in a weekly bulletin that summarizes them. (Institute national de la Propriété Industrielle, Paris 15°, Fr.)

Germany—Patentblatt (West Germany) has only lists of applications filed, patents granted, etc. (Deutsche Patentamt, Munich 2, Ger.) A companion publication, "Auszüge aus den Patentanmeldungen," issued by Wila Verlag für Wirtschaftwerbung in Munich, gives the main claim of all patents. East German patent rules are undergoing revision. It is proposed to publish applications almost immediately after filing.

Great Britain—The Official Journal (Patents) gives the titles of applications and notifications of acceptance. (The Patent Office, London WC2, Eng.)

Japan—The journal Tokkyo Kōhō is similar to the United States Official Gazette but carries abstracts of the published applications rather than abstracts of the granted patent. (Tokko Cho, Chiyoda-ku, Tokyo, Japan)

Netherlands—De Industrielle Eigendom has long-title, classed lists of applications open to inspection and of patents granted. (Bureau voor de Industrielle Eigendom, The Hague, Neth.)

Norway—Norsk Tidende for det Industrielle Rettsvern, Avdeling I; Patenter carries long-title, classed lists of patent applications open to inspection and of patents granted and abstracts of patents published about three weeks before. (Styret for det Industrielle Rettsvern, Oslo, Norway)

Russia—Byulleten' Izobretenii carries abstracts of patents or "author's certificates" and rewrites or reissues arranged according to class and numbered in classed order. (Komiteta po delam izobretenii i otkrytii, Moscow, U.S.S.R. or Tsentral'noe Byuro Tekhnicheskoi Informatsii, Moscow, U.S.S.R.) A cover-to-cover translation of Byulleten' Izobretenii is available from Derwent Information Service.

Switzerland—The Patent-Liste gives title of Invention, name of inventor, and other data but no abstracts. (Bureau fédéral de la propriété intellectuelle, Berne, Switz.)

Search Material—Abstracts

As E. Emmet Reid has pointed out, the abstracts are not patents in science or in law.[2] Wording in the patent itself may be very critical. Also, what the abstractor selects or the claim chosen for publication may not include the exact information available in the patent that the reader seeks.

Even with these limitations, patent abstracts can play important roles (a) in saving cost and time in preliminary searches for patents to be studied in connection with state of the art, patentability, infringement, or validity problems; (b) as indexes of new devices, processes, or products to be collected into bibliographies; and (c) as "straws in the wind," showing the direction of technical and market progress.

The most promising reference source for United States patents appears to be The National Catalog of Patents, Rowman and Littlefield, Inc., in which it is proposed to present information on all patents issued since 1790, in the form as described in the Official Gazette and grouped into the classes and subclasses of the Manual of Classification of the United States Patent Office. The initial volumes are being offered in two series, one covering Chemical and Related Patents and the other covering Electrical Patents (including communications and radiant energy). Coverage of other areas of patent subjects is projected. The publisher proposes to issue annual supplements to each unit to keep the information up to date. These will include changes in classification and other pertinent information that should be very effective for preliminary searching.

Patent abstracts may also appear in publications specializing in abstracts or in departments of periodicals where attention is called to important patents in their particular field of interest. Representative sources of the two types are given in Tables 3 and 4. These lists are of necessity not all-inclusive but will probably suggest additional sources. Chemical and allied fields are prominent in these lists, mainly because much attention has been given to the preparation of compilations of information on such patents.

Von Hohenhoff has published a bibliography of journals which list and abstract patents in various fields [3] and a similar bibliography of books and compilations.[4] (These have been reprinted by the Baltimore Special Libraries Association.) Worischek has published an article on searching foreign patents.[5] These three publications appeared in 1935 and 1936 and hence refer to patents that have now expired, but they are helpful on some of the older patents and may suggest additional sources of information on the more recent ones. An American Chemical Society publication lists possible sources of patent information with particular reference to chemical and allied fields.[6] Publications of Derwent Information Service are very useful for their information on recent and current foreign patents.[7, 8] Some of their abstract compilations are confined to a single country and a variety of subjects and some to a single category for several countries.

TABLE 3. ABSTRACTS AND INDEXES.

A. *Commonly Used*

Belgium Patents Report. Patents of chemical and allied interests. (Derwent Information Service, London WC1, Eng.)

British Patents Abstracts. Published in two parts, one of which covers Chemistry and Chemical Engineering and the other the remaining patent subjects. (Derwent Information Service, London WC1, Eng.)

British Plastics Federation Abstracts. Has abstracts of journal articles and patents from various countries on raw materials, processes, products, and applications of plastics. At present, lacks indexes, but there is a detailed grouping of abstracts according to subject. (British Plastics Federation, London WC1, Eng.)

Chemical Abstracts. This has coverage from 1907 and is very commonly used as the starting point for patent searches in chemical and allied fields. It is particularly useful for its annual and decennial indexes, which include separate indexes for patents. Libraries holding the periodicals abstracted are listed. (American Chemical Society, Washington 6, D.C.)

Chemische Zentralblatt. The oldest abstract journal devoted to Chemistry (from 1830). Before 1919, only German patents were covered. Its patent index is useful in locating equivalent patents in foreign countries. (Akademie-Verlag G.m.b.H., Berlin W8, Ger.)

Computer Abstracts. Abstracts of journal articles and patents. (Technical Information Co., Ltd., London WC2, Eng.)

Electronics Patent Service. (Radio-Electronics Patent Service, Washington 16, D.C.)

French Patent Abstracts. Patents of chemical and allied interest. (Derwent Information Service, London WC1, Eng.)

German Patent Abstracts. Published in two parts, one covering Chemistry and Chemical Engineering and the other the remaining patent subjects. (Derwent Information Service, London WC2, Eng.)

German Patent Applications. A digest of applications in the field of plastics. (Research Information Service, New York 5, N.Y.)

Indian Patent Abstracts. Included in alternate weekly issues of French Patents Abstracts. (Derwent Information Service, London WC1, Eng.)

International Patent Research Office. Prepares lists of titles and assignees of patents issued in the major countries, under a variety of headings. (The Hague, Nerthelands)

International Patent Service. Prepares bulletins covering patents issued in 18 countries in a variety of fields other than chemical. ('s-Hertogenbosch, Netherlands)

Japanese Patent Abstracts. Covers all patents in the seven groups. (Derwent Information Service, London WC1, Eng.)

Metallurgical Patents Journal, Abstracts of British, German, Belgian, French, South African, and Indian patents. (Derwent Information Service, London WC1, Eng.)

Metals Patents Bulletin. Abstracts of British, German, French, South African, and Indian patents. (Derwent Information Service, London WC1, Eng.)

Monatsregister Deutscher Patentanmeldungen. Patent titles, listed under subject, process, and use. (Wila Verlag für Wirtschaftswerbung, Munich, Ger.)

National Catalog of Patents. United States patents 1790 through 1961 by classes and subclasses with major claim. Chemical and Electrical units in process, other subjects projected. (Rowman and Littlefield, Inc., New York 11, N.Y.)

Nuclear Power Patents Bulletin. Abstracts of British, German, French, South African, and Indian patents. (Derwent Information Service, London WC1, Eng.)

Paper, Photography and Graphic Arts Patents Bulletin. Abstracts of British, German, French, South African, and Indian patents. (Derwent Information Service, London WC1, Eng.)

Research Information Service. Issues bulletins listing translations of German, Belgian, and Italian patents on various divisions of the field of plastics. (New York 5, N.Y.)

Russian Patents Report. Abstracts of patents of chemical and allied interest. (Derwent Information Service, London WC1, Eng.)

South African Patents Abstracts. In alternate weekly issues of the French Patents Abstracts. (Derwent Information Service, London WC1, Eng.)

Soviet Bloc and Mainland China Technical Journals. Includes abstracts from the patent journals and is issued in six series covering all subjects. (United States Department of Commerce, Washington 5, D.C.)

Uniterm Index. Provides a specialized index system covering United States patents on chemical and electronic subjects and a separate issue on Belgian chemical patents. (Information for Industry, Inc., Washington 6, D.C.) Discontinued 1964.

Univento. Issues lists of titles and assignees of patents of the major countries under various headings. (The Hague, Neth.)

B. Items Useful as Older References

Abstracts of Chemical Patents Vested in the Alien Property Custodian. Prepared by Chicago Section, American Chemical Society, 2 volumes (1944).

Bibliographies of Journals, Books and Compilations Which List and Abstract Patents. Von Hohenhoff, Elsa; J. Patent Office Society, Oct. 1935 to Feb. 1936.

British Abstracts. Outgrowth of abstracts of J. Chem. Soc. (from 1871) and J. Soc. Chem. Ind. (from 1882). Discontinued in 1953 but is still useful with its predecessors for locating older references.

Chemical Patents Index. Worden, E. C. (Chemical Catalog Co.) 1927-1934.

Fifty Years Subject Index 1861-1910 (British). (The Patent Office, London, Eng.)

Fortschritte in der Anorganische-chemischen Industrie. Bräuer, A. and D'Ans, J., Berlin 1872-1938.

Friedländer's Fortschritte der Teerfarbenfabrikation. Chemical patents of the last quarter of the last century and the first quarter of the present century, mainly German. (Julius Springer Verlag, Berlin, Ger.)

Subject Matter Index for Inventions (Brevets d'Invention) Granted in France from 1791 to 1876 Inclusive. (United States Commissioner of Patents, 1883)

Subject Matter Index of United States Patents, 1790 to 1873. (United States Patent Office)

TABLE 4. PERIODICALS LISTING SELECTED PATENTS BY TITLE ONLY OR WITH ABSTRACTS.

Acoustics
Journal of the Acoustical Society of America. (American Institute of Physics, New York 17, N.Y.)

Aircraft
Aircraft Engineering (Bunhill Publications, Ltd., London WC1, Eng.)

Carbon Black
Carbon Black Abstracts (Cabot Corp., Boston 10, Mass.)

Chemicals
American Dyestuff Reporter (Amer. Assoc. of Textile Chemists and Colorists, c/o Howes Publg. Co., Inc., New York 10, N.Y.)
Brennstoffe-Chemie (Verlag W. Girardet, Essen, Ger.)
Canadian Chemical Processing (Southam-Maclean Publns. Ltd., Don Mills, Ontario, Can.)
Chemiker-Zeitung (Alfred Huethig Verlag, Heidelberg, Ger.)
Chemische Weekblad (D. B. Centen's Uitbevers-Maatschappij, Hilversum, Netherlands)
Industrie Chimique Belge (Fédération des Industries Chimiques de Belgique, Brussels 4, Belg.)
Jahresberichte über die Leistungen der organi-

schen Chemie (Johann Ambrosius Barth Verlag, Leipzig Cl, Ger.)

Manufacturing Chemist (Hall Oak Press, London W6, Eng.)

SOCMA Patent List (Synthetic Organic Chemical Manufacturers Assoc., New York 17, N.Y.)

Chemical Specialties

Aerosol Age (Aerosol Publications, Inc., Caldwell, Inc., Caldwell, N.J.)

Drug and Cosmetics Industry (Drug Markets Inc., New York 1, N.Y.)

Soap and Chemical Specialties (MacNair-Dorland Co., Inc., New York 1, N.Y.)

Coatings

Abstract Review (National Paint, Varnish and Lacquer Assoc., Inc., Washington 5, D.C.)

Dairy Products

Dairy Industries (Dairy Industries, Ltd., London EC4, Eng.)

Designs

Design (Penton Publishing Co., Cleveland 13, O.)

Design News (Rogers Publishing Co., Inc., Englewood, Colo.)

Electrical

British Communications and Electronics (Heywood & Co., Ltd., London WC2, Eng.)

Electrical Communication (International Telephone and Telegraph Corp., New York 22, N.Y.)

Electrical Review (Iliffe Electrical Publications, Ltd., London SE1, Eng.)

Engineering

Engineering and Mining Journal (McGraw-Hill Publishing Co., Inc., New York 36, N.Y.)

General Motors Engineering Journal (General Motors Technical Center, Warren, Mich.)

Gas

Gas Abstracts. (Institute of Gas Technology, Chicago 16, Ill.)

Instruments

Instrument Practice (United Trade Press, Ltd., London EC4, Eng.)

Leather

Journal of the American Leather Chemists Assoc. (c/o University of Cincinnati, Cincinnati 21, O.)

Mechanical Handling

Mechanical Handling (Iliffe Industrial Publishers, Ltd., London SE1, Eng.)

Metals

The British Foundryman (The Institute of British Foundrymen, London SW1, Eng.)

Foundry (Penton Publishing Co., Cleveland 13, O.)

Iron Age (Chilton Co., Philadelphia 39, Pa.)

Metal Finishing (Metals and Plastics Publications, Inc., Westwood, N.J.)

Metalworking Production (McGraw-Hill Publishing Co., Ltd., London EC4, Eng.)

Stahl und Eisen (Verlag Stahleisen m.b.H., Düsseldorf, Ger.)

Technical Bulletin (Engelhard Industries, Newark 5, N.J.)

Miscellaneous

English Abstracts of Selected Articles From Soviet Bloc and Mainland China Technical Journals (Office of Technical Services, Department of Commerce, Washington 25, D.C.) Discontinued.

Science News Letter (Science Service, Inc., Washington 6, D.C.)

Nucleonics

Nuclear Abstracts (Office of Technical Services, Department of Commerce, Washington 25, D.C.)

Optics

Applied Optics (Optical Society of America, Inc., Washington 6, D.C.)

Packaging

Food Engineering (Chilton Co., Philadelphia 39, Pa.)

Modern Packaging (Modern Packaging Corp., New York 21, N.Y.)

Packaging Abstracts (Printing, Packaging and Allied Trades Research Assoc., Slurry, Eng.)

Paper

Abstract Bulletin (The Institute of Paper Chemistry, Appleton, Wis.)

Bibliography of Paper Making and United States Patents (Technical Association of the Pulp and Paper Industry, New York 17, N.Y.)

Petroleum

Bulletin of the American Association of Petroleum Geologists (Tulsa 1, Okla.)

Petroleum Management (The Petroleum Engineer Publishing Co., Dallas 2, Texas)

Photography

Ansco Abstracts (Ansco Division of General Aniline & Film Corp., Binghamton, N.Y.)

Photographic Abstracts (The Royal Photographic Society of Great Britain, London SW7, Eng.)

Plastics

Acrylo News (American Cyanamid Co., Wayne, N.J.)

Kunststoffe (Carl Hanser Zeitschriftenverlag G.m.b.H., Munich, Ger.)

Modern Plastics (Breskin Publications, Inc., New York 21, N.Y.)

Plastics Abstracts (Plastics Investigations, Welwyn, Hertfordshire, Eng.)

Plastics Technology (Plastics Technology Publishing Corp., New York 17, N.Y.)

Plastics World (Cleworth Publishing Co., Inc., Cos Cob, Conn.)

Polymer Reports (Institute of Polymer Industry, Inc., Tokyo, Japan)

Rubber

Bibliography of Rubber Literature (Division of Rubber Chemistry, American Chemical Society, Washington 6, D.C.)

Rubber Age (Palmerton Publishing Co., Inc., New York 1, N.Y.)

Rubber World (Bill Brothers Publishing Corp., New York 17, N.Y.)

Solar Energy

Solar Energy (Association for Applied Solar Energy, Phoenix, Ariz.)

Welding

Welding Journal (American Welding Society, New York 17, N.Y.)

Wood Products

Wood and Wood Products (Vance Publishing Corp., Chicago 3, Ill.)

Watch Services on Patents Issued

In order to keep up to date on new patents on specific items or in selected fields, many have found it advantageous to use the services of organizations established for the purpose. They report periodically on new United States and/or foreign patents as desired by the client with regard to inventions or fields of invention to be included, countries to be covered, and extensiveness of report. The extent may vary from only a list of titles and inventors or brief abstracts to an assembly of copies of the patents. A few examples of available services are given below.

TABLE 5. WATCH SERVICES.

Invention Inc. (Washington 4, D.C.). Reports weekly on United States, British, and Canadian patents of interest in specific fields.

Hiroshi Kataoka (Kyoto, Japan). Reports data on Japanese patents in specified fields and provides translations on request.

TD Nels (Berlin SW61, Ger.). Reports weekly on German applications and patents.

Patent Searching Service (Washington 5, D.C.). Covers United States patents.

Polyresearch Service (The Hague, Netherlands). Provides abstracts on designated subjects from Australian, Canadian, French, German, Mexican,

Dutch, South African, and United States patents and will include other countries if requested.

Research Intelligence Group (Philadelphia 2, Pa.). General topics.

Rotha Fullford Leopold and Associates (Melbourne, Australia). Digests of Japanese patents. Will translate, if requested.

United States Patent Office. Will supply patents in specified subclasses as issued and charge against a deposit account.

Patent Searching Procedures

Patent searching may cover a wide range in detail required but it is always painstaking and relatively slow, if it is to be effective. The following paragraphs suggest search procedures adjusted to the type of information required.

Patents on New Materials, Processes or Uses. Location of such patents usually involves a review of current official patent journals, technical abstracts and indexes (Table 3—Section A). If the subjects are not adequately covered by abstracts or indexes, the patent departments of appropriate periodicals can sometimes be of considerable help, although a search of periodicals can be time-consuming, as the patents are usually not indexed (Table 4). Reviews of official patent journals, on the other hand, are facilitated if pertinent classification numbers are known.

Patents Issued to a Specific Inventor or Assignee. A check of the name indexes of official patent journals and technical abstract periodicals may be all that is required in many cases. Foreign patents may, on occasion, give some trouble as they are frequently indexed only by the name of the assignee.

Patents Available for License or Sale. Such patents are neither listed nor indexed thoroughly. Most searching is apparently done through correspondence with patent owners. For a fee, the United States Patent Office will list a patent and publish the listing in the Official Gazette under the heading "Register of Patents Available for Licensing or Sale." The listing will also appear in the Decision Leaflet of the Official Gazette, which is sold separately. Patents so listed undoubtedly represent but a small fraction of those that might be made available. At intervals, lists of Government-owned inventions available for licensing and classified according to their industrial use are published through the United States Department of Commerce.

Foreign patents are frequently advertised as being available for licensing, in lieu of actual working of the patent, and may appear at times only in obscure publications. When there is real interest in obtaining license under foreign patents, inquiries to the proper companies or possibly through a reputable patent agent in the country in question are in order.

State of the Art Survey. Searches of this type can be very brief. They may be in abstract form or of varying degrees of complexity up to exhaustive reports giving full details together with a compilation of copies of all patents. In many cases, foreign patents may be as important as domestic ones, particularly if technical information is of major interest.

For many of these searches it is sufficient to review recent issues of the Official Gazette and other official patent journals, abstract publications, and indexes dealing with the subject. (Tables 2 and 3.)

If wider coverage is needed, the patent department of periodicals specializing in the particular field is reviewed for patents of interest. Lists of patents issued to inventors or corporations known to be active in that field may be checked for additional patents. Another fruitful source of information is the list of patents cited as references on patents already found to be of interest (if the latter were issued since February 4, 1947).

If the search is intended, for example, to provide a complete survey of applications of a particular type of synthetic resin, a comprehensive search of domestic patents and a search of foreign patents as extensive as possible with the help of official patent journals, abstract publications, and indexes is usually indicated. The American Chemical Society has published a compilation of articles which give the experiences of others in this type of patent search.[6]

Procedures for comprehensive searching are described in the next section.

Comprehensive Search of United States Patents. A search of this type generally starts with a selection of such classes and subclasses as may have a bearing on the subject of the search. Since United States patents are divided at this time among about 300 classes and over 50,000 subclasses, to which are added a separate list of 93 classes of design patents, a fully comprehensive search must be carefully planned. Full use of the classification information requires exercise of imagination and judgment. There are several procedures that may be used outside of Washington.

A request is filed with the Patent Office for a "Field of Search," to learn the pertinent classes and subclasses. It is essential that the request describe as fully as possible the nature of the invention or features of the subject matter to be searched. It may include such details as construction, mode of operation, process steps, intended uses, chemical nature, or other items as dictated by the subject matter and, in cases of design patents, type of ornamentation. Requests that are too general lead to unduly large numbers of subclasses and patents to be studied. On the other hand, a request that is too limited can exclude subclasses that properly belong on the list. It is well to check the list of subclasses supplied in the Field of Search against the Manual of Classification for possible omissions.

As an alternative to the foregoing, classes and subclasses are selected from the Patent Office Manual of Classification in the library. This selection requires imagination and preferably also an understanding of Patent Office indexing methods, including cross-referencing.

A less precise method, that it is sometimes expedient to use, involves the inspection of the annual volumes of the Index of Patents for patents issued to individuals or corporations known to be active in the field of interest and the scanning of recent copies of the Official Gazette, abstracts, books, patent notices on patented articles, and patent sections of periodicals for numbers of patents relating to the desired subject. The classification of these patents is determined by reference to the Index of Patents, the Official Gazette, and copies of the patents. The patents listed as references on patents and found to be of interest (if the patents were issued since February 4, 1947) are checked for their subclass numbers. The list of subclasses so found generally contains the more important ones, but it is not safe to depend upon them entirely; the Manual of Classification should be reviewed for other possibly relevant subclasses. Here again imagination is needed. There is a possibility of error, since a patent may have been reclassified after issuance. If there is doubt, the classification of a patent may be checked by writing to the Patent Office.

After a selection has been made of the subclasses to be searched, lists of *numbers* of all patents in each of those subclasses are purchased from the Patent Office. Orders for such lists specify both "original" and "cross-reference" lists. If desired, patent numbers for each subclass may be copied from lists on microfilm reels available in some libraries. The reels cover all patents, including design classifications, issued before September 23, 1959. Lists of patents obtained by either method are brought up to date by reference to the subclass lists in individual issues of the Official Gazette for the intervening period. Subclass lists issued in 1955 and later years are obtainable from the annual volumes of the Index of Patents and the latest issues of the Official Gazette. Here, again, is a chance for error if the classification has been changed since issuance of the patent.

Patents listed under the various subclass headings are next checked for applicability to the subject in hand. Preferably, this is done by reference to patents in the files of depository libraries or elsewhere. A preliminary screening is sometimes made through use of the Official Gazette but, if there is the slightest question about the information found there, the complete patent should be studied. When The National Catalog of Patents becomes available, it may serve better than the Official Gazette for preliminary screening, but the caution mentioned above in connection with use of the Official Gazette will still apply.

The study of important patents frequently raises questions as to the relationship between a patent and the prior art, reasons for apparent limitations of the claims, arguments used to support the claims, or other details. Such information is obtainable only from the Patent Office file of the patent, which contains specifications, drawings, and all papers relating to the case. Photocopies of the file may be purchased from the Patent Office.

Foreign Patents Search. For a full knowledge of prior art or of patent activities, foreign patents are also to be considered. They are not only important sources of technical information but in frequent instances are also related to domestic patent activities. In many cases, foreign patent applications are filed by domestic inventors subsequent to filing in the United States. The resulting foreign patents may be important in that (a) they may be published or at least open to inspection (particularly in Australia, Belgium, France and South Africa) before the United States patent appears, thus forewarning of patents being processed here; (b) they may disclose information that does not appear in the United States patent; or (c) a United States patent may never appear because of rejection or interference. Usually, it is necessary to search the patents of only a limited number of countries, such as those that publish early and those of particular interest from an industrial viewpoint, e.g., Germany, Great Britain, Italy, Japan, and U.S.S.R.

Classification of foreign patents differs from that of domestic patents. The outline of the system in use in a country is usually obtainable from the official patent journal of that country. The International Classification, used by a number of countries, has been described in the French and Belgian patent journals.[9, 10] The United States Patent Office may be able to supply information in some cases. Classification systems have been revised at times in the past in some of the countries and may cause difficulty if subclass numbers are used in searching.

In most countries, searching may be done by classification or by name of inventor or assignee. Classification and indexing are in general broader and less definite than United States practice. New patents may be followed by a review of the official patent journals of the countries selected and/or of patent translations and abstracts issued by patent information services. Searching of the older foreign patents involves the use of the sources indicated above for domestic patents, but there is less effective use of classification lists and more dependence on indexes, abstracts, and citations in journals, articles, and books.

Several foreign countries issue Patents of Addition or Improvement Patents, which add new material to the original patent. When such patents are located, the original is studied and a check is made for other related supplementary patnets, if the subject appears to be at all important.

When patents are filed in several countries by an inventor, disclosures thereof may appear at intervals over a period of years, because of variations in processing practices. Disclosures may be tied together and to the domestic patent in most cases by use of the convention date, which is used by all but a few countries. Kohnke and Lewenz have described an effective system for associating patents which they base on that date.[11] Some patent journals, such as the Belgian and Swiss give the name of the United States inventor as well as that of the assignee. Others, such as the French journal, are helpful in that they also include the serial number of applications originating in the United States.

References

1. Von Wimmersperg, Heinrich, 4 JPOS 172, 1960.
2. Reid, E. Emmet, "Invitation to Chemical Research," Franklin Publishing Co., 1961.
3. Von Hohenhoff, Elsa, 17 JPOS 808-825, 1935.
4. Von Hohenhoff, Elsa, 17 JPOS 971-992, 1935 and 18 JPOS 49-67, 139-150, 1936.
5. Worischek, Arthur, "Searching Foreign Patents," introduction to "Manual of Foreign Patents" by B. Severance, Patent Office Society, Washington, D.C., 1935.
6. Gould, Robert F., ed., "Searching the Chemical Literature," Washington, D.C., American Chemical Society, 1961.
7. "Derwent Patents Manual," London WC1, England, Derwent Information Service, 1962.
8. "Derwent Patent Abstracts," ibid.
9. "Bulletin Officiel de la Propriété Industrielle," number 3694 of 17 February 1955, Paris, France, Institut National de la Propriété Industrielle.
10. "Recueil des Brevets d'Invention," supplement to the first issue of 1953, Brussels, Belgium, Ministere des Affaires Economiques et de l'Energie.
11. Kohnke, E. L., and Lewenz, G. F., "Detecting Corresponding Patents from Different Countries," J. Chem. Doc. 1, 41-3, 1961.
12. Miller, A. L., "The Patent: Chemical Literature," 44 JPOS 133-141, 1962.

Cross-references: *Advance Information from Foreign Filings, Anticipation, Foreign Patents, Searching in Washington.*

SECRET INFORMATION—PROCEDURE IN ACCEPTING AND PROTECTION IN ITS USE

George S. Hastings

Manufacturing companies often receive unsolicited letters from the general public describing some improvement or new ideas for the company's products. Frequently, the letter will express the wish that the disclosure be held in confidence. Sometimes there is a request for compensation.

Once such a letter has been received, the company is faced with a problem which can be troublesome if it ever happens to use the unsolicited idea. Moreover, when the number of unsolicited ideas runs into the hundreds, there is a chance that whatever the company may do in the way of independently improving its product will come close to one of these disclosures, resulting in a possible law suit.

In the discussion to follow, attention will be given first to the problems of dealing with outside inventors. Possible solutions will then be explored with emphasis on methods that can be used effectively to minimize liability.

The following review of a court action (*Ackermans* v. *General Motors Corp.*, 96 USPQ 281, CA 4 1953) illustrates the pitfalls of such situations. Here, an independent inventor had submitted to a number of automobile manufacturers an improvement in automatic tops for convertibles. In this invention, a rubber pad operated by a folding pillar automatically closed the top at the rear side portion as a result of the automatic operation of the top.

The inventor had filed a patent application on this device. While the application was pending, he approached one of the large manufacturers and disclosed his invention with a view to selling or licensing its use. An official of the company expressed interest and asked the inventor to leave a copy of the application for patent. Shortly thereafter the inventor was advised by the company that the idea was not feasible. Some time later the manufacturer put out cars with a somewhat different form of device than that disclosed by the inventor but embodying the same principle of cushion closure operated by a folding pillar.

After the inventor's patent was issued, he sued the manufacturer for damages for infringement and for violation of confidential disclosure. The Circuit Court of Appeals, reversing the District Court, held the patent infringed. In addition, the court held that the manufacturer should pay damages for breach of confidential disclosure and for use of the invention for the period after disclosure and before issuance of the patent.

But the most significant feature of this case is that this decision was made in favor of the inventor under the following circumstances:

(1) The automobile manufacturer introduced oral testimony of its employees that it had the invention before disclosure. The court held that the burden of proof of earlier invention was heavily on the manufacturer and oral testimony of interested witnesses was insufficient.

(2) There was at no time any express request by the inventor, or any express agreement by the manufacturer, to hold the disclosure in confidence. The same invention also had been submitted to other automobile companies prior to the defendant. However, confidential agreement was implied from the circumstance of disclosure plus the inventor's evident desire for compensation.

(3) A patent application had been filed fully disclosing the invention, and what the manufacturer looked at was a copy of the patent application.

(4) There was clearly novelty of a definite, concrete type present.

(5) The original disclosure to the manufacturer was unsolicited but later the manufacturer asked the inventor to leave a copy of his patent application. The court referred to this as "inviting" a disclosure.

Whether other circuit courts will follow the decision in this case is not yet known.

The Problem

From the foregoing circumstances, it is clear that a company receiving outside ideas is faced with a hazardous problem. For its own protection, it must do something positive at the outset to negate the implication that it received the disclosure in confidence and should compensate the submitter, if it may later make use of the disclosure. For this reason, a number of corporations, if they can do so, refuse to receive disclosures from unknowns. They argue that they never get ideas worth the risk and that the poor public relations from refusing to receive outside ideas is less than would result from the necessary turning down of 99 per cent of the ideas received.

Even refusal to deal with outsiders does not completely solve the problem of the unsolicited letter setting forth in detail an invention for which the inventor desires compensation. It has been remarked that the only way a company can fully protect itself is by not reading its mail.

It is true that much of the risk can be avoided by simply refusing to receive outside submissions and by immediately returning them with a letter explaining that it is against the company's policy to receive them. For complete effectiveness, however, the return should be coupled with some systematic procedure by which the disclosures are segregated from any of the company's technical personnel.

But is that a good solution for either the company or the inventor or, for that matter, the country as a whole? A great deal, of course, will depend on the nature of the business of the company. For example, if the company confines itself to making piezoelectric crystals for stabilizing radio frequency, it is very unlikely that it is going to get anything from the public.

However, if a concern is making bicycles or bowling equipment with which millions of people are familiar, and it does not work out a way of receiving ideas from the public, it is going to cut itself off from a valuable source of corporate stimulation. It is also going to miss something worthwhile once in every 200 to 500 ideas submitted. A corporation which wishes to grow, which wants to insulate itself from the ups and downs resulting from being dependent on a few narrow lines of business, and which desires the higher margin of profit which comes from putting out something new, will want this one in 500 inventions, if it can obtain it with moderate risk.

An important point to be kept in mind is that it is quite possible to have large and well-stuffed engineering and research departments and still miss some pretty obvious and valuable product ideas. It is not too much of an exaggeration to state that the last company to develop a telephone would be the telegraph company and the last company to devise a new kind of transportation like the airplane would be a railroad transportation company. Important new weapons have almost always been the inventions of civilians like Simon Lake or the Wright brothers.

As a more graphic example of this point, the company that gave the public an Automatic Pinspotter was not the company that supplied eighty or ninety per cent of the bowling equipment in the country. It was instead a company whose main proprietary products were tobacco and bakery machinery. Moreover, that company got its start in this development from an outside inventor-designer in a paper-machinery factory who got disgusted with the lack of pin boys.

Each year from 1936 to the present, with remarkable consistency, 35 to 40 per cent of all U.S. patents are issued to individual inventors.

If the time comes when there is no place for the individual inventor because companies are unwilling to take the risks of considering their inventions, our economy as a whole, as well as individual corporations, will have lost a valuable source of stimulation. Also the U.S. patent system will have failed in a major respect and will become more vulnerable to political attack.

Thus, it is apparent that at least a tolerable solution to this problem of receiving outside ideas is important, and the solution may be promoted by analyzing the somewhat conflicting law on the subject.

Basic Concepts

Under the common law, the creator of an idea owns that idea. He can practice it in secret and will be protected in maintaining that secrecy. When and if he discloses his idea, however, the creator's rights depend upon the method of disclosure and the precautions taken in disclosing it. If he copyrights it, he retains the protection resulting from such registration. If he patents it, he retains the protection allowed by his claims. The broad rule is that there is no residual property interest protectible by law in an idea or disclosure which is communicated to third parties *without reservation*. To hold the recipient of his disclosure, the inventor must show (1) something more than the mere disclosure of his mental labors and (2) use for profit by the one to whom disclosure is made.

As Justice Brandeis stated in a Supreme Court decision:

"...[To] appropriate and use for profit, knowledge and ideas produced by other men, without making compensation or even acknowledgment, may be inconsistent with the finer sense of propriety; but with the exceptions (under copyright and patents statutes) or in cases of special relationship 'where the suit is based upon breach of contract or of trust or upon unfair competition' the law has heretofore sanctioned the practice." *International News Service* v. *Associated Press*, 248 U.S. 215, 1919.

The general rule is not very helpful. The problem lies in the exceptions and the cases of special relationship, depending on the circumstances under which the disclosure was made. There are several grounds for recovery.

Implied Contract. This relationship is the main source of difficulty. It generally includes two elements: (1) an implied agreement to keep confidential if no arrangement is made with the inventor and (2) an agreement to compensate if the idea is used. The second stipulation is generally implied from the agreement to keep confidential on the basis that the company should not be allowed to profit from its breach of confidence. The troublesome thing is that often there is no request for confidential treatment and no thought on the part of the company that it is agreeing to such a request. But the jury implies this from the circumstances, with consequences which the company never contemplated.

Unjust Enrichment. This premise generally requires willful and knowing appropriation of the idea or invention. Also the idea or invention ordinarily has to be novel. Although not relied on as much as the implied-contract theory, the unjust-enrichment argument is often used to buttress the implied contract basis for recovery.

Express Contract. This situation arises when the inventor asks for compensation and for the disclosure to be held confidential, and the company expressly assents. It is not of immediate concern. However, assuming the idea is unpatentable, it is easy for a company expressly to agree to hold confidential and, if the idea is later published or put into public use, find itself the only one in the world that cannot use the idea without paying for it.

This is the exact situation that developed in the *Listerine* case. Warner-Lambert and its predecessors developed the demand for the product and paid over 22 million dollars for the secret formula, over a period of some 75 years. During that period the formula was published in the U.S. Pharmacopeia, National Formulary, Journal of the American Medical Association and elsewhere in conformance with government agency requirements. Warner-Lambert eventually stopped payments, then at a rate in excess of 1.5 million dollars a year, on the ground that the formula was no longer a secret. In the decision on the suit that followed, the court noted that the original agreement and modifications thereof contained no provision to the effect that payments were to stop if the secret became available for free use by others. Although the disclosure obviously was no fault of Warner-Lambert, the court required continuance of the payments. *Warner-Lambert Pharmaceutical Co., Inc.* v. *John J. Reynolds, Inc.*, 123 USPQ 431, DC SNY 1959; aff. 126 USPQ 3, CA 2 1960.

Patent Protection. This point is of secondary importance to our discussion. If the patent is valid and infringed, a license may be negotiated. Anything not claimed is free to the public.

Degree of Risk

From this review of the different courses of legal action possible, it is apparent that several factors can influence the degree of risk to any company accepting outside ideas. There are certain "tests," based on previous court decisions, that can be used as a guide in determining the kinds of ideas or inventions which, when disclosed to a company, will not subject it to a successful suit for compensation.

(1) The disclosure must be concrete and specific and not expressed in general undeveloped form. Vagueness and indefiniteness are ordinarily fatal in the absence of an express contract.

(2) The chances of success in a court action are greatly decreased by lack of novelty in the disclosure. Certain cases, particularly in Illinois, state that novelty is not necessary where the idea is new to the party receiving it, and the circumstances are sufficient to show an implied or express agreement to keep the disclosure confidential, and thus not to use it without compensation. *Jones* v. *Ulrich*, 87 USPQ 331, CA 3 1950. However, the weight of decisions in other circuits is to require novelty in the absence of an express contract to hold confidential and to compensate. *Stevens* v. *Continental Can Co., Inc.*, 135 USPQ 111, 113, CA 6 1962. But such novelty does not have to be patentable novelty. Thus, it is quite possible for the claims of the patent to be held invalid, with the inventor re-

covering prior to patenting on the basis of use for profit of the submitted ideas disclosed in confidence, as occurred in a case originating in Indiana. *Booth* v. *Stutz Motor Car Co.*, 13 USPQ 12, CA 7 1932. In this case it was held that there should be recovery for that which was novel though not patentable, but no recovery for using those ideas disclosed in confidence which were not novel.

(3) If the idea becomes public, as by public use or publication, through the act of the inventor prior to use by the company, the company has been held not liable thereafter even though it received the idea in confidence before public use. *Northrup* v. *Reish*, 96 USPQ 78, CA 7 1953.

(4) If the company already has its own independently developed idea and uses that, it is not obligated to compensate an outside inventor even though the inventor gave the same idea in concrete form to the company prior to use of the idea. *Franke et al.* v. *Wilschek*, 292 F.2d 493, 99 USPQ 431, CA 2 1953. However, the burden of proof that the company had the idea first is heavily on the company.

It has also been held that if, before a disclosure is made, a corporation is careful to require the inventor to sign a document which provides in effect that the corporation is under no obligation to him respecting any use or disclosure, the corporation is protected. *Hisel* v. *Chrysler Corp.*, 94 F. Supp. 996, DC WM. 1951. The catch, however, is that quite often the corporation does not have a chance to get a signature. But this procedure is very worthwhile wherever there is an opportunity, as when the inventor states, "I have an idea," and the corporation jumps in and says: "Stop right there. Here's our waiver Form 356."

There is also authority for a similar procedure in the situation where the disclosure is received with sufficient concreteness, as through the mail, without opportunity to get a signature to a waiver agreement. If the corporation gives or forwards a statement of the conditions under which it can or will receive disclosures and states that it does not accept any disclosures on a confidential basis, or with any agreement to compensate, but requires that the inventor rely on his rights under the patent laws, then there is a serious impairment to the creation of a confidential relationship in such case. In a decision under such circumstances, the court rejected an attempt to imply an agreement to hold confidential. *Telechron, Inc. et al.* v. *Parissi*, 101 USPQ 144, DC NNY 1954. Furthermore, it stated that the essentials of breach of faith and use of confidential disclosure consist of (a) disclosure of something definite; (b) an understanding, express or (more often) implied, that there was to be compensation; and (c) that the invention was to be kept secret. This N.Y. case also required as essential (d) that the invention or disclosure be novel over what is known to the public, differing in this respect from holdings in the Illinois courts. It will be seen that anything which negatives the implication that a disclosure is intended to be confidential greatly decreases liability.

The Solution

A number of companies have considered this problem carefully and have decided that with suitable precautions it is worth the risk to receive outside ideas. They have set up a procedure somewhat as follows:

(1) Personnel likely to receive such disclosures are instructed to send them immediately to one nontechnical administrative person, often in the company patent department, who has the responsibility for handling such disclosures. Any letters that are recognized in the mail as being such disclosures are immediately forwarded to this administrative person. So far as possible, such disclosures are systematically kept segregated from technical or engineering personnel until the "ground rules" have been settled with the outside inventor.

(2) A waiver form is sent to the inventor and he is asked to sign and return it. An example of such a form is illustrated in Fig. 1. This sheet sets forth the basis on which the company will receive such disclosures. There are several essential conditions. The first negates a confidential relationship. Second, no commitment is made

While this Company is anxious to take every opportunity to improve its products and add profitable ones to its line, it has found certain precautions necessary in accepting disclosures. For example, its employees have varied and numerous ideas of their own, worked out in the past, or now being worked out, for the purpose of improving or adding to its many lines of products. Some of these ideas might, by chance, be similar to your own. Hence, in order to avoid any possible future confusion between your ideas and its own, and to prevent any misunderstanding as to what the rights and obligations of the inventor and the Company are, the Company's policies as to considering inventions are set forth below:

1. The Company cannot agree to hold your disclosure in confidence for the reason, among others, that it must disclose the invention to various employees and sometimes even to those outside of its employ, to determine its value to it, - and because agreements to hold in confidence have been found to entail other obligations not intended by either the submitter or the Company. It is understood therefore that no confidential relationship or agreement to compensate is entered into by reason of the Company considering your disclosure.

2. A full written disclosure, preferably the patent application drawing and specification, if there are such, or if not, a sketch or drawing (which need not be anything but a rough one provided it illustrates the invention so one skilled in the art can understand it), must be furnished to the Company, as the Company will otherwise have no way of telling whether or not it will be interested in your ideas.

3. The Company cannot ordinarily return any descriptions, drawings, or other disclosures sent to it, since otherwise it has no record of what was disclosed to it, though it may sometimes do so if allowed to make a copy. Therefore, you should keep a duplicate of any disclosure sent to the Company.

4. The Company is not under any obligation to reveal to you information of its own in the general or specific field to which the disclosure relates.

5. The Company wishes you to be satisfied that your interests are fully safeguarded as, for instance, by having filed an application for U.S. patent. If no such application has been filed, you should have the copy of your drawings which you retain signed, dated and witnessed.

6. Any disclosure to this Company is made on the understanding that the Company assumes no obligation to do more than consider the disclosure so far as in its judgment the disclosure merits and to indicate whether or not it is interested and that you rely only on your rights under the patent laws.

7. The Company receives no rights hereby, or as a result of considering this disclosure, under any patent rights you now have or may acquire to the subject matter of the disclosure.

8. The foregoing applies to any additional or supplemental disclosures relating to the same subject matter.

TO AMERICAN MACHINE & FOUNDRY COMPANY:

I am submitting herewith a disclosure of _____

_____

on the conditions set forth above.

SIGNED this _____ day of _____ , 19___.

_____ (L.S.)

Fig. 1. Disclosure submission conditions to those who submit disclosures to American Machine & Foundry Company.

that the idea or material will be kept secret. Third, the company does not agree to pay any compensation, but it gets no rights under any claims of a patent which may issue to the inventor. Fourth, the inventor agrees that his sole remedy is to enforce his rights under the patent. One company also adds that if it does use the idea submitted and the idea is unpatented, the top price that can be demanded and that will be paid by the company is $1000. As a matter of good public relations, the reasons for these conditions of submission are then set forth.

It may happen that a waiver form is signed, the disclosure received, and years later some of the company's engineers, completely independent of the disclosure, invent the same thing and incorporate it in the company's regular production. This presents a substantial hazard because it is difficult to convince a court or jury that one part of a company does not know what has happened in the past in another part of the company. Yet, it is a very natural occurrence in a large company, since it is difficult for any given person to know all that has happened in the past. While there is no sure-fire solution to this situation, possible causes can be greatly minimized if a system is set up by which outside disclosures are included in the search procedure when a new product is being contemplated. If it is found that an outside disclosure has been made on the same novel subject matter, negotiations can be entered into with the outsider prior to the commitment of the company and attendant sales publicity which would put the company in a poor negotiating position.

One might ask why the waiver doesn't solve the whole problem. Even if the inventor has agreed that the disclosure is submitted without any confidential agreement involved, if he has filed a patent application, the company still has a patent problem if it uses the invention. This, however, is far better than being faced with the implied agreement theory since the patent is definite, with claims which specifically define the invention, its validity can be determined and arms length negotiations entered into for a license.

Certain practical precautions should be observed in dealing with outside inventors. Arrange within the corporation to have outside disclosures channeled immediately to the person referred to below. If the discloser comes in person, avoid having him sit down and talk with company engineers working in the same field. This will happen unless advance precautions are taken. Have him talk first with some administrative nontechnical person who will give him the Waiver Sheet, and ask him to communicate his ideas in writing to the central patent person designated to receive it. If an immediate conference is to take place, arrange to hand him the disclosure agreement form and have it signed before disclosure.

Since ordinarily 200 to 500 of these submissions will be received for every acceptable and usable idea, a form letter will have to be worked out for rejection of impractical inventions. When submissions describing a concrete invention or ideas are rejected, retain copies of the disclosure so there can be no dispute as to what was disclosed. Because a public relations problem is involved, the rejection letter should be designed accordingly.

Wherever possible, get the waiver sheet to the inventor *before* he submits his idea in detail. Quite often the inventor will write in asking about the possibilities of an idea for accomplishing such and such result. Such disclosures are a pleasure to deal with. If he is asked to state simply what result or advantage he expects to get from his disclosure and what field of industry it relates to, the decision can quite often be made as to whether the corporation is interested without ever receiving a concrete disclosure. In any event, the company can get its waiver sheet in first.

One proposed solution is to have a completely independent consulting firm receive, process and screen disclosures, carry on any correspondence, and turn over the good ideas to the client corporation. There is a consulting firm which offered to do this but, of course, at a charge for the service.

Sometimes a corporation has submitted to it in considerable detail an idea which it is already working on and planning to use at some future date. The question then arises as to whether, in turning down the submitted material, the company should disclose the fact that it already has the same material developed. Perhaps as good a way as any of handling such situations is to include in the waiver sheet a paragraph stating that the company is under no obligation to reveal any information regarding its activities in the field to which the submitted idea pertains, even though the company has a similar idea under development.

Precautions with Respect to Company Employees

The fact that the inventor is a company employee under employment contract does not necessarily mean that the company is free from the problem of the outside inventor. If the invention is one which was made before the employment contract came into effect or is one of the class of inventions which was excepted from operation of the contract, the employment relationship has no bearing. In this case, the employee would be in the same situation as an outside inventor. Some companies take care of this by requiring, at the time the employee signs the usual patent employment agreement, a statement of all inventions made prior to coming with the company.

Another situation arises when a company hires from a competitor an employee who has had access to confidential and proprietary information of his former employer. This is a situation which requires considerable care to avoid being accused by the former employer of taking advantage of the employer's confidential information. One solution is to put the employee on projects other than those he may have worked on during his previous employment. At the very least, the employee should be clearly informed in writing that he should not utilize the secret and confidential information of his former employer. It would likewise be very imprudent to put him on work of exactly the same competitive type. A prime example is *Carter Products* v. *Palmolive Peet*, 104 USPQ 332, DC Md 1955; aff. 108 USPQ 383, CA 4 1956. In this case, a new

employee was assigned to the making of a pressure-foamed shaving cream when he had been working on that same project with his previous employer. The Court held that the new employer was under an obligation to take positive steps to avoid the transmission of confidential information.

Should a Company Solicit Ideas from Outside Inventors?

Corporate consensus on this question is emphatically no! One reason for this viewpoint is that solicitation increases the legal risk. Another reason is that any sort of solicitation tends greatly to increase the number of ideas to be screened without a corresponding increase in the number of useful ideas received.

Conclusion

If a company manufactures products about which the public is somewhat knowledgeable, it seems a mistake for it to cut itself off from the public's ideas relating to these products. Not only is it poor public relations, but sooner or later the company is going to miss an idea or invention that is worth all the risk and much more. The fact is that even the best of corporations may become a little ingrown on their proprietary lines of products, and anything that shakes up their routine thinking is valuable and well worth what it may cost in a compensation for outside inventions. *According to the experience of a number of corporate patent departments, not one of their companies has lost more on suits based on outside disclosures than the cost of operation of their research departments for a few weeks.*

In the author's opinion, not only is it good public relations to receive outside disclosures, but provided the precautions outlined above are taken, it is also good business.

A part of the information given herein is taken from the author's article in the August 22, 1957 issue of *Machine Design*.

For an independent study of this problem, reference is made to the Survey by the

National Industrial Conference Board, of the experience of industrial firms in receiving information from outside inventors, as reported by Carl G. Baumes and G. Clark Thompson, Business Management Record, p. 12, 15-18 (August, 1963).

Cross-references: *Secret Information and Employees' Responsibilities.*

SHOP RIGHT

Albert C. Nolte, Jr.

In the relationship between an employee-inventor and employer, there are two extreme situations. In one, the employee-inventor retains full ownership of his patented invention; in the other, the employer receives a full conveyance of the property in the employee's patented invention. Shop right falls between these extreme circumstances, in an area where equity recognizes some right of the employer to the invention, but not to such extent as to extinguish the inventor's right completely.

In a 1960 decision, the limits of the shop right doctrine have been defined as follows:

"Where an employee (1) during his hours of employment, (2) working with his employer's materials and appliances, (3) conceives and (4) perfects an invention for which he obtains a patent, he must accord his employer a nonexclusive right to practice the invention. United States v. Dubilier Condenser Corp., . . . 289 U.S. 178, 188, 17 USPQ 154, 158." *Banner Metals, Inc.* v. *Lockwood et al.,* 125 USPQ 29, 37.

The Court added: "[The] cost of the wire and other material [of the employer] used in the six wire models were negligible and in no substantial way contributed to the development of the receptacle."

The courts will find a shop right to lie in the employer if his assets were used in the development of the invention, or if the employee by his conduct created in his employer a justifiable reliance thereon and caused his employer to change his position. In the latter case, the employee is estopped to assert his patent rights as against the employer.

Use of Employer's Property

The basic doctrine that a shop right is vested in the employer, if the employee uses the former's property in the development of the invention (cost of patent application being included in this category), has been qualified in several aspects. If (1) no such use of the employer's property is found, *McNamara* v. *Powell,* 41 USPQ 47, N.Y. Supr.Ct. 1939, or (2) the employee-inventor has reimbursed the employer for the cost of the latter's assets used, *Doscher* v. *Phelps Guardant Time Lock Co.,* 153 N.Y. Supp. 710, Supr.Ct. 1915 aff. without opinion 172 App.Div. 954, no shop right accrues in the employer.

Partial Contribution by Employer. If, on the other hand, the employee has done work on his invention outside the scope of the employment, using his own time, tools, materials, at the beginning, and only in later stages of the development has used his employer's property, the employer is nevertheless entitled to shop right, *Wiegand* v. *Dover Mfg. Co.,* 292 F. 255, DC NOhio 1923.

Where the inventor wishes to demonstrate his invention to the employer for the mere purpose of satisfying the employer's curiosity as to the merits of the invention, and the inventor uses the employer's property to build suitable demonstration models or modify existing models to better suit the employer's purpose, no shop right will accrue to the employer. *Small* v. *Heywood-Wakefield Co.,* 28 USPQ 206, DC Mass 1936, aff. 32 USPQ 265, CA 1937, cert. den. 301 U.S. 698, 1937; *Shearer* v. *United States,* 37 USPQ 49, Ct. Cls. 1938, 60 USPQ 414, Ct. Cls. 1944, cert. den. 323 U.S. 676, 1944. The inventor's cooperation and assistance for the purpose of such demonstrations will not raise the inference of circumstances that would estop him later from asserting his patent rights.

The courts, when the employer's property used by the inventor was of very slight value, minimized the employer's contribution to the invention and denied shop rights to the employer. *Champayne* v. *Comr. Int. Rev.,* 26 T.C. 634, 110 USPQ 153, 1956. In this vein, use of $4.20 worth of the employer's material was found not to be enough to vest shop right in the employer. *Banner Metal, Inc.* v. *Lockwood,* 125 USPQ 29, Cal. DC of App. 1960.

Time of Final Development Immaterial. In *Elzwilaw Co.* v. *Knoxville Glove Co.,* 22 F.2d 962, CA 7 1927, the employee conceived of the invention prior to his employment, but developed it during his employment at his employer's expense, and filed a patent application thereon only after his employment had been terminated. During his employment, he conducted a considerable number of unsuccessful experiments at his employer's expense, subsequently left the employment, completed the development of his invention, and later was granted a patent thereon. The court found that, although the final steps which led to the successful invention were not taken until after the employee had left his employer, the employer should nevertheless not lose the benefit of his previous expenditures. The court implied to the inventor the intention to develop his invention for the benefit of his employer.

Estoppels Against Employee-Inventor

In numerous cases, the courts have refused to find estoppel even though the inventor-employee assisted the employer in putting the invention into practice, when the attendant circumstances allowed the inference that such assistance was merely for the purpose of demonstrating the operability or advantages of the invention to the employer. *Shearer* v. *United States,* supra; *Sanbo* v. *Bear Mfg. Co.,* 1 USPQ 45, DC SIll. 1929.

Estoppel *In Pais.* Shop right may vest in the employer on the basis of estoppel *in pais,* for a variety of reasons. In *Wiegand* v. *Dover Mfg. Co.,* supra, the Court found that the employer's operation became so geared to the employee's invention that

"If Wiegand's present contentions are sound, the result would be that he entered the company's employ in 1911 with nothing, and left in June, 1914, the practical owner of its electric sad-iron business...."

Similarly to the principle of shop right based on employer contribution to the invention, the courts have also limited and qualified the applicability of the shop right grant based on estoppel *in pais.* They have recognized, however, that certain safeguards have to be observed to prevent its indiscriminate application. In *Standard Sanitary Mfg. Co.* v. *Arrott,* 135 Fed. 750 CA 3 1905, Judge Gray stated:

"In the absence of expressly proved fraud, there can be no estoppel based on acts or conduct of the party sought to be estopped, where such conduct is as consistent with honest purpose or with an absence of negligence, as with their opposites."

Estoppel should not be found unless the failure of the plaintiff-inventor to file his complaint sooner damaged the defendant-employer or induced him to change his position; mere lapse of time does not by itself create estoppel. *Howe* v. *Howard,* 6 USPQ 255, DC SIll 1930, aff. 61 F.2d 577, 15 USPQ 93, CA 7 1932, cert. den. 289 U.S. 731, 1933.

By Laches. The employee's silence may, under certain conditions, also give rise to estoppel. Thus, if the inventor knows of the employer practicing his invention and does not assert a claim for compensation for such use within reasonable time, and if the employer has reasonably relied upon the employee's apparent acquiescence, the employee is estopped from asserting his rights. *Callahan* v. *Capron Co.,* 280 Fed. 254, DC RI 1922; *Dovel* v. *Sloss-Sheffield Steel & Iron Co.,* 139 F.2d 36, 60 USPQ 86, CA 5 1943.

By Encouragement of Employer to Use. Judge Dickinson, in *Mix* v. *National Envelope Co.,* 244 Fed. 822, DC Pa 1917, has stated another basis for granting shop right to an employer. The fact that the employee invites his employer by words or conduct to engage in its manufacture for use or sale, should be really based on the doctrine of dedication. In this case, the court has also given its thoughts on the underlying equitable considerations by stating that:

"The common sense of justice ... would condemn the action of an employee who first led his employer into making outlays to introduce to customers of the employer and to build up a valuable trade in a before untried invention, and, after the trade has been established, to take away from the employer, not only the right to make use of the invention, but the trade built up by the employer, and many of his old customers along with it."

Chief Justice Taft in *DeForest Radio & Telegraph Company* v. *United States,* 273 U.S. 236, 1927, has based the license on the contractual grounds that

"Any language used by the owner of the patent or any conduct on his part exhibited to another, from which the other may infer properly that the owner consents to his use of the patent in making or using it, or selling it, upon which the other acts, constitutes a license and a defensible action for a tort.... [The] relation between the parties thereafter in respect of any suit brought must be held to be contractual and not based on unlawful invasion of the rights of the owner."

Against Executive-Inventor. If the inventor is in a position, e.g., by being an executive of the employer company, where he could exercise pressure toward a favorable decision regarding the use of his invention, shop right on an estoppel basis will be implied. *Schmidt* v. *Central Foundry Co.,* 218 Fed. 466, DC NNJ 1914, aff. on other grds. 229 Fed. 157, CA 3 1916. The situation is similar if the inventor expressly consents to use of the invention by his employer or consents by conduct, such as supervising the employer's agents in practicing the invention. *Herman* v. *Herman,* 29 Fed. 92, Cir. S.D. N.Y. 1886; *Barber* v. *National Carbon Co.,* 129 Fed. 370, CA 6 1904.

An ample number of cases are available to the effect that a shop right will accrue to the employer in the invention of his executive-employee under the same, or similar circumstances, as in the case of the invention of any other employee. *Marshall* v. *Colgate-Palmolive Peet Co.,* 77 USPQ 69, DC Del 1948, aff. 175 F.2d 215, 81 USPQ 517, CA 3 1949); *Grip Nut Co.* v. *Sharp,* 40 F. Supp. 80 (DC NIll 1944), aff. 150 F.2d 192, CA 7 1945, cert. den. 326 U.S. 742, 1945. In *Dowse* v. *Federal Rubber Co.,* 254 Fed. 308, DC NIll 1918, the corporation president's invention became practically the only business of the corporation. The court found that the inventor, by agreeing to give

his entire time, thought and attention wholly and solely to the business, constructively agreed that he was employed to invent, his main responsibility being to make the business successful, and that, as he was an alter ego of the corporation, his invention belongs to his employer.

A corporation executive, while being in a fiduciary relationship with his employer, is not under duty to disclose his invention to his employer, unless he was hired to invent. *Talbot* v. *Harrison,* 270 N.Y. Supp. 171, Supr.Ct. NY. Cty. 1932; aff. without opinion 240 App.Div. 954, 268 N.Y. Supp. 875. The mere fiduciary relationship is not enough to estop the executive-inventor from asserting his patent rights as against his employer. *Doscher* v. *Phelps Guardant Time Lock Co.,* supra, aff. without opinion 172 App.Div. 957; *Detroit Testing Laboratory* v. *Robison,* 221 Mich. 442, 191 N.W. 218, 1922. Other jurisdictions are also in agreement with this rule. *Sanbo* v. *Bear Manufacturing Co.,* supra; *Banner Metal, Inc.* v. *Lockwood,* supra.

Conditions Defeating Estoppel. In *Ft. Wayne, C. & L. R. Co.* v. *Haberkorn,* 15 Ind. App. 479, 44 N. E. 322 (1896), a master mechanic employee of the railroad company had conceived, developed and patented certain inventions outside the scope of his employment. The employer, upon learning of these inventions, instructed the inventor to install them in the employer's railroad equipment. The court found that the investor's assistance in installing his inventions and the fact that he did not express demands for compensation did not create an estoppel situation since the employer knew that the employee had patents on the inventions. Furthermore, where an act is done or a service is rendered pursuant to a request, the law will imply a promise to pay what it is worth. The employer asked from the employee a valuable privilege to which the employer had no claim and, therefore, no estoppel was created.

Estoppel Against Employer

Where the employer rejects the employee's invention for reasons of impracticality, or the like, and the employee-inventor's further actions are in reliance on such a rejection, no shop right will be implied. A situation in which the employer was indifferent, or manifested a negative attitude when the employee tried to interest him in the invention, was not passed upon by the courts. *Moffett* v. *Fiske*, 51 F.2d 868, CA DistCol 1931, cert. den. 284 U.S. 662, 1931; *Maurice A. Garbell, Inc.* v. *Consolidated Vultee Aircraft Corp.*, 88 USPQ 59, DC SCal 1950, aff. 204 F.2d 946, 98 USPQ 4, CA 9 1953, cert. den. 346 U.S. 873, 1953.

In *Pure Oil Co.* v. *Hyman*, 95 F.2d 22, 36 USPQ 306, CA 7 1938, a former employer of the patentee attempted to assert a shop right against a former employee. The Court emphasized that the chain of events, which compelled it to find laches in the employer, was initiated by its assertion that the employee's patents were of no value.

Shop Right from Non-employees

The mere fact of employment is not enough to grant a shop right to an employer in his employee's invention. *General Time Corp.* v. *Padua Alarm Systems, Inc.*, 199 F.2d 351, 94 USPQ 350, CA 2 1952, cert. den. 345 U.S. 917, 1953.

On the other hand, in *Crom* v. *Cement Gun Co.*, 54 USPQ 129, DC Del 1942 the court stated:

"Under no circumstances can a shop right come into existence unless the inventor was an employee at the time when the invention was made and reduced to practice."

This appears to be a minority opinion, although in accord in New York with *Burden* v. *Burden Iron Co.*, infra, and *Burr* v. *De La Vergne*, 102 N.Y. 415, 7 N.E. 366, 1886. The majority of jurisdictions hold that shop right can accrue from relationships other than that between an employer and his inventor-employee, *Neon Signal Devices, Inc.* v. *Alpha Claude Neon Corp.*, 54 F.2d 793, 12 USPQ 339, DC WPa 1931; in the case of a partnership, *Gate-Way, Inc.* v. *Hillgren*, 81 USPQ 178, DC SCal 1949, aff. 181 F.2d 1010, 86 USPQ 140, CA 9 1950; and in the case of independent contractors, *McKinnon Chain Co.* v. *American Chain*

Co., 259 Fed. 873, DC MPa 1919, aff. on other grounds, 268 Fed. 353, CA 3 1920.

Royalties as Compensation for Shop Right

Although the general rule is that a shop right is gratuitous, an express agreement whereby the employer promises the payment of royalties to his inventor-employee would take effect even though the employer would have had a shop right in the employee's invention had the express agreement not been made. *Standard Sanitary Mfg. Co.* v. *Arrott*, supra; *Toner* v. *Sobelman*, 81 USPQ 304, DC EPa 1949; *Hazen Mfg. Co.* v. *Wareham*, 242 Fed. 642, CA 6 1917; *Dejur-Amsco Corp.* v. *Fogle*, 100 USPQ 304, DC NJ 1954, aff. 233 F.2d 141, 109 USPQ 263, CA 3 1956. An agreement between the employer and the employee for the payment of royalties for the use of the latter's invention can also be implied. *Deane* v. *Hodge*, 35 Minn. 146, 27 N.W. 917, 1886.

When the inventor has executed an assignment, even though the employer was not entitled to more than a shop right, in the absence of clearly provable fraud, the employer is entitled to the assignment. *Bowen* v. *B. F. Goodrich Co.*, 36 F.2d 306, CA 6 1929.

Shop Right for Limited Term

Similarly, an employee has the right to grant a shop right to his employer merely for the term of his employment. *Beecroft & Blackman, Inc.* v. *Rooney*, 268 Fed. 545, DC SNY 1920.

Shop Right Co-extensive with Business of Employer

Inventors have often interposed the defense, in suits for shop rights or assignments, that the employer under the given circumstances would be entitled to a gratuitous shop right license only for the particular machines, etc. that were made by the inventor during the term of his employment. Earlier opinions tended to uphold such defenses. *Barry* v. *Crane Bros.*

Mfg. Co., 22 Fed. 396, Cir. N.D. Ill 1884; *City of Boston* v. *Allen,* 91 Fed. 248, CA 1 1898; *Burden* v. *Burden Iron Co.,* 39 Misc. 559, Sup. Ct. 1903.

The courts have gradually moved away from such stiff interpretations and, as early as 1895, have stated that the implied license is co-extensive with the business requirements of the employer, *Withington-Cooley Mfg. Co.* v. *Kinney,* 68 Fed. 500, CA 6 1895. Accordingly, the employer under a shop right may use the employee's invention to such an extent or, if it is a particular machine or apparatus, he can build as many of them as his business may require. *Wiegand* v. *Dover Mfg. Co.,* supra, In *Tin Decorating Co. of Baltimore* v. *Metal Package Corp.,* 29 F.2d 1006, DC SNY 1928, aff. 37 F.2d 5, CA 2 1930, cert. den. 281 U.S. 759, 1930, the court stated:

"At one time it was thought that, if the invention pertained to a machine, the shop right extended only to the specific machine or machines made during the employment . . . but such authorities have little voice today."

In fact, in *Thompson* v. *The American Tobacco Co.,* 174 F.2d 773, 81 USPQ 323, CA 4 1949, it was held that the employer's rights include the right of reproducing the machine indefinitely.

Employer's Successor's Interest in Shop Right

Since a shop right license is created by operation of law, the employer's successor's shop right has been recognized under certain circumstances. A corporation, which is the entire successor to the previous shop right holder, assuming the assets, liabilities and good will of the predecessor, obtains the previous corporation's shop right.

"The suggestion that the right in and license to use said Letters Patent is a personal one, existing in favor of the James G. Wilson Manufacturing Company, and does not, in the absence of an express contract, pass to the defendant company, is not well taken, and cannot be maintained, for the reason that the defendant company is but a continuation of its predecessor company, and the complainant in good faith and fair dealing is as completely estopped from claiming the right here set up against one as the other. In a word, these patents were procured by the complainant while in the predecessor company's employ, with a view to the successful transaction of its business, and they are no less essential to the successor corporation's operation of its business than they were to the original company; and to allow the original company to sell and dispose of its stock and assets, which included these patent rights and privileges, and which added to the value of the assets, at a profit, and then to give the patents, or relinquish their privileges in them, to one having the relation to the business that the complainant had, would operate as a fraud upon the successor company." *Wilson* v. *J. G. Wilson Corp.,* 241 Fed. 494 (DC EVa 1917)."

In *Standard Parts Company* v. *Peck,* 264 U.S. 52, 1924, the court reached the same result, reasoning that it would be contrary to equitable principles to allow the patentee to enforce his patent rights against the entire successor of the shop right holder, while he could at the same time license business competitors under his patent. Similar results were reached in *Neon Signal Devices Inc.* v. *Alpha Claude Neon Corp.,* 54 F.2d 793, 12 USPQ 339, DC WPa 1931. Similarly, if a pre-existing partnership becomes incorporated and business is further continued by the same parties, no such transfer is involved that would terminate the shop right, *Rowell* v. *Rowell,* 122 Wis. 1, 99 N.W. 473, 1904.

Of course, if the employer was mistaken in believing that he has shop right, an entire successor cannot gain such rights since a vendor cannot confer greater rights on the vendee than he himself had. *American Stoker Co.* v. *Underfeed Stoker Co. of America,* 182 Fed. 642, Cir. W.D. Pa. 1910, aff. 188 Fed. 314, CA 3 1911.

Tests of Successorship. In recognizing the entire successor's equitable right, however, the courts have strictly construed the definition of the entire successorship. In *Hapgood* v. *Hewitt,* 119 U.S. 226, 1886, distinguished in *Lane & Bodley Co.* v. *Locke,* 150 U.S. 193, 1893, the court did not recognize the shop right of the new corporation, where the old corporation was dissolved and the new corporation was formed by the stockholders of the old corporation in another state through a receiver in the liquidation.

When an employer is merged, the shop right passes to the company effecting the merger. *Papazian* v. *American Steel and Wire Co.,* 115 USPQ 333, DC NOhio 1957.

However, when a corporation becomes the entire successor of another corporation, but maintains the other corporation in its former corporate entity, as a subsidiary, the shop rights of the subsidiary corporation will not accrue to the parent company. *General Paint Corp.* v. *Kramer,* 68 F.2d 40, CA 10 1933, cert. den. 292 U.S. 623, 1934.

A book in this field is that by Jasper S. Costa, "Law of Inventing in Employment," ed. by Joseph Rossman, New York, Central Book Co., 1953.

Cross-references: *Assignments, Employees' Inventions and Agreements, Estoppels in Patent Cases, Laches, Licenses.*

SOLICITATION. See ATTORNEYS AND AGENTS, PROSECUTION, and articles on each of the major arts

SOVIET PATENT LAW AND PRACTICE

P. J. Federico

In 1960, Mr. Robert C. Watson, Commissioner of Patents, Mr. Clarence A. Kalk, Director of Administration, and the author visited the Soviet office in Moscow which corresponds to a patent office and interviewed Soviet officials during a week. This article is a condensation of the more comprehensive report in 43 JPOS 5-96, 1961. It is primarily descriptive of the law and its administration with respect to securing rights to inventions. It utilizes explanations and information obtained from Soviet officials, as well as material derived from published sources.

Introduction

The basic principle which is followed is, fundamentally, to record the inventor's contribution and acknowledge his authorship by issuing to him a certificate which is called an "author's certificate" (or certificate of authorship), after an examination as to the novelty and usefulness of the invention. The invention represented by the certificate belongs to the State and the application for a certificate by the inventor constitutes an offer of his invention to the State; the State, by means of State establishment, is authorized to use the invention and, in fact, assumes some obligation to put the invention into use.

The law also provides for the issuance of patents for inventions. The patent parts of the law, particularly the subject matter that can be patented, and the conditions for patentability are similar in many respects to provisions in the patent laws of many other countries.

While the inventor may request either an author's certificate or a patent, except as to certain subject matter, the conditions are such that, for over twenty thousand author's certificates issued during the four years 1956-1959, there were only about a half dozen patents issued to Soviet citizens. The certificate of authorship entitles the holder to a certain compensation and also to certain privileges, with the State undertaking the utilization of the invention. This is not the case for a patent; the Soviet citizen would be left to his own resources in developing the invention and in the absence of private enterprise could not do much himself. Second, the author's certificate requires no fees of any kind, whereas in the case of a patent, fees are required for obtaining one and also for maintaining it in force. Also, if an inventor obtains a patent for one of his inventions, he becomes disqualified from receiving any of the privileges on any author's certificate he might obtain; he would still retain the right to compensation, however. Furthermore, in the case of inventions made during the carrying out of assigned duties and of inventions made with the assistance of the establishment or organization, the inventor is precluded from obtaining a patent, but a certificate of authorship may be obtained; there is no choice in this situation. There results, in effect, a complete State monopoly of practically all inventions and, by virtue of the law as a whole, government control over substantially all inventive activities in the Soviet Union.

The law provides that it is applicable to foreigners on the basis of reciprocity, which provision is interpreted to mean that, if the foreign country has a patent law which is applied to Soviet citizens, then the Soviet law will be applied to citizens of that country. Foreigners hence may obtain either author's certificates or patents in the USSR. The number of either obtained each year by foreigners is comparatively small. Most of the patents which are issued, which are very few in any event, are issued to foreigners.

The right conferred by a patent is the right to exclude others from utilizing the invention. Since there is no private enterprise, the patentee is reduced to negotiating with Soviet establishments or organizations and authorities for a license to use the invention.

Scope and General Nature of Statute

The statute (including the Regulation on Compensation) deals with three subjects, namely, (1) Discoveries, (2) Inventions, and (3) Innovation (Improvement) Proposals, and the main object of the statute is to protect the "right of authorship" in these fields according to the details of the law.

Discoveries. Discoveries relate to the establishment of existing but hitherto unknown laws of nature and qualities or phenomena of the material world. Geographical, archeological or paleontological discoveries, discoveries of mineral deposits and discoveries in the field of the social sciences are excluded from the statute. In connection with the discoveries which are included, "diplomas" are issued and the law provides for certain rewards to the discoverers.

Inventions. An invention is defined as the solution of a technical problem distinguished by its essential novelty, in any field of the national economy or culture, public health and national defense, which produces positive results. A few matters which might be protected as process inventions in the United States might be considered simply as discoveries under the Soviet law. Inventions are protected at the option of the inventor either by an author's certificate or by a patent, with certain exceptions.

Innovation Proposals. The law also relates to what is here translated as "innovation proposals." Under this heading are listed proposals for improvements of adopted technical equipment such as machines, appliances, instruments, devices, apparatus, assemblies; improvements in products, technology or production, methods of control, observation and research; methods of industrial safety and worker's protection, etc. These, in general, are technical improvements, and the term "improvement suggestions" will also be used in referring to them. Specifically excluded from this category are suggestions relating to organization and management. Improvement suggestions made by technical workers in the course of the performance of their official assignments are excluded from consideration under this law.

Promotion and Utilization of Inventions. The law contains provisions directed at the encouragement of inventing and improving. The Committee for Inventions is charged with general guidance in this field and, in cooperation with the All-Union Association of Inventors and Innovators, with work relating to the development of the inventiveness and innovativeness of the masses. Various levels of organization are also generally charged with guidance of development, down to the managers of shops who are required, in necessary cases and within the limits of their staff budget, to assign personnel to deal with inventing and improving.

The technical sections are divided according to, and named after, various fields of industry: Agriculture; Building and Building Materials; Chemistry, Fuel and Mineral Oil Products; Textile, Light and Food Industry; Machine Construction; Metallurgy and Mining Industry; Power and Electrical Engineering; Radio Engineering, Instrument Construction and Means for Automation; Transportation; Medicine and Medical Industry.

There are sections dealing with preliminary examination, information and publication, administration and service, patenting abroad, secrecy matters, inventor's rights, recording research projects, utilizing inventions in industry, and other matters.

The "Patent" Office

The administration of the features of the law dealing with author's certificates and patents, and other parts of the law, lies in a bureau or agency known as the "Committee for Inventions and Discoveries attached to the Council of Ministers of the USSR," which will be referred to as the Committee for Inventions or as the Committee.

The Committee has associated with it a separate Council of Experts, which considers appeals and other special matters which may be referred to it.

The Library is extensive. United States patents are subdivided and maintained in folders according to United States classes and subclasses.

Publications

Specifications of Author's Certificates and Patents. The most numerous publications of the office are the printed copies of specifications and drawings. They average about two and one-third pages.

The United States Patent Office began the exchange of copies of specifications early in 1959, the earliest one received by the Patent Office being No. 116,001. Of the earlier specifications, the U.S. Patent Office has copies from No. 1 of 1924 to No. 2496 of 1928; the Swedish Patent Office has copies of No. 1 to No. 59,308 issued in 1941. It should be noted that the arrangements for exchange of copies of specifications are purely bibliographical and library matters, public documents being exchanged to save the trouble of acquiring them in some other manner. Printed copies of United States patent specifications and also those of other countries, being published public documents, have always been available to anyone and the Soviet government obtained copies in the past in various ways.

Bulletin of Inventions. The office also publishes a journal corresponding to the Official Gazette of the United States Patent Office. It is called *Byulleten Izobreteniy—*

Bulletin of Inventions—and goes back to 1924 with variations in title and format. Copies from 1956 on are available in the Patent Office and the Library of Congress, with scattered earlier numbers. The Bulletin appears twice a month.

The bulk of the Bulletin is devoted to the publication of notices of author's certificates and patents issued. The listing includes number, name of the inventor, title of the invention, filing date and application number, and the text of the claim or claims (invention formula), which serve as abstracts; no illustrations are included.

The Bulletin includes notices of author's certificates which have been cancelled or amended, patents which have been cancelled, and, under the prior law, notices of allowed patent applications published for opposition. Also, from time to time, there may be announcements, items of information, decisions of the Council of Experts, notes concerning inventions which have been adopted, etc.

Specification Abstracts. Beginning late in 1959, the office began the publication of a series of "Compilations of Inventions"— pamphlets of abstracts of Soviet specifications relating to selected subjects, of which about two dozen have appeared or have been announced.

Information Pamphlets. A series of 18 brochures with the general heading "Information Concerning Inventions and Innovation Proposals for Workers" has been announced, but only one has been seen. This is called "Patent Literature and Its Utilization," the guide to the Patent Library which has been mentioned. There are also a small pamphlet on "How to Prepare the Application for an Alleged Invention," a booklet of "Instructions for Computing Savings Realized by Utilization of Inventions and Innovation Proposals," and a book containing the texts of the laws and administrative regulations.

Conditions and Procedure for Obtaining an Author's Certificate (or Patent)

The conditions and requirements for obtaining a patent are in general the same as those for obtaining an author's certificate and will be described generally with the author's certificate in mind; variations will be indicated.

Application. An application for the issuance of an author's certificate must be filed with the Committee for Inventions and Discoveries. The application must be filed by the inventor himself or by his heirs, or by the establishment or organization authorized by the inventor to do so. In the case of joint inventors, all the inventors must be named and they all receive the author's certificate. However, if an invention is the result of collective creative work in which the authorship of individuals cannot be established, the author's certificate is issued in the name of the establishment or organization in which the invention was made. In the case of a patent, the application may also be filed by the assignee with an indication of the true inventor.

The formal part of the application is made out by a one-page printed blank form which includes spaces for inserting the required information, names, addresses, place of employment, title of the invention, a declaration that the applicant or the person for whom the application is made is the true inventor of the proposal, etc. The application must contain a description of the invention and a drawing if the latter is necessary, so that its novelty may be ascertained and so that it would be possible to carry out the invention. What amounts to a claim or claims is also included at the end of the description. The application must be limited to a single invention and may not include independent variations of the construction or process. The application, i.e., the form, is filed in a single copy, but the description and drawings must be filed in triplicate. All copies must be signed. Supplemental material such as tests, reports, photographs, etc., may be submitted with the application.

The applicant may file amendments, in three copies, to his application within a period of one month provided they do not change the nature of the invention. Matter changing the nature of the invention can only be presented as a new application receiving a later date.

The printed specifications of author's certificates and patents show that the descriptions are usually rather brief.

Apparently, reliance is not always placed upon the description and drawing alone in carrying out the invention, as an inventor may be required to actively assist in the adoption and further development of his proposal as by supplying the organization or establishment which utilizes the invention with all available materials, explanations, and advice. (This requirement is said not to apply in the case of patents.)

Examination. When the applications are received by the office, they first go to a section which conducts a preliminary examination. This is not limited merely to a determination that the necessary papers are present and that all formalities have been complied with, but may go to other matters which are apparent on the face of the papers. If the application is refused acceptance for any reason, the applicant is informed and, depending upon the nature of the objection, he may correct it or file a new application, or file additional papers taking the later date. A period of one month is given for supplying deficiencies.

There are no interference proceedings as in the United States, as the inventor who files first is entitled to the author's certificate (or patent).

After the application has been accepted for examination, it is examined to ascertain the presence of novelty and usefulness.

Novelty. The examination for novelty is ordinarily conducted by the outside expert. This expert will make the search in the Patent Library of the office, and will turn in a report indicating presence or absence of novelty. Theoretically the report of the outside expert is not controlling and the technical section may make its own determination on the material supplied.

Novelty must exist at the time of filing the application and novelty may be defeated by prior author's certificates and Soviet, pre-Soviet, and foreign patents, as well as by prior publications either in the country or abroad, and other material.

It appears that previously filed applications are also used and matters which have been in public use presumably would also defeat novelty. There appears to be some use of prior knowledge which was not, in effect, generally available to the public, to defeat novelty.

Disclosure of the invention by the inventor himself in connection with the development of the invention, etc., during the four months preceding the filing of the application will not cause the loss of the right to an author's certificate; also, if the inventor's own invention was published or used by another without his knowledge during the year preceding the filing of the application, it will not cause loss of right to the author's certificate. However, prior publication or use of somebody else's invention of the same subject matter would do so, even if it occurred during the periods mentioned. The periods of four months and one year do not apply in the case of patents, where any publication or use before the filing of an application would cause the loss of right to a patent.

Usefulness. The other aspect of the examination is the determination of the "usefulness" of the invention. The application is looked at from the standpoint of whether or not the State would be apt to use the invention. Immediate practical utility and value is primarily controlling, but potential practical application in the near future is also taken into consideration when there is an indication of willingness to undertake research and development work. If the application is to be refused for lack of novelty, the referral and determination of usefulness is not always made. Where one particular way of doing something has been adopted and is in use, improvements in alternative ways would ordinarily be refused.

This requirement for usefulness is not applied in the same manner in the case of applications for patent.

Further Procedure. A decision is made by the technical section of the Committee on the basis of the reports on novelty and usefulness which have been mentioned. This action is required to be made in four months.

When the application is refused, the applicant must be supplied with the reasons, as is customary, and he has thirty days in which to object if he disagrees. The applicant is entitled to copies of the references, which must be supplied to him on request, free of charge in the case of an author's certificate, and the thirty-day period for reply dates from the sending of these copies. In the case of a reply there is a reconsideration by the technical section, which is required to be made within one month, and the applicant is informed of the results. There may also be an appeal, which is considered by the Council of Experts which has been mentioned. From this decision there is no further appeal.

Claims. If the action of the technical section is favorable, the letter to the applicant advising him of this fact includes the wording of the "formula" which is allowed. The information and publication section may revise the specification and prepare a draft of the "formula" for the technical section. The instructions to applicants require the description to conclude with a formulation of the subject of the invention explaining its characteristic features and distinguishing it from prior subject matter known to the inventor. This "formula" is supposed to be a concise, clear and complete outline of the nature of the invention; perhaps it is more analogous to the résumé in French patents than to claims, but some appear to be similar in form to claims in German patents. Normally there is just one "formula" or claim. If the applicant receiving a favorable action disagrees with the "formula" or claim which has been allowed, he may ask for reconsideration and have the matter decided on appeal by the Council of Experts which has been mentioned.

Issue. The certificate itself which is sent to the inventor consists of a folded sheet with the top page engraved. Between the folds is placed a copy of the specification and the two are ribboned and sealed.

The date the issue of the Bulletin of Inventions is approved for printing is considered as the date of publication of author's certificates and patents. An examination of the currently issued author's certificates listed in a single number of the Bulletin of Inventions (No. 8 of 1960) shows that half of them were issued in 9 months and 10 days, with 79 per cent issued within a year, after filing, but there were a substantial number with quite old filing dates.

The number of author's certificates and patents issued each year has also been increasing, as indicated in the following table:

	Filed	Issued
1956		2751
1957		5673
1958	36,300	6354
1959	44,134	8202

During the first half of 1960, the number issued was 4358. The patents included in these figures are only a fraction of one per cent.

The number of applications refused is over 75 per cent of those filed. About one-sixth are disposed of on the preliminary examination. Most of the remainder are refused for lack of novelty.

Revocation and Disputes as to Inventorship

Within one year from the date of publication of the issuance of the author's certificate (when not published, one year from the date of entry in the State Register of Inventions), any organization, establishment, or individual, may contest the certificate on the ground that the invention is not new or that some other person is the actual inventor. There is no time limit in the case of patents.

Disputes concerning inventorship or co-inventorship are decided by the courts. The general part of the statute provides that "Misappropriation of authorship, misappropriation of credit for co-authorship, giving credit for co-authorship to persons who did not participate in the creative work toward the discovery, invention, or improvement suggestion ... shall entail responsibility as determined by the laws of the constituent republics."

Secrecy

The Secrets Law of 1956 lists the following as representing State secrets:

14. Discoveries and inventions having considerable military significance.

15. Discoveries and inventions having considerable scientific and economic sig-

nificance, before the heads of the ministries and departments give permission to publish them.

Applications relating to secret and top secret inventions and discoveries are filed with and examined by the Committee for Inventions, except "the top secret pertaining to new means of armament, fighting technique and their tactical use." In the latter case, the application is filed with and examined by the Ministry of Defense, which will handle all matters except that, if an author's certificate is to be issued, the Committee for Inventions is notified and the certificate is issued and registered in blank.

Rights and Privileges Under Author's Certificates

Government establishments and organizations, as well as cooperative and public establishments and organizations, are entitled to use the invention, and the inventor has the right to compensation based upon the extent of use and may, in addition, obtain certain privileges specified in the law. An author's certificate can not be transferred to another, but it may be inherited by the heirs of the inventor; in this case the privileges do not descend, but only the right to remuneration. In general, the compensation to the inventor is calculated on the basis of the savings accomplished by the invention. The Regulation gives a table of ranges of savings and the percentages which are to be paid to the inventor, as tabulated below.

Features of Patents of Particular Interest to Foreigners

There are no fees of any kind in connection with author's certificates, whereas heavy fees are due in the case of patents. The application fee is 260 rubles, which, at the non-tourist official rate of exchange of four to one (in 1961), amounts to $65.00, one of the highest, if not the highest, application fee known. [Harold L. Roditi, in a private communication in 1963, compared the costs of filing ten applications in the USSR with the costs of 66 total filings of the same cases, each in 2 to 14 other coun-

Amount of Annual Savings (in rubles)	Compensation for Invention	Compensation for Innovation Proposals
Up to 100	25% of the saving but not less than 20 rubles	13.75% of the saving, but not less than 10 rubles
100-500	15% plus 10 rubles	7% plus 10 rubles
500-1000	12% plus 25 rubles	5% plus 20 rubles
1000-5000	10% plus 45 rubles	2.75% plus 45 rubles
5000-10,000	6% plus 250 rubles	2% plus 85 rubles
10,000-25,000	5% plus 350 rubles	1.75% plus 110 rubles
25,000-50,000	4% plus 600 rubles	1.25% plus 235 rubles
50,000-100,000	3% plus 1110 rubles	1% plus 360 rubles
Over 100,000	2% plus 2100 rubles, but not more than 20,000 rubles	0.5% plus 860 rubles, but not more than 5000 rubles

tries. The costs, including attorneys' and agents' fees, translations, drawings, legalization of documents and postage, averaged 14 per cent higher per case in Russia than in the other countries. Ed.]

There is also a fee of 260 rubles for recording an assignment and a fee of 130 rubles for taking an appeal. The patentee must also pay annual fees to maintain the patent in force. The amount of these fees, in rubles, is 220 for each of the first three years and rising thereafter to 2530 for the fifteenth year, making a total of 16,830 rubles. While most countries have an annual or periodical fee system for patents, with the amounts increasing with the years, the system in the USSR appears to be the highest of any other country, but the expected revised schedule will be less than in Germany. The fees given in this paragraph are those which have been in effect prior to and during 1960.

The law provides for an action to cancel the patent which may be filed with the Committee for Inventions and Discoveries by any person or organization, at any time during its term. This may be based on the ground that the patent does not comply with the law, i.e., lacks novelty, etc. The Bulletin of Inventions announced the cancellation of six patents in the 1959 issues. The prior law also provided for opposition proceedings in the case of patents, which were dropped in 1959.

The term of the patent is 15 years from the filing date, and the rights of the applicant begin from the same date. The owner may assign his rights or grant licenses and the instrument must be recorded with the Committee to be valid.

The statute states with respect to patents that "no one may use an invention without the consent of the owner." The word "use" is here used in a broad sense, and the various acts customarily considered as infringements of patents would be included. Importation of infringing articles would also constitute infringement and be forbidden. The statute on inventions and patents does not include any provisions relating to infringement, but an infringer would be subject to a suit for infringement by the patents and also to action by the State. It does not appear that any infringement suits have arisen, at least in recent years.

While the patent gives the right to exclude others from using the invention, inasmuch as there is no private enterprise, the patentee is left with the sole possibility of negotiating for a license with some organization or enterprise of the USSR. The negotiation must be conducted through a government agency. It is undoubtedly true that some licenses have been negotiated and as many as four or five specific instances have been mentioned.

If the invention is of particular importance to the State and if no agreement is reached between the ministry or department and the owner of the patent, the matter can be taken up by the Council of Ministers which can give permission to use the invention to the agency concerned and establish the amount of compensation to be paid. The previous law also provided for condemnation of a patent, i.e., taking over title by the State, in such instances, which provision was omitted in the law of 1959. There have been no instances of action under this section of the law.

The law provides for a right of prior user in the case of an establishment which, independently of the inventor, has been using the invention in the USSR prior to the filing of the application for patent; the establishment may continue to use the invention without charge. Such provision exists in the patent laws of some countries, for example, Germany, and indicates that mere use by others prior to the filing of the application might not be a bar to receiving the patent.

A patent which has not been assigned or licensed can be exchanged for an author's certificate. A patent cannot be obtained if the invention was made in connection with the work of the inventor in a government or public establishment or organization, or on assignment of such enterprise or organization, or when the inventor received pecuniary or other material aid in developing the invention.

The number of patents issued each year is rather small, although they have been increasing. The following table gives the number issued in a few recent years, with an indication of the country of origin.

TABLE 1. PATENTS ISSUED IN THE USSR.

Origin	1956	1957	1958	1959
USSR	1	1	2	1
East Germany	1	1	4	34
Czechoslovakia	3			20
Poland			1	
Hungary				7
Austria			1	1
Belgium				2
Canada				1
France			1	10
Germany		1	4	16
Great Britain	1		2	7
Italy			2	9
Sweden			1	1
Switzerland	1			
Total	7	3	18	109

While there are no patents in this list originating from the United States, it is understood that a number of applications have been filed recently.

As seen from the preceding table, most of the patents are obtained by foreigners. On the other hand, foreigners obtain relatively very few author's certificates in the USSR. The Bulletin of Inventions for 1959 shows a total of 72.

Foreigners who wish to apply for a patent or author's certificate in the USSR must deal through the All-Union Chamber of Commerce, which has a Patent Bureau that acts as the agent for the applicant. An agent's fee is charged and the Patent Bureau has a schedule of charges for filing various papers and for making translations. A ten-page publication in English called "General Information on the Procedure of Patenting Foreign Inventions and Registering Foreign Trade Marks in the USSR" is issued by the Patent Bureau, which supplies various forms.

Aside from the fact that an extension of the thirty-day period for response can be obtained in the case of foreigners, the procedure before the Committee for Inventions appears to be substantially the same as for natives, it being noted that applications for patent are not referred for a report on usefulness.

Russian Patenting in Foreign Countries

Soviet citizens have applied for and obtained rather few patents in foreign countries, but it appears that a policy has been adopted of increasing the rate of patenting in other countries.

The following shows the number of such applications in two countries:

	United States	Great Britain
1955	0	0
1956	0	0
1957	0	0
1958	3	3
1959	15	41

The first six months of 1960 show 27 applications in the United States.

Improvement Suggestions

Improvement suggestions (innovation proposals) are handled on a local basis. The author submits a description of the suggestion, with drawings or sketches if necessary, directly to the establishment or organization to whose activities it relates, or to a higher level organization if it has wider application.

Figures given for the number of suggestions made run in the millions. The Bulletin of Inventions in No. 8 of 1960 gives some round numbers and percentages from which the following table of rough approximations was calculated:

TABLE 2. IMPROVEMENTS AND INVENTIONS PROPOSED (*in millions*).

Year	No. of Persons	No. of Proposals	No. Adopted
1957	1.40	2.50	1.54
1958	1.74	2.97	1.82
1959	2.00	3.50	2.16

The same source states that the savings realized from the proposals adopted in 1959 were 11.727 billion rubles.

Discoveries

The author of a discovery receives a diploma. An application for the issuance of a diploma, formally similar to an application for an author's certificate, must be filed with the Committee for Inventions and Discoveries. There must be a description, drawings, if necessary, and a proposed claim (formula) giving a "concise, clear and complete outline of the nature of the" discovery. On the issuance of a diploma, the Committee for Inventions and Discoveries is to pay to the author an award in a lump sum of up to 5000 rubles (new scale).

The provisions relating to diplomas for discoveries appear for the first time in the statute of 1959. During the first year, two discoveries were published in the Bulletin of Inventions.

Bibliography

The article in 43 JPOS, on pages 50-84 or in footnotes elsewhere, gives a list of publications and authorities which the author has consulted or to which he refers and also translations of the Statute, the Decree promulgating it, and the Regulation on Compensation, and Information Pamphlet for Foreigners. The article also has a section on Soviet trademarks.

Cross-references: *Employee-Inventors' Patent Rights ... in Foreign Countries, Foreign Patents, Soviet Patent System—International Aspects.*

SOVIET PATENT SYSTEM— INTERNATIONAL ASPECTS

Harold L. Roditi

The invitation to write on Soviet patents for this Encyclopedia led eventually to a personal visit and discussions in Russia and to reports on the subject before the Patent Law Associations of New Jersey and Connecticut. During the two-year period of gathering the information, there has been a series of successive press releases relating to (1) study of the U.S. patent system by a team of visiting Soviet officials, (2) new patent regulations designed to promote protection of Soviet inventions abroad, (3) grant of the first U.S. patent in ten years to a resident of the Soviet Union, (4) the arrival of a Soviet representative to promote licensing of U.S. inventions for use in the Union, (5) statement of the intent to treat foreign licensors as favorably as domestic inventors, all signs that the Soviets are becoming internationally minded in patent matters.

In the modern age of industrial technology, the U.S.S.R. has emerged from her rudimentary industrial revolution. She has come to realize not only that she must make acquisitions at a higher scientific level, but also that she must have something to offer in exchange. In order to deal on an equal footing, she must trade the fruits of her own basic and applied research in a manner acceptable to the trading partner.

For detailed discussion of the Soviet patent system, see Robert C. Watson, 43 JPOS 6-8, 1961; P. J. Federico, *ibid.*, 8-96; S. P. Ladas, 49 T.M. Reporter 895.

Soviet Filings for Patents Abroad

In negotiations for rights to foreign inventions, the Soviets have found that they need, as trading material, ownership of patents abroad under which to exchange licenses. They have discovered, however, that patent applications filed by Russians in the U.S. have in the past been held up by means of red tape, even in the execution of the documents, because the applicants and their local attorneys were not familiar with the forms and were reluctant to go to the U.S. Embassy or Consulate to sign them. When the applications finally reached the U. S. Patent Office and were eventually rejected, most Russians were convinced that this was a symptom of the Cold War.

Recognizing the need for intake of knowledge and information and filing of patent applications by their inventors in other countries, the Russians have given orders to develop a regular flow of exchanges of licenses.

Although there is as yet no habit of successful negotiation, the immediate consequence has been a marked increase in the number of patent applications filed by Russians abroad. They have found that their earlier policy of giving credit to the originator, by scientific publication, was working against them. Many of their inventions were in fact barred from valid patenting by public disclosure too early. This form of credit by publication has now fallen into disfavor, therefore, and is being supplanted by securing patent rights. There is now pressure to withhold publication and public use until patent applications have been filed in all countries of interest. It is expected that Soviet Russia will soon apply for membership in the International Convention, and it is understood that a large staff of legal talent is carefully studying the treaties and the laws of all important countries in preparation for an imminent decision.

Filings by Foreigners in Soviet Union

It is common knowledge that the Soviets have been very active in buying printed copies of patents issued anywhere in the world, and this has usually been interpreted erroneously, and with deliberate tendentiousness, as evidence of the pirating of inventions. If the owners of those same inventions had protected themselves by filing patents in the U.S.S.R., the situation would have been entirely different, as most Europeans and even the Japanese recognize. Industrialists in all those countries deal with the Soviets and find them sophisticated in such transactions.

The Europeans who deal with the Soviets are not particularly afraid of having a prototype copied in Russia. Either the Europeans will have taken out patents and their initial contract to supply equipment will have included a license, possibly with a one-time down payment in lieu of royalty, or they estimate that it will take the Soviets so long to copy the unpatented prototype that the built-in obsolescence will be effective by the time newer and better models appear.

In order to deal as equals, the Russians must respect the distinction between that which has fallen into the public domain, through expiration or lack of timely protection, and that which is available for negotiation as a proprietary right. This means that they must either join the International Convention on patent rights or establish a two-way flow through bilateral treaties with individual countries. There is no point in their trying to sell national rights in a country to company A if those rights can be pirated with impunity in the same country by competitor B. They have to protect their inventions under the national law in every country where they want to sell them and, at the same time, make attractive the protecting and exploiting in the U.S.S.R. of inventions and know-how developed by outsiders.

It must be emphasized, for the benefit of those readers who may contemplate filing patent applications in Soviet countries, that, on paper at least, the task is no more difficult than in other lands. The legislative provisions and the implementing rules of practice are clearly laid down. See "Rules of Practice for Foreigners Filing Patent Applications in the U.S.S.R.," Patent Bureau of the U.S.S.R., Chamber of Commerce, Moscow, 1961. There is no more bargaining, in soliciting and prosecuting, than is likely to be encountered with our own examiners.

Costs. Costs have been analyzed on the basis of 10 different patent applications filed in 2 to 15 countries each, outside the Soviet areas. The average has then been compared with estimates of what the costs would have been in each of two major communist countries. The conclusion has been reached that for Poland the costs would have been 99 per cent of said average and for Russia, 132 per cent. The costs considered in arriving at these conclusions include attorneys' and agents' fees, translation, drawings, legalization of documents and postage. The nearness of the costs in Russia to the average becomes more significant on considering the large population over which the Russian patent rights extend. The appraisal shrinks as doubts, heretofore strong, arise as to enforceability of those rights.

Negotiating Licenses

The next logical step is the establishing of a network of local channels for negotiating of licenses. In the past, licensing has been through Amtorg, in offices opened by Soviet Russia in foreign countries as outposts of the Ministry of Foreign Trade for import and export. In the sphere of technology the activities of Amtorg have been unsatisfactory, however, and the Ministry has decided now that it must deal in each country with nationals who specialize in the work and are motivated by the profit incentive. The previous chain of command, from the Ministry, through Mas-Amtorg, to the Amtorg office in each country, and back again for information and decisions, was too unwieldy; each inquiry on reaching the Department had to be referred to the competent Trade Group for technical advice and there are about twenty-six such Groups, each having exclusive jurisdiction in its own technical sphere of industry such as electricity, railroads, building materials, textiles, chemistry, pharmaceuticals, medical appliances, steel, and optics.

The administrative channels have now been streamlined so that nationals in each country, when interested in acquiring Soviet technology, deal with a single autonomous body, Licensingtorg, established and directed by the Ministry of Foreign Trade to negotiate and settle the licensing terms with foreign nationals. (See Wall Street Journal, October 3, 1963.) It has technical and legal consultants on the staff and keeps the local Amtorg office in the foreign country informed, at each stage of the negotiations,

so that Amtorg may step in and sign the final text of agreement at the closing as the agent of Licensingtorg and of the particular Trade Group.

Some agreements have been concluded with U.S. concerns. They are of a fairly standard type acceptable to all the Trade Groups. One of the most difficult items to negotiate has been the arbitration clause, the Soviets insisting that any arbitration be submitted to the Supreme Soviet. A compromise was reached originally by distinguishing between plaintiff and defendant and submitting the case to a Soviet group if they are the defendants and to the American Arbitration Association if the U.S. party is defendant. This has been modified by providing for a Swedish arbitrator to settle disputes. The Wall Street Journal, *ibid.*, concludes that:

"Licensingtorg, a new Soviet Agency set up to handle licensing arrangements with the West, is relaxing terms to the point where they are about on a par with those offered in other foreign lands."

Several license agreements have reached the phase of preliminary implementation, plant visitations, delivery of know-how portfolios, and invitation and submission of bids. While the success or failure of these first ventures is locked in the future, a great deal of hard bargaining and careful psychological preparation are past. Delegations of American businessmen, engineers, top executives and corporation counsel have given repeated promotional talks to the various Trade Groups. Delays have been explained; an atmosphere of equality has been established across the bargaining table, and education and public relations have been applied to overcome road-blocks and to persuade the Soviets that they can sell only on the same terms as any other inventor and at competitive values. At the same time, the urge to "steal" has to be overcome on both sides, based as it was on the past practice of filing no patents and avidly reading the other's publications. And finally there has come conviction that it is better to respect the rights of others and pay a fee or royalty than to copy, make costly mistakes, redesign belatedly and become involved in law suits and bickering propaganda.

Cross-references: *Foreign Patents, Soviet Patents.*

STATE LAWS RELATING TO PATENTS

Hugo E. Weisberger

Many persons believe that because the Constitution vested in the Congress the power to secure to inventors the exclusive right to their inventions (Article I, Section 8), the individual states cannot grant patents of their own for inventions or enact legislation directly affecting patent rights under United States patents or the physical property produced under the protection of such patents. Moreover, these persons may believe that the ownership of a patent from the federal government entitles them to exemption from the operation of other state laws not aimed specifically at patents, but which are of general applicability to all citizens and their property within the state. These beliefs are erroneous. Supreme Court decisions of long standing have held that the mere facts that articles are patented and that a patent right is involved in a transaction do not exempt patent transactions from the operation of state laws.

There are in force at the present time, in many of the states including such industrially important ones as New York and Pennsylvania laws which prescribe the form and transfer of negotiable instruments given for patent rights and patented articles. Some other states require licenses to sell patent rights. It will be evident, therefore, that patent attorneys, business executives, inventors, and other persons who may undertake to sell or assign patent rights or patented property should become familiar with the laws of those states in which they intend to do business.

State Patents

In colonial times, several of the colonies granted patents. These patents were recognized by the Congress, following the ratification of the Constitution, in the first fed-

eral patent statute enacted in 1793, which provided that a state patentee could, by relinquishing his patent, apply for a United States patent. This meant that the owners of state patents were not deprived of their rights and that individual states could, if they chose, continue to grant patents concurrently with the federal government. The question arose in connection with the inventor Robert Fulton and the steamboat Clermont, in the interesting case of *Livingston and Fulton* v. *Van Ingen*, 9 Johnson (N.Y.) 507, N.Y. Court of Errors, 1812. The New York legislature had granted to Robert R. Livingston, later state chancellor, a patent on the exclusive right to make and use boats propelled by steam on the waters of New York state for 20 years. Livingston failed, but he joined forces with Fulton who succeeded with the Clermont. The original patent was extended to both inventors in 1803 for another 20 years. Van Ingen operated steam boats in the state, and Livingston and Fulton applied for a perpetual injunction, which was granted in the Appellate Court. Van Ingen appealed on the ground that the state patent was no longer enforceable since the Constitution had deprived the state of the power to grant patents. The Court disagreed with this view, holding that the federal constitution did not, in granting to Congress the power to grant patents, expressly prohibit the states from doing so.

As a practical matter, none of the states have continued to grant patents. A state patent would be of limited value because it would apply only in the granting state and might conflict with United States patents. In the well known case of *Gibbons* v. *Ogden*, 9 Wheat (22 U.S.) 1, 1824, which did not deal directly with this subject, the Supreme Court suggested, in passing, that the right of states to grant patents could not be exercised so as to restrain from intercourse among the states.

State Statutes Specifically Relating to Patents

These types of statutes relate to state licenses for selling patent rights and patented articles; the form, issuance, and transfer of promissory notes and other negotiable instruments given for patent rights; laws limiting the liability of states, counties, and municipal corporations for patent infringement or regulating their power to invite bids calling for the use of patented processes or articles.

The license and negotiable instrument laws relating to patents first came into existence in the decades following the Civil War, in order to protect the citizens of various states from fraudulent vendors of patent rights and patented articles. At that time, and particularly in rural areas, itinerant peddlers and hawkers of shoddy or worthless merchandise, such as "patent" medicines, lightning rods, watches, jewelry, and the like, included in their wares, patents to which they had obtained title from impecunious inventors for small sums. More often than not, the patents themselves covered worthless or inoperative products. The peddlers would sell to unwary farmers, the exclusive county or township rights in patented farm gates, lightning rods, hog troughs, and other devices, and obtain in return promissory notes. These notes would then be sold to innocent purchasers at a large discount; the farmer was without defense against such purchasers and had to pay the note. Another scheme was to exhibit to the farmer a patent for a gate or fence, inform him that he infringed, but that suit could be avoided by purchase of the patent. Other favorite places for the sale of patent rights were circuses, carnivals, and county or state fairs.

These activities led to the passage, particularly in farm states, of laws designated to curb such transactions and to protect their citizens. These laws took various forms. Some relegated vendors of patent rights to the status of peddlers and required them to obtain licenses. Other required registration of the patents with county clerks, together with the filing of affidavits attesting to their genuineness. The laws dealing with negotiable instruments required them to be marked "Given for a patent right," declared them subject to all defenses, and imposed fines and jail sentences upon vendors who accepted unmarked notes.

For a detailed discussion of the state laws, the reader is referred to the article entitled "State Control Over Patent Rights and Patented Articles" by this writer, 20 JPOS 182-316, 1938, portions of which have been adapted and brought up to date herein.

Fundamental to an understanding of this subject is the distinction between patent rights and patented articles. The term patent rights refers to the right given to the patentee or patent owner to exclude others from making, using or selling the invention covered by the claims. The patent right is treated by statute and decisional law as a kind of incorporeal and intangible personal property. It includes the patent itself and assignments, grants and licenses made thereunder. Patent rights are coextensive with the United States and are assumed by the courts to follow the person of the owner, and to be located at his place of residence.

The term patented article is used to represent tangible, physical property, such as a machine or device, brought into existence by the application of the patented discovery. As physical property, it is subject to the laws of the state in which it is situated, just as is any other personal property. *Patterson* v. *Commonwealth of Kentucky*, 97 U.S. 501, 1879.

The two kinds of state statutes which exist today and which regulate dealings in patent rights and patented articles are license laws and negotiable instrument laws. Until comparatively recently, penal laws were found, in Kansas and Indiana, making it a misdemeanor, punishable by fine or imprisonment, for any person to sell or offer to sell any patent right in any county without first filing with the county clerk duly authenticated copies of the patent, together with an affidavit of genuineness and of his authority to sell. Both of these statutes were expressly repealed by the state legislatures in 1951, and thus are no longer in force. They are mentioned here because the constitutionality of the Kansas registration statute was appealed to the U.S. Supreme Court, which, in one of the leading cases in this field, upheld the statute as a reasonable exercise of the police power of the state to protect its citizens. *Allen* v. *Riley*, 203 U.S. 347, 1906.

License Laws. Laws requiring the payment of a license tax or the obtaining of a license to sell patent rights or patented articles are found at the present time in certain states. A brief résumé of these laws follows.

TABLE 1. STATE LICENSE LAWS.

State	Latest Enactment	License or Tax
Mo.	1959	Semiannual license $3 to $20
N.C.	1957	Annual, $10 per county, municipalities extra
R.I.	1956, '60	$175 per license plus $2 issuance fee
Wis.	1957	Annual license $10 to $40

Three of these laws apply to the sale of patent rights or patented articles by peddlers or itinerant vendors. The constitutionality of this type of law was upheld in 1894, in a decision dealing with the original Missouri statute of 1889. *Emert* v. *Missouri*, 156 U.S. 347, 1894. The constitutionality of the similar laws of the other states may be regarded as settled, as recognized by their reenactment as recently as 1956-1960.

The provisions of the laws of the individual states are briefly summarized below. The taxes and other charges shown are generally annual, except where otherwise indicated.

Missouri. Rev. Stat. 1959, Chapter 150.-470—Whoever shall deal in the selling of patents, patent rights, patent or other medicines, lightning rods, goods, wares or merchandise going about from place to place to sell the same, is declared to be a peddler. Chapter 150.480—No person shall deal as a peddler without a license. Chapter 150.490 —Application for licenses is made to the collector of the county by paying the amount levied. Chapter 150.500—Rates of tax on licenses: $3 to $20 for every period of 6 months. Chapter 150.540—Penalty for violation: misdemeanor, fine $10 to $100.

North Carolina. Gen. Stat. 1957, Section 105-100, Patent Rights and Formulas— Every person, firm or corporation engaged in the business of selling or offering for sale any patent right or formula shall apply in advance and obtain from the Commissioner of Revenue a separate state license for each and every county where such patent right or formula is to be sold or offered for sale, and shall pay for each such separate license a tax of $10. Counties, cities or towns may levy a license on the business taxed in this section not in excess of the taxes levied by the state. Section 105-112—Application for license is to be made annually in advance before the first day of June each year.

Rhode Island. Gen. Laws 1956, Chapter 11, Hawkers and Peddlers. Section 5-11-3 (revised P.L. 1960, Chapter 76, par. 6) License for Patented Articles. Empowers the general treasurer of the state to issue a license for the whole state to a hawker and peddler for offering for sale and for selling any patented article upon the payment of $175, such license to describe the patented article, one license for each kind of article. Section 5-11-4 prescribes a license issuance fee of $2. Penalty for violation by peddling without a license is $10 to $20.

Wisconsin. Stat. 1957, Title 14, Regulation of Trade, Chapter 129, Peddlers, etc. Section 129.01 prescribes annual licenses for peddlers. Section 129.02 sets license fees at $10 to $40. Section 129.09 sets the penalty for violation at $25 to $50. Section 129.15, Selling Patent, requires that any person who shall sell or offer to sell any patent right or patented articles, goods, wares or merchandise by traveling from place to place for the purpose of such selling, must first obtain a license, or be subject to a fine of $20 to $100.

License laws of this type formerly existed in Kentucky, Georgia, Florida, Tennessee, and West Virginia. The Kentucky statute was declared unconstitutional by a state court in 1895. The laws of the other states in the group appear to have been repealed by omission from recent recodifications of the state statutes.

Negotiable Instrument Laws. Laws regulating the issuance and transfer of promissory notes and other obligations given for patent rights are in force at the present time in Georgia, New York, Pennsylvania, Tennessee, and Texas.

Similar laws were in force at one time in Arkansas, Illinois, Indiana, Kansas, Kentucky, Michigan, Minnesota, Nebraska, North Dakota, Ohio, South Dakota, Vermont, and Wisconsin. Many of the earlier enactments were held invalid by state courts. The Indiana and Kansas statutes were expressly repealed by the legislatures of those states in 1951. The law in Arkansas was expressly repealed in 1961. The statutes in North and South Dakota were repealed by omission in recent recodifications of the laws of those states. The Vermont law was repealed in 1959. The Nebraska and Ohio laws were repealed when the Uniform Commercial Code was adopted in those states in 1963 and 1961, respectively.

The existing laws are listed in Table 2 together with their salient provisions, and are summarized separately in the text below:

TABLE 2. NEGOTIABLE INSTRUMENT LAWS.

State	Kind of Instrument	Marking Provision	Type of Offense
Ga.	Note	Yes	Misdemeanor
N.Y.	Neg. Instr.	Yes	Misdemeanor
Penn.	Neg. Instr.	Yes	Misdemeanor
Tenn.	Note	Yes	Felony
Texas	Note	Yes	Misdemeanor

The states listed in the Table all include the Uniform Negotiable Instruments Act as the statute law dealing with bills, notes, and other instruments. The provisions pertaining to the execution of instruments given for patent rights are generally included as auxiliary sections. The penal statutes may be found either in the negotiable instruments laws or as part of the state penal codes.

In some states, the patent provisions apply to negotiable instruments of all kinds, while in others they mention only promissory notes. Negotiable instruments are defined in the statute as including both promissory notes and bills of exchange. The law defines a check as a bill of exchange drawn upon a bank. Accordingly in those states which regulate negotiable instruments given for patent rights, both promissory notes and checks are included. In Georgia, Tennessee and Texas, the laws mention only promissory notes, but it is possible that the wording might be construed broadly enough to include a check given in payment for a patent right. Whether the instrument is a promissory note or a check, the statutes

(1) require the vendor of the patent right to whom the instrument is given to designate the consideration on the face of the instrument, by marking it with the words "Given for a patent right" or similar indication and (2) render the vendor criminally liable for failure to do so. The maker of the note or check does not usually have this duty.

Most of the states subject the offender to the penalties of a misdemeanor, i.e., fine or imprisonment for less than one year. Tennessee makes the offense a felony and provides for possible imprisonment up to 5 years.

The purpose of these negotiable instrument requirements is to protect an innocent purchaser from acquiring them without knowledge of what they were given for and to put endorsees and transferees on notice of a possible failure of consideration. The statutes presently in force declare a marked note subject to the same defenses in the hands of any purchaser or holder as if in the hands of the original owner or holder. Where the instrument shows on its face that it was given for a patent right, there cannot be an innocent purchaser, and all defenses are available to the maker against any holder, for this is the express purpose of these laws. Such defenses may include, for example, the invalidity of the patent or breach of the contract for which the negotiable instrument was given. In the other states, such as Pennsylvania, New York, and Texas, a similar result has been attained by judicial interpretation.

When these negotiable instrument laws were first enacted in the 1870's and 1880's, they were challenged on the ground that they represented an unconstitutional attempt by state legislatures to direct the manner in which patent rights could be sold in the state and that they discriminate against patent owners, and many of the early laws were held invalid in the state courts.

In 1878, the Supreme Court of Pennsylvania in *Haskell* v. *Jones*, 86 Pa. St. 173, became the first state court to uphold such a promissory note statute, the Act of 1872, which is still in force in that state. Thereafter, the laws of Ohio, New York, Tennessee and Georgia were similarly upheld, in the highest courts of these states. The question of constitutionality of the negotiable instrument laws finally reached the U.S. Supreme Court, and two decisions were rendered in 1906 which settled the question. The Arkansas law, which was repealed about a year ago, was held valid in *John Woods & Sons* v. *Carl*, 203 U.S. 358, 1906, and in *Ozan Lumber Co.* v. *Union County National Bank*, 207 U.S. 251, 1906. In the latter case the Court said:

"The plain purpose of the whole statute is to create and enforce a proper police regulation. Its passage showed that the legislature was of the opinion that fraud and imposition were frequent in the sale of property of this nature. . . ."

Thereafter the Nebraska statute was held valid by the state supreme court.

The provisions of the negotiable instrument laws of various states presently in force are summarized below:

Georgia. Civil Code 1933, Bills and Notes Title 14.

Section 14-1804. Notes or contracts for the purchase price of a patent right or for the sale of any patented article or thing sold by a person, agent, company or corporation, shall have expressed on the face of such note or contract the consideration for the same.

Section 14-1805. Purchaser of a marked note takes it subject to all equities and defenses.

Section 14-9901. Violation is made a misdemeanor; fine—$1000, or sentence—six months, or both.

Act of 1897, pp. 81, 82, 83. Upheld in *Lee* v. *Hightower*, 3 Ga. App. 226; 59 S.E. 597, Ct.App.Ga. 1907.

New York. Owing to the commercial importance of this state, and because of recently enacted amendments to make the law conform to the Uniform Commercial Code adopted by the New York legislature, the law of New York will be discussed in some detail.

Two new laws relating to negotiable instruments in New York will take effect as of September 27, 1964, replacing present laws. The two statutes will then relate only

to the sale or transfer of a negotiable promissory note, the words "or other negotiable instrument" having been dropped from the old statute. The scope of the new laws will thus be left in part to judicial interpretation.

The Negotiable Instruments Law (Section 330) will then become Section 550 of the Uniform Commercial Code and will read:

"Notwithstanding article three of the uniform commercial code, a negotiable promissory note, the consideration of which consists wholly or partly of the right to make, use or sell any invention claimed or represented by the vendor at the time of sale to be patented, must contain the words 'given for a patent right' prominently and legibly written or printed on the face of such note above the signature thereto; and such note in the hands of any purchaser or holder is subject to the same defenses as in the hands of the original holder; but this section does not apply to a negotiable note given solely for the purchase price or the use of a patented article."

Section 1520 of the Penal Code has been amended correspondingly to read:

"A person who takes, sells or transfers a negotiable promissory note within article 3 of the uniform commercial code, knowing the consideration of such note to consist in whole or in part, of the right to make, use or sell any patent invention or inventions, or any invention claimed or represented to be patented, without having the words 'given for a patent right' written or printed legibly and prominently on the face of such note above the signature thereto, is guilty of a misdemeanor."

Pennsylvania. Purdon's Pa. Statutes 1930, title 56, par. 9 (Act of April 17, 1872, P.L. 60, No. 1). Whenever any promissory note or other negotiable instrument shall be given, the consideration for which shall consist in whole or in part of the right to make, use or vend any patent invention or inventions, claimed to be patented, the words "given for a patent right" shall be prominently and legibly written or printed on the face above the signature.

Paragraph 9a (P.L. 60, No. 2) provides that no person, knowing the consideration, shall take or transfer a note for a patent right which does not bear the required words, makes such a note subject to all defenses, and imposes for violation a fine of $500 or 60 days in jail or both.

The statute was originally held valid in *Shires* v. *Commonwealth*, 120 Pa. St. 368; 14 Atl. 251, Ct. of Quarter Sessions, Centre Co., Pa. 1888, and again in *Brown* v. *Pegram*, 125 Fed. 577, CA 3 1903.

Tennessee. Code 1956, Sections 601-604. Notes for purchase of patent rights or any interest therein or patent right territory, are subject to all defenses in the hands of any holder when the consideration appears on the face; it is unlawful to take such notes unless consideration is stated; violation is a felony, punishment 1 to 5 years in state penitentiary.

The original statutes of 1879 and 1897 held valid in *State* v. *Cook*, 107 Tenn. 499; 64 S.W. 720, S.Ct. Tenn. 1901.

Texas. Rev. Civil Statutes (1925), art. 578 (bills and notes). Notes or liens for patent rights or patent right territory must so state on face and are subject to all defenses.

It will be apparent that persons or companies which undertake to assign or license patent rights in the foregoing states and to accept payment in the form of negotiable instruments must take precautions to see that these statutes have been completely complied with.

States, Counties, and Municipal Corporations Liability for Infringement

The general rule is that a state, by reason of its sovereignty, is immune from suit. A state cannot be sued without its consent, either in a federal court or a state court, unless the state constitution so provides or unless the state legislature has provided an enabling statute. *Thingman* v. *Nebraska*, 125 Neb. 696; 251 N.W. 837; 20 USPQ 130, S.Ct. Neb. 1933, certiorari denied, 292 U.S. 56, 1934. A county is usually considered to be a local political subdivision of the state, and an agency of the state, and, as such, it is immune from suit unless a statute removes its immunity. In some instances, counties organized as corporations have been held liable for patent infringement,

but the local statutes must be consulted in any specific situation. A municipal corporation, such as city, town, village, borough, or the like, while in some respects also an agency of the state, is generally regarded as partaking of the character of a corporation and subject to suit for infringement in its corporate capacity.

Statutes Regulating Bids on Patented Articles or Processes. In many of the states, there exist statutes which limit or prohibit the power of municipal corporations to invite bids calling for the use of patented articles or processes. Typical of such laws is that of Ohio:

Ohio Revised Code 1958, Section 715-68. No municipal corporation shall adopt plans or specifications for a public improvement, required by law to be made by contract let after competitive bidding, which requires the exclusive use of a patented article or process.

General State Laws to Which Patent Rights and Patented Articles May Be Subject

As indicated earlier, all the states have general laws to which both patent rights and patented articles may be subject. The fact that patent rights are involved or that an article or process is patented does not provide exemption from such laws. Typical examples of state laws of general applicability are those in exercise of the police power, such as the sale of foods, pesticides, petroleum products and the like, and the practice of medicine; laws governing personal property; state taxation of personal property; state antitrust laws; and statutes affecting legal rights, such as the Statute of Frauds. Here also, the distinction between patent rights and patented articles, if kept in mind, helps to an understanding of the differing impact of these laws.

The Exercise of Police Power. It is well settled that the rights of patent owners are subordinate to the general authority of a state over all property within its borders. The principle involved was enunciated by the Supreme Court in 1879 in a leading case, *Patterson* v. *Commonwealth of Kentucky*, 97 U.S. 501. The Court said:

"[The] right which the patentee or his assignee possesses in the property, created by the application of a patented discovery, must be enjoyed subject to the complete and salutory power with which the States have never parted, of so defining and regulating the sale and use of property within their respective limits, as to afford protection to the many against the injurious conduct of the few.... The right to sell the Aurora oil was not derived from the patent; that right existed before the patent and, unless prohibited by valid local laws, could have been exercised without the grant of letters patent.... [The] tangible property which comes into existence by the application of the discovery is not beyond the control as to its use of state legislation, simply because the inventor acquires a monopoly in the discovery."

Statutes of this type must regulate all oils or other products equally and must not attempt to discriminate either in favor of or against patented products. A statute which did this would not be upheld as a valid exercise of the police power of the state. The guiding principle is that a statute regulating a commodity or requiring safeguards in its use must always describe them abstractly and by reference to the required qualities and must not name some specified patented article or the product of a particular manufacturer. *State* v. *Santee*, 111 Iowa 1; 82 N.W. 445, S.Ct. Iowa, 1900.

Other examples of the exercise of state police power are found in state pure food and drug laws and laws regulating the practice of medicine.

The broad principle applicable here was enunciated by the Supreme Court in the case of *Webber* v. *Virginia*, 103 U.S. 344, 1881, thus:

"...[The] right conferred by the patent laws does not take the tangible property...from the operation of the tax and license laws of the state.

"The patent for a dynamite powder does not prevent the state from prescribing the conditions of its manufacture, storage, and sale, so as to protect the community from the danger of explosion. A patent for the manufacture and sale of a deadly poison does not lessen the right of the state to control its handling and use."

The application of this principle in the food regulation field is well illustrated by a federal court case in Ohio decided shortly after the turn of the century. *Arbuckle* v. *Blackburn*, 113 Fed. 616, CA 6 1902; appeal dismissed, 191 U.S. 405, 1903. An Ohio law provided against the adulteration of food and drugs. It forbade the glazing or coating of coffee. Arbuckle Brothers manufactured and sold "Ariosa," a patented coffee in which ground coffee was roasted and sealed with eggs and sugar. The Ohio Food and Drug Commissioner held "Ariosa" coffee to be adulterated and prosecuted the makers under the Ohio statute. Arbuckle sued in the federal court for an injunction against the Commissioner. The fact that Arbuckle produced "Ariosa" under a patent was held not to exempt it from the operation of the statute and the bill for an injunction against the Commissioner was dismissed.

The present trend toward the enactment of state laws regulating the sale of drugs and pharmaceutical products lends emphasis to the importance of the principle in this field as well. The fact that a drug is patented does not exempt the manufacturer from the force of these laws. Neither does the fact that a person has a patent on a therapeutic preparation entitle him to administer the medicine to patients or to practice medicine without a license with respect thereto.

An early New York case makes this clear, in a situation not without its ironic aspects. In *Smith* v. *Tracy*, 2 Hall Superior Ct. Rep. N.Y. 501, Sup.Ct. N.Y. 1829, the plaintiff had a patent on a "botanic medicine" which was alleged to cure "most diseases to humanity," among which were mentioned gout, gravel, asthma, ulcers, St. Anthony's fire, consumption, and heart disease. Smith's recipe for these ailments was: Take one gallon of cider, half a pound of horse radish root, a quarter pound of white oak bark, two ounces of iron oxide, allow the mixture to stand for six days, and "it will be fit for use."

Smith, with no license to practice medicine as required by New York law, treated Tracy's wife. However, no cure was effected. A regular surgeon was called in before "the work was complete." Smith sued Tracy for the value of work and labor performed as "physician, surgeon and apothecary" upon the wife and for medicines furnished. The court denied recovery not only for the services, but even for the medicine furnished, saying:

"It is contended by the plaintiff, that the patent ...gives him the right to sell the medicines in question notwithstanding the provisions of the state law, and his general right to sell his medicines, as an apothecary, is not questioned in this case. The state law ... prohibits him from 'peddling his nostrums,' in the character of a physician, and inducing people to buy and use them, in consequence of their reliance on his pretended skill. Such practices the law of the state has declared to be dangerous to the public health, and if the patent in question had authorized him, in express terms, to vend his medicines in the manner in which he has done it in this case, I should have no hesitation in holding that the patent would be inoperative against the provisions of the law."

Similarly, where a device is prohibited by a state on the grounds of public policy or morals, such as a gambling machine, a patentee may be barred from its sale or use, despite his patent. In the interesting case of *Vannini* v. *Paine*, 1 Harrington (Del.) 65, Ct. of Errors and Appeals, Del. 1833, Vannini had a patent on a method of drawing lotteries and of designing lotteries on the permutation and combination principle. Other individuals designed a scheme for drawing a lottery under a certain Delaware law for the benefit of a school, adopting the plan of Vannini's patent. Lotteries were prohibited in the state at that time. Yates and McIntire, to whom Vannini had assigned his patent, sued for an injunction to restrain its infringement. The Court of Errors and Appeals, the highest state court, decided against the plaintiffs:

"[It] cannot be admitted that the plaintiffs have a right to use an invention for drawing lotteries in this State, merely because they have a patent for it under the United States. A person might with as much propriety claim a right to commit murder with an instrument, because he held a patent for it as a new and useful invention."

Another example of the right of a state to legislate with respect to property within its boundaries is found in public utility regulations. Here the public interest is held to be paramount, and the patent does not limit the power of a state to fix rates which public utility corporations may charge for the use of their facilities. In a leading case,

State of Ohio v. *Bell Telephone Co.*, 36 Ohio St. 296, S.Ct. Ohio, 1880, it was stated thus:

"... [W]here the beneficial use of patented property, or any species of property, requires public patronage and governmental aid, as, for instance, the use of public ways and the exercise of the right of eminent domain, the state may impose such conditions and regulations as in the judgment of the law-making power are necessary to promote the public good."

Laws Governing Personal Property

Patented articles represent physical property and, as such, are subject to the same legal principles and limitations as any other kind of tangible property. They are subject to the law of the place in which they are located.

The sale of a patented article is governed by the law of sales. In states in which the Uniform Sales Act is in force, there is a provision in this Act, dealing with implied warranties of quality, which reads:

"In the case of a contract to sell or a sale of a specified article under its patent or other trade name, there is no implied warranty as to its fitness for any particular purpose."

A corresponding provision does not appear in the implied warranty sections of the Uniform Commercial Code.

Patented articles, being physical property, are subject to the law of the place where they are located, or have their situs. Thus, they are subject to seizure and judicial sale on execution to satisfy a judgment against their owner.

Patent rights, however, being intangible, incorporeal property, stand upon a somewhat different footing.

Assignments. The manner in which patent rights may be assigned has been prescribed by the Congress and is set forth in 35 U.S.C. 261, which reads in part as follows:

"Subject to the provisions of this title, patents shall have the attributes of personal property.

"Applications for patent, patents, or any interest therein, shall be assignable in law by an instrument in writing. The applicant, patentee, or his assigns or legal representatives may in like manner grant and convey an exclusive right under his application for patent, or patents to the whole or any specified part of the United States."

An assignment of a patent is sufficient as to *form* if it meets these statutory requirements. But the *capacity* of persons, such as married women, guardians, or executors or administrators, to make assignments, depends upon the provisions of state laws. And the *effect* of such contracts is also determined by state law.

In a patent license agreement, there is a more limited transfer of patent rights, the owner retaining title to the patent, the rights and obligations of the parties being set forth in the contract. A patent license contract is a particular kind of contract subject to the general law of the states governing contracts.

The foregoing principles were aptly stated in a recent case in California, *Farmland Irrigation Co.* v. *Doppelmaier*, 48 Cal. 2d 208; 308 Pac. 2d 732, S.Ct. Cal. 1957. Here the plaintiff sought a declaratory judgment that it was entitled to manufacture and sell irrigation equipment under a patent license agreement and a declaration of its duties under the royalty provisions of the agreement. The Court said:

"It is contended that because a United States patent is the creature of a federal statute and can be assigned only in the manner provided by federal law, the assignability of rights under a patent license is also a federal question and in the absence of statutory provision is to be determined by the decisional law of the federal courts. This reasoning fails to distinguish patent rights, whose assignability is admittedly governed by a specific statutory provision, 35 U.S.C. par. 261, and rights created by a contract whose subject is exemption from a patent monopoly. It misconceives the policy of the federal patent statute and the relation between the federal and state law in the area of patent rights.

"Every action that involves, no matter how incidentally, a United States Patent is not for that reason governed exclusively by federal law.

"The plaintiff's cause of action arose under and was governed by the general common law of contracts . . . the law governing the elements of plaintiff's cause of action is state law—state law acting of its own force and not merely by incorporation into federal law."

Thus, the general statute and decisional law of states governing contracts applies with equal force to contracts involving patent rights. As one court expressed it:

"A patentee must observe the Sunday law as much as any other vendor; he must put his contract in writing under the same circumstances which require writings of others." *People* v. *Russell*, 49 Mich. 617; 14 N.W. 568, S.Ct. Mich. 1883.

The problem of whether a patent itself is subject to the operation of state laws, or to the jurisdiction of state courts, as a form of property, is one which has always presented difficulty. The question is not completely settled. Hence one must look to the laws and court decisions of the state concerned, usually the state of residence of the owner, be he an individual or a corporation.

The difficulty arises from the legal character of a patent. The courts have declared it to be incorporeal or intangible property, which does not exist in any particular state or district but is coextensive with the United States and has no locality. This, of course, refers to the legal rights represented by the patent grant and not to the patent document itself, the latter being merely evidence of the patent rights.

As a matter of practical necessity, therefore, the state courts had to work out a method of determining the location of patents and patent rights, in order to justify such established legal proceedings as execution of judgments, judicial sales, and insolvency proceedings with respect to patent rights.

Situs of Patent. A practical solution has been to look to the ownership of the patent. One approach is to consider the situs of the patent as being at the domicile of the owner. This approach is unsatisfactory because, within the United States, domicile would mean domicile within a particular state. But, as far as the states themselves are concerned, patents are coextensive with all the states and cannot exist solely in any particular one. Moreover, if the situs of a patent is deemed to be only at the domicile of the owner, no other state could subject the patent to its judicial proceedings. Therefore, the most workable solution has been to regard the patent as following the person of its owner and having its situs, if any, wherever he may be found, ordinarily at his place of residence.

However, it appears that where the inventor is a foreign inventor, the situs of patent rights is considered as being at his domicile, at least until an effective transfer of such rights to an assignee has taken place in this country. *Kent Jewelry Corp.* v. *Kiefer*, 119 N.Y. S. 2d 242, N.Y. Sup.Ct. 1952.

Seizure of Patents. Patent rights, being incorporeal, are not the kind of property which is subject to seizure and sale by execution at law to satisfy the debts of the owner, in the absence of express statutory authority. They may, however, be subjected to the payment of debts by a court of equity by way of a creditor's bill to subject the patent right to the payment of the judgment debt of the patent owner. The court must have personal jurisdiction of the patent owner, and the decree of the court directs him to assign the patent for the benefit of creditors to a trustee or master appointed by the court. Some states have statutes which provide a substitute procedure.

State Taxation of Patents. As indicated previously, the physical property brought into existence under the protection of a patent is private individual property, and as such, has its situs in a state, and is subject to state taxation as personal property.

Until as recently as 1932, the federal and state courts held that a state had no power to tax patents or patent rights either as property or in the form of income or royalties derived therefrom. The difficulty arose from the dual concept of a patent as having no situs and as being a federal franchise. As far back as the famous case of *McCulloch* v. *Maryland*, 4 Wheaton 432, Sup.Ct. 1819, where the doctrine was first enunciated, the Supreme Court has held that instrumentalities through which the federal government immediately and directly exercises its sovereign powers are immune from the taxing powers of the states. If it be assumed that a patent is a federal franchise and hence an instrumentality of the federal government, is it the kind of instrumentality which is entitled to exemption from state property taxation?

Justice Marshall, speaking for the Supreme Court in 1819, said:

"If the states may tax one instrument, employed by the government in the execution of its powers, they may tax any and every other instrument. They may tax the mail; they may tax the mint; they may tax patent rights; ... they may tax all the means employed by the government, to an excess which would defeat all the ends of government."

The criticism of the argument in *McCulloch* v. *Maryland* is that patent rights were not properly classified with taxing the mail and the mint, for while the latter constitute a means of government, patent rights do not; that the granting of patents by the federal government is not necessary to the execution of its powers, but simply extends to a private person a privilege to exploit his invention for his own benefit by excluding others. This is a privilege which, if it proves of value, should bear its proportion of the public burdens in the political subdivision having jurisdiction of the person and property of the inventor or owner. Nonetheless, for more than a century thereafter, wherever the courts, state or federal, had occasion to consider the subject or to refer to it, they considered it to be settled that patent rights were not assessable under the taxing powers of the states, as property.

However, in 1932, a New York corporation, engaged in the business of licensing copyrighted motion pictures in the State of Georgia, sued to restrain the collection of a state tax which was measured by gross receipts and hence was a direct charge on royalties. The Court, in *Fox Film Co.* v. *Doyal*, 286 U.S. 123, 1932, enunciated the following basic legal principles, which are considered as applying today to patents as well as copyrights:

"We are of the opinion that no controlling distinction can be based, in the case of copyrights, upon the character of the right granted. The argument that it is in the nature of a franchise or privilege bestowed by the Government, is met by the fact that it is not a franchise or privilege to be exercised on behalf of the Government or in performing a function of the Government.

"Copyright is a right exercised by the owner ... for his own profit and forms the basis for extensive and profitable business enterprises. ... after the copyright has been granted the Government has no interest in any action under it save the general one that its laws shall be obeyed ... a tax upon the gains derived from such operations is not a tax upon the exertion of any governmental function.

"We agree, however, with the contention that in this aspect royalties from copyrights stand in the same position as royalties from the use of patent rights, and what we have said ... applies as well ... to patents."

State Antitrust and Blue Sky Laws

Agreements for licensing and cross-licensing of patents, patent pools, and the like, were long regarded by state courts as outside the scope of state antitrust laws, merely because patents were involved. However, in recent years the tendency has been to hold at least some types of patent licensing agreements invalid under state antitrust laws. *Remington Rand, Inc.* v. *International Business Machines Corp.*, 35 USPQ 532, 532, N.Y. Sup.Ct. 1937.

Blue Sky Laws or State Securities Acts are found in most states and have as their purpose to protect investors by regulating the sale of securities. Licenses and permits are usually issued by a state securities commission after the necessary registration papers have been filed with it.

Many of these laws specify patent rights as among speculative assets. A good example is that of Oklahoma (Statutes 71-36) which states that if the information as to securities to be registered shall disclose that they have been or are intended to be issued for any patent right, they may be required to be delivered in escrow to the securities commission.

Blue Sky Laws have been held to be within the police powers of the states to protect the welfare of their citizens and not to constitute a burden on patent rights.

Cross-references: *Assignments, History of Patents —U.S., Licenses.*

SURVEYS. See MARKET SURVEYS AND PATENTS

T

TAXATION OF INCOME FROM PATENTS AND SECRET INFORMATION

Milam L. R. Wade

This article covers the application of the Internal Revenue Code of 1954 and related tax law to patent royalties and other income received from the transfer of patent rights, receipts by employees for assignments of patent applications and rights, spreading of income from an invention over several tax periods, compensatory damages for patent infringement, sale or license of secret information, sales or exchanges to or with controlled foreign corporations, and permissible deductions from gross income.

Special abbreviations are: "BTA" for Board of Tax Appeals; "TC," U.S. Tax Court; "TCM," Tax Court Memorandum Decisions; "Comm.," Commissioner of Internal Revenue; "Reg.," Regulations of Internal Revenue Service; "CB," Internal Revenue Cumulative Bulletin; P-H, Prentice-Hall, Inc.; "IRS," Internal Revenue Bulletin; and "IRC" or "Code," Internal Revenue Code of 1954.

Transfer of Patent Rights

Code Provisions (Section 1235)

"(a) A transfer (other than by gift, inheritance, or devise) of property consisting of all substantial rights to a patent, or an undivided interest therein which includes a part of all such rights, by any holder shall be considered the sale or exchange of a capital asset held for more than 6 months, regardless of whether or not payments in consideration of such transfer are

"(1) payable periodically over a period generally coterminous with the transferee's use of the patent, or

"(2) contingent on the productivity, use, or disposition of the property transferred.

"(b) For purposes of this section, the term "holder" means

"(1) any individual whose efforts created such property, or

"(2) any other individual who has acquired his interest in such property in exchange for consideration in money or money's worth paid to such creator prior to actual reduction to practice of the invention covered by the patent, if such individual is neither

"(A) the employer of such creator, nor

"(B) related to such creator (within the meaning of subsection (d))

"(c) This section shall be applicable with regard to any amounts received, or payments made . . . in any taxable year to which this subtitle applies, regardless of the taxable year in which such transfer occurred.

"(d) Subsection (a) shall not apply to any transfer, directly or indirectly, between persons specified within any one of the paragraphs of section 267(b); except that, in applying section 267(b) and (c) for purposes of this section:

"(1) The phrase '25 percent or more' shall be substituted for the phrase 'more than 50 percent' each place it appears in section 267(b), and

"(2) Paragraph (4) of section 267(c) shall be treated as providing that the family of an individual shall include only his spouse, ancestors, and lineal descendants. [As amended by P.L. 85-866, effective 9/3/58; for transfers on or before 9/2/58 the original section 1235(d) would apply.]

"(3) For special rule relating to nonresident aliens, see section 871(a)."

Meaning of "Patent" in Internal Revenue Code. The term "patent" means (1) a patent granted under 35 U.S.C., (2) a foreign patent with generally similar rights, (3) application for U.S. patent, and (4) the right an inventor has to apply for a patent.

Transfer by Sale, Exchange or Exclusive License. Section 1235 of the I.R.C. provides its own definition of sale or exchange.

The Senate Committee on Finance, in explaining the inclusion of transfers, where the consideration is contingent on the productivity, use or disposition of the property, within the concept of "sale or exchange," said:

"...exclusive licenses to manufacture, use and sell for the life of the patent, are considered to be 'sales or exchanges' because, in substantive effect, all 'right, title and interest' in the patent property is transferred (irrespective of the location of legal title or other formalities of language contained in the license agreement). Moreover, the courts have recognized that an exclusive license agreement ... may constitute a sale for tax purposes even where the right to 'use' the invention has not been conveyed to the licensee [along with right to make and sell], if it is shown that such failure did not represent the retention of a substantial right...."

The Regulations use the word "transfer" and avoid the expressions "sale" and "exchange" and the common law concepts of these words.

Where a transaction does not meet the tests of Section 1235, the resultant tax consequences are to be determined under other applicable provisions of the Code. Reg. Section 1.1235-1(b).

Intent, not Language of Transfer, is Controlling. In *Lockhart* v. *Comm.*, 258 F.2d 343, 119 USPQ 196, CA 3 1958, the right to manufacture and sell was specifically stated but "use" was not mentioned. The court said, "If the grantor has evidenced an intention to surrender to the transferee substantially all his rights in the patent, imperfections in draftsmanship, or the failure to use particular words do not control...." *Rollman* v. *Comm.*, 244 F.2d 634, 113 USPQ 356, CA 4 1957, states, "that it is not the name or form of an agreement but its true nature which controls its legal effect." In *Watson* v. *U.S.*, 222 F.2d 689, 105 USPQ 352, CA 10 1955, the court said, "The legal question ... must be determined by considering together the several provisions ..., not its title or the manner in which reference was made to the parties."

In another case the court ruled a transfer to be a sale notwithstanding the express statement: "This agreement shall be construed as a license of the aforesaid patents and not an assignment thereof." The court said in part: "[I]t is the operating intent of the parties that must control.... Thus the operative intent was plainly to pass all

the rights the plaintiff had. A transaction having such an intended effect was an assignment of the proprietary interest." *Pike* v. *U.S.*, 101 F. Supp. 100, 92 USPQ 105, DC Conn. 1951.

The courts have frequently considered parol evidence in getting at the true intent. Note this from *Magnus* v. *Comm.*, 259 F.2d 893, 119 USPQ 223, CA 3 1958: "The provisions for termination ... are ambiguous at best. But the agreement, as a whole, when viewed in the context of the declared intentions of the parties as testified to by taxpayer, leads us to the conclusion that the language used did not vest in taxpayer a right to terminate ... at will." In *Allen* v. *Werner*, 190 F.2d 840, 90 USPQ 133, CA 5 1951, the court said, "... the agreement, as to this feature, was ambiguous and uncertain in its terms and meaning and subject to explanation by parol evidence to show ... that the agreement should evidence a sale of all rights ..., subject to other provisions of the agreement."

In *Hans Jordan*, 27 TC 265, 1956, 111 USPQ 315, the Tax Court admitted oral testimony which had the effect of showing that the written agreement did not state the facts.

See, however, *Broderick* v. *Neale*, 201 F.2d 621, 96 USPQ 82, CA 10 1953, where the court said, "The intent and meaning ... must be determined from the language of the writing, and, if extraneous matter is to be considered, from the objective statements and acts of the parties and not from their subjective intentions, ... expressed after the contract was executed."

All Substantial Rights. The statute does not define this term.

The Senate Committee stated that

"...retention by the transferor of rights in the property which are not of the nature of rights evidenced by the patent and which are not inconsistent with the passage of ownership ... are not to be considered as such a retention as will defeat the applicability of this section.... a transfer terminable at will by the transferor would not qualify."

The Regulations say,

"...all substantial rights to a patent means all rights which are of value at the time the rights to the patent (or an undivided interest therein) are transferred. The circumstances of the whole transaction . . . shall be considered. . . . A transfer limited in duration . . . to a period less than the remaining life of the patent is not a transfer of all substantial rights. . . ." [Cf. 1964 amendment of section 39.117(q) of 26 CFR 1939.]

These rights may be retained: (1) legal title for the purpose of securing performance or payment, (2) retention of rights not inconsistent with the passage of ownership such as a security interest or a reservation in the nature of a condition subsequent; but the retention of other rights may or may not be substantial, depending upon the circumstances of the whole transaction. These others include (1) an absolute right to prohibit sublicensing or subassignment, (2) failure to convey the right to use or sell the patent property. Specifically, retaining a right to terminate a transfer at will "is the retention of a substantial right for the purposes of section 1235."

Retention by the vendor of legal title will not prevent the transfer from qualifying. *Arras* v. *U.S.*, 164 F. Supp. 150, 118 USPQ 10, DC Conn 1953; *Parke, Davis & Co.*, 31 BTA 427, 1934.

An exclusive license accompanied by an option to licensee to purchase the patent is not a transfer. In *Eterpen Financiera Sociedad* v. *U.S.*, 108 F. Supp. 100, 95 USPQ 191, Ct.Cls. 1952, the option agreement warranted that licensor was the sole and exclusive owner of the patent, i.e., after granting the license. The court held this situation distinguishable from *Myers*, 6 TC 258, 1946, 68 USPQ 346, and said that the license and option must be construed together.

A transfer of patent rights otherwise meeting the tests of section 1235 would not be denied capital gain treatment merely because of a geographical limitation. See *Rose Marie Reid*, 26 TC 622, 1956, 110 USPQ 145; *Dairy Queen* v. *Comm.*, 250 F.2d 503, CA 10 1957; *Comm.* v. *Celanese Corp.*, 140 F.2d 339, 61 USPQ 14, CA DC 1944; *Lamar* v. *Granger*, 99 F. Supp. 17, 90 USPQ 58, DC WPa 1951; and *Marco*, 25 TC 544, 1955, 108 USPQ 92. Section 1.1235-2(c) of the Regulations, in defining "undivided interest," states that such term would not include "a license limited geo-

graphically." The same statement appears in the Senate Committee report on section 1235. This expression does not appear at any other place in the Regulations respecting this section. In the *Waterman* case the Supreme Court held that the transfer of the exclusive right under a patent to make, use and vend within a specific part of the United States constituted an assignment. Apparently, therefore, the excerpt quoted from the Regulations covers only a nonexclusive license as distinguished from a conveyance of all rights.

In *U.S.* v. *Carruthers*, 219 F.2d 21, 104 USPQ 283, CA 9 1955, the licensee's rights to manufacture, sell and lease were limited to the tuna canning industry, but the court nevertheless held it to be a sale because the retained rights had no commercial value or their value was speculative. In *First National Bank of Princeton* v. *U.S.*, 136 F. Supp. 818, 108 USPQ 108, DC NJ 1955, the transfer was of the right to manufacture, use and sell only toothbrushes, the inventor retaining the right to use the patent on other brushes. The court said, "The reservation by Prof. Cooke here was like that in the Carruthers case—its monetary value was highly speculative." It has been held a sale for tax purposes where the transfer was an exclusive license to "2-sulfonamido pyrimidine" only under a patent which had claims to the genus "sulfonamido pyrimidines." *Merck & Co.* v. *Smith*, 261 F.2d 162, 119 USPQ 398, CA 3 1958. See, however, *American Chemical Paint Co.* v. *Smith*, 131 F. Supp. 734, 106 USPQ 361, DC EPa 1955. There the licensor reserved the right to manufacture, use and sell certain chemicals and processes under the patent, and the court said, "In the instant case, the patent rights were not designed for use solely in any particular industry. Therefore, the reservations . . . constituted substantial limitations on their use. . . ."

Waterman v. *Mackenzie*, 138 U.S. 252, S.Ct. 1891, is often cited, but the case did not involve taxes, and a number of the courts have declined to follow it in tax cases. *Lockhart* v. *Comm.*, supra, states the majority view: "We do not think, however. that the omission of the term 'use' [among the rights granted] was fatal. . . ." In *Mag-*

nus v. *Comm.*, supra, it was said, "But a more flexible rule has been applied by some courts . . . our inquiry is aimed at ascertaining only whether rights amounting to full and complete control were relinquished." Cf. *Schmitt et al.* v. *Comm.*, 271 F.2d 301, 123 USPQ 299, CA 9 1959.

A number of court decisions have applied to particular facts the expression "all substantial rights." Only a few have dealt with section 1235 of the 1954 Code or the similar section 117(q) of the 1939 Code, but they are cited because those sections are statutory recognitions of the then existing case law. The courts have held that retaining the following rights by the transferor would not involve transferring less than all substantial rights:

To defend or prosecute infringement suits, and dispose of recoveries. *Watson* v. *U.S.*, supra; *Roe* v. *U.S.*, 138 F. Supp. 567, 109 USPQ 246, DC STex 1956; *Graham*, 26 TC 730, 1956, 110 USPQ 454; and *Arras* v. *U.S.*, supra.

To use the patented apparatus in consulting work. *A.C. Ruge*, 26 TC 138 1956, 109 USPQ 300.

To terminate for nonpayment of royalty. *Storm* v. *U.S.*, 243 F.2d 708, 113 USPQ 305, CA 5 1957; *Magnus* v. *Comm.*, supra; *Lamar* v. *Granger*, supra; *Arras* v. *U.S.*, supra; and *First National Bank of Princeton* v. *U.S.*, supra.

To control quality of products produced under the patent or right. *Dairy Queen* v. *Comm.*, 250 F.2d 503, CA 10 1957.

To license others if the licensee fails to produce a stipulated quantity or amount. *Watson* v. *U.S.*, supra.

To terminate in event of dissolution or bankruptcy of licensee. *Comm.* v. *Celanese Corp.*, supra, and *Lamar* v. *Granger*, supra.

To cancel if the FTC issues a cease and desist order or the courts hold the patent invalid. *First National Bank of Princeton* v. *U.S.*, supra.

Retention by vendor of a royalty free license to use the patent. *Kavanagh* v. *Evans*, 188 F.2d 234, 89 USPQ 350, CA 6 1951.

Retention of an undivided part or share. *Kavanagh* v. *Evans*, supra; but see *Walen* v. *U.S.*, 273 F.2d 599, 123 USPQ 571, CA 1 1959.

To cancel if the patent is "shelved" or manufacture and sale discontinued. *Arras* v. *U.S.*, supra; *Storm* v. *U.S.*, supra.

Undivided Interest, Including a Part of All Substantial Rights.

This part of Section 1235 has not been extensively dealt with by the courts. The regulations say a person does not own an undivided interest unless "he owns the same fractional share of each and every substantial right"; and that a license covering some but not all valuable claims or uses would not qualify. In the Senate Committee report it was stated: "By 'undivided interest' a part of each property right represented by the patent (constituting a fractional share of the whole patent) is meant. . . ."

It has been said, although *obiter*, that: "Under the *Waterman* case and other cases, clearly a sale of an undivided share of the patent rights may be made, the remaining share being retained." *Crook* v. *U.S.*, 135 F. Supp. 242, 108 USPQ 117, DC WPa 1955.

Kavanagh v. *Evans*, supra, involved a conveyance with a license back to the assignor. The court said, "It was entirely lawful for him to retain an undivided part or share of his exclusive patent rights." But in *Walen* v. *U.S.*, supra, the court said, "We do not question that a taxpayer might sell a partial interest in an invention. However, to do so it should be of a measurable, identifiable share, and not an undefined one of elastic proportions dependent upon how many subsequent 'shares' the grantor might elect to create."

Disqualifying Retention of Substantial Rights. Rights that cannot be retained, if the transfer is to qualify as a transfer of all substantial rights under Section 1235, would include a grant for less than the whole period of the patent, the right to terminate the grant at the will of the transferor, and nonexclusiveness of the grant, as by nonexclusive license to another of the same subject matter in the same territory.

Definition of Holder. "Holder" is the individual whose efforts created the property and any other individual who acquired his interest for a consideration in money or money's worth paid prior to actual reduction to practice, but does not include the employer of the creator, spouse, ancestors and lineal descendants, corporations of which 25 per cent or more in value of the outstanding stock is owned directly or indirectly by or for the creator, or certain fiduciaries.

Primary "holder" is the individual who qualifies as the inventor.

The regulations do not define "money or money's worth" but state that "actual reduction to practice" has the same meaning as it has under Section 102(g) of Title 35, U.S.C. Reduction to practice for tax purposes may occur before or after the application; "actual practice" is defined to mean testing and operating the patent successfully under operating conditions.

The employee-owner of the residual rights, above his employer's shop right, may qualify as the holder of such residue. In *Hans Jordan*, supra, the Tax Court said such shop rights as petitioner's employer had did not dilute employee-petitioner's substantial rights in the patent within the meaning of Section 117(q) of the 1939 Code. See also *Herbert C. Johnson*, 30 TC 675, 1958, 118 USPQ 42.

The Regulations disqualify a partnership; however, each member is treated as a subholder as to his share of the patent. Both amateurs and professional inventors may be holders. The mere fact that title is held by one person does not prevent another from being considered as a holder if the latter was a joint developer of the patent.

Assuming reasonable grounds therefor, additional royalty payments in respect of patents previously transferred, provided for in a subsequent agreement, are still to be treated as consideration for the transfer. *Hofferbert* v. *Briggs*, 178 F.2d 743, 84 USPQ 36, CA 4 1949.

Holding Period. To qualify for long-term capital gain treatment, it is not necessary that the patent be held for more than six months or for any required period.

Payment to Employees for Assignment of Patent Applications or Patents. It is customary for employers to place those technical employees, in positions to make inventions, under contract to assign the inventions. Some concerns make nominal payments when the applications are assigned and also when the patents issue; these payments vary from a few dollars to 100 dollars or more in some instances. A small number of companies give bonuses of size related in some manner to the earnings or prospects from the use, sale or licensing of the patent.

There are two problems in these hiring situations. The first involves ownership of the inventions when made and the other the tax consequences.

Cases on shop rights include *Hapgood* v. *Hewitt*, 119 U.S. 226, 1958; *Solomons* v. U.S., 137 U.S. 342; *McAleer* v. *U.S.*, 150 U.S. 424; *Gill* v. *U.S.*, 160 U.S. 426; and *U.S.* v. *Dubilier Condenser Corp.*, 289 U.S. 178, 1933. The acquisition of shop rights by the employer would not involve a tax question; in rare instances only is the employee paid for the shop right and any payment would constitute ordinary income because the employer receives only a non-exclusive license.

The principal problem arises in applying the tax law under such circumstances as *Standard Parts Co.* v. *Peck*, 264 U.S. 52, 1923, holding that one employed to make an invention and who succeeds is bound to assign to his employer any patent obtained, even though the contract did not expressly provide that a patent would be solicited and assigned; *Marshall* v. *Colgate-Palmolive-Peet Co.*, 175 F.2d 215, CA 3 1949, where there was no contract but a showing of custom and practice which the employee knew of and acquiesced in; and *Air Reduction Co.* v. *Walker*, 118 Miss. 827, 195 NYS 120, 1921, where there was no express agreement to assign but the employee was hired to discover and invent some practical use for a product.

Section 1.1235-1(c)(2) of the Regulations provides that, in deciding whether sums received are attributable to a transfer of a patent (or an undivided interest therein) or represent compensation for services, all facts and circumstances will be considered. These include dependence of the payments upon the production, sale, use of, or value of the patent to the employer. As indicated in the cases discussed infra, it is difficult to determine what practical meaning the Revenue Service intends giving to this Regulation. The Courts, particularly the Tax Court, appear to believe that it should be construed liberally in favor of the employee-assignor.

A case that is important in itself and also in its review of the case law is *Roland Chilton*, 40 TC 552, 138 USPQ 336, 1963. The case involved income tax for the years 1954 to 1957. Chilton was hired as a "Consulting

Engineer" to "devote his whole time and apply his inventive ability [during business hours] to the problems, improvements, and developments relating to the Company's products and products similar to the Company's products referred to him by the Company." He agreed to assign his inventions, and the Company to pay him $15,000 as salary and 2½ per cent of the list price of articles made and sold under his patents as "additional compensation." After several years of reporting all income as ordinary, Chilton began reporting the royalties received as gain from sale of capital assets. The court noted that the employment contract called for "engineering work" and that the Company, having an option for 90 days to decide whether to accept assignment of Chilton's inventions, had not accepted all of them for patenting. The court held that Chilton was not "hired to invent" and the royalty income was capital gain.

Whether a scientist employed for industrial research can be considered as not hired to invent is a question that can be answered only on the basis of all facts and circumstances. While *Chilton* would seem to provide a guide, no invariable rule can be stated.

Chilton was followed by two other cases in both of which the employee-inventor prevailed. In *Thomas H. McClain*, 40 TC 841, the patent plan of Lockheed Aircraft Corporation was set out in detail. McClain agreed in his employment contract to assign all of his inventions, improvements and new methods of manufacture or process, and any patents issued thereon, in or relating to the field of aviation, whether made, discovered or produced during regular working hours or otherwise and whether or not at employer's suggestion. Under a plan, inaugurated subsequent to McClain's employment, employee-inventors received $50 upon assignment, $100 upon issuance of the patent, and a percentage of royalties or sums received from licenses or sales of rights. McClain invented a windshield construction that he conceived of while assigned as a layout draftsman to design window installations for the cockpit section of a new aircraft, but Lockheed had anticipated that McClain would use the existing state of the art, i.e.,

the then available materials and techniques. Citing Section 1.1235-1(c)(2) and the *Rose Marie Reid* and *Roland Chilton* cases, the Tax Court said:

"It is clear that petitioner was not hired to invent, and Lockheed . . . paid him the amounts in dispute in full compliance with its successive patent plans. . . . they were not mere wages, but were attributable to the transfer of the patent rights and at least a part of the consideration for such transfer. . . ."

T. Gardner Hill, TC Memo 1963-211, 22 TCM 1056, also involved the Lockheed plan, in effect when Hill was employed. Hill was required to assign his inventions. The Tax Court considered *Standard Parts Company* v. *Peck*, supra, and *Arthur N. Blum*, 11 TC 101, aff. in *Blum* v. *Comm.*, infra, all of which cases had been cited by the Commissioner. The Court held that these cases were not controlling, because Hill was not hired to invent, and said: ". . . Lockheed hired petitioner as a supervisor and manager at a certain salary, with the added agreement that certain patentable inventions would be transferred to Lockheed in consideration of certain payments (which had no connection with his salary payments) contingent upon Lockheed selling or licensing the invention. . . . [T]he payments in question . . . were consideration payments for his patent assignment."

Another case decided subsequent to enactment of Section 1235 is *Becker et al.* v. *U.S.*, 161 F. Supp. 333, 117 USPQ 226, DC WPa 1958. Becker, vice president and general manager for engineering and construction of Koppers Co., had no written employment contract. He was not hired to make inventions but, in a previous capacity, had assigned to the company eight minor inventions, voluntarily and without compensation. In 1920 he made an important invention, and in March, 1921, he agreed in writing with Koppers to assign all inventions for substantial payments at rates set in proportion to net earnings of his division, provided he was still employed. For several years Becker reported such payments as ordinary income, then claimed a refund on the capital gain theory. The court overruled the Commissioner's disallowance and said the "payments involved in this case constitute proceeds of a sale of a capital asset and are taxable as long-term capital gains."

In decisions under the former tax statute, i.e., before 1954, two were favorable to the employee-inventor and one held the additional payments to be ordinary income. In *Hofferbert* v. *Briggs*, supra, there was some question as to whether the corporation was entitled to the patents under the employment contract. The Court said,

"Even if it be thought that the corporation was entitled to the transfer under the terms of the original contract, certain it is that the transfer had not been made; and it was not made until after the contract of 1940 had settled the rights of the parties.... Whatever construction be put upon the terms of the original contract, the transfer for which the contract of 1940 provided was necessary ..., and the royalties here in question were unquestionably paid in consideration of the transfer.... Payment for the transfer of a capital asset does not suffer a change of character ... because made in addition to a prior consideration."

It is difficult to distinguish between *William M. Kelly*, 6 TCM 646, 1947, and *Blum* v. *Comm.*, 11 TC 101, 183 F.2d 281, 78 USPQ 272, CA 3 1950. In *Kelly* the additional payments were held to be taxable as capital gains and in *Blum* they were treated as ordinary income. In *Kelly* the decision apparently turned on the fact that, at the time the employee was hired as an inventor, he had already perfected the working model of his basic and most important invention, and the further observation "it is obvious that the corporation did not consider itself already the owner of the patents." In *Blum* the first contract appears ambiguous and was apparently so considered by the employee. Before the second contract was executed, which definitely provided for the assignment of the patents, Blum had perfected the chain saw. The Court, however, treated the three contracts as interrelated and constituting a single employment contract under which the employee was "... not only employed to invent but was specifically required to assign any patents obtained on his inventions to the Company." Moreover, the Court said the appeal did not "primarily involve a con-

struction of the tax statutes or regulations," but instead should be decided on the basis of patent law, citing *Standard Parts Co.* v. *Peck*, and *Marshall* v. *Colgate-Palmolive-Peet Co.*, supra. In view of Section 1235 and the regulations issued thereunder, it is conceivable that *Blum* would be ruled differently if decided today.

Blum was cited in *Cohen*, 15 TC 261, 1950, and *William B. Stout* v. *Comm.*, 185 F.2d 855, CA 6 1950, affirming TC Memo Decision, par. 49,265 P-H Memo TC, but in *Cohen* the real issue was whether receipts from a so-called royalty agreement were taxable to Cohen or to a trust, and in *Stout* the Tax Court found that petitioner did not actually sell any patents and that the "royalties" were ordinary compensation but were designated differently, to avoid comparison with salaries paid to other officers. *Blum* was cited unsuccessfully in the *Chilton* case.

Other cases holding income from assignments to be capital gain but involving unusual conditions are: *Herbert Johnson*, supra; *Raymond W. Hessert*, 6 TCM 1190, 1947; and *Rose Marie Reid*, supra.

As the case law now stands, probably the only payments to employees for assignments that would surely be ruled as ordinary income are those where the employee is specifically hired to invent and, in view of *Chilton*, perhaps only where he was employed to bring about invention in a particular field.

Employers who grant substantial bonuses for inventions would no doubt welcome an awards plan that meets the Code requirements for capital gains treatment, thus providing additional incentive for new and useful discoveries, if that could be done without loss of deductibility of the sums paid.

Spreading Income Over Tax Periods

Section 1302 of the 1954 Code is applicable only where an individual has income from an invention which is not taxable as a gain from the sale or exchange of a capital asset held for more than 6 months, either under the ordinary capital gain provisions of the Code or Section 1235.

The time of the work "from the beginning to the completion" of the invention must cover a period of at least 24 months, and the spreading is permitted only to income received by individuals who have "created" the inventions. It is frequently difficult to determine when an inventor begins to work on an invention, but it would undoubtedly be agreed that the time would start when an inventor began reducing his idea to drawings, models or written descriptions. Completion might and might not be the same as actual reduction to practice. Since a patent may be issued before actual reduction to practice, it is possible that eventually the courts would decide that completion would end when the patent is issued.

The beginning may not be pushed back to the germ of an idea or the taking of mental notice of passing data. The "beginning" must represent some demonstrative decision to take affirmative action to perfect the idea. *Beardsley* v. *U.S.*, 140 F. Supp. 541, 109 USPQ 27, DC Conn 1956.

The end of the period is the close of the taxable year in which the qualifying amounts are received or accrued. The total length shall be the shorter of (a) the period of work on the invention down to the close of the taxable year, or (b) 60 calendar months.

The income is to be allocated in equal portions to each calendar month which falls within the allocation period, i.e., the entire amount of gross income from the invention received or accrued in the current taxable year is divided by the entire number of calendar months included within the allocation period and multiplied by the number of such calendar months falling within a particular taxable year.

It is necessary to show that gross income from the invention includible in the taxable year will be 80 per cent of the income from the invention received or accrued in the taxable year, previous taxable years, and in the 12 months immediately succeeding the close of the taxable year.

The tax attributable to the Section 1302 gross income shall not exceed the aggregate of the taxes attributable to such income had it been received ratably over the allocation period. First a tax computation is

made for the taxable year in the usual manner disregarding Section 1302. Section 1302 is then brought into play and the resultant additional tax for the previous years is determined and a second computation is made for the taxable year including in the taxable year only the income allocable to that year under Section 1302. The series of computations producing the lesser aggregate tax will govern.

In *McEuen* v. *Comm.*, 196 F.2d 127, CA 5 1952, it was held that, in determining whether taxpayer received, in 1943, 80 per cent of the aggregate income from his invention within 36 months, it was proper to include in 1943 a payment only *constructively* received in that year. See also *Williams* v. *U.S.*, 84 F. Sup. 362, 81 USPQ 536, Ct.Cls. 1949.

In *Thompson* v. *Comm.*, 203 F.2d 820, CA 4 1953, dealing with the "spread back" of back pay, the court said, "the statute is remedial in nature and should be liberally construed...." Cf. *Sovik* v. *Shaughnessy*, 92 F. Supp. 202, aff. 191 F.2d 895, CA 2 1951.

The reasoning of the *Thompson* case was approved in *Sedlack* v. *Comm.*, 203 F.2d 825, CA 7 1953. *Young* v. *Comm.*, 269 F.2d 89, 122 USPQ 164, CA 2 1959, is also authority for a liberal construction. However, in *Van Hook* v. *U.S.*, 204 F.2d 25, CA 7 1953, the court, citing *Lindstrom* v. *Comm.*, 149 F.2d 344, CA 9 1945, said in part: "A taxpayer who claims the benefit of that section must show that he comes squarely within the letter and spirit of the Congressional grant." See also *Sloane* v. *Comm.*, 188 F.2d 254, CA 6 1951.

Commissions and other expenses paid in connection with income that is spread over several tax periods should be treated as if paid ratably over the same period. I.T. 3773, CB 1945, p. 151.

Compensatory Damages for Patent Infringement (Section 1304)

Compensatory damages for infringement represent "an amount awarded pursuant to a judgment or decree by a court as the result of a civil action for infringement of a patent (or contributory infringement) which action is authorized by title 35, U.S.C. 281," limited to that portion which represents damages to compensate for actual infringement sustained. They do not include "increased damages awarded by the court over and above the amount found adequate to compensate for the infringement, attorney's fees, interest or costs." Within these limits damages may include awards pursuant to a consent decree or judgment or the amount received or accrued in a settlement after decree or judgment, even though as to this last the amount is not made a part of the consent decree (but here taxpayer must show the portion which represents compensatory damages). Amounts received or accrued in a settlement where no judgment or decree is entered do not constitute compensatory damages. The damages must be in respect of a patent issued or granted by the United States pursuant to 35 U.S.C. 153. Reg. [Triple damages in antitrust suits are deductible. *New York Times*, 8/22/64, p. 26. Ed.]

Compensatory damages are allocated in equal portions to each calendar month including those of the current calendar year "which fall within the period during which the court has determined the infringement to have occurred." Reg. The tax for the current year is computed as follows: (1) Compute the tax for the current year by including the entire amount of compensatory damages as received or accrued in such year. (2) Compute the tax for the current year after excluding compensatory damage awards. (3) For each of the other years involved, recompute the tax by including compensatory damages allocated to that year. The tax for the current year shall be the lesser of the (a) tax for the current year as computed by including all compensatory damages as income of the current year, or (b) tax for such year after excluding compensatory damages allocated to the previous years plus the aggregate of additional taxes for the prior years attributable to allocated compensatory damages. Reg. Amounts allocable to each year, of awards received in respect of transactions within Section 1235, are considered as from the sale or exchange of a capital asset. Reg.

Special Rules Applicable to Spreading Income Over Tax Periods and Compensa-

tory Damages. Disregard a fraction of a month unless it amounts to more than half a month, in which case it is considered a month. These computations do not affect the tax on self-employment income. Amounts allocable to a particular year are considered income only of the person required to include the item in a separate return. Section 1307 of the Code.

Sale of Secret Information

Secret information, commonly referred to as "know-how," is a form of intellectual property. "It is well settled that secret processes may constitute property and be dealt with contractually as such." *G. E. Nelson* v. *Comm.*, 203 F.2d 1, CA 6 1953. It would seem, therefore, that sales of such property should be taxed in a manner similar to that for patents.

This point is discussed in *duPont* v. *U.S.*, 288 F.2d 904, 29 USPQ 473, 479, Ct.Cls. 1961. DuPont had transferred certain secret information to another party. The transfer, however, was not exclusive; the terms did not prevent duPont from disclosing the information to others or allowing others to use it. For this reason the transfer resembled a nonexclusive license under a patent. While the treatment of the income under an exclusive transfer of secret information was not at issue, the court considered *obiter* the different treatment that would have been accorded if the transfer had been exclusive and said in part:

"A person may pay the discoverer of a trade secret for its disclosure, but in fact the disclosure which is purchased carries with it the right to use the trade secret without liability to the owner. This is the instant case. Again, a person may pay the discoverer of a trade secret for disclosure (i.e., the privilege of using the trade secret) and in addition pay for the residual right possessed by the discoverer—the right to prevent unauthorized disclosure. And this right to prevent unauthorized disclosure is effectively, as stated above, the right to prevent anyone else from using the secret process. . . .

"When a patent owner gives not only the right to operate under the patent but in addition conveys all or a part of his remaining rights in the patent (particularly the right to exclude others from using the idea) in exchange for money, the disposition is complete. The transaction satisfies the 'sale' requirement of the Code, and any gain on the transaction may be entitled to capital treatment...."

The court then concluded that since duPont did not grant to the transferee the right to prevent further disclosure of the secret process, "the disposition of the trade secret did not meet the requirements of a 'sale.' Accordingly, the gain realized on the transaction must be taxed as ordinary income."

In Rev. Rul. 64-56, IRB 1964-8,9, the Internal Revenue Service has ruled that the unqualified transfer in perpetuity of the exclusive right to use a secret process, or the unqualified transfer of the exclusive right to make, use and sell an unpatented but secret process within a particular country, will be treated as the transfer of all substantial rights in the property in that country. This ruling provides some guides as to what is to be included in the transfer, but states that each case will have to be decided on its own particular facts.

Sales or Exchanges of Patents and Secret Information to Controlled Foreign Corporations

Section 1249 of the 1954 Code (added by P.L. 87-834) provides that:

"[Gain] from the sale or exchange after December 31, 1962 [but only if includible in a taxable year beginning after 12/31/62], of a patent, an invention, model, or design (whether or not patented) ..., a secret formula or process, or any other similar property right to any foreign corporation by any United States person (as defined in section 7701(a)(30)) which controls such foreign corporation shall, if such gain would [except for this section] be gain from the sale or exchange of a capital asset or of property described in section 1231, be considered as gain from the sale or exchange of property which is neither a capital asset nor property described in section 1231, ... control means ... the ownership, directly or indirectly, of stock possessing more than 50 percent of the total combined voting power of all classes of stock entitled to vote ... [The] rules for determining ownership of stock prescribed by section 958 shall apply."

Deductions from Gross Income

Research and Experimental Expenditures. Section 174, new in the 1954 Code, provides that such expenditures may be treated as expense or capitalized. Capitalized research and experimental expenditures may be amortized over a period to be selected by the taxpayer (of not less than 60 months), but this does not apply to capitalized patent costs.

The Regulations provide that the expenditures to which Section 174 applies may relate either to a general research program or to a particular project but they must be incurred in connection with the taxpayer's trade or business, must represent research and development costs in the laboratory sense and would include expenditures for the improvement of already existing property. Included are costs of obtaining a patent, such as attorney's fees and expenditures for research or experimentation carried on for taxpayer by another person or organization, but not the cost of acquiring another's patent, model, production or process.

Costs of land and depreciable property and improvements thereto are not deductible regardless of the fact that the property or improvements may be used in research or experimentation. However, depreciation of those facilities is considered as research or experimental expenditures for purposes of Section 174.

Such expenditures which result in the production of depreciable property to be used in the business (not including the labor and material costs of the property itself and installation costs thereof) may be claimed as current expenses under Section 174.

The Commissioner's consent is not required if taxpayer adopts the method of deducting these costs for the year he first pays or incurs such expenditures; he may, at any time, with the consent of the Commissioner, adopt that method but such consent may not be applied retroactively beyond the current year.

If the expense method is elected, which may be done notwithstanding different treatment on the books and in financial statements, all such expenditures should be claimed because they may not later be capitalized or amortized. Rev. Ruls. 58-74 and 58-78, CB 1958-1, p. 148.

In *Jno. F. Koons*, 35 TC 1092, 1961, the Tax Court declined to allow as an expense deduction under Section 174 some 45 thousand dollars spent to develop a patent because it found that the expenditures were not made in connection with an existing business. The invention was not patented until some 3 years after these expenditures were made. Cf. *Chas. H. Schafer*, TCM 1964-156 and *Martin Mayrath*, 41 TC #56.

Where expenditures are capitalized and amortized and a patent is later secured, the unamortized expenditures are treated as cost of the patent and said remaining sum is thereafter recovered by way of depreciation. Non-qualifying expenditures of a capital nature must be recovered by way of depreciation or at time of disposition. Reg. 1.1016-5(j).

Unamortized or undepreciated capitalized costs, whether or not under Section 174, on projects later abandoned, constitute deductible losses for the year of abandonment. *Dresser Mfg. Co.*, 40 BTA 341, 1938, and Reg., Section 1.1016-5(j). Cf. *Homer L. Strong*, 14 BTA 902, 1928. The basis for gain or loss and depreciation would apparently also include development costs deducted as expenses in a year as to which the taxpayer had no election to expense such items. *Goodell-Pratt Co.*, 3 BTA 30, 1925.

Litigation Expenses. If there is asserted a claim to a property interest in a patent and royalties already accrued, there would be a division of litigation costs between capital and income in the ratio of the remaining value of the patent at the time of the decree and the amount of the royalties involved. Cf. *Wm. A. Falls*, 7 TC 66 1946, 69 USPQ 557. In *Safety Tube Corp.* v. *Comm.*, 168 F.2d 787, 78 USPQ 312, CA 6 1948, the court said all such costs were capital expenditures, but no mention was made of Section 23(a) (2) of the 1939 Code. Where there is a recovery of damages for infringement, the expenses should be charged against such recoveries. If there is no re-

covery but simply a decree more perfectly establishing plaintiff's title, it would seem that the expenses should be capitalized.

Depreciation. As patents have a life of 17 years, the cost of each, if the research and development costs have been capitalized or represented capital expenditures under the law then in effect, should be deducted ratably over this life, i.e., 1/17th each year. Depreciation is allowed from the date the patent is granted. *John Douglas Co.*, 23 BTA 1308 1931 and *Ward* v. *U.S.*, 32 F. Supp. 743, DC Mass 1940. In *Kraft Foods Company*, 21 TC 513 1954, the Tax Court adopted a special method of computing depreciation where a group of patents were acquired for a lump sum and the cost of each was indeterminable. The ratio of the number of days of remaining life that expired in the taxable year to the number of days of unexpired patent life at the beginning of the taxable year for all patents was applied to the basis for all of the patents to arrive at the depreciation deduction.

Cross-references: *Accounting . . . , Incentives for Inventors, Profiting from Patents.*

TEACHING PATENT LAW TO ENGINEERING AND OTHER SCIENCE STUDENTS

Fred H. Rhodes

The scientist or engineer must look to the law of patents for the legal protection of his rights to any invention or discovery that he may make. For this reason, any program for training men for professional work in science or in engineering should include some instruction in patent law.

Nature and Importance of the Course

Such instruction will differ, in both extent and emphasis, from that provided for men contemplating professional careers as patent attorneys. The scientist or engineer is rarely, if ever, called upon to formulate the patent applications covering his inventions or to prosecute them in the Patent

Office. He is neither qualified nor expected to act as his own attorney in infringement suits or in other actions involving issued patents. For these reasons, the course in patent law offered to technical students should include no more instruction in the formal details of preparing patent applications or in the procedures in prosecuting patent actions than is required to provide a general acquaintance with the law of patents and of the protection afforded him under that law.

The technical man is greatly interested, however, in protecting his rights to his invention until his patent is issued and in securing to himself, in his patent, the full measure of protection that is properly his. He should know how to recognize an invention when he makes one; he should realize that sometimes a new idea that appears to him to involve the exercise of no very exceptional scientific imagination may have sufficient novelty to render it patentable and sufficient utility to make it valuable. Any program of instruction in patent law for technical students should emphasize keeping adequate records which can be made the basis for a proper patent application and will be admitted as evidence in patent actions and avoiding statements or acts that might jeopardize his right to the invention or any aspect of it. Such program should also prepare him to work in close accord with the patent attorney in the preparation and prosecution of the application and to provide the attorney with all available pertinent information.

Since many patentable inventions are now made by teams of men working together on phases of a general problem, some special attention should be paid to the granting of patents for inventions so made and to the rights of the individual inventors. Another topic of special present interest is that of the patentability of inventions made in government laboratories or in institutional laboratories under grants from government agencies.

Adequate instruction in patent law for technical students can be provided in a one-semester course of thirty or, preferably, forty-five one-hour lectures. A single such course can meet the requirements in the several branches of science and engineering, although a few of the topics are of special importance in the separate fields. For example, the law as it applies to plants is of particular interest to men in the plant sciences; students in chemistry and chemical engineering are especially concerned with the law as it relates to new chemical compounds or compositions, new processes of manufacture, or new uses for modified forms of previously known compositions.

Because of the limited time available for instruction in patent law in our technical curricula, any course in this subject almost necessarily consists of lectures with, of course, discussion of those cases that best illustrate and exemplify the significant points. There is not sufficient time for critical study of many cases by the students, and often the necessary source material is not conveniently at hand.

Since few universities offer such courses and since changes in the statutes and new rulings of the Patent Office and the courts make textbooks on patent law obsolescent rather rapidly, the market for such books is so limited and temporary that many publishers are reluctant to undertake their publication. In the curriculum in chemical engineering at Cornell University, Rhodes' "Elements of Patent Law" published in 1949 by the Cornell University Press has been used as a textbook, although changes in the statutes and their interpretation necessitate supplementing it with extensive notes.

Principal Topics

A course in patent law suitable for technical students should cover the following principal topics:

(1) *History of the American Law of Patents:* Origin of the English patent law and development to the time of the United States Constitution. Constitutional provision for the granting of patents. Progressive development of the patent statutes. Changes in the federal departments or agencies charged with administration of the statutes. Present organization of the Patent Office.

Patents as limited monopolies. Not granted because of an inherent right of the inventor to a monopoly of his invention but as means for encouraging progress in science and the useful arts.

(2) *Who May Apply for a Patent:* Right to apply personal to inventor. Applications by joint inventors. Extent of collaboration required to constitute joint invention. Subtracting or adding inventors' names on an application or an issued patent.

(3) *Invention and Discovery:* Definition of these terms. Requirement of unobviousness. Evidences of invention. Types of new devices usually held to lack inventive quality.

(4) *Utility and Novelty:* Definition. Requirements for patentability. Previous knowledge. Previous description in a printed publication. Previous public use. Previous secret use. Experimental use.

(5) *Classes of Patentable Invention:* Machine. Article of manufacture. Process. Composition of matter. Plants asexually reproduced. Patentability of new uses for previously known compositions. Patentability of new compounds of a previously known class or chemical series.

(6) *Abandonment:* Definition. Abandonment by express statement; by failure to claim; by lack of diligence in reduction to practice or in filing application; by undue delay or failure to reply properly to actions of patent examiner; by other means.

(7) *Date of Invention:* Definition. Proving date of invention. Date of reduction to practice. What constitutes reduction to practice. Importance of valid evidence in proving dates.

(8) *Form of the Application:* The specification. Completeness and clarity required. Drawings. Models. The claims. Extension of patent monopoly only to aspects of the invention covered by claims. Claims to be based on disclosures in the specifications. Subordinate and coordinate claims.

(9) *Prosecuting the Application:* Primary examination. Responses to findings in the first action. Later examinations and responses. Appeals. Amending the application. Accelerating or delaying action on the application.

Interferences.

(10) *Correcting a Patent:* Certificate of Correction. Disclaimer. Reissue patents.

(11) *Rights Conferred by a Patent:* Duration of patent monopoly. Voiding a patent by infringement suit decided in favor of infringer; by suit under Declaratory Judgment Act; by annulment action. Patent covers right to exclude others from making, using or selling the invention. Patentee not obligated to use his invention.

Patent as property. Assignment, grant, license. License by implication. Valid and invalid provisions in licenses; resale price, use with specified unpatented accessories. License agreements in contravention of the antitrust laws. Manner of compensation for license.

Individual rights of patentees under a joint patent.

(12) *Infringement Actions:* What constitutes infringement. Penalties for infringement. Contributory infringement. Obtaining evidence of infringement. Declaratory Judgment proceedings. Defenses against claim of infringement. Infringement actions against Federal Government. Against contractors employed by agency of government.

(13) *Relative Rights of Employees and Employers:* Conditions under which title to patent belongs to employer; to employee. Shopright. Ownership of patents on inventions made by employee of a federal agency; by employee working for a private institution on a grant to the institution from a federal agency; by an employee of a university or nonprofit organization.

(14) *Records of Invention:* Importance of proper records. Laboratory and field notes, adequacy and proper authentication. Progress reports. Record of experimental use before filing.

(15) *Foreign Patents:* Value. Special provisions in some countries.

(16) *Patent Policies.*

(17) *Special Topics:*

(a) Patents and the antitrust law.

(b) Special provisions relating to chemical patents.

(c) Special provisions relating to drugs and pharmaceuticals.

(d) Suggested changes in the patent statutes.

(e) Design patents, copyright, trademarks, brief discussion only.

Patent law for students in science or engineering may be offered at the graduate level or, preferably, as an undergraduate course in the third or a later year of the curriculum. Before the third year, the students lack adequate professional preparation for full benefit from the course.

For many years, the School of Chemical Engineering at Cornell University has offered such a course. Experience with it has been very satisfactory. The course has proved generally interesting to those enrolled in it. Many graduates report that it has been of definite value to them in their later professional work. Several men who have taken this course in their engineering curriculum have, after graduation, completed work leading to a degree in law and have become successful patent attorneys.

Cross-references: *Application Writing, Claim Drafting, Examiners,* Section on Training ..., *Information for Independent Inventor, Prosecution, Teaching Patent Practice.*

TEACHING PATENT PRACTICE

Robert Calvert

Experience as a student or teacher in three large metropolitan institutions leads to the conclusion that such instruction in patent practice is most helpful. It is, however, only a start in a difficult profession. Skill in analyzing data, uncovering the often concealed invention, presenting a complete and convincing disclosure in clear and concise English, and meeting the other exacting needs of the highly specialized profession requires a long and inquisitive contact with informed associates, inventors, patent examiners and, for those who will be engaged in litigation, the courts.

The Teacher

Many colleges and engineering schools do not feel justified in maintaining a full member of the staff who is qualified in patent law. They rely frequently on practicing attorneys. However, successful attorneys have little or no spare time. Also many of the prospective students are employed by day, as engineers, chemists, physicists, etc.,

in industry. As a result, evening courses in patent law are given in many large cities. Leading local attorneys provide the knowledge and enthusiasm that comes from current, front-line exposure to patent problems.

For this teaching, there is available a diligent coterie of attorneys with conspicuously objective attitudes toward their communities and profession. On the basis of vitas at hand from representative contributors to this Encyclopedia, it is estimated that at least one-fourth of them have taught at some time or are still teaching patent law. These are mostly the same attorneys whose names appear over and over again in the patent journals. To ask them to teach a course is to honor them appropriately.

Subject Matter to Be Taught

Subjects to be taught should include one or more lectures on each of the major titles in this book, taken in a logical order for teaching purposes. These would include a number of additions to those subjects listed in the immediately preceding article by Professor Rhodes who pioneered and early introduced the course in patent law for engineers at Cornell University.

A suitable length of course is about three hours or a single two-hour class weekly for a year or two.

One university, many years ago, gave no assignments in claim drafting during the entire first year. The teacher lectured on patent law, to a considerable extent on what he thought it should be. At another institution, the subject was the law as it is, and assignments to the students in claim drafting began with the first session and continued almost weekly throughout the year.

Teaching Claim Drafting. There is a difference of opinion as to whether the school should instruct the future attorney in claim drafting. Some patent lawyers, of outstanding success in the strictly legal areas such as agreements, licenses and litigation, hold that claim drafting need not be taught in the college course. Perhaps they feel that proficiency and special interest so established in the patent solicitation phase of the subject may tend to mire the attorney in that area. It might retard his progress, as they would call it, to the more exciting court activity and allied lines. Others believe, to the contrary, that the patent lawyer will be more effective, even before the courts as well as in other aspects of his calling, if he is knowledgeable in all the ramifications of the subject including writing applications and soliciting patents.

Private communications to the writer give answers from 30 selected patent practitioners, mostly patent lawyers, to the question: "Do you think that a college course in patent law, for one to acquire your experience, should include a significant amount of training in application writing or prosecution?" The answers were: "Yes" 80 per cent, "No" 20 per cent. A factor in the votes against such instruction may be attributed to (1) the desire to avoid overemphasis on application writing, (2) the feeling that inadequate instruction on a very difficult procedure is of doubtful value, or (3) the belief that claim drafting after all can be learned only by long personal experience with practising associates.

A good claim, it will be agreed, includes all that is both unobvious over the prior art and operable for the purpose and excludes all that does not meet these requirements. Those who teach its drafting should preferably have had their ideas tested and refined in the fire of experience.

Book List

An abbreviated list of primary reading matter, texts for students and also reference works follows. The reference works are arranged in approximate order of increasing price, which becomes considerable for some of the multivolume sets but not out of proportion to their value for the practitioner or patent library.

Primary Reading Matter. "Patent Laws," U.S. Government Printing Office, Washington 25, D.C. 30 cents.

"Rules of Practice of the U.S. Patent Office in Patent Cases," *ibid.*, 50 cents.

"Guide for Patent Draftsmen," *ibid.*

"Manual of Patent Examining Procedure," Ernest A. Faller, Editor, *ibid.*, $6.25.

George V. Woodling, "Inventions and Their Protection," New York, Clark Board-

man Co., Albany, N.Y., Matthew Bender and Co., 1954.

A. K. Berle and L. S. de Camp, "Inventions, Patents and Their Management," New York, D. Van Nostrand Co., 1959.

Roger Sherman Hoar, "Patent Tactics and the Law," New York, The Ronald Press, 1950.

Chester H. Biesterfeld, "Patent Law for Lawyers, Students, Chemists, and Engineers," New York, John Wiley & Sons, 1949.

Arthur M. Smith, "Patent Law: Cases, Comments and Materials," 2 vols., Ann Arbor, Mich., Overbeck Co., 1954.

Robert Calvert, "Patent Practice and Management," New York, Reinhold Publishing Co., 1950. Illustrated mostly by chemical subject matter. Available only at libraries or second-handed.

Reference Works. "Dynamics of the Patent System," William B. Ball, Editor, New York, Central Book Co., 1960.

"Patents, Research and Management," Howard I. Forman, Editor, *ibid.*, 1961.

Texts. Joseph Rossman, "Industrial Creativity; the Psychology of the Inventor," New Hyde Park, N.Y., University Books, 1964.

Ridsale Ellis, "Patent Claims" (1949), "Patent Licenses" (1958), "Patent Assignments" (1955), "Trade Secrets" (1953), Mount Kisco, N.Y., Baker Voorhis and Co.

C. W. Rivise and A. D. Caesar, "Interference Law and Practice," 4 vols., with forms, Charlottesville, Va., The Michie Company, 1948.

A. W. Deller, "Walker on Patents," 7 vols. kept up to date by annual pocket supplements, 1964–, New York, Baker Voorhis Co., 1937.

TESTIMONY IN PATENT CASES. See EXPERT TESTIMONY

TRADEMARKS IN RELATION TO PATENTS

Frances B. Bernstein

A trademark is a word, symbol, device or combination thereof adopted by a manufacturer or merchant and used on his goods, or in connection with them, in order to identify his products and distinguish them from those of others. Unlike a patent, a trademark is a common law right, acquired through prior use, not by statutory grant. The modern trademark performs three basic functions. It serves as an indication of origin, a guarantee of consistency of quality, and an aid to advertising and sales. In short, it symbolizes the goodwill attaching to the products on which it is used. In the marketplace, however, the chief value of a modern trademark is not identification of the source of the product—which is often anonymous in this era of mass distribution —but stimulation of sales of the goods upon which it appears.

"A dual theme runs through the law of trademarks—protection of the trademark owner and protection of the public interest. If an infringer uses another's mark on his goods, this may lead to confusion of purchasers who will buy the infringer's product thinking it emanates from the trademark owner. Thus the consumer is injured as well as the trademark owner. Courts frequently have pointed out this fundamental difference between patent litigations, where the owner seeks to protect only his own rights, and trademark and unfair competition cases which are "affected with a public interest." The latter are, "broadly speaking, grounded on the right of both dealer and purchasing public to be protected from frauds of which both are victims." *General Baking Co.* v. *Gorman*, 3 F.2d 891, 893, CCA 1 1925.

Speaking of trademarks before the American Bar Association in 1962, Judge Giles S. Rich said in part:

"Trademark law is, I think, immensely more complicated and subtle, as 'law,' than is patent law, involving, as it does, the intertwined fields of common law rights to use and to exclude others from using, the statutory right to register and the right to prevent others from registering. One can speak reasonably of the 'patent system' or the 'copyright system' but there is no such thing as a trademark 'system.'... We have a common law and statutory conglomerate." **52 Trademark Reporter 1185.**

This "intertwined" complex nature of the trademark law and its tendency to change have been demonstrated strikingly within the past few years in several areas of interest to the patent bar. In March, 1964,

the Supreme Court handed down two decisions which narrowly limit the common law right of protection for unpatented industrial designs against unfair competition. By contrast, the Patent Office, in recent years, finally has admitted that designs such as containers and configurations of goods can become valid trademarks susceptible of registration on the Principal Register, and has answered affirmatively the question whether simultaneous or consecutive protection is available for the same design under the design patent and trademark laws. In the field of trademark licensing, recent decisions have recognized that the need for quality controls may require the trademark owner to limit his licensee's suppliers in a manner which would be invalid in a patent license.

Trademark Registration of Designs

The Trademark Act of 1946, popularly called the Lanham Act, created two registers for trademarks used in interstate commerce: the Principal Register which provides substantial evidentiary and substantive benefits for registrants, and the Supplemental Register which creates no such rights. The differences in purpose and scope of protection of the two registers led to the inclusion of two different definitions of a trademark, a general definition appearing in Section 45 and a specific definition for purposes of supplemental registration in Section 23. The former defines a mark in terms of "any word, name, symbol or device or any combination thereof..." 15 U.S.C. 1127. The latter, far broader, says:

"For the purposes of registration on the supplemental register a mark may consist of any trademark, symbol, label, package, configuration of goods, name, word, slogan, phrase, surname, geographical name, numeral, or device or any combination of any of the foregoing, but such mark must be capable of distinguishing the applicant's goods or services." 15 U.S.C. 1091.

For more than a decade, the Patent Office held that the broad language of Section 23 was applicable only to supplemental registrations and that even if a container or configuration of goods had acquired secondary meaning, it could not be registered on the Principal Register as it was not within the traditional definition of a trademark as exemplified by that set forth in Section 45. However, Section 2 of the Act, which describes trademarks registrable on the Principal Register, states: "No trademark by which the goods of the applicant may be distinguished from the goods of others shall be refused registration on account of its nature" unless it falls into one of the several prohibited categories, none of which includes containers, etc. 15 U.S.C. 1052. Moreover, Section 27 of the Act specifically declares that a supplemental registration shall not preclude registration on the Principal Register. 15 U.S.C. 1095.

The logic of these two sections and repeated arguments that the Lanham Act had been intended to broaden the scope of trademarks finally led the Patent Office to accept the theory that a container could become a valid trademark acceptable on the Principal Register if, in fact, the container had come to distinguish applicant's goods from those of another, i.e., if it had acquired a "secondary meaning." The landmark decision was *Ex parte Haig & Haig, Ltd.*, 118 USPQ 229, Comr.Pats. 1958. The case for registration was particularly strong. Haig & Haig had adopted a unique "pinched decanter" bottle for their best whiskey and had used it for over fifty years. Until 1952, when applicant began to use the word "PINCH" on the bottles, the only way to request this particular whiskey was to describe the bottle. The record showed that the bottle had been adopted for the purpose of distinguishing applicant's goods and did so distinguish them.

The unique circumstances of the case do not impel the conclusion that the floodgates have been lowered, but since the time of that case there has been a trickle of favorable decisions. Thus, in April, 1960, the Patent Office granted a Principal registration for "the distinctively shaped contour, or conformation and design" of the Coca-Cola bottle. There was no written opinion, but the Coca-Cola Company had presented extensive evidence of secondary meaning. It showed inter alia that the bottles had been used since 1916, that over $6\frac{1}{2}$ billion of them had been manufactured in the United States alone, and that they had been placed in the hands of consumers as a package some 228 billion times. Other decisions rejecting applications have recognized that if a distinctive container does acquire a secondary meaning, it is entitled to registration on the Principal Register.

The Patent Office also has recognized that a unique configuration of goods may be accepted on the Principal Register if it has come to indicate origin. The configuration, however, "must be restricted to the configuration of a particular part or feature of an article and may not extend to the entire shape or design thereof." *In re Duro-Test Corp.*, 134 USPQ 137, 138, Trademark Trial and Appeal Board 1962. In *Duro*, this standard was applied to reject an application to register the configuration of a light bulb on the Principal Register. The Patent Office also will not register any feature of the goods which performs a utilitarian function even if it also identifies the applicant's product. In other words, such configurations will be held to be incapable of distinguishing as a matter of law, and will be denied trademark protection even if, in fact, the public has come to recognize them as identifying applicant's goods. Both rules apply also to the Supplemental Register, and similar rules limit the right to common law protection against unfair competition.

These rules, however, are relaxed with reference to applications for either register where applicant seeks to register the design of a container, not as a trademark for containers, but as a mark for the product contained. Then the application may be for the overall contours of the container, and the fact that the container performs the function of containing is not a barrier. However, those particular features of the container which, it is claimed, have rendered it distinctive, or capable of becoming distinctive, of applicant's goods, must not be functional; an ordinary, non-unique bottle cannot be turned into a trademark merely by picturing it on cartons and featuring it in advertising. *In re McIlhenny Co.*, 278 F.2d 953, CCPA 1960. (Application to register TABASCO bottle on Principal Register rejected.)

Effect of Design Patent on Trademark Registration. Until relatively recently, even supplemental registrations were denied to designs which were the subject of existing or expired design patents or even were of a nature subject to design patent protection. Now the CCPA has ruled that the existence of a design patent is no barrier to trademark registration on either register. *In re Mogen David Wine Corp.*, 140 USPQ 575, 1964.

This rule is based on a recognition of the fundamental difference in the character of protection provided by a design patent and a trademark. The former creates a monopoly under which the patentee can exclude all use of his design for any purpose for a specified term of years. The latter does not create a monopoly; it merely protects any goodwill attaching to the design as an indicium of source for a particular product and thereby protects the public from deception. The Trademark Trial and Appeal Board had taken the first step when it permitted supplemental registration of a contour of a bottle covered by an existing design patent. The Board had theorized that, since supplemental registration conveys no trademark rights, but only records a claim, and since the owner of a distinctive container for his goods will receive no protection in many foreign countries absent a United States trademark registration, there is no compelling reason for refusing such registration even during the life of the design patent. *In re The Pepsi-Cola Company*, 120 USPQ 468, TTAB 1959.

Principal Registration, however, does convey substantive trademark rights. The Board had, therefore, concluded that if the exclusive use which the patentee enjoys by virtue of his patent monopoly were to be considered the "substantially exclusive and continuous use" necessary to prove secondary meaning, then the trademark laws would indeed be serving "in effect, to extend the protection accorded the patented design contrary to the purpose and intent of the patent law." *In re Mogen David Wine Corp.*, 134 USPQ 576, 578, TTAB 1962. It was this decision which the Court of Customs and Patent Appeals reversed stating:

"We recognize the distinction between registrations on the Principal and Supplemental Registers and their legal effects. However, we can find no supportable reasons in the purposes or philosophies of patent and trademark law to support the conclusion the board bases on that distinction. In our opinion, trademark rights, or rights under the law of unfair competition, which happen to continue beyond the expiration of a design patent do not 'extend' the patent monopoly. They exist independently of it, under different law and for different reasons. The termination of either has no legal effect on the continuance of the other.... We know of no provision of patent law, statutory or otherwise, that guarantees to anyone an absolute right to copy the subject matter of an expired patent." 140 USPQ at 579.

The language of the court, particularly the last sentence quoted above, should be compared with that of the Supreme Court in the *Sears* and *Compco* cases, discussed below, which preceded this decision by a few days.

Designs Covered By Mechanical Patents. Although there has been no recent decision on the question, it appears that in the case of mechanical patents, the design of a patented machine or of an article made by a patented process is permanently dedicated to the public and not subject to recapture as a trademark by exclusive use after expiration. This is the effect of the decision in *Kellogg Co.* v. *National Biscuit Co.*, 305 U.S. 111, 1938, wherein it was held that the pillow-shaped design of the cereal produced on a patented machine was dedicated to the public, and the fact that the former patentee alone had sold cereal in this shape for fifteen years after expiration of its patent did not create any trademark rights in that shape. Even though the public identified the shape with one source, this was not the type of secondary meaning to which protection would be accorded.

That decision could be explained in terms of the fact that the shape was functional with relation to the patented process. However, in *Scott Paper Co.* v. *Marcalus Mfg. Co.*, 326 U.S. 249, 256, 1945, the Court took a broader view. It stated that the patentee may not "secure, to any extent, a continuation of his monopoly by resorting to the trademark law and registering as a trademark any particular distinctive matter appearing in the specifications, drawings or claims of the patent whether or not such matter describes the essential elements of the invention or claims." This seems to point to the conclusion that the rules granting trademark protection to the subject of existing or expired design patents will not be extended to the subjects of mechanical patents.

Design Protection Under the Law of Unfair Competition

Statutory trademark protection of a design such as a container or configuration of goods is relatively recent; the common law, however, long has afforded a remedy where one trader has imitated the goods of another in order to "pass off" his goods as those of the plaintiff. To succeed, plaintiff has to establish that his design is nonfunctional and has acquired secondary meaning. The traditional form of relief was an injunction.

During March, 1964, however, the Supreme Court handed down two landmark decisions which forbade states to enjoin copying of any designs not protected by patent, copyright or trademark on the grounds that this would interfere with the broad purposes of the patent laws. Such attempts by the states to protect unpatented designs from imitation would be contrary to the intent of the federal patent laws; these laws protect against copying only for a limited period of time and only when certain standards of invention and novelty have been met. States may, at most, impose labeling requirements or require "other precautionary steps" to "prevent customers from being misled as to the source of the goods." But "mere inability of the public to tell two articles apart is not enough to support an injunction against copying or an award of damages for copying that which the federal patent laws permit to be copied." Even where the particular feature copied has acquired "secondary meaning" and is "nonfunctional," injunctions are not permissible. *Sears, Roebuck & Co.* v. *Stiffel Co.*, 140 USPQ 524, and *Compco Corp.* v. *Day-Brite Lighting, Inc.*, 140 USPQ 528.

The ultimate effect these two decisions will have on the law of unfair competition is uncertain. There will be increased pressure for Congressional action to provide statutory protection, for a limited time, for designs which do not qualify for design patents. There is doubt as to whether these decisions will prevent injunctions against imitation of containers and other trade dress as opposed to imitation of the article itself. The resolution of these questions will take time; in the interim, it is probable that more and more merchants will seek to qualify their designs for protection under the existing statutes. See Casser, "Trade Regulation: Legal Protection of Commercial Design," 1959 Wis. L. Rev. 652, 50 TMR 135, 1939.

Name of Patented Product: The Problem of Becoming Generic

There can be no trademark rights in the common descriptive name, i.e., the generic name, of a product and this rule applies whether or not the product is or has been patented. Prior to 1962, the Lanham Act provided that a trademark could be cancelled "at any time if the registered mark becomes the common descriptive name of an article or substance on which the patent has expired ..." The "Housekeeping Amendments" passed that year eliminated the reference to patent expiration in recognition of the fact that this rule applies equally to all marks.

The *Kellogg* case, supra, and *Singer Mfg. Co.* v. *June Mfg. Co.*, 163 U.S. 169, 1896, frequently have been misconstrued as indicating that the trademark for a patented product is dedicated to the public upon expiration of the patent. Actually, the words "Singer" and "Shredded Wheat" were held to be dedicated precisely because they were not trademarks; they were the only words available to describe the patented articles themselves, i.e., they were generic. "Singer" was later restored to trademark status by long, continued and exclusive use.

These two cases do illustrate the special dangers with relation to the unique product, whether patented or not. If the originator fails to choose a product name, the mark inevitably will fill that function as there will be no other way for the public to identify the product. When others start to make it, they will be entitled to use the name. Similarly, if the product name is unwieldy and difficult to pronounce, like "acetyl salicylic acid," and the trademark is short and "catchy," like "Aspirin," the public will appropriate the mark as the product name and the protection will not survive the patent. See *Bayer* v. *United Drug Co.*, 272 Fed. 505, DC SNY 1921. Even if there is a short, easily pronounced generic name for a product, such as "vacuum bottle," if the generic term is ignored, and the trademark exploited, the public ultimately may come to treat the trademark, e.g., "Thermos," as the product name. *King-Seeley Thermos Co.* v. *Aladdin Industries, Inc.*, 321 F.2d 577, CA 2 1963.

If, however, the patentee, or innovator of a nonpatented product, chooses both a trademark and an appealing product name, exploits both, and educates the public to the fact that the first is the brand and the second the generic name, the trademark can survive indefinitely. See Restatement of the Law, Second, Torts, Sec. 735 (Tentative Draft No. 8).

The more popular the trademark is, the more it is tied in the public mind to a single product and the more it becomes "a household word," the greater is the chance of losing it. Avoidance of these problems is discussed in three excellent booklets of the United States Trademark Association: *"Trademark Management," "Trademark Selection"* and *"Trademarks in the Marketplace."*

Use of Trademarks in Patent Applications

Since a true trademark is not the generic name of a product, it is obviously inadequate to disclose the composition of a material or construction of an article. Use of a trademark to describe an ingredient in a formula, for example, does not constitute the type of full disclosure demanded by the patent laws and the Examiner will not accept the mark for a showing of the identity.

When a trademark is used in an application, the mark should be treated as a proper noun. Moreover, use of a trademark as a generic name can be protested by the trademark owner.

Where there are numerous alternatives for a particular trademarked product, the applicant should have no difficulty in disclosing his invention without describing any product by trademark. But if there is no obvious alternative and the mark is for a secret formula, the applicant may have considerable difficulty; when cooperation from the trademark owner is not forthcoming, applicant will need to discover for himself other materials which can be used to produce the same result. These he can then list, with the trademarked item also as an alternative, in the hope of being able later to furnish identification of it as of the date of filing the application.

This entire problem of improper trademark use in applications has been considered in an excellent article by Manuel C. Rosa, Executive Examiner, Patent Examining Operation, "Caution in the Use of Trademarks in Patents," 47 TMR 453, 1957. See also M.P.E.P. 608.01(v).

Trademark and Patent Licensing

Since a valid trademark, properly controlled, will survive the patent, combined trademark and patent licensing is highly advantageous. Because of the fundamental legal differences between patents and trademarks, however, the requirements of a valid licensing program for each are different.

The Requirement of Quality Control. The trademark is a symbol of goodwill; therefore, it cannot be assigned without a transfer of at least that part of the goodwill of the business connected with and symbolized by use of the mark. A "naked" assignment will be considered an abandonment of the mark. A trademark can be licensed, however, on the theory that the goodwill created by the licensee actually inures to the benefit of the licensor which remains, in legal theory, the "source of origin" of the trademarked goods. See *The Parkway Baking Co.* v. *Freihofer Baking Co.*, 154 F. Supp. 823, DC EPa 1957, *aff.* 255 F.2d 641, CA 3 1958.

The Lanham Act recognizes licensing and provides for registration of a mark used by a "related company" which is defined as a "person who legitimately controls or is controlled by the registrant or applicant . . . in respect to the nature and quality of the goods or services in connection with which the mark is used." 15 U.S.C. 1055 and 1127. In order to maintain his trademark rights, the licensor must provide definite standards of quality and strictly enforce them. If the licensor fails to provide such controls, he may be held to have abandoned his mark.

A patent owner may find it more profitable in the long run to make his trademark the central feature of any licensing system; then the royalties can survive the patent. The need for careful drafting to take advantage of this benefit is illustrated by the decision in *Ar-Tik Systems, Inc.* v. *Dairy Queen, Inc.*, 302 F.2d 496, CA 3 1962. The franchisees in that case each had paid a flat sum for a "Dairy Queen" franchise plus annual royalties on a patented ice-cream freezer. The agreements provided that the royalties were to be continued even after the patents had expired, but the court ruled that this was unenforceable. Had the royalties been linked to the trademark and trade name as in *Susser* v. *Carvel Corp.*, 206 F. Supp. 636, DC SNY 1962, the contract calling for continuing payments would have been legal.

The Antitrust Implications—Trademark Control as a Reason for Tie-ins. Another possible advantage in making the trademark the dominant feature of a license arrangement may be greater control by the licensor over his licensees. Certainly this is the fair implication of several recent decisions involving trademark franchises in which the courts have upheld licensing agreements which, inter alia, divided territories, required licensees to obtain materials from designated sources, and prevented licensees from dealing in competitive products. *Dennison Mattress Factory* v. *Spring-Air Co.*, 308 F.2d 403, CA 5 1962; *Engbrecht* v. *Dairy Queen Co. of Mexico*, 203 F. Supp. 714, DC Kan 1962; *Susser* v. *Carvel Corp.*, supra, aff. CA 2, 141 USPQ 609, 1964. In each case, the Court upheld the various restrictions as necessary to preserve the goodwill associated with the licensed trademark and/or trade name. By

parallel reasoning, in non-license contexts, other courts have upheld tie-in sales of services and products where necessary to maintain the goodwill of the supplying company. *United States* v. *Jerrold Electronics Corp.*, 187 F. Supp. 545, DC EPa 1960, aff. per curiam, 365 U.S. 567, 1961; *Dehydrating Process Co.* v. *A. O. Smith Corp.*, 292 F.2d 653, CA 1, cert. den., 368 U.S. 931, 1961.

The extent to which this reasoning will be applied where the tying product is patented is unclear. In the *Dehydrating Process* case, two patented items were tied together because there had been frequent customer complaints when the units were sold separately. This was upheld. The Court of Appeals for the First Circuit explained its decision in a later case, stating that "business arrangements which conceptually could be styled tie-ins might be exculpated from the reach of the antitrust laws if the arrangement was actuated by or could be explained on the basis of a legitimate business justification as opposed to an improper motive, e.g., desire to increase market control through the economic leverage supplied by the tying arrangement." *Beautyrest* v. *Simmons Co.*, 307 F.2d 458, 468, CA 1 1962. In *Beautyrest*, however, the tying product was not patented, and the court did not indicate any difference in its approach to the two situations.

On the other hand, in *Susser* v. *Carvel Corp.*, the lower court made specific mention of the fact that it considered the tying product to be an ice-cream freezer on which the patents had expired. The franchisees had asserted that the tying article was really a still-patented front assembly plate for the freezers which was leased to each franchisee, but the court rejected this contention. "This attempt to bring in an incidental patented article as a tying device as to which 'dominance' may be presumed is unrealistic and cannot be accepted." 206 F. Supp. at 644, note 7.

Susser was affirmed in May 1964. The Court split on the issue of the tying arrangements. The majority pointed out that such arrangements are not illegal per se, but are when the economic power with respect to the tying product is sufficient to restrain free trade appreciably. Here, Carvel had many competitors and only a small share of the overall ice-cream market. The dissenting judge found no such economic power in the package of trademarks, design patents and patents which were licensed together, but the majority disagreed. The patented items could not realistically be considered the focus of the arrangement. (No mention was made of the fact that the basic freezer patent had expired.) "The true tying item was rather the Carvel trademarks," and Carvel could justify the tying arrangements on the basis of its need to maintain the quality of the trademarked product. Although the decision was favorable to the trademark owner, the majority's concept of a trademark as a tying product, if accepted, could lead to appreciable restraints on trademark licensing. The dissent is even more foreboding. The dissenting judge flatly equated trademarks with patents, stating that both are Congressionally granted statutory monopolies, and that both generate the same economic power. The use of the "Carvel" trademark as the principal feature of the license system created, he said, the necessary economic power to make the tying arrangements illegal. This misconception of the nature and source of trademark rights is reminiscent of the ill-fated decision in *United States* v. *Guerlain*, 155 F. Supp. 77, DC SNY 1957, wherein the Court found the trademarked product itself to be the relevant market under the Sherman Act. That decision was bitterly attacked (see Handler, "Trademarks—Assets or Liabilities," 48 TMR 661, 1958) and the government ultimately dismissed the suit. 172 F. Supp. 117, 1959. The language of the dissent in *Susser*—indeed, the theory of the majority—is a reminder of the problems that can arise when trademarks are equated with patents, and of the unfriendly judicial attitude generated towards trademarks by such concepts.

Patent and trademark licenses both were involved in *Switzer Bros., Inc.* v. *Locklin*, 297 F.2d 39, CA 7 1961, cert. den., 369 U.S. 851, 1962. The court distinguished *Dehydrating Process* on the facts, thereby recog-

nizing the possibility of a "legitimate business justification" defense to tie-ins, but it indicated a hostile attitude towards conditioning the grant of a patent license upon the licensee's use of the licensor's trademark. That such conditioning, in some circumstances, can be a violation of the antitrust laws is illustrated by the fact that the United States sometimes has inserted in antitrust consent decrees the requirement that the defendant not condition patent licenses upon an agreement by the licensee to sell under the licensor's trademark. See *United States* v. *United States Pipe and Foundry Co.*, 1948-49 Trade Cases, Par. 62,285; *United States* v. *Electric Storage Battery Co.*, 1946-47 Trade Cases, par. 57,645. On the other hand, such joint licensing can be legal and is a common practice. Thus the question of permissible relationships between patent and trademark licenses still remains not entirely settled and awaits final clarification by the Supreme Court.

The cases already decided have focused attention on the antitrust implications of combined trademark and patent licensing and the problem of balancing the trademark owner's duty to control his mark with the public's right to unfettered competition. See LeBlanc, "Antitrust Ramifications of Trademark Licensing and Franchising," 53 TMR 519, 1963; Bisgaier and Price, "Quality Controls and the Antitrust Laws in Trademark Licensing," 72 Yale L.J. 1171, reprinted at 53 TMR 1130, 1963. Counsel should study the recent decisions carefully, both for what they say and what they omit and should frame license agreements accordingly.

Cross-references: *Antitrust Law and Patents, Design Patents, Licenses under U.S. Patent Rights, Misuse of Patents.*

TRADE SECRETS. See ABANDONMENT, KNOW-HOW

TRANSFER OF PATENT RIGHTS. See ASSIGNMENT, LICENSES, TAXATION

U

UNCLEAN HANDS DOCTRINE. See CLEAN HANDS

UNITED STATES PATENT PROCEDURE. See PATENT PROCEDURES, APPRAISAL FROM ABROAD

USE PATENTS

Robert Gottschalk

Recently, an experienced officer of the U.S. Air Force was disconcerted to find, after 50 minutes of flying a light plane, that strong headwinds had actually driven him backwards some eight miles behind his point of take-off. Years before, Admiral Peary, checking his position after a long hard day of driving his dogs towards the North Pole, found he was further south than when he started and only then did he realize that he was on a huge ice floe drifting rapidly to the South.

These illustrations are apt, for nowhere in the field of patents are the influence of environment and the force of external circumstance more strongly felt than in the field of "use patents." This applies to the determination of what we really mean by this term, the motivation which brings such patents into being, the ways in which they are used, and the legal and practical considerations and problems invariably involved in their exploitation and enforcement.

Meaning of Term "Use Patent"

In turning first to the definition, let us consider, by way of example, a new process for coating paper with starch. In the hands of a paper manufacturing company, a patent covering such a process would be an "operating" patent in the conventional and accepted sense. It would protect the manufacturer's own operations in the practice of the invention. It might or might not be licensed to other companies, enforced or not against competing paper manufacturers regarded as infringers. All of this would occur within the normal context of the every-day functioning of the patent system; and the patent would *not* be regarded as a "use patent."

However, suppose that a patent covering the same invention were owned by a starch company, which was engaged not in paper manufacturing, but rather in selling its starch to paper manufacturers. In the hands of such a company, this same patent *would* constitute a "use patent," and all of the factors surrounding its creation, utilization and enforcement would have to be viewed in a totally different light.

One of many "use patents" which have commanded the attention of the Supreme Court in recent years is that involved in the famous *Mercoid* [1] cases. It related to a furnace control system and claimed a combination of elements, including the control switch or thermostat manufactured and sold by the patentee. The patentee did not sell the other elements of the combination or install the systems covered by its patent. Had it done so, the patent in question would *not* have been a use patent; and the particular exploitation and enforcement problems which gave rise to this famous litigation would not have existed. Here again, the environmental situation, and not the specific nature of the patent itself, was the determining factor.

In short, then, we may define a "use patent" for present purposes as one owned or controlled by a patentee who does not himself practice the invention covered by the patent, but whose interests lie in the supply of a material or element employed in the practice of the patented invention. In the *Dry Ice* [2] case, it was solid carbon dioxide, used in a food package; in the *Barber Asphalt* [3] case it was asphalt, used in a concrete curing process; and in the *Morton Salt* [4] case, it was salt used in a food preserving process.

The questions arise as to whether such "uses" can be protected by patent, and if so, what are the incentives for doing so.

How Use Is Patented

Over the years, there has been an inordinate amount of confusion and controversy, on the part of bench and bar as well as the laity, as to the patentability of "new uses." It appears that much of this was really unnecessary, and could have been obviated by closer attention to the explicit language of the statutes which have always specifically designated the particular classes of inventions which alone could be patented under our laws. This remains as true today, under the Patent Act of 1952, as it was under the earlier statutes. The current statute provides, in Section 101:

"Whoever invents or discovers any new and useful *process, machine, manufacture,* or *composition of matter, or any new and useful improvement thereof,* may obtain a patent therefor...." (Emphasis added.)

The term "process" is defined, in Section 100(b), to mean:

"...process, art, or method, and includes a new use of a known process, machine, manufacture, composition of matter or material."

The essential provisions of the earlier statute, and their application, were excellently summarized by Judge Learned Hand in the *Old Town Ribbon* [5] case, as follows:

"...since 1793, unless a patent disclosed a 'new and useful art,' a new 'machine,' a new 'manufacture,' or a new 'composition of matter,' it has not been a valid patent. If it be merely for a new employment of some 'machine, manufacture or composition of matter' already known, it makes not the slightest difference how beneficial to the public the new function may be, how long a search

it may end, how many may have shared that search, or how high a reach of imaginative ingenuity the solution may have demanded. All the mental factors which determine invention may have been present to the highest degree, *but it will not be patentable because it will not be within the terms of the statute. This is the doctrine that a 'new use' can never be patentable....*" (Emphasis added.)

To be sure, the reference to a "new use" in the definition of process in the new statute touched off a fresh round of speculation and controversy, but the matter was soon laid to rest, as by this straightforward language of the Board of Appeals in the *Griffin* [6] case:

"The language used in Section 100(b) to define what is meant by the term 'process' is explicit. It, in our opinion, clearly indicates that it was the intent of Congress to authorize the grant of a patent for a new use, subject of course to the conditions and requirements of the act, *only when such use is claimed in the form of a process, act or method....*" (Emphasis added.)

And so the matter stands. [7]

Reasons for Use Patents

Granting that patents covering "new uses" can be obtained, why should they be? What incentives are there for doing so? What purposes are thereby served? Here again, our answers will depend not so much on the patents themselves as upon the environmental circumstances of the particular case.

The seller of starch, switches, dry ice, asphalt, or salt is naturally interested in stimulating the sales of his product. It is common, therefore, for suppliers of goods and products to attempt to develop new applications which would broaden the market and increase the demand for their wares. Then too, technical service of this kind to customers makes for good customer relations and hence for greater sales. To these ends, therefore, most supply companies conduct applications research and provide field service which leads, in many instances, to inventions which result in just such "use patents" as those to which we have referred.

Often, a major consideration in patenting new uses is a desire to invoke the defensive or protective power afforded by the patenting procedure. The objective may be simply to keep the market open on as wide and unrestricted a basis as possible. For example, suppose that the paper making process discussed above opened a new market or broadened an existing market for starch in the paper industry. It might then be in the interest of the starch company which made the invention to insure that no third party, by independently patenting the same invention, could foreclose any portion of that market and to obtain a "use patent" to provide that assurance. And having once obtained such a patent, the starch company might then dedicate it to the free use of the public, either implicitly, by failure to take action of any kind with respect to it, or expressly.

One might well conclude that such a "use patent" would then be serving essentially the same function as a publication of the invention in a trade or technical journal. In essence, this is so. In each case, the originating company would receive the benefits inherent in recognition by the public of its having made a valuable contribution to the development of the art and having gratuitously made it available for general use. The only real difference would be, of course, that the patenting process is usually regarded as offering more certain and complete defensive protection than would an ordinary publication. The respective merits of these two closely related procedures are outside the scope of the present article. Suffice it to say that for present purposes, they may be regarded as substantial equivalents and that, indeed, one might pursue both courses and thus capitalize on the best features of each.

However, mere defense and dedication may not be deemed enough. It may be determined to exploit the "use patent" more aggressively, in order to recoup costs, fund further development work, or provide additional income. It may also be desired to employ the "use patent" as a means for gaining a degree of market control, which the patentee would not otherwise possess, in connection with the supply of parts or materials used in practicing the patented invention.

Precautions in Utilizing Use Patents

What principles, problems and precautions are involved in such considerations?

Certain it is that much may be done along these lines. Many companies have pursued programs of active "use patent" exploitation with satisfactory results. But there is need, in any such case, to adopt a plan which will avoid the pitfalls that abound in this area, and then, in carrying out such a program, to resist the temptation to deviate from the plan.

The first hurdles to be overcome are generally practical and psychological, rather than legal. There is something about customers generally which seems to make them constitutionally indisposed to pay royalties to their suppliers. And, equally understandably, suppliers' salesmen would much prefer to offer bonus benefits to their customers than extract royalty payments from them. Any "use patent" program contemplating royalty payments, reporting, or any of the usual features of conventional patent licensing activities should take these basic and natural attitudes into account. This is not to suggest that such considerations need be regarded as controlling or dominant but, in view of them, sound business judgment dictates that every reasonable effort should be made to establish a program which places the fewest and least painful strains on the normal supplier-customer relationship.

In any case, however, if such a program is to be followed, it must be formulated and carried forward with scrupulous regard for the requirements imposed by law with regard to both the so-called misuse doctrine and the antitrust laws. The penalty for misuse is lack of enforceability of the patent; and antitrust violation, as is well known, subjects the offender to both treble damage civil suits and criminal prosecution as well. And on both counts, the courts and the Department of Justice have shown a fairly consistent and extremely sensitive concern for the "public interest."

Accordingly, if the patentee is to exploit his "use patent" without running afoul of this body of law, it is important for him to understand that he must exercise the greatest care "not only to be good, but also to seem good." He must avoid any use of his patent which may be said to represent an attempt to extend its monopoly beyond what it expressly covers or which tends to give him an improper advantage, based on his control of that patent, in the sale of unpatented articles or commodities used in the practice of the invention that the patent covers.

One of the surest ways to become quickly involved in this kind of difficulty is to "do what comes naturally," to say to customers, for example, "If you will buy your switches from me, this will automatically give you a free license under my furnace control patent covering a combination of which the switch is a part." Another invitation to involvement is to assert the patent only against those who, not being customers of the patentee, practice the patented invention or against competitors who, alleged to be contributory infringers, supply unpatented material for use in the unlicensed practice of the patented invention.

This, in effect, is exactly the kind of situation involved in the landmark *Mercoid*[1] cases and summarized in the 1955 Report of the Attorney General's National Committee to Study the Antitrust Laws, as follows:

"...the patent covered a home heating control system including furnace, room thermostat, and special but unpatented furnace control thermostat. The patentees, directly or by license, sold the unpatented furnace control thermostats which were specially designed for the purpose and gave to each purchaser a license to complete them and use the patented combination with the particular unit sold. Defendant, Mercoid, likewise sold the special furnace control thermostats but refused to take a license. The suits were brought against Mercoid as a contributory infringer. The Court found in the cases an effort to control commerce outside the scope of the patents and accordingly denied relief for patent infringement. In the second case, the alleged infringers were held entitled to treble damages for the patentee's violations of the antitrust laws."

The Court's decision rested squarely on its view that

"It is the public interest which is dominant in the patent system.... It is the protection of the public in a system of free enterprise which alike nullifies a patent where any part of it is invalid ...

and denies to the patentee after issuance the power to use it in such a way as to acquire a monopoly which is not plainly within the terms of the grant. The necessities or convenience of the patentee do not justify any use of the monopoly of the patent to create another monopoly.... The patent is a privilege. But it is a privilege which is conditioned by a public purpose...." (60 USPQ 21, 24, 1945)

The *Mercoid* decisions were regarded by many, including the writer[8] as extreme and excessive, and as virtually destroying the doctrine of contributory infringement. The Congress agreed and remedied this situation in the 1952 Patent Act. This Act defines infringement as including active inducement of infringement by another. 35 U.S.C. 271(b). It also defines and re-establishes contributory infringement as a living and effective doctrine of law. Section 271(c).

Despite the corrective influence of the current statute and the more reasonable line of court decisions which have followed in its wake,[9] it would appear that at least in the absence of unusual circumstances,[10] the only safe course for the holder of a "use patent" to follow in exploiting it is to *be sure that the right to practice the patented invention is not made dependent upon the purchases of supplies from the patentee or dependent upon any other kind of "tying" arrangement that would give the supplier, by reason of his patent ownership, an advantage over competing suppliers of unpatented supplies* used in practice of the patented invention.

If, for example, the patented invention is to be made available on a royalty basis, then licenses must likewise be available, on the same terms and conditions to all applicants, whether or not they are customers of the patentee. Nor may the patentee seek to accomplish results which would be unavailable to him in terms of direct dealing with customers and other licensees, through the bringing of suits for direct or contributory infringement. In this area, one would be well advised to err, if need be, on the side of conservatism and safety.

Licensing Procedures

Once it has been determined to afford equal opportunity to all applicants for licenses, a variety of specific procedures may be employed with substantially the same degree of legal and practical effectiveness. One very common approach in such cases is to set forth the royalty charge in the billing for the product, include a bold and explicit statement of both the royalty charge and the license right granted, and, at the time, offer the same kind of license, on the same terms and conditions, to non-customers as well. Alternatively, express written licenses may be entered into with all licensees, both customers and non-customers. And in any case, by both word and deed, the patentee-supplier should proclaim to the trade at large his willingness at all times to grant licenses, irrespective of the purchase from him of any supplies used in the practice of the patented invention.

Where the invention merits such arrangements, and if the matter is handled with understanding and care, the results of such a program can be satisfying to all concerned.

References

1. *Mercoid Corp.* v. *Mid-Continent Invest. Co.,* 320 U.S. 661, 1944. *Mercoid Corp.* v. *Minneapolis-Honeywell Reg. Co.,* 320 U.S. 680, 1944.
2. *Carbice Corp.* v. *American Patents,* 283 U.S. 27, 1931.
3. *Leitch Mfg. Co.* v. *Barber Co.,* 302 U.S. 458, 1938.
4. *Morton Salt Co.* v. *Suppiger,* 314 U.S. 488, 1942.
5. *Old Town Ribbon* v. *Columbia Ribbon,* 159 F.2 379; 72 USPQ 57, 1947.
6. *Ex parte Griffin,* 106 USPQ 388, 1953.
7. For a more complete discussion, see: Gottschalk, "The Term 'Process' Includes a New Use," 40 JPOS 451, 1958.
8. Gottschalk, "Further Comments on Recent Patent Decisions and Current Trends," 26 JPOS 151, 165 et seq., 1946.
9. See Davis, "Patent Licensing and the Anti-Trust Laws: Some Recent Developments," 46 JPOS 12, 17 et seq., 1964.
10. See *Binks* v. *Ransburg,* 126 USPQ 318, 1960. *U.S.* v. *Jerrold Electronics,* 187 F. Supp. 545, 1960; aff'd. 365 U.S. 567; *Dehydrating* v. *A. O. Smith,* 292 F.2 653, 1961.

Cross-references: *Act of 1952—Patents, Antitrust Law and Patents, Managing and Marketing Patents*—Section on Label License, *Unfair Competition.*

UTILITY OF INVENTIONS
Harry Goldsmith

"Whatever is beautiful is useful, because beauty gives pleasure, and pleasure is a kind of happiness, and happiness is a kind of utility." Quoted in *In re Nelson and Shabica,* infra.

General

The utility requirement for a patent is set forth in Title 35 U.S.C. as follows:

"Section 101. Inventions Patentable

"Whoever invents or discovers any *new* and *useful* process, manufacture, or composition of matter, or any *new* and *useful* improvement thereof, may obtain a patent therefor, subject to the conditions and requirements of this title." (Emphasis added.)

Another provision distinct from the mere *possession* of "utility," is the "how to use" requirement; to comply with the law a patent must adequately teach those skilled in the art *how to make and use* the invention. This is set forth as follows:

"*Section 112. Specification*

"The specification shall contain a written description of the invention, and of the *manner* and process of making and *using* it, in such full, clear, concise, and exact terms as to enable any person skilled in the art to which it pertains, or with which it is most nearly connected, to make *and use* the same, and shall set forth the best mode *contemplated* by the *inventor* of carrying out *his invention.*" (Emphasis added.)

In infringement suits, if the defendants use the inventions described in the patents sued on, they are estopped to deny utility. Also doubts relative to the question of utility are resolved in favor of the patentee and against the infringer; a patent is prima facie evidence of utility, and a patent ordinarily will not be declared void for lack of utility if it possesses any utility whatsoever.

In the Patent Office at one time utility was seldom questioned or a patent denied for lack of it except in cases of perpetual motion, cancer or bald head cures, or other obviously impracticable unworkable schemes or products. Starting about a dozen years ago and then with increasing frequency, however, the Patent Office began to question utility of the invention, particularly in chemical and pharmaceutical cases, as to the requirements of both Section 101 on the possession of utility and Section 112 on the description of it, in line with its interpretation of *In re Bremner et al.*, 182 F.2d 216, 86 USPQ 74, CCPA 1950. Many applications which by prior standards of the Patent Office, were legally adequate, were then held fatally defective as not complying with Section 112.

Nelson and Shabica Case

The issues were finally joined in *In re Nelson and Shabica*, 280 F.2d 172, 126 USPQ 242, CCPA 1960. In this landmark decision Judge Giles S. Rich for the Court considered thoroughly both being "useful" under Section 101 and disclosing "how to use" the invention under Section 112.

The particular subject matter in *Nelson and Shabica* involved steroid compounds which were stated to be valuable intermediates in the preparation of steroids having certain groups. The holding of the Court as to utility and disclosure of it and the principles established are of such general applicability that they are presented in detail below.

No Particular Degree of Utility Is Required. Speaking on the legal standards of utility the majority of the Court said:

"[Our] patent statutes, from the very beginning in 1790 to the latest act of 1952, have made it a prerequisite to patentability that the invention be new and useful. However, it has never been a requirement for patentability that there must be any particular degree of utility. (Citing many cases and authorities.)"

Nature of Utility. Considering, in *Nelson and Shabica*, whether the appellants' new compounds, the claimed C-19,14-hydroxy androstenes, are "useful" under the legal standards and on the basis of information given in the specification, the court concluded that the compounds were useful saying:

"Appellants' point is that new 'building blocks' *of value to the researcher* have been supplied which

have *utility as intermediates* in the search for cheaper and shorter routes to the synthesis of steroids having therapeutic or similar ultimate utility.

"The Patent Office position seems to have been that there must be a presently existing 'practical' usefulness to some undefined class of persons. We have never received a clear answer to the question 'Useful to whom and for what?' Surely a new group of steroid intermediates is *useful to chemists doing research* on steroids, and in a 'practical' sense too. Such intermediates are 'useful' under Section 101. They are often actually placed on the market before much, if anything, is known as to what they are 'good' for, other than experimentation and the making of other compounds in the important field of research. Refusal to protect them at this stage would inhibit their wide dissemination, together with the knowledge of them which a patent disclosure conveys, which disclosure the potential protection encourages. This would tend to retard rather than promote progress.

"The new androstenes, being *useful to research chemists* for the purposes disclosed by appellants, are clearly useful to society and their invention contributes to the progress of an art which is of great potential usefulness to mankind. They are new steroids which in known ways can be made into other steroids, thus furthering the development of this useful art.

"We conclude that the claimed compounds are 'useful' within the meaning of Section 101 and that there is a disclosure of the utility in the specification."

Thus, the Court held a compound is "useful" under the statute if it can be used for research purposes. There need not be a "presently existing 'practical' usefulness." Some different, or greater, or more commercial, or more mundane use than the one disclosed was not necessary.

Disclosure of Utility

"Of equal antiquity with the utility requirement of the statute," says the Court in *Nelson and Shabica*, "is that for a specification which, as provided by section 2 of the Act of 1790, was required to be of such particularity as would 'enable a workman or other person skilled in the art ... to make, construct, or use,' the invention.... No real alteration has been made in this law through the years."

The Nelson and Shabica specification contained the following statements about the use of the claimed compounds, the emphasis being the Court's:

"The cardiac glycosides, such as digitoxigenin and the like, comprise steroids which contain an OH-group in the 14-position. Important physiological properties are attributed to these steroids. *However, synthetically produced C-19 14-hydroxy-androstenes wherein the double bond is attached to carbon atom 5 have not heretofore been known.*

"*A primary object of the present invention is the embodiment of such synthetically-produced compounds,* corresponding to formula I supra. Formula 'I' is the general structural formula of the claimed androstenes set forth in the specification.

"*These new compounds are valuable intermediates in the preparation of steroids* wherein a hydroxyl group is present in the 14-position, and of steroids containing a 14,15-double bond, and of steroids the synthesis of which requires such groupings. . . .

"Conversion of the androstene compounds to produce analogous saturated 14-hydroxy steroids is effected by hydrogenating the Δ^5-double bond, for example by catalytic methods."

With respect to these statements about the use of the claimed compounds the Court stated:

"The sufficiency of a specification must be tested in the light of this fact and judged by what it conveys to those who *are* skilled in the art. The judge's task is to decide whether from the disclosure the man skilled in the art can make the invention and use it. If he can, this part of the statute is complied with, subject to the one further requirement that the inventor describe the best mode contemplated by him of carrying out his invention.

"Let us now examine what appellants have disclosed in their specification about their new compounds and how to use them. First, they have fully described their compounds and *how to make* them. No question has been raised as to this. Secondly, as to the 'best mode . . . of carrying out' their invention, their *invention* is the new compounds, not something to be done with them. The only apparent way in which it can be 'carried out,' it seems to us, is to make the compounds and no question has been raised but that the best way known to the appellants of doing this has been disclosed. Finally, we come to the description of how to use the invention, i.e. the C-19 14-OH-androstenes claimed. Appellants have said to those skilled in the art: Use them as intermediates to make other steroids having analogous structures; you can do this by hydrogenating the delta-5 double bonds by catalytic methods which you already know about. Similarly, with respect to other reactions, to which we

referred above, other hydrolysis and oxidation procedures were suggested and we have no doubt that those skilled in the steroid art would know of many other reactions in which they could use these intermediates in the course of their research. Are appellants entitled to a patent on this disclosure? We think they are. We are unable to see any fatal defect with respect to the disclosure of *how to use* the invention."

What a Specification Must Say About Utility and How to Use. Discussing *Bremner,* supra, on which the Board of Appeals and the Examiner relied to support the rejection, the Court stated:

"While eschewing any 'hard and fast' rule on disclosure of 'utility' in a specification, the court said [in *Bremner*] . . . it felt certain that the law required *an assertion of utility and an indication of the use or uses intended.*

"It is clear to us that the above 'rule' in the Bremner case has been fully met in appellant's application. They have *asserted* that their new steroid compounds are useful and they have *indicated* that the intended use is in the field of steroid chemistry wherein they have utility as intermediates in synthesizing other compounds."

In a footnote the Court made the following observation on the necessity for a mere assertion of utility in a specification:

"[The] opening statement of the Bremner et al. specification was that the invention was 'new *and useful.*' Upon reflection, we are now of the opinion that a *mere assertion* of utility in a specification is a meaningless formality and no more required by law than an assertion of novelty. We think it only reasonable to infer from the fact of filing an application that the applicant asserts that the invention is new and useful, for unless it is both he has no right to a patent. 35 U.S.C. 101."

Tests for Adequate Disclosure of Utility. The Nelson and Shabica decision continues:

"[The] test is what the application as a whole *communicates* to one skilled in the art. In some cases an applicant may, merely by naming his new instrument or material, indicate *what* its use is, as, for example, by saying he has invented a 'match,' 'hammer,' 'paint,' 'adhesive,' or 'detergent.' He may or may not have to go further in order to *enable* others to use the invention, depending on its nature and on how much those of ordinary skill in the art know. In other words, compliance with the law does not necessarily require specific *recitations* of use but may be inherent in description or may result from disclosure of a sufficient number of properties to make a use obvious; and where those of ordinary skill in the art will know *how* to use, the applicant has a right to rely on such knowledge. If it will not be sufficient to enable them to use his invention, he must supply the know-how. As this court has often said before, each case must be judged on its own facts."

But the court also included the following warning, on the basis of which the Patent Office relies for looking critically at disclosures of utility, particularly in cases involving chemical compounds:

"In holding, as we do, that appellants complied with section 112 in making a clear disclosure of use in steroid research, we do not mean to imply that applicants for patents on new compounds can now rest on an assumption that they are useful as intermediates and obtain patents without even suggesting *what* use may be made of them or *how* that use may be effected. We are not holding that *all* compounds are inherently useful as 'intermediates.' We have reason to believe some are not, and it is a question of fact to be determined in each case. Assuming, however, that a given compound would be so useful, it would still be incumbent on the applicant to disclose what is to be made from it and how it would be done. What the *Bremner rule* requires is that an application shall make known to those skilled in the art something that can be done with a new compound and not, through silence, leave the matter entirely to speculation or independent investigation."

Later Decisions

In *In re Johnson*, 282 F.2d 370, 127 USPQ 216, CCPA 1960, decided shortly after *Nelson*, the disclosure of utility for the claimed chemical compounds was as follows:

"The products of the aforesaid process are valuable as chemical intermediates of organic synthesis, for solvent use and for the preparation of toxic substances such as insecticides, fungicides, etc."

Holding that the disclosure was adequate to meet the requirement of Section 112, the Court stated:

"A reasonable compliance with Section 112 does not require that the earlier application here set forth a catalog of the specific insects and specific fungi against which the dimer is effective. It is sufficient if the product is disclosed as having toxic properties, and if one skilled in this art is informed,

as was done here, that the product is useful as an insecticide and fungicide."

In *In re Haven*, 289 F.2d 508, 129 USPQ 310, CCPA 1961 there was claimed the compound aminocyclopentadienyl (cyclopentadienyl) iron. The Court held adequate the following description of the utility and properties:

"Aminocyclopentadienyl (cyclopentadienyl) iron is a useful intermediate in the preparation of dyestuffs and also has antioxidant properties. The presence of the amino group attached to the dicyclopentadienyl iron structure permits conversion into other useful compounds, since a large number of other materials can react with the amino group."

In *In re Lorenz and Wegler*, 134 USPQ 312, 49 CCPA 1227, 305 F.2d 875, 1962, the Court of Customs and Patent Appeals decided that the following disclosure of utility for a chemical compound did *not* comply with Section 112.

"...A characteristic feature of the novel phosphoric acid esters is their low toxic effect against warm blooded animals, while at the same time they have a good effect against a very wide range of insects....

"It should have been an easy matter for appellants to have expressly described their compounds as insecticides but all they say is that their compounds have a 'good effect' against insects. We think that language, vague and nebulous as it is, would be equally applicable to a repellent or even an attractant."

In *In re Adams, Kirk and Petrow*, 137 USPQ 333, CCPA 1963 the Court had before it the following statement of how to use the invention:

"It is an object of the present invention to provide new 4-chloro-3-oxo-Δ^4-steroids of the androstane and the pregnane series which are of value on account of their biological properties or as intermediates in the preparation of compounds with useful biological properties....

"The process of the invention may be applied to a variety of 3-oxo-Δ^4-derivatives of the cyclopentenophenanthrene series. In particular, the process of the invention may be applied to steroid hormones containing the 3-oxo-Δ^4-system to give the 4-chloro-analogues of the aforesaid hormones, which new compounds will, in general, possess biological properties."

The Board had held the reference to appellants' compounds as having "biological properties" to be insufficient as a disclosure of utility.

The CCPA reversed, saying:

"We are of the opinion that when the *entire* disclosure, taken as a whole, is considered, [rather than the words "biological properties" only] one skilled in the art would be enabled to use the compounds. To take a specific example, it seems apparent that a steroid chemist would know that testosterone is the naturally occurring male hormone. It seems likely that the steroid chemist would then know how to use 4-chloro-testosterone. Whether or not the results in use are the same or inferior or superior, the specific field of use would be indicated to a steroid chemist. No further skill would be required to use the compound in the manner in which the naturally occurring analogue is used....

"The examiner and the Board of Appeals apparently were of the opinion that the method claims and the compound claims stand or fall together, since the two classes of claims have not been separately considered. However, the content of a sufficient disclosure need not be the same for a method as it is for a product. The disclosure of how the product is used is not required to be as complete in order to show how to use the method of making the product as it is with product claims. ... We have no doubt that the disclosure is sufficient, insofar as the method claims are concerned, to satisfy the requirements of 35 U.S.C. 112."

The *Wilke and Pfohl* decision, 136 USPQ 435, CCPA 1963, is of interest in that it rejected the Patent Office practice requiring "that the specification must teach a use for the product of a claimed process."

In this case both claims of the so-called Markush type to chemical products and claims to the process for making the products were recited. The Markush claim included four different carboxylic acid anhydrides. The Court allowed the process claims but held with respect to the Markush product claim that:

"[We] are unable to find *any* description of *how to use* two of the four addition products....We therefore affirm the rejection of claim 36 under 35 U.S.C. 112 as being based on an insufficient description of how to use the claimed products."

In affirming the rejection of the process claims, the Board had relied on a statement made by the Court in the Bremner case as follows:

"It was never intended that a patent be granted upon a product, *or a process* of producing a product, unless such product be useful." (Emphasis added.)

The Court, however, declined to apply this statement to the process claims involved.

This overruling of the so-called rule of Bremner, as applied to process claims, was confirmed in *In re Swarc*, 138 USPQ 208, 50, CCPA 1963.

The Court said:

"As stated in *In re Wilke* and *Pfohl*, a specification which teaches those skilled in the art how to use the process, i.e., by disclosing the manipulative steps of the process, the required operating conditions and the starting materials so that the process may be used by a person skilled in the art, meets the requirements of 35 U.S.C. 112. *It is not necessary to specify the intended uses for the product produced therein.*" (Emphasis added.) Cf. *In re Manson*, 142 USPQ 35, CCPA 1964, reaffirming this principle.

Operativeness and Utility

Operativeness has to do with the question of whether an alleged invention will work. If a device is useful, it is deemed operative; an inoperative device is inherently not useful. A device which is clearly incapable of being used for anything lacks utility as a result of inoperativeness. *In re Perrigo*, 48 F.2d 965, 9 USPQ 152, CCPA 1931.

A concoction of such things as bone marrow, aromatic oils and alcohol was held lacking utility for the specified purpose of growing hair. The Court noted that the "concoction ... belongs to a class of compositions which from common knowledge has long been the subject matter of much humbuggery and fraud." *In re Oberweger*, 115 F.2d 286, 47 USPQ 455 and 457, CCPA 1940. The applicant must demonstrate operability of the device disclosed if it conflicts with the principles of science. *In re Chilowsky*, 229 F.2d 457, 108 USPQ 321, CCPA 1956.

The patent sued on is invalid if the device disclosed is inoperative. *Hartford Empire Co.* v. *Obear-Nester Glass Co.*, 71 F.2d 539, 22 USPQ 270, CA 1934.

However, the general rule is that perfection of operation is not required.

In an infringement case involving Bell's famous telephone patents, the question of operability was raised. The facts showed that Bell had not and could not construct a telephone in accordance with his own teaching prior to the issuance of his patent, that the first Bell-type telephone was constructed by others in accordance with the patent disclosure, and that the speech reproduction was poor but intelligible. The U.S. Supreme Court said in *Telephone Cases*, 126 U.S. 1, 526, 1888 C.D. 321:

"The law does not require that a discoverer or inventor, in order to get a patent for a process, must have succeeded in bringing his art to the highest degree of perfection...."

Again in *Hildreth* v. *Mastoras*, 257 US 27, 1921 C.D. 372, the Supreme Court said:

"It is not necessary, in order to sustain a generic patent, to show that the device is a commercial success. The machine patented may be imperfect in its operation; but if it embodies the generic principle and works, that is, if it actually and mechanically performs, though only in a crude way, the important function by which it makes the substantial change claimed for in the art, is enough."

If there is occasional unreliability in operation without danger to persons and if the failure is without hazard to persons, is detectable and correctible with the exercise of merely the skill of the art and not of further invention, such deficiency will not otherwise defeat a meritorious invention. (See *Operability*)

But in a case involving a voting machine where it was proved that the machine failed to register correctly once in 100 times, the Court held the machine inoperative and worthless, since no electorate could afford to commit the registration of its electoral will to such a machine. *McKenzie* v. *Cummings*, 24 App. D.C. 137, 1904 C.D. 683. The same was held in the case of a cash register which failed to always give correct results. *Carlin* v. *Crumpton*, 45 App. D.C. 166, 1916 C.D. 211.

The Supreme Court, in *Coffin* v. *Ogden*, 18 Wall (84 U.S.) 120, 1873, and in *Dashiell* v. *Grosvenor*, 162 U.S. 425, 1896 C.D. 329, has held that a patent is presumptively for an operative device, and the rule of presumption of operability has been followed in many cases.

Since the Patent Office policy is generally to resolve doubts in favor of the applicant, in the normal case, it does not question operability unless the disclosed device is clearly inoperative on its face. Once the patent is granted the presumption of the *Coffin* v. *Ogden* and *Dashiell* v. *Grosvenor* cases attaches to it. The presumption of validity of an issued patent, 35 U.S.C. 282, also extends to the aspect of utility and operability. *In re Spence*, 261 F.2d 244, 120 USPQ 82, CCPA 1960.

Proof of Utility

While the Patent Office rarely raises a question regarding the operability or utility of a mechanical invention, it has become more stringent in recent years with respect to proving the utility of medical inventions, as in requiring proof of the therapeutic properties or action alleged.

Where the applicant was claiming a new compound per se, and disclosed in the specification some pharmaceutical or medicinal use, proof was seldom required, except perhaps for so-called controversial (incurable) diseases, for example, a cure for cancer, baldness or arthritis. However, where the claim recited the condition to be treated, as in the case of a preparation claim or process of treating claim, the practice had become well established until 1961 that applicant must produce proof of therapeutic qualities.

The policy followed by the Patent Office in 1957 was stated in *Isenstead* v. *Watson, Comr. Pats.*, 157 F. Supp. 7, 115 USPQ 408, DC DistCol 1957, as follows:

"Great care and scrutiny should be particularly taken in connection with applications for medical patents. While the granting of a patent does not legally constitute a certificate that the medicine to which it relates is a good medicine and will cure the disease or successfully make the test which it was intended to do, nevertheless, the granting of such a patent gives a kind of official imprimatur to the medicine in question on which as a moral matter some members of the public are likely to rely. In view of these circumstances, it is right and proper that the Patent Office should be very careful and perhaps even reluctant to grant a patent on a new medical formula until it has been thoroughly tested and successfully tried by more than one physician."

What kind of proof is necessary? The Patent Office said clinical proof, i.e., tests on human beings, even where no human use was disclosed in the patent specification. Experimental proof on mice, rats, rabbits or dogs was insufficient, since, according to the views of the Patent Office, curing or alleviating the disease in these animals was not the ultimate purpose—treatment of human beings was. Thus in the cases where applicants claimed a new compound and indicated that in animal tests the compounds show activity against tumors, such tests were not accepted as proof of utility, and the Patent Office rejected the application on the ground of "lack of utility" under 35 U.S.C. 101.

The issue finally reached the Court of Customs and Patent Appeals in the two cases of *In re Bergel and Stock*, 130 USPQ 205 and 206, 1961. The applications involved claimed the compound *p*-bis-(2-chloroethyl)-aminophenylalanine, processes for the manufacture thereof and the L-form.

The applicants' assertion of utility in the 206 case was:

"This invention relates to chemotherapeutic agents and has an object to provide an improved compound having tumor growth inhibitory action and process for the manufacture thereof....

"The L form has greater tumor growth inhibitory action than either the D form or the racemic form. All forms are, however, effective tumor growth inhibitors when tested against transplanted Walker rat Carcinoma."

The Board's ground of rejection was lack of utility—the utility asserted was not within the purview of 35 U.S.C. 101. The Board reasoned that "protection of rats, or mice, from the growth of cancer, specifically transplanted Walker rat Carcinoma, is not in itself a sufficient usefulness within the

purview of the patent statutes ... [and] the elimination of rodents themselves would be a more desirable objective."

A unanimous court reversed the Board and said:

"That appellants' compounds actually do inhibit the growth of the transplanted cancer strain is not questioned. In our opinion that achievement is sufficient to satisfy the express language of Section 101, and is in harmony with the basic constitutional concept of promoting the progress of science and the useful arts....

"Our conclusion is influenced by a background of common knowledge that cancer is one of the dreadest of all diseases; that for years untold measures of time, talent, and treasure have been devoted to a search for means to prevent its spread and discover a cure; and that as of now those measures have been largely unsuccessful."

In *In re Ross and Davis*, 134 USPQ 230, CCPA 1962, another "cancer" application, the Court reaffirmed its position in the *Bergel and Stock* cases.

Decided on the same day as the *Bergel and Stock* cases were the cases of *In re Krimmel*, 130 USPQ 215, 1961, and *In re Dodson*, 130 USPQ 224, 1961. Both of these CCPA cases claimed new chemical compounds as such. No allegation of utility in man was made, although appellants admitted in the argument presented to the Examiner "that the establishment of such a utility was desired."

The statement of use in the Krimmel specification was as follows:

"The compositions of the present invention can be advantageously employed in pharmaceutical applications.... [They] exhibit certain of the useful properties of the adrenocortical hormones. Thus, they are anti-inflammatory agents, as shown by their effectiveness in treating inflammation of the iris."

In the *Dodson case* the statement of utility was:

"The compounds of this invention are useful for the relief of conditions inimical to the well-being of the animal body. Specifically, the subject compounds manifest noticeable anti-iritic properties."

Both the Examiner and the Board held that experimentation with animals is insufficient to establish utility within the meaning of 35 U.S.C. 101, that clinical tests on humans were only valid to do this.

When the case reached the CCPA, the Court agreed with the solicitor of the Patent Office that the main issue was:

"...Whether a test restricted to a laboratory animal is sufficient to satisfy the utility requirement of the statute when a patent application discloses that claimed compounds are useful in the treatment of a condition which can occur both in man and in lower animals, and it is agreed that the disclosure does not exclude the treatment of man."

The answer of the unanimous court was a resounding "yes," that appellant "need do no more to satisfy the requirement of 35 U.S.C. 101 that the claimed invention is useful."

Said the Court:

"We do not agree with the solicitor that appellants' *immediate* aim was to use the compounds to treat human iritis. Even though there appears to be no question that the *ultimate* purpose was to do this, the lack of proof of the effectiveness of the compounds for this purpose is not determinative of the issues here.

"We wish to point out that this court is aware of the common practice of using 'experimental animals' in considerable variety for the evaluation of chemical compounds for possible pharmaceutical applications prior to clinical testing in humans. It is also our understanding that a demonstration that a compound has desirable or beneficial properties in the prevention, alleviation, or cure of some disease or manifestation of a disease in experimental animals does not necessarily mean that the compounds will have the same properties when used with humans. With this information in mind, we hold that when an applicant for a patent has alleged in his patent application that a new and unobvious chemical compound exhibits some useful pharmaceutical property and when this property has been established by statistically significant tests with 'standard experimental animals,' sufficient statutory utility for the compounds has been established. By 'standard experimental animals' we mean whatever animal is usually used by those skilled in the art to establish the particular pharmaceutical application in question. These may be mice in one case, rabbits in another, chickens in another, and monkeys in another."

The Court made short shrift of the *Isenstead* v. *Watson* decision discussed above, which both the Examiner and the Board cited as authority for their requirement that

appellant establish that his claimed compounds are "safe, effective and reliable" for treating human beings since the utility alleged did not exclude humans.

Regarding the above quotation from the *Isenstead* v. *Watson* decision, the Court said:

"Because we do not know the factual background which motivated this statement of the Court, we do not know what principle of law has been established and, therefore, the case cannot be the basis of our determination of the issues now before us."

The Court added:

"Although we have no doubt that the Patent Office has, in the case at bar, acted in good faith and with proper motives, the fact remains that the Patent Office has not been charged by Congress with the task of protecting the public against possible misuse of chemical patents. There is nothing in the patent statute or any other statutes called to our attention which gives the Patent Office the right or the duty to require an applicant to prove that the compounds or other materials which he is claiming, and which he has stated are useful for 'pharmaceutical applications,' are safe, effective, and reliable for use with humans. It is not for us or the Patent Office to legislate and if the Congress desires to give this responsibility to the Patent Office, it should do so by statute.

"We now hold only that appellant has established that his compounds have statutory utility even though he has not proven that they have the ultimate utility—prevention, alleviation, or cure of a disease in a human body. In this instance, appellant has proven sufficient utility to satisfy the requirement of 35 U.S.C. 101 (even though his immediate or ultimate *though unexpressed* aim be to use the claimed compounds to treat humans, as stated in the Dodson decision)."

The Patent Office was again reminded in *In re Hartop and Brandes*, 135 USPQ 419, CCPA 1962, that its authority and responsibility did not include Food and Drug administration and Federal Trade Commission activities. However, the Patent Office has resisted what many thought would be a liberalizing influence on the strict policy followed by the Patent Office in pharmaceutical cases regarding proof of utility. It still requires clinical tests if the disclosure of use mentions use on humans. Where humans are not mentioned, it has relied upon the words "statistically significant tests" in the *Krimmel* decision and now questions the animal tests as being statistically significant in the showings (affidavits) that are submitted. It would seem appropriate, therefore, that unless an applicant can supply clinical tests, he should shy away from any mention of human therapy in his application, and should be sure, in any showing submitted, to set forth tests that are statistically significant and to call them that.

Is the Examiner in cases of this type entitled to demand a showing of the veracity of the statement of utility? The question was raised at one time in the *Krimmel* case but was not listed as a specific error in the notice of appeal to the Court, since the issue was not before the Court and since evidence as to the utility had been submitted, the Court refused to decide expressly "whether an applicant must, in a situation as is now at bar, provide evidence or proof that claimed compounds are useful for a purpose stated in a patent application."

In the case of *In re Novak and Hogue*, 134 USPQ 335, CCPA 1962, just a year after the Krimmel case, the Court held that:

"When an applicant bases utility for a claimed invention on allegations of the sort made by appellants here, unless one with ordinary skill in the art would accept those allegations as obviously valid and correct, it is proper for the Examiner to ask for evidence which substantiates them. Here we find no indication that one skilled in this art would accept without question statements that carboxymethyl dextran has the alleged effects on the functioning of *any* base, physiologically active or not, and no evidence has been presented to demonstrate that the claimed product has those effects."

The claims involved in *Novak and Hogue* called for a carboxymethyl dextranate of an organic base, broadly and more specifically for a physiologically active base, for which both animal and human utility was alleged as well as certain properties for the carboxymethyl dextran group combined with the base. The applicant had argued that each component had been safely used but presented no evidence as to the utility claimed for the combined product which was regarded as an entirely different entity from its components. One may project that,

had the applicant omitted reference to human utility and presented some experimental evidence on animals, he might have won his case on the basis of *In re Krimmel* and of *Dodson*, which were not even mentioned in *Novak*.

However, in the *Hartop and Brandes* case, supra, decided about five months after the *Novak and Hogue* case, the Court held that "the disclosed utility of appellants' claimed invention relates to the treatment of humans" (in spite of appellants urging that their specification "has never alleged human use of their composition," and that there is "no specific representation of usefulness in humans"). But the Court ruled against the Patent Office requirement for experiments with humans, to prove the safety. Here the applicants claimed the stable concentrated solution of thiobarbituric acid dissolved in a nonaqueous solvent comprising parenterally acceptable lower aliphatic monohydroxy and polyhydroxy alcohols and an alkali metal alcoholate. The Court said:

"...We do not think that it is within the authority or responsibility of the Patent Office to demand such tests *in this* particular case in view of the evidence of record."

The tests submitted were with rabbits and mice, comparing the toxicity of the standard therapeutic aqueous dilutions of thiobarbituric acid (Pentothal) with dilutions of the claimed solution. These the Court held were sufficient.

With regard to the nature of "safety" in the field of drugs and medicaments, the Court said:

"We take judicial notice that many valued therapeutic substances or materials with desirable physiological properties, when administered to lower animals or humans, entail certain risks or may have undesirable side effects. True it is that such substances would be *more* useful if they were not dangerous or did not have undesirable side effects, but the fact remains that they *are* useful, useful to doctors, veterinarians and research workers, useful to patients, both human and lower animal, and so are useful within the meaning of 35 U.S.C. 101. The use of drugs in medicine is frequently a matter of balancing risks to save a life. Safety is a relative matter."

The Court felt the criterion for safety was whether appellants' solutions were *as safe as* the previously widely used and commercially acceptable solid form of Pentothal sodium. The Court felt that the test in rabbits was evidence of "safety" although no clinical tests were submitted. For support of its position, the Court turned to its decisions in many of the so-called reduction-to-practice cases in interference proceedings. The Court said that the same implied or expressed criterion was found in these cases.

"If the Court was convinced that *one skilled in the art* would accept a particular test or experiment as a 'possibility' or reasonable certainty or 'probability' or that it was 'reasonably predictable' that a tested invention would operate as alleged or have the utility alleged, a reduction to practice was found; otherwise the Court found no reduction to practice."

The majority of the Court held that the Patent Office had no authority or responsibility to demand clinical tests in this particular case, even though the disclosed utility, in their opinion, related to the treatment of humans. Yet the Court concluded its decision on the following warning note:

"However, no implication is intended here that clinical evidence should not be required by the Patent Office under different circumstances. Each case must be decided on its own facts."

Incredible or misleading statements of utility must be either removed or proved, the CCPA has held in *In re Citron*, 139 USPQ 516, 1963. Here the Court affirmed the rejection of claims to a serum for lack of proof of utility. No evidence either on animals or humans had been presented, the specification stating that the invention claimed was effective in human cancer. Distinguishing over *Krimmel* and *Dodson*, supra, the Court said that the latter cases "were decided on the basis of utilities established by credible evidence." See also infra.

May *in vitro* tests be used as evidence of therapeutic utility? The Board of Appeals, in the decision of *Ex parte Barnard*, 783 O.G. 6, 135 USPQ 109, 1961, in dicta said in effect "No." The application involved a composition of matter, adapted to be administered internally to the human body as an injectable medicinal. The Examiner rejected the claims, among other reasons, for lack of utility in the absence of tests on human beings. Applicant relied on *in vitro* and rabbit tests reported by him in an article.

The Board held:

"While we are aware that tests on animals may in some cases be sufficient to establish utility, as pointed out in the reply brief and as further indicated in the recent decision *In re Krimmel* [supra], we do not consider the reported tests in the instant case to be adequate. As to in vitro tests, we are not aware of any decision or authority which regards such tests as evidence of therapeutic utility. As for appellants' tests on rabbits, the results are equivocal and therefore fail to establish usefulness for the combination claimed; certainly not for the vast number of compositions encompassed by the appealed claims."

Suggestions for Meeting Utility Requirements

We can say that experimental utility, i.e., for research and experiment, meets the requirements of utility under 35 U.S.C. 101. In an infringement suit, operation of the device only in a laboratory was held sufficient proof of utility. *Electro-Dynamic Co.* v. *United States Light and Heat Corp.*, 278 Fed. 80, CA 2 1921. Use in experimental animals is useful even if the ultimate goal —human use—is not disclosed.

There must be a disclosure of the intended utility unless it is obvious to the man skilled in the art. To be on the safe side, the specification should spell out the various uses and the manner of practising them, even if considered obvious. Why invite an issue with the Examiner, the Board or the Court, as to what would be obvious in the way of use to the man skilled in the art?

If you face rejection on insufficient disclosure of utility, determine whether or not your use is among those decided by the Court as being obvious to the man skilled in the art. Perhaps you can find literature, prior patents, or earlier applications of your own, in which the utility of closely related compounds is disclosed and from which disclosure the utility of the new and claimed compounds would be obvious. *Ex parte Ladd et al.*, 112 USPQ 337, BdApp 1955; *Ex parte Wettstein et al.*, 140 USPQ 187, BdApp 1962; cf. *In re Adams, Kirk & Petrow*, supra. However, if you are relying on a third party's patent for a disclosure of utility to inure to your benefit, its granting date must be before your filing date. Board of Appeals in *Ex parte Lanham*, 135 USPQ 106, 783 O.G. 10, 1961.

In the same decision, the Board said that the disclosure that the products "are potentially useful" is insufficient; that the utility to support a patent must be certain and presently exist. So avoid the word "potential" in describing the utility, also the word "may" since some Examiners have criticized this as being equivocal and even the word "can." Say "is" or "are" and "have."

Do not specify human utility unless you can prove it. It seems from the CCPA decisions that you need not prove such utility unless it is alleged. Animal tests may be required and these may have to be "statistically significant."

If you are claiming a process which is adequately described, you need not disclose a use for the compound produced thereby. Nevertheless, it would be safer to do so. But if you claim the compound without such a disclosure, you may be denied the claim unless you have an adequate description of use or you can convince the Patent Office or Court that its use is obvious.

Amending Application to Disclose Utility. Can you amend the specification to disclose or amplify a utility disclosure which the Examiner says is insufficient? This was tried in both the *Nelson* and *Haven* cases, and the introduction was held to be new matter under 35 U.S.C. 132. So this approach is practically closed. However, where only a limited measure of utility and not a total cure was established for Actinomycin, the Board indicated the claims would be allowed if the disclosure of utility calling for "treatment" of the disease (which could be interpreted as involving complete cure) were amended to indicate that Actinomycin C is useful only for palliative

relief and temporary remission of the disease. *Ex parte Brockmann and Bohme*, 127 USPQ 57, BdApp 1960.

Sometimes you can save an application from the rejection of lack of utility, where several utilities have been disclosed, by cancelling out the disclosure of the utility which is questioned by the Examiner for proof. Thus, if you should disclose that your compound is useful as a herbicide, deweeding agent, and in addition as a tumor growth inhibiting agent, and the Examiner does not accept your proof of utility for the latter, you might cancel out the reference to tumor use and get your case allowed. On the other hand, if you do not, the disclosure of the other "acceptable" utilities will not obviate the rejection. *Ex parte Moore et al.*, 128 USPQ 8, BdApp 1960; *In re Citron*, supra. But see the earlier decision or *ex parte Lanham*, 121 USPQ 223, BdApp 1959, which permits retention of references to other proposed uses unless they are incredible or misleading.

In *In re Gottlieb and Amman*, 140 USPQ 665, CCPA 1964, the Court held that a disclosure of utility in treating a variety of plant fungi is sufficient to meet the requirements of 35 USC 101. The applicants having found that the antibiotic claimed was useful for some purpose, "it becomes unnecessary to decide whether it is in fact useful for the other purposes [treatment of humans and animals] 'indicated' in the specification as possibly useful."

The Court, however, stated that its decision did not preclude the Patent Office from making such requirements as to correction or cancellation of those statements concerning uses other than the control of fungal diseases. The Court further stated that the allegation of utility as a plant fungicide would not normally appear "to be incredible in the light of the knowledge of the art, or factually misleading," citing *In re Citron*, supra.

You can gain no benefit of your filing date if the specification is found fatally defective for lack of sufficient disclosure of utility. *Ex parte Buc*, 114 USPQ 552, BdApp 1957. If you refile the case having originally an inadequate statement of utility and an intervening reference appears, you may not use the earlier filing date to overcome the reference; but where, in the parent case, you disclosed one utility for the compound claimed and in the new application you disclosed a different utility, you are entitled to the date of the earlier case. *In re Kirchner*, 134 USPQ 324, 305 F.2d 897, CCPA 1962. Applicants and patentees have not been given the benefit of the disclosure of an earlier application which did not sufficiently describe an operative example to support the device claimed in the later filed case. *General Steel Products Co., Inc. v. Lorenz*, 132 USPQ 574, DC Fla 1962; *In re Smyth*, 189 F.2d 982, 90 USPQ 106, CCPA 1951; *Lavin v. Pierotti*, 129 F.2d 883, 54 USPQ 400, CCPA 1942; and *Whittier v. Borchardt*, 154 F.2d 522, 69 USPQ 382, CCPA 1946.

The CCPA did not give applicant the benefit of his foreign filing date because it held that his German application did not disclose sufficiently how to use his compounds. *In re Diedrich*, 138 USPQ 128, 1963.

In mechanical inventions, there is hardly any problem of disclosure of utility. But, to be safe, disclose the mode of operation of the machine and sufficient structure so that one who constructs it will have an operative device. *Philip A. Hunt Co. v. Mallinckrodt Chemical Works*, 177 F.2d 583, 83 USPQ 277, CA 2 1949. The device disclosed must be operative for the intended use.

Once the patent is granted, any infringer who attempts to have it held invalid on the ground that the disclosure of utility is inadequate or that it is useless, would have a difficult case in view of the presumption of validity and the fact that mere infringement attests to the utility. Of course, if the device or compound is inoperative for the disclosed use, but is infringed in other use, the plea of lack of utility may be properly made here.

Final Advice

Do not skimp on disclosure of utility. Be ready with proof of utility, particularly in pharmaceutical inventions and at least with animal experiments, in case the Examiner should have any reason for requesting proof.

Cross-references: *Operability, Pharmaceutical Patent Practice, Validity.*

V

VALIDITY

John F. Schmutz

What Is Validity?

Basically, validity deals with whether the exclusionary right sought by an inventor is justified when measured against the disclosure made by his patent and the primary purpose of the patent law of promoting science and the useful arts. In the courts, the question of validity usually arises as a defense in a suit for infringement, namely, that the patentee has no legally sufficient right under the claims of a patent to prevent the actions in question by the alleged infringer. In the daily practice of a patent attorney, validity always is considered, for example, in deciding whether an application can be filed, deciding when to file, drafting claims and specifications, selecting inventors, licensing and considering proposed commercial operations.

The vast majority of all validity considerations involve one or more of the following questions:

(1) Is there a patentable invention?

(2) Is the one claiming the invention, the inventor thereof?

(3) Has the inventor made timely claim to his invention?

(4) Does the patent adequately disclose and claim a patentable invention?

(5) Has the inventor by prior patents exhausted his right to the patent in question?

[For statistical studies and reviews of patents before the courts, on the issue of validity, see the separate article on adjudication.]

Validity v. Unenforceability—Misuse. Validity is to be distinguished from a cognate question, unenforceability.

The rights secured by a patent are de-fined by the claims of the patent. Each claim of a patent is considered as if it set forth a complete and independent invention. If a claim confers a legally sufficient right, it is valid; if not, it is invalid and void. 35 U.S.C. 253 provides that "Whenever, without any deceptive intention, a claim of a patent is invalid the remaining claims shall not thereby be rendered invalid."

If the claims of a patent are invalid, there are no patent rights for a patentee to enforce. However, the claims of a patent may be valid, but unenforceable, the most common reason for unenforceability being misuse. For the purpose of this discussion, misuse of a patent is an attempt to extend the powers incident to a patent beyond the exclusionary rights specifically granted. An illustration of misuse is the case of *Morton Salt Co.* v. *G. S. Suppiger Co.,* 314 U.S. 488; 52 USPQ 30, 1942, a suit for patent infringement. The defense was unenforceability of the patent because of misuse by certain tying-in clauses in licenses granted by the patentee. The plaintiff, Suppiger, licensed various canners under a patent to a machine for dispensing salt tablets, on the condition that licensees buy salt tablets for use therein from the plaintiff's subsidiaries. The defendant, Morton Salt Co., manufactured and sold such machines. The court denied recovery on the basis that the practice of requiring the purchase of unpatented salt tablets as a condition for licenses to use the machines was an attempt by the patentee to extend the powers incident to the patent beyond the exclusionary rights granted by the patent. Accord, *B. B. Chemical Co.* v. *Ellis,* 314 U.S. 495; 52 USPQ 33, 1942.

Other examples of patent misuse are *mandatory* package licensing of patents, *American Securit Co.* v. *Shatterproof Glass*

Corp., 268 F.2d 769; 122 USPQ 167, CA 3 1959, and resale price fixing of patented products. Apart from misuse, a patent also may become unenforceable, at least against certain parties, by laches, for example, where a patentee knows of infringement and inexcusably delays bringing suit to the prejudice of the defendant. *Potash Co. of America v. International Minerals and Chemical Corp.*, 213 F.2d 153, CA 10 1954.

Thus, validity differs from unenforceability in that validity deals with the patent as an entity, a legal document, while unenforceability is concerned with collateral actions by the patentee.

Is There a Patentable Invention?

Novelty — the First Requirement. 35 U.S.C. 102 provides:

"A person shall be entitled to a patent unless (a) the invention was *known or used* by others in this country, *or patented or described* in a printed publication in this or a foreign country, before the invention thereof by the applicant for patent...." (Emphasis added.)

If a process, machine, manufacture, or composition of matter is identical to something that has been publicly known or used before, there is no invention or discovery and a patent issued thereon is invalid because it is anticipated. However, very few patents are declared invalid because the invention claimed therein has been anticipated. P. J. Federico, "Adjudicated Patents, 1948-54," 38 JPOS 233, 248 1956. On the other hand, the vast majority of patents declared invalid are so declared because the invention claimed therein lacks invention over the prior art. Where there is no anticipation in the strict sense just noted, the issue in determining invention is simply: "Is the difference between that patented or sought to be patented and the prior art sufficient to constitute patentable invention?"

Unobviousness. Very early in the patent law the principle was introduced that the thing sought to be patented must be not only new but also unobvious to those skilled in the art. *Hotchkiss et al. v. Greenwood et al.*, Howard 248, 266, 1850.

If it were possible to determine by formula what is obvious and what is unobvious, that is, what is mere skill in the art and what is patentable invention, the patent law would be much simplified. However, the courts early recognized that there is no precise definition of a patentable invention. Thus, in *McClain v. Ortmayer*, 141 U.S. 419, 427, 1891, the Supreme Court stated:

"The truth is the word [invention] cannot be defined in such manner as to afford any substantial aid in determining whether a particular device involves an exercise of the inventive faculty or not ...but, whether the variation relied upon in a particular case is anything more than ordinary mechanical skill is a question which cannot be answered by applying the test of any general definition."

Perhaps, to emasculate the severe "flash of genius" test (*Pacific Contact Laboratories v. Solex Laboratories*, 209 F.2d 529, 1953; see also *Cuno Engineering*, infra) or perhaps, to set forth in the statute that which since *Hotchkiss et al. v. Greenwood et al.*, has been the law (*Lyon v. Bausch & Lomb Optical Co.*, 224 F.2d 530, CA 2 1955), 35 U.S.C. 103 provides, again negatively, that:

"A patent may not be obtained though the invention is not identically disclosed or described as set forth in Section 102 of this title, if the differences between the subject matter sought to be patented and the prior art are such that the subject matter as a whole would have been obvious at the time the invention was made to a person having ordinary skill in the art to which said subject matter pertains. Patentability shall not be negatived by the manner in which the invention was made."

Tests for Measuring Unobviousness. If the subject matter sought to be patented is, in the strict sense, anticipated, obviously there is no patentable invention. Conversely, if a startling discovery is made in an entirely new field of science, a patentable invention may be clearly indicated. But in the grey area in between these extremes, where the vast majority of all inventions lie, it is very difficult to tell with certainty whether, in fact, there is or is not invention in the difference between the thing sought to be patented and the prior art. The problem becomes particularly acute in crowded arts, for example, the paint industry, where very slight modifications in compositions may yield vastly different and improved results long sought by the trade. Yet, when compared constituent for constituent, the differences may seem minute. In the face of these difficulties, the courts in determining the issue of invention or lack of invention, that is, obviousness or unobviousness, have come to look not only at a literal comparison of the subject matter claimed and the corresponding subject matter in the art, but at the results obtained by the invention and commercial adoption of the invention by the art. For example, in *Expanded Metals* v. *Bradford,* 214 U.S. 485; 29 Sup. Ct. 652, 656, 1909, the Supreme Court stated:

"It may be safely said that if those skilled in the mechanical arts are working in a given field, and have failed, after repeated efforts, to discover a certain new and useful improvement, that he who first makes the discovery has done more than make the obvious improvement which would suggest itself to the mechanic skilled in the art, and is entitled to protection as an inventor."

A graphic illustration of the reasoning which a court employs in determining whether or not there is present in a patent this elusive thing called invention is *Eibel Process Co.* v. *Minnesota and Ontario Paper Co,* 261 U.S. 45, 1923. The *Eibel Case* involved an improvement in Fourdrinier machines which are used in making paper. In such machines, paper pulp is deposited on a moving screen or "wire" which passes through a series of rollers and suction boxes. While the pulp is carried by the screen, water is gradually removed therefrom and the pulp fibers are matted into a composite, coherent paper. The Eibel improvement consisted of pitching the screen at such a slope that the flow of the paper stock by gravity in the direction of movement of the screen would equal the speed of the screen. This permitted the screen to be run at a high rate of speed and still produce uniform paper. In the prior art Fourdrinier machines, the screen was substantially horizontal and, if the screen was run at a relatively high speed, it would tend to run faster than the pulp, thus causing ripples and nonuniformities in the wet pulp before it had finally set to form paper. The Eibel claims specified a Fourdrinier machine having the feed end of the screen maintained at a substantial elevation above the level, whereby the paper stock was caused to travel by gravity rapidly in the direction of the movement of the screen. The patent drawing showed the screen inclined at an angle of roughly 4 degrees or a feed end elevation on the order of 12 inches. In the prior art, for other reasons, the wire screen had been elevated slightly, for example, on the order of 3 inches near the feed end; but, as compared with the elevation used by Eibel, such prior art adjustment was clearly not substantial. After pointing out the differences between the prior art and the Eibel Fourdrinier machine, the Supreme Court pointed out several facts. First, the Court stated:

"The paper makers in this country, who do not use the Eibel pitch, therefore, are few.... The fact that the Eibel pitch has been generally adopted in the paper-making business and that the daily product in paper making has thus been increased at least 20 per cent over that which had been achieved before Eibel, is very weighty evidence to sustain the presumption from this patent that what he discovered and invented was new and useful." p. 56.

The Court also pointed out that when the Eibel machine was first introduced, those skilled in the art thought it so radical that they held back from adopting it until its usefulness was proved and that, where prior art machines were run at a rate of 500 ft/min., satisfactory product was obtained with the Eibel improvement at speeds up to 700 ft/min. and speeds of 1000 ft/min. were planned. Finally, the Court noted that:

"The invention was not the mere use of higher substantial pitch to remedy a known source of trouble. It was the discovery of the source not before known, and the application of the remedy for which Eibel is entitled to be rewarded in his patent. Had the trouble which Eibel sought to remedy been the well-known difficulty of too great wetness or dryness of the web at the dandy roll, and had he found that a higher rather than a lower pitch would do that work better, a patent for this improvement might well have been attacked on the ground that he was seeking a monopoly for a mere matter of degree. But that is not this case. On the other hand, if all knew the source of the trouble Eibel was seeking to remedy was where he found it to be, and also knew that increasing speed of the stock would remedy it, doubtless it would not have been inventive on his part to use the pitch of the wire to increase the speed of the stock, when such pitch had been used before to do the same thing, although for a different purpose and in less degree.... The fact that in a decade of an eager quest for higher speeds this important chain of circumstances had escaped observation, the fact that no one had applied a remedy for the consequent trouble until Eibel, and the final fact that, when he made known his discovery, all adopted his remedy, leave no doubt in our minds that what he saw and did was not obvious, and did involve discovery and invention." p. 68.

A substantial improvement had been obtained; the art had long sought this improvement to no avail; the prior art recognized the problem the improvement solved; and, once the improvement was pointed out, the art adopted it. In other words, the Court looked not only at the difference between the new and the old, but also at the result and the contribution afforded by such difference.

For similar reasoning since the enactment of 35 U.S.C. 103, see *Lyon* v. *Bausch & Lomb Optical Co.*, supra.

It is interesting to note, by contrast, that in *Cuno Engineering Corp.* v. *Automatic Devices Corp.*, 314 U.S. 84, 1941, from which the severe "flash of genius" test originated, the alleged infringing device had met with very great commercial success, but the device specifically shown in the patent, a cigarette or cigar lighter for automobiles, had never met with any commercial success. Thus, the patentee who had never disclosed a commercially successful embodiment attempted to assert his patent against one who had discovered a different and very successful commercial embodiment of his claimed genus.

Utility. For a discussion of utility, a further requirement for patentability and validity, reference is made to the article *Utility of Inventions.*

Is the One Claiming the Invention the Inventor Thereof?

At least theoretically, the validity of a patent might be contested on the basis that the patent was not issued to the correct inventor, or more precisely, the correct inventive entity, that is, that there had been a misjoinder or nonjoinder of inventors. However, 35 U.S.C. 256 provides that where a joint inventor has been omitted or an extra inventor has been incorrectly joined, by error and without any deceptive intention, such misjoinder or nonjoinder of inventors can be corrected. The Code also provides that a misjoinder or nonjoinder of joint inventors shall not invalidate a patent if such error can be corrected as provided in this section. However, at least one of the correct inventors must be named. (See *Inventors*) Also, one may not derive an invention from another and then obtain a valid patent thereon in his own name.

Normally, the question of inventorship and validity arise when a defendant in an infringement suit asserts inventorship in an entirely different inventive entity than that specified on a patent. An attack on a patent *under 35 U.S.C. 102(a)* is in reality an attack on inventorship. Thus, invalidity based on knowledge, use, patenting, or publication of an invention prior to the invention thereof by the patentee, all basically are grounded in the fact that the inventor on a patent is not the inventor of the subject matter patented. But a more direct attack on the validity of a patent can be made under what is now 35 U.S.C. 102(g) which provides that a person shall not be entitled to a patent if:

"(g) before the applicant's invention thereof the invention was made in this country by another who had not abandoned, suppressed, or concealed it...."

Where two adverse parties each are seeking or have obtained patent rights, this section of the Code provides the basis for interference practice under 35 U.S.C. 135 and suits to determine priority between interfering patents under 35 U.S.C. 291. In this section of this Article we are dealing mainly with the case where the defendant in an infringement suit sets up inventorship in another not the inventor named on the patent.

An example of a direct attack on inventorship is *Corona Cord Tire Co.* v. *Dovan*

Chemical Corporation, 276 U.S. 358, 1928, which involved a suit for infringement on a patent which claimed, inter alia, the use of diphenylguanidine (D.P.G.) as an accelerator in vulcanizing rubber. The basic issue in the case was who first discovered the use of D.P.G. as an accelerator. The patentee, Weiss, had made his invention in February, 1919. In November, 1921, he filed an application and later obtained a patent thereon. Kratz had conceived the accelerating effect of D.P.G. in 1916 and, at least by 1917, he had reduced his idea to practice. Between September 2 and 6, 1919, Kratz had read his findings to an A.C.S. meeting in Philadelphia. In April 1920, he published the results of his discovery. Kratz never sought to obtain a patent on his invention. In holding the Weiss patent invalid, the Supreme Court (pp. 383-385) stated:

"There was no abandonment in the sense that Kratz had given up what he was seeking for in demonstrating a new and effective accelerator in D.P.G. . . . It is a mistake to assume that reduction to use must necessarily be a commercial use. If Kratz discovered, and completed, as we are convinced that he did, the first use of D.P.G. as an accelerator in making vulcanized rubber, he does not lose his right to use this discovery when he chooses to do so for scientific purposes or purposes of publication or because he does not subsequently sell the rubber thus vulcanized or use his discovery in trade or does not apply for a patent for it. It is not an abandoned experiment because he confines his use of the rubber thus produced to his laboratory or to his lecture room. It is doubtless true that Kratz by his course in respect to his discovery as to the use of D.P.G. has abandoned any claim as against the public for a patent, but that is a very different thing from saying that it was abandoned as against a subsequent discoverer or patentee." Cf. *Lyon* v. *Bausch & Lomb Optical Co.,* supra.

As we have just seen, prior invention by another who does not abandon, suppress, or conceal the invention invalidates a patent. A specific instance of this principle is set forth in 35 U.S.C. 102(e) which provides that one may not obtain a valid patent if:

"(e) the invention was described in a patent granted on an application for patent by another

filed in the United States before the invention thereof by the applicant for patent." [Based on *Alexander Milburn Co.* v. *Davis Bournonville Co.,* 270 U.S. 390, 1926.]

The inventor to whom a patent can properly issue need not necessarily be the first inventor so long as he is an original inventor, that is, he made the invention through his own inventive faculties. Thus, if a prior inventor has abandoned or concealed his invention, such prior inventor will not bar a subsequent patent to another original inventor. *Gayler* v. *Wilder,* 51 U.S. 477, 1850.

Has the Inventor Made Timely Claim to His Invention?

Having made an invention, an inventor has several alternatives. First, he can exploit his invention without seeking patent protection and try to keep his invention secret. Second, he can seek patent protection and either exploit his invention or not, at his own discretion. Third, he can secrete his invention without exploiting it, with the hazard so incurred.

There may be good reasons for an inventor seeking to exploit an invention, yet trying to keep it secret. For example, the inventor may have invented a process which he can practice in secret but cannot describe in terms which would give him comprehensive patent protection commensurate with his disclosure. He may look to the law of trade secrets for his protection, not to the patent law, since the primary purpose of the patent law is promotion of science and the useful arts by disclosure to the public. If an inventor could exploit his invention for an unlimited period in secret, then file when the art begins to use it, the inventor might well prolong his patent monopoly for well in excess of the 17 years allowed. The law does not allow him an unlimited time to decide which of the alternatives he will choose. Furthermore, science and the useful arts are promoted best by bringing inventions to the public as soon as possible. On the other hand, an inventor often cannot file an adequate application before he has fully reduced his invention to practice and he should not be barred from exploiting his invention during a reasonable time necessary to file his application. Furthermore, when he first reduces his invention to practice, the inventor may not know whether his invention is worth patenting. In addition, the public itself may be benefited most by allowing to the inventor additional time for the invention to be further developed by the one most familiar with it, the inventor himself.

The foregoing considerations are brought together and balanced in 35 U.S.C. 102 which states:

"A person shall be entitled to a patent unless . . .

"(b) the invention was patented or described in a printed publication in this or a foreign country or in public use or on sale in this country, more than one year prior to the date of the application for patent in the United States. . . ." Once subject matter has been patented or described in a printed publication or in public use or on sale in this country for more than one year, the subject matter sought to be claimed is compared with that patented, published, or in public use or on sale. If there is no difference, that is the end of it. If there is not exact correspondence, then the difference should be measured by the standards of obviousness similar to those set forth in 35 U.S.C. 103 and discussed previously. This applies whether the disclosure be by way of printed publication or public use. *Standard Automatic Mach. Co.* v. *Karl Kiefer Mach. Co.*, 18 F.2d 326, DC NY 1925, aff. *ibid.* 331, CA 2 1927.

Actions by Others Prior to Filing. 35 U.S.C. 102(b) covers two general situations —cases in which a patent may be invalidated by the inventor's actions prior to assertion of his patent rights and cases in which a patent may be invalidated by the acts of others. With respect to the acts by others, the fact that patented or published subject matter and, for example, articles whose structure is readily discernible actually contribute to the *knowledge* of the art is undoubtedly an important reason for creating a one-year statutory bar under 102(b). But when the knowledge test is applied to a process to explain a public use bar under

102(b) some rather anomalous results are obtained because public use of a process which constitutes a bar does not necessarily disclose the process to the art. Furthermore, 102(b) does not require that, to be a bar, an invention must be sold, but merely that it must be "on sale." *Triplett* v. *Line Material Co.*, 53 USPQ 93, DC Ill 1942. Added problems result from confusion of cases of public use under 102(b) with cases of prior use under 102(a). In the latter case, the contribution to the sum of knowledge is of primary importance. Compare *Picard* v. *United Aircraft*, 128 F.2d 632, 635, CA 2 1942 with *Gayler* v. *Wilder*, supra.

It is submitted that much of the foregoing can be clarified if one views a primary reason for 102(b) to be that, once an invention has been made available to others or actually used by others, they should not be foreclosed from using such invention by the inventor's failure or delay beyond a reasonable period in asserting his claim thereto, irrespective of when the inventor actually made his invention. Otherwise, the art would be very reluctant to try any new inventions.

The foregoing dual aspect of 102(b)— use (or availability for use) coupled with unreasonable delay by the inventor—is illustrated by *Electric Storage Battery Co.* v. *Shimadzu*, 307 U.S. 5, 1939 and *Lorenz* v. *Colgate-Palmolive-Peet Co.*, 167 F.2d 423, CA 3 1948. The *Shimadzu* case involved a suit for infringement on a process patent and apparatus patent for making lead oxide for storage battery plates. The claimed inventions had been used by the defendant more than two years prior to the applications for the patents in question. In holding the patents invalid, the Court stated:

"The ordinary use of a machine or the practise of a process in a factory in the usual course of producing articles for commercial purposes is a public use.

"In the present case the evidence is that the petitioner, since June 1921, has continuously employed the alleged infringing machine and process for the production of lead oxide powder used in the manufacture of plates for storage batteries which have been sold in quantity. There is no finding, and we think none would have been justified, to the effect that the machine, process, and product were not well known to the employes in the plant, or that efforts were made to conceal them from anyone who had a legitimate interest in understanding them. This use, begun more than two years [one year is now sufficient] before Shimadzu applied for patents 1,584,150 and 1,-896,020, invalidated the claims in suit." 307 U.S. 5, 20, 1939.

In the above quotation, note the emphasis on normal commercial use and the apparent reluctance to foreclose the defendant from that rightfully done for over two years.

The aspect of delay by the inventor is illustrated by the *Lorenz* case which involved two interfering patents. It appeared that the plaintiff's invention, on which an application was filed more than two years after a public use, was fraudulently appropriated by the defendant, which had itself obtained a patent thereon. However, despite such mitigating circumstances, the court felt that the harm in not applying R.S. Section 4886, predecessor to 35 U.S.C. 102(b), strictly, outweighed the injustice which might be occasioned in circumstances such as the one in question. The court, quoting from *Eastman* v. *Mayor of New York*, 134 F. 844, CA 2 1904, stated:

"As Judge Coxe said in the Eastman case, isolated instances of injustice may result if the law be strictly applied, but the inventor's remedy is sure. He is master of the situation and by prompt action can protect himself fully and render the defense of prior public use impossible. 'If [the inventor] fails to take so simple and reasonable a precaution why should it not be said that the risk is his own and that he cannot complain of the consequences of his own supineness?' Moreover, it is apparent that if fraud or piracy be held to prevent the literal application of the prior-public-use provision a fruitful field for collusion will be opened and the public interest which R.S. Section 4886 is designed to protect will suffer." 167 F.2d 423, 430, CA 3 1948.

Although, as we have seen, public use does not necessarily involve common knowledge, the law still draws a distinction between public use as in the *Shimadzu* case, abandoned use as in the *Lyon* case, supra, or secret use as in *Gillman* v. *Stern*, 114 F.2d 28, 31, CA 2 1940. The latter case involved a suit for infringement on a patent for an invention by one Wenczel on a pneu-

matic device for quilting. Apparently, for several years before the application for the patent in question, one Haas had employed a very similar device commercially in his home, but always had taken great pains to keep its structure in utmost secrecy. The court, in holding the patent valid, stated:

"We are to distinguish between a public user which does not inform the art (Hall v. Macneale, 107 U.S. 90, 97) and a secret user; some confusion has resulted from the failure to do so. It is true that in each case the fund of common knowledge is not enriched, and that might indeed have been good reason originally for throwing out each as anticipations. But when the statute made any 'public use' fatal to a patent, and when thereafter the court held that it was equally fatal, whether or not the patentee had consented to it there was no escape from holding—contrary to the underlying theory of the law—that it was irrelevant whether the use informed the public so that they could profit by it. Nevertheless, it was still true that secret uses were not public uses, whether or not public uses might on occasion have no public value. Perhaps it was originally open to argument that the statute merely meant to confine prior 'public uses' to the prospective patentee and to be evidence of abandonment, and that 'first inventor' meant to include anyone who first conceived the thing in tangible enough form to be persuasive. But, rightly or wrongly, the law did not develop so, and it is now too late to change. Hence the anomaly that, by secreting a machine one may keep it from becoming an anticipation, even though its public use would really have told nobody anything about it."

Note the analogy between public v. secret use and 102(g) which negatives prior invention as a bar if there has been abandonment, suppression or concealment.

Actions by the Inventor. Bars to a patent created by use of an invention by the inventor appear to be the parent to and of the same genesis as the public use bars under 102(b) just discussed. *Electric Storage Battery Co.* v. *Shimadzu,* supra. Also, the period applied to such inventor-use bars has followed that applied to bars created by public use by others. Thus, one can reason that 102(b) applies to use by an inventor and the criteria of public use previously indicated should apply. However, the courts early treated inventor-use bars as if they were a constructive abandonment,

Egbert v. *Lippmann*, 104 U.S. 333, 1881, and in viewing the following cases the reasoning applied, rather than controlling statute, should be emphasized.

Exploitation by the Inventor. The law does not allow an inventor to exploit his invention indefinitely while keeping disclosure thereof from the public, because not only does this thwart the purpose of promoting science and the useful arts, but also it may unduly extend the inventor's monopoly. Thus, after completing his invention and having begun to exploit it, the inventor must claim his invention in an application within one year. A case in point is *Metallizing Engineering Co.* v. *Kenyon Bearing & A. P. Co.*, 153 F.2d 516, CA 2 1946. This involved an infringement suit on a process for conditioning the surfaces of metals so that additional metal could be more easily and securely bonded thereto. The inventor exploited his invention commercially for more than one year before he filed an application thereon. Judge L. Hand, in holding the patent invalid, stated in part:

"... [It] is a condition upon an inventor's right to a patent that he shall not exploit his discovery competitively after it is ready for patenting; he must content himself with either secrecy, or legal monopoly. It is true that for the limited period of two years he was allowed to do so, possibly in order to give him time to prepare an application; and even that has been recently cut down by half. But if he goes beyond that period of probation, he forfeits his right regardless of how little the public may have learned about the invention; ... it is part of the consideration for a patent that the public shall as soon as possible begin to enjoy the disclosure." *Ibid.*, 520; accord, *Huzar* v. *Cincinnati Chemical Works*, 172 F.2d 6, CA 6 1949.

Note that public use in this sense does not involve the question of public knowledge. Public knowledge is referred to in 35 U.S.C. 102(a) which deals with the date of invention, but not in 102(b) which deals with "statutory bars" by public use, sale and publication. Cf. *Elizabeth* v. *American Nicholson Pavement Co.*, 97 U.S. 126; 24 L.Ed. 1000, 1878. Thus, it is not the public knowledge of the invention that precludes the inventor from obtaining a valid patent, but his own exploitation of an invention fully completed. Note that 35 U.S.C. 102(a)

which refers to use *by others* does not mention sale, while 102(b) which includes use by the inventor refers to the time the invention is "on sale." With respect to the inventor, "on sale" in 102(b) has significance with respect to the time the invention is completed and exploitation by the inventor begins. Also, note that carrying the above reasoning to its logical conclusion vitiates the distinction between secret and public use in cases of use by an inventor.

Experimental Use as Anticipation. As previously indicated, the public is benefited by the inventor's complete development of his idea, for it is he who is in the best position to develop it and fully disclose it to the public. Furthermore, many inventions are not capable of development without some measure of commercial exploitation. Thus, in computing the one year period which bars a patent, periods of true experimentation are excluded even though some benefit may be incidentally obtained thereby. In *Elizabeth* v. *American Nicholson Pavement Co.*, supra, the inventor developed a new road surfacing or paving. Its durability and its surface qualities required testing under actual use conditions. Thus, the inventor paved a section of a toll road in Boston and frequently, almost daily, over a period of six years, tested and noted the performance of his surfacing. The Supreme Court held that such use was not a public use in the sense necessary to bar his patent, stating:

"It is sometimes said that an inventor acquires an undue advantage over the public by delaying to take out a patent, inasmuch as he thereby preserves the monopoly to himself for a longer period than is allowed by the policy of the law; but this cannot be said with justice when the delay is occasioned by a *bona fide* effort to bring his invention to perfection, or to ascertain whether it will answer the purpose intended. His monopoly only continues for the allotted period, in any event; and it is the interest of the public, as well as himself, that the invention should be perfect and properly tested, before a patent is granted for it. Any attempt to use it for a profit, and not by way of experiment, for a longer period than two years before the application would deprive the inventor of his right to a patent."

It should be noted that in this case the public knew of the invention and it was used publicly, but that throughout the period in question, the invention was actually tested and not exploited. It should be noted also that 35 U.S.C. (102(a) which refers to use *by others* does not mention sale, while 102(b) which includes use by the inventor refers to the time the invention is "on sale." With respect to the inventor, "on sale" in 102(b) has significance in relation to the time the invention is completed and exploitation by the inventor begins.

However, to qualify for the exclusion illustrated by the *Elizabeth* case, supra, the primary purpose of use must be experimental and not exploitation. Thus, in *Aerovox Corp.* v. *Polymet Mfg. Corp.*, 67 F.2d 860, CA 2 1933, the inventor developed a new condenser and process for making same, exploited his invention and sold condensers so produced commercially more than two years prior to his application. Although he did follow the performance of his condensers under actual service conditions, nevertheless it appeared that the invention was complete, not in the experimental state, and that the primary purpose was profit. Thus, the Court stated, p. 862:

> "It is not enough that he intends incidentally to test its value; he may not so reserve his rights; his primary purpose must be the test, though incidentally he may get what profit he can."

(See *Anticipation*)

Delay in Claiming. One further point should be mentioned. It is the assertion of a claim or claims to the invention which tolls the period of permissible public use. Thus, although in the normal case it is the period from the public use to the filing of the application which controls, this is not necessarily so. In *Muncie Gear Works* v. *Outboard, Marine & Mfg. Co.*, 315 U.S. 759, 1942, the inventor filed an application claiming one aspect of outboard motors. Subsequently, he sold motors described in the application and, more than two years after such sale and while his application was still pending, he abandoned claims as to the aspect of the motors originally claimed and claimed a different aspect of the motors sold. The Supreme Court held the patent

invalid essentially for the reason that the patentee did not assert claims to the invention ultimately covered in the issued patent until two years after the public use and sale.

An interesting application of the foregoing principles is found in *In re Ruscetta and Jenny*, 255 F.2d 687, CCPA 1958. In this case a parent application was filed for a method for etching tantalum capacitor electrodes. Subsequently, the application was refiled twice and, in the final application, the one in question, the case was broadened to include the production of electrodes of metals in addition to tantalum. More than one year prior to the filing of the last application, the British cognate of the parent application, disclosing only tantalum, was published. The court held that the British patent barred the generic claim in the final application and that the applicant was entitled only to so much as the original parent application disclosed and supported. In a sense, this case is analogous to the case wherein the applicant himself exploits an invention but fails to assert timely claim thereto. In the *Ruscetta case,* the applicant was limited to what he asserted as his invention within one year of the issuance of his British application. The court seemed to imply, relying on *In re Stempel*, 241 F.2d 755, CCPA 1957, that if the inventor had disclosed and claimed the genus in question prior to the expiration of one year from the date of publication of the British cognate, he might have validly claimed the genus.

The *Ruscetta* case is also analogous to bars by disclosures in printed publications generally, as well as public use by others in that the genus in question was rejected over the British patent on the basis that the added metals in the genus were obvious from the tantalum species. In a sense, the *Ruscetta* case is anomalous in that the inventor was entitled to what the art (his British patent) showed, but was not entitled to what the art did not show but in the court's opinion was obvious therefrom. However, when viewed in the light of the applicant's failure to make his claim to the "obvious" genus within one year of *his own* disclosure of his invention and the fact that he did not assert his claim within one year of the time that the art knew of his invention and could have acted thereon, it is not inconsistent with the principles previously enunciated. (See *Delay in Claiming* and *Laches*)

Foreign Patenting. One further ramification of the foregoing is set forth in 35 U.S.C. 102(d) which provides that a patent shall be invalid if the invention has been patented in a foreign country by the inventor or those deriving title from him prior to the date of application in this country on an application filed more than one year before the U.S. application. See, e.g., *General Steel Products Co.* v. *Lorenz,* 204 F. Supp. 518, DC Fla 1962. This section of the Code forces an inventor to seek patent protection in this country within one year of foreign filing or prior to foreign patenting or forever waive his claim thereto. Particularly where a first filed foreign application is in a quick issuing foreign country, for all practical purposes it forces U.S. filing within one year of the foreign filing date. Thus, 102(d) promotes disclosure in the U.S. just as does requiring an inventor to file within one year of commercial exploitation, use by others, or disclosure in a printed publication.

Does the Patent Adequately Disclose and Claim a Patentable Invention?

To insure that each patent teaches the public how to practice the patented invention and to insure that, during the term of the patent, the public can distinguish that area from which it is excluded from that area in which it is free to operate, 35 U.S.C. 112 provides:

"The specification shall contain a written description of the invention, and of the manner and process of making and using it, in such full, clear, concise, and exact terms as to enable any person skilled in the art to which it pertains, or with which it is most nearly connected, to make and use the same, and shall set forth the best mode contemplated by the inventor of carrying out his invention.

"The specification shall conclude with one or more claims particularly pointing out and distinctly claiming the subject matter which the applicant regards as his invention."

The underlying purpose of 35 U.S.C. 112 was clearly set forth by the Supreme Court in *General Electric Co.* v. *Wabash Appliance Corp. et al.,* 304 U.S. 364, 368-69, 1938. This case was actually decided under R. S. 4888, 35 U.S.C. 33 which, in substance, was the same as 35 U.S.C. 112. The Court stated:

"We may assume that Pacz has sufficiently informed those skilled in the art how to make and use his filament. The statute has another command ...Congress requires of the applicant 'a distinct and specific statement of what he claims to be new, and to be his invention.'...The inventor must 'inform the public during the life of the patent of the limits of the monopoly asserted, so that it may be known which features may be safely used or manufactured without a license and which may not.'"

Failure to meet the requirements of 35 U.S.C. 112 is a ground for invalidating a patent. Like most other defenses of invalidity, it is also a positive defense which must be pleaded. 35 U.S.C. 282(3). Courts often use different terms for their reasons for invalidating a patent under 35 U.S.C. 112. Often, for example, they invalidate functional claims as being indefinite. Rather than stating that the specification does not teach how to carry out the invention, courts may hold also that the specification is inoperative. Instead of stating that the claims are broader than the invention, courts may state that the claims encompass inoperative species or are inoperative.

For the purposes of the following discussion the main reasons for invalidating a patent for failure to comply with this section of the statute are:

(a) The specification fails to teach the public how to practice the invention,

(b) The claims are broader than the invention,

(c) The claims are functional, and

(d) The claims are indefinite.

The courts may combine two or more of these reasons.

Failure to Teach How to Practice the Invention. If a patent does not teach those skilled in the art how to practice the invention, then, in reality, the inventor has made no disclosure to the public and he should not be entitled to a patent. Although failure to teach in the specification how to practice the invention is not, perhaps, the most frequent ground for invalidating a patent under 35 U.S.C. 112, nevertheless this requirement is perhaps one of the most basic conditions precedent to patent rights. An illustration of invalidation of a patent on this ground is *Permutit Co.* v. *Graver Corporation*, 284 U.S. 52, 1931, which involved a patent on an apparatus for softening water. The Supreme Court held this patent invalid on two grounds, namely, that the specification did not teach how to practice the invention and the claims did not point out and distinctly claim the invention. As to this first ground, the Court stated (pp. 56 to 58):

"The apparatus described in the specification closely resembles sand filters long used. The elements enumerated above, alone and in combination, are confessedly old. The only invention seriously urged under claim 1 is the substitution of a 'free' for a 'locked' zeolite bed; a matter which is not referred to either in the specification or in the claim.... As the patentee has thus failed to give in the specification 'a written description' and has likewise failed particularly to point out and distinctly claim the free zeolite bed, as 'the part, improvement, or combination which he claims as his invention or discovery,' the patent is void."

Similarly, in *Plant Products Co.* v. *Charles Phillips Chemical Co.*, 96 F.2d 585, CA 2 1938, which involved a suit for infringement on a patent on a process for making milk of magnesia tablets, the Court stated (p. 586):

"We find it unnecessary to hold the patent invalid because it is inoperable.... [The] disclosure was in any event insufficient. All it said was that one should 'remove all of the moisture in the mass (except its water of constitution) without affecting its physical chemical or therapeutical properties'; it did not say at what temperatures this would take place and how long it would take; nor how one was to determine whether the 'properties' of the magnesium hydroxide had been 'affected.' But that is not all. The language on its face means what it says—'all of the moisture'—but to take it so, would be to miss the very kernel, which is absolutely vital to success. The obbligato, which gives its deeper meaning to this simple theme, is that a thin coating or jacket of water must remain around the colloidal clusters in the tablet in order to preserve their integrity."

In short, the patentee in the *Plant Products* case simply did not teach the art how to make his milk of magnesia tablets.

Claims Broader than the Invention. Passing on to the second paragraph of 35 U.S.C. 112 quoted hereinbefore dealing with the claims, a patent, or more properly, one or more claims of a patent, may be held invalid because they are broader than the invention made by the patentee. This section deals with claims which are too broad for reasons other than lack of invention.

Two points should be made at the outset about the breadth of claims. First, broad claims per se are not invalid, provided the inventor has truly made a generic invention and he discloses how to practice his generic invention. Second, an attack on claims on the ground of undue breadth should not be confused with an attack on claims on the ground of indefiniteness. A broad claim can be perfectly clear. Its metes and bounds can be precisely defined, but, nevertheless, it may be invalid because of undue breadth. Conversely, a very narrow claim can be invalid on the ground of indefiniteness, for example, for the reason that those skilled in the art cannot determine from the claim, albeit how narrow, the limits of the invention.

For the purpose of this discussion we can consider claims as being invalidated on the ground of undue breadth for three reasons.

(a) The contribution alleged does not apply to the full breadth of the claim.

(b) The claim includes inoperative species.

(c) The patentee has not disclosed any invention commensurate with the breadth of his claim.

Lack of Utility in Whole Area Claimed. An illustration of (a) above is *Georgia-Pacific Corp.* v. *United States Plywood Corp.*, 258 F.2d 124, CA 2 1958, which involved a suit for infringement on a patent for gouging relatively deep grooves in the surface of fir plywood in order to relieve stresses therein and prevent edge separation and cracking. The court held certain claims invalid, stating on p. 135:

"[S]ince panels made from wood dissimilar to Douglas fir have little tendency to check or separate at the edges, deep striation of such panels serves no utilitarian function of stress relief. Consequently, we conclude that claims covering all types of plywood are beyond the scope of the Deskey invention.

"Only one of the claims is properly limited to the scope of the Deskey invention. That is claim 1, which claims 'a plywood panel having a face ply of rotary-cut wood having pronouncedly different hard and soft growth, and consequent 'wild' graining when rotary-cut ...' Claims 2 to 7 are not so limited, and therefore we agree with Judge Herlands that they are invalid."

In short, the court held that the patentee's invention had no useful application to all woods. Thus, claims directed to all woods were broader than the invention and invalid.

Claiming Inoperative Species. The *Plywood* case is distinguished here from a case of inoperative species because in the *Plywood* case the problem remedied by the invention did not exist with all species claimed, that is, the treatment claimed served no useful purpose with all plywood. In a true case of inoperative species, the problem exists with all species, but a substantial number of species within a claimed genus do not solve it. An illustration of this second type of unduly broad claims is *Corona Cord Tire Co.* v. *Dovan Chemical Corp.*, supra, which involved a suit for infringement on a patent for a process for curing rubber with diphenylguanadine as accelerator. Certain claims in the patent covered curing rubber, not only with diphenylguanadine, but with all disubstituted guanadines. Such claims were declared invalid because it was shown that not all disubstituted guanadines cure rubber.

The reason for invalidating claims which include inoperative species is that 35 U.S.C. 112 places the burden *on the inventor* of pointing out and distinctly claiming his invention. He has the burden of pointing out those things that will work. The public should not be required to determine what within the area claimed will work and what is his invention.

Unfortunately, particularly in chemical cases, the justification for invalidating claims on the basis of inclusion of an inoperable species is not always as clear as it might at first blush appear. Goodman,

Herbert H., "The Invalidation of Generic Claims by Inclusion of a Small Number of Inoperative Species," 40 JPOS 745, 1958. If an inventor determines that one amine will work in a given process, should he then be entitled to claim the use of a class encompassing 100 amines? Perhaps not. But, suppose he tries a large number of amines representative of the different members of the class, all work, and he proceeds to claim the use of all members of the class. If at some later date it is discovered that for some peculiar reason a few members of the class do not work in the process, should the inventor be denied protection on the use of some or all of the other members that do work? To test all members of the class might be, for all practical purposes, impossible. Furthermore, to test them all might greatly delay disclosure of the invention. No case squarely answering this question has been found. But it would seem that the problem is somewhat alleviated (1) by the patentee drafting generic, subgeneric and species claims and refiling his application as tests proceed and (2) by the courts in so construing claims as not to include what one skilled in the art would obviously not use in view of the specification or giving a liberal construction to narrow the claims. *Graver Tank Co.* v. *Linde Air Products Co.*, 336 U.S. 271, 1949.

Narrow Disclosure v. *Broad Claims.* As to the final reason for invalidating claims on the ground of undue breadth, claims may be declared invalid because they are simply broader than the invention which is disclosed in the specification. In the Patent Office, this is the genesis of the very frequent rejection on insufficient disclosure. The invalidation of claims on this ground is illustrated by *Schering Corporation* v. *Gilbert*, 153 F.2d 428, CA 2 1946. This case involved a suit for infringement on a patent on certain chemical compounds used as contrasting agents in X-raying gall bladders. One compound, β-(4-hydroxy-3,5-diiodophenyl)-α-phenyl propionic acid, was shown to have very unique properties, to have been readily accepted by the art and achieved great commercial success. A claim directed to this specific compound was held valid. Another claim of the patent was directed to a broad genus of polyiodo derivatives of hydroxydiphenyl carboxylic acids. With respect to this claim the court (p. 433) said:

"Claim 4 covers by means of a broad elastic chemical formula which allows for the greatest number theoretically possible for molecular changes within the benzene ring, not only the compounds illustrated by way of examples in the specifications but also every possible variation of them which might result from further experiment. The specifications do not support that sort of claim but are no more at best than suggestions for experiment. Such experiment might be practically endless and futile as a matter of fact. And it might yield surprisingly useful results which, if this claim were valid, would be futile as a matter of law during the life of the patent. The claim is for an enormous number of as yet nonexistent compounds and is far broader than any disclosure in the patent. The specifications afford no adequate consideration for its grant and it must be held invalid for that reason."

An inventor need not exemplify everything claimed. But he must do more than invite experiment and he must lay down the guide lines by which others can practice his invention throughout the scope of the claims.

Functionality in Claims. Functional claims are claims which define a result to be achieved rather than the means of achieving such result. The main reason for invalidating such claims is that they really claim successful results instead of claiming *what* produces those results. An illustration of invalidation of objectionably functional claims is *General Electric Co.* v. *Wabash Appliance Corp. et al.*, supra, wherein the patentee claimed:

"A filament for electric incandescent lamps or other devices, composed substantially of tungsten and made up mainly of a number of comparatively large grains of such size and contour as to prevent substantial sagging and offsetting during a normal or commercially useful life for such lamps or other device."

In effect, the patentee claimed any filament which did not sag or offset, but did not point out or define which filaments did not sag or offset. In commenting on the claims, the court (on pp. 371-372) said:

"Claim 25 vividly illustrates the vice of a description in terms of function. 'As a description of

the invention, it is insufficient, and, if allowed, would extend the monopoly beyond the invention.' . . .

"A limited use of terms of effect or result, which accurately define the essential qualities of a product to one skilled in the art, may in some instances be permissible and even desirable, but a characteristic essential to novelty may not be distinguished from the old art solely by its tendency to remedy the problems in the art met by the patent. And we may doubt whether the language used in Claim 25, taken by itself, conveyed definite meaning to those skilled in the art of incandescent lighting."

What is functional and what is not functional is often not too obvious. Thus, in *Phillip A. Hunt Co.* v. *Mallinckrodt Chemical Works*, 177 F.2d 583, CA 2 1949, the court held invalid claims which used such terms as "resinous material," "filler," "adhesive powder," "lubricant powder," and "coloring material," not because the terms themselves were functional, but because, when one looked to the specification to determine what the terms meant, the definitions of the terms were functional. Thus, the claims read in the light of the specification were functional.

The essence of the problem of functionality is well illustrated in *S. D. Warren Co.* v. *Nashua Gummed & Coated Paper Co.*, 205 F.2d 602, CA 1 1953, which involved a suit for infringement on a patent for an adhesive containing a polymer and a crystalline plasticizer for the polymer. The polymer and the plasticizer were so chosen that at room temperature the polymer would be a hard solid and the plasticizer, a crystalline solid incompatible therewith. When the adhesive was heated, the plasticizer plasticized the polymer and made it sticky. When the adhesive began to cool, the plasticizer again crystallized very slowly and the adhesive again slowly became hard thus forming a firm bond. The advantage in the adhesive was that there was a considerable lag between the time the adhesive cooled and the time the plasticizer crystallized therefrom; thus, there was a considerable time in which the adhesive was sticky and, for example, labels coated therewith could be applied even though heat was removed therefrom. The claims contained such terms as "adhesive ... activatable to adhesiveness by heat," "materials substantially compatible to merge on heating to provide a substantially homogeneous mass," "amorphous, potentially viscous polymeric material," "potential plasticizer," "the polymeric material coexisting in physically independent individuality but merging on heating with release of the latent plasticizing property of the particles," "the plasticizer being present in significant proportion to provide after heating a merged mixture." The court on pp. 605-606 held these claims valid for the following reasons:

"Particularity of identification and clarity of statement are relative terms when applied to an invention. Some inventions are capable of description in terms of meticulous accuracy; others are not. And this is one of the latter class for there are a great many polymeric, potentially viscid, substances of a resinous nature, and there are also many crystalline plasticisers for the same. Moreover, there is uncontradicted evidence that new substances of both kinds are constantly being developed, and furthermore the proportions of the two basic ingredients can be varied at the user's will to produce heat activation at different imposed temperatures according to need. Thus Perry was confronted with a difficult problem. If he were meticulously specific, and listed every material of both kinds which he either knew about or could discover, his patent would be of no practical value almost as soon as he applied for it. On the other hand, he had to avoid the vice of being functional. In this extremity he took the only practical course available. He described the essence of his invention in detail and with particularity in his specification and he listed therein about forty illustrative examples of his film. Reading the claims in the light of the specification we think one skilled in the art could readily apprehend the precise nature of Perry's invention and the limits of its scope. This is all the law requires." *Huxler Brothers* v. *Sales Affiliates, Inc.*, 164 F.2d 260, CA 4 1947.

In comparing the *Warren* with the *Wabash* case, two facts should be noted. First, in the *Wabash* case, the claims did not distinguish structurally over the art. They read on the art except for stating that the claimed filaments did not have the disadvantage associated with the prior art. In the *Warren* case, the claims did not read on the art and did not specify any polymer-plasticizer mixture that would work; they really speci-

fied the properties or qualities of the polymer and plasticizer which resulted in the adhesive which would work. Second, in the specification in the *Wabash* case, the patentee did not describe structurally any filament which distinguished over the art. In other words, the specification did not teach the structure or properties which made the claimed filaments different aside from the fact that they did not have the problem associated with known filaments. In the *Warren* case, the patentee gave forty examples of compositions which were new, which distinguished over the art, and which functioned differently from the art's adhesives. Warren claimed a broad invention; but a broad invention was made, was fully described and, balanced against the injustice of requiring more particular claiming, was distinctly claimed. It would be very simple to state that any claim which is functional in terms should be invalid. But clearly, as set forth in the aforequoted section of the *Warren* case, this would not serve the ends of the patent system. For by invalidating all claims which at first blush have functional terms, inventors would be left with the choice of either inadequate protection or secrecy.

Indefiniteness. Now let us take up the final ground for invalidating claims under 35 U.S.C. 112—indefiniteness. Although this ground is often broadened to include, for example, functionality, we are using it here in the somewhat more limited sense of referring to claims which just do not point out what is the inventive feature, though they are not necessarily too broad or functional. An illustration of indefiniteness as a ground for invalidating claims is *United Carbon* v. *Binney & Smith Co.*, 317 U.S. 228, 1942, which involved an infringement suit on a patent which claimed "pure carbon in the form of commercially uniform, comparatively small, rounded, smooth aggregates having a spongy or porous interior." The carbon pellets were alleged to solve the problem of dusting of carbon black in rubber compounding. The pellets had to be hard enough so that they did not break and dust when they were handled, yet they had to be friable enough so that they could be mixed with the rubber in compounding. The

patentee never described in his specification or claims exactly what made his pellets useful where prior art carbon black was
not. He never defined, for example, how
strong they had to be, or what was commercially uniform. Thus, the claims did
not define the invention and one skilled in
the art could not tell precisely what the
claims covered. The Supreme Court held
the claims of the patent invalid stating:

"The statutory requirement of particularity and
distinctness in patent claims is met only where
they clearly distinguish what is claimed from what
went before in the art and clearly circumscribe
what is foreclosed from future enterprise. A zone
of uncertainty which enterprise and experimentation may enter only at the risk of infringement
[sic] claims would discourage invention only a
little less than unequivocal foreclosure of the field.
Moreover, the claims must be reasonably clear-cut
to enable courts to determine whether novelty and
invention are genuine.... An invention must be
capable of accurate definition, and it must be accurately defined, to be patentable." p. 236.

In *Binney* as in the *Wabash* case, the
patentee never described that feature which
made the claimed products work while the
art did not. There is some indication in
both of these cases that the court may have
reasoned, consciously or unconsciously, that
if the inventor had really made an invention and known what it was, he would and
could have described it. But in each case
the patentee never really determined what
he really invented. By contrast, in the *Warren* case, the patentee knew what he invented and claimed it, described in great
detail the essence of his invention, and illustrated it by 40 examples. He clearly taught
the art what he invented and how to practice his invention.

Summary. To summarize the question of
adequacy of disclosure and claims, one first
determines whether the patent teaches those
skilled in the art how to do a new, unobvious and useful thing. If it does, then one
compares the claims with what the patent
discloses. The claims cannot be broader
than the problem solved, or so vaguely
worded that others are unable to determine
what the claimed invention is or how broadly
the inventor believes his right extends.

Has the Right to a Patent Been Exhausted by a Prior Patent?

Patents can be declared invalid on the
ground that a prior patent has been granted
to the same inventor for the same invention,
that is, that there has been double patenting. The main reasons for declaring patents
invalid on the ground of double patenting
are: (1) that the grant of one patent on an
invention exhausts the power to grant any
further valid patents to the same inventor
on any invention which is not patentable
over the invention first patented, and (2)
that to permit the granting of two patents
on one patentable invention would permit
extension of the exclusionary rights provided
by 35 U.S.C. 154 beyond the 17 years there
specified.

The ground rules in the law of double
patenting were laid down by the Supreme
Court in *Miller* v. *Eagle Mfg. Co.*, 151 U.S.
186, 1894. For further discussion of the
subject, see *Double Patenting*.

Summary

Validity deals basically with the question
of whether the patent gives to the public
that disclosure which is necessary to support the exclusionary rights granted under
the patent.

The first condition precedent to validity
is that the inventor must have made a patentable invention, that is, a discovery that
is useful and not obvious from what the
public knew before he made it.

Having made a patentable invention, the
inventor normally must be the one to apply
for the patent thereon. He must apply for
the patent within one year of the time when
the public comes to use his invention, when
it is described in a printed publication or
patented, or when he elects to exploit his
invention.

In applying for his patent, the inventor
must describe and distinctly claim his invention so that those skilled in the art will
know how to practice it, the area in which
they are free to operate, and the area from
which they are excluded.

Having obtained a patent, the inventor
may not thereafter, by obtaining additional

patent(s), seek to prolong his exclusionary rights to the same invention.

If the inventor has met the foregoing requirements, he then is entitled, in the normal case, to the reward which causes inventors to bring their inventions to the public rather than secrete them, that is, to the protection conferred by a valid patent.

Cross-references: *Abandonment, Adjudication(s), Anticipation, Delay in Claiming, Laches, Licenses—Package, Patentability, Utility of Inventions.*

W

WORDS AND PHRASES. See CLAIMS, GLOSSARY

WRITING APPLICATIONS. See APPLICATIONS —ELECTRICAL AND ELECTRONIC, CLAIM DRAFTING, and each of the major arts, e.g., ATOMIC ENERGY, CHEMICAL, DESIGN, GENERAL AND MECHANICAL, MICROBIOLOGICAL, PHARMACEUTICAL, PLANT

Case and Author Index

The term "et al.", when it occurs as a part of the official case title, is omitted below.

Subject Index

A

"A", "an" interpreted, 152
Abandoned applications as anticipation, 45
Abandonment of invention and trade secret, 1-7
  by acquiescence in infringement, 6
  after and before reduction to practice, 4
  dedication, rebuttal of presumptive, 191-194
  by delay in filing, 6
  express, 3
  by failure to claim, 3
  by failure to record interference settlement, 4
  by misfiling, 4
  by patenting abroad, 4
  during prosecution, 3
  to the public, 1
  by publication or public use, 1
  by sale, 1
  by secret use, 2
  trade secret abandonment, 6
  by violation of secrecy order, 4
"About" interpreted, 151
Academy for patent training, 285
Accelerated prosecution, 657-663
Acceptance or rejection of secret information, 723-731
Access to patent application by assignee, 79
Accounting after infringement, 7-16
  attorneys' fees, 12
  costs, 12
  damages, 11, 457
    see Taxation, 758-768
  elements of recovery, 7
  interest accumulated, 11
  lost business, 12
  profits of defendant, 10
  royalty judicially determined, statistics, 8-14
    "reasonable," 7
Accounts, deposit, in patent office, 294
Acquisition of patent rights by government, 361
Acquisition of patents and antitrust law, 50
Act of 1952—patents, 16-19
  bar created by issuance of foreign patent, 16

correction of mistakes, 18
disclaimers, 18
"flash of genius" not required, 17
infringement, 19
  contributory, 19
knowledge abroad and invention date, 17
marking, 19
means claims, 17
misuse doctrine and contributory infringement, 19
non-obvious subject matter required, 17, 596-599
patentability, 593
reissues, 18
restriction, 17
rights of patent owner, 18
section 103 interpreted, 17, 595
"standard of invention" replaced, 596
Actions of patent office on applications, 276-282
Adding on or subtracting inventors' names, 489
Addition and petty patents abroad, 326
Adjudication of patents, 20-25
  by arts involved, 23
  by circuits, 21, 23
  declaratory judgment proceedings, 188-191
    court procedure, 459-460
  in district courts, statistics, 223
  grounds for invalidity, 22, 24
  infringement, 437-447
  of plant patents, 647-649
  statistics, 20-25
    meaning of, 20
  suits, 451-464
    low proportion of patents involved, 20
    time consuming, 22
    under 1952 Act, 20-22
  trend of decisions, 20
  validity, 21, 22, 24, 796-811
Administration of patent rights by government, 360, 375-380
Admissions of attorneys, in infringement suits, 454

832